THE GRAMMAR BOOK

An ESL/EFL Teacher's Course

SECOND EDITION

MARIANNE CELCE-MURCIA

DIANE LARSEN-FREEMAN

(WITH HOWARD WILLIAMS)

The publication of *The Grammar Book, Second Edition* was directed by the members of the Newbury House ESL/EFL team at Heinle & Heinle:

Erik Gundersen, Editorial Director
Charlotte Sturdy, Market Development Director
Maryellen Killeen, Production Services Coordinator
Stanley J. Galek, Vice President & Publisher
Amy Lawler, Managing Development Editor

Also participating in the publication of this program were:

Heide Kaldenbach-Montemayor, Assistant Developmental Editor
Mary Sutton, Associate Market Development Director
Mary Beth Hennebury, Senior Manufacturing Coordinator
PC&F, Inc., Interior Designer and Page Production
Ha Nguyen, Cover Designer
Jonathan Stark, Image Resources Director
Evelyn Nelson, Director Global ESL Training & Development
Amy Terrell, Global Market Development Director

Library of Congress Cataloging-in-Publication Data

Celce-Murcia, Marianne. Larsen-Freeman, Diane.
    The grammar book.

    Includes bibliographies and index.
    1. English language–Study and teachings–Foreign
speakers. 2. English language–Grammar–1950-
I. Larsen-Freeman, Diane. II. Title.
PE1128.A2C39   1999   428'.007   99-2267
                                                CIP

Manufactured in the United States of America.

ISBN: 0-8384-4725-2

Heinle & Heinle is a division of International Thomson Publishing, Inc.

10 9 8 7 6 5

To Caroline and her family
and
To Brent and Gavin

~ ACKNOWLEDGMENTS ~

Over the years we have received helpful feedback that has contributed to the revision process in creating this second edition. To students and colleagues who have taken the time to ask questions, make suggestions, and to challenge us, we are indebted. We have learned much from you and trust you will find satisfaction in our response to your feedback in this new edition.

More particularly, we would like to thank Professor Loretta Grey of Central Washington University, who piloted an early version of this second edition with her own students and gave us invaluable feedback. Also to be singled out for their assistance are colleagues Ray Clark, Kathleen Graves, Elizabeth Tannenbaum, and Elizabeth O'Dowd, and graduate students Gaby Solomon, Namhee Han, and especially Angela Burnett and Jo Hilder. Then, too, we need to acknowledge the following, who gave us specific feedback on portions of the first edition:

Elliot L. Judd
University of Illinois at Chicago

Professor Dorothy Disterheft
University of South Carolina,
Linguistics Program

Virginia Samuda
University of Leeds

H. Patricia Byrd
Georgia State University

Pat Killian
Florida International University

Carol Cargill
University of South Florida

Elizabeth Riddle
Ball State University

Susan Wright
Northern Arizona
University

Harry Solo
Mankato State University (MN)

Jean Zukowski/Faust
Northern Arizona University

Shelley Wong
Ohio State University

Elaine Hoter
Talpiot Teachers College, Tel Aviv

We also appreciate the efforts of the Heinle & Heinle team:
Erik Gundersen, Heide Kaldenbach-Montemayor, and Maryellen Killeen, and for the work of Elaine Hall at PC & F Inc.

We are very grateful to Howard Williams for doing the initial drafting of Chapters 24, 26, and 31–33. We had naively thought that writing a second edition would not be as time-consuming as the first. But when all was said and done, this was an enormous undertaking (on top of our full-time jobs), and Howard came to our rescue when it was clear we were going to miss yet another deadline without some assistance. We also found his feedback on other chapters helpful.

Finally, without the support of our spouses, Daniel and Elliott, this book would have been even longer in the making than it was. For their love and encouragement, we express heartfelt thanks.

We have included more material in this text than you can teach in a one-term course that deals with the structure of English for ESL/EFL teachers. To include less would have been unconscionable since we believe that ESL/EFL teachers need to be familiar with all the topics in this book. A one-term course should then aim not only to deal with a portion of the chapters in the text; it should also lay a foundation that will enable students to continue to make use of the book after the course is completed.

If you do not have a two-term sequence to deal with the structure of English, we recommend teaching certain introductory chapters and then filling out the term by choosing others that you and/or your students feel would be most useful. Any syllabus should include Chapters 1 through 6 in order to give students the tools they will need to work through the other material. Chapter 2 has been written to introduce students who have a limited background in grammar to some basic concepts and terminology. Students who are more knowledgeable about English grammar can skip this chapter.

Students less experienced with English grammar may require more guidance in determining what should be covered in the allotted time. It is our feeling that for these students, in addition to working on Chapters 1–6, a minimal core syllabus would include a thorough grounding in the following:

- verb tense-aspect system (Chapter 7)
- modal auxiliaries (Chapter 8)
- syntactic patterns of simple sentences (Chapters 10–13)
- chapters with basic structures that ESL/EFL students find particularly difficult (articles—Chapter 15, prepositions—Chapter 21, and phrasal verbs—Chapter 22)

Of course, it is also possible to expand upon the material in this text. There are many ways you can encourage your students to go beyond what you are able to do in class. Some examples may include encouraging students to:

- read from the "Suggestions for Further Reading" feature
- write short papers on some particular topic related to an English grammatical structure
- conduct usage studies on the distribution of a particular English structure in authentic discourse
- conduct surveys of native speakers of English to determine their syntactic preferences
- develop teaching suggestions for points not covered in class

One of the greatest challenges in teaching this course is helping students overcome the anxiety toward the study of grammar that they sometimes bring with them. One of the greatest rewards is watching students move from anxiety to curiosity. This does happen. We have been privileged to see it.

Happy teaching!

Marianne Celce-Murcia

Marianne Celce-Murcia
University of California,
Los Angeles

Diane Larsen-Freeman

Diane Larsen-Freeman
School for International Training
Brattleboro, Vermont

∼ PREFACE ∼

The Grammar Book, Second Edition, is designed to help prospective and practicing teachers of English as a Second or Foreign Language (ESL/EFL) enhance their understanding of English grammar, expand their skills in linguistic analysis, and develop a pedagogical approach to teaching English grammar.

Each chapter in *The Grammar Book, Second Edition,* is designed to lead readers systematically from an understanding of the grammar structure to an ability to use this understanding in the ESL/EFL classroom. After the first two introductory chapters, each chapter includes:

- a core presentation of one particular grammatical structure. Descriptions and examples draw upon the latest linguistics and applied linguistic research and include discussions of problems that ESL/EFL students regularly encounter.

- suggestions for teaching various aspects of each grammar structure to ESL/EFL students

- comprehension and application exercises that enable readers to assess their understanding of the material and practice their ability to apply what was been presented

- a list of references cited

- suggestions for further reading, consisting of ESL/EFL texts, grammar reference guides, and published linguistic research that provide further information regarding the analysis and teaching of the points covered

At the end of the text, we have also included a detailed appendix with suggested answers to the chapter exercises.

∼ NEW TO THE SECOND EDITION ∼

- A new organizational framework, which consists of a systematic presentation of the form, meaning, and use of each grammatical structure, improves readers' ability to access, assimilate, and make pedagogic sense of the material presented

- A new chapter (Chapter 2) introduces readers to foundational grammatical concepts and terminology, and provides a basis of understanding for readers with a limited background in linguistics

- Three new chapters expand the coverage of English grammar: Tense-Aspect-Modality in Discourse, Reference and Possession, and Adverbials

- Completely updated and rewritten chapters include newly synthesized linguistic and applied linguistic research, new exercises, and new references

- Updated teaching suggestions are coded to reflect their form, meaning, and/or use orientation and are connected to the organizational framework of the text

∾ CONTENTS ∾

Dedication   iii

Acknowledgements   iv

To the Course Instructor   v

Preface   vi

Chapters

Appendix

Indexes

INTRODUCTION

TWO APPROACHES TO TEACHING LANGUAGE

Over the years, language teachers have alternated between favoring teaching approaches that focus primarily on language use and those that focus on language forms or analysis. The alternation has been due to a fundamental disagreement concerning whether one learns to communicate in a second language by communicating in that language (such as in an immersion experience) or whether one learns to communicate in a second language by learning the *lexicogrammar*—the words and grammatical structures—of the target language. In other words, the argument has been about two different means of achieving the same end.

As with any enduring controversy, the matter is not easily resolved. For one thing, there is evidence to support both points of view. It is not uncommon to find learners who, for whatever reason, find themselves in a new country or a new region of their own country, who need to learn a new language, and who do so without the benefit of formal instruction. If they are postpubescent, they may well retain an accent of some kind, but they can pick up enough language to satisfy their communicative needs. In fact, some are natural acquirers who become highly proficient in this manner. In contrast, there are learners whose entire exposure to the new language comes in the form of classroom instruction in lexicogrammar. Yet they too achieve a measure of communicative proficiency, and certain of these learners become highly proficient as well. What we can infer from this is that humans are amazingly versatile learners and that some people have a natural aptitude for acquiring languages and will succeed no matter what the circumstances.

Of course, it is also true that for other learners, neither approach is entirely successful. Their language development may become arrested in an immersion environment, once their communicative needs have been met. For some, classroom instruction is unduly limiting. Perhaps a more important issue than whether to emphasize language use or language analysis in language teaching, then, is how to help all learners succeed to the extent they want or need. Moreover, we would hope to do so in a manner that improves upon or accelerates what learners are able to accomplish on their own. With regard to these aspirations, we can be less equivocal. We firmly believe that teachers will better prepared to meet their students' learning needs if they have a firm grounding in the grammar of the language they are teaching.

If the approach focuses on language analysis, the connection should be easy to make. The more teachers know about grammar, the more expeditiously they should be able to raise a learner's consciousness about how the language works. They should be able to focus learner attention on the distinctive features of a particular grammatical form in less time than it would take for the learner to notice them on his or her own. Teachers may accomplish this in an explicit fashion by giving students rules and exercises with the appropriate grammatical terminology, but they can also teach grammar implicitly as well.

Asking students to engage in particular tasks that require the use of certain structures is an implicit means of getting students to focus on and to practice form. In addition, a teacher might highlight properties of the grammatical structures by providing negative evidence—that is, helping students to see what is not possible in English. In this way, learners are encouraged to notice the gap between what they are producing and what the target language requires. Another example of teaching with an implicit focus on grammar is when teachers choose to "enhance the input" of their students by exposing them to language samples in which particular grammatical structures are highlighted or are more prevalent than they might be in ordinary communication.

However, even teachers who eschew implicit language analysis for their students— that is, those who favor teaching communication by having students communicate with no focus on form whatsoever—would be well served by their having a working knowledge of grammar. As teachers, they will have to answer students' questions about grammar; and any diagnosis of student errors or questions concerning whether or not to give feedback— and if so, what kind—will be enhanced by teachers' having a knowledge of how the grammar works. Indeed, even a communicative approach "involves a recognition of its [grammar's] central mediating role in the use and learning of language" (Widdowson 1988:154). Using language grammatically and being able to communicate are not the same, but they are both important goals. Thus, the language teaching field would be well served by finding a way to help learners accomplish both (Celce-Murcia 1992; Larsen-Freeman 1992).

A DEFINITION OF GRAMMAR SUITABLE FOR BOTH APPROACHES

THREE LEVELS INCLUDED

It is important, therefore, to define grammar in a way that suits both purposes—that is, a way that accounts for both the structure of the target language and its communicative use. In order to do so, we will need to take into consideration how grammar operates at three levels: the subsentential or morphological level, the sentential or syntactic level, and the suprasential or discourse level. Traditional structural accounts have dealt with grammar at the subsentential and sentential levels. For example, at the *subsentential* level, the level below that of the sentence, verb tenses have been described through the use of verb tense morphology. In the case of English, verb tense morphology consists of auxiliary verbs and certain suffixes or word endings such as *-ing*. Thus, we could describe the verb tense morphology of the past progressive tense in English as consisting of the past tense form of the auxiliary verb *be* and the *-ing* added to the base form of the main verb.

> *subsentential level:* past progressive = *be* (past tense) + base form of verb + *-ing*
> (*morphology*)   was/were + walk + -ing = was/were walking

At the sentential level such accounts would describe the syntax of the English sentence or its word order and show where the past progressive tense form of the verb would be located vis-a-vis the other words in the sentence.

> *sentential level:* One basic word-order rule in English is that verbs normally follow
> (*syntax*)   subjects and come before adverbials.
>
>   She was walking home from school that day.
>   subject   verb   adverbials

Sentence-level grammars would also indicate the placement of the *be* verb in questions. The tensed *be* verb is inverted with the subject to make a yes/no question:

Was she walking home from school that day?

They would also discuss the formation of negative sentences. In English the *not* follows the *be* verb and can be contracted to it:

She wasn't walking home from school that day.

This book, too, takes as its basic subject matter the morphology and syntax of English. However, whereas traditional structural accounts have often stopped at the level of the sentence, wherever possible we also include an analysis of how the morphology and syntax are deployed to effect certain discourse purposes at the suprasentential level. This level is particularly important in communication and is often overlooked.

suprasentential level: One discourse rule is that narratives often begin with the present
(*discourse*)   perfect tense as a "scene setter." Then the past and past progressive tenses are used to relate the specific actions that occurred in an episode.

She <u>has never been</u> so lucky as she <u>was</u> one day last May. She <u>was walking</u> home from
   present perfect   past   past progressive

school that day when she <u>ran</u> into a friend.
                    past

Although much is unknown about how English grammar operates at the discourse level, in this book we include what we do know and suggest research for what we don't.

ON THE NATURE OF GRAMMAR RULES

Probably the most common association with the word *grammar* is the word *rule*. In this book, we also use the term *rule*. But there are two qualifications we would like to make to the use of the term *rule* in connection with grammar. The first is that rules are not, as we shall see, airtight formulations; they always have "exceptions." While rules may serve a useful purpose, particularly in meeting the security needs of beginning language learners, it is important that teachers understand that almost every linguistic category or generalization has fuzzy boundaries. Language is mutable—organic, even; therefore its categories and rules are often nondiscrete (Rutherford 1987; Larsen-Freeman 1997).

The second qualification we make concerning grammar rules is that they often appear to be arbitrary formulations. For example, learners of English are told that it is possible to place a direct object after a certain kind of two-word, or phrasal, verb when the direct object is a noun, but not when the direct object is a pronoun. The asterisk before the second example is a linguistic convention used to indicate ungrammaticality:

I looked up a word in the dictionary. (Direct object *a word* is a noun.)
*I looked up it in the dictionary. (Direct object *it* is a pronoun.)

Such formulations do appear to be arbitrary; and yet, if one views this very same rule from a discourse perspective, we see that this rule is one manifestation of an important generalization concerning English word order, a generalization that we introduce first in Chapter 2 and then revisit throughout the remainder of the book. Therefore, at least some of the arbitrariness of rules disappears when we view language above the sentential level.

Another one of our firm convictions is that teachers (and consequently, their students) are helped by understanding English when generalizations can be made at the highest possible level of language. Indeed, what we seek to do in this book is to give *reasons, not rules,* for why English grammar functions as it does. Subsentential and sentential rules can sometimes appear arbitrary and make learning more difficult. Giving students reasons for why things are the way they are can aid students in learning English grammar, we believe. It also helps students see how grammar and communication interface, thus addressing, although not entirely solving, the common problem of students' not being able to activate their knowledge of grammar when they are engaged in communication.

THE THREE DIMENSIONS

Another major departure from some traditional analyses of English grammar, and one we feel is in keeping with attempting to view grammar with a communicative end in mind, is the recognition that grammar is not merely a collection of forms but rather involves the three dimensions of what linguists refer to as (morpho)syntax, semantics, and pragmatics. Grammatical structures not only have a morphosyntactic form, they are also used to express meaning (semantics) in context-appropriate use (pragmatics). We refer to these as the dimensions of *form, meaning,* and *use.* Because the three are interrelated—that is, a change in one will involve a change in another—it is helpful to view the three dimensions as a pie chart, with arrows depicting the interaction among the three.

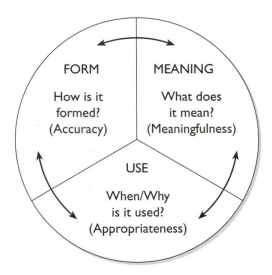

The question in each wedge of the pie provides further guidance in terms of defining what that wedge represents. In dealing with form, for instance, we are interested in *how* a particular grammar structure is constructed—its morphology and its syntax. When dealing with meaning, we want to know *what* a particular English grammar structure means, what semantic contribution it makes whenever it is used. Its essential meaning might be grammatical: for example, in our sample sentence, *She was walking home from school that day when she ran into a friend,* the past progressive signals a past action in progress. Or its meaning might be lexical (a dictionary definition); for example, the meaning of the phrasal verb *run into* used in our example means "to meet by chance."

Pragmatics, the domain of the use wedge of our pie, deals with issues concerning the choices that users of a particular language make when using the forms of language in communication. As such, it is a broad category. We use it in this book to mean the "relations between language and context that are grammaticalized, or encoded in the structure of a language" (Levinson, 1983:9). We can account successfully for the pragmatics governing the use of a particular grammar structure if we can explain *when* it is used or *why* it has been used instead of another structure with the same meaning. For instance, we would look to the use wedge of the pie to help explain why the narrator used the phrase *ran into a friend* instead of *met a friend by chance* (see Chapter 22). To elaborate on another example above, a pragmatic explanation would again be invoked to account for the difference between *I looked up a word in the dictionary* and *I looked a word up in the dictionary*, different versions of the same basic structure. ESL/EFL students need to know not simply how a structure is formed and what it means; they need to know why speakers of English choose to use one form rather than another when both forms have more or less the same grammatical or lexical meaning.

It is admittedly sometimes difficult to establish firm boundaries between the wedges in the pie, especially between the meaning and use wedges; as we have already pointed out, linguistic categories often have fuzzy boundaries. Nevertheless, we have found the three dimensions of the pie chart useful as a conceptual framework for teaching grammar. Since grammar does not deal simply with form, language teachers cannot be content with having students achieve a certain degree of formal accuracy. Language teachers must also help their students to use the structures meaningfully and appropriately as well. Thus, the three dimensions of form, meaning, and use make explicit the need for students to learn to use grammar structures *accurately, meaningfully,* and *appropriately.*

A PEDAGOGICAL GRAMMAR, NOT A LINGUISTIC GRAMMAR

In aggregating facts about accuracy, meaningfulness, and appropriateness concerning the grammar structures contained in this book, we have drawn from a number of different linguistic schools of thought. Whereas linguistic grammars strive for internal consistency, pedagogical grammars, such as this one for teachers, are eclectic. We feel that insights into the structure of English can be gleaned from different types of analysis. For instance, certain linguistic theories tend to be formal—most concerned with accounting for well-formed strings or sentences. They can be invoked for explaining sentence-level phenomena such as why the reflexive pronoun *himself* in the following sentence must refer to Paul and not to Steve. (See Chapter 16 for the explanation.)

> Steve said that Paul hurt himself in the lacrosse game.

Other theories are more functional, seeking to explain the occurrence of certain linguistic structures by exploring the communicative function they play in the organization of discourse. We had an example of this earlier when we looked at how the present perfect tense in English acts as a "scene setter." Since we are interested here in accounting for both sentential and discourse-level phenomena, we look to both formal and functional linguistic theories for helpful insights into English.

Then, too, linguistic grammars are often inaccessible except to those specially trained to work within a particular paradigm. We have tried to make available linguistic insights without requiring that our readers bring a great deal of linguistic background knowledge with them. We have adopted some formalism, however. For instance, in elucidating the form dimension we have employed our adaptation of transformational generative grammar trees. Although such trees are no longer as visible in the linguistics literature as they once were, we have found them to be a very effective parsing device in analyzing sentence-level syntax, and some linguists even claim that they describe sentences better than any other description of English to date (e.g., Lasnik and Uriagereka 1988:6). We also have turned to structural linguistics and corpus linguistics for observations relevant to the form dimension. For an understanding of the meaning dimension, we have drawn on insights in traditional, functional, lexical, cognitive, and case grammars. For the use dimension, our treatment comes from work in discourse and contextual analysis and in systemic functional grammar,[1] and again from corpus linguistics. In addition, many of the facts about English that we synthesize for each of the three dimensions originate with our own research and that of our students.

Finally, while many linguistic grammars go into great depth about a restricted set of structures, pedagogic grammars must be as comprehensive as possible in the number of structures they treat. We have tried, therefore, to cover the most frequently occurring structures with which ESL/EFL teachers have to deal in their classes. At the same time, we have been more selective about the amount of detail we include than a linguistic grammar might be. What we have compiled here is information that ESL/EFL teachers need in order to address the learning challenges of their students.

ACQUIRING SKILL AS WELL AS KNOWLEDGE

Many people are under the impression that the facts about a given language are all known. Nothing could be further from the truth. Much is not known about English, particularly at the level of discourse and in the dimension of pragmatics. Thus, one of the reasons we ask readers to work with the formalism and frameworks that we provide is to give them some tools to go beyond the facts presented in this book. We use linguistic terminology for the same reason. Besides giving us a metalanguage with which to investigate English, the use of linguistic terms will allow readers to consult reference grammars and other sources in order to augment their knowledge as new facts become known. We are interested, therefore, not only in readers' acquiring knowledge from our text but also in their developing the means to go beyond what has been presented here. Incidentally, the pie chart has been a useful tool for us personally in helping us expand our knowledge about English. We can map what we know about a particular grammar structure on a pie chart and create our own research agendas for what we don't know. Many linguistic conundrums await solutions. We call explicit attention to some of these throughout the text, and we encourage our readers to join us in the fun of trying to figure them out.

Before going on, though, it is important to underscore a point to which we alluded earlier. Grammar can be implicitly taught to language students. Therefore, the metalanguage and grammatical descriptions featured in this book are for teachers, who we hope will use them as aids in their teaching, not as the object of the teaching itself. What ESL/EFL teachers should be helping students do is *be able to use* the structures of English accurately, meaningfully, and appropriately. Thus, ESL/EFL teachers might better think of what they do as teaching **"grammaring"**—a skill—rather than teaching grammar as an area of knowledge (Larsen-Freeman 1991).

In the interest of balance, having said that grammar can be taught implicitly, let us also offer our view that the choice of ways of helping students use English structures accurately, meaningfully, and appropriately is contingent upon a number of factors, not the least of which are the learners' own particular cognitive styles. Teachers may help some students by giving them explicit grammatical descriptions and rules, but doing so may not help others. Our point here is simply that any explicit grammatical information should be a means to an end, not an end in itself. If a student can recite a rule but can't apply it, we will have failed in our "grammaring" efforts.

THE LEARNING PROCESS

No less important to language teachers than understanding the content of what they are teaching is an understanding of the process by which the content is learned. While it is beyond the scope of this book to treat the language acquisition literature in depth here (for books that do, see Larsen-Freeman and Long, 1991; Ellis, 1994), suffice it to say that with anything as complicated as language, it is not likely that the learning process will be a simple, invariant one. That is to say, we sincerely doubt that language acquisition could ever be accounted for by attribution to a single process such as habit formation or rule formation. On the contrary, it is intuitively appealing—to us, at any rate—to attribute language acquisition to a variety of processes, each of which is responsible for some particular aspect of language. For instance, we might hypothesize that habit formation or simple memorization plays a role in the acquisition of formulaic language (lexicogrammatical units such as "How are you?" and "I see what you mean"). On the other hand, hypothesis testing leading to rule formation is a plausible way to describe, although not necessarily explain, the acquisition of generalizations or principles that operate in the language, such as where to place *not* in an English sentence in order to express a negative message. While such attributions are speculative on our part, and we eagerly await the results of the concerted effort that is now being undertaken to research the efficacy of focusing on form,[2] we find the exercise useful for thinking about how one might go about teaching the three dimensions of language. Following the line of reasoning above, one might legitimately expect the different dimensions to be acquired through different means; therefore, it makes sense to think about using a variety of teaching techniques as well.

A MULTIFACETED TEACHING APPROACH

Please note that we do not argue simply for an eclectic teaching approach. Instead, we advocate a multifaceted approach—using different teaching techniques for teaching different aspects of the three dimensions. The choice will be conditioned by the learning challenge. For instance, what we are trying to achieve when we are teaching learners some structural aspect of English is their being able to accurately produce that structure on their own. We submit that what would assist learners to be able to do so is abundant practice with the particular target form. We might even go so far as to say that *purposeful, not rote,* repetition of a particular syntactic pattern, such as having students play "twenty questions" to practice yes/no question formation, should be incorporated into a lesson on some aspect of form.

When working on some part of the meaning wedge of the pie, however, purposeful repetition might be much less important in bringing about the desired objective of having students be able to use a particular form meaningfully. In the place of purposeful repetition, we might recommend an activity in which students are given an opportunity to associate a particular form with its meaning. An example that springs readily to mind is the technique teachers often employ to have students learn to associate the meanings of certain phrasal verbs with their forms. The students first watch the teacher and then, later, perform actions themselves signalled by the teacher's use of certain phrasal verbs: *Stand up, turn around, sit down.* Such a simple introduction allows the students to forge a meaningful bond between the form of each verb and its meaning.

To practice the use dimension, the activity should require students to make some choice within a context and to receive feedback on the appropriateness of their choice. For instance, after being introduced to the pragmatic difference between *look a word up* and *look up a word*, students might be asked to fill the blanks in a passage, choosing between the two forms with *look up* as well as the two forms with other phrasal verbs. Further examples of the application of these pedagogical principles will be offered for each structure we treat in this book.[3]

The three previous examples and most of the others we present in this book are practice activities, appropriate to the middle "p" in the "three p" teaching sequence of *present, practice, produce,* which has long guided teachers of grammar as well as teachers of other aspects of language. It should be acknowledged, however, that with the evolution of more communicative approaches, not all teachers adhere rigidly to this sequence. For instance, it might be that the need to teach grammar arises only when teachers notice that students are struggling to produce (the third "p") a particular grammatical structure during some communicative activity. At this point, a teacher might choose to conduct a practice activity, with or without initially presenting (the first "p") the structure. Alternatively, many teachers today subscribe to the practice of discovery or inductive learning, letting students figure out for themselves the generalizations about a particular grammatical structure. Thus, one teacher might have students engage in some meaningful consciousness-raising task or practice activity first in order for the students themselves to induce the rule that another teacher, following a more traditional approach, might have presented initially.

THE SYLLABUS FOR THIS TEXT

We do not deal explicitly with issues of syllabus design in this text. The issue of learnability, or student readiness to learn a particular aspect of the target language, has important implications for the selecting and sequencing of content for ESL/EFL students. Unfortunately, not enough is known about learnability at this point to move us to endorse one sequence of grammatical structures over another, although we do know that students do not master all aspects of one form before moving on to tackle another. The process of language acquisition is not a matter of simply aggregating one structure after another in linear fashion. The process is a gradual one; and even when learners appear to have mastered a particular structure, backsliding may occur as their attention is diverted to a new learning challenge. Thus, it makes sense to recycle various aspects of the target structures over a period of time: revisit old structures, elaborate on them, and use them for points of contrast as new grammatical distinctions are introduced. It also makes sense to think of a grammar syllabus as a checklist rather than an ordered sequence. In this case, it would be a teacher's responsibility to see that students learn the checklist of grammatical items by the end of a given course or period of time, but the choice of sequence would be left up to the teacher and would depend on his or her own approach and the students' needs.

Nevertheless, because this is a text for teachers and because we are teaching *about* the language and not teaching the language itself, we have sequenced the structures with which we deal in an order corresponding to their increasing complexity. While readers may not choose to make their way through the book in a strictly linear fashion, they should be aware that material that appears later in the text often builds upon what has been introduced in earlier chapters.

WHICH ENGLISH?

Another issue for which we should make our assumptions explicit has to do with "which English" we analyze here. English is not a single uniform language. Instead, many dialects of English are spoken around the world. As native speakers of North American English, we have chosen to focus our analysis on this dialect, although we acknowledge that many "Englishes" are spoken elsewhere. Though there may be some grammatical differences among dialects of English, they share a significant central core of grammatical units and relationships that enables us to speak of the grammar of English. We also, however, attempt to call attention to major exceptions to the generalizations we make when they do not apply to other dialects, especially to British English.

But even within a particular regional dialect there is variety. What we describe here is Standard English. Which dialect of English is considered Standard English is really more the result of historical sociopolitical factors than linguistic ones. Thus, there is no inherently superior dialect. It is true, however, that those who can use the standard dialect of any language enjoy access to opportunities that others lack. This alone is a good reason for helping students in an ESL context become bidialectal if Standard English is not their native dialect.

Even within Standard English, we encounter variability. The fact of the matter is that language is both an abstract system and a socially constructed practice. As a social construct, it is fluid, changing as it is used (Larsen-Freeman 1997). Since our grammar is descriptive of what English speakers do, it must reflect the variable performance of its users. We report the variability where we have usage studies that reflect what native speakers judge to be acceptable.

Finally, this is not a prescriptive grammar. We are not prescribing what *should* be said. We are more interested in accounting for what native speakers of English *do* say. Prescriptive grammars tell us to say *It is I*, not *It is me*. They also tell us always to use *whom* in object position. A prescriptive grammar can be abused by those who insist on outdated conventions or those who try to tell others what a form ought to mean rather than the meaning understood in general usage. Nevertheless, we feel that prescriptive grammar has its place in formal writing, at least, and students who are preparing to take standardized examinations like the TOEFL will need to know the prescriptive rules. Thus, while our grammar is mainly descriptive, we will call attention, whenever possible, to different norms where there is an obvious conflict between description and prescription.

All this variability manifests itself most often in gradient, rather than absolute, judgements of acceptability; that is, certain forms sound more acceptable than others. This is especially true of spoken, as opposed to written, discourse. However, we do not want to leave readers with the impression that anything goes in English. Despite the variation, there is still consistency of intuitions among speakers of English about what they consider grammatical concerning core grammatical structures in English.

This leaves us to define what ungrammatical means. In this book we restrict the use of the term "ungrammatical" to mean unacceptable to native speakers of English. For example, only the last form in the following list is ungrammatical:

> He did not say anything. (Standard Dialect of English—prescriptive for writing)
> He didn't say anything. (Standard Dialect of English—descriptive of writing and speaking)
> He didn't say nothing. (Nonstandard Dialect of English)
> *He no say. (Ungrammatical)

The last item on the list, its ungrammaticality signaled with an asterisk, is characteristic of the "interlanguage" produced by many ESL/EFL students. Such utterances provide important clues to what those students have yet to learn in English.

DEFINING THE LEARNING CHALLENGE

It is not possible to teach everything about English to ESL/EFL students. Further, as instructional time is usually so limited, it is not even possible to teach ESL/EFL students all that is presented in this book. Students will need to learn it, but it doesn't all have to be taught. Where we have attempted to be comprehensive, within limits, ESL/EFL teachers of grammar will have to be selective. Teachers have to, therefore, choose what to focus their students' attention on, trusting that students will be able to acquire on their own other aspects of English grammar. Thus, it is important that teachers define students' learning challenges: What is it that students most need to learn about a particular structure that they will not easily pick up on their own?

Knowing something about students' native dialect or language is very helpful in defining students' learning challenges. However, we can't devote sufficient space in this book to report all the findings from contrastive linguistics. What we do is to selectively include information about language typologies—that is, how other types of languages differ from English.

Students' learning challenges will depend not only on what knowledge they bring of their native language or dialect but also upon what they already know about English. Since the most effective instruction builds on what students already know, ESL/EFL teachers should continually assess what their students know about English and know how to do in English.

It also helps to define students' learning challenges by knowing where English is inherently difficult. Difficulties often arise when forms are exceptions to paradigms, when they are infrequent, marked, nonsalient, when one form has many functions, when there are semantic overlaps among forms, when the linguistic behavior of forms defies easy generalization, and so on. We hope to contribute to teachers' knowledge about these learning challenges by providing relevant facts about the form, meaning, and use of each major morphological and syntactic structure of English. With regard to these facts, we have attempted to be as comprehensive as space permits. Knowing, however, that instructional time is so limited, we conclude our treatment of each structure by discussing what our experience has led us to believe are the most challenging aspects of that structure.

THE ORGANIZATION OF THE CHAPTERS

Each chapter includes our analysis of the form, meaning, and use of a particular grammar structure or cluster of structures and any other pertinent information. Following the analysis, we provide teaching suggestions that illustrate ways of raising students' consciousness about certain aspects of English grammar and providing the necessary structured and communicative practice. We label each of these activities according to the dimension—form, meaning, or use—it addresses. We also include exercises of two types: The first allows readers to check their own comprehension of the material presented in each chapter, and the second asks readers to apply what they have learned to teaching issues. An example of the latter type of exercise is one in which we list actual errors made by ESL/EFL students and invite readers to analyze the errors and then suggest ways in which they might help learners bring their production to closer alignment with the target use. We also include sample answers to the exercises in an appendix at the end of the book. The final feature of each chapter is a list of references that allow readers to explore further the structure in focus.

YOU CAN LEARN GRAMMAR!

It has been our experience that some readers approach the task of learning grammar with some trepidation. While we understand this feeling, we have learned that by carefully reading the material in each chapter and conscientiously doing the exercises at the end, each reader does develop a working knowledge of English grammar. Moreover, some actually come away from the experience believing, as we do, that learning grammar is fun!

BIBLIOGRAPHY

References

Celce-Murcia, M. (1992). "A Nonhierarchial Relationship between Grammar and Communication: Part II: Insights from Discourse Analysis." In J. E. Alatis (ed.), *Georgetown University Round Table on Languages and Linguistics 1992*, 166–173. Washington, D.C.: Georgetown University Press.

Ellis, R. (1994). *The Study of Second Language Acquisition*. Oxford: Oxford University Press.

Grammar Dimensions: Form, Meaning, and Use (1997). [1st ed. 1993]. Four volumes. Boston, Mass.: Heinle & Heinle.

Larsen-Freeman, D. (1991). "Teaching Grammar." In M. Celce-Murcia (ed.), *Teaching English as a Second or Foreign Language* (2d ed.), 279–296. New York: Newbury House/HarperCollins.

Larsen-Freeman, D. (1992). "A Nonhierarchical Relationship between Grammar and Communication: Part I: Theoretical and Methodological Considerations." In J. E. Alatis, ed., *Georgetown University Round Table on Languages and Linguistics*, 158–165. Washington, D.C.: Georgetown University Press.

Larsen-Freeman, D. (1997). Chaos/Complexity Science and Second Language Acquisition. *Applied Linguistics* 18:2, 141–165.

Larsen-Freeman, D., and M. Long (1991). *An Introduction to Second Language Acquisition Research*. London: Longman.

Lasnik, H., and J. Uriagereka (1988). *A Course in GB Syntax*. Cambridge, Mass.: The MIT Press.

Levinson, S. (1983). *Pragmatics*. Cambridge: Cambridge University Press.

Rutherford, W. (1987). *Second Language Grammar: Learning and Teaching*. London: Longman.

Widdowson, H. (1988). "Grammar, Nonsense, and Learning." In W. Rutherford and M. Sharwood Smith (eds.), *Grammar and Second Language Teaching*. New York: Newbury House Publishers/Harper & Row.

Suggestions for Further Reading

For readers who would like to investigate different schools of linguistic thought, we can recommend the following:

Allen, J. P. B., and H. Widdowson (1975). "Grammar and Language Teaching." In J. P. B. Allen and S. Pit Corder (eds.), *Papers in Applied Linguistics* (vol. 2), 45–97. London: Oxford University Press.

Brown, K. and J. Miller (1996). *Concise Encyclopedia of Syntactic Theories*. Amsterdam: Elsevier Science.[4]

Edmondson, J., and D. Burquest (1992). *A Survey of Linguistic Theories*. Dallas, Tex.: The Summer Institute of Linguistics.

Herndon, J. (1976). *A Survey of Modern Grammars* (2d ed.) New York: Holt, Rinehart and Winston.

For readers who would like to investigate different issues for teachers of grammar to consider, we recommend:

Bygate, M., A. Tonkyn, and E. Williams (1994). *Grammar and the Language Teacher.* London: Prentice Hall International.

Harmer, J. (1987). *Teaching and Learning Grammar.* Essex: Longman.

Holisky, D. (1997). Notes on Grammar. Arlington, VA: Orchises Press.

Larsen-Freeman, D. (forthcoming). *Teaching Language: From Grammar to Grammaring.* In *TeacherSource* series. Boston, Mass.: Heinle & Heinle.

Odlin, T., ed. (1994). *Perspectives on Pedagogical Grammar.* Cambridge: Cambridge University Press.

Rutherford, W., and M. Sharwood Smith, eds. (1988). *Grammar and Second Language Teaching.* New York: Newbury House Publishers/Harper & Row.

For teachers' books containing ESL/EFL grammar teaching activities, we recommend:

Celce-Murcia, M., and S. Hilles (1988). *Techniques and Resources in Teaching Grammar.* New York: Oxford University Press.

Davis, P., and M. Rinvolucri (1995). *More Grammar Games.* Cambridge University Press. London: Longman.

Firsten, R., and P. Killian (1994). *Troublesome English.* Englewood Cliffs, N.J.: Prentice Hall Regents.

Hall, N., and J. Shepheard (1991). *The Anti-Grammar Grammar Book: A Teacher's Resource Book for Discovery Activities for Grammar Teaching.* Essex: Longman.

Kealey, J., and D. Inness (1997). *Shenanigames: Grammar-Focused Interactive ESL/EFL Activities and Games.* Brattleboro, Vt.: Pro Lingua Associates.

Madden, C., and S. Reinhart (1987). *Pyramids: Structurally Based Tasks for ESL Learners.* Ann Arbor, Mich.: The University of Michigan Press.

McKay, S. (1985). *Teaching Grammar.* New York: Pergamon Press.

Pennington, M., ed. (1995). *New Ways in Teaching Grammar.* Alexandria, Va.: TESOL, Inc.

Rinvolucri, M. (1985). *Grammar Games: A Resource Book for Teachers.* Cambridge: Cambridge University Press.

Ur, P. (1988). *Grammar Practice Activities: A Practical Guide for Teachers.* Cambridge: Cambridge University Press.

For more information on the sociopolitical aspects of dialect use and how social power relationships motivate choices of linguistic form, see:

Fairclough, N. (1989). *Language and Power.* London: Longman.

For a useful summary contrasting English with a number of other languages, consult:

Swan, M., and B. Smith, eds. (1987). *Learner English: A Teacher's Guide to Interference and Other Problems.* Cambridge: Cambridge University Press.

ENDNOTES

1. For those who would like to know more about these various grammars, we have listed some references at the end of this chapter.

2. Although to us, of course, it is an oversimplification to talk about focusing on form without also examining the meaningfulness and appropriate use of the form.

3. Additional examples can also be found in Larsen-Freeman (1991) and the four-volume series for ESL students, *Grammar Dimensions* (1993; 1997), for which Larsen-Freeman served as series director.

4. We are grateful to Francisco Gomes de Matos, personal communication, for recommending this reference.

GRAMMATICAL METALANGUAGE

INTRODUCTION

The purpose of this chapter is to introduce you to a metalanguage—a language to describe language. For many of you, the words in our metalanguage will be familiar, and you may wish only to skim this chapter. For some of you, this chapter provides an initial exposure to some common linguistic terminology, and you may need to study it more closely in order to become familiar with the new terms. Learning the vocabulary of any new language, however, takes time. Be patient. These new terms will become more meaningful as you encounter them in context throughout the book as you explore the grammatical structures of English.

Some ESL/EFL teachers choose not to use grammatical terminology with their students, feeling that it presents an additional learning burden. Other teachers find that by using the terminology, they can call their students' attention to certain aspects of English grammar more efficiently; thus, they conclude that students' time spent learning the terms is a worthwhile investment. Then, too, some teachers find that their students are more fluent in the metalinguistic terms than they are! As we stated in the previous chapter, we do not want to give the impression that knowing the terms is knowing the grammar. Nevertheless, for teachers, knowing the terms can be helpful in several respects.

First of all, the terms provide a discourse, a way of talking about grammar, that helps in the conceptualization of grammar. Use of the terms also serves a referential function, providing a means to identify these concepts when referring to them subsequently. Finally, by learning the metalinguistic terms, teachers will have better access to the many linguistic resources available to them apart from this text.

In the previous chapter, we discussed the three levels of grammar we address in this book: subsentential, sentential, and suprasentential levels. We use this ternary hierarchy in introducing the metalinguistic terminology in this chapter.

SUBSENTENTIAL TERMINOLOGY

THREE CRITERIA: SEMANTIC, STRUCTURAL, AND FUNCTIONAL

It may surprise some readers to learn that even identifying standard parts of speech is an enterprise fraught with difficulty. Consider, for example, the standard definition of a noun with which many of you are familiar: "A noun is the name of a person, place or thing." This definition works for the nouns *Kevin*, *Cincinnati*, and *eraser*, but it becomes problematic when we think about a word such as *blue*. Those of you conversant with part-of-speech terms may immediately identify *blue* as an adjective since it is a descriptive word. But one could argue that *blue* is the name of a "thing"—a color—and is, therefore, rightfully a noun. The structural or descriptive grammarians, eschewing such traditional *semantic,* or meaning-based, definitions of nouns as the one just given, chose instead to identify word classes through their *structural,* or formal, characteristics: their position in a sentence, adjacent function words, if any, and their constituents. For instance, common nouns in English typically occupy positions such as the following and are preceded by function words such as *the* or *their.*

> The _____ was very amusing.
> Did you notice their _____?

As for the constituents of nouns, a simple noun like *book* is a minimal unit; there is no way to break it down further. As such, we say it has one *morpheme.* A noun like *books,* on the other hand, has two morphemes, *book* and the grammatical morpheme *-s.*

There are two grammatical morphemes that can be used to mark nouns in English. Countable nouns have plural inflections to distinguish between "one" and "more than one" (*boy* vs. *boys*), and all nouns can have possessive inflections (*girl* vs. *girl's*) to signal possession or a number of other meanings (see Chapter 16). In addition to plural and possessive grammatical morphemes, English nouns often have derivational morphemes that mark nouns derived from other parts of speech (see Chapter 3). For example, adding *-ness* to the adjective *sad* gives us the noun *sadness.* There are several dozen noun deriva-tional morphemes, although some are used only in a few words, such as *-dom* as in *kingdom* and *wisdom* (Roberts 1958), whereas others like *-ness* are frequent and productive.

Not surprisingly, relying on structural criteria for identifying nouns can create problems. Not all nouns have distinctive noun-like morphemes, and even when they do, the words don't always function as nouns; for example, *wilderness* does not function as a noun in the compound *wilderness park.* Furthermore, many of the words without distinc-tive morphology would also appear to belong to more than one part of speech, such as *fly* as a noun or a verb and *orange* as a noun or an adjective.

Due to the inadequacy of identifying parts of speech based upon semantic and struc-tural criteria, a third criterion is sometimes employed. Known as a *functional* criterion, it defines a part of speech by the grammatical function it plays in a sentence. For example, from a functional perspective, a noun is a part of speech that can serve as a subject of a verb in a sentence. Thus, in the following sentence we know in part that the word *glass* is a noun because it is the subject of the verb *is.*

> The glass is dirty.

The problem here is that a noun such as *glass* can precede a verb and yet not function as subject, but rather can function as an adjective without changing its form (cf. its adjective form, *glassy*) as in

> The glass ashtray is dirty.

As can be seen, then, none of these definitions are complete by themselves. They all direct attention to different characteristics of nouns: their common meaning, their form/position, and their grammatical function. It is therefore better to think of a partic-ular part of speech as being determined by a cluster of criteria. Most linguists now acknowl-edge that it is not simple to define even the most elemental building blocks of grammar, the parts of speech. A further complication for ESL/EFL students is that sometimes there are cross-linguistics differences in parts of speech, for example, the English adjective *tall* has a noun equivalent in many West African languages. Some linguists would even say that categorizing a word as a noun or a verb is impossible in isolation, apart from the discourse in which it occurs (Hopper and Thompson 1984). Teachers should take heart from the observation, though, that most learners have no difficulty identifying parts of speech inductively when they have become familiar with a variety of typical examples. Ironically, it is not the recognition of a word's part of speech that appears to be problematic—it is the definition of the parts of speech that is elusive. In order to be as thorough as possible, we use all three criteria in defining the following parts of speech.

PARTS OF SPEECH

The parts of speech are usually grouped into two categories: the major and minor word classes. The major word classes—nouns, verbs, adjectives, and adverbs—are termed "major" because they carry most of the content or meaning of a sentence. Such classes are also "open" in that new words are added as they are coined. The other category, the minor word classes, plays a more structural role in a sentence and each of its classes is more "closed," in that normally no new words are added. Classes in this category include, but are not limited to, auxiliary verbs, prepositions, pronouns, determiners, and conjunctions. These words are sometimes also called "structure" words or "function" words, or even "functors." To contrast the two categories, notice the difference between the following two sentences:

> With the function words (content words deleted):
> *The* _____ *for* _____ *the* _____ *in the* _____ .

> With the content words (function words deleted):
> ___ broom ___ sweeping ___ floor belongs ___ closet.

Clearly, the central message can be grasped better when the content words are left in than when only the function words remain.

However, it is prudent to be cautious here too. As you saw just a moment ago, grammatical definitions are often not so airtight as they first seem. This observation holds here, too, in the division between the two word classes. To start with, the minor word classes do convey some meaning. Furthermore, not all the major word classes are truly open. Only certain adverbs can be added to the adverb class, namely the "manner" adverbs, which usually end in *-ly;* however, other types of adverbs are rather closed to new members. Then, too, as you have already observed, many words appear to belong to more than one category. A word like *few*, for instance, may function as a determiner (*There were few objections*) or a pronoun (*There were few*), both minor word classes. In spite of these concessions, we will retain the convenient division here and describe the major word classes first, followed by the minor ones.

Nouns

As we have already treated nouns earlier when illustrating the three criteria of defining parts of speech, much of what follows will either recapitulate or expand upon the earlier discussion. The notional, or semantic, definition of a noun is as you have seen—a noun is the name of a person, place, or thing. Some linguists add "or idea" to account for abstract nouns such as *democracy, environment,* and *life.*

As we also noted earlier, nouns have endings or derivational morphemes that formally indicate that a word is a noun; recall the *-ness* of *sadness.* They also have grammatical morphemes or inflections for plural and possessive. In terms of their position, they are frequently preceded by determiners, such as articles.

As pointed out earlier, nouns serve functionally as subjects of verbs. They can also, however, be:

> direct objects of verbs: *He watered his <u>lawn</u>.*
> subject noun predicates:[1] *We are all <u>learners</u>.*
> object noun predicates: *They elected Ann <u>president</u>.*
> indirect objects of verbs: *Ann gave the <u>people</u> confidence.*
> appositives: *Albany, <u>capital</u> of New York, is located on the Hudson River.*
> objects of prepositions: *Troy is also located on the <u>Hudson River</u>.*
> vocatives: *Let me tell you, my <u>friend</u>, grammar is just plain fun!*

Not all these labels may be familiar, but your intuitions alone should be enough to convince you of the multiple functions that nouns fulfill.

Another fact worth knowing about nouns is that there are three types. By far the most frequent in occurrence are *common nouns,* or nouns referring to a kind of person, thing, or idea. Common nouns themselves are divisible into two subcategories: *count* nouns, which take the plural inflection (e.g., *farmers*), and *mass,* or *noncount,* nouns, which don't (e.g., *air*).[2] In contrast to common nouns are *proper nouns,* or names for unique individuals or places (e.g., *Kevin; Cincinnati*). Proper nouns can be singular or plural (*Kevin Smith* vs. *the Smiths*). A small number of nouns that refer to groups are called *collective nouns.* Collective nouns seem to differ from other nouns in readily being able to take either singular or plural verb forms, depending on the interpretation given to the noun—that is, whether it is seen as a unit (*The family <u>is</u> together again*) or as a collection of individuals (*The family <u>are</u> all coming for the weekend*).

To conclude this section on nouns, we should note that gender is not an important feature of English grammar as it is in other languages. Gender is only marked in certain pairs of English nouns (e.g., *actor/actress; host/hostess; widow/widower*) and is evident in some personal pronouns such as *she* versus *he* and *him* versus *her.*

Verbs

The notional, or semantic, definition of a verb is that it is a word that denotes an action or state of being. Verb morphology in English is richer than noun morphology. Four inflections can be used with English verbs:

1. *-s* of third person singular present tense verbs: *Sue jog<u>s</u> every day.*
2. *-ed* of past tense verbs: *She jogg<u>ed</u> yesterday.*
3. *-en* of the past participle: *He has se<u>en</u> the movie three times already.*
4. *-ing* of the present participle: *I am teach<u>ing</u> three courses this term.*

In terms of their position, verbs follow nouns and may be followed in turn by adjectives, adverbs, or other nouns, as depicted in the following sentences:

> The authorities
> }_____ cautious.
> }_____ carefully.
> }_____ the plan.

Functionally, adding a verb to a noun is enough to complete a sentence:

> Pauline snores.

We discuss a number of different semantic verb types in Chapter 7. Here we simply categorize verbs by what follows them syntactically. According to Chalker (1984), there are six types:

intransitive verbs, which take no following object: *Mavis <u>smokes</u>.*
transitive verbs, which require an object: *Doug <u>raises</u> llamas.*
ditransitive verbs, which take two objects (indirect and direct): *I <u>handed</u> Flo the fax.*
linking verbs, where what follows the verb relates back to the subject: *We <u>are</u> teachers.*
complex transitive verbs, where what follows the object relates to the object: *They <u>considered</u> the project a waste of time.*
prepositional verbs, which require a prepositional phrase to be complete: *Steve <u>glanced</u> at the headlines.*

Two qualities verbs have are tense and aspect. We devote an entire chapter to discussing these characteristics of verbs; therefore, at this point let us simply note that *tense* traditionally refers to the time of an event's occurrence (hence the present, past, or future tenses), while a typical *aspect* distinction denotes whether or not the event has occurred earlier (perfect aspect) or is still in progress (progressive aspect). To illustrate aspect, compare the following two sentences, where the *have* verb + the past participle of the first sentence signals that the action is complete and the *be* verb + the present participle of the second sentence shows the action is in progress, i.e., uncompleted:

John *has written* his term paper.
Now he *is studying* for his final exams.

To conclude our discussion of verbs, we should point out that verbs, too, are marked for number, but only with subjects in the third person singular in the present tense or with the verb *be*. In such instances, subject-verb agreement occurs, and the verb is marked to agree with the singular or plural subject noun. For example:

present tense, subject in third person singular
Josh *loves* chocolate.
She *mows* the lawn on Saturdays.

be verb agreement with subject
I *am* surprised that you said that.
Jack *is* making the punch.
We *are* baking brownies.
Lloyd *was* absent.
They *were* frightened by the storm.

We investigate subject-verb agreement in more detail in Chapter 4.

Adjectives

The semantic definition of an adjective is that it describes or denotes the qualities of something. Adjectives commonly occur between a determiner and a noun, or after *be* or other linking verbs, although they can also follow a noun. Many adjectives have no typical form, but certain derivational morphemes are associated with adjectives, such as *-able* (like*able*), *-ish* (child*ish*), *-ful* (thought*ful*) and *-y* (lazy) (Chalker 1984).

English adjectives do not agree in number or gender with nouns as they do in some other languages; however, certain of them have inflectional morphemes for comparative and superlative forms such as *happy, happier, happiest.*

The function of adjectives is to modify or complement nouns. There are two adjective types: *attributive*, which precede nouns, and *predicative*, which follow linking verbs.

attributive: *The <u>old</u> bucket sprang a leak.*
predicative: *He became <u>angry</u> at the very thought.*

The semantic contrast between attributive and predicative adjectives is discussed in Chapter 20.

Adverbs

Adverbs modify verbs and contribute meaning of various sorts to sentences. Particularly common are adverbs of direction, location, manner, time, and frequency.

> direction: *Jim pointed <u>there</u>.*
> location: *Isabel shops <u>locally</u>.*
> manner: *The choir sang <u>joyfully</u> at the ordination.*
> time: *<u>Soon</u> Rachel will retire.*
> frequency: *We visit our friends in Detroit <u>occasionally</u>.*

As you can see, adverbs are quite flexible in terms of their location. They can occur in a sentence finally, medially, and initially. *Manner* adverbs are the only ones with distinctive inflections; they usually take the *-ly* ending.

The primary function of adverbs is to modify verbs, as in the previous examples, but they may also modify a whole sentence, as in the following:

> *Fortunately,* they arrived home before too much damage had been done.

Traditional grammars also distinguish adverbs of *degree,* which modify adjectives and other adverbs.

> It is *too* early to plant a garden.
> Ben was *very* late to school.

In our grammar, such modifiers are called *intensifiers* because they signal the degree of intensity of the following word.

Finally, we should note that many phrases and clauses can occupy the same position in a sentence as single-word adverbs and can convey the same meaning as adverbs. Due to their function in the sentence, these multiword constructions are called *adverbials.* For example:

> direction: *Jim pointed <u>at the constellation Pisces.</u>*
> location: *Isabel shops <u>at the mall</u>.*
> manner: *The choir sang <u>as if it was especially inspired</u>.*
> time: *<u>Next year</u> Rachel will retire.*
> frequency: *We visit our friends in Detroit <u>every once in a while</u>.*

The above discussion of adverbs and adverbials concludes our survey of the major parts of speech. What follows is a more abbreviated introduction to some of the members of the minor word classes.

Pronouns

Pronouns refer to or replace nouns and noun phrases within a text (e.g., "*my aunt, <u>she</u>* . . .") or as direct reference to an outside situation (e.g., in response to sudden loud noise, I can say, "*What was <u>that</u>?*"). They occupy the same position as a noun or noun phrase does. There are many different kinds of pronouns: subject (*I, you, he, she, it, we, they*), object (*me, you, him, her, it, us, them*), reflexive (*myself, yourself, himself, herself, itself, ourselves, themselves*), possessive (*mine, yours, his, hers, its, ours, theirs*), demonstrative (*this, that, these, those*), and others. The forms within each category are distinguished by number, person (first, second, and third), gender, and in the case of the demonstratives, by number and proximity. (See Chapter 16 for a fuller discussion.)

Determiners

Older grammars make no special reference to determiners, incorporating them into the adjective word class. We will use the term *determiner* to refer to that special class of words that limit the nouns that follow them. Various types of words fit into this category: articles (*the, a(n)*), demonstratives (*this, that, these, those*), and possessive determiners (*my, your, his, her, its, our, their*), to cite the major ones.[3] They precede an adjective if one is present; otherwise, they are positioned directly in front of a noun.

I put *my* backpack on *the* front porch, and now I can't find it.

Prepositions

Prepositions connect words to other parts of a sentence and have a close relationship with the word that follows, which is usually a noun. Together a preposition and noun comprise a prepositional phrase. Prepositions are usually one word (*in, to, at*), but sometimes can be two or three (*out of, on top of*). Prepositions prototypically signal spatial relationships, but certain prepositions can also signal the grammatical category of *case,* which is often displayed in other languages through morphological means. Case depicts the role relationship between words. For example:

dative case: Marge gave a donation *to* charity. (The preposition *to* marks the dative ("receiver") function of *charity.*)

ablative case: The charity received a donation *from* Marge. (The preposition *from* marks the ablative ("source") function of *Marge.*)

More is said about the way in which prepositions assign case in Chapter 21.

Conjunctions

Conjunctions are words that join. There are *coordinating conjunctions,* such as *and, but,* and *or,* which join elements that are grammatically equal. For example:

Marianne *and* Diane wrote this book.
Diane lives in Vermont, *but* Marianne lives in California.

And there are subordinating conjunctions, which we call *adverbial subordinators,* such as *because* and *although,* which join a subordinate clause to a main one:

It was hard to write a book together *because* they live so far apart.
Although Marianne and Diane live far apart, they are still friends.

We realize that we haven't defined *clause* as yet, but we will do so shortly. However, before doing so, we should briefly deal with one other grammatical concept at the subsentential level, namely *phrase.* A phrase is a group of words that function together. For example, if you were asked to divide the following sentence into phrases, you would probably not do so as follows:

The impatient/customer was acting very/cranky by the/time he was served.

Our grammatical intuitions tell us that these words grouped this way don't work together. Conversely, the following division is much more satisfying:

The impatient customer/was acting very cranky/by the time/he was served.
—or—
The impatient customer/was acting/very cranky/by the time/he was served.

In the last two versions of these sentences, the words between slash marks somehow cluster together better. If we take the last sentence as an example, we have divided it into four grammatical phrases and a clause. What makes *he was served* a clause is the presence of a subject-verb relationship. Any construction containing a subject-verb relationship is a clause. We have already noted that a noun and a verb together are sometimes sufficient to form a sentence. What is the difference between a clause and a sentence, then? Clauses that stand independently as sentences are called independent, or main, clauses; clauses that cannot are called dependent, or subordinate, clauses. The latter are typically preceded by an adverbial subordinator. Thus, in the sentence *"Although they live far apart, they are still friends,"* the first clause is a subordinate, or dependent, clause, and the second is the main, or independent, clause.

SENTENTIAL TERMINOLOGY

SIMPLE, COMPOUND, AND COMPLEX SENTENCES

A *simple sentence,* then, contains at least one subject and one verb and can stand alone as an independent clause. Notice that in the previous example, *"they are still friends,"* could stand alone as a complete sentence, whereas the first clause, *"although they live far apart,"* would be a sentence fragment.

There are five basic simple sentence patterns in English:

subject + verb	*The building collapsed.*
subject + verb + object	*They bought a new car.*
subject + verb + indirect object + direct object	*She wrote him a letter.*
subject + verb + subject predicate	*Janet's my friend.*
subject + verb + object + object predicate	*She makes me happy.*

In contrast to a simple sentence, a *compound sentence* consists of two or more clauses of equal grammatical importance. As we saw earlier, a coordinating conjunction connects the two clauses:

He went to the party, but I stayed home.

One type of *complex sentence* contains a main clause and one or more subordinate clauses. We have just considered one example describing Marianne and Diane. Here is another:

Peggy frequently calls because she wants to stay in touch.

In this sentence the main clause, *"Peggy frequently calls,"* is followed by a subordinate clause, *"because she wants to stay in touch."* As you can see in these examples, subordinate clauses are often, although not always, introduced by an adverbial subordinator.

In the second type of complex sentence, a dependent clause is embedded, or included, in an independent clause. Embedded clauses can take the place of a subject:

That he didn't want to go to the ballet was obvious. (*It* was obvious.)

or an object:

I argued *that it would be a mistake.* (I argued *my position.*)

or even of an adjective:

The person *who was responsible for the accident* fled. (The person *responsible* fled.)

Thus, when we move beyond the simple or monoclausal sentence, three processes are at work: *coordination,* or the joining of two clauses of equal grammatical stature; *subordination* of one clause to another; and *embedding,* when a dependent clause is included within a main or independent clause.

SENTENCE MOODS

English sentences are said to display three main moods—*declarative* (sometimes called indicative), *interrogative,* and *imperative*—and two minor moods: *exclamatory* and *subjunctive*. Mood conveys the speaker's attitude toward the factual content of the sentence. For instance, the subjunctive mood can indicate a speaker's uncertainty or the hypotheticality of the propositional content, or meaning of the clause. In the following sentence, the subjunctive mood is signalled by the use of the base form of the *be* verb, rather than the inflected form *is.*

If that be so, I'll leave now.

It can also indicate that something is contrary to fact, or counterfactual, here signalled by the use of the *be* verb in its third person plural past tense form:

If I were a bird, I wouldn't eat worms.

Four of the five moods have sentence type counterparts (see below), but the subjunctive in English can be marked only by using a different form of the verb from the form ordinarily called for. Usually, the subjunctive uses either the uninflected base form or *were.*

declarative (statement sentence type): *Today is Tuesday.*
interrogative (question sentence type): *What are you going to wear to the party?*
imperative (command sentence type): *Pass the milk, please.*
exclamatory (exclamation sentence type): *What a beautiful autumn it is!*
subjunctive (here realized with the *were* form): *I wish I were going with you.*

It has been said that the three main options in the English mood system correspond to the three main communicative functions of language: telling someone something, asking someone something, and getting someone to do something (Allen and Widdowson 1975:75). We should not lose sight of the fact, however, that a sentence type does not necessarily match its function. It is possible to ask someone to do something using any of the following three types, even though the first is a more indirect way than the other two:

statement: *I am thirsty. I wonder what is in the refrigerator to drink.*
question: *Could you bring something from the refrigerator for me to drink?*
command: *Please bring me something to drink from the refrigerator.*

It should be mentioned that the three main sentence types have negative forms as well:

negative statement: *I am not thirsty.*
negative question: *Couldn't you bring me something to drink?*
negative command: *Don't bring me anything to drink.*

It is interesting to see that among these, the negative question, at least, is still capable of accomplishing the same function as its affirmative counterpart. As we will see later in the book, context will determine when affirmative and negative yes/no questions are used.

THEME/RHEME

English has a fairly fixed word order compared with many other languages; still, some variation is possible. For example:

(a) The Cub Scouts held the carwash despite the rain.
(b) The carwash was held by the Cub Scouts despite the rain.
(c) Despite the rain, the Cub Scouts held the carwash.

The question that should come to mind is this: What is the difference among these three word orders? The sentences appear to have the same propositional content, or core meaning, so what purpose does word order variation serve?

A helpful concept to draw on in answering this question is the distinction that systemic-functional linguistics, following the Prague School of Linguistics, makes between *theme* and *rheme*. According to Halliday (1985:38), the theme provides the "point of departure of the message." In (a), it is the Cub Scouts; in (b), the carwash; and in (c), the rain. In other words, the theme provides the framework for interpreting what follows. What follows is the rheme, the remainder of the message in the clause.

English, then, typically uses word order to assign the roles of theme and rheme. Since English is a grammatical subject-predicate language—that is, every English sentence is composed of two major constituents, a *subject* and a *predicate*—it is commonly the case that the subject in English will be the theme and the predicate the rheme, as in (a) and (b) (we explicate (c) later).

The Cub Scouts	held the carwash despite the rain.
The car wash	was held by the Cub Scouts despite the rain.
subject	predicate
(here the theme)	(here the rheme)

Other languages use different means for making the theme-rheme distinction. For example, Japanese and Tagalog mark the theme with special particles. In Chinese, referred to as topic-comment language (see Chapter 5), the topic establishes that with which the clause is concerned,[4] but does not necessarily correspond to a grammatical subject:[5]

| My back, | it hurts. |
| topic | comment |

Since English does not strictly forbid such word orders, in speech at any rate, and since English even has other topic-like ways of establishing the theme (e.g., *As for fundraising, I prefer bake sales to carwashes*), Chinese and Japanese speakers will need a great deal of practice with subject-predicate sequences in order to avoid overusing such structures in English (Lock 1996).

MARKEDNESS

As we have just seen, English too, can thematize something other than the subject. Such is the case with (c) above, where the adverbial prepositional phrase *despite the rain* is the theme. Linguists use the term *marked* to refer not only to such instances of thematization of nonsubjects but also to refer to any exceptions from what is very typical, very predictable. It is perhaps better to think of markedness as a continuum from structures that are unmarked, meaning that they are typical, to highly marked structures that are exceptional.

VOICE

We have not yet accounted for the difference between sentences (a) and (b) above. Both sentences have subjects that are themes; both have the same propositional content or core meaning. The difference between the two lies in their *voice*. Sentence (a) is in the active voice; sentence (b) is in the passive voice. Voice is another linguistic device that languages employ to allow for different constituents to function as themes. In the active voice the subject functions as the theme and is most often the actor or agent of some action, as *the Cub Scouts* in our example. In the passive voice, the thing acted upon by the agent—*the carwash*—has been made the theme. There are other differences between (a) and (b) as well, and these are dealt with in detail in Chapter 18 on the passive voice. For our purposes here, it will suffice to say that the selection of the passive over the active allows the speaker or writer to thematize noun phrases other than agents.

SUPRASENTENTIAL TERMINOLOGY

So far we have been discussing terms that are useful for describing subsentence and sentence-level phenomena. We turn now to introducing terminology that applies to the suprasentential, or discourse, level of language.

BACKGROUNDING AND FOREGROUNDING

It has been observed that in a discourse narrative, certain sentences provide *background* information while others function in the *foreground* to carry the main storyline. What often distinguishes one from another are their verb tenses. For instance, in the following narrative, the past tense is used for the foregrounded information, the present tense for the background.

> Yesterday I went to the market. It has lots of fruit that I like. I bought several different kinds of apples. I also found that plums were in season, so I bought two pounds of them. . . .

In this bit of discourse, the forgrounded past narrative is interrupted by the second sentence with a present tense verb. This sentence provides information, here a statement about the market, that is general background information to the story.

COHESION

Another quality of English grammar at the suprasentential level that we might illustrate with this simple narrative is the fact that texts, units of spoken or written language at the suprasentential level, have an organizational structure of their own. It is not possible to put the second sentence first in the above narrative, for example, and have it mean anything. For the most part, we can no more move sentences around in a paragraph (unless we alter them in some way) than we can move words around in a sentence without making some other modifications.

Five linguistic mechanisms that Halliday and Hasan (1976) point to in order for texts to have *cohesion* or structure at the level of discourse are the following:

> reference: *The boy wanted a new bike. One day he . . .* (*he* refers back to the boy)
> ellipsis: *A: Who wrote the letter?*
>   *B: Marty.* (The response *Marty* elliptically signals that Marty wrote the letter.)
> substitution: *I plan to enter college next year. If I do, . . .* (*do* substitutes for *enter college*)
> conjunction: *Peter needed some money. He, therefore, decided to get a job.* (*therefore* makes explicit the causal relationship between the first and second sentences)
> lexical cohesion: (here through synonymy): *He was grateful for the money he had been given. He slipped the coins into his pocket and hurried down the street.* (*Coins* refer back to *money.*)

REGISTER

Another concept that applies at the suprasentential level is *register*. We used the word *register* in this book earlier to mean the level of formality of language. While this is true enough, it is something of a simplification. According to systemic-functional linguistics

(Halliday 1994), register actually involves three variables: field, tenor, and mode. *Field* refers to the social activity in which the language is being used and what is being talked about. Field is reflected in choices of content words. *Tenor* is concerned with the roles and relationships of interlocutors. For example, one's choice of sentence type to express a request—declarative, interrogative, imperative—would be conditioned by the nature of the relationship between the person making the request and the person being asked to fulfill it. The *mode* refers to the channel of communication, whether the language is written or spoken and, with regard to the latter, whether it is face to face or more remote. Cohesive ties in a text, among other things, will be affected by mode.

GENRE

A closely aligned linguistic concept to register is *genre*. Genre, too, refers to linguistic variation. Rather than variation due to level of formality, however, the variation is due to the communicative purposes to which the language is put. For example, the language used in a scientific research paper is different from that in a recipe or a letter of recommendation. They differ in their patterns of words, structures, and voice. For instance, in the interest of leaving no room for ambiguity, a legal document is often characterized by "very long sentences containing numerous and elaborate qualifications (all those elements beginning *notwithstanding, in accordance with, without prejudice to,* etc.)" (Swales 1990:63). Teachers whose job it is to teach English for special or academic purposes know full well the challenge of teaching students the necessary patterned structure of a particular genre. It might be said that professional training (including becoming ESL/EFL teachers) involves learning to speak and write a particular genre so that one can join a particular discourse community as a full-fledged member.

GIVEN/NEW

We conclude this discussion of suprasentential features by revisiting the theme-rheme distinction, which was introduced earlier. While theme-rheme has to do with the structure of clauses, there is a close relationship between this pair and the way information is distributed among sentences in a text. A common pattern of development in written texts is to introduce new information first in the rheme of one clause and then to treat it as given information in the theme or themes of a subsequent clause(s). *Given* information is that which is assumed by the writer to be known by the reader. This assumption is made either because the given information has been previously mentioned or because it is in some way shared between the writer and reader. *New* information, on the other hand, is "newsworthy"—not something the writer can take for granted that the reader knows.

Take, for example, the first five sentences that begin the previous paragraph. The words *theme-rheme distinction* occur in the rheme of the first sentence. They are echoed in the theme of the second sentence. In the rheme of the second sentence, the notion of *texts* is introduced and mentioned again in the theme of the third sentence. In the rheme of the third sentence, the concept of given information is introduced. Given infomation is treated in the theme of the fourth sentence. In the rheme of the fourth sentence, the words *which is assumed by the writer* occur. The theme of the fifth sentence picks up on this rheme by referring to *this assumption.* In this way, the information flows from rheme to theme, from sentence to sentence, from new to given.

The tendency to place new information toward the end of a clause is called *end focus.* End focus occurs in spoken discourse as well, although speakers have other means at their disposal in speech for flagging new information. Information units in the spoken language are defined by the tone group. Each tone group has a syllable made prominent by pitch movement.

> I went to the movies with LUcy.

One syllable in each tone group, the tonic syllable, functions to focus the attention of the listener. While the focus is typically at the end, it need not be.

> I went to the MOvies with Lucy.

However, when the prominent syllable is in nonfinal position, one typically interprets the stress as contrastive, that is,

> I went to the MOvies with Lucy. (not to the concert)

But while given/new and theme/rheme are related, they arise from a different perspective. Halliday (1985:278) puts it this way:

> The Theme is what I, the speaker, choose to take as my point of departure. The Given is what you, the listener, already know about or have accessible to you. Theme + Rheme is speaker-oriented, while Given + New is listener-oriented.
>
> But both are, of course, speaker-selected. It is the speaker who assigns both structures, mapping one on to the other to give a complete texture to the discourse and thereby relate it to its environment.

The speaker's (writer's) choices are thus predicated on what has gone before and what is to come. In this way, the structure of a single sentence both contributes to and depends on the physical context in which it occurs and the discourse around it. As you will see throughout this book, discourse and grammar have this symbiotic relationship in that grammar with lexis (words) is a resource for creating discourse, while the discourse context shapes grammar to accomplish very specific communicative goals.

CONCLUSION

This chapter by no means previews all the terms that you will find in this book. Its purpose is to lay a foundation upon which you can build. We regularly add terms to those we have introduced here. As we do so, we revisit what has been introduced here and provide you with opportunities to reinforce the understanding you have thus far acquired.

EXERCISES

Test your knowledge of what has been introduced.

1. Write an original sentence or short text that illustrates each of the following concepts. Underline and label the following pertinent word(s) in your sentence.

a. noun	**e.** pronoun	**i.** phrase/clause	**l.** coordination	**o.** genre
b. verb	**f.** determiner	**j.** subject/predicate	**m.** subordination	**p.** register
c. adjective	**g.** preposition	**k.** simple sentence	**n.** embedding	**q.** given-new
d. adverb	**h.** conjunction			

2. Identify the part of speech (noun, verb, determiner, etc.) of each word in the following sentences. Use semantic, structural, and functional criteria as necessary.

   a. John and Paul were fighting.

   b. John gave Paul a black eye.

   c. The principal sent them to his office immediately.

3. List the three major moods in English and write a sentence that corresponds to each type.

4. Illustrate the fact that a pragmatic function, such as a request, doesn't always correspond to a particular sentence type.

5. Give an original example for each of the five ways that Halliday and Hasan (1976) give to describe cohesion in discourse.

6. It is said that the theme is less important than the rheme in terms of its information-bearing status. Explain why this is so.

Test your ability to apply what you know.

7. Rearrange the sentences in the following short text. What other types of changes do you need to make to re-create the coherence of the original?

> There are only two ways to get to Culebra. One is to fly from San Juan. The other is to take a ferry from Fajardo. Unless, of course, you know someone with a boat. If you do, it will be easy.

8. Choose one of the following genres: a newscast, a newspaper article, or an advertisement in a newspaper or on the radio or television. Can you identify any special grammatical or lexical features of the genre you have chosen?

9. Discuss the following in terms of their themes:
   a. Out of nowhere came a giant blue heron.
   b. I was given a gold pen by my parents at graduation.
   c. Concerning homework, I don't believe in it.

10. It is said that language acquirers, whether acquiring their native language (Gruber 1967) or their second language (Givón 1979), go through an initial stage in which all of their utterances are of a topic-comment structure. This has been reported to be true regardless of the type of native or target language. Collect some beginning learner speech data and see if you find this to be the case as well. Consult Fuller and Gundel (1987) for some more background.

BIBLIOGRAPHY

References

Allen, J. P. B., and H. G. Widdowson (1975). "Grammar and Language Teaching." In J. P. B. Allen and S. P. Corder (eds.), *Papers in Applied Linguistics*. London: Oxford University Press, 45–97.

Chalker, S. (1984). *Current English Grammar*. London: Macmillan.

Fries, P. (1996). "Theme and New in Written English." *The Journal of TESOL France* 3: 1, 69–85.

Fuller, J., and J. Gundel (1987). "Topic-Prominence in Interlanguage." *Language Learning* 37: 1, 1–18.

Givón, T. (1979). *On Understanding Grammar*. New York: Academic Press.

Gruber, J. (1967). "Topicalization in Child Language." *Foundations of Language* 3: 37–65.

Halliday, M. A. K. (1985). [2d ed. 1994]. *An Introduction to Functional Grammar*. London: Edward Arnold.

Halliday, M. A. K., and R. Hasan (1976). *Cohesion in English*. London: Longman.

Hopper, P., and S. Thompson (1984). "The Discourse Basis for Lexical Categories in Universal Grammar." *Language 60,* 4: 703–752.

Lock, G. (1996). *Functional English Grammar.* Cambridge: Cambridge University Press.

Reid, W. (1991). *Verb & Noun Number in English.* London: Longman.

Roberts, P. (1958). *Understanding English.* New York: Harper & Row.

Swales, J. (1990). *Genre Analysis.* Cambridge: Cambridge University Press.

Suggestions for Further Reference

Crystal, D. (1985). *A Dictionary of Linguistics and Phonetics.* Oxford: Basil Blackwell.

Frank, M. (1993). *Modern English: A Practical Reference Guide* (2d ed). Englewood Cliffs, N.J.: Regents/Prentice-Hall.

Gordon, K. E. (1984). *The Transitive Vampire: A Handbook of Grammar for the Innocent, the Eager, and The Doomed.* Times Book.

Leech, G. (1989). *An A–Z of English Grammar & Usage.* London: Edward Arnold.

ENDNOTES

1. In traditional terms, these have been called subject complements, and for the next function, object complements. However, we refer to them as *subject and object noun predicates,* reserving the term *complement* for embedded clauses of various types (see Chapter 31 on complementation).

2. Actually, nouns have more flexibility in number than this traditional distinction reveals (Reid 1991). See Chapter 4 for further discussion.

3. Here we deal with one type of determiner, core determiners. Other types are introduced in Chapter 16.

4. Although similar, theme and topic are somewhat different concepts (see Fries 1996).

5. Some languages, such as Japanese and Korean, readily use both options—subject/predicate and topic/comment.

THE LEXICON

INTRODUCTION

In this chapter we briefly treat the lexicon of English. The lexicon has been characterized as a mental inventory of words and productive word derivational processes. We take a considerably broader view of the lexicon; we consider it to comprise not only single words but also word compounds and conventionalized multiword phrases. Despite increasing its breadth, our treatment of the lexicon must be cursory, although some grammarians might even be surprised to find this topic included in a grammar book at all. Traditionally, grammar and lexicon were seen to be two distinct components of language, and indeed they still are treated as such in some grammatical theories. From a pedagogical perspective as well, vocabulary and grammar have usually been viewed as two different areas of language. We believe, however, that it is better to conceive of grammar and lexicon as opposite poles of one continuum, and for this reason, following Halliday (1994), we prefer to think in terms of *lexicogrammar.*

There are three reasons for our preference. First is the interlingual argument: that which is accomplished grammatically in one language can be realized lexically in another. For example, Warao, a language from Venezuela, attaches a grammatical inflection to a verb that corresponds to the modal verb *can,* a separate lexical item in English (Dixon 1991). Second, from an intralingual perspective, in keeping with our broader scope of the lexicon, we note that many multiword lexical units conform to the grammar of a language; that is, they adhere to acceptable word order. For example, in English the lexical order is always *by the way,* not *way by the.* Recent work in computer analyses of large corpora of English texts suggests that these patterned multiword phrases are basic intermediate units between lexis (words) and grammar (Nattinger and DeCarrico 1992). Third, when we focus on the extremes at the ends of the continuum, the dichotomy between grammar and lexicon seems to hold. For instance, at the grammatical end of the continuum we could place the function words, such as the preposition *of* and the verb *be.* At the other end we could assign content words, such as *garden* and *grow.* If we leave it at this, the distinction seems sensible. However, we soon see that the differences are really matters of degree, and intermediate examples are easy to find. For example, a preposition such as *in* would seem to have more semantic content than a content word such as *thing.* Content words vary enormously in their concreteness of meaning and in their semantic specificity (Langacker 1987). Furthermore, it is our position, articulated in the first chapter of this text, that grammatical units express meaning, as well as having form and use. This is no less true of lexicogrammatical units, as we shall show.

We treat lexical units at three levels: (1) that of the individual word and its components, (2) that of word compounds and co-occurrences, and (3) that of conventionalized multiword phrases. It is not our intent here to teach ESL/EFL teachers how to teach vocabulary. Many excellent books do so, and we include a number of them in our suggested references at the conclusion of this chapter. Nonetheless, it is important that teachers know what a lexicon would consist of in the model of English grammar we are sketching. As we illustrate in our text, most lexical items appear in the basic structure of a sentence before the application of any rules. This reflects the fact that certain grammatical constructions are compatible with certain words and that a given word must often be used in special grammatical constructions. There are a few exceptions to this generalization about words appearing in the base, such as the addition of *do* in negative sentences and in questions where no auxiliary verb is present and one is needed. These exceptions are discussed at the appropriate time in the course of this book.

WHAT DOES IT MEAN TO KNOW A WORD?

A question we might reasonably pose to help us understand what is entailed in the lexicon is this: What does it mean to know a word? We might answer as follows. To really know a word, one needs to know its

- spelling (orthography)
- phonetic representation (pronunciation, syllabification, and stress [if multisyllabic])
- morphological irregularity (where applicable)
- syntactic features and restrictions (including part of speech)
- common derivations and collocations (i.e., words with which it co-occurs)
- semantic features and restrictions
- pragmatic features and restrictions

Consider, for example, the form of the word *child*. The knowledge of an English speaker would include its spelling, c-h-i-l-d, and its pronunciation, /čayld/. With respect to morphological irregularity, the speaker would need to know that the noun *child* has an irregular and idiosyncratic plural, *children*, which is not generated by the regular rules for forming plurals in English.[1] Syntactic features and restrictions would include the word's part of speech—a noun—and in particular, the fact that *child* is a common countable noun. Common derivatives include *childlike, childish,* and *childhood,* while common collocations include *child's play, child labor,* and *child psychology.*

Semantic information would include the concept *human* and also information indicating that the word is neutral regarding gender distinction. It would contrast the term *child* with similar terms for younger humans, such as *infant* and *baby,* and it would also contrast the word with parallel items denoting older humans, such as *adolescent* or *adult.*

Finally, from a pragmatic or use perspective, the speaker would be able to contrast *child* with other words with the same meaning—for example, an informal counterpart, *kid.* Notice that there is a pragmatic restriction on this form, however. While many speakers of English are quite comfortable using the plural version of this informal form, *kids,* they find that its singular form has a certain pejorative connotation:

> It's a snow day today. My kids are home from school. (acceptable)
> It's a snow day today. ?My kid is home from school. (questionable)

Many native speakers of English would prefer to use *son* or *daughter* or some other word when referring to one child.

Speakers of English use this lexical information in various ways. For example, we use orthographic information when we alphabetize words, phonological information when we make words alliterate or rhyme, and syntactic information when we match determiners and nouns appropriately. Here are some examples of the latter:

> this child   (not *these child)
> these children   (not *this children)
> many children   (not *much children)

Semantic information is used when we accept a lexical item in certain combinations as meaningful:

> The child slept for two hours.

But we reject it in others as nonsensical—at least in any literal sense:

> *The child evaporated two hours ago.

Semantic information also helps to distinguish among words with similar, but not identical, meanings. To truly know a word means to know both how it differs from and how it is similar to others. Pragmatic information is useful when we try to be sensitive to the appropriateness of the register of our lexical choices. It also helps us in the realm of usage—to identify patterns of words that collocate, or go together.

In order to truly know how to use a word appropriately in English, then, a speaker or writer would need to know much more than simply the general "meaning" of the word. We spend the next few sections looking at some of these attributes of words in more detail.

THE FORM OF WORDS

MORPHOLOGICAL AFFIXATION

Morphemes can be divided into two basic categories: freestanding words and morphemes that are bound or attached or affixed to other words. Each of these two major categories can be subdivided further into two types: those morphemes that have more lexical content and those that are more grammatical in function, although as we already submitted, the line between the two is sometimes hard to draw. The free morphemes with lexical content represent the major parts of speech: nouns, verbs, adjectives, and adverbs. The free grammatical functional morphemes include the minor parts of speech: articles, prepositions, and conjunctions, among others.

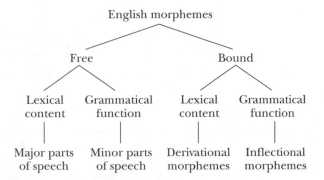

The bound morphemes consist of two kinds of affixes: derivational, which are more lexical in nature, and inflectional, which are more grammatical in nature. When a morpheme added to a word results in either a different part of speech or the same part of speech with a different lexical meaning, it is a *derivational* morpheme. Derivational affixes can be prefixes (e.g., <u>un</u>bend) and suffixes (e.g., argu<u>ment</u>). When the part of speech changes, as in our example when the verb *argue* becomes the noun *argument,* this is usually the result of adding a suffix rather than a prefix. We say more about derivational affixes in a later discussion of the productive processes of English word formation.

If a morpheme simply adds some element of meaning required by the grammar and changes the form of a word without changing its basic part of speech, then it is called an *inflectional* morpheme. An example of an inflectional ending would be the addition of *-ing* to the verb *watch* in *I am watching television*. *Watch* remains a verb after the *-ing* has been affixed, but the suffix adds a grammatical meaning, namely that the action is an ongoing one.

As you saw in the previous chapter, there are eight inflectional affixes in English:

Four of them involve verbs:

> present participle (*watching*)
> present tense—third person singular (*walks*)
> past tense (*jumped*)
> past participle (*eaten*)

Two are added to nouns:

> possessive (*John's*)
> plural (*books*)

And two of them come at the end of adjectives and adverbs:

> comparative (*clearer; faster*)
> superlative (*clearest; fastest*)

As you see, they are all suffixes. The only inflectional affixes that are not suffixes involve the irregular forms (plurals, past tenses, past participles, comparatives, superlatives), which can have internal vowel changes, no changes at all, or some completely different and historically unrelated (i.e., suppletive) form. For example:

internal vowel change:	*mouse* → *mice* (plural)
	ring → *rang* (past tense) → *rung* (past participle)
no change:	*one deer* → *several deer* (zero plural)
	hit → *hit* → *hit* (zero past tense and past participle)
suppletive form:	*go* → *went*; *be* → *was* (past tense)
	good → *better* (comparative) → *best* (superlative)
	bad → *worse* (comparative) → *worst* (superlative)

The pronunciation of several of the regular affixes changes depending upon the phonological environment in which they occur. The regular suffixes for plural, possessive, and third person singular, present tense, all pattern the same way:

	Plural	Possessive	Third person singular present tense
After /s/, /z/, /š/, /ž/, /č/, /ǰ/, the suffix is pronounced as /əz/	judges	Rose's	rushes
After all other voiced sounds, the suffix is pronounced as /z/	dogs	John's	runs
	toys	Jay's	cries
After all other voiceless sounds, the suffix is pronounced as /s/	cats	Mark's	walks

Similarly, the regular past tense and regular past participle suffixes (they take the same form) are pronounced /əd/ after /t/ and /d/ (e.g., *wanted, scolded*) but /d/ after all voiced sounds other than /d/ (e.g., *played, judged*), and /t/ after all voiceless sounds other than /t/ (e.g., *walked, kissed*).

SYNTACTICALLY RELEVANT LEXICAL FEATURES

Determiners/Adjectives Plus Nouns

Nouns, adjectives, and verbs all have syntactically important lexical features. Within noun phrases, determiner-noun restrictions are important because a few determiners co-occur only with uncountable nouns (e.g., *much* and *little*), other determiners co-occur only with singular countable nouns (e.g., *a/an, each*), and still others co-occur only with plural countable nouns (e.g., *these, many, few*). Note that some adjectives also co-occur only with plural nouns (e.g., *various, divergent*). There are, of course, also determiners that may occur with all nouns irrespective of countability or number (e.g., *the, my, his*). However, to ensure that only grammatical sequences are produced, the countability and number restrictions of all determiners and nouns must be explicitly stated in their lexical entries in the inventory of lexical items or the lexicon. Nouns have other features that influence syntactic behavior; for example, singular proper nouns referring to people (e.g., *John, Mr. Jackson, Albert Einstein*) do not co-occur with articles; however, common nouns referring to people do (e.g., *a man, the men, some men*). More is said about these matters in Chapter 15, which deals with article usage.

Adjective-Prepositional Phrase Restrictions

Adjectives that follow the verb *be* or some other copula are similar to verbs in that they may take objects (function transitively); however, unlike verbs, adjectives that take objects must have a preposition before the object noun. Some adjectives are inherently intransitive, which means that they are not usually followed by prepositions and noun objects:

> Joe is handsome.
> Mary is graceful.

Other adjectives are intrinsically transitive and cannot occur without an object:

> Sue is fond of sweets. (*Sue is fond.)
> John is related to Ralph. (*John is related.)

However, some adjectives can be used both transitively and intransitively without a change of meaning in the adjective itself—that is, the noun object limits the scope of the adjective but does not change its meaning. For example:

> Sally is nervous. Sally is nervous about the quiz.

All information about the transitivity or intransitivity of adjectives must be included in their lexical entries.

Verb-noun Restrictions

The most complicated lexical restrictions in English involve verbs. First, we must distinguish between verbs that take objects (i.e., transitive verbs) and verbs that do not take objects (i.e., intransitive verbs). This information is specified in the lexical entries of verbs.

The lexical feature (–transitive) for *disappear* and (+transitive) for *bring* allow us to accept these sentences as grammatical:

> The stain disappeared.
> The man brought a gift.

and help us explain the unacceptability of sentences such as these:

> *The drycleaners disappeared the stain.
> *The man brought.

Some verbs occur both transitively and intransitively with little or no change of meaning. These are ergative or change-of-state verbs, where the direct object in the transitive sentence is the same as the subject of the verb in the intransitive one:

> John opened the door. The door opened.
> Inflation increased prices. Prices increased.

These verbs would be marked (+/– transitive) in the lexicon.

There is also a special class of transitive verbs that permits the absence of a partially recoverable, understood noun object:

> Bill smokes cigarettes. Bill smokes.
> Harry drinks alcohol. Harry drinks.

Such verbs are, nonetheless, consistently transitive and would be marked as such in the lexicon with the added specification that a semantically recoverable object need not appear in the sentence containing such a verb. The semantic features of the partially recoverable object(s) must also be specified in the lexical entries of such verbs.

Finally, ditransitive, linking, complex transitive, and prepositional verbs (see previous chapter) all have qualities that would have to be indicated in the lexicon. For instance, the fact that prepositional verbs require an adverbial of location, direction, or a recipient (which can often be expressed either as a prepositional object or an indirect object):

> location: *The child lay on the bed.*   *The child lay.
> direction: *The boy headed home.*   *The boy headed.
> recipient: *I handed the note to John.*   *I handed the note.
>   (or, *I handed John the note*)

would also be indicated as a semantic feature of this category of verbs.

Co-occurrence Restrictions Involving Prepositions

Frequently, a verb or a transitive adjective must be followed by a particular preposition (e.g., *to rely on X, to distinguish X from Y, to be cognizant of X*). Similarly, a given noun phrase must be preceded by a given preposition (e.g., *in my opinion, to my mind, from my point of view*) and sometimes followed by one, too (e.g., *in lieu of, with regard to*). Whenever new words are introduced to ESL/EFL students, we recommend the prepositions with which they co-occur be introduced as well. With these and other co-occurring forms, ESL/EFL students will need a great deal of practice.

PRODUCTIVE LEXICAL PROCESSES

In addition to fairly structured lexical information such as we have given in the previous examples, the lexicon also contains rules governing three productive processes of English word formation; compounding, derivational affixation, and conversion. It is important to understand these as well, for these processes are responsible, in part, for new entries into the lexicon.

Compounding

Compounding, or putting together existing words to form a new lexical unit (*rain + coat = raincoat),* is a word-formation process that occurs in some languages. For example, the Germanic languages (this includes English) and the Chinese languages make rich use of compounding, whereas other languages make much less use of this process. According to the *Collins Cobuild English Grammar,* almost any noun can modify any other noun in English. Take the noun *house,* for instance. We have *household, housemate, house sitter, houseboat, house arrest, housebound, housebreaking, housebroken, houseguest, housefly, housekeeper, houselights, housewarming, housewife, househusband, housework,* and this list is not exhaustive, by any means. Many parts of speech can be combined in this way, sometimes ending up as one word, sometimes as two or more (e.g., *bathroom towel rack).*

Some of the most frequent English compounding patterns are:

noun + noun: *stone wall, baby blanket, rainbow*
noun + verb: *homemade, rainfall, lip-read*
noun + verb-*er: baby-sitter, can opener, screwdriver*
adj. + noun: *blackbird, greenhouse, cold cream*
adj./adv. + noun + -*en: quick-frozen, nearsighted, dim-witted*
prep. + noun: *overlord, underdog, underworld*
prep. + verb: *underestimate, undercut, overstep*
verb + particle: *makeup, breakdown, stakeout*

ESL/EFL students who speak a native language with little word compounding or with very different rules of word compounding may have trouble understanding and using compound words in English. Such learners may paraphrase and say "the sheet of the bed" instead of "the bedsheet" or may even reverse the order of elements in a compound and say "wine table" when they intend to say "tablewine."

As can be seen, the spelling of compound words proves a further complication because some are written as one word, some as two words, and some are hyphenated. Sometimes the same word is written in more than one way: *baby sitter, baby-sitter,* or *babysitter,* with the spelling as two words eventually coalescing into one compound word after a period of use. Students have to be taught to use their dictionaries when in doubt about the proper spelling.

Derivational Affixation

Earlier, we introduced the eight inflectional affixes of English. English words can also have derivational affixes, affixes that combine with stem (or base) forms to derive new words. Derivational affixes can be prefixes, which often change the meaning (<u>ex</u>patriate, <u>un</u>repentant), or suffixes, which usually change the part of speech of the word stem (wash<u>able</u>, child<u>ish</u>). In fact, it is possible for a word stem to have both a derivational prefix and suffix (<u>un</u>think<u>able</u>) or more than one suffix (govern<u>mental</u>).[2]

ESL/EFL teachers should help their students learn the most common and useful derivational prefixes (e.g., *anti-, bi-, inter-, intra-, pre-, un-*) and suffixes (e.g., *-able, -er, ism, -ist, -less, -ness*). This will help students expand their productive and receptive vocabularies. It is also worthwhile to spend some time on the common suffixes whose major function is to change one part of speech into another. For example, *-ous, -ary,* and *-ful* transform nouns into adjectives such as *famous, customary, successful;* and *-ness* and *-ity* transform adjectives into nouns such as *happiness* and *serenity.*

It should be noted, however, that which words take which affixes is not always predictable. Students will sometimes attempt a new form with a derivational suffix that does not work (*suggestment*) or will think that a word has a common prefix, when in fact the "prefix" is part of the root (e.g., *relay; resent*). There is also potential confusion (on native English speakers' parts as well) when having to choose between two words with different morphology that seem to be opposites, or at least different, but that actually have very similar meanings (e.g., *invaluable/valuable; slow up/slow down; admission/admittance; joyful/joyous*).

A final point to be made is that when both a derivational and an inflectional suffix are fixed to the same word, the inflectional suffix occurs last.

weaknesses   *weaksness

Conversion

The other important productive lexical process in English is conversion. This occurs when one part of speech is converted into another part of speech, without any derivational affixation. Most conversion in English takes place when the underlying verb has a very general meaning, and the meaning of a noun object (direct or prepositional) becomes incorporated into the verb to show that something has been (1) added, (2) taken away, or (3) used for something.

1. He put butter on his bread. → He *buttered* his bread.
   He poured water on the plants. → He *watered* the plants.
2. Jo removed dust from the desk. → Jo *dusted* the desk.
   I took the pits out of the dates. → I *pitted* the dates.
3. He cut the log with a saw. → He *sawed* the log.
   Sue gathered the leaves with a rake. → She *raked* the leaves.

This is a very productive process, and new words, or rather new functions for extant words, are always being coined. We recently heard someone say "That book was a good read!" and novel conversions often accompany innovations; for example, we now *e-mail* messages and *fedex* packages.

The example with *read* reminds us to mention that even though the dominant English conversion pattern occurs when noun meanings are incorporated into verbs, sometimes other parts of speech are involved. In the example, the verb *read* is nominalized.[3] In the following case, a prepositional meaning is incorporated into the verb:

Hal walked across the street. → Hal crossed the street.

HOMONYMY AND POLYSEMY

Finally, we should acknowledge here that sometimes words have the same form but different meanings, as in *bear* (an animal, to carry). With such homonyms, there is identity of spelling and sound, but it is possible to have identity with regard to only one of these. When it is sound, it is called *homophony* (*there, their, they're*), and when it is spelling, it is called *homography* (*wind blowing* versus *wind the clock*). Sometimes the part of speech is the same, but the meaning is different: <u>live</u> in *He lives* (= resides) *in Bangor* versus *He lives* (= is alive). In such cases, we have an example of *polysemy*, when one form with the same part of speech has a range of meanings.[4]

Homophones, homographs, and especially, polysemous forms represent problems for ESL/EFL students. Early on in their acquisition of vocabulary, students often adhere to the "one form, one meaning" principle. Since polysemous words are the most common words in the lexicon, confusion can reign. When students are struggling to understand a particular lexical item, sometimes it makes more sense to use a lower-frequency word to define it in order to avoid the ambiguity that can occur when using a word with more than one meaning. For example, we have found from our own teaching of beginning-level students, the polysemous adjective *hard* gets misconstrued, though the adjective *difficult* does not, when used to describe a question students find challenging.

An additional challenge in working with polysemy with ESL/EFL students is that sometimes a word in one language will share some of the meanings of the word in another language, but not all. Thus, a Spanish speaker learning English might be heard to speak of the *fingers* on his foot, as the Spanish word for fingers includes what English speakers have a separate lexical item for, *toes.* A related problem is the occurrence of *faux amis,* or false cognates—words that look as if they share the same meaning, but do not. For example, the French word *librairie* corresponds to *bookstore,* not *library* in English. These last two examples hint at the difficulties of relying on translation from the lexicon of one language to another. We will have more to say about this when discussing connotations of words.

THE MEANING OF LEXICAL ITEMS

As must have been apparent in part of our discussion of the processes of derivational affixation and conversion, and certainly in our explanation of polysemy, we have begun to cross the line from the form of lexical items to their meaning. In this section, we will first discuss other aspects of semantic features of words before turning to consider other issues involved with the semantics of the lexicon.

SEMANTIC FEATURES AND RESTRICTIONS

The information given in lexical entries also allows us to account for semantic well-formedness (or semantic incompatibility) in several types of constructions:

subject-verb:

1. a. The idea developed.   **b.** *The idea laughed.
2. a. The dog sneezed.   **b.** *The worm sneezed.

verb-object:

3. a. The harsh winter killed the plants.   **b.** *The winter killed the rocks.

adjective-noun:

4. a. The basement was mildewed.   **b.** *The government was mildewed.
5. a. The mare was pregnant.   **b.** *The stallion was pregnant.

We can account for the above incompatibilities in terms of a hierarchy of semantic features (going from low to high): common nouns are abstract or concrete, and concrete nouns are living or nonliving; living nouns are plant or animal, and animal nouns are human or nonhuman; finally, human and nonhuman animal nouns are masculine, feminine, or gender neutral.[5]

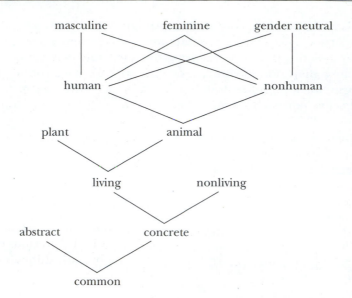

Our hierarchy is simplified, but it will suffice to demonstrate why sentences 1b through 5b are unacceptable. Nouns with features at the bottom of the hierarchy are excluded when a higher feature is required; for example, the verb *laugh* in 1b requires a human subject, so any noun lower on the features hierarchy is excluded semantically. Although not reflected in our hierarchy, it is probably necessary to divide nonhuman animals into higher and lower animals because dogs and horses can "sneeze" or be "intelligent" but worms and centipedes cannot (2b). Only living nouns can literally be killed, so that leaves 3b unacceptable; and only concrete (as opposed to abstract) nouns can literally be involved in action or processes such as falling, breaking, and mildewing, accounting for the unacceptability of 4b (although we admit it has appeal as a metaphor—see the next section in this chapter). Finally, the adjective *pregnant* modifies or describes a mature female animal, hence the unacceptability of 5b. All such semantic co-occurrence restrictions should be entered in the lexicon. The lexical entries of verbs must specify any semantic restrictions regarding the noun subjects and objects they normally take, and the lexical entries of adjectives must specify any semantic restrictions regarding the nouns they can modify.

Most of these semantic restrictions are probably universal and thus are not something we have to teach ESL/EFL learners;[6] however, they still constitute information that is included in the lexical entry of words and is part of lexical meaning. One of the most interesting things about these restrictions is that they are often violated in extension of meaning and figurative usage (e.g., *a pregnant pause, a broken heart*). And it is in these meaning extensions that languages differ.

MEANING EXTENSION

The lexicon is also where general processes of meaning extension should be described, since a great many word meanings are figurative or metaphorical rather than (or in addition to) being literal. Indeed, it is the deliberate violation of these semantic constraints that results in the rich imagery of poetic language. For example, the following examples show how descriptions of natural phenomena can be coded as actions without external agents or even as personified human-like action:

Nature as Action	Nature Personified
The wind blew.	The wind whispered.
The brook flooded.	The brook roared.
The saplings swayed.	The saplings danced.

Ascribing action and personification to nature represent common meaning extensions. Lakoff and Johnson, in their book *Metaphors We Live By*, show just how pervasive our use of metaphoric language is. For example the "container" metaphor is used frequently in English as a normal extension of meaning:

Literal	Metaphoric
Put it into the basket.	Put it into words.
He's in the garage.	He's in love.

Sometimes the same expression has both literal and figurative meaning, and the connection between literal and figurative use is not as obvious as in the previous examples. The nonobvious interpretation then becomes an *idiom*, a notoriously difficult type of lexical item for language learners:

> It's in the bag. (= the object is located in the bag)   *literal*
> (= the proposal is a reality/accepted)   *idiomatic*

Familiarity with the extensions of meaning, the metaphors, and the idioms commonly employed in everyday language (and also, of course, in fable, allegories, poems, etc.) can be a great asset to learners in acquiring a new language.

DENOTATIONS, CONNOTATIONS, AND CULTURAL ASSOCIATIONS

A word's *denotation* is its dictionary definition or referential meaning. For example, a cat is a feline quadruped. A *connotation* is the emotional association with a word. This association can be personal (as, for example, positive associations with the word for the month of your birth), or communal. With regard to the latter, Wierzbicka (1986) shows that while *only, merely,* and *just* all denote "It is not more than X" in the frame

$$\text{I am going to buy that pen. It is} \begin{Bmatrix} \text{only} \\ \text{merely} \\ \text{just} \end{Bmatrix} \text{50 cents.}$$

their connotations for English speakers are different. *Only* is more neutral, whereas *merely* is depreciative, and *just* is mildly positive. Another example from Wierzbicka shows this even better: the expression *just for fun* could be used as an advertising slogan, but *merely for fun* wouldn't work to sell much!

When it comes to the communal or shared connotations of lexical items, we can see how much our frame of reference influences the interpretations we give to words. Fillmore (1995) cites the tongue-in-cheek definition of *boy* from *A Feminist Dictionary*, compiled by Kramarae and Treichler (1985):

> **boy.** A male youth (cared for primarily by women) who is in training to support the institutions which state that his caretakers are kindly but otherwise inferior beings.

We can begin to appreciate how difficult it is to expect that a word in one language will have an equivalent in another. Wierzbicka (1988) points out that even concrete concepts such as *mouse* have culture-specific associations, determined by speakers' interests and attitudes as much as by any denotation. Although students will naturally resort to translating from their native language, as much as possible the lexical items of English should be learned in their own right and within context.

LEXICAL ASPECT: SEMANTIC CLASSES OF VERBS

Verbs in any language can be classified according to the type of action or state they describe (Vendler 1967). Some verbs, for example, are inherently punctual, such as *kick* or *hit*, meaning that the action is momentary, having no duration. Another category contains verbs that are inherently durative, such as *live* or *work;* use of these verbs implies that the action takes place over time. This semantic feature is often referred to as "lexical aspect," a topic we discuss in detail in Chapter 7, which deals with tense and aspect in English. What is significant about the lexical aspect of verbs is that they express different meanings when they combine with certain grammatical morphemes. For example, punctual verbs take on an iterative meaning when they combine with the progressive (*be . . . -ing*), whereas durative verbs take on a sense of "temporariness" with the progressive.

> She is hitting the rug with a stick in order to clean it. (repeatedly)
> She is working in Halifax for the summer. (temporarily)

We could cite many other categories of verbs in which the meaning of the verb affects other aspects of the sentence, such as what kind of complement structure—gerund or infinitive—follows the verb. We will deal with these categories as they arise in connection with particular grammar structures. For now, though, these observations should remind us of why the term *lexicogrammar* is an appropriate hybrid.

ARGUMENT STRUCTURE OF VERBS

Closely related to the noun-verb syntactic restrictions and the notions of transitivity we discussed above is the more semantic notion of "argument structure," a term used by linguists and philosophers to describe the number of nouns or participants (i.e., arguments) typically associated with a verb and the relationship that those nouns have with the verb. If a verb takes one argument, in English it is intransitive and the noun argument functions as the subject.

> *One argument:*   Milly jogs.

If the verb takes two arguments, one noun argument will function as the subject; however, the other noun argument could function as a direct object or as a locative prepositional phrase, or it could have some other role.

> *Two arguments:*   Lloyd drank the beer.
> Andrew lives in Richmond.

If the verb takes three arguments, one noun argument will function as the subject, one will function as the indirect object or recipient, and the other may function as a direct object; or the three arguments might function as subject, direct object, and locative prepositional phrase.

> *Three arguments:* Len gave me a book.
> Rhonda put the vase on the table.

Some arguments are optional. For example, a change-of-state verb like *open* must have as an argument the object that opens. Optionally, it can also have an argument that expresses the agent, or cause, of the opening:

> *One or two arguments:*   The door opened.
> John opened the door.

Finally, some arguments are inherent in the semantic structure of a verb but do not have to be expressed in a specific noun and can be interpreted very generally. For example, the verb *eat* always takes two arguments, but the direct object need not be overtly expressed:

> John ate a sandwich.
> John ate.

Fillmore's approach to distinguishing verb meanings (1968) shows one application of the notion of semantic features and argument structure of verbs that we have been discussing. Beginning with the following examples, Fillmore proceeds to elaborate the semantic distinctions that must be captured in the lexical entries of the verbs *touch, strike,* and *break.*

> **1.** Peter touched the window.   **3.** Peter broke the window.
> **2.** Peter struck the window.

Fillmore points out that *break* in 3 is different from *touch* in 1 and *strike* in 2 in that 3 has a related intransitive sentence that the other two verbs do not have—that is, one of the noun arguments is optional:

> **4.** *The window touched.   **6.** The window broke.
> **5.** *The window struck.

In addition, the verb *break* seems to require that its object be rigid, while *touch* and *strike* do not share this requirement. Consider these examples:

> **7.** Peter touched the dog.   **9.** ?Peter broke the dog.
> **8.** Peter struck the dog.

In 7 and 8, the dog can be a living animal, and the difference in meaning is one of relative intensity of impact: striking denotes a stronger, sharper impact than touching. In 9, however, the dog has to be an inanimate figure made of something breakable, such as plaster, ceramic, or glass.

Fillmore made several other useful generalizations about these verbs, but these examples demonstrate that understanding a lexical item entails, among other things, knowing precisely how it differs from other similar items. This brings us to the issue of semantic fields.

SEMANTIC FIELDS

As we have been attempting to show, words can often be really understood only in terms of their relationship to other words. On a very simple level, when an ESL student asks what *wet* means, perhaps the best explanation would be to use its *antonym,* or opposite, and reply, *not dry.* This explanation would not work, of course, unless the student knew the meaning of the antonym.

Another concept that is helpful in defining words in relation to other words is the concept of *semantic field,* a cluster of words that cover a particular semantic area and can best be understood in relation to one another. Examples of semantic fields most often cited are kinship terms and terms for colors in a language. The precise meaning of a color word can best be understood by seeing it in relation to other words that cover the spectrum.

Even though defining colors is difficult, as there isn't necessarily a one-to-one correspondence between languages, they can be illustrated more easily than words in other semantic fields. Take, for example, adjectives denoting physical attractiveness (*beautiful, lovely, pretty, attractive, good-looking, handsome,* etc.), items from the same semantic field, which therefore have some features in common. We could apply a semantic feature analysis (also called a componential analysis) by listing the features across the horizontal axis of a grid and the words belonging to the same semantic field along the vertical axis.

TABLE 3.1 A SEMANTIC FEATURE ANALYSIS	making a pleasant impression on the senses	close to an ideal	suggesting relative smallness	suggesting feminity or delicacy	arousing interest
beautiful	X	X			
pretty	X		X	X	
attractive	X				X

Adapted from Gairns and Redman (1986).

Even this abbreviated analysis of the semantic features shows that we can to some extent become more precise about the meaning of a word. These three words—*beautiful, pretty, attractive*—are not synonyms. Such an analysis, modified for the sake of comprehension, may assist ESL/EFL students who ask about the differences among words in a semantic field. Still, even this level of precision is not very satisfying. While such an analysis can assist us in being able to detect differences among these items, it should also be clear that this type of discrete feature analysis can also be misleading. For one thing, we may not agree on the exact defining features of a word. For another, it may be impossible to pin down all the semantic nuances of a word in sufficient detail. Leech (1981) suggests that most words have "fuzzy" meanings.

PROTOTYPICALITY

To explore further the fuzziness of meaning, consider the notion of prototypicality. It is well known that mammals have certain characteristics: They are furry, they give birth to live offspring, and they nurse their young, for instance. And yet, it is also well known that certain animals are classified as mammals even though they do not meet all the criteria (e.g., a platypus lays eggs but is considered a mammal). As Givón (1993) reminds us, membership in natural categories is not determined by rigid adherence to all criteria. Rather, membership is determined by a cluster of criteria. Further, some of these criteria are more central than others. Thus we might say that a bear is a more prototypical mammal than a platypus.

To take a linguistic example, there are many verbs of speaking: *say, tell, speak, talk, mention, remark, comment, shout, whisper,* and so on. Were we to perform a componential analysis of these verbs and others in their semantic class, we would find that some of the features are true of some of the verbs but not true of others. You saw this earlier with adjectives of physical attractiveness. We would also see, however, that some of the features are more central for membership in the class than others. For instance, that they all have to do with oracy is central, while the manner in which the oracy is performed is only encoded in two of the verbs and is therefore less central. If someone were to ask us to give an example of a prototypic verb of speech, we would most likely choose one of the first four on the list. We revisit the concept of prototypicality later in this book. As Lewis (1997) reminds us, considerations of prototypicality are very important when thinking of examples to give ESL/EFL students of a certain lexicogrammatical phenomenon.

THE USE OF LEXICAL ITEMS

You may be asking yourself why we have not yet mentioned true synonymy—two words with the same meaning. The reason is simple. Rarely will two linguistic forms mean exactly the same thing, for if they did, there would be little reason to have them both in the language. Thus, at best we can talk about partial synonymy. We do not mean to dismiss the use of synonyms, for giving a partial synonym is often the most efficient way of giving students the meaning of a particular word. It is important, though, to remain cognizant of the differences between words and, in the case of more intermediate and advanced students, to highlight the semantic differences. It is also true that what distinguishes words is not always their semantic differences; words can differ because of the area of their use: different dialects (e.g., British English *lorry* versus North American English *truck*); different registers (e.g., *friend* versus *buddy*); or they are age-graded, meaning that a certain age group will use them (e.g., adolescents using *cool* as an adjective of approval); or they are no longer fashionable (e.g., adolescents today would not accept *groovy* as a substitute for *cool*).

Whatever one learns about the meaning and formal requirements of a lexical item, one cannot ignore the context in which it is used. For example, Carter and McCarthy (1988) discuss the example of the word *stocking*, which takes on quite a different meaning when it refers to silk or nylon stockings as opposed to Christmas stockings. The former type of stockings are worn by women, but the latter type are worn by no one. They are simply stocking-shaped containers intended for small Christmas gifts or simply Christmas decorations attached to a fireplace mantle (or a wall or door).

COLLOCATION

Certain types of word co-occurrences that are governed by conventional use rather than form or meaning have long been studied under the label *collocation*. For example,

> adjective-noun: *a tall person or building* (not a "high" one)
> adverb-adjective: *statistically significant* (not "important")
> verb-direct object: *ask/answer a question* (not "say"/"tell")

Some collocations are more fixed than others: binomials, such as *high and dry, hat and coat,* and *pick and choose,* and trinomials, such as *a king's ransom, a handsome/pretty price,* and *a raw deal.* The difference between these fixed collocations and idioms has to do with the transparency of meaning. Idioms have meanings that are difficult to retrieve from the lexical items themselves (e.g., *kick the bucket* as a euphemism for *dying*), whereas words that go together in collocations still retain their lexical meaning. Collocations, therefore, should be decipherable, although here again it is probably better to think of them being on a cline—a continuum of idiomaticity (Fillmore, Kay, and O'Connor 1988).

Computer-assisted corpus research has demonstrated that a great deal of text in English is composed of words in common patterns or in slight variants of these patterns (Sinclair 1991). Gillian Francis (1996), reporting on the 320-million-word Cobuild corpus of British, American, and Australian English, claimed that researchers have identified over

700 patterns that are blends of lexical and grammatical elements. One such pattern, for example, consist of patterns with the verb *insist:*

> *insist (that)*
> *insist on*
> *insist on Verbing*
> *insist on Noun Phrase*
> *insist + quote*

One conclusion we can derive from this observation is simply that words don't occur randomly. Once you have chosen a word, you are severely limited in your choice of what comes next. The second point underscores what we have alluded to several times already. When it comes to performance, syntax and lexicon are intertwined.

Halliday and Hasan (1976) use the term lexical collocation in another sense. They refer to the expectation that other words will occur in a text (oral or written) once a particular word has occurred. Thus, if the word *professor* occurs in ongoing text, one might expect other words such as *lecture, university, teach,* or *publish* to occur. However, this is a much more general use of the term lexical collocation, and it seems to refer to related or associated vocabulary on a specific topic rather than the syntactically constrained collocations we have been discussing. One would expect the syntactically constrained collocations to appear as lexical information in the lexicon but not necessarily the more general topic-driven associations.

LEXICAL PHRASES, OR LEXICALIZED SENTENCE STEMS

Collocations are groups of words that occur together. Lexical phrases are also groups of words that co-occur; the difference is that lexical phrases serve specific functions. For example, the phrase *by the way* serves the function of enabling the speaker to shift the topic in discourse (Nattinger and DeCarrico 1992). As with collocations, some lexical phrases are more fixed than others: *at any rate* and *what on earth* are fixed; a phrase like *a _____ N [+ time] ago* is more open, allowing any noun of time (e.g., *day, week*) to fill the slot; also open is *as far as I _____* , allowing certain verbs such as *know* or *can tell,* to complete the lexical phrase.

While Nattinger and DeCarrico write of conventionalized form-function composites, Pawley and Syder (1983) use the term "lexicalized sentence stems" for regular form-meaning pairings.[7] They claim that English speakers know hundreds of thousands of such lexical units in which the grammatical form and lexical content are wholly or largely fixed but which are not true idioms.

Lexicalized sentence stems can be clause length or multiclausal:

Clause length:	What's for dinner?
	Need any help?
	You would ask that question.
Multiclausal:	I told him, but he wouldn't listen.
	Be careful what you're doing with that.
	If I'd known then, what I I know now . . .

In addition, according to Pawley and Syder, many semilexicalized (because they are less fixed) sequences possess permissible expansions or substitutions. In such cases, a formula can be extracted that consists of a nucleus of lexical and grammatical morphemes, which normally include the verb and certain of its arguments, as well as one or more structural elements represented by a category symbol such as TENSE, NP (noun phrase), or PRO (pronoun). For example, in the conventional expressions of apology for tardiness,

I'm sorry to keep you waiting.
I'm so sorry to have kept you waiting.
Mr. X is sorry to keep you waiting all this time.

a recurrent formula can be isolated together with a grammatical frame:

NP be-TENSE sorry to keep-TENSE you waiting

While lexical phrases and lexicalized sentence stems adhere for the most part to rules of English syntax, some are "extragrammatical" (Fillmore, Kay and O'Connor 1988) or "noncanonical" (Nattinger and DeCarrico 1992). Consider the phrases *sight unseen, all of a sudden,* and *so far, so good;* each has a grammatical structure, but not one predictable from the rules of English. Nevertheless, canonical and noncanonical phrases exist in other languages as well and perform the same functions as they do in English (Nattinger and DeCarrico 1992), so their existence and behavior should not come as a surprise to ESL/EFL students.

It has been known for some time that many beginning first and second language learners make use of large lexical units, giving them a fluency that they wouldn't ordinarily be capable of at such an early stage of acquisition. Bolinger maintains that a child learns collocations by hearing them in a variety of concrete contexts and later analyzing and abstracting the meaning of individual words (Bolinger 1976). Then, too, evidence suggests that by later analyzing the stock of formulas they have acquired, learners are able to induce the grammatical rules and regular patterns of the target language (Wong Fillmore 1976). In addition, no doubt, like native speakers of English, learners retain many of the lexical phrases and sentence stems as wholes because they conveniently fulfill certain functions or convey certain meanings.

DISCOURSE COMMUNITIES

We mentioned earlier the effect of cultural differences with regard to the connotation of words. Other linguistic differences have been viewed from a cultural perspective as well. For example, Atkinson and Ramanathan (1995) showed the disadvantage that nonnative speakers of English experience when their ESL writing instructors operate with a different set of cultural norms about what academic writing is than do instructors of writing classes for native speakers.

Other differences accompany divergent social practices or discourses (Gee 1990). Within each discourse community, certain norms exist concerning what constitutes appropriate ways of speaking or writing. For example, an educational adminstrator might say,

> *Prior to the administration of the assessment instrument, a skills-level analysis must be conducted to ascertain the critical level of preparedness of the target population.*

whereas a classroom teacher might say,

> *Before we give the test, we'd better find out if these particular students are ready for it.*

So, *assessment instruments are administered* and *tests are given.* The administrator's statement might seem wordy and obscure compared with the teacher's simple and direct way of saying the same thing. However, it is important to remember that language does not serve only to express propositional meaning. A particular discourse functions as "a sort of 'identity kit', which comes complete with [ways] to act, talk, and often write, so as to take on a particular social role that others will recognize" (Gee 1990: 42). Clearly, however, knowing a language is not simply knowing a phrase book.

It would seem that when language is formulaic, lexical items and conventions of use (i.e., collocations and lexical phrases) appear to be extremely important, whereas when language is more original and less formulaic, where precision and disambiguation are crucial, then the grammatical end of the continuum is more important than the lexical. As Nyyssönen (1995) notes, it follows that if the learner could make appropriate and effective use of the collocations and lexical phrases that are routinely employed by native speakers in large quantities, and if the learner could also make use of grammar to adapt the patterns as necessary and to achieve contextual fit, his or her language acquisition process would be well served.

CONCLUSION

The information that nonnative speakers of English must master regarding the lexicon is extensive. It is not sufficient simply to know many lexical items and their general meanings. For each item, nonnative speakers must master a network of related information about its form, meaning, and use if they wish to use the item accurately, meaningfully, and appropriately. Also, clearly, we can no longer think of the lexicon as a list of words having specified properties subject to combinatory rules. We must think of the lexicon as being composed of multiword units as well.

Despite the complexity of what we have presented here, we must introduce yet another level of difficulty. We have treated the lexicon as a static inventory. In fact, the lexicon is anything but static. It has been estimated that English increases by about 20,000 words annually. At a more local level, it has also been argued that many of the features and constraints that we have treated here as part of a lexical item, are in fact, mutable in dynamic discourse. For example, Thompson and Hopper (1997) have asserted that argument structure isn't a fixed property of predicates in the mental lexicon but rather is fluid and adaptable to conversational goals. Clearly, language is both product and process. While we deal more with language as product in this book, we acknowledge that both perspectives are necessary, and so we return to consider the dynamism of language at several points further on in this book.

TEACHING SUGGESTIONS

1. Form. When teaching vocabulary, it is good not just to teach words but to teach clusters of information that will help students to use the words correctly. For example: use *a/an* when introducing countable nouns (e.g., *a theory*); use *to* when introducing verbs (e.g., *to arrive*); show that verbs are transitive by adding an indefinite object such as *something* (*to propose something*); and use *to be* when introducing adjectives (e.g., *to be naive*). Also indicate any prepositions needed, where relevant (e.g., *to be interested in something*).

2. Form. Recommend to students that they use good learners' dictionaries to find grammatical information themselves. In addition, dictionary activities can ask students to find collocations either from the grammatical column of the *Collins Cobuild Dictionary* or from the examples in other dictionaries.
   a. Find two adjectives that can go before the noun *tone*.
   b. What two prepositions can be used after the noun *rejection*?
   c. Is *arouse* a transitive or intransitive verb? Find three nouns that go before or after the verb *arouse*.

3. Form. Nation (1990: 151) suggests an inductive method to draw students' attention to the form of words, using exercises like the following:
   a. Look at the word *insanity* in this sentence. What part of speech is it? Is it countable or uncountable? How do you know this?

He saw the beginning of insanity in her.

b. Look at *inhabit* in this sentence. What part of speech is it followed by?

Woodpeckers inhabit hollow trees.

4. Form. Low-intermediate ESL/EFL students often confuse the related forms of a word associated with different parts of speech. If a new vocabulary item has related forms in other parts of speech, these words should also be introduced with example sentences that make the parts of speech easily distinguished but that make the learner actively discriminate with the fill-in-the-blank process. For example:

a theory   to theorize   to be theoretical

Cynthia is very (1) _____ about everything. She has just developed a new (2) _____. She (3) _____ that the less one works, the more one will succeed at certain tasks.

5. Meaning. To encourage students to use productive word-formation processes that have been introduced to them, contextualized definition exercises such as the following can be useful:

   a. A _____ is a machine that detects smoke in a home, school, or office building and sounds an alarm.
   b. Someone who believes in and follows the ideas of Marx is called a _____.
   c. A person who employs others is an (1) _____; a person who is employed by someone else is an (2) _____.

6. Meaning. Intermediate to advanced-level students often confuse related derivations that have the same root and are the same part of speech, such as the following adjectives:

various	discriminating	identifying	fortunate
varied	discriminatory	identifiable	fortuitous

Exercises that teach students to distinguish such forms provide contexts that call for one or the other, but not both, such as the forms *discriminating* or *discriminatory:*

   a. The minority students complained because they felt some of the school regulations were _____.
   b. I knew that I could trust his judgment; he has _____ taste in such matters.

Students should understand why the words have the same root and part of speech (i.e., what the similarity in meaning is) yet why the words are different (i.e., what the crucial distinction is).

7. Use. For more controlled work on collocations, McCarthy and O'Dell (1994:5) suggest using "word forks" or matrices, such as the following:
   a. word fork

   original
   brilliant
   unusual   } idea
   great
   excellent

b. matrix

	a car	a motorbike	a bus	a horse	a plane
to fly					+
to drive	+		+		
to ride		+		+	

8. Use. Norbert Schmitt (in Nation 1994:148) suggests a game of collocation bingo, in which the teacher reads out a list of words, and students have bingo cards containing words that collocate with the teacher's words. Students write the word they hear in the same square as a word on their card that they think collocates with it. The normal game of bingo proceeds.

9. Use. As a consciousness-raising activity, bring in, or have your students bring in, several texts, two to three paragraphs in length, that all deal with the same topic in a particular discipline. Guide students in conducting a search for lexical patterns that appear to be norms of the particular discourse community from which the texts come.

EXERCISES

Test your understanding of what has been presented.

 1. Provide an original sentence illustrating each of the following terms. Underline the pertinent word(s) or word parts in your example.

   a. verbs requiring a locative prepositional phrase
   b. determiner requiring a mass noun
   c. conversion
   d. change-of-state verb
   e. compound word
   f. derivational affix
   g. inflectional affix
   h. transitive adjective
   i. semantic field
   j. transitive verb
   k. verb with three arguments
   l. irregular plural
   m. lexical phrase
   n. durative verb
   o. verb-direct object collocation
   p. co-occurrence with a preposition
   q. adjective-noun collocation
   r. polysemy

 2. Why are the following sentences ungrammatical?
   a. *The burglar lurked.
   b. *It fascinated the alarm clock.
   c. *I don't like these book.
   d. *There have to be some breaksthrough soon.
   e. *Anyone who is a good friend must be trustful.
   f. *My favoritism is for coffee, but I also drink tea.

Test your ability to apply what you know.

 3. If your students produce the following utterances, what errors are they making? How would you make them aware of these errors, and what exercises would you prepare to correct them?

a. *I got many *informations* from the book.
b. **In* my point of view, I think that's a bad idea.
c. ?They are remodeling the streets.
d. *People living in the United States use *crackerfires* on the Fourth of July.
e. *Photography has *passionated* me since I was a child.
f. *Solutions to reduce birth rates, especially within developing countries, need to be met.
g. *Mr. Wilson was not aware *to* his daughter's problems.
h. ?*By pure fortune*, we met on the train.

4. How would you answer an ESL/EFL student who asks you what the difference is among the following verbs: *see, look, watch, stare, peer,* and *glance?*

5. How would you answer an ESL/EFL student who asks you why *pretty*, which has to do with beauty, is used with *soon*, in the phrase *pretty soon.*

6. How would you answer an ESL/EFL student who asked you what the difference was between *owing to* and *due to?*

BIBLIOGRAPHY

References

Atkinson, D., and V. Ramanthan (1995). "Cultures of Writing: An Ethnographic Comparison of L1 and L2 University Writing/Language Programs." *TESOL Quarterly* 29: 3, 539–566.

Bolinger, D. (1976). "Meaning and Memory." *Forum Linguisticum* 1: 1–14.

Carter, R., and M. McCarthy (1988). *Vocabulary and Language Teaching.* London: Longman.

Dixon, R. M. W. (1991). *A New Approach to English Grammar, on Semantic Principles.* Oxford: Clarendon Press.

Fillmore, C. J. (1968). "Lexical Entries for Verbs." *Foundations of Language* 4, 373–393.

Fillmore, C. J. (1995). "Something to Look at while Listening to Discourse Features of Dictionary Definitions." *ILA* 40, March 11, 1995.

Fillmore, C. J., P. Kay, and M. C. O'Connor (1988). "Regularity and Idiomaticity in Grammatical Constructions: The Case of *Let Alone.*" *Language* 64, 3: 501–538.

Francis, Gillian (1996). "Grammar and Lexical Patterning." Paper presented at the 11th World Congress of Applied Linguistics. Perspectives on Lexical Acquisition in a Second Language. Jyväskylä, Finland.

Gairns, R., and S. Redman, (1986). *Working with Words.* Cambridge: Cambridge University Press.

Gee., J. (1990). *Social Linguistics and Literacies: Ideology in Discourse.* Bristol, Pa.: Falmer Press.

Givón, T. (1993). *English Grammar: A Function-Based Introduction.* Amsterdam/Philadelphia: John Benjamins.

Halliday, M. A. K. (1994). *An Introduction to Functional Linguistics* (2d ed.) London: Edward Arnold.

Halliday, M. A. K., and R. Hasan (1976). *Cohesion in English.* London: Longman.

Kramarae, C., and P. Treichler (1985). *A Feminist Dictionary.* London: Pandora Press.

Lakoff, G., and M. Johnson (1980). *Metaphors We Live By.* Chicago: University of Chicago Press.

Langacker, R. (1987). *Foundations of Cognitive Grammar: Theoretical Prerequisites* Volume I. Stanford, CA: Stanford University Press.

Langacker, R. (1991). *Foundations of Cognitive Grammar: Descriptive Application*. Volume II. Stanford, CA: Stanford University Press.

Leech, G. (1981). *Semantics* (2d ed.). Harmandsworth, England: Penguin.

Lewis, M. (1997). *Implementing the Lexical Approach*. Hove, England: Language Teaching Publications.

McCarthy, M., and F. O'Dell (1994). *English Vocabulary in Use.* Cambridge: Cambridge University Press.

Nation, I. S. P. (1990). *Teaching and Learning Vocabulary.* New York: Newbury House.

Nation, P., ed. (1994). *New Ways in Teaching Vocabulary.* Alexandria, Va.: TESOL.

Nattinger, J., and J. DeCarrico (1992). *Lexical Phrases and Language Teaching.* Oxford: Oxford University Press.

Nyyssönen, H. (1995). "Grammar and Lexis in Communicative Competence." In G. Cook and B. Seidlhofer (eds.), *Principles and Practice in Applied Linguistics: Studies in Honour of H. G. Widdowson.* Oxford: Oxford University Press, 159–170.

Pawley, A., and F. Syder (1983). "Two Puzzles for Linguistic Theory: Nativelike Selection and Nativelike Fluency." In J. Richards and R. Schmidt (eds.), *Language and Communication.* London: Longman, 191–226.

Ruhl, C. (1989). *On Monosemy.* State University of New York Press.

Sinclair, J. (1991). *Corpus Concordance Collocation.* Oxford: Oxford University Press.

Sinclair, J., and G. Fox (1990). *Collins COBUILD English Grammar.* London: Collins.

Thompson, S., and P. Hopper (1997). "'Emergent Grammar'" and Argument Structure: Evidence from Conversation." A presentation at UCLA, May 9.

Vendler, Z. (1967). "Verbs and Times." *Linguistics in Philosophy.* Ithaca, N.Y.: Cornell University Press.

Wierzbicka, A. (1986). "Precision in Vagueness: The Semantics of English Approximatives." *Journal of Pragmatics* 10: 597–614.

Wierzbicka, A. (1988). *The Semantics of Grammar.* Amsterdam/Philadelphia: John Benjamins.

Wong Fillmore, L. (1976). The Second Time Around: Cognitive and Social Strategies in Second Language Acquisition. Unpublished Ph.D. dissertation. Stanford University.

Suggestions for Further Reading

For references dealing with lexical formation in English, see:

Adams, V. (1973). *An Introduction to Modern English Word Formation*. London: Longman.

Austin, J. L. (1962). *How to Do Things with Words.* Oxford: Clarendon Press.

Jackson, H. (1988). *Words and Their Meanings.* Longman: London.

Makkai, A. (1972). *Idiom Structure in English.* The Hague: Mouton.

Marchand, H. (1969). *Categories and Types of Present-Day English Word Formation* (2d ed.). Munich: C.H. Beck'sche Verlagsbuch.

Searle, J. (1979). *Expression and Meaning.* Cambridge: Cambridge University Press.

For a thorough analysis of what it takes to know a lexical item, see:

Fillmore, C. J., P. Kay, and M. C. O'Connor (1988). "Regularity and Idiomaticity in Grammatical Constructions: The Case of *Let Alone.*" *Language* 64, 3: 501–538.

For exercises to work with English affixes, see:

Farid, A. (1985). *A Vocabulary Workbook: Prefixes, Roots, and Suffixes for ESL Students.* Englewood Cliffs, N. J.: Prentice-Hall.

Yorkey, R. (1970). *Study Skills for Students of English as a Second Language.* New York: McGraw-Hill.

For a list of verbs and adjectives followed by particular prepositions, consult:
Clark, R., P. Moran, and A. Burrows (1991). *The ESL Miscellany* (2d ed.). Brattleboro, Vt.: Pro Lingua Associates.

For a list and treatment of prepositional clusters, see:
Frodesen, J., and J. Eyring (1997). *Grammar Dimensions: Form, Meaning, and Use.* Book 4. (2d ed.). Boston, Mass.: Heinle & Heinle.

For many examples of compounding patterns, see:
Bolinger, D. (1975). *Aspects of Language.* (2d ed.). New York: Harcourt Brace Jovanovich, 114–115.

For a list of conversational lexical phrases, see:
Keller, R. (1979). "Gambits: Conversational Strategy Signals." *Journal of Pragmatics* 3: 219–237.

For an example of a pedagogical approach in which words are grouped into semantic sets (groups of related words), take a look at:
Seal, B. (1990). *American English Vocabulary Builder 1 and 2.* New York: Longman.

For pedagogical issues dealing with the lexicon, see:
Carter, R. (1987). Vocabulary. London: Allen and Unwin.
Carter, R., and M. McCarthy (eds.) (1988). *Vocabulary and Language Teaching.* London: Longman.
Coady, J., and T. Huckin (eds.) (1997). *Second Language Vocabulary Acquisition: A Rationale for Pedagogy.* Cambridge: Cambridge University Press.
French Allen, V. (1983). *Techniques in Teaching Vocabulary.* New York: Oxford University Press.
Gairns, R., and S. Redman (1986). *Working with Words: A Guide to Teaching and Learning Vocabulary.* Cambridge: Cambridge University Press.
Hatch, E., and C. Brown (1995). *Vocabulary, Semantics, and Language Education.* Cambridge: Cambridge University Press.
Lewis, M. (1993). *The Lexical Approach.* Hove, England: Language Teaching Publications.
Lewis, M. (1997). *Implementing the Lexical Approach.* Hove, England: Language Teaching Publications.
McCarthy, M. (1990). *Vocabulary.* Oxford: Oxford University Press.
Nation, I. S. P. (1990). *Teaching and Learning Vocabulary.* New York: Newbury House.
Nation, P., ed. (1994). *New Ways in Teaching Vocabulary.* Alexandria, Va.: TESOL.
McKay, S. (1980). "Teaching the Syntactic, Semantic, and Pragmatic Dimensions of Verbs." *TESOL Quarterly* 14, 1: 17–26.
Seal, B. (1991). Vocabulary Learning and Teaching. In M. Celce-Murcia (ed.), *Teaching English as a Second or Foreign Language.* 2d ed. New York: Newbury House, 296–311.
Taylor, L. (1990). *Teaching and Learning Vocabulary.* New York: Prentice-Hall.
Willis, D. (1990). *The Lexical Syllabus.* London: Collins COBUILD.

ENDNOTES

1. The only way that English nouns are morphologically irregular is with respect to plural formation. Only countable nouns, of course, would exhibit such irregularity.

2. Multiple prefixes are unusual but not impossible: *antidisestablishmentarianism.* Note that this word has two prefixes but four suffixes.

3. Interestingly, Langacker (1991) notes that there is crosslingual asymmetrical pattern whereby it is normal in languages for another part of speech to be nominalized—that is, made into a noun—without any apparent change in meaning, whereas when a noun is converted into a verb, some new meaning has been added. As we have indicated above, the new meaning might be "add noun" (*to salt*), "remove noun" (*to weed*), "use noun as an instrument" (*to glue*), "turn into noun" (*to liquefy*), and so on.

4. It should be noted as a counterpoint that the lexicographer, Charles Ruhl (1989), argues that virtually all polysemy is an illusion. He means that if you get abstract enough you can find a single "general" meaning for each word, which holds regardless of context. We will return to this notion when we consider prepositions, and will thus explore it more fully in Chapter 21.

5. Sometimes English speakers will assign feminine gender to nonliving nouns such as cars, ships, and countries.

6. Although English speakers will attest to the difficulty of learning the gender assigned to nouns in other languages.

7. Thus, although we treat them here in the use category, like single-word lexical items, they can be characterized by form and meaning as well.

Chapter 4

The Copula and Subject-Verb Agreement

INTRODUCTION

GRAMMATICAL DESCRIPTION

ESL/EFL learners are exposed to the forms of the copula *be* and the third person singular inflection almost immediately in their earliest English classes or in any English-speaking environment they might be experiencing. The forms are superficially simple to describe and understand, yet they pose problems for learners at all levels. The copula *be* poses the greatest problems at the initial stage. However, research on L2 morpheme acquisition has shown that the third person singular present tense *-s* inflection causes persistent problems for learners even at more advanced stages of proficiency.

In this chapter we will take a close look at these problem areas. They will reemerge regularly in the following chapters; however, we felt that a detailed treatment at this stage would be wise, given the pervasiveness of the learning challenges that these forms entail.

FORM: THE STRUCTURAL ROLES OF BE

Be functions as an auxiliary verb as well as a copula, so we should first take stock of these two distinct functions:

$$\textit{Copula: John is} \left\{ \begin{array}{l} \text{a teacher} \\ \text{tall} \\ \text{in Boston} \end{array} \right\}.$$

Auxiliary: John *is* talking to Susan (progressive aspect)

The copula links nonverbal predicates (i.e., nouns, adjectives, and certain adverbials[1]) with their subjects and serves as a carrier for tense and subject-verb agreement; that is, in the present tense the form of the verb *be* reflects the person and number of the subject noun as well as signaling present tense: *I am, he is, you are,* and so on.

This structural function of *be* as a copula is distinct from the use of *be* in the progressive aspect, where *be* combines with *-ing* to make the action denoted by the main verb more limited (see Chapter 7). Auxiliary *be* always occurs in conjunction with another verb, and it is thus referred to as an auxiliary verb. The progressive aspect is only one of several auxiliary verb functions that *be* has. It is also an auxiliary element in the passive voice (see Chapter 18) and in a number of phrasal modals (see Chapter 8).

WHY THE COPULA *BE* IS DIFFERENT FROM OTHER VERBS

The rule for expanding the verb phrase makes a clear distinction between copular verbs like *be* and all other verbs in English. There are at least four very good reasons for making such a distinction. First of all, *be*, which is the most frequent verb in English, has more distinct forms with respect to person, number, and tense than any other verb in English. The traditional paradigm for *be* compared with that for a lexical verb such as *walk* makes this clear:

COPULA BE				
	Present tense		*Past tense*	
Person	*Singular*	*Plural*	*Singular*	*Plural*
1st	I am	we are	I was	we were
2nd	you are	you are	you were	you were
3rd	he/she/it is	they are	he/she/it was	they were

VERB WALK				
	Present tense		*Past tense*	
Person	*Singular*	*Plural*	*Singular*	*Plural*
1st	I walk	we walk	I walked	we walked
2nd	you walk	you walk	you walked	you walked
3rd	he/she/it walks	they walk	he/she/it walked	they walked

a verb like *walk* has two present-tense forms and one past-tense form:

> *Present:* walks—third person singular
> walk—all other persons and numbers
> *Past:* walked—all persons and numbers

The verb *be*, on the other hand, has three distinct present-tense and two past-tense forms. Some of the forms are more restricted in their range than others, and this is represented in the following diagrams:

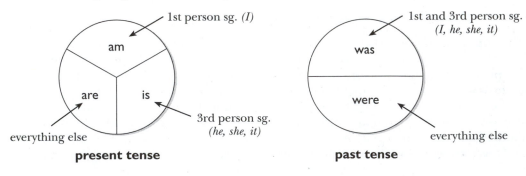

present tense   **past tense**

The multiplicity of forms explains why learners sometimes use the wrong form of the verb *be* in their speech or writing:

*You is late.   *We was on time.

Second, the copula *be* may be followed by adjective phrases, a defining characteristic that it shares with many other copular verbs (also called "linking verbs").[2] Although *be* is the most frequent and the semantically most neutral copula, there are three other types of copulas:

1. *perception copulas* (mental or sensory). The perceiver is sometimes expressed.

They $\begin{Bmatrix} \text{appear} \\ \text{seem} \\ \text{feel} \\ \text{look} \\ \text{smell} \\ \text{sound} \\ \text{taste} \end{Bmatrix}$ funny (to me).

2. *state copulas* (tend to take participial adjectives):[3]

They $\begin{Bmatrix} \text{lie} \\ \text{remain} \\ \text{rest} \\ \text{stand} \end{Bmatrix}$ protected.

3. *change-of-state copulas* (often only one or two adjectives go with a given copula):[4]

They $\begin{Bmatrix} \text{become} \\ \text{come} \\ \text{fall} \\ \text{get} \\ \text{go} \\ \text{grow} \\ \text{run} \\ \text{turn} \end{Bmatrix} \begin{Bmatrix} \text{tall.} \\ \text{true.} \\ \text{ill.} \\ \text{wild.} \end{Bmatrix}$

The copula *be* can be followed not only by adjective phrases but also by noun phrases and adverbial prepositional phrases (i.e., it is the grammatically most flexible copular verb):

Naomi is $\begin{Bmatrix} \text{attractive.} \\ \text{an actress.} \\ \text{in New York.} \end{Bmatrix}$

Most of the other copular verbs can be followed only by adjective phrases except for the change-of-state copulas *become*[5] and *turn*,[6] which can be followed by noun phrases as well as adjective phrases:

Naomi became $\begin{Bmatrix} \text{attractive.} \\ \text{an actress.} \end{Bmatrix}$

She turned $\begin{Bmatrix} \text{wild.} \\ \text{traitor.} \end{Bmatrix}$

Third, the syntactic behavior of the copula *be*, which behaves like an auxiliary verb and has operator function with regard to question formation (see Chapter 11), negation (see

Chapter 10), and other constructions, is very different from that of other verbs like *walk,* which require the addition of a *do* auxiliary as the operator if no other auxiliary verb is present.

Hal │is│ an engineer.   Hall walk│s│ to work.

│Is│ Hal an engineer?   │Does│ Hal walk to work?

Hal │is│n't a teacher.   Hal │does│n't walk home.

Like the main verb *walk,* copular verbs other than *be* take a *do* auxiliary in questions and negatives:

> Did he get taller?
> I don't feel well.

Finally, the copula *be* does not occur in all languages, but all languages have verbs. Especially in the present tense, many languages have nothing equivalent to the copula *be;* speakers of such languages simply express the literal equivalent of sentences like the three below, and this pattern readily transfers to English during their initial learning stage:

> *Hal engineer.   *Hal in next room.
> *Hal tall.

In sum, a verb is copular if it is followed by a noun phrase, an adjective phrase, or an adverbial that specifically predicates something about the subject of the verb.

MEANING

The lack of universality of the copula *be* is understandable if we consider that semantically it is not a necessary form; it is a linking element that carries tense—which can be marked only on verbs—and subject-verb agreement. In fact, children learning English as their mother tongue often omit the *be* copula in their early speech as do many second language learners of all ages when they are first learning English. Second language learners have been observed to omit the copula regardless of whether or not their native language has an equivalent form. All these phenomena are related to the fact that the copula *be* is a marked form.

However, we agree with Langacker (1991:65) that *be* is not merely a semantically empty grammatical operator, as some linguists have suggested. Langacker proposes that the meaning of *be* is primarily temporal and aspectual. It signals that an imperfective state is continuing through time as a stable situation. For Langacker, *be* is a true verb marking a stative relation. It is not semantically specific in any way regarding the relation between the subject noun phrase and the element following *be,* which may be adjectival, nominal, or adverbial (in the latter case, usually a prepositional phrase).

USE

Besides learning that sentences like the ones above with Hal require the *be* copula, the other use problem for ESL/EFL students is to realize that copula *be* does indeed function as an operator—it does not require the *do* auxiliary. Failure to recognize the special status of the *be* copula in the formation of questions and negative sentences sometimes results in errors such as the following:

> *Do they be happy? (for "Are they happy?")
> *We don't be teachers. (for "We aren't teachers.")

THE COPULA *BE* AS A LEARNING PROBLEM

For all the above reasons the ESL/EFL teacher must be sensitive to the problems that his or her learners will have with the copula *be*—especially if the learners are at the beginning level, since they may have a tendency to omit it. (For those students whose native language has no copula, this initial tendency will be even more pronounced.) The other problem, of course, involves use of the wrong form of *be*. Sufficient opportunity for meaningful practice can overcome both of these problems.

SUBJECT-VERB AGREEMENT

FORM

Third Person Singular Present

Standard grammatical treatments state that for verbs other than *be*, number agreement between the subject and verb (sometimes referred to as subject-verb concord) poses a problem only in the present tense, where third person singular forms are explicitly inflected while other forms are not.

NUMBER		
Person	*Singular*	*Plural*
*I*st 2nd 3rd	I speak French. You speak French. He/she/it (the parrot) speak-s French.	We speak French. You speak French. They speak French.

Some Typical Errors

Given the complexity of the choice, the beginning ESL/EFL learner tends to simplify and leave off altogether the third person singular inflection:

    *Sharon live in Seattle.   *Harry say he will come.

Occasionally, however, some learners will overgeneralize the inflection and apply it to uninflected forms, such as modal auxiliaries, or to verbs following modals (see Chapter 8):

    *Jack cans dance disco.
          or
    *Jack can dances disco.

They also may overuse it as an agreement marker with subjects of inappropriate person and/or number:

    *I
    *They } goes to Stanford.
    *You

Yet another reason why some learners overuse this form is that they interpret the *-s* ending as a plural marker on the verb to be used in agreement with plural subjects:

    *They
    *The boys } goes to the movies often.

Finally, it has also been observed that some Spanish speakers tend to initially overuse the verb + *-s* inflection with the second person singular pronoun because a similar form is used in their language when the subject noun reflects this person:

Spanish: Tu habla⌈s⌉ inglés.   *English:* *You speak⌈s⌉ English.

By far the most common error in subject-verb agreement is the first one we mentioned, that of the learner simply omitting the inflection for third person singular. Research in both language typology and second language acquisition can help us understand why this is so.

The languages of the world can be roughly divided into topic-prominent languages with pragmatic word order (e.g., Chinese, Japanese, Korean) and subject-prominent languages with grammatical word order (e.g., English, Spanish, Arabic); the former never mark subject-verb agreement, whereas the latter typically do. Thus it seems plausible that learners of English with a topic-prominent first language would find it more difficult to master subject-verb agreement than learners whose native language is subject-prominent like English. However, research in second language acquisition by Fuller & Gundel (1987) suggests that most learners pass through an early topic-prominent stage regardless of their first language. In analyzing the elicited oral narratives produced by low-intermediate learners of English, these researchers found no significant differences between native speakers of topic-prominent languages and those of subject-prominent languages in their use of subject-verb agreement in English. Most of their nonnative speakers made more than 10 errors demonstrating lack of agreement. Yet since speakers of topic-prominent languages are not prepared by their first language to expect the relationship between subject and verb to be marked in any way, it is likely to take them longer to master subject-verb agreement in English than speakers of subject-prominent languages. Further research is needed to see if this hypothesis is correct.

Agreement errors may be due to phonological or perceptual factors rather than syntactic or morphological differences. ESL/EFL teachers should be aware of the fact that some learners of English fully understand the third person singular present ending and can even produce it systematically when they write in English; however, they omit it frequently when they are speaking. One reason for this is because the sound system of their native language tends not to permit final /s/ sounds in particular or final consonants in general. Speakers of French and a variety of other languages have been observed to do this when speaking English.

Of course, other reasons for the slow and late acquisition of the third person singular present inflection on the verb—even when there is no phonological interference from the learner's native language—might be its lack of perceptual saliency[7] and its low frequency of occurrence in native speaker speech (Larsen-Freeman, 1976). The third person singular present tense inflection tends to be omitted for these reasons as well. Also, it is the only inflection in the present tense and has little communicative utility since the person/number is almost always clear from the subject noun phrase, just as it is with the other persons and numbers that do not take any inflection.

MEANING

Problems in Subject and Verb Number Choice

Whereas some cases of subject and verb number choice are puzzling mainly to nonnative speakers, several cases cause difficulty for native and nonnative speakers alike. We will now review many of the problematic areas in subject and verb number choice along with the more predictable and obvious rules.

The General Rule

In the most straightforward cases, the subject and verb number choice will agree: In the present tense we use the third person singular inflection (-*s* or the *be* form *is*) if the subject refers to one entity, whether it is a singular proper name, a singular common noun, a non-count noun, or a third person singular pronoun. Elsewhere—for nouns or pronouns referring to more than one entity[8] or for first or second person pronouns referring to one entity—no inflection is used in the present tense:

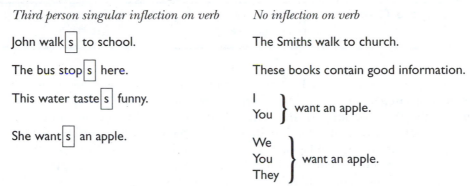

Third person singular inflection on verb   *No inflection on verb*

John walk s to school.   The Smiths walk to church.

The bus stop s here.   These books contain good information.

This water taste s funny.

She want s an apple.

To this formulation we should add that if the predicate of the sentence begins with an inflectable, tense-bearing auxiliary verb such as *be* or *have*, it is the auxiliary verb that indicates the third person singular inflection (not the main verb):

John is walking to school.

This water has boiled for 10 minutes.

Reid (1991) offers an excellent reanalysis of this problematic "rule." His arguments are based on meaning rather than form, and he emphasizes the fact that form follows from meaning; he believes that the subject-verb agreement "rule" is not grounded in syntactic automaticity but that its use reflects a series of semantic choices and decisions made by the speaker-writer. Reid proposes that all English nouns (in this case nouns that happen to function as subjects) have a number, which is either ONE or MORE THAN ONE. The number MORE THAN ONE can be encoded either lexically (e.g., *people, they*) or, more typically, morphologically with the inflection -*s*[9] (e.g., *several boys*). In some cases, lexical and morphological number can even co-occur and give new meaning to words (e.g., *peoples*).

Similarly, all English verbs have a number. Except for the verb *be*, which encodes number lexically even in the past tense, other English verbs encode number only in the present tense:

Present tense verb ending	Meaning	Example
–s	(ONE)	The boy runs.
–ø	(MORE THAN ONE)	The boys run.

Reid further proposes that the choice of number is made separately for both the subject noun and the verb (*be* or present tense lexical verbs) and that both choices contribute independently to the speaker's message. This perspective allows Reid to explain why the number of the subject noun and the verb, while most often the same, do not always agree since all combinations are possible though not equally frequent. The most frequent choices, i.e., the agreements, are the examples in the shaded boxes numbered 1 and 4:

		NOUN SUBJECT	
		One	**More Than One**
VERB	**One**	The boy likes candy. 1	Ten dollars is not a lot of money. 2
	More Than One	The family 3 are all here	The boys 4 like candy.

The examples in boxes 2 and 3 are unusual in that an overtly plural subject in 2 is reinterpreted as a singular lump sum, and an overtly singular subject in 3 is reinterpreted as a plural entity. We know this has been done by the speaker/writer because of the verb forms chosen: singular *is* in 2 and plural *are* in 3. The choice is complex, and for Reid it is based on the speaker's message and communicative intent in each case.[10]

We refer to Reid's system when we discuss several of the following problematic cases of subject noun and main verb number agreement/disagreement later in this chapter. We find his system appealing because it helps explain why the "rule" is so difficult for L2 learners to master and why even educated native speakers of English must constantly monitor their production in this area.

Examples of the general agreement rule are easy to understand and cause little or no difficulty—at least not at the conceptual level. However, there are so many special or difficult cases concerning subject and verb number that we must fill several pages with subrules and examples as we try to give you a complete picture of the problem.

Rules for Persistently Troublesome Cases

1. Collective nouns (see Chapter 17) like the one in box 3 of the preceding matrix may take either a singular or plural verb inflection depending on the meaning.[11] If the subject noun is conceived of as one entity, the verb carries the *-s* inflection; if the subject is felt to be more than one entity, the verb takes no inflection. (Note that other forms showing number agreement (e.g. determiners) may also change to reflect the number selected.)

> Our school team has won all its games. (= the team as a whole)
> Our school team have won all their games. (= individual team members)

2. Some common and proper nouns ending in *-s*, including *-ics* nouns and certain diseases, are always conceived of as a single entity and take a singular verb inflection.

> No news is good news.   Physics is a difficult subject.
> This series is very interesting.   Wales is lovely to visit.
> Measles is a contagious disease.

3. Titles of books, plays, operas, films, and such works—even when plural in form—take the singular verb inflection because they are perceived as a single entity.

> *Great Expectations* was written   *The Pirates of Penzance* is my
> by Dickens.   favorite operetta.

4. Nouns occurring in sets of two take the singular when the noun *pair* is present but take the plural when *pair* is absent—regardless of whether one pair or more is being referred to.

> A pair of trousers is on the sofa.   This pair of shoes needs new heels.
> Todd's trousers are on the sofa.   These shoes need new heels.

5. *A number of* normally takes the plural, while *the number of* normally takes the singular.

> A number of students have dropped that course.
> The number of students in this school is 2,000.

This generalization holds true most of the time because the noun *number* in the phrase *the number of* generally modifies or implies a single entity such as a sum or a totality, whereas the noun *number* in the phrase *a number of* normally modifies or implies more than one entity, much as the quantifiers *some*, *a few*, or *several* do. However, as Reid (1991) points out, authentic counterexamples do exist for this heuristic—especially if adjectivals that semantically support the opposite number interpretation are modifying the noun *number* so as to make "*(the) number (of)*" reflect more than one entity or make "*(a) number (of)*" reflect a single entity:

> "... the increased number of cancers were occurring at radiation exposure levels well below the official limit...." Reid (1991:219)

> "A smaller number of steps suggests a growing ability to organize." Reid (1991:282)

6. Fractions and percentages take a singular verb inflection when modifying a noncount noun and the plural verb inflection when they modify a plural noun; either the singular or the plural verb inflection may be used when they modify a collective noun, depending on the speaker's meaning.

> *noncount:*   One half of the toxic waste has escaped.
> Fifty percent of the toxic waste has escaped.
>
> *plural:*   Two thirds of the students are satisfied with the class.
> Sixty-six percent of the students are satisfied with the class.
>
> *collective:*   One tenth of the population of Egypt $\begin{cases} \text{is Christian.} \\ \text{are Christians.} \end{cases}$
>
> Ten percent of the population of Egypt $\begin{cases} \text{is Christian.} \\ \text{are Christians.} \end{cases}$

7. The nouns *majority* and *minority* are variously described as singular, plural, or collective, depending on which reference grammar one consults. The only satisfying description of these words that we found was in Fowler (1965: 349–350, 366). Fowler maintains that *majority* and *minority* have three related but slightly different meanings:

a. An abstract or generic meaning that refers to superiority of numbers; the reference can be human or nonhuman, but the number is always singular. For example:

> The great majority is helpless.

b. A specific meaning where one of two or more sets has a numerical plurality (*majority*) or numerical inferiority (*minority*); the examples make reference to political parties, and grammatically these cases are like collectives and can be either singular or plural. For example:

> The majority was/were determined to press its/their victory.

c. A specific meaning where most (*majority*) or less than half (*minority*) of an explicit set of persons is being referred to. Here, Fowler claims the number agreement should be plural. For example:

A majority of my friends advise it.

What we need is a usage study that will confirm or modify Fowler's classification. The limited data we have from studies of native speaker preference by van Shaik (1976) and Farhady (1977) support Fowler's (a) and (c) categories, respectively:

A majority of votes _____ needed to win. (van Shaik, 1976)
is—81%; are—19%

The majority of Democrats _____ opposed to local blackouts of the
are—80%; is—20%
Game of the Week. (Farhady, 1977)

Until we have more complete and definitive evidence, Fowler's analysis seems the best one available.

8. Plural unit words of distance, money, and time (like the example in box 2 of the matrix on page 60) take the singular verb inflection when one entity is implied but a plural verb inflection when more than one entity is encoded in the subject:

one	*distance:*	1,000 miles is a long distance
entity	*money:*	2 million dollars is a lot of money
	time:	5 years is a long time to spend on an M.A. thesis
more than	*distance:*	10 miles are to be added to this freeway next year
one entity	*money:*	2 dollars are on the table in the kitchen
	time:	3 years (i.e., 1602, 1649, and 1687) are missing from this set of calendars for the 17th century

9. Arithmetical operations (add, subtract, multiply, and divide) take the singular because they are perceived as reflecting a single numerical entity on both sides of the equation or equal sign. For example:

addition: One plus one $\begin{Bmatrix} \text{is} \\ \text{equals} \end{Bmatrix}$ two.

subtraction: Four minus two $\begin{Bmatrix} \text{is} \\ \text{equals} \end{Bmatrix}$ two.

multiplication: Two times two $\begin{Bmatrix} \text{is} \\ \text{equals} \end{Bmatrix}$ four.

division: Ten divided by two $\begin{Bmatrix} \text{is} \\ \text{equals} \end{Bmatrix}$ five.

10. The quantifiers *all (of), a lot of, lots of,* and *plenty of* take singular verb agreement if the subject head noun is noncount but plural verb agreement if the subject head noun is plural:

A lot of nonsense was published about that incident.
A lot of people were present when it happened.

Usage Issues in Subject-Verb Agreement

Since the choice of subject and verb number is a problem for learners at all levels and even puzzles native speakers at times, many reference grammars or style handbooks include a discussion of this topic. One of the most comprehensive treatments is in Crews (1980). He provides the reader with the preferred form as well as acceptable alternatives and covers more cases than most other sources. However, Crews tends to be more *prescriptive* than *descriptive* in his account; that is, he tells the reader what to do rather than documenting what native speakers do. Crews's prescriptions are sometimes useful teaching aids, since when one is presenting the rules for subject-verb agreement to a TOEFL (Test of English as a Foreign Language) preparation class, only the formal prescriptive rule corresponds to the correct answer. In our treatment, on the other hand, we try to be as descriptive as possible in our review of the rules of subject and verb number choice because we feel the ESL/EFL teacher must be aware of current usage as well as the traditional rules.

In discussing the usage preferences of native speakers with respect to subject and verb number, we have drawn heavily on studies done by van Shaik (1976), Farhady (1977), and Peterson (1990). They all surveyed the performance and preferences of a number of native speakers and pointed out discrepancies between traditional rules and the elicited performance of native speakers.

Obviously, not all cases of subject-verb agreement can be described as exclusively form-based or meaning-based. Some seem to be more a matter of usage and convention. The discussions below on quantifiers (*none, all, each, every*), relative-clause antecedents, clausal subjects, and heuristic principles are cases in point.

11. Rules conflict for *none,* and sometimes for *all, each,* and *every*. Many traditional grammars state that when used as a subject, *none* is always singular regardless of what follows in a prepositional phrase. The argument for this rule has been that *none* means *not one*. However, usage surveys give us a different picture of what native speakers are doing and thinking when they use *none*. When *none* refers to a noncount noun, the inflection is uncontroversially singular:

> *noncount:* None of the toxic waste has escaped.

> But when *none* refers to a plural noun—human or nonhuman—usage seems to be more or less equally divided between the singular and plural inflection. The percentages that we supply under the example sentences indicate the proportion of native speakers that favored each form in the survey cited.

> *plural (human):* None of those firemen _____ hearing the alarm go
>
enjoy—47%; enjoys—53%
> off. (van Shaik, 1976)

> *plural (nonhuman):* None of the costumes he has tried _____ him.
>
fit—50%; fits—50%
> (Farhady, 1977)

In a more recent survey, Peterson (1990:46) asked three groups with different socioeducational backgrounds (i.e., office workers, masters degree students, and Pepsi-Cola truck drivers) to respond to questionnaire items with *none* using a "Which do you prefer?" item-response format. Here are his results (the numbers for all of Peterson's sentences are ours, not his):

	Ofc. wrkrs. (N = 32)	M.A. stdnts (N = 36)	Truckdrvrs (N = 33)
1. a. None of the negotiations is likely to succeed.	44%	19%	24%
b. None of the negotiations are likely to succeed.	56%	78%	76%
		3%—either	
2. a. None even knows how to tie shoes.	44%	28%	61%
b. None even know how to tie shoes.	56%	69%	39%
		3%—either	

For both questionnaire items, *none* is notionally plural; in the second item, *none* is plural by elliptical reference since it points back (presumably) to some plural noun such as *children*. Except for the response of the Pepsi-Cola truck drivers to item 2, all respondents indicated their preference for plural verb agreement with *none* where *none* modifies or refers to a plural countable noun. Clearly, the traditional prescription that *none* is always singular is inadequate. Additional research based on analysis of tokens from current spoken and written English should be carried out to see if a more descriptively adequate rule of usage exists. In the meantime, ESL/EFL teachers must be aware of the fact that when the subject *none* refers to a plural countable noun, the plural verb inflection may well be used if current usage is any indication.

Although *none* is the most problematic quantifier with respect to subject-verb agreement, ESL/EFL learners also experience problems with the quantifiers *all, each,* and *every* (*one*).

The rules for subject-verb agreement with *all* are as follows: If the noun that *all* modifies is a noncount subject, then subject-verb agreement is singular:

> All (of) (the) water is polluted.

If *all* modifies a countable plural subject noun, subject-verb agreement is plural:

> All (of) (the) students have arrived.

A problem arises, however, when *all* is used to qualify a collective noun subject (see Chapter 17). Theoretically, one should be able to use either singular or plural subject-verb agreement in such cases. We tested such an item with 40 native speakers of English (graduate students and professors), and the results seem to support this theoretical duality:

> All of my family _____ present.
> *is*—55%; *are*—43%; no response—2%

Many style books, however, admonish us not to use the preposition *of* after the quantifier *all* in our writing. We thus administered a similar item, minus the *of* to the same group of people a week later. The results were as follows:

> All my family _____ present.
> *is*—68%; *are*—26%; used both—6%

Thus the presence or absence of the preposition *of* seems to have an effect on subject-verb agreement, since in the item without *of* our consultants favored singular agreement to a noticeably greater degree.

Peterson (1990:58) followed up on this observation and presented the following questionnaire items to his three groups of consultants:

	Ofc. wrkrs. (N = 32)	M.A. stdnts (N = 36)	Truckdrvrs (N = 33)
1. a. All of the class is restless today.	63%	89%	70%
b. All of the class are restless today.	37%	11%	30%
2. a. All of the team was caught drinking margaritas.	44%	66%	33%
b. All of the team were caught drinking margaritas.	56%	31%	67%
		3%—either	
3. a. All my family lives in Minnesota.	41%	66%	61%
b. All my family live in Minnesota.	59%	28%	39%
		6%—either	

Peterson did not test the same collective noun for items with and without *of;* however, his results suggest that factors other than the presence or absence of *of* are influencing or coloring these results. Analysis of spontaneous oral and written data showing different tokens of the same collective noun modified by *all (of)* with different types of subject-verb agreement would be useful in determining more precisely what the basis of this variation might be.

When the subject quantifier is *each* or *every (one)*, the rules are more straightforward. When the quantified subject noun is singular, there is no problem: the subject-verb agreement is always singular:

$$\left\{ \begin{array}{l} \text{Each} \\ \text{Every} \\ \text{Each and every} \end{array} \right\} \text{ student has a textbook.}$$

However, when the quantified noun refers to a definite plural set, there can be problems since the quantifiers are grammatically singular yet the set they are modifying is notionally plural:

$$\text{Each of his examples } \left\{ \begin{array}{l} \text{was} \\ \text{were} \end{array} \right\} \text{ out of context.}$$

$$\text{Every one of these athletes } \left\{ \begin{array}{l} \text{runs} \\ \text{run} \end{array} \right\} \text{ the mile in four minutes.}$$

The traditional prescriptive rule maintains that singular subject-verb agreement applies in such cases because *each* and *every (one)* are functioning as grammatically singular subjects. In these cases native speaker preference appears to closely mirror the prescriptive rule, since the same 40 consultants that reported divided usage for *all* were in agreement (93% or greater) that the verbs in the above two sentences should be *was* and *runs*. In contrast to our results, however, it is interesting to see what Peterson (1990:57) found when he surveyed his three groups:

	Ofc. wrkrs. (N = 32)	M.A. stdnts (N = 36)	Truckdrvrs (N = 33)
1. a. Each of them sees many advantages in that plan.	50%	83%	39%
b. Each of them see many advantages in that plan.	50%	11%	61%
		6%—either	

	Ofc. wrkrs. (N = 32)	M.A. stdnts (N = 36)	Truckdrvrs (N = 33)
2. a. Each of the children is happy today.	47%	58%	9%
b. Each of the children are happy today.	53%	39%	91%
		3%—either	
3. a. Every one of these four-door cars is ugly.	56%	64%	21%
b. Every one of these four-door cars are ugly.	44%	31%	76%
		5%—either	

Here we see the M.A. students showing a preference for singular agreement on the verb with *each* and *every* as subjects, while the Pepsi-Cola truck drivers strongly prefer plural agreement on the verb. The office workers are fairly evenly split between choosing singular and plural verb agreement. Peterson's results indicate that some consultants are indeed viewing *each* and *every* (*one*) as grammatically singular but that more are viewing these as notionally plural when a plural noun or pronoun intervenes between the quantifier and the verb. We will discuss reasons for this under our discussion of principles that influence subject-verb agreement.

12. Relative-clause antecedents: Subject-verb agreement is particularly problematic in certain types of relative clauses. In an example such as the following,

>Marsha is one of those rare individuals who _____ finished the M.A. early.
>
> *have/has*

traditional grammars maintain that the antecedent of *who* is *individuals* and thus *have* is the correct verb form. This antecedent rule conflicts with the nonintervention principle (see below); also it does not agree at all with the preferences of the native speakers that van Shaik and Farhady surveyed; most want the relative pronoun to agree with the predicate noun *one*, which they view as the antecedent of *who*:

>Jack is one of those rare individuals who _____ decided on a definite
>
> *have—16%; has—84%*
>
>career. (Farhady, 1977)

>He is one of the best students that _____ ever come to this school.
>
> *have—14%; has—86%*
>
>(van Shaik, 1976)

In fact, of the five survey items Van Shaik and Farhady used, only one was a bit weaker than the two above with respect to contradicting the traditional rule for this type of relative clause:

>I am one of those who _____ equal rights. (van Shaik, 1976)
>
> *favor—35%; favors—65%*

However, even in this example, where the presence of the *I* subject and pronominal use of *those* appear to be mitigating factors, the rule is still contradicted by an almost 2:1 margin. Clearly, most native speakers are using *one* as the antecedent of *who* or *that*, and the prescriptive rule should probably be revised to reflect actual usage more accurately.

13. Clausal and phrasal subjects: Traditional grammars tell us that when a clause functions as a subject, the subject-verb agreement is singular—regardless of any plural noun phrases that occur as part of the subject clause or the verb phrase. For example:

> That the children want friends doesn't surprise me.
> What they want is revolutions everywhere.

We do not have survey information on this type of agreement; however, we suspect that the second type of subject clause cited above causes some difficulty—even among native speakers. This seems especially true when the verb is followed by a plural noun phrase.

This rule also extends to phrasal subjects that are gerunds or infinitives because they also take singular verb agreement; however, they seem to cause fewer learning problems than clausal subjects.

> Reading books is my hobby.
> To err is human.

Two Heuristic Principles that Influence Subject-Verb Number Agreement

1. The proximity principle: For the correlatives *either . . . or* and *neither . . . nor*, traditional grammarians argue for a proximity rule; that is, subject-verb agreement should occur with the subject noun nearest to the verb:

Either my sister or *my brothers are* going to do it.	Neither the books nor *the movie was* helpful.
Either my brothers or *my sister is* going do it.	Neither the movie nor *the books were* helpful.

Do native speakers consistently follow the proximity principle? Not really, but they support it more strongly for *either . . . or* than they do for *neither . . . nor*.

Either your eyesight or your brakes _____ at fault (van Shaik, 1976)
was—31%; were—69%

Either the professor or her assistants _____ explain every lesson.
has to—33%; have to—67%

(Farhady, 1977)

Neither the students nor the teacher _____ that textbook.
likes—49%; like—51%

(van Shaik, 1976)

Apparently, *neither* can easily be perceived as a negative correlative referring to more than one entity, which would explain the slight preference for the plural form that van Shaik's questionnaire elicited.

Personal pronouns pose special problems when used with full correlatives, where the rule of proximity would have us produce *either you or I am, neither you nor he is,* and so on. In such cases, Farhady and van Shaik found even less agreement with the proximity principle than they did when correlatives involved lexical nouns:

Neither you nor he _____ able to answer the question. (Farhady, 1977)
was—40%; were—60%

Neither you nor I _____ trained for that job. (van Shaik, 1976)
am—12%; is—15%; are—73%

The immediately preceding example is especially interesting because *are* is a colloquial gap-filling substitute for *am* in some other constructions (*I'm going, too, aren't I? Aren't I lucky?*). *Am* is apparently perceived by native speakers as too limited a form for use in those correlatives where *I* is the second noun phrase constituent.

One other case where the proximity principle does in fact apply and where traditional grammar would not prescribe its use is in sentences beginning with *there* followed by conjoined noun phrases.[12]

Traditional rule: There are $\left\{\begin{array}{l}\text{a girl and two boys}\\\text{two boys and a girl}\end{array}\right\}$ in the room.

Proximity principle: There $\left\{\begin{array}{l}\text{is a girl and two boys}\\\text{are two boys and a girl}\end{array}\right\}$ in the room.

We have informally surveyed many native speakers, and a majority apply the proximity rule in such cases. So, again, we seem to have a situation in which the actual usage preference of native speakers differs from the traditional prescription.

2. The principle of nonintervention: Many reference grammars make a point of emphasizing that a singular subject noun or pronoun should take a singular verb inflection regardless of what else occurs between the subject and the verb; that is, the speaker or writer should ignore all plural forms in intervening prepositional phrases and expressions such as *together with, along with, as well as,* and *not others.*

When common or proper nouns are subjects, the nonintervention principle seems to be well supported:

The major cause of highway accidents in 1976 _____ drunk drivers.
was—93%; were—7%

(Farhady, 1977)

Peter, along with his brothers, _____ to open a store. (van Shaik, 1976)
plans—84%; plan—16%

The boy, not his parents, _____ being punished. (van Shaik, 1976)
is—88%; are—12%

However, when the subject followed by the prepositional phrase is *either* or *neither*, the nonintervention principle weakens because these forms can be perceived as signaling more than one entity—*neither* apparently more strongly so than *either.*

Neither of them _____ ready for marriage. (van Shaik, 1976)
is—66%; are—34%

Neither of them _____ enough money to afford a car. (Farhady, 1977)
has—50%; have—50%

However, van Shaik (1976) and Farhady (1977) surveyed only responses for *neither.* We suspected that similar problems might also arise with the usage of *either*, so we surveyed 43 consultants concerning the usage of *either* in a similar construction:

Either of the stories _____ going to be acceptable.
is—72%; are—24%; accepted both—2%

While there is also some weakening of the nonintervention principle in this item, it appears that *either* is perceived a bit more strongly as being singular than is *neither.* Peterson (1990) again found somewhat different results in his survey:

	Ofc. wrkrs. (N = 32)	M.A. stdnts (N = 36)	Truckdrvrs (N = 33)
1. a. Either of the dictionaries is good enough for this.	50%	61%	33%
b. Either of the dictionaries are good enough for this.	50%	33%	67%
		6%—either	
2. a. Either of mine is OK for your system.	63%	66%	36%
b. Either of mine are OK for your system.	37%	25%	64%
3. a. Neither of the salebooks was a good buy.	53%	66%	27%
b. Neither of the salebooks were a good buy.	47%	31%	73%
		5%—either	
4. a. Neither of hers is the same as mine.	53%	58%	42%
b. Neither of hers are the same as mine.	47%	31%	58%

While there are noticeable differences across the three groups, within each group consultants treated *either* and *neither* very similarly except for the office workers' response to item 2, where there was a clear preference for a singular interpretation of *either* that did not occur with the other three items.

One problem with all of the preceding data is that they represent elicited judgments and do not necessarily reflect actual use in situations where people are not made conscious of their production. Therefore, there is a clear need for further studies that examine spontaneous use of subject-verb agreement by native speakers for the problematic cases we have noted.

CONCLUSION

In many English sentences subject-verb number agreement is straightforward and noncontroversial. However, it is quite clear that a number of unresolved questions remain. In fact, we may well have inadvertently omitted other problems from this discussion. We do not claim to have exhausted the topic.

One of the reasons we have discussed the problems of subject-verb number agreement is that form, meaning, and use are associated with it. When a form is syntactically singular but notionally plural (or vice versa), there is a potential conflict. Agreement based on form is straightforward, but when agreement is driven by meaning or use, this gives rise to the possibility of variation among users. Here Reid's (1991) formulation, which holds that all co-occurrences of subject noun number and of verb number are possible, though not equally frequent, helps to explain many so-called problematic cases in that meaning-driven choices help lead the listener or reader to the intended interpretation.

Our advice to ESL/EFL teachers is that they be aware of the major traditional rules (see teaching suggestion (6) in the following list) and also aware of those instances where current usage seems to clearly deviate from the traditional prescription. Also, teachers should keep in mind that informal contexts permit a greater range of acceptable forms than formal contexts; therefore, they must be flexible about their correction standards, which should be different for formal writing than for informal writing or colloquial speech.

TEACHING SUGGESTIONS

I. Form. The copula *be* causes ESL/EFL students trouble because it is the most irregular verb in the English language. A lot of practice will have to be given to all its various forms:

present		*past*	
I *am*	we *are*	I *was*	we *were*
you *are*	you *are*	you *were*	you *were*
he, she, it *is*	they *are*	he, she, it *was*	they *were*

    a. One technique for practicing *am, are,* and *is* in context is to conduct a chain drill with your students' names:

> *Student 1:* I am Fatimah. Who are YOU?
> *Student 2:* I am José. You are Fatimah. Who are YOU?
> *Student 3:* I am Juan. You are José. She is Fatimah. Who are YOU?

Get the learners to contract "I am" to "I'm" as soon as possible.

    b. Sometimes the plural forms can be practiced using nationalities when two or more students in an ESL/EFL class are from the same country.

> *Student 1 to 2:* We are from Mexico. Are they from Mexico?
> *Student 2:* No, they aren't.
> *(to 3 and 4):* Where are you from?
> *Students 3 and 4:* We are from Iran.

Get the learners to contract "we are" to "we're" as soon as possible.

    c. The present tense forms of *be* should also be practiced with other adjectives and with prepositional phrases.

> *Teacher:* I am (I'm) tired today. Are you tired?
> *Student 1:* Yes, I am.
> *Teacher:* Is he tired?
> *Class:* Yes, he is.

> *Student 1:* I am in class. Are you in class?
> *Student 2:* Yes, I am. Is Ali in class?
> *Student 1:* Yes, he is. Is Miriam in class?
> *Student 2:* Yes, she is.

    d. To practice the past-tense forms of *be*, past-time contexts must be created. The teacher can set the pattern and then have students practice with each other, reminding them *be* does not contract in final position.

> *Teacher:* I was in class yesterday. Were you?
> *Student 1:* Yes, I was.
> *Teacher:* Were we in class yesterday?
> *Student 1:* Yes, we were.
> (Student 1 takes over the role of teacher.)

> *Teacher:* Was Carlos late today?
> *Class:* Yes, he was.
> *Teacher:* Was Kin Lee late?
> *Class:* No, she wasn't.
> *Teacher:* Were they late?
> *Class:* Yes, they were.
> (A student then takes over the role of teacher.)

2. Form. Badalamenti and Stanchina (1997:10) suggest using the names of famous people from all over the world to practice the copula *be* with country of origin and nationality. For example, the teacher can give one model and then provide only a name.

> Sophia Loren is from Italy. She's Italian.
> Arnold Schwarzenegger is from Austria. He's Austrian.
> Madonna is from the United States. She's American.
> Nelson Mandela is from South Africa. He's South African.

3. Form. The problematic area with regular present-tense verbs other than *be* involves the third person singular form of the verb. Since the third person singular form of the verb is the only one inflected for person and number agreement, ESL/EFL students frequently and persistently omit the necessary *-s* marker by simplifying or by overgeneralizing the basic pattern to third person singular. Practice with the present tense should thus put a great deal of focus on the third person singular inflection and on the contrast with all other persons. The teacher can introduce a fictional character *Jack* and talk about what he *does* every day.

> He gets up at 7 A.M.   He runs in the park at 5:00 P.M.
> He eats breakfast at 7:30.   He comes home at 6:00.
> He goes to work at 8:00.   etc.

Jack's schedule can be practiced by the class with the teacher using pictures and/or a clock with movable hands as prompts. Then, the practice can extend to classroom interactions, prompted by the teacher as needed.

> *Teacher:* What does Jack do at 7 A.M.?
> *Student:* He gets up.
> *Teacher:* When do you get up?
> *Student:* I get up at 8.
> *Teacher:* Ask Maria when she gets up and then tell us what you found out.
> *Student:* When do you get up, Maria?
> *Maria:* I get up at 6:30.
> *Student:* She gets up at 6:30.

Finally, pairs of students could interview each other about their daily schedules and report findings to the class.

4. Form. Riggenbach and Samuda (1997:9–11) suggest that job descriptions and names of occupations be first matched and then generated to practice the third person singular present tense.

  a. He wears a uniform and usually travels many miles a day. He serves food and drinks, but he hardly ever prepares them for himself. He's _____.

b. She wears a uniform and drives many miles a day. She never serves food or drinks. She's _____.

a flight attendant	a nurse
a teacher	a bus driver
a librarian	a student

Now students write similar descriptions for the job names that are still left.

5. Meaning. To practice with intermediate learners the notion that it is sometimes possible to use a plural or singular verb with a particular noun depending on how the noun is construed, give the students sentences and ask them to respond with "one" when the subject is singular and "more than one" when the subject is plural. They should also specify the entity or unit being referred to.

a. *Teacher:* The class is going to celebrate at the end of this term.
Students: one (class)

b. *Teacher:* The 20 minutes are going to pass quickly.
Students: more than one (minute)

c. *Teacher:* Twenty minutes is not a long time!
Students: one (time unit)

d. *Teacher:* My old school gang are meeting after work today.
Students: more than one (gang member)
etc.

6. Use. The following is a summary of traditional subject-verb agreement rules based on Frodesen & Eyring (1997:34–51) as well as in material in this chapter. The summary serves as a checklist of rules that ESL/EFL students need to learn or review for TOEFL (Test of English as a Foreign Language) preparation or for a formal academic writing course.

a. Noncount noun subjects take a singular verb:

(The food/John's advice) is good.

b. In most cases collective noun subjects take singular verbs, but if the group is viewed as individual members, use a plural verb:

The class is going on a field trip.
The class have been arguing about where to go.

c. Subject nouns that are derived from adjectives and describe people take plural verbs:

The rich are in favor of a tax cut.

d. Some proper noun subjects that end in -*s* such as names of courses, diseases, places, as well as book and film titles and the word *news*, take singular verbs:

Wales is a beautiful region.
Mathematics is a difficult subject.
Measles often has side effects.
The news was very good.

e. Plural subject nouns of distance, time, and money that signal one unit take a singular verb:

> Six hundred miles is too far to drive in one day.

f. Basic arithmetical operations (add, subtract, multiply, divide) take singular verbs:

> Four times five equals twenty.

g. For items that have two parts, when you use the word *pair*, the verb is singular, but without *pair*, the verb is plural:

> My pair of scissors is lost.
> My scissors are lost.

h. Clausal subject are singular even if the nouns referred to are plural:

> What we need is more reference books.

i. Gerund (verb + *ing*) and infinitive (*to* + verb) subjects take a singular verb:

> Reading books is my hobby.   To err is human.

j. With fractions, percentages, and the quantifiers *all (of), a lot of, lots of,* verb agreement depends on the noun coming after these phrases:

> 1) A singular noun, noun clause, or noncount noun takes a singular verb:
>
> > A lot of the (book/information) is about urban poverty.
>
> 2) A plural noun takes a plural verb:
>
> > A lot of computers need to be repaired.
>
> 3) A collective noun can take either a singular or plural verb depending on the meaning:
>
> > All my family (lives/live) in Ohio.

k. With *each, every,* and *every one* as subjects, use a singular verb:

> Every student has a lunch box.

l. With *a number of* as subject, use a plural verb:

> A number of students are taking the exam.

m. With *the number of* as subject, use a singular verb:

> The number of students taking the exam is 75.

n. With *none* as subject, use a singular verb:

> None of the magazines is here.

o. With *either* or *neither* as subject, use a singular verb:

> (Either/neither) was acceptable to me.

p. With correlative subjects *either . . . or* or *neither . . . nor,* the verb agrees with the closest subject:

> Either Bob or my cousins are going to do it.

Neither my cousins or Bob is going to do it.

q. With *there* subjects, the verb is singular or plural depending on whether the noun phrase following the verb is singular or plural:

There is one book on the table.

There are $\left\{\begin{array}{l}\text{three books}\\ \text{a book and a pen}\end{array}\right\}$ on the table.

Remember that many of these formal prescriptive rules have informal variants that are different and often more frequently used in informal speech and writing. The context in which language is being used and the discourse community of the participants will determine what is acceptable usage.

7. Use. Frodesen and Eyring (1997:49) suggest that teachers give students many statements and have them decide which items have verb forms that are appropriate for formal written contexts (i.e., the traditional prescriptive rule) and which would be acceptable for informal written or spoken contexts:

a. Neither of those political surveys are valid because the sample was not random.
b. In conclusion, either of the textbooks reviewed above is an excellent choice for an introductory chemistry course.
c. There's a number of errors in this report.
d. As far as we know, none of the experiment's results has been duplicated to date.

EXERCISES

Test your knowledge of what has been presented.

I. Provide an original example sentence illustrating each of the following concepts. Underline the pertinent word(s) in your example.
   a. the copular function of *be*
   b. a copular verb other than *be*
   c. an auxiliary function of *be*
   d. collective noun subject
   e. noncount noun subject
   f. third person singular present inflection
   g. the proximity principle
   h. the nonintervention principle
   i. subject-verb agreement with a clausal subject

2. What are two structural reasons for distinguishing the copula *be* from other verbs in English?

3. When does subject-verb agreement apply overtly? In other words, in what instances should your ESL/EFL students be aware that verbs must agree with subjects in person and number? Also, in what instances does subject-verb agreement not apply?

4. Name and illustrate two cases where a traditional subject-verb agreement rule is not supported by current usage.

Test your ability to apply what you know.

5. The following sentences contain errors that are commonly made by ESL/EFL learners. What is the precise nature of the error? How would you make the learners aware of these problems? What exercises would you use to practice the correct pattern and prevent such errors from recurring?

a. *Is you from Mexico?   d. *Nora wills read the book.
b. *Felix go to school every day. e. *They sings in a choir.
c. *I tired.   f. *I don't be angry anymore.

6. What will you say to a high intermediate ESL/EFL student who complains to you that you correct mistakes in his compositions when he writes sentences like this one but that he hears native speakers say things like this all the time?

   Either my roommates or my friend Bill are going to buy the refreshments.

7. How would you present the rules for fractions and percentages (see rule 10 on p. 62) to an intermediate-level high school ESL/EFL class? What contexts would you provide to help them have meaningful practice?

8. Some noun plurals are irregular (*men, mice*), and some have a change from *-f* (sg.) to *-ves* (pl.), such as *wife/wives*. How would you review irregular noun plurals with a low-intermediate ESL/EFL class?

BIBLIOGRAPHY

References

Badalamenti, V., and C. Henner-Stanchina (1997). *Grammar Dimensions.* Book 1 (2d ed.). Boston: Heinle & Heinle.

Crews, F. (1980). *A Random House Handbook* (3rd ed.). New York: Random House.

Farhady, H. (1977). "Subject-Verb Agreement in English: A Usage Study." Unpublished English 215 paper, UCLA.

Fowler, H. (1965). *A Dictionary of Modern English Usage* (2d ed., revised by Sir Ernest Gowers). Oxford: Clarendon Press.

Frodesen, J., and J. Eyring (1997). *Grammar Dimensions.* Book 4 (2d ed.). Boston: Heinle & Heinle.

Fuller, J. W., and J. K. Gundel (1987). "Topic-Prominence in Interlanguage." *Language Learning,* 37:1, 1–18.

Langacker, R. (1991). *Foundations of Cognitive Grammar. Vol II.* Palo Alto, CA: Stanford University Press.

Peterson, L. M. (1990). "Subject-verb Agreement with Select Subject Quantifiers: A Usage Study of All, Each, Every, Either, Neither, and None." Unpublished master's degree project, School for International Training: Brattleboro, Vt.

Reid, W. (1991). *Verb and Noun Number in English: A Functional Explanation.* London: Longman.

Riggenbach, H., and V. Samuda (1997). *Grammar Dimensions.* Book 2 (2d ed.). Boston: Heinle & Heinle.

van Shaik, J. D. (1976). "Subject-Verb Agreement in English: What the Books Say vs. Native Speaker Usage." Unpublished English 215 paper, UCLA.

Suggestions for Further Reading

Other reference grammars or handbooks on style or usage with useful descriptions of subject-verb agreement are:

Crew, F. (1980). A *Random House Handbook* (3d ed.). New York: Random House.

House, H. C., and S. E. Harman (1950). *Descriptive English Grammar.* Englewood Cliffs, N.J.: Prentice-Hall.

Irmscher, W. F. (1972). *The Holt Guide to English.* New York: Holt, Rinehart, and Winston.

Perrin, P. G., et al. (1962). *Handbook of Current English.* Glenview, Ill.: Scott, Foresman, & Co.

Quirk, R., et al. (1985). *A Comprehensive Grammar of the English Language.* London: Longman.

ESL texts with useful discussions and exercises for treating the copula be *and subject-verb agreement are:*

Alexander, L. G. (1988). *Longman English Grammar.* London: Longman.

Badalamenti, V., and C. Henner-Stanchina (1997). *Grammar Dimensions.* Book 1 (2d ed.). Boston: Heinle & Heinle.

Danielson, D., and P. Porter (1990). *Using English* (2d ed.). Englewood Cliffs, N.J.: Prentice Hall Regents.

Frodesen, J., and J. Eyring (1997). *Grammar Dimensions.* Book 4 (2d ed.). Boston: Heinle & Heinle.

Riggenbach, H., and V. Samuda (1997). *Grammar Dimensions.* Book 2 (2d ed.). Boston: Heinle & Heinle.

ENDNOTES

1. These adverbials typically are prepositional phrases and their substitutes (e.g., *in the room, there*).

2. Verbs that are not copulas can be followed only by adverbials and/or noun phrases. They do not take adjective phrases. In colloquial utterances like "He talks funny," *funny* is functioning adverbially (i.e., "in a funny manner") and not adjectivally.

3. Participial adjectives are derived from either the *-ing* present participle (e.g., *standing, walking, sleeping*) or the past participle, which takes the *-ed* ending in regular verbs and a variety of endings in irregular verbs (see Chapter 7) (e.g., *protected, forgotten, distraught*).

4. While *become, get,* and *turn* can take many different adjectives, the other change-of-state copulas tend to take only one or two fixed adjective completions, which we called "collocations" in Chapter 3, such as *fall ill, come undone, grow tall/old, run wild/amuck.*

5. It derives historically from *come to be.*

6. *Turn* is unusual in that it takes article-less nouns: *He turned traitor.* It also can take a preposition, in which case the noun object may take an article: He turned into a gentleman.

7. What is meant by the perceptual saliency of a form is whether or not it is easy for learners to hear. Because final consonants and consonant clusters tend to be more weakly articulated in English than initial consonants or clusters, this morpheme is in fact somewhat difficult to hear.

8. Remember that the verb *be* in the present tense would take the form *am* with a first person subject and *are* with a second person subject.

9. The regular morphological plural ending *-s* takes three different forms phonologically: /əz/ after sibilant consonants (consonants produced with friction forced through a narrow opening): *bushes, buses, mazes, peaches, badges;* /s/ after non-sibilant voiceless consonants (consonants where vocal cords are not vibrating): *books, hats, lips;* and /z/ after voiced non-sibilant consonants and vowels (sounds where the vocal cords are vibrating): *bags, gads, ribs, eyes, toes.*

10. However, we would like to point out that Reid's system does not properly explain why sentences like these are not acceptable under any circumstances:

> * The boy like candy.
> * The boys likes candy.

Some English nouns like *boy* are more individuated and countable than others like *gang, dollar,* or *number.* It is less-individuated nouns that have flexibility of number and support Reid's arguments. This is an issue we discuss further in Chapter 15 with reference to Keith Allan's (1980) work on noun number and countability.

11. In American English there still is a strong tendency to use the singular verb inflection with a collective noun subject. In British English plural inflections are frequently preferred.

> (Am. E.) My family is on vacation.   (Br. E.) My family are on holiday.
> The government is cheating us.   The government are cheating us.

Some collective nouns (i.e., *the police,* and those formed from adjectives that describe people: *the rich, the young, the privileged*) require a plural verb:

> The police are looking for that man.
> The rich are getting richer all the time!

12. It is of course informally acceptable to consider *there* a singular subject for agreement purposes (*There's two people in the room*) rather than referring to the logical subject for agreement (*There are two people in the room*). For further discussion of subject-verb agreement in *there* sentences with all plural subject nouns—not only nonconjoined subjects—see Chapter 23.

INTRODUCTION TO PHRASE STRUCTURE

WORD ORDER IN ENGLISH AND OTHER LANGUAGES

In English, word order within sentences is less flexible than it is in many other languages, or than it was in English 1,000 years ago. One reason for this is that English has lost most of its original Germanic system of inflections. This was a system of (1) suffixes on nouns and adjectives that reflected the gender, number, and case of every noun in a sentence and (2) suffixes on verbs that reflected past or present tense as well as the person and number of the subject noun. Without recourse to this full range of inflections to mark subjects (and objects of various kinds), English came to rely on a more fixed word order to distinguish subjects from objects. The basic underlying word order in an English sentence is subject-verb-object (S-V-O):

> Example: Joe   writes   poetry.
>   S   V   O

This rather fixed word order operates in conjunction with prepositions, which help to indicate the semantic functions of certain objects that are not direct objects. For example, in the following sentence the preposition *with* signals that its object noun *Sarah* is in some sense the source of Joe's agreement:

> Example: Joe   agrees   with   Sarah.
>   S   V   Prep   O

Thus we say that English is an S-V-O language, like French, Spanish, and many other languages. However, a major difference exists between English and French, on the one hand, and Spanish, on the other: both English and French require that a subject noun of some sort appear in all but certain imperative sentences, whereas Spanish does not have this requirement for sentences with pronominal subjects. For example:

> I speak English.   Je parle français.   (Yo) hablo español.
>   (I speak French.)   (I speak Spanish.)

In fact the most frequent version of the Spanish example omits the first person subject pronoun, *yo*. Spanish can delete pronominal subjects because it has a rich system of verb inflections that unambiguously indicate the person and number of the subject. If you have studied only languages like English, Spanish, and French, you might assume that all languages more or less follow S-V-O word order; in fact, several languages unrelated to English, Spanish, and French, such as Cantonese and colloquial Egyptian Arabic, are also S-V-O languages.[1]

However, S-V-O is only one of three major orders for sentence constituents in the languages of the world, S-O-V and V-S-O being the two alternatives to S-V-O.[2] Some major languages that follow the S-O-V pattern are Japanese, Korean, Turkish, and Farsi (Persian). Some languages that use the V-S-O pattern are the classical versions of Semitic languages such as Hebrew and Arabic, and Celtic languages like Irish, Welsh, and Breton.

In addition to these sentence-level ordering differences, there also seem to be cross-linguistic differences in word order at the phrasal level depending on whether the object noun precedes or follows the verb (Jacobs, 1995:36 ff.). Jacobs points out that in languages like English, where the verb precedes the object, auxiliary verbs normally precede verbs, prepositions precede their objects, and relative clauses follow the nouns they modify. In contrast, in languages like Japanese and Korean, where objects precede verbs, auxiliary verbs normally follow main verbs (in the form of inflections), postpositions follow their objects, and relative clauses precede the nouns they modify. Such phrase-level ordering differences can also cause problems for learners; we discuss them further in the following chapters where relevant.

PHRASE STRUCTURE RULES

In this chapter and the next, we will introduce a set of phrase structure rules for English. These rules describe the sentence-level and sub-sentence-level structures of the language. We agree with Jacobs (1995:34 ff.) that phrase structure rules provide us with a parsing device to make explicit three important basic properties of sentence grammar: linearity, hierarchy, and categoriality. The property of linearity accounts for the fact that the words and morphemes of any English sentence need to be produced in some sort of sequence since they cannot all be produced at once. The basic S-V-O word order for English is an example of linearity. The property of rule hierarchy accounts for the fact that it is not sufficient to simply specify the words and morphemes of an English sentence and give their linear order; some words group together, and these groups in turn contribute to other groups and ultimately to a larger whole. Thus in the following sentence,

The child ate some cookies.

we can see that two words—*the* and *child*—function together as the subject noun phrase while the remaining words—*ate some cookies*—function together as the predicate. Within the predicate we have the verb *ate*, while the other two words, *some* and *cookies*, form the object noun phrase. Now we have something resembling the following in terms of the hierarchy of our sentence (the exact names of the nodes in the hierarchy will be specified later in the rules):

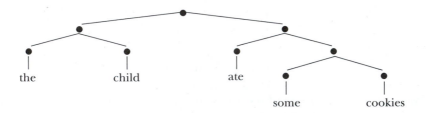

The remaining property, categoriality, accounts for the fact that some words and groups of words behave grammatically in very similar ways and in ways that are different from other words or groups of words. Words may be similar in their distribution (i.e., in the position they can fill in a sentence) or in the inflections they can take. For example, a countable noun, such as *child* or *cookie*, can take a plural inflection and can function as either a subject or object. A transitive verb, such as *eat*, *buy*, or *want*, co-occurs with both a subject and an object and can be inflected for past tense (*ate*, *bought*, *wanted*). Such nouns and verbs are lexical categories (traditionally referred to as parts of speech). However, there are also phrasal categories such as noun phrases, verb phrases, and prepositional phrases that we account for in our rules.

What is the larger lexico-grammatical system within which the phrase structure rules function?

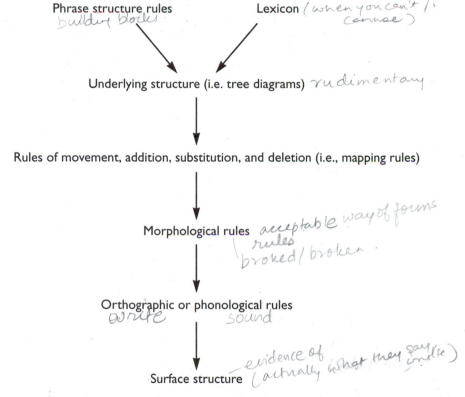

Phrase structure rules *building blocks*   Lexicon *(when you can't /. cannse)*

Underlying structure (i.e. tree diagrams) *rudimentary*

Rules of movement, addition, substitution, and deletion (i.e., mapping rules)

Morphological rules *acceptable way of forms rules broked/broken*

Orthographic or phonological rules *write   sound*

Surface structure *—evidence of (actually what they say/...)*

The phrase structure rules and the lexicon produce the underlying structure, or tree diagrams. The underlying structures first undergo mapping rules of movement, addition, substitution, and deletion as may be needed, and then the resulting structures take morphological rules as needed. Finally, either orthographic or phonological rules, which we do not treat in any detail in this grammar and thus omit from our mappings, are needed to produce a written or spoken surface form.

Through a series of phrase-structure rules, we analyze in greater detail the basic structure of English sentences. The rules are arranged in a hierarchy so that the first rule tells us what the largest unit, the sentence, is composed of. The next rule takes one of the constituents of the sentence and further breaks it down to reveal its composition. In this chapter and the next, we provide a descriptive account of most basic English sentences.

These two chapters differ from those that follow in that phrase structure rules give us a description of language form only, but they are the starting point for our descriptions of the meaning and use of language forms in later chapters.

It is important that you be able to do phrase structure analysis if you wish to develop a thorough understanding of the basic structural units of English. Your students often tend to commit errors of a fundamental nature because they have not yet gained an appreciation for which components of a sentence or phrase in English are obligatory and in what order both obligatory and optional constituents must appear.

Let us now consider our first phrase structure rule:

1. $$S \rightarrow \left\{ \begin{array}{l} (sm)^n \ S' \\ SUBJ \ PRED \end{array} \right\}$$

The arrow means that *S* (sentence) is expanded (or rewritten) in one of two ways, which is indicated by the use of the curly brackets to the right of the arrow. In the first instance, *S* is expanded to include one or more optional sentence modifiers *sm*—the parentheses indicate the optionality of this constituent—and an obligatory sentence core, represented here as *S'*. For now we will limit the term *sentence modifier* to words like *perhaps, maybe, yes,* and *no*. These are sentential adverbs—that is, adverbs that modify an entire sentence. Later, other types of sentence modifiers such as the question marker *Q* and the negation morpheme *not* will also be introduced. This is why the (sm) symbol has the superscript *n*, which allows us to generate any number of sentence modifiers. The capital letters used for the *S* to the left of the arrow and the *S'* to the right indicate that if *S* is expanded as (*sm S'*), the *S'* should be viewed as the main constituent and the (*sm*), which is in lower case, as the modifier.

In the second instance, *S* is expanded in rule 1 as the traditional subject (SUBJ) and predicate (PRED). Rule 2 simply makes explicit the fact that *S'* is also expanded as subject and predicate in those cases where (sm) has been selected in applying rule 1:

2. $S' \rightarrow$ SUBJ PRED

A more graphic way of representing these rules is in a tree diagram. Using the example sentence (e.g., *Perhaps the man works at home*) to illustrate our first two rules, we can construct a tree as follows:

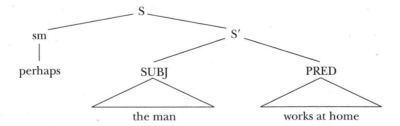

The triangles under SUBJ and PRED indicate that we have not yet completed our analysis of these constituents and must ultimately apply additional rules to complete the task.

THE INTERNAL STRUCTURE OF NOUN PHRASES

The third phrase structure rule rewrites SUBJ as NP (or noun phrase):

3. SUBJ $\rightarrow$ NP

The fourth rule rewrites NP in two quite different ways:

4. $$NP \rightarrow \left\{ \begin{array}{l} (det)^3 \; (AP) \; N \; (\text{-pl}) \; (PrepP) \\ pro \end{array} \right\}$$

In the second instance, NP can be rewritten as a pronoun: *I, you, he, she,* and so on. The first option is more complex in that it allows NP to be expanded in any number of ways. Minimally, it is expanded as an uninflected lexical noun such as *book, rice,* or *Nancy,* for example. Optionally, it can be expanded:

- as a noun with a plural inflection: *books, children*

- as a noun with up to three determiners: *all his other money*

- as a noun with a preceding adjective phrase:[3] *a very blue sky*

- as a noun with a following prepositional phrase: *a man of honor*

- as a noun with various combinations of the above options:

    the famous city of New York

    all the little children

    many very colorful Jack-o-lanterns

The determiner slot in rule 4 can take up to three words. This seems to be more or less the upper limit in English: *all the other, my other two, the first four.* The determiner slot itself consists of three subcategories: (i) predeterminers (words like *all* and *both*), (ii) core determiners (articles like *a* and *the,* demonstratives like *this* and *that,* and possessives like *my* and *his*[4]), and (iii) postdeterminers (quantifiers like *three* and comparative reference terms like *other,* both of which may occur in either order). There is a more detailed discussion of the different kinds of determiners in Chapter 16.

Since determiners are modifiers of nouns, they are often restricted with respect to the number and/or countability of the head nouns with which they can co-occur. In other words, there are some determiners that occur only with singular count nouns like *a, one, another* and many determiners that occur only with plural count nouns: *these, those, many, both, two, three,* and so on. A few determiners occur only with uncountable nouns: *much, (a) little;* and some determiners occur with either singular or uncountable nouns such as *this* and *that.* There are also determiners that occur with either plural nouns or uncountable nouns: *some, all, no, other.* Some determiners, such as the following, of course, can occur with any kind of common noun and thus are not restricted with regard to the number and countability of the head noun: *the, my, his.* As pointed out in Chapter 3, these agreement features are important information about determiners and nouns that should be included in their lexical entries.

The optional prepositional phrase in rule 4 accounts for those prepositional phrases that cannot have a predicate relationship with the head noun (e.g., *a man of honor, the city of Chicago, two pounds of sugar,* etc.). In other words, we cannot paraphrase such NP + PrepP combinations with an intervening *be* copula: **a man is of honor;* **the city is of Chicago.* This contrasts with those prepositional phrases that are semantically predicative, such as *the flowers in the vase* (= the flowers are in the vase), *the books on the table* (= the books are on the table), which have another source.

Noun phrases function in one of three ways in English: as subjects, as objects, and as predicates. Rule 3 accounts only for subject NPs. In the next chapter, we clarify this three-way distinction by showing that where the NP is generated in the sentence determines its grammatical function as a subject, object, or predicate.

Let us now redraw the tree diagram for our example sentence *(Perhaps the man works at home)* using rules 1 through 4 to see the greater specificity we can provide for the subject NP:

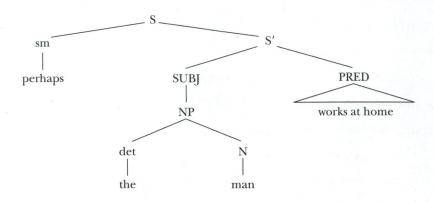

Rule 5 allows us to expand any optional adjective phrase (AP) that we may have selected as part of our expansion of NP in rule 4:

5.　AP → (intens)^n ADJ^n (PrepP)

The term *intens* stands for the optional but potentially multiple intensifiers that can precede an adjective to specify the degree or extent to which the adjective applies. Sometimes the same intensifier is repeated, which is referred to as reduplication, and sometimes different intensifiers are selected:

| very, | very | interesting | news | | really | very | nice | clothes |
| intens | intens | ADJ | N | | intens | intens | ADJ | N |

Rule 5 also indicates that multiple descriptive adjectives can occur before head nouns (e.g., the *big old yellow* bus). The ordering of these adjectives is discussed in some detail in Chapter 20.

The optional prepositional phrase in rule 5 occurs most often with adjective phrases generated in predicate position—a structure we discuss in the following chapter; however, this type of expansion does occasionally occur before the head noun in noun phrases and is usually represented orthographically as a hyphenated complex adjective when it does occur:

| My | good-for-nothing | cousin |
| det | ADJ　PrepP | N |

Let us now expand our example sentence to *Perhaps the very old man works at home* in order to see how the addition of rule 5 affects our tree diagram:

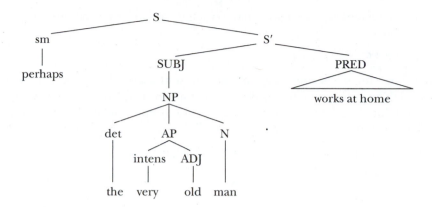

Rule 6 simply expands prepositional phrases as prepositions followed by noun phrases:

    6.   PrepP → Prep NP

Since NP (noun phrase) has already been expanded in rule 4, we would go back and reapply our earlier rule for NP expansion whenever we have a prepositional phrase.
    With the addition of rule 7, we begin to expand the PRED (predicate) constituent:

    7.   PRED → AUX VP (Advl)^n

This means that the predicate of any English sentence obligatorily consists of an auxiliary constituent (AUX) followed by a verb phrase (VP). In addition, any number of optional adverbials may occur in sentence-final position. We leave the discussion of the auxiliary and the verb phrase for the following chapter and conclude this chapter by considering the types of optional adverbials we can have in sentence-final position in English.

THE INTERNAL STRUCTURE OF ADVERBIALS

Rule 8 provides us with three syntactic possibilities for each sentence-final adverbial generated by rule 7:

$$8.\quad \text{Advl} \rightarrow \begin{Bmatrix} \text{Advl CL} \\ \text{Advl P} \\ \text{PrepP} \end{Bmatrix}$$

An example of each structural possibility follows:

    Advl CL: The boys left **before their father could find them.**
    Advl P: The boys work **very quickly.**
    PrepP: The boys eat lunch **in the city.**

Remember that the curly brackets indicate that for each adverbial generated, one, but only one, of the three choices must be selected—an adverbial clause (Advl CL); an adverbial phrase (Advl P); or a prepositional phrase (PrepP).

An adverbial clause can be expanded to include an adverbial subordinator (adv sub) followed by a new sentence (S):

    9.   Advl CL → adv sub S

This rule reintroduces S, a constituent already present in rule 1. To expand the new S, we would go back to rule 1 and begin the process all over again. In other words, phrase structure rules are recursive and can be applied as often as needed. Let us consider the tree diagram for a sentence with an adverbial clause:

Perhaps the boys left before their father could find them.

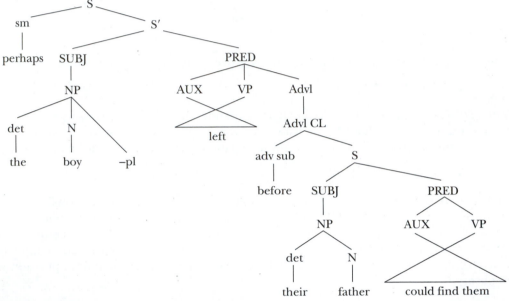

Another possible expansion of the adverbial in rule 8 is an adverbial phrase (Advl P), which is rewritten as follows:

    10. Advl P →   (intens)^n ADV

This rule means that an adverbial phrase contains an obligatory adverb, ADV, optionally preceded by one or more intensifiers, *intens*. An intensifier occurs not only before adjectives—as you saw earlier in rule 5—but also before adverbs. The following sentence and tree diagram illustrate a case where the optional intensifier has been selected to modify an adverb:

Perhaps the boys worked very quickly.

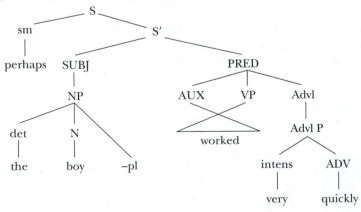

The superscript *n* after the optional intensifier allows for more than one intensifier to occur. As is also the case with adjective phrases in rule 5, some intensifiers may be repeated, while other series of intensifiers can consist of different lexical items:

> very, very quickly
> really quite eagerly

Finally, an optional adverbial may also be expanded as a prepositional phrase. Rule 6, which was introduced earlier and which is repeated here, would apply in such a case:

> 6.   PrepP → Prep NP

We are now in a position to more fully specify the tree diagram for the following sentence:

> Perhaps they eat lunch in the city.

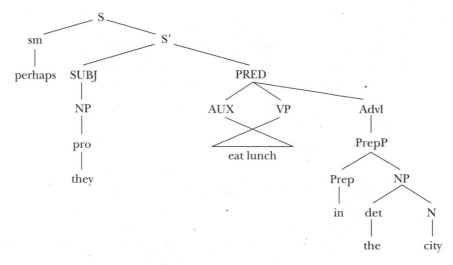

STRUCTURAL VARIATION IN PREPOSITIONAL PHRASES

Note that in sentence-final adverbials, prepositions are used to give adverbial function to nouns with temporal or locative meaning. As a general rule, nouns do not function on their own as adverbs in English. For example, take the following sentences, where the nouns *Monday* and *home* become adverbial with the help of the preceding prepositions:

> Max will stay *until Monday.*   Mr. Green works *at home.*
>   Prep   N   Prep N

However, in some sentences, such as the following, prepositions are optionally deletable:

> I've lived in New York (for) many years.   I'll get the wine (on) Thursday.

And in some sentences, for a variety of reasons, prepositions simply do not occur in English before certain nouns that function adverbially:

> Jack went home.   He will return tomorrow.

To preserve the integrity of our phrase structure rules and to show that the adverbials in all three types of sentences above are very similar in their semantic function, we use similar underlying representations for all of them to acknowledge that in some environments prepositions are optional and in others they do not occur:

| (Max will stay) until Monday | (I've lived in NY) (for) three years. | (Jack went) ø home. |

(a)

```
        PRED
         |
        Advl
         |
        PrepP
        /    \
     Prep     NP
      |        |
    until      N
               |
            Monday
```

(b)

```
          PRED
           |
          Advl
           |
         PrepP
         /    \
      Prep     NP
       |      / | \
     (for)  det N  \
            |   |   \
          three year  -pl
```

(c)

```
        PRED
         |
        Advl
         |
        PrepP
        /    \
     Prep     NP
      |        |
      Ø        N
               |
             home
```

We emphasize that the previous examples (b) and (c) of optionally deletable and obligatorily suppressed prepositions, respectively, are the exceptional cases. Normally, a sentence in which a noun functions adverbially must have a preposition:

> *Aaron was born a leap year. (in)
> *Your belongings are the table. (on)

For further discussion of prepositions, see Chapter 21.

THE ORDERING OF SENTENCE-FINAL ADVERBIALS

The final point to make about sentence-final adverbials is that when more than one occurs, the ordering is not random. To understand the order, it is important to first establish that there are many semantically different types of sentence-final adverbials (the following list is not exhaustive):

> *manner adverbial:* John runs *quickly.*
> *direction adverbial:* John ran *to the store.*
> *position adverbial:* John is *at home.*
> *time adverbial:* Judy eats lunch *at noon.*
> *frequency adverbial:* Judy eats lunch *every day.*
> *purpose adverbial:* Harry works *to earn money.*
> *reason adverbial:* Harry works *because he has to pay bills.*

Some generalizations seem to apply most of the time when more than one adverbial occurs:

Re: Adverbials of Manner, Direction, and Position:
1. Direction and manner have variable order with respect to each other.
2. Manner and position have variable order with respect to each other.
3. Direction tends to precede position, and they tend to be adjacent.

Example:

He ran
{
quickly around the track at the park. [manner → direction → position]
around the track at the park quickly. [direction → position → manner]
?around the track quickly at the park. [direction → manner → position]
}

Re: Adverbials of Time and Frequency:

1. Time and frequency tend to follow manner, direction, and position.

2. Time and frequency are variable in order with respect to each other.

> Example: She eats lunch *quickly (every day at noon/at noon every day)*.
>   manner frequency time   time frequency

Re: Adverbials of Purpose and Reason:

1. Purpose and reason tend to follow all other adverbials.

2. Purpose tends to precede reason.

> Example: She eats lunch *quickly every day* $\left\{ \begin{array}{l} \textit{in order to have time to read.} \\ \quad\quad\quad\text{purpose} \\ \textit{because she likes to have time to read.} \\ \quad\quad\quad\text{reason} \end{array} \right\}$
>   manner frequency

> Jane went to Ohio *to visit her uncle because she hadn't seen him for years.*
>   purpose   reason

> ?Jane went to Ohio *because she hadn't seen her uncle for years to visit him.*
>   reason   purpose

The ordering of sentence-final adverbials thus exhibits some variability, yet it is far from being random, since sequences such as the following are awkward if not ungrammatical:

> ?Marcia walked this morning to the shopping center.
> ?Jane fixes dinner every day quickly.
> ?Harry goes jogging in order to stay fit at noon.

Many nonnative speakers of English order multiple adverbials in unacceptable ways. They also make other common word-order mistakes involving adverbs, such as putting an adverb between the verb and object noun in a verb phrase, which is ungrammatical in English:

> *Mary speaks fluently French.
> *Judy eats quickly lunch.

We will come back to the topic of adverbial ordering in Chapter 25.

CONCLUSION

This concludes our introduction to some important notions that underlie word order and phrase structure in English. We introduced 10 rules and will complete our inventory of the basic phrase structure rules of English in the next chapter, which focuses on the auxiliary and the verb phrase.

TEACHING SUGGESTIONS

As we said earlier, not only do ESL/EFL students have to learn all the parts of an English sentence, they also have to master the order in which these constituents appear. As an ESL/EFL teacher, you would not want to present the phrase structure rules with the formalism used here; however, you certainly can make use of this information to point out to your students that a constituent has been omitted or rule of order violated.

1. Form. For beginning-level students, it might be useful to do some sentence unscrambling, especially if their first languages have S-O-V or V-S-O word order. Stress the basic S-V-O + (advl)^n word order in English for a variety of statement-form sentence types, giving a scrambled sentence to each pair of students (each major constituent group is on a separate slip of paper).

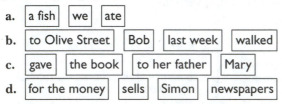

a. | a fish | we | ate |

b. | to Olive Street | Bob | last week | walked |

c. | gave | the book | to her father | Mary |

d. | for the money | sells | Simon | newspapers |

Each pair unscrambles their sentence and writes it on the board for the class to confirm or correct.

2. Form. One rule that you would probably want to teach in a lesson is the rule governing the usual order of sentence-final adverbials. The following is one way in which this might be accomplished (an idea suggested by Robin Abramson):

Step 1: The teacher makes a statement containing one or two adverbials about himself or herself and asks a question of a student that will elicit the same type of statement.

Example questions:
a. *Teacher:* I drove to school today. How did *you* get here?
   Student: I took the bus (here).
b. *Teacher:* I come to English class every day. How often do you come (to class)?
   Student: I come (to English class) every day.
c. *Teacher:* I eat lunch in the cafeteria at noon every day. Where do you eat lunch?
d. *Teacher:* Do you know why I come here at 8:00 every morning? I come here at 8:00 every morning because I want to teach English. Why do you come here?

Step 2: The teacher puts the following sentence on the blackboard:

1   2   3   4   5

Aza comes <u>here</u> <u>promptly</u> <u>at 8:00</u> <u>every day</u> <u>because she wants to learn English</u>.

Step 3: The teacher tells students that each part she or he has underlined is called an adverbial. The teacher then asks students:

a. What does number 1 describe? ([to] where—direction)
b. What does number 2 describe? (how—manner)
c. What does number 3 describe? (when—time)
d. What does number 4 describe? (how often—frequency)
e. What does number 5 describe? (why—reason)

Step 4: The teacher divides the class into three groups. The teacher then passes out a handout. Each handout contains sentences with scrambled adverbials. Each group is to work on one set of sentences and correct any improper order of adverbials. Students may refer to the model on the blackboard. (If more than one order is acceptable, both orders should be given as answers.) For the purposes of this exercise, only postverbal ordering of the type illustrated in the example in Step 2 should be discussed. Later (in Chapters 25, 27, and 30) we show that some adverbials occur sentence-initially for information management or emphasis (e.g., Because of the bad weather we stayed at home). A few examples of sentences to use for the handout might be:

a. Mary studies daily there.
b. The prime minister visited three times last week the United Nations.
c. She ate lunch because she was hungry quickly in the cafeteria.

Step 5: When the groups are finished, students in each group give their answers, and the class or the teacher corrects where necessary.

3. Form. Another grammatical point introduced in this chapter is the agreement required between certain determiners and the number of the noun that follows them. Thus, the sequences below on the left are acceptable, while the sequences on the right are not:

this rod	*these rod
these rods	*this rods
that rod	*those rod
those rods	*that rods

The Cuisenaire rods of various lengths and colors, a tool used in the Silent Way approach (see Gattegno, 1976), provide an excellent device for teaching these agreement patterns once all the colors have been learned.

Step 1: *Teacher* (holding the rod—one in one hand, two in the other):

This rod is yellow. These (rods) are red.

Students (holding the rods—practice using all colors until the agreement pattern is established):

This rod is blue. These (rods) are black. This rod is white. These (rods) are orange.

Step 2: *Teacher* (holding one rod and having placed another rod of another color off at a distance):

This rod is light green. That $\left\{ \begin{array}{c} \text{rod} \\ \text{one} \end{array} \right\}$ is brown.

Students manipulate rods of various colors and practice the agreement pattern until it is established.

Step 3: *Teacher* (holding two rods of one color and having placed two others of another color off at a distance):

These rods are red. Those (rods) are yellow.

Students manipulate rods of various colors and practice the pattern until it is established.

Step 4: *Teacher* stands at a distance from the students to elicit the use of distinct demonstratives based on proximity. Teacher is holding one rod and one student is holding another.

> *Teacher:* What color is this rod?
> *Student:* It's yellow.
> *Teacher:* What color is that rod?
> *Student:* It's red.

Students manipulate rods and practice with each other until the pattern is established. The same thing can then be done for the plural (*Teacher:* What color are these rods? *Student:* They're black) followed by extended student practice in pairs or small groups.

Step 5: Students ask teacher questions while they and teacher hold rods of various quantities and colors.

> *Student:* What color is this rod?
> *Teacher:* It's dark green.
> *Student:* What color are those rods?
> *Teacher:* They're brown.

Step 6: Students manipulate rods and structures (numbers and distance) in any combination or sequence they wish and communicate with each other in pairs or small groups using these patterns. Tea.cher merely supervises at this stage.

EXERCISES

(*Note:* Since we feel it is often more important for you to provide your students with good examples than with verbal definitions, we ask you to do exercises like the first one below throughout the text.)

Test your knowledge of the structures introduced.

1. Provide an original example sentence illustrating each of the following concepts. Underline the pertinent word(s) in your example:
   - **a.** noun phrase
   - **b.** adverbial of reason
   - **c.** adverbial of frequency
   - **d.** adverbial of manner
   - **e.** adverbial of direction
   - **f.** subject
   - **g.** predicate
   - **h.** sentence modifier
   - **i.** adverbial clause of time
   - **j.** intensifier
   - **k.** prepositional phrase
   - **l.** deletable preposition
   - **m.** adjective phrase

2. Draw partially specified tree diagrams for the following sentences using the rules given in this chapter:
   - **a.** The girls talked after the teachers left.
   - **b.** Surely John exercises on Sunday.
   - **c.** The little baby cried because she was hungry.
   - **d.** Fortunately his two brothers work very quietly.
   - **e.** Perhaps Mary studies Latin in the library.

Test your ability to apply what you know.

3. The following sentences contain errors commonly made by ESL/EFL learners. How would you make the learners aware of these errors, and what exercises or activities would you provide to help the learners correct the errors or avoid them in the future?

    a. *He took his brother yesterday to the store.

    c. *John ran for shelter because was raining.

    b. *Those woman are striking for peace.

4. What are the similarities and differences in the structure of the time adverbials in these sentences?

    a. We'll eat at 10 o'clock.

    c. I'm going to Dallas next week.

    b. I've studied English for ten years./ I've studied English ten years.

5. A student asks you why it's okay to say, "I went to school," "I went to church," or "I went to work," but not okay to say "I went to home." How will you answer this question?

BIBLIOGRAPHY

References

Gattegno, C. (1976). *The Common Sense of Teaching Foreign Languages.* New York: Educational Solutions, Inc.

Jacobs, R. A. (1995). *English Syntax: A Grammar for English Language Professionals.* New York: Oxford University Press.

Suggestions for further reading

Other versions of the phrase structure rules for English can be found in the following sources (the last two references are less formal than the first three):

Akmajian, A., and F. Heny (1975). *Introduction to the Principles of Transformational Syntax.* Cambridge, Mass.: MIT Press.

Baker, C. L. (1989). *English Syntax.* Cambridge, Mass.: MIT Press.

Culicover, P. (1976). *Syntax.* New York: Academic Press.

Keyser, S. J., and P. M. Postal (1976). *Beginning English Grammar.* New York: Harper and Row.

Van Riemsdijk, H., and E. Williams (1986). *Introduction to the Theory of Grammar.* Cambridge, Mass.: MIT Press.

Some good suggestions for teaching the order of adverbials are found in:

Danielson, D., and P. Porter with R. Hayden (1990). *Using English Your Second Language* (2d ed.). Englewood Cliffs, N.J.: Prentice Hall Regents. (see especially pp. 189–195)

ENDNOTES

1. Recall that in the previous chapter we distinguished subject-prominent languages from topic-prominent languages. For purposes of the very gross word-order differences we describe here, *subject* and *topic* can be considered roughly equivalent notions.

2. This three-way typology cannot be used too strictly. For many languages, qualifications must be made regarding this typology to explain basic word order patterns. For example, German has mixed word order (S-V-O in main clauses; S-O-V in subordinate clauses), and both Mandarin and Vietnamese appear to have word orders that are shifting from S-V-O to S-O-V. In addition, linguists have found a small number of languages that seem to follow other orders.

3. Someone has pointed out to us that adjective phrases (AP), like descriptive adjectives, seem to occur in strings of two or more. For example:

> -a rather old, quite round, very shiny plate (adjective phrases)
> > versus
> -an old round shiny plate (simple descriptive adjectives)

However, we feel that such multiply-occurring adjective phrases derive from conjunctions (see Chapter 24), but that many instances of multiply-occurring descriptive adjectives do not (see phrase structure rule 5 in this chapter as well as Chapter 20).

4. Articles, demonstratives, and possessive determiners are mutually exclusive in English, though not necessarily so in other languages.

MORE PHRASE STRUCTURE RULES

The preceding chapter introduced 10 rules that specified the form of sentences, noun phrases, and adverbials in English. In this chapter we turn our attention to the phrase structure rules for predicates. The core elements of predicates are auxiliary elements (AUX) and verb phrases (VP).

THE STRUCTURE OF THE ENGLISH VERB SYSTEM

The verb system of English can be discussed in terms of its forms—or it can be discussed in terms of how it encodes meaning. In this chapter we present only the forms of the verb system (the meanings and uses of the forms are discussed in Chapters 7 through 9).

The tense forms of any language are a selective rendering of the many distinctions—both direct and indirect—that one can make with reference to time, and speaker perspective on time, in the real world. The system is selective because *tense*, in the morphological sense, refers only to the inflections one can use with finite (i.e., inflectable) verbs. Given this perspective, English has only two tense forms—past and present (or as some like to say, "past and nonpast," where "past" includes reference to remote events as well as past time, while "nonpast" includes references to present and future time as well as cases in which timelessness is intended, such as "two plus two equals four").[1] If we exclude the irregular verb *be* for the moment, the past tense may be realized through either regular suffixation:

We *walk*⎢ed⎥ to school. (*walk*)

or other irregular vowel and consonant changes:

We *saw* the principal. (*see*)　We *bought* some books. (*buy*)

The present tense is explicitly marked only in the case of third person singular subjects:

He walk⎢-s⎥ to school.

It is expressed implicitly with a lack of marking for all other subjects:[2]

I
you
they ⎬ walk ⎢ø⎥ to school.
we

The verb *be* is more highly inflected than other verbs in English and can express the present through three forms: *am, is, are,* and the past through two forms: *was, were.* (See Chapter 4 for details.)

Every nonimperative English sentence must have either a modal auxiliary (e.g. *can, must, will*) or a grammatical tense—past or present. In addition, English has two optional structural markers of aspect—the progressive and the perfect aspect, which were introduced in Chapter 2 and are further elaborated in Chapter 7.

1. I am walk ing to school.
   be . . . -ing (progressive aspect)

2. I have see n the principal.
   have . . . -en (perfect aspect)

What we need to remember about the progressive and perfect aspects is that the auxiliary verb and the inflection are discontinuous. This is indicated by the three dots in their phrase structure representations. The inflection immediately moves over the following verb to eventually combine with it.

PHRASE STRUCTURE RULES FOR THE AUXILIARY

The English verb thus has many potential auxiliary elements that must be accounted for in our phrase structure rules. Consider the following sentences:

1. John wrote a book.   **4.** John is writing a book.
2. John should write a book. **5.** John is going to write a book.
3. John has written a book.   **6.** Write a book!

If we consider the auxiliary (AUX) as everything in the predicate but the verb phrase and cite the verb phrase in its uninflected base form, *write a book*, we see that the auxiliary + the verb *write* in each of the sentences above consists of the following elements:

1. past tense + write = *wrote*
2. modal *should* + write = *should write*
3. pres tense + perfect *have . . . -en* + write = *has* writt*en* (*-en* = past participle)
4. pres tense + progressive *be . . . -ing* + write = *is* writ*ing* (*-ing* = present participle)
5. pres tense + the phrasal modal *be going to* + write = *is going to write*
6. imperative mood + write = *write*

As we previously mentioned, nonimperative English sentences obligatorily take grammatical tense (-past, -pres) or a modal (e.g., *will, can, must, shall, may*). If some auxiliary verb other than a modal is present, it carries the tense. Beyond tense or a modal, three different optional auxiliary verb types may be present: a phrasal modal[3] (e.g., *be going to, have to, be able to*); the perfect aspect (*have* plus the past participle); and the progressive aspect (*be* plus the present participle). If no tense-bearing auxiliary verb is present, the main verb will carry past or present tense (e.g., sentence 1 above).

Sometimes much more than tense or a modal auxiliary occurs in the AUX of a single sentence. For example:

1. John had to be writing a book. (AUX = past tense, phrasal modal, and progressive aspect)
2. John has been writing a book. (AUX = present tense, perfect and progressive aspects)
3. John should have written a book. (AUX = modal and perfect aspect)
4. John will have been writing a book. (AUX = modal, perfect and progressive aspects)
5. John will have to have written a book. (AUX = modal, phrasal modal, and perfect aspect)
6. John had to have been writing a book. (AUX = past tense, phrasal modal, perfect and progressive aspects)

Not all the combinatory possibilities are illustrated here. We discuss others in subsequent chapters. The tree diagram for the sixth example sentence above is

John had to have been writing a book.

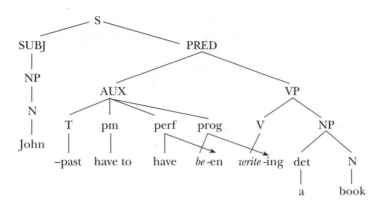

As we have just seen, whenever three or more auxiliary elements occur together, the perfect precedes the progressive, and a phrasal modal precedes either of the two aspects. A modal can precede a phrasal modal and also either of the two aspects. If two or more potentially tense-bearing auxiliary verbs are present, only the first of these auxiliary verbs will carry the tense.

These relationships can be summed up in the following rule:

$$11. \quad \text{AUX} \rightarrow \left\{ \left\{ \begin{matrix} \text{T} \\ \text{M} \end{matrix} \right\} \quad \text{(pm) (perf) (prog)} \atop \text{-imper} \right\}$$

Here the auxiliary is AUX. It is made up of either -imper (imperative mood) or tense (T) or a modal (M), if (T) or (M) is selected; it can be followed by the other optional auxiliary elements: phrasal modal (pm) and the perfect (perf) and progressive (prog) aspects. (Imperative mood is a tenseless verb form in English, which will be explained in detail in Chapter 12.)

You have already learned that morphological tense in English is either past or present. This choice is stated in phrase structure rule 12:

$$12. \quad \text{T} \rightarrow \left\{ \begin{matrix} \text{-past} \\ \text{-pres} \end{matrix} \right\}$$

The perfect and progressive aspects are expanded into their auxiliary verbs and accompanying grammatical inflections in rules 13 and 14 respectively:

13. perf → have . . . -en   *Past Participle*
14. prog → be . . . -ing   *Present participle*

Notice that we are using the -*en* as a symbol for the past participle. Past participles in English are not always formed with an -*en*, as the following examples show:

-en[4]	Vowel alternations	Look the same as the past tense form
written	sung	learned
eaten	drunk	read
seen	swum	taught

ESL/EFL students will need ample practice using the various past participles in order for them to master the many forms.

We have been asked why we have a separate node for the auxiliary elements in our phrase structure rules for English. We do this because the auxiliary is syntactically very important in forming interrogative and negative sentences. It also carries tense, mood, modality, and voice and accounts for most of the morphological complexity in English. The subject and verb phrase, on the other hand, account for the propositional content of sentences—a distinction we will return to in later chapters.

PHRASE STRUCTURE RULES FOR THE VERB PHRASE

Leaving the auxiliary elements aside for the moment, we know that English verb phrases also can be complicated. Consider the following sentences:

a. John is a teacher.	**e.** Judy studies mathematics.
b. Alice is very pretty./Alice is very, very pretty.	**f.** He gave the money to Sally.
c. The students are in the room.	**g.** He gave Sally the money.
d. Steve snores.	**h.** Gaby is allergic to cats.

A phrase structure rule that would allow us to account for all such structural possibilities follows:

$$15. \quad VP \rightarrow \left\{ \begin{array}{l} cop \left\{ \begin{array}{l} NP \\ AP \\ PrepP \end{array} \right\} \\ V \quad (NP)^2 \ (PrepP) \end{array} \right\}$$

(*cop* refers to a copular verb[5])

Can you determine which instance of the above rule would be used to generate each of the above eight sentences? For example, the first three sentences could be accounted for by the following subrules contained within rule 15:

a. VP → cop NP
b. VP → cop AP
c. VP → cop PrepP

See if you can figure out the phrase structure for the verb phrases in sentences (d) and (e). Sentences (g) and (h) convey propositionally equivalent information but are generated by slightly different phrase structure rules for the verb phrase:

g. VP → V NP PrepP
h. VP → V NP_1 NP_2

When option (g) is selected, a special rule of interpretation applies so that we know the first noun phrase is the indirect object and the second the direct object. There is further discussion of this in Chapter 19, which treats sentences that have indirect objects in addition to direct objects. Here is the tree diagram for sentence (h):

Gaby is allergic to cats.

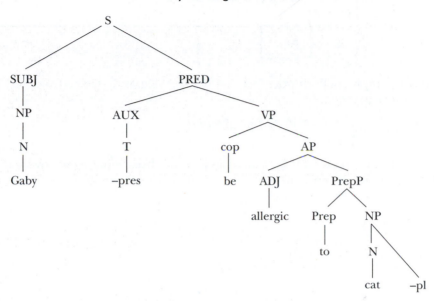

OBJECT NOUN PREDICATES[6]

To complete our basic phrase structure rules, we need to discuss one further sentence type: sentences with object noun phrases that take nouns, adjectives, or adverbial prepositional phrases as predicates. Consider the following examples:

	direct object NPs	*object predicates*
	↓	↓
1. We elected	Sam	treasurer.
2. Lola considers	Forrest	stupid.
3. Sally placed	the book	on the table.

The constituents following the direct objects in these three sentences are the same constituents that can follow a copular verb; however, when they directly follow a copular verb, they refer back to the subject NP (e.g., *Sam is the treasurer*). In the sentences above, the underlined constituents refer to the object NP and predicate something with respect to that object noun phrase:

       1′ Sam is treasurer.
       2′ Forrest is stupid.
       3′ The book is on the table.

To account for this type of sentence, where there is no explicit verb but where a predicative relationship is nonetheless present, we need one further rule[7] that generates such predicates:

$$\text{NP} \rightarrow \text{NP}' \begin{Bmatrix} \text{NP} \\ \text{AP} \\ \text{PrepP} \end{Bmatrix}$$

Actually, this rule is an expansion of rule 4, introduced in the preceding chapter. Rule 4 is now as follows:

4. NP → $\left\{ \begin{array}{l} \text{(det)}^3 \text{ (AP) N (-pl) PrepP} \\ \text{pro} \\ \text{NP}' \left\{ \begin{array}{l} \text{NP} \\ \text{AP} \\ \text{PrepP} \end{array} \right\} \end{array} \right\}$

Our final rule simply spells out the fact that NP′ gets expanded exactly the way NP has been previously expanded:

16. NP′ → $\left\{ \begin{array}{l} \text{(det)}^3 \text{ (AP) N (-pl) (PrepP)} \\ \text{pro} \end{array} \right\}$

These rules allow us to account for sentences like the three sentences above with object predicates. Below, we diagram the first such sentence as an example:

We elected Sam treasurer.

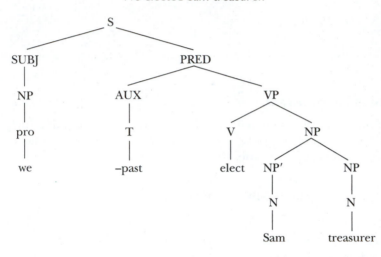

There is one condition on the third option in rule 4; it applies only to prototypical NP objects (e.g. direct objects). Indirect objects, for example, do not take this type of object noun predication.

SYNTACTIC ROLES OF NPS IN PRED (PREDICATE)

This is a good time to review the two syntactic roles that noun phrases can have under the predicate (PRED) node. This is in contrast to the noun phrases directly generated under the subject node (SUBJ), which function only as subjects. Under the predicate node (PRED), NPs can function as objects or predicates. They function as three types of objects:

direct objects: Jim read <u>a book</u>.
indirect objects: Sara gave <u>me</u> some flowers.
objects of prepositions: Sam lives in <u>a big house</u>.

Noun phrases function as predicates of subjects when they occur after a copular verb. They function as predicates of objects when an object noun phrase is expanded, (i.e. the third possibility in rule 4 above) to include an object noun predicate:

subject noun predicate: Jan is <u>a teacher</u>.
object noun predicate: We elected Sam <u>treasurer</u>.

SYNTACTIC ROLES OF PREPOSITIONAL PHRASES

Perhaps the most ubiquitous constituent that we have introduced in our phrase structure rules is the prepositional phrase (PrepP). Prepositional phrases can be generated as parts of noun phrases, verb phrases, adjective phrases, adverbials, or object noun predicates:

PrepP in NP: a man <u>of honor</u>, an ounce <u>of vodka</u>
PrepP in VP: be <u>in the house</u>, give the book <u>to Mavis</u>
PrepP in AP: fond <u>of cats</u>
PrepP in advl: do laundry <u>on Saturday</u>
PrepP in object noun predicate: put the flowers <u>on the table</u>

The three structures with prepositional phrases that are most difficult to distinguish structurally are those where the PrepP is part of the verb phrase, those cases where the PrepP functions as the object noun predicate, and those cases where the PrepP is generated after the verb phrase as an adverbial modifying the whole sentence.

We are going to generate prepositional phrases under the verb phrase only in the following cases:

1. where the PrepP follows the copular verb *be* and predicates something of the subject NP, such as:

   John is <u>in his room</u>.

2. where the PrepP is needed to complete the argument structure of a verb. For example:

   a. *intransitive verb:* The baby lay <u>in the crib</u>.
   b. *ditransitive verb:*[8] Sue handed the letter <u>to Mr. Blake</u>.

Other verbs like *lay* are *lurk, live* (= reside), *head* (= set out for), and *arrive*. The verbs *come* and *go* are also of this type; however, the adverbial (often a PrepP) is frequently not explicitly stated because it is understood from the context. Some other verbs like *hand* are *give, tell, explain, send, transfer, show,* and *deliver*. We normally generate PrepP as the object noun predicate only with verbs like *put, place, set,* or *stand* and verbs like *elect* and *consider* when they are followed by *as:*

   We put the vase <u>on the table</u>.
   We elected Tim <u>as the interim chair</u>.

Again, what distinguishes object noun predicates from other object-like constituents is that they predicate something of the direct object: *The vase is on the table; Tim is interim chair.*

All other cases where the PrepP follows the verb are adverbial in origin and are generated under the adverbial node (Advl):

   Mrs. Symms teaches kindergarten <u>in Dallas</u>.
   Jack sells auto parts <u>for a living</u>.
   We canceled the picnic <u>after the thunderstorm</u>.

SENTENCE DERIVATION

Thus far, the only rules that we have applied are phrase structure rules. They generate the basic structure to which lexical items are added to complete the representation of the sentence. In many cases, minor changes must be made on the output of the phrase structure rules in order to produce grammatical English sentences. This process is called mapping, and the changes are called mapping rules (as opposed to phrase structure rules). Consider the following sentence and its tree diagram:

John has to have been working in the library.

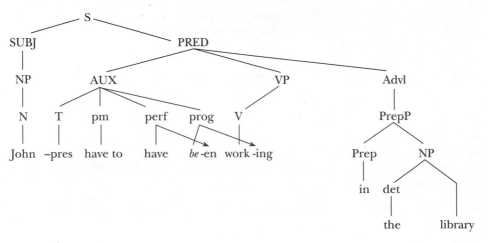

The output of the tree (i.e., the phrase structure rules) is

output: John -pres have to have be -en work -ing in the library

The first mapping rule that we apply to any sentence with a tense morpheme is to copy the person (i.e., 1, 2, or 3) and number (i.e., sg or pl) of the subject NP on the tense; this ensures correct subject-verb agreement. We want to emphasize that subject-verb agreement can apply only to sentences that have a tensed auxiliary.[9] In actual fact, though, no verbs other than *be* ever require subject-verb agreement if past tense appears in the AUX rather than present tense. We abbreviate the operation of copying the subject person and number on the tense by writing simply "copy s/t":

copy s/t: John -pres [+ 3 + sg] have to have be -en work -ing in the library

Finally, morphological rules apply to produce the correct surface form.

morphological rules: John has to have been working in the library.

Let us consider another example with a less complex auxiliary:

Sheila ate the cookies.

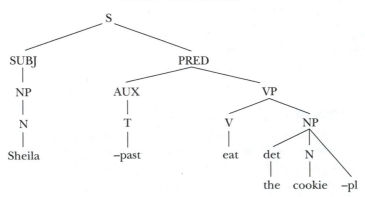

Here, the output of the phrase structure rules is

output: Sheila -past eat the cookie -pl

We again copy the person and number of the subject NP on the tense morpheme; however, since the tense is -past and the verb is not *be*, this will not have any morphological consequences in terms of overt subject-verb agreement:

copy s/t: Sheila -past [+ 3 + sg] eat the cookie -pl

Then we apply morphological rules and get

morphological rules: Sheila ate the cookies.

We provide many more tree diagrams and mappings in subsequent chapters.

SUMMARY OF THE PHRASE STRUCTURE RULES

At this point we think it would be useful to list all the phrase structure rules we have introduced and discussed in this chapter and the preceding one:

1. $S \rightarrow \begin{Bmatrix} (sm)^n \ S' \\ SUBJ \ \ PRED \end{Bmatrix}$

2. $S' \rightarrow SUBJ \ \ PRED$

3. $SUBJ \rightarrow NP$

4. $NP \rightarrow \begin{Bmatrix} (det)^3 \ (AP) \ N \ (-pl) \ (PrepP) \\ pro \\ NP' \begin{Bmatrix} NP \\ AP \\ PrepP \end{Bmatrix} \end{Bmatrix}$

5. $AP \rightarrow (intens)^n \ ADJ^n \ (PrepP)$

6. $PrepP \rightarrow Prep \ \ NP$

7. $PRED \rightarrow AUX \ \ VP \ \ (Advl)^n$

8. $Advl \rightarrow \begin{Bmatrix} Advl \ CL \\ Advl \ P \\ PrepP \end{Bmatrix}$

9. $Advl \ CL \rightarrow adv \ sub \ S$

10. $Advl \ P \rightarrow (intens)^n \ ADV$

11. $AUX \rightarrow \begin{Bmatrix} \begin{Bmatrix} T \\ M \end{Bmatrix} \ (pm) \ (perf) \ (prog) \\ -imper \end{Bmatrix}$

12. $T \rightarrow \begin{Bmatrix} -past \\ -pres \end{Bmatrix}$

13. $perf \rightarrow have \ldots -en$

14. $prog \rightarrow be \ldots -ing$

15. $VP \rightarrow \left\{ \begin{array}{l} cop \left\{ \begin{array}{l} NP \\ AP \\ PrepP \end{array} \right\} \\ V \quad (NP)^2 \ (PrepP) \end{array} \right\}$

16. $NP' \rightarrow \left\{ \begin{array}{l} (det)^3 \ (AP) \ N \ (-pl) \ (PrepP) \\ pro \end{array} \right\}$

These rules can also be summarized in a tree-like fashion following Clark (1997):

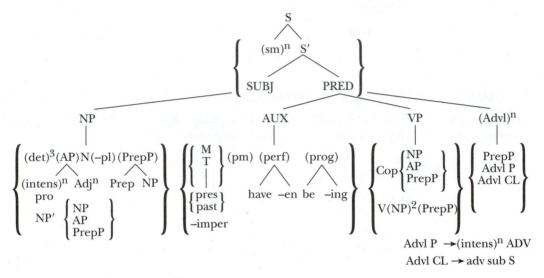

Advl P → (intens)^n ADV
Advl CL → adv sub S

CONCLUSION

This concludes our presentation of the basic phrase structure rules of English grammar. Additional rules and further expansions of the rules will be added from time to time in subsequent chapters as needed. To conclude this chapter we refer back to the diagram presented in the preceding chapter which showed how the phrase structure rules—in combination with lexical choices—can describe the underlying structure of all English sentences. The addition of mapping rules and morphological rules, as needed, account for the more familiar surface structure of these sentences. This flow of rules represents the sequence of rules we will be using in this text.

TEACHING SUGGESTIONS

1. Form. The important thing to stress with the progressive and perfect aspects is that both are formed with two constituents that are not next to each other in the surface structure:

> progressive—a form of *be* plus the present participle *(-ing)* attached to the main verb
> perfect—a form of *have* plus the past participle *(-en)* attached to the following verb

A common error committed by ESL/EFL students is to omit one of the two necessary constituents when forming one of the aspects (i.e., the auxiliary verb or the participial inflection). To help your students better understand this fact, ask them to memorize three sentences that you have written on the blackboard. Make sure that the sentences contain perfect and progressive aspects. Ask the students to close their eyes. While they are not looking, erase certain words or inflections. When the students open their eyes again, they have to guess what is missing. Repeat this procedure several times with different sentences (maybe some of the students can suggest example sentences).

2. Form. Another problem arises when the ESL/EFL student has to learn to deal with all the irregular past tense and past participle forms. The regular past participle forms, like the regular past tense, cause no undue hardship. This is because both are formed with the addition of the *ed* inflectional affix for all persons and numbers:

I walked	we walked	I have walked	we have walked
you walked	you walked	you have walked	you have walked
he/she/it walked	they walked	he/she/it has walked	they have walked

However, many different irregular forms of past tense verbs and past participles will have to be presented as separate vocabulary items—a few introduced from time to time in a 10-minute portion of a class hour.

A good way of organizing such a lesson is to introduce together those past tense verbs and past participles that conform to the same phonological pattern. For example:

> Verbs that pattern like *blow, blew, blown*
> pres past past participle

These can all be presented together. The following is one way this could be accomplished:

a. Teacher writes the following paragraph on the blackboard and then reads it out loud.

> Yesterday the wind <u>blew</u> very hard. It had never <u>blown</u> that hard before. I <u>knew</u> when it first began that it would be bad for my garden. The plants that <u>grew</u> out in the open were hurt badly. Only a few which had already <u>grown</u> strong survived the windstorm. If I had only <u>known</u>, I would have planted them closer to my house.

b. Teacher has students read the paragraph once out loud and discusses with class any new vocabulary. Teacher calls particular attention to the past tense and past participle forms of the underlined verbs:

> blow   blew   blown
> grow   grew   grown
> know   knew   known

c. Teacher gives students an exercise where students have to supply the correct form of a given infinitive verb for a number of sentences. For example:

> (to grow) I have never _____ tulips before.
> (to throw) After waiting a moment, the pitcher _____ the ball to the catcher.

3. Form. Olson and Shalek (1981) suggest that game-type activities be used to practice past participles. One of their ideas is to use a tree with many branches as a visual prop for a verb conjugation game. Each tree branch has several pockets for cards, and on each branch the pocket closest to the trunk has been filled with a card that gives one example of the verb conjugation pattern that the branch represents. The class (or a group) is then given a stack of cards that must be put into the remaining pockets in the tree branches. Sample cards are as follows (note that all three verb forms should be visible even when the card is placed in the pocket):

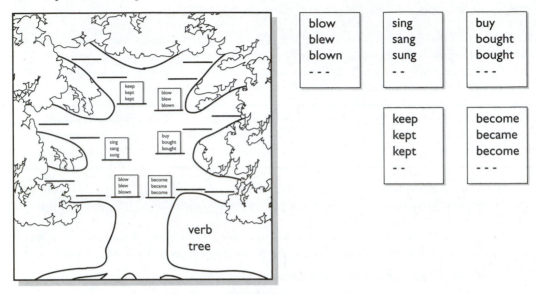

blow
blew
blown
- - -

sing
sang
sung
- -

buy
bought
bought
- - -

keep
kept
kept
- -

become
became
become
- - -

4. Form. With regard to verbs that take an obligatory predicate adverb of direction or position, Valerie Sandoval (personal communication) suggests two exercises:

a. Have students identify and complete any ungrammatical sentences, such as the following:

1. John put the books
2. Here are the flowers
3. The baby cried
4. The tired old woman lay

b. Have students complete sentences using visual aids such as the following:

The baby lay. . .

Ann put the flowers. . .

Roy hung his coat. . .

EXERCISES

Test your knowledge of the structures introduced.

1. Provide an original example sentence illustrating each of the following terms. Underline the pertinent word(s) in your example.
   - **a.** imperative
   - **b.** modal
   - **c.** verb with two objects
   - **d.** phrasal modal
   - **e.** perfect aspect
   - **f.** progressive aspect
   - **g.** object noun predicate

2. Draw tree diagrams for the following sentences, using the phrase structure rules and mapping rules given in this chapter:
   - **a.** The quiet girls talked after the teachers left.
   - **b.** Surely John exercises on Sunday.
   - **c.** The baby cried because she was hungry.
   - **d.** Ian is going to take that class next term.
   - **e.** Anne could have been doing her homework.
   - **f.** Fortunately his brothers work very quietly.
   - **g.** Perhaps Mary has been studying in the library.
   - **h.** We gave some candy to the children.
   - **i.** Ralph put the chairs in the hallway.

Test your ability to apply what you know.

3. The following sentences contain errors that are commonly made by ESL/EFL learners. How would you make your students aware of these problems? What exercises would you use to practice the correct pattern and prevent such errors from recurring?
   - **a.** *She can swims very fast.
   - **b.** *Jane is jump rope.
   - **c.** *Bob will to come tomorrow.
   - **d.** *The man been to Chicago twice.
   - **e.** *Sarah put the books.

4. Although phrase structure rules should not be presented to ESL/EFL students in the forms given in this chapter, they do yield important insights into English structure. One of the insights that should be emphasized in grammar classes has to do with the composition of the progressive aspect. In light of the following errors by different ESL learners attempting to form the progressive aspect, what should be emphasized for each of them?
   - **a.** *She running now.
   - **b.** *She is run now.

5. One of your students asks you why a certain grammar text claims that English has no future tense. This student feels that English *has* a future tense. How would you answer this question?

BIBLIOGRAPHY

References

Clark, R. (1997). Class notes, English Structures. School for International Training, Brattleboro, Vt.

Olson, C., and S. Shalek (1981). Games and Activities Based on Grammatical Areas Which Are Problems for the Intermediate ESL Student. Unpublished manuscript, School for International Training, Brattleboro, Vt.

van Riemsdijk, H. and E. Williams (1986). *Introduction to the Theory of Grammar.* Cambridge, Mass: MIT Press.

Suggestions for further reading

For the historically original form of phrase structure rules written within a transformational grammar of English, see:
Chomsky, N. (1957). *Syntactic Structures*. The Hague: Mouton.
Chomsky, N. (1965). *Aspects of the Theory of Syntax*. Cambridge, Mass.: MIT Press.

For useful lists of verbs with irregular past tense and past participles, see:
Clark, R., P. Moran, and A. Burrows (1991). *The ESL Miscellany* (2d ed.). Brattleboro, VT: Pro Lingua Associates. 60–64.

For a list of phonologically similar irregular verbs, see:
Celce-Murcia, M., D. Brinton, and J. Goodwin (1996). *Teaching Pronunciation*, New York: Cambridge University Press, 382–385.

ENDNOTES

1. From a morphological point of view, English has no future tense, since future time is not expressed inflectionally but periphrastically, using auxiliary verbs (e.g., *John will go*) or adverbs of time in combination with the present tense (e.g., *John goes tomorrow*) instead of a morphological future tense.

2. The symbol ø represents zero. Here it means no inflection.

3. Modal auxiliaries and phrasal modals and their combinations and interactions with aspect are discussed further in Chapter 8.

4. Those verbs that add *-en* are often phonologically and/or orthographically irregular.

5. As discussed in Chapter 4, the most common English copular verb is *be;* however, other verbs may also have a copular function (i.e., may link subjects with nominal, adjectival, and adverbial predicates); for example: *become, seem, appear, sound.*

6. Some traditional grammars refer to the constructions we discuss here as "object complements."

7. Many linguists (van Riemsdijk & Williams, 1986:323ff.) refer to such structures as "small clauses" and offer more complicated rules to account for them. We will keep the simpler notation of expanded rule 4 and note that this rule can be used not only to generate predicates of NP objects but also to generate verbless predicates of subject NPs (the man *responsible* is Ralph) and NP objects of prepositions (I talked to those *responsible* for the incident).

8. Recall that ditransitive verbs either require or allow two object noun phrases to complete their argument structure (or meaning). Often there is also a paraphrase of such sentences without the prepositional phrase: *Sue handed Mr. Blake the letter.*

9. In those cases where there is no tense in AUX (i.e., the AUX is a modal (M) or -imper, there can never be any subject-verb agreement, since such agreement is possible only in sentences that have a tensed auxiliary.

7

THE TENSE AND ASPECT SYSTEM

INTRODUCTION

In Chapter 6 we presented a form-oriented account of tense and aspect in English and introduced the following phrase structure rule:

$$\text{AUX} \rightarrow \left\{ \begin{matrix} \left\{ \begin{matrix} T \\ M \end{matrix} \right\} \text{ (pm) (perf) (prog)} \\ \text{-imper} \end{matrix} \right\}$$

According to this rule, the auxiliary of a non-imperative English sentence must have either a modal or a tense marker (which a later rule specifies as either *past* or *present*), and it may have several optional components: phrasal modals, perfect aspect, and progressive aspect. The expression "future tense" was viewed as a misnomer since in English finite verb stems[1] are not inflected to express future time, as they are in certain other languages, such as most Romance and Slavic languages. Of course, this does not mean that English speakers cannot talk of future events. They do so by using other means, such as modals, phrasal modals, and adverbials of time, rather than by placing a formal marking on the verb itself.

However, as we have already seen, language teachers need to deal with meaning and use as well as form. It is not enough to say to ESL/EFL students, "English does not have a future tense," and be done with the matter. Therefore, in this chapter we start by inventorying the forms that English *does* use to deal with the three time periods: present, past, and future. We also discuss perfect and progressive aspects, leaving most of the discussion of modals and phrasal modals to the next chapter. Because the exact mapping of form, meaning, and use varies considerably from language to language, mastering the English tense-aspect system requires considerable effort on the part of ESL/EFL students. Because of its importance and its challenge, we devote two chapters to its consideration. In this first chapter we explore the form, meaning, and use of the English tense-aspect system at the sentence level. Sentence-level use is perhaps the way most teachers first introduce the forms. To really understand how the system functions, however, it is necessary to appreciate its application at the suprasentential, or discourse, level. Without this perspective it is impossible to fully explain the various patterns of tense-aspect combinations that occur, which we do in Chapter 9.

One point we wish to underscore here for teachers is that even at the sentence level a system is operating. We have sometimes seen teachers introduce a tense, yet fail to show students how that tense contrasts with others, let alone how it fits into the system as a whole. In order to see how the system operates, we first describe its form. Next, we propose a core meaning for each of the tenses and aspects of the system and illustrate how the core meaning applies when tenses are used by themselves and when they are combined with one or both aspects. Finally, we contrast the uses of some of the most commonly confused combinations.

THE FORMAL CHARACTERISTICS OF THE TENSE-ASPECT SYSTEM

Over the years, the important distinction between tense and aspect has become blurred. Instead, English has been said to have 12 "tenses." We have tried to be careful in the preceding discussion to talk about the *tense-aspect* system and *tense-aspect* combinations. We feel that if the natural division between tense, which relates to *time,*[2] and aspect, which has to do with the internal structure of the action occurring *at any time,* are dealt with separately at first, the system that results from their subsequent combination is much easier to see and, therefore, easier to learn. We do this in the following chart by listing the two tenses, present and past, along the vertical axis. We include the future on this list of tenses as well, for although there is no verb inflection for future time, any description of the English tense-aspect system needs to account for what form-meaning combinations *do* exist that relate to future time. The four aspects—simple (sometimes called zero aspect), perfect, progressive, and their combination, perfect progressive—are arrayed along the horizontal axis. We illustrate the tense-aspect combinations with the irregular verb *write* and the regular verb *walk*.

	Simple	**Perfect**	**Progressive**	**Perfect Progressive**
	ø	*have + -en*	*be + -ing*	*have + -en be + -ing*
Present	*write/writes*	*has/have written*	*am/is/are writing*	*has/have been writing*
	walk/walks	*has/have walked*	*am/is/are walking*	*has/have been walking*
Past	*wrote*	*had written*	*was/were writing*	*had been writing*
	walked	*had walked*	*was/were walking*	*had been walking*
Future	*will write*	*will have written*	*will be writing*	*will have been writing*
	will walk	*will have walked*	*will be walking*	*will have been walking*

You can see in the chart that the traditional 12 "tenses" are actually 12 combinations of tense and aspect. They are named by combining a tense with an aspect or aspects, such as present perfect or past perfect progressive. Only the forms in the first column receive their names by first specifying the aspect—simple—and then the tense, such as simple present.[3]

The simple present remains in its base form (*write, walk*) with one exception—the third person singular form, which is made by adding an *-s* to the verb (*writes, walks*). The present perfect is formed with the verb *have* (*has* for third person singular) and the past participle, here symbolized by *-en*. It is important to remember that *-en* is only a symbol. Sometimes the past participle does indeed end in *-en*, as does our example irregular verb, *written*. Other times, the past participle is identical to the past tense form of the verb, as you can see in our other example, where the regular verb *walk* has the past participle *walked*. The present progressive form (sometimes called the present continuous) combines a form of the *be* verb (*am, is, are*), depending on the person and number of the subject, with the present participle, an *-ing* form.[4] Finally, the present perfect progressive can be seen to be a combination of the perfect form with *have + -en* and the progressive form with *be + -ing*. In this case, the *be* verb of the progressive carries the *-en* perfect ending; in other words, it is in its past participle form, *been*.

Reading down the chart, you can see that the various combinations with past tense and aspect pattern in much the same way as the present tense. The past tense in its simple form in English is formed by using its past irregular form, as in the irregular verb in our chart, *wrote,* or with a regular verb such as *walk* by adding an *-ed* to give us *walked.* One difference from the simple present is that the form of the simple past remains invariant for all persons and numbers. The past perfect form is made with the past form of the *have* verb (i.e., *had*) followed by the past participle of the main verb. The past progressive form combines the past form of the *be* verb, here in two forms—first and third person singular form *was* and all the other persons and numbers with *were*—followed by the present participle. The past perfect progressive is formed with the past form of the *have* verb (i.e., *had*) followed by the past participle of the *be* verb (i.e., *been*) and the present participle of the main verb, here *writing* or *walking.*

For the future line in our matrix, we use the modal *will,* since there is no future tense that appears as a marking on the verb in English. As we have also already noted, however, English uses a number of ways in addition to the use of *will* to indicate that an action or event is to take place in the future. (We discuss these in the section on The Use of the Tense-Aspect System later in this chapter). The future adheres to the same patterns as the present and past in terms of its combination of aspect markers: *will* with the base form for the simple future, *will + have + -en* for the future perfect, *will* with *be + -ing* for the future progressive, and *will + have + -en + be + -ing* for the future perfect progressive.

Thus, one of the reasons for displaying the tense-aspect combinations in this manner is to demonstrate that the 12 "tenses" are simply combinations of tense and aspect. Since the perfect and progressive aspect markers contribute consistent meanings regardless of tense, in effect, ESL/EFL students have to learn only the form and meaning of the three tenses (in their simple form) and the two aspects (perfect and progressive) to develop an understanding of the tense-aspect system of English. This is why we say that by viewing the tenses and aspects as a system, the learning burden is lessened.

If we think of this matrix as a map of the territory that the tense-aspect system of English covers, we can make some further observations that have pedagogical import. For example, the traffic on our map is focused more in the northwest (including the present progressive) than in other areas. In other words, the frequency with which these tense-aspect combinations are used is greater than in other regions of our map. Such observations can help teachers to decide where to put the limited time they have to best advantage. The southeast, for example, receives very little traffic and consequently should probably not receive as much attention as those combinations in the northwest.

Another point worth making in viewing the semantic territory covered by the tense-aspect system as a map is that the borders between the various regions of the map which prove to be most problematic. Where, for example, does the semantic domain of the past tense end and the present perfect begin? If you were to draw circles on our map to connect those areas with troublesome boundaries, you would find that there are a few that prove particularly challenging to ESL/EFL students. You may wish to try to do this now. We revisit these difficult distinctions in a later section on the use of the tense-aspect system.

MEANING IN THE ENGLISH TENSE-ASPECT SYSTEM

This is an exceedingly important dimension in helping students manage the tense-aspect system. If students are able to develop a feel for the meanings conveyed by components of the system, they will have a tremendous advantage in learning to cope with the boundary problems introduced above and discussed in detail below. In this section, therefore, we attempt to capture the semantic core of each of the components of the system—the three tenses with simple aspect and the two other aspect markers used independently and in tandem.

As we have asserted earlier, understanding the semantics of the tenses in terms of time is inadequate. For instance, if we label the *-ed* marker as a past-tense marker that denotes past time, then we have a hard time explaining its presence in sentences such as the following:

> If I walked home after school today, it would take me all afternoon.
> They said that they loved grammar.
> *Host to guest:* Did you want something to eat before the game?
> *Sales clerk to customer:* What sort of price did you have in mind?

In the first sentence, the action is hypothetical and hasn't taken place, so obviously the *-ed* is not signifying past time. In the second sentence, an example of reported or indirect speech, the verb in the embedded clause is in past tense, but the expression of their affection for grammar could well still apply—that is, it may not be over and done with. In the third example, the irregular form of the past tense of the verb *do* is used in a present offer; in the fourth, it is used in a question pertaining to the present. We could cite many other examples. The point is that in order to understand the meaning of the tenses, you must go to a deeper level of abstraction than that of temporal meaning. By so doing, you will see what core meaning underlies the use of the past tense in the preceding example sentences and in all other sentences in which it occurs. The *core meaning* of a particular form is the meaning that is most central, primary, or invariant (Hatch and Brown 1995). We begin by analyzing the core meanings of the tenses with simple aspect.

SIMPLE ASPECT

Hirtle (1967) explains that simple aspect refers to events that are conceptualized as complete wholes. The events are not presented as allowing for further development. This aspect stands in contrast to progressive aspect, which is incomplete or imperfective— where the event or state is viewed as some portion of a whole and where there is room for further development or change. We can see this difference by comparing examples with the simple present tense and present progressive:

> Susan and Carl live in Newark.
> Susan and Carl are living in Newark.

The simple present in the first sentence presents the fact that Susan and Carl live in Newark as a whole event, not allowing for further development, and with no suggestion of change. The present progressive in the second sentence suggests that their living in Newark may be temporary, thus allowing for the possibility of change. In the second sentence, Susan and Carl's living in Newark is some portion of the whole, in the sense that we understand that they may have lived elsewhere before moving to Newark and will likely in the future move again.

With this explanation of the core meaning of simple aspect as a backdrop, let us consider what core meaning each of the tenses adds.

Simple Present Tense

The present tense conveys immediate factuality (Lewis 1986):

> I skim the *New York Times* at breakfast.
> The earth rotates around the sun.
> My mother loves daisies.
> It is a beautiful day.

Let us now show how the core meanings of the simple present, its complete or unchanging nature, and its immediate factuality, apply.

a. Habitual actions in the present:

> He walks to school every day.

b. General timeless truths, such as physical laws or customs:

> Water freezes at 0 degrees centigrade.
> Spaniards eat dinner late.

c. With *be* and other stative verbs to indicate states:

> There is a large house on the corner.
> I know Mr. Jackson.
> The car belongs to Bill.

or even the inception of states:

> Now, I understand.

d. In the subordinate clauses of time or condition when the main clause contains a future-time verb:[5]

> After he finishes work, he'll do the errands.
> If Cindy passes the bar exam, she'll be able to practice law.

e. Expresses future (when a scheduled event is involved, usually with a future-time adverbial):

> I have a meeting next Wednesday at that time.

f. Present event/action (usually in sporting events or demonstrations/procedures of some sort):

> Here comes the pitch; Vaughn swings and misses.
> Now I add three eggs to the mixture.

g. Present speech acts (where the action is accomplished in the speaking of it):

> I resign from the commission.

h. Conversational historical present (used to refer to certain past events in narration):

> "So he stands up in the boat and waves his arms to catch our attention."

It can be seen then, how each event being reported on in the simple present is complete; we can infer there will be no change. Further, each use is an immediate factual report. Next, let us consider the simple past tense. The same general semantic character for simple aspect holds for the simple past as well. Simple past describes events as wholes, ones not conducive to change or development.

Simple Past Tense

The simple past also states facts. What the core meaning of the past tense adds is a sense of remoteness (Knowles 1979). The event can be remote in time:

> The Toronto Blue Jays won the World Series in 1992.

And even if the event is a recent one, such as

> I finished my term paper!

the "remoteness" comes in the feeling that the event is over and done with. As we saw earlier, the feeling of remoteness can apply even to notions other than time:

> If I walked home from school, it would take all afternoon.

Here, the remoteness is due to the conditional, hypothetical nature of this statement. In fact, this is an imaginary conditional (see Chapter 27), and remote from reality.[6] In the example sentence given earlier, "They said that they loved grammar," the remoteness comes from the fact that this is a report of what some other people originally said. It is indirect, not their actual expression of affection. And, in the host's offer, "Did you want something to eat before the game?" the use of the past-tense form of the *do* verb makes the offer more indirect than it would be if the present-tense form *do* were used. Here indirectness can be a sign of politeness. This same interpretation explains why the clerk used the past tense in his question to the customer about the price she had in mind. Another example of indirectness as social distance conveyed by the past tense occurs in the following preliminary to a request:

> I am calling because I wanted to ask you a favor.

Let us now examine uses of the past tense to see how these notions of completeness and remoteness apply:

a. A definite single completed event/action in the past:

> I attended a meeting of that committee last week.

b. Habitual or repeated action/event in the past:

> It snowed almost every weekend last winter.

c. An event with duration that applied in the past with the implication that it no longer applies in the present:

> Professor Nelson taught at Yale for 30 years.

d. With states in the past:

> He appeared to be a creative genius.
> He owed me a lot of money.

e. Imaginative conditional in the subordinate clause (referring to present time—discussed in Chapter 27):

> If he took better care of himself, he wouldn't be absent so often.

f. Social distancing:

> Did you want to sit down and stay a while?

So as we can see, the simple past is used when the speaker conceptualizes a complete event factually, but as remote in some way.

Simple Future Tense with *will* (or Contracted *'ll*)

We have already made the point several times that there are many ways to talk about the future in English. We discuss the alternatives later in this chapter and then again in Chapter 9. For now, the picture we have been painting for simple aspect holds for the simple future as well. In other words, simple future is used when the event is conceptualized as a whole. One difference in its core meaning is that events in the future time cannot be factually knowable in the same way as those in the past or present can. Therefore, because, strictly speaking, the future can't be reported on factually, *will* is said to be used for strong predictions, not factual reports:

> We will cover the first half of the book this term.

> We will never know what cures tropical plants possess if we don't become serious about preserving the forests in which they grow.

Will has other meanings as well, and these are dealt with in the chapter on modals. Let us now see how its core meaning of strong predictability applies:

a. An action to take place at some definite future time:

> Joel will take the bar exam next month.

b. A future habitual action or state:

> After October, Judy will take the 7:30 train to Chicago every day.

And even for present habits, about which strong predictions can be made:

> Erik is so funny. He'll wake up, and before coming downstairs, he'll start playing with his trains. (example from Lori Gray)

c. A situation that may obtain in the present and will obtain in the future but with some future termination in sight (notice here it is not the *will* that suggests the limitation on the event, but the subordinate clause):

> Nora will live in Caracas until she improves her Spanish.

d. In the main (result) clause of future conditionals:

> If you go, you'll be sorry.

Here again, we should be able to see that the simple tense allows us to talk about events as wholes. Before moving on, then, let us summarize. Simple aspect allows us to talk about events as not open to development or change and to make factual statements or strong predictions about them. This is true despite the tense and is true for both specific facts and general ones.

Specific	*General*
Joe misses Susie.	Leap year comes every four years.
You slept till noon!	Dinosaurs roamed the earth for millions of years.
I'll be home by 6 P.M.	Oil will float on water.

PERFECT ASPECT

The core meaning of the perfect is "prior," and it is used in relation to some other point in time. For instance, present perfect is used retrospectively to refer to a time prior to now:

> Have you done your homework?

The past perfect offers a retrospective point of view on some past time:

> He had left before I arrived.

The future perfect offers a retrospective point of view on some future time:

> Mark will have finished all his chores by the time we get there.

Next, we examine in detail the combination of the perfect with the three tenses to see how this core meaning obtains.

Present Perfect

a. A situation that began at a prior point in time and continues into the present:

> I have been a teacher since 1967.

b. An action occurring or not occurring at an unspecified prior time that has current relevance

> I have already seen that movie.

c. A very recently completed action (often with *just*):

> Mort has just finished his homework.

d. An action that occurred over a prior time period and that is completed at the moment of speaking:

> The value of the Johnson's house has doubled in the last four years.

e. With verbs in subordinate clauses of time or condition:

> She won't be satisfied until she has finished another chapter.[7]
> If you have done your homework, you can watch TV.

Past Perfect

a. An action completed in the past prior to some other past event or time:

> He had already left before I could offer him a ride.
> She had worked at the post office before 1962.

b. Imaginative conditional in the subordinate clause (referring to past time):

> If Sally had studied harder, she would have passed the exam.

Future Perfect

a. A future action that will be completed prior to a specific future time:

> I will have finished all this word processing by 5 P.M.

b. A state or accomplishment that will be completed in the future prior to some other future time or event:

> At the end of the summer the Blakes will have been married for 10 years.

Thus, you can see that when it interacts with each of the three tenses, perfect aspect allows us a retrospective point of view from a particular point in time: present, past, and future.

PROGRESSIVE ASPECT

We have already made the case for the core meaning of progressive aspect as being imperfective, meaning that it portrays an event in a way that allows for it to be incomplete, or somehow limited. You saw how this core meaning was manifest in the contrast between an event of a temporary nature:

> Susan and Carl are living in Newark.

in contrast with an ongoing state:

> Susan and Carl live in Newark.

Another difference is that while the simple tenses can be used to make generic statements:

> Weeds grow like wildfire.

progressive aspect is always specific:

> Weeds are growing like wildfire (in my garden).

Here are uses of the tense-progressive combinations, so you can see how the core meaning of the progressive holds for all the tenses:

Present Progressive (Sometimes Called Present Continuous)

a. Activity in progress:

> He is attending a meeting now.

b. Extended present (action will end and therefore lacks the permanence of the simple present tense):

> I'm studying geology at the University of Colorado.

c. A temporary situation:

> Phyllis is living with her parents.

d. Repetition or iteration in a series of similar ongoing actions:

> Henry is kicking the soccer ball around the backyard.

e. Expresses future (when event is planned; usually with a future-time adverbial):[8]

> She's coming tomorrow.

f. Emotional comment on present habit (usually co-occurring with frequency adverbs *always* or *forever*):

> He's always delivering in a clutch situation. (approving)
> He's forever acting up at these affairs. (disapproving)

g. A change in progress:

> She's becoming more and more like her mother.

Past Progressive

a. An action in progress at a specific point of time in the past:

> He was walking to school at 8:30 this morning.

b. Past action simultaneous with some other event that is usually stated in the simple past:

> Karen was washing her hair when the phone rang.
> While Alex was traveling in Europe, he ran into an old friend.

c. Repetition or iteration of some ongoing past action:

> Jake was coughing all night long.

d. Social distancing (which comes from the past tense and the tentativeness of the progressive aspect):

> I was hoping you could lend me $10.

Future Progressive

a. An action that will be in progress at a specific time in the future:

> He will be taking a test at 8 A.M. tomorrow.

b. Duration of some specific future action:

> Mavis will be working on her thesis for the next three years.

PERFECT PROGRESSIVE ASPECT

As its name implies, this aspect combines the sense of "prior" of the perfect with the meaning of "incompleteness" inherent in the progressive aspect.

> He has been working hard on a special project.

We understand that the event being reported here was begun prior to now and that his hard work is limited—that is, it will not continue indefinitely. Next, we examine how these two core meanings work in tandem for each of the tenses.

Present Perfect Progressive

a. A situation or habit that began in the past (recent or distant) and that continues up to the present (and possibly into the future):

> Burt has been going out with Alice.

b. An action in progress that is not yet completed:

> I have been reading that book.

c. A state that changes over time:

> The students have been getting better and better.

d. An evaluative comment on something observed over time triggered by current evidence:

> You've been drinking again!

Past Perfect Progressive

a. An action or habit taking place over a period of time in the past prior to some other past event or time:

> Carol had been working hard, so her doctor told her to take a vacation. She had been trying to finish her degree that year.

b. A past action in progress that was interrupted by a more recent past action:

> We had been planning to vacation in Maine, but changed our minds after receiving the brochure on Nova Scotia.

c. An ongoing past action or state that becomes satisfied by some other event:

> I had been wanting to see that play, so I was pleased when I won the tickets.

Future Perfect Progressive

Durative or habitual action that is taking place in the present and that will continue into the future up until or through a specific future time:

> On Christmas Eve we will have been living in the same house for 20 years.
> He will have been keeping a journal for 10 years next month.

We can sum up our observations so far concerning the core meanings of the English tense-aspect system with this diagram:

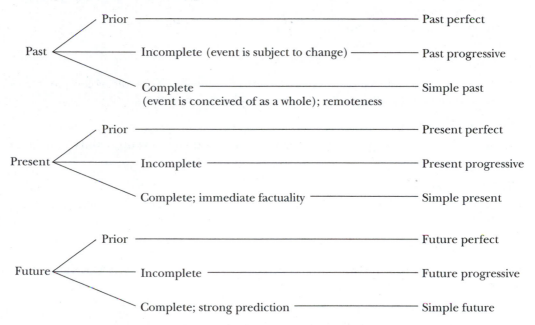

While this approach accounts, we feel, for much of the core semantics of the system, it does need some refinement at a more local level. For one thing, the meaning of the grammatical aspect can be affected by the choice of verb since verbs have their own inherent lexical aspect.

THE LEXICAL ASPECT OF VERBS

As you saw in Chapter 3, verbs have not only grammatical aspect but lexical aspect as well. Verbs can be divided into four categories based on their inherent lexical aspect (Vendler 1967).

Activity	*Accomplishment*	*Achievement (punctual)*	*State*[9]
run	paint (a picture)	recognize (something)	have
walk	make (a chair)	realize (something)	contain
swim	build (a house)	lose (something)	seem
live	write (a novel)	find (something)	want
study	grow up	win the race	like

Activities, accomplishments, and achievements all involve changes of state. Activity verbs are durative and describe an ongoing action. They each have an undefined beginning and end point. Accomplishment verbs, on the other hand, share with activity verbs their durativity but each has a well-defined end point, when the particular action described in the verb phrase is—or is not—completed. Achievement verbs also each have a well-defined end point; however, they have no duration. They are punctual. Stative verbs do not involve change. They depict a stable situation that is assumed to last more or less indefinitely. Often stative verbs are broken down into the following subcategories, with several verbs appearing in more than one category depending on their meaning:

Sensory perception: *smell, see, hear, taste, feel*
Mental perception: *know, believe, think, understand, mean, doubt*
Possession: *possess, have, own, belong*
Emotions, attitudes, and opinions: *like, love, hate, dislike, want, desire, need, prefer, appreciate, doubt, feel, wish*
Measurement: *equal, measure, weigh, cost*
Relationship: *contain, entail, consist of*
Description: *be, resemble, sound, appear, seem, look*

How these four main categories of verbs—activity, accomplishment, achievement, and state—interact with the aspects we have just considered is as follows:

With Simple Aspect

The simple tenses can express either specific or general facts, events, habits, and states with all four verb types.

With Perfect Aspect

Activity verbs are not as commonly used with perfect aspect as some of the other categories of verbs. When they are used with perfect aspect, they describe a prior experience or activity.

I have run before.

Accomplishment and achievement verbs go easily with perfect aspect and signal prior events that are completed:

John Updike has written many novels.
The true meaning of that holiday has been lost.

Stative verbs with perfect aspect signal a state that may or may not have ended at the time of speech:

I have owned a Rolls Royce $\begin{cases} \text{before.} \\ \text{since 1987.} \end{cases}$

With Progressive Aspect

Activity verbs readily take the progressive, which reinforces the fact that the action has duration:

Meg is washing her car.

Accomplishment verbs also take the progressive, but in this case the progressive focuses on progress toward a particular end that has not yet been completed:

The contractors are building the new civic center.

With achievement verbs, because they are punctual, the progressive gives the meaning of iteration:

He is nodding his head in agreement.

or inception of an event:

Joe is realizing his mistake.

Alternatively, by stretching out the moment, the speaker can place emphasis on the action associated with the achievement:

> The plane is landing right on schedule.

It has been said that stative verbs do not normally take the progressive because of a fundamental semantic conflict between a grammatical aspect that denotes a limited duration and a lexical aspect that expresses a stable state.

> *I am knowing the answer.

However, such an unqualified generalization discounts the frequently made observation that the progressive can occur with stative verbs to achieve certain effects. (See Kesner Bland 1988 for discussion). The progressive turns states into events. As such, "progressive statives" can be used to

a. intensify the emotion expressed by the verb:

> I'm hating this assignment.
> I hate this assignment.

b. indicate current behavior as opposed to general description:

> He's being rude.
> He's rude.

c. introduce change in states by focusing on differences in degree across time:

> I'm understanding less and less about life, the older I get.

Other uses of progressive statives found by Gavis (1997) are to:

d. show limited duration

> "Are you understanding this?"

e. emphasize conscious involvement:

> "What we are seeing is a red dwarf star."

f. show vividness

> "One night in the middle of the night, I'm hearing dripping."

g. express politeness

> "Are you liking it?" (cf. "Do you like it?")

h. mitigate criticism

> "I like the first piano notes, but I'm not liking it where the strings come in."
> (cf. . . . "but I do not like it . . .")

i. avoid imposition

> "I was just wanting to invite you to a gathering . . ." (answering machine message)

The other difficulty we run into in claiming that stative verbs do not take the progressive is that many stative verbs, even the classic verb of state, the copula *be*, have nonstative counterparts that are active in meaning and that may occur with the progressive.

State *(subject is not the agent)*	Action *(subject is the agent)*
The steak weighs 12 ounces.	The butcher is weighing the steak.
You are a fool.	You're being a fool.
I taste cinnamon in these rolls.	We'll be tasting wine at the vineyard.

All this means that we have to think in terms of stative "meanings" rather than stative "verbs" to correctly understand and explain restrictions on the use of the progressive aspect in English.

With Perfect Progressive Aspect

With activity verbs, perfect progressive aspect implies that the action began in the past and has duration at the present time:

> Mike has been running for two hours.

or is iterative and/or habitual:

> Mike has been running for years.

With accomplishment verbs, the perfect progressive indicates that the action has been going on for some time and is not yet complete:

> They have been repairing that bridge for months.

With achievement verbs, perfect progressive aspect is a bit strange if only one action is intended, due to the fact that achievement verbs are punctual:

> ?Mike has been winning that race for hours.

but not if the achievement is iterative:

> Mike has been winning that race for years.

With stative verbs, perfect progressive aspect often appears to be more compatible than progressive aspect alone:

> ?I am wanting to see you.
> I have been wanting to see you.

Here, the perfect adds the notion of inception prior to present time and thus signals that the state has history, or duration.

Besides the obvious implication that lexical aspect interacts with grammatical aspect to affect meaning, another point we should make is that lexical aspect influences the acquisition of the simple tenses as well. Researchers in second language acquisition have discovered that the acquisition of past tense is not a unitary phenomenon but rather proceeds in stages. Typically, learners use the past tense with achievement (punctual) verbs first and then, later, its use spreads to accomplishment verbs and, finally, to activities and states. Another trend is for learners not to use past tense with adverbs of frequency, such as *never* and *always* (Bardovi-Harlig and Reynolds 1995). These observations regarding the acquisition of past tense have implications for the selection of example sentences. Teachers may well want to supplement the natural input to which students are exposed and to focus their attention on the use of past tense with activity and stative verbs and its co-occurrence with adverbs of frequency (Bardovi-Harlig and Reynolds 1995).

ADVERBS OF TENSE AND TIME

To conclude our discussion of the meanings associated with the verb tense-aspect system in English, we should point out that because of the semantics of the tense-aspect combinations, certain adverbs of indefinite time (*still, yet, soon, already, anymore,* and *just*) often co-occur with particular combinations. Consider how they all could be used as different answers to the following question:

Has Chris finished her M.A. thesis?

1. Yes, she has *just* finished it.   4. No, but she'll finish it *soon*.
2. Yes, she has *already* filed it.   5. No, she's *still* working on it.
3. No, she hasn't finished it *yet*.   6. No, she's not working on it *anymore*.

In answer 1, *just* signals recent completion, while in 2, *already* is used to signal a result that occurred previously—perhaps earlier than anticipated. In 3, the adverb *yet* indicates noncompletion. All three occur with the present perfect, although American English, unlike Standard British English, also permits simple past tense to occur with these three adverbs. For example:

1. Yes, she *just* finished it.
2. Yes, she *already* finished it.
3. No, she didn't finish it *yet*.

Like 3, answer 4 also signals noncompletion; however, future completion is implied in *soon*, whereas it is less certain in *yet*. The present progressive with *still* in 5 signals a state of affairs that is somehow persisting in the present—perhaps longer than anticipated—while answer 6 indicates noncompletion, and one is led to believe that the task has been abandoned.

Consider also the following situation. A parent may ask his or her child either

> Have you done your homework *already*?
>   or
> Have you done your homework *yet*?

The question with *already* suggests that the parent expects a positive answer but perhaps is surprised because he or she did not expect completion that early. The question with *yet* is more neutral, or it may be used to signal that the parent does not expect the homework to be finished but wants to make the child feel as though it should be.

Note also that *just* and *soon* appear to be complementary retrospective and future markers—signaling recent completion and expected completion in the immediate future, respectively:

> Joe has *just* finished his assignment, and I will finish mine *soon*.

A final point is that *anymore*,[10] which negates the past, can be viewed as complementary to *still*,[11] which affirms continuation of the past in the present:

> Helen's *still* living in Omaha, but she doesn't go to school *anymore*.

The semantically incomplete connotations of *yet*, *anymore*, and *still* and the semantically complete (or about to be completed) nature of *just*, *soon*, and *already*—as well as the tenses with which these forms co-occur most frequently—are facts about English that you should be prepared to convey to your students. Of course, some of these adverbs have other nontemporal meanings as well, which we discuss in Chapter 25 and elsewhere. We leave the meaning dimension of the tense-aspect system now and turn to the use dimension.

THE USE OF THE TENSE-ASPECT SYSTEM

In ways that are not true for other structures, the meaning/use distinction in the tense-aspect system is difficult to discern. What we have therefore attempted to do is to anticipate the troublesome boundaries for ESL/EFL students, to which we alluded earlier, and to elucidate the differences by calling upon both semantic and pragmatic resources. Chapter 9 in its entirety is devoted further to issues of use.

UNDERSTANDING DIFFICULT CONTRASTS IN TENSE-ASPECT COMBINATIONS

1. Simple Present Versus Present Progressive

The present progressive is used for limited action in progress, while the simple present is more compatible with states. Thus, this distinction is manifest in the following ways:

a. Action happening at the moment of speaking versus a habit:

> Why are you wearing glasses? (moment of speech—i.e., right now)
> Why do you wear glasses? (habitual)

b. Temporary event versus permanent situation:

> Linda is living with her parents. (temporary—until she gets a better job)
> Linda lives with her parents. (permanent—because it costs her too much to live alone)

c. Specific event versus general situation:

> What are you doing for Thanksgiving? (one specific Thanksgiving holiday—the forthcoming one)
>
> What do you do for Thanksgiving? (the holiday each year)

d. Activity versus state (two different lexical entries required):

> I am thinking about the answer. (mental activity)
> I think it is 144. (mental state/report)

2. Present Perfect Versus Present Perfect Progressive

The present perfect progressive emphasizes activity as compared with achievement with the present perfect. Thus, the following distinctions may occur:

a. Specific and possibly still ongoing activity versus prior event:

> I have been visiting my great-grandmother. (possibly still ongoing)
> I have visited my great-grandmother. (prior event)

b. Strong implication of continuation versus continuation being only a possibility:

> I have been teaching for 25 years. (and I can't imagine doing anything else)
>
> I have taught for 25 years. (so now it's time to think about doing something else)

Notice, in fact with this pair, that the present perfect progressive implies continuation unless it is contradicted by another clause:

> I have been teaching for 25 years, but now I want to do something else.

c. Single accomplishment, incomplete, versus a completed one:

> Gail has been remodeling her home. (incomplete)
> Gail has remodeled her home. (complete)

3. Simple Past Versus Present Perfect

This distinction is extremely difficult for many ESL/EFL students to make. You could call their attention to some sentence-level contrasts, but this distinction is often best sorted out at the level of discourse (see Chapter 9). One thing is certain: Even though one is a present tense and the other a past, the choice is not dependent upon the time at which the event took place. As Inoue (1979) has pointed out, the truth value of the present perfect is identical to the past. For example, in the following pair of sentences, the time at which Sheila joined is not different:

> Sheila has joined the Sierra Club.
> Sheila joined the Sierra Club.

If the time of her joining is the same, what accounts for the difference? We might say that the use of the present perfect has more to do with our present perspective on the event rather than on the actual time at which it took place. This concept is difficult to get across to ESL/EFL students. Therefore, some additional sentence-level ways to help students determine whether to use the present perfect or the simple past tense are the following:

a. The simple past often occurs with specific past-time adverbials. Recall that the core meaning of the past tense is remoteness. The use of specific past-time adverbials (e.g., *yesterday, last year, 1990*) makes the past tense obligatory. As we have already seen, the use of certain more general temporal adverbials is commonly associated with the perfect (e.g., *already, since, yet*).

b. Even if a past-time adverbial isn't explicit, the remoteness may be defined elsewhere in the context or simply implied:

> John Lennon was a creative genius.

c. The past tense is used for a completed historical period versus an incomplete one:

> My father lived here all his life. (complete—implies the father has left or is dead)
> My father has lived here all his life. (incomplete—the father still lives there)

d. The present perfect is used for an indefinite versus a definite query:

> Have you ever gone to Phoenix?

> Did you go to Phoenix? (You said that you traveled to the Southwest last summer)

In fact, you would almost have to have some shared knowledge with your listener to use the specific past tense in such situations. Use of the present perfect in such a context does not presume shared knowledge.

e. Citing Joos (1967), Knowles (1976) gives us another way to view the differences between the simple past and present perfect. According to Knowles, the function of the present perfect is to change the nature of the relationship between the subject and predicate—it emphasizes the predicated event's result on the grammatical subject. In the following example,

> I've been to Japan twice already, but I still don't speak much Japanese.

the speaker is not so much talking about an event as characterizing "I" at the time of the discourse. To know the time of the trips requires additional questions and answers. Thus, the present perfect functions as a "scene setter," a topic we return to in Chapter 9.

4. Simple Past Versus Past Progressive

a. The past progressive indicates incomplete versus complete action:

> He was drowning in the lake, so the lifeguard raced into the water. (incomplete)
> He drowned in the lake. (complete)

b. Simple past sees the event as a totality with no room for change; past progressive indicates that an event has already begun and extends the event in time and thus allows for a change or its interruption:

> He left when I came in.

> He was leaving when I came in. (and so may have changed his mind and stayed.)

c. Permanent versus temporary state:

> They lived in Baltimore all their lives. (past permanent)
> They were living in Baltimore during the seventies. (past temporary)

5. Simple Past Versus Past Perfect

a. The past perfect is used to mark the completion of some event before a past time period:

> By the end of the 1920s, women in the United States had won the right to vote.

or before another past event that is in the simple past:

> Pat had blamed them for the problem before he considered all the evidence.

However, it is possible to report this same sequence with two events using just the simple past tense for both since the time adverbial *before* makes clear the sequence (cf. endnote 7):

> Pat blamed them for the problem before he considered all the evidence.

Even without a time adverbial, the simple past tense can be used with both clauses if the sequence of the clauses follows the sequence of events:

> Marion worked in an insurance company for 20 years and retired in 1997.

Only when the clauses report two events out of sequence and there are no time adverbials that indicate the actual order is the past perfect necessary:

> When Marion became a photographer, she had finished her degree in fine arts.

b. Sometimes the past perfect appears to mark the later rather than the earlier of the two events in a two-clause sequence (G. Stevens, personal communication):

> I answered before she had asked.
> She collected it before I had finished.

Notice here, though, the event in the subordinate clause was not actually completed. In this case, it appears that the past perfect is a kind of implied counterfactual, suggesting that the event in the subordinate clause was not completed or did not occur. Here again, a simple past tense will often do without a change in meaning:

> I answered before she asked.

6. Simple Future (*will*) Versus Other Ways of Indicating Futurity

a. Simple future with *will* is used for the following:

Future predictions:

> Belinda will be 40 next year.

Spontaneous decision when the person has control over the action:

I'll get the phone.

b. *Be going to* is used for the following:

Future predictions (more informal than *will*):

Belinda's going to be 40 next year.

Future intentions (based on prior decision):

Randy and Joyce are going to get married in October.

Future certainty based on current condition or present evidence:

Pauline's going to have a baby.
It's going to rain today.

c. Present progressive is used for the following:

Future plans that have already been made:

I'm marching in the parade next week.

d. Simple present is used for the following:

Fixed scheduled events:

We get paid next Friday.

Subordinate clauses of time (i.e., those beginning with *when, after, before,* etc.) or condition (i.e., *provided that, if, as long as,* etc.):

If the train arrives on time, we'll beat rush hour getting home.

Some of these uses are very close, and difficulties may arise accordingly. Here are some observations that may help to distinguish some uses:

a. The distinction between future scheduled events and future plans is sometimes indiscernible, and the same event can be referred to either way—simple present or present progressive. However, the simple present is more formal and impersonal and is not very common except with travel arrangements and fixed timetables.:

Aunt Jeanne arrives today.
Aunt Jeanne is arriving today.

b. The present progressive is very common and sometimes overlaps with *be going to.* The present progressive, however, emphasizes that the arrangements have already been made, whereas *be going to* focuses more on the speaker's plans or intentions:

I'm staying at the Marriott.
I'm going to stay at the Marriott.

Of course, the present progressive is not likely to be used to express the future with stative verbs or where the subject is inanimate:

*The red car is belonging to me tomorrow.
 The red car is going to belong to me tomorrow.
*That tree is falling tomorrow.
 That tree is going to fall tomorrow.

or any time when no planning or preparation can guarantee the outcome:

> *We are winning the tennis match next weekend.

c. *Will* and *be going to* are sometimes interchangeable when *be going to* expresses the speaker's certainty and *will* is used to make a strong prediction. However, since *be going to* is a present-tense form, it is used especially when there is evidence in the present to support the prediction; this is not necessarily the case with *will*.

> Mark is going to be tall like his dad.
> ?Mark will be tall like his dad.

And they also differ in that *will* is used for quick, "on-the-spot" decisions, whereas *be going to* is used with more premeditated ones:

> What can I give Jill for her birthday? Oh, I know. I'll get her that new novel.
>   Oh, I know. ?I'm going to get her that new novel.

Finally, when they occur together, the *be going to* tends to come first, to introduce the event, with details supplied with *will* (see Chapter 9).

> Tomorrow night we're going to have a cookout. Our guests'll bring something to grill, and we'll supply the rest.

7. Simple Future Versus Future Progressive

The future progressive allows for the possibility of change with regard to some future event:

> We'll go to Everglades National Park on our vacation. (definite plan)
> We'll be going to Everglades National Park on our vacation. (less definite in that it allows for a change in plans; i.e., We'll be going to Everglades National Park unless we run out of time)

> We will offer that class next semester. (more definite)
> We will be offering that class next semester.[12] (more tentative in that it allows for change—i.e., its cancellation if not enough students enroll in it)

8. Simple Future Versus Future Perfect

As do the other perfect aspects, the future perfect marks an event/activity that is complete prior to some other time (in this case, future), or complete prior to some other future event:

> By the year 2008, the information superhighway will have become accessible to all.
> Megan will have moved by the time she completes her studies.

Simple future alone suggests that the event/activity begins with the time mentioned:

> The information superhighway will become accessible to all by the year 2008.
> Megan will move when she completes her studies.

Some Additional Facts Regarding Use

In the next chapter, we deal comprehensively with the modal system of English. It is worth calling attention at this point, however, to some modals and phrasal modals whose functions relate to the uses of the tense and aspect markers. There are three observations that we would like to make here.

1. Although we have already shown a number of ways to talk about future events and states, many modals, in addition to *will,* and phrasal modals, in addition to *be going to,* can be used for this purpose as well. Here are just a few of them:

may, could, might	It *may/could/might* rain tomorrow. (less certain than *will*)
be to	The recruit *is to* report at 7 A.M. tomorrow morning.
be about to	Look out! You *'re about to* step in a puddle.
be supposed to	We *'re supposed to* go on a field trip tomorrow, but the weather forecast doesn't look good.

Of course, meanings differ among these, and we explore them in the following chapter on modals.

2. We can use the phrasal modal *used to* and the modal *would* to express past habits. When they occur together, *used to* tends to frame the discourse, and *would* serves to elaborate (see Chapter 9).

> When we were children, we *used to* swing on the lawn swing for hours. We *would* stop only when we were called for dinner.

3. The past form of the phrasal modal *be going to* can be used to talk about failed future plans from a past perspective:

> Pam *was going to* play tennis this weekend, but she sprained her ankle.

CONCLUSION

This ends our analysis of the form, meaning, and use of the verb tense-aspect system as it operates at the sentence level. We hope this treatment has helped demonstrate some of the systematicity underlying what might seem at first to be disparate facts. Much more of the systematic nature of English tense-aspect is revealed when we examine the use of the tense-aspect system at the discourse level in Chapter 9.

From our perspective, the long-term challenge of learning the English tense-aspect system centers around what we have termed "the boundary problem." In this regard it is very important that as new tense-aspect combinations are introduced, they are contrasted with what has been presented previously. We have spent time examining the core meanings of the aspects and tenses because we feel that some of the difficulty of discerning the differences between pairs of tense-aspect combinations can be dispelled if students can first be taught to associate the core meanings with the forms; then, they can be helped to understand the more peripheral uses that are not easily explicable from a core-meaning perspective. Furthermore, while it is commonplace to introduce the present progressive by teaching students to associate its core meaning with events that are happening this very minute, this is only part of the story of the present progressive. If teachers are sensitive to the core meanings of the various forms that compose the tense-aspect system, perhaps they will assist their students to develop an understanding of the wider usage of these forms.

TEACHING SUGGESTIONS

1. Form. An inductive approach to teaching the form of English tense-aspect combinations is to provide students with naturalistic data in which the input has somehow been enhanced (Sharwood Smith 1993) in order to make the verb endings more salient. You might try, for example, giving your students short reading passages with certain verb endings boldfaced or italicized. You could do this for a period of time before ever formally drawing their attention to any particular tense-aspect combination.

2. Form. ESL/EFL students will need to learn the irregular past tense and past participle forms. One suggestion for practicing these is to play the game of concentration. Each group of four or five students will need a set of 30 cards. On 15 of the cards, write the base form of the verb; on the other 15 cards, write the past tense and/or past participle.

Shuffle the cards and place them face down, forming a grid of six cards down and five across. Students take turns turning over two cards at a time. If the two cards make a match—that is, if the base form and past tense and/or past participle are of the same verb—the student keeps the pair of cards. If they do not match, the cards must be replaced, face down, in their original spots. When all the pairs have been matched, the student with the most cards wins. This game can be replayed from time to time as new verbs are introduced.

3. Meaning. To teach meaning, we want students to *associate* a form and its meaning. For example, you might bring in a color wheel, or draw one on the board, for practicing the unchanging fact/state core meaning of the simple present tense. Have students make statements about how to form other colors from the primary ones and other combinations:

> T: What do red and blue make?
> S: Red and blue make purple.
> T: What do black and white make?
> S: Black and white make gray.
> T: What do all the colors together make?
> S: All the colors together make black.
> T: Now make as many sentences as you can with English words for colors.

4. Meaning. One way of getting students to associate forms and meanings is to teach them certain adverbials that frequently occur with particular tenses. For example, give students a list of three adverbials that commonly go together with the present tense-aspect combinations:

Simple Present	*Present Perfect*	*Present Progressive*
every (day)	for X days	this day; these days
once a week	up until now	at the moment
on (Wednesday)	since (Monday)	today

Next, give them a blank monthly calendar for the current month. Read to them a paragraph, such as the following, with Jill's activities and appointments for the month. Ask the students to pencil them in.

> During the month of _____, Jill is very busy. She goes to class every weekday and studies on the weekends too. She has tests once a week on Fridays. These days she is also working. She works on Monday, Wednesday, and Friday evenings after school. She is not working this evening (Wednesday), though, because she is not feeling well. She has been sick since Monday. She has missed school and work for two days. . . .

Finally, give students new blank calendars and have them work in pairs to write down their partner's monthly activities.

5. Meaning. To teach students to associate meaning with verb forms, you can use a real or imaginary biography that details the events in someone's life. This can be effectively presented in the form of a scroll, which you can slowly unwind as you ask students questions. For example, you might ask questions such as the following that help students understand the meaning of the perfect progressives:

- **a.** Present perfect progressive: It's 1970. (For) how long has Diana been living in Chicago?
- **b.** Past perfect progressive: In 1976, (for) how long had Diana been attending the University of Illinois?
- **c.** Future perfect progressive: In 1987, (for) how many years will Diana have been working on her Ph.D.?

Students can create scrolls of their own lives and ask and answer each other's questions.

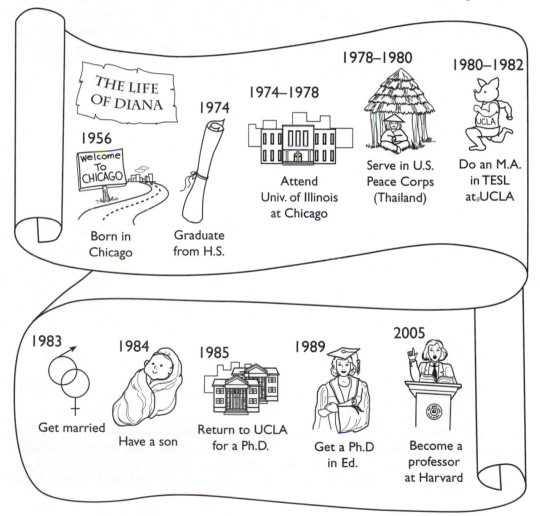

6. Use. Learning to use the tenses appropriately seems to be the greatest challenge that ESL/EFL students face. To have students see the difference between the simple past and the past progressive, have them think of a famous historical event that took place during their lifetimes. For example, the shooting of Anwar Sadat, the tearing down of the Berlin Wall, the Kobe earthquake. Ask a student to say what their event was, and then ask other students to tell what they were doing at the time. Have them use the following frame:

> When I heard about X, I was Y.
> When I heard about Anwar Sadat, I was driving in my car.

7. Use. Another problem students commonly wrestle with is choosing between *will* and *be going to* appropriately. Dalglish, Joshee, and Holzer (personal communication) recommend that the teacher write the following two sentences on the board:

> She is going to dive into the water.
> She will dive into the water.

Show students a picture of a woman perched on the end of a diving board and lean forward, and ask students which sentence correctly describes the picture. The students may intuitively know that the use of *will* in this context is not appropriate. Help them to see that *be going to* here is more appropriate because the woman's posture and position at the end of the diving board indicates a preplanned activity for which there is evidence. *Will*, on the other hand, expresses intention at the immediate moment of decision when the person has control over the action. Next ask students to create appropriate contexts for each sentence of each pair below:

  a. I'll sell my car.
  I'm going to sell my car.
  b. I'll buy her a necklace.
  I'm going to buy her a necklace.
  c. I'll have an omelette and a salad.
  I'm going to have an omelette and a salad.

8. Use. To help students practice one difference in usage between the simple past and the present perfect, Gene Parulis and Fiona Cook (personal communication) suggest students role-play a job interview.

> A: Have you ever { taken shorthand / done any computer programming / written advertisements before } ?
>
> .
> .
> .
>
> B: { No, I haven't, but I have edited a newsletter. I worked . . . / Yes, I have. I worked . . . }

For students who are less advanced, you could work on the same use difference between present perfect and past by asking each student to think up one question to ask another student in the class, using the frame *Have you ever. . . ?* If the student to whom the question is asked answers affirmatively, then the first student asks a follow-up question. For example:

> A: Have you ever eaten cous-cous?
> B: Yes, I have.
> A: Really? When did you eat it?
> B: I ate some last week at a restaurant.

EXERCISES

Test your understanding of what has been presented.

1. Provide original example sentences to illustrate the following terms. Underline the pertinent word(s) in your examples:

   a. simple future   **d.** past perfect   **g.** accomplishment verb

   b. present perfect   **e.** stative verb   **h.** present perfect progressive

   c. past progressive   **f.** simple present

2. Do the following sentences differ at all with regard to the ordering of events?

   a. I had finished my homework before I practiced the piano.

   b. I finished my homework before I practiced the piano.

   Give a reason for your answer.

3. The word *since* does not usually occur with the simple past tense. Why do you think this is so?

4. Compare and contrast the following pairs of sentences:

   a. I have read the book.   I have been reading the book.

   b. Stan sells vacuum cleaners.   Stan is selling vacuum cleaners.

   c. Did you go to Yankee Stadium?   Have you gone to Yankee Stadium?

Test your ability to apply what you know.

5. Why are the following sentences ungrammatical? If your students make these errors, how would you make them aware of the errors, and what activities would you provide to help students avoid these errors?

   a. *William has bought it last Saturday.

   b. *I'm believing you.

   c. *Help! I will fall.

   d. *When Larry will come, I will go.

   e. *Phyllis was lived with her parents for 20 years.

6. ESL/EFL teachers often associate "now" with the present progressive, but consider the following:

   He goes to the store now.   Now you've done it!

   What interpretation can you give to these sentences that will explain the tense use?

7. Consider the following verbs of internal sensation: *hurt, ache, feel, itch*. Although sometimes these are considered a subcategory of stative verbs, we have not included them because of their special nature with regard to progressive aspect. Explain.

8. Apart from the British and American dialect difference mentioned under Adverbs of Tense and Time, *just* and *already* can occur with the present perfect and/or the simple past. Is there a difference? Would these sentences occur in different contexts?

   a. Did you just hear the news about the flooding in Georgia?

   b. Have you just heard the news about the flooding in Georgia?

9. In American English, sometimes the past participle *gotten* appears to be used the same way as *got*.

   Has he gotten/got over his illness?

Other times they appear to have different meanings:

He has got the following ingredients.
He has gotten the following ingredients.

Can you explain the difference?

10. If a student asks you what the difference between the following two sentences is, how would you answer?
   a. I have been hearing that melody over and over again.
   b. I have been listening to that melody over and over again.

BIBLIOGRAPHY

References

Andersen, R., and Y. Shirai (1994). "Discourse Motivation for Some Cognitive Acquisition Principles." *Studies in Second Language Acquisition* 16:2, 133–156.

Badalamenti, V., and C. Henner Stanchina (1997). *Grammar Dimensions: Form, Meaning, and Use.* Book 1 (2d ed). Boston, Mass.: Heinle & Heinle.

Bardovi-Harlig, K., and D. Reynolds (1995). "The Role of Lexical Aspect in the Acquisition of Tense and Aspect." *TESOL Quarterly* 29:1, 107–131.

Dowty, D. (1979). *Word Meaning and Montague Grammar.* Dordrecht: Reidel.

Gavis, W. (1997). "What Factors Influence the Use of Stative Verbs in the Progressive Form?" Paper presented at the American Association of Applied Linguistics Meeting, Orlando.

Hatch, E., and C. Brown (1995). *Vocabulary, Semantics, and Language Education.* Cambridge: Cambridge University Press.

Hirtle, W. (1967). *The Simple and Progressive Forms: An Analytical Approach.* Quebec: Laval University Press.

Inoue, K. (1979). "An Analysis of the English Present Perfect." *Linguistics* 17:561–589.

Joos, M. (1968). *The English Verb (Form and Meanings).* Madison, Wis: University of Wisconsin Press.

Kesner Bland, S. (1988). "The Present Progressive in Discourse: Grammar versus Usage Revisited." *TESOL Quarterly* 22:1, 53–68.

Knowles, P. L. (1976). "A Different Approach to the English Verb." *Cross Currents,* autumn, 112–128.

Knowles, P. L. (1979). "Predicate Markers: A New Look at the English Predicate System." *Cross Currents* 6:2, 21–36.

Lewis, M. (1986). *The English Verb.* Hove: Language Teaching Publications.

Sharwood Smith, M. (1993). "Input Enhancement in Instructed SLA: Theoretical Bases." *Studies in Second Language Acquisition* 15:2, 165–179.

Vendler, Z. (1967). *Linguistics and Philosophy.* Ithaca: Cornell University Press.

Suggestions for further reading

For a discussion of aspect, see:

Bouscaren, J., and J. Chuquet, with L. Danon-Boileau (1992). *Introduction to A Linguistic Grammar of English: An Utterer-Centered Approach.* Translated and adapted by R. Flintham and J. Bouscaren. Paris: Ophrys.

Comrie, B. (1976). *Aspect: An Introduction to the Study of Verbal Aspect and Related Problems.* New York: Cambridge University Press.

Hirtle, W. (1967). *The Simple and Progressive Forms: An Analytical Approach.* Quebec: Laval University Press.

McCoard, R. W. (1978). *The English Perfect Tense Choice and Pragmatic Inferences.* Amsterdam: North Holland Publishing Comany.

Scheffer, J. (1975). *The Progressive in English.* Amsterdam: North Holland Publishing Company.

Smith, C. (1983). "A Theory of Aspectual Choice." *Language* 59:3, 479–501.

For useful descriptions of the English tense-aspect system, consult the following sources:

Allen, R. L. (1966). *The Verb System of Present-Day American English.* The Hague: Mouton.

Comrie, B. (1985). *Tense.* New York: Cambridge University Press.

Joos, M. (1968). *The English Verb (Form and Meanings).* Madison, Wis.: University of Wisconsin Press.

Leech, G. (1987). *Meaning and the English Verb* (2d ed.). London: Longman.

Lewis, M. (1986). *The English Verb.* Hove: Language Teaching Publications.

Palmer, F. R. (1968). *A Linguistic Study of the English Verb.* Coral Gables, Fla.: The University of Miami Press.

For a discussion of the differences between will *and* be going to, *see:*

Binnick, R. (1971). "*Will* and *Be Going To.*" Papers from the 7th Regional Meeting, Chicago Linguistic Society. Chicago: Chicago Linguistic Society.

Binnick, R. (1972). "*Will* and *Be Going To*" (vol. 2). Papers from the 8th Regional Meeting, Chicago Linguistic Society. Chicago: Chicago Linguistic Society.

For an in depth study of stative progressives, see:

Gavis, W. (Forthcoming). Stative Verbs in the *Be + -ing* Progressive Form. Unpublished Ph. D. Dissertation. Teachers College, Columbia University.

For helpful pedagogical analyses, see:

Feigenbaum, I. (1981). "The Use of the English Perfect." *Language Learning* 31:2, 393–408.

Martin, M. (1978). "Future Shock: A Pedagogical Analysis of *Will* and *Be Going To.*" In C. Blatchford and J. Schachter (eds.), *On TESOL '78. Washington, D.C.:* TESOL, 183–190.

Richards, J. (1979). "Introducing the Perfect: An Exercise in Pedagogic Grammar." *TESOL Quarterly* 13:4, 495–500.

Richards, J. (1981). "Introducing the Progressive." *TESOL Quarterly* 15:4, 391–402.

Riddle, E. (1986). "The Meaning and Discourse Function of the Past Tense in English." *TESOL Quarterly* 20:2, 267–286.

For pedagogical suggestions, take a look at:

Badalamenti, V., and C. Henner Stanchina (1997). *Grammar Dimensions: Form, Meaning, and Use.* Book 1 (2d ed.). Boston, Mass.: Heinle & Heinle.

Kesner Bland, S. 1996. *Intermediate Grammar: From Form to Meaning and Use.* New York: Oxford University Press.

Koustoff, L. (1993). "Teaching Perfective Forms Using Cuisenaire Rods." *The Language Teacher* 17:12, 23–27.

Riggenbach, H., and V. Samuda (1997). *Grammar Dimensions: Form, Meaning, and Use.* Book 2 (2d ed.). Boston, Mass.: Heinle & Heinle.

ENDNOTES

1. Finite verbs are verbs that can stand alone in independent or main clauses; nonfinite verb forms, such as infinitives, occur on their own only in embedded or subordinate clauses.

2. This is the dictionary definition of tense. But as you have already seen, by noting the absence of a future tense in English, there is no one-to-one correspondence between tense and time. Indeed, in the section on meaning you will see that the past tense is used for more than past time, the present tense is also used for future time, and so on.

3. In some British English grammars, though, the pattern is preserved by referring to tense first and then aspect, i.e., "present simple."

4. For a list of the spelling rules that apply to forming the present participle, see Badalamenti and Henner-Stanchina (1997).

5. Even though the whole sentence expresses future, the present tense is used in the subordinate clause. This follows a general principle of historical linguistics that holds that historically older inflectional/grammatical forms and word orders are preserved in subordinate clauses longer than in independent clauses. Since Old English had only two tenses (present and past) and used the present tense to express future time, this principle seems to apply here.

6. Here and with the host's offer and sales clerk's question, the past-tense marker has taken over the subjunctive function in English.

7. Notice, though, that the simple present (*finishes*) could also work here (Lori Gray, personal communication). This is in keeping with the fact that the use of perfect aspect is sometimes optional when its notion of prior can be made explicit by other means—here, the use of *until*. You will encounter the optionality of the perfect again when we contrast the simple past with the past perfect.

8. It is difficult to see how the core meaning applies to the uses of the progressive in e and f. Perhaps this is because these are more marked uses of the progressive—that is, using a present tense to speak about a future event in e and using the progressive with habits as in f, normally the domain for simple aspect.

9. This chart has been somewhat altered from the one that appeared in Andersen and Shirai (1994). Dowty (1979) has shown that there is overlap between the accomplishment and activity categories with certain verbs such as *draw* in sentences such as the following:

> a. He drew the picture in an hour. (accomplishment)
> b. He drew the picture for an hour. (activity)

For this reason, Dowty argues that classification should occur with the whole verb phrase. While we would not quarrel with his assessment, for our purposes this categorization of verbs is sufficient.

10. There is a dialect of North American English, spoken mainly in the South, that uses *anymore* to mean *lately* or *these days* (Jaimie Scanlon, personal communication).

> I don't have time to read the newspaper. I only read books for school anymore.

11. Although it affirms the persistence of the past in the present, *still* often implies a negative evaluation:

> Is Harold still writing his thesis? (He shouldn't be; he should have finished it long ago.)

12. Example from Norbert Gross, personal communication.

Modal Auxiliaries and Related Phrasal Forms

Introduction

In Chapter 7, all the components of our phrase structure rule for expanding the auxilary (AUX) in nonimperative sentences that we introduced in Chapter 6 were discussed except for the modal auxiliary (M) and the phrasal modal (pm) forms:

$$\text{AUX} \rightarrow \left\{ \begin{matrix} \left\{ \begin{matrix} \text{T} \\ \text{M} \end{matrix} \right\} \ \text{(pm) (perf) (prog)} \\ \text{-imper} \end{matrix} \right\}$$

This chapter completes our discussion of the constituents that compose the AUX, or auxiliary, in nonimperative sentences by describing the form, meaning, and use of modal auxiliaries and some of their most frequent phrasal forms.

The Form of Modals

Modal auxiliaries are among the more difficult structures ESL/EFL teachers have to deal with. One of the reasons for this is the form of modals. Some of your students, who have been told time and time again that present-tense verbs with third person singular subjects require an *-s* ending, overgeneralize this rule to modals— for example, *He cans play tennis. This overgeneralization results in errors because in English modal auxiliaries (*can, may, shall, will,* etc.) are distinguished from other auxiliary verbs (*be, have, do*) as well as from ordinary verbs by their lack of tense and their resultant lack of subject-verb agreement; that is, modals do not inflect.

In English, modals are derived from verbs that *did* carry tense and take agreement markers during a much earlier stage of the language. Other languages, such as German, French, and Spanish, still carry out tense-marking and/or agreement operations on their equivalents of English modal verbs. It is thus important to emphasize to learners that English no longer inflects modals for tense and number.

Another formal property of modals that may cause your students some trouble is that modals directly precede a verb without the intervening infinitive *to* that is required when two ordinary verbs follow each other in sequence:

Modal + Verb   *Verb + Verb*
I can go.   I want to go.
*I can to go.   *I want go.

Many of your students will treat modals like ordinary verbs and produce errors by using a superfluous infinitive *to: *Jack must to study harder; *We should to return the book.*

Another source of difficulty with the form of modals, of course, may be your students' native language(s). Not all languages have modal auxiliaries; in those that do not, regular verbs or adjective/adverbs are used to express the meanings and functions that modals have in English. Students speaking such a first language may feel the need to inflect English modals as if they were ordinary verbs.

In this grammar we describe modals formally as tenseless auxiliaries that take no subject-verb agreement and no infinitive *to* before the following verb. However, we acknowledge that modals do derive historically from ordinary verb forms inflected for either present or past tense because this historically-based relationship still has some semantic implications (see our discussion of meanings of modals below)

Historical Present Tense	*Historical Past Tense*
can	could
will	would
may	might
shall	should
∅ ◄——————	must, (had to)[1]

Many linguists argue, using data such as the following, that the preceding forms are still marked for present or past tense:

Direct Speech	*Indirect (i.e., Reported) Speech*
Joe: I can go.	Joe said that he could go.
May: I will leave.	May said that she would leave.
Jim: Shall I stay?[2]	Jim asked if he should stay.
Bill: May I smoke?	Bill asked if he might smoke.
Ann: I must work.	Ann said that she had to work.[3]

The direct-to-indirect speech tense shift is the main piece of evidence cited to support the assignment of tense to modals. However, we demonstrate in Chapter 33, which deals with indirect speech, that the so-called rules of tense shifting are not always followed by native speakers. This is especially true for modals; thus such evidence is somewhat weak. While it is true that the historically present-tense modals *can* and *will* still resist being used in past time frames whether they involve reported speech or not (e.g., **He can leave yesterday; *She told me on March 25 last year that she will leave the following day*), their so-called past tense counterparts, *could* and *would,* don't always work in past-time frames (**He could leave yesterday*), and they often occur with reference to present time (*Would/Could you pass me the salt?*). Perhaps the strongest current support—other than reported speech—for a semantic relationship between present time and remote past time obtains between *can* and *could* when *could* is used to express ability in the remote past:

I can't speak French now, but I could when I was a child.

However, this is a semantic, not a syntactic, relationship, and it does not hold for other modal pairs; in fact, in some cases so-called present-tense modals refer to past time:

Jim may have been late last night. (past meaning)

Also, in many other cases, so-called past-tense modals refer to present or future time:

That could be Sara. (present meaning)
You should see a doctor. (future meaning)

Given the fact that the "present tense" modals would be the only present tense verb auxiliaries in English that do not take the third person singular inflection, there are few valid syntactic reasons for maintaining the historical description and ascribing past or present tense to modals.

MODALS AND THEIR PHRASAL MODAL COUNTERPARTS

Multiword forms ending in infinitive *to*, which function semantically like true modals (in certain of their meanings), are called phrasal modals (they are also called periphrastic modals, pseudo modals, or quasi-modals). Every modal seems to have at least one phrasal counterpart, and some modals have several:

Modal	*Phrasal Modal*
can, could	be able to
will, shall	be going to, be about to
must	have to, have got to
should, ought to[4]	be to,[5] be supposed to
would (= past habit)	used to
may, might	be allowed to, be permitted to

Notice that the phrasal modals do not exhibit the same formal properties as the true modals in that the subject-verb agreement rule must be applied (except for *used to*, which is an inflected past tense[6]) and that all phrasal modals require that a *to* infinitive precede the main verb; that is, the phrasal forms behave syntactically much more like ordinary verbs than they do like true modals.

$$
\text{She} \left\{ \begin{array}{l} \text{is able to} \\ \text{is going to} \\ \text{is allowed to} \\ \text{has to} \\ \text{has got to} \end{array} \right\} \text{go to Fresno tomorrow.}
$$

In fact, phrasal forms developed in part because the original class of modals lost their connection to time, and the phrasal forms gave English users a way to mark tense and express modality on one and the same verb form. Phrasal modals, however, differ from lexical verbs in speech in that they have assimilated with *to* and often pronounce *to* as if it were part of a single word with the verb: *gotta, gonna, hasta, hafta,* and so on. Also, it is much more difficult to put an adverb between the verb and the *to* of a phrasal modal than between a regular verb and an infinitive *to:*

? I have often to study.
I try often to study.

In addition to the true modals and phrasal modals, there are some other modal-like forms in English, such as the following: (*had*) *better* or (*had*) *best* (advisability), *would rather*, *would prefer* (preference), and *would like* (= desire in statements and offers in questions). These must be included in a comprehensive treatment of modals and phrasal forms, and we return to them later.

Another point should be made regarding the formal properties of modals and their phrasal equivalents: The order of these constituents with respect to each other is fixed. Consider the following examples:

1. *We can should study hard.
2. He will have to improve his work.
3. *I am able to must do the job.

4. I might be able to go there.
5. He is going to have to improve his pronunciation.

While further study is needed to determine what all the possible combinations are in standard English, we see in example 1 that modal plus modal[7] cannot occur and in example 3 that phrasal modal plus modal cannot occur. Sequences of three phrasal modals seem to be the upper limit (Sara Weigle, personal communication):

> I'm gonna have to be able to do that by Saturday.

We can thus add a superscript three to the (pm) in the AUX rule to describe the upper limit on possible sequences of phrasal modals.[8] However, we still lack a precise description of the combinations of modals and phrasal modals that can occur versus those that cannot.

Another point to make about the form of so-called phrasal modals is that they occasionally appear to take perfect or progressive aspect (Barbara Strodt, personal communication):

> I'm having to work harder to lose weight now.
> Lately he's been able to run the mile in five minutes.

Our current phrase structure rule does not account for such an order of constituents. Such cases reflect the fact that phrasal modal verbs are tensed and inflected like ordinary verbs. Their relation to modal auxiliaries is a semantic one. When they occur with the aspectual markers, we must treat them syntactically as ordinary verbs taking infinitives rather than as phrasal modals. Many phrasal modals seem to be hovering somewhere between a regular verb and a true phrasal modal.

Phrasal modals have a variety of internal structures. Some of them look like another construction that consists of *be* + adjective + preposition + verb [gerund]:

> I am able to go there. (pm + verb [infinitive])
> I am used to going there. (be + adj + prep + verb [gerund])

with the result that some learners overgeneralize the pattern with the phrasal modal and produce errors like:

> *I am used to go there

These superficially similar but structually very different constructions must be properly distinguished for more advanced learners to help them avoid such errors.

To sum up what we have said about the form of modals, and phrasal modals, let us apply the phrase structure rules and mapping rules to one sentence:

> I might be able to finish the work by Friday.

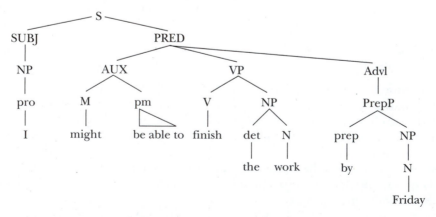

The interesting thing about this example is that the mapping is complete without the need for any additional rules. There is no tense morpheme, so we do not copy the person and number of the subject on the tense. There are no bound inflectional morphemes to map onto the appropriate lexical item. There is no morphology. The output of the phrase structure rules—in this particular case—produces a grammatical surface structure.

THE MEANINGS OF MODALS

While all of the formal properties above may seem rather complicated, an additional problem in the teaching of modals arises when you attempt to convey to ESL/EFL students the meanings of modals, phrasal modals, and modal-like forms.

Traditional grammar books tend to list or summarize the form and meaning of the modals one by one. Such presentations give a rather fragmented view of modals, since they suggest that they should be learned and taught form by form and meaning by meaning. In our description of the modals (as in our descriptions of tense and aspect) we want to give at least as much consideration to the semantic systems that modals reflect as we do to their individual forms and meanings.

The first thing to notice about the meaning of modals is that they form a semantic opposition with ordinary tensed verb forms. When English speakers use a modal, they interject their own perspective and view a proposition more subjectively than when they simply use present or past tense:

Tense	*Modal*
John is a teacher.	John may be a teacher.
John was a teacher.	John may have been a teacher.

Modals are used for several reasons: to give a proposition a degree of probability, to express one's attitude, and to perform various social functions, such as expressing politeness or indirectness when making requests, giving advice, or granting permission.

Many linguists and semanticists (Hofmann 1966 and Palmer 1990, among others) have discussed modals as having at least two distinctly different functions: (1) an epistemic meaning expressing logical probability and (2) a deontic function expressing a use related to social interaction. (We will use the terms "logical probability" and "social interaction" here.) Consider the following examples:

You may leave the room. (*may* expresses granting of permission and thus accomplishes a social interaction)

It may rain tomorrow. (*may* expresses a degree of logical probability that is weak rather than strong)

When modals are used for social interaction, the person using them must take into account the relevant features of the social situation. For example, in "You may leave the room," the speaker should have sufficient status and authority to be able to grant permission to the interlocutor(s). Furthermore, the situation should be formal rather than informal, or the speaker would have used "can" instead of "may" for granting permission. Knowing all the relevant features of the social situation allows the speaker to select the appropriate modal auxiliary in any given interaction. In contrast, in the sentence "It may rain tomorrow," knowledge of the social situation would have little or no effect on the modal selected. What the speaker is intending to convey is his or her assessment that the probability of rain the following day is relatively low. The speaker would likely use *may* regardless of the interlocutor(s) or the situation.

Like *may*, virtually all the modals can express both logical probability and social interaction. ESL/EFL students should be made aware of this and be given some guidance in working with the systems operating within both dimensions. In this chapter, we consider the logical probability of modals to be *meaning* and the social function of modals to be *use*.

LOGICAL PROBABILITY MEANINGS OF MODALS

The logical meanings of the modals typically deal with the speaker making an inference or prediction. For example:

> *Wilbur:* Someone's knocking at the door.
> *Gertrude:* It may be Sydney.

In fact, we can establish a hierarchy for the logical meanings of modals. What increases is the degree of certainty regarding our inference:

> *Wilbur:* Someone's knocking.
> *Gertrude:* That must be Sydney.[9]   High certainty
> (That will be Sydney.)
> That should be Sydney.
> That may be Sydney.
> That could/might[10] be Sydney.   Low certainty

Only the first two options have informal phrasal equivalents (e.g., *It has to/has got to be Sydney; It's gonna be Sydney*) since, in general, phrasal forms seem to be selected more readily to express social interaction than logical probability. Of the modals in the logical probability hierarchy, *will* and *should* are the most limited in that they do not work well for all situations:

> A: I have flushed cheeks and a slight fever.
> B: You (could/might/may/must/?will/*should) be coming down with something.

It appears that the speaker requires some special personal knowledge to make a present inference using *will* or *should* as opposed to the other more neutral modals of probability (i.e., *could/might/may/must*).

Present inference can also be stated in negative terms, but this is much less frequent, and the selection and order of forms is somewhat different:

> *Wilbur:* Someone's knocking at the door. I believe it's Sidney.
> *Gertrude:* That might not be Sydney.   Low possibility
> That may not be Sydney.
> That won't/wouldn't be Sydney.
> That can't/couldn't be Sydney.   Impossibility

Should and *must* are absent from the negative inference scale since they are typically used for social functions in the negative—to advise and order others on what not to do:

> They shouldn't do that.
> You mustn't arrive late.

Notice that adjectives and adverbs can often be used to paraphrase the logical uses, but only rarely the social uses, of modals:

must	—necessarily, very certain(ly)	High certainty
will	—fairly certain(ly)	
should	—probable, probably, likely	
may	—perhaps, maybe, quite possible/ly	
could, might	—possible, possibly	Low certainty

The same set of modals can be used for past as well as current inference with the addition of perfect aspect *have* (*have* + *-en*):

Wilbur:	Someone was asking for you.	
Gertrude:	That must have been Sydney.	High certainty
	That (will/would) have been Sydney.	
	That should have been Sydney.	
	That may have been Sydney.	
	That (could/might) have been Sydney.	Low certainty

Addition of perfect aspect (*have* + *-en*) follows the discussion of tense and aspect in Chapter 7, where the perfect aspect is a marker of anteriority when used with each tense. It further argues for modals being described as "tenseless" since, like infinitives, modals need perfect aspect to express past inference, whereas the semantically parallel adverbs and adjectives can be used with simple past tense verbs to express the same notions:

> It's very certain that was Sydney.
> It's fairly certain that was Sydney.
> It's probable/likely that was Sydney.
> It's quite possible that was Sydney.
> It's possible that was Sydney.

Again, *should* and *must* do not seem to play a role in expressing negative past inference for the same reasons noted above for negative present inference:

Wilbur:	Someone was asking for you. I believe it was Sydney.	
Gertrude:	That might not have been Sydney.	Low possibility
	That may not have been Sydney.	
	That won't/wouldn't have been Sydney.	
	That can't/couldn't have been Sydney.	Impossibility

Prediction

All of the forms above can be used to express degrees of prediction, with the exception of *must*, perhaps because *must* historically was a past tense verb form and is thus not well suited for prediction, or perhaps because predictions cannot be as strong as current and past inferences:

> Question: What did the weatherman say?

		Degree of probability
Response:	It will rain tomorrow.	High
	It should rain tomorrow.	
	It may rain tomorrow.	
	It (could/might) rain tomorrow.	Low

Of these, only the first sentence has an informal phrasal equivalent: *It's going to rain tomorrow.*

Again, paraphrases with adverbs or adjectives are available (note that the modal auxiliary in the propositional *that* clause is *will* in all four cases):

> It is certain that it will rain tomorrow.
> It is probable/likely that it will rain tomorrow.
> It is quite possible that it will rain tomorrow.
> It is possible that it will rain tomorrow.

In the above *that* clauses, *will* seems to be a future tense as much as a logical modal. Also, the use of an adverb with a modal can reinforce or weaken the meaning of the modal; for example, *It probably/possibly will rain.* On the negative predication scale, the forms occur in reverse order, but *could* drops out. Apparently, *couldn't* is more strongly associated with past time frames or present negative inference rather than negative prediction, which has a future time frame:

> A: The weatherman said it will rain tomorrow. Do you agree?
> B: (No), it might not rain tomorrow   Low possibility
>   it may not rain tomorrow
>   it shouldn't rain tomorrow
>   it won't rain tomorrow
>   it can't rain tomorrow   Impossibility
> because this new weather pattern is moving in.

Necessity

Another reason why *must* is not used for prediction may be that, along with phrasal *have to,* it is often used to express necessity, which—according to Palmer (1990)—can be internal or external in origin:

> Internal: I have to see my doctor about this rash.
> External: You must fill out the top of this form.

General necessity (the equivalent of a condition) is also often expressed with *must:*

> Fully qualified applicants must have a bachelor's degree.

MODALS AND NEGATION

Modals and phrasal forms interact with *not* in interesting ways. Usually the negation of a modal and the negative of the corresponding phrasal modal have parallel semantic effects:

> I cannot do it. / I'm not able to do it.
> He will not do it. / He's not going to do it.
> You should not lie. / You're not supposed to lie.

However, the following are clearly distinct:

> You must not go. / You don't have to go.[11]

In the two immediately preceding examples, the modal expresses prohibition, while the phrasal form offers the addressee a choice (i.e., you can go, but it's not necessary).

THE USE OF MODALS AND PHRASAL FORMS

SOCIAL FUNCTIONS OF MODALS

Making Requests

One major system in the social use of modals entails making requests. These can be requests of a general nature,

> Will/Would
> Can/Could } you help me with this math problem?

or specific requests for permission:

> May/Might
> Can/Could } I leave the room now?

Although both historical present and past forms of these modals can be used in making requests, only the historical present tense forms are likely to be used in responses to requests:

To general requests:	Yes, I can/*could; No, I can't/*couldn't.
	Yes, I will/*would; No, I won't/*wouldn't.
To requests for permission:	Yes, you may/*might; No, you may not/*might not.
	Yes, you can/*could; No, you can't/*couldn't.

The reasons for this distinction is that the historical past forms of modals are considered more polite and less presumptuous than the historical present forms, and thus the person making the request will often use the historical past tense forms to "soften" the request; however, the person being addressed is expected to respond directly and thus uses the less deferential historical present forms. Also, the person responding to a request usually does not want to make the response sound conditional, which is a possible result if the historical past form of the modal is used:

A: (Can/Could) you help me with this math problem?
B: Yes, I could (if you would wait a few minutes while I finish this work).

Many ESL/EFL students, even at an advanced level, do not recognize that they are often perceived by native speakers of English as being abrupt and aggressive with their requests, given the social circumstances. If they learned to soften requests by employing the historical past tense forms of the modals, they might find their requests being better received. For example,

Could (instead of *Can*) I talk to you for a minute?
Would (instead of *Will*) you open the door?

There seems to be a subtle difference between *can/could* versus *will/would* in making requests such as those above in that the former seems to ask "is this possible?" whereas the latter seems to query the willingness of the addressee. Further data-based research, however, is needed to show us precisely in what contexts each form is preferred and why.

Requests for Permission. When asking for permission, the selection of *may* or *can* is socially significant:

Can/May I talk to you for a minute?

The greater the addressee's degree of formal authority (as perceived by the speaker or projected by the addressee), the more likely the use of *may*. In North America there are many situations where there is a lack of clearly defined authority, and *can* tends to be much more widely used than *may* and is often perceived as more polite than *may*: *You (can/may) go now* (Bailey, 1997).

Note that while modals can be used in making requests, phrasal modals are generally used not to make requests but to ask literal questions:

Will/would you open the door? (possible request)
Are you going to open the door? (literal question)

There is, however, a modal-like phrase which can be used to make a polite request:

Would you mind turning down the volume on that radio?

The interesting thing here is that *do* serves as an informal, more direct, and less polite substitute for *would* in this phrase, whereas *will* is ungrammatical:

Do you mind turning down the volume on that radio?
*Will you mind turning down the volume on that radio?

As Ney (1978) points out, all request modals show differences in meaning when the negative *not* is contracted to the modal as opposed to when it is uncontracted and precedes the main verb.

> Won't you please get into the pool? (Please do get in.)
> Will you please not get into the pool? (Please do not get in.)
> Couldn't I please go to the party? (I want to go; please let me.)
> Could I please not go to the party? (I don't want to; please don't force me.)

When the negative is contracted with the modal, it serves to amplify or strengthen the request that something should be done; however, if the negative is uncontracted and precedes the verb, the request has the opposite meaning: that something not be done.

Giving Advice

The other major system in the social interactional use of modals involves the giving of advice. Notice that the systematicity lies in the fact that we can order the modals according to the speaker's degree of authority or the urgency of the advice. For example:

> You must see a doctor.   (Speaker's authority or urgency of
> You (should/ought to) see a doctor.   the message increases, not
> You (might/could) see a doctor.   necessarily in equal increments.)

The top two options on the above continuum have informal, rough phrasal equivalents (differences in meaning and use are discussed later):

> You (have to/have got to/need to) see a doctor.
> You (had) better/best see a doctor.
> You (might/could) see a doctor. (no equivalent)

In some situations an offer or invitation initially refused can be recast as urgent advice to make it more emphatic:

> You must have another piece of pie!

Advice can, of course, be negative as well as positive. Less formal and weaker expressions of negative advice often involve *should* or its phrasal counterparts with *not,* although other forms are possible:

> You (had) better/best not say things like that.   Stronger negative advice
> You ought not (to) say things like that. (rare)
> You shouldn't say things like that.
> You're not supposed to say things like that.
> You don't $\left\{\begin{matrix} \text{have} \\ \text{need} \end{matrix}\right\}$ to say things like that.   Weaker negative advice

From our experience, introducing modals in this relative fashion to ESL/EFL students is far more enlightening than simply introducing each form individually and ascribing a number of distinctive meanings and functions to it.

OTHER MEANINGS AND USES OF
MODALS AND MODAL-LIKE FORMS

Here are some other meanings and uses expressed by modals and modal-like forms that do not fit into the logical meanings and social uses described above:

Potential realization—*can, be able to:*

1. "ability" for animate subjects:

> I can speak Indonesian.
> Superman is able to leap tall buildings with a single bound.

2. "potentiality" for inanimate subjects:

> This business can be reorganized.
> The car is able to go faster with this fuel.

Desire—*would like (to)* (normally takes a statement form):

> Sarah would like to travel around the world.
> Ralph would like an apple.

Offer/invitation—*would you like (to)* (normally takes a question form):

> Would you like something to drink?
> Would you like to dance?

Preference—*would rather* (X than Y), *would prefer to:*

> Brad would rather study languages than mathematics.
> Joe would prefer to go to school instead of working.

One could argue that *would like (to)* and *would prefer (to)* are simply sequences describable as: modal + verb + infinitive. For pedagogical purposes, however, we advise teaching these as frozen modal-like lexical chunks to emphasize the unchanging nature of *would* in these expressions to avoid ESL/EFL errors such as:

> *I will prefer to stay here.   *Will you like some cake?

CONTEXTS OF MEANING AND USE FOR SOME MODALS AND PHRASAL FORMS

Different degrees of formality tend to hold between use of a modal or a corresponding phrasal form, the latter being more informal, especially when phonologically reduced. Often other word choices in the sentence also reflect this difference in degree of formality:

> The United States must conserve its resources. / It has to (hasta) / have got to (gotta) conserve our resources.

> The exam will be 50 percent of your grade. / It's going to (gonna) be half your grade.

> You should tell your parents about this. / You ought to (oughta) tell your folks.

Can Versus Be Able To

The principal exception to the above tendency is *can/be able to*. Here the phrasal form is much less frequent and seems more formal than the modal:

> Can you do it?   Are you able to do it?

One reason for the informality of the modal may be the fact that *can* is often the modal first acquired by both native and nonnative speakers of English. It is very necessary for informal conversational English. Additionally, a data-based study (Polio 1988) indicates that in most instances where *be able to* is used, structural constraints prohibit the use of *can:*

—after other modals:

> Will you be able to join us?

—after perfect forms (i.e., *be able to* is more like a regular verb in such cases):

> I've been able to knit for a long time.

—in gerunds, participles, and infinitives:

> Being able to swim is a requirement for this job.
> I'd like to be able to swim.

Along with the greater formality of *be able to,* these constraints help explain why *can* is more frequent in the spoken language and is more informal. Zemach (1994) in another data-based study points out that *can* and *be able to* seem equivalent only in those cases where the meaning of "ability"—or "lack of ability" in the negative—is being expressed. This also holds for *could* and past forms of *be able to:*

> I left my books at school, so I (couldn't/wasn't able to) do my homework.

Other uses of *can* or *could* that signal potentiality, permission, choice, and so on, cannot be paraphrased with *be able to,* which occurs quite rarely in comparison with *can.* In fact, Zemach's data show that the best environments for use of *be able to* are those that convey special effort or frustration on the part of the grammatical subject (= the agent):

> After waiting for an hour, I _____ see the doctor.
> a. was finally able to (strongly preferred)
> b. could finally
> c. both (a) and (b)

Going back to Zemach's earlier example about "books" and "homework," we can now see that the reading with *couldn't* sounds more neutral or matter-of-fact, whereas the reading with *wasn't able to* expresses more concern and frustration about the speaker's inability to complete the work. There is also an asymmetry in the present and immediate past time uses of *can/could* versus *is able to/was able to,* which may result in learner errors:

> Today I $\left\{ \begin{array}{l} \text{can} \\ \text{am able to} \end{array} \right\}$ go to Disney World. (= The possibility exists. I may or may not actually go.)

> Yesterday I was able to go to Disney World. (= Strongly implies I did go.)
> ?Yesterday I could go to Disney World. (= unclear—did I go or not?)

Learners often say or write the last sentence with "could" when what they want to say requires "was able to." If they truly want to say only that the possibility existed, then a very careful paraphrase—or the addition of perfect aspect—is needed instead of the version with *could:*

> Yesterday, the possibility existed for me to go to Disney World.
> Yesterday, I could have gone to Disney World. (= implies I did not go.)

Note that for expressing remote past ability—in contrast to immediate past—both forms are acceptable:

> I $\left\{ \begin{array}{l} \text{was able to} \\ \text{could} \end{array} \right\}$ speak German fluently when I was a child.

Interestingly, when negated, both forms seem acceptable for expressing immediate past-time uses:

Yesterday I wasn't able to go to Disney World.
Yesterday I couldn't go to Disney World. } = I did not go. The possibility did not exist.

Shall

One modal we have not discussed in any detail is *shall*. Since it is used infrequently in North American English, we prefer to teach this form to most of our students for reception rather than production. For advanced students, we point out that when *shall* does occur, it is usually found in requests for a decision or for advice from the addressee, in tags with *let's*, or in statements establishing new topics:

Shall I call her? *(should can also be used here)*
Let's go, shall we?
Next we shall discuss the difference between *X* and *Y*.

Shall does occur in some frozen formulas where it signifies an invitation or a suggestion. In such cases, *should* cannot be substituted for *shall* without a change of meaning:

Shall we dance? (= would you like to dance? i.e., an invitation)
Should we dance? (= is it advisable? i.e., a question)

In formal commands—both affirmative and negative—one occasionally encounters *shall*:

You shall report promptly at 0500 hours.
You shall not wear sandals in the mess hall.

Certainly the old prescriptive rule—i.e., use *shall* to express future time with *I* and *we;* use *will* elsewhere—no longer holds true for North American English.

Will Versus Be Going To

Often the choice between semantically similar modals or between modals and phrasal forms will be a matter of usage preference rather than meaning per se. For example, for deciding whether to use *will* or *be going to,* some general guidelines come from work by Stafford (1975), McCarthy and Carter (1995) and others.

First of all, *be going to* is more informal and interpersonal than *will,* which is more formal and neutral as an expression of future time. Thus, one of two friends at a restaurant says to the other friend, "I'm gonna have the mushrooms." However, several minutes later the same speaker says to the waiter, "I'll have the mushrooms." Likewise, an army officer would say to a superior officer, "The war will be over soon" rather than "The war's gonna be over soon" to maintain a proper level of formality.

Secondly, *be going to* is closely tied to action already begun in the present or immediately imminent, given evidence available in the present but over which the speaker has no control (or has lost control). Thus English speakers say things like:

"Help! I'm going to fall."
"Look, it's gonna rain soon."

The equivalents with *will* would sound strange in such statements. The form *will* occurs in conditions and other statements where future outcome is contingent on some other result, is more distant, or involves speaker control:

"If you put your pawn there, he'll win the game."
"Go to the cafe at 9 P.M., and I'll meet you there."

In the immediately preceding example, *will* (*'ll*) conveys a sense of promise or commitment in the statement, but use of *be going to* would convey a plan or intention instead.

Should, Ought To, and Be Supposed To

Sometimes more than two choices are possible. When *should, ought to,* and *be supposed to* are compared, one can argue that some sort of expectation or standard—moral or otherwise—is being invoked. Using examples from written discourse, Bouscaren et al. (1992) argue that with *should* the moral judgment stems from the speaker's/writer's own personal criteria, whereas with *ought to* the judgment is based on external rules (social conventions, institutions):

> "I felt that I ought to be showing these people where to find food. But should I? If I were to lead them . . ."
> —J. Wyndham, *The Day of the Triffids* (context: humanity has become blind except for the narrator who is a witness to the disaster).[12]

Gaskill (1978), citing transcribed oral data, argues that the difference between *should* and *be supposed to* is that *should* invokes internal authority or a higher authority, whereas *be supposed to* invokes a very special type of impersonal external authority, an appeal to some predetermined schedule, plan, or perspective:

> A: Physics is, they say, formula plugging—whenever you say that it's formula plugging the teachers always get mad at you and say you're not supposed to look at it like that.

> B: Well, if you'll notice, most teachers say you should, uh, take an interest in your subject—you should apply it to life. And you try to, but somehow it doesn't work in most cases. (Carterette and Jones 1974, p. 406, punctuation added)

It seems both Bouscaren et al. and Gaskill argue that *should* expresses someone's internal moral judgment or a higher moral authority; the difference between the external force of *ought to* and *be supposed to* is that *ought to* is a marker of some general external moral or social standard, whereas use of *be supposed to* refers to explicit, externally agreed-upon standards, schedules, or expectations that may be restricted to a certain group (e.g., members of Al Capone's gang were *supposed to* kill people).

Must, Have To, and Have Got To

Melrose (1983) found in her study of *must, have to,* and *have got to* in spoken American English that most native speakers of American English reserve the use of *must* for expressing inference (present and past):

> You must have the wrong number!
> John must have been joking when he said that.

The form *have to* is used in speech to express both external and internal social necessity:

> You have to wait here till the doctor gets back.
> Excuse me. I have to go to the powder room.

What Melrose found that was extremely interesting was that the form *have got to,* rather than having its own discrete meaning(s) in opposition to *must* and *have to,* was used to express affect on the part of the speaker. The speaker would use *(have) got to,* often reduced to *gotta,* to express either inference or social necessity with a special degree of urgency (real or feigned):

> You gotta be kidding me![13]
> You've gotta lend me $10. I'm broke!

Thus we have a new use for certain modal forms—the expression of affect or special attitudes or overtones. This use seems to account for the difference between *should* and *(had) better/best;* the latter conveys special affect by sometimes suggesting the possibility of unpleasant consequences, whereas *should* is much more neutral:

> You should return that book to the library.
>
> You had $\left\{ \begin{array}{l} \text{better} \\ \text{best} \end{array} \right\}$ return that book to the library.

The use of *had better/best,* however, does not always imply negative consequences; this is especially true if the utterance is self-directed: *I'd better do the dusting before the vacuuming.*

Use of *Can* Versus No Modal

Sometimes the use of a modal conveys special affect in contrast to the absence of a modal. Park (1993) argues for such an analysis in a study of *can* with verbs of perception and cognition:[14]

> I can see your point.
> I see your point.

By doing a qualitative study of many contextualized examples drawn from transcribed conversation, Park found that the use of *can* (or *can't*) was preferred in contexts that were more interactional, affective, and empathy building:

> "Yeah, I can understand where she's coming from."

The use of the present tense, on the other hand, is preferred in contexts that are factual, direct, and sometimes abrupt or even argumentative:

> "I understand your point. Anything else?"

Sometimes the negative form of *can* with these types of verbs expresses surprise at a fact rather than conveying any literal negation of ability or possibility:

> "It's your birthday? I can't believe it!"

The use of *I don't believe it,* which can also express surprise, is preferred in contexts that are more factually-oriented, where the speaker is being direct; it would be used rather than *can't* in those cases where the speaker does not accept the statement as true.

Used To Versus *Be Used To* and *Get Used To*

Sometimes modal-like forms are easily confused with other forms. Students may confuse *used to* (the phrasal equivalent of *would* in its past habitual meaning)[15] with *be used to* and *get used to.* While *used to* suggests a factual report of past habit, *be/get used to* expresses a more affective stance, expressing familiarity and possibly some positive attitude. In *be/get used to* the word *used* = "accustomed." Compare the following sentences:

I used to eat hot food when I was in Thailand.	(factual report of past habit)
I got used to eating hot food when I was in Thailand.	(change of habit or circumstance in past)
I am used to eating hot food.	(current circumstance or habit)

Note that while *used to* expresses only past habit, *be used to* and *get used to* can refer to any time frame by changing the tense of *be* or *get.* Note also that *used to* is followed by bare infinitives, while *be used to* and *get used to* are followed by gerunds.[16]

CONCLUSION

This concludes our overview of the modal auxiliaries in English. We freely admit that it is far from complete. For example, we have not fully discussed archaic or shifting modals such as *dare* and *need*. We have not discussed the hypothetical use of the modals *would, should, could,* and *might*, since this is discussed later in Chapter 27, which deals with conditional sentences. We wish to emphasize again that very few languages have modal auxiliaries in the extreme form that English does—that is, as a separate verbal class that has very different syntactic properties from those of normal verbs.

We have also not discussed in any detail the dialect differences that modals display. For example, *must* is used much more frequently for social uses in British English than in North American English:

> You must come over for dinner soon.
> We must correct that problem as soon as possible.

In North American English, *have to* is generally used in such environments, while *must* is reserved for logical inference in the spoken language:

> This must be the correct answer.
> He must have heard the news.

Sometimes phrasal modals also exhibit dialect differences. For example, the Southern U.S. form *be fixing to* indicates a much more immediate future than *be going to:*

> (speaker with pen and paper in hand): I'm fixing to write a letter.

Although we have a fairly good understanding of the form and meaning of modals and their phrasal forms, we are very far from understanding all there is to know about their uses. English speakers use modals in extremely subtle ways to try to advise or control others, to express affect (positive and negative), to mark attitude or stance, to show authority, and for other purposes. We now need further research on the interactional uses of modals in a variety of different social and institutional settings to make progress in this area.

TEACHING SUGGESTIONS

1. Form. To accustom students to the fact that modal auxiliary verbs are followed directly by the lexical verb without *to*, an adaptation of a technique suggested by Ur (1988) can be used. The teacher can describe an object, animal, or person with sentences using modals, and the students have to guess what it is. This allows them to hear the correct form repeatedly. Writing some of the sentences on the board and drawing students' attention to the form can provide additional reinforcement.

An example in Ur (1988:172), focusing on *can* and *can't*, is the following (where the subject to be guessed is "koala bear"):

> It can climb trees.
> It can carry its baby.
> You can't buy one in a shop.

Sentences using other modal verbs could also be used. After this pattern has been established, the technique could be carried out in the way Ur suggests, in which only one student is not told what the chosen subject is, and all the other students participate in giving clues, using modal verbs to do so.

Students could also write their own descriptions, following the same pattern, and the teacher or other students could guess the subjects.

2. Form/Meaning. The communication activity "Find someone who . . ." can be used for practice in the production of modal verbs in questions (Een & Badalamenti, 1993). Each sentence should use a modal verb. For example:

> Find someone who can play tennis.
> Find someone who might go to Europe one day.
> Find someone who thinks they should do more exercise.

Each student has a worksheet with a list like the above and moves around the classroom asking questions of their classmates and writing down the name of the person who fits the description in each sentence. To add more interest, this can also be done using a grid, with a sentence in each square. The game is then played like bingo—the first student to get a straight line of squares with a different name in each is the winner.

3. Meaning. Teach the modal verbs in systems so that the relationship between them is clear.
    a. One of the uses of the logical probability modals is to predict something such as the chance of rain tomorrow. Show your students what degree of prediction is expressed by each modal (or combination of modal and adverbs[s]):

(possibly)	weak, outside chance	It could/might rain tomorrow.
(perhaps)	stronger chance	It may rain tomorrow.
(probably)	even stronger chance	It may very well rain tomorrow.
(very likely)	very strong chance	It will very likely rain tomorrow.
(certainly)	certainty	It will rain tomorrow.

For oral practice, have students express (using a modal) situations such as the following with the degree of prediction suggested by the context:

> 1) There's a 30 percent chance of rain tomorrow.
> 2) There's an 80 percent chance of rain later today.
> 3) The probability of good weather this coming weekend
> 4) The probability of man landing on Mars within the next 20 years

For written practice, have students read a paragraph or essay using modals predictively. Get them to describe in their own words the degree of each prediction. Have them write their own essay on a parallel topic.

    b. The other main use of the logical modals is to make inferences (guesses) about current or past states/situations. Give your students a modal paradigm for the present or the past, Example (for the present):

> Someone's knocking at the door.
>
> | | |
> |---|---|
> | weak inference: | That could/might be Mary. |
> | stronger inference: | That may be Mary. |
> | strong inference: | That should be Mary. |
> | very strong inference: | That must be Mary. |

For oral practice, have students react (using a modal) to situations such as the following:

> 1) Student X is not in class today.
> 2) Student Y is falling asleep/is thinking of something else.
> 3) The local football star has not been playing as well as usual.

In academic writing, this use of modals shows the degree of certainty about a statement. Cooper (1979:42) sets this in the context of discussion of cause and effect, using the topic of erosion as one example:

> The erosion may have been caused by the wind.
> The erosion must have been caused by the wind.

Study of texts that use modals in this way can be followed by writing tasks that require similar patterns. Contexts in which there is some kind of mystery to explain (even a picture to speculate about) are also valuable for eliciting the use of modals to express degrees of certainty (see Riggenbach and Samuda (1997:70–75) for examples).

4. Meaning. Modals are frequent in a discussion or written description of job openings that need to be filled. Ur (1988:175) and Thewlis (1997:75–76) each suggest exploiting this situation by asking students to describe a suitable candidate for a particular job, possibly after examining some advertisements from the newspaper. Students could also write their own want ads or job descriptions. For example, Thewlis (1997:80–82) provides three job advertisements and asks the students to identify

1) the things that an applicant must be able to do
2) the things he or she should be able to do (although they may not be absolutely required)
3) some things that are neither required nor recommended but are still characteristics that "the perfect candidate" might have
4) what an interested candidate has to do in order to apply for the position

He then asks students to discuss why any of the jobs would or would not interest them.

5. Meaning/Use. Appropriate social uses of modals can be practiced with brief role-plays in which students are given hypothetical situations to respond to. They would have to decide whether (a) the situation is formal or informal and (b) which degree of strength is called for. Ask, for example, "What would you say if . . . ?"

1) you are a teacher who wants to let a certain student know that it is essential to come to class on time
2) you want to tell a close friend who needs money for an emergency that one possibility is for him to sell his car
3) a fellow professor is not being paid the proper salary, and you think it would help if he saw the dean

6. Use. To practice the use of modals for politeness, Ur (1988:178) suggests presenting a brief dialogue that is abrupt and direct, for example:

> A: Hey, you! Open this door!
> B: It's locked. Want me to get the key?
> A: Yeah. Get it. Fast.

Discuss how it could be made more polite using modals. For example:

> A: Excuse me, would you open this door?
> B: I'm afraid it's locked. Shall I get the key?
> A: Please, if you wouldn't mind, as quickly as you can.

Students can then be asked in groups to compose two parallel dialogues such as the above for different situations (such as getting someone to lend you some money or asking someone to go out with you) and to perform them for the rest of the class.

7. Use. For the use of modals in offers, Paula Hidalgo (personal communication) suggests a card game that uses a set of cards containing pairs of problematic situations and suitable solutions that could be offered; for example, a picture of a thirsty person would be matched with one of a glass of water.

Students play in groups of three or four, and each student receives a number of cards, the remainder to be left in a stack. One player calls out a problematic situation for which he or she holds the card (e.g., "I'm thirsty!"), and another player who has the card for a suitable solution is required to make a polite offer (e.g., "Would you like a glass of water?"). The pair of matching cards is then discarded. If the offer is not made politely, play passes to another player to call a situation. If no student has the card for the solution, each of the players (except the one with the problem) picks up a card from the stack until someone gets the solution card. If a player holds both the problem and the solution cards, they immediately discard them.

The winner is the first one to get rid of all their cards. While luck is involved, the students' correct production of polite offers also affects their chances of winning, and this motivates the students to monitor one another's performance. If the offer is not politely made, it is in their interest to point this out so that they have a better chance of winning.

8. Use. To teach the different usages of *will* and *be going to,* give your students situations such as the following, which were taken from a paper by Stafford (1975), and ask them to choose (1) or (2). Discuss their choices with them, and they should begin to become sensitive to the differences.

a. You are on a tour of Disneyland with your friends. As you step off one of the rides, you suddenly lose your balance and shout:

(1) "Help! I will fall!"   (2) "Help! I'm going to (gonna) fall!"

Difference: Be going to is the preferred form, since it is used with actions or events beyond the control of the subject that are just about to happen.

b. An army officer is talking to a superior officer. He says,

"Well, sir, if our strategies continue to be successful, the war
(1) is going to soon be over."   (2) will soon be over."

Difference: Will is the preferred from when a more formal register is called for.

c. A shy 17-year-old boy calls up a girl he's been admiring all year. He says,

(1) "Will you meet me at the show this Friday?"
(2) "Are you going to meet me at the show this Friday?"

Difference: Will is used for requests/invitations; *be going to* is inappropriate in such contexts.

EXERCISES

Test your understanding of what has been presented.

I. Provide original example sentences that illustrate the following concepts. Underline the relevant word(s) in your examples.

    a. phrasal modal

    b. social use of a modal

    c. logical probability meaning of a modal

    d. a combination of more than one modal or phrasal modal

    e. polite form of a request

    f. literal question with a phrasal modal

2. Explain the ambiguity of the following sentence:

    His mother says he may go.

3. Explain the semantic difference between the two sentences in each of the following pairs:

    a. It must be nighttime.   It must have been nighttime.

    b. Will you help me with this problem?   Would you help me with this problem?

    c. I was able to go to the library last night.   I could have gone to the library last night.

    d. The ground is wet. It may have rained last night.   The ground is wet. It must have rained last night.

    e. You should do your homework.   You had better do your homework.

4. The meaning of the affirmative sentences in the following pairs is similar. Explain the semantic difference between the negative sentences:

    a. That might be important. → That might not be important.

    b. That could be important. → That couldn't be important.

Test your ability to apply what you know.

5. Students of yours have made the following errors. In each case explain the nature of the error and state what activities you would provide to correct it.

    a. *You will can go there.

    b. *May you cash this check, please?

    c. *We should study a lot for that class last term.

    d. *They could be easily to reach the goal.

    e. *I must to speak English.

    f. *This action will good for workers.

    g. ?Excuse me, Mr. Smith, you gotta give us our homework back.

    h. Would you please close the window? *Of course I would.

6. What is the difference in meaning in each of the following pairs of sentences? There may be differences in the presuppositions of the speaker.

    a. Could you tell me how to get to the bus stop?

    b. Would you tell me how to get the bus stop?

    c. Sam should introduce the guest speaker.

    d. Sam is supposed to introduce the guest speaker.

    e. The principal said Joe may go.

    f. The principal said Joe may have gone.

7. Consider the verb forms *need* and *dare:*

    a. I need to see him.   **d.** Need I bring anything?

    b. You needn't worry.   **e.** I dare you to do that.

    c. Do we dare think that?

Are they modals, phrasal modals, regular lexical verbs, or a mixture of these forms?

8. Sometimes, when referring to ability in the past, one can use the phrasal modal but not the true modal:

> I was able to pick up the tickets last night.   *I could pick up the tickets last night.

At other times, both the phrasal modal and the true modal are acceptable:

> I could read at an early age.   I was able to read at an early age.

Furthermore, even the ungrammatical sentence above is acceptable when it is negated:

> I couldn't pick up the tickets last night.

Can you think of a generalization that would account for these restrictions on the use of *could?*

BIBLIOGRAPHY

References

Bailey, C.J. (1997). You and Your English Grammer. Unpublished manuscript

Bouscaren, J. and J. Chuquet, with L. Danon-Boileau (1992). *Introduction to a Linguistic Grammar of English: An Utterer-Centered Approach.* Translated from the French by R. Flintham and J. Bouscaren. Paris: Orphys.

Carterette, E., and M. Jones (1974). *Informal Speech.* Berkeley: University of California Press.

Cooper, J. (1979). *Think and Link: An Advanced Course in Reading and Writing Skills.* London: Edward Arnold.

Een, J., and V. Badalamenti (1993). Workshop in teaching grammar thematically (TL4174) given at Columbia Teachers College, fall 1993.

Gaskill, W. (1978). "*Should* versus *Be Supposed To.*" Unpublished English 215 paper, UCLA.

Hofmann, T. R. (1966). "Past Tense Replacement and the Modal System." Computational Laboratory, Harvard University, NSF Report 17.

McCarthy, M., and R. Carter (1995). "Spoken Grammar: What Is It and How Can We Teach It?" *ELT Journal* 49:3, 207–218.

Melrose, S. L. (1983). "*Must* and Its Periphrastic Forms in American English Usage." Unpublished M.A. thesis in TESL, UCLA.

Ney, J. W. (1978). "Practical Suggestions for Teaching the English Modals," *Cross Currents* 5:2.

Palmer, F. (1990). *Modality and the English Modals* (2d ed.). London: Longman.

Park, Y. Y. (1993). "A Discourse Analysis of *Can* versus Its Absence with Verbs of Perception and Cognition in Spoken English." Unpublished MA thesis in TESL, UCLA.

Polio, C. (1988). "The Uses of *Can* and *Be Able to* in American English." Unpublished English 252K paper, UCLA.

Riggenbach, H., and V. Samuda (1997). *Grammar Dimensions: Form, Meaning, and Use.* Book 2 (2d ed.). Boston: Heinle & Heinle.

Stafford, C. (1975). "Expressing the Future: *Will* vs. *Going To.*" Unpublished English 215 paper, UCLA, Fall, 1975.

Thewlis, S. (1997). *Grammar Dimensions: Form, Meaning, and Use.* Book 3 (2d ed.). Boston: Heinle & Heinle.

Ur, P. (1988). *Grammar Practice Activities: A Practical Guide for Teachers.* Cambridge: Cambridge University Press.

Walker, C. (1993). "Double Modal Usage in Intimate Conversation in an Alabama Dialect." Unpublished M.A. thesis in TESL, UCLA.

Zemach, D. E. (1994). "A Contextual Analysis of the Difference between *Can* and *Be Able to* to Express Ability." Independent Professional Paper, School for International Training, Brattleboro, Vt.

Suggestions for further reading

For useful traditional descriptions of English modal auxiliaries, see:

Close, R. A. (1981). *English as a Foreign Language* (3d ed.). London: Allen and Unwin, 110–131.

Ehrman, M. (1972). *The Meaning of the Modals in Present-Day American English.* The Hague: Mouton.

Frank, M. (1993). *Modern English: A Practical Reference Guide* (2d ed.). Englewood Cliffs, N.J.: Regents/Prentice-Hall, 95–108.

Leech, G. (1971). *Meaning and the English Verb.* London: Longman, 69–98.

For a useful discussion of differences between will *and* going to, *see:*

Martin, M. (1978). "Future Shock: A Pedagogical Analysis of *Will* and *Going To*," in J. Schachter and C. H. Blatchford (eds.), *ON TESOL '78.* Washington, D.C.: TESOL.

For interesting accounts of English modals and for perspectives on the root (social)/epistemic (logical) distinction that differ somewhat from the one presented here, see:

Cook, W. A. (1978). "Semantic Structure of the English Modals," *TESOL Quarterly* 12:1, 5–15.

Diver, W. (1964). "The Modal System of the English Verb," *Word* 20:3, 322–352.

Palmer, F. R. (1990). *Modality and the English Modals.* London: Longman.

Tregidgo, P. S. (1982). "Must and May: Demand and Permission," *Lingua* 56:1, 75–92.

For good suggestions on the teaching of modal auxiliaries, consult:

Badalamenti, V. and C. Henner Stanchina (1997). *Grammar Dimensions: Form, Meaning, and Use.* Book 1 (2d ed.). Boston: Heinle & Heinle, 256–271.

Bowen, J. D., and C. F. McCreary (1977). "Teaching the English Modal Perfects." *TESOL Quarterly* 11:3, 283–301.

Danielson, D., and P. Porter, with R. Hayden (1990). *Using English: Your Second Language* (2d ed.). Englewood Cliffs, N.J.: Prentice-Hall Regents, 76–111.

Frodesen, J., and J. Eyring (1997). *Grammar Dimensions: Form, Meaning, and Use.* Book 4 (2d ed.). Boston: Heinle & Heinle, 58–74.

Riggenbach, H. and V. Samuda (1997). *Grammar Dimensions: Form, Meaning, and Use.* Book 2 (2d ed.). Boston: Heinle & Heinle, units 3, 7, 8, 14, 15, and 24.

Thewlis, S. (1997). *Grammar Dimensions: Form, Meaning, and Use.* Book 3 (2d ed.). Boston: Heinle & Heinle, units 5, 20, 21, 31.

Ur, P. (1988). *Grammar Practice Activities: A Practical Guide for Teachers.* Cambridge: Cambridge University Press, 172–180.

ENDNOTES

1. Note that *must,* originally the past tense of Anglo-Saxon *motan,* has no historically related present form. What happened in modern English is that *must* became largely "present" in terms of its meaning potential; as a result, explicit marking of past necessity is

often expressed with the phrasal *had to,* past tense of *have to. Had to* was the first phrasal modal to develop in English, and it arose at a time when *must* and *should* had lost their connection to past time and no longer took direct objects.

2. *Should* can be viewed as the past tense of *shall* only if the speaker is asking for advice. When *shall* is used to express the future, *would* functions as a past-time equivalent in North American English:

> Joe: I shall see you later.
> Joe said that he would (*should) see us later.

3. See Endnote 1 above for an explanation for the *must/had to* alternation seen here.

4. The form *ought to* is intermediate between a true modal (it doesn't inflect) and a phrasal form (it takes *to*); one can classify it either way. Historically, *ought* is a past form of *owe;* in current usage *ought* may lose its *to* in negative sentences and look more like a true modal, but this does not work for all speakers of North American English:

> You oughtn't *(to)* do that. We ought not *(to)* stay longer.

5. Although we indicate that *be to,* which is rare in any case, is a phrasal equivalent of *should,* as in What am I to do?, *be to* can also be a phrasal equivalent of *will* (I *am to* leave tomorrow) and *must* (You *are to* report here at 6 A.M.).

6. There is some dialectal variation here in that native speakers represent questions and negatives with *used to* differently. Some write the prescriptively favored "Did you use to?" "You didn't use to" while others write "Did you used to?" "You didn't used to." For the second group, *used to* is on its way to becoming more of an intermediate frozen form like *ought to,* whereas the first group still views *used to* as a normally inflected past-tense form. The second group is probably indicating a future change.

7. There are Southern dialects of North American English where certain modal-plus-modal sequences are possible:

> We might could do that.

See Walker (1993) for further discussion.

8. Three also seems to be the limit on multiple modal sequences in those Southern dialects that allow them: *might should ought to* (Steve Nagle, personal communication).

9. Following Halliday (1985), these scales and those that follow present *must* as stronger than *will* or *be going to.* Not everyone will agree with this. In fact, *will* is used only rarely in North American English as an epistemic modal. Such usage sounds British to American ears.

10. An anonymous reviewer has indicated to us that for him/her *might* is the equivalent of *may* rather than *could.* We recognize that such differences are dialectally and idiolectally possible, especially with more rarely used modals such as *might.*

11. Another possible, though less frequent, equivalent for *You don't have to go* is *You needn't go. Need* is unusual in that it can function as a modal in negatives and occasionally in questions *(Need I say more?),* but it very rarely if ever functions as a modal in affirmative statements in North American English; instead it functions like an ordinary verb or a phrasal modal *(We need to go).* Another form that is sometimes like a modal in questions and negatives and more often like a regular verb in affirmatives is *dare: Dare we ask?* We *don't dare ask! He dared to be brave.*

12. Cited in Bouscaren et al. (1992: 68).

13. The omission of *have* in *have got to* and of *had* in *had better/best* makes the speaker sound more informal and colloquial.

14. Many grammarians claim there is no difference between use of *can* and simple present tense with such verbs.

15. The patterns of usage for *used to* and *would* to express past habit are described in Chapter 9.

16. This indicates that different structures are involved: *I used to eat:* PM + V; *I was/got used to eating:* BE/GET + adj + prep + gerund.

THE TENSE-ASPECT-MODALITY SYSTEM IN DISCOURSE

INTRODUCTION

A limitation of sentence-based accounts of English tense, aspect, and modality—even if well contextualized—is that such accounts fail to capture the fact that certain tenses, aspect, and modality combinations tend to occur together in discourse whereas others do not. To help us understand the uses of the tense-aspect-modality system in English discourse, the early work of Bull (1960) is an insightful starting point. After presenting Bull's framework, we also briefly discuss a proposal by Chafe (1972) concerning tense sequences in discourse. The bulk of this chapter, however, reports on a number of more recent data-based studies that are beginning to help us better understand the functions of the tense-aspect-modality (TAM) system in English discourse, both spoken and written. The various approaches we discuss with respect to analyzing TAM in discourse do not necessarily fit together in a unified way; they all, however, offer useful perspectives.

This chapter thus complements the previous two in that it builds on what we have learned about tense and aspect at the sentence level in Chapter 7 and about modal auxiliaries and phrasal modals at the sentence level in Chapter 8 in order to examine the special uses that many of the forms discussed earlier can have at the discourse level. Such an examination of TAM is important because "tense-aspect-modality is one of the major devices coding the connectedness/coherence of sentences in their wider discourse context" (Givón, 1984:269). This whole chapter is thus dedicated to describing the use of TAM in discourse.

First, let us examine some data. Consider the two following narratives:

> A. I have a splitting headache that I've had for two hours. I'm going to take some aspirin.[1]
> B. ?I have a splitting headache that I had for two hours; I will take some aspirin.

In the first example, we find the *present* tense in the first clause, the *present* perfect in the second clause, and *be going to* with a *present* tense *be* in the final clause; that is, the tenses have an orientation to the present throughout the sequence. Unmotivated changes in the tense sequence are not felicitous and, if made, may produce a less coherent piece of discourse. This is what occurs in B above, where the unmotivated tense-switching from present to past to future results in the relative incoherence of the second narrative (i.e., the simple past *had* is used where the present perfect *have had* is preferred).

Similar observations can be made about samples of discourse concerning events reported in past time. Consider the following:

    C. The little girl cried her heart out. She had lost her teddy bear and was convinced she wasn't ever going to find him. (possible substitution: "would never" for "wasn't ever going to")

The first clause is simple past, the second clause is the past perfect, and the third is the *be going to* future but with a past tense *be;* that is, a past orientation is maintained throughout the episode. Again, if we make unmotivated changes in the tenses used in the narrative as in D below, these changes may well have negative consequences for the flow of the discourse:

    D. ?The little girl cries her heart out. She lost her teddy bear and is convinced she won't ever find him.

The version in D of the past narrative is comprehensible and not obviously incoherent, but it comes out sounding somewhat disjointed and awkward when compared with the original in C because one does not normally jump from present tense to past tense to future tense in a short piece of discourse. Yet this is precisely what many nonnative speakers of English do when they speak and write in English. One reason for this may be that they have learned the English tense system bit by bit at the sentence level without ever learning how the bits interact in longer pieces of discourse. This chapter directly addresses this teaching/learning problem.

THE BULL FRAMEWORK

In 1960, William Bull first proposed a framework to describe tense in Spanish; however, he intended that the system be very general and applicable to any language. In this chapter, we apply Bull's framework to English. His framework posits four axes of orientation, or points of view, with respect to time: future, present, past, and hypothetical. We do not deal with Bull's hypothetical axis here but save it for Chapter 27 on conditionals. Bull's framework is quite radical in presenting three distinct time axes (four if we count the hypothetical line); most other accounts of English tense and aspect assume one timeline and try to illustrate all tense-aspect forms in terms of this single line:

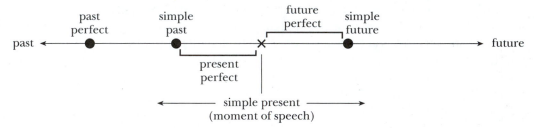

Bull forces us to make a conceptual shift and to think in terms of viewing the tense-aspect system as a resource for taking different temporal perspectives on actions, events, and states of affairs. For example, if asked the question:

    Would you like something to eat?

one can answer either (a) or (b):

    (a) No thanks. I've already eaten.
    (b) No thanks. I already ate.

The time of the speaker's meal does not necessarily differ in (a) and (b). Both responses report past events, but the choice allows the speaker to add his/her perspective on the current relevance of the response; this perspective is what conditions the choice rather than any real linear sense of time: (a) is not necessarily more recent within real time than (b).

What (a) signals is the current relevance that the response is believed to have, whereas (b) does not signal any assumption of current relevance. In fact, (b) puts the speaker's last meal squarely in the past rather than the present. Another example that suggests Bull is correct to take us away from a linear perspective on tense and aspect to a three- or four-tiered system is to consider the future perfect, which asks the listener to step into the future and look back. It is quite possible, as the following example shows, for an event/action described with a future perfect (1) to have occurred before one described with the simple past (2):

1. He will have finished all that work months ago. [You don't know John the way I do]
2. I saw John at the market yesterday.

Each axis in Bull's framework has a neutral or basic time slot in the middle and two possible marked slots—one on the left signaling a time before the basic time of the axis and the other on the right signaling a time after the basic time of that axis. Based on this semantic framework, each "tense" of any language can then be placed in the appropriate slot on the appropriate axis. It is quite likely, however, that any given language will not fill each possible slot with a unique form and that any given language might turn out to have some overlap or substitutability of forms across slots.

See Table 9.1 for our interpretation of Bull's axes applied to English and their corresponding verb tense forms (with input from Houts Smith [1993]):

		TABLE 9.1 THE BULL FRAMEWORK	
Axis of orientation	**A time *before* the basic axis time**	**Basic axis time corresponding to the moment of reference**	**A time *after* the basic axis time**
Future	By 5:00, he will have finished all the chores. (future perfect)	He { will / is going to } eat dinner at 5:00. (simple future)	Upon completion of this work, he { will / is going to } watch TV. (no distinct form— use simple future)
Present	He has played golf since 1960. (present perfect)	He plays golf. (simple present)	He is going to play golf next Sunday. (future of the present) Note: *Will* may be used as a formal substitute
Past	When he left to play golf, he had finished all his chores (past perfect)	He played golf on Saturday afternoon (simple past)	Having finished his golf game, he went out to dinner with his golf buddies. or Having finished his golf game, he would go out to dinner. (= habitual)

This framework helps us understand quite explicitly why two of the preceding narratives were smoother or more coherent than their alternatives: In the preferred samples of discourse, the author stayed within one axis of orientation—that is, present or past—and made "before" and "after" time references that were appropriate to that axis; the author did not jump from one axis to the other.

Although the present- and past-time axes are the two axes most frequently used in English, we should at this stage also provide a discourse sample that illustrates the application of the Bull framework to the future axis, which is another temporal point of view the speaker/writer can take:

> E. John will (possible substitution: *is going to*) travel to Europe this summer. Before doing that he will have completed his B.S. in Math. When he returns to the States, he will begin graduate work in Management.

Here, the tense sequence moves from *future* to *future perfect*, and the text once again ends with *future*. In the subordinate clause beginning with "when," the tense is "present" but the whole sentence still expresses future time.[2] The overlap of *will* and *be going to* in both the future axis for the core tense and in the present axis for the "future of the present" is due to many factors, including register (*will* is more formal) and interaction (*be going to* has more interactive immediacy); however, the ability of *be going to* to inflect for present tense and the greater relative ease of combining *will* with perfect aspect in the future axis suggest that the underlying assignment of *will* to future axis and of *be going to* to present axis is indeed valid despite the areas of overlap.

Another unique feature of Bull's framework is that the so-called perfect aspect in English is shown to be much more closely associated with tense than is the progressive aspect. The perfect aspect signals the "before time" in each axis, (called "prior" time in Chapter 7) whereas the progressive aspect is a truly independent aspectual form that can express notions such as duration, noncompletion, or iteration in combination with all the tense-aspect-modality forms in Table 9.1. By including the be going to form, we now have 14 distinct tense-aspect combinations in English instead of the traditional 12:

Bull System Forms	*Bull Forms plus Progressive Aspect*
will V (will talk)	will be V -ing (will be talking)
will have V + -en (will have talked)	will have been V -ing (will have been talking)
V -pres (talk(s))	Be -pres V -ing (is/are/am talking)
have V + -en (have/has talked)	have been V -ing (has/has been talking)
Be-pres going to V (is/am/are going to talk)	Be -pres going to be V -ing[3] (is/am/are going to be talking)
V -past (talked)	Be -past V -ing (was/were talking)
had V + -en (had talked)	had been V -ing (had been talking)

THE BULL FRAMEWORK VERSUS PREVIOUS ACCOUNTS

Teachers might wonder whether the Bull framework differs substantially from previous analyses of the English tense-aspect system, and if so, how. We feel that the Bull framework permits an analysis that is like traditional accounts such as Jespersen's (1924), in that meaning has priority over form and also that it retains much of the traditional grammatical terminology for describing the tenses. Bull's system, however, is considerably more complex in that not just one but three parallel time lines (i.e., the three axes of orientation) are used to illustrate and explicate the tense system—*tense*, in any language, is a grammatical system that uses notions of time to reflect the user's perspective on events. Bull's system begins to account for tense sequences in discourse as well as accounting for tense in isolated sentences, and teachers can refer to the axes to show students how tenses should relate to each other in discourse; that is, students should perhaps learn the tenses one axis at a time rather than one form at a time. Bull's framework is also more sophisticated and subtle than the usual structural account of the English tense-aspect system in that it shows clearly how the so-called perfect aspect consistently functions as a marker of "a time before" with respect to the basic English tense in each of the three axes, with the result that the progressive appears to be a more flexible and genuine marker of aspect than the perfect in English because it interacts with each form in Bull's matrix to signal duration, noncompletion, or iteration and is not restricted to "a time before."[4]

CHAFE'S OBSERVATIONS ON TENSES IN DISCOURSE

To provide a more complete accounting for tense sequences in discourse, Chafe (1972) introduces the notion of generic tenses—which we describe in Chapter 2 as backgrounding. He provides the following piece of discourse (pp. 48–49) along with his accompanying tense analysis:

F. *Discourse Sequence*	*Chafe's Tense Analysis*
a. I went to a concert last night.	a. past
b. They played Beethoven's second.	b. past
c. You don't hear that very often.	c. generic
d. I enjoyed it.	d. past
e. Next Friday I'm going to another concert.	e. future
f. They're playing something by Stravinsky.	f. future

Using this illustration, Chafe makes several important points: When a tense or time has been established in a piece of discourse, this tense must be maintained unless:

1. A "generic" tense (usually the simple present) is used for a comment or aside, as in (c) above and temporarily suspends the past tense requirement followed in (a), (b), and (d).
2. A new explicit time marker—or a clearly implied shift—is introduced into the discourse, which terminates the old tense and replaces it with another, as happens with "Next Friday" initiating clause (e) with a subsequent new tense in (e) and (f).

In discourse sequence F, we would like to point out that Chafe uses "future" to label the tense forms in (e) and (f) that are considered "present" in Bull's framework. Using *will*, a more general marker of the future that is not tied to the present axis, would sound much less appropriate than the present axis forms Chafe actually used in (e) and (f). This is because the time phrase *Next Friday* is deictic (i.e., its interpretation is tied to the speaker's here and now, like *this* and *that*) and thus depends on the time of speaking (i.e., present time) for its interpretation. Also, in Chapter 2, Chafe's generic tense as in line (c) was described as backgrounding in narrative. In what follows we refer to tenses used for backgrounding instead of using Chafe's term, i.e., generic tenses.

The following is an authentic example of the simple present used to provide background in oral narrative to provide evaluation and express speaker stance (lines 2 and 3) in between two past-tense forms that are the foreground and represent the main story line (lines 1 and 4):[5]

G. "Skiing over a cliff"
1. So my front skis bent down
2. Interestingly enough, when something like this happens
3. all these thoughts flash in your mind
4. I managed to flash my whole life in front of me.

LABOV'S STRUCTURE FOR NARRATIVE

To better explain tense shifts in narrative, we refer from time to time to Labov's (1972) narrative structure, which posits six elements for any narrative, three of which are obligatory and bulleted and thus more important than the others in parentheses, which are optional:

Six Elements of Narrative[6]	Description of Each Element
(the abstract)	who and what the narrative is about
• orientation	the background for the narrative
• complicating action	the conflict or problem in the story
(evaluation)	asides or comments from the narrator
• result or resolution	the outcome of the narrative
(coda)	an epilogue or the moral of the story

A simple constructed example of this narrative sequence follows:

abst.: This is about a prince, a witch, and a princess.
orient.: Once upon a time there was a handsome prince.
compl.: A wicked witch turned him into a frog.
eval.: That's not nice, is it?
resol.: A beautiful princess broke the witch's spell by kissing the frog.
coda: The prince and princess lived happily ever after.

Different parts of a narrative tend to be realized with different tenses. For example, an evaluation, as we have seen above in lines 2 and 3 in the skiing story in G and in the fourth line of the fairy tale above, will often be in the simple present because it is background, whereas the result or resolution tends to occur in the simple past because it is foreground (i.e., part of the main story line).

HISTORICAL PRESENT TENSE AND TENSE SHIFTING

An additional complication in understanding tense sequencing is a particular function of the simple present tense known as "the historical present" (see Chapter 7). It uses the present tense to relate a past event and is very common in oral narrative. Labov (1972), Schiffrin (1981), Wolfson (1981), and Baquedano-López (1994) have all examined the role of the historical present tense. It is different from the backgrounding use of the present tense discussed in texts F and G above in that it refers to a specific event in the past, not a background statement or evaluation, and is a stylistic device employed by the speaker to accomplish any of several things. Both the historical present and backgrounding present occur in the following authentic oral narrative:

H. "Driving home"[7]
1. So Dad decides that he's gonna pass these cars
2. And, uh, he pulls out in the other lane
3. And starts passing them.
4. And all of a sudden we see this big truck, you know, this truck coming for us.
5. And, uh, this guy was going pretty fast
6. And we had passed one car
7. And there's no way we can get over
8. And this trucker's coming
9. And he's just sort of bearing down on us honking his horn
10. He wasn't slowing down.
11. So you know it gets to the point where you're halfway past the second car

12. And it becomes apparent that we might hit this truck.
13. You know, my mom was sitting in the front seat
14. And my sister and I are in the back seat
15. And all of a sudden we see this truck
16. And thought for sure we were gonna hit it.
17. And I went "Well this is it," you know
18. And my sister and I just started yelling
19. And we ducked.

In this narrative, the historical present tense is used initially in lines 1–4 and then the tense switches to the past progressive in line 5 (and even the past perfect in line 6) to signal an ongoing complicating action. A tense shift back to historical present (simple or progressive) in lines 7–10 continues the story line. A backgrounding present tense in lines 11 and 12 interjects the speaker's evaluation before he switches the tense back to past progressive in line 13 and the historical present in lines 14 and 15 to get back to the story line. The remaining lines (16–19) switch back to past tense and relate the thoughts, words, and actions of the participants. Note that the reported speech in line 17 is present tense but the reporting verb *went* is past tense.

The historical present and backgrounding present can occur in the same episode since lines 11 and 12 above are arguably backgrounding present, given the pronominal shifts from previous references to *he* (= dad) or *we/us* (= family) to the line 11 reference to *you* (= whoever is trying to pass a line of cars on a road). Examples such as the above demonstrate that tense shifts in authentic oral narrative are extremely complex. As Baquedano-López (1994) points out, they can mark boundaries between elements within the narrative itself, but they also can function much more locally to mark contrasts such as main story vs. speaker aside, agent x vs. agent y, or narrative storyline vs. reported speech/thought, etc.

SUH'S FRAME-ELABORATION HYPOTHESIS

A rather different perspective on the use of tense-aspect-modality sequences in discourse is taken up in Kyung-Hee Suh's research. Drawing on a number of existing databases, Suh (1992a) noticed that in the course of constructing oral narratives, English speakers often use one tense-aspect-modality form to very generally introduce (or sometimes to close) a type of narrative or an episode, and then they switch for the remainder of the episode to another form to elaborate the episode and provide the details.

Tense and Aspect Sequences

In this regard, one pattern Suh noticed was that the present perfect tense can be used to either introduce or sum up a habitual present-tense narrative. Observe how this pattern is illustrated in the following two examples:

   I. Jazz musician[8]
     1. There's been a lot of untruths told about improvisation.
     2. Men just don't get up on the stage and improvise on things they're not familiar with.
     3. True improvisation comes out of hard work.
     4. When you're practicing at home, you work on a theme, and you work out all the possibilities of that theme.
     5. Since it's in your head, it comes out when you play.
     6. You don't get out on the stage and just improvise,
     7. Not knowing what the hell you're doing.[9]
     8. It doesn't work out that way.

J. "Now that dad has retired"[10]

    1. When my father gets up, he showers and shaves.

    2. Then he eats breakfast and reads the newspaper while he slowly drinks his coffee.

    3. After that he walks the dog.

    4. That's the way it's been ever since he retired.

In narrative I, the present perfect initiates the episode in line 1, and the simple present—interrupted by two present progressives in lines 4 and 7 that seem to be background information—completes the episode. In narrative J, the simple present occurs in all but the final clause of line 4, where the present perfect serves to tie the details together and relate the entire episode to the moment of speech.

    Suh (1992a) noticed even more cases in oral narrative where the present perfect provides a transition from the moment of speaking (i.e., Bull's present axis) and introduces or frames a specific past experience, the details of which are then reported in the simple past. Two narratives exemplifying this frame-elaboration pattern follow:

K. "Gas-meter reader"[11]

    1. I've been bit once already by a German shepherd.

    2. And that was something.

    3. It was really scary.

    4. It was an outside meter the woman had.

    5. I read the gas meter and was walking back out and heard a woman yell.

    6. I turned around, and this German shepherd was coming at me.

    7. The first thing I thought of was that he might go for my throat, like the movies.

    8. So I sort of crouched down and gave him my arm;

    9. Instead of my neck, he grabbed a hold of my arm, bit that, turned around.

    10. My arm was kinda soft so I thought I'd give him something harder.

    11. So I gave him my hand, a little more bone in that.

    12. So he bit my hand.

    13. I gave it to him so that he wouldn't bite my throat.

    14. I didn't want him to grab hold of my face.

L. "Airline stewardess"[12] [*Note*: The first two lines are simply background]

    1. . . . . Here I'm thinking, what if I die today? I've got[13] too much to do.

    2. I can't die today. I use it as a joke.

    3. I've had emergencies where I've had to evacuate the aircraft.

    4. I was coming back from Las Vegas and being a lively stewardess.

    5. I'd stayed up all night, gambled. We had a full load of passengers.

    6. The captain tells me we're going to have an emergency landing in Chicago because we lost[14] a pin in the nose gear.

    7. When we land, the nose gear is gonna collapse.

    8. He wants me to prepare the whole cabin for the landing, but not for two more hours.

    9. And not to tell the other stewardesses.

    10. Because they were new girls and would get all excited.

    11. So I had to keep this in me for two more hours,

    12. Wondering, "Am I gonna die today?"

In both of the excerpts above, the present perfect introduces or frames the specific past event and the simple past (or historical present) is used to elaborate and give the details. The immediately preceding example, L, is especially interesting since the stewardess' thoughts, fears, and her reported inner speech are all in the historical present tense (lines 1, 2, and 12) with progressive aspect added to express duration in lines 1 and 12.

Also, what the captain tells the stewardess to do is reported with the historical present (lines 6–9), while causes or reasons for his orders are simple past (lines 10 and 11). Such tense shifts help to separate thoughts and reports from the sequence of more specific events pertaining to the emergency itself. The *going to* and *gonna* tokens in lines 6, 7, and 12 are considered present tense (future of present) forms in the spirit of the Bull framework. They reflect possible future consequences of the events being reported.

Modal and Phrasal Modal Sequences

In addition to tense and aspect sequences like the two illustrated above, Suh's frame-elaboration hypothesis also works for two other interesting cases that involve modals and phrasal modals: the use of *used to* and *would* for past habitual narratives and *be going to* and *will* for future scenarios.

Previously, researchers have had problems distinguishing *used to* and *would* at the sentence level, for it seemed that pairs such as the following were more or less equivalent in terms of stating habitual actions or states in the past:

> M. a. My father used to exercise every morning.
>   b. My father would exercise every morning.

Certainly one difference is that (a) can signal only habitual past action whereas (b) can also be conditional given appropriate context (i.e., "If he had time"). However, without further context, (a) and (b) cannot be distinguished at the sentence level. In collecting many instances of spontaneous oral narratives with past habitual time references, Suh (1992b) noticed that the temporally more explicit *used to* tends to mark an episode boundary or set up a frame for a past habitual event, whereas the more contigent form *would* (or *'d*) marks the details or elaborates the topic, with the simple past also occurring as an alternative to *would*. Consider the following examples:

> N. "Farm worker"[15]
> 1. The bad thing was they used to laugh at us, the
> 2. Anglo kids. They would laugh because we'd bring tortillas
> 3. and frijoles to lunch. They would have their nice little
> 4. compact lunch boxes with cold milk in their thermos and
> 5. they'd laugh at us because all we had was dried tortillas.
> 6. Not only would they laugh at us, but the kids would pick fights.

> O. "Cabdriver"[16]
> [Note: The cabdriver was formerly in the Merchant Marines. The first four lines are background to the target episode, which starts in line 5.]
> 1. The big topic at sea is still exploits with women.
> 2. Because there's always loneliness. A traveling salesman,
> 3. he has a means of picking up a phone. But a seaman is one
> 4. month to three months before he'll get a letter from his wife.
> → 5. I used to phone my wife three, four times every
> 6. trip. In Calcutta I waited five hours to get a phone
> 7. call through. If I didn't get it through one night,
> 8. I'd call again and wait three, four hours the next morning.
> 9. The feeling you get, just hearing her voice. . .
> 10. I'd stand on the phone and just actually choke up.
> 11. My wife would be crying on the other end, and I'd say,
> 12. "Woman, listen, I'm spending too much money on this phone call.
> 13. Stop crying."

Note the backgrounding present tense used in line 9 in the preceding text for expressing the seaman's emotions, the simple past tense used in lines 6 and 7 for the specific events that happened once when he was in Calcutta, and also the quoted speech of the last two lines marked by present tense. Other than these forms, the frame with *used to* and the elaboration with *would* alternating with past tense account for the tense-aspect-modal sequences in both of the two texts above.

In contrast to the relatively longer texts in the habitual past that Suh (1992b) described, such as the two above, many shorter texts exist in which patterns with *used to* are also discernible. In the following examples in P, *used to* occurs in the first clause and is followed by a second and possibly third clause in the present, present progressive, present perfect, or present perfect (progressive) tense. These noninitial clauses typically follow *but* and contrast with and negate the past habitual event or state expressed in the first clause with *used to:*

> P. a. Alice used to be a kindergarten teacher, but she doesn't work anymore. She's now a mother and homemaker.
>   b. Jack used to live in Chicago, but since 1992, he's been working in Los Angeles.

We feel that such shorter frames should also be identified, described, and presented and practiced pedagogically.

Suh (1992a) also found many examples of future narratives that lend further support to her frame-elaboration hypothesis. She found that oral narratives that express possible future scenarios tend to be framed by *be going to,* which makes a bridge from the present moment of speaking to the future. These narratives are then elaborated with *will* (*'ll*), which express more remote future contingencies. Consider the following examples:

> Q. "Gastric restriction"[17]
>   [A doctor informally explains the surgical procedure he performs on the morbidly obese.]
>   1. They're going to go in and, uh, have their gut
>   2. slit open, their stomach exposed, and have it stapled off
>   3. so that there'll be two pou—/ an upper pouch in the
>   4. stomach which will hold about two ounces of food,
>   5. it's got a little hole right in—in the middle of that
>   6. pouch where—where food when it's finally ground up
>   7. will slowly go through.

> R. White House transcripts (1974), p. 68 [John Dean is speaking.]
>   1. I think what is going to happen on the civil
>   2. case is that the judge is going to dismiss the complaint
>   3. that is down there right now. They will then file a new
>   4. complaint which will come back to Ritchie again. That will
>   5. probably happen the 20th, 21st, 22nd. Then 20 days will
>   6. run before any answers have to be filed and the depositions
>   7. will be commenced. So we are eating up an awful lot of time.

In passage Q the initial *be going to* holds for the first two lines, after which the speaker switches to *will* (*'ll*) except for the background aside given in the simple present in lines 5 and 6. In passage R, the frame (i.e., *be going to*) occurs twice in the first two lines, which happens occasionally especially in a case like this where a *wh*-cleft occurs (see Chapter 30) and the same tense tends to appear on both sides of *be*. The elaborations then occur with *will* until the final clause in line 7, which switches to the present progressive to give the speaker's personal evaluation of the ongoing situation rather than projecting any additional future events.

In contrast to these longer future scenarios described by Suh (1992a), we would also like to point out shorter texts where *be going to* expresses a future planned action; the subsequent clause often begins with *so* and is elaborated with *can* or *will* to express the justification, purpose, or expected outcome of the planned action:

> S. a. Patrick O'Brien is going to marry his American girlfriend so he can get a green card.
>
> b. I'm going to study in Spain for a year next year so I'll be fluent in Spanish.

Once again, we feel that such shorter frames, when they can be described and documented, are also very useful for pedagogical purposes. Their brevity makes them accessible even to beginners, who can understand them and create meaningful short texts by referring to frames like these early in their language-learning experience.

Perhaps it would be useful at this stage to summarize the various frames that Suh and the authors have described above for oral narratives:

habitual present narrative	(frame: present perfect elaboration: simple present)
specific past narratives	(frame: present perfect elaboration: simple past)
past habitual narratives	(frame: *used to* elaboration: *would* ('d) sometimes simple past)
short contrasts (past vs. present)	(frame: *used to* conjunction: *but* elaboration: present (progressive and/or perfect aspect acceptable, too))
future scenarios	(frame: *be going to* elaboration: *will* ('ll))
short future plan + expected outcome	(frame: *be going to* conjunction: *so* elaboration: *can* or *will*)

These discourse frames are of course not the only way these types of oral narratives can be accomplished; however, they are sufficiently frequent and salient in English speakers' spontaneous discourse to merit pedagogical attention.

TENSE-ASPECT-MODALITY AND INTERACTION IN ORAL DISCOURSE

The patterns discussed above were for more or less monologic oral narrative. When two or more speakers are engaged in conversation, however, the dynamics are often different such that we can note other ways in which tense-aspect-modality forms are used.

For example, Suh (1992a) noticed that when an interrogative structure with present perfect tense is inserted in the middle of a story-telling sequence, the speaker is often checking the interlocutor's knowledge before proceeding further.[18]

> T. Conversation data used by Suh (1992a:94).
>
> Ken: We went down into Juarez and through El Paso, and oh, we had a ball.
>
> Louise: Really?
>
> Ken: Yeah. Have you ever been t— have you ever hearda Juarez?
>
> Louise: I've hearda both of 'em because my girlfriend's old boyfriend was stationed in El Paso.
>
> Ken: Well we went to Juarez . . .

In this example, Ken uses the present perfect in his second turn to interrupt his past-tense narrative in order to check Louise's knowledge of the places he is talking about. Louise also uses the present perfect in her response in order to display her knowledge. Here the shift from simple past to present perfect is interactionally motivated rather than being driven by the structure of the narrative Ken is relating.

McCarthy and Carter (1995) have noticed that some instances of variation between *be going to* and *will* are interactionally driven in that *be going to* expresses greater personal involvement on the part of the speaker, whereas *will* is a more neutral, detached and formal option. One of their examples is:

> U. "BBC radio weather forecast"
> Temperatures will be below freezing, and it's going to be icy on those country roads, so do take care if you're driving.
> (McCarthy and Carter 1995:24)

Here, McCarthy and Carter feel that their interactional explanation describes the form shifts occurring in such informal weather forecasts given on radio and TV, where *will* is used for neutral prediction whereas *be going to* signals the forecaster's more interpersonal evaluation. We noted in Chapter 3 that argument structure is more fluid in conversation than in written discourse. Similarly, McCarthy and Carter conclude, ". . . real spoken data pushes us away from considerations of the semantics of time and more towards interactive interpretations of verb-form choices" (1995:114).

In a study of related interest, Schwarz (1988) had consultants place 24 oral and written texts along a continuum ranging from "involved, interactive" to "detached, no interaction" and found that the frequency of the progressive aspect was much higher in texts that demonstrate interaction and involvement than in texts that do not. Here are the numbers for four texts representing the two extremes on the continuum:

Text	Frequency of progressive
conversation between good friends	30/1,000 words
personal letters to friends	20/1,000 words
phonetics textbook	1.3/1,000 words
economics textbook	1/1,000 words

There was near perfect correlation between where the texts fell on the continuum and the frequency of the progressive aspect, which means that native English speakers make systematic use of the progressive to signal involvement and interaction or to signal detachment, formality, and lack of interaction by not using the progressive.

Batstone (1995) argues that tense and aspect are used covertly in written discourse to signal pragmatic notions such as negative attitude (e.g., past tense = "this idea is passé") or positive attitude (e.g., present tense = "this idea is relevant"). Similarly, he proposes that a simple tense by virtue of signaling a neutral, unchanging situation can bring about different results from the same tense with progressive aspect, which signals potential for change:

> a. Sheila says she doesn't want to come.
> b. Sheila is saying she doesn't want to come.

In Batstone's data, the (b) version occurred in the conversation, and the two interlocutors quickly shifted to a discussion of how to get Sheila to change her mind. Had the (a) version occurred, Batstone feels the speaker would have signaled that Sheila's position was not open to change and a different conversation would have ensued.

We agree with Suh (1992a), McCarthy and Carter (1995), Schwarz (1988), and Batstone (1995) concerning the importance of examining oral language in interaction for special uses of tense-aspect-modality forms. However, by referring to our earlier discussion of the Bull framework, we point out that it is not accidental that present-axis forms (present perfect and *be going to* future) are frequently used to accomplish interactive functions. Interaction relates to the "here and now," in contrast to the simple past, which relates past events, or the form *will,* which makes neutral future predictions.

Two Other Types of Tense Patterning in Written Discourse

Sentence-level accounts of tense and aspect tell us that the past perfect generally marks an event occurring prior to some other time or event in the past (e.g., *Before John came, I had finished my dinner.*)[19] However, in informal written discourse we have found that the past perfect can be used to mark a climax—that is, to state a purpose for relating a prior series of actions and events narrated in the simple past. This function is probably an instance of the "result/resolution" in Labov's narrative structure. Consider the two following examples:

> V. "The convocation"[20]
> The students sat in the bleachers of Pauley Pavilion watching the faculty enter in their caps and gowns. Dignitaries continued to arrive while the band played a festive melody for the onlookers. To the cheers of the crowd, President Clinton came in and took his assigned seat on the podium . . . UCLA's 75th anniversary *had begun.*

> W. "The case of Koko"[21]
> In the 1980s, researchers at Stanford University were trying to teach American Sign Language to Koko, a gorilla. Koko was well cared for and was surrounded by interesting objects. Her caretakers continually exposed her to signs for the foods and toys in her environment. Koko particularly loved eating bananas and playing with kittens. One day she was hungry but couldn't find any bananas. She went to the researcher and made a good approximation of the sign for "banana." Koko was rewarded with a banana and the research team knew that Koko *had made* the connection between a sign and the object it represented.

This pattern is thus similar to the six that Suh (1992a) and the authors identified above; however, here the past perfect is used to terminate a narrative episode given in the simple past rather than to initiate the narrative episode because it is functioning to mark the outcome or resolution. It is certainly not being used to mark a prior action or event.

Another systematic use of tense shift in written discourse has been noted by Brinton (1994), who prepared grammar exercises to accompany an introductory college-level psychology text by Huffman, Vernoy, and Vernoy (1994). Brinton noticed that the authors of this psychology text frequently presented a real-life illustration of a phenomenon in a paragraph written in the past tense:

> X. In 1848, Phineas Gage suffered a bizarre accident when an explosion happened at his work place. As a result of the explosion, an iron rod entered his skull and pierced his frontal lobe. Phineas recovered physically from this accident, but his personality changed forever.   (Brinton 1994:9)

The story or anecdote then becomes the basis for the authors' discussion in the following paragraph of the significance of the anecdote and other similar events. This more general discussion invariably occurs in the present tense:

> Y. From the case study of Phineas Gage, it appears that the frontal lobe controls much of our individual personality and defines our ability to make decisions. We now know that the frontal lobe helps us to plan and change actions.   (Brinton 1994:9)

Although the order above is preferred for presenting anecdotes and generalizations in this particular textbook, sometimes the reverse order occurs—the generalization paragraph comes before the anecdote paragraph:

> Z. The difference between an obsessive-compulsive disorder (OCD) and milder forms of compulsion is that OCD behaviors are much more extreme, appear irrational to almost everyone, and interfere considerably with everyday life. Individuals with OCD sometimes wash their hands hundreds of times a day or spend hours performing senseless rituals of organizing and cleaning. Billionaire Howard Hughes provides an example of obsessive-compulsive behavior.
>
> (Huffman, Vernoy, and Vernoy 1994:522)

After this general description of OCD, the following paragraph provides the specific case description (i.e., Howard Hughes):

> Z. Due to his unreasonable fear of germs, he made people who worked with him wear white gloves, sometimes several pairs, when handling documents he would later touch. When newspapers were brought to him, they had to be in stacks of three so he could slide the middle one out by grasping it with Kleenex. To escape contamination by dust, he ordered that masking tape be put around the doors and windows of his cars and houses.   (Huffman, Vernoy, and Vernoy, 1994:522)

Whichever order occurs, the real-life illustration is in the simple past tense, which includes historically past-tense modal forms (e.g., *would* and *could*), and the authors' generalizations and discussion are in the simple present tense. This discourse-level use of these tenses is in fact similar to their sentence-level uses since simple past tense is often used to relate a past event and the simple present is used to express generalizations. If this pattern occurs widely enough in other social science textbooks, it is one that can and should be taught explicitly to ESL/EFL readers and writers who are using such a textbook in their content classes.

CONCLUSION

All the findings reported above suggest that the uses of the tense-aspect-modality forms described in this chapter can be fully grasped only when we consider their discourse-pragmatic and interactional features as well as their formal and semantic features. The challenge of the English TAM system, as represented in this chapter, is on *use*. It provides a way of helping learners see where one form is preferred over another, especially in cases where two or more forms can often be used at the sentence level to "mean" essentially the same thing:

pres perfect/simple past
be going to/will
used to/would

The findings reported above have pedagogical implications because the patterns of use reported here have the potential to serve as templates or discourse "scripts" regarding certain discourse functions of these forms. Such information can readily be applied in materials development. Teachers (and learners) will encounter authentic materials that contain segments conforming to a large extent to the patterns we have described. Suh found them occurring frequently in comic strips and novels as well as transcribed conversational data. There are of course other patterns as well; Lori Gray (personal communication) has reminded us that teachers of English for specific purposes might be interested in knowing how tenses are used in different disciplines. In a science report, for example, the introduction is usually in the present tense, whereas the methods section is normally written in the past tense. For an art class, a student would use the present tense to describe a painting. Other tense patterns will occur in other disciplines.

Teachers need to help learners understand how the English tense-aspect-modality system works in relation to different discourse types and to realize that it operates differently in different languages; that is, the discourse conventions of learners' native language tense-aspect-modality system will most likely not transfer positively to English. In fact, in examining tense choice in essays and cloze passages completed by native and nonnative speakers of English,[22] Hinkel (1997) found that the past-tense selections of these two groups differed significantly due to different styles of rhetorical development and temporal organization as well as culturally different ways of framing events. She concludes that the way past time frames are conventionalized in English is not always obvious to nonnative speakers because boundaries of objective time and tense are conventionalized differently within discourse frames in different cultures.

Finally, further research is needed to help complete and refine the very preliminary sketch we have given here of the uses of tense-aspect-modality in English discourse. The studies we have presented constitute neither a complete nor a unified account; however, they do constitute a useful beginning that we hope others will be able to extend and refine.

TEACHING SUGGESTIONS

Note: All focus on use.

1. Celce-Murcia and Hilles (1988:80) suggest that students bring in postcards of scenic places in their country (or pictures of any places they would like to visit) to elicit discussion of travel plans. The teacher should have some extra postcards and pictures available. Each student presents a card or picture (or several) and gives a short narrative about travel plans or suggestions using *be going to* to frame and *will/'ll for elaboration;* the student should also give a reason and can use *because* to signal the reason. The teacher should model a sample narrative for the class, using appropriate postcards or pictures:

> I'm going to visit the Tuscany region of Italy on my vacation. I'll go to Florence, Pisa, and Arezzo because these are interesting old towns with beautiful art and historical architecture.

2. Making explicit use of the Bull framework, Kathi Bailey (personal communication) devised a lesson for simultaneous review of the past perfect and the future perfect for high-intermediate students. In this lesson, Bailey used many examples to show the semantic relationships and adverbial markers that the two tenses share in the past axis and future axis respectively. For example:

> Monday (future axis): John will arrive at 9 P.M. tomorrow. (By that time/Before then) I will have finished reading the book you lent me.

> [Tuesday: John arrives at 9 P.M.]

> Wednesday (past axis): John arrived at 9 P.M. yesterday. (By that time/Before then) I had finished reading the book you lent me.

3. Have each student make a list of 10 things they did when they were 10 years old. Next, ask them if they still do each of these things now. For every item on the list that states something they no longer do, students should generate short texts with *used to* marking the past habitual action or state and with the simple present tense and/or the present perfect expressing the present contrast. For example,

> I used to rollerskate when I was 10 years old, but I no longer do.

> I used to speak Spanish when I was 10 years old, but now I can't. I've forgotten my Spanish.

4. Ask students to write a brief story about an experience they had in the past. They should be told to stay in the past axis when they write. For example:

> In 1968, I spent the summer with my uncle, who lived on a farm. I learned to milk cows, bring in the hay, and feed the chickens. It was a very good experience.

After getting feedback and correction from the instructor or from peers, the students should then rewrite their story in either the present or the future axis, changing time markers as appropriate.

5. Students can be given several texts (at least three) that exhibit the same pattern, for example, the *used to . . . would ('d)* framework-elaboration pattern often used in past habitual narrative. They should work in pairs or small groups in order to figure out the function of *used to* and *would/'d* in the narratives. The reports of the various groups, with appropriate input from the teacher, should result in an informal version of Suh's (1992b) framework-elaboration hypothesis. Here are example texts you might use:

   a. My older brother used to do most of the fighting for us, and he'd come home with black eyes all the time.   (Terkel 1974:32)
   b. We used to joke about him in the office. We'd call him Mr. Straight because he was Mr. Straight—a man who'd never invite me to have a drink after work. He would never invite me to lunch alone. Would never, never make an overture to me.   (Terkel 1974:107)
   c. We used to have these things when I was a kid up in Northern California. The flowers—after the flower would wilt—this little pea-like structure would come, and it would form kind of a coil, and the seed would grow inside it. . . .
                              (transcribed conversation cited in Suh 1922b:8)

EXERCISES

Test your understanding of what has been presented.

 1. Provide original example sentences that illustrate the following concepts. Underline the relevant word(s) in your examples. You may need to write a short series of sentences for some of the terms.
   a. historical present
   b. backgrounding tense
   c. past time axis
   d. future time plus progressive aspect
   e. interactive use of the present perfect
   f. frame-elaboration pattern for
      (i)—specific past events
      (ii)—past habitual narrative
      (iii)—future scenario

2. Explain the difference in meaning between the italicized parts of the following two sentences:
   a. *I see him* every day at school.
   b. The other day, I'm walking home from school and *I see him* coming up the road.

3. Explain the problem with the following sequence of sentences:

   > When I was little, I would take my brother to school each day. I used to hate it.
   > I've taken him for three years and I walk really slowly.

4. Analyze the following passage from a short story in terms of both Bull's framework and Suh's frame-elaboration hypothesis. Divide the passage into episodes. Look for patterns within each small episode of the narrative:

   > In those days we went into the wild to hunt. I had come from the city to stay with my grandparents in Zitilchen for my holidays, and I'd already made some friends. From the low hill that rises south of town, Chidra, the half-breed Mayan, would first go to call for Crispin. When he reached the house, he gave a long whistle and out Crispin came: short, nervous, cunning. Then they came to fetch me. . . .
   > When they got to our farm Chidra whistled again, and my grandfather would come to the door to let them in. Chidra lived in the wild, and had eaten no food. Not so Crispin. He lived a few streets away, and I knew he had had a good breakfast. Both, however, accepted the hot chocolate and rolls my grandmother offered them. While we ate, my grandfather, tall but stooping, joked gravely with us, as was his manner. With Crispin particularly: the old man was very fond of Crispin. He used to call him "Don Crispin," and every now and then he'd suggest jobs for him inspired by his diminutive stature and resilient character. (Zavala 1989:148)

5. Explain the reason for the tense changes in the following excerpt from a short story:

   > There's a man in the habit of hitting me on the head with an umbrella. It is five years to the day since he began hitting me on the head with his umbrella. At first I couldn't stand it; now I've grown accustomed to it.
   > I don't know his name. I know he's an ordinary man, with a plain suit, graying at the temples, and a nondescript face. I met him one sultry morning five years ago. I was sitting peacefully on a bench in Palermo park, reading the newspaper in the shade of a tree. All of a sudden I felt something touch my head. It was this same man who now, as I write, automatically and impassively keeps striking me blows with his umbrella.
   > That first time I turned around full of indignation (I become terribly annoyed when I'm bothered while reading the paper); he went right on, calmly hitting me.
   > (Sorrentino 1989:233).

6. What difference in effect is there in the following excerpt from a short story when the simple past tense is changed to the historical present?

   > I was a little girl, nine years old, in 1961. You'd left my father and me only two years before. Four months after leaving, you sent me—always me, never him—your first postcard, of a turnpike in the Midwest, postmarked Enid, Oklahoma. You called me "My little angel" and said that the sunflowers by the side of the road were tall and very pretty. (Kaplan 1989:85)

   > I am a little girl, nine years old, in 1961. You've left my father and me only two years before. Four months after leaving, you send me—always me, never him—your first

postcard, of a turnpike in the Midwest, postmarked Enid, Oklahoma. You call me "My little angel" and say that the sunflowers by the side of the road are tall and very pretty.

7. What tense is used as a marker to show the shift in topic in the following extract of oral narrative?

When I was a little kid I wanted to be a baseball pitcher. I went through Little League, Pony League, and went to college for a year and a half, when I got drafted. Baseball would have been nice. Good yearly sum (laughs). The gas company's really been good with the pay. Out of every two weeks I'll make about $250 clear after taxes—which isn't bad. (Gas-meter reader in Terkel 1979:369)

Test your ability to apply what you know

8. Students of yours have written the following problematic tense sequences in their essays. In each case, explain the nature of the problem and state what activities you would provide to correct it.
   a. ?Now that John had won the nomination, he is going to campaign for the election.
   b. ?*Fatal Attraction* was a film that had affected the way that I thought about marriage.
   c. ?Some people could handle societal change, but could not handle economic change, especially when the stock market was introduced. People will lose their minds.
   d. ?After I learned this, I suddenly realize that my working thesis was too large in scope.
   e. ?I have come from China in 1991 and I am here for six years. I have some problems. My biggest problem was English. I used to hate speaking, and I used to just sit quietly. I used to go to English class every day, but I didn't learn much. The teacher used to ask me questions, but I used to hate it. Now, I'm much better at speaking and I will talk in class today.

9. A student is unsure about the tense changes she has used in the following section of an essay she is writing. She asks you to correct her tenses. How will you respond?

After 1978, a great number of Asian women came to the United States and looked for jobs to support their families. The garment industry has become a place where these Asian are oppressed because garment workers do not need to speak English and do not even have to be U.S. citizens.

10. Explain the difference in meaning between the following:
   a. I'm going to study in Spain for a year next year, so I'll be fluent in Spanish.
   b. I'm going to study in Spain for a year next year, so I'm going to be fluent in Spanish.

BIBLIOGRAPHY

References

Baquedano-López, P. (1994). "A Preliminary Study of the Shift in Tense and Aspect as a Cohesive Device in Spoken Narrative." Unpublished 250 paper, UCLA Department of TESL & Applied Linguistics, spring, 1994.

Batstone, R. (1995). "Grammar in Discourse: Attitude and Deniability." In *Principle and Practice in Applied Linguistics. Studies in Honour of G. G. Widdowson.* G. Cook and B. Seidlhofer (eds.). Oxford: Oxford University Press, 197–213.

Brinton, D. (1994). *Handbook for Non-native Speakers to Accompany Psychology in Action* (3rd ed.). New York: John Wiley & Sons.

Bull, W. E. (1960). *Time, Tense, and the Verb: A Study in Theoretical and Applied Linguistics, with Particular Application to Spanish.* Berkeley and Los Angeles: University of California Press.

Celce-Murcia, M., and S. Hilles (1988). *Techniques and Resources in Teaching Grammar.* Oxford: Oxford University Press.

Chafe, W. (1972). "Discourse Structure and Human Knowledge." In J. B. Carroll and R. O. Freedle (eds.), *Language Comprehension and the Acquisition of Knowledge.* Washington, D. C.: V. H. Winston & Sons, 41–69.

Givón, T. (1984). *Syntax.* Amsterdam: John Benjamins.

Hinkel, E. (1997). The Past Tense and Temporal Verb Meanings in a Contextual Frame. *TESOL Quarterly* 31:2, 289–313.

Halliday, M. A. K., and R. Hasan, (1989). *Language, Context, and Text: A Social Semiotic Perspective.* Oxford: Oxford University Press.

Houts Smith, L. (1993). "An Investigation of the Bull Framework: One Teacher's Personal Inquiry into the English Tense System." Independent Professional Project, School for International Training, Brattleboro, Vermont.

Huffman, K., M. Vernoy, and J. Vernoy (1994). *Psychology in Action* (3d ed.). New York: John Wiley & Sons.

Kaplan, D. M. (1989). "Love, Your Only Mother." In R. Shapard, and J. Thomas (eds.), *Sudden Fiction International: 60 Short-Short Stories.* New York, London: W. W. Norton, 85–88.

Keenan, E. O., and T. L.Bennett, (eds.) (1997). "Discourse across Time and Space." Occasional Papers in Linguistics. SCOPIL No. 5, University of Southern California.

Labov, W. (1972). "The Transformation of Experience in Narrative Syntax." *In Language in the Inner City: Studies in the Black English Vernacular*, 354–405. Philadelphia: University of Pennsylvania Press.

Larsen-Freeman, D., and M. Long, (1991). *An Introduction to Second Language Acquisition Research.* London: Longman.

McCarthy, M., and R. Carter, (1995). "Spoken Grammar: What Is It and How Can We Teach It? *ELT Journal* 49:3, 207–218.

Schiffrin, D. (1981). "Tense Variation in Narrative." *Language* 57:1, 45–62.

Schwarz, S. (1988). "The Progressive Aspect in American English Usage." Unpublished M.A. thesis in Teaching English as a Second Language, UCLA.

Sorrentino, F. (1989). "There's a man in the habit of hitting me on the head with an umbrella" (translated by N. T. di Giovanni and P. D. Cran). In R. Shapard and J. Thomas (eds.), *Sudden Fiction International: 60 Short-Short Stories.* New York, London: W. E. Norton, 233–236.

Suh, K. H. (1992a). *"A Discourse Analysis of the English Tense-Aspect-Modality System."* Unpublished Ph.D. dissertation in Applied Linguistics, University of California, Los Angeles.

Suh, K. H. (1992b). Past Habituality in English Discourse: "*Used to* and *Would*." *Language Research* 28:4, 857–882.

Terkel, S. (1974). *Working.* New York: Ballantine Books.

Tregidgo, P. S. (1979). "Tense Subordination." *English Language Teaching* 33:3, 191–196.

White House Transcripts (1974). New York: Bantam Books.

Wolfson, N. (1982). *The Conversational Historical Present in American English Narratives.* Dordrecht, Netherlands: Foris Publications.

Zavala, H. L. (1989). "Iguana Hunting" (translated by the author with A. C. Jefford). In R. Shapard, and J. Thomas (eds.), *Sudden Fiction International: 60 Short-Short Stories.* New York, London: W. E. Norton 148–153.

Suggestions for further reading

For an alternative interpretation of the Bull framework, see the following:

Houts Smith, L. (1993). "An Investigation of the Bull Framework: One Teacher's Personal Inquiry into the English Tense System." Independent Professional Project, School for International Training, Brattleboro, Vermont.

Tregidgo, P. S. (1974). "English Tense Usage: A Bull's Eye View." *English Language Teaching* 28:2, 97–107.

For a comprehensive introduction to the historical present tense, see Wolfson (1982) in the references above.

For pedagogical suggestions on teaching tense-aspect-modality (and other features of oral grammar) to language learners, see McCarthy and Carter (1995) in the references above.

For creative pedagogical suggestions for applying the Bull framework to exercises and activities for ESL learners, see:

Frodesen, J. and J. Eyring (1997). *Grammar Dimensions: Form, Meaning, and Use.* Book 4 (2d ed.). Boston: Heinle & Heinle, 1–33.

Thewlis, S. (1997). *Grammar Dimensions: Form, Meaning, and Use.* Book 3 (2d ed.). Boston: Heinle & Heinle, 6–12 and 23–26.

ENDNOTES

1. One can substitute I *will* or *I'll* for *I'm going to* in this narrative. However, such a substitution expresses a future action contingent upon the present circumstances and is less clearly tied to the present than *I'm going to.*

2. This follows a general principle of historical linguistics which holds that historically older forms and word orders are preserved longer in subordinate clauses than in independent clauses. Old English had only two tense forms (past and present) and used the present tense to express future time; this principle thus seems to apply here. For further discussion of tense subordination, see Tregidgo (1979).

3. Some readers have questioned the validity of this combination; however, we have seen and heard many examples of it, such as "I'm gonna be visiting my cousin next week."

4. Recall that the perfect aspect signals a "before time" not just with the basic tenses but also with modals, infinitives, and other nonfinite forms.

5. This is only a short excerpt from a longer narrative. It is from data collected by Keenan and Bennett (1977) for a research project.

6. According to Halliday and Hasan (1989), only the orientation and complicating action are obligatory because many authentic oral narratives have no clear result or resolution.

7. From the database used to produce the research reported in Keenan and Bennett (1977).

8. This is from Terkel (1974), *Working:* 598–599.

9. The first *-ing* form in this line *(knowing)* is a participle, not a progressive (See Chapter 25). The second *(doing)* is a progressive form.

10. This is from data the authors have collected.

11. This is from Terkel (1974), *Working:* 365–366.

12. This is from Terkel (1974). *Working:* 80.

13. *I've got* looks like the present perfect but it is not; it is merely the formulaic *I have got . . .* in the present tense.

14. Note that according to the Bull framework, this should be *have lost* not *lost;* however, in informal usage, Americans often simplify and use the simple past instead of the present perfect.

15. This is from Terkel (1974), *Working:* 32.

16. This is from Terkel (1974), *Working:* 267.

17. This passage is from the UCLA oral corpus, an in-house database.

18. Larsen-Freeman and Long (1991) call these "confirmation checks." They are common in discourse between native and nonnative speakers, where they are cited as an example of interactional modification employed by native speakers.

19. There are, of course, cases where the past perfect marks some later noncompleted event (Gini Stevens, personal communication); e.g., *The instructor collected the papers before I had finished the exam.* In such cases we say that the past perfect is signaling a counterfactual clause in that "before I had finished = I did not finish."

20. Excerpted and adapted from the UCLA *Daily Bruin,* May 25, 1994.

21. Author data.

22. The nonnative speakers in Hinkel's study had only first languages that do not mark verbs for tense, such as Chinese, Thai, Yoruba.

10

NEGATION

INTRODUCTION

Negation in English is a very broad topic, it affects words, phrases, and sentences. Many of our comments here are restricted to the simple sentence level; that is, to the means of constructing negative rather than affirmative (also known as positive) simple English sentences:

Affirmative		*Negative*
Cynthia likes to fish.	→	Cynthia *does not/doesn't* like to fish.
Danielle is an editor.	→	Danielle *is not/isn't* an editor.
Robby can cook well.	→	Robby *cannot/can't* cook well.

although we discuss lexical and phrasal negation as well. We also, of course, deal with the meaning and use of negation in English. In this chapter we mention only in passing negative questions, negative commands, and negative compound/complex sentences. Those negative structures are examined in detail in other parts of this book.

PROBLEMS FOR ESL/EFL STUDENTS

Many of your ESL/EFL students will find syntactic negation problematic, especially if they are at the beginning level. One reason is that different languages tend to place their negative particle in different positions in the sentence:

Spanish (preverbal):   Juan   *no*   habla   inglés. "John doesn't speak English."
(John) NOT (speaks) (English)

German (postverbal):   Johann geht *nicht* zur Schule. "John doesn't go to school."
(John) (goes) NOT (to) (school)

English (postauxiliary): John $\left\{ \begin{matrix} \text{will} \\ \text{does} \end{matrix} \right\}$ *not* talk to Judy.

Also, many languages allow multiple negation in one sentence, which was historically acceptable in English but which today, depending on the scope of the negation, usually produces nonstandard sentences such as "I did*n't* say *no*thing to *no*body!"

An additional problem involves the form of the negative particle. Some languages do not have distinct forms for expressing their equivalents of English *not* and *no*. Some have more than two negative particles.[1] Finally, English usually contracts *not* in speech and in informal writing, which few other languages do with their negative particle. This makes it harder for learners to understand and acquire *not* than if it were consistently produced as a separate, uncontracted word.

THE NEGATION SYSTEM: ITS FORMS

THE LEXICAL LEVEL

At the word, or lexical, level, one can simply use a negative affix in English to convey negativity. The way to make many adjectives and adverbs negative is to add a negative derivational prefix to a word:

happy	→	*un*happy	happily	→	*un*happily
appropriate	→	*in*appropriate	appropriately	→	*in*appropriately
possible	→	*im*possible	possibly	→	*im*possibly
logical	→	*il*logical	logically	→	*il*logically
relevant	→	*ir*relevant	relevantly	→	*ir*relevantly
ordered	→	*dis*ordered	orderly	→	*dis*orderly
typical	→	*a*typical	typically	→	*a*typically

The variety derives in part from the fact that different affixes were borrowed from different languages. For example, while *un-* is a native English prefix, *in-* with its allomorphs (different forms of the same morpheme), *im-/il-/ir-*, come from Latin, *dis-* comes from Greek, and *a-* from Greek through Latin.

Other parts of speech can also take some of these prefixes to make them negative; for example, *dis-* combines with verbs to make *dislike* and *distrust*.

The negative prefix *non-* is used to form certain negative nouns and adjectives:

Nouns	*Adjectives (non- + verb)*
non- + sense = *non*sense	*non-* + drip = *non*-drip (as in *non*-drip paint)
non- + intervention = *non*intervention	*non-* + stick = *non*-stick (as in *non*-stick surface)[2]

Some of these prefixes can have more than one meaning. *Un-*, for instance, does not always indicate negativity. Consider verbs such as *unfasten* and *unwrap*, in which the *un-* means a reversal of the process denoted by the stem. The use of the *un-* to signal this other meaning, however, is not as frequent as the use of the *un-* prefix to mean "not" with all the gradable adjectives (those denoting a property that can be possessed in varying degrees) as in *unreasonable, unwise,* and *unkind.* Nevertheless, *un-* is still subject to various restrictions; in particular, it is not used where some etymologically unrelated opposite is available (we say *bad,* not * *ungood*), where some other less-productive prefix is established (*disloyal* rather than * *unloyal*), or with "strong" adjectives—that is, adjectives that express the same notion to a stronger degree (*unhappy,* but not * *unecstatic*).

Determining which prefix to use with which stem is not always predictable. Further, the rules about which negative prefix to use when more than one is possible are not absolute, but we can make the following generalization: *in-, dis-,* and (less so) *un-* tend to be pejoratively evaluative of the stems to which they attach, while *non-* and *a-* prefixes are more descriptive or objective (Horn 1989). Some minimal pairs that illustrate this contrast are:

Pejorative/Evaluative	*Descriptive/Objective*
irrational	nonrational
disbeliever	nonbeliever
disfunctional	nonfunctional
unprofessional	nonprofessional
unprofitable	nonprofit
untheoretical	atheoretical
immoral	amoral

The choice of *in-, im-, il-* or *ir-* is phonologically conditioned by the consonant which follows it. *In-* is most common, but *im-* is used if the following consonant is a bilabial (*b, p, m*), *il* - with a stem beginning with *l,* and *ir-* when the adjective begins with *r.*[3]

There is also a negative suffix, *-less,* which can be used to negate nouns by expressing their absence or nonexistence, thus forming adjectives such as *hopeless, penniless, speechless, lifeless,* and *shameless.* Howell (personal communication) has pointed out that there is a similar suffix *-free* with a more positive connotation (cf. *careless* vs. *carefree*): s*moke-free workplace, fat-free foods.*

Certain indefinite pronouns and an adverb beginning with *no-* can also be used to give a negative meaning:

no + thing = nothing	*Nothing* has been done.
no + body = nobody	*Nobody* is home.
no + one = no one (two words)[4]	*No one* seems concerned.
no + where = nowhere	They were *nowhere* to be seen.

However, not all words can be made negative with the use of affixes. Lexical gaps exist; some words have no single-word negative counterparts. For instance, we say *not unique,* not **ununique.* It works the opposite way as well. Some words exist in negative forms that have no affirmative counterparts, as the following humorous excerpt from Jack Winter's essay in the *New Yorker,* (July 25, 1984, volume 75, page 82) entitled "How I Met My Wife" makes clear:

> It had been a rough day, so when I walked into the party I was very chalant, despite my efforts to appear gruntled and consolate.
> I was furling my wieldy umbrella for the coat check when I saw her standing alone in a corner. She was a descript person, a woman in a state of total array. Her hair was kempt, her clothing shevelled, and she moved in a gainly way.

Other formally negative items are the negative adverb of frequency *never* (*not + ever*), the negative coordinating conjunction *nor (and + not),* and the negative correlative conjunctions *neither . . . nor* (*not + either*). Functional items that are not formally marked for negation but that connote negativity are the quantifiers *little* and *few,* as opposed to the positive quantifiers *a little* and *a few,* the negative adverbial subordinator of conditionals *unless,* the negative adverb of time *yet,* the negative intensifier *too,* and adverbs of frequency *seldom, rarely, scarcely,* and *hardly.* There are also lexical items that Jespersen (1917) calls "inherent negatives." These are content words that have a negative meaning but that appear positive in form—for example, *fail, forget, lack, exclude,* and *absent.* All these lexical and functional items are dealt with later in this chapter or in other places in this book.

THE PHRASE LEVEL

At the phrase level, *no* can function as a negative determiner in a noun phrase:

> I am surprised that *no* alternative was proposed.
> *No* plans have been made.

Many idioms take this form; for example, *no way, no wonder, no sweat.* Another common idiomatic phrase with *no* is *no + gerund,* which may be used to indicate that something is prohibited—*no smoking, no parking, no running*—or unexpected, such as, *no kidding, no fooling.*

Before infinitive verbs in infinitive phrases (i.e., a sequence of *to + verb* that follows an inflected verb), *not* is used to make the phrase negative:

> Marge has decided *not* to pay her income tax this year.

Although prescriptively prohibited, we have noticed that many native speakers of English will split the infinitive with the negative particle in an infinitive phrase, presumably to emphasize the negative action in the phrase:

> Marge has decided to *not* pay her income tax this year.

THE SENTENCE LEVEL

Not is the main sentence-level negator:

	Not	*Not, Contracted* (more common)
Statements	John is not at home.	John isn't at home.
Questions:	Are you not going?	Aren't you going?
Commands:	Do not move!	Don't move!
Exclamations	Is that not grand!	Isn't that grand!

However, *no* can also make a sentence negative, especially when it negates the subject:

> No one was home to sign for the package.

No and *not* are also negative substitutes. *No* can be a negative substitute for an entire sentence:

> A: Are you going to town after class?
> B: No. I have got to meet Larry in the library.

and *not* can substitute for a negative subordinate clause (parallel to *so* substituting for an affirmative subordinate clause):

> Are you coming? { If not, please let me know.
> { If so, please bring something to drink.

> Are you coming? { I think not.
> { I think so.

SUMMARY

The following table summarizes the basic formal markers of negation in English.

A SUMMARY OF BASIC NEGATIVE FORMS IN ENGLISH		
Affix-Negation	**No**-Negation	**Not**-Negation
a-	*no*	*not, -n't*
dis-	*nothing*	*never (not + ever)*
in-/im-/il-/ir-	*nobody*	*neither (not + either)*
non-	*no* one	*nor (and + not)*
un-	*nowhere*	
-less		
-free		

A SYNTACTIC ANALYSIS OF SENTENCE-LEVEL NEGATION

Here we deal with negation in statements, returning to negation in other simple sentence types as well as compound and complex sentences (in examples of reported speech) in later chapters.

With Auxiliary Verbs

Consider the following sentences:

1. (a) I can swim.   (b) I cannot swim.
2. (a) It is going to rain on Monday.   (b) It is not going to rain on Monday.
3. (a) We have done our homework.   (b) We haven't done our homework.
4. (a) Philip is taking a nap.   (b) Philip isn't taking a nap.

It is clear that what distinguishes the form of the (b) sentences from the form of the (a) sentences is the presence of the negative particle *not* or its contracted and suffixed form *-n't*. As we noted above, English has postauxiliary negation, and these sentences illustrate that generalization. Auxiliary verbs such as modals, phrasal modals, the perfect *have*, and the progressive *be* are all followed by the *not* particle. Moreover, if more than one auxiliary verb is present, as in 5 (*have* and *be*), it is the *first* auxiliary verb that is followed by the negative particle.

5. (a) Pam has been working hard.   (b) Pam hasn't been working hard.

Following Quirk et. al (1985), we call the first or only auxiliary verb the "operator," in that this verb performs several operational functions in English that involve relating major syntactic structures.[5]

Since in all of our sentence-level examples thus far the negation applies to the entire sentence, not just the auxiliary verb, we depict *not* as a sentence modifier.

A schematic representation of this would be as follows:

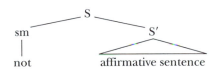

To be more precise, the basic structure for sentences 2(b) and 5(b) are as follows:

2. (b) It is not going to rain on Monday.

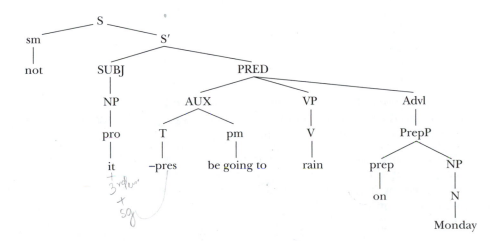

5. (b) Pam hasn't been working hard.

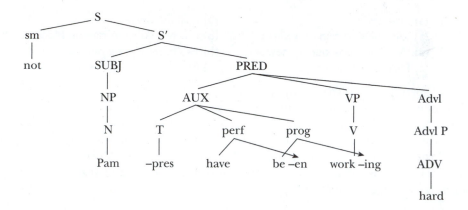

Not Placement

To derive the surface structure from the base we must call upon the *not* placement rule. Its function is to place the *not* particle in its proper position in English—after the operator.

It is not going to rain on Monday.

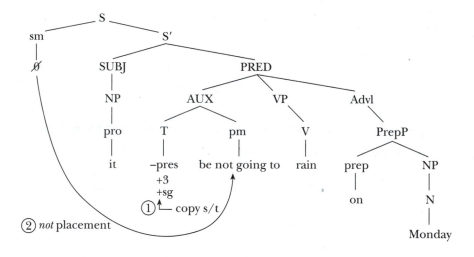

What would also have to happen is for subject features to be copied on the tense before *not* placement and then for morphology (which includes subject-verb agreement) to apply after it. The rules would apply in this order:

output of base: not it -pres be going to rain on Monday
copy s/t: not it -pres [+ 3 + sg] be going to rain on Monday
not placement: it -pres [+ 3 + sg] be not going to rain on Monday
morphology: It is not going to rain on Monday.

Not Contraction

We also need an optional rule[6] that reduces *not* to *-n't* and attaches it to the appropriate verb. This rule will account for the contracted form of *not* found in sentences 3(b), 4(b), and 5(b). Many combinations of *-n't* with an auxiliary verb are regular, but some are irregular:[7]

Regular—disyllabic negatives
did + n't → didn't
would + n't → wouldn't
have + n't → haven't
etc.

Irregular (orthographically and/or phonologically)—monosyllabic negatives
will + n't → won't ("ll" is lost, vowel changes)
can + n't → can't (one "n" lost)
do + n't → don't (vowel sound changes)

With this *not* contraction rule we can now also produce sentences such as 3(b), 4(b), and 5(b). For example, here is the tree for sentence 3(b):

We haven't done our homework.

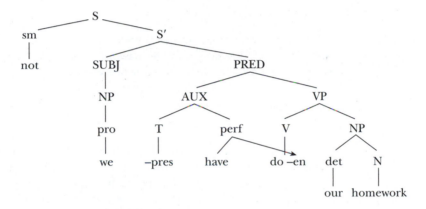

And now this is what it would look like after copy s/t and *not* placement:

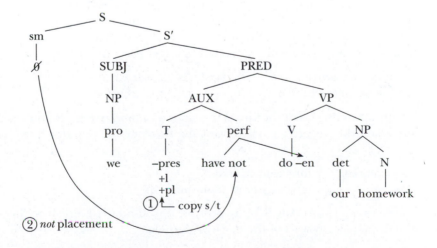

and *not* contraction:

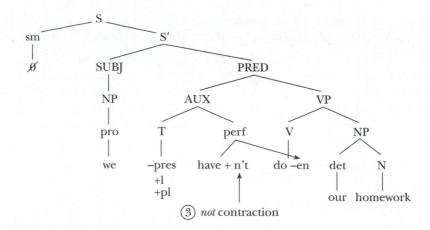

③ *not* contraction

Here is the order in which the rules would apply:

output of base: not we -pres have do -en our homework
copy s/t: not we -pres [+ I + pl] have do -en our homework
not placement: we -pres [+ I + pl] have not do -en our homework
not contraction: we -pres [+ I + pl] have + n't do -en our homework
morphology: We haven't done our homework.

With the *Be* Copula

So far we have accounted for the placement of the negative particle when a sentence contains an auxiliary verb. But, of course, not all sentences have such a verb. Two other types of verbs are possible: the *be* copula and all main verbs other than *be*.

You may have wondered why in our phrase structure rules we made a distinction between the *be* copula and other main verbs. Actually, the *be* copula is distinctive for a number of reasons. One of the main ones is that the *be* copula patterns very much like the auxiliary verbs in that it, too, can be an operator. For instance, to make a sentence with the *be* copula negative, we place the *not* after the *be* just as we did with the first or only auxiliary verb. This is not true with other main verbs as you will see later. In 6 the *not* is placed after the *be* copula operator, and in 7 the *not* is placed after the *be* copula operator (via *not*-placement) and is optionally contracted to it (via *not* contraction).

6. (a) Brad is a teacher.   (b) Brad is not a teacher.
7. (a) The beach is crowded.   (b) The beach isn't crowded.

The only exception to this worth noting is the stigma in modern-day Standard English against contracting the negative particle with the first person singular form of the *be* verb, *am*.

8. (a) I am tired.   (b) I am not tired.
              (c) I ain't tired. (non-standard)

Of course, a contracted form of 8(b) is possible in Standard English if the *be* verb contracts with the subject instead of the negative particle.

           (d) I'm not tired.

With Other Main Verbs

Another aspect of English that has changed over the years is the fact that it is no longer grammatical, as it was in the Elizabethan period, to place the negative particle after a main verb other than *be*.[8]

> *I go not.

Instead, the *do* verb of modern English, already extant in the fifteenth century, had become standard for forming negatives by the seventeenth:

> I do not go.

Thus, in modern English, when there is no other operator in a negative sentence, we insert the auxiliary verb *do* to perform the function of operator, to carry the tense and permit the negative to attach to it in contracted form.

> 9. (a) Muriel plays the piano. (b) Muriel does not/doesn't play the piano.
> 10. (a) Shirley smoked. (b) Shirley did not smoke/didn't smoke.

This type of sentence negation is accomplished through a mapping rule called operator addition. Here's an example of a tree for a negative sentence with *do*:

> Shirley didn't smoke.

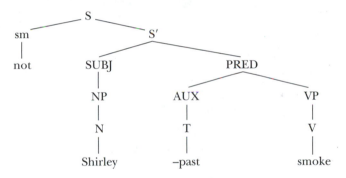

Here's how it looks after copy s/t and operator addition:

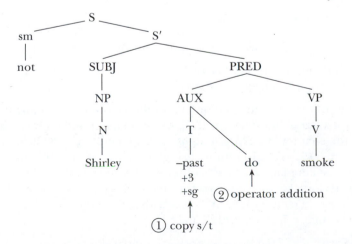

After *not* placement and *not* contraction, the tree would look like this:

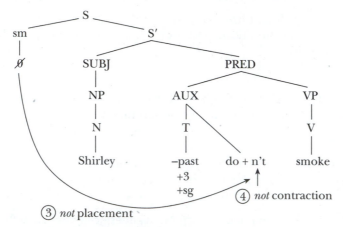

③ *not* placement

④ *not* contraction

Here's how the mapping rules would apply:

output of base: not Shirley -past smoke
copy s/t: not Shirley -past [+ 3 + sg] smoke
operator addition: not Shirley -past [+ 3 + sg] do smoke
not placement: Shirley -past [+ 3 + sg] do not smoke
not contraction: Shirley -past [+ 3 + sg] do + n't smoke
morphology: Shirley didn't smoke

One dialect difference that we should note is that in the stative possessive use of the verb *have*, American English prefers the *do* auxiliary in negatives while British English treats the *have* verb itself as an auxiliary:

Audrey doesn't have a clue. (American English)
Audrey hasn't a clue. (British English)

A more colloquial form of this sentence used in both dialects employs **have got** where the *have* behaves as an operator.

Audrey hasn't got a clue.

THE MEANING OF NEGATION

Logicians would say there is a symmetry between affirmative and negative propositions:

affirmative statement: It is the case that . . .
negative statement: It is *not* the case that . . .

As you will see in this section and the one that follows, however, the meaning and use of negatives are not as straightforward as this analysis makes it seem. Accordingly, we begin this section of the chapter by acknowledging that the negative particle can have different meanings. Bloom (1970), in her pioneering study of the acquisition of negation by children whose first language is English, observed that most children in her study learned the word *no* rather quickly (certainly by the "terrible two's"!), but used it for a variety of meanings/purposes. For instance, in the data that Bloom collected, the children said *"No"* for nonexistence, rejection, and denial:

"No pocket."	[There are no pockets]	(nonexistence)
"No dirty soap."	[I don't want . . .]	(rejection)
"No truck."	[This isn't a truck.]	(denial)

While acknowledging that a developmental psychologist might need to distinguish the meaning of nonexistence from denial, linguist Tottie (1991) sees nonexistence as a subcategory of denial. Saying something doesn't exist is denying the (at least implicit) assertion that it does exist. In other words, "No truck," is a denial of the (possibly implicit) assertion "This is a truck." Denials, then, may be either explicitly expressed or contextually inferred. Compare the following from Tottie (1991:21):

> A: John is married.   X: John's wife is a teacher.
> B: John isn't. (married)   Y: John isn't even married.

B denies what A has just explicitly stated, but Y merely denies the implicit presupposition of X, the belief of X that John is married. Thus, we may sum up Tottie's treatment of the meaning of negation in English in the following way. There are two meanings of negation in English, rejection and denial, with denial being either explicit or implicit.

1. Rejection (including refusals)   A: Would you care for scotch?
                                       B: No, thanks. I don't drink.

2. Denial   a. Explicit   A: That dress must have been very expensive.
                                B: It wasn't (expensive). In fact, I bought it at a sale.
                 b. Implicit   A: Bill seems to have got lost.
                                B: Yeah. He must not have driven this way before.

Tottie also mentions a category she calls "supports," in which listeners signal that the information speakers are giving them is received.

> A: but I left that out because
> B: yes
> A: it wasn't typical
> B: no

This category, however, represents only about 8 percent of Tottie's data.

As his own refinement of the denial category, Horn (1989) notes that by denying something, a person can be denying (1) the truth value of the previous proposition or (2) its form. Horn calls examples of the latter "metalinguistic" (p. 371):

> "I didn't manage to trap two mongeese, I managed to trap two mongooses."

where the morphological form of the prior assertion is challenged, and

> "Grandpa isn't feeling lousy, Johnny, he's just a tad indisposed."

where the register or stylistic level is being corrected.

THE SCOPE OF NEGATION

When we are concerned with the meaning of the negative in English, we must also be concerned with its scope. It is usually said that what is negated in a sentence is everything that comes after the negative particle until the end of the clause.[9] Thus, there is a meaning contrast in the following pair of sentences:

> Joe obviously hasn't understood a word. (It is obvious that he did not.)
> Joe hasn't obviously understood a word. (It is not obvious that he did.)

It follows then that typically the subject of an English sentence will be outside the scope of sentential negation, but it can, of course, be negated with the negative determiner *no*.

> *Not anyone was planning to come.
> No one was planning to come.

We have already pointed out that negation can occur at three levels. Thus, the first sentence in the following set exemplifies lexical negation, the second sentence illustrates phrasal negation, and the third sentential negation.

1. Harry is uncoordinated.
2. Marge has decided not to pay her taxes.
3. John is not at home.

We can demonstrate that only the third sentence has negation that is sentential in scope by adding a tag question to each. When tag questions in their unmarked form are negative, the sentence is affirmative; when they are affirmative, the sentence is negative.

1. Harry is uncoordinated, isn't he?
2. Marge has decided not to pay her taxes, hasn't she?
3. John is not at home, is he?

The same question tag test can show that while *no* is only a determiner, its scope can be sentential.

> No one came to fix the plumbing, did they?

The same is true for the other negative forms associated with *no*:

> Nothing is going right, is it?

and with *not*:

> They never answered, did they?

We have already noted that unlike other languages, Standard English does not permit double negation.

> I didn't buy no books. (non-standard)

This is a somewhat simplified rule, however, because although it isn't possible to have two negatives that are sentential in scope, it is possible to have a lexical with a phrasal negative or a phrasal or lexical negative with a sentential negative. Here are two examples: the first from the autobiographical account *Crossing to Avalon* (Bolen 1994: 105), and the second from the sports pages of a local newspaper (1/16/95). We have added the italics.

> *Unable to not go on*, she was then confronted with the necessity of accomplishing a series of initially impossible tasks.

> [National Football League cornerback] Darrien Gordon said, "The one thing you *don't want to feel is not respected.*"

A SHIFT IN MEANING

Usually, when you negate something, the basic meaning of the proposition is maintained in its negative form. In English, however, this is not true in at least three cases:

1. In the affirmative, *must* can convey obligation, as can its phrasal counterpart *have to*:

> We *must* be on time. (obligation)
> We *have to* be on time. (obligation)

In the negative, however, the meaning of *must* shifts.

> We *mustn't* be at school until 9:00. (It's prohibited that we arrive before 9:00.)
> We *don't have to* be at school until 9:00. (no obligation)

2. Although there can be synonymy between affixal and nonaffixal negation,

> I dislike lima beans. = I don't like lima beans.

often they are not semantic equivalents. Semantic nonequivalence occurs when there is a middle condition:

> He is unhappy. ≠ He is not happy. (He could be not happy, and not unhappy too.)

or when there is an adverbial intensifier:

> This is totally untrue. ≠ This is not totally true.
> His laugh was so unreal. ≠ His laugh wasn't so real.

Semantic nonequivalence can also occur in the interaction of *not*- versus *no*-negation with quantifiers:

> All the guests didn't drink wine. ≠ All the guests drank no wine.

between sentential negation and negation in prepositional phrases,

> My aerobics class isn't continuing for any clear reason. ≠ My aerobics class is continuing for no clear reason.

and before "non-pejorative" nouns (Bailey 1997):

> He's not a doctor. ≠ He's no doctor.

Here *no*-negation assumes that he is a doctor, but not a very satisfactory one.

3. Finally, there is semantic nonequivalence between positive comparatives and negative equatives with negative polarity adjectives:[10]

> Fran is older than Emily. (positive comparative)
> Fran is not as young as Emily. (negative equative)

With the comparative we have no real idea about the age of the two people involved. They could be young or elderly or any age in between. With the negative equative, however, the implication is that both people are young. We will have more to say about negative equatives in the section of this chapter on the use of the negative system.

SOME VERSUS ANY

The last area we need to deal with regarding meaning and the system of negation has to do with words that accompany the negative particle. Many textbooks point out that following a negative particle, *some* in an affirmative sentence changes to *any* in a negative one.

> Laura bought *some* cheese.   Laura didn't buy *any* cheese.

This is true even when *some* is part of an indefinite compound pronoun:

> Stan has *something* to wear to the party.   Stan doesn't have *anything* to wear to the party.

While this is probably a useful generalization to offer beginning-level students, more advanced-level students should know that this is not always the case. *Some* and *any* have actually two main meanings, and one of the meanings is compatible with negation. It is, in fact, possible for *some* to occur in a negative sentence when a meaning of identity is invoked:

> I don't eat *some* foods—lima beans, for example.

In a negative sentence, the *some* is stressed. When *some/any* refer to an indefinite quantity or amount (such as in the sentences above with Laura and Stan), *some* is weakly stressed and occurs with positive sentences. It is not used with ordinary negative statements. It is also possible for stressed *any* to occur in an affirmative sentence:

> *Anyone* can do that.

Here, *any* refers to a person of such unspecified identity that it refers to virtually all persons.

USE OF THE NEGATIVE SYSTEM

SOCIAL FUNCTIONS

It is said that while affirmatives and negatives often have a logical semantic symmetry, they have a functional asymmetry: while affirmatives are standardly used to introduce propositions, the chief use of negatives is directed at a proposition already in the discourse (Horn 1989: 202–203). The claim is that negatives are used more to respond than to initiate. In social interaction, then, a negative assertion can be a contrary, denying speech act (Givón 1993: 193). As such, we might expect its use to vary with regard to the relative social position of interlocutors; and when there is a marked difference between them, we might expect the subordinate-status speaker to use other means of registering disagreement, such as "Perhaps you may wish to consider an alternative."

This expectation was supported by Yaeger-Dror (1985), who has shown that when the negative utterance can be construed as showing disagreement, it is generally realized with reduced intensity and nonprominent pitch on the negative elements. Although one might expect that the negative, being new information, would receive prominent stress, in fact the stress is reduced to mitigate the disagreement, presumably in the interest of maintaining social harmony. Interestingly enough, when negatives are used in disagreeing with oneself or when agreeing with the previous speaker, they are realized with prominent pitch on the negative, often accompanied by enhanced intensity. Here is an example of a prominent negative showing agreement, adapted from Yaeger-Dror (1985:216):

> A: You see the fault I am getting at with the schools, they haven't got an answer to the problem.
> B: No! They don't.
> A: But they think they do.
> B: I agree with you.

This is an apt time to remind readers that speech acts come in many forms. For example, we have seen that one of the meanings of the negative is refusal. It does not follow, though, that all refusals have to be negative in form. In investigating refusals made by English and Arabic speakers, Stevens (1993) found very few outright *no*'s in the responses of native-speaking subjects in either language. Nonetheless, there were "pragmatic failures" among the refusal strategies adopted by Arabic speakers speaking in English. For instance, the chiding strategy (reprimanding someone as a way of refusing an offer) that works in Arabic is pragmatically inappropriate in English.

> Don't make me mad; keep your money with you. (a refusal to another's offer to pay his/her own share of a movie admission)[11]

Similarly, Snipp (1992), studying refusal strategies of Japanese EFL speakers, found that the speakers' intended refusals were sometimes misconstrued by native English speakers because of their indirectness.

For instance B, a native Japanese speaker, is indirectly refusing A's request. A, an English speaker, does not neccessarily understand that she is being refused.

> A: Nice scarf! Can I borrow it to wear to the dance tomorrow?
> B: It is new.
> A: Yes. I didn't think I saw you wearing it before.

Not only can negatives seem to be too direct for certain speech acts; paradoxically, negatives can be used to soften other speech acts in the presence of a perceived social status gap:

> Won't you come in, please?   (Come in.)
> I don't suppose you've had the chance yet. (Have you had the chance yet?)

NOT VERSUS NO

Earlier, we spoke of the semantic nonequivalence of the negative particles *not* and *no* in certain structures, such as those with quantifiers. At other occasions, though, it is difficult to discern a meaning difference between them.

> I don't have any time to help this weekend.
> I have no time to help this weekend.

What, then, constitutes the difference?

From an examination of the conversations in the London-Lund Corpus and of written prose in the Lancaster-Oslo/Bergen Corpus,[12] a significantly different distribution of the two types of negation in the spoken and written samples was found. The proportions of *not*-negation and *no*-negation were almost exactly reversed in speech and writing. In speech there was 66 percent *not*-negation and 34 percent *no*-negation, and in writing, there was 37 percent *not*-negation and 63 percent *no*-negation. This difference is significant at $p < .001$ (Tottie 1991:321).

The reason for this discrepancy is presumably due to the fact that *no*-negation antedates *not*-negation, and thus the older form is preserved in writing, which is more formal and conservative than speech. When *no*-negation occurs, it is often in collocations such as *see no reason; no more, no less; no longer;* in implicit denials in existential constructions (*There is no milk in the house*) as compared with contrastive *not*-negation in explicit denials (*There isn't any milk in the house*); and in object noun phrases of high-frequency lexical verbs such as *have* (stative possessive), *make, give,* and *do* (as a main verb)—for example, *She has no excuse.*

A contextual analysis of North American English by Tai (1995) bears out Tottie's findings. Although they are trends, not absolutes, *not any* is more likely to occur in speaking and explicit denials. Tai also found the trends to hold for the distribution of *not anything* and *nothing* (i.e., *not anything* tended to be found more in speaking and explicit denials), although the trends were somewhat weaker. What was an additional factor with this pair, though, was syntatic complexity. While *not anything* goes with shorter modifiers, *nothing* goes with long modifiers.

> Most mail these days could consist of nothing that could truly be called a letter.
> It's just as well, because we can't do anything with it. (Tai 1995)

AFFIXAL VERSUS NONAFFIXAL NEGATION

The most pertinent finding in Tottie's study on the usage difference between affixal and nonaffixal negation was that affixal negation was far more prevalent in writing than in speech. In fact, two-thirds of the negatives in the written sample were affixal negatives, whereas two-thirds of the negatives in the spoken sample were nonaffixal. A great many of the affixal negatives were prenominal adjectives, such as *impossible* as in *the impossible dream.* Tottie attributes this finding to the fact that different discourse strategies are used in speaking and writing due to differences in production conditions, such as online production under time pressure in conversation, in contrast to more planning time available in the writing process. Because of the greater pressure imposed on speakers, they tend to produce utterances where one idea follows another in a fragmented discourse, whereas writers typically have more time to combine and superimpose ideas and can, therefore, mold their thoughts into a more integrated discourse (cf. Chafe, 1982). The use of prenominal or attributive adjectives constitutes "the single most prevalent feature of written language," according to Chafe (1982:42). Even when they use adjectives as subject predicates (*The dream is impossible*) rather than as premodifiers, writers prefer to use the more integrated type with affixal negation.

Another reason that affixal negation is favored in writing is that it is used in conjoined structures (*difficult and unbearable/*difficult and not bearable*), and conjoined phrases and complex clauses are more characteristic of writing than speaking.

CONTRACTED VERSUS UNCONTRACTED NEGATIVES

A way to give prominence to the negative is to keep it in its uncontracted form:

> Maureen hasn't decided to sell her house.
> Maureen has not decided to sell her house.

In addition to giving the negative more emphasis, the sentence with the uncontracted *not* is considered more formal. This formality is the reason for the prescriptive rule warning against the use of contractions in writing. It seems, though, that American English is becoming more accepting (at least compared with British English) when it comes to using contractions in writing (cf. Biber 1988), and we have chosen to use them in this text.

An informal way of still giving prominence to the negative would be to contract the subject and the auxiliary verb rather than the auxiliary verb and *not:*

> They're not going to be able to make it.

Because the negative is retained in its full form, it is more emphatic than its contracted *not* counterpart. For this reason, uncontracted *not* is often used in statements that contradict or correct a misunderstanding.

> (Two people looking at a photograph)   A: And that must be your brother.
> B: That's not my brother—it's my cousin.

NEGATIVE EQUATIVES

Returning briefly to our discussion concerning the contrast between comparatives and negative equatives, we should comment on their potential different uses. In general, it is considered more tactful to use negative equatives rather than comparatives, when the adjective has negative polarity. For example, in the following, the negative polarity adjective *dumb* is very rude in the comparative, whereas its positive polarity counterpart in a negative equative is considered more indirect and less rude:

> Moe is dumber than Curly.
> Moe is not as intelligent as Curly.

FUNCTIONAL NEGATIVES

We conclude this use section of the chapter by pointing out that just as words need not be marked affixally in order to convey negativity (cf. Jespersen's inherent negatives), so, too, can positive statements and questions have negative meaning, depending on the discourse context.

> *Joe:* Did you ace the final, Ray?
> *Ray:* Are you kidding? I'm lucky I passed!

In other words, although the question and statement in Ray's response are formally positive, they function as negatives.[13]

CONCLUSION

This chapter provides an introduction to the negative system in English. As you no doubt can tell, because of the many words and structures that are included in the system, you will encounter the topic of negation repeatedly in the chapters that follow. Students will need a great deal of practice with the form of the negative, which in our experience represents their greatest long-term challenge.

TEACHING SUGGESTIONS

1. Form. When students are first learning to place the negative particle *not* in its correct position in sentences, it is useful for them to practice unscrambling sentences with auxiliary verbs and the copula *be*. Write 12 to 15 sentences. Put one word of each sentence on a card or slip of paper.

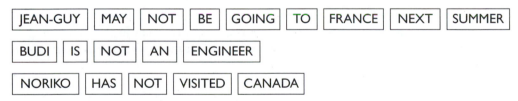

Shuffle the cards for each sentence and give three sets of shuffled cards to each small group of students. The students' task is to unscramble each of the three sentences and put them in grammatical order. When the groups are finished, they should mix the cards for each sentence again and swap cards with another group. The procedure should be repeated several times so that each group gets to practice unscrambling at least 12 sentences. Afterwards, you can ask the students to make their observations concerning the placement of the *not* in sentences with auxiliary or *be* verbs.

2. Use. Tell students the sentences they made are accurate, but an English speaker would probably not use the full form of the negative. Have students remove the card with the *not* on it in each of the final set of three sentences they were working on, turn it over and write the contraction *-n't* on the reverse side. Students should put the contraction next to the verb to which it is attached. They should then read the sentences out loud. You can correct their pronunciation of the contracted form as needed.

3. Form. As a presentation activity, to introduce your students to the need for the operator *do,* a flannelboard with words and inflections on slips of paper or an overhead projector with words and inflections on individual pieces of plastic comes in handy. Present the class with the following:

| JOHN | | CAN | | SWIM |

Next, put strips of paper or plastic with NOT and DIVE above the sentence and ask students to place them in the sentence properly. After practicing a few of these familiar sentences with the *be* verb or other auxiliary verbs, you can introduce the *do* beginning with plural subjects such as the following:

| CHILDREN | | LIKE | | CANDY |

Then CANDY is changed to HOMEWORK, and DO and NOT are placed above the new sentence. Students are asked where the new words go. You should help students see that the *do* verb is carrying the tense and showing number agreement with the subject. This might become clearer when you introduce the next sentence:

| MARIA | | SPEAKS | | S | | SPANISH |

After | SPANISH | has been changed to | CHINESE |, the | DO | and | NOT | are again placed above the sentence and students asked to put them in the right position in the new sentence. Then the | S | on speaks is moved over to follow | DO | (the first verb form in the sentence), at which point a newly introduced form, | DOES |, can be substituted for the two strips | DO | and | S |. Students should have an opportunity to practice several more of these sentences together before doing them on their own.

Notice that even when working on form, we don't ignore meaning. By changing the sentence from "John can swim" to "John cannot dive," rather than "John cannot swim," the truth value of the negative is upheld.

4. Meaning. Students can practice contradicting when you or other students deliberately make statements about members of the class that are not true (along with a few that are true). For example:

> *Teacher:* Maria comes from China.
>
> The class answers:
> *Students:* No, she doesn't. She comes from Argentina.
> *Teacher:* The person behind Paulo is Jorge.
>
> The class answers:
> *Students:* No, it isn't. It's Wu Min.
> *Teacher:* Boris is married.
> *Students:* Yes, Boris is married.

5. Meaning. Show students two pictures that have differences between them. Ask students to find the differences and use negative sentences to define them. In other words, they have to say what is not in one picture as contrasted with another. Later, divide the group into pairs and give each student a picture, which the student is not allowed to show. Each student has to converse with his/her partner to discover the differences between their pictures without showing the pictures (adapted from Ur 1988). For example:

> *A:* There are two cars in picture A.
> *B:* There are not two cars in picture B. There is one car.

6. Form. While students will need practice in producing all the contracted forms of negation, one form that may give them special difficulty in listening is the colloquial English *don't* in *I da wanna go* and *I dunno.* Another is *can't,* since English speakers distinguish *He can come* from *He can't come* more from its rhythmic structure and vowel quality than from its other segmental sounds.

> He can come [hiy kən kʊm]
> He can't come [hiy kæn kʊm]

Give students practice listening to you say one or the other of these with regard to a particular skill. You can hold up contrasting pictures and ask students to point to the one that shows what she says.

> *T:* (holds up two pictures) He can play the piano.
> Students point to one of the pictures.
> *T:* Yes. (holds up two new pictures) He can't swim.
> Students point to one of the pictures.
> etc.

7. Meaning. In practicing the difference between *don't have to* and *must not,* students could be asked to make comparative statements about classroom manners in the countries they come from and the United States. For example:

> In Malaysia, you must stand when the teacher enters the classroom, but in the United States, you don't have to.

> In Malaysia, you mustn't speak unless the teacher calls on you. That's sometimes true in the United States too.

8. Use. Intermediate-level students could learn to make tactful comparisons using negative equatives. They could be asked to bring in one or two pictures of famous people that they cut out of magazines. They could then hang the pictures up and make statements like the following:

> Madonna is not as talented as Meryl Streep.
> Arnold Schwarzenegger's new movie is not as good as his last one.
> etc.

EXERCISES

Test your understanding of what has been presented.

1. Provide original example sentences to illustrate the following terms. Underline the pertinent word(s) in your examples:
   - **a.** sentence-level negation
   - **b.** phrasal negation
   - **c.** lexical negation
   - **d.** operator addition
   - **e.** *not* contraction
   - **f.** *no* determiner
   - **g.** negative equative
   - **h.** negative indefinite pronoun

2. Draw the trees and say which mapping rules apply:
   a. Alice doesn't laugh at my jokes.   d. I can't understand the lyrics.
   b. They have no children.   e. The boys aren't playing football this year.
   c. Meg is not about to listen to you.

3. In what way are the following sentences in each set related? How are they different?
   a. Sam is not working these days.   c. Trudy doesn't remember anyone.
      Sam's not working these days.   Trudy remembers no one.
      Sam isn't working these days.   d. I would say that is inadvisable.
   b. Bill is shorter than Richard.   I would say that is not advisable.
      Bill is not as tall as Richard.

Test your ability to apply what you know.

4. If your students produce the following sentences, what errors have they made? How will you make them aware of the errors, and what exercises will you prepare to correct them?
   a. *That boy no like me.   d. He don't worry. (nonstandard)
   b. *I not understand.   e. I didn't do nothing. (nonstandard)
   c. *Seth is very unpatient.   f. *Not any students will come to school today.

5. What is the difference between the following two sentences:

   They might not have tried before.
   They might have not tried before.

6. A few years ago, a way of negating in English was jokingly used in the movie "Wayne's World":

   You're my best friend . . . not.

   Actually, this form has been around for a number of years (Sheidlower and Lighter 1993). How does this form of negation differ from Standard English and what is its purpose?

7. A student tells you that he has been told that *any* is always used in place of *some* in a negative sentence, but that he heard another teacher say the following: *I can't recall some of their names.* The student asks you if this is grammatical. What would you say?

8. Many relatively advanced ESL/EFL students systematically refuse to contract the negative particle in their speech. How would you teach them the fact that contraction is normally used in speech and informal writing?

9. Early on in this chapter we listed some verbs that are inherently negative. Besides the semantics of verbs like *fail*, what sort of syntactic evidence can you adduce that would demonstrate their negativity?

BIBLIOGRAPHY

References

Bailey, C. J. (1997). "You and Your English Grammar." Kea'au, Hawaii: Orchid Land Publications.
Biber, D. (1988). *Variation across Speech and Writing.* Cambridge: Cambridge University Press.
Bloom, L. (1970). *Language Development: Form and Function in Emerging Grammars.* Cambridge, Mass: The MIT Press.

Chafe, W. (1982). "Integration and Involvement in Speaking, Writing, and Oral Literature." In D. Tannen (ed.), *Spoken and Written Language: Exploring Orality and Literacy.* Norwood, N.J.: Ablex, 35–53.

Close, R. A. (1992). *A Teachers' Grammar.* Hove: Language Teaching Publications.

Givón, T. (1993). *English Grammar: A Function-Based Approach.* Amsterdam/Philadelphia: John Benjamins.

Horn, L. (1989). *A Natural History of Negation.* Chicago: University of Chicago Press.

Jespersen, O. (1917). *Negation in English and Other Languages.* Reprinted in *Selected Writings of Otto Jespersen.* London: Allen and Unwin.

Quirk, R., S. Greenbaum, G. Leech, and J. Svartvik (1985). *A Comprehensive Grammar of the English Language.* London: Longman.

Sheidlower, J., and J. Lighter (1993). "A Recent Coinage . . . NOT!" *American Speech* 68, 2:213–219.

Snipp, K. (1992). Refusals in Japanese and English: "A Contrastive Linguistic Study of the Language Used in the Refusal of the Requests of Peer Acquaintances." Independent Professional Project, School for International Training, Brattleboro, Vt.

Stevens, P. (1993). "The Pragmatics of 'NO!': Some Strategies in English and Arabic." *IDEAL* 6:87–112.

Tai, S. (1995). "A Contextual Analysis of NOT + ANY and NO in American English." Unpublished M.A. in TESL thesis, UCLA.

Tottie, G. (1991). *Negation in English Speech and Writing: A Study of Variation.* San Diego: Academic Press.

Yaeger-Dror, M. (1985). "Intonational Prominence on Negatives in English." *Language and Speech* 28:197–230.

Suggestions for Further Reading

For a classic early transformational treatment of negation, see:

Klima, E. (1964). "Negation in English." In J. Foder and J. Katz (eds.), *The Structure of Language.* Englewood Cliffs, N.J.: Prentice-Hall, 246–323.

For another helpful analysis of negation, see

Dahl, O. (1979). "Typology of Sentence Negation." *Linguistics* 17:79–106.

For pedagogical help with basic negative formation, see:

Badalamenti, V., and C. Henner Stanchina (1997). *Grammar Dimensions: Form, Meaning, and Use.* Book 1 (2d ed.). Boston, Mass: Heinle & Heinle.

For pedagogical suggestions with negative equatives, see:

Riggenbach, H., and V. Samuda (1997). *Grammar Dimensions: Form, Meaning, and Use.* Book 2 (2d ed.). Boston, Mass: Heinle & Heinle.

ENDNOTES:

1. For example, in Bahasa Indonesia, *bukan* is used to negate a nominal; *tidak* negates verbs, adjectives, and adverbials; and *belum* negates a past action, event, or state and could be glossed as "not yet."

2. A similar sort of pattern is the use of *no-* as an adjective-forming prefix as in, for example, *no-fault insurance, no-wax floors, no-good rascal, no-win situation,* and so on.

3. Sometimes this assimilation is overgeneralized to other parts of speech where the same *in-* is not used as a negative prefix. For example, you may hear people say /impʊt/ instead of /inpʊt/ for *input.*

4. Readers might expect to see *none* on this list. Actually, *none* is foremost a quantifier (see Chapter 17) and only incidentally pronominal.

5. Close (1992) identifies six such operations:

   a. To make negatives: *I haven't done my homework.*
   b. To make questions: *Have you done your homework?*
   c. To make negative questions: *Haven't you done your homework?*
   d. To make tag questions: *You've done your homework, haven't you?*
   e. To emphasize: *I háve done my homework.*
      (the operator is stressed)
   f. To substitute for the whole predicate: *My brother hasn't done his homework, but I have.*
      (in order to avoid repetition)

6. A mapping rule that must be applied to produce a grammatical sentence is "obligatory." Such is the case with *not*-placement. A mapping rule that may be applied to a grammatical sequence to produce a stylistic variation is "optional."

7. And some are rarely if ever contracted; e.g., ** mayn't, ?oughtn't*. Horn (1989:480) argues that for this reason, as well as for others, contracted auxiliary verbs should be analyzed as separate lexical items rather than syntactic combinations of sentential *not* and the first auxiliary verb. While Horn's contention has linguistic merit, for ESL/EFL pedagogical reasons it seems to make sense to treat the contracted auxiliary verb as being syntactically derived from *not* + auxiliary verb.

8. One exception is its use in stylized rhetoric. Remember John F. Kennedy's exhortation when he was inaugurated President of the United States: "Ask not what your country can do for you; ask what you can do for your country." It is also used in certain other formulaic utterances, such as, *I kid you not, She loves me not.*

9. As Givón (1993) points out, it is possible for negation of a main clause or negation of a complement clause to yield similar, if not identical, meanings:

   I don't think that she came.
   I think that she didn't come.

This is not true for all verbs, however. Common verbs that follow this pattern are *believe, expect, feel, imagine, intend, plan, propose, reckon, suppose, think, want,* and *wish.*

10. *Old* is perceived as positive and *young* as negative for age in that we always ask, "How old are you?" See the discussions in Chapters 20 and 34 for more on the polarity feature of adjectives.

11. Stevens attributes this strategy to the fact that it is not culturally appropriate in Arab society to go "Dutch treat."

12. These are British-English corpora but the findings are believed to hold for American English as well, with the possible exception that American English favors *not*-negation even more than British English.

13. Conversely, some formal negatives function as ironic positive statements rather than negatives—for example,

   I can't believe it!

Chapter 11

YES/NO QUESTIONS

INTRODUCTION

Yes/no questions are often defined as questions for which either "yes" or "no" is the expected answer:

Are you going to the party? $\begin{cases} \text{Yes (I am).} \\ \text{No (I'm not).} \end{cases}$

A syntactic rule inverting the subject and operator gives rise to the characteristic form of yes/no questions in English

Lucille is studying in Ypsilanti this semester.
Is Lucille studying in Ypsilanti this semester? [+ inversion + rising intonation]

Inversion such as this is relatively rare among the world's languages. A few languages other than English use inversion in making questions—German, for example—but on the whole, most languages do not use inversion to form questions. Instead, as Ultan (1978) reports in a typological study of 79 languages from differing language families and areas of the world, most languages use a distinctive intonation pattern for questions.[1] The second most popular option among the languages Ultan studied was the inclusion of a special interrogative particle either at the beginning or end of the question to signal its interrogative status.

It is not surprising, then, that inversion in English yes/no questions is problematic for ESL/EFL students. Inversion has not always been used in English questions, however. At an early stage in the history of English, questions were made with the use of rising intonation alone. Only much later did inversion in question formation come into being. And the earliest form of this inversion was with the subject and the verb:

Know you the way to Ipswich?

It took much longer for the rule requiring subject and operator inversion to become standard.

Todeva (1991) has pointed out the parallelism between the evolution of the English language and the acquisition of English as either a first or second language: learners of English are known to first use rising intonation; only after several more stages do they completely master inversion to signal that they are asking a question. The following is the developmental pattern that has been observed for ESL learners, whose pseudonyms are in parentheses (Hatch and Wagner-Gough 1976):

Stage I: Rising intonation   You go? (Zoila)

(either transferred from the learners' first language, the L1, or the result of an interlanguage communicative strategy)

Stage II: Tag questions   George come school, no? (Ken)
Stage III: Modal inversion   Can I play? (Paul)
Stage IV: *Be* inversion   Are you play? (Homer)
Stage V: *Do* support   Do you like ice cream?

Of course, as with all second language (L2) data, these stages are not discrete or categorical, and within each there is certainly individual variation. Nonetheless, it can generally be said that the rule of inversion is the major formal challenge for students, and its mastery takes a while. The challenge is no doubt made more difficult by the fact that native speakers frequently do not invert questions in conversational English; hence, the input to which ESL/EFL learners are exposed is heterogeneous with regard to inversion. We return to this point later.

In this chapter, then, we begin by examining the inversion rule in English under the heading of form. Other comments about form are made with regard to the intonation pattern of yes/no questions and the structure of short answers. As is our custom, we also comment on the meaning of yes/no questions and their formal variants: negative yes/no questions, focused yes/no questions, and uninverted yes/no questions. Next, we revisit the distinction between *some* and *any* that we introduced in the previous chapter. In the section on use, we make some observations about short answers to yes/no questions. We also discuss contraction in negative questions and the use of elliptical questions. We conclude this chapter by pointing out other functions that yes/no questions can fulfill. In Chapter 13, we deal with *wh-* questions that ask for information. Later in the book, in Chapter 33, we discuss embedded questions.

THE FORM OF YES/NO QUESTIONS

SUBJECT-OPERATOR INVERSION

With an Auxiliary Verb

Consider the following questions:

1. Will they be in Reno on Friday?   3. Has Alice gone home?
2. Was she able to finish in time?   4. Are you doing anything tomorrow?

Each of these four questions begins with an auxiliary verb. The mapping rule that accounts for the auxiliary verbs at the head of each sentence is a movement rule called subject-operator inversion. This rule moves the operator and the tense marker, if there is one present, to a position before the subject. Here is an example of how the rule operates when it is applied to the base structure underlying the first question:

Will they be in Reno on Friday?

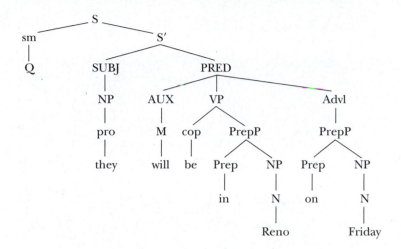

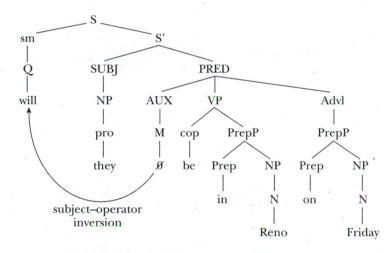

subject–operator
inversion

The Q marker is treated as a sentence marker because its scope applies to the whole sentence. You can think of it as a device that triggers subject-operator inversion and ensures acceptable yes/no question intonation (which we discuss below).

Notice that if this sentence had two auxiliary verbs—for example, if we were to add *be* + *ing* to the *will* in question 1—it is only the *first* auxiliary verb in the auxiliary string, the

Will they be gambling in Reno on Friday?

operator, that is inverted with the subject. Furthermore, if the auxiliary has more than one element, as does the phrasal modal in question 2, then it is only the *first* of the elements in the first auxiliary verb, again the operator, which, along with the tense marker, if there is one, is inverted with the subject. Here are the trees for question 2 as an illustration of this last point.

Was she able to finish in time?

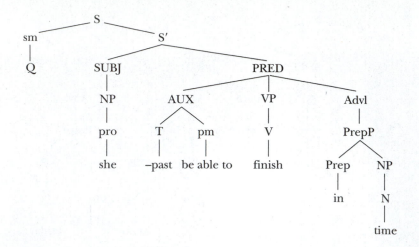

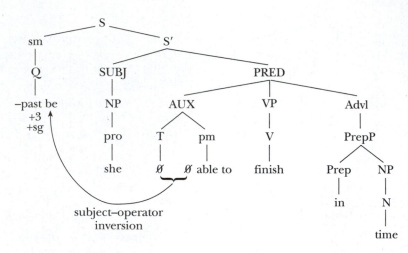

subject–operator
inversion

Here is how it would look with all the mapping rules:

output of base: Q she -past be able to finish in time
copy s/t: Q she -past [+ 3 + sg] be able to finish in time
subject-operator inversion: -past [+ 3 + sg] she be able to finish in time
morphology: Was she able to finish in time?

With the *Be* Copula

As you saw in the previous chapter on negation, the negative particle (adverb) *not* is placed after the first auxiliary verb. In this chapter you have learned that it is also the first auxiliary verb that is involved in question formation. Similarly, just as the *not* follows the *be* copula verb when no auxiliary verb is present in negative sentences, so does the *be* copula verb serve as the inverted operator when no auxiliary verb is present in yes/no question formation.

Pamela was a graduate student at the time.
Was Pamela a graduate student at the time?

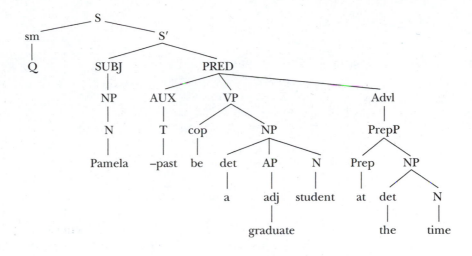

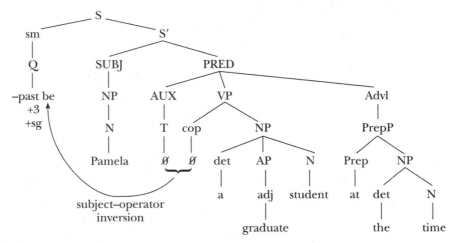

With Other Verbs

When a sentence has no auxiliary or *be* verb, a different condition obtains. Notice that we cannot simply invert the subject and the verb as we did with the *be* verb to form a grammatical question:

> Arlene plays the organ on Sunday.
> *Plays Arlene the organ on Sunday?

Although, as we have already noted, such forms were acceptable in historically earlier forms of English, and their equivalents are grammatical in certain languages today, such as the German and Scandinavian languages, main verb inversion with the subject is not grammatical in modern English.[2]

Once again we can point to the parallelism between negation and yes/no question formation. Recall that to make a sentence negative when it has no auxiliary verb or *be* verb, the verb *do* is introduced as an operator, We can invoke the same rule—namely, operator addition—to introduce the *do* to function as an operator in yes/no questions for which there is no auxiliary verb or *be* copula verb to perform this function.

> Does Arlene play the organ on Sunday?

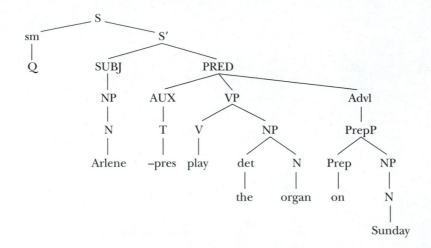

This is how it looks after copy s/t and operator addition:

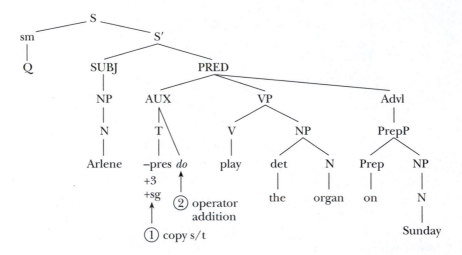

and then after subject-operator inversion:

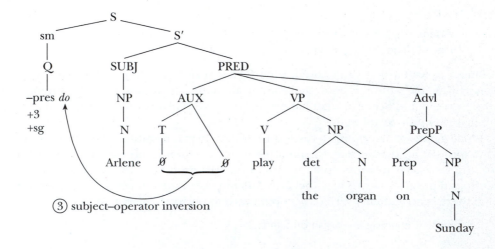

Since subject-operator inversion cannot apply without some auxiliary verb or *be* copula that can function as an operator, the *do* verb is added to make subject-operator inversion possible.

Here is the sequence of mapping rules:

> output of base: Q Arlene -pres play the organ on Sunday
> copy s/t: Q Arlene-pres [+ 3 + sg] play the organ on Sunday
> operator addition: Q Arlene -pres [+ 3 + sg] do play the organ on Sunday
> subject-operator inversion: -pres [+ 3 + sg] do arlene play the organ on sunday
> morphology: Does Arlene play the organ on Sunday?

Operator addition is also needed for a few phrasal modals:

used to   Did you use to go skiing when you lived in Vermont?
have to   Does Brent have to work on weekends?

In most cases, however, the first element in phrasal modals is the operator and inverts with the subject when subject-operator inversion is applied:

be to   Are you to report tomorrow?

Notions such as subject-operator inversion and using *do* as a surrogate operator help us to gain insight into the process of question formation in English. We would not necessarily be doing our ESL/EFL students a service, however, by using such terminology. What generalizations about the form of yes/no questions can we make, then, that would be useful for our students?

ESL/EFL students need to know that in a yes/no question the first auxiliary verb in the sentence should appear before the subject and carry the tense of the question (if there is tense). If there is no auxiliary verb, the *be* copula should be moved before the subject. If there is no auxiliary verb or *be* copula, then *do* must be introduced in the auxiliary to make subject-operator inversion possible.

INTONATION IN YES/NO QUESTIONS

In addition to inverted word order and sometimes the addition of the *do* operator, English also uses intonation to mark yes/no questions. Yes/no questions typically display a raised, nonterminal intonation.[3] To understand how this is articulated, consider that statement intonation in English usually rises on the last stressed syllable of the last content word and then falls on that word in the sentence. For example:

②   ③①
Muriel is learning to use a computer.

Unmarked yes/no question intonation typically rises through the same stressed syllable and then stays high.

②   ③③
Is Muriel learning to use a computer?

SHORT ANSWERS TO YES/NO QUESTIONS

It is unlikely that the response to a yes/no question will be in the form of a full sentence:

Is Ramon an engineering student?

Yes. $\begin{Bmatrix} \text{He is} \\ \text{He's} \end{Bmatrix}$ an engineering student.

No. He isn't an engineering student.

Although these answers are possible, such replies may give the listener the impression that the speaker is annoyed by the question. ESL/EFL teachers should be aware of the possible negative affect expressed by a full-sentence answer to a yes/no question and not always insist on their students answering questions with full sentences, as teachers sometimes do. A more common form of answer, although this too is restricted in its distribution, as you will see in a later section on use, is the short answer:

Is Ramon an engineering student?
Yes, he is.
No, he isn't.

If the yes/no question begins with the copula *be*, as in our example sentence, the short answer is formed with the same form of the *be* verb that appeared in the question. Notice that *be* cannot be contracted in an affirmative short answer. All affirmative short answers must be followed by at least one other word, or else the full form of *be* must be used.

*Yes, he's.
Yes, he's studying electrical engineering.
Yes, he is.

When the yes/no question contains an auxiliary verb, that operator is used in the short answer.

With a modal	Can she go?	$\begin{cases} \text{Yes, she can} \\ \text{No, she can't.} \end{cases}$
With a phrasal modal (the first element)	Is she able to go?	$\begin{cases} \text{Yes, she is.} \\ \text{No, she isn't.} \end{cases}$
With perfect aspect	Has she gone?	$\begin{cases} \text{Yes, she has.} \\ \text{No, she hasn't.} \end{cases}$
With progressive aspect	Is she going?	$\begin{cases} \text{Yes, she is.} \\ \text{No, she isn't.} \end{cases}$

If the sentence contains more than one auxiliary verb, the short answer may also contain an auxiliary verb in addition to the operator, although when the second or third auxiliary verb is some form of *be*, the speaker usually omits it; for example,

With modal and perfect	Will she have gone?	Yes, she	$\begin{cases} \text{will have.} \\ \text{will've.} \end{cases}$
		No, she	$\begin{cases} \text{won't have.} \\ \text{won't've.} \end{cases}$
With modal, perfect, and progressive	Will she have been worrying?		Yes, she will have (been). No, she won't have (been).

If *do* is the operator in the question, it is also used in the short answer with the same tense used in the question:

> Does she go there often?   Yes, she does.
>   No, she doesn't.

THE MEANING OF YES/NO QUESTIONS

Although not all linguists agree (cf. Bolinger 1978), most feel that an acceptable paraphrase of a yes/no question might be "Is it the case that . . . ?", in which the speaker is asking for confirmation or denial of a proposition. Such an analysis implies that yes/no questions are neutral questions—that is, there is no presupposition regarding whether an affirmative or negative reply is likely. Chalker (1984), for example, calls them "open questions" because the speaker has an open mind about the answer. Such is not the case with negative yes/no questions.

NEGATIVE YES/NO QUESTIONS

Negative yes/no questions have a different orientation. In this example,

> Is Josh playing soccer this year?
> Isn't Josh playing soccer this year?

The first question is neutral with regard to speaker expectations, but the negative question signals that the speaker has reason to believe that something he or she had previously thought was true might not be so. Here, in using the negative question, the speaker is signaling that he or she expected that Josh would be playing soccer but, because of new evidence, now realizes that this may not be true. The speaker may be hoping for a positive answer but not really expecting one. Because the prior expectation tends to be aligned with the speaker's wishes, Quirk et al. (1985) add that negative questions can express disappointment or annoyance because the speaker's earlier wishes/expectations now seem to be no longer true.

> Aren't we going to the movies? (I thought we had agreed to.)

> Didn't you say that the test would be next week? (I thought that was what you had announced.)

Negative yes/no questions create semantic problems for many ESL/EFL learners (Bevington 1979). For example, native speakers of most Asian and West African languages react to a negative yes/no question in a literal manner in their own language—they agree or disagree with its form.

> Don't you have bananas? $\begin{cases} \text{Yes (we have no bananas).} \\ \text{No (we have bananas).} \end{cases}$

The native speaker of English, on the other hand, reacts to negative yes/no questions as if they were affirmative ones with a presuppositional difference:

> Don't you have bananas? $\begin{cases} \text{Yes (we do).} \\ \text{No (we don't).} \end{cases}$

While negative questions are not all that frequent, the miscommunication that results from not understanding the underlying presupposition warrants teaching ESL/EFL students how to reply to them.

FOCUSED YES/NO QUESTIONS

So far we have been considering yes/no questions where the whole state, activity, or event is being queried. Sometimes, however, yes/no questions can be more focused in their query. A proposition may be thought to be true in general, but one of its specific components—subject, verb, object, adverbial—may be still in doubt. The uncertain element is then queried in a focused way. Consider, for example, questions below where contrastive stress is used to mark the focused elements (Givón 1993:247–248). Unlike unmarked yes/no questions, which are open with regard to the proposition being expressed, the truth of the presupposition in a focused question is presupposed but contains an indeterminate element in the focused position.

> Did *Megan* play a practical joke on Pat? (or did *someone else?*)
> Did Megan *play* a practical joke on Pat? (or only *plan* one?)
> Did Megan play *a practical joke* on Pat? (or did she play *something else,* such as a trick?)
> Did Megan play a practical joke *on Pat?* (or was it played *on someone else?*)

When an optional adverbial is present in the question, it automatically attracts and focuses attention in yes/no questions, because of its final position in the clause (see Chapter 2). Thus, the following focused questions query the adverbial:

> Did Megan play a trick on Pat *deliberately?* { (or was it *an accident?*)
> { (*or did she not do it?*)

> Did Megan play a trick on Pat *last Sunday?* { (or was it on *Monday?*)
> { (*or did she not do it?*)

> Did Megan play a trick on Pat *at the mall?* { (or was it *somewhere else?*)
> { (*or did she not do it?*)

That the interrogative focus is attracted to optional constitutents is further supported by the fact that when an optional adverbial is present, stressing the optional adverbial is natural. In contrast, stressing another constituent in the clause is odd:

> Did Megan play a trick on Pat *deliberately?* (or was it an accident?)
> Did *Megan* play a trick on Pat deliberately? (?or did someone else do it deliberately?)

Two observations have emerged from our discussion so far regarding meaning and yes/no questions. The first is that speakers may differ in their expectations of negative or positive responses concerning the entire proposition. The second is that speakers have varying reasons for uncertainty about the proposition. The use of contrastive stress is one device speakers can resort to to identify more specifically the locus of their uncertainty.

UNINVERTED QUESTIONS

Another structure that speaks to the first observation—a speaker's presupposition with regard to an expected reply—is a statement-form, or uninverted, question. This type of question is also marked in the sense that the speaker who poses the question is anticipating confirmation of either a positive or a negative presupposition:

> A: I just got back from San Francisco.
> B: You had a good time there? (expecting confirmation of positive presupposition)

B's reply with accompanying rising question intonation suggests that B's hunch was that the answer would be "yes." Had B chosen instead to use the unmarked, neutral, inverted question, we might assume that B had uncertainty about what A's reply would be:

> A: I just got back from San Francisco.
> B: Did you have a good time? (uncertain expectation)

A negative uninverted question could reflect the fact that new information has just been received that runs counter to an earlier presupposition:

> (Person A returns home early from a shopping trip)
> B: The stores weren't open late? (expecting confirmation of negative presupposition)

A's early return contradicts B's presupposition that A would be shopping until later.

Weber (1989) and Williams (1989) both report that uninverted questions are much more common than one might suppose.[4] In her analysis of face-to-face and telephone conversations, Weber found that as many as 41 percent of all the questions in the data were either uninverted, of the sort we have just considered, or nonclausal forms such as the following (Weber 1989:181):

> A: I've got so much work that I don't believe it, so I'm just not thinking about that.
> B: In school, you mean?

In this nonclausal example, B questions with a prepositional phrase plus the clause tag *you mean*. Uninverted forms with rising intonation, with and without tags, serve, as we see in this example, as comprehension checks (Williams 1990).

In addition to comprehension checks, nonclausal questions often function as "next turn repair initiators" (Schegloff, Jefferson, and Sacks 1977:367). *Repair* refers to the efforts of participants to deal with trouble in hearing or understanding, and *next turn* indicates that the repair occurs in the conversational turn after the "trouble source" turn. Here is another example from Weber (1989:170):

> A: What's the dark green thing?
> B: Pardon?
> A: What's this?
> B: That's Japanese eggplant.

In this example, B's production of *pardon*, a next turn repair initiator, displays some trouble with hearing or understanding A's entire question. A recasts her somewhat modified question. This time its meaning is clear, and B responds to the question. Williams (1989) contributes evidence from her own investigation that full clausal uninverted questions also function as clarification requests.

One variant of an uninverted question is an *echo question*, which simply repeats, or modifies in some minor fashion, a previous utterance with rising intonation. If the intonation is rising, as it is for unmarked yes/no questions, then the purpose for using the echo question would simply be to seek confirmation of the preceding speaker's remark:

> A. My sister is going out with Lou.
> B: { Your sister is / She's } going out with Lou? (seeking confirmation that the previous remark has been understood)

If, on the other hand, the pitch of the intonation rises beyond the usual range, then the echo question can express counterexpectation—surprise, or disbelief (see VanderBrook, Schlue, and Campbell 1980 for further discussion):

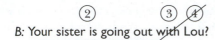

B: Your sister is going out with Lou?

SOME VERSUS ANY

The last point in our discussion of the meaning of yes/no questions has to do with the use of *some* and *any*, a contrast you first encountered in the previous chapter on negation. Many ESL/EFL grammar texts say that *any* is used in questions as well as negatives. This is true with regard to open or unmarked questions, such as:

> Do you have *any* paper I can borrow?

However, you also saw in the chapter on negation that weakly stressed *some* suggests a positive quantity. It is therefore used in questions that in some way expect a positive answer, such as with an offer:

> A waiter to a customer in a restaurant: Would you like *some* dessert? (to encourage the answer "yes")

Just as we saw in our discussion with negatives, we must therefore be cautious about what we say about the distribution of *some* and *any* as they can both occur with different question types, depending on the meaning (partly based on Chalker 1984:15):

> Is there some news?   (expecting the answer "yes")
> Is there any news?   (open or neutral question)
> Isn't there some news?   (Surely there is.)
> Isn't there any news? ⎤
> Is there no news?   ⎦ (I had hoped there would be.)

ISSUES OF USE CONCERNING YES/NO QUESTIONS

We now turn to our last section, where we deal with issues pertaining to use: when speakers have two or more question forms with the same meaning to choose from, what factors condition their choice—that is, why do they prefer one form to another?

THE USE OF SHORT ANSWERS

Earlier we discussed the form of standard short answers in English (*Yes, it is. No, it isn't*). While these short-answer forms are worth teaching ESL/EFL students, one should bear in mind that even these forms do not occur frequently as responses to yes/no questions. In Richards (1977), replies to yes/no questions containing auxiliary or verb repetition made up less than 20 percent of the written corpus and less than 10 percent of the spoken English corpus. Similarly, in a discourse analysis of speech samples collected from a wide variety of contexts, Winn-Bell Olsen (1980) found that standard short forms were used rather infrequently by native English speakers—in fact, only 8 percent of the time—as answers to yes/no questions in her data (26 out of 329 instances).

She discovered that native speakers were much more likely to answer questions with a direct "yes" (or its colloquial variants, e.g., "yup," "yeah," "uh huh") or a direct "no" (or its variants, e.g., "nah," "nope," "uh uh," "not yet"), each often followed by some sort of expansion. Indirect affirmations, denials, or hedges (e.g., "Does it make you uncomfortable to talk about this problem?" "I guess maybe it does.") accounted for a rather large percentage of the answers, as well. Finally, a significant portion of the answers were formulaic expressions of confirmation or denial (e.g., "I doubt it."). Since 23 out of 26 occurrences of standard short-form answers in her data were found in conversations between strangers or in self-conscious speech, Winn-Bell Olsen hypothesizes that the more distant the relationship between speakers or the more uncomfortable the situation, the more frequently speakers tend to use standard short-form answers.

UNINVERTED YES/NO QUESTIONS

The use of uninverted yes/no questions might also be said to relate to issues of social familiarity or distance. Recall that uninverted questions are used when the speaker expects confirmation of a positive or negative presupposition. Using an uninverted question thus suggests that the person asking the question knows the other person well enough to predict the other's answer. Such intimacy often may not exist, and the use of uninverted questions could then appear to be presumptuous.

> Worker to supervisor: You're going to the dance?

ELLIPTICAL QUESTIONS

At some point, teachers will want to expose their intermediate- and advanced-level students to informal yes/no questions that occur without an overt initial auxiliary. Such questions are fairly frequent in informal conversations between native speakers and are different from uninverted yes/no questions in that they presuppose no answer or express no particular emotion.

> (Are) You going to the movies?
> (Has) She been feeling better?
> (Do) You know Fred Callahan?

If *you* is the subject, it can also be deleted in most cases, along with the operator.

> (Do you) Wanna study together?

In such questions, the operator and subject are optionally deletable because they are recoverable from other grammatical and lexical information in the question and from the discourse context. It would probably not be of high priority for your students to practice using such elliptical yes/no questions, but they should develop comprehension of this form and perhaps an ability to automatically supply the missing operator or operator and subject.

CONTRACTED VERSUS UNCONTRACTED NEGATIVES IN NEGATIVE QUESTIONS

In English negative yes/no questions, the negative may appear in both contracted and uncontracted forms. Only the contracted form, however, may appear sentence-initially as part of an operator;

> Isn't it appropriate to ask?
> Is it not appropriate to ask?

The question with the uncontracted negative after the subject is more formal than its counterpart with a question-initial contracted negative.

In a usage study, Kontra (1981) has documented the occurrence in contemporary English of uncontracted negative questions such as the following:

> Is not linguistics a branch of psychology?

Here, the *not* appears before the subject in its uncontracted form. While such questions do occasionally occur, we view this type of question as a stylistically formal and somewhat archaic vestige of an earlier stage of English. Evidence for our position comes from the fact that the uncontracted *not* in pre-subject position has a rather limited distribution; for example, the subject of such a question can rarely be a pronoun:

> *Is not it a branch of psychology?

Nevertheless, Kontra (1993) has found evidence of the existence of even this form in British English. Such a question, Kontra believes, is used when the speaker is inviting the listener to agree with the speaker's assumption that the expressed proposition is self-evidently true. One example he cites is the following excerpt from a discussion in the British Parliament: (Kontra 1993:340)

> Is not it an outrage that the Minister has not even tried to answer the question? . . .
> Does not the Minister think that he has a duty to tell people the facts before they vote?

This word order would be highly unusual in North American English.

THE USE OF *AREN'T* AS A GAP-FILLER

A final note on contracted negative yes/no questions concerns the lexical gap that occurs in the first person singular. All of the following are acceptable contracted negative questions and short answers:

> Isn't he/she/it?   He/she/it isn't.
> Aren't we/you/they?   We/you/they aren't.

However, we cannot contract the verb *be* and the *not* in *I am not* unless we use nonstandard *I ain't*. What speakers of English do in negative yes/no questions (but not in short answers) is to substitute *are* for *am* and contract. Thus:

> Aren't I?   I am not.
>   I'm not.

This illogical gap-filler arose because there were strong social and educational stigmas against the use of *ain't*. *Aren't I* is mainly a colloquialism, but it may puzzle ESL/EFL students when they encounter it; so you should be prepared to explain why sometimes *aren't* is used with the first person singular pronoun in negative yes/no questions.

OTHER FUNCTIONS

We have been dealing with questions whose function is primarily to seek new information or to clarify or confirm given or shared information. Yes/no questions can perform a number of other functions, of course. You have already seen in Chapter 8 how questions with modal forms can be used in requests for assistance:

> Can I get a ride home with you? (direct request)

As we also saw in the chapter on modals, the "past-tense" form of *can* softens this a bit:

> Could I get a ride home with you? (less direct)

An even more polite form of request uses an embedded question (about which we have more to say in Chapter 33):

> I wonder if I could get a ride home with you. (least direct, therefore most polite)

You also saw in Chapter 8 how yes/no question forms could be used in making offers or invitations:

> Would you like to sit for a while?

They can also be used as commands:

> Would you please stand up straight?

as reprimands:

> Aren't you a little old to be doing that?

as complaints:

> Have you ever stayed home all day with a two-year-old?

and many other functions. Clearly, the function of a yes/no question is going to depend on the context and the speaker's intention.

CONCLUSION

As we have indicated, the main challenge for most ESL/EFL students will be to learn about inversion in yes/no questions—both the syntactic rules and the social conditions in which they are appropriate. Because the *do* operator is not a morpheme with many equivalents in the languages of the world, its use in yes/no questions may require some special attention. Students may also need some understanding of how to respond to yes/no questions as well, particularly negative yes/no questions. Finally, we should remember that not all yes/no questions are inverted. As you have seen in this chapter, many conversational yes/no questions are uninverted, elliptical, or nonclausal in form. While we might not specifically teach ESL/EFL students to produce these forms, students may be confused by them, and you may need to help them understand their use.

TEACHING SUGGESTIONS

1. Form. To expose students to yes/no questions before they are asked to form them on their own, surveys can be used. Surveys in which students learn something about themselves and their classmates work well. Depending on the ages and backgrounds of your students, you can use various survey themes: for example, health habits (Do you exercise?), eating habits (Do you eat rice for breakfast?), or study strategies (Do you speak English with your friends?). You can give students a survey form that you have prepared, or they can create one with you. They then complete the survey themselves and ask the questions of one or more other students.

2. Form. As suggested in the chapter on negation, a flannelboard or overhead projector is a useful device for presenting rules for the addition of function words and syntactic movement. To introduce inversion in sentences containing an auxiliary verb or *be,* you can substitute a question-mark card for the period card and then move the first auxiliary verb or *be* verb card to sentence-initial position.

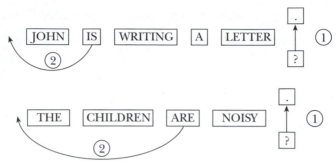

Later, in order to introduce students to the formation of yes/no questions without an auxiliary verb or *be*, you will need to place a DO card at the front of a sentence after substituting a question mark card for the period card. For example:

Next, you can explain to students that the *do* verb carries the tense for the question. This can be demonstrated by replacing the DO card with DID and the ATE card with EAT after substituting the ? for the . Thus:

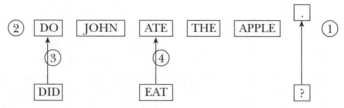

Cards could also be used to show that the *do* carries the tense and person markings with the simple present tense.

① Put these on the flannelboard. JOHN EAT S APPLES .

② Substitute ? at the end of the sentence and introduce DO to the front.

③ Show that the S of *eats* gets moved to the initial DO by moving the S from its position after EATS to a position following DO . Immediately replace DO S

with a new card DOES explaining that rewriting *do* plus third person singular present as *does* is a convention in English. After several examples have been done, it is good to have student volunteers come up and practice forming questions by moving and substituting the cards. To give students additional practice, prepare (or have students prepare) pieces of paper with the words, question marks, and morphemes for each student (or pairs of students) to manipulate at his or her desk.

3. Form. It is often easier to make up activities in which students answer yes/no questions than activities in which students practice asking the questions. Guessing games can give students good practice in both asking and responding to questions.

a. For example, the game "Twenty Questions" provides an engaging way to practice forming and answering yes/no questions. The rules are simple. Someone thinks of an animal (including human beings), a vegetable (any living nonanimal), or a mineral (anything inanimate). The other players then can use up to 20 yes/no questions in an attempt to guess what it is the person is thinking of. If they can't guess after using all 20 questions, the person wins.

A more concrete version for younger learners would be to have someone put an object in a paper sack, out of sight of the other players. They then get 20 yes/no questions to guess what is in the sack. For example:

> *T:* I have put something in this sack. Try to guess what it is, using questions that can be answered only with a *yes* or *no.*
> *S1:* Is it round?
> *T:* Yes, it is.
> *S2:* Is it hard?
> *T:* No, it isn't.
> *S3:* Is it a ball?
> *T:* No, it isn't.
> *S4:* Can we eat it?
> *T:* No, you can't.
>   etc.

The person who guesses correctly can be the person to hide the next object. If students are in the early stages of learning to form yes/no questions, you may want to restrict the questions to those with modals and the *be* verb. Also, if they are beginners, they might need some help from you in accurately forming the questions they want to ask.

b. Another guessing game that encourages the use of yes/no questions is "What's My Line?", in which members of the class select occupations for themselves, and the rest of the class must try to guess the occupation.

c. A similar game is one in which students play "Who Am I?", where a class member pretends to be a well-known contemporary or historical figure. The other members of the class ask yes/no questions to guess the identity of the figure.

4. Form. Each student is given an assignment on a card. The assignment is to find someone in the class who is characterized by the particular trait written on the card. For example, one card might say, "Find someone who can play the drums." Another might say, "Find someone who is a good cook." Students must ask each other yes/no questions to find at least one person in the class for whom the trait is true.

5. Form. Getting students to ask each other questions about their native countries, academic majors, hobbies, favorite foods, and so on can be useful for practicing questions and helping students to get to know one another better. One of the techniques of the method "Suggestopedia" that encourages fluency is to have a student pose a question and then toss a ball to another student. That student catches the ball, answers the question, poses another question, and tosses the ball to a third student.

> *S1:* Are you from Mexico? (tossing the ball to S2)
> *S2:* (catching the ball) No; I am not. I am from Guatemala.
> *S2:* Do you study engineering? (tossing the ball to S3)
> *S3:* (catching the ball) Yes, I do.
> *S3* Do you enjoy disco dancing? (tossing the ball to S4)
> *S4:* (catching the ball) No, I don't.
>   etc.

For students with a low level of proficiency in English, this same activity can be done in a chain-drill form, in which the same question is asked of and answered by every student in the room, one by one, thereby creating a chain; for example:

> *S1:* Are you from Mexico?
> *S2:* No. I'm not. I am from Guatemala.
> *S2:* Are you from Vietnam?
> *S3:* No, I'm not. I am from Laos.
> *S3:* Are you from Morocco?
> *S4:* Yes, I am.
> etc.

6. Form. Sometimes reciting verse or poetry can be a pleasant way to practice the intonation and grammatical form of yes/no questions. Of course, the verse would have to be something that could be made comprehensible to students. Several of Christina Rossetti's poems make repeated use of yes/no questions. They lend themselves to reading aloud in pairs or groups—one can ask the question, the other can answer it.

7. Meaning. To give students the necessary practice in asking and answering negative yes/no questions as native speakers of English do (responding to the presupposition, not the form), you can tell students a short story twice. During the second telling, change a few of the details. The students' task is to listen to the story intently and, after you have told it twice, to use focused negative yes/no questions to ask about details in the second telling that did not coincide with the first. For instance:

(First story) *T:* A man walked out the front door and tripped over his son's wagon. He scolded his son and told him to put the wagon in the garage. The boy did this. A while later, the man went into the garage and tripped over his son's wagon again.

(Second story) *T:* A man walked out the back door and tipped over his son's bicycle. He scolded his son and told him to put the bicycle in the shed. The boy did this. A week later, the man went into the shed and tipped over his son's bicycle again.

> *S1:* Wasn't it the *back* door?
> *T:* Yes, it was.
> *S2:* Wasn't it a *wagon*?
> *T:* Yes, it was.
> *S3:* Didn't the father *trip* over the wagon?
> *T:* Yes. he did.
> *S4:* Wasn't it a *day* later?
> *T:* No, it wasn't.
> etc.

Students will need to make up and tell their own versions of two stories to receive practice in answering the focused negative yes/no questions of their classmates.

8. Use. To give students practice in using yes/no questions in making polite requests, have students write down five requests they would like to make. They should each then make the request of another student in the class. Only if the request is in a polite form, should the second student agree to comply with the request. For example:

> *S1:* Hey, Pablo, can I have some scrap paper?
> *S2:* Sorry. No.
> *S1:* Pablo, could I borrow some scrap paper, please?
> *S2:* Sure. Here's some.

EXERCISES

Test your understanding of what has been presented.

1. Provide original example sentences that illustrate the following concepts.
   - **a.** unmarked yes/no question
   - **b.** negative yes/no question
   - **c.** *some* in a yes/no question
   - **d.** uncontracted negative yes/no question
   - **e.** yes/no question with *do*
   - **f.** uninverted question
   - **g.** focused yes-no question
   - **h.** standard short-form answer
   - **i.** formulaic short answer
   - **j.** yes/no question with phrasal modal and *do*
   - **k.** echo question (showing surprise)
   - **l.** elliptical yes/no question
   - **m.** nonclausal question as a next turn repair initiator

2. Give the basic structures and state which mapping rules apply to derive the following questions:
   - **a.** Was she in class yesterday?
   - **b.** Did he write the letter?
   - **c.** Will her brother come to the party?
   - **d.** Have you been living in Tampa?

3. What rules have been violated as the following questions were formed?
   - **a.** *Do she went?
   - **b.** *Could have he gone?
   - **c.** *Runs he fast?
   - **d.** *Do they be happy?

4. What do the *not* placement rule and the subject-operator inversion rule have in common?

Test your ability to apply what you know.

5. If your students produce the following questions, what errors have they made? How will you make them aware of the errors, and what exercises will you prepare to correct them?
   - **a.** *Saw you the movie?
   - **b.** *Did you threw the ball?
   - **c.** *Is not she intelligent?
   - **d.** Do you like ice cream? *Yes, I like.

6. Negative yes/no questions present an interesting problem with regard to the application of mapping rules. Draw the tree for the first question below. Which order of the three rules (*not* placement, *not* contraction, subject-operator inversion) works to generate the first two questions—but not the third—as acceptable negative yes/no question forms in English?

   > Can't you wait?
   > Can you not wait?
   > *Can not you wait?

7. You have a student who never inverts yes/no questions but simply uses an uninverted question with question intonation. When you tell him that he should invert, he replies that he often hears native speakers use uninverted questions. What would you say to this student?

8. An old joke arises from the fact that yes/no questions can serve more than one function. A wants to know the time and sees that B is wearing a wristwatch.

   > A: Do you have a watch?
   > B. Yes. (and keeps on walking)

   Explain the misunderstanding.

BIBLIOGRAPHY

References

Bevington, G. (1979). "On Being a Negative ESL Teacher." *TESOL Newsletter* 13:2, 20–22.

Bolinger, D. (1978). "Yes/No Questions Are *Not* Alternative Questions." In H. Hiz (ed.), *Questions*. Dordrecht: Reidel.

Chalker, S. (1984). *Current English Grammar*. London: Macmillan.

Cruttenden, A. (1986). *Intonation*. Cambridge: Cambridge University Press.

Givón, T. (1993). *English Grammar: A Function-Based Approach* (vol. 2). Philadelphia: John Benjamins.

Hatch, E., and J. Wagner-Gough (1976). "Explaining Sequence and Variation in Second Language Acquisition." *Language Learning*, Special Issue No. 4, 39–57.

Kontra, M. (1981). "On English Negative Interrogatives." In J. E. Copeland and P. W. Davis (eds.), *The Seventh Lacus Forum 1980*. Columbia, S.C.: Hornbeam Press.

Kontra, M. (1993). "Do Not People Say Such Things?" In V. Becker Makkai (ed.), *The Twentieth Lacus Forum 1993*. Chapel Hill, N.C.: The University of North Carolina.

Quirk, R., S. Greenbaum, G. Leech, and J. Svartvik (1985). *A Comprehensive Grammar of the English Language*. London: Longman.

Richards, J. (1977) "Answers to Yes/No Questions." *English Language Teaching Journal* 31:2, 136–141.

Schegloff, M., G. Jefferson, and H. Sacks (1977). "The Preference for Self-Correction in the Organization of Repair in Conversation." *Language* 53:2, 361–382.

Todeva, E. (1991). "Language Change Factors in a Broader Perspective." In N. Boretzki, W. Enninger, B. Jebing, Th. Stolz (eds.), *Sprachwandel und seine Prizipien*. Bochum: Universitatsverlag Dr. N. Brochmeyer, 71–85.

Ultan, R. (1978). "Some General Characteristics of Interrogative Systems." In J. Greenberg (ed.), *Universals of Human Language* (vol. 4). Stanford: Stanford University Press.

VanderBrook, S., K. Schlue, and C. Campbell (1980). "Discourse and Second Language Acquisition of Yes-No Questions." In D. Larsen-Freeman (ed.), *Discourse Analysis in Second Language Research*. Rowley, Mass.: Newbury House, 56–74.

Weber, E. (1989). "Varieties of Questions in English Conversation: A Study of Morphosyntax in Declarative and Nonclausal Forms." Unpublished Ph.D. Dissertation, UCLA.

Williams, J. (1989). "Yes/No Questions in ESL Textbooks and Classrooms." *IDEAL* 4, 149–156.

Williams, J. (1990). "Another Look at Yes/No Questions: Native Speakers and Nonnative Speakers." *Applied Linguistics*, 11:2, 159–182.

Winn-Bell Olsen, J. (1980). "In Search of Y/N S-AUX: A Study of Answers to Yes-No Questions in English." Paper presented at the 6th Annual Meeting of the Berkeley Linguistics Society, February.

Suggestions for further reading

For discussion of interrogatives in other languages, see:
Chisolm, W. (ed.) (1984). *Interrogativity*. Philadelphia: John Benjamins.

For a functional classification of questions, see:
Tsui, A. (1992). "A Functional Description of Questions." In M. Coulthard (ed.), *Advances in Spoken Discourse Analysis*. London: Routledge, 89–110.

For pedagogical exercises, see:

Danielson, D., and P. Porter (1990). *Using English: Your Second Language* (2d ed.). Englewood Cliffs, N.J.: Prentice-Hall, ch. 4.

Riggenbach, H., and V. Samuda (1997). *Grammar Dimension: Form, Meaning, and Use.* Book 2 (2d ed.). Boston, Mass.: Heinle & Heinle.

ENDNOTES

1. English does this as well in its "statement-form," or uninverted, question (*"You're a teacher?"*). However, such questions serve a different purpose than do ordinary unmarked yes/no questions in English. This is discussed in the portion of this chapter devoted to meaning.

2. It can be done, though, in British English with the main verb *have* as in *Have you the time?* and in some lexicalized sentence stems in American English, such as, *Have you any idea . . . ?*

3. It should be acknowledged that there is no *unique* question intonation, although some tones may be more common in questions than others (Cruttenden 1986:59).

4. Of the 637 questions in Weber's data, 108 were uninverted forms and 153 were nonclausal forms.

Chapter 12

IMPERATIVES

INTRODUCTION

In Chapter 2 we established the fact that there are three main moods for English sentences: declarative (sometimes called indicative), interrogative, and imperative. We have examined aspects of the first two moods when dealing with basic word order in declarative sentences (Chapter 5) and with yes/no questions (Chapter 11). Obviously, there is a great deal more to say about qualities of these two main sentence moods; however, before we proceed to do this, it is time to introduce the final main sentence mood, that of the imperative. In Chapter 2 we also made the point that there are a number of syntactic ways that the communicative function of "getting someone to do something" can be accomplished; nevertheless, the sentence type that is normally associated with the imperative mood is the command.

When we examine commands such as

Go away.   Be quiet.

we are struck by the fact that there is no obvious (overt) subject noun phrase. Such sentences would seem to be in violation of one of our fundamental phrase structure rules, which indicates that every English sentence must have both a subject (i.e., NP) and a predicate (i.e., everything that follows the subject NP in a sentence—AUX VP (Advl):

S → SUBJ PRED

Another idiosyncrasy of imperatives is that they are tenseless and take no modals. Notice that to capture this fact, our phrase structure rule for the auxiliary offers a choice between tense/modal and -imper:

$$\text{AUX} \rightarrow \left\{ \begin{matrix} \left\{ \begin{matrix} T \\ M \end{matrix} \right\} \text{(pm) (-perf) (-prog)} \\ \text{-imper} \end{matrix} \right\}$$

This rule also indicates that -imper occurs with no pm, -perf, or -prog. While this is true for the most part, it is possible, though rare, to have an imperative with progressive aspect:

Be watching tomorrow night for the conclusion to the show.

We must also address the question, "When is it appropriate to use imperatives in English?" The traditional answer to this question offered in many ESL/EFL texts is that imperatives are used when there is a status difference between the speaker and listener such that the speaker has the power to order or command the listener to do something. For example, the military officer is often portrayed as "barking commands" at service personnel of lesser rank, using imperatives such as "Listen up!"

Given our attempt in this teacher's text to be comprehensive, we intend to show that the status difference between speaker and listener is only one of the factors that plays a role in determining when imperatives are used. The late rock idol Elvis Presley's plea to "Love me tender" seems a far cry from a military bark; nonetheless, his plea and the military order above share a common syntactic form. Sociolinguistic factors governing use of imperatives are investigated in the use section, which follows our analysis of their form and meaning.

THE FORM OF IMPERATIVES

You have just seen how the fact that imperatives are subjectless presents us with a dilemma as far as our phrase structure rule for S. We could, of course, modify our phrase structure rule for S by putting parentheses around the SUBJ, thus signifying its optionality. However, our intuition tells us that a subject actually does underlie imperative sentences; it simply does not usually surface.[1]

Traditional grammarians have referred to the underlying subject of imperative sentences as the "understood *you.*" In other words, the subject of an unmarked form of an imperative is the second person singular or plural subject pronoun, *you.*

(You) listen up!

While such an explanation is intuitively satisfying, we can go even further and use syntactic evidence to corroborate the traditional grammarians' assertion that an understood *you* is the subject of an imperative. Athough we do not fully examine reflexive pronouns until Chapter 16, suffice it to say here that the object of a reflexive verb must be identical in reference to the subject of the same sentence; that is, in the following sentence, *Ann* and the reflexive pronoun *herself* are co-referential—they refer to the same person:

Ann prided *herself* on her accomplishments.

Now notice the form of the reflexive pronoun when it occurs in object position in an imperative.

Watch yourself!　Watch yourselves!

If basic structure subjects other than second person singular or plural were possible in imperative sentences, the following imperatives would also be acceptable; however, they are not:

*Watch myself!　*Watch itself!
*Watch himself!　*Watch ourselves!
*Watch herself!　*Watch themselves!

Thus, this syntactic evidence supports our intuition that the subject of imperative sentences is *you.* Here is the tree for *Be quiet!* to illustrate this point.

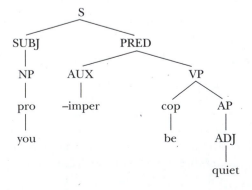

The tree illustrates another point we should make about the form of imperatives. Recall that our phrase structure rule draws a sharp distinction between imperative and nonimperative sentences based on the contention stated earlier in this chapter that imperative sentences are "tenseless." The strongest evidence in favor of this analysis are those imperatives formed with the copula *be*:

> You be quiet!   Be on time!

If these sentences had a "present tense" instead of an -imper auxiliary in their basic structure, we would expect to find the second person form of the *be* verb, *are*, after subject-verb agreement and morphological rules have applied:

> output of base: you pres be quiet
> copy s/t: you pres [+2+sg] be quiet
> morphology: You are quiet.

Since such strings do not occur as imperatives, we can assume that imperatives do not contain a tensed auxiliary and that the morphology rule joins -imper to the following verb to produce the base, or uninflected, form, i.e., *be*.

Finally, since *you* sometimes is present in an imperative (e.g., *You take care, now*), we need to call upon an optional subject deletion rule to delete the *you* only in derivations where the subject is not present on the surface.

> Be quiet.

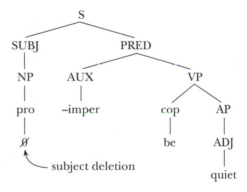

NEGATIVE IMPERATIVES

With *Do*

Negative imperatives are somewhat more complicated than their affirmative counterparts. Three types of negative imperatives occur:

1. Don't you run! (contracted negative; subject present)
2. Don't run! (contracted negative; subject absent)
3. Do not run! (uncontracted negative; subject absent)

A fourth combination, with an uncontracted negative and subject present, does not occur:

4. *Do $\left\{ \begin{array}{l} \text{not you} \\ \text{you not} \end{array} \right\}$ run!

The three grammatical negative imperatives all derive from a common basic structure:

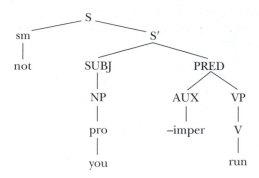

Then, by applying our derivation rules, we can produce the three acceptable forms:[2]

	Sentence 1	Sentence 2	Sentence 3
output of base:	not you -imper run	not you -imper run	not you -imper run
operator addition:	not you -imper do run	not you -imper do run	not you -imper do run
not placement:	you -imper do not run	you -imper do not run	you -imper do not run
not contraction:	you -imper do + n't run	you -imper do + n't run	(does not apply)
subject-operator inversion:	-imper do + n't you run	(does not apply)	(does not apply)
subject deletion:	(does not apply)	-imper do+n't run	-imper do not run
morphology:	Don't you run!	Don't run!	Do not run!

By making sure that the *not* contracts with the *do* before subject-operator inversion applies, the ungrammatical forms in 4 above could never be produced.

With Be

An examination of the following set of sentences reveals that the rule of *not* placement operates differently in negative imperatives from the way it operates in negative declarative sentences and in interrogatives.

5. Don't you be late!
6. Don't be late!
7. Do not be late!

8. *Do $\left\{ \begin{array}{l} \text{not you} \\ \text{you not} \end{array} \right\}$ be late.

Even when the copula *be* is the main verb, there is a *do* verb. This is a departure from our earlier observation in the chapter on negatives and again in the one on yes/no questions —that English declarative sentences treat copula *be* as an operator, and therefore, sentences with copula *be* do not require the addition of the *do* operator to carry the tense.[3] With negative imperatives, the operator-addition rule must apply because the -imper auxiliary cannot combine with the particle *not*. It must attach to an operator, so the operator *do* is needed to fill this void. Here's an example of a tree and the derivation of the sentence in 6 above:

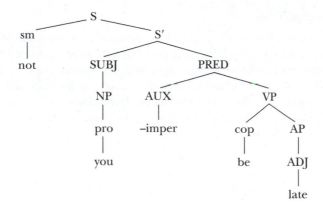

With operator addition:

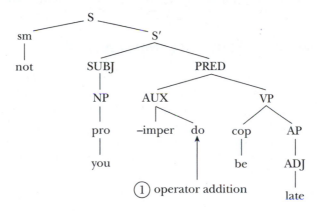

With *not* placement, *not* contraction and subject deletion:

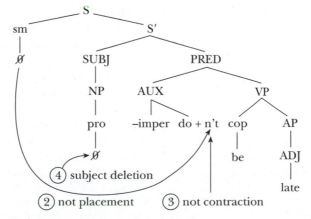

The related imperative with an uncontracted *not* particle (i.e., 7, "Do not be late!") would share the set of rules above except that the optional rule for *not* contraction would be omitted. To produce 5, subject-operator inversion would take place after *not* contraction. Note that if the *not* is uncontracted, then the *you* must be omitted, or else the ungrammatical forms found in 8 would result.

A final observation is that it is possible to produce a negative imperative by using the preverbal adverb of frequency, "never," in initial position without the *do* verb:

Never be late again!   (Don't you ever be late again!)

ELLIPTICAL IMPERATIVES

As in other structures you have seen, imperatives can be used in truncated fashion in normal conversational interaction. Kuehn (1993) reported that in three hours of transcribed conversation among employees and between the supervisor and employees in a dishwashing room of a small-town college, of the 25 imperatives that occurred, fewer than half (11) were in their full form. In the 14 others, verbs or objects were deleted. Deletion was especially prevalent where an object was being held or something was being demonstrated.

Kuehn offers the following examples:

Trays!   (Put your trays on the conveyor belt.)
These two.   (Put these two trays together.)
Switch!   (Switch garbage disposal covers with me.)

As Kuehn points out, certainly for workers in a noisy work environment with a fairly standard work routine, even elliptical imperatives with such deletions would be quite clear.

MEANING AND THE ENGLISH IMPERATIVE

Earlier, we said that imperatives are commands, also known as directives, whose function is to get someone to do something. It is time now to revisit the question of who that someone is. We have made the case for imperatives having second person subjects; that is, the command is directed at the "you" present in the environment. There are, however, several other addressees of imperatives. In addition, we want to be specific about when and when not to use *you* in English imperatives. These issues seem to us to relate more to meaning than to use, although the line between the two is admittedly more permeable here than elsewhere.

YOU: ITS RETENTION AND ITS DELETION

As you have seen, when we use an imperative without a subject, we might be addressing one or more persons. If we want to make it clear that we are speaking to someone in particular, we can add an unstressed *you* (e.g., *You wait here for a moment*). For the same reason, the *you* is also often retained when one is giving instructions to a particular child and wants to be explicit, such as saying, "You come here" (with a gesture to indicate which child). To further reduce ambiguity, a vocative, here the addressee's name, can also be used before the imperative, such as, "Mr. Holmes, you sit over there." Notice that *you* is still the subject of this imperative, with *Mr. Holmes* having the distinctive rising-falling intonation of English vocatives. It is also possible to move the vocative to the end of the sentence, "You sit there, Mr. Holmes." Unlike these other examples, if the *you* subject is being stressed, annoyance is conveyed; for example: "*You* cut that out!"

DIFFUSE IMPERATIVES

Related to the issue of addressee is a special kind of imperative called the *diffuse imperative.* Diffuse imperatives are directed at anyone and everyone who is present:

Somebody open the door.   (*somebody* = one of you here)
Don't anybody move!   (*not* + *anybody* = none of you here)

Note that diffuse imperatives would be inappropriate if two people were conversing. A speaker alone, however, who is addressing an imaginary or wished-for audience can use a diffuse imperative (e.g., "Somebody help me!"). Note that diffuse imperatives are different from more specific imperatives that begin with a vocative, the name of the person being addressed:

> Mac, open the door.

In such cases a *you* can also occur, as we have just seen:

> Mac, you open the door.

However, this cannot be done with diffuse imperatives because their subjects are indefinite third person pronouns, not the definite second person pronoun:

> *Somebody, you open the door.

LET'S

In addition to the imperatives above, some grammarians describe an *inclusive imperative,* an imperative that includes the speaker with the addressee(s):

> Let's go to the movies.

And here is its negative form:

> Let's not stay here any longer.
> (or, less likely) Don't let's stay here any longer.

These, of course, function often as suggestions, not commands. They can be seen as functioning more like commands, however, when the *us* is not contracted and the *Let us* is seen as an exhortation to follow the speaker's instructions or to agree with the judgment that the speaker expresses:

> Let us pray.
> Let us never forget the brave men and women who made the ultimate sacrifice.

Finally, another kind of imperative-like sentence that makes use of the *let* but is not inclusive (contains no *us*) is the kind of proclamation that only a deity, a sovereign or an authority figure is allowed to make; that is, the mere fact that such a power or authority would utter the proclamation ensures that what is said will occur:

> Let there be light!   Let the word go forth.

A weaker form of this *let* can mean *may,* as in the following toast:

> Let this be a new start for both of us.

THE USE OF IMPERATIVES

FUNCTION AND FORM

At the risk of redundancy, we once again acknowledge that the form and function link between imperatives and directives is not a categorical one—that is, one can command or, less forcefully, request without using an imperative form:

> Imperative: *Help me, please.*
> Declarative: *I need some help.*
> Interrogative: *Could/Can you give me a hand?*

And, conversely, the following list illustrates some of the functions in addition to commands that imperatives can be used for, depending on the situational context:

Other Uses of Imperatives (in addition to commands)
Offers: *Have another biscuit.*
Suggestions: *Let's go to a movie tonight.*
Requests: *Close the door, please.*
Advice: *Don't forget Mother's Day.*
Directions: *Go left at the next corner.*
Prohibitions: *Do not pick the flowers.*
Warnings: *Watch out!*
Procedures: *Add a teaspoon of baking powder to the flour.*
Invitations: *Come in.*
Threats: *Watch your step.*
Wishes: *Have a great day!*

POLITENESS AND THE USE OF THE IMPERATIVES

With regard to the three moods, what advice might we be able to give ESL/EFL students on when to use the imperative mood in giving commands or making requests and when to use other forms? Carrell and Konneker (1981) found considerable agreement among native speakers and learners of English as to which forms were considered the most polite in making requests. The forms varied among three dimensions: sentence mood (declarative, interrogative, and imperative), presence or absence of a modal, and the tense used. Here is their hierarchy of politeness, around which there was considerable native-speaker/nonnative-speaker consensus:

Least Polite (most direct)	Imperative—elliptical	A glass of water.
	Imperative	Give me a glass of water.
	Declarative—no modal (*want/need*)	I want a glass of water.
	Declarative—historically present tense modal[4]	I'll have a glass of water.
	Declarative—historically past tense modal	I'd like a glass of water.
	Interrogative—no modal	Do you have a glass of water?
	Interrogative—historically present tense modal	Can you give me a glass of water?
Most Polite (least direct)	Interrogative—historically past tense modal	Could you give me a glass of water?

According to the subjects in Carrell and Konnecker's study, sentence mood contributes the most to the order of the politeness hierarchy: interrogative—most polite; declarative—next most polite; imperative—least polite. Presence of modals contributes next to politeness; modals don't add much to the politeness of the already-very-polite interrogative, but they do contribute more to the politeness of the not-as-polite declarative. Finally, if the modal is in historically past tense, this adds a small additional degree of politeness.

Increasing the politeness

While Carrell and Konnecker did not explicitly examine the politeness contribution of *please*, it could be noted that the effect of adding *please* to an imperative does contribute to its being more polite. Compare, for example,

> Give me a glass of water.
> *versus*
> Please give me a glass of water. *or* Give me a glass of water, please.

Notice that if there is a *you* subject, the addiction of *please* seems odd:

> *Please you give me a glass of water.
> ?You please give me a glass of water.
> ?You give me a glass of water please.

Kindly can also be used to make an imperative more polite.

> Kindly hand me the wrench.

Another way to enhance the politeness of imperatives when they are used as offers, wishes, or invitations is to use the *do* auxiliary verb, which makes the wish or offer more emphatic:

> Have a good time.   Come in.
> Do have a good time.   Do come in.

In contrast to polite imperatives with *please*, imperatives with *just* adds affect that can be either negative, as in *Just (you) wait and see*, or positive, as in *Just be patient; everything will work out.*

On Politeness and Rudeness

To provide some balance here, we must also acknowledge that although we want to help our students to be as polite in English as they want to be, we do not want to give ESL/EFL students the impression that they should *always* opt for the most polite form possible. Beebe (1996P), for instance, advises teaching students how to be rude so that they can deal with people appropriately when the situation calls for it—for instance, when they feel they are being taken advantage of. Moreover, undue politeness can have a distancing effect of its own. Perhaps the rule of thumb here should be the principle that Ervin-Tripp (1982) laid out with respect to the use of imperatives. It is not so much that a power differential between speaker and listener conditions the use of an imperative; it is more the case that imperatives are used when "cooperation is assumed." For example, it can be assumed that a private in the army will cooperate with an officer; accordingly, an imperative is appropriate. If the cooperation of one's peers can be assumed, imperatives are also appropriate. For instance, telling someone to "Pass the catsup" at the dinner table is perfectly acceptable because there is no reason to assume lack of cooperation. Of course, the use of *please* is almost always appropriate (as parents are forever telling their children). To cite another example, when giving a warning, such as *Watch out!*, cooperation can certainly be assumed. And we would prefer to receive such a warning in the shortest possible form rather than a longer one with all the politeness markers intact. Wouldn't you?

CONCLUSION

Learning the form, meaning, and use of the imperative mood is challenging for ESL/EFL students. Except for negative imperatives, form is perhaps less challenging because students need not concern themselves about typical verb morphological problems such as tense and subject-verb agreement. Nevertheless, the subtle distinctions among English imperatives require that students receive practice in using their forms appropriately. Giving students help with understanding commands might be important as well. Considering the variety of forms that are used to give a command, it is not surprising that nonnative speakers struggle to understand them. Kuehn (1993) cites the example of the nonnative speaker of English who did not recognize "Can you take this and load it?" as a command from his supervisor and who replied that he didn't know how. While the worker was no doubt speaking honestly, Kuehn notes that the supervisor's question was not a yes/no question, as this young and inexperienced employee seemed to think it was, nor was it a polite request, as demonstrated by the fact that the supervisor next said, "Better learn!"

Regarding use, helping students be as polite as they want to be without appearing obsequious or standoffish is no easy feat. Whatever help in the form of direct instruction or feedback in the appropriate use of the imperative that ESL/EFL teachers can provide their students will be valuable.

TEACHING SUGGESTIONS

1. Form. James Asher (1977) has developed a methodology for teaching a second language that he calls "Total Physical Response." Within this methodology, the second language learner carries out commands issued solely in imperative form in the target language by the teacher. By gradually building up a syntactic and lexical repertoire, the learner is increasingly able to respond appropriately. We find that when students act out commands as a first step in learning imperatives, it helps them associate the syntactic pattern with action. Commands such as "Stand up," "Turn around," "Turn left," "Turn right," "Point to the board," "Sit down," and so on could be taught from the very earliest days of instruction. Later, to get practice in production, students can give commands with which the teacher and the other students are asked to comply.

2. Form. For practice in using both affirmative and negative imperatives, the class can play an adaptation of the children's game "Simon Says," in which students have to do whatever is commanded unless the negative is present (note that the pace must be quick in order to make this a bit of a challenge). Here's an example:

> T: Simon says, "Stand up." (Students stand up.)
>
> T: Simon says, "Turn around." (Students turn around.)
>
> T: Simon says, "Don't sit down."

Anyone who sits down after this third command is eliminated from the game, which continues until the class has one or two "winners" remaining.

This game can also give students practice in forming negative imperatives. After students become more proficient in forming negatives, students can lead "Simon Says."

3. Meaning. To practice comprehension and then production of imperatives, the teacher can ask students to follow certain procedures; later, students direct similar procedures. The following steps in an "operation" (a simple, self-contained procedure) are suggested by Pat Moran:

a. The teacher models a chain of commands and accompanying actions that perform an "operation." For example, an operation might be to write and mail a letter. The steps would be to pick up a pen, write a letter, sign the letter, fold the letter, address the envelope, put the letter into the envelope, seal the envelope, put a stamp on the envelope, and mail the letter.

b. The teacher repeats the operation once again, pantomiming the steps and giving the commands.

c. Students then "perform" the operation in response to commands from the teacher.

d. Students give the directions to the teacher.

e. Students give the directions to each other.

4. Use. As we pointed out in this chapter, students will need to learn when a request is being made of them. This is particularly challenging when the syntactic form of the request seems to suggest that some other function is being communicated. To begin to address this challenge, teachers might read a list of sentences (including interrogatives and imperatives) to their students. After each one, students should respond not to the *form*, but to the *function* of the sentence. For example:

> *T:* Felipe, do you have a pen I can use?

Felipe should learn, of course, that this is a request to borrow a pen, not a request for information. Thus, in this exercise, he should offer a pen to the teacher.

> *T:* Miquel, how do you like the weather here in Winnipeg?

Miquel needs to recognize that this is a request for information and respond accordingly—"It's cold."

> *T:* Somebody, turn off the lights.

Here everyone should attempt to comply, or at least those sitting near the light switches.

> *T:* Phiang, should you be chewing gum in class?

Phiang needs to know to take out the gum.

5. Use. To give students practice with polite commands, ask students to pair up, and give each member of each pair a task that he or she will ask the other member of the pair to do. Also assign each a role. For example, in the first pair, A is told that B is her friend and that she wants B to help her with her homework. B is told that she is A's friend and that she would like A to give her a ride home after school.

The pair of students then role-play this simple interaction. Students are told to agree to the other's request only when they are satisfied that the other has been sufficiently polite. For example:

> *A:* Help me with my homework, please.
> *B:* Sorry. I can't.
> *A:* I need some help with my homework.
> *B:* Sorry. I can't.
> *A:* Could you please help me with my homework?
> *B:* All right/Okay/No problem/Certainly/Of course.

Notice that this sort of exercise also gives students practice in responding to the requests that others make.

EXERCISES

Test your understanding of what has been presented.

   1. Provide original example sentences that illustrate the following concepts. Underline the pertinent word(s) in your examples.

   a. imperative
   (i) affirmative
   (ii) negative

b. inclusive imperative

c. diffuse imperative

d. *let* (noninclusive) imperative

e. elliptical imperative

f. *you* retention

g. *you* deletion

h. imperative with *please*

i. emphatic *do* to add politeness

2. Give the basic structures and then state which rules would apply to derive the following sentences:
   a. Take a break.
   b. Don't forget her birthday.
   c. Don't be mad.
   d. You come here.

3. Why are the following sentences ungrammatical?
   a. *She go away.
   b. *Don't angry.
   c. *Leaves the room.
   d. *Do not you take offense.

Test your ability to apply what you know.

4. Review the syntactic arguments for claiming that imperatives are tenseless. Do likewise for the syntactic arguments that underlying imperatives is an understood *you*. See if you can explain these arguments in your own words.

5. As you saw in the chapter on yes/no questions and as Schaffer (1993) points out, a number of different types of sentences in colloquial, spoken English are subjectless, such as the following:

Nice day.	(It's a nice day.)
Going to the party?	(Are you going to the party?)
Got too much work to do.	(I've got too much work to do.)

   What is the difference between these subjectless sentences and the subjectlessness of the imperative in English?

6. Sometimes ESL/EFL teachers have difficulty convincing students to use imperatives because the students feel that they are rude. What would you do to convince your students that imperatives are often appropriate?

7. We have discussed a number of ways through which imperatives can be made more polite. List those we have already mentioned. Then see if you can add any more.

8. Some transformational analyses of the imperative (e.g., Liles 1971) have suggested that the underlying structure of all imperatives contains *will* because *will* often occurs in imperative tags—for example, *Come in, won't you?* The output of the base for *Be quiet* in such an analysis would be *you will be quiet*. One could make both a semantic and a syntactic argument against such an analysis, however. Can you figure out what those arguments are?

BIBLIOGRAPHY

References

Asher, J. (1977). *Learning Another Language through Actions: The Complete Teacher's Guidebook*. Los Gatos, Calif: Sky Oaks Productions.

Beebe, L. (1996). "Loose Language: Pragmatic Strategies for Responding to Rudeness." Paper presented at the New York TESOL Convention, November.

Carrell, P., and B. Konneker (1981). "Politeness: Comparing Native and Nonnative Judgements." *Language Learning* 31, 1:17–30.

Ervin-Tripp, S. (1982). "Ask and It Shall Be Given to You: Children's Requests." In H. Byrnes (ed.), *Georgetown University Round Table on Languages and Linguistics.* Washington, D.C.: Georgetown University Press, 232–245.

Kuehn, K. (1993). "Requests and Commands in the Workplace." A term paper written at the University of Minnesota for Linguistics 5741, winter, 1993.

Liles, B. (1971). *An Introductory Transformational Grammar.* Englewood Cliffs, N. J.: Prentice-Hall.

Schaffer, K. (1993). "Subject omission in Written English."A paper written in partial fulfullment of the requirements for the M.A. degree in Linguistics at the University of Minnesota, June 10, 1993.

Suggestions for further reading

For a good summary and evaluation of all the various linguistic analyses that have been proposed to account for imperative sentences, see this source:

Stockwell, R., P. Schachter, and B. Partee (1973). *The Major Syntactic Structures of English.* New York: Holt, Rinehart and Winston, 663–670.

For additional ideas on using "operations" to practice imperatives, see:

Nelson, G., and T. Winters (1980). *ESL Operations: Techniques for Learning While Doing.* Rowley, Mass: Newbury House.

For classroom exercises on recognizing appropriate commands and requests, see:

Badalamenti, V., and C. Henner Stanchina (1997). *Grammar Dimensions: Form, Meaning, and Use.* Book 1 (2d ed.). Boston, Mass: Heinle & Heinle.

Danielson, D., and P. Porter (with R. Hayden) (1990). *Using English: Your Second Language* (2d ed.). Englewood Cliffs, N.J.: Prentice-Hall Regents, 82–85.

ENDNOTES

1. In the meaning section we discuss the conditions for its appearance.

2. We use three different notations to show derivations in this book. One is to show how trees are changed by the application of mapping rules (as you saw with *Be quiet* after subject deletion). A second is to simply mention the mapping rules that apply, and a third is to use a line-by-line list of the various rules, as we do in what follows. We do this in order to accommodate readers' different learning styles.

3. Notice that the copula *be* used in affirmative imperatives is not really stative because here it means something like "become" (e.g., *Be strong*) or "act like" (e.g., *Be a dear and get me something to drink*). We cannot use copula *be* with its stative meaning in imperatives (e.g., **Be thin*). Negative imperatives with *be* are less limited and therefore more common (e.g., *Don't be mad*). Other normally stative verbs can be used in the imperative mood when they have a more dynamic meaning, such as *Love it or leave it.*

4. Carrell and Konnecker did not test for any distinction among the modal verbs themselves, since the hierarchy was based on syntactic rather than semantic markers. For the same reason, the use of *please* and other lexical distinctions were also omitted from the hierarchy.

13

WH-QUESTIONS

INTRODUCTION

Wh-questions are very important structures for ESL/EFL students. They are used to request specific information, so the need to use them arises often. For instance, *wh*-questions are used in social interaction (*What's your name?*), for getting directions (*Where's the post office?*), in seeking explanations (*Why is the plane late?*), for eliciting vocabulary (*What's this?*), and so forth. Notice that while yes/no questions query an entire proposition, *wh*-questions are used when the speaker is missing one specific piece of information.

> *Did someone walk the dog?* (general query about the truth of the proposition)
> *Who walked the dog?* (speaker is asking for the name of the person who walked the dog)

The nature of the missing piece of information conditions the selection of the question word, which most often, although not always, begins with *wh*.

Second language acquisition research tells us that English *wh*-questions, despite their usefulness, are not acquired especially early. This is presumably due to their variety and to the fact that English has two basic structures for *wh*-questions—one requiring inversion and one not. Thus, students struggle with inversion, and errors such as **Where you are going?* are common even at intermediate stages of acquisition.

It is also true, however, that *wh*-questions sometimes appear accurately in the interlanguage of language learners long before the learners have mastered the syntactic rules for their formation, presumably because learners have memorized frequently occurring question forms as lexicalized units (e.g., *How are you? Where are you from?*). Because of their usefulness and their frequency, we feel *wh*-questions should be taught from the very beginning of instruction, even if holophrastically at first.

THE FORM OF WH-QUESTIONS

As we stated above, there are really two fundamental issues to be aware of regarding the form of *wh*-questions. The first has to do with the variety of constituents that can be queried with *wh*-questions. The second has to do with the two basic word orders for unmarked *wh*-questions.

VARIETY OF CONSTITUENTS

Consider the following sentence:

> Lee wrote an angry memo to his boss before he quit.

A variety of constituents can be queried in a *wh*-question:

Subject NP: *Who wrote an angry memo to his boss before he quit? (Lee)*
Object NP: *What did Lee write to his boss before he quit? (an angry memo)*
Object of the prep.: *To whom did Lee write an angry memo before he quit?(his boss)*

or

Who(m) did Lee write an angry memo to before he quit? (his boss)
Verb phrase: *What did Lee do before he quit? (He wrote an angry memo to his boss.)*
Determiner: *Whose boss did Lee write an angry memo to before he quit? (his boss)*
Adjective: *What kind of memo did Lee write? (an angry memo)*
Adverbial: *When did Lee write the angry memo to his boss? (before he quit)*

As can be seen, the scope of what is being queried can range widely—from a whole verb phrase, for instance, to part of a noun phrase (as small as a possessive determiner, for example). The focus of inquiry in a *wh*-question is narrower than that of a yes/no question, however. In fact, we might almost say that *wh*-questions are statements with an information gap. The fact that English *wh*-questions have the same intonation pattern as statements supports this contention.

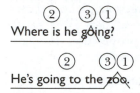

Underlying a *wh*-question is the assumption that some event/action has taken place or some state of affairs exists. The proposition expressing this assumption forms the basis for the tree diagram. For example, the tree structure for a question where the information gap is represented by the subject is as follows, with the Q marked *wh* to reflect its more limited scope.

Who wrote a memo to his boss before he quit?

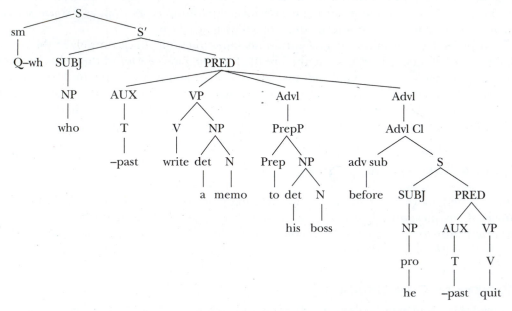

Here's another one. The information gap for this question exists in the object NP.

What did Lee write to his boss before he quit?

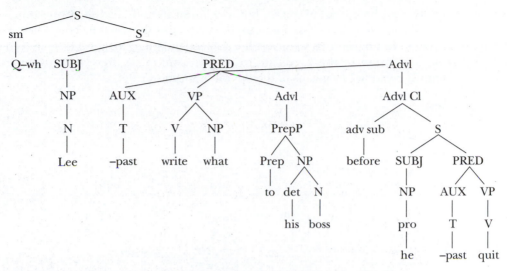

SUBJECT *WH*-QUESTIONS VERSUS PREDICATE *WH*-QUESTIONS

Notice the fundamental difference between the two previous example questions. The derivation of the first one is straightforward. Since it is the subject that is being queried, and since the subject is already in initial position in a sentence, only the rules to copy subject person and number on tense, and morphology are needed to derive the surface structure.

> Who wrote a memo to his boss before he quit?

> output of base: who -past write a memo to his boss before he -past quit
> copy s/t: who -past [+ 3, + sg] write a memo to his boss before he -past [+ 3, + sg] quit
> morphology: Who wrote a memo to his boss before he quit?

It is a different story with the second question, where it is the object NP that is being queried. In this tree, we see that the information gap is in the predicate; thus, the *wh*-question word is not in the position it normally occupies in English. In order to deal with this matter, we will have to move the *wh*-question word to the front of the sentence, applying the derivation rule of *wh*-fronting.

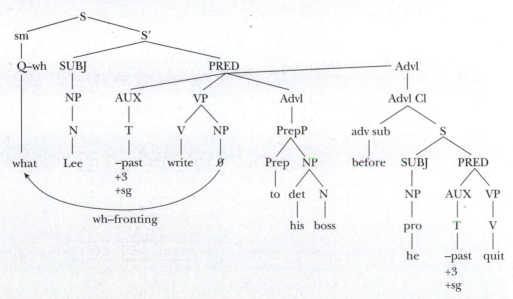

We cannot apply morphology at this point, however. You will note that every question we generated above, save the subject-based *wh*-question, contains the *do* verb. This is because of the requirement in English that we invert the subject and operator if we have moved a *wh*-word from a position in the predicate to initial position. If there is no operator present, one must be added by means of the operator addition rule.

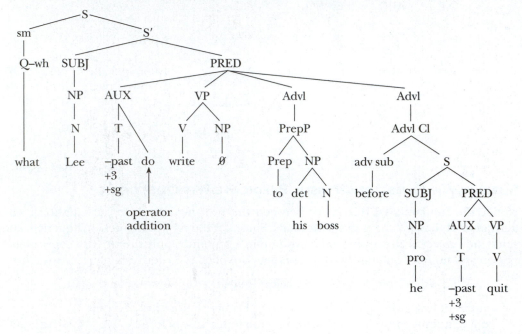

Then, subject and operator can be inverted:

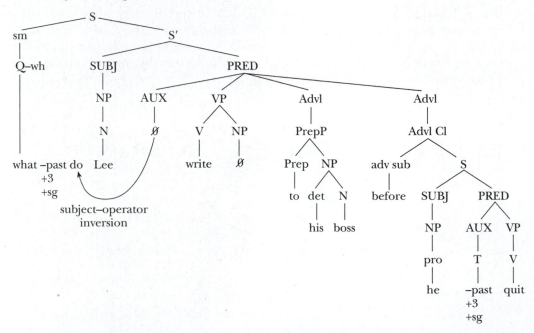

Here's another example of a derivation where the missing information occurs in the predicate position in the underlying proposition—the adverbial of time is being queried:

When did Lee write a memo to his boss?

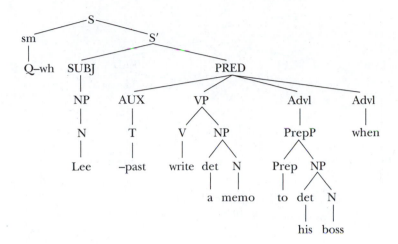

With copy s/t, *wh*-fronting, operator addition, and subject-operator inversion, this is how the tree would look:

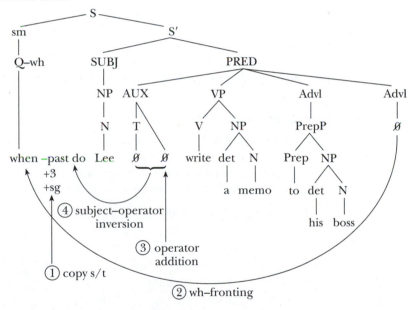

Here is the order of the mapping rules:

output of base: Q -wh Lee -past write a memo to his boss when

copy s/t: Q -wh Lee -past [+ 3 + sg] write a memo to his boss when

wh-fronting: when Lee -past [+ 3 + sg] write a memo to his boss

operator addition: when Lee -past [+ 3 + sg] do write a memo to his boss

subject-operator inversion: when -past [+ 3 + sg] do Lee write a memo to his boss

morphology: When did Lee write a memo to his boss?

Of course, if an auxiliary verb is present, then it will move when subject-operator inversion is applied. It will carry the tense, and operator addition will be unnecessary.

Where are you going?

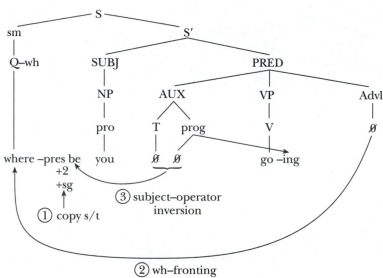

In sum, then, *wh*-questions in which some constituent in the subject is being queried are simpler syntactically than those in which something in the predicate is being queried. The former requires merely selecting the appropriate *wh*-question word (see below), given the inquiry focus. The latter involves the additional operations of fronting the *wh*-word, inverting the subject and operator, and adding the operator *do* if no other operator is present.

SPECIAL CASES INVOLVING *WH*-FRONTING

The *wh*-fronting rule introduced above is a rule that has some special cases and exceptions. One such case involves determiners and intensifiers. If a determiner or intensifier is the focus of a *wh*-question word, the consitutent it modifies must be moved to the front of the string along with the determiner or intensifier. This can be seen in the following question:

Whose boss did Lee write the memo to?

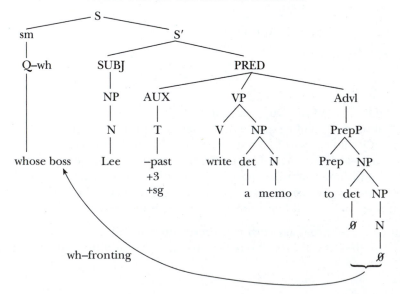

Because it is the possessive determiner that is being queried, the determiner and the constituent it modifies (here, the noun head *boss*) must be moved to the front of the sentence with *wh*-fronting.

The same holds true when it is an intensifier that is being queried:

How diligently had Lee worked at the firm?

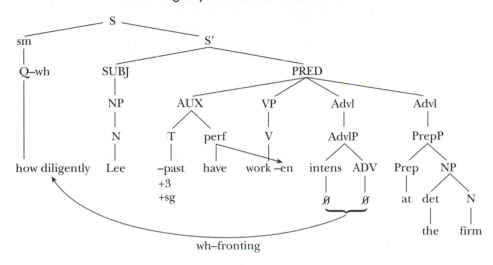

Diligently moves along with the intensifier being queried, i.e., *how*, through *wh*-fronting. Notice also in this question that there is no need for operator addition since the auxiliary verb *have* is there to serve as operator for subject-operator inversion.

Another special case exists when the object of the preposition is the unknown element. When *wh*-fronting is applied, the preposition may either be left behind or be moved up to the front of the string along with the NP. While this choice is syntactically optional, you will note a difference in register depending on its application, with the first option being more formal than the second:

> To whom did Lee write an angry memo before he quit?
> Who(m) did Lee write an angry memo to before he quit?

Finally, we occasionally encounter a *wh*-question where the question word is the object of a preposition within another prepositional phrase:

> By virtue of what authority did Lee do that?

In such a case, the entire prepositional complex must be fronted; the preposition *of* or the words *by virtue of* cannot be left behind when *wh*-fronting takes place.

WH-QUESTIONS WITH THE COPULA BE

Before concluding our analysis of major *wh*-question types, let us also consider this example:

> What is that object?

Some of you may think at first that the subject NP is being questioned. However, you should ask yourselves what the underlying proposition is—that is, whether it more closely resembles proposition a or b:

> a. That object is a stethoscope.   b. A stethoscope is that object.

The answer of course is a; the predicate noun, not the subject noun, is being questioned. The correct basic structure for this question is:

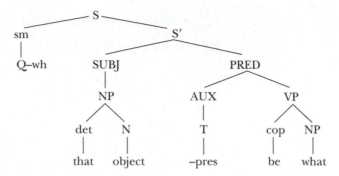

There is no need for operator addition for we have seen that the copula *be* can serve as an operator. Thus with copy s/t, *wh*-fronting, and subject-operator inversion we get:

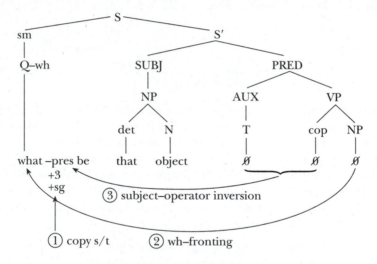

Here is the list of mapping rules:

output of base: Q -wh that object -pres be what
copy s/t: Q -wh that object -pres [+ 3 + sg] be what
wh-fronting: what that object -pres [+ 3 + sg] be
subject-operator inversion: what -pres [+ 3 + sg] be that object
morphology: What is that object?

The lesson here is that one must always fully reconstruct the underlying proposition when analyzing the meaning and derivation of a *wh*-question.

THE MEANING OF *WH*-QUESTIONS

CHOOSING A *WH*-QUESTION WORD

One of the areas concerning meaning is one's choice of a question word. The determination is really a lexical choice which involves selecting the appropriate *wh*-question word depending on the semantic character of the inquiry focus. The following is an inventory of common *wh*-words and their syntactic/semantic correspondences:

Subject NP [+ human]	→	who	Who did it?
Subject NP [– human]	→	what	What went wrong?
Subject Noun Predicate [+ human]	→	who	Who is that?
Subject Noun Predicate [– human]	→	what	What is that?
Object NP [+ human]	→	who(m)[1]	Who(m) did you tell?
			To whom did you tell the story?
Object NP [–human]	→	what	What did she say?
det [possessive]	→	whose + NP	Whose idea was it?
det [demonstrative]	→	{ which + NP / what + NP }	Which excuse did they give? / What alibi did they use?
det [quantifier; – count]	→	how much + (NP)	How much (money) did they get?
det [quantifier; + count]	→	how many + (NP)	How many thieves were there?
det [quantifier] + measure word[2]	→	how long	How long did it take them?
ADJ [quality]	→	{ how / what . . . like }	How did they look? / What did they look like?
ADJ [type]	→	what kind of (NP)	What kind of mask did he wear?
ADJ [color, size, nationality]	→	what + NP	What color was it?
intensifier	→	{ how + / how + } ADJ / ADV	How calm did they seem? / How fast did they work?
VP	→	what . . . do	What did they do next?
Advl [means]	→	how	How did they get away?
Advl [direction]	→	where	Where did they go?
Advl [position]	→	where	Where did they hide?
Advl [time]	→	when	When were they discovered?
Advl [manner]	→	how	How did she take the news?
Advl [reason]	→	why	Why did they confess?
Advl [purpose]	→	what . . . for	What did they do that for?
Advl [frequency]	→	how often	How often does it end this way?

Several observations need to be made about the list above. First of all, as we said, these are general *wh*-words. It is also possible to ask very specific *wh*-questions about the same semantic domains. For instance, if we want to make a general query about the time of a specific event, we could ask,

> When is the concert?

but we could also ask about the time of a specific event, using more specific *wh*-questions:

> What date is the concert?
> Which day is the concert?
> What time is the concert?

Similarly, we could ask a question about direction using *where*, but we could also ask a more precise question using *which way*:

> Where did they go?
> Which way did they go?

The same is true at the clausal level. We can ask a very general *wh*-question about an event:

> What happened?

Or we can ask more specific questions about the event:

> What did the thieves do?

Or even just about the action—that is, the verb:

> What did the thieves do to the bank teller?

UNINVERTED *WH*-QUESTIONS

As with yes/no questions, it is also possible to have uninverted *wh*-questions. For such *wh*-questions, both *wh*-fronting and subject-operator inversion would be suppressed. Sometimes these are just "echo" questions in which the listener is signaling to the speaker that he or she didn't hear a part of what just was said:

> *A:* I expect to be going to Hawaii for the holidays.
> *B:* You expect to be going where for the holidays?
> *A:* To Hawaii.

Or just the *wh*-question word can be used as a repair to signal that something was not heard (Weber 1989):

> *A:* I expect to be going to Hawaii for the holidays.
> *B:* Where?
> *A:* To Hawaii.

However, if B's reply had been said with pitch above the normal range (especially on *where*), then A would have interpreted B's uninverted question as expressing surprise or disbelief:

> *A:* I am going to Hawaii for the holidays.
> *B:* You're going *where* for the holidays?
> *A:* I know. Lucky me!

It is even possible to mark more than one constituent + Q -wh (e.g., *Who* said *what* to *whom?*) in uninverted *wh*-questions.

EMPHATIC QUESTIONS WITH *EVER*

English speakers use *ever* with *wh*-questions to make them emphatic. Such questions express a variety of emotions:

> Dismay: *Wherever did you get that idea?*
> Admiration: *However did you manage it?*
> Perplexity: *Whatever does she see in him?*

We use *ever* after all *wh*-question words except *which* and *whose,* and we often put heavy stress on it in spoken questions:

> *Wherever* did you pick that up?

NEGATIVE *WH*-QUESTIONS

We have already seen the semantic difference between negative and affirmative yes/no questions. Such can be the case with *wh*-questions as well. Negative questions can be neutral, like affirmative *wh*-questions:

> Who hasn't gotten their assignment back?

However, they can also connote a negative judgment:

> What did John say? (unmarked neutral question)
>
> What didn't John say? (could imply that he talked a great deal or that he withheld
> information)
>
> Why didn't you answer when I called? ⎫ (They accuse the interlocutor of an
> Why haven't I been invited?   ⎭ omission.)
>
> Where didn't you go?   (You seemed to go everywhere.) ⎫ (They comment on the
> What didn't happen?   (Everything seemed to happen.) ⎭ lack of any omission.)

Notice also, as with yes/no questions, there are two acceptable forms of negative *wh*-questions depending on whether *not* has been contracted:

> When isn't it a good time?
> When is it not a good time?

THE USE OF *WH*-QUESTIONS

YES/NO QUESTIONS VERSUS *WH*-QUESTIONS

As mentioned in the introduction, yes/no questions query a whole proposition, and *wh*-questions query a specific part of the proposition. In other words, the pragmatic context for using most *wh*-question words is one in which the speaker already assumes that the listener knows the proposition. If this knowledge cannot be assumed, the speaker would use a yes/no question to establish the proposition. Once this is done, *wh*-questions would be employed to provide specific details:

> A: Did you go to the concert last night?
> B: Yeah.
> A: How was it?

Notice that if A had incorrectly assumed shared knowledge of the proposition, and thus began with a *wh*-question, a communication breakdown might have occurred. Had A assumed too much, this would have necessitated some sort of communicative repair:

> A: How was the concert?
> B: What concert?

SOCIAL USES

Of some pedagogical import is the fact that certain fixed formulaic *wh*-questions serve social functions. These would certainly seem to be candidates for the holophrastic learning of which we spoke in the Introduction. Among them are certain combinations with *how* and *what*:

Introductions: *How do you do? What do you do?*
Greetings: *How are you? How have you been? What's new? What's up? What's happening?*
Eliciting personal reactions: *How was the X?* (e.g., *How was the test?*)

and one with *why*:

Making suggestions: *Why don't you X?* (e.g., *Why don't you ask?*)

A subset of these formulaic questions might be called truncated *wh*-questions (Schonbeck 1982) because they are actually question fragments, which appear to be used for particular functions in informal conversations. While they may not be used exclusively for these functions, the following are common:

Making a suggestion: *How about X?* (e.g., *How about a movie?*)
Responding positively to a suggestion: *Why not?*
Expressing exasperation: *What now?* or *Now what?*
Seeking another's opinion: *How about you?*
Challenging another's opinion: *How come? What for? Since when?*
Expressing perplexity: *What to do?*
Asking for clarification/expansion: *What about it?*

UNINVERTED WH-QUESTIONS

In Chapter 11 we made the point that uninverted questions can seem offensive because they imply a certain level of social familarity. Anecdotal evidence suggests that caution would be in order when using uninverted *wh*-questions as well. One ESL teacher told us that he had taught uninverted *wh*-questions to his students. One of them was called to the dean's office soon thereafter. The dean talked about something he had done recently, and the student asked for clarification with *"You did what?"* The dean told the student that he was being rude by asking the question this way, and the ESL teacher reports that the student returned to class feeling somewhat betrayed!

ELLIPTICAL QUESTIONS

In very informal conversations it is also possible to encounter *wh*-question fragments that focus on the predicate and have a deleted auxiliary, such as these:

Question	Deleted Auxiliary
Where you been hiding?	(have)
What you (Whatcha) doing?	(are)
How we going to (gonna) do that?	(are)

Like the elliptical yes/no questions, these *wh*-questions have auxiliaries that are recoverable from other information in the sentences. In very informal contexts, redundant function words such as auxiliaries tend to be deleted, and other phonological reductions take place.

WHO/WHOM

Earlier, we noted that *who* is the *wh*-question word that queries the subject and *whom* queries the object. While this is prescriptively correct, your ESL/EFL students will encounter *who* being used for both roles. It is common for native speakers of English to use *who* for both when speaking:

> Who asked? (subject focus)
> Who did you tell? (object focus)

However, when the *wh*-question word is querying the object of a preposition, and the preposition has been fronted through *wh*-fronting, *whom* should be used:

> To whom was the message delivered?
> *To who was the message delivered?

DISPLAY QUESTIONS

Teachers and parents/caretakers are fond of using uninverted *wh*-questions with their students or children. Such questions are referred to as display questions in that teachers and caretakers use them to ask students and children to display their knowledge.

> Teacher: So this story is about what?

The teacher already knows the answer to the display question, but uses it as a device to elicit students' response so their comprehension can be checked:

> So you have learned what about *wh*-questions?
> They are used when?
> They are formed how?
> They are different from yes/no questions in which ways?

Display questions can, of course, also take the form of inverted *wh*-questions:

> Teacher: What is the capital of Virginia?

and this is the common form of display questions used in writing conferences (Hilder 1997):

> Teacher: Why might we want to use a transition word here?

CONCLUSION

We started out in this chapter by making the claim that *wh*-questions should be taught early on to ESL/EFL students, even if only formulaically. We think so because *wh*-questions serve many useful purposes in general and, more specifically, can be used by language students to advance their knowledge further. Aside from problems with inversion, we expect beginners to have few problems in acquiring some rudimentary questions and in learning to reply to certain others. More advanced students need to be systematically introduced to the more marked forms such as negative, uninverted, and elliptical *wh*-questions. For them, the challenge lies in mastering their meaning and use.

TEACHING SUGGESTIONS

I. Form. When working with beginning students, it is advisable to do some early work with subject NP focus in *wh*-questions so that they can become familiar with some common *wh*-words without worrying about subject-operator inversion at the same time:

> Who is writing on the board?   What happened?

One way of practicing such questions is to ask everyone in the room to keep doing something different from the others. The teacher can then establish the pattern with the present progressive:

> *T:* Who is opening the windows?   *T:* Who is tapping her pencil?
> *Ss:* Ramon (is).   *Ss:* Michele (is).

Then the students can take over the activity:

> *S1:* Who is drawing pictures?   *S2:* Who is sleeping?
> *S2:* Ali (is)   *S3:* Yen-Mai (is).

2. Use. As we said in this chapter, students at the beginning levels of instruction will probably learn inverted questions as lexicalized units. Useful questions of this type to teach are those that students can use to further their knowledge of English. We have in mind such questions as these:

> What is the meaning of *X*? or What does *X* mean?
> How do you spell *X*?
> How do you pronounce *X*?
> How do you say *Y* in English? (where *Y* = something in the student's L1)

A teacher might give students practice with these by giving each student in class a vocabulary word and its definition on a card. Students have to circulate and ask questions and take notes on each other's vocabulary items. For example:

> *S1:* What is your word?
> *S2:* Butcher.
> *S1:* How do you spell "butcher"?
> *S2:* B. . u. . t. . c. . h. . e. . r.
> *S1:* What does "butcher" mean?
> *S2:* (reading) A person who sells meat.

3. Form. The easiest and most frequent *wh*-questions involving subject-operator inversion contain the *be* copula. To facilitate practice of this pattern, the teacher can bring in several bags of kitchen utensils and gadgets. Each small group of students is given a bag. Beginning-level students will not likely have full control of the vocabulary. Students can work in small groups, and individuals can ask others in the group questions such as:

> *S1:* What's this? (holding up something he or she has picked from the bag)
> *S2:* A can opener. (selecting something else)
> *S2:* What's this?
> *S3:* A funnel.
> *S3:* What are these?
> *S4:* Measuring spoons.

If no one in the group can identify one or more items, they will need to ask other groups for assistance. They should identify all the objects in the bag that they can and then get together with another group to teach them the names of things they might not know and to ask them for help with the names of things that they have not yet identified.

4. Form. The biggest problem for beginning students—and often intermediate students too—is forming a *wh*-question that requires subject/operator inversion with a main verb other than the *be* copula.

Nancy Reed (personal communication) has developed a useful strategy for relating information students have already learned about subject-operator inversion in yes/no questions to the generation of *wh*-questions. Using charts or a flannelboard or the overhead projector to provide visual as well as aural reinforcement, she asks students yes/no questions and then follows up each yes/no question immediately with a more specific *wh*-question structurally related to the yes/no question. Here's an example:

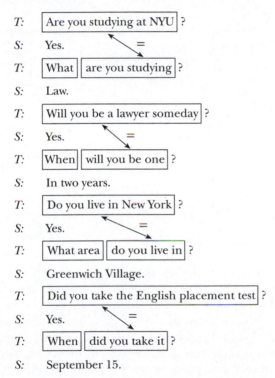

Using these paradigms, Ms. Reed then cues a student to ask another student a yes/no question, which he or she then follows up with another appropriate *wh*-question that the teacher can cue if necessary; for example:

    T: Juan, ask Ming-Lee if she is increasing her English vocabulary.

    J: Are you increasing your English vocabulary ?

  M-L: Yes.

    T: Ask her *how* she's doing it.

    J: How are you doing it ?

  M-L: By reading.

Eventually, the students are able to carry on such dialogues without cues, and they get a lot of practice using *wh*-questions that require subject-operator inversion and, where needed, the addition of *do*. The relationship between yes/no questions and these types of *wh*-questions has been made explicit. And the recurrence of common question formation errors such as *What you are doing?* can thus be reduced.

5. Meaning. Information-gap activities are ideal for working with the meaning of a variety of *wh*-question words. The teacher prepares a class information sheet with the names of categories on the horizontal axis and the names of some students on the vertical axis. Some of the cells of the grid are completed, but not all of them. One half of the class is given this sheet. A similar sheet is prepared for the other half of the class. On this sheet the cells missing the information on the first sheet are filled, but other cells are empty. In pairs, students have to ask and answer each other questions in order to complete their class information sheets. For example:

Sheet A

Student	Native Country	Native Language	How long studying English	Major
Ketut Sudha	Indonesia		10 years	
	Mexico			Nursing
	Japan	Japanese	12 years	

Sheet B

Student	Native Country	Native Language	How long studying English	Major
Ketut Sudha		Indonesian		Biology
Nina Rojas		Spanish	8 years	
Eiko Watanabe				Music

> S1: What language does Ketut speak?
> S2: Indonesian. Where does Nina come from?
> S1: Mexico. Who comes from Japan?
> S2: Eiko. How long has she been studying English?

6. Meaning. Write a number of *wh*-questions down one side of a piece of paper and their answers down the other side. Cut the paper apart vertically, so the answers are separate from the questions. Now cut the answers up and scramble them, and do the same with the questions. Have each student take one slip of paper from each pile. The students must go around the room asking the question on their pieces of paper to each other until they find an answer that matches. When a student has found a match for both answer and question, he or she should come to you and get a new pair. Do this until all of the questions and answers have been matched (adapted from Ur 1988).

7. Use. Role plays are helpful for practicing the social use of truncated *wh*-questions. For example, a teacher might set up a situation where three friends are trying to decide what to do that evening. We might expect language of the following sort to be used:

> A: How about a movie?
> B: Sounds good to me. How about you, C?
> C: Sure. Why not? What about the one at the Paramount?
> A: I have seen it already. Why don't we try the First Cinema?

EXERCISES

Test your understanding of what has been presented.

1. Provide original example sentences that illustrate the following concepts.
   a. *wh*-question focusing on the subject
   b. *wh*-question focusing on an object of a preposition (Give both versions.)
   c. *wh*-question focusing on a determiner:
      (i.) possessive
      (ii.) demonstrative
      (iii.) quantifier
   d. uninverted *wh*-question
   e. negative *wh*-question
      (i.) contracted
      (ii.) uncontracted
   f. formulaic *wh*-question (lexicalized unit)
   g. *wh*-question with ellipsis of the auxiliary

2. Draw tree diagrams and state the mapping rules that would apply to form each of the following *wh*-questions:
   a. How is your father today?
   b. Whom should we invite to the party?
   c. How long is the table?
   d. What did you understand?
   e. Where does your brother study physics?

3. Why are the following sentences ungrammatical?

   *Which did he buy car?   *Whose did he steal handbag?

4. The general *wh*-question word for Advl [position] is *where*.

   Where do you live?

   What are some specific *wh*-questions we use to ask about position?

Test your ability to apply what you know

5. If your students produce the following sentences, what errors have they made? How will you make them aware of the errors, and what exercises will you prepare to correct the errors?
   a. *Where you are going?
   b. *What you want?
   c. *To whom did he say that to?
   d. *Where Benny?

6. It has been suggested that *why, what . . . for,* and *how come* are *wh*-question words that all may be used to ask the same question.

   Why did he say that?   What did he say that for?   How come he said that?

   What are some differences in structure, meaning, and register among these expressions? Cite cases where they cannot be used to paraphrase one another.

7. The following *wh*-questions have been written on the blackboard of an ESL/EFL classroom. The object of the class is to review *wh*-questions in the simple past.
   a. What did you do yesterday?
   b. Where did you go?
   c. What happened?
   d. Who went with you?
   e. When did you get home?

   One of the students asks the teacher why three of the questions have a *did* while the other two do not. If you were the teacher, how would you answer this student's question?

8. See if you can draw the tree and derive the surface structure for the negative *wh*-question: *Why didn't you buy the car.* (Hint: Apply all the mapping rules involving the negative particle first.)

9. A student asks you why there are two *do* verbs in *What do you do?* How would you answer?

BIBLIOGRAPHY

References

Hilder, J. (1997). "Problem Identification in ESL Writing Conferences: Instructor Questions and Student Responses." MA in TESL Thesis, UCLA.

Schonbeck, G. (1982). "Other Questions." Term paper for the course English Applied Linguistics, School for International Training.

Weber, E. (1989). "Varieties of Questions in English Conversations: A Study of the Role of Morphosyntax in Declarative and Nonclausal Forms." Unpublished Ph.D. dissertation, UCLA.

Suggestions for Further Reading

For a useful linguistic description of wh-questions, see:

Bolinger, D. (1975). *Interrogative Structures of American English (The Direct Question).* Publication 28 of the American Dialect Society. Tuscaloosa, Ala: University of Alabama Press.

Chisolm Jr., William (ed.) (1984). *Interrogativity.* Philadelphia: John Benjamins.

For suggestions on how to teach wh-questions, see:

Abbott, G. (1980). "Teaching the Learner to Ask for Information." *TESOL Quarterly* 14:1, 21–38.

Pennington, M. (ed.) (1995). *New Ways in Teaching Grammar.* Arlington, Va.: TESOL, 155–167.

Riggenbach, H., and V. Samuda (1997). *Grammar Dimensions: Form, Meaning, and Use.* Book 2 (2d ed.). Boston, Mass.: Heinle & Heinle.

ENDNOTES

1. See later discussion of *who/whom* in the section on the use of *wh*-questions.

2. Other common measure words in combination with *how* are: *deep, old, high, long, big, far.* Answers to such questions would be in appropriate units, such as *feet, years, miles.*

OTHER STRUCTURES THAT LOOK LIKE QUESTIONS

INTRODUCTION

In this chapter we discuss four structures that look like questions but that function differently from the yes/no and *wh*-questions we have examined in Chapters 11 and 13, respectively. The four structures are tag questions, alternative questions, exclamatory questions, and rhetorical questions. Despite the "question" label, you will see that these structures really are not necessarily used to seek information. They are common enough, though, that ESL/EFL students should be able to recognize them and learn how to respond to them appropriately. Indeed, these structures may cause as many problems for ESL/EFL students in comprehension as they do in production.

TAG QUESTIONS

AN ANALYSIS OF THE FORM OF TAG QUESTIONS

Why the Form of Tag Questions Is Problematic

A tag question is a short question form appended to a statement. The tag question generally contrasts in polarity with the statement; that is, when the statement is affirmative, the tag is negative, and vice versa.

> Your aunt *is* visiting from Tennessee, *isn't she?*
> Your aunt *isn't* visiting from Tennessee, *is she?*

While most other languages have a structure equivalent to the English question tag, the equivalent is often invariant and thus is far simpler to master than the English tag. For example, French has *n'est-ce pas,* German has *nicht wahr,* and Mandarin Chinese has *ma,* spoken with a rising tone. Consequently, native speakers of such languages have been known to overgeneralize one frequently occurring tag in English:

> *She's coming today, isn't it?

In some languages the tag-formation convention consists merely of adding to a statement the equivalent for *no* or *yes* with rising intonation. Translated literally into English, this convention produces utterances like the following, which are not uncommon among ESL/EFL learners:

*We don't have homework today, yes?[1]

Then, too, not all languages use clause-final tags. For example, question tag particles may appear before the clause in Polish, after the first constituent in Ute, or after the focused constituent in Russian (Weber 1989).

The Syntax and Morphology of Tag Questions in English

In English, tag questions are normally clause final. When a sentence is written, a comma separates the main clause from the tag. If a tag question is sentence medial, commas set off the tag, and the terminal punctuation is still a question mark:

> It's human, isn't it, to hope that peace among all people in the world is possible?

Tag questions are syntactically like abbreviated unmarked yes/no questions in that they require subject-operator inversion.

> They can't do that, *can they?*   (*they can?*)
> He's the one you wish to speak to, *isn't he?*   (*he isn't?*)

When there is no auxilary verb or *be* verb in the main clause, then a *do* verb must be introduced as an operator to carry the tense.

> She assigned homework, *didn't she?*

Unlike yes/no questions, however, additional steps must be taken to form tag questions. First of all, as you have already seen, if the main clause is affirmative, the tag is negative; if the main clause is negative, the tag is affirmative.[2] The main clause can be negative by virtue of having a negative preverbal adverb of frequency, such as *never:*

> Budi has never seen snow, has he?

Negative tags have two forms. By far the more common is the contracted form. It is also syntactically possible, although stylistically formal, to have a full, uncontracted negative; in this case, however, the negative must be separated from the verb:

> You have missed a lot of practices, haven't you?
> You have missed a lot of practices, have you not?
> *You have missed a lot of practices, have not you?

Second, if the subject of the main clause is not a pronoun, then it must be pronominalized in the tag.

> Megan is quite a basketball player, isn't *she?* (*isn't Megan?*)

The only word that can be used as the subject in the tag that is not a personal pronoun is the nonreferential *there* (see Chapter 23).

> *There* are a lot of social events at this time of year, aren't *there?*

The Intonation of Tag Questions

Two different intonation patterns are used with tag questions:

1. Rising-falling: Ethan wanted to play, didn't he?

2. Rising: Ethan wanted to play, didn't he?

We discuss the differences between these forms in a later section on meaning.

Idiosyncratic Tag Questions

One further note should be made here with regard to the form of tag questions. Certain tags are idiosyncratic:

> Let's go, shall we? I am going, aren't I?
> We ought to go, shouldn't we? Open the door, won't you?[3]

Also, numerous unsystematic lexical-type tags are used informally:

> You aren't going, right? You are going, O.K.?
> You aren't going, huh? You are going, eh?[4]
> You are going, no?

All of these unsystematic tag questions occur with rising intonation.

Responding to Tag Questions

As we hinted in the Introduction to this chapter, it may be more important for ESL/EFL students to know how to reply to tag questions than to be able to produce the full form accurately. It is worth noting, then, that tag questions are rarely responded to with short answers in discourse between native speakers. In other words, the following response to a tag question is somewhat unusual:

> A: She's a brilliant chess player, isn't she?
> B: Yes, she is.

Out of 80 tag questions in her extensive corpus of oral and written data, Brown (1981) found only three instances of such a traditional short answer, and only one of these consisted simply of a *yes* or *no* and the short form. In her corpus, 30 percent of the tags received no answer at all. Others received affirmative answers, such as *That's right*, or some reply in which additional information would be offered:

> A: Science is your favorite subject, isn't it?
> B: Has been since I was five. (Carterette and Jones 1974:262, cited in Brown 1981)

When listeners disagreed with the speaker, they would give an explanation for the disagreement:

> A: . . . They can't get that big, can they, Wendy?
> B: Well, when they stretch, yes.

The forms of responses to tag questions are mentioned not only for their pedagogical implications but also because they hint at one of the differences between tag questions and other "confirmers." We have more to say about this when we discuss the use of tag questions. First, we should make some comments about their meaning.

THE MEANING OF TAG QUESTIONS

The meaning of tag questions is reflected in their form: A tag question is a question attached to a statement. In other words, something is being asserted to which the listener is invited to respond. Quirk et al. (1985) suggest that it is important to distinguish the assumption underlying the main clause from the expectation expressed in the tag question. These two intersect with the two intonation patterns introduced earlier to give us four possible combinations:

Polarity		Intonation	Assumption	Expectation
Main Cl.	*Tag*		*Main Cl.*	*Tag*
affirm.	neg.	rising	positive	neutral
neg.	affirm.	rising	negative	neutral
affirm.	neg.	rising-falling	positive	positive
neg.	affirm.	rising-falling	negative	negative

Huang (1980) provides a succinct explanation for these two intonation patterns. He feels that the speaker's intonation indicates how strong his or her presupposition is that the assumption—positive or negative—will be confirmed by the listener. If the speaker uses rising intonation, the expectation is weak. If he or she uses rising-falling intonation, the presupposition of confirmation is strong.

Tag questions thus enrich the scale of the certainty of the truth of the underlying proposition in both directions:

> *Strongest bias toward negative certainty*
> ▲ Sally didn't finish her report, did she? (rising-falling intonation)
> │ Sally didn't finish her report, did she? (rising intonation)
> │ Did Sally finish her report?
> │ Didn't Sally finish her report?
> │ Sally finished her report, didn't she? (rising intonation)
> ▼ Sally finished her report, didn't she? (rising-falling intonation)
> *Strongest bias toward positive certainty*[5]

Marked Tag Questions

Although far less common than their unmarked counterparts, marked tag questions, instead of having a polar contrast in the affirmative-negative or negative-affirmative marking of the main clause and tag, have a main clause and tag that are nonpolar, or noncontrasting:

> *affirmative*   *affirmative*
> You're an accountant, are you?[6]
> You call yourself a writer, do you?
>
> *negative negative*
> So I can't, can't I?

In order to make sense of these nonpolar tags in North American English, we interpret them as conveying some additional nuance of meaning. For example, the first could be a confirmation check expressing some doubt or reservation; the second might be sarcasm; the third could be a dare. Thus, it seems that marked tags in North American English have emotional overtones.

THE USE OF TAG QUESTIONS

As we have already asserted, tag questions are generally not used to seek information, regardless of their intonation. According to Huang (1980), intonation makes a difference only in presuppositional strength, not in actual function. What, then, is the purpose of a tag question?

First of all, we should note that tag questions occur much more frequently in oral discourse than in written discourse. In Brown's 1981 corpus of oral and written data, she found nine times as many tags in spoken discourse as in written, and the latter included mainly tags in reported language (see Chapter 33).

Brown also found that tag questions fulfilled five major functions:

1. Indicating inference (43 instances): *So, therefore, that proves malice, doesn't it?*
2. Seeking agreement (43): *They keep coming back, don't they?*
3. Inviting confirmation (36): *Science is your favorite subject, isn't it?*
4. Expressing doubt (27): *They can't get that big, can they?*
5. Expressing opinion (21): *But that makes a mockery of belief, doesn't it?*

and six minor functions:

Keeping the conversation going (5 cases)	Beginning a conversation (3)
Expressing interest (5)	Making a polite request (3)
Expressing humor or sarcasm (5)	Expressing surprise (3)

Thus, according to Brown, tag questions seem to be a way that the speaker has of seeking confirmation of his or her assertion. This explains why there are more negative than affirmative tags in Brown's data: speakers use negative tags to invite correction. Another fact about form that this function helps explain is the infrequent use of the first person. A person is the best source of information about opinions or inferences about himself or herself; consequently, he or she would generally not seek confirmation of such information from another, although people occasionally add tags like the following, perhaps inviting disconfirmation:

I'm being silly, aren't I?

Difference Between Tags and Other Confirmers

English speakers can also employ other confirmers, including complete sentences:

A: The moon is supposed to be full tonight. *Isn't that right?*
B. Yeah, that's right.

Speakers apparently use full-form confirmers when they want explicit confirmation that what they said is correct. All the full-sentence confirmers in Brown's corpus were answered, compared with the 30 percent of the tags in Brown's corpus that went unanswered.

ALTERNATIVE QUESTIONS

YES/NO VERSUS ALTERNATIVE QUESTIONS

Variously referred to as alternative questions, choice questions, and *or*-questions, this questionlike form offers listeners a choice between two alternatives:

A: Would you rather study physics or chemistry next semester?
B: Chemistry, I think.

While the syntax is that of a yes/no question, the intonation pattern is not. Clearly, therefore, a *yes* or *no* answer would be inappropriate, yet this is often the response given by ESL/EFL students.

A: Would you like regular or decaf?
B: *Yes, please.

ESL/EFL students need to learn the intonational differences between yes/no questions with conjoined objects and true alternative questions. Whereas the former rise in intonation at the end, the latter rise on the first of the two alternatives and have rising-falling on the second:

Yes/No Question	Alternative Question
A: Would you like coffee or tea?	A: Would you like coffee or tea?
B: Yes, please.	B: Coffee, please.

Lest we leave readers assuming that only near-identical alternatives can be conjoined, consider the following alternative question with different subjects:

Did you buy it, or did someone give it to you?

Three conjuncts are also possible with rising tone on each of the alternatives except the last:

Did you buy it, did someone give it to you, or did you find it?

And even clauses with different tenses and subjects can appear as alternatives:

Did you buy it, or am I going to have to?

It is also possible to have an alternative question where the second of the two alternatives is an elliptical negative clause:

Did you buy it, *or not?*

As use of a yes/no question already presumes the inevitability of one of these two alternatives, the alternative question form with the redundant *or not* seems to be petulant. The degree of speaker irritation appears to increase with the amount of redundancy expressed in the second alternative:

Did you buy it, or not?
Did you buy it, or didn't you?
Did you buy it, or didn't you buy it?
Did you buy it, or did you not buy it?

However, the connotation of petulance is speculative on our part. Intonation would also be a factor, and we would need to do a discourse analysis of questions like these to determine the differences among them.

In sum, we note that alternative questions result when listeners are given a choice between two or more options and when the truth value of only one of the two or more alternatives is presumed. This is different from a yes/no question with objects conjoined by *or*, which does not necessarily exclude either alternative. The semantic difference is signalled by an intonational difference.

ALTERNATIVE *WH*-QUESTION COMBINATIONS

While probably few ESL/EFL students will speak languages that have alternative questions of the type we have just examined, they will likely be familiar with the kind that takes the form of a *wh*-question combined with an elliptical alternative question:

What would you like—coffee, tea or milk?
Where do you live—in Queens or Brooklyn?

In many languages of the world, only this form of alternative question is permitted. Perhaps introducing this alternative *wh*-question hybrid first will ease your students into the new forms of alternative questions they will encounter most frequently in English.

EXCLAMATORY QUESTIONS

An exclamatory question is not really a question at all. It is an exclamation. It gets its name from the fact that like questions in English, it undergoes subject-operator inversion.

> Isn't that grand!

Notice, however, that in writing, it is usually punctuated with an exclamation mark.

Quirk et al. (1985:811) liken exclamatory questions to tag questions with falling intonation. While exclamatory questions are more emphatic than tag questions, they both invite confirmation of the underlying proposition. Compare:

> Wasn't she angry! (exclamatory question)
> She was angry, wasn't she? (tag question with falling intonation)

It is also possible to have exclamatory questions that look like *wh*-questions:

> What a good idea (that is)!
> How silly (it all seems)!

As can be seen in the two examples, these usually take the form of *what a* + noun + (clause) or *How* + adjective + (clause).

As Tsui (1992) notes, it is also possible to use exclamatory questions that do not seek confirmation:

> Am I hungry!

Since such exclamations report a personal experience, they would be only acknowledged (e.g., *Dinner will be ready soon*), not confirmed.

RHETORICAL QUESTIONS

A rhetorical question is similar to an exclamatory question in that it is interrogative in form but not in function. It is used by the speaker to assert something without anticipating a response from the listener.

> Just because you've failed the first test, is that any reason to give up?

The speaker's message here is *"Surely, no—that is no reason to give up."* Sometimes the speaker actually answers the question as part of a monologue. Sometimes the answer is merely implicit. In either case, the speaker is not asking the listener for information or for a *yes* or *no* response.

According to Frodesen and Eyring (1997), rhetorical questions may be employed by a speaker or writer for two main purposes:

To introduce/shift a topic:	Can the Democrats save Medicare?
	Remember the great fluoride debate?
To focus on a main point:	Haven't we had enough wars?
	How much longer can we ignore the signs of global warming?

Interestingly, the authors point out that the second function of rhetorical questions can be paraphrased by tag questions with rising-falling intonation:

We've had enough wars, haven't we?
We can't ignore the signs of global warming any longer, can we?

This is presumably because both rhetorical questions and tag questions with rising-falling tone are used to seek agreement.

CONCLUSION

By comparing tag questions with exclamatory questions and rhetorical questions, we have come full circle in our discussion of other structures that look like questions. Admittedly, some of these (e.g., alternative questions and question tags with rising intonation) are more question-like in their function than others (e.g., question tags with rising-falling intonation, exclamatory questions, and rhetorical questions). Nevertheless, they all share certain syntactic features with the yes/no questions and *wh*-questions we discussed earlier.

We conclude by pointing out that ESL/EFL students will at least need to recognize the fact that although these structures look like questions, they do not necessarily function as questions; having learned the difference, students will be able to respond to them appropriately. Analyses of foreigner talk discourse (Long 1981) have revealed that questions are very common in native speaker input to nonnative speakers of English. In the analysis of his data, Long discovered that whereas statements made up 83 percent of the discourse among native speakers, questions of all types dominated foreigner talk discourse, where they accounted for 66 percent of all t-units.[7] His analysis reveals that native speakers addressing nonnatives used significantly more alternative questions than did native speakers in conversation with other native speakers.

Presumably, native speakers in conversations with nonnative speakers used more questions in an attempt to lighten the nonnative speakers' interactional burden. However, from examples such as the following (excerpted from Long's data),

> *Native speaker:* Aha. Do you study?
> or   *Nonnative speaker:* No.[8]
> do you work?

it is clear that ESL/EFL students will need practice in learning to recognize what the speaker's intention is and in responding more appropriately on a pragmatic level to native speakers' questions.

TEACHING SUGGESTIONS

I. Form. After introducing your students to the concept of tag questions, you might focus their attention on the variety of tag question forms that exists in English. One way to do this is to divide the class into small groups. Give each group an envelope containing 40 pieces of paper. On 20 of them you have written main clauses, and on the other 20 you have written tag questions. Students have to match the main clause with the correct tag. Be sure to include a variety of statements and tags with both negative and affirmative forms.

2. Use. Tag questions are typical of conversation, so one way to have students practice their use is in dialogues. By working with dialogues, students will also become acquainted with responses to tag questions. In constructing such dialogues, it would be wise to keep in mind some of the form-frequency patterns Brown (1981) found in her study. Tag questions are overwhelmingly in the present tense, and they occur most often with the copula *be* or with the operator *do*. Most subjects are third person singular or second person, and 75 percent of all tag questions have an affirmative statement with a negative tag.

> *Hal:* Hi, Sue. Good to see you again. It's a nice day today, isn't it?
> *Sue:* Hi, Hal. It sure is. Say you look good. You've lost some weight, haven't you?
> *Hal:* I'm trying hard. What have you been up to?
> *Sue:* I've been studying for my midterm exams in economics and calculus.
> *Hal:* Wow! You take tough courses, don't you?
> *Sue:* Yeah, but I enjoy the challenge.

3. Form/Meaning. To help your ESL/EFL students become familiar with the intonation pattern of alternative questions and to make them aware of the contrast between it and the intonation of syntactically similar yes/no questions, you can give your students a worksheet with 10 pairs of answers. Next, read a question and ask your students to circle the letter of the appropriate corresponding pair of answers. In order to answer correctly, your students will have to recognize whether the question you are giving them has the intonation of an alternative question or a yes/no question. Here's an example:

> Teacher reads out loud: 1. Are you studying English or history?
>
> Students circle correct reply: 1. A. Yes, I am.
>   B. Just English now.

4. Meaning. You can give your students practice in producing alternative questions by giving them "breakfast menus" that you have prepared. For each category, there might be two or three items from which to choose; for example:

Cold Beverages: Orange Juice	Hot Beverages: Coffee
Grapefruit Juice	Tea
Entrees: Scrambled Eggs	Side Dishes: Hash Brown Potatoes
Pancakes	Bacon
Oatmeal	Ham

Pairs of students take turns role-playing servers and restaurant customers. The server might ask a yes/no question, such as

> Would you like a cold beverage?

>   or

> Would you like orange juice or grapefruit juice?

or an alternative question:

> Would you like orange juice or grapefruit juice?

Depending on the type of question, the "customer" would give an appropriate answer. For instance, if it was the yes/no question, the customer would reply,

> Yes, please. I'll have orange juice.

If, on the other hand, the server used the intonation of an alternative question, the customer would answer:

> Orange juice, please.

5. Use. After explaining what rhetorical questions are and providing a number of examples, ask your intermediate or advanced ESL/EFL students to find and bring to class one example of a rhetorical question from a newspaper editorial or advertisement, a published speech, a textbook, or an essay. Ask the class to decide why the speaker or writer used a rhetorical question. See if the students can figure out the implied answer for any rhetorical question that the speaker or writer does not answer himself or herself.

6. Use. If possible, ask each student to tape-record a conversation between him or her and a native speaker of English. Have the student pick out and categorize the different questions the native speaker uses. Are they all "questions," or are some of them the structures discussed in this chapter that only *look* like questions?

EXERCISES

Test your understanding of what has been presented.

1. Provide original example sentences that illustrate the following terms. Underline the pertinent word(s) in your examples.
   - **a.** tag question
     - (i.) unmarked
     - (ii.) idiosyncratic
     - (iii.) marked
   - **b.** alternative question
   - **c.** alternative *wh*-question combination
   - **d.** exclamatory "question"
   - **e.** rhetorical question

2. Why are the following sentences ungrammatical?
   - **a.** *John wants to go, didn't he?
   - **b.** *Susan never laughs, doesn't she?
   - **c.** *He left, did not he?
   - **d.** *Is not that wonderful!

3. What would the complete form of these utterances be?
   - **a.** Is Janet blue-eyed or not?
   - **b.** Looking forward to vacation, aren't you?
   - **c.** Was it Bill or was it Bob who wrote this letter?

Test your ability to apply what you know.

4. If your students produce the following sentences, what errors have they made? How will you make them aware of their errors, and what exercises will you prepare to help your students correct these errors?
   - **a.** *We're going, isn't it?
   - **b.** *This is nice music, yes?
   - **c.** Native speaker: Would you like coffee or tea?

     ESL/EFL student: *Yes.

5. Under what circumstances might an English speaker utter question 2 rather than question 1 in the following pairs? Discuss both options in your response.
   - **a.** 1. It is going to rain, isn't it?   **2.** It isn't going to rain, is it?
   - **b.** 1. Do you want to go or not?   **2.** Do you want to go or do you not want to go?
   - **c.** 1. You did, didn't you?   **2.** You did, did you?
   - **d.** 1. There isn't much to do, is there?   **2.** There isn't much to do, is there?
   - **e.** 1. Isn't that good?   **2.** Isn't that good!
   - **f.** 1. Max sings well, doesn't he?   **2.** Max sings well, don't you think?

6. John Henry Newman wrote a famous essay entitled "What Is a University?" Why do you suppose he chose a question for his title?

7. If an ESL/EFL student asks you what the difference is between the following, how would you answer?

> Open the door, won't you?
> Open the door, will you?

BIBLIOGRAPHY

References

Brazil, D. (1984). "Tag Questions." *Discourse Analysis*, special issue of *IIha do Desterro* 11, 93–108.

Brown, C. (1981). "What Discourse Analysis Reveals about Tag Questions." Paper presented at the Annual TESOL Conference, Detroit, March.

Frodesen, J., and J. Eyring (1997). *Grammar Dimensions: Form, Meaning, and Use.* Book 4 (2d ed.). Boston, Mass.: Heinle & Heinle.

Givón, T. (1993). *English Grammar: A Function-Based Introduction.* Amsterdam/Philadelphia: John Benjamins.

Huang, J. (1980). "Negative Yes/No Questions in English: Forms and Meanings." Unpublished English 215 paper, UCLA.

Long, M. (1981). "Questions in Foreigner Talk Discourse." *Language Learning* 31:1, 135–157.

Quirk, R., S. Greenbaum, G. Leech, and J. Svartvik (1985). *A Comprehensive Grammar of the English Language.* London: Longman.

Tsui, A. (1992). "A Functional Description of Questions." In M. Coulthard (ed.), *Advances in Spoken Discourse Analysis.* London: Routledge, 89–110.

Weber, E. (1989). "Varieties of Questions in English Conversation: A Study of the Role of Morphosyntax in Declarative and Nonclausal Forms." Ph.D. dissertation in Linguistics, UCLA.

Suggestions for Further Reading

For an analysis of tag questions, see:

Hintikka, J. 1982. "Tag Questions and Grammatical Acceptability." *Journal of Nordic Linguistics* 5:2, 129–132.

For exercises on intonation of tag questions and alternative questions, see:

Celce-Murcia, M., D.Brinton, and J. Goodwin (1996). *Teaching Pronunciation: A Course for Teachers of English to Speakers of Other Languages.* New York: Cambridge University Press.

Riggenbach, H., and V. Samuda (1997). *Grammar Dimensions: Form, Meaning, and Use.* Book 2 (2d ed.). Boston, Mass.: Heinle & Heinle.

For pedagogical suggestions on how to work with rhetorical questions, see:

Frodesen, J., and J. Eyring (1997). *Grammar Dimensions; Form, Meaning, and Use.* Book 4 (2d ed.). Boston, Mass.: Heinle & Heinle.

ENDNOTES

1. It is possible in informal English to use *no* as a tag with an affirmative main clause: e.g., *We have homework today, no?* but not *yes* with a negative main clause.

2. There are exceptions to this convention, which we discuss later in this chapter when we deal with marked tag questions.

3. Notice that tags are sometimes added to imperatives to soften them or to make them more like requests or invitations: e.g., *Come in, won't you?*

4. The *eh* tag—often pronounced /ey/—is commonly used in Canadian English.

5. This scale has been adapted from Givón (1993).

6. Affirmative main clauses and tags are apparently used in unmarked ways in British English to verify the proposition expressed in the first clause.

7. A t-unit is an independent clause and any subordinate clauses or nonclausal structures associated with it.

8. Utterances by two speakers printed on the same line indicates an overlap.

Chapter 15

ARTICLES

INTRODUCTION

The English articles (i.e., definite *the*, indefinite *a/an*, and unstressed *some* /səm/—as well as the use of no article at all) are part of a larger system of reference and determination that we continue to discuss in the next chapter. However, the learning difficulty and frequency of the articles[1] has convinced us to treat them as a separate topic before taking on the larger systems in which they function.

Articles are understandably problematic from a cross-linguistic perspective: most Asian and Slavic languages and many African languages have no articles. Even those languages that do have articles or article-like morphemes (e.g., French, Spanish, Farsi, the Scandinavian languages, and the Semitic languages) often use these morphemes in ways that differ from English. For example, many of these article-using languages mark the generic use of an abstract noun with their equivalent of the definite article. Thus, instead of saying *Beauty is truth*, as the English poet Keats did, the literal equivalent of this sentence in many of these languages would be **The beauty is the truth*. Also, some of these languages (e.g., Farsi and some Scandinavian languages) can indicate definiteness or indefiniteness with a suffix or morpheme following the noun, as opposed to the invariant prenominal position that articles have in English.

You may be wondering at this point how languages without articles can signal definiteness or indefiniteness. The most common means is word order; that is, the noun in topic position is definite, whereas a noun in comment position tends to be indefinite.[2] Thompson (1978) gives us a functional explanation for the evolution of the English article system: She says that languages like English that use word order to signal grammatical relations such as "subject" and "object" tend to develop articles because given versus new information cannot be consistently signaled through word order, as they are in topic-comment languages like Russian and Chinese, which tend not to have articles. In topic-comment languages, word order signals given versus new information: the topic comes first, signaling given information, and the comment comes later, signaling new information. Thus as was pointed out in Chapter 2, the definite and indefinite articles in languages like English help us to identify new and given information: given information, tends to take the definite article, while new information, somewhat independently of word order, tends to take the indefinite article.

The historical development of articles in English is similar to that of most other languages that have developed an article system: the definite article *the* derives from the demonstrative signaling distance (i.e., *that*), while the indefinite article derives from the numeral *one*; it is in fact still possible to use *one* as a stressed emphatic variant of *a/an*:

That's one big bug!

FORM: STRUCTURAL FACTS ABOUT ARTICLES

PRONUNCIATION OF THE ARTICLES

Although the definite article has an invariant spelling, *the*, it has four different pronunciations. The two pronunciations that are most frequent and occur in normal speech in unstressed form are:

/ðə/ *before consonant sounds* [3]	/ðiy/ *before vowel sounds (less preferred /ðəʔ/ also occurs)*
the book	the apple
the unit	the orange
the song	the elephant

The third and fourth pronunciations—stressed /ðʌ/ and stressed /ðiy/—are the stressed versions of the above forms, which alternate as possible citation forms. Emphatic use of the definite article is pronounced as stressed /ðiy/:

Citation:　The word *the* has four pronunciations. (stressed /ðʌ/ or /ðiy/)
Emphatic:　I met THE Elizabeth Taylor. (the actress, not someone else with the same name) (stressed /ðiy/)

The history of the indefinite article *a/an* helps explain why, before a word with an initial vowel sound, its form is *an*, and before a word with an initial consonant sound, its form is *a*—that is, the *n* sound in *one* and *an* are historically related:

/ə/ *before a consonant sound* [4]	/ən/ *before a vowel sound*
a book	an apple
a unit	an idea
a student	an ear

The stressed form of the indefinite article is /ey/ and is usually a citation form:

> The indefinite article is most frequently realized as *a*.

However, on rare occasions this stressed form also occurs as an emphatic or contrastive form in natural speech, as in the Peanuts cartoon script we cite later on p. 281 (Not "A" dog . . . "The" dog).

The plural counterpart of *a/an* (*some*) is generally unstressed /səm/ when used as an article. This article function should be distinguished from three other determiner functions of *some* that are stressed:

Partitive/quantifier:　Some of the people left early. (*some = part of the set*)
Emphatic:　That was some party!
Presentative:　Some guy came to the door and tried to sell me a vacuum cleaner.
　　　　　　(*some = a certain one and often conveys negative affect.*)

CLASSIFICATION OF NOUNS

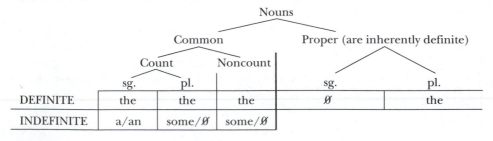

	Common			Proper (are inherently definite)	
	Count		Noncount		
	sg.	pl.		sg.	pl.
DEFINITE	the	the	the	Ø	the
INDEFINITE	a/an	some/Ø	some/Ø		

Most of the strictly form-based information about English articles depends on the English noun classification system. All English nouns are classified as either common nouns (e.g., *a boy, a country, a planet*) or proper nouns (e.g., *Bob Robertson, Denmark, Saturn*). In addition, all common nouns can be further classified as noncount nouns (e.g., *water, clothing, luggage*) or count nouns (*a beverage, a shirt, a suitcase*). Noncount nouns are singular in number for purposes of subject-verb agreement but cannot take the indefinite article and the plural inflection as common count nouns do:

Noncount	Count (common)
*a water, *some waters	a beverage, some beverages
*a luggage, *some luggages	a suitcase, some suitcases

Noncount nouns and plural count nouns do, however, share the possibility of taking the zero article or indefinite *some*:

Noncount	Count (plural)
water	suitcases
some water	some suitcases

Proper nouns are a special case: they are like common count nouns because they are countable, but they are different because they are inherently definite and thus never take the indefinite article when they function as true proper nouns. When they take the plural inflection, they require the definite article to retain proper noun status:[5]

Count (proper)
Mr. Wayne, *a John Wayne, the (two) Waynes (= John and Patrick)
America, *an America, the (two) Americas (= North and South, or Anglo and Latin)

Even though both the proper/common and the count/noncount classifications seem to overlap in certain cases, the conceptual distinctions involved are basic to mastery of the English article system.

The Count-Noncount Distinction

The lexical classification of English common nouns into count and noncount nouns is a very important preliminary to correct use of articles. It is a conceptual distinction that accounts for many systematic patterns in article usage. The distinction is problematic for ESL/EFL learners in that many languages make use of a similar concept; however, what is countable and what is uncountable is somewhat arbitrary and varies to some extent from language to language. For example, *information* and *furniture* are noncount nouns in English but count nouns in French and Spanish, and *chalk* is a noncount noun in English but a count noun in Japanese. Also, even within English itself many nouns can be used either as count or noncount nouns, which is something we discuss below.

Most English nouns, however, tend to be viewed as either uncountable (e.g., *bacon*) or countable (e.g., *boy*). Examine the following paradigms:

Noncount (*a* to *e* are ungrammatical)
a. *The bacon (a singular unit) is lying next to another one.
b. *A bacon fell onto my plate.
c. *The bacons got cold.
d. *Some bacons were in the cupboard.
e. *Bacons are for eating.
f. The bacon was too salty.
g. Some bacon was found in the cupboard.
h. Bacon is naturally salty.

Count (*f* to *h* are ungrammatical)

a. The boy played in the street.
b. A boy played in the street.
c. The boys played in the street.
d. Some boys played in the street.
e. Boys are made of snails and puppy-dog tails.
f. *The boy (uncountable amount) wasn't enough for the scout troop.
g. *Some boy made up the scout troop.
h. *Boy is made of snails and puppy-dog tails.

These paradigms are useful and help clarify the difference between archetypical noncount nouns such as *bacon* and archetypical count nouns such as *boy*. However, the paradigms and the count/noncount terminology suggest a strict dichotomy where there is very likely a continuum of sorts. Allan (1980), for example, applies a series of syntactic "tests" to demonstrate that the noun *car* is more countable than the noun *cattle*, which has no singular form, and that the noncount noun *mankind*, which has a collective sense, is less of a noncount noun than the noun *equipment*, which does not. Allan, in fact, argues for eight discrete levels of countability. However, despite our basic agreement with Allan's analysis, we continue, for pedagogical reasons, to view nouns as either basically countable (i.e., singular, plural) or basically uncountable.

As an extension of our simplified count/noncount analysis, we note that there are many abstract noncount nouns (e.g., *beauty, truth, crime, law, education*) that we can conceive of in a more individuated way and thus we make them countable without substantially changing the meaning:

> life (the general notion):
> > Life can be beautiful. (the noncountable use)
> a life (a human being as a specific instance of the general notion):
> > The quick-thinking police officer saved a life. (the countable use)

With their dual count-noncount function, such nouns can be used in every slot in the paradigm we cited above to structurally differentiate *bacon* and *boy*:

Noncount → Count

count
{
a. The life of the old man was forfeited.
b. A life is not proper payment for that.
c. The lives lost in the war were wasted.
d. Some lives were saved.
e. Lives are always lost in war.
}

noncount
{
f. The life in the old man was fading fast.
g. Some life could be detected in the old man.
h. Life can be difficult at times.
}

It is useful to distinguish abstract noncount nouns from more concrete, substance-like noncount nouns. Therefore, in the rest of this chapter we distinguish abstract noncount nouns (*life, beauty, education*, etc.) from mass noncount nouns (*cheese, coffee, bacon*), often referring to them simply as abstract nouns or mass nouns.

Mass-to-Count Noun Shifts

In addition to the above noncount-to-count shift that many abstract nouns can undergo, a number of other similar mass→count shifts[6] involve more concrete noncount mass nouns.

If we conceive of such a noun as "a kind or a type of," we make it countable, as in the following example:

Mass	→	Count	
(generic)		(type)	
cheese		a cheese	cheeses
wine		a wine	wines
tea		a tea	teas

Likewise, if we conceive of the mass noun as "a unit or a serving of" we make it countable, as in the following examples:

Mass	→	Count	
(substance)		(unit or serving)	
coffee		a coffee	two coffees
aspirin		an aspirin	two aspirins
chocolate		a chocolate	some chocolates

Often the same mass noun can occur with both of the above count noun interpretations, depending on the context; for example:

> How many different teas do they sell here? (types)
> We'll have two teas with lemon. (servings)

Of course, many idiosyncratic meaning relationships involving mass noncount and count nouns must be learned independent of any such regular semantic shifts; in these cases, the meaning change is not predictable, so the combinations and their meanings must be learned as individual lexical items:

Mass	Count—Singular	Count—Plural
air (the atmosphere)	an air (melody)	airs (mannerisms)
glass (the silicate-based substance)	a glass (water tumbler)	glasses (spectacles)
iron (the metal)	an iron (for pressing clothes)	irons (golf clubs)

Distinguishing Between Proper and Common Nouns

Proper nouns, which include personal names, geographical names, and some other minor categories, also pose a few special problems in terms of noun classification and category shifting. Proper nouns are always definite, yet with the exception of a few instances, which can be accounted for as borrowings (e.g., *The Hague, The Matterhorn*), they do not take the definite article in the singular unless the speaker is being extremely emphatic and using stressed *the* (e.g., *THE Elizabeth Taylor* [to distinguish the actress from all other women with the same name]). Plural proper names always take the definite article: *the Johnsons, the Azores,* and so on. and are semantically collective. In fact, some proper collective nouns, such as *The United Kingdom* or *The Vatican* take the definite article without an explicit plural. (See Chapter 17 for further discussion of collective nouns.)

Shifts Involving Proper and Common Nouns

When proper nouns are used in common noun patterns, they are no longer functioning as true proper nouns; they have become common nouns by virtue of an understood head noun; for example, *the man called George→the George.* All the following sentences contain proper nouns that are being used as common nouns:

> The George that called yesterday called again today.
> Some Ernests can surely be found in this crowd!

A Robert spoke to me all night long at the party.
Nine Marys were on the list.

Personal names are not the only proper nouns that can shift to common noun use. Trade names are also a common source of such a shift:

Kleenex	→	a kleenex (= a paper tissue)
Xerox	→	a xerox of something (= a photocopy)
Kodak	→	a kodak (= a camera)

If we turn to geographical names, the opposite shift seems to occur just as often. Geographical names can experience a shift over time whereby unique common nouns—that is, nouns which take *the* because of their cultural or situational uniqueness—become proper nouns. This has happened in some cases where regions or territories have become countries:

Unique Common Noun[7]	→	*Proper Noun*
the Sudan	→	Sudan
the Gambia	→	Gambia
the Ukraine	→	Ukraine

This shift has also happened in the case of local geographical names (or place names). When English speakers become personally acquainted with a geographical term and hear it mentioned frequently, they tend to drop the definite article and thereby create a proper name:

Unique Common Noun	→	*Proper Noun*
the green park	→	Green Park
the river road	→	River Road
the Brookfield Zoo	→	Brookfield Zoo

In such cases, two alternatives sometimes exist side by side (e.g., *the Brentwood Country Club; Brentwood Country Club*); the unique common noun is used by speakers who are less personally familiar with the place concerned, and the proper name is used by those who have close affiliation with and make frequent mention of the place.

In rare cases, it is possible for the same speaker to refer to the same entity as either a proper noun or a unique common noun:

Earth → the earth

Used as a proper name, "Earth" fits the same paradigm as the other planets in our solar system—*Venus, Mars, Saturn,* and so on; it is also used poetically or in personifications as a proper noun: (*Mother*) *Earth.* Used as a unique common noun, *the earth* relates to *the sun, the moon, the land, and the sea* as part of our immediately visible environment. Thus speakers can sometimes have different frames of reference for one and the same entity, and they reflect this in their article usage, a topic we discuss further under the use of articles.

The important thing to remember about both noncount-count shifts and common-proper shifts is that the lexical classification of English nouns is important information for article usage but that there is always a degree of flux that can be explained by speaker reconceptualization of a classification and by usage in context.

THE SYNTAX OF ARTICLES AND OTHER DETERMINERS

The definite article, like demonstratives and possessive determiners, is considered a core determiner and thus can optionally be preceded by one predeterminer and followed by one or two postdeterminers (recall that the upper limit on total number of determiners seems to be three):

Predeterminer	Core	Postdeterminer	Head Noun
all	the	other	boys
	the	first, three	cars

The indefinite article *a/an* has a more idiosyncratic distribution because it derives from a number (*one*). The following are some common patterns involving the co-occurrence of *a/an* with other determiners (see also Chapters 16 and 17):

I. In fractions and frequencies in the sense of *each, every, per*:

> half a gallon
> twice a day

2. After *what* and *such* and before singular nouns in exclamations:

> What a day!
> Such a nuisance!

3. Before the quantifiers *few* and *little* to impart a positive rather than a negative sense of quantity:

> Jake has (a) few friends.
> (A) little money was missing.

4. A necessary part of *lot of, number of, great/good deal of* when these are used as quantifiers:

> a lot of energy
> a (large) number of boats
> a great deal of money

THE MEANING OF ARTICLES

Each of the articles can signal a number of meanings. To understand the meanings, it is helpful to begin with some basic concepts. First of all, articles can convey *generic* meaning, in which all or most members of a set are referred to.

> The lion is a ferocious animal.
> A lion is a ferocious animal.
> ø Lions are ferocious animals.

The article + noun in these sentences tell us that it is the lion species that is being commented upon. We discuss the differences among these generic forms in the Use section of this chapter.

Far more common, however, is the *nongeneric* meaning of articles, in which one or more individual members of a set are being referred to.

> The lion escaped from the zoo.
> A lion escaped from the zoo.
> ø Lions escaped from the zoo.

In these examples, we understand that an individual animal or animals are being commented upon—not all lions.

To distinguish among the nongeneric uses of articles, we need to make the distinction between specific and nonspecific noun phrases. A *specific* noun phrase is one in which the identity of individual member(s) is clear. In the example *The lion escaped from the zoo,* a particular lion is being referred to; for instance, there may have been only one lion in the zoo so its identity is clear. A *nonspecific* noun phrase is one where the identity of a member of the set is not clear, e.g.:

>   Have you ever seen a lion in the wild?

THE MEANING OF THE INDEFINITE ARTICLES

Nonspecific noun phrases can only be marked with indefinite articles (*a/an, some,* ø):

>   Let's rent *a* movie or listen to *some/ø* music.

The identity of the movie or music is not clear.

>   I need *some/ø* stamps.

In other words, the speaker is saying that any stamps will do.

The difference between *some* and ø here can be accounted for by noting that the zero article expresses a nonspecific, semigeneric meaning:

>   I need stamps.

The speaker is concerned with the qualitative meaning of the noun, i.e. the quantity is irrelevant (Christophersen 1939). Use of *some* seems to impose a limit on the number of stamps needed, even though the precise number of stamps remains unspecified.

>   I need some stamps.

Another difference between *some* and ø exists when a subject noun predicate is being used to classify, i.e., to represent a particular type or class as opposed to another type or class. To classify, the singular indefinite article is used:

>   John is a teacher.
>   This is a pencil.

However, with a plural subject noun predicate, only the ø article can be used.

>   John and Bill are teachers.   These are pencils.
>   *John and Bill are some teachers.   *These are some pencils.

Sometimes the status of an NP preceded by an indefinite article is ambiguous. This is because it is possible to use an indefinite article when the noun being referred to by the speaker is either specific or nonspecific:

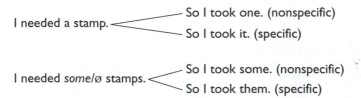

The situational context or the discourse context may help to disambiguate whether nonspecific or specific meaning is intended.

Finally, as we have already seen in our examples with the lion, the indefinite singular noun and the zero article can be used generically. This is not true of *some*.

> A stamp can be very valuable.
> Dolphins are intelligent. (plural count noun)
> Water sustains life. (noncount noun)
> *Some dolphins are intelligent. (Notice that here *some* is being used as a quantifier. See Chapter 17.)
> *Some water sustains life.

We will have more to say about the zero article after our discussion of the meaning of the definite article.

THE MEANINGS OF THE DEFINITE ARTICLE

The definite article *the* can also signal a generic function like the singular indefinite forms and the zero article. With singular nouns, this generic usage of *the* is formal and abstract:

> The lion is the king of beasts.

With plural or collective nouns, the definite article signals a sense of generic collectivity:

> The Germans now realize that reunification has come with problems. (plural)
> The clergy are divided on that issue. (collective)

Most instances of *the* are nongeneric, and Hawkins (1978) provides a useful perspective on the nongeneric meaning of the definite article in English. He argues that a number of definite article types that people have claimed to be different are simply instances of the same strategy. He proposes his "location theory" to account for all instances of nongeneric *the*: When a speaker/writer uses *the*, he instructs the hearer/reader to locate the referent in the same shared mental set of objects. The instruction to locate may have a situational-cultural, a textual, or a structural basis.[8]

Examples of situational-cultural instructions to locate the referent include the five following subcategories, which have often been proposed as distinct uses of *the*:

1. *General cultural* use (the referent is unique for all members of the speech community):

> the sun, the moon, the earth

2. *Immediate situational use:*

> Don't go in there. The dog will bite you.

3. *Perceptual situational use* (the referent is uniquely visible, audible, etc.):

> Pass me the salt, please.

4. *Local use* (general knowledge—unique for members of the same family or village):

> the car, the church, the pub

5. *Local use* (specific knowledge—unique for members of a specific community):

> [In the town of Halifax,] there is a type of gallows called the gibbett, which exists nowhere else.

There are three textual subcategories for use of *the*, which can all be grouped together as instructions to the listener or reader to locate the co-referent in the text:

1. *Anaphoric use* (prior mention):

> Fred left a book on his desk this morning. He returned home in the afternoon to get *the book*.

2. *Deductive anaphoric use* (prior mention of a schematically-related notion):

> Fred bought a book at Duttons. He later spoke to *the author* about it.

3. *Cataphoric use* (subsequent mention of something related):

> Here's *the bottom line*: you don't get to take the exam again.

The two structurally based instructions to locate the referent are:

1. *Usage with post-modifiers* (relative clauses, prepositional phrases, appositives):

> *The* person (he dated) was nasty to him.
> I remember *the* beginning (of the war) very well.
> *The* number (seven) is considered lucky.

2. Usage with ranking determiners and adjectives:

> *The* first European in America was Scandinavian.
> What is *the* next book you plan to read?

Some idiomatic and formulaic usages are difficult to explain in terms of any principle of form, meaning, or use:

> That's *the* ticket!
> He's right on *the* mark.

Halliday and Hasan's account (1976:74) for the nongeneric meaning of *the* is quite similar to that of Hawkins:

> Its meaning is that the noun it modifies has a specific referent, and that the information required for identifying this referent is available. . . it does not say where the information is to be located. It will be found somewhere in the environment, provided that we interpret "environment" in the broadest sense: to include the structure, the text, the situation, and the culture.

In other words, article "meanings" and the uses to which articles are put are very abstract and general with a potential for change from one context to another. Also, some uses are truly culture bound, which makes them particularly difficult for learners who do not share the culture behind the language.

CONTRASTING ZERO ARTICLE WITH *A/AN* AND *THE*

Master (1997) reminds us that there are really two "zero" articles in English. One occurs with nonspecific or generic noncount and plural nouns (e.g., *milk, eggs*) and is referred to as the zero article (Chesterman 1991), and the other occurs with certain singular count and proper nouns (e.g., *London, lunch*) and is referred to as the null article. The zero article is the most indefinite of English articles, whereas the null article is the most definite (the following countinuum is adapted from Chesterman 1991):

(least definite) zero→some→a/an→the→null (most definite)

The zero article seems to alternate with the indefinite article in several contexts where the zero article is more general and the indefinite article more individuated:

1. Zero signals noncount, and *a/an* signals count:

    The boys ate (a) chicken.

2. Zero signals general, and *a/an* particular:

    He sells (a) cheese of uncommon flavor.

3. Zero signals abstract, and *a/an* concrete:

    (A) Prison dehumanizes its inmates.

The null article seems to alternate with the definite article in three contexts with slightly different meanings being expressed (Master, 1997):

1. Null article names, and *the* describes:

    Mr. Phillips was appointed (the) treasurer.

2. Null article is vague, while *the* is focused:

    It usually snows here in (the) winter.

3. Null article is familiar, while *the* is less familiar:

    (The) Lunch was quite uneventful.

USES OF THE ARTICLES

Ultimately, articles must be understood in terms of their use more than their structure or meaning. Their use is not simply an independent decision made by the speaker/writer but rather a reflection of shared knowledge between the interactants in any act of ongoing communication. The speaker/writer must assess the interlocutor's background knowledge and make a series of assumptions regarding the information he or she shares (or does not share) with the interlocutor. Pica (1983) notes that in the sentence-level examples given in grammars and textbooks, *a* and *the* can often be interchanged without any loss of grammaticality; however, in natural data that are grammatically acceptable, she notes that communication breaks down when articles are used with reference to items that exist in one participant's experience but not in the other's. Here is an example we have found of the phenomenon that Pica discusses:

    A: Where's the dessert?
    B: What dessert?
    C: You were supposed to bring the dessert.

Differences in the perspectives or experiences of participants can also be a source of humor:

    "Peanuts" cartoon:
    Frame 1: Girl standing at front door with Snoopy says:
        There's a dog here who wants to come in.
    Frame 2: Snoopy thinks:
        Not "A" dog . . . "The" dog!

USE OF NONGENERIC COMMON NOUNS IN INTERACTION AND DISCOURSE

Brown (1973) gives us a good way of visualizing the interaction of the speaker/writer and the listener/reader with regard to article usage of nongeneric common nouns in English:

		Speaker (Writer)	
		specific referent	nonspecific referent
L i s t e n e r ⌒ R e a d e r ⌣	specific referent	definite: Can I have the car?	indefinite: There's a spy hiding in your cellar. I heard you once wrote an article on X.
	nonspecific referent	indefinite: I saw a funny looking dog today	indefinite: I don't have a car. I need a new belt.

As Brown's matrix indicates, the definite article is used properly only when the noun being discussed has a specific, identical referent (from the speaker/writer's point of view) within the speaker/writer's and the listener/reader's knowledge base.

The usage described in Brown's matrix is generally reflected in realistic dialogues. Read the following dialogue (adapted by Linda Chan-Rapp from usages she observed) and try to choose the appropriate article by applying Brown's matrix to each blank:

> *Student:* How did I do on (1) _____ test?
> *Teacher:* Well, actually you didn't do very well. Don't you have (2) _____ tutor?
> *Student:* Yes. Mary's been tutoring me for two weeks now. It's been difficult to meet though, because I don't have (3) _____ car. Mary does have (4)_____ small Toyota, but it isn't always reliable.

Here, only the first blank takes the definite article because the test is specific for both the speaker and the listener. Each of the other blanks takes *a/an*, with each reflecting a different quadrant in Brown's matrix (2—nonspecific for speaker; 3—nonspecific for both; 4—nonspecific for listener).[9]

FIRST VERSUS SUBSEQUENT MENTION IN NARRATIVES

Often, specific discourse genres develop their own conventions of article usage. For example, in traditional narratives, it is common to introduce participants with an indefinite article and to use the definite article or a personal pronoun for subsequent mentions of the same participant. This first mention→subsequent mention principle often works well in simple narratives such as those found in fables or folktales. In the following rendition of the "Fox and Crow" fable from Aesop (adapted from Celce-Murcia and Hilles 1988:152–153), the key noun participants are: *crow, cheese, tree,* and *fox.* The first mention→subsequent mention principle works well for these nouns:

> There was once *a crow* who stole *a wedge of cheese* from *a kitchen window.* She flew off with *the cheese* to *a nearby tree. A fox* saw what *the crow* had done, and he walked over to *the tree.*

"Oh, Mistress Crow, you have such lovely black feathers, such slender feet, such a beautiful yellow beak, and such fine black eyes! You must have *a beautiful voice.* Would you please sing for me?"

The crow felt very proud. She opened her beak and sang CAW-CAW-CAW. Of course *the cheese* fell down, and *the fox* snatched it up and ate every bite.

Other forms of discourse can be much more complicated in terms of article usage. The "Fox and Crow" fable by Aesop is a good example of a "canonical" use of articles in written discourse. A more complicated example that seems to break the rules; is the opening paragraph from William Faulkner's (1931) *Sanctuary* (p. 3):

From beyond the screen of bushes which surrounded the spring, Popeye watched the man drinking. A faint path led from the road to the spring. Popeye watched the man— a tall, thin man, hatless, in worn gray flannel trousers and carrying a tweed coat under his arm—emerge from the path and kneel to drink at the spring.

Right from the beginning, the reader gets *the man* and *the spring* and *the road*; after the person is called <u>*the*</u> *man* in line 1, he is referred to as <u>*a*</u> *man* in line 3. This sort of opening (which is common in literature), rather than alienating the reader (as the hearer is alienated in the "dessert" example on p. 281), is actually intended to draw the reader *into* the story, as if he or she were already familiar with the participants and locale.[10]

Whatever type of text is used to illustrate article usage, it is, however, imperative that discussions of usage go beyond the sentence level to include discourse and context.

USE OF GENERIC NOUNS IN DISCOURSE

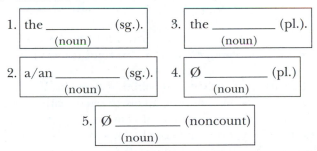

Many reference grammars and ESL/EFL texts (e.g., Quirk and Greenbaum, 1973) cite examples such as the following that state that all four patterns express generic meaning— the implication being that they share the same meaning and use:

1. The German ⎱ is a good musician.
2. A German ⎰
3. The Germans ⎱ are good musicians.
4. Germans ⎰

The examples above deal only with countable nouns. Noncount nouns can also be used generically and this would add a fifth pattern to the above list:

5. Water is essential for life.

However, since this fifth pattern is the only one we can use for noncount nouns, there is less variation according to usage and context unless a mass-to-count shift occurs, which is the case in the study by Bergsnev (1976) that we report below.

Research by Stern (1977) indicates that the four generic patterns for countable nouns have very different distributions in discourse and that a great deal depends on whether generic statements are being made about humans, animals, plants, historical inventions/devices, or less significant inanimate objects and whether the context is formal or informal.

The first pattern $\boxed{\text{The _____ (sg.)} \atop \text{(noun)}}$ represents formal usage. It describes generically classes of humans, animals, body organs, plants, and countable inanimate objects that are presented as human inventions whose origins can be traced: the gaslamp, the can opener, the laser, the computer, and so on. It is not appropriate as a generic pattern for countable inanimate objects that gradually developed over time and are not thought of as having been invented: the book, the window, the table, the chair, the bottle, and so forth.[11]

> *The book fills leisure time for many people.

To express such a proposition, either pattern 2 $\boxed{\text{a _____ (sg.)} \atop \text{(noun)}}$ or

4 $\boxed{\emptyset \text{ _____ (pl.)} \atop \text{(noun)}}$ would be appropriate:

> A book fills ⎫
> Books fill　⎬ leisure time for many people.
> 　　　　　 ⎭

Pattern 1 $\boxed{\text{the _____ (sg.)} \atop \text{(noun)}}$ occurs, for example, in informative or technical writing on plants, animals, musical instruments, and complex inventions or devices. Words like *class, symbol, representation, image,* and *stereotype/prototype* also tend to occur in discourse making use of this pattern.

In a relevant study of article usage in articles published in *Scientific American,* Master (1987) found that the first pattern was the one most likely to occur with noun subjects and to mark the topic of the essay; this pattern was also more likely to occur in first sentences of paragraphs and in introductions and conclusions of essays than elsewhere. Master (p. 165) felt that these usages "appear to reflect the . . . focused . . . nature of generic *the*" in contrast to the other more descriptive generic patterns.

Stern (1977) found that the third pattern above $\boxed{\text{the _____ (pl.)} \atop \text{(noun)}}$ is the most limited of the four. It usually expresses generic facts about human groups[12] that have a religious, political, national,[13] linguistic, social, or occupation/professional basis. Group affiliation is critical. This was not true in pattern 1, where science-based class membership rather than social group affiliation was the criterion. Thus the following are not acceptable as generic statements (they are, however, acceptable as specific statements):

> *The tigers are ferocious beasts.
> *The roses need water.
> *The pianos are splendid instruments.

However, any of the other three patterns for countable nouns (i.e., 1, 2, and 4) would produce acceptable generic statements for these examples. Some grammarians would claim that pattern 3 is not really generic, that it applies to plural proper names that express a collective meaning. Nonetheless, since this form is often used in formal writing in the social sciences instead of pattern 1, and since the pattern can be used with both specific and generic meaning, we believe it should be discussed and considered along with the other three patterns.

The pattern illustrated in sentence 4 $\boxed{\varnothing \underline{\hspace{2cm}} \text{ (pl.)} \atop \text{(noun)}}$ above is slightly less formal

than the pattern in 1 $\boxed{\text{the } \underline{\hspace{2cm}} \text{ (sg.)} \atop \text{(noun)}}$. In speech, it definitely occurs more

frequently than pattern 1. In fact, it can be used in almost all the discourse environments where pattern 1 occurs; in addition, it can be used to make generic statements about simple inanimate objects:

> Books fill leisure time for many people.

It is more concrete and frequent than pattern 1 in that it generalizes via pluralization rather than abstract classification. It is important because it can be used in virtually all contexts and because it ranges from semiformal to informal register.

Pattern 2 $\boxed{\text{a/an } \underline{\hspace{2cm}} \text{ (sg.)} \atop \text{(noun)}}$ is the most concrete and colloquial way of

expressing a generality. It is used most appropriately when the context is specific:

> (Mrs. X to Mrs. Y) I don't know about you, but I think *a husband* should help out with the housework.

It can be used to express informal generalities for all semantic contexts except those where collectivity or group cohesiveness is being expressed. In other words, one could substitute "husbands" or "the husband" for "a husband," and the register would change but not the meaning.[14]

Related to Stern's observations on the distribution of article and noun number patterns in generic usage, Bergsnev (1976) showed that abstract nouns deriving from verbs and adjectives often have both a noncount and a count form[15] with *a/an* available to express a generality; for example:

> Dependence on drugs is increasing.
> A dependence on drugs is increasing
> Increase in input produces dramatic changes in output.
> An increase in input produces a dramatic change in (the) output.

Some of the other abstract nouns that Bergsnev noted being used both ways include: *acceleration, achievement, deceleration, decrease, demand, depression, emphasis, equilibrium, expenditure, growth, priority, retardation, strain,* and *success*.

Noting that written texts in the hard sciences seem to prefer the abstract zero-article use, whereas written texts in the humanities seem to favor the countable form use with *a/an*, Bergsnev concluded that hard-and-fast rules were not realistic but that some guidelines were possible: The more concrete and informal the context, the better the countable form sounds with the indefinite article:

> Bill, don't you know that doctors say weight gain can put (a strain/?strain) on your heart?

Conversely, the more abstract and formal the context, the better the version without the article sounds:

> Demographic change often causes (population dispersion/?a population dispersion).

TOPIC-SPECIFIC USES OF ARTICLES

Patterns of article usage are sometimes relatively fixed for given disciplines and topics, which is of some comfort to those who teach English for specific purposes. For example, in medicine, anatomy, and biology, only two patterns seem to be used for both specific and generic references to organs or parts of the body:

BODY PARTS

Pattern 1 (the + noun)	*Pattern 3 (the + noun + pl.)*
(for singular body parts)	(for plural or paired body parts)
the heart	the ears
the liver	the eyes
the stomach	the lungs
the bladder	the teeth

The names of physical ailments and diseases, however, present a much greater learning problem because of the variety of article patterns and the singular and plural forms they take; they run the whole gamut of article and noun number patterns, the only overlap being the option of using either pattern 3 or pattern 4 for certain diseases:

DISEASES

Pattern 1	*Pattern 2*	*Pattern 3*	*or*	*Pattern 4*	*Pattern 5*
the + noun	*a/an + noun*[16]	*the + noun + pl.*		*noun + pl.*	*mass noun*
the flu	a cold	(the) bends			influenza
the gout	a hernia	(the) mumps			pneumonia
the plague	a headache	(the) measles			malaria
:	an earache	(the) chickenpox			cancer
:	a backache	(x = ks)			:
	:	:			

Occasionally, the same disease has two different names occurring in two different patterns:

> *Pattern 1*: the flu
> *Pattern 5*: influenza

Thus, the use of articles with body parts can involve the teaching of a system; however, the name of a disease and its article and noun number usage pattern should be mastered as a lexical unit if ESL/EFL students are to avoid making recurring errors when they refer to ailments and diseases, because no straightforward system underlies their usage.

Geographical Names

Geographical names are usually proper nouns and, as such, occur with no article if they are singular and with the definite article if they are plural and/or collective. Here are the major semantic categories for singular geographical proper names:

continent: Asia, South America, Africa, . . .
country: Canada, France, Nigeria, . . .
county: Nassau County, Cook County, . . .
city: Dallas, London, Tokyo, . . . (exception: The Hague)
mountain: Mount Whitney, Mount Aetna . . . (exception: The Matterhorn)
lake: Lake Michigan, Lake Baikal (exception: The Great Salt Lake) . . .
island: Catalina Island, Staten Island, . . .
point: Point Dume, Point Mugu, . . .
bay: San Francisco Bay, Tampa Bay, . . .
cape: Cape Cod, Cape Canaveral, . . .
park: Yosemite National Park, Douglas Park, . . .
region: Appalachia, Alsace, Siberia, . . .
street, road, avenue, boulevard, and so on: Downing Street, Wilshire Boulevard, Fifth
     Avenue, . . .
square: Trafalgar Square, Union Square, . . .

For plural or collective geographical names, the following categories are relevant and are consistent with plural proper noun conventions, which require use of *the*:

countries (if viewed as unions, federations, collections of islands): the U.S.A., the
     United Kingdom, the Philippines, . . .
lakes (if they form a geological group): the Great Lakes, the Finger Lakes, . . .
mountain ranges: the Rocky Mountains (or the Rockies), the Alps, the Andes, . . .
islands (if viewed as a group): the Canary Islands, the Azores, the Bahamas, . . .

However, a number of singular geographical names function as unique common nouns (as opposed to true proper nouns) and take the definite article. Consider the following list; the head noun is indicated in parentheses when deletion is possible:

regions: the Caucasus, the Crimea, the Rousillon, . . .
deserts: the Sahara (Desert), the Mohave (Desert), . . .
peninsulas: the Monterey Peninsula, the Iberian Peninsula, . . .
oceans and seas: the Pacific (Ocean), the Black Sea, . . .
gulfs: the Gulf of Mexico, the Persian Gulf, . . .
rivers: the Mississippi (River), the Amazon (River), . . .
canals: the Erie Canal, the Suez Canal, the Panama Canal, . . .

With the exception of "regions," which seem to be divided between proper names and unique common nouns, geographical names seem to pattern fairly neatly according to their geographical features. The unique common nouns in the last set, according to Hewson (1972), seem to be harder to define than the proper nouns. They are large and hard-to-define bodies of water (e.g., oceans, seas, gulfs—as opposed to lakes). Still others represent flowing water or strips of water used for navigation or irrigation (e.g., rivers and canals). The remaining categories are land masses or areas that are hard to define. For example:

regions—as opposed to countries or cities (where exactly does a given region begin
     or end?)
deserts—as opposed to arable land (where exactly does the desert end and the
     arable land begin?)
peninsula—as opposed to an island or the mainland (where exactly does the
     peninsula end and the mainland begin?)

While Hewson's generalization is useful, it is not perfect, since one might well wonder why oceans, seas, gulfs, and peninsulas—which are unique common names—are harder to define than bays, points, and capes, which are proper names. Perhaps, as Hewson suggests, size is a factor here, and smaller places are more likely to be familiar and to have proper names. In any case, Hewson's observations may help learners recall geographical names properly. Correct article usage with place names depends on correct assignment to the proper noun category (singular or plural/collective) or to the unique common noun category.

RESIDUAL PROBLEMS INVOLVING ARTICLE USAGE

In this chapter, we have established that for countable common nouns the definite article can be predicted in those cases where a noun referent is specific for both the speaker and the listener owing to situational uniqueness, textual co-reference, or structural and lexical information. It can also be explained if a noun is being used as a plural proper name or used generically in formal exposition to refer to a noun class. In this section, we want to mention briefly two uses of the definite article that do not appear to fit any of these categories very neatly.

Mechanical Inventions and Devices

Consider the following examples:

> We listened to the news on *the radio*.[17]
> I talked to Burt on *the phone*.
> I took *the train* to Boston.

In such cases, the hearer does not know the specific, radio, phone, or train that is being referred to (sometimes even the speaker does not know); however, it is clear that a specific radio, phone, or train has to be involved if these events take place in real time. We would thus expect an indefinite article here (we assume there has been no prior mention in the given communication), yet the definite article is being used in a way that seems to approach generic usage. However, this is quite different from true generic usage (e.g., the world's largest land mammal is *the elephant*) where no specific entity is involved. Perhaps this type of usage is close to the diseases we discussed above, since when we say,

> John has the flu.

we mean that John has an instance of the flu. Likewise, when we say,

> Alice took the train to Boston.

we mean that Alice took one specific instance of the noun class TRAIN to Boston.

Locations Associated with Activities

Examples such as the following are also problematic in a similar way:

$$\text{I'm going to} \begin{cases} \text{the store/mall.} \\ \text{the doctor/the} \begin{Bmatrix} \text{doctor's} \\ \text{dentist's} \end{Bmatrix} \text{office.} \\ \text{the bank.} \\ \text{the park.} \\ \text{the movies (Br.: the cinema).} \\ \text{the beach.} \end{cases}$$

In such cases, the hearer may well know but does not need to know the specific store, office, bank, and so on that is involved. For communication, such specificity does not seem to be essential; so why is the definite article used instead of the indefinite article or no article? Perhaps we are again approaching generic usage here, for when we say,

> I'm going to the store.

We actually mean that we are going to the store that we typically or habitually go to for shopping. We can, of course, also say:

> I'm going to a store.

but that would occur in much more constrained contexts such as the following:

> I'm going to a store $\begin{cases} \text{that Nancy recommended.} \\ \text{I've never been to before.} \end{cases}$

where the speaker in all likelihood is not yet familiar with the location being referred to.
Closely related to the above examples are those few cases where no article is used:

> I'm going to school/church/temple, . . .[18]

In such sentences, we are focusing on the activity (i.e., studying/learning; worshiping/praying) rather than the location. Focus on the physical location itself would require the use of an article:

> I'm going to a/the school.

We recognize that our explanations for the above residual usages of articles are tentative; however, such expressions do occur frequently, and at some point every ESL/EFL teacher must find a way to present and explain them to his or her students.

CONCLUSION

Much more, of course, needs to be said about article usage in English. We hope that this chapter provides a foundation. We discuss article usage again from time to time when it overlaps other grammatical topics. For example, in Chapter 4 under subject-verb agreement, we discussed the difference between phrases where the use of *a* or *the* often triggers a difference in number:

> a number of people are . . .   the number of people is . . .

Likewise, in Chapter 17 under quantifiers, we discuss the difference between pairs such as these where the presence of an indefinite article changes the meaning:

> few/a few   little/a little

Then, in Chapter 23, we observe that most sentences with *there* in subject position contain noun phrases with *a/an* or other indefinite determiners after the copula *be*:

> There's a snake in the bathtub!
> There is another problem we should discuss now.

We also mention articles again when we discuss the superlative degree in Chapter 35, since the definite article typically co-occurs with this construction:

> Tom is *the tallest (one)* in the class. We own *the oldest house* on the block.

In other words, article usage cannot be compartmentalized. Articles are everywhere in English, and the definite article is the most frequently used word in the English language (Francis and Kučera 1982). As an ESL/EFL teacher, you must be prepared to cope with the varied learning problems that your students will have related to the use of articles.
Some applied linguists (Dulay, Burt, and Krashen 1982) argue that the English articles are unteachable and can be acquired only through exposure. Others (Master

1994) have shown that focused instruction (i.e., systematic presentation in a hierarchy of manageable segments with built-in recycling) can make a difference and can help learners improve their use of articles. We agree with Master. Although the article system in English is extremely complex, many aspects of it are teachable. In the teaching suggestions that follow, we provide some exercises that we have found to be useful.

TEACHING SUGGESTIONS

1. Form. To practice the difference between count and noncount nouns, use a grid with count and noncount headings and ask learners to sort the words into the proper columns, instructing them to put words that describe things as wholes under "Noncount" and words that can be counted under "Count."

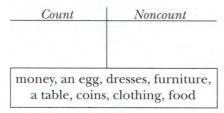

Count | *Noncount*

money, an egg, dresses, furniture, a table, coins, clothing, food

(adapted from Badalamenti and Henner-Stanchina 1997)

2. Form/Meaning. Indefinite article:
  a. Use the indefinite article to teach identification—first to distinguish *a* from *an* and then the singular form from the article-less plural.

> This is a(n) _____. (sg.) (orange, book)
> This is a(n) _____. (sg.)/These are _____s. (pl.) (a book/books)

For advanced students, Master (1990:198–199) suggests focusing on the use of the indefinite article with "classifying" or "defining" postmodification, in contrast to the use of the definite article with "identifying" postmodification, suggesting that these predictable patterns (among others) "might provide students with easily applied rules of thumb." Master gives the following examples:

> "classifying"   A thermometer is <u>an</u> instrument *that measures temperature.*
> "identifying"   <u>The</u> water *in this glass* is dirty.

  b. To stress normal indefinite noun usage—as opposed to the predicate noun usage shown above in suggestion 2a—have your students practice describing their possessions using *a/an* for singular nouns and unstressed *some* for mass or plural nouns.

> I have a _____. What do you have? I have some _____. What do you have?

3. Form/Meaning. Modified cloze dialogs such as the following can be used for both teaching and testing purposes (developed by Linda Chan-Rapp (personal communication)—based on Brown's matrix):
  Instructions: Fill in the blanks with *the* or *a/an.*

> *Son:*   Hey, Dad, can I have (1) _____ car Friday night? I want to take Sally to (2) _____ school dance.
> *Dad:*   Well, that depends. Don't you have (3) _____ paper to write?

> *Son:* Yeah, but it's almost done, and besides, (4) _____ friend told me
> Miss Fittich postponed it to next Friday.
> *Dad:* Well, okay. But be back by 12:30.
> *Son:* Thanks, Dad. Er . . . by the way, could I go buy (5) _____ new shirt for
> (6) _____ dance?

Cloze passages of academic prose can be valuable for advanced students.

4. Form/Meaning. After a range of article uses have been introduced, a common activity which uses authentic materials is to ask students to expand newspaper headlines into complete sentences. This would then be followed by a discussion of the articles chosen. Riggenbach and Samuda (1997:307) give the example: "Blizzard of '96 paralyzes East Coast," which can be expanded to "The Blizzard of '96 paralyzes the East Coast." Other headlines could be "Man bites dog" (which would use indefinite articles), or "UFO lands on White House," (which would use an indefinite and a definite article).

5. Form/Meaning. Give students a checklist for editing their own writing, such as the following:
  a. Underline all the nouns in your writing.
  b. If you have no article before the noun, is it
     i) a noncount noun (e.g., enrollment growth)?
     ii) a plural count noun (e.g., student numbers)?
     iii) a proper noun?
  c. Draw boxes around the nouns with the article *the*.
  d. If you have the article *the* + noun, does this refer to someone or something that is specified by
     i) the context (including common shared knowledge)?
     ii) previous mention?
     iii) mention within a noun group?
  e. Circle the nouns with the article *a*.
  f. If you have the article *a* + noun, does this refer to someone or something that is singular and:
     i) is not specified?
     ii) is being mentioned for the first time?
     iii) is being classified? (e.g., This piece of apparatus is *a Bunsen burner*.)

6. Meaning. Give your students practice in expressing generic usage with the zero article (especially abstract nouns) with the following activities, suggested by Ur (1988) and by Riggenbach and Samuda (1997), respectively:
  a. Have the class write a "cooperative poem." Give students a poetic title that is likely to be rich in associations (Ur suggests "Night" and "Home"). Ask students to write a noun phrase that describes an association that the topic has for them and write the suggestions up on the board to form a poem. This provides a great deal of repetition of the noun chosen with correct article usage.
  b. Ask students to interview people about what they think is most important for achieving happiness. Prior to the activity, elicit from students or provide them with a list of possible abstract nouns such as *love, romance, money, success, health, religion*. Discuss the appropriateness of zero article usage. Students then report their results to the class, monitoring themselves and being monitored by their peers for correct article usage.

7. Meaning. Give your students practice in category shifting from mass (generic) to count (specific) nouns:

tea   →   a tea/teas

Tea is a healthy beverage.   This is a nice tea. Try it.

Sri Lanka produces many teas.

Other nouns that could be used are: *wine, coffee, cheese, beer, bread, pasta,* and so on.

8. Use. Give your students practice in expressing generic concepts appropriate to different registers:

> cue: elephant/gigantic

    a. Formal—*The elephant* is gigantic/a gigantic land mammal.
    b. Less formal—*Elephants* are gigantic/gigantic animals.
    c. Colloquial—*An elephant* is huge.

9. Use. Develop students' awareness of the article system at higher levels, especially for academic purposes, by studying texts from the students' disciplines together in class. This can uncover specific patterns of usage, such as the patterns of use for medical language.

10. Use. Master (1995) suggests systematic consciousness raising to improve the article usage of advanced students. Providing constant feedback on article usage in students' written work, having brief class discussions of article usage patterns, and asking students to keep records of their article errors—these are all methods he has used.

11. Use. Howard Williams (personal communication) suggests that teachers of academic English spend some time teaching those common nouns or descriptions that are unique by definition and where *the* works practically 100 percent of the time:

Draw a line with 10 points along it on the board and draw students' attention to these mathematical concepts:

the first point	the second to the last point
the last point	the next point
the second point	the previous point

    .

    .

    .

    the tenth point

By drawing a loop from one point back to that point illustrate:

    the same point

Show students that these "points" can be rhetorical as well as literal/mathematical and that one can use these determiners with many other head nouns: *argument, example, draft, case, page, line, paragraph,* and so on.

12. Use. The informal generic use of the indefinite article could be practical and taught using dialogs like these:

> *Teacher:*   If you could be anything or anybody in the world, what or who would you want to be?
> *Student:*   I'd want to be an eagle.
> *Teacher:*   Why would you want to be an eagle?
> Student: Because eagles soar.

EXERCISES

Test your understanding of what has been presented.

1. Provide original example sentences that illustrate the following terms. Underline the relevant word(s) in your examples. You may need to write more than one sentence to properly illustrate some terms:

   a. noncount noun
      (i) mass noun
      (ii) abstract noun
   b. count noun
   c. definite article
      (i) —with textual co-reference
      (ii) —with situational/cultural reference
      (iii) —with structural reference
   d. first mention/subsequent mention principle
   e. indefinite article
      (i) —with generic usage
      (ii) —with predicate noun
   f. indefinite noun
      (i) —specific
      (ii) —nonspecific
   g. idiomatic article usage
   h. zero article use with generic meaning
   i. null article use with definite meaning

2. Develop your own example sentences for each quadrant of Brown's matrix.

3. Classify the following definite articles according to Hawkins' classification system— (1) situational/cultural reference; (2) textual reference; (3) structural reference:
   a. I went to New York City last week. *The* traffic is awful.
   b. Hurry up and put *the* car in *the* garage!
   c. I did a grammar course last year. My friend is going to do *the* course next year.
   d. *The* brick house on the corner is mine.

4. Explain the ungrammaticality of the following sentences:
   a. *She has a coffee on her dress.
   b. *They gave us many informations.
   c. *I have examination in French today.

Test your ability to apply what you know.

5. Students of yours have made the following errors. In each case, explain the nature of the error, and state what activities you would provide to correct it.
   a. *Change takes a long times.
   b. *This is an exclusive product in Taiwan travel industry.
   c. *We have to make the detailed travel plan.
   d. *Nowadays, personal computer isn't luxury anymore.
   e. *When I went to the Europe . . .
   f. *I enjoy writing the poetry. It's my hobby.
   g. *My brother is student.

6. In what two ways can the following sentence be interpreted?

   John is interested in buying a car.

7. Explain the different speaker conceptualizations for the noun *coffee* in the following sentences:

   a. Coffee is a stimulant.
   b. I'd like a coffee, please.
   c. The coffee here is good.
   d. This café has dozens of different coffees.

8. Imagine you are writing a letter home to your family from a foreign country that no one in your family has ever visited. Under what conditions would you write each of the following:

   a. I went to the beach today.
   b. I went to a beach today.

BIBLIOGRAPHY

References

Allan, K. (1980). "Nouns and countability." *Language* 56:3, 541–567.

Badalamenti, V. and C. Henner Stanchina, (1997). *Grammar Dimensions*. Book 1 (2d ed). Boston: Heinle & Heinle.

Bergsnev, L. (1976). "Variations in Article Usage with Abstract Nouns." Unpublished English 215 paper, UCLA, fall, 1976.

Brown, R. (1973). *A First Language*. Cambridge, Mass.: Harvard University Press.

Chesterman, A. (1991). *On Definiteness: A Study with Special Reference to English and Finnish*. Cambridge: Cambridge University Press.

Christophersen, P. (1939). *The Articles: A Study of Their Theory and Use in English*. Copenhagen: Einar Munksgaard.

Covitt, R. (1976). "Some Problematic Grammar Areas for ESL Teachers." M.A. thesis in TESL, UCLA.

Dulay, H., M. Burt, and S. Krashen (1982). *Language Two*. New York: Oxford University Press.

Francis, W. N., and H. Kučera (1982). *Frequency Analysis of English Usage*. Boston: Houghton Mifflin.

Hawkins, J. (1978). *Definiteness and Indefiniteness*. Atlantic Highlands, N.J.: Academic Press.

Hewson, J. (1972). *Article and Noun in English*. The Hague: Mouton.

Master, P. (1987). "Generic *the* in *Scientific American*." *English for Specific Purposes* 6:3, 165–186.

Master, P. (1994). "Effect of Instruction on Learning the English Article System." In T. Odlin (ed.), *Perspectives on Pedagogical Grammar*, 229–252. New York: Cambridge University Press.

Master, P. (1995). "Consciousness Raising and Article Pedagogy." In D. Belcher and G. Braine, (eds.), *Academic Writing in a Second Language: Essays on Research and Pedagogy*. Norwood, N.J.: Ablex.

Master, P. (1997). "Acquiring the Two Zero Articles in English." Paper presented at the Annual AAAL Conference. March 9, Orlando, Fla.

Pica, T. (1983). "The Article in American English: What the Textbooks Don't Tell Us." In N. Wolfson and E. Judd (eds.), *Sociolinguistics and Language Acquisition*, 222–233. Rowley, Mass.: Newbury House.

Riggenbach, H., and V. Samuda (1997). *Grammar Dimensions: Form, Meaning, and Use*. Book 2 (2d ed.). Boston: Heinle & Heinle.

Quirk, R., and S. Greenbaum, (1973). *A Concise Grammar of Contemporary English.* New York: Harcourt Brace Jovanovich.

Stern, S. (1977). "Generic Use of Articles in English." Unpublished English 215 paper, UCLA, fall, 1977.

Swan, M. (1980). *Practical English Usage.* London: Oxford University Press.

Thompson, S. A. (1978). "Modern English from a Typological Point of View: Some Implications of the Function of Word Order." *Linguistische Berichte* 54:1, 19–35.

Ur, P. (1988). *Grammar Practice Activities: A Practical Guide for Teachers.* Cambridge: Cambridge University Press.

Suggestions for further reading

For the best traditional account of the English article system, see:

Christophersen, P. (1939). *The Articles: A Study of Their Theory and Use in English.* Copenhagen: Einar Munksgaard.

For a good recent synopsis of article use in English with excellent exercises, see:

Berry, R. (1993). "Articles." *Collins COBUILD English Guides No. 3.* London: HarperCollins.

For a somewhat alternative perspective on articles and many good teaching suggestions, see:

Master, P. (1990). "Teaching the English Articles as a Binary System." *TESOL Quarterly* 24 :3, 461–498.

Master, P. (1996). *Systems in English Grammar.* Englewood Cliffs, N.J.: Prentice-Hall. See especially pp. 215–228 for both explanation and exercises.

ENDNOTES

1. Covitt (1976) did a survey of ESL teachers in the Los Angeles area in the mid seventies and found that article usage was their number one teaching problem. We feel that this result would still be true today if the survey were repeated.

2. Another way to signal given vs. new information in many languages (both topic-prominent and subject-prominent) is through contrastive stress; e.g. JOHN took the money. Here, the fact that John rather than someone else was the agent is new information because of contrastive stress, even though the noun in the subject position often is old or given information.

3. Note that this rule applies to the initial *sound* of the following word, not the initial *letter*, which may be a vowel letter representing a consonant sound.

4. See footnote 3.

5. Historically significant eras often take the definite article and pattern very much like plural proper names (i.e., the head noun is either plural or singular but semantically collective in meaning): the 1990's, the Roaring Twenties, the War Years, the Great Depression, the Renaissance.

6. We focus on mass-to-count shifts here. The opposite shift (count-to-mass) is, of course, also possible: e.g., an egg→He's got egg on his tie. However, our emphasis reflects the higher frequency of mass-to-count shifts; this tendency occurs perhaps because the countable common noun is the prototypical or unmarked "noun" class toward which the other noun types tend to shift in English.

7. These cases normally have a capital letter both as a unique common noun and as a proper noun because both refer to geographical territory.

8. In the following discussion, we draw on Hawkins' theory as well as many of his examples but have added a few subcategories and examples of our own to make the account as comprehensive as possible.

9. Whatever exercises the teacher provides, the native-like acquisition of articles is extremely difficult. A learner might actually put *the* in the second blank of Chan-Rapp's exercise on the assumption the teacher and student know there is just one tutor. But *the* will not work as idiomatic English here because the teacher does not know who the tutor is. This is the kind of mistake learners can make when trying to apply the "rules."

10. This style may be somewhat regional; people from the South or other rural areas in the United States have a tendency to refer to objects and places and people in the presence of a newcomer as if they were already familiar to the newcomer.)

11. Such simple inanimate objects can, however, be used with *the* by anthropologists or historians who present them as a significant invention: for example, "The wheel represented a step forward for this culture/mankind."

12. On rare occasions, plants or animals will attain the necessary group status and affiliation to merit use of pattern 3:

> Save the whales.
> The redwoods must be preserved forever.

Such cases, however, appear to be exceptions.

13. Generally, the adjective form of a nationality is used with the definite article to function as the generic collective nouns in pattern 3 (e.g., The Germans). If the adjective ends in *n* or *i*, then a regular plural ending is added: the Canadians, the Israelis, the Saudis. If the adjective ends in a sibilant sound (e.g., *s, z, (t)ch, dge, sh*), no plural ending is added: the English, the Chinese, the Welsh, the Dutch). If the adjective ends in *-ish*, usually the stem minus the suffix is used with a plural ending to form the generic collective noun: Polish/the Poles, Swedish/the Swedes, Finnish/the Finns. However, "English" appears to be an exception to the *-ish* pattern in that we say "English/the English;" i.e., the sibilant pattern applies here.

14. Someone has pointed out to us that the meaning potential would indeed change in cultures where a wife can have more than one husband. In such cases, there would be a difference in meaning between a generic statement with "a husband/the husband" vs. "husbands" vs. "the husbands." This again points out the role of shared cultural knowledge in article use and interpretation.

15. This would correspond to a choice between pattern 2 and pattern 5.

16. In British English, all of the *-ache* compounds in this pattern except *headache* can also occur without the indefinite article, such as, *Joe has earache;* however, there is considerable variation from region to region. The interested reader should consult Swan (1980) for discussion of British usage in this area.

17. Note that television is treated differently in British and American English. In British usage we see a program "on the television (the telly, the tube)" but in American usage we see it "on television (on TV)."

18. Note that "mosque" is an exception to this pattern. We would say "I'm going to the mosque" not *I'm going to mosque," which suggests that English speakers classify *mosque* as a building (similar to their use of *cathedral, tabernacle,* etc.). However, we have been told that English-speaking Muslims are likely to say, "I'm going to mosque," so this may well be a matter of what one's religion is.

16

REFERENCE AND POSSESSION

INTRODUCTION

In this chapter, we describe the forms, meanings, and uses of the grammatical resources that express reference and possession in English. Referential forms point to people or objects in the real world or to other forms called "antecedents" and include the various types of personal pronouns, the demonstratives, and a number of other referring forms. Possession can be expressed inflectionally (*'s*), periphrastically (*x of y*), or referentially (via possessive determiners or pronouns). We will first treat reference, topics under which are diagrammed below:

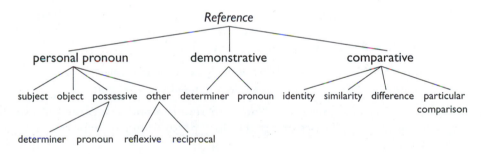

FORMS THAT EXPRESS REFERENCE

Halliday and Hasan (1976) distinguish three types of reference in English: personal reference, demonstrative reference, and comparative reference.

PERSONAL REFERENCE

The personal pronouns in their various permutations constitute the personal reference system in English.

Subject and Object Pronouns

The following are the subject and object forms of the personal pronouns in English:

	SUBJECT		**OBJECT**	
	singular	*plural*	*singular*	*plural*
Ist person	I	we	me	us
2nd person	you	you	you	you
3rd person	she/he/it	they	her/him/it	them
	(one)[1]		(one)[1]	

The subject pronouns function as subject NPs; the object pronoun forms can function as direct, indirect, or prepositional objects.

Both the subject and object pronouns can function as subject predicate nouns:

> A: Who's there?
> B: It is I./It's me.
>   (subj.   (obj.
>   pro.)   pro.)

In this environment, the subject pronoun is the historically older and formally prescriptive form, but the object pronoun is currently more frequently used and is certainly favored in informal speech. There is more discussion of this issue later in the section on meaning and use.

Possessive Determiners and Pronouns

The possessive pronoun forms are also part of the personal reference system in English. They perform two syntactic functions: a possessive form can serve as a possessive determiner before a noun, or it can replace an entire possessive NP. (In the former case, it is called a possessive adjective in traditional grammars):

> This is Sheila's book. → This is *her* book. (possessive determiner)
> This book is Sheila's. → This book is *hers*. (possessive pronoun)

Depending on whether it precedes a noun or stands alone as a pronoun, two slightly different forms exist in all cases except the third person singular masculine form, which does not change:

	DETERMINER FUNCTION		**PRONOMINAL FUNCTION**	
	singular	*plural*	*singular*	*plural*
Ist person	my	our	mine	ours
2nd person	your	your	yours	yours
3rd person	her/his/its	their	hers/his/ø[2]	theirs
	one's		ø[2]	

As mentioned earlier in Chapter 5, the possessive determiners are core determiners like the definite article and the demonstratives and thus can be preceded by a predeterminer and followed by a postdeterminer:

pre	core	post	noun head
all	*his*	*other*	*books*

The possessive pronouns, however, replace an entire noun phrase and can function as subjects or objects:

> A: Hal has an excellent word processing program.
> B: Really? *Mine* has more options.
>   (subject)

> A: Do you like Joe's new car?
> B: I prefer *yours*.
>   (object)

The *wh*-question word routinely associated with these referential possessive forms is *whose*; it is used most frequently as a determiner but occasionally occurs as a pronoun:

> Whose (umbrella) is this?

Reflexive Pronouns

The other major set of forms that function as personal reference pronouns are the reflexive pronouns:

	SINGULAR	*PLURAL*
1st person	myself	ourselves
2nd person	yourself	yourselves
3rd person	herself, himself, itself	themselves
	oneself	

Can you see anything unusual about the forms of the pronouns that precede the stem *self/selves*? It should be apparent that the third person masculine singular reflexive pronoun *himself*, the third person plural reflexive pronoun *themselves,* and the neutral, formal third person pronoun *oneself* are formed differently from the others in that they contain the object form of the personal pronoun + *self/selves*, whereas the others consist of the possessive determiner + *self/selves*. This is a possible source of error for ESL/EFL students who imagine the paradigm to be regular and thus erroneously produce **hisself* and **theirselves*, forms that also occur in some nonstandard dialects of English.

When used in their underlying reflexive sense, reflexive pronouns replace NP objects that have the same referent as the subject of the sentence:

> (subject)   (object)
> Sally   cut   *herself.*

Reciprocal Pronouns

Two other phrasal forms routinely used to express personal reference are the reciprocal pronouns, *each other* and *one another*. Like reflexive pronouns, both replace NP objects that typically refer back to NP subjects in the same sentence. However, for these forms the subject must be conjoined or plural:

> Bob and Dick can't stand *each other.*
> The five children in that family helped *one another* throughout their lives.

DEMONSTRATIVE REFERENCE[3]

The demonstrative determiners of English vary along two dimensions: proximity and number.

	SINGULAR	PLURAL
Near	this	these
Far	that	those

Like the possessives, the demonstratives can also function as pronouns as well as determiners and can represent an entire subject or object NP. Thus, one can say,

Please fill $\left\{ \begin{array}{l} \text{this form} \\ \text{these forms} \end{array} \right\}$ out. (determiner function)

or, if the context makes the noun "form(s)" clear, simply say,

Please fill $\left\{ \begin{array}{l} \text{this} \\ \text{these} \end{array} \right\}$ out. (pronominal function)

Like the possessive determiners and the definite article, the demonstrative determiners are core determiners that can co-occur with a predeterminer and a post determiner:

pre   core   post   head noun
all   *these*   *other*   *issues*

The *wh*-question word most closely associated with demonstratives is *which*; it can readily serve either a determiner function or a pronominal function:

Which (dress) did Margaret buy?

Sufficient context is required for the pronominal use to be interpretable.

COMPARATIVE REFERENCE

A rather amorphous set of forms come together under the rubric of Halliday and Hasan's (1976) comparative reference. This type of reference includes forms that express identity, general similarity, difference, and particular comparison.

Identity

The forms expressing referential identity—*same* and *self-same*—are used mainly as determiners:[4]

The young vagrant loitered on the corner.

The $\left\{ \begin{array}{l} \text{same} \\ \text{self-same} \end{array} \right\}$ young man had been there the day before.

General Similarity

The referential forms expressing general similarity—*such, so,* and *likewise*—have different grammatical functions. *Such* is a determiner. As shown by the three different ways of continuing the dialogue started by speaker A, it can directly precede noncount nouns

(B1) and plural count nouns (B2), but it is unusual among determiners in that it must be followed by *a/an* when it modifies a singular count noun (B3):

> A: Did you like Professor Grogan's lecture?
> B1: No, such argumentation tends to bore me.
> B2: No, such lectures bore me.
> B3: No, such a lecture tends to bore me.

The referential form *so*, when used to express general similarity, is quite parallel to *this* used adverbially:

$$\text{Our table is } \begin{Bmatrix} \text{so} \\ \text{this} \end{Bmatrix} \text{ long.}$$

$$\text{Do it like } \begin{Bmatrix} \text{so.} \\ \text{this.} \end{Bmatrix}$$

Both *this* and *so*, when used as comparative referential forms, generally co-occur with some sort of physical gesture or demonstration on the part of the speaker. *Likewise* is a referential adverb expressing general similarity; it often co-occurs with the pro-verb *do*, and together they refer to a previously occurring verb phrase:

> Mrs. Allison made a generous donation to the Cancer Society. We were hoping you would do likewise.

Difference

The referential forms of difference are *other*—including its related forms (*the*) *others* and *another*—and *else*,[5] and are frequent and important words in English. They tell the listener/reader that one speaker/writer is referring to some target item other than the antecedent:

> 1. Have you had a cookie? Yes? Have another!

> 2. I needed some help, and I couldn't find Ralph, so I looked for someone else.

In 1, *another* is used referentially to mean "another cookie," that is, something in addition to but different from the antecedent (i.e., *a cookie*). In 2, *else* in combination with *someone* refers back to *Ralph* but means "a person other than or different from Ralph."

Particular Comparison

The particular comparatives (e.g., *more, less, better, worse,* etc.) can be used like pronouns or adverbs to refer to something in prior discourse:

> 3. I finished my coffee. Amy offered me more.
> 4.   A: How are you feeling?
>   B: Better.

In 3, the "more" means "more coffee," in addition to what the speaker had finished, and in 4, the response "better" means "I'm feeling better than before." Note that many of the comparative reference forms allow us to say something more elliptically and concisely; thus, we can avoid repetition.

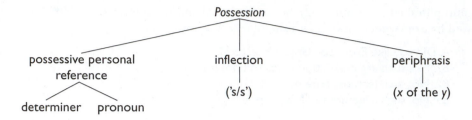

POSSESSIVE FORMS[6]

In addition to the possessive determiners and possessive pronouns already discussed above, as part of reference, there are two other major ways of signaling possession in English:

In writing, the first is by inflecting regular singular nouns and irregular plural nouns not ending in *s* with *'s*, as in

> the baby's crib   the women's room

or by adding an apostrophe after the *s* ending of regular plural nouns and singular forms that already end in the sound *s*:

> the boys' trip   Kansas' farmlands[7]

The apostrophe added to regular plural nouns and singular nouns ending in *s* does nothing to alter the pronunciation of the word; however, the addition of the *'s* to singular and irregular plural nouns is realized in speech as /s/ when it occurs after voiceless consonants, /z/ when it follows voiced consonants and vowels, and /əz/ after sibilants (i.e., /s/, /z/, /š/, /ž/, /č/, and /ǰ/):

> Mac's   /mæks/
> Sam's   /sæmz/
> Grace's   /greysəz/

The other way of signaling possession is by using the periphrastic *of* possessive form where the possessor and thing possessed are inverted if one compares this order with that of the inflected *'s* form.

> the man's name → the name of the man

From the example above, you might infer that the *'s* possessive and *of* possessive forms are interchangeable. This is not usually the case, as you will see below when we discuss this contrast again under use.

When the nouns involved are relatively short, double possessive inflections are possible:

> Bob's brother's car

Double and even triple periphrastic possessives are also possible, regardless of whether the nouns involved are long or short:

> the cover of the folio of the sonnets of Shakespeare

Syntactically, we treat a noun inflected with the possessive *'s* as a determiner, but a possessive determiner would always precede a possessive noun determiner. (recall that up to three determiners are possible):

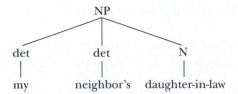

The periphrastic possessive with *of* is generated as a noun phrase with a modifier prepositional phrase following the head noun:

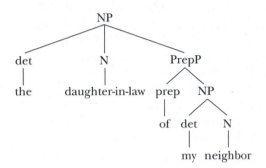

One of the most interesting structural facts about the possessive inflection is that it may be an inflection on complex or compound noun phrases as well as on simple nouns:

the mayor of San Diego 's car

Sally and John 's new baby

THE SCOPE OF REFERENTIAL FORMS

The basic difference between the reflexive and reciprocal pronouns and all the other personal pronouns is that the antecedent for reflexive and reciprocal pronouns must be in the same sentence or clause:

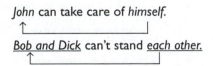

For possessive pronouns, the antecedent can be either within the same clause/sentence or in an earlier clause:

Greg loves *his* dog. (same clause)

Do you know *Greg?* I walk *his* dog. (prior clause).

Subject and object personal pronouns, however, typically refer to an antecedent in a preceding clause:[8]

Do you know *Sara? She's* just moved to Atlanta.

Do you know *Sara?* Yes, I've been acquainted with *her* for ten years.

THE MEANING, ACQUISITION, AND USE OF SUBJECT AND OBJECT PRONOUNS

Subject and object pronoun forms do not usually cause undue learning hardship for ESL/EFL students, since the English pronominal system is far simpler than that of many other languages. There are only a few problems that ESL/EFL teachers need to be aware of. Many non-English speakers have told us that they find the presence of only one second personal pronoun form—*you*—disconcerting and too direct. English has no way to be either formal or intimate linguistically and no way to explicitly mark singular or plural number. Another source of initial confusion, due to the simplicity of the English pronoun system, might occur for students whose native language has inclusive and exclusive forms of the first person plural pronoun. Having two such forms is typical of languages of the Malayo-Polynesian family. Indonesian speakers, for example, use *kita* to mean *we* when the person addressed is included, as in

We should (all) go to the movies next Saturday.

whereas *kami* means *we,* excluding the person addressed:

Are we late? (addressed to person who has been waiting)

Since inclusive and exclusive meanings are both contained in the English first person plural pronouns, students who distinguish these forms in their native languages should have no problems once they recognize that one form is used to express both meanings in English.

A more serious problem arises for students whose native language makes no gender distinction for third person singular pronouns. Such students understand the use of *he* or *she/him* or *her,* of course, but since they are not accustomed to observing the distinction in their mother tongue, they often use the English third person pronouns inappropriately. Mere rule explication will probably do little to aid in this area; however, contextualized practice in using the various third person pronouns should help heighten student awareness. This same problem, of course, applies to the third person singular possessive and reflexive personal pronouns.

SOME ODDITIES OF SUBJECT AND OBJECT PRONOUN USE

ESL/EFL students will have to learn that certain inanimate objects are sometimes referred to with a feminine pronoun form, although the use of *it* is more common today. This has been true for ships, countries, cars, and until recently, hurricanes, which now are given alternative masculine and feminine names and referred to as *he* or *she* as appropriate. (Note that once an animal or anything else has been given a gender-marked proper name, the appropriate feminine or masculine pronoun tends to be used.)

Of course, the controversy continues as to whether or not it is sexist (or discriminatory) to use the third person singular masculine form when one intends to include both the meaning of *he* and *she,* as in

When a person first arrives in a new country, he has many adjustments to make.

For now, this controversy will have to be resolved by each individual. Even if you yourself do not find such references offensive, you might explain to your ESL/EFL students that some people do and that stylistic alternatives are possible and often preferred. (The use of "singular" *they* in such cases is discussed later.)

> When a person first arrives in a new country, he or she has many adjustments to make. (use of "he or she")

> When people first arrive in a new country, they have many adjustments to make. (use of plural)

In verbless or elliptical utterances, the object pronoun sometimes replaces the subject form, which would be expected in a complete sentence or in a partially reduced sentence with a verb form.

> Who received the letter? $\begin{cases} \text{I received the letter.} \\ \text{I did.} \\ \text{Me.} \end{cases}$

As mentioned previously, in full sentences with the copula *be*, personal pronouns functioning as subject noun predicates used to take the subject form in formal English:

> It is I.   This is she.

This usage is now changing even in formal English, and in informal English, the object form of the pronoun is definitely preferred:

> It's me.
> That's her.

However, the desire to use formal English and be "correct" has led some native speakers to use *I* even as a conjoined direct object or a conjoined object of a preposition.

> ?This concerns only you and I.   ?The article was written by Nancy and I.
> ?Between you and I, he's a fool.

These forms are becoming colloquially acceptable, and they are occurring with ever-increasing frequency even though they are prescriptively incorrect.

INDEFINITE PRONOUNS

Even though the so-called indefinite pronouns are not referential in and of themselves, they often serve as antecedents for referential forms or co-occur with referential forms like *else*. We introduce them here in order to discuss some interesting features of use associated with these forms:

The indefinite pronouns occur as compound forms:[9]

	some	*any*	*no*	*every*
-body	somebody	anybody	nobody	everybody
-one	someone	anyone	no one	everyone
-thing	something	anything	nothing	everything

Notice that they all are written as single words except for the phrase *no one*. *-Body* and *-one* mean "person" in general. *-Thing*, however, refers to an inanimate or abstract concept, or to an entity not clearly identifiable as a person (e.g., "Shhh! *Something* moved"). Whenever *one* is used to mean the cardinal number, however, an indefinite pronoun or compound no longer results. In this case there is a two-word sequence with the number *one* receiving stress. Compare:

> Anyone could have gotten in free.
> Any one of us could have gotten in free; the other two would have had to pay.

The Use of Plural Pronouns to Refer to Singular Nouns

All the compound indefinite pronouns prescriptively require singular verbs. Nevertheless, the use of a formally plural pronoun such as *they, them,* or *their* to refer back to the following singular compounds is acceptable in informal usage, such as:

$$\left.\begin{matrix} \text{Everyone} \\ \text{Everybody} \end{matrix}\right\} \text{ has } \left\{\begin{matrix} \text{his} \\ \text{their} \end{matrix}\right\} \text{ own way of doing things.}$$

Based on a conversational analysis she conducted, Nesbitt (1980:60) reports that the "*everyone . . . their* combination actually occurred far more frequently than "the 'sexist' *his* form and the wordy *his* or *her* form." Presumably this same preference will carry over to the other indefinite pronouns and will result in their increasing acceptability in combination with plural pronouns:

> Somebody is driving without their lights.   Nobody had a good time, did they?
> Has anybody brought a watch with them?

Lagunoff (1992, 1997) extends Nesbitt's study beyond indefinite pronouns to include other antecedents as well. In fact, she documents the use of singular *they* in written as well as spoken English from the fifteenth century to the present. She proposes that an antecedent allowing co-reference with singular *they* must be unspecified in some way (i.e., number, gender, referentiality) and that singular *they* is an unmarked pronoun. Some of the interesting examples she cites follow (page numbers cited are from Lagunoff [1992]):

> Someone left their sweatshirt here. (p. 6)
> No one sends their children to public school anymore. (p. 7)
> Has anyone lost their pen? (p. 9)
> Who ever gets to imagine that they might become an artist? (p. 12)
> Every (parent/mother/father) thinks their baby is cute. (p. 17)[10]

Lagunoff concludes that teachers can certainly present singular *they* as an option that students can use for co-reference with certain types of antecedents in informal spoken and written contexts.

Indefinite Pronouns and Other Indefinite and Generic Noun Phrases

Bolinger (1977:14–15) hypothesized that *-one* and *-body* compounds do not occur in free variation. He suggests that *-one* signals nearness in both a spatial and psychological sense and that *-body* signals distance. Thus:

$$\text{This present is for } \left\{\begin{matrix} \text{someone} \\ \text{?somebody} \end{matrix}\right\} \text{ very dear to me.}$$

$$\text{"Who should introduce the speaker?" I asked. "Oh, } \left\{\begin{matrix} \text{anybody} \\ \text{?anyone} \end{matrix}\right\} \text{," he replied disinterestedly.}$$

To test Bolinger's hypothesis, Roth (1991) examined over three hundred contextualized tokens of *someone* and *somebody* occurring in written and spoken English sources and largely confirmed but also extended Bolinger's proposals. She found that *somebody* occurred with significant frequency in contexts that were hypothetical, general, distant, and where the speaker/writer expressed neutral or negative stance towards the NP. *Someone*, on the other hand, occurred with significant frequency in contexts that were concrete, proximate, intimate, and where the speaker/writer expressed positive stance towards the NP. Roth also found something Bolinger had not hypothesized: *someone* occurred very frequently with verbs of communication such as *say* and *tell* in her oral data:

> Years ago when I worked in Hollywood, someone said, "You don't understand. This town is run on fear." (Roth, p. 19)

THE MEANING OF DEMONSTRATIVES

When we introduced the demonstrative determiners, we said that *this/these* had a sense of "nearness" and *that/those* a sense of "distance." What we did not explain was that the nearness or distance being conveyed could be spatial, temporal (*this* = now vs. *that* = then), psychological (*this* = more preferred vs. *that* = less preferred), or simply sequential (*this* = first mention vs. *that* = second mention):

spatial:	I like this car better than that one [11] over there.
temporal:	I like this movie better than that concert last night.
psychological:	I like this candidate, which is why I didn't vote for that one.
sequential:	This dress is less attractive than that one.

Further functions of the demonstratives in discourse are discussed below.

USE OF DEMONSTRATIVES IN DISCOURSE

Demonstratives seem to follow somewhat different patterns of use in spoken and written English. Strauss (1993) looked at spoken data, where it is important to distinguish situational (i.e., deictic or exophoric [reference to people and things outside the text]) uses of demonstratives from textual (i.e., anaphoric [backwards pointing] and cataphoric [forward pointing]) uses. Using 37 different data sets and over 40,000 transcribed words, Strauss concluded that it was necessary to include *it* along with *this/these* and *that/those* to give an accurate account for her data. Her overall analysis follows:

FORM(S)	DATA FREQUENCY	MEANING	HEARER	REFERENT
this/these	15%	high focus	new information (not shared)	important
that/those	30%	med. focus	↕	↕
it	55%	low focus	old information (shared)	unimportant

By "focus," Strauss, drawing on Kirsner's (1979) work, means the degree of attention the listener should pay to the referent. Strauss found that *that/those* and *it* were used overwhelmingly with anaphoric textual reference in her data (91% and 97%, respectively):

[Caller to a radio talk show on gardening]

Hi. I have a very old kind of a vine-type rose. I think that *it* grows—*it's* actually in my next-door neighbor's vacant yard and, uhm, I don't really know how to prune *that* thing. *It* gets—seems like a floribunda type.

(Strauss 1993:407)

This/these, on the other hand, were used anaphorically in her oral corpus only 51 percent of the time since these forms also are used in the following ways (examples from pp. 405–407):

Cataphorically (7%) (to point forward):
[another radio talk show]
Again we come back to *this*: Murder is the act of killing someone. . . .

Exophorically (22%) (to point outside the text at something):
[teacher is lecturing]
Yeah. The border states, specifically [pulls down map] we've looked at *this* before. . . .

Nonreferentially (20%) (to introduce or present new information like *a/an*):
Bee: They stuck us in *this* crazy building that they juh—they're not even finished with it.

The other interesting pattern that Strauss found was that *this/these* occurred as determiners about 60 percent of the time and as pronouns about 40 percent of the time, whereas *that/those* occurred as pronouns about 70 percent of the time and as determiners only 30 percent of the time. Strauss feels that this reinforces her analysis of *this/these* as high-focus, new-information signals where the whole noun referent tends to be mentioned; however, *that* is more like *it* and occurs more often pronominally to signal a lower degree of focus and a greater degree of shared information.

The use of demonstrative determiners and pronouns in written English was the focus of a study by Nishimura (1995). She compared published book notices and short essays by native English-speaking authors published in the *TESOL Quarterly* and found that use of demonstratives was highly constrained in the book-notice genre. The vast majority of tokens were modifier uses of *this/these* with very few tokens of *that/those*: *this text, this book, this level,* and so forth. The short essays, however, followed a different pattern. Demonstratives were used not only to refer to prior noun phrases but to whole clauses and groups of clauses.[12] Although *this/these* still occurred more often that *that/those*, the essay had a greater variety of functions for and a higher number of *that/those* tokens; pronominal uses occurred alongside the more frequent determiner uses:

In *these* comments I have expanded on DuFon's discussion of the sixth area of the TESOL guidelines. Research has a world view. It can be dishonestly executed to serve the aims of others, although . . . I believe *that* is truly rare. . . .

(Davidson 1993:162, cited in Nishimura 1995)

The determiner *these* above is in the opening sentence of a final paragraph and refers to the author's own entire essay (i.e., *these comments*). Then the demonstrative pronoun *that* is used to refer to an entire proposition, "[research can be] dishonestly executed to serve the aims of others." Nishimura concluded that because the use of demonstratives was so constrained in the book-notice genre while the academic essay genre allowed room for rhetorical effect and personal style suggests that demonstrative usage may be quite genre specific in written discourse. This area needs further study.

INTERACTION OF DEMONSTRATIVES, PERSONAL PRONOUNS, AND ARTICLES

Frodesen and Eyring (1997:108) point out that it is important to understand how the demonstratives and personal pronouns interact with the articles. They give the following examples to show that these forms are often equally grammatical choices but that the choice depends on the speaker's or writer's intentions or what she or he expects the listener/reader to know:

$$\text{Oh, I've heard } \left\{ \begin{array}{l} \text{that joke} \\ \text{the joke} \\ \text{it} \end{array} \right\} \text{ before.}$$

$$\text{Moya told us } \left\{ \begin{array}{l} \text{the jokes.} \\ \text{those jokes.} \\ \text{them.} \end{array} \right\}$$

With the following two example sets, Frodesen and Eyring show that demonstratives give the referent more emphasis (or "focus" as Strauss says) than use of an article or pronoun:

> I heard a speaker on campus this afternoon . . .
>   (1) *The speaker* was talking about the dangers of nuclear power.
>   (2) *This speaker* was the best I've heard regarding the nuclear power issue.

Here the definite article in (1) emphasizes the topic of nuclear power while the demonstrative in (2) emphasizes the speaker.

> I'm not sure if I'll type my paper myself . . .
>   (3) If I do, *it* will probably take all day.
>   (4) I have more important things to do than *that*!

The *it* in (3) gives less emphasis to the antecedent—type my paper myself—and more to the fact that it will take all day; the *that* in (4) gives the antecedent more emphasis, which is reinforced by the sentence-final position of *that*.

   The other point that Frodesen and Eyring make is that personal and demonstrative pronouns are often used to avoid repetition and wordiness when antecedents are in adjacent clauses:

> (5) I asked my instructor if I needed to submit a bibliography with my draft.
>
> She told me $\left\{ \begin{array}{l} \text{that} \\ \text{?the bibliography} \end{array} \right\}$ would be unnecessary.
>
> (6) This paper is the best I've written. I'm sure my classmates will
>
> enjoy $\left\{ \begin{array}{l} \text{it} \\ \text{?the paper} \end{array} \right\}$.

THE MEANING AND USE OF REFLEXIVE AND RECIPROCAL PRONOUNS

A potential cross-linguistic problem derives from the distinction English makes between plural reflexive pronouns and reciprocal pronouns.

The children hit themselves.

The children hit each other.

Many languages (e.g., Spanish and Yoruba) can use virtually the same forms to refer to both the reflexive and reciprocal meaning and allow the context to disambiguate. Learners speaking such first languages may unintentionally produce English sentences such as the following:

>*After ten years, she and Ted were happy to see themselves again.

ASYSTEMATIC USES OF REFLEXIVE PRONOUNS

In a series of studies, Staczek (1986, 1987) has made observations about unpredicted uses of reflexive pronouns in English.

First, the reflexive pronoun seems to be alternating with subject and object pronouns in ways that are not semantically reflexive.[13]

> What about yourself?
>> (= you)
>
> We expected yourself to take the lead.
>> (= you)
>
> The text was first copyedited by my mother and myself.
>> (= me)
>
> Mr. Dennison, Mr. Pappas, and myself have spent hundreds of hours . . .
>> (= I)
>
> On behalf of myself and Delta Airlines, . . .
>> (= me)

From a syntactic view, such uses of reflexives are a form of asystematic variation, according to Staczek. They may at times reflect the speaker's or the writer's insecurity over whether to use the subject or object pronoun or a reflexive pronoun, or their desire to use a phonetically more salient form in juxtaposition with one or more proper names. These may also be instances where a first-person narrator is interacting with several other people and uses "ourselves" instead of "us" to capture the interactive, dual, speaker-listener role that everyone is experiencing:

> I'd like to remind ourselves . . . (Staczek 1987:118)

Second, Staczek (1988) has looked at the variation in the use of the plural reflexives -self/-selves and suggests that increasing colloquial use of the -self forms as plural reflexives—which he documents (examples below)—is evidence that English is undergoing a change and that the now prescriptively required -selves forms may eventually be lost:

> How we portray ourself influences the way we behave.
> I'm sure many of you have played this head game with yourself.
> We encourage people to give themself credit for the labor in remodeling.

These examples are reminiscent of Lagunoff's (1992, 1997) work on singular "they."

THE USE OF RECIPROCAL PRONOUNS

Prescriptive tradition and some current grammar books (e.g., Cook and Suter 1980) state that the rule for distinguishing the two reciprocal pronoun phrases, *each other* and *one another*, is dependent on the number of participants involved: *each other* should be used with two participants and *one another* with more than two:

> Bob and George dislike each other.
> The three sisters are devoted to one another.

Quirk et al. (1985) reject this rule and offer an explanation based on register rather than number: *each other* is informal, and *one another* is used in more formal contexts. The American Heritage Dictionary (1992) states that *one another* is preferred over *each other* in temporally ordered series of events or things:

> The waiters followed one another into the room.

Amundson (1994) analyzed 55 authentic tokens of reciprocal pronouns (46—*each other*; 9—*one another*) and was able to demonstrate that neither the number of participants nor the temporally ordered sequence of items offered any valid explanation for her naturally occurring data. She noted that modality may offer a partial explanation in that only one of nine tokens of *one another* came from a spoken source, whereas there were 16 spoken tokens and 30 written tokens of *each other*. The written mode, therefore, seems more amenable to the use of *one another* than the spoken mode, whereas modality seems to be much less of an issue in the case of *each other*, which appears to occur freely in both speech and writing.

Another factor in the use of reciprocal pronouns appears to be the animacy—or even humanness—of the referents. For *one another*, all nine sets of subject participants were animate and eight were human,[14] whereas nine of the 46 sets of participants were inanimate in the case of *each other*.

> These sentences have nothing to do with each other.

We feel there is a case to be made for certain genres favoring the use of *one another*; for example, passages from the Bible frequently favor the use of *one another*:[15]

> I give you a new commandment, that you love one another. Just as I have loved you, you also should love one another. By this everyone will know that you are my disciples, if you have love for one another.
>
> —*John* 13:34 and 35[16]

To sum up, *each other* is clearly the more frequent and flexible reciprocal pronoun; in fact, it seems to be used by some English speakers and writers to the exclusion of *one another*.

THE MEANING AND USE OF POSSESSIVE FORMS

What does the "possessive" inflection or form mean?

In many traditional grammars, the possessive inflection is referred to as the genitive case. This is perhaps appropriate given that the *'s* inflection or a possessive form, while often expressing possession:

- POSSESSION: John's car   her book

can also be used to express many other meanings:

- AGENCY/SOURCE: Shakespeare's   his ideas
                           sonnets
- HUMAN RELATIONSHIPS:
    a. kinship   Bob's cousin   my father
    b. professional: Joe's teacher   their doctor
    c. other social: Anne's neighbor   your girlfriend

- TRAITS (PHYSICAL :
    OR OTHER)   Sue's eyes   her ego
- REPRESENTATION: John's portrait   his statue
           (= a portrait of John)   (= a statue of him)
- EVALUATION: the project's importance   its value
- NAMED AFTER: St. Paul's cathedral
- MEASUREMENT: an hour's time
- SUBJECT +
    NOMINALIZED VERB: the earth's rotation   his actions
           (= the earth rotates)   (= he acts)

This list does not exhaust the meaning potential of possessive inflections and forms in English. The construction is highly ambiguous from a semantic perspective since a phrase such as the following can mean several different things:

> John's portrait
> **a.** possession: the portrait that John owns
> **b.** agency: the portrait that John painted.
> **c.** representation: the portrait of John

In most cases the context will help disambiguate the intended meaning. However, it is important to keep in mind that Han's (1996) research shows us that possession and agency are the two most frequent meanings (in that order) and that they account for a majority of the possessive forms occurring in spoken English discourse. It is quite possible that the frequency of any of the above meanings is somewhat dependent on discourse genre: for example, critics of art, music, theater, etc. may tend to use possessive forms expressing agency or evaluation rather than those expressing possession.

THE USE OF POSSESSIVE FORMS

A problem in using possessive forms may arise for learners whose first language has grammatical gender. English has notional gender, in which the gender of the possessive determiner or pronoun agrees semantically with the gender of the possessor:

> Paul lost his book.
> Paula lost her book.

In some languages with grammatical gender (e.g., French, Spanish, etc.), the possessive determiner agrees grammatically with the object possessed. Thus in French one says:

> Paul/Paule   a   perdu   son   livre.
> Paul/Paule (has)   (lost)   (his/her) (book)

Livre is a masculine noun in French, and the possessive determiner *son* must agree with the possessed noun *livre* regardless of whether the possessor is Paul (M) or Paule (F). This is an initial problem for learners to sort out if their L$_1$ has this type of grammatical gender.

Also, although all languages have a way of signaling possession, they don't all regard the same things as possessable. In Spanish, for example, one refers to parts of the body using the definite article, whereas in English, we would use a possessive form.

> Compare: Spanish (literal translation):   I have broken the leg.
>   English: I have broken my leg.

Thus, one of the areas you may have to work on with your students is to help them become familiar with those semantic or lexical domains where the English possessive forms normally occur.

We should also mention two special syntactic constructions—one using the possessive determiner, the other using the possessive pronoun—which appear similar yet are slightly different in meaning:

> Philip is one of our friends.   Philip is a friend of ours.

The first sentence means that we have an unspecified number of friends and that Philip is one of them. The second sentence makes no reference to our other friends but instead means that Philip is our friend and suggests that he may also be a friend of other people. Some reference grammars and ESL/EFL texts erroneously state or imply that such sentences are completely synonymous.

Nouns marked with the possessive inflection have two main uses: (1) they may be definite determiners, such as

> my cousin's father
> some people's opinions

or (2) they may be a modifier more closely associated with the head noun and behave much like part of a compound noun:

> several women's universities
> a ship's doctor

Han (1996) in a data-based study of possessives in spoken English found that about 70 percent of her more than 250 tokens were definite determiners and about 23 percent had the more lexicalized modifier function (with the remaining 7 percent representing four other minor functions). We will focus here on the definite determiner use and see how such possessives[17] are used in discourse.

What types of nouns most typically occur together as inflected possessive determiners and head nouns in oral discourse? In her oral corpus, Han found that the possessive determiners modifying head nouns were of three types:

- personal names (71%), e.g. *Bob, Mr. Smith*
    example: <u>*Bob's*</u> *house*
- personal roles (19%), e.g. *teacher, child*
    example: <u>*the teacher's*</u> *report*
- collective or institutional nouns (10%), e.g. *team, the company*
    example: <u>*the company's*</u> *report*

The head nouns modified by possessive determiners were of five types in Han's corpus:

- nouns of internal possession (26%), e.g., *information, problem, opinion*
    example: *Bob's* <u>*problem*</u>
- personal roles (26%), e.g., *doctor, secretary, wife*
    example: *Mr. Smith's* <u>*doctor*</u>
- locative nouns (19%), e.g., *lawn, office, garage*
    example: *the teacher's* <u>*office*</u>
- physical objects (14%), e.g., *desk, box, book*
    example: *the professor's* <u>*book*</u>
- other (15%) includes partitive nouns, animals, and institutional and collective nouns
    example: *Billy's* <u>*dog*</u>

Thus, personal names used as possessive determiners followed by head nouns that refer to an internal possession or a personal role accounted for the majority of noun phrases that were inflected for possession in Han's oral corpus.

Most possessive determiners (along with their head nouns) signal new information and tend to occur in the predicate (i.e., toward the end of the sentence) and function as direct objects, objects of prepositions, and predicates of subject nouns. In Han's oral corpus, about 77 percent of the NPs inflected for possession perform these various predicate functions, while about 19 percent function as subjects.[18] However, she found that the NPs inflected for possession that were subjects tended to repeat or summarize previously mentioned (i.e., given) information and thus were anaphoric in nature.

The following excerpt from a radio broadcast (CBS, August 4, 1997) illustrates some typical discourse functions of possessives:

> Jeanne Calment, who had the distinction of being
> the world's oldest person,
> died today in Arles, France, at the
> age of 122. . . . Born on February 21 in 1875,
> Calment was Arles' greatest attraction
> since Vincent Van Gogh, who spent a year
> there in 1888. She met him when he
> came to her uncle's shop to buy paints. . . .

This excerpt from the news bulletin contains three noun phrases inflected for the possessive:

> the world's oldest person
> Arles' greatest attraction
> her uncle's shop

All three noun phrases are in predicate position and provide new information for listeners not previously familiar with Jeanne Calment, her age, and her life. The third token is instructive in that it shows us that a possessive determiner can precede and modify a noun inflected for possession and that together they form a complex possessive determiner modifying the head noun. The fact that superlatives are included as post-determiners in two of the noun phrases can be explained by virtue of Jeanne Calment's record age.

One final observation that should be made about the *'s* possessive form is that, like possessive pronouns, the noun that follows the inflected noun may be deleted if it can be inferred from context:

> Where is your car?
> It's being repaired, so I borrowed *Ted's*. (i.e., Ted's car)

The Use of Inflected Versus Periphrastic Possessives

Many ESL/EFL texts will tell the learner to use the *'s* form with human head nouns and the *of* form with nonhuman head nouns. Such a rule accounts for examples like these:

> Martine's *husband* (human head noun)
> *the end* of the road (nonhuman head noun)

but not for these:

> The works of Shakespeare fill an enormous volume.
> The dog's tail is wagging.

According to a study conducted by Khampang (1973) in which he tested native English speakers' preference for the *'s* possessive versus the *of* form, the native speakers preferred the *'s* form whenever the head noun was animate. Moreover, the native speakers preferred the *'s* form even with inanimate head nouns when the noun could be viewed as performing an action. For example,

> The train's arrival was delayed.

was preferred over

> The arrival of the train was delayed.

To these fairly general applications of the *'s* possessive, we should add a few less common ones, such as

double possessives:	Hank's brother's car
nouns of special interest to human activity:	the game's history
	London's water supply
natural phenomena:	the earth's rotation

The *of* possessive, on the other hand, is preferred in all other instances, most commonly with inanimate objects:

> He stood at the foot of the bed.   *He stood at the bed's foot.

But, according to Khampang, the *of* possessive may be used even with human head nouns when the modifier noun is long.[19] For example,

> He's the son of the well-known politician.

was preferred over

> He's the well-known politician's son.

or with long double possessives which, when short, normally both take *'s* (e.g., Hank's brother's car); for example,

> What can I do for the husband of Dr. Smith's daughter?

was preferred over

> What can I do for Dr. Smith's daughter's husband?

Likewise, if formality is desired, the *of* possessive is preferred, whereas *'s* signals informality where both versions are possible:

> Shakespeare's sonnets (informal)   the sonnets of Shakespeare (formal)

Thus, the fact that there are these two ways to signal possessive forms in English and the fact that the rules for distinguishing their usage are not clear-cut may be some reasons why ESL/EFL students often use possessive forms incorrectly. Another reason may be that the *'s* form occurs relatively infrequently in English compared with other inflectional morphemes such as the plural, the past tense, and the progressive; that is, we know that when a morpheme is of low frequency in the input that learners receive, it is acquired later than the more frequently occurring morphemes are (Larsen-Freeman 1976). Yet another reason may be interference from the student's native language. Regardless of the source of difficulty, two typical patterns of error are overgeneralization of the *of* form:

> *The car of my friend is new.

and simplification, when students omit the *'s* altogether and simply signal possession by juxtaposition of two NPs.

> *My friend car is new.

SOME USES OF POSSESSIVE DETERMINERS

It would be useful to have a data-based analysis of the possessive determiner forms (*my, your, his, her, one, their*) similar to Han's study of lexical nouns with the possessive inflection. We know that these determiners can be used both for sentence-internal reference to avoid repetition (John lost his keys) and for cross-sentential or cross-clausal reference as in the last sentence of the text above about Jeanne Calment. Note that there are four mentions of Calment, who is the topic of the news bulletin:

> Jeanne Calment
> Calment
> She
> her uncle's shop

In the last mention, the possessive pronoun is used not only for purposes of topic continuity but also as a means of introducing a new noun phrase (the uncle's shop) into the discourse. It would be useful to know how frequently possessive determiners are used in this and other ways and which of their uses are most typical.

Social Uses of Possessive Determiners

We do know from work by Staczek (forthcoming) that at least two possessive determiners, *your* and *our,* are used in nonliteral, socially motivated ways in spoken English in a variety of settings. It seems that speakers are trying to identify with and engage the listener(s)[20] through these special uses of *your* and *our*:

> You get your fan, your temperature gauge . . . These are your fog lamps in the front. [Volvo salesman to potential customer] (p. 3)
>
> The chicken is not your real hot Mexican food. [chef to TV audience on PBS cooking program.] (p. 6)
>
> Here's a look at your local weather. [local meteorologist on the All Weather Channel] (p. 9)
>
> We're gonna go ahead and put our fertilizer down. [radio gardening expert to caller] (p. 2)
>
> What are we going to do with our certificate of deposit? [bank officer to customer] (p. 2)

In most of these cases, the possessive determiner can be paraphrased with either a definite article or no article at all.[21] Staczek notes that he has found such uses of *your* and *our* in instructional settings, sales/marketing situations, scripted TV comedies, weather forecasts, and even in fifteenth-century cookbooks ("*and cover them with thy lids and let them bake . . .*" [p. 12]). We feel that nonpossessive pronominal forms (especially, *we*) can also be used similarly:

> [doctor to patient]: How are we today?

The use of *we* in the preceding sentence and of *our* in the bank officer's question above, respectively, can sometimes be perceived by the listener as condescending speech on the part of the user, i.e., the bank officer and doctor appear to be treating the bank customer and the patient like children. Where the speaker clearly has the right to instruct someone or demonstrate something (i.e., the gardening expert), the use of *we/our* and *your* seems less condescending and more in the nature of building informal relationships.

CONCLUSION

The English pronoun system is not as complicated as that of many other languages. Nevertheless, there is considerable detail for your students to master in learning the forms and uses of the pronoun system and of English demonstratives, possessives, and other referential forms. Your job will require that you give your students continued exposure and meaningful practice to aid them in their acquisition and use of these forms.

TEACHING SUGGESTIONS

1. Form/Meaning. Cuisenaire rods can be very useful for introducing and practicing subject and object pronouns, since the rods can make the meaning clear. (Recall that a teaching suggestion using these rods to teach demonstratives was presented in Chapter 5.)

Subject Pronouns	*Object Pronouns*
Give a green rod to Pheng.	Give a green rod to her.
What did Esteban do?	Give it to Antonella.
He gave a green rod to Pheng.	
	Give two blue rods to him.
Give two blue rods to Paolo.	Give them to Paolo.
What did Antonella do?	
She gave two blue rods to Paulo.	Take the red rods from them.
	Take them from Paolo and Antonella.

2. Form/Meaning. A good way for children to practice the possessive determiners with parts of the body is to play "Simon Says" and to amplify the game with questions. For example:

> T: Simon says, touch your head.
> T: What did you (sg.) do?/What did you (pl.) do?
> S1: I touched my head./We touched our heads.
>   or
> T: What did he do?
> S2: He touched his head.

3. Meaning/Use. Kealey and Inness (1997:80–83) suggest the following activity for practicing possessive forms. Students are each given a sentence with possessives in it and are asked to memorize it (individually, in pairs, in groups—depending on the size of the class). The sentences are all descriptions of a child's face. The students are given a family picture with the child's mother and father clearly depicted but with the child's face missing. They have to circulate around the room and tell each other their sentences in order to complete the child's face and thus the family portrait. Sample sentences: He has his mother's hair. He has his father's eyes. He has his mother's chin.

4. Form. A substitution drill may be useful for demonstrating and practicing the correspondence between possessive determiners and pronouns.

Your book is red	→	Yours is red.
My book is blue.	→	Mine is blue.
My car is green.	→	Mine is green.
Their car is orange.	→	Theirs is orange.

5. Form/Meaning. Penny Larson (1977) suggests preparing flash cards as an aid to teaching the 's possessive form. On each flash card (no smaller than 5 by 8 inches), paste a picture of a person and a picture of an item (Larson says "The Sears catalog is good for pictures of people and any discount catalogs are good for pictures of items"). Print a name on the card under the picture of the person. Use common American names or the names of your students. Be sure you have both singular and plural items and people. Then teach the new pattern by holding up a flash card and asking:

T: What's this?	Students: It's a book.
T: Who's this?	Students: It's John.
T: Whose book is this?	Students: It's John's book.
	or
	It's John's.

Go through the cards once with the teacher asking and the students answering. Then, ask the students to ask you the "Who's/Whose" questions. When they are comfortable with the pattern, they can ask and answer each other. Pass out the cards, keeping a couple yourself so they can practice *this/that*.

6. Use. Give your students a passage in which the possessives followed by head nouns have been replaced with a blank line and two NPs in parentheses. Have them write the correct form of the possessive on each line, inflectional or periphrastic, explaining why they made the choices they did. For example:

> Last Saturday I went shopping. It was (1) _____ (my friend/birthday) and I
> wanted to buy a gift. I drove (2) _____ (my father/car) to town. When I arrived,
> I realized (3) _____ (the center/shopping district) was already quite crowded. . . .

7. Meaning. To practice distinguishing *his* and *her*, Celce-Murcia and Hilles (1988) suggest giving learners a black-and-white sketch of a boy and girl (or man and woman, if learners are adults). The male and female are similarly dressed (in T-shirts and shorts). Each learner should have a small box of crayons. The teacher then gives a series of commands (learners are told not to look at any sketch but their own): Color his hair red; color her hair brown; color her shorts green; color his shorts black; and so on. When the exercise is finished, the learners can compare their results.

8. Use. Have pairs of students work at completing short dialogs with blanks where *this/these*, *that/those*, or *it* is required. The students should be prepared to explain their choices:

a. X: Let's go camping next weekend.
    Y: _____ 's a great idea! I like _____.

b. X: Listen to _____: Mark won the lottery!
    Y: What's he going to do with all _____ money?

   c. *X:*   [two women at a store] Which of _____ two dresses should I buy?

      Y: _____ dress looks nicer on you than _____ one.

9. Form/Meaning. As a way of introducing students to the syntactic and semantic elements inherent in the use of the reciprocal pronoun *each other*, Marie Bedell (personal communication) suggests the following procedure. (The sentences should be written on the board after they have been produced orally.)

> *Teacher:*   (introduces a sentence) I saw Albert.
> (Teacher asks a student to reverse the action.)
> *Student 1:*   Albert saw me.
> (Teacher asks another student to combine the two sentences.)
> *Student 2:*   I saw Albert and Albert saw me.

Teacher explains that whenever we have two sentences that are the reverse of each other, we can avoid the repetition by conjoining the subjects and using *each other* as a substitute for the objects;

> Albert and I saw each other.

The teacher then provides several other sentences that the students can (a) reverse, (b) combine, and (c) paraphrase with *each other*;

> Phil hit George.   Sally likes Sam.

10. Use. Sports commentators make frequent use of reciprocal pronouns during their broadcasts.

> "The Boston Celtics have faced the New York Knicks many times before, but never have they played each other with the fervor we've seen tonight."

If you are in a situation where your students can listen to English language sports broadcasts, have them collect examples of reciprocal pronouns used in such contexts.

    In an EFL (or ESL) situation, supply your students with a nonpictorial visual aid (Shaw and Taylor 1978) such as a summary of the results of the last two decades of World Cup Soccer championships. Have them generate sentences with reciprocal pronouns based on the information they've been given; for example:

> Brazil and Italy have never played each other in a championship game.
> Uruguay and England have faced each other twice recently.

(*Note:* Be aware that in informal usage even native English speakers sometimes use reflexive pronouns in sentences where the meaning is clearly reciprocal: ?The players congratulated *themselves* after they had won such a close game.)

EXERCISES

Test your understanding of what has been presented.

  1. Provide your own sentences to illustrate the following terms. Underline the word(s) illustrating the term:

a. subject pronoun	**e.** demonstrative pronoun	**i.** indefinite compound pronoun
b. object pronoun	**f.** demonstrative determiner	**j.** singular "they"
c. possessive pronoun	**g.** reciprocal pronoun	**k.** *'s* possessive
d. possessive determiner	**h.** reflexive pronoun	**l.** *of* possessive

2. Explain the ungrammaticality or awkwardness of the following sentences:

a. ?The room's walls are dirty.

c. *This *Time* magazine is mines.

b. *Him and she are going to Akron next weekend.

d. *There's no one here besides I.

Test your ability to apply what you know.

3. If your students produce the following sentences, what errors have they made? How will you make them aware of the errors, and what exercises will you prepare to correct them?

a. *The house of my friend is on the corner.

b. *He kicked hisself for not remembering her name.

c. *This is Mary bicycle.

d. *Everybody from all the classes are going.

e. *Leo and Hugo hit themselves, and Hugo got injured.

4. Second language morpheme acquisition studies have found that the *'s* possessive form was supplied far less accurately than many other morphemes in obligatory contexts by ESL/EFL students (Dulay and Burt, 1974). We have already mentioned several reasons why the *'s* form causes problems for learners. Can you think of any other feature(s) of this structure that would account for its frequent misuse or omission?

5. In English there are constructions called noun compounds, which consist of two nouns juxtaposed to create a compound word. The noun in attributive position functions much as an adjective would; for example:

> jewelry store   table leg
> stone wall

As Andersen (1979) points out, the Spanish construction for both the English *'s* possessive form and noun compound is often the same:

> *possessive*—Milly's garden—el jardín de Milly
> *noun compound*—a baseball player—un jugador de beisbol

Given these facts, what sort of problems would you expect a Spanish speaker to have with English *'s* possessives? What two types of errors involving the possessive form in English would you expect these learners to commit?

6. We have already seen how the indefinite pronoun *one* can mean "everyone" in a general sense, as in

> One never knows who real friends are until times like these.

What other pronoun (or pronouns) in English can also more informally mean "everyone in general"?

7. In this chapter we have mentioned the objection some people raise these days to using the third person singular masculine pronoun in reference to people of both genders. Many people reject the solution of using slash lines, as in *his/her* or *s/he* because they feel it is stylistically awkward. Aside from creating a new neuter pronoun, which is a solution some have suggested, what are other acceptable ways of circumlocuting the usage of *he, his,* and *him* when these forms are used in a general sense?

8. One of your students heard a native speaker of English say, "This prize was given to Edgar and I." Your student asks you if this sentence is okay. What will you reply?

BIBLIOGRAPHY

References

Amundson, M. (1994). "A Data-Based Contextual Analysis of Reciprocal Pronouns in English." Unpublished paper. University of California, Los Angeles, Department of TESL & Applied Linguistics, dated December 13, 1994.

Andersen, R. (1979). "The Relationship Between First Language Transfer and Second Language Overgeneralization: Data from the English of Spanish Speakers." In R. Andersen (ed.), *The Acquisition and Use of Spanish and English as First and Second Languages.* Washington, D.C.: TESOL.

Bolinger, D. (1977). *Meaning and Form.* New York and London: Longman.

Celce-Murcia, M., and S. Hilles (1988). *Techniques and Resources in Teaching Grammar.* New York: Oxford University Press.

Cook, S. J., and R. W. Suter (1980). *The Scope of Grammar.* New York: McGraw-Hill.

Dulay, H., and M. Burt (1974). Natural Sequences in Child Second Language Acquisition. *Language Learning* 24:1, 37–54.

Frodesen, J., and J. Eyring (1997). *Grammar Dimensions.* Book 4 (2d ed.). Boston: Heinle & Heinle.

Halliday, M., and R. Hasan (1976). *Cohesion in English.* London: Longman.

Halliday, M., and R. Hasan (1989). *Language, Context, and Text.* Oxford: Oxford University Press.

Han, N. (1996). "The Meanings of Inflected Genitives in English: A Spoken Data-Based Analysis." Unpublished paper. UCLA, Department of TESL & Applied Linguistics, dated December 11, 1996.

Kealey, J., and D. Inness (1997). *Shenanigames: Grammar-Focused Interactive ESL/EFL Activities and Games.* Brattleboro, Vt.: Pro Lingua Associates.

Khampang, Phon (1973). "A Study of the *s*-Genitive and the *of*-Genitive in English." Unpublished English 215 paper, UCLA, fall, 1973.

Kirsner, R. S. (1979). "Deixis in Discourse: An Exploratory Quantitative Study of Modern Dutch Demonstrative Adjectives." In T. Givón (ed.) *Syntax and Semantics Vol. 12: Discourse and Syntax.* New York: Academic Press, 355–377.

Lagunoff, R. (1992). "A Description of *They* as a Singular Pronoun." Unpublished M.A. thesis in Teaching English as a Second Language, UCLA.

Lagunoff, R (1997). Singular *they.* Unpublished Ph.D. dissertation in Applied Linguistics. UCLA.

Larsen-Freeman, D. (1976). "An Explanation for the Morpheme Acquisition Order of Second Language Learners." *Language Learning* 26:1, 125–134.

Larson, P. (1977). "Teaching Possessives." *CATESOL Newsletter* 8:4.

Nesbitt, L. S. (1980). "Problems in Teaching Oral American English to ESL Students: A Conversation Analysis and ESL Textbook Review." *CATESOL Occasional Papers,* 6.

Nishimura, C. (1995). "Demonstratives in Academic Written Discourse." Unpublished M.A. thesis in Teaching English as a Second Language, UCLA.

Quirk, R., and S. Greenbaum (1973). *A Concise Grammar of Contemporary English.* New York: Harcourt Brace Jovanovich.

Quirk, R., S. Greenbaum, G. Leech, and J. Svartvik (1985). *A Comprehensive Grammar of the English Language.* London: Longman.

Roth, S. (1991). "Functional Differences Between *Somebody* and *Someone* in American English." Unpublished M.A. thesis in Teaching English as a Second Language, UCLA.

Shaw, P., and J. B. Taylor (1978). "Non-Pictorial Visual Aids." In S. Holden (ed.), *Visual Aids for Classroom Interaction.* London: Modern English Publications.

Staczek, J. (1986). "The English Pronominal Reflexive: An Aspect of Usage Variation." *Studia Anglica Posnaniensia* 19:119–128.

Staczek, J. (1987). "Sentential and Discoursal Reflexives in English: A Matter of Variation." *Studia Anglica Posnaniensia* 20:115–121.

Staczek, J. (1988). "Variation in the Plural Reflexive in Spoken English: Preliminary Evidence for Merger." In A. R. Thomas (ed.), *Methods in Dialectology.* Clevedon, England: Multilingual Matters.

Staczek, J. (forthcoming). "Social Uses of Possessive Adjectives in English." To appear in M. Montgomery and G. Little (eds.), *Centennial Volume of Usage Studies,* published by American Dialect Society.

Strauss, S. (1993). "Why *This* and *That* Are Not Complete Without *It.*" In *CLS* 29. Papers from the 29th Regional Meeting of the Chicago Linguistic Society. Eds. K. Beals, G. Cooke, D. Kathman, S. Kita, K. McCulloch, and D. Testen, 403–417.

Suggestions for further reading

For the best single descriptive source dealing with all the forms introduced in this chapter, see:
Quirk, R., S. Greenbaum, G. Leech, and J. Svartvik (1985). *A Comprehensive Grammar of the English Language.* London: Longman.

For extensive theoretical treatment of pronouns and possessives, consult:
Stockwell, R., P. Schachter, and B. Partee (1973). *The Major Syntactic Structures of English.* New York: Holt, Rinehart and Winston, Chaps. 4, 11.

For treatments of reference, see:
Brown, G., and G. Yule (1983). *Discourse.* Cambridge: Cambridge University Press.
Gundel, J. K. et al. (1993). Cognitive Status and the Form of Referring Expressions in Discourse. *Language* 69:2, 274–307.
Halliday, M., and R. Hasan (1976). *Cohesion in English.* London: Longman.
Wales, K. (1996). *Personal Pronouns in Present-Day English.* Cambridge: Cambridge University Press.

For a treatment of asystematic reflexive pronouns in British English, see:
Baker, C. L. (1995). "Contrast, Discourse Prominence, and Intensification with Special Reference to Locally Free Reflexives in British English." *Language* 71:1, 63–101.

For an account of anaphoric pronoun use from the perspective of cognitive grammar, see:
van Hoek, K. (1995). "Conceptual Reference Points: A Cognitive Grammar Account of Pronominal Anaphora Constraints." *Language* 71:2, 310–340.

For explanations and exercises of various pronouns and possessive forms, see:
Badalamenti, V., and C. Henner Stanchina (1997). *Grammar Dimensions.* Book 1 (2d ed.). Boston: Heinle & Heinle.
Danielson, D., and P. Porter (1990). *Using English: Your Second Language* (2d ed.). Englewood Cliffs, N.J.: Prentice Hall Regents.
Rutherford, W. E. (1977). *Modern English* (2d ed., vol. 2). New York: Harcourt Brace Jovanovich, 45–71.

For a unit on demonstratives in discourse and another on possessives, see:
Thewlis, S. (1997). *Grammar Dimensions.* Book 3 (2d ed.). Boston: Heinle & Heinle.

For a unit on referential words and phrases and their use in discourse, see:
Frodesen, J., and J. Eyring (1997). *Grammar Dimensions.* Book 4 (2d ed.). Boston: Heinle & Heinle.

ENDNOTES

1. The personal pronoun *one* is a formal, general third-person pronoun that neutralizes the gender distinction in *she/he* or *her/him*. Since it is formal, it is of lower frequency than the other personal pronouns.

2. For all practical purposes, there are no possessive pronouns *its* and *one's*. The possessive determiners *its* and *one's* in the following sentences do not have pronominal counterparts.

> The cat is going to eat its dinner. One should take care of one's health.
> *This dinner is its. *Regarding health, one should take care of one's.

The acceptable version in the pair on the right is more typically British than American. In American English, we would more likely say "One should take care of his health" or—to avoid sexist language—"People should take care of their health."

3. Halliday and Hasan (1976) also include the definite article *the* (which derives etymologically from *that*) and the pro-adverbs (i.e., pro-forms that replace and refer to adverbials) *here, there, now,* and *then* as part of demonstrative reference.

4. When "(the) same" functions pronominally, there is usually no co-reference; instead, there is substitution for a member of the same class (or what Halliday and Hasan [1989] refer to as co-classification).

> A: I'll have a hamburger and fries.
> B: I'll have the same.

5. *Else* has a related adverbial form *elsewhere,* which is used to direct the listener or reader away from the antecedent and to some other place or condition: *If the answer to the problem isn't in the back of the book, you'll have to find it elsewhere.*

6. In other grammatical descriptions, this form is sometimes called the genitive inflection, since many other meanings besides possession are signaled by it, as we indicate later in this chapter.

7. When singular nouns ending in *s* are monosyllabic and used informally, one now also sees spellings such as *Bess's, Russ's,* which more closely mirror pronunciation. Some writers now use *'s* after all singular nouns ending in *s.*

8. Initial subordinate clauses followed by main clauses may either follow this pattern or reverse it:

> When Sara moved to Atlanta, she started a new job.
> When she moved to Atlanta, Sara started a new job.

This flexibility of referential direction is not possible when the subordinate clause follows the main clause; in this case, the antecedent must precede the referring form:

> Sara started a new job when she moved to Atlanta.
> *She started a new job when Sara moved to Atlanta.
> (* = *she* and *Sara* are not co-referential)

9. These indefinite "pronouns" are not true pronouns; syntactically, they behave much like regular nouns and take adjectives and prepositional phrases: *a certain someone, somebody with a gun.* There are also related indefinite pro-adverbs:

> Somewhere/someplace anywhere/anyplace nowhere/noplace everywhere/everyplace

10. This last example is interesting in that we can see that use of nouns with overtly masculine or feminine gender (mother/father) does not preclude use of singular *they* so long as they are used generically.

11. The nominal substitute *one* (pl. *ones*) often co-occurs with referential determiners to avoid repetition of lexical nouns. For more information on the nominal substitute *one*, see Halliday & Hasan (1976:91–105).

12. Halliday and Hasan (1976:66ff) also point out that *this, that,* and *it* can be used for extended reference to refer to an entire clause or extended passage of text, not just to noun phrases.

13. Other semantically nonreflexive uses of reflexives are for emphasis (1) and used adverbially to mean "alone," "without assistance" (2):

> 1. John himself will tell you the news.
> 2. The child wanted to solve the puzzle by himself.

14. The one nonhuman, animate example referred to "horses" in a context that one could argue involved personification.

15. This so-called genre-based use of *one another* probably is something more general than Biblical style; the one oral token of *one another* that Amundson (1994) found came from a transcript of a marital counseling session and occurred in a question asked by the marriage counselor of the couple undergoing the counseling:

> How do you support and love one another?

This suggests the larger genre—or speech activity—is one of prescribing or facilitating moral behavior and love between human beings that are associated through marriage, religion, or in some other way.

16. This passage was taken from a Sunday service Bible reading insert prepared by the U.S. Lutheran Church, Missouri Synod.

17. We say "possessives," and indeed, Han (1996) found that possession was the most frequent meaning of this inflection in her oral corpus (i.e., about 46 percent). However, she also found that agency was expressed for about 26 percent of the tokens and description in about another 11 percent. The remaining 17 percent of tokens represented measurements, appositives, and several other minor relationships.

18. The remaining 4 percent of tokens occurred in fragments where the precise grammatical function (subject, object, etc.) was hard to identify.

19. Notice the reverse can also be true: that is, the *'s* possessive can be used with inanimate nouns, where it normally would not occur, in order to avoid an awkward sequence of two *of* phrases:

> Many of the book's pages were torn.

was preferred over

> Many of the pages of the book were torn.

Here the motivation for the preference appears to be stylistic or prosodic (i.e., rules and constraints related to stress and rhythm of spoken language) rather than semantic.

20. Examples and page numbers are from Staczek's manuscript.

21. Staczek notes the opposite pattern also may occur: the definite articles can be used where the possessive determiner is expected: *I forgot to buy the wife a gift* (p. 14); however, he gave no explanation or analysis for this use.

17

PARTITIVES, COLLECTIVES, AND QUANTIFIERS

INTRODUCTION

Being able to communicate the quantity or amount of something is an important human need that we satisfy through language. If we need to be precise, we can refer to quantities by using numbers of various types:

> Cardinal number: We have class for *two* hours a day.
> Fraction: I have to leave in (*a*) *half* an hour.
> Percentage: *Fifty percent* of the class was out with the flu.[1]
> Multiplier: They have offered to *double* my salary if I join their firm.

But due to the importance of this concept, we employ many other linguistic devices for quantification besides numbers. To illustrate this, here is a partial inventory of the different linguistic means English speakers use to express *approximations* of quantity (based on Kennedy 1987).

- First of all, we have terms in each of the four major parts of speech:
  Nouns: *average, estimate, neighborhood, vicinity*
  Verbs: *say, guess, verge on*
  Adjectives: (*50*)-*odd, inexact, approximate*
  Adverbs: *approximately, roughly, nearly*

- Then, too, minor parts of speech can be used to give an approximation of quantity:
  Prepositions: *about, around, near*
  Determiners: *some* (*50*) . . .

- Plural numbers: *dozens of, hundreds of*

- Affixes:
  Suffix: (*50*)-*ish*
  Prefix: *quasi-universal*

- Phrases:
  Conjoined prepositional phrases: *from* (*50*) *to* (*60*), *between* (*50*) *and* (*60*)

Lexicalized phrases: *more or less, or so, or more, or thereabouts, something like, within a
hair's breadth of, within spitting distance of, at (the) most, on the order of*

• Clauses: *If you said (50), you wouldn't be far wrong.*

Finally, three linguistic devices exist purely to deal with issues of quantification—how
we can talk about quantity, amount, or proportion and how we can impose limits on
wholes. Here is an example of each type of device as it used for approximation:

Partitives: *the best part of*
Collectives: *group*
Quantifiers: *almost all*

These last three syntactic constructions are the focus of this chapter.

PARTITIVES

We have already seen how English distinguishes between nouns that can be made plural
(count nouns) and those that can't (noncount nouns). This does not mean, however, that
there is no way of quantifying noncount nouns.

Both count and noncount nouns can be modified by partitive constructions—that is,
constructions denoting a part of a whole. A partitive is a phrase, typically consisting of a
count noun followed by *of* that precedes another noun.

> *(det) noun of*
>   a grain of

The same pattern can be used to quantify noncount nouns:

> (det) _____ of _____   e.g., a drop of water
>   [partitive noun]   [noncount noun]   two drops of water

and to delimit the quantity of count nouns as well:

> (det) _____ of _____   e.g., a deck of cards
>   [partitive noun]   [count noun]   two decks of cards

Partitives can modify both nonspecific nouns:

> I need *a deck of cards* to show you my new magic trick. (any deck—nonspecific)

and specific nouns:

> Will *a deck of these cards* do?

When the partitive noun is part of the subject, the verb agrees with it. If the partitive
noun is singular, the verb is singular. If the partitive noun is plural, the verb is also plural:[2]

> A mountain of dirty laundry was piled up after our vacation.
> Mountains of dirty laundry were piled up after our vacation.

In order to capture the array of common types of partitives, we group them by categories (although some may overlap).

• Precise measure phrases (Many ESL/EFL students are more familiar with metric
  measure phrases):

> a gallon of gas   a yard of fabric
> two cups of sugar   two spoonfuls of cough syrup

- Container-based:[3]

  | a bottle of catsup | a jar of jam |
  | two cartons of books | two cans of oil |

- Portion-based:

  | a slice of bread | a dollop of whipped cream |
  | two helpings of potatoes | two servings of ice cream |

- Individual members of a category (of course more than one can be referred to when a number is used):

  | a word of advice | an item of information |
  | two pieces of luggage | two articles of clothing |

- Parts or fractions:

  | a segment of society | a part of life |
  | two portions of the budget | two sections of the newspaper |

- Shape of:

  | a ball of yarn | a column of smoke |
  | two streams of water | two sticks of butter |

- Pair of:

Some plural count nouns without a singular form are viewed strictly as pairs—things having two equal parts—and the partitive count noun *pair*[4] is used with these nouns; for example:

$$\text{a pair of } \left\{ \begin{array}{l} \text{trousers} \\ \text{scissors} \\ \text{tongs} \end{array} \right\} \qquad *\text{a} \left\{ \begin{array}{l} \text{trouser} \\ \text{scissor} \\ \text{tong} \end{array} \right\}$$

- Idiomatic partitives:

Vegetables	*Other food items*
a head of $\left\{ \begin{array}{l} \text{lettuce} \\ \text{cabbage} \end{array} \right.$	a bunch of grapes
	a loaf of bread
an ear of corn	a clove of garlic
a stalk of celery	a sprig of parsley
Animals	*People*
a herd of cattle	a gang of thieves
a flock of birds	a troupe of actors
a school of fish	a team of ball players
a pride of lions	a crew of helpers

- *The whole of, the rest of, the remainder of:*

These three partitives, with a definite determiner, are used to express an entire thing (the whole of) or some specific part thereof.

$$\text{I'd like } \left\{ \begin{array}{l} \text{the whole of} \\ \text{the rest of} \\ \text{the remainder of} \end{array} \right\} \text{ that piece of meat.} \qquad \text{(Quirk et al. 1985)[5]}$$

The whole of Quebec is francophone.

In $\begin{Bmatrix} \text{the rest of} \\ \text{the remainder of} \end{Bmatrix}$ the country, English is spoken.

- *A majority of, the majority of, a minority of:*

These partitives are used to show proportion of some explicit set. *A majority of* and *the majority of* are used with quantities greater than half. *A minority of* is used to signal less (or fewer) than half.

A majority of the people feel that educational reform is a priority.

- A few "partitives" can even be used to express a quality or subtype, rather than quantity, of a particular thing:

a sort of appliance   new kinds of media
a type of bird

EXCEPTION WITH NUMBERS

Certain numbers can be used as nouns in partitive constructions as well, with one important structural difference. When the number is specific, and the second noun is not, no *of* is used. This is a small point, but it does cause ESL/EFL students understandable difficulty.

hundreds of people (nonspecific plural number; as you already have seen, nonspecific plural numbers can be used to approximate)[6]
*a hundred of people (specific numbers preceding nonspecific nouns cannot be followed by of)
a hundred people

Compounding the problem is the fact that *of* must be used when both the partitive number noun and the noun being modified are specific:

a hundred of the old people   three hundred of them

Note that *hundred* remains singular with a specific number even when the number preceding it is more than one.

*three hundreds of them

We return to consider the use of the word *of* later in this chapter.

COLLECTIVES

COLLECTIVE NOUNS

One special group of nouns rightfully belong with any discussion of partitives. These are the collectives. The count nouns that can be used in partitive constructions to refer to groups of people and animals (see above) are one type of collective noun.

a team of ball players   a flock of birds

Collective nouns are the exception to the normal rule of subject-verb agreement, to which we referred earlier, in that, as subjects, they may take either singular or plural subject-verb agreement.

The team has been outstanding this year.
The team have been outstanding this year.

Although American English speakers favor the singular form, in British English plural subject-verb agreement occurs much more frequently. In both dialects, however, speakers can choose to interpret the noun as a whole unit or as the individual members or components that compose the unit:

A flock of birds was circling the field. $\left\{ \begin{array}{l} \text{It was looking for prey.} \\ \text{They were looking for prey.} \end{array} \right.$

The duality of number is, of course, also observable in other anaphoric forms, such as reflexive pronouns, possessive determiners, and relative pronouns;

The committee blamed $\left\{ \begin{array}{l} \text{itself.} \\ \text{themselves.} \end{array} \right.$

The committee blamed $\left\{ \begin{array}{l} \text{its} \\ \text{their} \end{array} \right\}$ chairperson.

My audience, $\left\{ \begin{array}{l} \text{which was} \\ \text{who were} \end{array} \right\}$ very supportive, . . .

Although modern English prefers more general collectives for animals (e.g., *herd, flock, swarm*), older forms of English had many more of these idiomatic collectives for animals, *a brace of partridges, a gaggle of geese, a pod of whales, a leap of leopards,* and so on.

According to Celce (1970), there are actually three main types of collective nouns. The first comprises common collectives, some of which can enter into partitive constructions, as you have just seen. They might be referred to as "particularizing" nouns because they talk about a particular collection of people or animals. The other types are the unique collectives, which represent the sole member of a particular set, and the generic collectives, which refer to all members of a class.

1. Common Collectives	*2. Unique Collectives*	*3. Generic Collectives*
(a/the) class	the Vatican	the clergy
(a/the) team	the Kremlin	the bourgeoisie
(a/the) herd	(the) Congress	the intelligensia
(a/the) government	(the) Parliament	the aristocracy

Thus, each of these collective nouns can be seen to be a single entity or a collection of individuals. One's perspective, in North American English, at least, is most frequently signalled by the use of singular or plural anaphoric reference.

Collective Nouns Derived from Adjectives

In addition to these three types of collective nouns, a number of adjectivally derived nouns in English may be considered as generic collectives. Nouns like *the meek, the dead, the rich,* when they have human reference, resemble generic collective nouns in a number of ways: they are always preceded by *the,* they are not overtly singular or plural, and they may refer to a whole group in general terms rather than to a particular or unique group.

An important difference between these collective nouns derived from adjectives and the other categories of collective nouns is that the adjective-based collectives always take plural verbs.[7]

The elderly are increasingly asserting their rights.
*The elderly is increasingly asserting its rights.

QUANTIFIERS

As we have already noted, a third syntactic construction is used when we want to talk about amount or quantity. Quantifiers indicate a nonspecific amount or quantity of the noun that follows.[8] Quantifiers can be determiners or when the referent is clear, pronouns.

> A: I want some ice cream.
> B: I want some too.

It is helpful to arrange quantifiers showing increasing amounts along two continua— one positive and one negative.[9] The diagonal lines connect items or sets of items that logically contradict each other. Quantifiers that modify count nouns are above the horizontal lines; those used with noncount nouns are below the lines. Where there are no lines, the quantifier can be used with count and noncount nouns alike. We explore each of these distinctions in more detail below the continua.

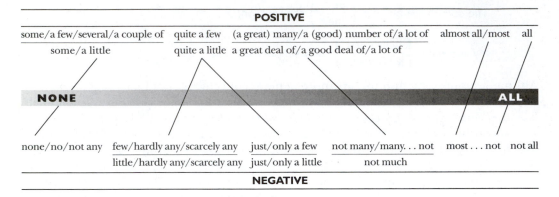

DIFFERING AMOUNTS

Going from left to right on the continua are increasing amounts of the noun being modified. To illustrate this, here is one progression from along the positive continuum.

> Some packages have been brought in from the car.
> Quite a few packages have been brought in.
> A lot of packages have been brought in.
> Almost all packages have been brought in.
> All packages have been brought in.

We said earlier that quantifiers can be determiners or pronouns. This is easily seen in all these example sentences save the middle one. *A lot of* cannot be a pronoun, but *a lot* can.

> Some have been brought in from the car.
> Quite a few have been brought in.
> A lot have been brought in.
> Almost all have been brought in
> All have been brought in.

POSITIVE AND NEGATIVE CONTINUA

The reason for the two continua is that the negative quantifiers not only convey quantity but also convey a negative assessment of the quantity. The speaker or writer's negative stance is overtly marked by the negative particle *not* in many of the negative quantifiers:

All people were created equal.
Not all people were created equal.

With other quantifiers on the negative continuum, there is no negative particle; nonetheless, they have a negative connotation. These examples make the connotations explicit:

He took *a few* (= some, several) biscuits, with the result that *few* (= hardly any) were left for the rest of us.
He then took *a little* (= some) butter, with the result that *little* (= hardly any) was left for the rest of us.

As our continua show, the quantifiers in these pairs (*a few* vs. *few*; *a little* vs. *little*) do not directly contradict each other but rather convey different meanings. Notice that the way to capture the negative connotation in the second quantifier in each of the pairs above would be to paraphrase *few* and *little* as *hardly any* or *scarcely any*.

Another difference between *a few* or *a little* and *few* or *little* is that the former can occur in the first utterance in a discourse; for example:

Do you have $\left\{ \begin{array}{l} \text{a few minutes} \\ \text{a little time} \end{array} \right\}$?

There are a few apples in the kitchen if you'd like one.
There's a little cake in the kitchen if you'd like some.

Few and *little*, however, generally require more context, because a negative or contradictory tone must be established:

Harold was lonely and desperate; he had few friends and little money.

Many ESL/EFL students omit the indefinite article when they use *a few* or *a little*. While the result is not necessarily an ungrammatical sentence, the listener or reader is likely to be confused by the use of an implicitly negative quantifier when a positive one seems to be required by the discourse:

?I have few good friends back home. They write to me often.

Details such as these are subtle; however, they are understood and used by all native speakers of English and will, therefore, have to be taught and practiced in the ESL/EFL classroom.

MINIMAL CONTRADICTIONS WITH QUANTIFIERS

As we have stated, the diagonal lines indicate the quantifiers that express a minimal contradiction with respect to each other. Here are some examples:

A: There were *some* musicians at the party.
B: That's not true. There were *no* musicians.

A: He has *quite a few days* of vacation.
B: Not really. He has *only a few* more than most people do.

A: Jason must have *a lot of* friends.
B: No, actually, he doesn't have that *many*.

A: *Almost all* of our tomatoes have ripened.
B: Really! I'd say *most* of ours haven't.

A: *All* the dancers wore red shirts.
B: No, *not all*. Some wore yellow shirts.

It is, of course, possible to use more than the minimum logical contradiction if the facts warrant a stronger response.

A: All Republicans are conservative.
B: That's not true. *Most* of the Republicans I know are *not* conservative.

QUANTIFIERS WITH COUNT/NONCOUNT NOUNS

As you have seen, some quantifiers occur only with count nouns; others with noncount nouns; and still others with both.

Count: There weren't *many* people at the soccer game due to the inclement weather.
Noncount: There wasn't *much* food left after the football players ate.
Both count and noncount: There weren't *a lot of people* at the soccer game.
                            There wasn't *a lot of food* left.

When *much* and *many* are used as pronouns, the verb form associated with each reflects the difference: *many* requires a plural verb, whereas *much* agrees with a singular verb.

Many are called every year.
Much is done by nonprofit organizations.

With *a lot of,* the verb agrees with the number of the noun being quantified.

A lot of people were there.   A lot of time was wasted.

QUANTIFIERS ARE DETERMINERS

You may already have noticed that some of the quantifiers take the form of a partitive construction—a phrase consisting of a noun of quantity followed by *of* and preceded by the indefinite article: *a lot of, a number of, a great deal of, a couple of.*

Notice that these phrasal quantifiers are not true partitives, however, for several reasons:

- They convey a nonspecific number:

  Quantifier: The bulldozer has already cleared a lot of land at the construction site.
  Partitive: The bulldozer has already cleared 10 acres of land at the construction site.

- Their nouns can't be quantified in the same way that partitive nouns can:

      They lost a good deal of money in the pyramid scheme.

      *They lost { two good deals of money / two lots of money } in the stock market.

      There were a number of problems with the show.

      *There were { two numbers of problems / two couples of problems } with the opening act.

- Like other quantifiers, they can precede partitives:[10]

  A couple of pounds of sliced turkey should last for a while.
  Several wagonloads of hay should see us through the winter.

- Finally, when they modify a subject, the main verb agrees with the noun that follows them:[11]

      A lot of effort goes into these productions.
      A lot of students have returned from recess.

In other words, these phrasal quantifiers are determiners, as we have already observed, not the partitive noun + *of* construction.

USING OF BEFORE SPECIFIC NOUNS

Notice that just as you saw earlier with numerals, the quantifiers can be made to modify specific noun phrases, too, by adding *of* and the definite article before a specific noun phrase:

a few sophomores	**a few of sophomores*
a few of the sophomores	**a few the sophomores*

This change of form changes the meaning:

some first-year students	(a small number of nonspecific students)
some of the first-year students	(a segment of a specific group of students)

Prescriptive grammarians have insisted that it is unneccessary to use the *of* after the quantifiers *all* and *both* (we deal with the latter below) except when they precede a pronoun, in which case *of* is required. It is true that neither *all* nor *both* need *of* to signal a specific noun following them, because the semantics of *all* and *both* demand that the noun be specific.

> *All (the) juniors will register tomorrow.*
> *All of them*
> *Both (the) seniors were inducted into the Honor Society.*
> *Both of them*

However, the use of *of* with *all* and *both* is quite common, especially in North American English, as you saw in Chapter 4, presumably by analogy with the other quantifiers.

> *All of the juniors will register tomorrow.*
> *Both of the seniors were inducted into the Honor Society.*

COMPARATIVE QUANTIFIERS

We have much to say about comparatives later in this book, but it is appropriate at this juncture to point out that even though they are determiners or pronouns and not adjectives, several quantifiers have comparative and superlative forms like adjectives.

	Comparative	*Superlative*
much	more	most
many	more	most
few	fewer	fewest
little	less	least

Whereas many of the quantifiers on the continua above are absolute, the comparative and superlative forms are relative.[12]

> Many people are telecommuting these days.
> Still, more people prefer to work in an office in the company of others.
> And most people don't have a choice.
>
> I have few homework assignments these days.
> I have fewer homework assignments than I did at the beginning of the term.
> I have the fewest homework assignments of anyone I know.[13]

Note that although prescriptively speaking, *less* is reserved for noncount nouns, *less* is increasingly used for both count nouns and noncount nouns, especially in informal discourse.

> This beer has fewer calories.
> ?This beer has less calories.

We have more to say about the use of these quantifiers in Chapters 34 and 35.

QUANTIFIERS WITH SPECIAL SEMANTIC CHARACTERISTICS

Other quantifiers are excluded from our continua because of their special semantic nature: *any, both, each, every, either, neither,* and *enough.*

- *Any,* as you saw in earlier chapters, is used in negatives and questions as a counterpart to the unstressed article *some. Any* can also be used in affirmative statements as a quantifier, and when it is, it refers to "one or more, no matter which."

(Jespersen 1933:181)

> Any of those answers will do.
> Any household detergent works.

Bolinger (1960) notes that such sentences are related to conditionals; that is, *if something is a household detergent, it will work.* The conditional sense of *any* extends to sentences such as:

> Any of the pasta left at the end of the meal will be put in a casserole.

A paraphrase of this example would be *pasta, if there is any.*

- *Both* is a predeterminer having a dual number. As such, it can be followed only by plural nouns signaling quantities of two.

> Two boys and a girl were accused of setting off a false alarm. Both (of the) boys felt ashamed of what they had done.

- *Each* refers to all members of a group, but does so individually, rather than collectively. It therefore modifies a singular noun and takes a singular verb.

> Each one of the special effects was created by a different computer programmer.

- *Every* is much like *each* in its meaning but is more collective. It too takes a singular verb. Unlike *each,* however, *every* must be followed by a noun or *one;* i.e., it can never function as a pronoun.

> Every one of the special effects was created by a different programmer.
> Each of the special effects was created by a different programmer.
> *Every of the special effects was created by a different programmer.

- *Either* and *neither* are like *both* in that two members of a set are being considered. In fact, sometimes *either* can substitute for *both.* However, both *either* and *neither* take singular verbs (see Chapter 4).

> Either date is preferable to September 7. (i.e., both dates are preferable)

Either can also offer a choice between two alternatives:

> When you are through, you can ask either of us to help you clean up.

- *Neither* means "not one and not the other." Like the other quantifiers, it can be a determiner or a pronoun:

  Neither one of us ever remembers to bring the sun lotion.
  Neither of the twins has ever married.

- *Enough* means sufficient. As a determiner:

  We have enough volunteers to finish building the playground.

As a pronoun:

  He eats enough to kill a horse.

THE ORDER OF DETERMINERS IN A NOUN PHRASE

Although we have not considered all the possible forms that can serve as determiners in English, in the last few chapters we have dealt with the most important types. Thus, it is appropriate now to revisit a point we first made in Chapter 5 when we introduced the phrase structure rule for the noun phrase. We said then that there are three subcategories of determiners to consider when sequencing determiners before a noun. The following is a chart (based on Quirk et al. 1985) that distributes most of the determiners we have explored thus far into one of the three subcategories.

Predeterminers	*Core Determiners*	*Postdeterminers*
quantifiers: *all,*	articles	cardinal numbers
both, half	possessives	ordinal numbers
multipliers: *double,*	demonstratives	general ordinals:
twice, three times, etc.	quantifiers: *some, any,*	*next, last , another,* etc.
fractions	*no, each, every, either,*	quantifiers: *many, much, (a)*
such a, what a	*neither, enough*	*few, (a) little, several, more,*
		less, most, least
		phrasal quantifiers:
		a great deal of, a lot of, a
		good number of, etc.

It is possible to sequence determiners in an English noun phrase by picking one determiner from the predeterminer column, one from the core determiner column, and one or more from the postdeterminer column. Here are some examples:

  pre core post   core
  All our many hopes were kept alive by her encouraging words.

  core post post
  These next two weeks before school starts will be hectic.

Not all combinations are possible, of course. For instance, quantifiers may be present in all three positions, but they cannot always be combined.

  *Half every paycheck goes to pay off our mortgage.

When a predeterminer quantifier is used as a pronoun, with the partitive *of* phrase following it, though, it is possible to have one quantifier from each of the first two columns combined.

  Half of every paycheck goes to pay off our mortgage.

ISSUES OF USE WITH QUANTIFIERS

MUCH AND MANY WITH QUESTIONS AND NEGATIVES

Grammar books will often say that *much* has a restricted use—that it is used in questions and negatives, but *a lot of* is preferred in affirmative statements.

Does Jake have many friends?	Does Jake have much fun?
Jake doesn't have many friends.	Jake doesn't have much fun.
Jake has many friends.	*Jake has much fun.
Jake has a lot of friends.	Jake has a lot of fun.

While this is a good rule of thumb for beginning and low-intermediate-level ESL/EFL students, it is not the whole story. Neumann (1975) found that in formal written contexts, *much* can be used in affirmative statements.

> (in a job application) I have much experience in the skills you have listed as required for the position.

Even here, though, Neumann found that native speakers preferred *a great deal of* in such a context. She also reports that native speakers prefer *many* over *a lot of* in formal contexts, even in affirmative statements.

> Today, more people are raising children alone, and many individuals are discovering that the act of being the sole parent can be very difficult.

Notice, too, that unmodified *much* and *many* cannot readily be used in short answers to questions:

How much money does it cost? $\left\{\begin{array}{l} \text{*Much.} \\ \text{Not much.} \\ \text{A little.} \end{array}\right\}$

How many books do you have? $\left\{\begin{array}{l} \text{?Many.} \\ \text{Not many.} \\ \text{(Quite) A few.} \end{array}\right\}$

REGISTER WITH PARTITIVES

We have already alluded to the matter of register in discussing the use of *many* and *much* in affirmative sentences. Register has an impact on the use of partitives as well. The partitives we have listed so far would presumably be appropriate for most registers. However, there are clearly other partitives that have a distinctively informal flavor. Here, for example, are some informal partitives equivalent in meaning to *a lot of*:

> When I win the lottery, I'll have a lot of money. (appropriate in all but the most formal contexts)

When I win the lottery, I'll have $\left\{\begin{array}{l} \text{lots of} \\ \text{plenty of} \\ \text{heaps of} \\ \text{oodles of} \\ \text{truckloads of} \\ \text{etc.} \end{array}\right\}$ money. (informal contexts)

DISCOURSE CONSIDERATIONS IN THE USE OF QUANTIFIERS

In a contextual analysis of *some*, (*a*) *few*, and (*a*) *little*, Hsu (1995) found that these quantifiers were distributed differently, depending on genre. For example, Hsu investigated *some*:

- In its protypical use as a quantifier:

  (from a novel)   They had let *some* reporters use their phone, but they would no longer.

- In its partitive use:

  (from a mathematics text)   In concluding this section, we should like to give an example which illustrates *some* of the ideas of the primary decomposition theorem.

- As a pronoun for its quantifier use:

  (from a government document)   Some weapon systems have become obsolescent while still in production, and *some* while still under development.

- As a pronoun for its partitive use:

  (from a novel)   The yards, front and back, were narrow; *some* were trash dumps, *some* had flower gardens.

- As an indefinite determiner (not a quantifier):

  (from a social science text)   . . . to their own future family life stages, various crises which could be expected to confront them at *some* time or other.

- As an approximator (not a quantifier):

  (from a social science text)   *Some* 30,000 completed schedules with 20 items . . . have been tabulated.

What Hsu found is that mathematics texts used *some* considerably more often as an indefinite determiner than as a quantifier. The opposite was true for social science texts. *Some* as a quantifier was also more prevalent than *some* as an indefinite determiner in government documents and letters to the editor. The least degree of difference was found in novels, where quantifier and nonquantifier uses were more closely balanced.

Hsu conducted a similar type of analysis with (*a*) *few* and (*a*) *little*. Perhaps, not surprisingly, given its greater scope as a quantifier, total tokens and tokens of quantifier *some* far surpassed tokens of (*a*) *few* and (*a*) *little*. Further, while overall (*a*) *little* occurs more often than (*a*) *few*, (*a*) *few* is more often used as a quantifier, since *little* is used more frequently as an adjective.

CONCLUSION

Our treatment of the linguistic devices English speakers use in quantification has been limited. Still, it is apparent that there is a lot to learn. We hope that it has also been clear that these devices are quite common. Indeed, we found that we have used a lot of (!) quantifiers, collectives, and partitives to talk about quantifiers, collectives, and partitives! We should also point out that while the core quantifiers constitute a closed class, partitives are an open class. Indeed the pattern for partitives is very productive, which means it can be extended to create new expressions all the time.

ESL/EFL students should have no trouble grasping the semantic concepts of these linguistic devices in general. They will, however, struggle with some of the details of form, the difference in positive and negative connotations as depicted on our two continua, and perhaps with the development of a large enough repertoire of these expressions to provide both variety and appropriateness in the ways in which they express quantification in English.

TEACHING SUGGESTIONS

1. Form/Meaning. To have students practice partitives, play the "(super)market" game. A student starts the game by saying "I went to the supermarket and I bought . . . " completing the sentence with a partitive and a noun beginning with the letter A; for example, "a bag of **a**pples." The second student must repeat the sentence and add to it with a partitive and a noun beginning with the letter B; for example, "I went to the supermarket and I bought a bag of **a**pples and a bunch of **b**ananas." The third student might add: "I went to the supermarket and I bought a bag of **a**pples, a bunch of **b**ananas, and a box of **c**ookies." The game continues until all students have had a chance, or all 26 letters have been used, or when the teacher and students are stumped in finding examples!

2. Form/Meaning. Have your students bring in their favorite recipes and share them with one another. This will give them good practice in using measure quantifiers. Collect the recipes and "publish" a class cookbook. If possible, prepare some of the recipes together.

3. Form/Meaning. Plan a party with your class. Have students figure out what they would like to serve and how much they will need of each item. Draw up a shopping list. If practical, go on a shopping trip together, using the opportunity to introduce some of the idiomatic partitives for fruits and vegetables you find.

4. Form/Meaning. Nancy Marwin (personal communication) suggests the following scenario for practicing collective nouns in a context. First, divide the class into small groups and then distribute a handout with the essential material for a story-writing exercise.

> The setting is a courtroom where a gang of thieves, all members of the same family (the Braysons), are on trial. Outside, a crowd of people have gathered: a group of reporters, a crew of photographers, and dozens of bystanders. Inside are the other participants: a team of lawyers, the judge, and the jury.

The groups of students are then instructed to write a story using this material, including the collective nouns, and to focus on both units and individuals where appropriate. They are told to be careful to use correct number agreement based on the meaning when they refer to collective nouns.

5. Meaning. Here are two books that students might enjoy perusing. Intended for children, they have great lists of collective nouns:

- *Beasts by the Bunches,* by A. Mifflin Lowe (Garden City, New York: Doubleday), in which the author has written a poem for each collective noun.

- *A Cache of Jewels and Other Collective Nouns,* by Ruth Heller, 1987 (New York: Scholastic, Inc.), which has great illustrations and which also shows the variety of collective nouns that can be used for the same animal group.[14]

6. Form/Meaning. For fun, have your students create their own collective nouns. Readers of *National Wildlife* magazine were asked to write in and suggest names for groups of animals. Here are some they came up with:

> a union of carpenter ants
> a pinch of crabs
> a battery of electric eels
> a syndicate of killer whales

See also Thewlis (1997) for a similar idea as applied to groups of humans, such as, *a scoop of journalists, a rash of dermatologists.*

7. Meaning. To work on the semantic differences among the quantifiers, ask the students to paraphrase the quantifier in one sentence with that of another. For example:

> *T:* 1a. There was little money left after the shopping spree.
> *SS:* 1b. There wasn't much money left after the shopping spree.
>
> *T:* 2a. A majority of the items we bought were purchased in the first hour.
> *SS:* 2b. More than half of the items we bought were purchased in the first hour.
>
> *T:* 3a. However, a few items were purchased later.
> *SS:* 3b. However, some items were purchased later.

8. Use. Ask students to conduct a survey of their classmates' preferences. In small groups, students should decide which preferences they would like to survey, such as type of music, type of book, food, movie, and so on. Staying in their small groups, students should design a questionnaire to collect the information they wish to learn. After the questionnaires have been distributed and completed, the group should compile the information and report their findings to the rest of the class. They should use quantifiers first and then use percentages to be more precise. For example:

> Our survey shows that some students in our class prefer rock music, some prefer classical music, and a few prefer jazz. Forty percent chose rock music, . . .

EXERCISES

Test your understanding of what has been presented.

1. Provide an original sentence illustrating each of the following terms. Underline the pertinent word(s) in your example.
   a. partitive noun
   b. idiomatic partitive noun
   c. collective noun
   d. collective noun derived from adjective
   e. quantifier
   f. quantifier with negative connotation
   g. quantifier for count nouns
   h. phrasal quantifier

2. Account for the ungrammaticality or semantic problems in each of the following sentences:
   a. *Chalk are on blackboard tray.
   b. *A lot people were at the garage sale.
   c. *Although he had few close friends, he was very lonely.
   d. *He has a deal of energy today.
   e. *Almost people like Chinese food.

3. Explain the difference between (1) and (2) in each of the following pairs of sentences.
   a. (1) Many of the workers at the plant lost their jobs due to downsizing.
       (2) Many workers lost their jobs due to downsizing.
   b. (1) The class didn't quiet down; it was in a boisterous mood.
       (2) The class didn't quiet down; they were in a boisterous mood.
   c. (1) Thanks a lot.
       (2) Thanks lots.
   d. (1) I got a speck of dust in my eye.
       (2) I got a piece of dust in my eye.

Test your ability to apply what you know.

4. The following sentences contain errors that ESL/EFL students sometimes make. Account for the ungrammaticality or awkwardness of each sentence, and explain how you would make your students aware of such errors.
   a. *I still have much problem in learning English.
   b. *Larry bought a dozen of eggs.
   c. *Peg needs to get some informations for her term paper.
   d. ?We have much homework tonight.
   e. *Some my friends are going camping this weekend.
   f. *Katie likes the song "Five Hundreds Miles."
   g. *I need a couple a minutes.
   h. *Some of books on the table may be yours.

5. How are the following partitive nouns the same? How are they structurally different?

   a head of cattle
   a head of lettuce

6. Explain the plural use of the number-based noun in the following newspaper headline:

   Greece: A Centuries-Old Framework for Contemporary Living

7. A student asks you to explain why in one instance *several* is followed by *of* and in another instance it isn't. How would you explain? Note that you can use suprasentential information to help you.

   The Chinese have given a pair of pandas to the Bronx Zoo. They have had several offspring. Several of the offspring have been sent to other zoos around the country.

8. There are two ways of making a noun specific when it is preceded by a partitive. One is to use a definite determiner with the partitive noun. Alternatively, a definite article can be used with the following noun.

   Will $\left\{ \begin{array}{l} \textit{this deck of cards} \\ \textit{a deck of these cards} \end{array} \right\}$ do?

   What is the difference between them? It will help to answer this question if you generate some of your own examples.

BIBLIOGRAPHY

References

Bolinger, D. (1960). "Linguistic Science and Linguistic Engineering." *Word* 16: 374–391.
Celce, M. (1970). "The Duality of Collective Nouns." *English Language Teaching* 24:2.

French, E. (1992). "A Clove by Any Other Name . . ." Unpublished term paper for Linguistics 5741, University of Minnesota.

Hsu, K. (1995). "A Contextual Analysis of *Some, Few,* and *Little:* Implications for ESL." Unpublished Ph.D. qualifying paper, UCLA.

Jespersen, O. (1933). *Essentials of English Grammar.* London: Allen and Unwin.

Kennedy, G. (1987). "Quantification and the Use of English: A Case Study of One Aspect of the Learner's Task." *Applied Linguistics* 8:3, 264–286.

Langacker, R. (1991). *Cognitive Grammar: Descriptive Application.* Vol. II. Stanford, Calif: Stanford University Press.

Neumann, R. (1975). "Much Confusion." Unpublished English 215 paper, UCLA.

Quirk, R., S. Greenbaum, G. Leech, and J. Svartvik (1985). *A Comprehensive Grammar of the English Language.* London: Longman.

Thewlis, S. (1997). *Grammar Dimensions.* Book 4 (2d ed.). Boston, Mass.: Heinle & Heinle.

Suggestions for further reading

For linguistic analyses of quantification, see:

Hintikka, J. (1974). "Quantifiers and Quantification Theory." *Linguistic Inquiry* 5: 151–157.

Hogg, R. (1977). *English Quantifier Systems.* Amsterdam: North Holland Publishing Company.

For a usage study on quantifiers, see:

Behre, F. (1967). *Studies in Agatha Christie's Writings: The Behavior of* A Good (Great) Deal, A Lot, Lots, Much, Plenty, Many, A Good (Great) Many. Gothenberg Studies in English. Göteborg: Elanders Boktryckeri Aktiebolag.

For pedagogical suggestions in teaching partitives and quantifiers, consult:

Badalamenti, V., and C. Henner Stanchina (1997). *Grammar Dimensions.* Book 1 (2d ed.). Boston, Mass.: Heinle & Heinle.

Danielson, D., and P. Porter (1990). Using English: *Your Second Language* (2d ed.). Englewood Cliffs, N.J.: Prentice Hall Regents.

Riggenbach, H., and V. Samuda (1997). *Grammar Dimensions.* Book 2 (2d ed.). Boston, Mass: Heinle & Heinle.

For pedagogical ideas for teaching quantifiers and collective nouns, see:

Byrd, P., and B. Benson (1989). *Improving the Grammar of Written English: The Handbook.* Belmont, Calif: Wadsworth.

Thewlis, S. (1997). *Grammar Dimensions.* Book 3 (2d ed.). Boston, Mass: Heinle & Heinle.

ENDNOTES

1. You may wish to review the rules presented in Chapter 4 for subject-verb agreement for fractions and percentages.

2. Some partitive nouns are always singular.

> A bit of humor always improves the classroom ambience.
> *Twenty bits of humor always improve the classroom ambience.

Here *a bit of* means a small amount. *A bit of* can also mean *a piece of,* in which case, the partitive noun is plural.

> Bits of paper were strewn about the street as if there had been a tickertape parade the day before.

3. You can add *-ful* to partitives of containers:

> a boxful of chocolates   a bagful of chips

You can also add *-ful* to some other partitives:

> a mouthful of food   a houseful of company

Notice that some measure words require it:

> a spoonful of medicine
> *a spoon of medicine

4. The count noun *pair* also occurs with other nouns that are usually in pairs, but these nouns may also occur in the singular:

> a pair of shoes   an old shoe
> a pair of earrings   a jade earring

5. The difference between *the whole of* and the quantifier *all* is very complicated. See Quirk et al. (1985) for the details.

6. Notice that with large nonspecific numbers, such as

> Tens of thousands of fans sought tickets to the rock concert.

the partitive is preceded by another number + *of*.

7. Other nouns that have no plural marking but are used as plurals are *police, people, cattle, vermin*. These are not normally considered collective nouns, however.

8. Except for *all* and *none*, which are at the extreme ends of the scale.

9. The quantifiers on the continua are among the most frequently used. Not all quantifiers are represented. We discuss others with special semantic character later in this chapter.

10. Normally, partitives don't follow other partitives, although it is possible for a quantity partitive to be included within the scope of a quality partitive:

> Two types of bars of soap
> *Two bars of types of soap

11. As you saw earlier, this is not the case with the true partitives, whose nouns determine number agreement with the verb when the partitive is in subject position.

> A pile of dishes was in the sink.
> Two piles of dishes were in the sink.

12. Another quantifier that is relative is *all*. *All* is relative in the sense that it specifies a quantity in relation to a reference quantity. Langacker (1991) shows that in response to a question asking *how many* an absolute quantifier would be acceptable, but a relative one would not:

> How many California condors still exist?
> Several   *All
> A few   (absolute quantifiers)   *Most   (relative quantifiers)
> Nineteen   *Each

13. Since *fewest* is a superlative form, it requires the definite article. See Chapter 35.

14. This is true of other quantifying expression as well. For instance, French (1992) shows that some English speakers prefer the partitive *a clove of garlic*, others *a bulb of* and still others make a distinction between the two, with *bulb* used for several *cloves* clumped together.

Chapter 18

THE PASSIVE VOICE

INTRODUCTION

In this chapter, we look at a linguistic device that is different from the others we have explored thus far. It is the grammatical feature of *voice*, which pertains to who or what serves as the subject in a clause. You are well acquainted with the active voice because it is the one we have been investigating to this point. In the active voice, the subject of a clause is most often the agent, or doer, of some action.

> Darwin studied the fauna of the Galapagos Islands.

At other times, speakers/writers of English will have reason to put the receiver or undergoer of the action into subject position. One way to do so is to use the passive voice.

> The fauna of the Galapagos Islands was studied by Darwin.

As Langacker (1987) has pointed out, the difference between active and passive is a focal adjustment analogous to the difference between:

> The cat is under the blanket.
> The blanket is over the cat.

In other words, using the passive allows speakers to make a kind of figure/ground reversal.

Most languages in the world employ different voices to put different constituents in initial position. For example, in the Bantu languages, the passive is used if the agent is inanimate and the patient or receiver is animate. Thus, many Bantu languages would avoid the equivalent of the active voice in a statement such as:

> The election bothered Nancy.

and would strongly prefer the passive voice, thus:

> Nancy was bothered by the election.

Another example comes from Japanese. Japanese is said to have an adversative passive, in which the subject is adversely affected by the action portrayed in the verb (Wierzbicka 1988). For example:

> John   ga   ame   ni   fur-are-ta.
> John (topic marker) rain   by   fall (passive) (past)

The literal translation of this sentence, *John was fallen by rain*, is interpreted to mean that John was adversely affected by rain. Although "neutral" passives are possible in Japanese, adversative passives are common enough that Japanese students may puzzle over when to use the passive voice in English.

Indeed, although many ESL/EFL grammar books make it seem that the learning challenge for the passive is its form, this is not true from our perspective. Our experience has shown us that it is learning when to use the English passive that presents the greatest long-term challenge to ESL/EFL students. Nonetheless, as with all structures, students will have to learn its forms and their meanings, so it is to these we turn first, before concluding the chapter by fully explicating the use of the passive voice.

FORMS OF THE ENGLISH PASSIVE

As we have just noted, the passive allows the thing or person that receives the action of the verb to occupy subject position. Here is a tree to illustrate a passive sentence:

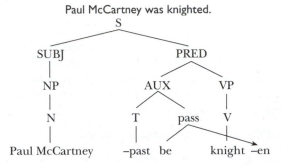

Paul McCartney was knighted.

Note that the normal word order of English still holds, but the auxiliary has been expanded to include the passive morphology: a form of the *be* verb + the past participle—*be . . . -en*. We will obviously need to elaborate our phrase structure rule for the auxiliary to accommodate the passive:

$$AUX \rightarrow \left\{ \begin{Bmatrix} T \\ M \end{Bmatrix} \text{(pm) (perf) (prog) (pass)}^{1} \atop \text{-imper} \right\}$$

And the phrase structure rule specifying what the passive is composed of is

pass → *be . . . -en*

As can be seen in our example sentence, the agent is not the subject of the sentence. In fact, usually in passive sentences, the agent is not mentioned at all. If the agent is mentioned, it appears in a prepositional phrase marked with the preposition *by*. Here is how a tree looks with the agent expressed.

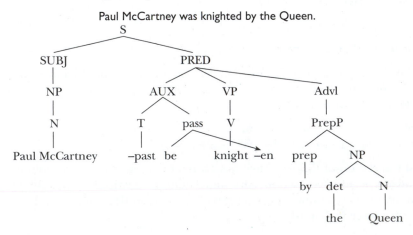

Paul McCartney was knighted by the Queen.

THE PASSIVE WITH TENSE AND ASPECT

What we have illustrated so far is the simple passive. It is also possible for the passive voice to interact with other elements in the auxiliary.[2] For illustrative purposes, here are a few of the combinations that exist:

- With modals:

    Diamonds can be mined in South Africa.

- With simple present:

    Diamonds are mined in South Africa.

- With present perfect:

    Diamonds have been mined in South Africa.

- With present progressive:

    Diamonds are being mined in South Africa.

- With simple past:

    Diamonds were mined in South Africa.

- With past progressive:

    Diamonds were being mined in South Africa.

- With *be going to* for future:

    Diamonds are going to be mined in Botswana.

The perfect progressive forms of the *be*-passive are possible for some speakers of North American English, but rare, since the two *be* verbs in a row make this combination difficult to process:

    Diamonds have been being mined in South Africa for years.

Notice that in all of the above, the passive was the last verb to appear in the string, thereby earning its position in our phrase structure rule as the final optional auxiliary element.

OTHER PASSIVE VERBS

It is important to recognize that although *be* is the prototypical auxiliary verb of the passive, it is possible to have other verbs fulfill this function.

Get

The *get*-passive is quite common in informal, conversational English. Here's an example in the simple past.

    Barry got invited to the party.

In order to account for such examples, our phrase structure rule will have to include *get* as an alternative to *be*. One important structural difference to note between the *be*-passive and the *get*-passive is that *get* does not function as a true auxiliary in questions and negatives the way that *be* does. As a result of this, *do* must serve as an operator for *get* in questions and negatives:

be-passive	*get-passive*
A: Was Bruno arrested?	A: Did Bruno get arrested?
B: No. He wasn't even caught.	B: No. He didn't even get caught.

Another difference that exists between the *be*-passive and the *get*-passive is that the latter can occur more readily with the perfect progressives:

> His plans have been getting sidetracked for years.
> ?His plans have been being sidetracked for years.

The *get*-passive should not be confused with the main verb *get* followed by an adjective when it is used to mark a change of state.

> Unfortunately, Lou got sick just before the big game.

Sometimes the adjective is in the form of a past participle, which makes it more difficult to distinguish main verb *get* from passive auxiliary verb *get*.

> Unfortunately, Lou got indisposed just before the big game. (get is main verb followed
> by a past participle, which is an adjective)

We return to this point later in this chapter.

Have

It is also possible for *have* to function as a passive auxiliary. When it does, we refer to it as the experiential *have* to distinguish it from the causative *have*, which we examine in Chapter 32.

Mary had her purse snatched

> passive (experiential—The purse-snatching happened to her. It was beyond her control.)

> causative (Mary arranged for someone to snatch her purse—perhaps to file a fraudulent insurance claim.)

Note that the *have*-passive is a bit more complicated than the *be*-passive and the *get*-passive in that the pattern for the *have*-passive includes an intervening noun phrase: *have . . . NP . . . -en.*

Be (in complex passives)

The *be*-passive can also interact with complements such as *that*-clauses and infinitives, producing complex passives.

> It is rumored that he will get the job.
> That he will get the job has been decided.
> John is thought to be intelligent.

We consider these fully in Chapters 31 and 32 .

PASSIVE ONLY

The passive is more limited than the active voice in that only transitive verbs may be in the passive. In fact, some passive sentences in English have no active voice counterpart, such as

> Mehdi was born in Tehran.
> ?His mother bore Medhi in Tehran.

There is of course the active verb "*to bear,*" as in "*The lioness bore three cubs.*" However, for all intents and purposes, there is no active voice counterpart to *to be born* to talk about facts concerning human birth. Other verbs that occur commonly in the passive are *be deemed, be fined, be hospitalized, be jailed, be scheduled, be shipped, be staffed, be suspended.*

Similarly, some verbs readily enter into complex passives that have no variant in the active voice:

> It is rumored that he is on his way out.
> *Someone rumors that he is on his way out.

For these reasons, and for reasons we give in the meaning and use sections, we feel justified in positing a base structure for passive sentences that is different from active sentences.

THE MEANING OF THE PASSIVE

The passive can be said to have a grammatical meaning rather than a lexical one. It is a focus construction that exists to put the patient, i.e., the receiver or undergoer of an action, in subject position. The subject is acted upon and is thus "passive." Indeed, Shibitani (1985) has shown that the passive "defocuses" the agent. No matter when it is used or what its form, then, it will always have this core meaning. However, there are issues related to this core meaning about which ESL/EFL students need to know. In the remainder of this chapter, we address these.

SEMANTIC CONSTRAINTS ON USING THE PASSIVE

As stated earlier, the passive requires a transitive verb. This is not to say, however, that every passive sentence with a transitive verb is acceptable. Langacker (1987), for example, shows that the acceptability of passive sentences is influenced by several factors:

1. The more definite the subject is, the more acceptable the sentence in passive form is:

> This poem was written by Henry Wadsworth Longfellow.
> ?Poems were written by Henry Wadsworth Longfellow.

2. With stative verbs, the more indefinite the object in the *by* phrase is, the more likely it is to be acceptable in its passive form.

> Arthur Ashe was liked by everybody.
> ?Arthur Ashe was liked by me.
> The movie has been seen by everyone in town.
> ?The movie has been seen by Jim.

3. The more the verb denotes a physical action, as opposed to a state, the more acceptable its use in a passive sentence is:

> The ball was kicked over the goalposts.
> ?The ball was wanted by the other team.[3]

Notice, though, that if factors 1 and 2 are honored, then a stative verb like *want* can more easily be used in the passive voice.

> This old jalopy of mine must be wanted by somebody!

Presumably the first two observations can be accounted for by recognizing that the information status of constituents appearing in initial position and in predicate position in English sentences is different. As you have already seen several times in this book, the subject NP is typically more definite than any predicate NP because it represents given information—what the predicate is about. We have more to say about this in the section on use.

The third observation stems from the fact that the subject of a passive sentence needs to be somehow affected by the action of the verb. Thus, certain transitive verbs, when used statively, are not likely to occur in the passive voice.[4] This is true, for example, of the following verbs:

- verbs of containing (e.g., *contain, hold, comprise*):

    *Two gallons of water are held by the watering can.

- verbs of measure (e.g., *weigh, cost, contain, last*):

    *Five dollars is cost by the parking fine.

- reciprocal verbs (e.g., *resemble, look like, equal*):

    *Lori is resembled by her father.

- verbs of fitting (e.g., *fit, suit*):

    *He is suited by the plan.

- verbs of possession (e.g., *have, belong*):

    *A car is had by him.

and others.

MEANING DIFFERENCE BETWEEN THE ACTIVE AND PASSIVE

At other times, both active and passive voice can be used, but there is a difference in meaning. This is especially true when numerals or quantifiers are used and in generic statements:

Everyone in the room speaks two languages. (i.e., any two languages per person)
Two languages are spoken by everyone in the room. (i.e., two specific languages that everybody speaks)   (Chomsky 1965)

Few people read many books. (i.e., There are few people in this world who read lots of books.)
Many books are read by few people. (i.e., There are many books that are read by few people.)   (Lakoff 1968)

Moles dig tunnels. (A true statement about all moles)
Tunnels are dug by moles. (This is not true. Not all tunnels are dug by moles.)

BE-PASSIVES VERSUS *GET*-PASSIVES

We offered an explanation for the difference between the passive *have* and the causative *have* by saying that the passive *have* talks about the subject as experiencer. Next, we turn to the semantic distinction between *be* and *get*.

As we said earlier, the *be*-passive is the prototypical passive verb. It is unmarked and thus semantically neutral, which is not true of the *get*-passive. According to Carter and McCarthy (1997), the English *get*-passive, like the Japanese passive, overwhelmingly tends to be used adversely (124 of 139 occurrences in their corpus of slightly over one million running words of informal spoken English). Here are some examples from their data:

A: And er she had gone in the house because I gave her the key.
B: Yeah.
A: And for some reason don't ask me why but she couldn't get out.
B: Oh no. She *got locked in.*

A: And I lost my second eldest brother.
B: Ahh yeah yeah
A: He was er sergeant and er
B: [Yes, mm]
A: [*he got killed* [B: Mm] trying to save some other man, some other soldier.]

The adversative nature of the *get*-passive was also borne out in a contextual analysis by Yim (1998). Yim found that the *get*-passive occurred with verbs from semantic categories such as physical assault (*get hit*), hindrance (*get trapped*), transference (*get snatched*), and verbs of emotional or mentral strain (*get punished*). Yim suggests that the *get*-passive's affinity for affective connotations is consistent with its colloquial nature.

Other characteristics of the *get*-passive noted by Carter and McCarthy were its lack of expressed agent (130 of 139 *get*-passives had no explicitly stated agent; and likewise, in Yim's data 119 of 125 *get*-passives had no *by* phrases) and the fact that *get*-passives could not replace *be*-passives with nondynamic verbs:

This bed had not been slept in.
*This bed had not got slept in.
Joe hasn't been seen for years.
*Joe hasn't got(ten) seen for years.

Yim's data support this observation. It appears that *get*-passives are predominantly associated with verbs that emphasize actions or processes. Consequently, they are also more likely to occur with adverbs of frequency:

This man continually got wiped out.

Finally, Yim notes that the overwhelming majority of *get*-passives in her data had human subjects (90.4%), which is not true of *be* passives.

PAST PARTICIPLES: ADJECTIVES OR PASSIVE?

Most of the time the distinction between a past participle functioning as a passive verb and one serving as an adjective will be obvious. However, the distinction is not always clear-cut. Willis (1994) points out that in a sentence such as:

The windows were broken.

the past participle *broken* could be regarded as either adjectival or passive.

The house was a mess. The paintwork was peeling and the windows were *broken.*
(participle is adjectival)
The windows were *broken* by the force of the explosion. (participle is passive)

In the first interpretation, the past participle is descriptive, or stative, and thus adjectival. In the second, the past participle is dynamic and thus passive. However, you will see in Chapter 20 that adjectives can sometimes be dynamic. Thus, in the end, in cases of ambiguity, the only distinguishing sentence-level feature we are left with is the use of *by* with a noun phrase to mark an agent in the passive voice, if there is one:

The beans were *refried.* $\begin{cases} \text{by someone (passive)} \\ \text{present state of the beans (adjective)} \end{cases}$

The fact that not all adjectival and passive participle pairs are homophonous, even though their spelling makes them appear so, suggests that adjectives and passives have a different origin:

The suspect was *alleged* to have taken the money. [ə l ɛ ǰd]
The *alleged* thief . . . [ə l ɛ ǰɪ d]

This was confirmed by Dubinsky and Simango (1996), who note that in Old English there were two distinct affixes that have merged into the modern spelling -*ed.*

The congregation was blessed. $\begin{cases} \text{verb [b l ɛ s t]} \\ \text{adjective [b l ɛ s ɪ d]} \end{cases}$

A MIDDLE VOICE

We hinted in the introduction to this chapter of the existence of a means besides the passive to put a nonagentive NP into subject position. There is, in fact, a "middle voice," intermediate between active and passive voices. The middle voice allows the subject of a sentence to be nonagentive, as in the passive voice, but the morphology of the verb to be in the active voice.

1. Her high C shattered the glass. (active voice)
2. The glass was shattered by her high C. (passive voice)
3. The glass shattered. (middle voice)

As Lock (1996) puts it, English allows a representation of processes not only in terms of actions (1 and 2) but also in terms of happenings (3). Other languages, of course, can report happenings as well. Some do so with the use of reflexives (examples from Shibatani 1985):

Spanish	*French*	*Russian*
Se abriò la puerta.	La porte s'est ouverte.	Lekcija načalas'.
(Refl. open the door.)	(the door Refl.-is opened.)	(lecture began Refl.)
The door opened.	The door opened.	The lecture began.

Instead, English uses special verbs to express spontaneous occurrences. Such verbs, which allow the object of a transitive clause to be a subject of an intransitive clause without changing voice, are called ergative, or change-of-state, verbs. Ergative verbs, such as *shatter,* can appear in all three voices and thus take either agents or undergoers of the action (sometimes called patients or themes) as subjects. There are several hundred ergative verbs, common enough so that students will encounter them frequently.

Many ergative verbs, like *shatter,* suggest changes of state: *age, begin, bend, break, burst, change, close, cool, condense, decrease, develop, drop, dry, empty, end, evaporate, finish, grow, increase, melt, open, sink, slow, spread, start, stop, tear,* and others.

Three other categories of ergative verbs are mentioned in *Collins Cobuild English Grammar:*

• Verbs of cooking *(bake, boil, cook, defrost, fry, roast, thicken,* etc.):

I'm baking a cake.
The cake is baking.
The cake is being baked by her friends.

- Verbs of physical movement (*move, rock, shake, spin, swing, turn,* etc.):

  The boy spun the top.
  The top spun.
  The top was spun by the boy.

- Verbs that involve vehicles (*drive, fly, park, reverse, run, sail,* etc.):

  She drove the car.
  The car drives well.
  The car was driven all the way to Tallahassee.

Rutherford (1987) tells us that ESL/EFL students, for whom the idea of an ergative verb is new, sometimes object to such sentences as

  The window broke.

The students argue that windows can't break themselves, and thus they feel obliged to use the passive or express an agent.

  The window was broken.
  Someone broke the window.

While such sentences are not wrong, of course, the active voice sentence with a nonagentive subject is perfectly permissible in English with ergative verbs. The difference between the two options is that the passive sentence suggests the existence of an agent, even if the agent is not explicit. The verb used ergatively does not permit an agent. This can be shown by the addition of a *by* phrase

  The window was broken. (passive)   The window broke. (ergative)
  The window was broken by the gang.   *The window broke by the gang.

Thus, the following are situations in which agentless "change-of-state" sentences are preferred to passive sentences with an explicit or implicit agent:

1. When the focus is on the change of state, and the agent is irrelevant.

  The bank closes at 5 P.M.

2. When the writer's or speaker's objective is to create an aura of mystery or suspense—that is, things seem to be happening without the intervention of an agent:

  We were sitting quietly after dinner, when suddenly the door opened.

3. When the subject is something so fragile or unstable that it can break, change, dissolve, and so on without any apparent intervention on the part of any agent:

  Left hanging on the fence, the red balloon suddenly burst.

4. When it is natural to expect change to occur (i.e., physical, social, or psychological "laws" seem to be involved):

  The ice on the pond melted earlier than usual.

5. When there are so many possible causes for a change of state that it would be misleading to imply a single agent:

  Prices increased due to a variety of factors.

Another challenge for ESL/EFL students is to learn which verbs are ergative. Lock (1996) notes that students may make errors such as

*Many of the old buildings in the center of town have recently demolished.

—not because they have trouble with the passive voice, but rather because they have incorrectly assumed that the verb *demolish* can be used ergatively.

In addition to verbs that can occur in all three voices, the middle voice can also be expressed by intransitive verbs that take the focus of the process as subjects.

- Verbs of occurrence: *happen, occur, take place*

    The incident occurred before anyone knew what was happening.

- Verbs of inherently directed motion (Rosen 1984): *arrive, fall, rise, emerge, go*

    The dough rose.

- Verbs of description: *appear, disappear, vanish*

    The trail disappeared into the woods.

Since these verbs have no transitive counterparts, they do not occur in the passive voice. These intransitive verbs in the active voice with nonagentive subjects cause problems for ESL/EFL students who sometimes overgeneralize the passive voice and write:

*The accident was happened last night.

Yip (1995) reports that these errors occur in Chinese students' interlanguage possibly because students have been taught that sentences with grammatical subjects that are not the agent require the passive in English. This is simply not the case, and ESL/EFL students will need to learn about this middle voice.

Other languages treat the thing or person who has been affected or has undergone the process with case endings (e.g., Japanese) or word order (e.g., Italian) to distinguish subjects of active intransitives from subjects of intransitives that are events or happenings (Zobl 1989).

Giovanni telefona. Giovanni telephones.	(The subject-verb order indicates that the subject of the intransitive verb is an agent, therefore, the verb denotes an action.)
Arriva Giovanni. Giovanni arrives.	(The verb-subject order indicates that the subject is nonagentive, denoting a happening, not an action.)

English, with its restricted word order, will not permit such permutations, of course. Nevertheless, it does have a middle voice, which affords English speakers yet another option for achieving theme-rheme requirements in discourse (Rutherford 1987).

THE USE OF THE PASSIVE

Rutherford's observation provides a convenient segue into a discussion on the use of the passive. Two matters concern us here: knowing when English speakers use the passive, as opposed to the active, or middle voice; and knowing when they include an explicit agent in a passive sentence. As you will see, these two issues overlap considerably.

ACTIVE VERSUS PASSIVE

Again, we should remember that most languages have a means of shifting focus in a sentence. The English passive is not unique in this regard. What will be problematic, though, is that not all languages use the passive or equivalent focus constructions for the same reasons. We have already noted that most often the Japanese passive is adversative. While the English passive can be used to report adversity as well (especially the *get-*passive), the passive in English has a wider distribution than in many other languages. Nevertheless, the passive is the marked voice; English speakers normally select the agent as subject and use the active voice. Just when, then, is the passive preferred?

We have already indicated that the passive is used when we want to defocus the agent. The following are three specific times when this might be warranted (Thompson 1987).

1. The passive is used when the agent is not to be mentioned because

- it is redundant or easy to supply:

    Pineapples are grown in Hawaii.

- it is unknown:

    The bank was robbed yesterday.

- it is very general (example from Hayes 1992):

    By the end of the 1960s, the United States could no longer be described as a white, Anglo-Saxon, Protestant nation.

- the speaker/writer is being tactful:

    Margaret was given some bad advice about selecting courses.

- the speaker is being evasive:

    An error was made in the budget.

2a. The passive is used when the nonagent is more closely related than the agent to the theme of the text (i.e., what it is about):

> I was a young Columbia man while I worked in a cafeteria from 6:30 A.M. to 3:00 P.M. *I was much respected by the management,* even though I drove the people I worked with insane, because I had standards they couldn't cope with.
>
> (Example from Terkel's *Working,* found in Thompson 1987:503. Italics added.)

The nonagent *I* in the italicized clause is more thematic than the agent *the management.* In other words, the passive topicalizes the patient or receiver/undergoer of the action.

Here is another example where the thematic status of the agent and nonagent is critical to the decision to use the passive:

> The ends of a spindle were suspended from a bracket protruding to one side of the sledge frame.
>
> We suspended the ends of a spindle from a bracket protruding to one side of the sledge frame.

The first sentence in the passive voice, which has been adapted from Banks (1997), was culled from a corpus of 11 research articles having to do with oceanography. The second sentence is one that Banks constructed. Banks argues that scientists choose to use the passive not so much due to their desire to sound objective as to the fact that the theme of scientific writing deals with the apparatus or results of a study rather than the person conducting the investigation.[5]

2b. The passive is used when the nonagent is a participant in the immediately preceding sentence. Here is an example, again cited in Thompson 1987:506, taken from *The Explorers of the Mississippi*, page 145.

> Lorenzo arrived in Paris as a down-at-heel political refugee without friends or money; luckily for him, *France at that time was ruled by an Italian,* Cardinal Mazarin . . .

In this example, France is not the theme of the passage, but it does relate to Paris in the previous clause. You saw in Chapter 2 how new information is introduced in the rheme of one sentence and then becomes the theme of the next sentence. As we noted at the end of the section on meaning, passive and middle voices are devices that promote this thematic cohesion. Thus, as Thompson points out, strategies 2a and 2b above are related. They are illustrations of the same cohesive principle of thematic unity with strategy 2a simply applying to a larger stretch of text than strategy 2b. Thompson (1987:501) concludes:

> It appears that users of English are content to code the agent as subject unless broadly thematic or more local cross-clausal considerations require an alternative coding.

Not surprisingly, distributions of the passive differ among genres. Where more focus is on the outcome or what happened, such as with scientific or journalistic writing, passives are more frequent than with fictional and conversational English. Pioneering work by Huddleston (1971) and Shintani (1979) attest to this.

It is worth noting that although not as many passives occur in conversations as in written genres, there is a way in informal English to defocus the agent without using the passive voice. Interlocutors often use the nonanaphoric *they* with active voice where the passive would also be possible (Thompson 1987):

> They forecast a snowy winter this year.
> A snowy winter was forecast this year.

The *they* is nonanaphoric because it has no antecedent. The exact identity of the agent is unimportant. Thus, the discourse function of nonanaphoric *they* can be said to overlap partially with agentless passives. This brings us to the question of the conditions governing naming an agent. As we said earlier, reasons for when to use the passive overlap considerably with issues concerning whether or not to mention the agent. This is the other major use issue concerning the passive voice.

AGENTED PASSIVES

Since the function of the passive is to defocus the agent (Shibatani 1985), we may rightfully inquire as to when the agent does appear. In fact, the answer is that it appears surprisingly infrequently. Most analyses show that only about 15 to 20 percent of the passives occurring in texts explicitly include agents. Because of their infrequency, Shintani (1979) suggests that we teach our ESL/EFL students when and why to retain the agent in those approximately 15 percent of passive sentences that have explicit agents—rather than trying to give them rules for omitting the agent in those 85 percent of passives that are agentless. She examined a large number of agents that were overtly expressed in passive sentences occurring in written and spoken discourse, and she concluded that almost all these agents could be explained by one of three generalizations.

Agented passives are used:

1. When the agent is new information:

   While Jill was walking down the street, her purse was snatched by *a young man.*

2. When the agent is nonhuman (i.e., we expect agents to be human):

   All the lights and appliances in the Albertson household are switched on and off daily by *this electrical device.*

3. When the agent is a well-known personage and should be included as propositional information:

   The Mona Lisa was painted by *da Vinci.*

Several issues concerning the use of the passive were researched by Tomlin (1985). Tomlin investigated the relationship between information structure and clausal grammar by studying ice hockey broadcasts.

Here is an excerpt from one sportscast:

   Quick pass ahead to Errol Thompson, trying to work past Lapointe, it came back to Polonich. Polonich never got the shot away, checked by Lapointe. (1985:70).

Confirming what you have seen so far, the passive is used in the last clause (*checked by Lapointe*) because the subject of this passive clause (i.e., Polonich) is nonagentive and thematic both in terms of the whole event—Polonich as the person with the puck and thus a potential scorer—and in terms of Polonich's being a participant in the previous clause. An agented passive is used because the agent (Lapointe) is new information in the discourse; that is, the fact that it was Lapointe who did the checking is new information that listeners need to know in order to follow the flow of the game.

CONCLUSION

Early transformational grammar accounts and many ESL/EFL texts tended to treat the passive voice as if it were a syntactic variant of the active voice. We have attempted to argue against this characterization of the passive. In fact, use of the two voices is motivated by different reasons. One would find a passive in a discourse for which an active voice sentence would not be appropriate. For this reason, we think that it is misleading to students to present the passive as if it were derived from the active voice. Learning when to use the passive is a challenge to ESL/EFL students, who will tend to over- or under-use it depending on its frequency of occurrence and its functions in their native languages. Therefore, it is better from the start to introduce the passive as a grammatical structure with a particular use of its own.

TEACHING SUGGESTIONS

1. Form. Willis (1994) suggests that since the *be* + past participle pattern will be familiar to students from the pattern for copular verbs followed by adjectives, this pattern can be used as a starting point for teaching students the passive voice. Ask students to look around the room and choose five objects. Then they are to ask classmates what they are made of. For example:

A: What is the desk made of?
B: The desk is made of wood.
B: What are the windows made of?
C: The windows are made of glass.
C: What are the chairs made of?
D: The chairs are made of plastic and metal.
D: What is the blackboard made of?

Next, to introduce the passive, ask students to talk about what they are wearing or carrying with them and where it was made. For example:

My shoes were made in Italy.
My blouse was made in the Philippines.
My calculator was made in Japan.

To reinforce the dynamic sense of the second set of statements, you can point out to students that the second set of sentences is used in the past tense and can be followed by a *by* phrase with the agent or doer of the action.

My shoes were made in Italy by shoemakers.

However, the sentences in the first set cannot be followed by the agent because the past participle is being used adjectivally—that is, to describe the state of the object, not the result of a process.

*The desk is made of wood by furniture makers.

2. Form. (present perfect passive) Ask students to close their eyes. Change five things about the room. Ask students to open their eyes and to guess what changes have been made. For example:

The lights have been turned off.
The desk has been cleared off.
The chair has been turned upside down.

3. Form. (past passive) Have students play the card game "Concentration." Make 12 pairs of cards. On one card of each pair, put the name of a famous painter, author, inventor, for example. On the other card in the pair, put the name of the painting, book, invention, and so on for which the person is famous. Make up pairs of cards such as the following:

Agatha Christie	Murder on the Orient Express
Beethoven	The Moonlight Sonata
Shakespeare	Romeo and Juliet
Alexander Graham Bell	The telephone
Picasso	Guernica

Give each small group of students a deck of cards that has been shuffled and ask them to place the cards face down. Students should take turns. The first student should turn over two cards. If the cards match, the student should make an active or passive sentence—an active voice sentence if the agent was the first card that the student turned over, or a passive voice sentence if the agent was the second card. If the student is able to make a match and a correct sentence, he or she keeps the pair of cards and can turn over another pair. If not, both cards are turned face down again and it is the next student's turn to try. The game continues until all the pairs have been matched. The student with the most matched pairs wins the game.

4. Form/Meaning. To have students practice the *get*-passive, as it is used adversatively, tell students to imagine that they are children. They have had some friends over. The friends have left, but the place is a mess. Their parents have returned, and the "children" have to explain what happened. Give students a list of problems to explain or have them brainstorm a list themselves. Have them role-play the parent-child interaction. For example:

> *Parent:* What happened to the curtain?
> *Child:* It got stepped on.
> *Parent:* And what happened to the rug?
> *Child:* It got spilled on.

5. Meaning. Show students two photographs of the same place—one taken many years ago and one taken recently. Ask them to say what changes have occurred.
  Then ask them to predict what changes they think will occur in the future.

> A new highway was opened.
> New houses will be built.

6. Meaning. To familiarize students with change-of-state verbs, have them conduct or imagine conducting an experiment that demonstrates that water evaporates when heated and condenses when cooled. Have them write up or talk through the steps of the experiment.

7. Use. Ask students to pretend that they are newspaper reporters. They have been called to the scene of a fire. Describe the scene to them, or have them imagine one of their own. Ask them to write a newspaper account of the incident. For example:

> Late last night, a fire broke out at 212 Main Street. All of the people who lived there were rescued, but unfortunately, two pets were killed by the smoke. Firefighters were called shortly before midnight. When they arrived . . .

8. Use. Find a short article on science from a publication such as *Science News*. Ask students to read the article, locate the passive sentences, and say why they think the author used the passive. Also, they should try to explain why an agent has been mentioned, if it has.

EXERCISES

Test your understanding of what has been presented.
  1. Provide an original sentence illustrating each of the following terms. Underline the pertinent word(s) in your examples:

a.	active voice	**e.**	a verb that is always passive
b.	passive voice	**f.**	a verb that is never passive
c.	passive voice with agent	**g.**	middle voice (ergative)
d.	the *get*-passive	**h.**	an intransitive verb with a nonagent subject

  2. Draw tree diagrams for the following sentences:
    a. The report is being studied by the committee.

   b. The work isn't going to be completed on time.

   c. Was the play written by O'Neill?

   d. John got arrested yesterday.

3. Why are the following sentences ungrammatical or at least unacceptable?

   a. *Horace will be had tested on his Spanish proficiency.

   b. *Two liters were contained by the bottle.

   c. *In the bus was eaten a sandwich by Bill.

   d. ?Three cars were bought by the customer.

4. When there are two *be* verbs in a row in a passive sentence, one of them is passive. Which one is the passive *be* and how do you know?

> The food for the festival has been being prepared for days.

Test your ability to apply what you know.

5. Examine the directions following the examples in Teaching Suggestion 3. Explain why the passive was used where it was.

6. If your students produce the following sentences, what errors have they made? How will you make them aware of the errors, and what exercises will you prepare for your students to correct them?

   a. *I born in Seoul in 1970.

   b. *The song was sang several times by the choir.

   c. *Brazil was slowed down its inflation.

   d. *She got hurted by his remarks.

   e. *My cat must have been died by a car.

   f. *It was disappeared two weeks ago.

7. In light of what has been discussed in this chapter, see if you can account for the difference between the following pairs of verbs, infamous for causing native speakers of English problems.

     rise   raise

     lie   lay

     sit   seat

8. One of your students asks you to distinguish between *be married* and *get married*. What would you say? How about *have married* and *have been married*?

9. Although we didn't specifically discuss how the length of the *by* phrase affects the choice of active or passive, it clearly does. Remember, though, that we are looking for *reasons* to give our students. What is the reason for a lengthy *by* phrase and how does its length affect a decision to use the passive? Here is an example, cited in Gilbert (1992), from Annie Dillard's *A Trip to the Mountains* (*Harper's*, August 1991).

> That night, on the journey to the Skagit village, he was wakened in his blanket by the dark force of something he had heard and neglected to consider.

BIBLIOGRAPHY

References

Banks, D. (1997). "On the Structure of Scientific Information." *The News: Teachers of English to Speakers of Other Languages*—France *15: 15–18.*

Carter, R., and M. McCarthy (1997). "*Get* Passives in a Conversational Corpus." Paper presented at the American Association of Applied Linguistics, Orlando, March.

Chomsky, N. (1965). *Aspects of the Theory of Syntax.* Cambridge, Mass.: MIT Press.

Dubinsky, S., and R. Simango (1996). "Passive and Stative in Chichewa: Evidence for Modular Distinctions in Grammar." *Language* 72:4, 749–781.

Gilbert, S. (1992). "Passive Voice Constructions in Literature." Term paper written for Linguistics 5741, University of Minnesota.

Hayes, C. (1992). "Use of the Passive Voice in the Editorial/Opinion Page of Major Newspapers." Term paper written for Linguistics 5741, University of Minnesota.

Huddleston, R. (1971). *The Sentence in Written English.* London: Cambridge University Press.

Lakoff, G. (1968). "Repartee: Negation, Conjunctions, and Quantifiers." Unpublished paper, Harvard University.

Langacker, R. (1987). *Foundations of Cognitive Grammar,* Vol. I. Stanford, Calif.: Stanford University Press.

Lock, G. (1996). *Functional English Grammar.* Cambridge: Cambridge University Press.

Rosen, C. (1984). "The Interface between Semantic Roles and Initial Grammatical Relations." In D. Perlmutter and C. Rosen (eds.), *Studies in Relational Grammar 2.* Chicago, Ill.: University of Chicago Press, 38–77.

Quirk, R., S. Greenbaum, G. Leech, and J. Svartvik (1985). *A Comprehensive Grammar of the English Language.* London: Longman.

Rutherford, W. (1987). *Second Language Grammar: Learning and Teaching.* London: Longman.

Shibatani, M. (1985). "Passives and Related Constructions." *Language* 61:4, 821–848.

Shintani, M. (1979). "The Frequency and Usage of the English Passive." Unpublished Ph.D. dissertation in Applied Linguistics, UCLA.

Sinclair, J., and G. Fox (1990). *Collins COBUILD English Grammar.* London: Collins.

Thompson, S. (1987). "The Passive in English: A Discourse Perspective," In R. Channon and L. Shockey (eds.), *In Honor of Ilse Lehiste.* Dordrecht: Foris Publications, 497–511.

Tomlin, R. (1985). "On the Integration of Syntactic Subject, Thematic Information, and Agent in English." In J. Wirth (ed.), *Beyond the Sentence: Discourse and Sentential Form,* Ann Arbor, Mich.: Karoma Publishers, 61–80.

Warner, A. R. (1995). "Predicting the Progressive Passive: Parametric Change within a Lexicalist Framework." *Language* 71:3, 533–557.

Wierzbicka, A. (1988). *The Semantics of Grammar.* Amsterdam/Philadelphia: John Benjamins.

Willis, D. (1994). "A Lexical Approach," In M. Bygate, A. Tonkyn, and E. Williams (eds.), *Grammar and the Language Teacher.* London: Prentice Hall, 56–66.

Yim, B. (1998). The *Get* Passive. Unpublished M.A. thesis, UCLA.

Yip, V. (1995). *Interlanguage and Learnability: From Chinese to English.* Amsterdam/Philadelphia: John Benjamins.

Zobl, H. (1989). "Canonical Typological Structures and Ergativity in English L2 Acquisition." In S. Gass and J. Schachter (eds.), *Linguistic Aspects of Second Language Acquisition.* Cambridge: Cambridge University Press, 203–221.

Suggestions for further reading

For further information on the roles of participants in English sentences, see:

Dowty, D. (1991). "Thematic Proto-Roles and Argument Selection." *Language* 67:3, 547–619.

Roca, I. M. (ed.) (1992). *Thematic Structure: Its Role in Grammar.* Berlin and New York: Foris.

For more on ergativity, also known as unaccusativity, see:
Balcom, P. (1997). "Why Is This Happened? Passive Morphology and Unaccusativity." *Second Language Research:* 13, 1.
Levin, B. (1993). *English Verb Classes and Alternations.* Chicago: University of Chicago Press.
Levin, B., and M. Rappaport Hovav, (1995). *Unaccusativity: At the Syntax-Lexical Semantics Interface.* Cambridge, Mass.: MIT Press.
Van Valin Jr., R. (1990). "Semantic Parameters of Split Intransitivity." *Language* 66:2, 221–260.

For additional references on the get-*passive, consult:*
Givón, T., and L. Yang (1994). "The Rise of the English *Get*-Passive," In B. Fox and P. Hopper (eds.), *Voice: Form and Function.* Amsterdam and Philadelphia: John Benjamins, 119–149.
Vanrespaille, M. (1991). "A Semantic Analysis of the English *Get*-Passive." *Interface* 5:2, 95–112.

For pedagogical suggestions, see:
Byrd, P., and B. Benson (1992). *Applied English Grammar.* Boston, Mass.: Heinle & Heinle.
Danielson, D., and P. Porter (1990). *Using English, Your Second Language* (2d ed.). Englewood Cliffs, N.J.: Prentice Hall Regents.
Frodesen, J., and J. Eyring. (1997). *Grammar Dimensions.* Book 4 (2d ed.). Boston, Mass.: Heinle & Heinle.
Riggenbach, H., and V. Samuda (1997). *Grammar Dimensions.* Book 2 (2d ed.). Boston, Mass.: Heinle & Heinle.
Thewlis, S. (1997). *Grammar Dimensions.* Book 3 (2d ed.). Boston, Mass.: Heinle & Heinle.

For pedagogical suggestions, particularly for teaching ergative verbs, see:
Pennington, M.(ed.) (1995). *New Ways in Teaching Grammar.* Alexandria, VA: TESOL

ENDNOTES

1. This rule works to account for the structure of most passive sentences. It does fail, however, to produce passive imperatives, which are rare but possible in English (Quirk et al. 1985), although it could be argued that *seated* is an adjective participle:

>   **Be seated.**

If we were to move -imper up into the curly brackets with T and M, we could account for passive imperatives, but other problems would arise. For now, therefore, we will stick with this rendition of the phrase structure rule.

2. Warner (1995) shows that the progressive passive is relatively new to English, the first attested instance appearing in the latter half of the eighteenth century. He goes on to claim that the progressive passive did not originate from the merging of the passive voice with progressive aspect, but rather resulted from other changes in the auxiliary.

3. Notice that in *Butch Cassidy was wanted by the law, want* has a special meaning.

4. The reason we say *certain* stative verbs do not take the passive voice is that some stative verbs that involve mental states passivize easily, such as *be believed to, be thought to.*

SENTENCES WITH INDIRECT OBJECTS

INTRODUCTION

Traditional grammars define an indirect object as a second noun object that tells us *to whom* or *for whom* the action expressed in the verb is being carried out. This second noun object occurs in addition to the direct object, which identifies the thing or person being acted upon. There are also some indirect objects that tell us *of whom* the action expressed in the verb is being requested. (Admittedly, there are far fewer indirect objects of this third form in English than there are of the first two.)

Joe gave	*a book* direct object	to	*Sally.* indirect object
Joe made	*a bookcase* direct object	for	*Sally.* indirect object
Joe asked	*a question* direct object	of	*Sally.* indirect object

Notice that another form of these sentences is also possible with the recipient NP in immediate postverbal position:

Joe gave Sally a book.
Joe made Sally a bookcase.
Joe asked Sally a question.

We discuss the analysis of sentences of this type below.

Furthermore, many verbs taking both a direct and indirect object have a second option for the subject noun phrase of a passive sentence. In the active voice, the agent NP of such verbs serves as the subject (*Joe gave a book to Sally*). However, in the passive voice either the NP being acted upon or the recipient NP can serve as the subject:

The book was given to Sally (by Joe).
Sally was given the book (by Joe).

PROBLEMS FOR ESL/EFL STUDENTS

Why do sentences with indirect objects sometimes cause problems for ESL/EFL students? First of all, students must be able to sort out whether a given verb takes an indirect object preceded by a *to, for,* or *of* when the indirect object occurs in a prepositional phrase. Then they must learn which English verbs permit indirect object alternation. Those students whose native languages allow the indirect object to occur rather freely next to the verb (e.g., French and Spanish) may produce ungrammatical sentences such as "*John opened me the door" instead of "John opened the door for me." Many students will be confused by the fact that one of two verbs with similar meanings does not allow the indirect object to occur next to the verb. Thus by analogy with

> He told me the answer.

students will incorrectly produce

> *He said me the answer.

In fact, according to Mazurkewich and White (1984), children acquiring English as their first language also seem to have some problems learning all the constraints on indirect object alternation.

THE FORM OF SENTENCES WITH INDIRECT OBJECTS

THE SURFACE GRAMMAR OF VERBS THAT TAKE INDIRECT OBJECTS

The verbs that take indirect objects in English share certain similarities and differences. One important difference is that for some of these verbs, the indirect object is indispensable to the meaning and the structure of the sentence; for example:

> *Joe gave a book.[1]
>
> Joe gave { a book to Mel. / Mel a book. }
>
> *Morgan handed the letter.
>
> Morgan handed { the letter to Peter. / Peter the letter. }

In other instances the meaning of the entire sentence, not just the verb, must be considered, since the indirect object may not be structurally required, but the sentence will have a different meaning depending on whether or not the indirect object is present; for example:

> Mr. Jensen found { a job for me. / me a job. } ≠ Mr. Jensen found a job. (i.e., for himself)

Verbs with Implied Indirect Objects

There are also many cases where the indirect object is not structurally essential but where it is strongly implied and thus seems to be present semantically. In addition, the meaning of these sentences does not change markedly if the indirect object is not overtly expressed; for example:

> Sam sold the car. (i.e., to someone)
> Barbara asked a question. (i.e., of someone)

Verbs with Optional Post-Prepositional Indirect Objects

In the above two examples with *give* and *hand,* we can say that the indirect object is closely associated with the meaning of the sentence as a whole and the verb phrase in particular. However, in contrast to such cases, there are also instances where the indirect object is optional both structurally and semantically. In such a case we would have a complete sentence without the indirect object. If the indirect object is not explicitly stated, it is not even strongly implied. The two following sentences, for example, have optional indirect objects that seem much less closely related to the rest of the sentence than those in the two immediately preceding examples:

> Bob made a bookcase (for Sally).   The teller cashed the check (for me).

Verbs with Optional Indirect Objects in Postverbal Position

There are also cases where a postverbal indirect object seems to be optionally and redundantly added to sentences to indicate that there is a specific recipient of the action involving the direct object (this is often the speaker or a group including the speaker):

> Go find (*me*) a pencil.
> Get (*me*) a bumper sticker.

Verbs with Obligatory Versus Deletable Direct Objects

As a related matter, we must also consider the role of the direct object in sentences that contain both a direct and an indirect object. First, there are cases where the direct object cannot be deleted whether or not the preposition preceding the indirect object is present; for example:

> Peter gave the book to Alice.   *Peter gave Alice. (≠ donate)
> *Peter gave to Alice. (≠ donate)

In such a case, both the direct and indirect object are interdependent, indispensable elements in the sentence. Second, in some cases, the direct object can be deleted, but only if the indirect object comes directly after the verb and before the understood direct object.

> We paid the money to Harry.   *We paid to Harry.
> We paid Harry (the money).

Furthermore, there are cases where the direct object can be deleted, but the preposition preceding the indirect object must be retained. If the preposition is not retained, the meaning of the sentence changes, since the direct object is a required or understood constituent and the indirect object is optional or additional (i.e., the indirect object is reinterpreted as a direct object when it is the only object in postverbal position).

> Sara cooks (dinner) for us.   ≠   ?Sara cooks us.

In such instances we can say that the direct object is implied whether overtly stated or not, and the indirect object is not as closely linked to the meaning of the verb as it was in the two preceding cases with *give* and *pay*. Rather, the role of the indirect object is optional and similar to what it was in one of the sentences in the introduction:

> Joe made   a bookcase   for Sally.
>   [direct object]   [indirect object]

Subcategorization of English Verbs that Take Indirect Objects

Many common English verbs can take indirect objects in two different syntactic configurations:

postverbal position (V NP_x NP)

> John gave *Mary* the book.

postprepositional position (V NP Prep NP_x)

> John gave the book *to Mary*.

Other verbs that behave like *give* are *hand, tell, pass, sell, send, get, show, throw, lend, teach, offer, fax,* and *wire,* among others.

Many verbs can take indirect objects only in the postprepositional position:

> *I explained Mary the problem.
> I explained the problem to Mary.

Other verbs that behave like *explain* are *donate, announce, recommend, reveal, confess, introduce, narrate, describe, transmit, refuse, deny,* and so on.

Finally, a small number of verbs take only the immediate postverbal position and allow no indirect object in postprepositional position:

> The book cost me $10.
> *The book cost $10 to me.

A few other verbs that seem to behave like *cost* are *bill* and *(over)charge.*

Therefore, verbs taking indirect objects need to be marked in the lexicon according to which syntactic configuration(s) they may or may not occur in. In general, monosyllabic verbs—which are generally of Germanic origin—take indirect objects in immediate postverbal position more readily than do multisyllabic verbs, which tend to be of Latinate origin and which tend not to allow indirect objects in postverbal position.

THE SYNTAX OF SENTENCES WITH INDIRECT OBJECTS

Even if verbs are properly subcategorized, we will still need to generate indirect objects in different ways. For verbs that either permit or require the immediate postverbal position for indirect objects, the following structure applies:

John sent me a letter.

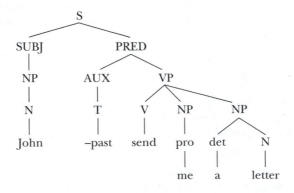

This structure also works for sentences like:

> The book cost me a fortune.
> Joe gave Sue some candy.
> The boy handed me a telegram.

For verbs that require an indirect object and either permit or require the indirect object to occur after the direct object in a prepositional phrase, the following structure applies:

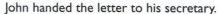

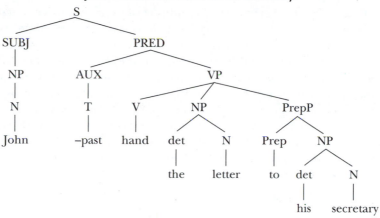

The structure also works for sentences like:

> Mr. Smith gave a note to his neighbor.
> Joe passed the salt to Susie.
> My mother lent her ballgown to Sarah.

Finally, for verbs that optionally allow but do not require prepositional indirect objects in order to complete their argument structure, the following structure applies:

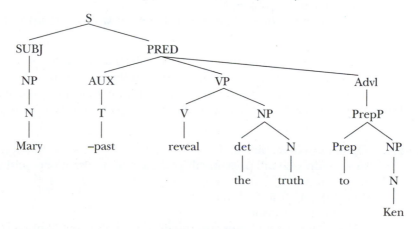

This tree structure also works for sentences like:

> The teacher explained the problem to the students.
> The magician performed a trick for us.
> The lawyer announced the news to his colleagues.

We shall see later that the syntactic differences between the last two structures become helpful in understanding whether or not the recipient NP can function as the subject of a passive voice sentence.

MEANING ISSUES WITH INDIRECT OBJECTS

THE MEANING OF VERB–INDIRECT OBJECT COMBINATIONS

Jacobson (1966) arranges the verbs that take indirect objects[2] into three semantic groups: "dative"[3] verbs such as *give*, "benefactive" verbs such as *make*, and "eliciting" verbs such as *ask*. Each group of verbs can be associated with the type of prepositional phrase that follows it.[4] ESL/EFL students would learn, then, that they must select *to* + NP in the case of the dative verbs (*give, say, sell, explain*, etc.), *for* + NP in the case of the benefactive verbs (*make, buy, cook, prepare*, etc.), and *of* + NP in the case of the "eliciting" verbs (*ask, request*, etc.). The "dative" verbs compose the largest category, the "eliciting" verbs the smallest. Of course, students must learn to take into account the meaning of the verb as it is used in sentences, because some verbs will occur in more than one of Jacobson's semantic categories, depending on how they are used; however, in such cases two different meanings of the verb form are involved; for example:

> I'll get this to him. (dative) = "deliver"
> I'll get this for him. (benefactive) = "fetch, obtain"

The Ambiguity of *for* Phrases

One related point to consider is that sentences with prepositional objects preceded by *for*, such as the following, may be ambiguous:

> John bought the book for me.

There are two possible interpretations of this sentence:

Proxy:	John bought it for me (i.e., he acted on my behalf) because I didn't have time to buy it myself.
Benefactive:	John bought it for me because my birthday was coming up and he wanted to give me a gift.

However, if the indirect object occurs directly after the verb in the above sentence (i.e., *John bought me the book*), only the benefactive interpretation seems to be possible.

This double meaning of *for* helps explain why the indirect object can come immediately after the verb *open* in the first sentence below (where *for* is benefactive) but not the second:

Benefactive:	Open me a beer, please. (The addressee will presumably open a can/bottle of beer and give it to the speaker.)
Proxy:	Open the door for me, please. *Open me the door. (The addressee does not give the door to the speaker, but merely opens the door on his/her behalf.)

Semantics of Verbs Followed by Indirect Objects

Wierzbicka (1988)—drawing on Green (1974)—offers a detailed set of eight semantic subcategories for verbs that can be immediately followed by indirect objects.[5]

1. Verbs of transfer (e.g.: *throw, buy, send, lend, sell, give, hand, pass,* etc.)

   Jim threw Betty an apple.
   I passed Joe the salt.

2. Verbs that speak of the recipient's future possession or nonpossession of something (e.g.: *promise, offer, allow, allot, refuse, deny,* etc.)

   Bill promised Sue a watch.
   Jack refused Jill an ice cream.

3. Verbs of making or creating (e.g.: *bake, knit, carve, make, fix, draw, write,* etc.)

   Jill knitted Jack a sweater.
   I'll draw you a picture.

4. Verbs of preparing something for use (e.g.: *fry, roast, grill, iron, butter, peel,* etc.)

   I'll grill you a trout.
   Daddy peeled Sally an orange.

5. Verbs of entertaining (e.g.: *read, sing, tell, play,* etc.)

   Read me a story.
   Sing me a song.

6. Verbs of telling or transmitting messages (e.g.: *phone, wire, fax, tell, telex,* etc.)

   Bill wired Sue the news.
   I'll fax you that letter.

7. Verbs of teaching someone to do something (e.g.: *teach, show,* etc.)

   Sam taught Fido a trick.
   I'll show you the solution.

8. Verbs of showing something so someone can see it (e.g.: *show*)

   Tim showed Sam a picture.

As the last four of Wierzbicka's subcategories make clear, a verb form can belong to more than one subcategory:

   Tell can be a verb of entertaining or a verb of transmitting messages.
   Show can be a verb of teaching or of showing (i.e., making visible).

Of course there are also many verbs semantically related to one of these eight subcategories that do not take an immediate postverbal indirect object because the verb concerned takes only prepositional indirect objects:

(telling a message)	*She announced them the news.
	She announced the news to them.
(entertaining)	*The magician performed the boys a trick.
	The magician performed a trick for the boys.
(preparing for use)	*He decorated her the room.
	He decorated the room for her.

In these cases the etymology and syllable structure of the verbs concerned seem to override their semantic properties. Wierzbicka also argues that the indirect object seems much less essential with such verbs, since the sentences are perfectly complete with no indirect object:

She announced the news.
The magician performed a trick.
He decorated the room.

However, to this we would add that many of the sentences above in the eight subcategories taking postverbal indirect objects also seem complete without the indirect object:

I'll draw a picture.
I'll grill a trout.
I'll sing a song.

Semantics Governing Postverbal Position for Indirect Objects

Going beyond the semantic categorization of verbs to the interpretation of sentences, Goldsmith (1980) and Stowell (1981) have proposed that postverbal position for indirect objects is limited semantically to cases where the indirect object is "animate" and is a "projected possessor" of the direct object. Thus we can explain the acceptable and unacceptable alternations in the following sets:

1. **a.** Joe sent a letter to Sue.
   b. Joe sent Sue a letter.
   c. Joe sent a letter to Cincinnati.
   d. *Joe sent Cincinnati a letter.

2. **a.** I opened a beer for Sam.
   b. I opened Sam a beer.
   c. I opened the door for Sam.
   d. *I opened Sam the door.

In 1b *Sue* is the animate, projected possessor of the letter, whereas in 1d, *Cincinnati* is merely the location of the letter. In 2b, *Sam* is the animate, projected possessor of a beer, whereas in 2d, *Sam*, while animate, is not the projected possessor of the door.

ISSUES OF USE

EXPLANATIONS FOR INDIRECT OBJECT ALTERNATION

We have already given several examples in this chapter of the alternation of the indirect object in postverbal or postprepositional position. In this section we will discuss the function of indirect object alternation.

Function of Indirect Object Alternation

Erteschik-Shir (1979) has proposed a discourse principle, which is useful for understanding the function of indirect object alternation. It is the concept of *dominance*. Basically, a dominant constituent in a sentence is the one that a speaker has chosen to highlight, to call to his or her listener's attention. It is this constituent in a sentence that will probably be the topic of further conversation if there is to be any. Furthermore, in the string:

$$\text{V} \quad \text{NP1} \quad \begin{Bmatrix} \text{to} \\ \text{for} \\ \text{of} \end{Bmatrix} \quad \text{NP2,}$$

NP2 (i.e., the indirect object) is the dominant noun phrase. If the speaker wants to give prominence to NP1 (the direct object) instead, the alternate pattern is selected, if lexically possible, and NP2 precedes NP1, allowing NP1 to be the dominant noun phrase (the preposition drops out in this case).

To illustrate, the only context where

Pass the salt to me, please.

$$V \quad NP1 \left\{ \begin{matrix} to \\ for \end{matrix} \right\} NP2$$

would be appropriate is one in which the speaker's request is directed to a listener who is (1) holding a salt shaker and (2) obviously not knowing to whom to pass it. The listener might then reply, "Oh, I heard the request for the salt, but I didn't know who said it." Most contexts define the important part of the sentence as being the speaker's desire for salt, and therefore one more frequently hears:

Pass me the salt, please.

or—since the speaker is generally the indirect object by implication—simply:

Pass the salt, please.

If the person who complies with this request says anything at all, he or she would be likely to comment upon the direct object—the salt—not upon the one who initiated the request, that is, "Sure. Here it is."[6]

CONDITIONS ON INDIRECT OBJECT ALTERNATION

Erteschik-Shir's notion of dominance helps us understand why certain conditions such as the following are placed on indirect object alternation:

1. For many, though not all dialects of English, the indirect object cannot be postverbal if the direct object is a pronoun (especially *it*) and the indirect object is a noun.

> **We sent it to John.**　　　***We sent John it.**[7]

On the other hand, when the indirect object is a pronoun and the direct object is a noun (especially an indefinite one), the alternate pattern is likely to be selected.

> **We sent him a package.**

These observations can be explained by noting that pronouns are, as a rule, less dominant than nouns. Since pronouns usually have an anaphoric referent or a referent in the immediate physical environment, it is unlikely that a speaker would need to direct attention to them—their meaning is already clear from the text or context. This is not to say that an indirect object that is a pronoun would never occupy the dominant position, but when this does occur, a different interpretation would be necessary—for example, a contrastive one.

> **We sent a package to *him*. (not *her*)**

All other noun-pronoun combinations of direct and indirect objects are syntactically possible, although the intentions of the speaker will dictate the order.

> **We sent John the book.**
> **We sent him ('im) it. (acceptable to most if the indirect object is phonologically reduced)**

2. If the direct object is a long complex phrase or clause (i.e., dominant), a postverbal indirect object is necessary to avoid awkwardness:

> **?/* I told that John would be coming to his girlfriend.**
> **I told John's girlfriend that he would be coming.**

Clauses are always more dominant than NPs, and so the clausal direct object moves to the dominant position. On the other hand, if the indirect object is heavily modified, postverbal position is less likely:

> I bought a present for my new little niece, the first daughter of my eldest brother.
> ?/* I bought my new little niece, the first daughter of my eldest brother, a present.

The speaker who elaborates either the direct or indirect object has already given it dominance. Such objects, therefore, move to the dominant final position if the verb permits the preferred order.

3. The main verb must belong to the class of verbs permitting both postverbal and postprepositional position for indirect objects. Verbs like *give, send, ask, sell, pay, tell, hand, lend, show, offer,* and *teach* all readily accept the above conventions; however, *explain, reveal,* and *announce,* for example, do not.

> Explain the answer to me.
> *Explain me the answer.

All verbs that take indirect objects have to be marked in the lexicon according to whether or not they occur in postverbal position, postprepositional position, or both.

+ alternation	+ postprepositional position only	+ postverbal position only
give	announce	cost
send	explain	charge
lend	describe	bill
teach	say	.
tell	mention	.
.	.	.
.	.	.

We should note here that some of those verbs that do not allow postverbal position do, in fact, still allow the indirect object to precede the direct object, especially if the latter is elaborated (e.g., is several phrases long or is a clause). In such a case, however, the indirect object always retains its preposition so we know that some stylistic option other than indirect object alternation has occurred in such cases:

> They mentioned the new restaurant on Putney Road to me.
> *They mentioned me the new restaurant on Putney Road.
> They mentioned to me the new restaurant on Putney Road.

Authentic examples of this stylistic option are rare and almost always occur in writing rather than speech (Williams, 1994).

4. Lakoff (1969) notes that in conjoined sentences there are also constraints on indirect object alternation. If the verb is deleted in the second sentence, both sentences must have their indirect objects in the same position:

> I gave John a book, and Bill a bicycle.   *I gave John a book, and a bicycle to Bill.
> I gave a book to John, and a bicycle to Bill.   *I gave a book to John, and Bill a bicycle.

If the verb is retained in both parts of the conjunction, this constraint does not hold.

> I gave a book to John, and gave Bill   I gave John a book, and gave a bicycle to
> a bicycle.   Bill.

WHERE IS THE INDIRECT OBJECT MOST LIKELY TO OCCUR?

Thompson (1988) examines the problem of dative alternation[8] more narrowly than Erteschik-Shir (1979) with her principle of dominance. Specifically, Thompson focuses on the recipient (the indirect object) and makes two proposals concerning English sentences with indirect objects (we have reworded Thompson's proposals to conform to our terminology[9]):

1. Indirect objects are more topic-like[10] (i.e., more like subjects) than direct objects.
2. Postverbal indirect objects are more topic-like than postprepositional indirect objects.

Generally, the most topic-like constituent (i.e., the constituent with given information) in an English sentence occurs in subject position; however, in sentences where there are three NP participants, the second participant (i.e., the one in immediate postverbal position) is generally more topic-like than the third participant, which occurs at the end. For Thompson, a constituent is topic-like if it has as many of the following features as possible: animacy, pronominality, specificity, identifiability, proper noun status, short length, and activated status (i.e., presumably in the addressee's consciousness at time of utterance).

Using a written database consisting of two mystery novels and one personal narrative (nonfiction), Thompson tested her two hypotheses against 196 tokens of sentences having both direct and indirect objects and grammatically allowing both the postverbal and postprepositional position for indirect objects. She found that the indirect objects as a group were indeed much more topic-like than the direct objects.

By eliminating 11 sentences that had the postverbal direct objects *it* and *them*, pronouns that seem to occur categorically in this position, Thompson had 185 potentially flexible tokens to analyze. Of these, 132 sentences had indirect objects (i.e., the more topic-like of the two object constituents) that occurred in postverbal position with the direct objects occurring at the end. Of the remaining 53 tokens where the indirect object was in postprepositional position (with the direct object in postverbal position), the indirect object tended to be a full noun phrase that was not a proper noun, or it tended to occur at the end because it was nonspecific, inanimate, nonactive, or inordinately long (or a combination of these factors). Indirect objects in postprepositional position were pronouns (other than *it* or *them*) or proper names only when used contrastively:

> She had chosen to tell her story *to me*.
> He made that shoe for *Mr. Alexis*.

Thus Thompson concludes that indirect objects are indeed more topic-like than direct objects and that indirect objects in postverbal position are more topic-like than those occurring in postprepositional position. These conclusions led Thompson to make two additional suggestions: (1) postverbal position is a favored site for topic-like nonsubjects, and (2) grammatical regularities may be shaped by extragrammatical factors, such as the way speakers manage the flow of information.

SENTENCES WITH INDIRECT OBJECTS IN THE PASSIVE VOICE

We have already noted that English has more passive voice alternatives for sentences with indirect objects than some other languages do. Thus the active voice sentence "Alice gave John the book," has two passive voice paraphrases; one option selects the direct object as the subject of the passive:

The book was given to John (by Alice).[11]

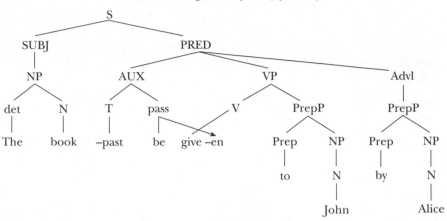

The other option selects the indirect object as the subject of the passive:

John was given the book (by Alice).

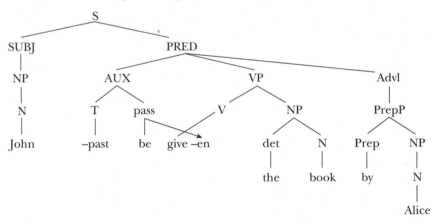

Some languages resist selecting the indirect object as the subject of a passive sentence. For example, the literal translation of "John was given the book (by Alice)" would be ungrammatical in German. (In German the direct object or accusative case can become the nominative subject of the passive; however, the dative case cannot.) Students coming from such language backgrounds will need practice in forming English passive sentences where dative, benefactive, and eliciting NPs function as subjects.

Not all sentences containing indirect objects allow two passive paraphrases as readily as the preceding one. When indirect objects are structurally optional constituents in an active sentence, they do not easily serve as the subject of a passive sentence. For example, the active sentence "Mary revealed the truth to Ken" readily accepts the direct object as subject of a passive counterpart:

The truth was revealed to Ken (by Mary).

However, many native speakers of English find that if the indirect object is the subject of the passive, the sentence becomes awkward if not ungrammatical:

?Ken was revealed the truth (by Mary).

Some readers will speculate that since *reveal* does not permit postverbal indirect objects, this may account for the questionable nature of the passive sentence above. However, there are also cases where the active voice counterpart permits alternation:

> Arlene made Sandra this dress.
> Arlene made this dress for Sandra.

And the passive counterpart with the direct object as subject is fully acceptable:

> This dress was made for Sandra (by Arlene).

However, the version with the indirect object as subject is much more questionable:

> ?Sandra was made this dress (by Arlene).[12]

Those sentences where the indirect object is an obligatory component of a ditransitive verb readily allow the indirect object to serve as the subject in the passive voice; however, in those sentences where the indirect object is optional—that is, the verb is transitive but requires only a direct object—the indirect object cannot readily serve as the subject of the passive. This is why we put such indirect objects outside the verb phrase in tree diagrams such as the third one in this chapter for "Mary revealed the truth to Ken." There are disagreements among native speakers regarding the acceptability of such sentences because the closeness of the association between the indirect object and the verb often is a matter of degree rather than a categorical obligatory or optional distinction.

CONCLUSION

As we have seen many times before, the more closely we examine a structure, the more complicated it seems to become. As usual, more research is needed; for example: is there a principle (or set of principles) to help us better determine which verbs allow indirect object alternation and which do not?

In the meantime, it would seem sensible for you to concentrate your efforts on the following three teaching challenges: (1) whether verbs take dative, benefactive, or eliciting indirect objects and (2) which verbs do—and which do not—allow both indirect object patterns and (3) the fact that only verbs taking dative *to*, benefactive *for*, and eliciting *of* as their prepositions can have postverbal indirect objects in English that retain the same meaning as the paraphrase with the preposition. It will also be helpful if you can give your students some understanding of the discourse principle of dominance so that they have some guidance when trying to decide whether to put the indirect object in postverbal position or in postprepositional position in those cases where both structures are possible.

TEACHING SUGGESTIONS

1. Form. To develop your students' sense of when indirect object alternation is appropriate or inappropriate, group them in pairs to manipulate and discuss sentences with words such as the following written on cards or strips. Then ask students to decide whether or not the *to* can be deleted and what any subsequent word order changes would be.

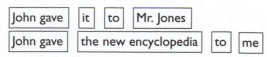

| Mary described | the movie | to | me |

| Sam told | that the meeting was postponed | to | us |

This exercise can also be done very effectively with the entire class by using an overhead projector and strips of transparency for the words or groups of words.

2. Use. Sketch pictures or clip pictures from magazines that naturally elicit indirect objects; such as the following:

Jill   Nancy

Teacher: What is Jill doing?

Student: She's giving { Nancy (some) flowers. / (some) flowers to Nancy. }

(Either word order would be an appropriate response.) With more advanced students, the teacher should continue:

Teacher: (removes card from view) Do you think Nancy is happy?
Student: Yes.
Teacher: Why?
Student: Because Jill gave her flowers! (The word order with *to* would be less appropriate.)

3. Form. To help students develop a sense of using the *to* preposition in those contexts where the indirect objects is emphasized in a response, try a drill like this:

a.   S1:   Would you lend me your car?
       S2:   I can't. I've already promised to lend it to Harvey.
b.   S1:   Would you lend me your textbook?
       S2:   I can't. I've already promised to lend it to Judy.

4. Form. Using verbs like *buy* and *make,* you can elicit addition of a benefactive *for phrase* in the following manner:

a.   T: John bought some candy.   **b.**   S2:   Sarah made a dress.
       S: Who did he buy it for?   S3:   Who did she make it for?
       T: Himself.   S2:   Me.
       S: Oh, he bought it for himself!   S3:   Oh, she made it for you!

5. Form. To practice the use of direct objects as passive subjects, students can give things—that the teacher provides—to each other with an appropriate follow-up question (Who was the _____ given to?):

    a.   *T:*   Paolo, give the candy to Maria.   **b.**   *T:*   Said, give the ruler to Roberto.
          S1:   Who was the candy given to?   *S3:*   Who was the ruler given to?
          S2:   It was given to Maria.   *S4:*   It was given to Roberto.

6. Form. To practice the use of indirect objects as passive subjects, use consumer gripes as a context. One student can role-play the consumer affairs officer and the others can state their complaints.

    a.   *S1:*   What's your $\begin{Bmatrix} \text{complaint} \\ \text{problem} \\ \text{gripe} \end{Bmatrix}$?

          S2:   I was sold a bad car by AZ Used Cars.
    b.   *S1:*   What's your _____?
          S3:   I was sold a defective TV set by Jones Appliances.
    c.   *S1:*   What's your _____?
          S4:   I was sold a fake diamond by Bijou Jewelers.

7. Meaning. To help learners practice deciding whether verbs take *to*, *for*, or *of* with indirect objects, have students paraphrase sentences like the following so that the indirect object becomes the most important (i.e., new or dominant) information. They should imagine dialogues where *A* first says the indirect objects very softly or mumbles them.

    A: I gave Mary the book.
    B: Who?
    A: I gave the book to *Mary*.

    A: I baked Harry a pie.
    B: Who?
    A: I baked a pie for *Harry*.

Other sentences that could be used for this exercise are:

    I asked Bill a question.
    I sold Jane my car.
    I read Susie a story.

EXERCISES

Test your understanding of what has been presented.

    1. Provide original example sentences to illustrate the following terms. Underline the pertinent word(s) in your examples.

        a. direct object   **g.** indirect object alternation
        b. eliciting indirect object   **h.** benefactive *for*
        c. benefactive indirect object   **i.** proxy *for*
        d. dative indirect object   **j.** verb of transfer
        e. passive with indirect object as subject   **k.** verb of future possession
        f. dominance

2. Give tree diagrams and mapping rules for the following sentences:

   a. I handed Sue the note.
   b. He was offered a job by the supervisor.
   c. The information was given to him yesterday.
   d. We bought Horace a watch.
   e. Did Martha ask George a question?

3. Why are the following sentences ungrammatical (or at best awkward)?

   a. *John hasn't sent his brother it.
   b. *Mary bought for me the book.
   c. *Roger asked a question to Phyllis.

4. List all the active and passive sentences—with and without indirect object alternation—that would be related to the following information.

   a. verb: send (past tense); agent: mother; direct object: the parcel; directional indirect object: Bob.
   b. verb: bring (past tense); agent: Bill; direct objects: some flowers; benefactive indirect object: Agnes.

Test your ability to apply what you know.

5. If your students produce the following sentences, what errors have they made? How will you make them aware of the errors, and what exercises will you prepare to correct the errors?

   a. *Explain me that rule again, please.
   b. *Are you going to give to me an answer?
   c. *Why didn't you open him the door?
   d. *We didn't know, so we asked to Harry.
   e. *Please excuse me my poor English.

6. Bruce Fraser (personal communication) has suggested that the indirect object alternation rule for verbs taking the preposition *to* is based on phonological considerations and will apply *only* if the verb is:

   a. monosyllabic; or
   b. disyllabic with stress on the initial syllable; for example:

      Tell John the answer.   *Explain John the answer.
      Offer us something else.   *Communicate Ann the answer.
      ?Whisper Ann the answer.

Can you think of any exceptions to this rule? What about verbs that take the prepositions *for* and *of*?

7. ESL/EFL students sometimes have difficulty in distinguishing pairs such as the following—especially when they are listening. Think of ways that would help students learn what to watch for to clearly distinguish such sentences.

   Mary was giving a sweater to John
   Mary was given a sweater by John.

8. One of your students asks you what kind of verb *beg* is (dative? benefactive? eliciting?) and whether or not it can take an indirect object. How will you respond?

BIBLIOGRAPHY

References

Erteschik-Shir, N. (1979). "Discourse Constraints on Dative Movement," In T. Givón (ed.), *Syntax and Semantics* (vol. 12: *Discourse and Syntax*). New York: Academic Press.

Fillmore, C. J. (1968). "The Case for Case." In E. Bach and R. Harms (eds.), *Universals in Linguistic Theory.* New York: Holt, Rinehart and Winston.

Goldsmith, J. (1980) "Meaning and Mechanism in Grammar." In S. Kuno (ed.), *Harvard Studies in Syntax and Semantics* (vol. 3).

Green, G. (1974). *Semantic and Syntactic Regularity.* Bloomington, Ind.: Indiana University Press.

Jacobson, R. (1966). "The Role of Deep Structures in Language Teaching." *Language Learning* 16:3 & 4, 151–160.

Lakoff, R. (1969). "Manual for Teachers of English as a Foreign Language." Unpublished manuscript.

Mazurkewich, I., and L. White (1984). "The Acquisition of the Dative Alternation: Unlearning Overgeneralizations." *Cognition* 16, 261–283.

Stowell, T. (1981). "Origins of Phrase Structure." Unpublished doctoral dissertation. MIT, Cambridge, Mass.

Thompson, S. (1988). "Information Flow and 'Dative Shift' in English Discourse." In *Santa Barbara Papers in Linguistics* (vol. 2 ,"Discourse and Grammar"). S. A. Thompson (ed.), Santa Barbara: University of California, 141–163.

Wierzbicka, A. (1988). *The Semantics of Grammar.* Amsterdam: John Benjamins (see pp. 353–389).

Williams, R. S. (1994). "A Statistical Analysis of Double Object Alternation." *Issues in Applied Linguistics* 5:1, 35–59.

Suggestions for further reading

For excellent discussions of the interaction of the passive voice and indirect object alternation, see:

Fillmore, C. J. (1965). *Indirect Object Constructions in English and the Ordering of Transformations.* The Hague: Mouton.

Fillmore, C. J. (1968). "The Case for Case." In E. Bach and R. Harms (eds.), *Universals in Linguistic Theory.* New York: Holt, Rinehart and Winston.

For good traditional discussion of indirect objects, see:

Frank, M. (1993). *Modern English* (2d ed.). Englewood Cliffs, N.J.: Prentice-Hall Regents.

Jespersen, O. (1964). *Essentials of English Grammar.* University, Ala.: University of Alabama Press, 111–116.

For two useful articles dealing with the use of indirect objects (R. S. Williams) *and their acquisition* (W. D. Davies) *see the* June, 1994 (vol. 5:1) *Issues in Applied Linguistics.*

For a study focusing on the L2 acquisition of dative alternation in English by speakers of Chinese and Japanese, see:

Inagaki, S. (1997). Japanese and Chinese Learners' Acquisition of the Narrow-Range Rules for Dative Alternation in English. *Language Learning* 47:4, 637–669

For good lists and patterns for verbs taking indirect objects, see:

Praninskas, J. (1975). *Rapid Review of English Grammar.* Englewood Cliffs, N.J.: Prentice-Hall, 202–203.

For some examples of exercises for teaching indirect objects, see:

Badalamenti, V., and C. Henner Stanchina (1997). *Grammar Dimensions: Form, Meaning, and Use.* Book 1 (2d ed.). Boston: Heinle & Heinle (unit 13, pp. 187–204).

Brinton, D., and R. Neuman (1982). *Getting Along: English Grammar and Writing* (bk. 2). Englewood Cliffs, N.J.: Prentice-Hall, 138.

Celce-Murcia, M., and S. Hilles (1988). *Techniques and Resources in Teaching Grammar.* New York: Oxford University Press, 10, 92–93.

Danielson, D., and Porter, P. (1990). *Using English: Your Second Language* (2d ed.). Englewood Cliffs, N.J.: Prentice-Hall Regents, 262–269.

Rutherford, W. E. (1975). *Modern English* Vol. 1 (2d ed.). New York: Harcourt Brace Jovanovich, 175–177.

ENDNOTES

1. Here we interpret *give* as the specific transfer of something from one person to another —not as the general *give*, which means "to donate." In this latter general sense, of course, an explicit indirect object, while possible, is not required. These two meanings of *give* would have separate lexical entries.

2. Jacobson, however, does not refer to them as verbs that take indirect objects; rather, he considers them verbs that take direct objects plus complements.

3. "Dative" is the term used by Fillmore (1968) for such indirect objects, while Jacobson refers to them as "directional." You may want to consider following Jacobson's terminology for pedagogical purposes.

4. Students have asked us why objects of *from* and *with* in sentences like the following are not also considered indirect objects:

    a.   I took the book from her.
    b.   I left the book with her.

In sentence (a), *from her* expresses the source, not the recipient of the book. We would not be able to say "I took her the book" and have the same meaning as in (a). In (b) the *with her* expresses the location of the book rather than receivership or possession of it. If we say "I left her the book," what we really mean is "I left the book for her," where she is indeed the intended recipient. From examination of sentences such as these, it can be concluded that only verbs taking the prepositions *to, for,* and *of* can have indirect objects in English. The students' first language may often be the source of these questions and of the related errors they make in English. For example, in German it is possible to have a postverbal— in this case postauxiliary—indirect object expressing the equivalent of "steal from": *Er hat mir das Auto gestohlen* = *He stole the car from me.* Literally, this is *He has me the car stolen,* which can be more freely translated as *He stole me the car.* In English this sentence would mean, "He stole the car for me," not "He stole the car from me."

5. Wierzbicka's term for this construction is "internal dative," but since she includes benefactive and eliciting verbs along with dative verbs, we feel that "internal dative" is a syntactic rather than a semantic notion.

6. Of course, "dominance" can also be achieved by phonological means (i.e., stress) just as it can through syntax. For example, contrary to Erteschik-Shir's syntactic principle, one could say:

    Pass *the salt* to me. (i.e., not the pepper!)   Pass *me* the salt. (i.e., not Roger!)

7. Sentences of this form are apparently much more acceptable in British than American English.

8. "Dative alternation" is called "dative shift" by Thompson.

9. Thompson refers to "recipients" rather than indirect objects and to "patients" rather than direct objects.

10. Thompson's term here is "topicworthy."

11. In some dialects of English—especially British—*The book was given John (by Alice)* is another acceptable version of this sentence. In American English, retention of the preposition *to* is preferred.

12. Again, several native speakers of British English have indicated to us that this sentence is acceptable in their dialect. For most speakers of American English, this is not the case.

Chapter 20

ADJECTIVES

INTRODUCTION

As you saw in Chapter 2, adjectives are words that describe a quality of a noun. Adjectives remain invariant in form, no matter what position they occupy in a sentence.

> The moon is *full* tonight.
> The *full* moon shone brightly.

The forms of adjectives in English are not as complicated as they are in some other languages. Although they once did, English adjectives no longer inflect for gender, person, or number.

Although this seems easy enough, ESL/EFL learners do have to learn certain things about English adjectives. Some adjectives can occur only before a noun; others only after a copular verb. Many adjectives can occupy more than one position, but depending on where they are placed, they may convey different meanings. Finally, when more than one adjective is used, as in

> A *spectacular full* moon seemed to rise from the sea.

they often must be sequenced a particular way, which may cause problems for students.

THE FORM OF ADJECTIVES

As we saw in Chapters 2 and 3, adjectives do not have any typical form; however, derivational affixes commonly associated with adjectives include *-al* (*mental, special*), *-able/-ible* (*commendable, possible*), *-ar* (*particular, popular*), *-ful/-less* (*hopeful, hopeless*), *-ic* (*scientific, basic*), *-ive* (*attractive, expensive*), *-ous* (*dangerous, delicious*), and *-y* (*pretty, dirty*) (Leech 1989).

Adjectives also have two inflectional morphemes: the *-er* of the comparative (*larger*) and the *-est* (*largest*) of the superlative. We will say no more at this point about these inflectional morphemes because we devote two full chapters to issues of comparison and degree (Chapters 34 and 35).

The syntax of adjectives is another matter. As we saw in our phrase structure rules, there are two basic positions for adjectives in a sentence:

I. Attributive position (before a noun)

> NP → (det) (AP) N (-pl) (PrepP)
> the *funny* clowns
> a *perfect* match

2. Predicative position (after *be* copula and other copular or linking verbs—*seem, appear, feel, look,* etc.)

> VP → cop AP
> The clowns are *funny.*
> The weather turned *cold.*

Sometimes the copular verb is deleted, here in its infinitive form, so that the adjective follows a noun directly; the same string can be directly generated as an object noun predicate:

> They considered Stuart [to be] *mad.*

A predicative adjective in postnominal position can also result from a reduced relative clause (discussed below):

> The news [that is] *available* at this time is not good.

In the following sections, we go into further detail with regard to the two basic positions of adjectives in English clauses.

ATTRIBUTIVE ADJECTIVES

Prenominal, or attributive, position is the most characteristic position for English adjectives. Although many adjectives can appear in both positions, certain ones, called reference adjectives, must occur prenominally. The following list details the eight categories of adjectives that occur exclusively in attributive position (based on Bolinger 1967).

Reference Adjectives

1. Those adjectives that show the reference of the head noun has already been determined:

the { very / particular / same / self-same / exact } man I was seeking

2. Those adjectives that show us the importance or rank of the head noun:

their { main / prime / principal / chief } faults

3. Those adjectives that show the head noun is recognized by law or custom:

the { lawful / rightful / legal / true } heir

4. Those adjectives that identify the reference of the noun itself—that is, they tell us (in part) what the noun means—and that may not occur after the copula *be*:

a medical doctor	*a doctor is medical
an atomic physicist	*a physicist is atomic
a reserve officer	*an officer is reserve

5. Those adjectives that qualify the time reference of the noun:

> the future king the former chairperson
> the present monarch the previous occupant

6. Those adjectives that qualify the geographical reference of the noun:

> a Southern gentleman the urban crisis
> a rural mail carrier

Two other subcategories that are mentioned but not specifically defined by Bolinger are:

7. Those adjectives that intensify or emphasize the head noun:

> a total stranger a mere child
> sheer fraud utter nonsense

8. Those adjectives that show the uniqueness of the head noun:

> the sole survivor
> the only nominee
> a single individual

There are probably some additional minor subcategories as well.

Of course, saying that the adjectives are prenominal simply means that they occur before a noun. Thus, wherever nouns can occur, so can adjectives. They can modify both subjects and objects.

> subject: *Thoughtful* guests
> indirect object: give their *deserving* hosts
> direct object: *personal* gifts
> object of the preposition: of *special* value.

PREDICATIVE ADJECTIVES

Once again, most adjectives can appear in several different positions in a sentence.[1] Like exclusively attributive adjectives, however, certain adjectives can only be predicative. There are three such categories:

1. Adjectives that begin with an *a-* prefix:[2]

> The boy is *asleep*. *the asleep boy
> The boat is *adrift*. *the adrift boat

2. Health adjectives (Chalker 1984):

> Larry feels *faint*.
> He is not *well*.

3. Adjectives that must be followed by prepositional phrases or infinitives (i.e., ones that are more complex syntactically):

> He's *bound* for China.
> Debbie seems *inclined* to agree.

As we have already seen, predicative adjectives can also occur directly after a noun when the copular verb has been deleted. There are two kinds. The first kind of postnominal adjective consists of adjectives modifying object nouns:

> They considered Stuart mad.

This pattern occurs only with certain verbs. One group are verbs showing mental assessments or personal preferences, such as *consider, like, think, prefer, declare, report, believe, imagine, hold, want, call,* and so on.

> Sandy thought it odd.
> They declared him sane.
> They held him accountable.

As we observed earlier, the adjective occurs directly following the NP because an object noun predicate has been generated or because the copula in its infinitive form has been deleted. The pattern with the infinitive is discussed further in Chapter 31 on complementation.

Another group of verbs that permit the adjective to follow the object directly are certain causative verbs such as *make, turn, get, keep:*

> Hay fever makes me crazy.
> The frost turned the leaves brown.
> His diet kept him healthy.

No deleted infinitive copula is posited for such sentences. Notice, however, that these sentences can be paraphrased by inserting the verb *cause* and a copula infinitive:

> Hay fever causes me to be crazy.
> The frost causes the leaves to turn brown.
> His diet causes him to keep healthy.

See Chapter 32 for more on the special characteristics of causative verbs.

The second kind of postnominal adjective can be said to be derived from relative clauses (see Chapter 29). Suffice it to say here that they follow the noun directly, having lost the relative pronoun and the *be* verb of the relative clause:

> The news available at this time is not good.
>   ↑
>   [that is]

Here are two more examples:

> People strong in character should run for political office.
>   ↑
>   [who are]

> Join the committee concerned with local development issues.
>   ↑
>   [that is]

It should be apparent why relative clauses are sometimes called adjective clauses. Adjectives and relative clauses serve similar functions in providing qualifying information about nouns.

As with the other positions, a few categories of adjectives always occur in postnominal position (Chalker 1984).

1. Adjectives in phrases of measurement:

> He is six feet *tall.*
> The ruler is twelve inches *long.*

Note that entire adjectival measure phrases can appear before a noun, but when they do, the noun is in its singular form, regardless of the cardinal number expressed:

> They have a one-year-old child.
> He is a six-foot-tall man.
> It is a twelve-inch-long ruler.

Actually this is true of more than measure phrases. Nouns serving to modify other nouns are unmarked for number in prenominal position. This is a minor point, but a source of errors for ESL/EFL students.

> I need an egg carton.   This shoe box will do.
> *I need an eggs carton.   *This shoes box will do.[3]

2. Adjectives in certain fixed expressions (mostly borrowed from French):

> attorney *general*   heir *apparent*
> president-*elect*   notary *public*

3. Adjectives following indefinite pronouns, where the adjective derives from a reduced relative clause:

> Let's do something [that is] *more interesting.*
> I can't think of anything [that is]*exciting* to do.

PARTICIPLES

You may have noticed that the adjectives in our last two examples end in *-ing.* We have encountered this form previously only as progressive aspect, where we knew it as a present participle. It is indeed a present participle here as well, although here it serves an adjectival, as opposed to a verbal, function. As such, it can be found in the positions that other adjectives can fill:

> Attributive: *He has led an interesting life.*
> Predicative: *His life has been interesting.*
> Predicative: *Marshall has made life interesting.*
> (post-nominal)

Before we distinguish present participles functioning as adjectives from present participles functioning as verbs, remember in the chapter on passives we saw that the past participle (*-en*) can also function both adjectivally and verbally. You may have noticed this in the use of past participial adjectives in some of the examples above, such as *concerned* and *inclined.* Past participles functioning as adjectives can occupy the same positions as many other adjectives:

> Attributive: *The well-worn book was a favorite of all the children.*
> Predicative: *The book was well worn.*
> Predicative: *The book, well worn from much use, was a favorite.*
> (post-nominal)

In addition, both present and past participles can be modified by nouns or adverbs to create compound participial adjectives:

> noun + present participle—*a man-eating tiger*
> noun + past participle—*a flea-bitten dog*
> adverb + present participle—*a fast-rising star*
> adverb (intensifier) + past participle—*a much-loved story*

Distinguishing Adjectival Participles from Verbal Participles

-ing adjective: The magician is *amazing*.
-ing verb: The magician is *amazing* us with his magic tricks.

-en adjective: The security guard was *relieved*. (i.e., he stopped worrying)
-en verb: The security guard was *relieved* by the night watchman. (i.e., replaced)

One way to differentiate adjectival participles from verbal participles is to add the intensifier *very* before the italicized forms in the above sentences. Since we know that intensifiers can precede adjectives but not verbs, sentences having verbs with intensifiers before them are ungrammatical.

> The magician is very amazing.
> *The magician is very amazing us with his magic tricks.
> The security guard was very relieved.
> *The security guard was very relieved by the night watchman.

This test is more successful in distinguishing identical *-ing* forms than it is identical *-en* forms, however, as there appears to be increasing acceptance of the use of intensifiers with a *by* phrase that would normally mark a passive use of the past participle.

> Her behavior shocked all of us.
> We were all (very) shocked by her behavior.

In other cases, where there is only one form, the intensifier test works to identify past participles serving as passive verbs:

> I was paid for my efforts.

> *I was very paid for my efforts. ⎫ (past participle is verbal: it fails the intensifier test,
> I was well paid for my efforts. ⎬ but can be modified by the adverb *well*, which in
>   ⎭ turn can be modified by *very*.)

> I was very discontented with my pay. (past participle is adjectival)

Some adjectives look as if they were past participles, but they actually aren't:

> the one-legged man   the crooked lane
> the naked truth   the wicked witch
> the green-eyed monster   the bearded iris

As we saw in Chapter 18, the pronunciation of certain of these adjectives (*legged, crooked, naked, wicked*) is distinctive. Where phonological rules wouldn't predict it, the *-ed* is pronounced syllabically as /ɪd/. Sometimes the only thing that determines whether an attributive adjective is a past participle or not is its pronunciation:

> a learned behavior   a learned scholar
> (/lərnd/ is a past participle)   (/lərnɪd/ is not a past participle)

The intensifier test will also work to distinguish postnominal participles that are adjectives from postnominal participles that are verbal. Here are some participles that result from reduced relative clauses but fail the intensifier test and, therefore, are not adjectival participles:[4]

> Who is that person waving at us?
> *Who is that person very waving at us?
> The man, robbed of his passport, went immediately to the embassy.
> *The man, very robbed of his passport, went immediately to the embassy.

An additional test to determine whether the *-en* form is adjectival or verbal is to look at the preposition following it. *-En* forms functioning as adjectives take a variety of prepositions (e.g., *amazed at, interested in,* etc.), whereas *-en* forms functioning as passive verbs normally take only the *by* phrase; although, as you saw above, having a *by* phrase is no guarantee that the past participle is a verb.

> adjective: *We were amazed at his success.*
> adjective/verb?: *We were (very) amazed by his performance.* (no explicit agent in *by* phrase)
> verb: *He was greeted by his many fans after the show.* (explicit agents in *by* phrase)

The identity of form can sometimes create ambiguous sentences.

> *Martha Stewart is entertaining.*
> adjective: *She is an entertaining person.*
> verb: *She is entertaining guests.*

> *We were relieved.*
> adjective: *We felt a sense of relief.*
> verb: *We were relieved by other workers. (i.e., they came to take our places.)*

Of course, when these sentences occur in context, it's highly unlikely that they will be perceived as ambiguous.

Other Structural Facts

As you can see in our phrase structure rule

$$AP \rightarrow (intens)^n \; ADJ^n \; (PrepP)$$

an adjective can be optionally preceded by one or more intensifiers:

> Lennox china is *very* expensive.
> Wedgewood china is *really very* expensive.

And a predicative or postnominal adjective can be followed by a prepositional

phrase:

> I was really surprised *at her appearance*.
> She got me interested *in quilting*.

For certain adjectives, the prepositional phrase is obligatory:

> *He was averse.
> He was averse to my suggestion.

Some adjectives always co-occur with the same preposition (e.g., *conscious of*); others take a variety of prepositions, often with a shift of meaning, such as *good with, good to, good for, good at.*

We also know from our phrase structure rules, that some noun phrases can also take prepositional phrases:

> a man of honor

These seem very similar semantically to attributive adjectives:

> an honorable man

The function of prepositional phrases following nouns is adjectival, unlike that of prepositional phrases in the verb phrase, which is adverbial.

THE MEANING OF ADJECTIVES

ATTRIBUTIVE VERSUS PREDICATIVE POSITION

Now that we have shifted our attention to semantic considerations, it is time to investigate the meaning of adjectives. As we said earlier, many adjectives can appear in both attributive and predicative position; however, with a few adjectives, there is a change in meaning.

> That responsible person. (trustworthy)
> That person is responsible. (trustworthy, or to blame)

Bolinger (1967) noted that there is often something semantically more permanent or characteristic about the attributive adjectives that directly precede nouns than the postnominal adjectives that directly follow nouns, which tend to reflect temporary states or specific events; for example:

> The stolen jewels (a characteristic of the jewels)
> The jewels stolen (identified by a specific act—maybe they were recovered later)
>
> The only navigable river (usual fact about a given region)
> The only river navigable (temporary state due to a drought or some other event)
>
> The guilty people (a characteristic, classifying modifier of the people)
> The people guilty (the people are described in terms of one act or event)

Predicative adjectives are potentially ambiguous, since if we say:

> These jewels are stolen.
> The river is navigable.
> These people are guilty.

we cannot tell whether the adjective is being used to describe something that is permanent and characteristic of the subject noun or something that is temporary or occasional. Changing the adjective to either attributive position or immediate postnominal position can disambiguate in such cases. As Bolinger points out, attributive position tends to reject the temporary and the occasional; for example:

> The house was pink in the sunset ≠ The pink house

This is further borne out by the fact that health adjectives are usually used predicatively, as you have seen.

> He is sick.

If we change the adjective to attributive position, the quality is construed as much more enduring:

> He is a sick man.

Attributive position also favors negatives that characterize:

> the departed relative   *the arrived relative
> your absent friend   *your present friend

Compound attributive adjectives formed with present participles tend to reflect habitual or customary action as opposed to isolated events;[5]

> Your friend writes plays. → Your play-writing friend
> The man broke a leg. → *The leg-breaking man

Carnivores are animals that eat meat. → Carnivores are meat-eating animals.
My brother bought a house. → *My house-buying brother

Other languages use adjective position to mark meaningful differences, of course. In Spanish, for instance, prenominal or postnominal adjectives can differ in meaning.

El viejo amigo describes a friend you have had for a long time.
El amigo viejo describes a friend who is elderly.

Compare this with the three-way ambiguity of the English phrase *"an old friend,"* which obliges English speakers to paraphrase it with a relative clause to make its meaning clear.

an old friend {
a friend who is old
a friend whom I have had for a long time
a former friend (i.e., a person who is no longer my friend)

PARTICIPLES (PRESENT VERSUS PAST)

A problem for many nonnative speakers of English is the adjectival use of *-ing* and *-en* participles derived from "emotive" verbs. The term "emotive" is used to refer to verbs such as the following:

aggravate	bore	convince	frighten	mislead	shock
alarm	calm	defeat	insult	mystify	stagger
amaze	captivate	disappoint	interest	overwhelm	surprise
amuse	charm	disturb	intrigue	please	terrify
annoy	comfort	embarrass	intrigue	puzzle	tire
astonish	concern[6]	encourage	love	satisfy	worry
bewilder	confuse	excite			

A tendency that many nonnative speakers have is to overgeneralize the *-ing* participle and produce sentences such as the following:

*I am interesting in sports. (i.e., *interesting* for *interested*)

Students have to learn that when they want to use an adjective to refer to the experiencer—the one experiencing the emotion—then the *-en* participle should be used. If they want to use an adjective to refer to the cause of the experience, the *-ing* participle should be used. There is a semantically related sentence that contains the emotive verb without a participial form.[7]

Emotive Verb	-en participle refers to the experiencer (the object of the active sentence with the emotive verb)	-ing participle refers to the cause (the subject of the active sentence with the emotive verb)
Sports Interest Francis.	Francis is interested in sports.	Sports are interesting to Francis.
Ethnic jokes don't amuse Kowalski.	Kowalski is not amused by ethnic jokes.	Ethnic jokes aren't amusing (to Kowalski).
Ted's loud stereo annoys his neighbors.	Ted's neighbors are annoyed by his loud stereo.	Ted's loud stereo is annoying (to his neighbors).

STATIVE/DYNAMIC

Givón (1993) places the major parts of speech on a continuum, saying that nouns tend to encode the most static lexical meanings, verbs the least static, with adjectives (and related adverbs) somewhere in between.[8]

Nouns ——————— Adjectives/Adverbs ——————— Verbs
most static meanings   least static meanings

Most English adjectives are like nouns in that they describe fairly permanent inherent qualities. This is especially so, as you saw, when they are in attributive position. This observation helps explain also why it is odd to use progressive aspect or imperatives with adjectives.

> The Earth is round.
> *The Earth is being round.
> *Be short.

Some adjectives, however, can be used predicatively to refer to a temporary state, a change in progress, or something immediate:

> She is just being stubborn.
> He is looking stronger. (with the comparative form of the adjective)
> Be careful.

It is also possible to give a more dynamic sense to certain adjectives by using the copular verb *get* + adjective to indicate a change of state, as opposed to *be* + adjective, which indicates a condition or a state.

> He was dry. → [It rained.] He *got wet.* → He is wet.

RESTRICTIVE/NONRESTRICTIVE

Semantically, adjectives can be either restrictive or nonrestrictive. The former are necessary for defining which noun is being referred to:

> I live in a *brick* house.
> The house *decorated* by the Johnsons is quite unusual.

Nonrestrictive adjectives merely add additional information without being essential for identification:

> I live in the corner house, which is *brick.*
> The house, *decorated* for the holidays, is quite unusual.

This is even true of some prenominal adjectives, such as

> our distinguished speaker
> our clever receptionist

where there is only one speaker or receptionist.

We go into this distinction in greater detail in Chapter 29, where we discuss restrictive and nonrestrictive relative clauses.

POLARITY

Earlier, in Chapter 10, we spoke of adjectives of negative and positive polarity. Polarity merely refers to positive and negative contrasts in a language. Thus, adjectives can be paired by contrasting poles:

Positive Polarity (unmarked)	*Negative Polarity (marked)*
big	small; little
old	young
old	new
long	short
good	bad
hard	soft
fast	slow
tall	short
wide	narrow
high	low
loud	quiet
rough	smooth

The adjectives with positive polarity are unmarked because they are used more frequently in a given language, learned earlier by children, and used in neutral contexts, such as

How old are you?

The adjectives of negative polarity, on the other hand, are marked, meaning that they are less frequently used, being reserved for unusual contexts.

You say that your daughter is too young to pay full fare. Just how young is she?

Notice the asymmetry is also displayed in answers to questions with adjectives of different polarity.

How old are you? $\left\{ \begin{array}{l} \text{Very old.} \\ \text{Very young.} \end{array} \right.$
(unmarked)

How young are you? $\left\{ \begin{array}{l} \text{*Very old.} \\ \text{Very young.} \end{array} \right.$
(marked)

We say more about the polarity of adjectives in the discussion of comparisons.

GRADABILITY

Earlier in this chapter, we suggested that the intensifier test could be used to test to see if a participle was acting as a verb or adjective. In fact, many adjectives can be placed on a continuum of intensity, with the intensity increasing or decreasing depending on the intensifier chosen.

[less intense]   [more intense]
somewhat rare, rare, quite rare, very rare, extremely rare

While this works well for many adjectives, not all adjectives can be so modified. Some adjectives, in fact, are not gradable, such as the following:

I. Reference adjectives:

> *The very former senator from the state of Washington
> *The very symphonic concert

2. Adjectives with an absolute meaning:

> *A very alternative way of looking at the matter

3. Adjectives of nationality

> *She is very Scottish. (We can say, of course, "She is very Scottish," if we are referring to some aspect of her behavior, such as her pronunciation. [Chalker 1984])

ISSUES OF USE

ORDER OF ATTRIBUTIVE ADJECTIVES

Our phrase structure rule for defining adjective phrases allows for more than one adjective in a sequence:

> AP → (intens)^n ADJ^n (PrepP)

The order of two or more attributive adjectives is a point of English grammar that is a minor source of error for nonnative speakers of English. This is partly so because not all languages follow a prenominal order the way English does. For instance, some languages, like French, have a mixed order: some attributive adjectives referring to age, size, and evaluation precede the noun, while other attributive adjectives referring to color or origin follow. For example:

> une grande voiture jaune   une vieille femme Italienne
>   (big)   (car) (yellow)   (old) (woman) (Italian)
> "a big yellow car"   "an old Italian woman"

In certain cases, two adjectives may precede a noun in French and one may follow:

> une   jolie   petite   voiture   jaune
> (pretty) (little)   (car) (yellow)
> "a pretty little yellow car"

French also seems to permit no more than two adjectives following a noun:

> une voiture Japonaise   jaune
>   (car) (Japanese) (yellow)
> "a yellow Japanese car"

Even this seems stylistically awkward to many French speakers, who would prefer to avoid such a construction altogether.

In Arabic, according to Svatko (1979), *all* attributive adjectives come after the noun, and up to three adjectives are possible in this position; however, Svatko adds that the Arabic ordering system is less rigid than the English one; as a result of all these differences, Arabic speakers beginning their study of English make adjective ordering errors in their English speech and writing; for example,

> *an American interesting movie   *a wooden big bowl

In her study Svatko found that more advanced Arabic speakers of English made fewer errors of this type and were able to more closely approximate the English system.

Adjective order has been discussed by traditional and structural linguists for some time. Sledd (1959), for example, in his structurally based introduction to English grammar, gives the following order (which we have adapted somewhat) for elements in a noun phrase:

1. predeterminer
2. core determiner
3. post determiner
4. intensifier
5. descriptive adjective
6. noun adjunct or modifier
7. head noun (the noun being modified)

Some example sentences making use of this order are:

1	2	3	4	5	6	7
All (of)	the	dozen	very	long-stemmed	American-beauty	roses
Both (of)	John's	last	quite	rare	history	books

Kathleen Bailey (1975), in an empirical investigation of attributive adjective ordering in English, points out that Sledd's fifth category (descriptive adjectives) has several subcategories, some of which are:

a. coloration
b. measurement (*tiny, short*)
c. shape (*irregular, round*)
d. subjective evaluation (*nice, sweet*)

Bailey's data, which included (1) analysis of both transcribed speech and written texts, (2) a card-sorting task, and (3) speech samples that were elicited with visual prompts, show that most of these subcategories have a relatively fixed ordering with respect to one another that is seldom violated. This ordering of elements in the noun phrase is as follows:

1. determiner
2. subjective or evaluative adjective
3. measurement adjective
4. coloration adjective
5. material adjective
6. head noun

Examples:

1	2	3	4	5	6
The	poor	little	pink	plastic	doll
An	ugly	old	gray	wooden	statue

Svatko's (1979) study of adjective ordering in English starts with the description given in Praninskas (1975:262), which Svatko selects as the best one available. It is more detailed than Bailey's in that seven rather than four distinct semantic categories of descriptive adjectives are listed. (Note, however, that material adjectives are not distinguished from geographical origin—Indonesian, Egyptian, etc.—adjectives in this system.)[9]

det	opinion	size	shape	condition	age	color	origin	noun
an	ugly	big	round	chipped	old	blue	French	vase

Both Praninskas and Svatko point out that sequences of more than three adjectives seldom occur in speech or writing and that two-adjective sequences are the most typical ones. When more than one occurs, however, they should follow this order.

Svatko's study tested Praninskas' ordering rule by using a series of questionnaires with items such as the following, which presented two, three, or four adjectives that respondents were then asked to order with respect to each other in a given context:

This is a/an _____, _____, _____ car.
large
American
red

This is a/an _____, _____ test.
short
easy

Based on the responses of 30 native speakers of English, correlations were calculated to determine the strength of the relationship between the predicted position (i.e., Praninskas' order) and the observed position (i.e., the order emerging from the responses of the native speakers) for each semantic category of prenominal adjectives. The results were as follows:

opinion	size	shape	condition	age	color	origin	noun
.80	.96	.66	.79	.85	.77	1.0	

For adjectives referring to origin, speaker performance matched order prediction 100 percent of the time; that is, there was a perfect correlation. Adjectives of size exhibited a strong correlation, while adjectives of age, opinion, condition, and color also exhibited fairly strong correlations. Adjectives of shape exhibited the weakest correlation between the predicted and the observed order. These results indicate that while the established order is valid, it is not equally fixed for all types of adjectives.

Another point we should mention about adjective order is that attributive adjectives are sometimes conjoined with *and* when there are two adjectives from the same category that both partially modify the same noun (i.e., using either of the two adjectives alone would be semantically misleading):

an orange and white marble
a wooden and metal implement

Also, two or more attributive adjectives are sometimes separated by commas in writing if there is repetition (intensification) or if the two adjectives are from the same class and are not incompatible (i.e., it would not be semantically misleading to use only one of them); for example:

a big, big ice cream cone
a charming, attractive host

CASES WITH VARIABLE ORDER

Certain adjectives Bailey (1979) described have a variable order:

1. Proper adjectives[10] and the way they order with material adjectives such as *wooden, brick,* and *glassy*; for example:

These { wooden Japanese / Japanese wooden } chests   A large { porcelain Chinese / Chinese porcelain } vase

2. Proper adjectives and adjectives of color, such as

A { German white / white German } wine

3. Adjectives denoting shape—such words as *round, oblong, wide,* and *flat*— may, in combinations with other adjectives, be rearranged according to the demands of the context:

a { large / yellow } oblong box / an oblong { large / yellow } box

a round { blue / small } table / a { blue / small } round table

Further study is needed to determine the semantic constraints and discourse contexts that will explain the variable order for these types of adjectives.

THE PRIMARY STRESS RULE

Another interesting finding of Bailey's study is that subjects produced strings such as the following in two different contexts with different stress patterns:

> Context 1: Three large triangles—one blue, one red, and one yellow—produced *"the large YELLOW triangle."*
> Context 2: Three yellow triangles—two small and one large—produced *"the LARGE yellow triangle."*

That is to say, the ordering of measurement and color adjectives is more or less fixed, but English speakers assign primary stress to one adjective or the other depending on context; that is, the adjective that most clearly limits and defines the noun with respect to the other nouns in the same context gets primary stress.

CONCLUSION

Although English adjectives aren't complicated, compared with those in other languages, some teachable points can help ESL/EFL students master them more efficiently. Primary among these are matters of meaning and use, particularly the meaning of adjectives associated with particular positions, the meaning differences between present and past participles, and the sequencing of descriptive adjectives of different types when using more than one in attributive position.

TEACHING SUGGESTIONS

1. Form. Tim Butterworth and Darlene Schultz suggest that a teacher who wants to have students practice adjectives should put on a desk a number of different objects. Then the teacher tells students to concentrate on the objects. After a few minutes, the teacher covers the objects with a cloth. Students are then asked to remember as many of the objects as they can and describe them; for example:

> a gold(en) cufflink
> a little blue stuffed animal

2. Form. Firstin and Killian (1994) recommend a role play in which one person plays the role of a traveler at an airport or train station who has lost his or her luggage, while another student plays the role of an agent in the "Lost-and-Found" office. The agent has to ask very specific questions about the lost luggage and its contents, and the traveler has to be able to answer the question in great detail.

3. Form. To work with the need to hyphenate prenominal measure phrases, tell students to treat the hyphens as if they were parentheses in math, where the inner (i.e. hyphenated) material is interpreted first, before the larger phrase.

> four year old children
> four [year-old] children
> [four-year-old] children

Have them hyphenate other measure phrases depending on the meaning, such as

> five hundred pound wrestlers (Hyphenate this to describe sumo wrestlers.)
> two foot long hot dogs (Hyphenate this to show what is so famous about hot dogs from Coney Island.)

4. Meaning. In order to give high-intermediate or advanced ESL/EFL students a feeling for attributive versus postnominal position of those adjectives that can occur in both positions, exercises such as the following should be provided. The students should be asked to put the adjective specified in attributive position if a characteristic or permanent meaning is conveyed, and in postnominal position if a temporary or specific interpretation is called for.

    a. *available.* We didn't purchase any new equipment last month because there was so little (1)_____ money (2)_____.

    b. *elected.* At the beginning of each board meeting, the chairperson introduces the (1)_____ officers (2)_____.

    c. *assigned.* Jack has decided to take History 100 instead of History 121 next semester because the professor teaching History 100 says there will be no (1)_____ term projects (2)_____.

5. Meaning. To help students understand the meaning of present participle versus past participle adjectives, Steve Thewlis (1997) says to give students a short list of some common emotions or feelings, such as boredom, confusion, depression, excitement, and embarrassment. They then form groups and make two lists—(1) situations that may cause them to feel this way and (2) their reactions when they do. For example, *boredom*:

Boring Situations	*Bored Reactions*
long meetings	doodle

movies I have seen already   fall asleep
some lectures   think about other things

The groups then compare their responses and discuss similarities and differences.

6. Form/Meaning. For more advanced students, give them the following passage from Mark Twain's *Life on the Mississippi.*

> After all of these years I can still picture that old time to myself now, just as it was then: the town drowsing in the sunshine on a summer's morning; the streets empty, or pretty nearly so; one or two clerks sitting in front of the Water Street stores with their splint-bottomed chairs tilted back against the walls, chins on breasts, hats slouched over their faces, asleep . . . ; two or three wood flats at the end of the wharf, but nobody to listen to the peaceful lapping of the wavelets against them; the great Mississippi, rolling its mile-wide tide along, point above the town and the point below, bounding the river-glimpse and burning it into a sort of sea, and withal a very still and brilliant and lonely one.

Ask students to identify the adjectives and discuss their position.

7. Meaning. The teacher might try a variation of "Mad-Libs." To do this the teacher writes a passage, leaving blanks where adjectives belong. Without showing the passage to the class, the teacher elicits an adjective of color, an adjective of shape, a proper adjective, an adjective with *-ing,* an adjective with *-en,* an adjective that can be preceded by *very,* and so on. Then the students fill in the blanks using the adjectives that have been elicited. Usually, a humorous story results. Following this class exercise, the students prepare their own similar passages (individually or in groups) and have other students supply them with adjectives to fill in the blanks.

8. Use. Penny Ur (1988) suggests giving each student a copy of several grids. Across the horizontal axis are two adjectives of different types in the correct order plus a noun. In each column of the grid are adjectives of the same type. Students have to choose an adjective from each of the first two columns and a noun from the third column. They check one box in each column. Then, they try to find their "twin"—someone else in the class who has made the same choices. For example:

Grid 1
I have a . . .

big	black	dog
small	brown	mouse
fat	white	cat

Student A: Do you have a big white cat?

Student B: No, I don't.

Grid 2
I have some . . .

expensive	French	paintings
cheap	Spanish	vases
rare	Italian	glasses

Student A: Do you have some expensive

Italian vases?

Student B: Yes, I do. You're my twin!

9. Use. Have each student in the class write a sentence that describes another student, using two or more adjectives. The other students have to guess who is being described; for example:

He is an athletic, eighteen-year-old Mexican student.

EXERCISES

Test your understanding of what has been presented.

1. Provide an original sentence illustrating each of the following terms. Underline the pertinent word(s) or word parts in your example.
   - **a.** attributive adjective
   - **b.** predicate adjective
   - **c.** postnominal adjective
   - **d.** reference adjective
   - **e.** present participle adjective
   - **f.** past participle adjective
   - **g.** restrictive adjective
   - **h.** gradable adjective

2. Why are the following sentences ungrammatical?
   - **a.** *The asleep children can have lunch later.
   - **b.** *This problem is main.
   - **c.** *An overly fond of chocolate person is called a "chocoholic."
   - **d.** *Jessica is my thirteen-years-old friend.

3. How is the following sentence ambiguous?

   Hazel is trying.

4. Explain the difference:

   Tom Sawyer painted the fence white.
   Tom Sawyer painted the white fence.

Test your ability to apply what you know.

5. If your students make any of the following errors, how would you help them become aware of the errors, and what exercise could you develop to help students correct them?
   - **a.** *She received a big nice bunch of roses for Valentine's Day.
   - **b.** *Snowball is my white hairs cat.
   - **c.** *I am boring in algebra class.

6. Why is the following amusing?

   A: How good are the Boston Red Sox this year?
   B: (disgusted fan) You mean how bad are they.

7. A student asks you to explain why she heard a native speaker say,

   She avoided things unfamiliar. . . .

instead of

   She avoided unfamiliar things.

How would you answer?

8. Examine the following. How is *quite* different from other intensifiers?

Erik was quite generous.   Erik was quite a generous man.
Erik was very generous.   Erik was a very generous man.
Erik was extremely generous.   Erik was an extremely generous man.

9. A student asks you to explain the difference between *used to* and *be used to*. What test could you use?

I used to eat spicy Indian food.
I am used to spicy Indian food.

BIBLIOGRAPHY

References

Bailey, K. M. (1975). "The Ordering of Attributive Adjectives in English: A Preliminary Study." Unpublished English 215 paper, UCLA.

Bolinger, D. (1967). "Adjectives in English: Attribution and Predication," *Lingua* 18, 1–34.

Chalker, S. (1984). *Current English Grammar.* London: Macmillan.

Firsten, R., and P. Killian (1994). *Troublesome English.* Englewood Cliffs, N.J.: Prentice Hall Regents.

Givón, T. (1993). *English Grammar.* Amsterdam/Philadelphia: John Benjamins.

Leech, G. (1989). *An A–Z of English Grammar & Usage.* London: Edward Arnold.

Praninskas, J. (1975). *Rapid Review of English Grammar* (2d ed.). Englewood Cliffs, N.J.: Prentice-Hall.

Sledd, J. (1959). *A Short Introduction to English Grammar.* Chicago: Scott, Foresman.

Svatko, K. (1979). "Descriptive Adjective Ordering in English and Arabic." Unpublished M.A. thesis in TESL, UCLA.

Thewlis, S. (1997). *Grammar Dimensions.* Book 3 (2d ed.). Boston, Mass.: Heinle & Heinle.

Ur, P. (1988). *Grammar Practice Activities.* Cambridge: Cambridge University Press.

Suggestions for Further Reading

For discussions of the attributive and predicative functions of adjectives in English, see:
Bolinger, D. (1967). "Adjectives in English: Attribution and Predication," *Lingua* 18, 1–34.
Bolinger, D. (1972). *Degree Words.* The Hague: Mouton.

For a discussion about the complexity of adjective order in English, see:
Gruber, J. (1967). *Functions of the Lexicon in Formal Descriptive Grammars.* Santa Monica, Calif.: System Development Corporation.

For explanations and exercises on the ordering of attributive adjectives, see:
Danielson, D., and P. Porter (1990). *Using English: Your Second Language* (2d ed.). Englewood Cliffs, N.J.: Prentice Hall Regents.
Thewlis, S. (1997). *Grammar Dimensions.* Book 3 (2d ed.). Boston, Mass.: Heinle & Heinle.
Winer, L. (1995). "Adjective Order with Buttons." In M. Pennington (ed.), *New Ways in Teaching Grammar,* Alexandria, Va.: TESOL.
For exercises that work on the differences between present participle and past participle adjectives, consult:
Riggenbach, H., and V. Samuda. (1997). *Grammar Dimensions.* Book 2 (2d ed.). Boston, Mass.: Heinle & Heinle.

ENDNOTES

1. What we mean is that it is syntactically possible. Presumably, for any given sentence the information status of the adjective would influence where it is placed. For instance, when the quality of a noun is new information, the adjective modifying it is likely to be included in the predicate.

2. There are even a few adjectives that don't have the same etymology, but by analogy, are treated in the same way:

> The children were afraid of the thunderstorm.
> *The afraid children

3. There are, however, a few exceptions. We do say, for example, *the parts department.*

4. We should acknowledge that not all postnominal adjectives can be said to derive from reduced relative clauses.

> The Johnsons have bought a house resembling a barn.
> *The Johnsons have bought a house that is resembling a barn.
> The man in line in front of me purchased several items totaling $205.
> *The man in line in front of me purchased several items that were totaling $205.

See Chapter 29 for further discussion.

5. We agree with Bolinger (1967) that customary action is one source of compound adjectives, but would also cite isolated events as another source, provided they have some historical significance or newsworthiness and are not mundane isolated events such as those in the starred sentences cited below:

> He batted in the run that won the game. → The game-winning run
> Her time in the race broke a record. → Her record-breaking time

6. *Concern* and *involve* appear as adjectives only in their past participle form.

7. It may also be useful to point out to students that both the *-ing* and *-en* forms can function as manner adverbs if an *-ly* suffix is added:

> Ted's stereo is annoyingly loud most of the time.
> Corey stared excitedly at the hand he had just been dealt.

8. Givón's continuum provides a functional explanation for the notion of parts of speech, and also helps to explain cross-linguistic differences in parts of speech, such as, why the English adjective *tall* has a noun equivalent in many West African languages, why Japanese inflects some adjectives the same as verbs, and why many adjectives in English can also function as nouns (*Blue is my favorite color*). In other words, adjacent categories may overlap in certain ways.

9. Note also that size can be an opinon or evaluative category as well. When this is the case, size can appear earlier in the sentence separated by other opinion adjectives with a comma:

> Atlanta is a big, welcoming city. (The positive quality is reflected in *big*.)
> A big, ugly beetle had somehow gone undetected. (Here the size is interpreted as negative.)

10. Proper adjectives—"adjectives of origin" in the Praninskas system—refer to nationalities, religions, geographical regions, and directions (sometimes even cities—*Venetian*), months, seasons of the year, etc. They are often written with a capital letter.

21

PREPOSITIONS

INTRODUCTION

Prepositions are notoriously difficult to learn. Long after ESL/EFL students have achieved a high level of proficiency in English, they still struggle with prepositions. Why do such little words as *in, on,* and *at,* cause so many problems?

One answer to this question lies in the fact that the work of prepositions is often performed in other languages, such as German, Russian, and Latin, through inflections. We alluded to this point in Chapter 2 when we pointed out that English, having lost many of its inflectional affixes over the years, has assigned to prepositions the function of showing role relationships. For example, we noted in Chapter 16 that the preposition *of* can mark possession; in Chapter 18, we showed that it was the responsibility of the preposition *by* to mark a particular noun as the agent in a passive sentence; and in Chapter 19 we examined three prepositions—*to, for,* and *of*—that mark indirect objects. ESL/EFL students, therefore, have to learn new forms for familiar functions.

Second, in their spatial meaning, prepositions do not always match up well from one language to another.

> English *to* = German *zu*   English *at* = German *an* (or *in* or *bei*)
> (but) John is at home. = Johann ist zu Hause.
> English *to* = French *à*   English *for* = French *pour*
> (but) a glass for cognac = un verre à cognac

In addition, there are language-specific gaps when expressing some universal spatial meanings. For instance, Zelinsky-Wibbelt (1993) notes that compared to English and French, German is underdetermined with respect to expressing spatial relations with prepositions. Not having correspondence from one language to the next becomes even more problematic when the meaning of prepositions is extended beyond expressing spatial relations to establishing relationships of a more abstract nature.

Then, too, even proficient English speakers exhibit variable performance with regard to which prepositions they use for a particular meaning. For instance, do you say *going out to lunch* or *going out for lunch*? Variation in the input data can cause much confusion on the part of ESL/EFL students, especially when the use of prepositions by native speakers departs from what the prescriptive rules dictate. A nonnative speaker of English shook his head in exasperation recently when he learned that it was possible to say *symbol for something,* whereas earlier he had been taught always to use *of* in such a context.

Since these three problem areas correspond to the three dimensions of form, meaning, and use, we now proceed directly to our tridimensional analysis.

The Form of Prepositions

Basic Characteristics

You have encountered prepositions in prepositional phrases many times thus far in this book. You have seen that prepositions make nouns adverbial (*He gets off work at night.*) and create noun modifiers (*the mayor of Philadelphia*). You have also seen that prepositional phrases follow verbs (*She is in school.*) and adjectives (*She is good at math.*). By reviewing the phrase structure rule for a prepositional phrase, we can make several observations about the form of prepositions.

$$PrepP \rightarrow Prep\ NP$$

First of all, English prepositions are free morphemes, not bound inflectional affixes as they are in many other languages. The reason that prepositions have the name they do is that they precede nouns—they are *pre*-positions. This contrasts with other languages, such as Japanese, that have postpositions, which follow nouns. This is not to say that English prepositions must always come before nouns. As you have already seen in Chapter 13, it is possible for a preposition to be "stranded" when a wh-question word is fronted:

> Who(m) are you speaking to?

Second, the rule tells us that prepositions are followed by NPs. Since the NP is the "object" of the preposition, if it is a pronoun, it is an object pronoun.

> for us / to me

Third, the symbol Prep in our rule does not necessarily represent a single word. Although many prepositions are single words, some complex prepositions consist of two or more words that function as single prepositions, such as *because of, out of, on top of, in front of.*[1] In fact, some prepositions that once existed as two words have coalesced: *into* and *onto* are examples that spring readily to mind.

The other phrase structure rules that are relevant to our discussion of the form of prepositions are the ones that demonstrate that prepositional phrases follow copular verbs and certain intransitive verbs and transitive adjectives, where they are needed to complete the VP and AP, respectively:

> Cop + Prep: *The car is in the garage.*
> Verb + Prep: *He lay on his side.*
> Adj + Prep: *I am averse to the idea.*

Co-occurrence with Verbs, Adjectives, and Nouns

We have already pointed out in Chapter 3, but it bears repeating here, that a number of verbs and adjectives co-occur with particular prepositions. As such, they should be taught along with the verbs and adjectives. Here are some examples:

Verb + Prep[2,3]	Adj + Prep
to rely on	*to be dependent on*
to detract from	*to be free from/of*
to consist of	*to be afraid of*
to substitute for	*to be sorry for*
to part with	*to be content with*

Sometimes the same verb with two different prepositions will have significantly different meanings; for example:

> *provide for:* You should provide for your old age now. (make provisions for)
> *provide NP with:* The Red Cross provided us with blankets. (gave blankets to us)

However, sometimes two different prepositions can be used with the same verb with little or no change of meaning:

> Joe competes $\begin{Bmatrix} \text{with} \\ \text{against} \end{Bmatrix}$ his older brother too much.

Finally, it is possible for some verbs to be optionally followed by a preposition:

> I believe that.   It wasn't at all what she had planned.
> I believe in that.   It wasn't at all what she had planned on.

Here, however, there is a meaning difference. Further, the preposition has the effect of lessening the transitivity of the verb creating a distance between the verb and its arguments (O'Dowd 1994).

In addition, if certain noun phrases are preceded or followed by a preposition, there may be only one possible option; examples are *in my opinion, to my mind, from my point of view, objection to, awareness of, belief in.* Sometimes, noun phrases are both preceded and followed by prepositions to form multiword clusters, such as *with respect to, at odds with, in return for.* Some of these multiword preposition clusters include the following combinations (based on Frodesen and Eyring 1997):

in + noun + *of*	*on* + noun + *of*	*in the* + noun + *of*	*on the* + noun + *of*
in case of	on account of	in the course of	on the advice of
in charge of	on behalf of	in the habit of	on the basis of
in favor of	on grounds of	in the name of	on the strength of

LEXICAL COMPOUNDING

We cited an example of a lexical compound with prepositions in Chapter 3—preposition + noun, such as *underdog.* As a reminder of the frequent employment of prepositions in compounding, we offer here four prepositions commonly involved in verb compounds; for example:

out + verb	*over* + verb	*under* + verb	*down* + verb
outdo	overdo	underestimate	downplay
outrun	overrate	underrate	downgrade
outlast	overeat	underscore	downshift
outgrow	overcome	underwrite	downsize

DELETION OF PREPOSITIONS

Again, as we have seen before, it is possible to delete the preposition. Sometimes the deletion is optional; at other times, the preposition must be deleted.

Optional deletion:

- When the preposition *for* expresses a span of time:

> We have lived here (for) 12 years.
> (For) how long have you owned this house?

- When the preposition *on* is used before days of the week (when the day is used alone or when the day of the week modifies another temporal noun such as *morning, afternoon, night*):

    Brent went cross-country skiing (on) Saturday.
    He bought a new pair of skis (on) Friday night.

This is not an acceptable option in British English.

- In responses to questions that would cue temporal use of *in, at, on,* or *for*:

    How long have you lived here?   (For) two years.
    When do you wake up?   (At) 6 A.M.

Obligatory deletion:

- When the temporal noun phrase contains a determiner used deictically (i.e., as seen from the perspective of the speaker such as *last, next, this*[4]) or when the head noun of the noun phrase contains *before, after, next, last,* or *this* as part of its meaning (e.g., *yesterday, tomorrow, today, tonight*).

    I was busy (*on) last Friday.
    We will be in Eugene (*on) tonight.

- When the temporal noun phrase contains a universal quantifier like *every* or *all*:

    We stayed in Provo (*for) all week.

- When a locative noun, such as *home* or *downtown,* or the pro-adverbs *here* and *there* are used with a verb of motion or direction:[5]

    We went (*to) home.
    Phyllis walks (*to) here every day.

THE MEANING OF PREPOSITIONS

ON ABSTRACT DEFINITIONS VERSUS PROTOTYPES

As we indicated earlier, one of the greatest learning challenges presented by prepositions is their meaning, since languages carve up semantic territory in different ways. Moreover, even within a particular language, it is sometimes difficult to ascribe a meaning to a preposition that would account for all its instantiations. Prepositions are indeed polysemous (Taylor 1993). For example, what possible meaning could *in* have that would hold in all of the following possible instances?

    Stephanie is *in* the room.
    The room is *in* a mess.
    Seth is *in* trouble.
    In running out of the room, he knocked over the vase.
    He'll be back *in* an hour.

Linguists have in fact been able, in most cases, to abstract from particular instantiations of a preposition its general meaning, or a few fundamental meanings. For instance, for all instances of *in* above we might say that *in* conveys a general notion of boundedness within an enclosure. The enclosure is more literal in the first instance, but more abstract, metaphorical, or extended in the other instances. It should be clear that a problem with giving such abstract definitions to ESL/EFL students is that the definition is often more difficult to comprehend and apply than the form itself! Sometimes a more helpful alternative is to use concrete examples, rather than definitions.

It is time to keep the promise we made in Chapter 3 to return to the concept of prototypicality. You will recall that prototypical examples are the best exemplars of characteristics that the members of a particular category have in common. Thus, for example, a robin, to North American English speakers at least, would be a more prototypical bird than a penguin. Relating this observation to our present concern, we note that many prepositions prototypically deal with locating objects in space. While often their meanings are extended beyond space, experience has shown that anchoring the meaning of prepositions in spatial relationships is the first step to helping students learn to deal with areas where the meaning is more abstract. Associating spatial schemata with prepositions, where possible, also helps teachers avoid a common pitfall, which is to define a preposition using other prepositions. Therefore, we begin by delving into the underlying semantics of common prepositions in the spatial domain.

LOCATING OBJECTS IN SPACE

Locating an object in space involves two or more entities. For example, in our first example with *in* above, the two entities are *Stephanie* and *room*. Taylor (1993) notes that the relationship between the two entities is inherently asymmetrical, in that one entity is selected for foregrounding, while the other entity serves as a background. The former has been variously referred to as the figure, or trajector, and the latter is called the ground, or landmark.

The analysis below comes from Dirven (1993).[6] According to Dirven, *at*, *on*, and *in* are the basic and most general place prepositions:

- *at* denotes place as a point of orientation

    Meet me at the corner.

- *on* denotes physical contact between trajector and landmark, necessitating viewing the landmark as a one-dimensional space (a line) or two-dimensional space (a surface)

    Don't sit on the desk.

- *in* denotes the enclosure of the trajector in the landmark and, therefore, views the landmark as two- or three-dimensional space (a surface or a volume)

    Stephanie is in the room.

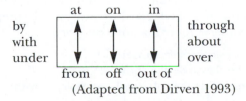

(Adapted from Dirven 1993)

The three source prepositions: *from*, *off*, and *out of* involve the notion of separation from place and hence are connected by two-pointed arrows with the basic place prepositions in the diagram. For example:

- *from* denotes separation from a point of orientation

    He took it from me.

- *off* denotes separation from contact with a line or surface

  The vase fell off the table.

- *out of* denotes separation from inside of a landmark

  The water spilled out of the vase.

By and *with* are the proximity prepositions, which are adjacent to *at* on the diagram because they locate the trajector in relation to a point of orientation, just as *at* does.

- *by* denotes the idea of "connection"[7]

  Doug lives by me.

- *with* denotes both a point of orientation and the idea of connection but may do so in a more abstract way to mean association and/or accompaniment. In its spatial sense, *with* can occur only with animate nouns as a landmark.

  He walks with me to school.

Through and *about* require the landmark to be seen as a surface or a volume and are therefore positioned on the diagram next to *in*.

- *through* structures space as a tunnel or channel

  Take the first path through the woods.

- *about* denotes spatial movement in any direction

  He walked about the room searching for where he had left his keys.

Under and *over* are vertical space prepositions.

- *under* denotes a trajector that is at a lower point than a landmark

  Don't sit under the apple tree with anyone else but me.

- *over* denotes a trajector that is at a higher point than a landmark

  We peered over the fence.

Under and *over* don't fit as neatly as the other prepositions in the picture that Dirven draws; nevertheless, Dirven justifies their inclusion and their placement on the bottom of the vertical axes by noting that *over* can overlap in some domains with *through* and *about*; that *under* is similar to *from, off,* and *out of* in that all four denote a negative polarity; and that *under* negates the positive polarity preposition *over.*

It is important to note that many prepositions can be used to describe not only stative relationships but also dynamic ones. In keeping with this observation, Taylor (1993) suggests that three categories of relations[8] are expressed by prepositions: place, path, goal. Some prepositions can serve more than one category.[9]

> The picture is over the sofa. (place)
> The crop duster flew over the cornfield. (path)
> Hang the picture over the sofa. (goal—endpoint of path)

Taylor also allows for a fourth category, source, based on Dirven's analysis:

> The catsup flowed out of the bottle. (source)

Not all prepositions can serve all of these relationships. For example, *toward* is exclusively a path preposition. Nonetheless, these four categories might provide additional semantic hooks for ESL/EFL students to hold onto when dealing with the amorphous nature of space.

MEANING EXTENSIONS OF SPATIAL PREPOSITIONS

Dirven's and Taylor's analyses can be used to support our longstanding contention that while the spatial sense of these prepositions is most prototypical, their spatial meanings can be extended metaphorically from physical to mental space. Further, the "extensions of meanings of a preposition from physical space via time into more abstract domains do not occur in any haphazard way but follow a path of gradually increasing abstractions, whereby the link with each prior meaning remains obvious and may account for most, if not all, co-occurrence restrictions between trajector and landmark" (Dirven 1993:76).

Thus, when prepositions are used in a nonspatial sense, their meanings are not random but rather are highly motivated. We will first attempt to demonstrate this by analyzing the meaning of one preposition. Then, we will provide analyses of an additional nineteen prepositions arrived at using the same general approach.

We begin with *at*. Dirven shows how *at* extends from an orientation point in space to one in time, and then beyond into state, area, manner, circumstance, and cause:

a. point as place: *at the station*
b. time point: *at six o'clock*
c. state: *at work*
d. area: *good at guessing*
e. manner: *at full speed*
f. circumstance: *at these words (he left)*
g. cause: *laugh at, irritation at*

The notion that *at* involves some sort of orientation point is easily perceived in the dimensions of space (a) and time (b). Furthermore, this core meaning can also obtain in the less prototypical extensions into state (c), such as *at play, at work, at rest*, and with regard to area (d), in which area is construed as a context or field within which an event is seen. Thus, one can be good within the field of guessing. *At* can denote a point along a scale exemplified above in its use in manner (e). More abstract is the use of *at* in circumstances (f), where human actions become the reference point. Such a relationship is made explicit in the causal use of *at* (g), where the object of the preposition is the cause or trigger of an emotional state.

Although her work was done earlier, Hudson's (1979) findings are consistent with Dirven's observations. Hudson reviewed linguistic studies and the lexical entries of unabridged dictionaries. By collapsing categories and synthesizing definitions, Hudson came up with seven meanings for *at* that she felt were optimally general but detailed enough to make all the important distinctions:

1. Used to locate an object in space

The paper was lying at my feet.

2. Used to locate an object in time

He was here at one o'clock.

3. Used to indicate a state, condition, or engagement in a particular activity

I'm never at ease when taking a test.

4. Used to indicate a cause or a source of an action or state

She wept at the bad news.

5. Used to indicate direction toward a goal or objective

> The man over there is pointing at us.

6. Used to express skill (or lack of it) in relation to a particular activity or occupation

> She's a whiz at poker.

7. Used to indicate relative amount, degree, rate, value, ordinal relationship, or position on a scale

> He retired at 65.

Having identified 305 common so-called idioms using *at*, which Hudson had drawn from several sources, Hudson asked 20 native speakers of English to sort these idioms into one of nine categories—the seven categories given above and the two following:

8. Does not mean the same as or fit any of the categories.
9. I do not understand or use this expression.

Of the 305 items using *at*, 216 were put into the same category by the 20 subjects at the $p<.005$ level of significance.

Then, in a reverse of this procedure, Hudson took the seven lists of significant items identified by her 20 subjects, and she asked 10 other subjects if they could describe the meaning of *at* for each of the seven lists. With the exception of the definition for category 4, which Hudson later recommended changing to "Used to express a reaction to someone or something," good approximations of the other six definitions were reconstructed 80 percent of the time or more. Thus, six of Hudson's seven meanings were verified, and the seventh underwent a minor adjustment.

One could come away after reading this sort of research by concluding that since the tiny word *at* is so polysemous, it is hopeless to expect ESL/EFL students to ever learn all of the meanings of the prepositions. While we would understand this interpretation, that is not our message. First of all, not all the meanings of prepositions are equally important. Certain meanings are more frequent than others. Parker (1993) and Heitzman (1993) surveyed written texts to see how Hudson's meanings of *at* were distributed. Parker and Heitzman both found that the locative meaning predominated—in a psychology text (Parker) and in an issue of *Newsweek* magazine (Heitzman). The position-on-a-scale meaning (7 in the list above) was used most often in a linguistics text, although this result is skewed by the fact that the collocation *at least* accounted for 54 percent of the tokens illustrating scalar position (Parker 1993). It bears repeating, then, that one of the meanings of a preposition is usually more central, more prototypical, and that the others somehow derive from it.

Lakoff (1987), in a reanalysis of Brugman's (1981) study of *over*, shows how the central sense of *over* combining elements of both *above* and *across* can be depicted in an image schema such as the following:

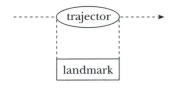

(Adapted from Lakoff 1987)

While this schema occupies a central position, one can imagine radiating from this central schema a system of links that are sometimes defined by shared properties with the central schema but that are often connected metaphorically to account for uses of *over*, such as

> She has a strange power over me.

Given the notion of a central schema or a more prototypical meaning for prepositions, it would perhaps make sense to portray the meaning of prepositions as a series of concentric circles—with the spatial sense being most central. If we were to rearrange Dirven's observations about *at*, they might look something like this:

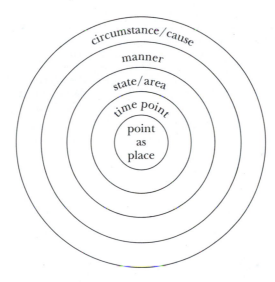

In the interest of space, however, let us instead display in chart form the various meanings of common prepositions.[10]

Prep.	Space	Time	Degree	Other (includes idiomatic usages)
at	*point/intersect:* meet at the corner	We met at 1:00.	Water freezes at 0⁰C.	
	target: Look at John./ Throw the stone at the wall.			He works at keeping in shape.
	general area: Meet me at the theater.	It rains at night there.		She's good at dancing.
about	*all around:* He ran about the yard.	*approx:* about 1:00	*approx:* about $1 about 70 degrees	*concerning:* a book about mathematics
above	*higher than:* above the picture (on the wall)		above $5 above freezing above average	above suspicion above reproach
against	*contact:* to lean against the wall	*conflict:* to work against the clock	*conflict:* two against four	*internal:* against one's will *external:* against all odds
around	*state:* The fence is around the house. *action:* The children run around the yard.	*approx:* around 1:00	*approx:* around $2 around 4 miles	

Prep.	Space	Time	Degree	Other (includes idiomatic usages)
before	*in front of:* before the mast He stood before us.	*earlier than:* before 1960 before the accident		
below	*lower than:* below the surface		below zero below average	
between	*at an intermediate point in relation to two entities:* between the house and the street	between 1 and 2 o'clock	between 100 and 110 lbs.	between you and me
by	*nearness:* chair by the desk	*no later than:* by 5 P.M.	*reduplication -* (*gradual increase*): little by little; inch by inch *degree of failure:* miss the target by a mile; miss the train by 3 minutes	*without help:* do by oneself
for	*goal:* set out for Alaska *distance:* for 7 miles	*duration:* for 7 years	*exchange:* buy for $4	*reason:* California is famous for its wines. *goal/purpose:* fish for trout
from	*a starting point:* We traveled from N.Y. to L.A. *origin:* man from New York	work from 9 to 5	from 60 to 80 degrees from 5 to 7 dollars	*source:* paper is made from wood *cause:* wet from the rain
in	*enclosure:* The man is in the room.	*in a period:* WW II ended in 1945. *future appt.:* Come in 10 minutes		*currency:* Pay me in dollars. *language:* Write/say it in English.
of	*names of geog. loc. or institutions:* the city of N.Y. the state of Texas the Univ. of Calif.	*before:* a quarter of ten	*fraction, portion:* one of the boys	*posses./assoc.:* a friend of mine *source:* a table made of wood
on	*contact:* on the wall *along:* on the Po; I live on this street.	*day, date:* on Sunday on Nov. 9th		*communication:* on the radio; on TV/the telly *concerning:* a book on magic; a lecture on modern art
over	*state of being above (with or without contact):* carry a sweater over his shoulder; the roof over our heads *action above:* jump over the fence	*spanning time:* over the weekend	*more than:* over an hour over $2 over 0°C	*communication:* over the radio, TV
through	*penetrate:* through the window; through the forest	*duration:* through the years		*endurance:* through thick and thin

Prep.	Space	Time	Degree	Other (includes idiomatic usages)
to	*direction:* go to the movies	*until:* work from 9 to 5 *before:* a quarter to eleven	He is wise to that extent./He is wise to such an extent that	*accompany:* dance to the music
toward(s)	*in the direction of:* walk toward the wall	toward morning	the temperature moved steadily toward 0°C	toward a lasting peace
under	*below (state):* be under the house *below (action);* crawl under the house	*less than:* in under an hour	under $1 under 10 men under 70 degrees	*condition:* under duress (stress)
with	*alongside, near:* even with the wall	*together:* He grew wiser with the years. He rises with the chickens.	*equal standing or ability:* rank with the best; run with the fastest	*in regard to:* pleased with the gift *manner:* spoke with ease

The chart above is only a partial systematization of prepositions. An unabridged dictionary will provide you with other definitions for each preposition listed.

THE MEANINGS OF NONSPATIAL PREPOSITIONS

Two of the most common prepositions, *of* and *for*, don't have as obvious a spatial sense as do the other frequently used ones.[11] We know of no study that has focused on the meaning(s) of *for* in authentic texts; however, *of* has been investigated by Thompson (1992). In reviewing the history of *of*, Thompson found that *of* does, in fact, have a spatial connection. Thompson states that until a few centuries ago, *of* and *off* represented different pronunciations of the same word. Dirven (1993) also mentions the common origin of *off* and *of*, with *off* reduced to *of* in its area or causal meaning:

> Place: *He has stepped off the platform.*
> Area: *Talk of the devil (and he is sure to appear).*
> Cause. *He died of cholera.*

We have also seen that *of* co-occurs with *out* in a spatial sense to mean departure from an enclosure, which can be extended metaphorically to an emotional state:

> Place: *He walked out of the house.*
> Cause: *He killed himself out of despair.*

However, in other instances of the use of *of*, it is more difficult to discern any spatial meaning. Thompson (1992) analyzed 200 tokens of *of*—100 from written texts and 100 from oral texts—in light of the three definitions she had distilled from her search of relevant literature:

1. concerning; about

> a story of a princess
> They told of her heroism.

2. derived or coming from (*X* of *Y*)

> the President of the United States
> the headlights of the car

3. having (*Y* of *X*)

> a man of courage
> a mother of two

Thompson was able to assign 61 percent of the instances of *of* to one of the three primary meanings. When *of* was spoken, it was most often used for the second meaning. The written samples had a wider distribution of use—although still the second meaning was used in the majority of samples, followed by the first and then the third. Of the instances of the second meaning, most common was its possessive or genitive use (e.g., *the views of the chairman, the umbrellas of Christo*) and its partitive use (e.g., *a can of worms*), accounting for 42 percent of the samples, followed by its originating use (e.g., *the people of Israel*), which made up 25 percent of the samples. We can see from these last three "meanings" that *of* could just as easily be classified as a syntactic marker as it could a word with a lexical meaning.[12] We might say that *of* has grammaticized as a linking element. Indeed, Thompson points out that the remaining 39 percent of the occurrences of *of* in her data, which couldn't be assigned to one of the three primary meanings above, could be described only in terms of their function or syntax, a point to which we return in the Use section of this chapter.

SEMANTICS OF CASE

Another approach to the meaning of prepositions is to examine the second of their major functions. In addition to expressing spatial relationships and their extended meanings, prepositions can be used to assign case, i.e., to mark roles that relate sentence constituents. Fillmore (1968) describes many uses of prepositions as being caselike in nature. We have borrowed his cases and have added a few others that we feel are useful. Note that a preposition may assign more than one case[13] and that only highly frequent prepositions signal cases. We do not claim that this list is an exhaustive one for English cases:

1.	*by* (agentive)	It was composed by Tchaikovsky.
2.	*by* (means)	We went there by bus.[14]
3.	*for* (benefactive)	I bought the gift for Marty.
4.	*for* (proxy)	He manages the store for the Bakers.
5.	*from* (ablative, source)	Sherry bought the car from Dave.
6.	*of* (eliciting)	He asked a favor of us.
7.	*of* (separation)	They cleared the field of trash.
8.	*of* (genitive)	The hood of the car was dented.
9.	*to* (dative)	I gave the hat I was knitting to my best friend.
10.	*to* (direction, goal)	We drove to Charlotte, North Carolina.
11.	*with* (instrument)	He broke the window with a rock.
12.	*with* (comitative)	I went to town with Jack.
13.	*with* (joining)	The storm covered the mountains with snow.

In some types of sentences, the order of cases is significant with respect to the prepositions that occur:

> Unmarked order: Craig planted beans in his yard. (= somewhere in his yard)
> agent   patient   loc.
>
> Marked order: Craig planted his yard with beans. (= all over his yard)
> agent   loc.   patient

Here, the noun functioning as patient, or the thing affected by the action of the verb (i.e., *beans*), normally does not take a preposition; however, it does take *with* when a marked order of cases occurs, altering the meaning of the sentence somewhat. Conversely, the locative *in his yard* takes the preposition *in* when the normal order of cases is followed, but it does not when the marked order occurs. The following pair is another example of this phenomenon:

> Unmarked order: Meg emptied the groceries out of the bag. (= one by one, no rush
>   agent   patient   loc.   implied)

> Marked order: Meg emptied the bag of groceries. (= quickly, all at once)
>   agent   loc.   patient

The verbs and the underlying cases of the nouns remain the same. However, the meaning of the sentence changes slightly. In each of the marked orders, the action emphasizes the completeness of the patient with regard to the location—*with* signals that the patient completely covers the location, and *of* separates the patient completely from the location.

REVIEWING SEMANTICALLY RELATED CASE FUNCTIONS TOGETHER

Frequently, two or more case functions can be usefully reviewed in sets. Four examples of sets follow:

1. Dative, benefactive, and eliciting—these are all semantic cases associated with indirect objects. These were discussed in Chapter 19.

   > I mailed the package to my pen pal.
   > I bought the tickets for Mary.
   > I asked a question of the speaker.

2. Dative and ablative (there are often two related verbs of transfer; one dative and the other ablative (Gruber 1965)):

   to (dative) *from* (ablative)

   > *sell/buy*
   > *give/take*
   > *lend/borrow*
   > *talk/write/read*
   }
   Native Germanic vocabulary (two forms)

   e.g., Sam sold the car to Jennie.
          Jennie bought the car from Sam.

   > *rent/rent*
   > *lease/lease*
   }
   French origin vocabulary (one form)

   e.g., Mr Bains leased the apartment to us.
          We leased the apartment from Mr. Bains.

3. Joining *with* and separating *of*:

   > The cashier filled my bag with groceries.
   > When I got home, I emptied the bag of groceries.

   verbs of joining *(with): fill, cover, shower, anoint,* etc.
   verbs of separating *(of): empty, rob, strip, clear,* etc.

4. Agentive *(by)* and instrumental *(with)* with passives:

   > The window was broken by Bruce.
   > It was broken with a rock.

THE USE OF PREPOSITIONS

VARIATION IN USE

As we noted at the outset of this chapter, there are issues of use as well concerning prepositions. For one thing, there appear to be instances where more than one preposition with the same meaning is acceptable in a given context:

1. spatial proximity: *a house near/by the lake*
2. time/degree approximation: *happened around/about 10 o'clock; cost around/about $100.*
3. telling time: *a quarter to/of ten* (*of* for telling time is not used in British English)
4. telling time: *a quarter after/past ten*
5. location along something linear: *the towns on/along the Rhine*
6. in a time period: *It happened in/during 1998.*
7. temporal termination: *work from 9 until/till/to 5.*
8. location lower than something: *below/beneath/under/underneath the stairs*
9. location higher than something: *above/over the table*
10. location in/at the rear of something: *behind/in back of the door*
11. location adjacent: *next to/beside the stream*

Throughout this book, we have been invoking the linguistic principle that a language will not tolerate having more than one form with exactly the same meaning and use. Therefore, we may indeed find that members of a given set are not equally acceptable in all contexts. For example, while *above* and *over* can be interchangeable in three-dimensional space,

> The plane flew above the storm clouds.
> The plane flew over the storm clouds.

a semantic distinction can exist in two-dimensional space:

> Hang the picture above the mirror. (location on a flat, vertical surface)
> Hang the picture over the mirror. (could mean "Cover the picture with the mirror")

Members of other sets may be distinguished by use issues—register, for instance. *Underneath* may occur in a more formal context than *under*, for example. Then, too, no doubt some dialect variation occurs; that is, not all proficient speakers of English will accept all the alternatives we proposed above. Finally, it is possible that the principle we have been operating with does not always apply synchronically. For while languages do not permit the uneconomic situation of having more than one form with the same meaning and use, languages do change, and at any one point in time, it is possible that one or more of the redundant forms is in the process of dying out with the other(s) remaining. More research needs to be done to determine which, if any, of these explanations serve to distinguish between seemingly equivalent prepositions.

PREPOSITIONS IN DISCOURSE

The other issue of use that we should deal with is the discourse in which prepositions occur. According to Kennedy (1991), it is important to study the "linguistic ecology" of prepositions. One way to do so is to use computer corpora. Kennedy examined the Lancaster-Oslo/Bergen (LOB) corpus for incidence of the prepositions *between* and *through.* Although their meanings sometimes overlap, analysis revealed that there was a striking difference between the words that these two prepositions co-occur with. Kennedy found that nouns typically precede *between* (*difference between*), whereas verbs are the most common word class preceding *through* (*flash through*).[15]

Both *between* and *through* are most commonly used in their locative senses; however, other nonphysical relations are also very frequent—involving, for example, interaction (*communication between management and employees*), comparison (*there is little to choose between the two*), similarity (*the important parallel between Handel and Beethoven*), difference (*the discrepancy between expected and observed scores*), means (*through the medium of the English language*), or causation (*dilapidation through lack of maintenance*). Kennedy goes on to point out that while grammars and dictionaries already provide descriptively adequate accounts of the grammatical functions and possible meanings in context of *between* and *through*, corpus study goes beyond systemic possibility by adding to linguistic description a statistical dimension based on use in context.

A more far-reaching implication, which is a reprise of a theme we first introduced in Chapter 3 and mentioned in this chapter in conjunction with the grammaticization of *of*, is the question of whether it really makes sense in all cases to teach prepositions as meaningful words unto themselves. What could be the meaning of *by*, for example, in the expression *by and large*? Some applied linguists would submit that some of the most frequently occurring prepositions are delexicalized (Lindstromberg 1996) and that it therefore makes sense to think not only about teaching their meanings but also about teaching their recurring combinations. Kennedy (1990), for instance, in studying the preposition *at*, found that 142 collocations beginning with the word *at* accounted for 43 percent of its 2576 tokens. The most frequent collocation, *at least*, which we have already encountered in our discussion of Parker's study, is very telling in that like other frequently occurring collocations, its basic locative meaning does not stand out. Kennedy suggests that to treat prepositions as roughly substitutable parts of speech can be very misleading. As we noted in Chapter 3, we may not have as open a choice in grammatical frames in the words we use as we think. It may be then that we shouldn't teach certain prepositions in isolation but rather teach them as in relation to their occurrence with other words.

PREPOSITIONS: A MULTILEVEL STRATEGY

Another finding from Kennedy (1991) will allow us to segue to our final point in this chapter. Kennedy observes that the traditional rule that tells English speakers to use *between* with two entities and *among* with more than two is not observed in the LOB corpus. *Between* is frequently used where *among* might be expected; for example:

> [he] would help to establish an enduring peace between nations

In keeping with the previous discussion on the value of using corpora to conduct linguistic research, Todaka (1996) analyzed instances of *between* and *among* in the Brown corpus. Todaka agrees that the traditional prescriptive rule has some influence but says it does not fully reflect the distribution of these two prepositions in the data. Therefore, Todaka recommends a multilevel strategy. At the word level, the central sense that differentiates the two prepositions is that objects with the semantic features of [+ explicit, + separable] always take *between*; when the objects are conceived as [+ collective], *among* is used.

> *A quarrel between the six attorneys . . .* (the attorneys are explicit and are seen as individuals)
>
> *Among the recipients of the Nobel prize for literature, more than half are practically unknown to readers of English.* (the recipients of the Nobel prize are seen collectively)

At the phrase/sentence level it is possible to account for some of the instances that cannot be explained through the semantic feature analysis by examining their occurrence in collocations. For one thing, *between* takes leftward collocations and *among* takes rightward collocations:

a relation between	*among others*
a distinction between	*among* + plural noun + *on the whole* (e.g., *among English-speaking people on the whole*)
a distance between	*among* + ranking adjective (e.g., *among the best*)

Then, according to Todaka, at the level of discourse, what determines the choice of prepositions, when it can't be explained by semantic features or collocations, is whether or not the object's individual members are identifiable from the discourse context. When they aren't, *among* is more likely to be used.

> among all western hemisphere languages (the individual languages are not identifiable from the context)

When the object's members are identifiable, *between* is used.

> ... And lastly, with hypnotherapist and client, there rarely is an affective bond established, whereas in faith healing there almost always is a terrific bond that forms immediately between people.

The object, *people,* is [− explicit]. However, *between* is used because it is clear from the context that the people to whom the speaker is referring are the faith healer and the people consulting the healer. As such, the individuals referred to in the object are identifiable, while not explicit.

CONCLUSION

It may be more obvious now that you've read the chapter why prepositions cause such difficulty for ESL/EFL students. Even relatively advanced-level students continue to make errors of omission, as in

> *I served the Army until June 1964.
>   (in)

or use the wrong preposition, as in

> *It is predicted that the degree to social adaptation will determine . . .
>   (of)

or use a superfluous preposition, as in

> *I studied in biology for three years.
> (ø or majored in?)

Nonetheless, the situation is not hopeless. As we have tried to show in this chapter, there is some systematicity in how the core meaning of certain prepositions is extended beyond representing spatial relationships. Calling attention to it where it exists will doubtless lighten the learning burden.

While learning the various meanings and meaning extensions of prepositions is perhaps the greatest challenge, a pedagogical strategy that enables students to pay attention to their co-occurrence, collocational, and discourse behavior in addition will no doubt facilitate learners' acquisition of these difficult lexico-grammatical forms.

TEACHING SUGGESTIONS

1. Form. At the beginning and intermediate levels, it probably suffices to make sure that when new verbs or adjectives are introduced, any prepositions that occur with them are also taught. At the advanced level, it would be helpful to systematically review the particular patterns of verb + preposition and adjective + preposition clusters that are common. For example, Frodesen and Eyring (1997) recommend an exercise that gets students to practice verb + *for* combinations by having them discuss different immigrant groups to the United States. The students are given certain information and are asked to use it to say why they think that different groups immigrated. For example:

> The Pilgrims longed for freedom from religious persecution.
> In the 1840s and 1850s, the Irish hoped for freedom from hunger.
> In the late 1800s, the Scandinavians yearned for farmland.

2. Meaning. Using a matrix, such as the one we have adapted from Quirk et al. (1985:674) below, will help students in learning the spatial meaning of prepositions as contrasting sets rather than independent lexical items.

	Positive Direction	*Position*	*Negative Direction*	*Position*
point	to $\rightarrow X$	at $\bullet X$	(away) from $X \rightarrow$	away from $X \bullet$
line or surface	on (to)	on	off (of)	off
area or volume	in (to)	in	out of	out of

Perhaps a chart like this could be placed in the classroom for students' reference and to foster any peripheral learning.

3. Meaning. There is a children's game that affords practice with prepositions. It is called "A Bear Hunt." The narrator tells a story about going to hunt bears, and as the story is told, the narrator mimes the corresponding actions in an exaggerated fashion. The listeners repeat the words and actions after each sentence. For example:

> Let's go on a bear hunt. First we go out the door (mimes action). Then we go under the fence (mime action). We have to walk through some deep grass (narrator makes swishing noise by rubbing hands together). Next, we have to wade across a stream (narrator picks feet up in an exaggerated fashion as if walking through water). Then, we have to walk on a path to the forest (narrator slaps hands on thighs, alternating left and right, in order to make a "clopping" sound). In the forest, we have to go through a swamp. . .

When a bear is sighted, the narrator leads the group through all the steps again, this time in reverse order, so as to get everyone safely home. Such stories may not be appropriate for older learners, but some enjoy them, and they can be entertaining ways of associating forms with meaning.

4. Meaning. Lindstromberg (1996) outlines a systematic approach to teaching the prototypical meanings of the prepositions,[16] and how to treat their more abstract meanings derived by metaphorical extensions. He illustrates his approach with the preposition *on*. We don't have the space to report every step of the approach, but here is a synopsis.

Lindstromberg first uses classic approaches, such as the use of Total Physical Response and schemata, to make the protypical place and goal meaning of a preposition clear; for example:

Put it on the table.

Later, also using pictures, he introduces more metaphorical extensions:

- *on* = about or *concerning*: *An article on holidays in France*

- the burden metaphor: *The engine died on us.*

- the basis metaphor: *The argument is based on copious data.*

- the vehicle metaphor: *It's hard to get through the day on one sandwich.*

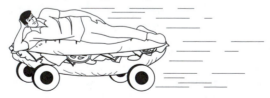

Finally, along the way, Lindstromberg contrasts prepositions with overlapping meanings, such as *on top of* versus *on*.

As Lindstromberg himself notes, the use of schemata to represent prepositional meaning long predates prototype theory. However, what may be innovative is to use a schemata series to show how the prototype meaning holds throughout its metaphorical extensions.

5. Meaning. Several groups of prepositions are frequently confused by learners. These include the spatial and temporal meanings of *in, on,* and *at*. As we have pointed out in this chapter, *at* is used to show one-dimensional relationships; *on*, two-dimensional; and *in*, three-dimensional. Another way to think about these relationships is that they differ with regard to their specificity. For example, with addresses and dates, *at* is most specific, *on* is less so, and *in* is most general.

a. Addresses: From most specific to most general

I live at 252 Linden Street.
I live on Linden Street.
I live in Bellmore.
I live in Nassau County.
I live in New York State.
I live in the United States.

b. Dates: From most specific to most general

Our daughter was born at 6:30 A.M.
Our daughter was born on (a) Friday.
Our daughter was born on October 27, 1972.
Our daughter was born in the morning.
Our daughter was born in October.
Our daughter was born in 1972.
Our daughter was born in the 70s.

Students can interview each other about when they were born and where they live. The first answer each interviewee should give should be very general. With repeated questioning, the interviewee should get more specific.

A: Where do you live?
B: In Brazil.
A: Where do you live in Brazil?
B: In São Paulo.
A: Where do you live in São Paulo?
B: On Alameda Lorena.

6. Meaning. A fairly common way of getting students to associate spatial meaning with prepositions is to make use of maps. Create a simplified map of the town you are living in or of your school. Give each student a copy of the map and ask students to trace the path you are following with their pencils as you describe it. For example:

I am *at* the bank *on* Main Street, and I want to go *to* the market. I go *out of* the bank, and I make a right turn. *At* the corner, I go *across* Main Street. I turn right again. The market is two blocks *down* the street, *on* Elliott Street. It is *next to* the laundromat. I go *in* the front door.

Later, you can give them your starting point and some directions. See if they can figure out where you are after following the directions. When they are ready, they can take turns asking for and giving directions to each other.

7. Meaning. Another widely used technique for giving students practice in using prepositions to express spatial relationships is to ask students to draw pictures or manipulate bits of paper to create designs. Give each student five pieces of paper in the shapes of a triangle, square, circle, star, and rectangle. Then ask students to pair up. Ask Student A to arrange the shapes in any pattern he or she likes. Student B does not watch. Then Student B has to try to construct the same pattern that Student A has created following A's description. The students are seated back to back. When the five pieces of paper have been placed, the students should compare A's original to B's copy. Then it is B's turn to describe a new pattern to A.

8. Use. Kennedy (1991) encourages us to help students learn about prepositions by learning about "the company they keep." To this end, advanced learners could be assigned to explore the collocations of particular prepositions in a variety of texts. Different students could choose to examine different prepositions in the same text and report on their findings to the rest of the class. Another possibility is to have different students investigate the same preposition in a variety of texts. In addition to noting collocational patterns, students could be encouraged to describe the use of prepositions from the several different perspectives we have presented here—their meanings, their collocations, and anything in the discourse that favors the use of one preposition over another.

EXERCISES

Test your understanding of what has been presented.

1. Provide an original sentence illustrating each of the following terms. Underline the pertinent word(s) or word parts in your example.

   a. verb + preposition co-occurrence   **d.** complex preposition
   b. deletable preposition   **e.** source preposition
      (i) optional   **f.** metaphorical extension of *in*
      (ii) obligatory   **g.** genitive use of *of*
   c. co-occurring nonadjacent prepositions   **h.** collocation with preposition

2. Explain the ungrammaticality of the following sentences:
   a. *You can rely me.
   b. *In case someone phones, I'll be back during 15 minutes.
   c. *He is interested by good books.
   d. *It is underneath one's dignity.

Test your ability to apply what you know.

3. If your students produce the following sentences, what errors have they made? How will you make them aware of the errors, and what exercises will you prepare to correct the errors?
   a. *We discussed about our plans.
   b. *Stuart lives on 160 Western Avenue.
   c. *Because of the teacher gave us a lot of homework, I can't go.
   d. *After my evening class, I went to home.
   e. I live in Washington, D.C. *I like living in here.

4. A student asks you what the meaning of *of* is in the following sentence. What would your answer be?

     Don't forget to buy me a pad of paper.

5. There are several pairs of prepositions that ESL/EFL students often confuse:

Source meanings of *from* and *out of*:

     Paper is made from wood. (source not visibly obvious)
     This table is made (out) of wood. (source visibly obvious)

Temporal meaning of *in* and *within*:

     Come back in 30 minutes. (30 minutes from now)
     Come back within 30 minutes. (between now and 30 minutes from now)

Since/For to express spans of time:

> I have lived here since 1960. (refers to beginning of span)
> I have lived here for decades. (refers to duration of span)

Choose one of these and create an exercise that would help students to detect the difference and be able to use them correctly.

6. Describe two prepositions other than the 20 listed in the large chart in this chapter that do not express case functions and that have meanings that can be extended from one dimension into others.

7. How is the following sentence ambiguous?

> I'll tell you the story in five minutes or less.

BIBLIOGRAPHY

References

Brugman, C. (1981). "The Story of *Over*." Masters thesis, University of California, Berkeley. Later published in 1988 as *The Story of Over: Polysemy, Semantics, and the Structure of the Lexicon.* New York: Garland.

Dirven, R. (1993). "Dividing Up Physical and Mental Space into Conceptual Categories by Means of English Prepositions." In C. Zelinsky-Wibbelt (ed.), *Natural Language Processing (vol. 3, The Semantics of Prepositions).* The Hague: Mouton de Gruyter, 73–97.

Fillmore, C. J. (1968). "The Case for Case." In E. Bach and R. Harms (eds.), *Universals in Linguistic Theory.* New York: Holt, Rinehart and Winston, 1–90.

Francis, W. N., and H. Kučera (1982). *Frequency Analysis of English Usage.* Boston: Houghton Mifflin.

Frodesen, J., and J. Eyring (1997). *Grammar Dimensions.* Book 4 (2d ed.). Boston, Mass.: Heinle & Heinle.

Gruber, J. (1965). "Studies in Lexical Relations." Ph.D. dissertation in Linguistics, MIT.

Hawkins, B. (1984). "The Semantics of English Spatial Prepositions." Ph.D. dissertation, University of California, San Diego.

Hawkins, B. (1993). "On Universality and Variability in the Semantics of Spatial Adpositions." In C. Zelinsky-Wibbelt (ed.), *Natural Language Processing (vol. 3, The Semantics of Prepositions).* The Hague: Mouton de Gruyter, 327–349.

Heitzman, S. (1993). "*At*: Frequency of Its Function in *Newsweek*." Term paper for Linguistics 5741, University of Minnesota.

Hudson, J. K. (1979). "Towards a Systematization of the Idiom List: A Sample Method with *AT*." Masters thesis in TESL, UCLA.

Johnson, M. (1987). *The Body in the Mind. The Bodily Basis of Meaning, Imagination, and Reason.* Chicago: University of Chicago Press.

Kennedy, G. (1990). "Collocations: Where Grammar and Vocabulary Teaching Meet." In S. Anivan (ed.), *Language Teaching Methodology for the Nineties.* Singapore: RELC, 212–229.

Kennedy, G. (1991). "*Between* and *Through*: The Company They Keep and the Functions They Serve." In K. Aijmer and B. Altenberg (eds.), *English Corpus Linguistics.* London: Longman, 95–110.

Lakoff, G. (1987). *Women, Fire, and Dangerous Things.* Chicago: University of Chicago Press.

Lakoff, G. (1987). *Women, Fire, and Dangerous Things.* Chicago: University of Chicago Press.

Lindstromberg, S. (1996). "Prepositions: Meaning and Method." *ELT Journal* 50:3, 225–236.

O'Dowd, E. (1994). "Prepositions and Particles in English: A Discourse-Based, Unifying Account." Ph.D. dissertation in Linguistics, University of Colorado.

Parker, J. (1993). "Function and Frequency of 'At' in Academic English." Term paper for Linguistics 5741, University of Minnesota.

Quirk, R., S. Greenbaum, G. Leech, and J. Svartvik (1985). *A Comprehensive Grammar of the English Language.* London: Longman.

Rauh, G. (1993). "On the Grammar of Lexical and Nonlexical Prepositions in English." In C. Zelinsky-Wibbelt (ed.), *Natural Language Processing (vol. 3, The Semantics of Prepositions).* The Hague: Mouton de Gruyter, 99-149.

Taylor, J. (1993). "Prepositions: Patterns of Polysemization and Strategies of Disambiguation." In C. Zelinsky-Wibbelt (ed.), *Natural Language Processing (vol. 3, The Semantics of Prepositions).* The Hague: Mouton de Gruyter, 151–175.

Thompson, B. (1992). *"Of:* Common, Complex, and ?Definable." Independent Professional Project. School for International Training.

Todaka, Y. (1996). *"Between* and *Among:* A Data-Based Analysis."* Word* 47: 1, 14–40.

Zelinsky-Wibbelt, C. (ed.) (1993). *Natural Language Processing (vol. 3, The Semantics of Prepositions).* The Hague: Mouton de Gruyter.

Suggestions for Further Reading

For linguistic analyses of English prepositions in addition to those cited above, see:

Herskovits, A. (1986). *Language and Spatial Cognition. An Interdisciplinary Study of the Prepositions in English.* Cambridge: Cambridge University Press.

Rauh, G. (ed.) (1991). *Approaches to Prepositions.* Tübingen: Gunter Narr Verlag.

Talmy, L. (1983). "How Language Structures Space." In H. Pick and L. Acredolo (eds.), *Spatial Orientation: Theory, Research, and Application,* New York: Plenum Press, 225–282.

For helpful resources on collocations, see:

Benson, M., E. Benson, and R. Ilson (1986). *The BBI Combinatory Dictionary of English.* Amsterdam: John Benjamins.

Sinclair, J. (ed.) (1987). *Collins Cobuild English Language Dictionary.* London: Collins.

For useful diagrams representing the spatial meanings of prepositions, see:

Firsten, R., and P. Killian (1994). *Troublesome English.* Englewood Cliffs, N.J.: Prentice Hall Regents.

For pedagogical suggestions, see:

Badalamenti, V., and C. Henner Stanchina (1997). *Grammar Dimensions: Form, Meaning, and Use.* Book 1 (2d ed.). Boston, Mass.: Heinle & Heinle.

Frodesen, J. and J. Eyring (1997). *Grammar Dimensions: Form, Meaning, and Use.* Book 4 (2d ed.). Boston, Mass.: Heinle & Heinle.

Murphy, R. (1989). *Grammar in Use.* Cambridge: Cambridge University Press.

ENDNOTES

1. O'Dowd (1994), noting that we can't use *out* alone as a source preposition—that is, to mean "from" *(*I took it out the box)*—argues that the sequence *out of* is actually a particle followed by a preposition. We will be discussing particles in the next chapter when we deal with phrasal verbs.

2. In the next chapter we deal with constructions consisting of verb + particle, such as *write off*, which appear to be the same as verb + preposition co-occurrences, but which function differently.

3. Some verbs can take an object NP before the preposition, e.g., *accuse someone of, charge someone with, prefer something to, protect someone from.*

4. These determiners can be preceded by a preposition in nondeitic use; for example, in *on the last Sunday of the month*, *last* means "final," not the Sunday before the moment of speech. For the same reason, *that* isn't included in our list since it is usually used anaphorically (e.g., *I was ill on that Sunday*), not deictically.

5. Note that the concept of motion or direction is important since *home* may take the preposition *at* with a stative verb:

Is Jackie (at) home?

Also, *here* and *there* can take prepositions in other environments:

Yes. She is (in) there.

6. We are using Dirven's analysis for illustrative purposes. There are more prepositions that express spatial relationships than are presented here. Also, for a different type of semantic analysis of spatial prepositions, see Hawkins (1993).

7. Hawkins (1984) notes that in addition to the denotation of prepositions, there is also an implicit frame of reference that must be accessed in order to understand the full meaning of a preposition. For instance, implicit in *by* is the notion of a scale of distance. The prepositions *up* and *down* access a domain of oriented physical space, in which they denote positive and negative polarity, respectively.

8. Or what Johnson (1987) calls "image schemas." See the discussion of Lakoff (1987) that follows.

9. In fact, Taylor states that "In general, prepositions that denote the place of a tr [trajector] can also denote a goal, i.e., a place where the tr comes to occupy with respect to the lm [landmark]" (Taylor 1993:161). This place-goal polysemy can cause ambiguity:

He jumped on the wall. (place or goal)

10. According to Francis and Kučera (1982), the most common prepositions in decreasing order of frequency are: *of, in, to, for, with, on, at, by, from.*

11. In fact, by some estimates, *of* is the second most frequently used word in the English language, second only to the definite article.

12. For example, *of* in its genitive use is equivalent to the apostrophe syntactic marker.

13. Rauh (1993) notes that indeed it is the prepositions that assign roles themselves and not just that prepositions express roles assigned by verbs, as is often assumed.

14. Note that *on foot* and *on horseback* are exceptions to *by bus, by car, by taxi, by train, by plane,* etc. Also, there are other prepositions such as *through* which also express means, e.g.:

She has accomplished a great deal through hard work. (i.e., by working hard)

15. Although, as Kennedy notes, looking only at adjacent words can be misleading since discontinuous collocations, sometimes several words apart, are quite common. For instance, in the following example from Kennedy's data, there is more of a collocational association between the verb *move* and the preposition *through* than there is between the pronoun *it* and *through*.

I found that I had moved, without realizing it, through the gateway.

16. Although he also includes what we call particles, which we discuss in the next chapter.

22

PHRASAL VERBS

INTRODUCTION

Consider the following sentences and their analyses adapted from O'Dowd (1994). How would you describe the role of *up* in each?

> **a.** She walked up the street to get a bite to eat.
> **b.** I live up in Springfield.
> **c.** When are you going to clean up your room?
> **d.** I am sorry that I messed you up.

The most generally agreed upon interpretation would be that *up* is a preposition in the first two sentences. In (a) it is the preposition in the adverbial PrepP of direction *up the street*. In (b) it is once again a preposition. This time its object, presumably "north," has been deleted. In (b) the PrepP *up north* is an adverbial of position.

The *up's* in (c) and (d) are different, structures with which we have not yet dealt in this text. These *up's* we will call particles, which when combined with the verbs *clean* and *mess*, form phrasal verbs. Despite sharing the same form, the meaning of *up* in (c) is quite different from that of (d). In (c), the *up* is syntactically optional, and its contribution to the meaning of the sentence is quite modest. The verb could stand on its own with almost the same meaning; that's not true with the particle in (d). In this sentence, *up* seems to form an integral part of the verb (*mess up*) despite its separation from the verb by the intervening pronominal direct object *you*.

It may already be obvious that we are once again dealing in this chapter with a structure that is very difficult for ESL/EFL students. For one thing, the meaning of phrasal verbs is often noncompositional; that is someone can know the meaning of the verb and the apparent meaning of the particle, but when they are put together, a unique meaning is derived.

> Jennifer gave up. (*to give up* = to surrender)

For another thing, there are very few non-Germanic languages[1] that have phrasal verbs. Thus, most ESL/EFL students will find such verbs strange and difficult. Yet they are ubiquitous in English; no one can speak or understand English, at least the informal register, without a knowledge of phrasal verbs. Because they don't realize this, some nonnative speakers of English have a tendency to overuse single lexical items where a phrasal verb would be much more appropriate; for example:

> **a.** I arose early this morning.
> **b.** I got up early this morning.

While sentence (a) is accurate and meaningful, it is not appropriate usage in conversation.

A final learning challenge involves the conditions governing optional or obligatory separation of the verb and the particle for phrasal verbs used transitively.

a. Turn out the lights.   Separation optional (direct object is not a pronoun)
b. Turn the lights out.

c. Turn them out.   Separation necessary (direct object is a pronoun)
d. *Turn out them.

While most analyses of phrasal verbs highlight the pronominal status of the direct object to account for the ungrammaticality of (d), we go beyond this explanation to invoke a pragmatic principle in the use section of this chapter to explain why (d) is unacceptable. We do this heeding the advice we offered in Chapter 1—to give students "reasons, not rules."

FORM OF ENGLISH PHRASAL VERBS

SYNTACTIC ANALYSIS OF PHRASAL VERBS

As you have just seen, a phrasal verb (PV) is made up of two (or more) parts that function as a single verb. Phrasal verbs are sometimes called two-word verbs because they usually consist of a verb plus a second word, the latter often referred to as an adverb. We will refer to the second part of the phrasal verb as a particle, to show its close association with the verb, and to distinguish it from prepositions and other adverbs, although we acknowledge that, as you have just seen with *up,* the same word can fit into more than one category.[2]

To be able to analyze sentences with phrasal verbs, we need to refine our phrase structure rule for the VP by generating a PV as an alternative to V.

$$
VP \rightarrow \left\{ \begin{array}{l} \text{cop} \left\{ \begin{array}{l} \text{NP} \\ \text{AP} \\ \text{PrepP} \end{array} \right\} \\[2em] \left\{ \begin{array}{l} \text{V} \\ \text{PV} \end{array} \right\} (NP)^2 \, (PrepP) \end{array} \right\}
$$

The PV category is then expanded in a new phrase structure rule as a verb and particle (Prt):

$$PV \rightarrow V \; <<Prt>>$$

The symbols on either side of the particle indicate that although the particle is part of the phrasal verb, it need not be contiguous with it. Here is the basic structure of a sentence in which the particle follows the verb directly.

Jamie turned out the light.

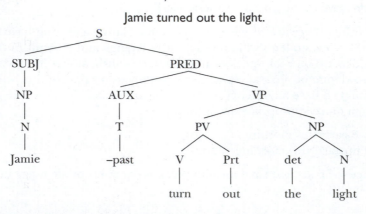

Now here is a tree where the particle is not contiguous with the verb but rather is separated from it by an intervening direct object.

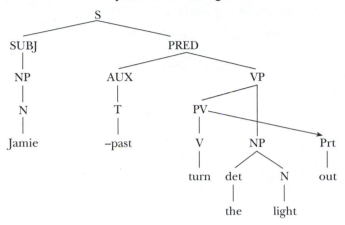

Jamie turned the light out.

SYNTACTIC FEATURES OF PHRASAL VERBS

Transitive and Intransitive Phrasal Verbs

Like single-word verbs, phrasal verbs can be transitive:

> Harold turned on the radio.
> Barbara passed out the new assignment.[3]
> I called off the meeting.

(Others: *do over* (repeat), *look over* (examine), *fill out* (complete), *find out* (discover), etc.)

Phrasal verbs can also be intransitive.

> My car broke down.
> He really took off.
> The boys were playing around in the yard.

(Others: *come back* (return), *come over* (visit), *make up* (reconcile), *pass out* (faint), etc.)

Of course, just as some regular ergative or change-of-state verbs (e.g., *open, increase*) may be either transitive or intransitive depending on the role of the agent, some phrasal verbs can have this dual function, too; for example:

> An arsonist burned down the hotel. (transitive)
> The hotel burned down. (intransitive)

Phrasal Verbs that Require Prepositions

Also like single-word verbs, adjectives, and nouns, many phrasal verbs take a specific preposition. Examples of this type of construction are:

put up with	*get along with*	*cut down on*	*close in on*
look in on	*check up on*	*catch up with*	*make away with*
look down on	*check out of*	*stand up for*	*make up for*
get away with	*go in for*	*keep up with*	*drop in on*
get down to	*come up with*	*end up with*	*run up against*
get back to	*give in to*	*pick up on*	*break up with*

In these expressions the phrasal verb and preposition must be learned as a unit.[4]

The only thing that can be added to such a string is an adverb or adverbial phrase between the particle and the preposition:

> I haven't kept up fully with the work.
> Mort has cut down almost completely on his smoking.

Here's how a tree would look with a "three-word phrasal verb" (i.e., a phrasal verb that takes a preposition).

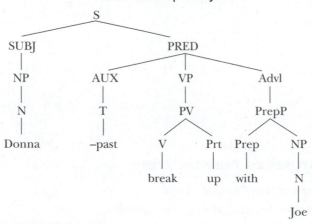

Donna broke up with Joe.

The Separability of Phrasal Verbs

Thus far we have been discussing characteristics that phrasal verbs share with regular verbs; however, there is one syntactic characteristic peculiar to transitive phrasal verbs: sometimes the particle can be separated from the verb by the direct object and sometimes it cannot. Separation is obligatory when the direct object is a pronoun.

Separable Phrasal Verbs

Mark threw away the ball.   *Mark threw away it.
Mark threw the ball away.   Mark threw it away.

Rachel looked up the information.   *Rachel looked up it.
Rachel looked the information up.   Rachel looked it up.

(Others: *take up* (discuss), *leave out* (omit), *pass out* (distribute), *bring back* (return), *turn down* (refuse), etc.)

The largest, most productive category of phrasal verbs are these transitive separable ones. However, we also posit a smaller category of inseparable phrasal verbs, where the particle cannot be separated from its verb. Some linguists would argue that the inseparability is due to the fact that what we are calling a particle is really a preposition, and thus would naturally precede its object. Because the two words appear to have a syntactic affinity (see the section on syntactic tests later) and together have a meaning beyond what each word contributes individually, we feel that it makes good pedagogic sense to have a category of inseparable phrasal verbs.

Inseparable Phrasal Verbs

I came across an interesting article last night.   I came across it last night.
*I came an interesting article across last night.   *I came it across last night.

Josh ran into an old friend.   Josh ran into him.
*Josh ran an old friend into.   *Josh ran him into.

(Others: *get over* (recover), *go over* (review), *look into* (investigate), *go for* (attack), etc.)

We have already illustrated the two trees for the separable phrasal verb *turn out.* Here's a tree for a sentence with an inseparable phrasal verb. Since the particle must follow the verb directly in an inseparable phrasal verb, only one tree is possible.

Angela ran across a classmate.

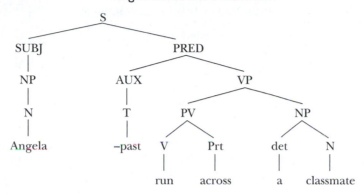

Phrasal Verbs That Are Always Separated

A few phrasal verbs seem to occur only with the verb and particle separated:

How can I get $\begin{Bmatrix} \text{the message} \\ \text{it} \end{Bmatrix}$ through to him? (*get . . . through* = convey; transmit)

*How can I get through the message to him?

We'll see $\begin{Bmatrix} \text{this ordeal} \\ \text{it} \end{Bmatrix}$ through together. (*see . . . through* = survive)

?We'll see through this ordeal together.

The reason for the obligatory separation is presumably to avoid the ambiguity with the inseparable phrasal verbs that have the same form but a different meaning:

get through the lesson (*get through* = finish)
see through his excuse (*see through* = not be deceived by)

Such phrasal verbs that are always separated compose a small subcategory of phrasal verbs. Their lexical entries would have to indicate the fact that the verb and particle are always separated.

DISTINGUISHING PHRASAL VERBS FROM VERB + PREPOSITION SEQUENCES

Syntactic Tests

At the begining of this chapter you saw that a particular word can behave as a preposition in some contexts and a particle in others. Despite the overlap, there is reason to try to arrive at a common understanding of what distinguishes its prepositional use from that of its particle use in a phrasal verb. The following are some of the tests that have been applied (adapted from O'Dowd 1994:19).

Only prepositions (not particles) allow:

Adverb insertion   We turned quickly off the road.
*We turned quickly off the light.

Phrase fronting	Up the hill John ran.
	*Up the bill John ran.
Wh-fronting	About what does he write?
	*Up what does he write?

Only particles in separable phrasal verbs (not prepositions) allow:

Passivization[5]	The light was turned off.
	*The road was turned off.
Verb substitution	The light was extinguished.
	(= the light was turned off.)
NP insertion	We turned the light off.
	*We turned the road off.

The rationale for many of these tests is the fact that a preposition makes a natural unit with the NP object that follows it, whereas a particle makes a natural unit with the verb that precedes it. For instance, when we apply *wh*-fronting:

   About what does he write?

we produce a somewhat stilted but nevertheless grammatical question because we have fronted a natural unit consisting of a preposition and its object. When we apply this same test to a sentence containing a phrasal verb, the question is ungrammatical:

   ***Up what does he write?**

because it is not possible to separate the particle *up* from the verb *write*, with which it forms a natural unit.

   Since we are positing a three-way distinction among separable PVs, inseparable PVs, and verb-plus-preposition sequences, we recommend adopting the following hierarchy of tests. Consider the following examples:

   Peter looked up the new word.
   Peter looked at the newspaper.
   Peter looked into the matter.

1. Can you put the object noun between the verb and the "P"?

   Peter looked the new word up.   → Yes = Separable PV (*look up*)

   {*Peter looked the newspaper at.}
   {*Peter looked the matter into. } → No = Inseparable PV or V + Prep

2. Can you front the "P" in a *wh*-question?

   At what did Peter look? →   Yes = V + Prep (*look at*)
   *Into what did Peter look. (*look into* = investigate) → No = Inseparable PV (*look into*)

   Another reason for the difficulty in distinguishing particles from prepositions is that their syntactic roles are evolving (O'Dowd 1994); that is, some of the items O'Dowd calls "Ps" are becoming more particle-like and some more preposition-like. For now, let us say that it is perhaps more helpful to view phrasal verbs and verbs taking prepositions as opposite ends of a continuum rather than as a categorical dichotomy. Indeed, O'Dowd (1994) rejects the hard-and-fast distinction between prepositions and particles; she also, however, acknowledges the tendency for particular "P's" to specialize in one syntactic role or another.

Used more as prepositions ————————————————————————————Used more as particles

with, of, for, from	to, in, on, about, by	through, around, over,	up, out, down, away, back
		off, across, along	

Just as Hopper and Thompson (1984) have made the case that the discourse context plays a decisive role in determining whether to construe a particular form as a noun or verb, O'Dowd (1994) suggests that it may be impossible to distinguish a particle from a preposition apart from the way it behaves in a particular context. O'Dowd hypothesizes that the preposition-particle distinction is evolving as a two-way extension from a single element corresponding to what Bolinger (1971) called an "adprep." The specialization of certain "Ps" as either prepositions or adverbial particles reflects their greater degree of grammaticization in one direction or another.

Phonological test

Another formal difference between a verb + preposition and a phrasal verb is that a particle may receive stress, whereas a preposition usually doesn't:

> He loòked uṕ the word. (phrasal verb)
> He loóked uṗ the road. (verb + preposition)

Although this test often works to disambiguate prepositions from particles, again there are enough exceptions or marked cases where the preposition is stressed:

> He loòked uṕ the road, not down.

that the test is not always reliable.

Another problem for ESL/EFL students is that they have been taught to put stress on the content word. Therefore, they tend to stress the head verb rather than the particle (Dickerson 1994):

> *I planñed to tuŕn it doẃn.

MEANING OF ENGLISH PHRASAL VERBS

THE PRODUCTIVITY AND IDIOMATICITY OF PHRASAL VERBS

Certain particles such as *over, off, up, out, down, away,* and *back* can readily form phrasal verbs by combining with common verbs such as *be, come, go, do, make, take, put* and *give.* Phrasal verbs are a highly productive lexical category in English. Indeed, Bolinger (1971:xi) refers to the constant new coinage of phrasal verbs as "an outpouring of lexical creativeness that surpasses anything else in our language."

However, we have no way of knowing in advance exactly which verb will join with which particle to form a new phrasal verb. Furthermore, there is also a certain unpredictability as to what the meaning of a new phrasal verb will be since many of them are noncompositional or idiomatic—their meanings are different from what combining the meaning of the verb with the meaning of the particle would lead you to expect. For example, knowing the meaning of *run* and the meaning of *out* doesn't provide much of a clue to the meaning of their combination in a phrasal verb where *to run out* means "to exhaust." To make matters worse, what might appear to be its antonym, *run in,* has one completely unrelated meaning of "to send to jail" when it is separated.

> I am going to run him in for violating his parole.

One pedagogical strategy resulting from the apparently hopeless task of deciphering the meaning of phrasal verbs has been to ask ESL/EFL students to commit to memory long lists of such verbs along with their meanings. Fortunately, this is not the only answer. There is some systematicity in how meaning is represented in phrasal verbs, and to exploring this, we now turn.

SEMANTIC CATEGORIES OF PHRASAL VERBS

First of all, the systematicity that does exist becomes easier to perceive when phrasal verbs are not treated monolithically. At least three categories of phrasal verbs can be discerned: literal, aspectual, and idiomatic.

Literal Phrasal Verbs

The first category is comprised of verbs that appear to be a combination of a verb and a directional PrepP. Nevertheless, for pedagogical purposes, we will classify them as phrasal verbs because they function syntactically like verb-particle constructions. Since the particle retains its prepositional meaning, the result is a phrasal verb whose meaning is fully compositional (Jackendoff 1997). Some examples of literal phrasal verbs are: *sit down, stand up, hand out, take down, carry out, throw away, climb up, fall down, pass through*. These should not be especially difficult for ESL/EFL students to comprehend and to produce.

Aspectual Phrasal Verbs

The second category is one where the meaning is not as transparent, but it is not idiomatic either. This category consists of verbs to which certain particles contribute consistent aspectual meaning. (Recall our discussion of the aspectual meaning of verbs, such as of accomplishment and activity verbs in Chapter 3, and of aspect, e.g., punctual versus continuous in Chapter 7.) This category in turn can be subdivided into a number of semantic classes, depending on the semantic contribution of the particle.[6]

- Inceptive (to signal a beginning state)

   John took off.

   (Others: *set out, start up*)

- Continuative (to show that the action continues)

   —use of *on* and *along* with activity verbs

   Her speech ran on and on.
   Hurry along now.

   (Others: *carry on, keep on, hang on, come along, play along*)

   —use of *away* with activity verbs with the nuance that the activity is "heedless"

   They danced the night away.

   (Others: *work away, sleep away, fritter away*)

   —use of *around* with activity verbs to express absence of purpose

   They goofed around all afternoon.

   (Others: *mess around, play around, travel around*)

   —use of *through* with activity verbs to mean from beginning to end

   She read through her lines in the play for the audition.

   (Others: *think through, skim through, sing through*)

- Iterative (use of *over* with activity verbs to show repetition)

    He did it over and over again until he got it right.

    (Others: *write over, think over, type over*)

- Completive (uses particles *up, out, off,* and *down* to show that the action is complete)

    —turns an activity verb into an accomplishment

    He drank the milk up.

    (Others: *burn down, mix up, wear out, turn off, blow out*)

    —reinforces the sense of goal orientation in an accomplishment verb

    He closed the suitcase up.

    (Others: *wind up, fade out, cut off, clean up*)

    —adds durativity to a punctual achievement verb

    He found out why they were missing.

    (Others: *check over, win over, catch up*)

In short, there is some consistency of meaning for certain particles. Nonetheless, we should also acknowledge that even here ESL/EFL students can have problems. For example, *burn up* and *burn down* are not antonyms. *Up* has a positive "goal completion" meaning versus *down* or *out*, which have a more negative "complete extinction" meaning (O'Dowd, personal communication). And even if the aspectual particles signal certain meanings consistently, they cannot be assigned freely to any verb. Certain aspectual particles co-occur with certain verbs. *Fade out* is acceptable, but **fade up* is not (Brinton 1988:182). This brings us to the last category—noncompositional, or idiomatic, phrasal verbs.

Idiomatic Phrasal Verbs

As we have been saying, many phrasal verbs are idiomatic, such as *chew out, tune out, catch up, put off*. It seems difficult, if not impossible, to figure out the meaning of the verb by combining the separate meanings of its parts. This is not to say that the situation is hopeless, however. Stauffer (1996) makes the point that native speakers coin novel phrasal verbs and can understand phrasal verbs that they have never before encountered because they understand the underlying logic of the language. For example, earlier we contrasted a phrase with a verb + preposition sequence *run up the hill* with one with a phrasal verb, *run up the bill*. Stauffer demonstrates how in each sentence *run* contributes a sense of motion entailing change and *up* contributes the meaning of higher vertical direction on some path. When *run* and *up* occur together with what appears to be an incompatible object since it is [– place] (i.e., *the bill*), the listener can use logic to infer that if one is running up a bill and something is going to change, then what is going to change is the amount of money. Since the direction is up, it means that the amount of money will increase.

Pelli's (1976) statistical analysis of 14,021 verb-particle constructions has shown that the vast majority rely at least in part on the literal spatial or aspectual meaning of the particle. Thus, it would behoove teachers to guide their ESL/EFL students through some "idiomatic" phrasal verbs by analyzing their component parts and then looking for a logical relationship within a specific context.[7]

POLYSEMOUS PHRASAL VERBS

A final point concerning the meaning of phrasal verbs is that as with other verbs, phrasal verbs can be polysemous. A verb such as *check out*, for instance, can have many meanings. A partial inventory might include:

1. I need to check out by 1 P.M.
2. I went to the library to get a book, but someone had already checked it out.
3. Be sure to check it out before you buy it.
4. Check it out!
5. If you have fewer than 10 items, you can check out in the express lane.

While the meanings of some of these verbs are related, they illustrate the point of the polysemy. Furthermore, they show how the two-word sequence can be literal, aspectual, or idiomatic. Just as one form can have many meanings, we know that it is also possible to have more than one form with the same or similar meanings. This brings us to the question of use.

THE USE OF PHRASAL VERBS

REGISTER

Level of Formality

When we discussed matters of form, you learned that the verb substitution test could be used to identify phrasal verbs. Indeed, although like the other tests it is not failproof, many phrasal verbs do have single-verb counterparts, words derived from Latin.[8] One factor that makes English speakers prefer phrasal verbs such as *put off, call off*, and *show up* to their Latinate counterparts[9] *postpone, cancel*, and *arrive*—is presumably a question of register. As we indicated in the introduction to this chapter, phrasal verbs are common in informal registers, although not completely absent from formal discourse (Cornell 1985).

Field

Another use of the term register is relevant here. As we saw in Chapter 2, register can also refer to the social activity in which the language is being used and what is being talked about. Certain phrasal verbs are associated with a particular field for which there are no concise alternatives. For instance, *check out* in example 1 above will likely be understood to mean check out of a hotel room. It would be difficult to describe the same action using any other verb. A paraphrase of *check out* in this context might be that "upon leaving a hotel, I have to go to the front desk, give the clerk my key, and pay my bill." No other verb exists that has this precise meaning.

Conversely, airline personnel often favor Latinate verbs over phrasal verbs, perhaps to assist nonnative speakers of English comprehend announcements. For instance, in the days when cigarette smoking was permitted on all airplanes, passengers were requested to "extinguish all smoking material," prior to landing, rather than the more common "put out your cigarette." Thus, the field-specific use of the term register is pertinent in explaining the use or non-use of phrasal verbs in certain contexts.

THE ISSUE OF PHRASAL VERB SEPARABILITY

Principle of Dominance Revisited

Erteschik-Shir's (1979) principle of dominance, which we discussed with regard to indirect objects in Chapter 19, applies to account for when separable phrasal verbs require that an NP direct object intervene between the verb and particle. If the direct object is a pronoun, its referent has already been made clear in the discourse context, and it would therefore be nondominant. By virtue of its nondominance, it does not occupy the final position in the sentence if this can be avoided, and thus a pronoun direct object is put between the verb and its particle.

> He poured out his heart.　(direct object is a noun—either order is
> He poured his heart out.　syntactically possible)

> He poured it out.　(direct object is a pronoun—*it* must be placed
> *He poured out it.　between the verb and particle)

On the other hand, if the direct object contains a significant amount of new, complex, or unpredictable information, its insertion between the verb and the particle would interrupt the cognitive unity of the verb and particle and make processing very difficult.

> ?He poured a brand new can of green paint that was on sale out.

Thus, if the direct object is not a pronoun, and especially if it is a long and elaborate NP, it would occupy the more dominant position after the particle. You will recall that this is the conventional position for new, discourse-salient information.

> He poured out a brand new can of green paint that was on sale.

Of course if the direct object is not dominant, then the particle can occupy the dominant position.

> He cried his eyes out.

The ability of the particle to occupy this position is in keeping with the fact that it can bear primary stress. Phrasal verbs thus afford English speakers the opportunity to put part of the verb into end-focus position. Such syntactic flexibility does not exist for Latinate verbs where all the semantic features are conflated into a single word (O'Dowd, personal communication).

Sentences with Separable Phrasal Verbs, Direct and Indirect Objects

We also noted in Chapter 19 that indirect objects that are nondominant are likely to precede direct objects. In the following, the indirect object—*the country singer*—marked by the definite article as having already been introduced into the discourse, is nondominant.

> The Mayor of Nashville gave the country singer a tour of the city.

What happens when the direct object and indirect object occur in a sentence with a separable phrasal verb? As you might expect, the order of particle, direct object, and indirect object depends on the dominance of the objects.

If the indirect object is dominant, then the sentence could occur with the particle directly following the verb and the indirect object in sentence-final position:

> John paid back his loan to the bank.

To reinforce the dominance of the indirect object, the direct object could be followed by the particle, separating the direct and indirect objects:

> John paid his loan back to the bank.

If, on the other hand, the direct object is the dominant NP, then the order would be:

> John paid the bank back his loan.

It is not likely that the verb and its particle would occur contiguously in such a sentence because it would be in conflict with the fact that the indirect object is nondominant:

> ?John paid back the bank his loan.

Finally, it is possible to have a sentence order in which the particle follows both the direct and the indirect objects:

> John paid the bank his loan back.

Here the direct object, *his loan,* is more dominant than the indirect object, *the bank,* but *his loan* is still less dominant than when it was in sentence-final position. It's the particle *back;* which is in sentence-final position, and therefore dominant.

In short, while there is nothing wrong with the rule that says that if the direct object is a pronoun it goes between verb and the particle, it is simply incomplete and offers no explanation for why the object should be placed in this position. Furthermore, it offers no explanation for why one word order is preferred over another when there is a syntactic choice—that is, when the direct object is a noun. We now know that there is a reason for the rule and a greater generalization to be made. The rule is not arbitrary, but rather it reflects the higher-order principle regarding the ordering of constituents with different information status: when an object is nondominant, it will be placed between the verb and particle of a separable phrasal verb.

CONCLUSION

Phrasal verbs are not unique to English, but they are different enough from verbs in many languages of the world, and common enough in English, to pose a significant learning challenge. Perhaps the most challenging dimension is in the meaning, for while there is some semantic systematicity, there is still enough idiomaticity to cause difficulty for ESL/EFL students. Furthermore, the meaning of idiomatic phrasal verbs is not only obscure, it is often deceptive because while one expects to be able to figure out the meaning because the words look so familiar, knowing the meaning of the parts does not necessarily aid comprehension. In other words, part of the challenge of phrasal verbs is recognizing when you are dealing with compositional as opposed to noncompositional meaning.

ESL/EFL students will also have to make appropriate choices when it comes to the dimension of use—when to use a phrasal verb versus a single-word verb and when to split the particle from its verb.

TEACHING SUGGESTIONS

1. Form/Meaning. Many teachers like to begin to introduce the concept of phrasal verbs using Total Physical Response. Giving commands such as *stand up, turn around, turn on the light, turn off the light, go back to your chair, sit down,* and so forth will get students used to the fact that certain verbs in English are composed of two forms, and the exercise will have students begin to associate meaning with certain common forms.

2. Form/Meaning. Certain routines can be pantomimed in which a number of different phrasal verbs can be incorporated. The teacher reads the routine the first time and mimes the actions with the students. Later, the students can give the routine and mime it. Here are two examples:

Morning Routine:
My alarm goes off at 6 A.M. I wake up. I turn off my alarm. I stretch in bed and then I get up. I go to my closet and take out my slippers. I put them on . . .

Telephone Routine:
I want to call up my classmate. I look up her number in the telephone book and I write it down. I pick up the receiver and I dial the number. The line is busy so I hang up. I will call back later.

3. Form/Meaning. Prepare 20 verb cards and 20 particle cards (some can be repeats) for each small group of students. Have the students shuffle the verb cards and place them face down on a desk or table. Then they should do the same for the particle cards. The first student in each group turns over one verb card and one particle card. If there is a phrasal verb match, the student should give a sentence using the phrasal verb to show that the student knows its meaning. If there is no match, the student should say that. Students take turns turning over two cards at a time and helping each other decide if a match has been made and what the meaning and syntactic properties of the match are.

4. Meaning. Margaret Olin suggests creating a "phrasal verb wall." Whenever the class or an individual student discovers a new phrasal verb, someone should write the phrasal verb on a chart and indicate whether it is transitive/intransitive, separable/inseparable. Next, a picture should be drawn illustrating its meaning. Finally, a sentence in which it is used should be added. The chart should be mounted on the wall (or on a long roll of paper if the teacher is more mobile) and added to throughout the term.

5. Meaning. Drehmel (1997) reports that one of her Swiss friends once remarked that "English is such an easy language. All you have to know is the word *get.*" Intrigued by this observation, Drehmel wrote a passage entitled "*Gotcha.*" It begins thus:

> *This morning I got up at 7 A.M. After getting showered and shaved, I got dressed. Then I got my own breakfast since none of my roommates had gotten back from vacation yet. . . .*

Not all the uses of *get* involve phrasal verbs, of course. However, Drehmel's suggestion that students try to rewrite the passage without *get* gives students an opportunity to learn which do and which don't.

6. Meaning. Ivins (1986) has a good way to practice the literal and aspectual meaning of certain particles. The teacher makes a grid with five verbs along the side and five particles along the top.

	on	out	up	away	off
take					
put					
get					
turn					
give					

Students have to make up sentences for every phrasal verb combination possible.

Then, they should see if they can figure out the underlying literal or aspectual meaning of the particles.

7. Use. Linnea Henry and Lauren Parker have created a dialogue that uses forms that are accurate and meaningful but are not what a native speaker of English would probably say. The students are asked to first listen to the dialogue and then to read it, rewriting the verbs so that they are more appropriate for conversational English. Here is our adaptation of their dialogue.

> *Linnea*: Hey, Lauren, I heard that guy finally asked you for a date.
> *Lauren*: Yeah, well, actually, Pam arranged the meeting.
> *Linnea*: How did it go?
> *Lauren*: Well, first he telephoned me at 8 in the morning, and it was necessary for me to leave my bed. I was quite annoyed. It was Saturday morning. Then he said he wanted to have a date with me that night.
> *Linnea*: So, what happened?
> *Lauren*: Well, he was supposed to arrive at 7, but he didn't. He stumbled when he entered. I think he may have been drinking. He came an hour late because he said that his car had stopped working. Then he said there was no more gas in it.
> *Linnea*: I would have abandoned him.
> *Lauren*: Yeah. I told him to leave. I said that I couldn't take any more.

8. Use. In order to give students practice with the constraints governing verb-particle separability, Riggenbach and Samuda (1997) suggest asking students to read items in which the particle is sometimes correctly placed vis-a-vis the verb and sometimes isn't. When the particle is in the wrong position, students are to circle the particle and to draw an arrow to show its correct position. For example:

> Last June, after school was over, I decided to clean up my office. I had been putting off it for as long as I could. I started with my filing cabinets. I threw all the papers I had been keeping since graduate school out.

EXERCISES

Test your understanding of what has been presented.

1. Provide original example sentences to illustrate the following terms. Underline the pertinent word(s) in your examples:
   a. verb + preposition
   b. transitive phrasal verb
   c. intransitive phrasal verb
   d. separable phrasal verb
   e. inseparable phrasal verb
   f. phrasal verb plus preposition
   g. literal phrasal verb
   h. aspectual phrasal verb
   i idiomatic phrasal verb
   j. phrasal verb that is always separated

2. Give tree diagrams for the following sentences:
   a. Graeme warmed the soup up.
   b. Anne puts up with murder.
   c. Deidre brought the cart back to the market.
   d. Rachel looked up the tree.

3. Explain why the following sentences are ungrammatical or, at least, awkward.
   a. *We called our neighbors on.
   b. *I looked the report that Phyllis wrote in Dallas last week over.

    c. *I gave back Larry the money.
    d. ?He showed just as all the work was done.
    e. ?Amber placed back the things that had fallen down from the shelf.

Test your ability to apply what you know.

4. If your students produce the following sentences, what errors have they made? How will you make them aware of the errors, and what exercises will you prepare to correct the errors?
    a. *Donna can't put up the noise anymore.
    b. ?We discontinued our engagement.
    c. *After two hours the candle had burned off.
    d. *Kim worked out her muscles at the gym.
    e. *The child ate up it.

5. Why is the term "two-word" verb somewhat inaccurate?

6. Apply the syntactic tests in this chapter to the following sentences to determine if the verb + "P" is a phrasal verb or a verb + preposition.

> When we *got to* the station, the train had already left.
> My brother and I always *fought over* the prize in the box of cereal.

7. In the last chapter, we contrasted the prepositions of English with the postpositions of other languages like Japanese and Korean. Consider the following examples. Is it really accurate to say that English has no postpositions? Explain your answer.

> Bonnie ran over the field.
> Bonnie ran the field over.

8. Make up a routine like the two examples we gave in Teaching Suggestion 2, which takes place at the library.

9. We gave *check out* as an example of a verb that really has no single verb paraphrase in its use in a hotel context. Can you think of any other phrasal verbs that have no single verb counterparts?

BIBLIOGRAPHY

References

Bolinger, D. (1971). *The Phrasal Verb in English*. Cambridge, Mass: Harvard University Press.
Brinton, L. (1988). *The Development of English Aspectual Systems*. Cambridge: Cambridge University Press.
Clark, R. (1995). "Course Materials for English Applied Linguistics." School for International Training, Spring Term.
Cornell, A. (1985). "Realistic Goals in Teaching and Learning Phrasal Verbs." *International Review of Applied Linguistics in Language Teaching* 23: 4, 269–280.
Dickerson, W. (1994). "Discourse Stress and Phrasal Verbs." *Ideal* 7: 56–66.
Drehmel, C. (1997). "*Gotcha.*" *TESOL Journal* 6:4, 30.
Erteschik-Shir, N. (1979). "Discourse Constraints on Dative Movement." In T. Givón (ed.), *Syntax and Semantics* (vol. 12: *Discourse and Syntax*). New York: Academic Press.

Fraser, J. B. (1976). *The Verb-Particle Combination in English.* New York: Academic Press.

Hopper, P., and S. Thompson (1984). "The Discourse Basis for Lexical Categories in Universal Grammar." *Language* 60:4, 703–752.

Ivins, K. (1986). "A Communicative Approach to Teaching Phrasal Verbs." Independent Professional Project, School for International Training.

Jackendoff, R. (1997). "Twistin' the Night Away." *Language* 73:3, 534–559.

O'Dowd, E. (1994). "Prepositions and Particles in English: A Discourse-Based, Unifying Account." Ph.D. dissertation, University of Colorado.

Pelli, M. (1976). *Verb-Particle Constructions in English: A Study Based on American Plays from the End of the 18th Century to the Present.* Zurich, Switzerland: Francke Verlag Berne.

Riggenbach, H., and V. Samuda (1997). *Grammar Dimensions.* Book 2 (2d ed.). Boston, Mass.: Heinle & Heinle.

Stauffer, D. (1996). "Phrasal Verbs." A paper presented at the XXIII MEXTESOL National Convention. Zacatecas, Mexico.

Suggestions for Further Reading

For a diachronic view of phrasal verbs, see:

Martin, P. (1990). *The Phrasal Verb: Diachronic Development in British and American English.* Ph.D. dissertation, Columbia University.

For reference works dealing with phrasal verbs as well as prepositions, consult:

Cambridge International Dictionary of Phrasal Verbs. 1997. Cambridge: Cambridge University Press.

Courtney, R. (1983). *Longman Dictionary of Phrasal Verbs.* London: Longman.

Crowell, T. (1960). *A Glossary of Phrases with Prepositions.* Englewood Cliffs, N.J.: Prentice-Hall.

Dixson, R. (1983). *Essential Idioms in English.* Englewood Cliffs, N.J.: Prentice-Hall.

Heaton, J. B. (1982). *Prepositions and Adverbial Particles.* London: Longman.

Hill, L. A. (1968). *Prepositions and Adverbial Particles.* London: Oxford University Press.

Hook, J. N. (1981). *Two-Word Verbs in English.* New York: Harcourt Brace Jovanovich.

MacArthur, T., and B. Atkins (1976). *Dictionary of English Phrasal Verbs and Their Idioms.* London: Collins.

Meyer, G. (1975). *A Dictionary of Verb-Preposition Phrases in American English.* The Hague: Mouton.

Moore, D. (1985). *Getting on with Phrasal Verbs.* Oxford: Basil Blackwell.

Reeves, G. (1975). *Idioms in Action.* Rowley, Mass.: Newbury House.

For another work that discusses information status and separability, see:

Chen, P. (1986). "Discourse and Particle Movement in English." *Studies in Language* 10:1, 79–95.

For teaching suggestions, see:

Danielson, D., and P. Porter (1990). *Using English: Your Second Language* (2d ed.) Englewood Cliffs, N.J.: Prentice Hall Regents.

Gunn, C. (1997). "Defining the Challenge of Teaching Phrasal Verbs." ThaiTESOL Bulletin 10: 2, 52–61.

Riggenbach, H., and V. Samuda (1997). *Grammar Dimensions.* Book 2 (2d ed.). Boston, Mass.: Heinle & Heinle.

ENDNOTES

1. The Germanic languages include English, German, Dutch, Flemish, and the Scandinavian languages. Some Bantu languages apparently also have phrasal verbs (Paul Schachter, personal communication).

2. Others have tried to accommodate the overlap among adverbs, prepositions, and particles by referring to a certain word that follows the verb as an "adprep" (Bolinger 1971), a "prepticle" (Clark 1995), and even just a "P" (O'Dowd 1994).

3. Sometimes a phrasal verb can be used both transitively and intransitively with different meanings, e.g.:

> Barbara passed out the papers. (distributed)
> Maxine passed out. (fainted)

It is best to consider such homophonous items as two different phrasal verbs with two separate lexical entries.

4. Although the overwhelming majority of phrasal verbs taking prepositions are intransitive, there are also a few idiomatic transitive phrasal verbs that take prepositions where the direct object pronoun *it* intervenes between the verb and the particle, e.g.:

> She *put* it *over on* him. (= She deceived/fooled him.)
> I'll *make* it *up to* you. (= I'll return the favor/good deed.)

5. This test refers to the passivization of direct objects. We know from Chapter 19 that it is possible for objects of prepositions that are indirect objects to be subjects of passive sentences:

> Dan's organization was awarded the contract.

6. We have drawn from the following sources to compile this list: Fraser (1976), Brinton (1988), O'Dowd (1994), and Jackendoff (1997).

7. Only 6 percent of Pelli's verb-particle sequences were classed in the idiomatic group. All the others were semantically recoverable as compositional sequences.

8. Of course, Latinate verbs are not true synonyms. Neither, for that matter, are other verb + adverb sequences. As we saw in the discussion of the meaning of phrasal verbs, the particle often connotes some aspectual sense. For instance, in *check out* in sentence 3 above, the particle conveys a sense of goal orientation (the goal being the speaker's satisfaction), which is lost in a paraphrase like *examine* or even the verb + adverb sequence *check thoroughly*.

9. Of course, as O'Dowd (1994) shows, the Latinate verbs themselves are frequently made up of the same sort of morphological composition as verb-particle combinations. For instance, one of the paraphrases of the phrasal verb *check out* might be "examine," which in and of itself carries the Latin directional preposition *ex-* ("out of," "from") as its prefix.

NONREFERENTIAL *IT* AND *THERE* AS SUBJECTS

INTRODUCTION

You have already seen that the forms that we treat in this chapter fill other functions. In Chapter 16, *it* was called a personal pronoun, the same form being used for both subject and objects:

> A: Has anyone seen the newspaper?
> B: The last time I saw *it, it* was in the living room.

In Chapter 21, we referred to *there* as a pro-adverb, since it can be a paraphrase of another type of adverbial, namely a prepositional phrase.

> A: Where exactly did you see it?
> B: (Pointing) I saw it *there* (on the coffee table).

While the forms themselves, then, may not be new, their meanings and uses as nonreferential subjects are different and, therefore, warrant a special treatment of their own.

These subjects have gone by many names: nonreferential, dummy, empty, and so forth. What these terms have tried to capture is that, unlike the referential *it* and *there* we have just exemplified, these subjects appear to have no clearly definable antecedent.

> It's raining. (What is the *it* that is raining? What does *it* refer to?)
> There's a lot of noise here. (Where is *there*? What does *there* refer to?)

Without a clearly identifiable referent, *it* and *there* are free to serve very useful purposes in English. Consequently, they occur frequently.

CHALLENGES FOR ESL/EFL STUDENTS

Despite their common occurrence, nonreferential *it* and *there* can cause difficulties for ESL/EFL students. Speakers of Spanish and Italian, for instance, who speak languages that do not require a surface subject the way English does (for every nonimperative and nonelliptical sentence), may produce sentences that are ungrammatical in English, such as the following:

> *Is raining.

Speakers of Cantonese might translate literally from their language into English and say:

> *Rain is plentiful.

Speakers of topic-comment languages—Japanese, for example—may preserve the topic-comment structure of their native language and instead of producing sentences with nonreferential *there*, such as

> There are 27 students in Taro's school.

produce sentences such as:

> *Taro's school is 27 students.
> *Taro's school students are 27.
> *In Taro's school students are 27.

(Examples from Sasaki 1990)

Another strategy speakers of Japanese employ is to use the English verb *have*, which allows for the topic-comment word order of Japanese while generating well-formed sentences in English. But even this type of sentence is not as acceptable as a sentence with a nonreferential *there* in subject position.

> ?Taro's school has 27 students.
> There are 27 students in Taro's school.

Another problem for speakers of topic-comment languages is the formation of "pseudo-relatives" (Yip 1995). It has long been known that Chinese students use the nonreferential *there* frequently (Schachter and Rutherford 1979:3). Many of these sentences with nonreferential *there* subjects appear to be missing a relative pronoun.

> *There were lot of events happen in my country.

It is understandable why an ESL/EFL teacher might be inclined to correct sentences like this by supplying the relative pronoun *that*, in addition to making other modifications.

> There were a lot of events that happened in my country.

However, as Rutherford (1983) shows, such ungrammatical learner utterances do not stem from omission of the relative pronoun, but rather conform to Chinese grammar. The *there* is presumably seen by learners to correspond to a topic introducer in Mandarin Chinese, which goes before a subject.

Then, too, the fact that English has two nonreferential subjects, *it* and *there*, is a potential source of confusion to those ESL/EFL students who have no such structure—or to those whose languages have only one such form, the meaning of which may overlap with the meanings of English *it* and *there*. This state of affairs sometimes results in students producing errors such as

> *There is very nice in Korea.

Any similarities that the two nonreferential subjects share are far outweighed by many obvious differences: *it* and *there* occur in different contexts and have different meanings.

Finally, nonnative speakers of English struggle with matters of use, such as when it is appropriate to say

> There's a book on the table.

rather than

> A book is on the table.

By now you know to look for a use difference between these last two sentences. The guiding principle we follow in this book is that if there are two forms in a language with the same propositional meaning, there must be a difference in their use. We therefore explore in this chapter when *there* is used and when it is not.

Because *it* and *there* overlap only in the fact that they both have the same syntactic function, we depart from our usual means of organizing chapters and instead treat each of these separately.

NONREFERENTIAL *IT*

FORM

The form of the nonreferential *it* is fairly straightforward. Since nonimperative sentences require a subject in English, *it* fills this function. This form therefore acts as a subject, always taking a singular verb, usually *be*:

> *It* was a very blustery autumn day.
> What time is *it*?

MEANING

Chafe (1970) and Bolinger (1977) refer to the nonreferential *it* as "ambient." Ambient *it* is grammatically necessary, but lexically vague. The meaning of ambient *it* derives from the rest of the sentence, which makes it clear to the listener/reader what is being discussed. It is found commonly in expressions of:

- Time
  It is six-thirty.   It is early.   It will be my birthday.
  It is August 28.   It is Wednesday.   It was 1880.

- Distance
  It is about 100 miles to Boston.   It is not far to Portland.
  It is just two stops on the Metro.

- Weather
  It is cloudy.   It's getting dark.   It's 20 degrees!
  It is freezing.   It's going to snow.   It's windy.

- Environment   It is never crowded at the Pontiac Hotel.
  It gets a little rowdy on the ninth floor.

At first glance, these *its* may appear to be referential. It is true that we could ascribe noun antecedents to some of these. We could say that in the sentence

> It is six-thirty.

the *it* is a personal pronoun replacing the noun phrase *the time*:

> The time is six-thirty.

However, this analysis won't explain the *it* in an associated *wh*-question:

> What time is it?
> *What time is the time?

And the same anomaly holds for other corresponding questions; for example:

> It/The day is Saturday.   What day is it?
> *What day is the day?

Moreover, it is impossible to find referents for some cases of *it* above:

> It is raining.

What is raining? (?The clouds are raining. *The rain is raining.[1] ?The weather is raining.)

> It gets a little noisy, especially when everyone is warming up.

What gets noisy? (The room gets a little noisy. ?The space gets a little noisy. ?The ambience gets a little noisy.)

Therefore, for both these reasons—first, the fact that unlike the personal pronoun *it*, nonreferential *it* requires no antecedent or anaphoric referent, and second, there is often no conceivable referent for the *it*— linguists conclude that the nonreferential *it* takes its meaning from the ambience/environment in which it occurs. "We can therefore acknowledge the rationale for calling *it* a dummy—its meaning is too unspecific to articulate, and speakers have no clear conception of its referent. But that precisely is its crucial semantic property . . . ." (Langacker 1991:377). By virtue of *it* being a linguistic chameleon, it is extremely versatile in that this form can be identified with many different aspects of the linguistic or situational context.[2]

USE

As we have seen, nonreferential *it* occurs in a number of simple statements and questions in English dealing with time, distance, weather, and other environmental features. Use of nonreferential *it* allows such a question or statement to be shorter and less redundant than it would be if content nouns such as "time" and "weather" were used instead. Note that certain nouns do exist to deal with these notions, which, when used, make a statement more formal or more precise.

> The time is (now) 10 o'clock.
> The weather today will be fair and cool.

Such formal statements are sometimes used in television or radio broadcasts. The issue of when speakers of English use a content noun like *time* or *weather* versus when they use nonreferential *it* would be a good topic for a future research study.

There is another nonreferential *it* that is used in subject position as well, one that has an important discourse management function:

> It is human to err; it is divine to forgive.

However, we prefer to call this *it* by another name, the anticipatory *it*, because its referent is established cataphorically—that is, by something that follows: in this case, the clause that comes at the end of the sentence. This *it*, therefore, has a different function, one that we address in Chapter 31 on complementation.

NONREFERENTIAL *THERE*

FORM

As we mentioned earlier, you have encountered *there* before as a pro-adverb. As a pro-adverb it can be used anaphorically (*Let's go to London. There we can see the crown jewels.*) and deictically—its meaning is understood within the context in which it occurs. One of the manifestations of this deictic meaning is that it is usually accompanied by some gesture, such as finger pointing. It is also stressed.

THERE is the little boy who looks after the sheep.

Deictic *there* calls attention to a location relative to the speaker. Contrast deictic *there* with the unstressed *there* in the next sentence.

There is a little boy who looks after the sheep; his name is Little Boy Blue.

The *there* in this second sentence does not refer to any specific location. It is not accompanied by any typical gesture, and it does not bear stress; in fact, its vowel may well be reduced [ər]. The *there* in the second sentence is called the nonreferential *there*.

In addition to its phonological and nonverbal differences, the nonreferential *there* has certain syntactic properties that the deictic *there* does not share. One is that the nonreferential *there* is the subject of the clause; the deictic *there* is not. To prove this, we can see that the deictic *there*, since it is an adverb, can be moved to another position in the sentence. This is not true of the nonreferential *there* because as the subject, it is always clause initial:

Deictic *there:* The little boy who looks after the sheep is THERE.
Nonreferential *there:* *A little boy who looks after the sheep is there. (Sequencing the words in this fashion forces a deictic interpretation to the *there;* that is, such an order is not possible with nonreferential *there.*)

Lakoff (1987) offers additional syntactic tests to distinguish the two forms of *there:*

- Question tag test

    Deictic *there:* *There's the little boy who looks after the sheep, isn't there?
    Nonreferential *there:* There is a little boy who looks after the sheep, isn't there?

Recall that question tags are made with the subject of a sentence. Only the nonreferential *there* can be used in the question tag, demonstrating that it is indeed a subject.

- Negation test

    Deictic *there:* *There isn't the little boy who looks after the sheep.
    Nonreferential *there:* There isn't a little boy who looks after the sheep.

Only sentences with nonreferential *there* can be negated.

- Deictic *here* test (substitute *here* for *there*)

    Deictic *there:* Here's the little boy who looks after the sheep.
    Nonreferential *there:* *Here's a little boy who looks after the sheep. (forces a deictic interpretation)

Deictic *here* can alternate syntactically with deictic *there*, but not with nonreferential *there.*
There are other tests that could be applied as well. The results of these should suffice to demonstrate that nonreferential *there* is a subject, therefore a noun phrase, not an adverb.

There and Subject-Verb Agreement

As a subject, *there* is followed by a verb, most often the copula verb *be*. In terms of subject-verb agreement, nonreferential *there* is much more problematic than nonreferential *it*, which is always followed by a singular verb. In contrast, in sentences with nonreferential *there* subjects, the verb may be singular or plural depending on the form of the noun phrase following the *be*.

There is a book on the table.
There are two books on the table.

Here is the tree and the derivation for the second sentence.

There are two books on the table.

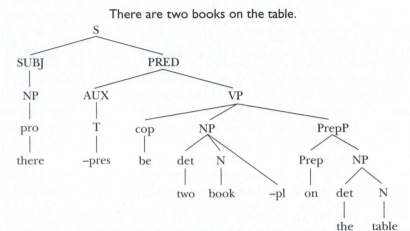

output: there -pres be two book -pl on the table
copy s/t: [with nonreferential *there* in subject position, the person and number of
the NP following the verb is copied onto the tense marker]
there -pres [+3 +pl] be two book -pl on the table
morphology: There are two books on the table.

It is rather strange that the NP following the verb determines the form of the verb in that a basic property of subjects in English is their power to govern the agreement of the verb. The explanation for this phenomenon is that the noun phrase following the verb would have been the subject of the sentence rather than *there* had other considerations not intervened. We discuss these other considerations in the Use section in this chapter. For now, the point is that the NP following the verb is not an object but rather is notionally, although not morphosyntactically, the subject.[3] Sometimes such an NP is referred to as the logical subject, as opposed to the grammatical subject.

To make matters more complex, there is also considerable variation from speaker to speaker with regard to the form of the verb, with many speakers opting for a singular verb when the verb is contracted with *there*, no matter what the number of the following noun is.

There's problems here.

This preference might arise because speakers are treating nonreferential *there* as analogous to nonreferential *it*, which is always followed by a singular verb. In other words, they are copying the number of *there* onto the tense instead of the number of the logical subject. Another explanation is that speakers choose the singular form of the verb due to the awkwardness of articulating two consecutive weak syllables with final "r" sounds, which the choice of contracting the plural form of the verb necessitates.[4]

There're problems here.   (there're = /ðʌrər/)

It may also be the case that *there* and *is* have become fused into a single formula (Breivik 1981). Whatever the reason, in a study of spoken discourse, Celce-Murcia and Hudson (1981) confirmed that *there's* predominates in informal speech, even when a plural noun phrase follows the verb.

Therefore, it is probably unrealistic of ESL/EFL teachers to expect their students to maintain the traditional subject-verb agreement rule in their speech when many native speakers of English ignore it. ESL/EFL students should probably be taught the contrast *there is* versus *there are* since the number-agreement distinction is still expected in formal—

especially written—usage; however, they should also realize that, when speaking, native speakers of English often use *there's* with following plural nouns.[5] Another strategy might be to teach ESL/EFL students to say *there's* instead of *there is* because the contraction definitely makes the lack of agreement more acceptable:

> There's too many term papers for this course.
> ?There is too many term papers for this course.

A related issue, which was discussed in Chapter 4, is that the proximity principle tends to apply when conjoined noun phrases follow *there*, with the result that the verb *be* agrees with the number of the nearest noun phrase rather than the number of both noun phrases combined, which was the older prescriptive agreement rule. This tendency occurs even in writing:

> There are two boys and a girl in the room. First conjunct is plural.
> There is a girl and two boys in the room. First conjunct is singular.
> ?There are a girl and two boys in the room. Traditional prescriptive agreement now sounds strange to many native speakers of English.

Verbs Other Than *Be* with Nonreferential *There*

Even though *be* is by far the most frequent verb following nonreferential *there*, it is by no means the only one. Other groups of intransitive verbs can occur with nonreferential *there*:

- Verbs of existence or position: *exist, live, dwell, stand, lie, remain,* etc.

> There exist several alternatives.
> At the edge of the forest there dwelt a troll.

- Event verbs that describe something happening, developing, or materializing: *develop, arise, appear, emerge, ensue, happen, occur,* etc.

> There arose a conflict.
> There ensued a dispute.

- Verbs of motion or direction: *come, go, walk, run, fly, approach,* etc.

> There came three suspicious-looking men down the street.
> Along the river there walked an old woman.

The Use of the Indefinite Determiner with the Logical Subject

You may have noticed, in the example sentences beginning this discussion of *there*, that the only morphological feature that distinguished the sentence with deictic *there* from the sentence with nonreferential *there* was the choice of determiner before *little*.

> There's the little boy who looks after the sheep. (deictic *there*)
> There's a little boy who looks after the sheep. (nonreferential *there*)

The indefinite article in the sentence with the nonreferential *there* indicates that the noun following the verb—that is, the logical subject, *boy*—is not specific. Some reference grammars state that only logical subjects with indefinite determiners occur with nonreferential *there*. As a matter of fact, all the example sentences we have presented thus far in our chapter agree with this condition. As you will see a little later, however, it is possible to use the definite article with the logical subject. Nevertheless, this "rule" requiring use of the indefinite determiner with the logical subject provides a clue as to the meaning of the nonreferential *there*.

MEANING OF NONREFERENTIAL *THERE*

Although we introduced the nonreferential *there* by contrasting it with deictic *there*, we should also acknowledge that it is not mere coincidence that the two share a form. Lakoff (1987) invokes the notion of prototypicality to explain the identity of form between deictic and nonreferential *there*. As we saw with spatial prepositions, it is assumed that the deictic or spatial notion of *there* is a core meaning, while the meaning of the nonreferential *there* is an extension of it. As opposed to physical space, the nonreferential *there* designates a mental space in which some entity is to be located. The common use of the indefinite determiner with the logical subject supports the notion that the *there* functions to introduce something into mental awareness (Bolinger 1977); for this reason, it has sometimes been called the *existential there*. Bolinger claims that asserting the location of something or asserting the existence of something are opposite sides of the same coin—i.e., if you locate something, it exists; if something exists, it is located somewhere.

It is clear then, that although *there* is not a content word of the usual order, to call *there* a dummy subject ignores the fact that it does serve a function other than simply filling the subject slot. Also, if *there* merely existed to fill the subject slot, this would leave us with no explanation for why two well-formed sentences, such as the following, exist.

> a. There is a pen on the table.
> b. A pen is on the table.

To answer such a question, we must turn to use.

THE USE OF NONREFERENTIAL *THERE*

The Presence and Absence of *There* Contrasted

- Logical subject in subject position

While Langacker (1991) prefers to say that *there* designates an abstract setting as opposed to some mental space, he concurs that the basic function of a *there* clause is a presentational one; that is, a *there* clause brings an element into awareness. *There* serves as a signal to the addressee to direct his or her attention toward an item of new information (Breivik 1981). The result of *there* being in clause-initial position, then, is that everything that follows the verb can be accorded new information status, including the logical subject. In other words, by using *there* as the subject, the usual distribution of given and new information in a clause can be maintained.

While in some cases, such as with sentence (b) above, the use of *there* may seem syntactially optional,[6] presumably the discourse context would favor one sentence over another in a given instance. For example, one can imagine staging a play and being given stage directions describing a scene, one sentence of which might be "A pen is on the table." If I am on the telephone, on the other hand, and express the need for a writing implement to someone in the room, I would be put off by the use of this marked descriptive sentence. I would find the use of sentence (a), with *there* in subject position, much more appropriate, as the entire predicate gives me the information I am seeking. In other words, the use of *there* may be syntactically optional in certain cases, but it is not discoursally optional.

In fact, in his search of the Survey of English Usage, a corpus of 450,000 words of spoken text and 300,000 words of written texts of modern, educated, British English usage, Brevik (1981) was able to find very few instances of sentences such as (b), where the logical subject with an indefinite determiner occupied subject position. One example he did find occurs in a text describing the interior of a department store selling electronic equipment.

> The first floor houses the real heart of the store—the hi-fi departments—but there is much else here also . . . A headphone bar is also on the first floor.

The last sentence in this text, one that illustrates what we have been calling the stage-direction use, presumes the existence of the first floor and provides one visual detail about it. The clause with *there* after *but* in the text above asserts the existence of something—here *much else,* which is then elaborated on with a concrete detail, the one provided in the last sentence. Sentences like these without *there,* then, appear to be very restricted in use, limited to providing details for a scene whose existence has already been established or can be presupposed.

- Preposed locative adverbials

Although we will have more to say about this in the chapter on adverbials, for now we should note that it is also possible to move a locative prepositional phrase to initial position in a sentence:

> On the table is a pen.

This word order has the effect of treating the logical subject as new information, in the same way that the use of *there* does. This word order is still marked, however, not unlike the stage-direction use. Also, moving a phrase to initial position without *there* can be done only with locative phrases.

> ?This month are a lot of holidays.
> This month there are a lot of holidays.
> There are a lot of holidays this month.

Finally, we should also note that *there* is still syntactically optional when the adverbial locative phrase is preposed:

> On the table is a pen.
> On the table there is a pen.

But *there* is more likely to be used if the logical subject is more abstract:

> ?In the house was no sign of life.
> In the house there was no sign of life.

As Bolinger (1977:96) notes, "The less vividly on stage an action is, the more necessary *there* becomes."

Various Uses of *There*

Since the function of the nonreferential *there* is to focus the listener on what follows the verb, the information status of this part of the clause must somehow be new in the moment; that is, the listener must have been unaware of the referent, or must have forgotten about it and needs to have his or her memory "reactivated" (Chafe 1970). The following uses of *there* fall out from this deduction (based in part on Lakoff 1987):

- Presentational use (introduces a new referent to the discourse, which then becomes the topic):

    There are several alternatives. We could go shopping first and then take in a movie . . .

- Locative use (introduces the logical subject and its location):

    There are several books on the table.
    There used to be a tree behind the garage.

- Ontological use (strongly asserts the existence of something where the verb *exist* can appear instead of *be*, and the main verb bears stress):

    There exist five prime numbers below twelve.
    There is a Santa Claus.[7]

- List:

    A: What is there to see in Tucson?
    B: There's the Sonora Desert Museum, a Saguaro cactus, the Biosphere, a dude ranch . . .

B's reply seems to violate the constraint we mentioned earlier about logical subjects with *there* in subject position needing to take indefinite articles. Rando and Napoli (1978) explain this phenomenon by saying that what is being asserted in such a conversation is the existence of a list, leaving the items on the list free to take definite or indefinite determiners depending on their uniqueness. The way Ward and Birner (1995) explain the use of definite articles here is to say that the speaker is presumably giving the listener new information about things to see in Tucson, so the NPs are still nonspecific to the listener, with the choice of definite or indefinite article determined by the uniqueness of the noun referred to.

- Reminder (Speaker is reminding listener of the existence of someone or something; a verb like *remain* can easily serve this function):

    A: Before we leave on vacation, there remains the problem of what to do with the dog.
    B: Oops. I almost forgot.

A variation of a reminder is when something is acknowledged by the listener as new in the moment:

    A: I feel depressed, and I am not sure why.
    B: I am sorry, but remember, you often feel this way in mid-winter.
    A: Yes. Well, there is that.

In this example, it is not that the link between the season and A's feelings is unprecedented in A's life; it is just that in the moment, A accepts B's explanation as a plausible account for why A is feeling depressed, an explanation that apparently did not occur to A until B raised it. In other words, B's explanation was interpreted by A as new-in-the-moment information, what we earlier noted as a status required of an NP in this position in a sentence with *there* as a subject. The NP itself may be specific, as is *that* above, but what it represents is a new or reactivated awareness to the listener (Abbott 1997; Ward and Birner 1997).

- Narrative use (In narratives, *there* is used to introduce a new element into the narrative, while simultaneously sketching a scene or background to the story):

    There once lived an old woodsman in a little cottage deep in the woods.

With narrative use, it is possible to have an entire VP, not just a verb, precede the logical subject:

> Suddenly, there burst onto the scene the entire volunteer fire department.

For discourse reasons involving the need to elaborate new information, which are now familiar to you, the logical subject cannot be preceded by a lengthy VP unless it itself is of sufficient length.

> ?Suddenly, there burst onto the scene a firefighter.

* Suggestion (Jo Hilder, personal communication)

  > A: Where is he going to sleep?
  > B: Well, there's the couch.

Other Uses of the Definite Determiner with the Logical Subject

Contrary to what some reference grammars indicate, it is further possible to use a definite determiner with the logical subject, even when it is not on a list. Bolinger (1977) and Rando and Napoli (1978) have pointed to the existence of sentences such as the following:

> 1. There's the/a most unusual man standing over there.
> 2. There will soon appear the definitive edition of "Hamlet."
> 3. There never was that problem in Austin.

In each case, however, there is an explanation for the use of definiteness. In the first sentence _the_ or _a_ is used because of an odd fact about certain English superlative adjectives that permit either a definite or indefinite article to be used in such a context to mean "very unusual" (see Chapter 35 for more details). In the second sentence the uniqueness explanation applies (there can only be one "definitive" edition of any work); and, in the third explanation, _that problem_, the _that_ is being used anaphorically to refer to something previously mentioned.

The point of all of this is that it is too simplistic to say that the logical subjects always take indefinite determiners.

There in Oral Discourse

Much of what has been presented in this chapter is a sentence-level analysis. Our treatment would not be complete if we did not also examine the use and distribution of _there_ at a level above the sentence as well. Sasaki (1991) has done so for spoken American English. Sasaki's data are taken from oral transcripts representing three different speech genres: informal conversations, radio show discourse, and oral narratives. Transcripts were analyzed for topic continuity using a modified version of Givón's method (1984) of measuring referential distance. Although there were qualitative differences among the three different genres, the general trends Sasaki observed obtained for all three genres.

* Logical subjects in sentences with _there_ tended to have low topic continuity. They were not previously mentioned. This finding is consonant with our observation that logical subjects represent new information and thus tend to be the topic of subsequent clauses, not previous ones.
* Although the logical subjects introduced specific new information, it was often a subcategory of some previously mentioned topic.
* The elements following the logical subject of nonreferential _there_ sentences were found to have high topic continuity; that is, their central referents had been previously mentioned in the discourse. In this way, the postlogical subject element was

functioning as what Fox (1987) calls an "anchor" or a "linker" between the new topic introduced by the logical subject and the preceding part of the discourse.

Here is an example from Sasaki's data (recorded earlier by Jan Frodesen) to illustrate the third trend as manifest in an interview with a Great Lakes shipping captain:

> Well, the thing is, that when you see the boat at the dock and you see all
> that steel and all that riveting, you think well, *there's* nothing gonna harm
> this boat, and when you're out on a big storm, you're wondering what's
> keeping it all together.

In this extract, we see that the central referent of the postlogical subject element, *this boat* in line 3, connects *the boat* in line 1 to *it* in line 4. It is this postsubject element that contributes to the cohesion of the discourse.

Sasaki's is the only study we know of that examined the use of *there* in oral discourse. There has been much more study of *there* in written discourse, and it is to this research that we turn next.

There in Written Discourse

Huckin and Pesante (1988) examined a corpus of 100,000 words taken from 29 written English texts representing a variety of genres, ranging from reference books to magazines. They found four purposes for *there* clauses in written discourse. The basic function was to assert existence, the other three being more specific extensions from the notion of asserting existence: (1) presenting new information, either as setting a new topic or (2) making isolated topic shifts, and (3) using *there* sentences to summarize.

Ahlers (1991), building on the work of Huckin and Pesante and Sasaki, examined 100 tokens of *there* gathered from 18 sources–undergraduate college readings from a variety of disciplines, as well as other academic writing. Ahlers found that there were two primary ways that *there* functions in academic expository writing: general–particular and listing. The general–particular function is one where a new topic is introduced in a general statement beginning with *there*, which is followed by clauses which offer supporting details or elaboration. Here is an example from Clyde Kluckhohn's *Mirror for Man* taken from Ahlers' data. Prior to this excerpt, Kluckhohn has been discussing various differences among cultures.

> All this does not mean that *there* is no such thing as raw human nature. The members
> of all human groups have about the same biological equipment. All people undergo the
> same poignant life experiences, such as birth, . . .

Kluckhohn makes a generalization with a *there* statement and then provides other details in subsequent supporting statements.

Fully three quarters of the tokens of *there* in Ahlers' data fit into subcategories of the general-to-particular function. The other one quarter of the examples exemplified the listing function, which you have already become familiar with at the sentence level. Here's an example from Ahlers' data of the listing function as the author uses it in discourse to list places in Portugal. This is an example from the Eleanor Perenyi's "Escape to the Past," *Atlantic Monthly,* February 1982, pages 39–42.

> Portugal abounds in old Ritzes. I use the term generically; *there* is a real Ritz in Lisbon,
> a modern one with no atmosphere at all, and we didn't stay at it. Our choice was the
> Avenida Palace, which fills the bill by being very grand (tapestries, red plush, chande-
> liers) and rather shabby. Grander, less shabby, and twice the price is the Infante de
> Sagres at Porto. Its high-Edwardian decor is appropriate to a city where the wine

trade has been so heavily involved with England that *there* is even an English club, founded in 1785 . . .

The final study of written discourse that we shall summarize here is one of research reports published in journal articles (Thomas and Hawes 1994). The authors of this study did not focus exclusively on nonreferential subjects, being more generally interested in the syntactic choices available to writers for making reporting statements. Of the 129 reports they analyzed, approximately 10 percent had nonreferential *it* or *there* as subjects followed by the *be* verb. A reporting statement with *there*, in particular, was used to assert the existence of evidence. It seemed to be used when the writer was submitting evidence of a certain kind in connection with a point he or she was making. These themes co-occurred with nouns like *evidence* and *support*, such as *There is increasing support for the hypothesis.* Here is an example from their data.

> Chronic bronchitic patients do seem to suffer from high levels of psychiatric disorder, and a close liaison between chest physicians and psychiatrists or clinical psychologists may contribute to the effectiveness of patient management. There is some evidence that alleviation of psychiatric symptoms is associated with a reduction of breathlessness.

The first sentence is making a tentative claim by the writer. The writer then brings in evidence in the form of a report as the basis for making the claim. The structure allows the foregrounding of the word *evidence* and the clause qualifying it, so that the relationship between the two sentences—the claim and the supporting evidence—is highlighted.

All of the examples of *it* used in reports are anticipatory *it,* a structure with which we deal in Chapter 31.

CONCLUSION

We have seen that the scope and complexity of sentences with nonreferential subjects is far greater than what most reference grammars would lead us to believe. It has been claimed in some traditional grammars that such forms as nonreferential *it* and *there* are mere fillers, to be avoided in any formal writing. What our investigations in this chapter have suggested instead is that *it* and *there* serve important, albeit unconventional, functions. While they may not be semantically rich themselves, the semantic chameleon nature of nonreferential *it* and the focusing function of nonreferential *there* equip these structures to be important grammatical devices in discourse management. It is not good advice, in our opinon, to tell ESL/EFL students to avoid them in writing.

It is difficult to pinpoint the challenge for these structures in general. Perhaps the greatest challenge lies in the one to which we have devoted the most space—the use of *there*. Teachers have to help ESL/EFL students get beyond simply using the *there* + *be* + NP + LOC construction. It may be the easiest to teach this to beginning-level students, but it is not what is used most. The other general challenge lies in helping students to understand the distinction between these two nonreferential forms, *it* and *there*.

TEACHING SUGGESTIONS

1. Form/Meaning. Ask students to listen to a weather report before coming to class. Ask them to report what they have heard. Alternatively, bring into class a weather report cut out from a local newspaper and guide students in making statements with nonreferential *it* using the weather information.

It was hot yesterday.
It was 80 degrees Farenheit.
It was dry.
It was windy.

2. Form/Meaning. Use a calendar to get students to practice asking and answering questions concerning the day, month, year, and date.

What day is it?	It's Friday.
What month is it?	It's March.
What year is it?	It's 1999.
What is the date?	It's March 19, 1999.

3. Form/Meaning. Bring a map into class and ask students to make statements about distances and travel times.

How far is it from Pittsburgh to Cleveland?	It is about 100 miles.
How long does it take to drive by car?	It takes about two hours.

4. Form. Stevick (1982) offers the following activity. Have students describe a place that has special significance to him or her. As the student describes the scene, he or she places cuisenaire rods on a table to indicate the location of things in the scene. Each statement by the student is repeated by the teacher. If the student makes a grammatical error while describing the scene, the teacher does not correct it but rather repeats the student's statement using the correct form. For example:

S: I am thinking of a place in my hometown. It is the plaza in the middle of the town. It has a big fountain. (The student places a rod down to mark the fountain.)
T: I see. There's a big fountain in the center of the plaza.
S: Yes, and it has bench around the fountain. (The student places rods around the first rod to represent benches.)
T: There are benches around the fountain.

When the student has finished describing the scene, the teacher can repeat the entire description using the rods to recall the various aspects of the scene. At this point, another student can be called upon to describe the same scene. After this, the students can form small groups, with each group having rods and the task of reconstructing and describing the scene.

5. Form. Have students pair off. Each pair of students gets a different picture of a city scene. Only one student in each pair gets to look at it. Identical pictures are placed on a desk at the front of the room. Student A describes the picture to Student B, who has to guess which city it is and then has to run up to the desk at the front of the room and find the picture that Student A has described. Then the roles are reversed. For example:

A: There are skyscrapers. There is a bridge. There is a building next to the water. It is white. It looks like a shell.
B: Is it Sydney?

6. Form/Meaning. Have your students conduct a survey. Shaw and Taylor (1978) suggest one with the signs of the zodiac. After the students have learned each other's astrological signs, they should tally the numbers for each sign and make summary statements. For example:

There are five Capricorns in the class.
There is one Libra.

7. Use. Badalamenti and Henner Stanchina (1997) suggest showing a picture of someone's apartment to a class and then asking students to figure out the characteristics of the apartment dweller. They need to make a claim and support it with evidence. For instance, a student might make the statement:

> S: The person is a tennis player.
> Another student or teacher could ask:
> T: How do you know?
> S: Because there is a tennis racket in the closet.

8. Use. Frodesen and Eyring (1997) suggest giving students different categories such as:

- **a.** types of books you like best
- **b.** things that you think make a good movie or TV program
- **c.** steps for performing a procedure that you know how to do

Students should write a general statement to introduce the topic and then write two or three sentences to develop the particular statements; for example:

> There are three secrets to making good sushi. First, you need the right kind of rice. Second, it is important to use very fresh fish. Third, you need a sharp knife.

9. Use. Kathi Bailey suggests that composing a letter or creating an audiotape to send home after moving to a new place provides a good context for reinforcing the differences between nonreferential *it* and *there*. If the students are of a low level, the letter could be given to them with just the words *it* and *there* missing.

> Dear_____,
> It's raining again today, so I'll take the time to write some letters. My new dorm room is okay. It is pretty noisy here. There are four people living in each room.

EXERCISES

Test your understanding of what has been presented.

1. Provide an original sentence illustrating each of the following terms. Underline the pertinent words.
   - **a.** nonreferential *it*
   - **b.** referential *it*
   - **c.** deictic *there*
   - **d.** nonreferential *there*
   - **e.** ontological use of *there*
   - **f.** narrative use of *there*

2. Why are the following sentences ungrammatical?
   - **a.** *It are four o'clock.
   - **b.** Who's going?
     *There's Harry and I.
   - **c.** There is sunny today.
   - **d.** ?In the month of February are 28 days.

3. An early transformational grammar approach to the existential *there* was to insert *there* in subject position after the logical subject had been moved to a position after the verb.

   > A book is on the table. → There is a book on the table.

   What are some problems with this analysis?

Test your ability to apply what you know.

4. If your students produce the following errors, what errors have they made? How will you make them aware of the errors, and what exercises will you prepare to help your students?

    a. *Is windy.

    b. *A lot of noise is in the street.

    c. *There are many tourists visit there.

    d. ?My family has a lot of people.

    e. *There has been a long time since I have seen you.

5. What is the difference among/between the following sentences:

    a. (i) A ball was in the street.   **b.** (i) The time is nine o'clock.

    　　(ii) In the street was a ball.　　　　　　(ii) It is nine o'clock.

    　　(iii) There was a ball in the street.

6. One of your ESL/EFL students comes to you and says, "I heard an English speaker say, "There's usually a lot of empty rooms on the weekend." The student asks you why the English speaker didn't say "There are . . . ." How will you answer?

7. Lakoff (1987:557) notes that there is a lack of symmetry with regard to the following:

    a. There's a Japanese executive in the waiting room.

    b. A Japanese executive is in the waiting room.

    c. There's a Japanese executive in our company.

    d. *A Japanese executive is in our company.

    Can you figure out why (d) is ungrammatical?

BIBLIOGRAPHY

References

Abbott, B. (1997). "Definiteness and Existentials." *Language* 73:1: 103–108.

Ahlers, E. (1991). "A Discourse Analysis of Nonreferential *There* in Academic Writing." MA thesis in TESL, UCLA.

Badalamenti, V., and C. Henner Stanchina (1997). *Grammar Dimensions*. Book 1 (2d ed.). Boston, Mass.: Heinle & Heinle.

Bolinger, D. (1977). *Meaning and Form*. London and New York: Longman.

Breivik, L. (1981). "On the Interpretation of Existential *There. Language* 57:1, 1–25.

Celce-Murcia, M., and J. K. Hudson (1981). "What '*There*' Is to Subject-Verb Agreement." Paper presented at the annual TESOL Convention, Detroit.

Chafe, W. (1970). *Meaning and the Structure of Language*. Chicago: University of Chicago Press.

Fox, B. (1987). "The Noun Phrase Accessibility Hierarchy Reinterpreted." *Language* 63:4, 856–870.

Frodesen, J., and J. Eyring (1997). *Grammar Dimensions*. Book 4 (2d ed.). Boston, Mass.: Heinle & Heinle.

Givón, T. (1994). "Universals of Discourse Structure and Second Language Acquisition." In W. Rutherford (ed.), *Language Universals and Second Language Acquisition*. Amsterdam: John Benjamins, pp. 109–133.

Huckin, T., and L. Pesante (1988). "Existential *There*." *Written Communication* 5:3, 368–391. Sage Publications, Inc.

Lakoff, G. (1987). *Women, Fire, and Dangerous Things.* Chicago: Chicago University Press.

Langacker, R. (1991). *Foundations of Cognitive Grammar (vol. 2). Stanford: Stanford University Press.*

Rando, E. and D. Napoli (1978). "Definites in *There* Sentences." *Language* 54:2, 303–313.

Rutherford, W. (1983). "Language Typology and Language Transfer." In S. M. Gass and L. Selinker (eds.), *Language Transfer in Language Learning.* Rowley, Mass.: Newbury House Publishers, pp. 358–370.

Sasaki, M. (1990). "Topic Prominence in Japanese EFL Students' Existential Constructions." *Language Learning* 40:3, 333–368.

Sasaki, M. (1991). "An Analysis of Sentences with Nonreferential *There* in Spoken American English." *Word* 42:2, 157–178.

Schachter, J., and W. Rutherford (1979). "Discourse Function and Language Transfer." *Working Papers in Bilingualism 19:* 1–12.

Shaw, P., and J. B. Taylor (1978). "Non-Pictorial Visual Aids." In S. Holden (ed.), *Visual Aids for Classroom Interaction.* London: Modern English Publications, pp. 15–19.

Stevick, E. (1982). *Teaching and Learning Languages.* New York: Cambridge University Press.

Thomas, S., and T. Hawes (1994). "Thematic Options in Reporting Previous Research." *IDEAL* 7: 13–28.

Ward, G., and B. Birner (1995). "Definiteness and the English Existential." *Language* 71:4, 722–742.

Ward, G., and B. Birner (1997). "Response to Abbott." *Language* 73:1, 109–112.

Yip, V. (1995). *Interlanguage and Learnability: From Chinese to English.* Amsterdam/Philadelphia: John Benjamins.

Suggestions for further reading

For other linguistic treatments of existential there, *see:*

Abbott, B. (1993). "A Pragmatic Account of the Definiteness Effect in Existential Sentences." *Journal of Pragmatics* 19: 39–55.

Hannay, M. (1985). *English Existentials in Functional Grammar.* Dordrecht: Foris Publications.

Jenkins, L. (1975). *The English Existential.* Tübingen: Niemeyer.

Lumsden, M. (1988). *Existential Sentences: Their Structure and Meaning.* London and New York: Routledge.

McNally, L. (1992). "An Interpretation for the English Existential Construction." Ph.D. dissertation, University of California, Santa Cruz.

Milsark, G. (1974). *Existential Sentences in English.* Ph.D dissertation, MIT.

Prince, E. (1978). "On the Function of Existential Presuppositions in Discourse." *CLS 14:* 362–376.

For other corpus-based research on existential there, *consult:*

Erdmann, P. (1976). *"There": There Sentences in English: A Relational Study Based on a Corpus of Written Text.* Muenchen: Tudeuv-Verlagsgesellschaft.

Lloyd-Jones, M. (1987). "A Contextual Analysis of Nonreferential *There* in American English Usage." MA thesis in TESL, UCLA.

For good pedagogical treatment of nonreferential subjects, see:

Badalamenti, V., and C. Henner Stanchina (1997). *Grammar Dimensions.* Book 1 (2d ed.). Boston, Mass.: Heinle & Heinle.

Benson, B., and P. Byrd (1989). *Improving the Grammar of Written English: The Handbook.* Belmont, Calif.: Wadsworth.

Frodesen, J., and J. Eyring (1997). *Grammar Dimensions*. Book 4 (2d ed.). Boston, Mass.: Heinle & Heinle.

Ur, P. (1988). *Grammar Practice Activities*. Cambridge: Cambridge University Press.

ENDNOTES

1. Such a sentence is possible in Arabic, but not in Engish.

2. Langacker points out that this is true to a somewhat lesser extent for other pronouns. For example, the first person plural personal pronoun *we* can have a specific meaning of *my partner and I*, but it can also refer to a larger set that is not so readily delineated, such as *We have a lot of coyotes around here.* This is also true of the third person plural personal pronoun, *they*, as in *They say you can never have too much life insurance.*

3. Notice, for instance, that object, not subject, pronouns are used.

> A: Who's going tonight?
> B: Well, there's Sheila, you, and me, at least.

4. In this regard note that deitic *there, here,* and the *wh*-question word *where* sometimes exhibit the same subject-verb behavior in informal speech (i.e., *there're, here're* , and *where're* tend not to occur):

> There's the two people I was talking about.
> Where's the earrings you wore last time?
> Here's the two books I promised you.

5. This is an obvious case of language change in progress. The written language, which maintains the old forms, is more conservative than the spoken language, which shows us where the language is heading.

6. In many cases, of course, *there* is not syntactically optional.

> There was a collective sigh.
> *A collective sigh was.

Such an example demonstrates why a transformational analysis that suggests that *there* is inserted through an optional syntactic rule after the subject is moved out of initial position cannot account for the data.

7. Note the use of the indefinite determiner with the logical subject even though it is a proper noun. The indefinite article is appropriate, of course, because it is indicating that the information is new in the moment for the listener/reader.

Chapter 24

COORDINATING CONJUNCTION

INTRODUCTION

Conjunction, or *coordination,* is the process of combining two constituents of the same type to produce another, larger constituent of the same type. In traditional grammar, this has been called *compounding;* for example, two sentences that are combined by means of a comma plus a connecting word make a "compound sentence"; two subject NPs that are combined with the word *and* are called a "compound subject."

There are several options for conjunction available in English. One is simply to combine like constituents with a coordinating conjunction, such as *and.* For example, two object NPs are conjoined in the following sentence:

> We enjoyed wine *and* cheese.

This is referred to as simple coordination. Another option exists when redundancies in the VP are eliminated. This option is called *ellipsis.* In the following example, the verb in the first VP has been omitted, or elided in the second VP and *too* has been added.

> We could see Orion and they could too.

A third option exists, which involves use of a pro-form:

> Annie plays softball, and she plays soccer too.

Again, in this sentence the subjects in both clauses are identical. The substitution of the pronoun *she* for the repeated subject, *Annie,* eliminates the redundancy. The adverb *too* has been added to mean "also."

In addition to simple conjunction, there is also complex conjunction, consisting of two-part correlative structures, here exemplified with *both . . . and.*

> Cecilia is *both* energetic *and* ambitious.

First, we will treat the form of each of these major syntactic options for conjunction in turn, drawing attention to the similarities and differences within each option. Next, we will treat together the meaning and use of the various coordinating conjunctions. Finally, we will consider other matters of use as they pertain to conjunction.

Form: Syntactic Options for Simple and Complex Conjunction

Combining Like Constituents with Coordinating Conjunctions

Perhaps the easiest way to begin a discussion of conjunction is by mentioning the most common signal used to conjoin: the coordinating conjunction *and*, which seems to mean much the same as the "plus" sign in arithmetic. Consider some of the constituents that *and* may conjoin:

[bread] and [butter]	(noun + noun)
[the bread] and [the butter]	(NP + NP)
[big] and [strong]	(adjective + adjective)
[very big] and [extremely strong]	(AP + AP)
quickly [run] and [hide]	(verb + verb)
[run fast] and [hide quickly]	(VP + VP)
[over the field] and [into the trees]	(PrepP + PrepP)
[neatly] and [effectively]	(adverb + adverb)
[very neatly] and [rather effectively]	(AdvP + AdvP)
[She got in the pool,] and [she began to swim.]	(S + S)

You should have no difficulty constructing sentences in which such sequences naturally occur; for example:

> The children ran and hid.
> The problem was solved neatly and effectively.
> The police saw nothing unusual, and they left the scene.

On the other hand, we find difficulty conjoining two constituents that are not of the same type:

> *bread and strong
> *very big and hide
> *The police saw nothing unusual and effectively.

Consistent with the adage "You can't add apples and oranges," simple conjunction standardly involves the coordination of constituents of the same type marked by at least one coordinating conjunction, where the meanings of the conjuncts (i.e., the individual constituents conjoined) are distinct from each other.[1] Coordinate structures might be generated in a number of possible ways, but we will assume that simple conjunctions are generated directly in the base in their normal position between constituents of identical categories. Our phrase structure rules will be revised accordingly to read:

$$X \rightarrow X \text{ Conj } X \text{ (Conj } X)$$

where *X* represents any constituent of a given category. Thus, simple conjoined constituents in a tree would look like this:

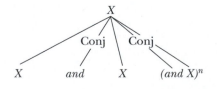

Such an analysis assumes that conjoined constituents form a superconstituent of the same category. For example, two conjoined noun phrases are assumed to be a "super-NP" with the properties of any other NP. This is a reasonable assumption to make, since a conjunction of two noun phrases seems to behave syntactically exactly as a single, simple noun phrase: it can figure as subject, direct object, indirect object, object of preposition, and so on:

subject:	*[John] bought a stereo.*	*[John and Fred] bought a stereo.*
direct object:	*Let's get [some coffee].*	*Let's get [some coffee and a cake].*
indirect object:	*I sent [Russ] a gift.*	*I sent [Russ and Kevin] a gift.*
obj of prep:	*They worked with [a hammer].*	*They worked with [a hammer and an ax].*

We must, of course, allow for the possibility of multiple conjoined structures, as in *Let's get [some coffee, a cake, and a bottle of wine];* the material inside the parentheses in the rule is intended to capture this fact, as exemplified in the three-part coordination in the following tree:

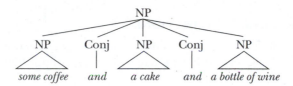

The NP "super-node" is of course used only for illustration; as we have seen, cases of multiple conjunction occur with adjectives (*a big, high, fearsome wave*), with prepositional phrases (*they ran out of the house, across the yard, and into the street*), or any other constituent type. The constituents inside the parentheses in the phrase structure rule must be allowed to repeat in order to create still longer chains of conjoined elements.

We must also take into account that such cases of multiple coordination usually involve an overt conjunction only between the last two conjuncts:

> They had vegetables, rice, and beans.
> ?They had vegetables, rice, beans.
> *They had vegetables and rice, beans.

An optional deletion rule that deletes all conjunctions except the one between the last pair of conjuncts will generate the acceptable sequences. Rising intonation, reflected in writing with commas, appears on all items on a list except the final one, which is marked by falling intonation. An orthographic convention allows an optional comma before the conjunction that precedes the last conjunct.

> They had vegetables, rice, and beans.

Finally, we should point out that coordination can occur at different levels of the tree. It is not the case that any sequence of the form "NP and NP and NP" is a case of coordination of three constituents at syntactically equal levels. In fact, certain cases may be ambiguous:

> We had red beans and rice and fish.

Here, one may interpret red beans and rice either as separate food items on a plate or as the famous New Orleans dish by that name. The two relevant segments of the tree would be those below:

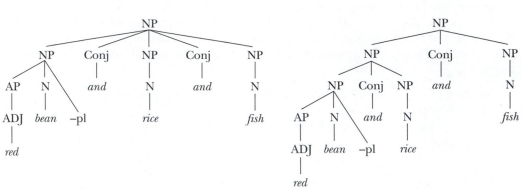

This type of ambiguity is relatively common in everyday speech.

SIMPLE COORDINATING CONJUNCTIONS

Other than *and*, the traditionally labeled simple coordinating conjunctions include *or, nor, so, but, yet,* and *for.*[2] As we saw with *and,* each of these conjoins two like constituents, placing them at syntactically equal levels:

> We will have coffee or tea. We will have coffee, or we will have tea.
> He is friendly but/yet vain. He is friendly, but/yet he is vain.
> She arrived early at the market, so she got the freshest food.
> They closed the shop, for there was no other choice.

Not all of these coordinating conjunctions are as amenable to conjoining the full range of constituents as is *and.* For instance, *for* seems able to coordinate only full clauses, as in the last sentence above. While *so* can join nonclause conjuncts, this is not common:

> The ring is [expensive so unaffordable].

However, such facts do not seem to invalidate the overall syntactic classification of these words.

The conjunction *nor* is a special case (we discuss below its occurrence with *neither*). First of all, *nor* connects two negative clauses. Second, *nor* cannot connect two negative clauses without additional syntactic changes:

> *John will not stay at his job, nor he will leave town permanently.
> John will not stay at his job, nor will he leave town permanently.

Subject-operator inversion must apply to the second clause, which has its negative marker incorporated into the *nor.* If there is no modal verb, *have,* or copula *be* in the second clause, operator addition applies:

> John did not stay at his job, nor did he leave town permanently.

But why does inversion occur at all? Notice that it does not occur where *or* is used:

> *John will stay at his job, or will he leave town permanently.
> *John stayed at his job, or did he leave town permanently.

One explanation is a historical one: the inversion here is a special case, a remnant of a process in older stages of English: whenever something other than the subject occurred in first position in the sentence, a verbal element had to be in second position. In modern English, inversion is required when a negative/restrictive element precedes the subject. More is said about this phenomenon in Chapter 25.

Ellipsis

Uninverted Affirmative Form

We noted in the introduction to this chapter that a second syntactic option exists to accomplish simple coordination. Ellipsis, or deletion, occurs frequently in English and will be encountered elsewhere. Here, we view it in the context of coordination. Consider the set of sentences below:

(a) ?Birds can fly, and I can fly.
(b) Birds can fly, and I can fly too.
(c) Birds can fly, and I can too.
(d) *Birds can fly, and I too.

Sentence (a) is the result of the simple addition of a coordinating conjunction, the process we have just discussed. Simple addition of a coordinating conjunction in clausal conjunction, when there is redundant material in the second clause as in sentence (a), results in a rather strange sentence. It is improved considerably with the addition of the adverb *too*, placed in the normal adverbial position at the end of the clause, as in (b).

Birds can fly, and I can fly too.

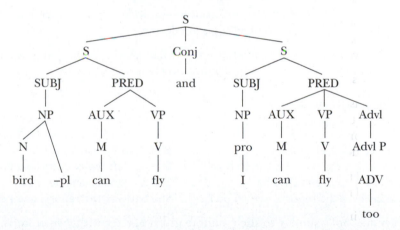

The improvement that results from the presence of *too* presumably stems from the consistency between the redundancy of the information in the second clause and the meaning of *too*: "also" or "in addition." Perhaps an even better solution is to elide or eliminate the redundancy, or part of it, as in (c).

We might be tempted to hypothesize that the grammaticality of (c) and the ungrammaticality of (d) is due to some rule in English that makes it possible to omit the main verb but not the auxiliary verb when both are redundant. While plausible from the data we have considered thus far, our hypothesis fails to explain the data in the next set of sentences:

(a) ?She has left the country, and I have left the country.
(b) She has left the country, and I have left the country too.
(c) *She has left the country and I have the country too.
(d) She has left the country, and I have too.
(e) *She has left the country, and I too.

It appears that the entire VP must be elided, as in (d), not just the main verb, as in (c). Sentence (e) reinforces our observation that if there is a redundant auxiliary verb, it must remain in the clause. But what if the VP is redundant but there is no auxiliary verb? Such is the case with the next set of sentences where the *be* copula is the main verb and there is no auxiliary verb:

(a) ?She is a citizen, and he is a citizen.
(b) She is a citizen, and he is a citizen too.
(c) She is a citizen, and he is too.
(d) *She is a citizen, and he too.

As we have come to expect with the *be* copula, in the absence of auxiliary verbs, it can function as the operator. Its presence makes (c) grammatical; its absence makes (d) ungrammatical. Finally, as we have also come to expect, when there is no other operator, the *do* verb serves this function.

(a) ?She believes the reports, and I believe the reports.
(b) She believes the reports, and I believe the reports too.
(c) She believes the reports, and I do too.
(d) *She believes the reports, and I too.

Observe that it does not seem to matter how much material is elided in the verb phrase:

She believes [the reports that the politician was lying about his involvement with space aliens during his first term of office], and I do too.

So long as the material deleted is identical to that which already appears in the first clause, no meaning is lost in the second, elliptical clause.

Inverted Affirmative Form

Now let us look at the following examples:

Birds can fly, and so can I.	*Birds can fly, and I can so.
She has left the country, and so have I.	*She has left the country, and I have so.
She is a citizen, and so is he.	*She is a citizen, and he is so.
She believes the reports, and so do I.	*She believes the reports and I do so.

Here the syntax looks similar to the example given earlier with *nor*—that is, sentences such as *John did not quit his job, nor did he leave town permanently*, where subject-operator inversion occurs—with the difference that in the four cases above, the sentences are affirmative rather than negative. We will simply assume that *so* is an adverb like *too*. *So* has a special requirement, however. It must be in clause-initial position, thus triggering subject-operator inversion. The new mapping rule is called "*so*-fronting." We'll assume that it obligatorily moves *so* to initial position in its clause.[3]

Birds can fly, and so can I.

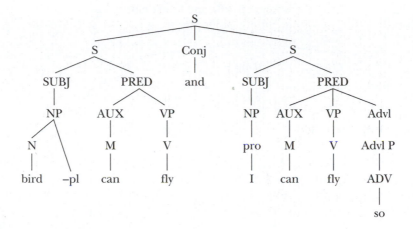

output of base: [bird -pl can fly] and [I can fly so]
ellipsis: [bird -pl can fly] and [I can ø so]
so-fronting: [bird -pl can fly] and [so I can]
subject-operator inversion: [bird -pl can fly] and [so can I]
morphology: Birds can fly, and so can I.

Uninverted and Inverted Negative Forms

The negative counterparts of the sentences above are derived in essentially the same manner, with the addition of the mapping rules needed to place negative elements properly.

(a) Turkeys can't fly, and I can't fly either.
(b) Turkeys can't fly, and I can't either.
(c) Turkeys can't fly, and neither can I.

(a) She hasn't left, and I haven't left either.
(b) She hasn't left, and I haven't either.
(c) She hasn't left, and neither have I.

(a) She doesn't believe the reports, and I don't believe them either.
(b) She doesn't believe the reports, and I don't either.
(c) She doesn't believe the reports, and neither do I.

The (b) sentence in the first of these sets can be derived as follows:

output of base: [not turkey -pl can fly] and [not I can fly either]
not placement: [turkey -pl can not fly] and [I can not fly either]
ellipsis: [turkey -pl can not fly] and [I can not ø either]
not contraction: [turkey -pl can + n't fly] and [I can + n't either]
morphology: Turkeys can't fly, and I can't either.

The tree for (b) looks like this:

Turkeys can't fly, and I can't either.

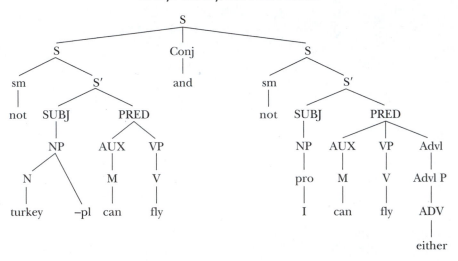

Sentence (c), *Turkeys can't fly, and neither can I*, adds the steps of (1) combining *not + either* to form *neither*, (2) the fronting of *neither* to clause-initial position in the second clause, and (3) subject-operator inversion, which is forced by the existence of the negative element in presubject position in the clause.

> output of base: [not turkey -pl can fly] and [not I can fly either]
> ellipsis: [not turkey -pl can fly] and [not I can ø either]
> *not + either:* [not turkey -pl can fly] and [I can fly neither]
> *neither* fronting: [not turkey -pl can fly] and [neither I can fly]
> subject-operator inversion: [not turkey -pl can fly] and [neither can I]
> *not* placement: [turkey -pl can not fly] and [neither can I]
> *not* contraction: [turkey -pl can + n't fly] and [neither can I]
> morphology: Turkeys can't fly, and neither can I.

You can try to apply the mapping rules to the remaining sets of sentences with perfect *have* and simple present; the latter, of course, will involve the insertion of the operator *do*.

One last brief alternative with *too/so/either/neither* ellipsis concerns the clipped forms, used as rejoinders; for example:

> I play tennis. Me too!
> I don't play squash. Me (n)either.

As is well known, these forms are often frowned on by prescriptive grammarians. Exactly how these forms are generated need not concern us. What is interesting about them formally is the fact that the pronouns, which in the other elliptical forms above appear in subject form, are here in object form. We do not hear

> *I too.
> *I (n)either.

In addition, only the uninverted forms may appear in this way. We do not hear

> *So me.
> *(N)either me.

USING PRO-FORMS

In addition to ellipsis, another syntactic option exists for avoiding redundancy. This is the possibility of substituting a pro-form for a redundant constituent. In fact, pro-forms often occur in tandem with ellipsis. We could, for instance, say that the operator in the sentence sets we have just considered, be it an auxiliary verb, the copula *be*, or the *do* is really a pro-form or substitute for the entire VP. There are some times, however, that pro-forms are used in compound sentences without ellipsis. This is the case with pronouns and substitute words:

> She has left the country, and I have left it too.
> She believes the reports, and I believe them too.
> She is a citizen, and he is one too.

and also pro-adverbs:

> He graduated in '95, and she graduated then too.
> He graduated from Tulane, and she graduated from there too.

GAPPING

An additional type of ellipsis, called *gapping*, which occurs medially in conjoined structures, is worth looking at briefly. Gapping may occur provided the conjoined sentences have (a) nonidentical subjects and (b) at least one nonidentical predicate constituent apart from the verb. Here are some examples:

> John trimmed the tree, and Mary the hedge.
> My uncle works in Ann Arbor, and my aunt in Detroit.
> The wind was brisk, the sun bright, and the ocean calm.

Derivation of gapped sentences seems to proceed in much the same way as the derivation of those with deleted VPs:

> output of base: [John -past trim the tree] and [Mary -past trim the hedge]
> copy s/t: [John -past [+ 3 + sg] trim the tree] and [Mary -past [+ 3 + sg] trim the hedge]
> gapping: [John -past [+ 3 + sg] trim the tree] and [Mary ø ø the hedge]
> morphology: John trimmed the tree, and Mary the hedge.

The major difference in the case of gapping is that the deleted part of the sentence lies in the middle rather than at the end of the second clause.

PHRASAL VERSUS SENTENTIAL CONJUNCTION

A question worth addressing at this point is whether all conjunction might be derived from two or more full sentences that are then conflated into a single sentence by deletion rules, leaving only the coordinated constituents in the tree. Why not derive a sentence like *John trimmed the tree and the hedge* from the two sentences *John trimmed the tree* and *John trimmed the hedge?* Then, following the pattern of ellipsis, the repeated constituents can be deleted and a single sentence created as a result. This was, in fact, an earlier treatment of conjunction in generative grammar, but certain problems arose as a result of this type of analysis. For example,

> John, Bill, and Harry met in Vienna.

cannot be derived from

> *John met in Vienna, Bill met in Vienna, and Harry met in Vienna.

The key seems to be that one feature required of the verb *meet*, when used intransitively, is a plural NP or coordinate NP subject. Likewise, the normal reciprocal interpretation of *John and Mary got married*—that is, they married each other—is lost if the sentence is expanded to *John got married and Mary got married*. Cases like these led linguists to assume that conjunction can occur directly at many levels in the base rather than always as a result of deletion rules applied to conjoined sentences or clauses. Most of the sentences we have considered in this chapter are examples of sentential conjunction; however, *John, Bill, and Harry met in Vienna* and *John and Mary got married* are examples of phrasal conjunction.

SENTENCES WITH *RESPECTIVELY*

We conclude this section on simple conjunction with mention of the adverb *respectively*. It seems again that few other languages have an equivalent word; it is used only where conjunction occurs in at least two places in the sentence, and it serves the purpose of resolving interpretation problems. For example, in the sentence

> Mary bought a Honda Accord, and John bought a Volkswagen.

there is no doubt as to who bought which car. However, in the sentence

> Mary and John bought a Honda Accord and a Volkswagen.

it is less clear whether each person bought one or more cars individually or whether the two cars were purchased jointly by John and Mary. Although the sentence seems fully grammatical, an interpretation problem may arise—a problem that the addition of the adverb *respectively* can solve because it clarifies that Mary bought the Honda and John bought the Volkswagen.

> Mary and John bought a Honda Accord and a Volkswagen, respectively.

Respectively is a word that is capable of appearing in different structural positions. The sentence below is synonymous with the one above:

> Mary and John, respectively, bought a Honda Accord and a Volkswagen.

While *respectively* serves mainly to disambiguate, correlatives serve both to disambiguate and to emphasize as well. We turn to correlative conjunction next.

CORRELATIVE CONJUNCTION

Though the syntax of simple coordination is not an area of English grammar that causes many ESL/EFL learning problems, students often have difficulties with complex coordination—two-part correlative structures where one part precedes the first conjunct and the other precedes the second. The correlative conjunctions include *both . . . and, either . . . or,* and *neither . . . nor*. An additional correlative conjunction pair, *not only . . . but also*, will be taken up in the exercises.

Both . . . And

The correlative conjunction pair *both . . . and* shows a wide range of possibilities available for constituent coordination. The correlative elements appear just prior to the coordinated constituents:

Both [Mary] and [John] arrived early.
Mary is both [energetic] and [ambitious].
John did his work both [quickly] and [enthusiastically].
John did his work both [with speed] and [with enthusiasm].
John did his work with both [speed] and [enthusiasm].
John wants both [to stay at his job] and [to leave town permanently].
John both [wants to stay at his job] and [wants to leave town permanently].

Almost any pair of constituents can be joined by *both . . . and*, with the exception of full-sentence coordination—that is, with clausal conjunction, some kind of ellipsis is necessary:

*Both [John wants to stay at his job] and [he wants to leave town permanently].

We will simply generate such structures by a rule that places the two parts of the correlative directly into a sentence:[4]

$$X \rightarrow both \ X \ and \ X$$

The rule will apply to constituents below the clausal level, thus accounting for the ungrammaticality of the last example sentence above. *Both* does not always occur, however, directly before the first conjunct. Note the following sentences with their respective synonymous variants:

Both [John] and [Mary] arrived early. = [John] and [Mary] both arrived early.
Joe is both [energetic] and [ambitious]. = Joe is [energetic] and [ambitious] both.
John did his work with both [speed] and [enthusiasm]. =
    John did his work both with [speed] and [enthusiasm].
John wants both to [stay at his job] and to [leave town permanently]. =
    John both wants [to stay at his job] and [to leave town permanently].
John wants both to [stay at his job] and [leave town permanently].

In the second versions of these sentences, the first correlative does not occur immediately before a constituent type identical to the one before which the second occurs. Stockwell, Schachter, and Partee (1973) related these sentences by a rule called "correlative movement." While we will not attempt to debate the order in which such movements occur or present the details of the authors' original arguments, it is important to make note of the fact that the variants exist and that some are more informal and perhaps less widely accepted than others.

Either . . . Or and Neither . . . Nor

Correlatives with *either . . . or* and *neither . . . nor* are parallel to *both . . . and* in that they generally place the conjunctive elements directly before the options mentioned:

Either [Mary] or [John] arrived early.
Neither [Mary] nor [John] arrived early.

Mary is either [energetic] or [ambitious].
Mary is neither [energetic] nor [ambitious].

John did his work either [quickly] or [enthusiastically].
John did his work neither [quickly] nor [enthusiastically].

> John wants either [to stay at his job] or [to leave town permanently].
> John wants neither [to stay at his job] nor [to leave town permanently].

However, there are variants of the sentences in the last one of these pairs in which the first correlative element appears in a different position. The corresponding affirmative/negative sentences below are synonymous with the last two above:

> John wants either to [stay at his job] or [leave town permanently].
> John wants neither to [stay at his job] nor [leave town permanently].
> John either wants [to stay at his job] or [to leave town permanently].
> John neither wants [to stay at his job] nor [to leave town permanently]

We will assume that these variants are also related by some type of correlative movement, which is basically stylistic in nature.

It is worth noting that *either . . . or* is different from *neither . . . nor* and *both . . . and* in that correlative conjunction is possible at the clausal level as well as below the clausal level.

> Either he does what is expected of him, or he'll lose his job.

It may have occurred to you that the last few topics we have dealt with under the heading of form straddle the border with meaning. We now turn to fully explore the areas of meaning and use.

The Meaning and Use of Coordinating Conjunctions

A straightforward account of the meaning of the coordinating conjunctions might look like this:

Conjunction	Meaning	Example
and	plus	Lloyd and Mark are going into business together.
but	shows contrast	Lloyd is hardworking, but Mark is lazy.
yet	but at the same time	Mark is lazy, yet well intentioned.
so	therefore	Neither man had much money, so they decided to collaborate.[5]
for	because	I hope they succeed, for this has been a dream come true for both men.
or	one or the other of two alternatives is true	They are determined to make it or to go bankrupt in the process.
nor	conjoins two negative sentences, both of which are true	Lloyd doesn't give up easily, nor does Mark.

While this account may well be satisfactory for low-level ESL/EFL students, its straightforwardness is deceptive. The question of what conjunctions "mean" is a difficult area for linguists. It has been explored on the one hand by logicians and on the other by researchers in pragmatics; the two groups have in the past come to different conclusions, with the former generally favoring what Posner (1980) calls a "meaning-minimal" account and the latter a "meaning-maximal" account. Let us take a brief look at the two views and, in the process, attempt to characterize the nature of the conjunction *and*. We then, in turn, look at *but, yet, or,* and *so*. We do not discuss *for* here because as we mentioned in note 2, the use of *for* as a coordinating conjunction is somewhat archaic. We also do not deal with *nor* further here, as it occurs much more frequently with its correlative counterpart *neither*, which we address later on. It is important to emphasize that linguists by no means agree over what constitutes "semantic meaning" and what constitutes "pragmatic meaning" in this area of language.

AND

The meaning of the word *and* has inspired lively debate. Below, we sketch some of the ways the question has been approached.

And as Logical Operator

Most linguists agree that conjunctions have certain logical properties. Branches of linguistics that are oriented toward mathematically formal description, such as logical semantics, speak of the truth-conditional properties of connective elements. The general idea is that the truth of the statement

> Stu is a cook and Fred is a waiter.

is a function of the truth of each individual conjunct. So long as each conjunct is true, then the entire conjoined statement is true; if one conjunct is false, the statement is false. Since this truth-conditional meaning seems to be constant across all uses of *and*, that is often thought to be its central, prototypical, or essential meaning.

As it turns out, *and* seems to convey many additional meanings in English, not all of which are conveyed by its roughly equivalent word in other languages. If *and* is really only a logical operator, it ought to be possible to reverse all clauses that are conjoined by *and* without any loss of meaning—after all, in logic and mathematics $(X + Y)$ is equivalent to $(Y + X)$. And, indeed, it does not seem to matter how we order the two major parts of the sentence below:

> Tokyo is the capital of Japan, and Paris is the capital of France.
> Paris is the capital of France, and Tokyo is the capital of Japan.

However, once we get beyond such stilted-sounding sentences to ones which are likely to be uttered more frequently, problems arise:

> Fred fell down, and he hurt his foot badly.
> ?Fred hurt his foot badly, and he fell down.

The problem in the second sentence does not lie in the question of whether *and* is truth-conditional or not: after all, it is true that if Fred fell down and hurt his foot, then Fred did hurt his foot, and he did fall down. The problem is that the hearer concludes in the first case that Fred's hurting his foot was a result of his having fallen. If the order of clauses is reversed, as in the second example above, we do not come to that conclusion; if anything, we might conclude the opposite: that his falling was the result of his foot injury. What is responsible for these different interpretations?

And as Marker of Many Meanings

One solution is to take the "meaning-maximal" route and say that *and* has two meanings—one simply the truth-conditional meaning of logic, and the other a richer meaning that includes the idea of "as a result." There would therefore be ambiguity in the word *and;* as in other cases of lexical ambiguity, the listener or reader simply has to figure out from the context of utterance whether one meaning or the other is intended (as happens when one says, "I went to the bank"—have we been talking about money, or are we now in the middle of a fishing trip?). Yet this solution has its own problems. As Posner (1980:186) shows, the same sort of juxtaposition of sentences with *and* can yield many additional readings:

a. Annie is in the kitchen, and she is making doughnuts. (*and there . . .*)
b. Annie fell into a deep sleep, and her facial color returned. (*and during this time . . .*)
c. The window was open, and there was a draft. (*and coming from it . . .*)
d. Peter married Annie, and she had a baby. (*and after that . . .*)
e. Paul pounded on the stone, and he shattered it. (*and thereby . . .*)
f. Give me your picture, and I'll give you mine. (*If you give me your picture, I'll give you mine.*)

All seem frequent uses of the conjunction. The number of possible senses of *and* grows with such a list, which may still be incomplete. For example, in a sentence like *I gave them everything they wanted, and they still didn't thank me, and* could be replaced by *but*. In principle, the meanings of *and* shade into one another in such a way that they could become too numerous to list; this is not a problem we encounter with ordinary lexical ambiguity. When we say "bank," we might mean a place to deposit our money or a place from which to fish, but we are certainly not tempted to interpret the word as some combination of these two meanings—say, as a safety deposit box alongside a river.

And as Inferential Connective

This sort of problem has led those who work in the field of pragmatics and who look for general principles of language use to the conclusion that these so-called "meanings" of *and* are actually not meanings at all but aspects of use—where "use" means that the context of utterance determines exactly how the word will be interpreted. Blakemore (1992) argues that when we use the conjunction *and*, we may intend to draw the listener's/reader's attention to something over and above what is expressed by the individual conjuncts; the use of *and* is motivated, in other words, by the desire to have the listener/reader draw an inferential connection, one that is not stated but implied. If we are simply making a grocery list, there is no mystery to the use of *and* to connect items in a parallel way. However, if someone utters, *John fell down and hurt his knee*, the listener/reader is implicitly being invited to seek some other relevant connection between the conjuncts. Given what we know about the possible effects of a fall upon the human body, we are led to the most likely connection—a causal one. Since we assume that the speaker/writer is equally aware of the possible connection, we will feel almost betrayed in the event that no such connection was actually intended—in the case that, for instance, John did fall down but had actually hurt his knee from some other cause prior to or later than that.

And as Marker of Speaker Continuation

Another, much different, presentation of *and* by Schiffrin (1987) examines its use in conversational discourse beyond the ideational, or content, level. She calls it a mark of "speaker-continuation," with which a speaker signals that the discourse to follow is in some way connected with what has come before. The connection may be a way to seize back a conversational turn that has been interrupted by someone else, thereby indicating that the original speaker has not finished. A speaker who wishes to continue a monologue, but needs to catch his or her breath, does well, then, to signal this wish by ending with an uttered *and* just prior to the pause. This use of *and* goes beyond the usual ideational conjunctive uses and places it into the category of what have come to be known as "discourse markers"—a category that contains words like *oh* and *well*, expressions that cannot well be defined without reference to a speaker's role in conversation at a given moment. The study of discourse markers has not traditionally played much of a role in ESL/EFL pedagogy but may soon do so, in view of the growing linguistic and second-language literature on the subject. Discourse markers certainly should have a role in the teaching of oral communication skills.

As was the case with the syntax of simple conjunction, the meaning and use of *and* are not especially problematical aspects of English for ESL/EFL students. This is so despite the fact that although most languages may have a word that is translatable as *and*, this word may not be as free in its syntactic occurrence or potential interpretations as is the English word. Mandarin Chinese, for example, may coordinate NPs with the word *han*, but sentences are coordinated by other words such as *er* or *che*.[6] At least one of these would fit into most of the slots filled by *and* in Posner's example sentences above but would make no sense at all in the warning, *Do that, ____ I'll hit you!* A comparative study of distribution will show that in general, English is quite broad with respect to the contexts in which *and* may be used; most ESL/EFL students may not make full use of the options available to them.

BUT AND YET

But is often described as logically equivalent to *and*. That is, if the sentence "It is raining, but I am happy" is true, it is also true that it is raining and I am happy. However, *but* clearly means more than this, and this "more" is generally said to be contrast of some sort.[7] *But* signals two types of contrast, while the conjunction *yet* is generally limited to a single type of contrast.

But/Yet in Denials of Expectations

One type of contrast is usually called "denial-of-expectation." This use, often called "adversative," has to do with the violation of reasonable expectations: what is expected after a reading of the first conjunct turns out not to be true from a reading of the second. Some examples are the following:

> He is friendly but/yet introverted.
> He worked slowly but/yet diligently.
> They tried for three hours to steer the boat from the storm, but/yet the boat sank.
> They've had a terrible time up to now, but/yet they'll probably succeed in the end.
> She told us that Athens was in this direction, but/yet she's mistaken.

As such examples show, *but/yet* may be used where the violation of expectations is not especially strong; in the last example above, it is not necessary that we expect the directions that people give to be correct all the time. However, we do tend to trust others' directions, and we find our trust misplaced if the directions are faulty; so the issue of expectation probably plays a part in the choice of conjunction.

But as Marker of Semantic Contrast

The other major use of *but* involves a real semantic contrast, one in which exactly two entities or qualities are set adjacent to each other in order to focus on one or more semantic differences in them. Most often they may involve polar opposition, but the following examples show that they need not do so:

> Winter is warm in Miami but cold in Moscow.
> John likes skiing, but his sister prefers tennis.
> This is not a rose but a geranium.
> Nimbus clouds threaten rain, but cirrus clouds do not.
> She likes an occasional visit to the desert, but he wants to relocate there.

Although it is possible to imagine circumstances in which some of these sequences might involve denials of expectations (which would then also permit *yet*), in general no real denials of expectations need be present here; for instance, we cannot expect or predict anything at all about Moscow weather from information about Miami weather. Sometimes, the semantic contrast is not exhibited in a specific pair of words like *warm/cold* or a clear negation word, but rather in an implied ideational contrast such as that between *occasional visit* "stay a short time" and *relocate* "stay a long time" in the final example above.

But as Marker of Speaker-Return

There seems to be a clearly distinct third way in which *but* is used in discourse, especially conversational discourse, one that has been described by Schiffrin (1987). When seen as a discourse marker, *but* can be, among other things, a sign of speaker-return: when one party to a conversation has strayed for some reason from the main point of a monologue, *but* (or *anyway*, or *but anyway*, or *but anyway, as I was saying*) can be used to mark the attempt to recover the lost point. This use of *but* differs greatly from the two ideational uses.

As was true with *and*, languages other than English tend to have some sort of expression like *but* to mark contrast; ESL/EFL students do not seem to experience great difficulties with the use of *but*. Again, these other languages may have two or more noninterchangeable words which cover the uses of the English word. Modern Hebrew distributes these uses across two words, *aval* and *ela*. One Mandarin Chinese equivalent of *but*, the expression *tan-she*, is actually a correlative with which one can express denial of expectations, but not semantic contrast, which can be marked by another word, *er*.[8] German has one word, *aber*, which covers both denial and contrast except in the case of explicit contradictions as in *This is not a rose but a geranium*, in which case the word *sondern* is used. As with *and*, the task of the student learning English in such cases, where many native-language words coalesce into one, seems much simpler than that of the English-speaking student learning one of these languages, in which he or she might tend to generalize just one of the forms to inappropriate cases.

OR

Arguments over the true meaning of *or* are parallel to those we summarized above concerning *and*. In presenting them, we will cover the major uses of this conjunction.

Inclusive *Or*

The meaning of the conjunction *or* has been characterized by logically-oriented linguists in a truth-conditional way: any sentence "*X* or *Y*" is true so long as one of its conjuncts is true. If both of the conjuncts are false, then the statement is false; if both are true, the statement is true. Thus if someone says,

> We'll serve carrots or (we'll serve) peas.

without a specific commitment to doing only one of these things, one might normally say that the conditions of the statement are fulfilled as long as we do one or both of these things; it is unlikely that if we serve both carrots and peas someone would accuse us of having spoken falsely. Logic and reality seem to work in parallel ways here.

Exclusive *Or*

However, it is clear that when we use *or*, we do not always intend it in this way. In some cases, we clearly intend to convey the exclusive rather than the above inclusive meaning. Suppose that during the sale of an automobile the seller says,

> You can pay us ten thousand dollars in cash, or you can give us a money order for that amount.

In this case, the buyer clearly expects that the seller intends the exclusive reading to hold; neither buyer nor seller would consider the inclusive reading as even a remote possibility. In other cases, it seems that real-world conditions dictate an exclusive reading regardless of our intentions, as in the case of the sentence

> Right now our relatives are in London, or they are in Paris.

In others, logic dictates such a reading as in

> It is snowing outside, or it is not snowing outside.

Logicians might then insist, as those in Gamut (1991) do, that such problems are matters of context, not of word meaning: whatever the world is like, it still holds that the semantic meaning of simple *or* is the logical one. The conjoined sentence *Right now we are in London, or we are in Paris* is still true so long as at least one of its conjuncts is true. The fact that in this case both of its conjuncts cannot be true at the same time is a problem for the world, not for logic, and as long as we are in one of the two cities at the time of the utterance, the sentence is true and the meaning of *or* remains constant.

We thus seem to have a problem similar to that for *and*, where semantic meaning and pragmatic meaning are confounded. Since ambiguities can arise through mismatched intentions, English does have a correlative form *either . . . or*, which seems, for most speakers, to have the exclusive reading. The sequences

> (a) either *X* or *Y* but not both . . . (= exclusive)
> (b) either *X* or *Y* or both . . . (= inclusive)
> (c) *X* and/or *Y* . . . (= inclusive or exclusive)

serve the same purpose in an even more emphatic way.

Or as Warning

Or may have additional senses that go beyond the inclusive-exclusive distinction. One involves an imperative, or quasi-warning, sentence followed by a statement of consequence:

> Stop that loud music, or I will call the police.
> Buy me that toy, or I will scream.
> You have to fix the car, or we can't go on our trip.

In such cases *or* may be paraphrased lexically as *otherwise*. These sentences may also be naturally paraphrased syntactically with such conditional structures as

> If you do not stop that loud music, (then) I will call the police.
> If you do not buy me that toy, (then) I will scream.
> If you do not fix the car, (then) we can't go on our trip.

Once again, given a more fully explicated form of the imperatives (as in *Either you will stop that loud music, or I will call the police*), a logician would likely hold *or* to the constant semantic meaning while leaving the pragmatics to others.

Or in Paraphrases

A further use of *or* is somewhat more puzzling:

> This is a matsutake, or pine mushroom.
> The boards have to be mitered, or cut at an angle.

Or is frequently used in this way at the phrasal level in definitions or paraphrases. At first glance, the situation seems complementary to that of *It is snowing, or it is not snowing* as far as logic is concerned. While the reading of *or* in that sentence is necessarily exclusive, in the two sentences above, the reading seems necessarily inclusive: we cannot have a matsutake without also having an exotic mushroom called by the common English name "pine mushroom." (This kind of all-inclusion is, after all, part of what makes a good definition.) Yet the logician could still tell us that the usual definition of *or* holds true. Pragmatically, there seems to be something metalinguistic happening in such sequences. In the first part of each sentence, in uttering the words *matsutake* or *mitered*, we may seem to be referring to things (objects or events) in the world. In the second part, however, we retroactively call attention to those words as words, rather than as representations of objects or events. This metalinguistic intention shows up in spoken discourse by means of special emphatic stress on the word to be defined or paraphrased; it shows up in written discourse by means of italics or quote marks. Thus, the speaker seems to be saying,

> You can refer to this object as a "matsutake" or as a "pine mushroom."

> The action that must be performed on the boards can be called either "mitering" or "cutting at an angle."

Since there is a possibility here of choosing one option, the other option, or both, the logician's definition still seems to hold true.

Or as Self-Correction Device

At the clausal level, this metalinguistic version of *or* shows up in what often appear as self-corrections when a speaker has not expressed himself or herself satisfactorily. For example:

> We have to help the children. Or, more precisely, we have to help them to help themselves.

> You are a joy to be around. Or, to put it another way, I love you.

Here, the *or* may be interpreted in reference to the prior statement itself in such a way as to suggest, "What I intended by the first sentence was . . ."

These uses of *or* do not necessarily match the full range of uses of any single word in other languages. Although the correspondence between English *or* and German *oder* is rather neat, Mandarin Chinese is quite different: Mandarin speakers use the expression *huo zhe* for yes/no questions, while the expression *hai she* is used for alternative questions (see Chapter 14); the two are not interchangeable. In the case of the imperative-warning use of *or*, only the expression *fo ze* (i.e., "otherwise") is available. None of these three may be used to express metalinguistic-paraphrase *or*, which is typically marked with an expression that we can translate as "that is to say"; in this kind of metalinguistic paraphrase, the English use may seem quite bizarre to Chinese learners.

So

The conjunction *so*[9] might be seen essentially as a marker that relates causes with results, as in

> The rope broke, so the box fell down.
> She has a cold, so she won't be coming with us today.

However, Blakemore (1988) calls *so* more generally an inferential marker—that is, a conjunction that relates an inference in the second clause to a proposition in the first. (Since propositions are typically rendered in sentence form, we may have an explanation for why *so* finds practically no use as a phrasal conjunction.) For Blakemore, the causal reading is what she calls an "enriched" interpretation. It is possible to use *so* where no expression of cause is desired, but where logical inferences are strong, as in examples like:

> There's five dollars in my wallet, so I didn't spend all my money, then.
> The car's in the garage, so Susan must be here.

This use of *so* can be used across interlocutors, where one supplies the initial proposition and the other supplies the inference:

> A: The LGB Corporation has just gone out of business.
> B: So we've lost our investment.

So may even be used, as Blakemore points out, where no prior utterance at all has occurred: Suppose that someone is wondering who has taken a freshly made cake and then sees the family dog with frosting on its face. A likely reaction would be to say, *So YOU ate it!* If the baker of the cake had not already noticed that the cake was missing (and hence not had at least the proposition, *The cake is missing*, already in mind), the baker could not, on seeing the dog's face, attach *so* to the exclamation. What unifies all of these uses of *so* is that while logical inferences may or may not always be present, the listener/reader will always be cued to the construction of some kind of inference as his or her main task.

Looking at extended conversational interactions, Schiffrin (1987) illustrates situations in which a speaker marks a transition in the conversation by use of *so*, thereby offering the listener the chance to become a speaker and either carry the topic further or change topics. One of the speakers whom she recorded is quoted as saying,

> "We're considered the . . . more or less . . . the oppressors. So ah . . . take it from there."

Often, when a conversation seems played out, an interlocutor will utter *so . . .* , often with fading intonation, apparently as a signal that the discussion agenda is being opened or, perhaps, that the conversation is nearing an end. It is worth investigating to what extent this conversational device can be seen as an extension of the ideational one described by Blakemore.

AND/*OR* ALTERNATION IN AFFIRMATIVE AND NEGATIVE STRUCTURES

One final comment on the meanings of conjunctions has to do with the alternation between *and* and *or* in conjoined structures in affirmative and negative statements, respectively. Consider the following sets:

> a. They have a house and a car.
> b. They don't have a house and a car.
> c. They don't have a house or a car.

Most native speakers of English will tend to find the proper negation of the proposition expressed in (a) to be (c), not (b), although negation seems to have operated on (b) in the normal way.

What sentence (c) expresses is:

> It is not true that they have a house. It is also not true that they have a car.

In contrast to that, the typical logical interpretation of the (b) sentence is:

> It is not true that they have both a house and a car. It is true that they have either a house or a car.

We find a parallel in a structure already presented in Chapter 10: the alternation between *some* and *any*. Recall that the standard negation of

> She has some books.

is the sentence:

> She doesn't have any books.

Recall, too, that the sentence:

> She doesn't have some books.

admits of the interpretation:

> There are some books that she doesn't have.

implying that there are some books that she does have. As is true with the *some/any* distinction, the *and/or* alternation is likely to be the source of many learner errors; the two structures may even merit treatment together in class.

OTHER ISSUES OF USE WITH CONJUNCTION

SIMILARITIES AND DIFFERENCES BETWEEN STRUCTURES WITH *TOO/EITHER* AND *SO/NEITHER*

In many English grammar textbooks, the affirmative expressions *I do too* and *so do I* and the negative expressions *I don't either* and *neither do I* are presented as synonymous forms that can be freely substituted one for the other.

	Uninverted	Inverted
Affirmative	I do too	so do I
Negative	I don't either	neither do I

They are similar in that the words *too* and *so* serve to provide new information in affirmative statements while cueing the listener/reader that identical components of the first clause may need to be inferred to fill in syntactic gaps and flesh out the full meaning. The words *either* and *neither* serve the same purpose for negative statements. All four phrases can also be seen as devices to shortcut the repetition of sentence elements primarily in the expression of agreement between interlocutors.

We earlier presented *too* as similar to *so*, and *either* as similar to *neither*, differing only in their relative syntactic positions and in the fact that subject-operator inversion occurs with a fronted *so* or *neither*. In fact, they often do seem interchangeable, but they are not equivalent in all contexts since the *too*-form permits the addition of new information within the predicate, while the *so*-form does not. For example:

> Matt plays second base, and he pitches, too.
> *Matt plays second base, and so does he pitch.

> You can fish from the bridge, and you can dive from it too.
> *You can fish from the bridge, and so can you dive from it.

In contrast, the corresponding forms with *either/neither* are both possible, although the second of these tends to sound somewhat awkward:

> I don't like broccoli, and I don't like squash either.
> I don't like broccoli, and neither do I like squash.
>
> You can't fish from this bridge, and you can't dive from it either.
> You can't fish from this bridge, and neither can you dive from it.

When one wants to add new information in subject position, however, all the forms are suitable:

> Matt plays second base, and so does Lou.
> Matt plays second base, and Lou does too.
>
> I don't like broccoli, and neither do you.
> I don't like broccoli, and you don't either.

When new information is added both to the subject and the predicate position, however, or when multiple pieces of information are added to the predicate, speakers express reservations about the appropriateness of any of these forms:

> ?I play first base, and my sister pitches too.
> ?I don't play first base, and my sister doesn't pitch either.
>
> ?You can fish from this bridge, and you can dive from that one too.
> ?You can't fish from this bridge, and you can't dive from that one either.

However, Celce-Murcia (1980) provides evidence from discourse analysis that such sentences do occasionally occur in informal conversations.

A second difference worth pointing out is that when these forms are used as rejoinders, only the uninverted forms may be shortened and used without an auxiliary verb. Also, when these forms are shortened, any subject pronoun involved must be changed to an object form:

> A: I'm sorry that Cleveland lost the World Series.
> B: So am I. / I am too. / Me too!
>
> A: I wasn't paying attention.
> B: Neither was I. / I wasn't either. / Me neither.

These rejoinder forms, in addition to being of a highly informal register, seem almost completely restricted in use to the expression of personal agreement between interlocutors. Evidence for this lies in the fact that only the first person pronoun *me* regularly appears in this structure:

> A: She wants to wear a sweatshirt today.
> B: So does he. / He does, too. / ?Him too.
>
> A: I don't want to stand in line all day.
> B: Neither do they. / They don't either. / ?Them neither.

In other words, one cannot talk about other people's agreement with these forms. Nor are they regularly used with the first person pronoun in a monologue:

> ?She wants to go, and me too.
> ?She doesn't want to go, and me neither.

Therefore, *me too* and *me (n)either* seem tied to a very specific and restricted discourse function.

By using a questionnaire, Shayne (1975) was successful in isolating a third context where the uninverted forms were strongly preferred over the inverted forms. This is where the "tag" is preceded by a logical connector such as *because, since, although,* or *in spite of the fact;* for example:

> Macy's offers a lot of good buys, although
> a. so does Gimbel's.
> b. Gimbel's does too. (strongly preferred)
> c. no preference

You have seen several contexts above where the uninverted forms were necessary or were preferred over the inverted forms. The opposite also occurs. In a usage study, Celce-Murcia (1980) showed that native speakers preferred the inverted forms over the uninverted forms in those cases where an insult was intended. (The numbers in parentheses refer to the number of respondents completing a questionnaire who preferred a given form.) For example:

> You're a rotten egg and
> (74) a. so is your father.
> (31) b. your father is too.
> (8) c. no preference

The uninverted forms are more frequent and versatile overall than the inverted forms; however, there are important discourse differences. While this area of grammar could stand more investigation, it is an oversimplification to treat the two affirmative (and two negative) forms as mere paraphrases of each other.

COORDINATE CLAUSES WITHOUT CONJUNCTIONS

Coordination, or conjunction, presumably exists as a syntactic operation to ease language processing. In many cases, redundancy is eliminated and more efficient communication is achieved. In addition, conjunction serves to clarify the relationship between sentences. When conjunctions are not used, the clause sequence may be ambiguous.

> It was bitter cold. It was snowing.

The most likely interpretation of the relationship between these two sentences might be an additive one:

> It was bitter cold and snowing.

Without conjunctions, however, we have no way of telling the relationship from the syntactic evidence. People who live in snowy climates, for example, know that bitter cold days and nights are often the clearest—that is, it doesn't often snow when it is bitter cold. Therefore, we could give another interpretation to this pair of sentences:

> It was bitter cold, yet snowing.

Many other interpretations are possible. The point is that conjunctions serve to disambiguate the relationship between sentences and thus clarify intended meaning. In Chapter 26 we will consider logical connectors, where this is even more the case.

CONCLUSION

Conjunction presumably exists to help speakers and writers avoid repetition of identical constituents and to avoid ambiguity. We have seen that this can be done by adding coordinating conjunctions, and through the use of ellipsis and pro-forms. Correlative conjunctions can serve this same purpose, while emphasizing the coordination of grammatically similar constituents.

One of the fascinating aspects of conjunctions is the chameleonlike way in which they may behave as simple logical operators at one extreme, and as discourse markers at the other. While the study of discourse markers does not play a large role in this book, teachers should be aware that many of the uses of conjunctions, particularly conversational ones, fall into this linguistic type. For ESL/EFL teachers, much having to do with conjunctions is fairly unproblematical for students. Nevertheless, the processes of coordination will have to be taught so that ESL/EFL students can learn to produce acceptable conjoined structures.

TEACHING SUGGESTIONS

I. Form. A focus on coordination in English is a good context in which to deal with grammatical parallelism—that is, the coordinating of sequences of NP-NP-NP, VP-VP-VP, and so on, while avoiding the coordination of unlike elements. Lack of parallelism is often seen as a problem in native student writing as well, but with a difference: ESL/EFL students often have difficulty internalizing and automatizing differences among word forms such as *important/importance* or *real/really/reality*; they also may have difficulties in recognizing larger phrasal units. Engaging students in coordination work is an excellent way to practice these forms even at advanced class levels. Students can be presented with sentences from a text like the following or shown samples of their own or other students' work; they can be asked to determine whether the sentences are properly formed and to fix those that are not:

> Weather is the effect of four forces: temperature, humid, wind, and the fourth force is pressure.

> Warm air rises, it cools, and forms clouds.

> The climate of northern Africa is hot and dry, in southeast Asia is hot and wet, and cold in northern Europe.

Creating parallel structures is strikingly like the addition of fractions: one cannot add fractions unless a common denominator exists. The idea that the process of forming parallel structures is exactly like that of finding common denominators may in fact be interesting to students who enjoy doing math.

2. Form/Meaning. The following exercise can be used to create the contexts for practicing *so/too/either/neither* forms. Students in pairs can draw up individual lists in which they describe their most and least favorite activities, their most and least favorite subjects in school, the things that they have never done that they would like to do, or the jobs that they would most and least like to have. (You might think up other possibilities, but the idea is to elicit points of agreement of both positive and negative types.) Students then compare lists and make note of the areas in which they agree. They then report to the class on the content of their lists; students take turns reading items where there is agreement:

Maria: Tomomi wants to visit Las Vegas, and so do I.
Tomomi: Maria would not like to major in engineering, and neither would I.

3. Form/Meaning. In the context of a discussion of world geography or cultures, students may be presented with a map of the world. One student can go up to the map and point to two countries, then ask another student to make a statement that is true of both countries. For example, if the student points to Russia and Canada, possible answers might be:

Russia is in the far northern part of the world, and Canada is, too.
Both Russia and Canada reach from one end of a continent to the other end.
Russia does not have banana trees, and Canada does not have them, either.

The student who answers with a true statement may then go up to the map and point to two countries of his/her own. Students take turns in this way until every student has asked and answered a question.

4. Form/Meaning. Shaw and Taylor (1978) have suggested that nonpictorial visual aids can be very useful stimuli for encouraging use of conjoined sentences in communicative exchanges among class members. For example, a baseball box score clipped from the previous day's newspaper could provide an opportunity for relevant practice. The statistics could allow for conjoined sentences, such as:

The Boston Red Sox scored eight runs, but they didn't win the game.
One player hit a single, a double, and a home run.
The Red Sox didn't make an error, nor did the Yankees.

5. Form/Meaning. The use of coordination with *too/either/neither* takes practice for ESL/EFL students to master. This is so partially because of structural difficulties; for *either/neither,* it is so also for another reason. Many languages—east Asian languages, for example—show agreement with a negative statement by asserting affirmation rather than negation. As we saw when discussing negative yes/no questions, when the question tag "You aren't from Japan, are you?" is used, the speaker will agree by saying "Yes" (meaning, "No, I am not from Japan"). This potentially confusing difference carries over to *neither* structures, where one student will say, "I am not finished with my studies," and a second student will comment, "So am I" (or "Me, too" meaning "Neither am I"). It is therefore highly desirable to spend time on this type of sentence-pairing.

One possibility is to have one student make a statement about a like or dislike, about his or her studies, or about another topic and have a second student comment on the statement with respect to himself or herself in the following manner:

S1: I don't like liver.
S2: I don't like liver, either.

A third student can then comment on the information given by students 1 and 2, saying:

S3: Neither Mariko nor Ali likes liver.
   Mariko doesn't like liver, and Ali doesn't like liver, either.
   Mariko doesn't like liver, and neither does Ali.

Should a sequence like that below occur:

S1: I don't like liver.
S2: So do I.

and if Student 3 cannot recognize and acknowledge it as an unacceptable response, the teacher can step in and model a more appropriate response.

6. Form/Meaning. A variation of the above exercise, useful for writing, has the students making lists of their likes and dislikes with regard to the city they are staying in, and then comparing lists like those below. This works well as a pair activity:

Ali	Mariko
1. I don't like the weather.	1. I don't like the food.
2. I don't like the dirty air.	2. I don't like the weather.
3. I don't like the subways.	3. I don't like the noise.
4. I like the food.	4. I like the people.
5. I like the people.	5. I like the school.
6. I like the museums.	6. I like the subways.

From this list, Ali, for example, may derive the following comparisons:

> I don't like the weather, and neither does Mariko.
> I don't like the subways, but Mariko does.
> I like the food, but Mariko doesn't.
> I like the people, and so does Mariko.

7. Form/Meaning. Ur (1988) describes an activity that gives students practice with correlative conjunctions. Students first are given a list of activities, such as painting a picture, playing basketball, helping to move heavy furniture, singing a high part in a song, and so on. Next, students receive brief descriptions of a few people. Students then are asked to say which people are likely to be able to do the activity; for example:

> Either Teresa or Joanna could paint a picture.
> Neither Umberto nor Ramón could sing a high part in a song.

8. Use. Thewlis (1997) suggests working with students on avoiding run-on or run-together sentences, in which coordinating conjunctions are omitted or sentences containing them are incorrectly punctuated. Give students a paragraph in which you have intentionally run together certain sentences, and ask them to correct it.

Alternatively, gather run-on sentences from students' compositions, and ask the students to correct the errors. Note that if you follow the latter alternative, there should be at least one error from most everybody in the class so as to avoid stigmatizing certain students.

9. Use. Tape-record a conversation and bring it to class. Ask students to listen to it and to make note of the coordinating conjunctions that they hear. Which of them are used as discourse markers? Can the students figure out their function?

EXERCISES

Test your understanding of what has been presented

1. Provide example sentences that illustrate the following terms. Underline the pertinent words in your examples.

   a. coordination
   b. coordinating conjunction
   c. conjunct
   d. correlative conjunction
   e. correlative movement
   f. *respectively*-addition
   g. ellipsis
   h. gapping

2. Draw trees for the following sentences and talk about how to map them onto surface structures:
   a. They were invited for dinner with Paul and Paulette.
   b. She likes Billy Joel's music, and so do I.
   c. She does not believe the reports, and neither do I.
   d. Jun wore a dress, and Ken a suit.

3. Explain by means of trees the ambiguity in the following sentence:

   Pam drinks coffee and milk.

4. *Do* could really be called a pro-VP, not a pro-verb. Explain.

Test your ability to apply what you know.

5. Suppose that your students produce the following sentences. What errors have they made? How might their attention be drawn to the errors?
   a. *Either Helen or Judy are going to be the president next year.
   b. *I couldn't go to a university in my country, and my sister couldn't go too.
   c. *The doctor couldn't be found anywhere, and the nurse either.
   d. *You didn't ask me, neither I asked you.
   e. *Bill can play tennis, and John can.
   f. *Fred paid Bill and Bill paid Fred, respectively.

6. While this chapter gives examples of many types of coordinated constituents, no examples of coordinated prepositions were listed. Can two prepositions be coordinated? If so, provide some examples.

7. An additional item frequently cited as a correlative conjunction is the sequence *not only . . . but also*. Construct your own example paradigm of its use.
   a. Can *not only . . . but also* coordinate successfully at all word and phrase categories? Will additional changes be necessary in some cases?
   b. Can you find an acceptable example of the use of this sequence at the clause-to-clause level?

8. Consider the following sentences:

   The police found him penniless and without visible means of support.
   They finished the freeway construction, and quickly.

Do these sentences seem to pose any problem for the analysis of coordination? Is there in fact a problem in each case, and if so, what? Can you think of a possible solution which takes ellipsis in a new direction that has not been covered in this chapter?

9. Suppose that a student tells you that he or she has heard the following sentence spoken by a native speaker of English:

   I'm neither going to make a salad or anything else today.

Having learned that *neither* should be followed by *nor*, the student is confused and asks for an explanation. What would you tell the student?

10. A writing student produces an essay, an excerpt from which appears below:

> It was a warm day, and we were feeling like nothing could happen to us because we were young and everything looked so beautiful in the mountains, and we went to pick up my brother because he was coming with us. We began our bicycle trip from my brother's house, and he lived not so far from the mountains, and so we rode directly in the direction of the mountains, and we felt the warm breeze on our faces and bodies, and after about one half-hour we reached the mountains, and it was cooler there. . . .

There are many possible ways for a teacher to respond to descriptive writing. Would you respond to the student's frequent use of *and* in this excerpt? If so, what might your response be? If you would rather not respond directly, what general comment can you make on the use of *and* in this piece?

BIBLIOGRAPHY

References

Bayer, S. (1996). "The Coordination of Unlike Categories," *Language* 72:3, 579–616.

Blakemore, D. (1988). "*So* as a Constraint on Relevance." In R. Kempson (ed.), *Mental Representations*. Cambridge: Cambridge University Press.

Blakemore, D. (1992). *Understanding Utterances*. Oxford: Blackwell.

Celce-Murcia, M. (1980). "A Discourse Analysis of *I do too, So do I*." In J. Povey (ed.), *Language Policy and Language Teaching: Essays in Honor of Clifford Prator*. Los Angeles: English Language Services.

Gamut, L. T. F. (1991). *Logic, Language, and Meaning* (vol. 1). Chicago: University of Chicago Press.

Lakoff, G., and S. Peters (1969). "Phrasal Conjunction and Symmetric Predicates." In D. Reibel and S. Schane (eds.), *Modern Studies in English: Readings in Transformational Grammar*. Englewood Cliffs, N.J.: Prentice-Hall.

Lunsford, A., and R. Connors (1995). *The St. Martin's Handbook* (3d ed.). New York: St. Martin's Press.

Posner, M. (1980). "Semantics and Pragmatics of Sentence Connectives in Natural Language." In J. Searle, F. Kiefer, and M. Bierwisch (eds.), *Speech Act Theory and Pragmatics*. Dordrecht: Reidel.

Schiffrin, D. (1987). *Discourse Markers*. Cambridge: Cambridge University Press.

Shaw, P., and J. B. Taylor (1978). "Nonpictorial Visual Aids." In S. Holden (ed.), *Visual Aids for Classroom Interaction*. London: Modern English Publications.

Stockwell, R., P. Schachter, and B. H. Partee (1973). *The Major Syntactic Structures of English*. New York: Holt, Rinehart, and Winston.

Tsai, P. (1980). "Neither Jane nor I are happy?" *English Teaching Forum* 18:1, 19–24.

Suggestions for Further Reading

For articles on conjunction in the generative tradition, see:

Baker, C. L. (1989, 1995). *English Syntax*. Cambridge: MIT Press.

Gleitman, L. (1969). "Coordinating Conjunctions in English." In in D. Reibel and S. Schane (eds.), *Modern Studies in English: Readings in Transformational Grammar*. Englewood Cliffs, N.J.: Prentice-Hall, pp. 80–112.

Lakoff, R. (1971). "*Ifs, Ands,* and *Buts* about Conjunction." In C. Fillmore and D. T. Langendoen (eds.), *Studies in Linguistic Semantics*. New York: Holt, Rinehart, and Winston.

For one of the first articles that addresses the interface between logic and pragmatics, see:
Grice, H. P. (1975). "Logic and Conversation." In P. Cole and J. Morgan (eds.), *Syntax and Semantics 3: Speech Acts.* New York: Academic Press, pp. 41–58.

For an overview of conjunctivity from the viewpoint of Systemic Grammar, see:
Martin, J. R. (1992). *English Text.* Philadelphia: John Benjamins.

For treatments of individual conjunctions, consult:
Blakemore, D. (1988). "Denial and Contrast: A Relevance-Theoretic Analysis of *But*." *Linguistics and Philosophy* 12, 15–37.
Blakemore, D. (1988). "*So* as a Constraint on Relevance." In R. Kempson (ed.), *Mental Representations.* Cambridge: Cambridge University Press.
Dascal, M., and T. Katriel (1977). "Between Semantics and Pragmatics: The Two Types of *But*—Hebrew *Aval* and *Ela*." *Theoretical Linguistics* 4, 143–172.

For a study that looks at the effect of discourse markers on ESL/EFL audiences, see:
Flowerdew, J., and S. Tauroza (1995). "The Effect of Discourse Markers on Second-Language Lecture Comprehension." *Studies in Second Language Acquisition* 17:4, 435–458.

For some practical suggestions on the teaching of conjunctions, especially correlatives, see:
Frodesen, J., and J. Eyring (1997). *Grammar Dimensions.* Book 4 (2d ed.). Boston: Heinle & Heinle.
Rutherford, W. (1975). *Modern English.* New York: Harcourt Brace Jovanovich.

For teaching punctuation of compound sentences, see:
Bryd, P., and B. Benson (1989). *Improving the Grammar of Written English: The Handbook.* Belmont, Calif.: Wadsworth.
Raimes, A. (1990). *How English Works.* New York: St. Martin's Press.

Many good usage manuals offer exercises on grammatical parallelism; for one that is accessible to both ESL/EFL and English native speakers, see:
Glazier, T. F. (1990). *The Least You Should Know About English.* New York: Harcourt Brace College Publishers.

ENDNOTES

1. A discussion is found in Bayer (1996) of various instances where unlike categories may be coordinated, such as

> Jermaine is boring and a fool.

2. *For* is used in writing, and somewhat archaically in speech, to mean "because":

> The flight was diverted to Philadelphia for the weather was bad in New York.

3. In another environment not discussed in this chapter, *so* need not move. This is typically called the *do so* construction, as in

> They asked me to move the car, and I did so.

4. Stockwell, Schachter, and Partee (1973), in a classic treatment, assumed a rule of "correlative addition," whereby the word *both* is inserted optionally; this rule captured the essential synonymy of identical sentences one of which contained *both* while the other did not: *John and his brother are mechanics* versus *Both John and his brother are mechanics. Both* may be used to put special focus on the fact that "not just one but two brothers are mechanics."

5. The *neither* in this sentence is a quantifier, not a correlative conjunction. Although both forms are identical and obviously related semantically, remember from Chapter 17 that quantifiers function as determiners, as *neither* does here, or pronouns.

6. For judgments on Mandarin, thanks go to Regina Wu and to the Taiwanese students in the Summer 1997 Academic English Program at UCLA.

7. *But* also has the meaning of "except," as in

> We had everything but what we needed.

This is an historically old use of the word; in this context it seems to function more as a preposition than as a conjunction and is usually treated as such in descriptive grammars. *But* may also be used in a second seemingly noncontrastive context where it often combines with *instead.*

> The rain did not go away but (instead) came down harder than ever.

In this use, *but* most often coordinates VPs rather than full clauses.

8. This fact seems, incidentally, to be the source of frequent production errors among Chinese ESL/EFL students who attempt to combine *although* at the beginning of an initial clause with *but* at the beginning of the second.

9. Note that the conjunction *so* is generically distinct from the *so* discussed earlier in this chapter as a marker of VP-deleted material:

> I can swim, and so can you.

25

ADVERBIALS

INTRODUCTION

Adverbials are morphologically and syntactically the most diverse grammatical structures in English. Traditional grammarians define *adverbs* as words that modify a verb, an adjective, or another adverb. However, in this chapter we will show that adverbials, which may be words, phrases, or clauses, are just as likely to modify entire sentences or clauses as they are to function according to the traditional definition of adverbs. We have already discussed adverbs and adverbials briefly in Chapter 2 (grammatical metalanguage) and Chapter 5 (phrase structure rules) and again in Chapter 21 (prepositions). In this chapter we provide an overview of adverbials in terms of their major phrasal and clausal types, including participles functioning as adverbials, complementing the section in Chapter 20 (adjectives) that examined participles functioning as adjectivals. We also examine what types of adverbials occur in sentence-final and in sentence-initial position, and we give special attention to preverbal adverbs of frequency[1] (e.g., *sometimes, often, never*) since they occur primarily—though not exclusively—in sentence medial position.

As mentioned above, this chapter is a general overview. Other specific topics involving adverbials are covered in later chapters: Conjunctive adverbs are covered in Chapter 26 and adverbial conditional clauses in Chapter 27. Relative adverbials are discussed in Chapter 29, and adverbials of degree are treated in Chapters 34 and 35.

We begin this chapter with a review and expansion of the rules stated in Chapter 5 for sentence-final adverbials; then we treat sentence-initial adverbials before considering some issues of form and use that pertain to both sentence-final and sentence-intial adverbials. We then turn to participles functioning as adverbials before treating preverbal adverbs of frequency.

FORM, MEANING, AND USE OF SENTENCE-FINAL ADVERBIALS

FORM OF SENTENCE-FINAL ADVERBIALS

As shown in our PRED expansion rules in Chapter five, sentence-final adverbials occur in the form of adverbial clauses, adverbial phrases, or prepositional phrases:

$$\text{PRED} \rightarrow \text{AUX VP (Advl)}^n$$

$$\text{Advl} \rightarrow \left\{ \begin{array}{l} \text{AdvCl} \\ \text{AdvP} \\ \text{PrepP} \end{array} \right\}$$

> Adverbial clause: Mary danced *while John played the piano.*
> Adverbial phrase: Mary danced *very gracefully.*
> Prepositional phrase: Mary danced *in the living room.*

Here is an example tree diagram of a sentence with two final adverbials; we can generate such sentences using our phrase structure rules from Chapters 5 and 6:

Jason ate dinner at four o'clock because he was hungry.

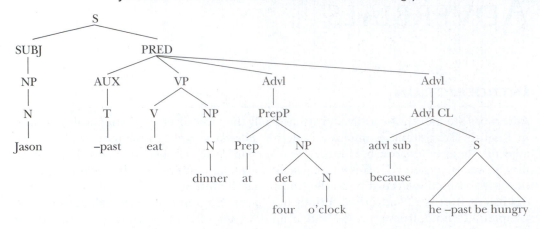

MEANING OF SENTENCE-FINAL ADVERBIALS

Not every form combines with every semantic sub-type of sentence-final adverbial, as demonstrated by the several empty spaces in the matrix in Table 25.1, which is intended to be representative rather than exhaustive in terms of sentence-final adverbial types:

Table 25.1　　Form and Meaning of Sentence-final Adverbials

MEANING OF ADVERBIAL	FORM OF SENTENCE-FINAL ADVERBIALS		
	Adv. Clause	**Adv. Phrase**	**Prep. Phrase**
Direction	—	northwards	to the store ø[2] there
Position	where Main St. crosses First Ave.	(quite) locally	in the garden ø here
Goal	—	—	at the station
Manner	just as I do	(very) quickly	with gusto
Time	after he saw the report	(quite) recently	at six o'clock ø next week
Frequency	as often as you can[3]	(almost) always	ø every Monday
Purpose	in order to finish the job[4]	—	for the glory
Reason (Cause)	because we were able to go there	—	because of the weather[5]

USE OF SENTENCE-FINAL ADVERBIALS

Although these adverbials can also occur in sentence-initial position—an option we discuss later—sentence-final position is certainly the more frequent and unmarked position for them. As we pointed out in Chapter 5, when more than one sentence-final adverbial occurs, there are unmarked orders that tend to be followed; for example:

- direction or goal comes before position
- manner comes before time or frequency
- purpose and reason come last after other adverbials

There are also some variable orders for sentence-final adverbials:
- manner and direction + position can occur in either order
- time and frequency can occur in either order

This information allows us to propose the following rule of thumb regarding the unmarked ordering of sentence-final adverbials:

$$\begin{Bmatrix} \text{direction} \\ \text{goal} \end{Bmatrix} + \text{position} \longleftrightarrow \text{manner} + \text{time} \longleftrightarrow \text{frequency} + \begin{Bmatrix} \text{purpose} \\ \text{reason} \end{Bmatrix}$$

Fortunately, the use of sentence-final (and clause-final) adverbials has been studied by Miller (1991), who examined a database of 50,000 words (roughly half spoken and half written); he found 2,901 tokens of clause-final adverbials. Approximately 75 percent of these tokens were prepositional phrases while adverbial phrases, adverbial clauses, and nonfinite adverbials accounted for the remaining 25 percent in that order. Miller found the following totals and percentages with respect to single and multiple strings of sentence-final adverbials in his corpus (all but the last example come from Miller's database but are not cited in his thesis):

one final adverbial   1,597   (73%)

    (e.g. The machine worked <u>properly</u>.)

two final adverbials   486   (22%)

    (e.g. They raced <u>up the slope to the steppes beyond</u>.)

three final adverbials   87   (4%)

    (e.g. Noriega shouted <u>at his supporters in the town of Santiago on Thursday</u>.)

four final adverbials   14   (less than 0.5%)

    (e.g. The attempted overthrow was launched <u>in a hail of gunfire at about 8 A.M.</u> <u>(on)</u> <u>Tuesday by a Panamanian major and 100 rebel soldiers</u>.)

five final adverbials   3   (less than 0.1%)

    (e.g. Mary Morris is resting <u>comfortably at her Buttonwillow home to finish her recuperation after her doctors released her earlier this morning</u>.)[6]

What we can conclude from Miller's numbers is that strings with more than three sentence-final adverbials—while possible—are extremely rare. Multiple adverbials of two or more occurred 13 times per 1,000 words in Miller's written corpus but only 7.6 times per 1,000 words in his oral corpus, supporting the intuition that such structures occur more in written than in spoken English discourse. Furthermore, within the written corpus, Miller found that the fiction portion of his database was richest in clause-final adverbials (85 per 1,000 words), followed by popular philosophy/history, technical writing, and journalism.

While adverbial prepositional phrases occurred in all positions in a string of multiple adverbials in Miller's data, adverbial phrases tended to occur first in a string (61 percent of the time) and adverbial clauses tended to occur last (78 percent of the time). This confirms that shorter constituents tend to come before longer constituents in a string of multiple adverbials.

The semantically based sequences that were strongly confirmed by Miller's study were the following:[7]

Direction occurs before position (92 percent of tokens)

> (e.g. I last saw Phil walking across the street in Atlanta.)

Manner before time or frequency (75 percent of tokens)

> (e.g. Mrs. Lee worked very quickly yesterday.)

Position or direction before time or frequency (80 percent of tokens)

> (e.g. Tourists travel to the Caribbean every December.)

Goal before time or frequency (95 percent of tokens)

> (e.g. The train arrived at the station before dinner.)

Reason or purpose come last (more than 75 percent of tokens)[8]

> (e.g. Kuniko studies hard to get good grades.)

Miller also found that manner and position occur in either order with equal frequency as do time and frequency:

Manner/Position: Bill weeded $\begin{cases} \text{energetically in his garden.} \\ \text{in his garden energetically.} \end{cases}$

Time/Frequency: Sarah jogs $\begin{cases} \text{at 6 A.M. every morning.} \\ \text{every morning at 6 A.M.} \end{cases}$

All of these findings support the rule of thumb we presented earlier on page 493 of this chapter.

FORM, MEANING, AND USE OF SENTENCE-INITIAL ADVERBIALS

FORM OF SENTENCE-INITIAL ADVERBIALS

Like sentence-final adverbials, sentence-initial adverbials can be phrasal (which includes single words), prepositional, or clausal, although the shorter phrasal adverbials tend to occur more frequently in this position:

> phrasal: *Fortunately,* Helen won the election.
> prepositional: *With our help,* Helen won the election.
> clausal: *After we held a recount,* Helen won the election.

In order to account structurally for the possibility of generating one or more adverbials directly in initial position, we allow the sentence modifier (sm) to generate adverbials as one of many possibilities (i.e., along with *not, Q,* etc.).

With such a capability for "sm," we can then expand "Advl^n" to directly generate all the adverbials that readily occur in sentence-initial position before the subject and predicate. As Quirk et al. (1985) point out, initial adverbials "are syntactically more detached and in some respects 'superordinate' in that they have a scope that extends over the sentence as a whole" (p. 613).

Here is an example tree diagram for a sentence with this type of adverbial:

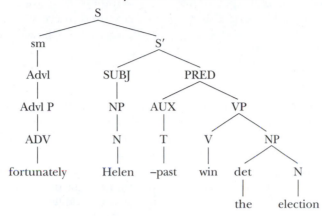

Fortunately, Helen won the election.

We could change the sentence modifier so that instead of being a single phrasal adverb like "fortunately," it is a prepositional phrase (e.g., *of course, with our help*) or an adverbial clause (e.g., *if/whenever we all voted; after we held a recount*). (With the exception of *of course*, the other sentence-initial adverbials that are prepositional phrases or adverbial clauses do not express speaker stance and attitude.[9] However, like the single-word adverbs, their scope also includes the entire following sentence. We say more about the use of sentence-initial adverbials in a later section.)

MEANING OF SENTENCE-INITIAL ADVERBIALS

Sentence-initial adverbials have been classified by different analysts as being "epistemic" (Lyons 1977), "evaluative" (Ernst 1984), "evidential" (Chafe and Nichols 1986; Palmer 1988), "factive" (Koktova 1986a,b), and "attitudinal" (Greenbaum 1969). We find it useful to refer to Halliday's (1994) four functional categories for sentence-initial adverbs, all of which refer to a different facet of speaker attitude:

Probability: *maybe, perhaps, certainly, surely*
Usuality:[10] *usually, generally, typically, occasionally*
Presumption: *of course, obviously, clearly, evidently*
Desirability: *(un)fortunately, luckily, hopefully, regrettably*

With the exception of the prepositional phrase *of course*, these lexical adverbs are all generated as adverbial phrases consisting of a single adverb.

USE OF SENTENCE-INITIAL ADVERBS.

The most comprehensive data-based study of the use of sentence-initial adverbs of probability, usuality, presumption, and desirability has been done by Lee (1991). She examined over 300,000 words each of written and spoken data (a total of more than 675,000 words) and found 736 tokens of sentence-initial adverbs that were distributed as follows (percentages are rounded off) across the four categories:

probability	280/736	38 percent	(e.g., *maybe, perhaps*)
usuality	199/736	27 percent	(e.g., *sometimes, often*)
presumption	200/736	27 percent	(e.g., *of course, obviously*)
desirability	57/736	8 percent	(e.g., *(un)fortunately*) (Lee 1991:29)

While the first three categories were well represented in Lee's corpus, the fourth occurred much more rarely. Lee decided to look at seven words in detail because she had a sufficient number of tokens to make generalizations about their use at the discourse level and felt that they represented best how these adverbs are used in everyday discourse: *maybe* (136), *perhaps* (169), *sometimes* (77), *of course* (125), *obviously* (37), *unfortunately* (34), and *fortunately* (19)—497 tokens altogether.

Maybe Versus Perhaps

On the surface, *maybe* and *perhaps* seem to be very similar sentence-initial adverbs. However, while *maybe* occurred twice as often in speech as in writing, *perhaps* had the reverse pattern in Lee's corpus, suggesting that *perhaps* is the more formal of the two. Lee found that both *maybe* and *perhaps* are used to rule out previously made assertions and to contrast two or more arguments—both co-occurring frequently with *but* or equivalent terms (e.g., *except*). *Maybe* tended to cluster with other tokens of *maybe*, emphasizing the speaker's uncertainty as well as the different alternatives possible:

> [G. recounts his war experiences in Vietnam]
> G: . . . So *maybe* just *maybe* I could work my way, because at night there was artillery from Da Nang. And if I just followed that direction, just *maybe* I could come upon one of the patrols or something. *Maybe* I'd just luck out, you know.
>
> (Lee 1991:46)

This led Lee to suggest that *maybe* is weaker in terms of probability than *perhaps*, which was reinforced by the fact that *maybe* co-occurred with overt negatives more frequently than *perhaps*:

> [oral narrative about faith-healing]
> . . . *maybe* there was *no* divinity in this whole thing at all. *Maybe* there was *no* force falling, *maybe* there was *nothing* except just the change of attitude on the part of the recipient.
>
> (Lee 1991:48)

Tokens of initial *perhaps*, on the other hand, rarely clustered and tended to collocate with positive superlatives; Lee suggests that this is a strategy used by the writer to strengthen the truth of the following proposition or inference or to recommend the writer's judgment to the reader regarding the alternative presented. Alternatively, we suggest *perhaps* is used by the speaker to persuade the reader of the truth of the following proposition:.

> [from a feature in *Newsweek*]
> Seven out of 10 families eat dinner together twice or more times a week. . . . *Perhaps* the *most* hopeful sign for the future of America's dinnertime is that couples with young children seem especially determined to have their evening meal together.
>
> (Lee 1991:54)

Sometimes

Of the 77 tokens of *sometimes* in Lee's corpus, 56 were used in speech and 16 of these tokens occurred in clusters (i.e., sometimes *x*, sometimes *y*). This sentence-initial adverb occurred most often (of the seven studied by Lee) with first and second person NP subjects, reinforcing its strong interpersonal force. Lee found that the discourse functions of *sometimes* varied according to whether it occurred initially, medially, or finally in the paragraph or episode:

Used paragraph-initially (22/77 tokens), it presents the topic and provides a transition with what preceded:

> *Sometimes* the truth itself is better than fiction. An almost illiterate man served three years in jail for a warehouse robbery he insisted he didn't commit. His defense was that he was a mile away in a shopping plaza, but he had no witnesses.
>
> (Lee 1991:58)

Used paragraph- or episode-medially (42/77 tokens), *sometimes* elaborates upon or restates the preceding argument:

> Well, there are some aspects that overlap. *Sometimes*, say, for instance, the matter of point of view will come up in a poem. . . . It's crucial in fiction, and it's not something you think a lot about in poetry. . . .
>
> (Lee 1991:60)

Used paragraph- or episode-finally (13/77 tokens), *sometimes* is used to sum up the preceding arguments, to show the result of a process or some change, or to offer a final alternative, as in the last sentence of the following speaker turn:

> "It used to be," said my friend, Beth, grieving the death of her middle son, "that whenever I'd catch myself in repose, I'd be aware that I wasn't happy. . . . Somewhere along the way, there has been a change. I'm no longer feeling that ever-present sorrow. I feel comfortable again in moments of repose. *Sometimes* I feel very happy."
>
> (Lee 1991:60–61)

Of Course Versus *Obviously*

For both sentence-initial *of course* and *obviously*, the proposition's truth value is so unarguable from the speaker/writer's perspective that he or she projects strong certainty to the interlocutor. Of Lee's 125 tokens for *of course*, 93 were spoken and 32 written. For *obviously*, there were many fewer tokens (i.e., 37) but a better balance between the spoken (20/37) and the written (17/37) corpus. Lee characterizes *of course* as having a persuasive rhetorical function while presuming the listener shares the opinion expressed by the speaker: it marks a point of departure from the argument in the prior discourse and simultaneously provides another perspective that contrasts with the prior discourse; often a version of the first argument is once again subsequently reasserted following *but* (or an equivalent form):

> As recently as the early 1970s, when I was doing the research for a book on the lives of young working-class families, many of the men still said stoutly, "No wife of mine will ever work; she belongs at home with the kids." *Of course,* many working-class women have always worked outside the home, and many of those I met then did also. *But* the men in those families felt it as a stigma, a public admission of their inadequacy . . .
>
> (Lee 1991:67)

While following much the same pattern of argumentation as *of course*, *obviously* (according to Lee) tends to reinforce a more negative or self-effacing perspective rather than marking a more positive, or self-enhancing perspective as *of course* does; it also does not presume that the listener agrees with the speaker and thus requires less context than *of course* to support its use (the following example contains several of these adverbs):

> [from the White House Transcripts]
> HP—And I see the problem in two dimensions and, *of course,* I see it in this respect as a neophyte. *Obviously* you and Bill Rogers are much more experienced in these affairs than I, *but* maybe because I am a neophyte and one of the public I see it perhaps more clearly—at least from a different point of view. (Lee 1991:79)

Fortunately Versus Unfortunately

Both of these two sentential adverbs occurred almost twice as frequently in the written corpus as in the spoken one, and *unfortunately* occurred almost twice as frequently as *fortunately*. The speaker/writer signals negative assessment and regret about circumstances when using *unfortunately*, which tends to co-occur with other grammatical and lexical items indicative of a negative or problematic situation:

> [in a review of P. Skira's *Still Life: A History*]
> [The genre of still life] has suffered from relative scholarly *neglect* in spite of the almost hypnotic appeal exerted by many of the images . . . produced by . . . our greatest artists. . . .

> → *Unfortunately*, this volume *fails* to fill the void. It does *not* supersede Charles Sterling's "Still Life Painting . . . " (1959), which, *regrettably*, was reprinted in 1981 with *only* black-and-white illustrations.

> (Lee 1991:83)

"In contrast to *unfortunately*, which foregrounds problems, a main function of *fortunately* is its problem-solving scope (Lee 1991:91)." After a problem has been stated, use of *fortunately* indicates the speaker's conviction that the reality of things is in fact less negative and more positive than prior information might lead one to expect:

> [from a review of a restaurant]
> The Cactus Café is the front end of a comedy nightclub, The New Improvisation in Santa Monica. But these ungainly air ducts hanging down from the ceiling aren't funny . . .

> → *Fortunately,* though, the Cactus Café is a pretty comfortable room, with its surprisingly high ceiling and mirrors. It's a pleasant place to sit and eat . . .

> (Lee 1991:87)

ADDITIONAL COMMENTS ON INITIAL AND FINAL ADVERBIAL CLAUSES

REDUCED FORMS OF ADVERBIAL CLAUSES

Some adverbial clauses of time, both initial and final, may appear in subordinate clauses in which the subject and sometimes also the auxiliary verb seem to have been deleted. Thus we can have synonymous pairs like the following:

> When the barber was finished with the haircut, he took the customer's money.
> When finished with the haircut, the barber took the customer's money.

> Until I came to this city, I did not know what excitement was.
> Until coming to this city, I did not know what excitement was.

> He did his homework while he was listening to music.
> He did his homework while listening to music.

> When she saw a seagull, she always smiled broadly.
> When seeing a seagull, she always smiled broadly.

These reductions are actually types of *participial* constructions, which are to be discussed later in more depth.[11]

The concessives *although, even though, though,* and *while* may also appear in reduced clauses:

Although he was rather late to the party, he was still able to get some food.
Although rather late to the party, he was still able to get some food.

While it was not the best season for wildflowers, it was certainly not a bad season.
While not the best season for wildflowers, it was certainly not a bad season.

When teaching such reductions, the principle by which we may infer the identity of the deleted subject should be kept in mind. Most typically, it is the subject of the main clause that is identical with the deleted subject of the reduced subordinate clause.

PUNCTUATION WITH ADVERBIAL CLAUSES

In written English, a sentence-initial adverbial clause is normally followed by a comma whereas a sentence-final adverbial clause normally is not preceded by a comma although there is some variation here:

After Professor James finished the lecture, he asked for questions from the audience.
Professor James asked for questions from the audience after he finished the lecture.

These punctuation conventions reinforce the more salient role in discourse that sentence-initial adverbials have.

Sometimes, if a sentence-final adverbial clause is viewed as an afterthought; it; too, is set off with a comma:

Professor James was willing to answer questions, provided the audience wanted to ask any.

USE OF INITIAL AND FINAL ADVERBIAL-CLAUSES IN CONVERSATION

Ford (1993), drawing on the earlier work of Thompson (1985), Schiffrin (1987), and others, examined a fairly large corpus of transcribed conversations and found 194 adverbial clauses. These are the types of adverbial clauses Ford found:

Temporal: *When an old man reaches* 77, they have this big ceremony. (p. 29)
Conditional: *If you wanna go home*, Donna, I'll take you. (p. 43)
Causal: You don't like it,[12] *because you didn't think of it.* (p. 94)
Concessive: He's getting a knee replacement, *even though he's not so active anymore.*[13]

These adverbial clauses are distributed as shown in Table 25.2, according to position and type (Ford 1993:24).

Table 25.2   Adverbial Clause Tokens in Conversations from Ford (1993)

	TYPE OF ADVERBIAL CLAUSE				
Position	**Temporal**	**Conditional**	**Causal**	**Concessive**	**Totals**
Initial	21	26	—	1	48 (25%)
Final	40	18	75	2	135 (69%)
No main clause	2	8	1	—	11 (6%)
Totals	63	52	76	3	194 (100%)

The figures in Ford's table show us that adverbial clauses occur sentence-finally in conversation much more often than sentence-initially (except for conditionals, which are discussed in detail in Chapter 27); causal adverbials—especially—tend not to occur initially. In a small number of cases (6 percent), there is no main clause. We can also see that concessive adverbial clauses seem to be rather rare in informal conversation.

Ford also noted that conversation is very different from writing since in conversation sentence-final adverbials can follow a main clause spoken with continuing intonation or they can follow a main clause that has been spoken with final intonation—that is, the adverbial clause can have its own separate intonation contour. This latter option of a separate contour occurred 18 percent of the time for sentence-final temporal clauses, 33 percent of the time for final conditionals, and—most surprisingly—53 percent of the time for causal adverbial clauses. Leaving aside conditional clauses for the moment, since they are discussed in detail in Chapter 27, what did Ford find with respect to initial and final adverbial clauses in conversation?

Sentence-initial adverbial clauses are "pivotal points in the development of talk" (p. 62). They present explicit background for what follows in the discourse; they also tend to tie back to previous discourse. Sentence-initial temporal adverbial clauses, for example, introduce time frames and also signal shifts in time (from general/nonspecific to specific or vice versa). The following segment shows a shift from a specific time reference to a time that is nonspecific (adapted from Ford 1993:37–38):

> E: So you're not gonna go up this weekend?
> C: Nuh, I don't think so.
> E: How about the following weekend?
> C: That's the vacation, isn't it?
> E: Oh. All right. No hassle . . . we'll make it for another time then. Just let me know when you're gonna go.
> C: Sure.
> → E: Whenever you have intentions of going, let me know.
> C: Right.

According to Ford, sentence-final adverbial clauses with continuing intonation serve to provide new information that qualifies, locates, or completes the meaning of preceding utterances, but they do not create discourse links or shifts the way that the sentence-initial ones do. In the following example, the temporal adverbial clause completes the meaning of the preceding main clause:

> [G. is talking about the car of an acquaintance]
> G: In two weeks, he's taking it t' Florida.
>   He's gonna pull it down there,
>   Just to goof around with,
> → While he's down there on vacation.

(adapted from Ford 1993:69)

However, sentence-final adverbial clauses produced with their own separate intonation contour have altogether different functions, according to Ford. Such adverbial clauses are used either by the same speaker (to self-edit in response to a perceived problem) or by another speaker (to negotiate understanding). Segments exemplifying both of these cases follow:

> [A is telling R about his work situation at a TV studio]
> A: But the thing is, they might get their project canceled. (pause)
>   → Because ABC got bought out. Did you hear about that?

(adapted from Ford 1993:111)

[J shows his understanding and agreement with P, whose roommates are out for the
  night]
P: I've got the apartment to myself, and I'm gonna take advantage of it by going to bed
  early.
J: Oh.
P: An' they come home, they gonna talk about it. And I'm gonna go to bed.
→J: Before they get there, yeah.

(adapted from Ford 1993:126)

In summary, Ford (1993) shows us how the operation of the turn-taking system in conversation and the more general management of information in discourse both help to explain the initial and final placement of adverbial clauses in conversations and the difference between sentence-final clauses that are intonationally linked to the preceding main clause versus those that function as separate utterances with their own intonation contours.

PARTICIPLES FUNCTIONING AS ADVERBIALS

In addition to adverbial clauses, adverbial phrases, and adverbial prepositional phrases, we also need to discuss another structure not directly generated by our rules: adverbial participles. For example, we discussed reductions such as the following earlier in the chapter:

Until I came to this city, I did not know what excitement was.
Until coming to this city, I did not know what excitement was.

Not all adverbial participials retain an adverbial subordinator; in fact, many simply begin with an -*ing* verb form or an -*en* verb form:

Turning the corner, John was surprised to see Alice walking toward him.
Written in Spanish by his grandmother, the letter was incomprehensible to José.

THE FORM OF ADVERBIAL PARTICIPLES

The -*ing* participle has three possible forms:

1. Basic form: *working* (signals a time overlapping with the time expressed in the main clause), such as

Working diligently on his paper, John began to type up the bibliography.

2. Perfective form: *having worked* (signals a time preceding the time expressed in the main clause), such as

Having worked on his paper since 4 P.M., John stopped at 8 to watch the DePaul basketball game.

3. Perfective-progressive form (rare): *having been working* (signals an action in progress at a time preceding the time expressed in the main clause), such as

Having been working on his paper for more than a week, John decided he would turn it in without further revision.

The *-en* participle also has three possible forms:

1. Basic form: *worn out* (signals a reason for the result expressed in the main clause), such as

> Worn out from all the work, John decided to relax.

2. Progressive form: *being worn out* (much like the basic form but with stronger emphasis on the fact that the participle gives a reason or cause for the result expressed in the main clause), such as:

> Being worn out from all the work, John decided to relax for the evening.

3. Perfective form: *having been worn out* (signals that the action in the participle is completed before—and is also the reason for—the result expressed in the main clause), such as:

> Having been worn out from three days' work on his paper, John decided to relax over the weekend.

The basic form is by far the most frequent one for both the *-ing* and the *-en* participle. The other forms do occur, however, and grammar texts sometimes erroneously refer to the progressive and perfective forms of the *-en* participle as instances of the *-ing* participle because of the initial *-ing* forms.

SENTENCE-INITIAL ADVERBIAL PARTICIPLES

The adverbial use of *-ing* and *-en* participles in clause-initial position is a potential problem for native as well as nonnative speakers of English. Errors such as the following are traditionally referred to as "dangling modifiers" or "dangling participles," and they are the bane of many a high school English teacher's existence:

> *Laughing hysterically and unable to answer Miss Fiddich, she sent poor Tom to the principal's office.

> *Torn and bent beyond recognition, I received my mother's letter.

In such cases, the subject of the participle should also be the subject of the main clause. Whenever this is not the case—as in the two examples above—a dangling participle (i.e., an ungrammatical sentence) results.

Danielson and Porter (1990) have pointed out that such participles can usefully be viewed as reduced forms of adverbial clauses; however, they caution that the reduction is grammatically acceptable only if both clauses have the same underlying subject. With this condition in mind, we can now correct the above sentences:

> Because Tom was laughing hysterically and unable to answer Miss Fiddich, Tom was sent to the principal's office (by Miss Fiddich).→Laughing hysterically and unable to answer Miss Fiddich, Tom was sent to the principal's office.

> After my mother's letter had been torn and bent beyond recognition, my mother's letter was delivered to me yesterday.→Torn and bent beyond recognition, my mother's letter was delivered to me yesterday.

Both native and nonnative users of English should be given ample opportunity to reduce sentence-initial adverbial clauses to participle clauses when the same subject condition is met. Students should also be able to identify clauses that cannot be reduced to participles. Some teachers find it useful to point out to their students the unintended humor that occurs when a dangling participle is interpreted literally; for example:

> *Following the recipe carefully, my cake was a great success. (= my cake followed the recipe carefully!)

> *Flattened out of shape by Dmitri's serve, we could no longer play with the old volleyball. (= we were flattened out of shape by Dmitri's serve!)

The same subject participles discussed above are the most common type of sentence-initial adverbial participle; however, it is also possible to have a sentence-initial adverbial participle with a subject that is different from the subject of the main clause; in such a case the subject of the participle must be overtly stated:

> The bus drivers being on strike, many people had to get to work using other means of transportation. (Since the bus drivers were on strike, . . .)

When *-en* participles are used in this type of construction, only the progressive or perfect form of the participle occurs:

> The house having been constructed poorly, the new owners had to cope with many unexpected repairs. (Since the house had been constructed poorly, . . .)

Many grammarians refer to the two preceding sentences as absolute constructions, which they carefully distinguish from participle clauses. We see no need to do this, since the semantic function of the two clause types is parallel.[14] The only difference is whether the subjects of the two clauses are the same or not.

SENTENCE-FINAL ADVERBIAL PARTICIPLE CLAUSES

A sentence-final participle clause is normally detached from the main clause by a comma in writing or by special features in speech, such as a pause before the lowered pitch on the participle clause; for example:

> Laura looked at him, consumed with contempt for what he represented.

> An old woman shouts out a long apocalyptic interpretation of the Bible, prophesying the immediate arrival of the Messianic Kingdom.

While the use of a sentence-final participle clause seldom leads to ungrammatical sentences in the way that the use of the "dangling modifier" does, a potential for ambiguity exists in those cases where there is more than one noun in the main clause that could be the antecedent of the underlying subject in the participle clause:

> ?Meg met Tom in the corridor, laughing heartily about what had happened in class.

In the absence of additional context, either *Meg* or *Tom* could be the underlying subject of the participle clause in this sentence. Such ambiguity, however, rarely occurs. First of all, the main clause may have only one noun phrase:

> Betty danced joyfully, never suspecting what was about to happen.

Second, for many main clauses with two or more noun phrases, there is usually only one noun phrase that qualifies semantically as the subject of the participial clause:

> Sheila ignored the dog and the TV set, deeply engrossed in the new book-of-the-month that had come in the mail.

Even though the main clause in this example contains three noun phrases (i.e., *Sheila, the dog, the TV set*), only *Sheila* can serve as the underlying subject of the participial clause—that is, someone who is deeply engrossed in reading a book.

Note that all the examples we have given above of sentence-final adverbial participles are of same noun phrase variety—the subject of the participle clause is identical in reference to one of the noun phrases in the main clause. As shown before with sentence-initial clauses, not all sentence-final participle clauses conform to this pattern; some have an overt subject that is not identical in reference to any noun phrase in the main clause.

> They decided to wait for dawn, *each hiker taking his two-hour turn at watch.*
> She walked along hurriedly, *her purse clutched tightly in her arms.*

Again, we feel that there is no significant difference in structure or function between the examples involving identical noun phrases and non-identical noun phrases. The identical noun phrases have simply been deleted with the remainder of the clause being reduced to a participle.

THE DISCOURSE FUNCTION OF ADVERBIAL
-*ING* PARTICIPLE CLAUSES

In carrying out an extensive study of -*ing* participle clauses, Thompson (1983) found that they occurred most frequently in descriptive prose and very rarely in factual, scientific writing. For example, she compared 10,000 words of text from two different sources—a historical narrative and a pharmacology text—and found that the former contained 74 -*ing* participle clauses while the latter contained only five. (We feel that a similar ratio would obtain for -*en* participle clauses if such a count were carried out.) Thompson feels that the differences in frequency can be explained by the discourse function of these participle clauses; namely, they evoke a visual image in the mind of the listener or reader. Thompson's term for this function is "depictive." She adds that the more formal the language and the more descriptive the discourse, the higher the frequency of participle clauses. A corollary of this functional principle is that participle clauses do not occur frequently in speech, since conversation leaves little opportunity for the planning required to make one's language evoke images in the listener's or reader's mind, which is the function of this construction.

FORM, MEANING AND USE OF
PREVERBAL ADVERBS OF FREQUENCY

Background

In Chapter 5 we mentioned the adverbials of frequency that usually occur at the end of a sentence. Some of these adverbials express a specific and others a general sense of frequency:

> Bob does his laundry *once a week.* ⎫
> I brush my teeth *every day.* ⎬ specific frequency

> Helen does the dishes *once in a while.* ⎫
> You should write your parents *every now and then.* ⎬ general frequency

If we want to be more precise, we can refer to such adverbials as "adverbials of specific or general frequency."[15] Although these adverbials tend to occur at the end of the sentence (i.e., the activity is in focus), they may also occur initially if the adverbial of frequency is in focus:

Once a week Bob does his laundry.
Every now and then you should write your parents.

FORM OF PREVERBAL ADVERBS OF FREQUENCY

In contrast to these adverbials of specific or general frequency, English also has a class of preverbal adverbs of frequency (PAFs) that tend to occur most naturally in the middle of a sentence:[16]

Josh *never* writes his parents.   Bill has *often* forgotten to make his bed.
Mary is *always* late for class.   I can *usually* do my shopping on Saturday.

As you will see below, the preferred position for such adverbs of frequency is somewhat complicated but predictable. Because of the complexity, however, misplacement of these forms is a common problem for ESL/EFL learners, who produce ill-formed sentences such as the following:

**Always Mary is coming late to class.   *Bill has forgotten often to make his bed.

THE SCOPE OF PREVERBAL ADVERBS

Perhaps the most important generalization to make about preverbal adverbs is that in any given sentence, they modify the entire sentence in which they occur. The following paraphrases make this clear:

Barry frequently drives faster than the speed limit. (It is frequently the case that Barry drives faster than the speed limit.)

Cynthia never smiles at strangers. (It is never the case that Cynthia smiles at strangers.)

We can expand our basic phrase structure rule to optionally generate preverbal adverbs of frequency (PAF) and other adverbials such as the conjunctive adverbs to be discussed in Chapter 26 between the SUBJ and the PRED node:

$$\begin{Bmatrix} S \\ S' \end{Bmatrix} \rightarrow \text{SUBJ (Advl) PRED}$$

This rule accounts for all indicative and imperative sentences with preverbal adverbs that do not have auxiliary verbs:

Gerald seldom goes to church.
Joan always jogs in the morning.
Never talk with your mouth full.

The rule also accounts for all cases where there is an operator (i.e., an auxiliary verb or copula *be*) that carries emphatic or contrastive stress; that is, the preverbal adverb always precedes a stressed auxiliary or copula:

You never *are* ready on time!   Jim never *did* talk to Raymond![17]
I never *have* met the president!

This rule also accounts for reduced sentences where the operator occurs in final position, and thus cannot take reduced stress the way it might if it occurred in a complete sentence, e.g.:

A: Is Mr. Franks strict?   A: I want to be class president.
B: Yes, he often is.   B: You never will (be).
(cf. Yes, he is often strict.)   (cf. You will never be class president.)

However, we need to adjust the output of our rule to account for the many cases where a complete sentence contains an unstressed operator (auxiliary verb or *be* copula). In such cases, a rule of adverbial movement will move the PAF directly after the operator (and before *not* if syntactic negation with *not* is involved—see the discussion on *not* in the meaning section):

| Mary is always late for class. | Bill has often forgotten to make his bed. |
| I can usually do my shopping on Saturday | Mickey has always been on time. |

Let us look at the tree diagram and mapping rules for one of these sentences:

I can usually do my shopping on Saturday.

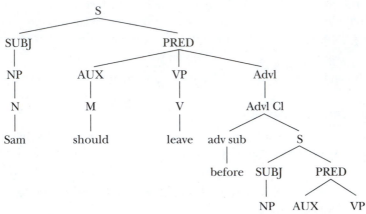

The one mapping rule required for a grammatical surface structure is the adverbial movement rule since this sentence requires no morphological rules:

    Output: I usually can do my shopping on Saturday.
    Advl movement: I can usually do my shopping on Saturday.

Some of the preverbal adverbs of frequency fall into Halliday's "usuality" category for sentential adverbs (i.e., *sometimes, occasionally, frequently, usually, generally, regularly*)[18] and thus can also be generated directly in initial position. The PAFs that can occur easily in sentence-final position and can be generated there are: *sometimes, occasionally, often,* and *frequently*. The other PAFs are awkward (*usually, rarely, seldom*) or ungrammatical (*never, always*) in final position. Therefore, we need a stylistic and lexically specific rule that allows generation of *sometimes, occasionally, often,* and *frequently*—but not the other PAFs—in final position.

    However, all preverbal adverbs of frequency can be generated between the subject and the predicate and then adjusted for surface position with respect to the operator, as necessary.

    A good piece of evidence for claiming that PAFs are generated sentence-internally and preverbally are the negative PAFs, which express zero or low frequency: *never, seldom, rarely, scarcely ever,* and *hardly ever*. When they are moved to initial position for stylistic reasons, it is necessary to invert the subject and the operator in response to the fronting (adding *do* if no operator is present) to ensure grammaticality.[19]

$$\text{We have} \begin{cases} \text{never} \\ \text{seldom} \\ \text{rarely} \\ \text{scarcely ever} \\ \text{hardly ever} \end{cases} \text{seen such a sight!}$$

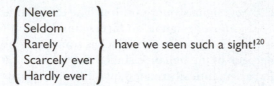

$\left\{\begin{array}{l}\text{Never} \\ \text{Seldom} \\ \text{Rarely} \\ \text{Scarcely ever} \\ \text{Hardly ever}\end{array}\right\}$ have we seen such a sight![20]

If the negative PAFs could be directly generated in initial position, there would be no subject-operator inversion, i.e., the inversion is a reaction to the fronting of the negative adverbial, which has been generated medially.

Statements and Questions with *Ever*

The particle *ever*[21] interacts with preverbal adverbs of frequency in a number of ways. As shown above, it is generally used phrasally with *scarcely* and *hardly* when they function as preverbal adverbs of frequency:

Joan has $\left\{\begin{array}{l}\text{scarcely} \\ \text{hardly}\end{array}\right\}$ ever gone to bed after midnight.

*Joan has $\left\{\begin{array}{l}\text{scarcely} \\ \text{hardly}\end{array}\right\}$ gone to bed after midnight.

In such cases, *scarcely ever* or *hardly ever* would be generated as phrasal preverbal adverbs in the base and follow the same rules of adverbial movement discussed above.

Ever can also be used in yes/no questions as the most general (i.e., least presupposing) of the PAFs:

Does Mark $\left\{\begin{array}{l}\text{ever} \\ \text{sometimes} \\ \text{often} \\ \text{usually} \\ \text{always}\end{array}\right\}$ sing in the shower?

The *wh*-question for all expressions of frequency (including PAFs) is "how often":

How often does Mark sing in the shower?

THE MEANING OF PREVERBAL ADVERBS OF FREQUENCY

Resemblance to Quantification

Similar to the quantifiers described in Chapter 17, preverbal adverbs of frequency fall along either the positive or the negative continuum of a scale on which *always* constitutes the positive extreme and *never* the negative one. Again, there are several pairs of positive and negative terms that logically contradict each other. (See the diagonal lines in the diagram.)

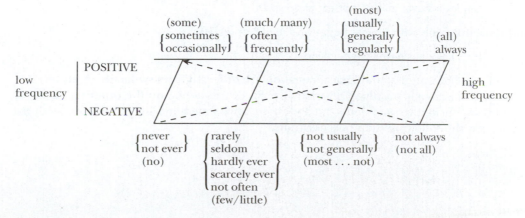

Note: The dotted line between *never* and *always* signals an opposition. The dotted line and arrow going from *not always* to *sometimes/occasionally* signals an inverse implication (e.g., saying that Jack is not always on time is the same as saying that Jack is sometimes not on time or that Jack is sometimes late).[22] Because of the semantic similarities between quantifiers and preverbal adverbs of frequency, a semantically related quantifier is indicated in parentheses at each point in the diagram.

Many sentences with preverbal adverbs can in fact be paraphrased with sentence-final adverbials containing semantically related quantifiers:

> John *always* gets up at 7 A.M.   John gets up at 7 A.M. *all the time.*
> Bob *sometimes* reads the paper.   Bob reads the paper *some of the time.*
> Students *often* drink beer.   Students drink beer *on many occasions.*

Likewise, the *wh*-question of frequency "How often?" has its quantifier-based counterpart in "How many times?"

> How often have you gone to Boston?   How many times have you gone to Boston?

Negation and Preverbal Adverbs

As Klima (1964) has pointed out, we can verify the negative or affirmative nature of preverbal adverbs by observing their behavior in unmarked tags, since an affirmative preverbal adverb co-occurs with a negative tag and vice versa.

$$
\text{Jason is} \left\{ \begin{array}{l} \text{always} \\ \text{often} \\ \text{sometimes} \end{array} \right\} \text{late, isn't he?}
$$

(i.e., these are affirmative preverbal adverbs)

$$
\text{Mavis} \left\{ \begin{array}{l} \text{never} \\ \text{seldom} \\ \text{scarcely ever} \end{array} \right\} \text{goes out, does she?}
$$

(i.e., these are negative preverbal adverbs)

Interaction with *Not*

The semantically strongest negative preverbal adverb of frequency (e.g., *never*) may not co-occur with the negative particle, *not,* if the *not* derives from the sentence modifier:[23]

> *Jim is not never on time.

It does occasionally occur with the *not* expressing phrasal negation (see Chapter 10):

> Sandra is never able to not eat chocolates.

and it occurs freely with lexical negation (see Chapter 10):

> Mrs. Beck has never been unkind.

(Recall that both phrasal and lexical negation are different from syntactic negation.)

The semantically positive preverbal adverbs of frequency, on the other hand, occur not only in affirmative statements but also in negative statements in combination with *not* (or *-n't*), as the following examples illustrate:

1. a. Florida often $\begin{Bmatrix} \text{isn't} \\ \text{is not} \end{Bmatrix}$ cold in winter.

   b. Florida is often not cold in winter.

   c. Florida $\begin{Bmatrix} \text{isn't} \\ \text{is not} \end{Bmatrix}$ often cold in winter.

2. a. Professor Potter usually $\begin{Bmatrix} \text{hasn't} \\ \text{has not} \end{Bmatrix}$ attended faculty meetings.

   b. Professor Potter has usually not attended faculty meetings.

   c. Professor Potter $\begin{Bmatrix} \text{hasn't} \\ \text{has not} \end{Bmatrix}$ usually attended faculty meetings.

Our current syntactic rules for negation and for PAF generation and movement account for sentences like (1a and b) and (2a and b). In these sentences, the *not* and the PAF are independently generated, placed, and moved, if needed. In the case of (1c) and (2c), the *not* appears to be part of a phrasal negative PAF (i.e., *not often, not usually*) that has been generated medially and moved to post operator position. Other phrasal PAFs that are a result of combining with *not* in this way are: *not always, not ever,* and *not generally.*

SOME OBSERVATIONS ON THE USE OF PREVERBAL ADVERBS OF FREQUENCY

Frequency in Oral Discourse

Not all preverbal adverbs occur with equal frequency in oral discourse. We examined about 23,000 words of transcribed English conversation (American, 14,000 words; British, 9,000 words). Altogether, there were 79 occurrences of preverbal adverbs, distributed as follows:

never—32	ever (in questions)—9	usually—2
always—19	occasionally—3	generally—1
sometimes—13		

The only thing that surprised us about this count was the fact that *often* did not occur even once in the approximately 23,000 words. It would be interesting to have comparable data from a written corpus to see what, if any, register differences there are.

Interaction with Tense and Aspect

Praninskas (1975) points out that since preverbal adverbs of frequency are used to express approximately how many times a habitual action or condition is repeated, they are typically not used with the progressive aspect. Instead, the simple present tense, the present perfect tense, and the simple past tense (in its habitual sense) tend to co-occur with these adverbs:

Professor Johnson is always busy.   Joe often studied until midnight.
I have never visited Japan.

In fact, we would add that all adverbials of frequency—not just the preverbal adverbs—tend to co-occur with tenses that are used to express habitual action:

Horace goes to the movies once a week.
Alberta drank champagne every now and then.

While we agree in principle with Praninskas' generalization, we would, however, point out that the progressive aspect may co-occur with preverbal adverbs of frequency when the speaker's message carries emotional overtones:

> Orville is always hearing noises. (i.e., he hallucinates)

Compare this with the less emotional, more objective sentence:

> Orville always hears noises. (i.e., he has a keen sense of hearing)

The preverbal adverb of highest frequency, i.e., *always*, also closely resembles certain adverbs that express iteration or duration, although *always* is less emphatic than *continually* or *constantly*:

$$
\text{Sydney is } \left\{ \begin{array}{l} \text{always} \\ \text{continually} \\ \text{constantly} \end{array} \right\} \text{ grouchy.} \qquad \text{Martha } \left\{ \begin{array}{l} \text{always} \\ \text{continually} \\ \text{constantly} \end{array} \right\} \text{ loses things.}
$$

(durative: a continuing state of affairs)　　(iterative: a series of events)

Sentence-initial Use of PAFs

Several—though not all—preverbal adverbs of frequency sometimes occur in initial position. What does such initial position signal? Close (1981) suggests that logical contradiction is a likely environment for a sentence-initial preverbal adverb:

> A: Peter is always on time.
> B: No, Peter isn't always on time. *Sometimes* he's late.

While this seems to be a reasonable suggestion, Lee's (1991) research on *sometimes*—reported above—certainly argues that sentence-initial use of PAFs can signal other important discourse organizing functions, especially if they occur at the beginning of a paragraph or episode.

Some Other Discourse Considerations

Many reference grammars and ESL/EFL textbooks state that *how often* begins a *wh*-question that asks about frequency. What they usually do not point out is that such questions tend to elicit responses containing specific (or general) adverbials of frequency rather than preverbal adverbs of frequency. In fact, a response with a preverbal adverb could be considered vague, evasive, or even rude:

A: How often do you go to the movies?　B: $\left\{ \begin{array}{l} \text{I go about once a week.} \\ \text{?I go (fairly) often.} \end{array} \right.$

A: How often do you study in the library?　B: $\left\{ \begin{array}{l} \text{I study there every night.} \\ \text{?I always study there.} \end{array} \right.$

The above questions begin with "How often do you . . . ," and they are asking about the frequency of current habitual activities. There are other questions beginning with "How often . . . " that involve the perfect of experience; a specific or general frequency is expected in the response. Again, most preverbal adverbs are inappropriate, and *always* is impossible.

A: How often have you been to Acapulco?

B: $\left\{ \begin{array}{l} \text{Three times.} \\ \text{Many times.} \\ \text{?Seldom.} \\ \text{?Frequently.} \\ \text{*Always.} \end{array} \right.$

Yes/no questions with *ever*—like the above "How often . . . ?" questions—may ask about either specific experiences or the frequency of habitual actions:

Specific experience: Have you ever been to Acapulco?
Frequency: Do you ever study in the library?

Yes/no questions with *ever* that ask about specific experiences tend to elicit specific responses—again, responses with a preverbal adverb of frequency are too vague:

A: Have you ever been to Acapulco?

B: $\begin{cases} \text{Yes, for one week back in 1971.} \\ \text{?Yes, I } \begin{cases} \text{sometimes go} \\ \text{usually go} \end{cases} \text{ there.} \end{cases}$

On the other hand, yes/no questions with *ever* that ask about the frequency of habitual actions readily elicit responses with a preverbal adverb of frequency, and they are the only questions with *ever* that can do this:

A: Do you ever study in the library?

B: I $\begin{cases} \text{always} \\ \text{usually} \\ \text{often} \\ \text{sometimes} \\ \text{rarely} \\ \text{never} \end{cases}$ do.

Therefore preverbal adverbs are not normally elicited by wh-questions and can be naturally elicited by only one type of yes/no question (i.e., questions about the frequency of habitual actions). This observation has ramifications for teaching, since we want our students to practice using preverbal adverbs in contexts that are as natural as possible. Clearly we need a comprehensive discourse analysis of the use of preverbal adverbs in English speech and writing that will give us some of the information we have about other adverbials, based on the research of Lee (1991), Miller (1991), and Ford (1993).

CONCLUSION

This chapter has expanded on our brief earlier discussions about adverbial phrases, prepositional phrases used adverbially, and adverbial clauses. We have shown that these three adverbial structures can be generated both sentence-finally and sentence-initially, with very different implications for the organization of discourse.We also included a discussion of participles functioning as adverbials to complement our earlier discussion of participles functioning as adjectives in Chapter 20. In the final section of this chapter we introduced preverbal adverbs of frequency (PAFs), an important sub-class of adverbials, which overlap semantically with the quantifiers presented in Chapter 17. All PAFs are generated medially between the subject and the predicate; many of them can also be generated sentence-initially where they function as sentence modifiers reflecting speaker stance, and a few of them can occur sentence-finally as verb phrase modifiers.

Adverbials will be the topic of the following two chapters on logical connectors, Chapter 26, and conditionals, Chapter 27. We will encounter adverbials again as a special type of relative clause in Chapter 29 and in the two chapters that deal with degree constructions (Chapters 34 and 35).

TEACHING SUGGESTIONS

1. Form. Miller (1991:75–77) suggests having learners unscramble sentences putting the adverbials after the verb; each scrambled sentence contains two adverbials for which a clear ordering preference has been established; for example:

> sometimes/John/to the beach/goes
> jumped/the cat/into the car/through the window
> in the spring/salmon/upstream/swim
> Mr. Chaves/from Peru/immigrated/ten years ago

2. Form/Meaning. To help learners see the semantic relationship between adjectives and adverbs of manner, have them convert sentences with adverbs to sentences with adjectives, and vice versa:

> John is a careful worker → John works carefully.
> Sheila dances gracefully → Sheila is a graceful dancer.

3. Use. Provide students with contexts that would allow them to respond with sentential adverbs in order to show their attitude and stance:

Context	*Response(s)*
The American Cancer Society estimates that at least 20 percent of all cancers could be prevented by proper diet.	Perhaps that's an understatement.
	Of course, if you include tobacco as part of diet, the percentage goes way up.
	Sometimes I wonder what these people base their numbers on.

4. Meaning/Use. Danielson and Porter (1990:195) suggest providing students with a text where the adverbials come at the end of each sentence in parentheses in a scrambled order. The students have to rewrite the paragraph inserting the adverbials in appropriate places:

> San Francisco is cool (in the summer, usually). The skies are overcast, and the fog rolls off the bay to cover the city (in the morning, almost always, completely, often). However, the weather turns warm and sunny (sometimes). . . .

5. Meaning/Use. Thewlis (1997:25) suggests that students complete sentences about themselves (the prompts contain sentence-initial or preverbal adverbs and/or the beginning of a sentence-final adverb):

> I often think about my problems when . . .
> While I was growing up . . .

6. Form/Meaning. Ask students—based on their personal experience—to qualify statements that the teacher provides by selecting the appropriate preverbal adverb of frequency from a list and then placing the adverb correctly in the sentence:

> (list of adverbs: *always often sometimes seldom never*)
> *T:* Juan is late for class.
> *S1:* Never.
> *S2:* Juan is never late for class.

7. Meaning. Sharon Voss (personal communication) suggests that the teacher prepare large flashcards—each with a preverbal adverb of frequency. When each student has a flashcard, the class members must first arrange themselves into a positive group and a negative group. Then, within each of the two groups, they should order themselves from high to low frequency according to the meanings of the preverbal adverbs of frequency on their flashcards. Each student then says an original sentence using his or her preverbal adverb of frequency and, if necessary, receives comments and corrections from peers. The teacher should also get the students to discuss the appropriateness of the sentences containing the preverbal adverbs (e.g., Would an alternative sound better?).

8. Use. Have students work in groups to describe events that surround some notable event such as an earthquake, an election, the Olympics, or the World Cup. Ask them to use preverbal adverbs of frequency to describe the related events. For example:

> an earthquake
> Some animals always know when an earthquake is going to occur.
> People sometimes panic during an earthquake.
> Homes and buildings are often damaged by an earthquake.

EXERCISES

Test your understanding of what has been presented.

1. Provide original sentences that illustrate the following terms or rules. Underline the pertinent word(s) in your examples.
   a. sentence-initial
      (i) adverbial phrase
      (ii) prepositional phrase
      (iii) adverbial clause
   b. sentence-final
      (i) adverbial phrase
      (ii) prepositional phrase
      (iii) adverbial clause
   c. specific or general adverbial of frequency
   d. preverbal adverb of frequency
      (i) positive
      (ii) negative
   e. phrasal preverbal adverb of frequency
      (i) positive
      (ii) negative
   f. adverbial participle

2. Why are the following sentences or dialogues ungrammatical?
   a. *Is not he ever going to finish his degree?
   b. *Marvin does often not dance.
   c. A: Are you ever late to class?
      B: *I am never.

Test your ability to apply what you know.

3. If your students produce sentences like these, what error(s) have they made? How will you make them aware of the errors, and what activities will you provide to correct these errors?
   a. *José can play sometimes handball after work.
   b. *Rarely we can eat outside in the garden.
   c. *I speak fluently French.
   d. *We enjoy going in Boston to seafood restaurants.
   e. *Crying hysterically, the mother tried to calm the little girl down.

4. What is the difference in meaning, if any, between the sentences in each of the following pairs?

    a. Alice uses dental floss.
       Alice always uses dental floss.

    b. Sometimes we need to think before we act.
       We sometimes need to think before we act.

    c. When I think about Sybil, I get very angry.
       I get very angry when I think about Sybil.

5. What, if anything, is inappropriate with the responses to these two questions? What is the explanation for any problem you detect?

    a. *A:* How often do you go to the beach?
       B: Usually.

    b. *A:* Have you ever been to Europe?
       B: Sometimes.

6. A student asks you if there is any difference between these two sentences, and if so, when he should use one form rather than the other. What will you say?

    a. I have always told the truth.
    b. I always *have* told the truth.

7. A student asks you which of these two sentences is correct. What will you say?

    a. I watch the news at 10 P.M. every day.
    b. I watch the news every day at 10 P.M.

BIBLIOGRAPHY

References

Chafe, W., and J. Nichols (eds.) (1986). *Evidentiality: The Linguistic Coding of Epistemology.* Norwood, N.J.: ABLEX.

Close, R. A. (1981). *English as a Foreign Language* (3d ed.). London: Allen and Unwin.

Danielson, D., and P. Porter (1990). *Using English.* (2d ed.) Englewood Cliffs, N.J.: Prentice Hall Regents.

Ernst, T. B. (1984). *Towards an Integrated Theory of Adverb Position in English.* Bloomington, Ind.: University of Indiana Linguistics Club.

Greenbaum, S. (1969). *Studies in English Adverbial Usage.* London: Longman.

Halliday, M. (1994). *Introduction to Functional Grammar.* London: Edward Arnold.

Jacobs, R. (1995). *English Syntax: A Grammar for English Language Professionals.* Oxford: Oxford University Press.

Klima, E. (1964). "Negation in English." In J. Fodor and J. Katz (eds.), *The Structure of Language.* Englewood Cliffs, N.J.: Prentice-Hall, 243–323.

Koktova, E. (1986a). *Sentence Adverbials in a Functional Description.* Amsterdam: John Benjamins.

Koktova, E. (1986b). Remarks on the Semantics of Sentence Adverbials. *Journal of Pragmatics* 10:1, 127–40. Cambridge: Cambridge University Press.

Lee, D. K. (1991). "A Discourse Analysis of Seven English Sentential Adverbs." Unpublished M.A. thesis in TESL, UCLA.

Lyons, J. (1979). *Semantics* (vol. 2). Cambridge: Cambridge University Press.

Miller, D. O. (1991). "A Discourse Analysis of Clause-Final Multiple Adverbials." Unpublished M.A. thesis in TESL, UCLA.

Palmer, F. R. (1988). *Mood and Modality*. Cambridge: Cambridge University Press.

Praninskas, J. (1975). *Rapid Review of English Grammar*. Englewood Cliffs, N.J.: Prentice-Hall.

Quirk, R., S. Greenbaum, G. Leech, and J. Svartvik, J. (1985). *A Comprehensive Grammar of the English Language*. London: Longman.

Schiffrin, D. (1987). *Discourse Markers*. Cambridge: Cambridge University Press.

Thewlis, S. (1997). *Grammar Dimensions*. Book 3 (2d ed.). Boston: Heinle & Heinle.

Thompson, S. A. (1983). Grammar and Discourse: The English Detached Participial Clause. In F. Klein (ed.), *Discourse Perspectives on Syntax*. New York: Academic Press, 46–65.

Thompson, S. A. (1985). "Grammar in Written Discourse: Initial vs. Final Purpose Clauses in English." *Text* 5:1, 55–84.

Suggestions for further reading

For useful overviews of linguistic and grammatical analysis of adverbials, see:

Buysschaert, J. (1982). *Criteria for the Classification of English Adverbials*. Brussels: Paleis der Academien.

Ernst, T. B. (1984). *Towards an Integrated Theory of Adverb Position in English*. Bloomington, Ind.: University of Indiana Linguistics Club.

Nilsen, D. L. F. (1972). *English Adverbials*. The Hague: Mouton.

For useful information on usage, see:

Ford, C. E. (1993). *Grammar in Interaction: Adverbial Clauses in American English Conversation*. Cambridge: Cambridge University Press.

Greenbaum, S. (1969). *Studies in English Adverbial Usage*. London: Longman.

Koktova, E. (1986). *Sentence Adverbials in a Functional Description*. Amsterdam: John Benjamins.

For information on negative preverbal adverbs of frequency, see:

Klima, E. (1964). "Negation in English." In J. Fodor and J. Katz (eds.), *The Structure of Language*. Englewood Cliffs, N.J.: Prentice-Hall, 246–323.

For suggestions on how to teach adverbials, see:

Danielson, D, and P. Porter (1990). *Using English: Your Second Language* (2d ed.). Englewood Cliffs, N.J.: Prentice Hall Regents, 181–196.

For explanations and exercises for learners on adverbial phrases and clauses and also on using adverbs and aspect to indicate time relationships, see:

Thewlis, S. (1997). *Grammar Dimensions*. Book 3 (2d ed.). Boston: Heinle & Heinle, 27–43 and 360–374.

ENDNOTES

1. The term "preverbal adverb of frequency" comes from the work of Klima (1964).

2. All the ø symbols represent obligatorily or optionally deleted prepositions of the types described in Chapter 21.

3. This is an equative degree clause functioning adverbially (see Chapter 35), not the usual subordinate adverbial clause consisting of an adverbial subordinator followed by a full sentence.

4. Note that this is a nonfinite adverbial clause, different from the usual adverbial clause (an adverbial subordinator followed by a full finite sentence). Jacobs (1995:67) points out that nonfinite subordinate clauses often lack an overt subordinator: *She locked the door (so as) to prevent any more intrusions.*

5. Recall that *because of* is a complex preposition of the type described and diagrammed in Chapter 21.

6. This example is adapted from Thewlis (1997:36) because we could not locate one of the three tokens with five final adverbials in Miller's database.

7. These examples have been constructed by Miller or the authors.

8. This result could also be due to constituent length: reason or purpose adverbials tend to be clauses, which are almost always longer than phrases.

9. The other major syntactic means of introducing speaker stance and attitude toward propositions in English is via the short introductory clauses that can precede noun clause complements: *It's possible* he was injured; *I think* you're right. (See Chapter 31.)

10. This includes "frequency," which we treat in our discussion of preverbal adverbs of frequency. Some of the preverbal adverbs of frequency, such as *sometimes*, can also function as sentence-initial adverbs.

11. These should not be confused with gerund constructions, which we discuss in Chapter 32. The *-ing* forms that appear here do not make the verbs into nouns. If the *-ing* forms after *until* and *when* were really nouns, it would be possible to question it as a "what?": (*When what did she always smile broadly?)

12. The comma in these examples and other data from Ford (1993) does not reflect orthographic convention but intonation following the notation used in conversation analysis, where a comma means level intonation, a period (full stop) means falling intonation, and a question mark means rising intonation.

13. This is a constructed example. We could not find a concessive example in Ford (1993).

14. The semantic function of all these adverbial participle clauses is either temporal (i.e., *after x, y,* or during *x, y)* or causal (i.e., *because of x, y, or given x, y).*

15. We have not provided phrase structure descriptions for many general and specific adverbials of frequency, such as *once a week, once in a while, every now and then,* because their analysis is simply too complicated to be worth doing. *Once a week,* for example, would have an underlying structure corresponding roughly to

$$\text{`` } \left\{ \begin{matrix} \text{ø} \\ \text{on} \end{matrix} \right\} \text{ one time } \left\{ \begin{matrix} \text{during} \\ \text{in} \end{matrix} \right\} \left\{ \begin{matrix} \text{every} \\ \text{each} \end{matrix} \right\} \text{ week''}$$

Such a string would require a series of lexicalizations and syntactic reductions before we finally arrived at *once a week.*

16. Note that whereas adverbials of specific or general frequency tend to be phrases (with exceptions such as *weekly, yearly, daily, hourly*), preverbal adverbs of frequency tend to be single words, although they may take intensifiers and thereby form adverbial phrases (e.g., *very often, almost always*). Sometimes both types of adverbs of frequency occur in statements of habitual action, e.g., *I usually do my laundry once a week.* When this happens, the preverbal adverb is modifying the specific adverbial of frequency; in other words, preverbal adverbs of frequency modify the entire sentence—they do for the sentence what quantifiers do for the noun phrase—whereas general or specific adverbials of frequency modify the activity expressed in the verb phrase.

There are also some prepositional phrases semantically similar to the preverbal adverbs *generally* and *usually* that typically occur in initial position:

$$\left\{ \begin{matrix} \text{As a rule} \\ \text{In general} \end{matrix} \right\} \text{ Sara walks her dog after dinner.}$$

17. Note that in this example the auxiliary verb *do* has been added via operator addition to carry the emphatic stress as well as the tense. For further discussion of this function of *do*, see Chapter 30. Also, with emphatic *do* as operator, there is one other possible ordering in strong agreement rejoinders that the rules do not predict: Yes, she *does* always do that!

18. For some reason, *often* is more awkward than these other adverbs when used sentence-initially (?Often Mary jogs in the morning) even though it is in the same semantic category. The somewhat archaic equivalent form *oftentimes* seems to work better in initial position than *often*.

19. Negative preverbal adverbs are not the only negative forms that cause subject/operator inversion when fronted. Most, if not all, negative constituents have this effect in English:

Not since Hiroshima has mankind seen such devastation.

20. Note that not all sentences containing *never, rarely,* etc., may undergo this change of word order. The speaker or writer typically must be expressing an exclamation of sorts; if not, the fronting of the negative PAF and the inversion are strange:

John has never washed his socks.   ?Never has John washed his socks.

21. *Ever* can function on its own as a PAF in questions and after *not/-n/t*.

22. *Ever* is not listed on the semantic continua for preverbal adverbs of frequency (see p. 507) because it is midway between the positive and negative lexical items. It occurs mainly in questions or in negatives as a part of phrasal combinations with *not, hardly,* or *scarcely*.

23. This impossible combination may be due to the fact that historically *never* is a lexicalized form of *not + ever*.

Chapter 26

LOGICAL CONNECTORS

INTRODUCTION

In Chapter 24, we presented an overview of coordinating conjunctions, which were said (a) to conjoin syntactically equivalent constituents and (b) to lead the listener/reader to certain interpretations of the way that clauses relate to each other meaningfully. These interpretations might be available without the use of conjunctions, but their use strengthens the likelihood that the listener/reader will understand the connections as the speaker/writer intended them. In Chapter 25, we considered adverbials in general, noting the variety of forms that they take and syntactic positions that they occupy.

In this chapter, we focus on adverbial expressions, which in a great many cases serve a purpose similar to coordinating conjunctions—that is, they allow a listener/reader to infer connections between two segments of discourse—usually adjacent sentences. We also mention a few other lexical means for achieving the same purpose. Together, these expressions are often called logical connectors, and they chiefly include what are traditionally called *subordinating conjunctions* (what we have called *adverbial subordinators*) and *conjunctive adverbials*.[1] Like some uses of coordinating conjunctions, logical connectors are typically said to be types of cohesive devices, lexical expressions that may add little or no propositional content by themselves but that serve to specify the relationships among sentences in oral or written discourse, thereby leading the listener/reader to the feeling that the sentences "hang together" or make sense.

TYPES OF LOGICAL CONNECTORS

CLAUSES WITH ADVERBIAL SUBORDINATORS

We have already encountered in this book what traditional grammarians have called subordinating conjunctions. We have referred to them as adverbial subordinators because they function to subordinate one clause to another and they have the force of an adverbial. We first introduced them in Chapter 5, where we saw that one of the grammatical forms that adverbials take in English is clausal (rule 8), and that adverbial clauses are in turn composed of sentences that are introduced by adverbial subordinators (rule 9).

$$
8. \quad \text{Advl} \rightarrow \left\{ \begin{array}{l} \text{Advl Cl} \\ \text{Advl P} \\ \text{PrepP} \end{array} \right\}
$$

$$
9. \quad \text{Advl Cl} \rightarrow \text{adv sub S}
$$

Simple Adverbial Subordinators

A list of simple adverbial subordinators or subordinating conjunctions includes the following:

after	lest	when(ever)
although	once	where(ver)
as	since	whereas
because	though	while
before	until	
if	unless	

We should point out immediately that many of the words listed above also fit other part-of-speech categories, in which they would not be called adverbial subordinators. You have seen how *where* and *when*, for instance, function as *wh*-question words (Chapter 13). As you will see later, they also function as markers of relative clauses (see Chapter 29).

One test for whether or not a form is serving as an adverbial subordinator is to move the clause into different positions in the sentence, for adverbials typically can occupy clause-final, initial, and medial positions.

final: A whole crowd came out to see him *when he arrived.*
initial: *When he arrived,* a whole crowd came out to see him.
medial: A whole crowd came out, *when he arrived,* to see him.

Adverbial subordinators double in other contexts as prepositions in prepositional phrases:

adv sub: *Before/After the play ended,* many patrons were crying.
Prep: *Before/After the play,* we had coffee.

adv sub: *Since the day you talked to me about it,* I've become convinced.
Prep: *Since Monday,* it has been terribly hot.

adv sub: *Until it cools off,* I am not doing any yardwork.
Prep: We will not have our next class *until the end of the week.*

Notice that what distinguishes these uses is what comes after the adv sub or Prep. If it is an adv sub, it will be followed by a clause; as a Prep, it is followed by an NP.[2]

An additional possible point of confusion concerns the word *as.* This word falls into the class of subordinators provided that it is used in the causal sense of *since,* as below:

She left soon, as she saw no reason to remain.

As is also used extensively in comparative structures; it is discussed in that context at some length in Chapter 34.

Complex Adverbial Subordinators

We will add to the list of expressions certain other fixed lexicalized units that also follow the pattern of preceding a subordinate clause, where the combination of [complex adverbial subordinator + clause] is able to appear in various positions in the sentence—before, after, and occasionally in the middle of, the main clause:

so/as long as	inasmuch as	in that
as soon as	in case (that)	now that
even if	in order that	provided that
even though	insofar as	so that
given that		

final: You can stay with us *as long as you bring your own bedding.*
initial: *As long as you bring your own bedding,* you can stay with us.

final: Bring an umbrella *in case it rains.*
initial: *In case it rains,* bring an umbrella.

The Syntax of Sentences with Adverbial Clauses

When the adverbial subordinator + subordinate clause appears in final position in the sentence, the tree looks like the following:

Sam should leave before Larry objects.

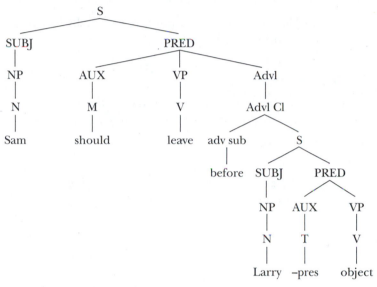

When the adverbial clause appears at the beginning of the sentence, the adverbial clause is considered a sentence modifier, as you saw in the previous chapter. The reasons for the different architecture between sentence-initial and sentence-final position are discussed later in the section on use.

Before Larry objects, Sam should leave.

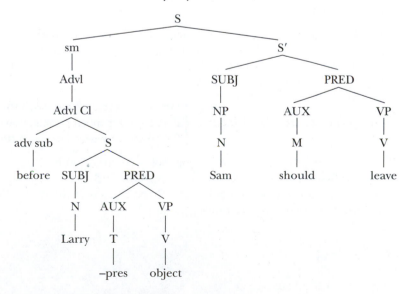

It is somewhat more difficult for adverbial clauses to appear medially; when they do so appear, they are typically separated in speech by heavy pauses:

final: You can see as far as Orcas Island *when the sky is clear.*
initial: *When the sky is clear,* you can see as far as Orcas Island.
medial: You can, *when the sky is clear,* see as far as Orcas Island.

Note again a parallel with other adverbial options, here a prepositional phrase:

final: We plan to take the trip *during the summer.*
initial: *During the summer,* we plan to take the trip.
medial: We plan, *during the summer,* to take the trip.

Thus, we see once again that adverbials as a whole are unusually free in their placement options in comparison with other constituents.

CONJUNCTIVE ADVERBIALS

Conjunctive adverbials, unlike adverbial subordinators, are complete adverbials unto themselves. They do not subordinate a clause; rather, they connect independent clauses.

Sam should leave; *however,* Larry will object.

The inventory of English conjunctive adverbials is considerably larger than that of adverbial subordinators. A fairly complete list is given below. Some are individual words, and some qualify as lexicalized units:

additionally	furthermore	likewise
after all	however	moreover
also	in addition	nevertheless
alternatively	in any case/event	on the contrary
as a result	indeed	on the other hand
in contrast	in fact	otherwise
consequently	in other words	rather
conversely	in particular	similarly
despite that	in spite of that	still
first . . . second . . . finally	in sum	that is
for example/instance	in turn	therefore

Like other adverbials, most of these conjunctive adverbials are capable of appearing in different places in a clause; they may be found at the beginning, in the middle, or at the end of the independent clauses with which they occur. (We will discuss the punctuation of sentences with logical connectors below.)

Raccoons and bears are related animals. {
However, raccoons are much smaller.
Raccoons are much smaller, however.
Raccoons, however, are much smaller.

Because these adverbials relate independent clauses, two completely separate trees are drawn—one for the first sentence (without the adverbial) and one for the second (with the adverbial).[3] Following the first tree below are three trees that illustrate the variable positioning of *however* in the second sentence:

Raccoons and bears are related animals.

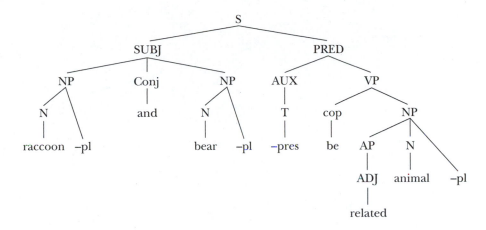

However, raccoons are much smaller.

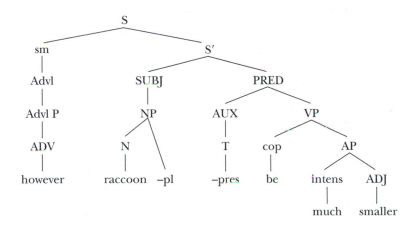

Raccoons, however, are much smaller.

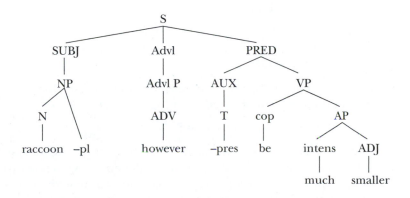

Raccoons are much smaller, however.

```
                         S
            ┌────────────┴──────────────┐
          SUBJ                         PRED
           │                     ┌──────┴───────┐
          NP                    AUX            VP
         ┌─┴──┐                  │       ┌──────┼─────────────┐
         N    │                  T      cop    AP            Advl
         │    │                  │       │    ┌─┴──┐          │
      raccoon –pl              –pres    be  intens ADJ      Advl P
                                             │     │         │
                                            much smaller    ADV
                                                             │
                                                          however
```

It is also possible for conjunctive adverbials to follow coordinating conjunctions and to relate grammatical categories below that of the full sentence:

> This is a possum and therefore a marsupial. (NP *and therefore* NP)
>
> You can raise the car or, alternatively, lower it to remove the engine. (VP *or alternatively* VP)
>
> She is on the one hand very helpful and on the other hand completely untrustworthy. (AP *and on the other hand* AP)

They work with the coordinating conjunctions to join syntactically equivalent constituents.

PUNCTUATION

Let us first look at the punctuation patterns found across the three types of connectors we have so far described. As a sample case, we will use the contrastive words *but* (a coordinating conjunction), *although* (an adverbial subordinator), and *however* (a conjunctive adverbial). While these connectors may not be completely interchangeable in context, they are close enough in their contribution to discourse to be usefully comparable when looking at form.

Coordinating Conjunctions

English writers tend to punctuate coordinated clauses in three ways—with periods before them, commas before them, and no punctuation at all.

> They had just arrived at their vacation retreat. But already they wanted to leave.
> They had just arrived at their vacation retreat, but already they wanted to leave.
> They had just arrived but they wanted to leave.

For many of you, the last sentence may seem improperly punctuated. However, you may be more willing to accept no punctuation in the following sentence:

> They had just arrived and dinner was served.

Quirk et al. (1985) report that there is a tendency on the part of English speakers to be more accepting of no punctuation when *and* is the coordinating conjunction than when *but* is used to mark a contrast. They also point out that independent sentences are more frequently introduced by *but* than by *and*. It is likely that the tendency to use commas is partly also a function of the relative length of the connected clauses. When the clauses are short, no punctuation may be required.

Adverbial Subordinators

With subordination, the options are somewhat more limited. Our example adverbial subordinator is *although.*

> He could not steer the boat out of the storm although he tried every means possible.

Usually, the two-clause sequence of main clause + subordinate clause does not require comma punctuation. An exception to this occurs when the adverbial clause has an after-thought quality—when there is a separation or juncture between it and the main clause, reflected in writing by the comma.

With the combination of subordinate clause + main clause, a comma is almost always used between the clauses in written texts.

> Although he tried every means possible, he could not steer the boat out of the storm.

In written texts, main clause + subordinate clause or subordinate clause + main clause combinations are not separated by a period (full stop), nor falling intonation between the clauses in oral production:[4]

> *He could not steer the boat out of the storm. Although he tried every means possible.

> *Although he tried every means possible. He could not steer the boat out of the storm.

Traditionally, cases of subordinate clauses that are punctuated as full sentences have been termed *sentence fragments*—that is, partial sentences masquerading as complete sentences.

Conjunctive Adverbials

When we turn to the conjunctive adverbial *however,* we see that it is preceded by a period or semicolon.[5] When *however* is in the clause-initial position of the second of two clauses that it connects, it is always followed by a comma. The comma is somewhat dependent on which conjunctive adverbial is used. *Nevertheless,* for example, does not need a following comma. Neither do *thus* and *rather.*

> He tried every means possible. However, he could not steer the boat out of the storm.
> He tried every means possible; however, he could not steer the boat out of the storm.
> He tried every means possible. Nevertheless he could not steer the boat out of the storm.

We do not see punctuation like the following:

> *He tried every means possible, however, he could not steer the boat out of the storm.

Traditionally, such written sentences are termed a type of *run-on sentence* or *comma splice*—that is, two sentences masquerading as a single sentence. It is possible, however, to bracket a conjunctive adverbial in commas when it falls in the middle of a clause, as in the following example:

> He tried every means possible; he could not, however, steer the boat out of the storm.

This rule depends somewhat on the particular conjunctive adverbial. A conjunctive adverbial like *also,* for example, need not be set off with commas.

> He tried every means possible. His partner also tried.

When the conjunctive adverbial falls at the end of the sentence, punctuation is not usually necessary.

> We could invite John. He's too busy though.

However is the exception to this rule, requiring a comma before it even when it is in clause-final position.

> He tried every means possible. He could not steer the boat out of the storm, however.

Punctuation Problems for ESL/EFL Students

The punctuation of sentences with coordinating conjunctions, adverbial subordinators, and conjunctive adverbials is one area where ESL/EFL learners might benefit from work with prescriptive grammar of the type that native English speakers receive, at least those in grade schools where a traditional prescriptive curriculum is followed. Yet the problems ESL/EFL learners face in punctuation are even greater for a number of reasons:

- Because the three classes of connectors are functionally so similar, students may consider them grammatically equivalent as well.
- Not all languages distinguish three classes of connectors in the way that English does, and for some that do have more than one class, there is a different correspondence between meaning and class than exists in English. Japanese, for example, has a single word that translates as "because," which may begin a clause that is freestanding both orthographically and intonationally. This situation may lead to the frequent production of sentence fragments in written English when a *because*-clause follows a main clause. Similarly, not all languages that have commas use them in quite the same way that English does; transfer from the native language in the area of punctuation may be strong in this area.
- Many conjunctive adverbials such as *nevertheless* and *consequently* are relatively uncommon in oral production, with the result that input providing cues to intonation is not normally available.

All these problems suggest that in teaching logical connectors, teachers should draw students' attention to issues of punctuation.

OTHER ESL/EFL FORM PROBLEMS WITH LOGICAL CONNECTORS

There are a few issues of form specific to individual logical connectors that arise for ESL/EFL students:

Because Versus Because Of

Confusion occurs between forms that are semantically and functionally similar but grammatically distinct. There is in English a prepositional construction *because of* that requires a noun object; it is often confused with the adverbial subordinator *because*, resulting in sentences like

> *We were late because of we had car problems.

A parallel problem holds for the expressions *as a result* and *as a result of*. Then, too, often the synonymous prepositional constructions *due to* and *on account of* are mistakenly pressed into service by learners as adverbial subordinators, as in the sentence

> *I couldn't finish my homework due to it was too hard.

For Example Versus Such As

Another common area of confusion concerns the semantically similar expressions *for example* and *such as*. The former functions as a conjunctive adverbial, while the latter functions as a complex preposition.

> We like beaches that have good surf. For example, we like Hapuna and Rincon.
> We like beaches that have good surf. *Such as, we like Hapuna and Rincon.

Such as is best presented as a prepositional construction: in normal use, it is most often followed by a noun, not by a full clause:

> We like beaches that have good surf, such as Hapuna and Rincon.

For example, as a conjunctive adverbial, may semantically connect constituents smaller than full clauses, including nouns. However, when it is used in this way, it is most often set off from the main clause by a dash or a colon:

> We like beaches that have good surf—for example, Hapuna and Rincon.
> We like beaches that have good surf: Hapuna and Rincon, for example.

During Versus While

Finally, let us mention the confusion that occurs between *while*, an adverbial subordinator, and *during*, which acts as a preposition. Teachers will often see sentences like the following:

> *During I was making the dinner, the phone rang.

Semantically speaking, the ideas expressed by *while* and *during* are the same. However, *during* can appear only before noun phrases:

> During the course of the day, four meals were served.
> During 1979, I was working in Europe.

While cannot appear before noun phrases. In ESL/EFL oral and written production, although one often sees errors like the one above, where *during* appears in a context where *while* should occur, *while* used in place of *during* is uncommon:

> *While 1979, I was working in Europe.

Teachers will find many student errors in connection with all of these functionally similar but grammatically distinct expressions. To the extent that a teacher wishes to draw attention to them, they may merit classroom treatment on a one-by-one basis.

THE MEANING AND USE OF LOGICAL CONNECTORS

TRUTH CONDITIONAL VERSUS INFERENTIAL

Much of what was said in Chapter 24 about the meaning and use of coordinating conjunctions applies equally to logical connectors. Though we would like to say that logical connectors all have "meanings" in just the same way as other words and expressions and sentences have meanings, an examination of a large percentage of the connectors soon reveals that they "mean something" in a way much different from the common truth-conditional sense used in most semantic analyses. To see how this is so, we will look first at the cases where the meanings are quite clear—in the cases of expressions that mark temporal (time) relationships (*before, after, until, when*), place relationships (*where*), or causal relationships (*because, consequently*). The distinction can be illustrated with two examples. Here is the first:

> Julius Caesar's career was finished long before Napoleon rose to power in France.

If the adverbial subordinator *before* is replaced with *after,* the resulting sentence is simply false. The words *before/after* contribute something to the truth or falsehood of the sentence; one can respond to the sentence with *after,* "That's not true! Napoleon lived almost two millennia after Caesar!" This illustrates that explicit temporal logical connectors, like *before* and *after*, contribute something to the main propositional content of the sentences with which they are associated. The same can be said where place subordinators and causal subordinators are used.

However, not all connectors contribute to propositional content in this way. Compare the following sequence with the one above:

> Caesar was a strong Roman leader; ??thus, Napoleon powerfully ruled France.

We cannot say that this sequence says anything false, but we can say that something seems wrong in the way that the word *thus* is used. We are asked to infer a certain connection between the sentences that does not make sense at all. To understand exactly what the problem is, let us first ask what purpose inferential connectors serve in discourse.

THE FUNCTION OF INFERENTIAL LOGICAL CONNECTORS IN DISCOURSE

The need for inferential logical connectors is in some ways parallel to the need for coordinating conjunctions like *and*, as we discussed in Chapter 24. It may be illustrated by looking at the pair of adjacent sentences below, taken from Blakemore (1992:136):

> Barbara isn't in town. David isn't here.

Why would a speaker set these sentences side by side? What has been said prior to the utterance, or what both speaker and listener already share as background knowledge may make the reason clear. But contexts may not always be available or obvious enough to make intentions transparent. For this reason, in Blakemore's view, languages tend to create expressions whose primary purpose is to clarify these intentions. In English these sentences might be joined with four separate connectors, each of which makes the speaker's intention much clearer:

> a. Barbara isn't in town. So David isn't here.
> b. Barbara isn't in town. After all, David isn't here.
> c. Barbara isn't in town. Moreover, David isn't here.
> d. Barbara isn't in town. However, David isn't here.

It is certainly possible for the speaker to achieve the same effects in periphrastic ways. For example, we could say in the (a) and (b) cases,

> David isn't here. The reason I know that is that Barbara isn't in town.
> Barbara isn't in town. The reason should be clear to you: it's because David isn't here.

However, connectors enable us to achieve the same effects more economically. It goes without saying that speaker intentions can easily be lost, or badly misunderstood, if no connector is used or if the wrong connector is used. In reading, where there are no paralinguistic cues (e.g., tone of voice) or extralinguistic cues (e.g., gestures) to aid the reader in comprehension, writer intentions may be missed even more easily without proper connector use. As with some uses of conjunctions, the proper use of connectors plays a vital role in leading readers/listeners to accurate inferences about the writer's/speaker's intentions. We therefore say that there are two types of connectors:

a. Truth-conditional connectors like *before/after*, which contribute to propositional content and the truth-falsity of the sequences in which they occur

b. Inferential connectors like *thus* and *therefore*, which do not contribute to truth or falsity but which do clarify the logical relationship the speaker/writer intends

We make note of this distinction in the discussion to follow, especially in the discussion of conjunctive adverbials.

The Meanings of Adverbial Subordinators

According to Thompson and Longacre (1985), all languages seem to have some means to use clauses to modify other clauses in a way consistent with English adverbial clauses. The authors further claim that the types of clausal modifiers come from a relatively small set:

time	reason	concessive
location	circumstantial	substitutive
manner	simultaneous	additive
purpose	conditional	absolute

English has adverbial subordinators that fall into most of these categories as follows. Most of them are truth-conditional:

> Time: *after, as long as, as soon as, before, since, when, whenever, until*
> Location: *where, wherever*
> Manner: *as* (e.g., *Do that as your brother does it.*), *in that*
> Purpose: *so that, in order that*
> Reason: *since, because, as* (e.g., *He left, as it was late.*), *inasmuch as, now that*
> Circumstantial: —
> Simultaneous: *while* (e.g., *While she sang, he played.*), *as* (e.g., *As I was leaving, I saw her.*)
> Conditional: *if, even if, as long as, in case, provided that*
> Concessive: *although, even though, though, while*
> Substitutive: —
> Additive: —
> Absolute: —

Those types that have no adverbial subordinators associated with them are expressed by other means in English. For circumstantials, this includes the *by + -ing* construction, as in *They knocked down the coconuts from the tree by throwing rocks at them.* Substitutives are expressed by the complex prepositions *instead of* and *rather than* as well as by the conjunctive adverbial *rather*. Additives in English are marked with coordinating conjunctions (*and*) and conjunctive adverbials (e.g., *in addition, moreover, furthermore*), and absolutes come into English as participial constructions, already discussed in Chapter 25.

The meanings of most of these expressions are rather straightforward, and most ESL/EFL students have little difficulty with them. The Concessive and Reason types, however, do merit some discussion here.

Concessives

The concessives—*although, even though, though,* and *while*—fall within the class of inferential connectors. A concession is a special variety of contrast where the sense conveyed is "Yes, but . . . ": where concession occurs, the speaker/writer wishes to grant the truth of one proposition while asserting the truth of another proposition in such a way as to make the first proposition seem of lesser importance:

> Even though that is a good restaurant, I still think we should try this one.
> Although she has done good paintings, she is not a real artist.

While *but* might be used to substitute for the subordinator in either one of these sentences, neither *although* nor *even though* is appropriate simply to mark semantic contrasts in the way that *but* often is used:

> New York is huge, but my hometown is small.
> ?Although New York is huge, my hometown is small.

The use of concessive expressions involves a functional sort of contrast; the material in the main clause is normally intended as the primary focus, and it is the concessive expression that draws the reader/listener to that inference.

Two Types of *Because*

The word *because*, placed in the Reason category above, is used in two distinct ways that are often distinguishable in speech by intonation patterns and in writing by punctuation conventions. The more common of the two meanings clearly contributes to truth-conditions in specifying a cause; there is no intonation drop until the end of the complete sentence:

> a. My friend was fired because he didn't come to work on time.
> b. The poplar tree died because it was attacked by a disease.

The idea in sentence (a) is that being late led to the dismissal; similarly, the idea in (b) is that the disease caused the tree to die.

Used in a different, more colloquial, sense, *because* is an inferential connector that signals warrant for a particular belief. When the word is intended in this sense and when the main clause comes first, the main clause is often followed by a comma in print, reflecting a complete sentence intonation contour in the main clause and another in the second:

> c. My friend was probably fired, because I don't see him anywhere.
> d. I think this is a poplar tree, because the leaves are pointed at the top.

In sentence (c), the speaker is saying that his/her inability to find the friend constitutes evidence for the belief that the friend has been fired; in (d), the speaker is justifying his/her belief that the tree is a poplar. In neither case is causation being asserted, unlike in the previous examples (a) and (b).

THE MEANINGS OF CONJUNCTIVE ADVERBIALS

Conjunctive adverbials are frequently classified according to broad discourse-functional criteria. Halliday and Hasan (1976:242–3)[6] create four broad categories for them, which we present in simplified form below:

Additive
emphatic: *in addition, moreover, furthermore, besides, also*
appositional: *that is, in other words, for instance*
comparative: *likewise, similarly*

Adversative
proper adversative: *however, nevertheless, despite this, in contrast*
contrastive: *in fact, actually, however, on the other hand, at the same time*
correction: *instead, rather, on the contrary, at least*
dismissal: *in any case, anyhow, at any rate*

Causal
general causal: *therefore, consequently, for that reason, thus*
causal conditional: *then, in that case, otherwise*

Sequential
then, next, first, second, last, finally, up to now, to sum up

"Additive" is presented as involving new information; "adversative" is defined as "contrary to expectations"; "causal" involves both true causes and logical inferences; "sequential" concerns either real-time relationships or sequential relationships in a text. ESL/EFL texts often present logical connectors in a schematic form similar to Halliday and Hasan's.

While such a classification is useful at the global level to sort out possible meaning relationships into types, it presents problems for the definitions of individual connectors (and frequently leads to erroneous word choices for second language learners). One problem is that the expressions within each category are often not interchangeable. For example, we cannot use *nevertheless* or *despite this* in every case in which we can use *however*.

> Calvin wanted to fly to the moon. However, he did not know how.
> Calvin wanted to fly to the moon. ??Nevertheless, he did not know how.
> Calvin wanted to fly to the moon. ??Despite this, he did not know how.

Another problem is that certain expressions may find acceptable paraphrases in more than one conjunction: we can say (*but*) *in any case*, (*and*) *in any case*, as well as (*or*) *in any case*, depending on the context of utterance:

> We can take this apartment, or we can take the other one.
>   (But) in any case, we have to take something soon!

> We may not be able to take our vacation as planned. The area is under six feet of snow.
>   (And) in any case, we just don't have enough money.

> We may not be able to take our vacation as planned.
>   (Or) in any case, we won't be able to make it a long one.

A final problem is that functional labels such as "adversative" are not always accurate: the use of *however* below can hardly be said to mark something that is "contrary to expectations":

> Calvin wanted to fly to the moon. However, he did not know how.

PROPOSITIONAL FRAMES FOR CONJUNCTIVE ADVERBIALS

In a study of conjunctive adverbials, Williams (1996) claims that classifying these connectors according to notional ideas such as "additive" and "adversative" gives at best only a vague approximation of their meaning. An additional element, independent of these functions, is required in order to come to adequate definitions. What the majority of these expressions do, in Williams' view, is call attention to propositional frames that are either explicitly or implicitly encoded in the text. If they are only implicit, the listener or reader will have to reconstruct the frames from the meaning of the clause. Nearly all the conjunctive adverbials then fall into the category of inferential connectors rather than truth-conditional ones. We consider some of these frames below. First, the adversatives:

In Any Case

What brings together all of the uses of *in any case* is the frame

> X implies Y, or not X implies Y

Applied to one of the examples above, *In any case, we have to take something soon,* this means:

> If we take this apartment, it is true that we must take something soon.
> Or if we do not take this apartment, it is true that we must take something soon.

The use of *in any case* allows this frame to be mentally constructed without the need to verbalize it in a wordy way as in the above paraphrases.

Nevertheless

The conjunctive adverbial *nevertheless* is said to imply a propositional structure like the following:

> X implies Y, and X is true, but Y is not true.

That is, *nevertheless* requires a situation in which one is led to expect one thing but finds something different to be true. Williams' data showed that in the following pairs of sentences, *nevertheless* found strong acceptance among 30 native-speaker judges for only the first pair:

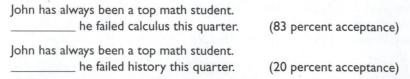

> John has always been a top math student.
> _____ he failed calculus this quarter.   (83 percent acceptance)

> John has always been a top math student.
> _____ he failed history this quarter.   (20 percent acceptance)

If someone is a good math student, we expect that person to be good at calculus, but we have less strong expectations about how well that person will perform in a history class. For both pairs, the adverb *however* was considered acceptable at rates approaching 100 percent. It seems that it does not matter much for the use of *however* whether "adversativity" is present—that is, whether one's expectations are being flouted—while this is the essence of the meaning of *nevertheless*.

In Contrast

In the case of *in contrast*, what is needed is a propositional frame like the following:

> X (a) in contrast Y (b)

The frame specifies that two different topics or subjects are different in at least one respect. We can say,

> South Carolina is mild in the winter. In contrast, South Dakota is frigid.

because we are contrasting South Carolina with South Dakota and mild with frigid. This explains why we can't use *in contrast* with the Calvin example (*Calvin wanted to fly to the moon. *In contrast, he didn't know how*): the required propositional frame is not present.[7]

On the Other Hand

Another connector, one in which propositional frames are often only implicitly given, is *on the other hand*. Here, it is only necessary to have a single subject or topic, which is then contrasted with respect to two contrasting qualities.

> X (a) on the other hand X (b)

Often these qualities are of the "good/bad" sort:

> Minnesota is bitterly cold in the winter. On the other hand, it is one of the more scenic states. (i.e., Minnesota is bad in one way, but good in another.)

> Real estate sales can be a thrilling business to be in. On the other hand, people aren't buying homes today the way they used to. (i.e., Real estate sales are good in one way but bad in another, so real estate sales might not make a perfect career.)

However

However may be used almost generically wherever attention is drawn to a difference. This difference may be between expectations and reality. It may equally be between what is uncertain and what is certain, between antonyms or other kinds of lexical opposition. It may even be used in a way similar to the way *but* is used as a discourse marker to change topics in conversation (see Chapter 24):

Certainty versus uncertainty:

> We may go to Hawaii, or we may go to California. However, we have to find a way to escape the snow this winter.

Semantic opposition:

> Jill doesn't do well in school. However, her sister is a straight A student.

Topic change marker:

> I lost $20,000 in Las Vegas last week. However, let's talk about something else.

Some of the connectors traditionally categorized as additive may be roughly described as follows, based on an examination of textual data and native speaker judgements on pairs of constructed sentences:

Also

Also is practically interchangeable with *and,* with a preference for identical subjects in the two clauses:

> He threshed the wheat. Also, he hoed the corn. (Or, more commonly: He also hoed corn.)

In Addition

In addition is practically interchangeable with *and,* with a preference for nonidentical subjects:

> He threshed the wheat. In addition, his children hoed the corn.

Moreover

Moreover is used primarily in arguments where several premises are used to support a conclusion of some sort:

> Smith probably committed the crime. He had a guilty look on his face. Moreover, the police found a gun under his bed.

Furthermore

Furthermore is used like *moreover,* except that it tends to preface third or fourth premises where more than two premises exist:

> The working classes, for example, had multiple grievances. The long deskilling of the craft worker that had begun in the 1820s accelerated during the Second Empire. It was coupled with yet another strong surge of rural migration into the city, and the diminution of any collective power over labor-market conditions. *Furthermore,* the struggle to reverse those conditions through the formation of a social and political republic in 1848 was roundly defeated. . . . (from D. Harvey, "The Urban Face of Capitalism" (1991). In J. F. Hart (ed.), *Our Changing Cities.* Baltimore: Johns Hopkins Press)

Similarly, Likewise

Similarly and *likewise* are used when there is some semantic similarity across two predicates and when the two clauses in some way support a conclusion as supporting examples:

> The Sudstrom family are not miserly when it comes to buying clothes.
> John Sudstrom wears only Ralph Lauren shirts. *Similarly,* his brother Fred buys only designer pants.

The description of *similarly/likewise* runs somewhat counter to a common description of these two words, which says that these adverbials are used when a speaker or writer wants "to show a similarity." In fact, they are almost never used solely for this purpose in written discourse; rather, they are used to provide parallel examples for illustrative purposes. *Similarly* seems to occur across clauses with two separate subjects, while *likewise* tends to prefer just one:

> Her eating habits are extravagant. She drinks expensive French wines. *Likewise,* she has caviar at least once a week.

The connectors often described as causal invite the listener/reader to assume a direct inferential relationship between the propositions in the first and second clauses. The generalizations below seem to hold for some of these expressions:

Consequently

Consequently is used to signal a real causal relationship between two events or conditions:

> Greta won the lottery; consequently, she bought a Ferrari.

Although listeners/readers who don't know Greta cannot predict what she will do with her money, they can easily understand the causal connection between the lottery win and the purchase.

Therefore

Therefore, when used with causes, tends to be used when listeners/readers are in a much better position to come to the conclusion on their own:

> She won the lottery; therefore, she was happy.

Therefore is also used in such a way as to invite listeners/readers to construct an inference of a noncausal type, which is again likely to be easy for them to construct based on the facts given:

> The gun was under the bed; Smith had a guilty look on his face; *therefore,* it is likely that Smith committed the crime.

Thus

Thus is used much like *therefore,* but *therefore* tends to be used more often where there is a chain of premises in an explicit argument. *Thus* may be used for parenthetical "asides," where no explicit argument is intended. It seems to be used in the same way as *so,* except that the register is more formal and the word is found mostly in written prose.

PROBLEMS IN CHOOSING BETWEEN CONNECTORS WITH SIMILAR MEANINGS

ESL/EFL students often have trouble determining which connector conveys the intended relationship between sentences. *In contrast* is often confused with *on the contrary,* as in the following:

> I like skiing. ?On the contrary, my partner likes fishing.

The problem is that *on the contrary* is most usually used to deny a proposition, whether inferred or explicit, that has come before; *in contrast* is used to compare two things.

Moreover and *furthermore* are often used in more formal ESL/EFL writing in contexts where they would not ordinarily appear in native prose:

> My mother went to the dry cleaners. ?Moreover, she shopped for clothes.

The problem here is that *moreover/furthermore* are used when some sort of conclusion is expected from the connection of the two clauses. If the student intends only to make a list of what his/her mother did, *and* would be more appropriate.

An especially frequent misuse of a connector involves the word *therefore*. Under normal circumstances, this adverbial is used when the speaker/writer expects to argue for something when all the information necessary to follow the argument is either provided by the speaker/writer or easily available to the listener/reader from prior knowledge. It does not work well in cases like the following:

> We had not eaten all day. ?Therefore, we decided to have dinner at McDonald's.

Does the listener/reader naturally expect McDonald's to be a likely choice of restaurant for someone who has not eaten all day? It is not impossible that the speaker/reader has already said that he/she goes to McDonald's whenever he/she is especially hungry. However, in the absence of such information, the use of *therefore* seems inappropriate.

OTHER ISSUES OF USE CONCERNING LOGICAL CONNECTORS

REGISTER

Partly because teaching materials are often quite vague in the area of logical connectors, students may frequently misuse connectors or overuse them in their writing in ways that seem strange. With conjunctive adverbials, this is frequently because many of the adverbials occur chiefly in highly formal registers, or styles of speaking in different social circumstances, that are not appropriate in other types of writing. A teacher may find, in a narrative of the student's childhood, a sentence like

> My father said, "Let's go to the beach on Saturday. Moreover, let's rent a boat."

There is, of course, nothing in the sound or grammar of the word *moreover* itself that would naturally indicate to a nonnative speaker that the word is almost never used in speech or in personal narrative writing this way. Part of the problem is that the nonnative speaker is unaware that *moreover* tends to be used in a register different from the one that a parent is likely to use with a child. A more appropriate (if lexically less precise) connector is *and*, a coordinating conjunction.

PLACEMENT OF ADVERBIAL SUBORDINATE CLAUSES IN A SENTENCE

Another issue of use has to do with the placement of an adverbial subordinate clause within a sentence. As we mentioned in the section on the form of adverbial clauses, these clauses generally appear either before or after the main clause, although they can also appear clause medially. One may ask whether there is a difference in overall effect if the clause is placed in one position rather than another. What determines which order below will be chosen?

Main clause + subordinate clause:

He always brought flowers when he visited.

Subordinate clause + main clause:

When he visited, he always brought flowers.

There is a strong tendency, according to Ramsay (1987), for initial subordinate clauses to be thematically linked with the material that has come before in discourse, while subordinate clauses in second position seem to be more closely linked with their main clauses. This is our justification for treating sentence-final subordinate clauses as we would any other adverbials, but classifying a sentence-initial adverbial clause as a sentence modifier. It is a sentence modifier in that it acts as a "discourse pivot," establishing links between what has come before the sentence and the main clause of the sentence it is in. To take a simple constructed example:

The rivers dried up during the drought. Because there was so little water, the city imposed a water rationing program. It worked rather well.

It would seem somewhat less natural to reverse the order of the two clauses in the second sentence if uttered in the context of the first sentence. A possible result of this linking tendency is the fact that subordinate clause + main clause ordering tends to occur more toward the beginnings of paragraphs (though need not, as in the example above), while main clause + subordinate clause order tends to be found later in the paragraph. By using such ordering in initial sentences, it is possible to establish more solid links between paragraphs. In this way, sentence-initial adverbial clauses can provide an "advance organizer" for what is to follow in the main clause and indeed in the paragraph.

PLACEMENT OF CONJUNCTIVE ADVERBIALS IN A SENTENCE

Similarly, as we have seen, conjunctive adverbials are comparatively free to occupy several different positions in a sentence. Placement in sentence-initial position makes them most salient, and by reasoning similar to the arguments we have used for adverbial subordinate clauses, we have accorded sentence-modifier status to sentence-initial conjunctive adverbials. The next most salient position for conjuncitve adverbials is presumably clause medial, with the least salient position being sentence final.

This claim has been borne out in a study of logical connector placement by Salera (1978). Salera hypothesized that the adversative connectors, *however, nevertheless,* and *instead,* would occur:

1. Clause initially if the situation calls for an emphatic, contrary-to-expectation expression.

The fire swept down Mandeville Canyon. We were forced to evacuate, convinced that we would return to find ashes.

predicted as the preferred choice →   **a.** Instead, we found our home
    for the next clause   completely untouched.
                                b. We found, instead, our home
                                  completely untouched.
                                c. other _____

2. Cause medially if the situation calls for a strong contrastive relationship (but one that is not emphatically counter to expectation) or one that expresses a reservation about a previous clause.

> Jack is a magazine columnist who is concerned that people aren't using words correctly. He notices that words sometimes mean different things to different people. This condition, he believes, could be corrected if people would use their dictionaries more often.

predicted as the preferred choice →
    for the next clause

  a. He knows, however, that they won't.
  b. He knows that they won't, however.
  c. other _____

3. Clause finally if the situation calls for a contrastive comment or afterthought that is not as important as what went on before.

> Miriam has been running for over a year. Two months ago she went into training for a 15-kilometer race by running the hilly perimeter of UCLA. The week before the race, she knew she was ready—she was running smoothly and easily. When she got to the race, she found the course more hilly than she expected.

predicted as the preferred choice →
    for the next clause

  a. She nevertheless ran a good race.
  b. She ran a good race nevertheless.
  c. other _____

In general, the results of Salera's study revealed a confirmation of her hypotheses, although agreement among native speakers with regard to the preferred sentence position of the logical connectors was by no means unanimous. More usage studies dealing with the placement of logical connectors would be helpful.

OVERUSE OF LOGICAL CONNECTORS

Sometimes the problem for ESL/EFL students is not the underuse of logical connectors; it is the overuse. It is important to emphasize that logical connectors do not always fulfill a useful purpose if they are intended to lead listeners or readers to the understanding of relationships that are already transparent from the discourse context. The effect of the overuse of connectors can be much like the effect of endless repetition of facts already present in the minds of listeners or readers. When used judiciously, however, logical connectors play a useful role, especially in written prose. Teachers should be aware of both the positive and the negative aspects of their use.

CONCLUSION

In the ESL composition literature of the late 1970s and 1980s, partially as a result of the influence of Halliday and Hasan's work on cohesion in written text, a great deal of attention began to be paid to the need for connectors as a means of achieving cohesion in ESL writing, and composition texts began routinely to include a section on these "transitional expressions." Students were given lists of expressions to use for addition, contrast, and so on and told to make use of them in their writing.

After a number of years, however, teachers began to realize that something was not right. Students received the implicit message in their classes that it was only necessary to fill in a connector of some sort between each pair of sentences to create a truly cohesive essay. The result was often highly stilted-sounding prose that was so filled with these connectors that it seemed almost overcohesive. An additional problem was that students often misused the connectors and thereby sent the wrong message about the relationships of ideas in their writing.

To be proficient writers, ESL/EFL students do need to know about the use of logical connectors. They need to know how to place and punctuate them, what propositional frames they occur in, and when to—and when not to—use them.

TEACHING SUGGESTIONS

1. Form. Students need to be aware of the different patterns of connected clauses. A teacher might construct pairs or sets of sentences that have connectors that are semantically or functionally similar in order to illustrate the syntactic differences (and resulting differences in punctuation):

> They couldn't play ball because the dog ate the ball.
> The dog ate the ball. As a result, they couldn't play ball.
>
> They tried to catch the train, but they woke up too late.
> They tried to catch the train. But they woke up too late.
> Although they tried to catch the train, they were too late.
> They tried to catch the train. However, they were too late.
>
> The train had gone, so they left the station.
> The train had gone. So they left the station.
> The train had gone. Consequently, they left the station.

If teachers, in modeling the sentence sequences, accentuate the relevant intonation heavily each time, it may create a classroom atmosphere that makes such repetitive exercises not only bearable but amusing. Teachers may ask individual students to repeat a sentence-pair and then ask the other students whether they "heard" a comma, period (full stop), or no punctuation at all. In this way, the relation between intonation and punctuation may be highlighted.

2. Meaning. Give students a scrambled paragraph. Some of the sentences should contain logical connectors. Ask the students to unscramble the sentences and reconstruct the paragraph.

3. Form/Meaning. It is worthwhile, especially in intermediate to advanced composition classes, to teach grammar functionally when the topic of expressing reasons arises and to take an inventory of the many ways in which reasons may be expressed. This might be done, for example, in the context of writing cause-effect essays. Consider the ways below, which are only some of the possibilities:

> Because/Since air inversion occurs in the Los Angeles Basin, pollution is high.
>
> Pollution is high in the Los Angeles Basin because of / due to / on account of / as a result of air inversion.
>
> Air inversion occurs in the Los Angeles Basin. As a result, pollution is high.

> Pollution is high in the Los Angeles Basin due to the fact that there is air inversion.
>
> Pollution is high in the Los Angeles Basin. The reason is that there is air inversion.
>
> The existence of air inversion causes pollution to be high in the Los Angeles Basin.
>
> Air inversion exists in the Los Angeles Basin. Consequently, pollution is high.

Students might be given pairs of grammatically unconnected sentences and asked to para-phrase each pair in three ways that show the cause-effect relationship. Then, they can be asked to incorporate these ways into their own writing on a topic that naturally involves a cause-effect relationship (for example, "What are the effects of bringing up a child in the city versus the country?" or "What will happen if drugs are legalized?" or similar topics).

4. Meaning/Use. A modified cloze exercise is a good way to get students to practice using logical connectors. Tom Gorman and Marjorie Walsleben offer the following text for completion, followed by a list of expressions to fill in the blanks:

> (1)_____, we may observe that animal communication systems are closed, (2) _____ human systems are open-ended. (3)_____, even though bees communicate, they will only be able to exchange variants of the same message—in what direction the nectar is and how far away. Apes cannot communicate freely about anything for which they do not have a specific signal, and even in those cases the possibilities are extremely restricted. People, (4)_____, can talk about anything they can observe or imagine. (5)_____, what they say on almost any topic is almost unlimited.
>
> *moreover   finally   on the other hand   whereas   for example*

The exercise above is appropriate for an intermediate class. The technique can be adapted for a much more advanced class with a different cloze passage and a list of connectors that are much more similar to each other in meaning and use, where finer discriminations must be made (*however, nevertheless, on the other hand, in contrast, on the contrary*). It can also be done with no list at all, where the students must supply the connec-tors themselves.

5. Meaning. Teachers can highlight the meaning differences among the connectors by creating single sentences and then asking students to continue the sequence beginning with a variety of connectors. For example,

> The paper was too large to use on the typewriter.
> Therefore, . . .
> In addition, . . .
> Moreover, . . .
> In other words, . . .
> Nevertheless, . . .

This activity can be expanded and contextualized in a story format. The teacher can supply the first few sentences of a story, and then write one or two additional sentences with blank spaces left for connectors. Students can then choose, by means of their connector choices, the direction in which they want to take the story. (Teachers may be surprised at the interesting variety of stories that will result!)

6. Use. A way to make students sensitive to register differences might be to have them substitute a logical connector of one register with one from another—for instance, to have them change each of the following example sequences with informal or universally acceptable connectors to ones with formal connectors:

> Possums have sharp claws and teeth. Also, they are not easily trained.
> So they do not make good pets.
> (*Also → Moreover; So → Therefore, Consequently, Thus*)

> The team was losing the game badly. But they decided to continue to play their hardest.
> (*But → Nevertheless, However*)

> They wanted a Rolls-Royce. I mean, they wanted the best car they could possibly find.
> (*I mean → That is*)

7. Use. To practice putting the clauses in an order that will promote cohesion within a text, give students a passage in which certain sentences in the passage are presented in two forms: a. Subordinate clause + main clause; and b. Main clause + subordinate clause. When they come to such a choice, students should choose order (a) or (b) and explain why they chose as they did.

EXERCISES

Test your understanding of what has been presented.

1. Provide an original sentence illustrating each of the following terms. Underline the pertinent words in your example.
   a. adverbial subordinator
   b. conjunctive adverbial
   c. a concessive connector
   d. a time connector
   e. a purpose connector
   f. a causal connector
   g. an inferential connector

2. Draw trees for the following sentences:
   a. The business did not have enough employees; therefore, they hired more.
   b. You can try that route to San Francisco; you will never get there, however.
   c. Mary is always punctual. Her sister, in contrast, never arrives on time.
   d. When you go in that direction, you will come to a fork in the road.
   e. They bought the blue car even though they preferred the red one.

3. Account for the unacceptability of the following sentences:
   a. *You see lots of trees in Oregon; on the contrary, there are few in Arizona.
   b. *We took the extra class, as a result, we understood the material completely.
   c. *I saw the movie, although, I wouldn't recommend it to most people.
   d. *Crystal glasses are very fragile; nevertheless, plastic glasses are stronger.
   e. David was working hard in the garden. *While George was napping in the hammock.

Test your ability to apply what you know.

4. There is increasing use of the word *plus* in everyday American speech in ways like those below:

> They had to drive five miles out of the way. Plus, they had to drive through mud.
> There are three midterms in the class. Plus, you have to write a 10-page paper.

This word is normally not found in lists of conjunctions or logical connectors. How would you characterize this word—as a coordinating conjunction, an adverbial subordinator, a conjunctive adverbial, or none of these? Make your case by constructing relevant acceptable and unacceptable examples and providing syntactic arguments.

5. The following error types are frequent in ESL/EFL writing. Suppose that you are faced with the following sentences in student compositions. Assuming that you want to offer some rationale for correction, how would you explain the problems below?
   a. *Although I wanted to attend that college, but it was too far away from home.
   b. *The rain came down in torrents, as a result we had to cancel the picnic.
   c. *My sister loves to go to movies in the afternoon; on the contrary, I hate that.
   d. *If he tells me how to get there, so I will follow his directions.
   e. *Even you gave me the money, I wouldn't go to see that movie.

6. Suppose that you have said in a writing class that subordinate clauses cannot stand alone but need a main clause attached in order to create a properly formed sentence. A student approaches you with the following advertisements and asks for an explanation:

   > Caffall, the caffeine tablet. When you can't get that morning cup of coffee.
   > Use Sanofresh deodorant. Because you can't afford to worry about body odor.

   Such fragments are quite common in the media, especially in advertising. How would you respond to such questions?

7. The following is adapted from a student essay:

   > My family decided to take our usual family vacation at my grandparents' home in the northern part of the island. At that time, my family consisted of me, my mother, my father, and my brother and sister. Also, one of my cousins was going on the trip. So we packed up our car with food; in addition, we took camping supplies. Moreover, we also brought scuba-diving equipment; however, only my brother and I were really interested in that. Therefore, we had a car which was full of equipment, and in addition to that, we did not have enough room for all of us. Consequently, we had to decide what we should do. . . .

   In what way might you respond to the student's use of connectors?

BIBLIOGRAPHY

References

Blakemore, D. (1992). *Understanding Utterances.* Oxford: Blackwell.

Emonds, J. E. (1972). "Evidence That Indirect Object Movement Is a Structure-Preserving Rule." *Foundations of Language* (vol. 8), pp. 545–561.

Halliday, M. A. K. (1994). *An Introduction to Functional Grammar* (2d ed.). London: Edward Arnold.

Halliday, M. A. K., and R. Hasan (1976). *Cohesion in English.* London: Longman.

Martin, J. (1992). *English Text: System and Structure.* Philadelphia: John Benjamins.

Quirk, R., S. Greenbaum, G. Leech, and J. Svartvik (1985). *A Comprehensive Grammar of the English Language.* London: Longman.

Ramsay, V. (1987). "The Functional Distribution of Preposed and Postposed 'If' and 'When' Clauses in Written Discourse." In R. Tomlin (ed.), *Coherence and Grounding in Discourse.* Amsterdam: John Benjamins.

Salera, C. (1978). "The Mobility of Certain Logical Connectors." Unpublished English 215 paper, UCLA.

Thompson, S., and R. Longacre (1985). "Adverbial Clauses." In T. Shopen (ed.), *Language Typology and Syntactic Description* (vol. 2). Cambridge: Cambridge University Press.

Williams, H. (1996). "An Analysis of Conjunctive Adverbial Expressions in English." Unpublished doctoral dissertation in Applied Linguistics, UCLA.

Suggestions for Further Reading

For an extensive discussion of interclausal coherence, see:
Givón, T. (1990). *Syntax: A Functional-Typological Introduction* (vol. 2). Amsterdam: John Benjamins.

For a reference that inventories adverbial subordinators in 50 European languages, see:

Kortmann, B. (1996). *Adverbial Subordination: A Typology and History of Adverbial Subordinators Based on European Languages.* Berlin and New York: Walter de Gruyter.

For an alternative view of connectors that is grounded in cognitive psychology and the theory of relevance, see:
Blakemore, D. (1992). *Understanding Utterances.* Oxford: Blackwell.

For an extended treatment of clause combining that is accessible to intermediate to advanced ESL/EFL students, consult:
Collins Cobuild English Grammar (1990), Ch. 8. London: Collins.

For a discussion of the misuse and overuse of connectors, see:
Crewe, W. J. (1990). "The Illogic of Logical Connectives." *ELT Journal* 44:4, 316–325.

For ESL/EFL textbooks that devote substantial attention to logical connectors, consult:
Frodesen, J., and J. Eyring (1997). *Grammar Dimensions.* Book 4 (2d ed.). Boston: Heinle & Heinle.

Raimes, A. (1990). *How English Works.* New York: St. Martin's Press.

ENDNOTES:

1. There is no reason why the conjunctions treated in Chapter 24 could not also be considered *logical connectors,* especially when considered at the clause-connecting level.

2. Data like these led Emonds (1972) to the conclusion that many if not all of these subordinators are, in fact, better seen as prepositions that take clausal objects. One reason supporting his claim was that just as some verbs take phrasal, clausal, or either phrasal or clausal objects, so may prepositions take different object types; the lexical overlap in the common words in the above pairs of sentences may be no accident. While Emonds' arguments are quite convincing, we continue to use the traditional terms *subordinating conjunctions* or *adverbial subordinators.*

3. We do not draw a line connecting the two independent clauses as we did for clauses conjoined by coordinating conjunctions in Chapter 24. The reason is that while there is a meaning relationship between the clauses, there is no special syntactic relationship.

4. An exception might be the case of "afterthought clauses," where a speaker appends the subordinate clause as if suddenly realizing that the thought that has just been expressed is incomplete.

5. A semicolon and a period are associated with the same end-of-sentence falling intonation. The chief difference between the two types of punctuation is often said to be that when one uses a semicolon, one is attempting to show that the two sentences are more strongly integrated in some way. There is, in fact, a strong correlation between the use of semicolons and the use of conjunctive adverbials.

6. Halliday (1994) and Martin (1992) use a somewhat different classification system, but still do not attend to the meaning of individual adverbials.

7. *In contrast* may work below the propositional level as well:

> She likes to listen to Bach in winter; in contrast, she likes Mozart in summer.

This frame distinguishes *whereas* as well:

> Chicago is a fun place, whereas Centerville is dead.
> *Chicago is a fun place, whereas it is an expensive place.

CONDITIONAL SENTENCES

INTRODUCTION

In a survey of the most serious teaching problems encountered by ESL teachers in the Los Angeles area, Covitt (1976) found that conditional sentences ranked fifth.[1] This is not difficult to understand. Conditional sentences consist of two clauses, a subordinate clause and a main clause, and are therefore more complex syntactically than many other structures. Moreover, the semantics of all the various types of conditional clauses are subtle and hard to understand even for native speakers. Good comprehensive descriptions are not readily available. Furthermore, ESL/EFL students need a good grasp of the English tense-aspect system as well as the modal auxiliaries and negation before they can cope with the full range of conditional sentences in English.

In addition to the general problems noted above, we must point out that ESL/EFL textbooks and reference grammars typically provide highly oversimplified information. For example, numerous texts introduce and practice only three conditional structures (the labels used to describe these structures vary):

1. *Future conditional:* If I have the money, I will take a vacation.
2. *Present conditional:* If I had the money, I would take a vacation.
3. *Past conditional:* If I had had the money, I would have taken a vacation.

Several reference grammars refer to the first sentence as a "real" or "possible" conditional as opposed to the second and third sentences, which refer to the "unreal/hypothetical" present and past, respectively.

Another problem is that ESL/EFL students, who have learned to associate past tense with past time, often find it hard to believe that sentences like the second one above refer to present and not past time. They become confused because they hear and read many types of conditional sentences that are not included in the three structures usually taught. In fact, one of the problems with such descriptions is that they do not treat the most frequent (and also the simplest) conditional sentence type in English:[2]

> If you boil water, it vaporizes.
> If Bobby goes swimming, he catches a cold.

In this chapter we provide a description of conditional sentences that should help the ESL/EFL teacher better understand this problematic topic.

FORM OF CONDITIONALS

A SYNTACTIC ANALYSIS OF CONDITIONAL SENTENCES

A conditional sentence is a complex sentence that consists of a main clause and a subordinate clause; the latter typically begins with the adverbial subordinator *if*. We agree with Quirk and Greenbaum (1973:323) that conditional sentences express the dependence of one set of circumstances (i.e., the result clause) on another (i.e., the *if* clause). Furthermore, in most cases, two clause orderings are possible.

> If I go, George will go. If Dracula returns, we will scream.
> George will go if I go. We will scream if Dracula returns.

In either order, the *if* clause sets up the condition, and the main clause gives the result or outcome. We will therefore treat the *if* clause as an adverbial clause of condition. By so doing, we can generate conditional sentences in final position using the system of phrase structure rules and mapping rules presented in Chapters 5 and 6.

George will go if I go.

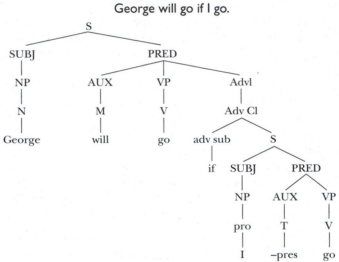

In order to account for the *if* clause in initial position, we generate the adverbial clause under the sentence modifier (sm), as was discussed in Chapter 25:

If I go, George will go.

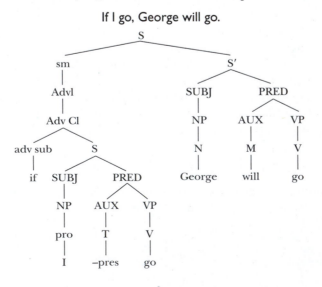

Other than the two orderings of the clauses, the same mapping rules apply. However, one new option is possible. When the *if* clause occurs in initial position, it is possible to optionally add *then* before the main clause. Let us assume we wanted to account for:

> If I go, then George will go.

We would start with the same base rules used above for the second tree diagram and the mapping rules would be as follows:

> Output: If I -pres go, George will go.
> Copy s/t: If I -pres [+ 1 + sg] go, George will go.
> *then* addition: If I -pres [+ 1 + sg] go, then George will go.

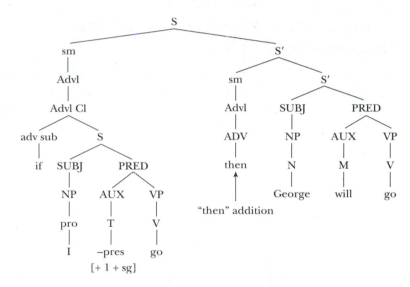

> Morphological rules: If I go, then George will go.

Note that *then* insertion is an optional rule that tends to be applied only if the conditional clause is generated in initial position; that is, the rule is much less likely to be applied when the *if* clause follows the main clause:

> ?Then George will go if I go.

There would have to be a great deal of prior context or shared information, and the speaker would have to be making an inference based on such shared information, for a sentence like the one above to be acceptable. It would be helpful to have an empirical study describing specifically when and where the optional *then* occurs in conditional sentences.

We have not included rules concerning tense-modal sequencing as part of our syntactic analysis of conditional sentences. We feel that such sequences are determined by semantic rather than syntactic constraints. Even so, there is great syntactic diversity.

OTHER SYNTACTIC DETAILS

Subject/Operator Inversion in Conditionals

In hypothetical conditionals with initial *if* clauses containing certain auxiliary verbs such as *had* or *should,* it is possible to delete the initial *if;* however, when such a deletion takes place, subject/operator inversion must follow:

> If I had known that, I wouldn't have said anything.
> Had I known that, I wouldn't have said anything.

If the guests should arrive early, no one will be here to greet them.
Should the guests arrive early, no one will be here to greet them.

Conditional Clause Pro-forms

As Halliday and Hasan (1976) have pointed out, and as we mentioned in Chapter 10, certain pro-forms can be used to replace the entire conditional clause following *if: so* is used if the clause is affirmative; *not* is used if the clause is negative. For example:

Would you like to make a class presentation? { If so, volunteer. If not, you don't have to. }

THE MEANING OF CONDITIONAL SENTENCES: A SEMANTIC OVERVIEW

English conditional sentences express three different kinds of semantic relationships: factual conditional relationships, future (or predictive) conditional relationships, and imaginative conditional relationships (see Figure 27.1). We will discuss each of these types with its sub-types in turn.

Figure 27.1
A Semantic Hierarchy of
Conditional Sentence Types

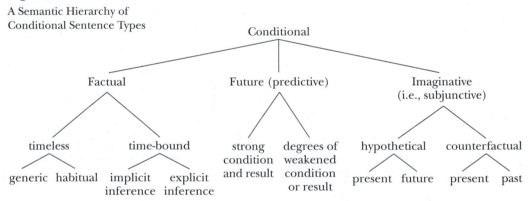

FACTUAL CONDITIONAL SENTENCES

Factual conditional sentences are of high frequency in everyday English, and yet they are overlooked altogether in many ESL/EFL textbooks. Factual conditionals include four types: generic, habitual, implicit inference, and explicit inference.

Generic Factual Conditionals

Generic factual conditionals express relationships that are true and unchanging; for example:

If oil is mixed with water, it floats.   If you boil water, it vaporizes.

Because of their unchanging truth value, these conditionals normally take a simple present tense in both clauses. They are especially frequent in scientific writing, since the sciences are often concerned with such absolute relationships.

Habitual Factual Conditionals

Habitual factual conditionals resemble generic factuals in that they also express a relationship that is not bounded in time; however, the relationship is based on habit instead of physical law. Habitual factuals express either past or present relationships that are typically or habitually true; for example:

Present: If I wash the dishes, Sally dries them.
Past: If Nancy said, "Jump!" Bob jumped.

This type of conditional sentence is frequent in conversation. Both clauses usually have the same tense: simple present in both clauses if the habitual relationship refers to extended present time; simple past in both clauses if the sentence refers to a past habit.

Note that for both generic and habitual conditionals it is possible to substitute *when* or *whenever* for *if* and still express more or less the same idea:

When(ever) you boil water, it vaporizes.
When(ever) I wash the dishes, Sally dries them.

Implicit Inference Conditionals

Factual conditionals that express an implicit inference are different from generic or habitual factuals in that they express inferences about specific time-bound relationships. As such, they make use of a much wider range of tense and aspect markers, and they also occur with certain modal auxiliaries. Schachter (1971:70) provides some examples of what we refer to as implicit inference conditionals:

If smog can be licked in L.A., it can be licked anywhere.
If the radicals haven't made the government more responsive, they have wasted their time.
If there was a happy man in the world that night, it was John Tunney.

To these we add a few more examples of our own:

If it's freezing outside, my roses are dying.
If it's Tuesday, it's Sam's birthday.

Implicit inference conditionals, like their habitual counterparts, are conversational in flavor, and like generic and habitual factuals, implicit inference factuals tend to maintain the same tense and aspect or the same modal in both clauses—even though they make use of a much wider range of tenses and auxiliary verbs. However, implicit inference factuals differ from generic and habitual factuals in that *when* or *whenever* cannot substitute for *if* without changing the meaning and often making the sentence ungrammatical or, nonsensical:

?When(ever) it's Tuesday, it's Sam's birthday.

The lack of semantic congruity here is due to the fact that this type of conditional is expressing a more specific time-bound or location-bound inference rather than a generic or habitual relationship.

Explicit Inference Factual Conditionals

The final type of factual conditional, the explicit inference conditional, is the only case where there is no strict parallelism of tense, aspect, or modal in both clauses. This is because the conditional (i.e., the *if* clause) is used as the basis for making an explicit inference; the result clause thus contains an inferential modal—typically *must* or *should*:

If someone's at the door, it must be Peter.
If anyone has the answer, it should be Rod.

Explicit inferential factuals are similar to implicit inference factuals in that both refer to more specific time-bound events or states in the *if* clause. Also, both involve making inferences; however, only the explicit inference factual conditional overtly marks the inferential process with a modal. Explicit inference conditionals, however, are more limited in range, since they cannot occur with the same variety of tense and modal combinations that implicit inferences do. Like implicit inference conditionals, explicit inference conditionals can refer to past as well as present time. Recall (Chapter 8) that past inference with *must* or *should* is expressed by adding *have . . . -en* after the modal:

Past implicit inference:	If he was there, he saw the painting.
Past explicit inference:	If he was there, he must have seen the painting.

FUTURE (OR PREDICTIVE) CONDITIONAL SENTENCES

Strong Condition and Result

Many other authors have discussed "future conditionals." For example:

> If it rains, I'll stay home.

Such sentences express future plans or contingencies. The normal pattern for this type of conditional is simple present tense in the *if* clause and some explicit indication of future time (e.g., *will* or *be going to*) in the result clause:

> If you finish your vegetables, I'm going to (gonna) buy you an ice cream cone.
> If Steve comes to class, he will get the answers to the quiz.

Degrees of Weakened Condition or Result

The above examples reflect the only type of future conditional most ESL/EFL texts mention. However, sometimes the future outcome expressed in the result clause is not sufficiently certain to warrant use of *will* or *be going to,* in which case a weaker modal of prediction such as *may* or *should* can be used:

> If you finish your vegetables, I may buy you an ice cream cone.
> If Steve comes to class, he should get the answers to the quiz.

Thus, the prediction scale that we outlined for modals in Chapter 8 also applies to the result clauses of future conditional sentences:

will, be going to =	certain (strong result)
should =	probable
may =	possible (stronger than *might*)
might =	possible (weaker than *may*)

(progressively weakened result from *will* to *might*)

There is also a way to weaken the condition expressed in the *if* clause of a future conditional sentence by using the modal *should* or the verb *happen*—or both of them together.

$$\text{If it} \left\{ \begin{array}{l} \text{should} \\ \text{happens to} \\ \text{should happen to} \end{array} \right\} \text{rain, I'll stay home.}$$

Therefore, we feel that it is an incomplete treatment of the future conditional to present only one form to students (e.g., *If it rains, I'll stay home*)—especially if the students are at the intermediate or advanced level in their study of English, since they regularly will be encountering the "weakened" versions of this construction in the speech and writing of native speakers.

IMAGINATIVE CONDITIONAL SENTENCES

The imaginative conditional sentences are perhaps the most problematic of the three main types in our description.[3] There are two subtypes of imaginative conditionals—hypotheticals and counterfactuals. Hypothetical conditionals express what the speaker perceives to be unlikely yet possible events or states in the *if* clause:

> If Joe had the time, he would go to Mexico. (present hypothetical)

The *if* clause is not strongly negated here. There is an outside chance that Joe has (or will have) the time. Counterfactual conditionals, on the other hand, express impossible events or states in the *if* clause:

> If my grandfather were alive today, he would experience a very different world.
> (present counterfactual)

The *if* clause is strongly negated (i.e., my grandfather is not alive today nor will he be alive in the future).

In hypothetical conditionals the negative quality of the *if* clause can be even further weakened so that the possibility of the result occurring becomes stronger:

$$\text{If Joe} \begin{Bmatrix} \text{should have} \\ \text{happened to have} \\ \text{should happen to have} \end{Bmatrix} \text{the time, he would go to Mexico.}^4$$

Such weakening does not happen in a counterfactual conditional since the *if* clause is strongly negated and the condition remains impossible:

$$\text{?If my grandfather} \begin{Bmatrix} \text{should be} \\ \text{should happen to be} \end{Bmatrix} \text{alive today, he would experience a very different world.}$$

Hypothetical conditionals can refer to the future as well as the present (they are open to change in the present or future):

Present: If Joe had the time, he would go to Mexico.
Future: If Joe were to have the time, he would go to Mexico.

Counterfactual conditionals refer to impossibilities with reference to the present or the past (we don't know what (im)possibilities the future holds):

Present: If my grandfather were alive today, he would experience a very different world.
Past: If my grandfather had still been alive in 1996, he would have been 100 years old.

The problem with imaginative conditionals arises in the tense used.[5] The past tense refers to the present time, and the past perfect tense refers to past time. Furthermore, we have a vestige of the Old English subjunctive mood[6] in the use of *were* with singular first and third person subjects where *was* is the expected form:[7]

> If my grandfather were here now, he would be angry.
> If I were the President, I would make some changes.

Even rarer in current English than the use of *were* to express the subjunctive mood in imaginative conditionals is the occasional use (now slightly archaic) of subjunctive *be* in present conditionals; for example:

> If it be inappropriate to have said this, I humbly apologize.

Sometimes the difference between using a future conditional and a hypothetical conditional is a matter of speaker choice:

Future: If it rains, I will stay home.

Hypothetical: If it $\left\{\begin{array}{l}\text{were to}\\ \text{should}\end{array}\right\}$ rain, I would stay home.

The choice reflects the degree of confidence in the speaker's mind concerning the fulfillment of the condition: the future conditional—if not weakened, as discussed above—expresses a greater degree of confidence that the condition is a real possibility than does the hypothetical conditional.

Summary

We realize that the above semantic taxonomy of conditional sentences, while more comprehensive than most other descriptions available, still does not account for every possible conditional sentence in English. However, we feel that it provides a sufficiently rich set of distinctions to present to ESL/EFL students, since the most frequently occurring types have been included. Our semantic description is summarized in Figure 27.2 with verb forms added:

Figure 27.2

Summary of Conditional
Sentence Types

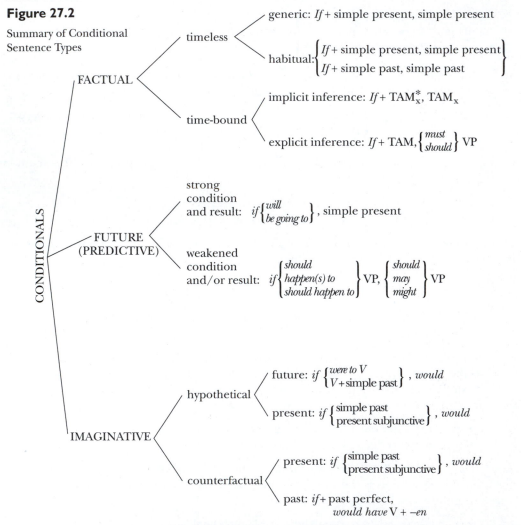

*TAM = any possible combination of tense, aspect, modals, and phrasal modals.

THE BULL FRAMEWORK REVISITED

In Chapter 9 we introduced Bull's (1960) universal framework for describing tense systems, and we presented his present, past, and future axes. We did not treat his hypothetical axis but promised to revisit this topic when discussing conditionals. Both Tregidgo (1974) and De Carrico (1986) have attempted to apply Bull's hypothetical axis to English. For Tregidgo there is a shift whereby simple present in real time becomes simple past in hypothetical time, and simple past becomes *would have V-en* in hypothetical time. De Carrico (1986) adds a "hypothetical past time" axis to the grid we presented for the Bull framework on page 163. However, our preceding discussion has shown that we need two imaginative time lines for English so that we can account for both hypothetical present and future time and counter-factual present and past time. Also we feel that the two imaginative axes are somewhat unique in that there is no "time before," simply a basic time and a time after (the perfect forms have other functions in these axes because hypotheticals and counterfactuals are shifted back in time to convey unreality). Thus we would represent the two imaginative axes as follows:

	A Time Before	Basic Time	A Time After
present/future hypothetical or present counterfactual	(no distinct form)	If you mowed my lawn, [simple past]	I would give you $5. [*would* + V]
past counterfactual	(no distinct form)	If you had mowed my lawn, [past perfect]	I would have paid you $5. [*would* + *have* + V + *-en*]

Here we feel that the *if* clauses convey the basic imaginative shifted time in each axis and the result clauses convey the time after through *would* (with the perfect aspect added to *would* for the past counterfactual).

SOME OTHER MEANING DISTINCTIONS: CONDITIONAL AND RELATED CONNECTORS

Only If and Unless

Compare the following sets of sentences:

> I will stay home if it rains.
> I will stay home only if it rains.[8]

> Don't apply for the job if you don't have an M.A.
> Don't apply for the job unless you have an M.A.

Both *only if* and *unless* mark conditions that are exclusive; that is, no other condition will bring about the stated result. *If* and *if . . . not,* on the other hand, express weaker or more neutral conditions in that they do not exclude the possibility that other conditions might also bring about the same result. Thus we have the following semantic relationships expressed by conditional adverbial subordinators in English:

	Affirmative	Negative
open (unmarked) conditions	if	if . . . not
exclusive (marked) conditions	only if (sometimes: *if* and *only if*)	unless (= except if)

Most reference grammars and ESL/EFL textbooks equate *unless* with *if . . . not*. This is misleading, as Whitaker (1970) and Quirk and Greenbaum (1973) have pointed out, since there are cases where such a substitution produces an ungrammatical sentence:

> If it hadn't been for Zeke's daring rescue, we wouldn't be here.
> *Unless it had been for Zeke's daring rescue, we wouldn't be here.

Also, there are other contexts where substitution results in a change of meaning:[9]

> I couldn't have made it on time unless I'd had an executive jet.
> I couldn't have made it on time if I hadn't had an executive jet.

It is possible to interpret the first sentence as meaning that the speaker didn't have an executive jet and that he didn't arrive on time. The second sentence, however, can mean only that he did have such a jet and thus did arrive on time.[10] Even in less complicated contexts, there always seems to be a difference between *unless* and *if . . . not*:

> If I can't go, I'll call you.
> (= I think I'll be able to go, so I probably won't call you.)
>
> Unless I can go, I'll call you.
> (= I don't think I'll be able to go, so I'll probably won't call you.)

Thus we conclude that ESL/EFL teachers should refrain from teaching *unless* as the equivalent of *if . . . not*. In fact the only reasonable paraphrase relationship involving the above four subordinators exists between *only if* with an affirmative result and *unless* with a negative one:

> Apply for the job only if you have an M.A.
> Don't apply for the job unless you have an M.A.

Even Though and Even If

Consider the following examples:

> You should visit Vienna even though it is expensive.
> You should visit Vienna even if it is expensive.

In the first sentence the speaker knows that Vienna is expensive (i.e., the state of affairs exists) but advises that the addressee visit it despite the cost. In the second sentence the speaker doesn't know definitely whether or not Vienna is expensive—there is a possibility that Vienna is expensive (i.e., it is unclear whether or not the state of affairs exists)—but in any event, the advice is to visit the city.

Thus, *even though* expresses a concession. It is an emphatic form of *although*. *Even if* is conditional—in this case an explicit inference conditional—and it is an emphatic counterpart to *if*.

As the following example demonstrates, *even if* can also function emphatically in hypothetical conditionals:

> I wouldn't marry you if you were the last person on earth!
> I wouldn't marry you even if you were the last person on earth!

Note that the *even if* clause can readily occur initially but that, in the absence of extremely marked exclamatory intonation, the *if* clause is strange if it occurs initially in this type of exclamatory conditional:

> ?If you were the last person on earth, I wouldn't marry you!
> Even if you were the last person on earth, I wouldn't marry you!

Thus it appears that we have isolated a context in which the *if* clause is usually not in initial position. We will discuss some other cases below in the section on use, where ordering of clauses seems critical.

Whether . . . or Not

Thus far we have examined sentences in which the adverbial subordinator indicates that the condition is unmarked, exclusive, emphatic, negative, or exclusive and negative:

> I will stay home *if* it rains. (unmarked)
> I will stay home *only if* it rains. (exclusive)
> I will stay home *even if* it rains. (emphatic)
> I will stay home *if* it doesn't rain. (negative)
> I will stay home *unless* it rains. (exclusive negative)

English has yet another adverbial subordinator, *whether . . . or not,* which indicates that the condition can be explicitly eliminated from playing any role in determining the outcome expressed in the result clause. Thus we can refer to such cases as irrelevant conditions:

> I will stay home *whether or not* it rains.

Our reason for indicating the potential separation of *whether* and *or not* in irrelevant conditions is that with short conditional clauses, the *or not* may also occur at the end of the clause separated from the *whether:*

> I will stay home *whether* it rains *or not.*

However, the longer the clause, the less preferred such a separation becomes:

> ?I will stay home *whether* Professor Dickinson agrees to give the graduate students a lecture on plasma physics *or not.*

RELATED VERBS

Hope and Wish

The verb *hope* is similar to future (predictive) conditionals in that the same clauses that follow *hope* can also function either as the *if* clause or the result clause of a future conditional. For example:

> I hope (that) $\left\{ \begin{array}{l} \text{John finishes his work.} \\ \text{John will come.} \end{array} \right.$

> If John finishes his work, he will come.

Both of these sentences imply that it is possible that John will finish his work and that he will come.

   The verb *wish,* on the other hand, is similar to counterfactual conditionals in that the same clauses that follow *wish* can also function either as the *if* clause or the result clause of a counterfactual conditional:

> I wish (that) $\left\{ \begin{array}{l} \text{John had finished his work.} \\ \text{John could have come.} \end{array} \right.$

> If John had finished his work, he could have come.

In both sentences we know that John didn't finish his work and that he didn't come. Also, the subjunctive forms that can occur in imaginative *if* clauses also occur after *wish:*

> I wish I were a millionaire.   If I were a millionaire . . .

Related to the verb *wish*, there is also the more formal and slightly archaic expression *would that*, which can be used in exclamatory imaginative conditionals to express wishes:

> Would that I had a Rolls Royce! Would that I could fly!
> (I wish I had a Rolls Royce!) (I wish I could fly!)

Besides *wish* and *hope*, English makes use of several other verbs of imagination such as *imagine*, *pretend*, and *suppose*, all of which should be included in a comprehensive description of imaginative clauses:

> Let's imagine that we had a new president. (present counterfactual)
> Pretend that you could fly. Do you think you would own a car? (present counterfactual)
> Suppose we went to Europe next summer. How much would it cost? (future hypothetical)
> (Thewlis, 1997: 277)

THE FREQUENCY AND USE OF CONDITIONAL SENTENCES

THE MOST FREQUENT CONDITIONAL STRUCTURES

Hill (1960) has claimed that English conditional sentences may contain 324 (i.e., 18×18) distinct tense-modal sequences. However, Hwang (1979) analyzed a corpus of English speech (63,746 words) and writing (357,249 words) representing diverse discourse types and concluded that in addition to general rules of consistency in tense sequencing (e.g., *If* present, present; *If* past, past, etc.), only two statements can be made about ungrammatical forms in conditional sentences: (1) logical uses of *might* do not occur in *if* clauses; (2) subjunctive *were* and *were to* do not occur in result clauses:

> *If it might rain, we would need our umbrellas.
> *If the weather got too hot, I were not feeling well.

Furthermore, Hwang found that seven patterns—out of a total of about 70 patterns that naturally occurred—accounted for two-thirds of the conditional sentences in her corpora. Furthermore, she found that these seven patterns—with minor ranking differences—were most frequent in both the spoken and the written corpus.

Table 27.1 on the following page reproduces the most important frequency data reported by Hwang (1979: 63).

Although Hwang identified 45 additional structures for the spoken corpus and 57 more for the written one, these all occurred with frequencies lower than 2 percent except for the eighth ranking structure in the written corpus, which occurred 21 times (i.e., 2.2 percent):

$$\text{Structure H:} \quad \text{If + -past,} \quad \left\{ \begin{array}{l} \text{would} \\ \text{could} \\ \text{might} \end{array} \right\} \quad \text{have + -en}[11]$$

While it is impossible to compare Hwang's structures with our semantic hierarchy in any exact way, the above table does show us that present tense factual conditionals (i.e., structure A) are by far the most frequent type of conditional sentence in both speech and writing. They are followed by the classic future conditional (structure B), which is also represented in weakened form at the bottom of the table (structure G). Present imaginative conditionals are represented in structures C and E,[12] and past counterfactuals are represented in structures F and H. Structure D seems to be a mixed bag including both inferential factuals (*must, should*) and weakened future conditionals (*can, may*).

We feel that Hwang's study indirectly validates our semantic hierarchy, and this assures us that we have indeed accounted for the most frequent conditional structures in English. More importantly, however, Hwang's study helps to establish more realistic priorities for the

TABLE 27.1   A FREQUENCY RANKING OF CONDITIONAL SENTENCE TYPES

Structure	This Book's Terminology	Speech (266 conditionals)	Ranking	Writing (948 conditionals)	Ranking
A: If + pres., pres.	generic factual	51 (19.2%)	1	156 (16.5%)	1
B: If + pres., will/be going to	future (predictive)	29 (10.9%)	2	118 (12.5%)	2
C: If + past, {would / might / could}	present hypothetical or counterfactual	27 (10.2%)	3	95 (10%)	4
D: If + pres., {should / must / can / may}	explicit inference factual or future with weakened result	24 (9%)	4	114 (12.1%)	3
E: If + {were / were to}, {would / could / might}	present or future hypothetical or present counterfactual	23 (8.6%)	5	57 (6%)	6
F: If + {had + en / have + en}, {would / could / might} have	past counterfactual	10 (3.8%)	6	31 (3.3%)	7
G: If + pres., {would / could / might}	future with weakened result	7 (2.6%)	7	58 (6.1%)	5

Note: This chart accounts for only those conditional sentences in Hwang's corpora that followed the most frequent syntactic patterns; i.e., 171 of the total 266 conditional sentences in the spoken corpus and 629 of the total 948 conditional sentences in the written corpus.

ESL/EFL teacher. Present-tense factual conditionals should be taught first and introduced early, followed by future conditionals. Imaginative conditionals should be taught at a later time—after students have learned enough about perfect tenses, modals, and negation to provide the proper syntactic and semantic foundation for using such structures.

USES OF CONDITIONAL SENTENCES

Conditional sentences with initial *if* clauses, which account for almost 80 percent of conditional sentences, perform four functions in both oral and written discourse, according to Ford and Thompson (1986), who did a corpus analysis of conditionals in English. These functions, in order of frequency, are (1) to propose options for future scenarios, (2) to introduce contrasts, (3) to provide examples following generalizations, and (4) to make inferences based on previously mentioned assumptions.

Let us examine a discourse segment illustrating each of these uses.

Proposing Options for Future Scenarios

> [from a phone call discussing the fact that B will be visiting his sister V]
> B: I'll probably leave there, at the latest ten . . . so I'll probably be there at your place, at the latest midnight.
> V: Okay, well if I go to bed, I'm gonna leave the door open.
> B: Oh okay.
> V: Okay? 'Cause I usually go to bed early.
>
> [adapted from Ford and Thompson, 1986]

In this oral segment, V uses a future conditional, ". . . *if I go to bed, I'm gonna leave the door open*," to tell her brother what the scenario will be if he arrives late and she goes to bed early.

Introducing Contrasts

> There is another intellectual virtue, which is that of generality or impartiality. . . . When, in elementary algebra, you do problems about A, B, and C going up a mountain, you have no emotional interest in the gentlemen concerned, and you do your best to work out the solution with impersonal correctness. But if you thought that A was yourself, B your hated rival, and C the schoolmaster who set the problem, your calculations would go askew, and you would be sure to find that A was first and C was last.
> [Russell (1950:31), cited in Ford and Thompson (1986)]

In this text, Bertrand Russell uses a present hypothetical conditional preceded by *but* (a typically co-occurring connector) to describe the contrasting set of circumstances—that is, negative emotional involvement as opposed to the unemotional impartiality that is expressed earlier in timeless simple present tense.

Providing Examples Following Generalizations

> Any solution . . . acid, base or salt . . . will act chemically more readily on one electrode than it will on the other. For example, if electrodes are placed into an orange, a potential difference will appear between electrodes.
> [Randall (1968:47), cited in Ford and Thompson (1986:358)]

Here the future conditional sentence is preceded by the connector *for example* and serves to present a specific illustration of the generalization in the immediately preceding discourse.

Making Inferences Based on Previously Mentioned Assumptions

> A: Joyce went there last night.
> B: Well, if Joyce went there, she saw what happened.
> [author data]

In this segment, speaker B uses a past factual conditional in the *if* clause to reiterate the information previously mentioned by speaker A in order to make an inference in the result clause.

Other Uses of Conditionals in Oral Discourse

Sentence-initial *if* clauses have several other functions in oral discourse that one rarely finds in written discourse (unless the writing is simulating oral discourse). We will mention a few of these predominantly oral discourse functions:

Giving Polite Directives

> [tour guide to the people on her bus]
> TG: If you look out the left side, you'll see Mann's Chinese Theater. You'll have a chance to walk back there and take photos in a few minutes.

Using *if* conditions to present directives can be viewed as polite in that, like a suggestion, it leaves the option of performing the condition to the listener(s).

Speaking Humorously or Sarcastically

> If he's intelligent, then I'm Albert Einstein!
> If you had half a brain, you'd be dangerous.

Tautologisms—where the same words are repeated in both clauses—are a special subcategory of this case:

> If she's not coming, she's not coming!

In the three above examples, initial position of the *if* clause is virtually obligatory since much of the humor or sarcasm would be lost if the two clauses were reversed; and the tautologism seems completely unacceptable if reversed:

> ?She's not coming if she's not coming.

In sum, conditionals are commonly used for many social functions in the spoken language that rarely occur in formal written discourse. A few other such "speech act" conditionals are:

Offer:	If I can help you in any way, just let me know.
Command:	If you're not here to help, please leave!
Apology:	If I've offended you in any way, I'm very sorry.
Advice:	Don't take English 120A unless you've already completed English 20.
or	
Instructions:	Take Introduction to Symbolic Logic only if you're willing to work very hard for a B.

USES OF SENTENCE-FINAL *IF* CLAUSES

Only 23 percent of the *if* clauses in Ford and Thompson's (1986) written corpus were in final position. They found that the following observations accounted for most of their sentence-final *if* clauses:

a. When a conditional clause occurs within a nominalization, an infinitive, or a relative clause, it tends to occur in final position; for example:

> Imagine the difficulty of understanding this information if it were presented one word at a time.
>
> [Terrace (1979:10), cited in Ford and Thompson (1986:359)]

b. English speakers sometimes prefer to introduce strong arguments and interesting topics in the main clause, which may necessitate final position for the subordinate conditional clause; for example:

> The Soviet government would have been less fierce if it had met with less hostility in its first years.
>
> [Russell (1950:109), cited in Ford and Thompson (1986:360)]

c. Long and involved conditional clauses tend to occur in final position; for example:

> . . . Lana would not receive any apple if she pressed such incorrect sequences as: *please machine apple give* or *machine please give apple.*
>
> [Terrace (1979:24), cited in Ford and Thompson (1986:361)]

Even fewer (i.e., 18 percent) of the conditionals in the oral corpus were noninitial than in the written corpus. Many of the examples could be explained with reference to the three strategies cited above for written discourse; however, in oral discourse Ford and Thompson found sentence-final conditionals also fulfilling some other functions. Sentence-final conditionals functioned as afterthoughts or reminders, and these could come from the interlocutor as well as occurring in a continuation by the same speaker:

Student:	Is it practically impossible to have that? [a certain demand curve]
Instructor:	If you have this base.

Sometimes final oral *if* clauses are used deferentially:

> Let's do the dishes later, if that's okay with you.

and sometimes they follow an evaluation which the speaker presents first for emphasis:

> I think it would be better if you came after all.

Perhaps one of the most interesting observations made by Ford and Thompson is that 19 percent of final (but only 5 percent of initial) conditional clauses occur with questions:

> Well, why doesn't he say something, if he has a solution?

Ford and Thompson suggest that these post-question conditional clauses may be functionally related to the "afterthought, reminder" type of conditionals already described above.

Our description of conditionals has focused on *if* and certain related forms. Some other words, phrases, and constructions that signal conditionals are:

whatever	provided that	so long as
who(m)ever	given that	The more, the merrier.
wherever	assuming that	To know him is to love him.
however	no matter *wh-*	Put up your hands or I'll shoot.
whenever	as (if)	

A comprehensive study of conditionals would have to account for these items—and others—and show precisely what relationship they have to the conditional sentences discussed in this chapter.

CONCLUSION

We are the first to admit that one could say much more about conditional sentences in English; however, the analysis above has covered the essentials and has shown that these structures are used in a vast array of contexts, ranging from scientific and mathematical writing to polite directives, verbal insults, and other functions in informal conversation. Hwang (1979) points out in fact that conditional sentences are even more frequent in speech (4.2 per 1,000 words) than in writing (2.7 per 1,000 words).[13] This is true no doubt because spoken English uses conditionals for sarcasm, insults, politeness/deference, and other affectively loaded social functions, as well as using them for the more straightforward inferential and hypothetical functions that predominate in the written language.

It should be obvious from our discussion that conditionals are too vast a topic for any ESL/EFL teacher to cover with one class. Therefore, if you are teaching conditionals, it is important that you teach your students those conditional sentences they are prepared to handle—both structurally and semantically. If you don't present too much information at once, and if you always present and practice conditionals in realistic contexts, you will be able to avoid many of the problems that learners typically experience with conditionals.

TEACHING SUGGESTIONS

1. Form/Meaning. The factual generic conditional, which is often used to express physical laws, is important for students majoring in the sciences. If the condition is satisfied, the result is automatic. Note that the simple present tense is used in both clauses—that is, without modals. For example:

> If you lower the temperature of water to 0°C, it freezes.
> If you raise the temperature of water to 100°C, it boils.

Given the following conditions and results, have groups of students first match the appropriate A and B items and then generate all the possible factual generic conditional sentence(s):

A: Conditions	B: Results
fly west/east	it curdles
mix milk with lemon juice	it floats
pour oil on water	you lose/gain time

> Example: If you fly west, you gain time.

2. Form/Meaning. As well as expressing general truths, factual conditionals may also deal with inferences based on the speaker's prior knowledge. The frequent use of *should* and *must* in such result clauses reinforces their inferential nature; for example:

> If it's 10 o'clock, then Grady (is/must be) taking a coffee break.
> If it's Tuesday, then this must be Belgium.

Given part of Philip's daily schedule, make inferences about what he is doing based on the time:

6:30	—	get up	1:00–2:00	—	lunch
7:00	—	read the newspaper, have coffee	.		
8:00	—	go to work; sell furniture	.		
.			5:00	—	go home
.			6:00	—	eat dinner
10:30	—	coffee break	7:00	—	watch TV
.			.		
.			.		

> Example: If it's 7 o'clock, Philip must be { reading the newspaper.
>   having coffee.

This exercise can also be reversed so that the class can make inferences about the time based on what Philip is doing; for example:

> If Philip is reading the newspaper, it must be 7 o'clock.

3. Form/Meaning. The future or predictive conditional is often used to make plans for the future based on various contingencies. One good context for introducing this structure is a chart with information about pupils: their names, their grades. These pupils will either (a) pass, (b) fail, or (c) skip a grade at the end of the school year. The class can practice all the logical possibilities.

Pupil	Current grade	Possibilities at End of Year	Grade Next Year
Sam	5	Pass (normal promotion)	?
Sally	4	Fail "flunks" (no promotion)	
Kurt	3		
Edith	6	Skip (double promotion)	

Example:
T: What will happen if Sam passes?
S1: If Sam passes, he will be in grade 6 next year.
T: What if he flunks?
S2: If Sam flunks, he will still be in grade 5 next year.

4. Form/Meaning. We use a past habitual conditional to talk about past habits or fixed past schedules that are no longer true. In this context *if* becomes similar to *when* or *whenever*, although it is never exactly the same as *when(ever)*. The following exercise can bring out this similarity.

Mr. Nelson, a retired high school history teacher, thinks about his experiences. He worked with many different types of students and had to handle many different situations:

a. a bright class . . . make lessons challenging
b. a slow class . . . present the basic facts carefully
c. an exceptionally intelligent student . . . give special attention
d. a student with behavior problems . . . contact the parents
e. a student with a physical disability . . . treat as normal

Describe what Mr. Nelson did over the years; for example:

If / When } Mr. Nelson had a bright class, he made his lessons challenging.

5. Form/Meaning. The present counterfactual conditional (impossible, subjunctive) uses past tense and a special subjunctive form:

$$\left(\text{If} + \left\{\begin{array}{l} I \\ she \\ he \end{array}\right\} \text{ were X}, \ldots \right)$$

This is a common and frequent construction and should be practiced in a variety of contexts:

a. Have pairs of students work at imagining that they are famous contemporary people and describing what they would or could do if they were these people. The teacher can provide cue cards with pictures of famous people, and students can make up sentences such as

If I were the President, I would/could . . .

b. Have pairs of students imagine that they have something that they don't really have, or can do something that they really can't do. The teacher may provide cue cards with written or visual cues, such as

| $1,000,000.00 | Picture of a Rolls Royce | Picture of a pilot flying a plane | Picture of a driver racing in a Grand Prix event |

Example:
If I had a million dollars, I would/could . . .

If I $\left\{ \begin{array}{l} \text{could fly} \\ \text{flew} \end{array} \right\}$ planes, I would . . .

c. To make the situation emphatically counterfactual, completely imaginary, Barbara Hawkins suggests that the teacher prepare cue cards with pictures of animals and objects—one for each student or, alternatively, five or six that the whole class can choose from. Then each student should imagine that he or she is the animal or object in question and write as many sentences as possible, which can then form the basis of a short composition.

| Picture of a tree | Picture of an elephant | Picture of a bottle of champagne | Picture of an eagle |

Example:
If I were an eagle, I would be able to fly very high in the sky.

6. Form/Meaning. Many popular songs and folk songs use the imaginative present. The ESL/EFL teacher can take advantage of this by teaching and singing one of these songs to introduce or reinforce the pattern:

"If I Had a Hammer" "If I Were a Carpenter"
"If I Were a Rich Man" "If I Had the Wings of an Angel"

7. Form/Meaning. For practicing past counterfactuals, use the concept of "hindsight." Have each student imagine himself or herself to be a famous person (now deceased) and describe what they would have done or would not have done; for example:

If I had been Napoleon, I would not have fought the British at Waterloo.

8. Meaning. Underlying each past counterfactual conditional sentence, there are indirect messages about what really happened or what was really the case. Ask your students to work in small groups to figure out the reality underlying counterfactual conditionals like these (note that negative markers have been added to several of them to make them more difficult):

If Suzie hadn't been so lazy, she could have passed her history final.
(Suzie was lazy; Suzie didn't pass her history final.)

If I hadn't come early, I wouldn't have been able to help Joan.
(I came early; I helped Joan.)

If Bob had a million dollars, he wouldn't be poor.
(Bob doesn't have $1,000,000; he is poor.)

9. Meaning/Use. To contextualize past counterfactuals, have the class talk about Harry and everything that went wrong for him yesterday.

"Harry's Bad Day"

a. Harry did not get up on time. → He had to rush to get to work.
b. He was in a hurry. → He did not lock his door properly.
c. He did not catch his bus. → He was late for work.
d. Harry's boss was angry. → The boss fired Harry.
e. A burglar entered Harry's apartment. → All of Harry's belongings were stolen.

Have students work in pairs and write out all the things that might have happened/not have happened if Harry had not made any mistakes yesterday. For example:

> If Harry had gotten up in time, he would not have had to rush to get to work.

> If Harry had locked his door properly, the burglar would not have entered his apartment.

10. Form/Meaning. The following series of contextualized exercises for reviewing and relating various forms of the conditional to each other has been inspired by Edmonson (1975), who provides the ESL/EFL teacher with a number of interesting contexts in his article.

a. Familiarize the class with Gary's options for next summer:

Condition	Result
stay in Chicago	work for his father (shoe store)
go to San Francisco	work for his uncle (restaurant)
go to Urbana, Illinois (Univ. of Illinois)	study physics in summer session
go to Green Bay, Wisconsin	work as a camp counselor

Then have students practice the future conditional in small groups, constructing sentences such as

> If Gary stays in Chicago, he will work { for his father
> in his father's shoe store.

b. Using the same situation as in (a), ask the students to switch to the present counterfactual (i.e., the subjunctive) by imagining that they are in Gary's shoes:

> If I were Gary, I would go to San Francisco and work for my uncle.

c. Again refer back to the chart about Gary's summer, but now say that summer is over. Gary went to Wisconsin and worked as a camp counselor. Past counterfactual conditions can now be generated for everything else in the chart; for example:

> If Gary had stayed in Chicago, he would have worked for his father.

After all the sentences have been generated, be sure to have the class interpret them too. For example, the above sentence means:

> Gary didn't stay in Chicago. Gary didn't work for his father.

11. Meaning. The following exercises contain suggestions for teaching *unless* and *only if:*

a. Make your students aware of the fact that *unless* is frequently used along with negative imperatives if the speaker is giving an ultimatum or a warning. The

unless precedes the condition that is necessary for neutralizing the negation in
the imperative;

Don't run in a marathon unless you run long distances regularly.
(affirmative implication: If you run long distances regularly, you can run in a marathon.)

Have your students advise each other not to do the following things unless a necessary
condition—which they are to specify—is met. Have them also indicate what the affirmative implication is in each case.

apply for admission to graduate school go to a party the night before an exam
join the army open up a restaurant
accept a job in Alaska work for a low salary

Examples:
Don't apply for admission to graduate school unless you have at least a 3.25 GPA.

(affirmative implication: If you have at least a 3.25 GPA, you can apply for admission to
graduate school.)

b. You can familiarize your students with the use of *only if* by referring to the same
situations listed above. Emphasize that although the advice is overtly positive in
this case, the implication is negative; that is, if the necessary condition is not met,
the advice in the result clause no longer applies. For example:

You (can/should) apply for admission to graduate school, only if you have at least a
3.25 undergraduate GPA.
(negative implication: If you don't have at least a 3.25 undergraduate GPA, don't apply
for admission to graduate school)

c. At some point your students also need to understand that an *unless* clause can be
used with an affirmative result clause, too. This is particularly true if future plans
are being discussed; for example:

We will vacation in Hawaii unless our schedule changes between now and May.
(implication: We expect to vacation in Hawaii but our schedule might change between
now and May. If it does, we won't go.)

Have your students make up their own sentences using *unless* clauses with the plans below
to express the idea that other things could intervene. Have them paraphrase their
sentences to show the implication, too.

I'll see you next Sunday.
I will withdraw from my physics class.
Let's plan on going to the movies this weekend.
Gary will travel to Europe in July.
Sylvia is going to work part-time at a restaurant.

Example:
I'll see you next Sunday unless I have too much homework to do.

(implication: I'll see you next Sunday, though I may have too much homework to do,
and if I do, I won't see you.)

EXERCISES

Test your understanding of what has been presented.

1. Provide example sentences that illustrate the following terms. Underline the pertinent word(s) in your example.
   - **a.** factual conditional
     - **(i)** generic
     - **(ii)** implicit inference
   - **b.** future conditional
     - **(i)** weakened result clause
     - **(ii)** weakened *if* clause
   - **c.** counterfactual conditional
   - **d.** contrastive use of a conditional
   - **e.** subjunctive use of *were*
   - **f.** *then* insertion
   - **g.** *if* deletion with subject/auxiliary inversion
   - **h.** conditional clause pro-form
   - **i.** sarcastic use of conditional
   - **j.** hypothetical conditional

2. Draw the tree diagrams and state the mapping rules that are needed:
   - **a.** If I had the time, I would go to Europe.
   - **b.** If John had studied, then he would have received an A.
   - **c.** I will not stay at the meeting if he is there.
   - **d.** Don't go for an interview unless you want the job.

3. Why are the following sentences ungrammatical (or at best awkward)?
   - **a.** *If she had been there, she did the work.
   - **b.** *If John might be free, I'll invite him.
   - **c.** ?I'm a monkey's uncle if she's only 22 years old!
   - **d.** ?Then he'll keep his word if he made a promise.

Test your ability to apply what you know.

4. If your students produce the following sentences, how will you make them aware of their errors, and what exercises and activities will you provide to correct the errors?
   - **a.** *If I were an American, I were speaking better English.
   - **b.** *What happens if I pushed this button?
   - **c.** *Why had some Americans said, "Gesundheit," if someone sneezes?
   - **d.** *Only if you help me, I will study for the quiz.

5. One of your advanced students has heard native speakers say conditionals like these, and he or she wants to know whether they are correct or not. What will you say?

   > If I was the Dalai Lama, I'd do the same thing.
   > I would be less nervous if you would stop staring at me.

6. Select a passage or article and identify all the conditional sentences. Try to account for the sentences using the semantic hierarchy provided on page 548 in this chapter. Are there any sentences that cannot be explained according to the hierarchy? If so, try to provide your own analysis or explanation of the sentence(s).

7. Use the semantic description of conditionals provided in this chapter and decide where a sentence such as the following one belongs:

   > If the gardener doesn't come tomorrow, Father will have to mow the lawn.

BIBLIOGRAPHY

References

Bull, W. (1960). *Time, Tense, and the Verb: A Study in Theoretical and Applied Linguistics, with Particular Attention to Spanish.* Berkeley, Calif.: University of California Press.

Covitt, R. I. (1976). "Some Problematic Grammar Areas for ESL Teachers." Unpublished M.A. thesis in TESL, UCLA.

De Carrico, J. (1986). "Tense, Aspect, and Time in the English Modality System." *TESOL Quarterly* 20:4, 665–682.

Edmonson, W. J. (1975). "Contrasts in Conditional Sentences." *The Art of TESOL*, Part I, in A. Newton (ed.), Selected Articles from the *English Teaching Forum.* Washington, D.C.: USIA.

Ford, C. E. (1993). *Grammar in Interaction: Adverbial Clauses in American English Conversations.* Cambridge: Cambridge University Press.

Ford, C. E., and S.A. Thompson (1986). Conditionals in Discourse: A Text-Based Study from English. In E. Trangott et al (eds.) *On Conditionals.* Cambridge: Cambridge University Press.

Halliday, M., and R. Hasan (1976). *Cohesion in English.* London: Longman.

Harsh, W. (1968). *The Subjunctive in English.* University, Ala.: University of Alabama Press.

Hill, L. A. (1960). "The Sequence of Tenses with *If* Clauses." *Language Learning* 10:3 and 4, 165–178.

Hwang, M. (1979). "A Semantic and Syntactic Analysis of 'If' Conditionals." Unpublished M.A. thesis in TESL, UCLA.

Quirk, R., and S. Greenbaum (1973). *A Concise Grammar of Contemporary English.* New York: Harcourt Brace Jovanovich.

Randall, R. K. (1969). *Auto Engine Tune-up.* Indianapolis, Ind.: Theodore Andel.

Russell, B. (1950). *Unpopular Essays.* New York: Simon & Schuster.

Schachter, J. (1971). "Presupposition and Counterfactual Conditional Sentences." Unpublished Ph.D. dissertation in Linguistics, UCLA.

Terrace, H. (1979). *Nim: A Chimpanzee Who Learned Sign Language.* New York: Washington Square Press.

Thewlis, S. (1997). *Grammar Dimensions: Form, Meaning, and Use.* Book 3 (2d ed.). Boston: Heinle & Heinle.

Tregidgo, P. S. (1974). "English Tense Usage: A Bull's Eye View." *ELT Journal*, 28:2, 97–107.

Whitaker, S. F. (1970). "Unless." *English Language Teaching Journal* 24:2, 154–160.

Suggestions for Further Reading

For useful general information on conditional sentences, see:

George, H. V. (1966). "If" (1) and "If" (2). *English Language Teaching Journal.* 20:2, 113–119, and 3: 232–239.

Jespersen, O. (1940). *A Modern English Grammar on Historical Principles* (vols. V, VII). Copenhagen: Einar Munksgaard.

Leech, G., and J. Svartvik (1975). *A Communicative Grammar of English.* London: Longman.

Quirk, R., S. Greenbaum, G. Leech, and J. Svartvik, (1985). *A Comprehensive Grammar of the English language.* London: Longman.

For a cross-linguistic, cross-disciplinary account of conditionals, see:
Jackson, F. (ed.) (1991). *Conditionals.* Oxford: Oxford University Press.
Traugott, E., A. ter Meulen, J. S. Reilly, and C. A. Ferguson, (1986). *On Conditionals.*
    Cambridge: Cambridge University Press.

For excellent suggestions on how to present conditionals to ESL/EFL secondary school students, see
Edmonson (1975) in the references above.

For one of the few ESL texts that properly distinguishes hypothetical and counterfactual conditionals, see:
Rutherford, W. (1977). *Modern English.* Vol II (2d ed.). New York: Harcourt Brace
    Jovanovich.

For excellent suggestions for teaching hope *and* wish, *as well as conditional sentences, see:*
Danielson, D., and P. Porter (1990). *Using English: Your Second Language* (2d ed.).
    Englewood Cliffs, N.J.: Prentice-Hall.

For a unit that introduces factual conditionals to high-beginner ESL/EFL students, see:
Badalamenti, V., and C. Henner Stanchina (1997). *Grammar Dimensions: Form, Meaning,*
    and Use. Book 1 (2d ed.). Unit 25. Boston: Heinle & Heinle.

For a unit that introduces hypothetical (present and past) and future conditionals to low intermediate
ESL/EFL learner, see:
Riggenbach, H., and V. Samuda (1997). *Grammar Dimensions: Form, Meaning, and Use.*
    Book 2 (2d ed.). Unit 25. Boston: Heinle & Heinle.

For a unit that contrasts real and hypothetical conditionals for intermediate learners, see:
Thewlis, S. (1997). *Grammar Dimensions: Form, Meaning, and Use,* Book 3 (2d ed.). Unit 17.
    Boston: Heinle & Heinle.

For a review of conditionals for advanced students, plus exercises dealing with only if, unless, even
though, even if, *see:*
Frodesen, J., and J. Eyring (1997). *Grammar Dimensions: Form, Meaning, and Use.* Book 4
    (2d ed.). Unit 15. Boston: Heinle & Heinle.

ENDNOTES

1. The five most serious problems were ranked as follows:
      articles
      prepositions
      phrasal verbs
      verbals (infinitives, gerunds, participles)
      conditionals

2. Hwang (1979) demonstrates that ESL/EFL students cannot produce or interpret these simple, present-tense conditionals as well as they can future conditionals—very probably as a result of incomplete and misleading instruction.

3. We are indebted to Schachter (1971) both for the term "imaginative" and also for much of the following description and terminology.

4. In colloquial North American English, such an *if* clause sometimes contains a *would*:

    If Joe would have the time, he would go to Mexico.

This results in a double "would" construction, which many prescriptive usage manuals rule out as unacceptable in formal English.

5. Hwang (1979) demonstrates that ESL/EFL students confuse hypothetical and counterfactual conditionals and cannot interpret them properly even when they are able to select the correct form on a multiple-choice test item. Many students interpret hypotheticals as if they were counterfactuals—thus ignoring a subtle but important semantic distinction in English.

6. See Harsh (1968) for a comprehensive description of the subjunctive in English.

7. In colloquial English *was* in fact often occurs in such imaginative conditional sentences in lieu of *were.*

8. Note that when the *only if* clause is fronted, this forces subject/operator inversion in the main clause:

$$\text{Only if it rains,} \begin{cases} \text{will I stay home.} \\ \text{*I will stay home.} \end{cases}$$

We believe that this occurs because of the negative implication that *only if* conveys as part of its exclusive meaning; i.e., no other condition will bring about the result.

9. Such conditional sentences highlight another problem for ESL/EFL students. Hwang (1979) shows that they have severe problems interpreting conditionals with one or two negatives—so this must be an area to which the teacher gives special attention.

10. Both the ungrammatical example with *unless* and the difference in meaning in the executive jet examples can be explained by the fact that *unless* is incompatible with a counterfactual interpretation. *Unless* can be used hypothetically but not counterfactually.

11. Note that this structure might be a simplification of structure F:

$$(\text{If} + \text{had} + \textit{-en,} \begin{cases} \text{would} \\ \text{could} \\ \text{might} \end{cases} \text{have} + \textit{-en})$$

if the simple past is replacing the past perfect in the *if* clause.

12. Structure E contains *were to* as well as *were,* which means that future hypotheticals are included here, too.

13. This ratio is confirmed by Ford and Thompson (1986), who found twice as many conditionals occurring per 1,000 words in their oral corpus than in their written one.

28

INTRODUCTION TO RELATIVE CLAUSES

INTRODUCTION

You'll need to know a great deal about relative clauses as a teacher of ESL/EFL. This construction is—first and foremost—a type of complex postnominal adjectival modifier used in both written and spoken English. For example:

> San Antonio is a city *that has experienced very rapid growth.*

In this example, the italicized relative clause gives us additional information about San Antonio. In English it would be very awkward, even ungrammatical, to convey the same information using an attributive adjective phrase:

> *San Antonio is an experiencing very rapid growth city.

It would be possible, but more wordy and less elegant, to express the same information as two independent clauses:

> San Antonio is a type of city; it has experienced very rapid growth.

Relative clauses thus give us a means to encode complex adjectival modifiers that are easier to process than complex attributive structures and that are less wordy than two independent clauses.

In this chapter we will consider the form, meaning, and function of restrictive relative clauses like the one in the example above. The other major type of relative clause, the nonrestrictive type, will be dealt with in the following chapter along with some other relative clause constructions.

THE FORM OF RELATIVE CLAUSES

A relative clause derives from a basic structure consisting of more than one sentence. Actually, as early as Chapter 5, and then again in Chapter 25, you saw that one basic structure sentence could be subordinated to another when preceded by an adverbial subordinator; for example:

> The baby walked before she crawled.
> (S1 + adv sub + S2)

This, of course, was also the type of subordinate structure we used to derive some of the conditional sentences in the preceding chapter.

In Chapter 24 we analyzed sentences with two or more basic structure sentences that are conjoined; for example:

> The children dressed up for Halloween, and they carved jack-o-lanterns out of pumpkins.
> S1 + conj. + S2

The basic structural relationship among the sentences that we consider in this chapter is different from that of subordinating or coordinating conjunction. It is a relationship brought about by a process called *embedding*, which is the generation of one clause within another higher-order or superordinate clause such that the embedded clause becomes a part of the superordinate main clause. In the case of restrictive relative clauses, the embedding consists of a clause embedded within an NP and modifying that NP. For example:

> The fans [who were attending the rock concert] had to wait in line for three hours.
> (NP[S])

Here we have the sense that the embedded clause "who were attending the rock concert" is closely associated with the head NP, "the fans." In fact, we find that the clause has a modifying function much like an adjective; it tells us which "fans" had to wait in a long line. Perhaps now it is apparent why such clauses are called "restrictive" (or in some grammars "defining" or "limiting" or "adjective" clauses). They restrict or identify for us which noun(s)—of all nouns in the same set we are speaking about (i.e., anybody who could be called "a fan").

Keenan and Comrie (1972; 1977) help us better understand the restrictions that obtain in any language on NPs that can be relativized, i.e., replaced by relative pronouns. They posit the "noun phrase accessibility hierarchy," which lists the most "accessible" type of NP at the top and the least accessible type at the bottom:

> subject NP (most accessible or most able to become a relative pronoun)
> direct object NP
> indirect object NP
> oblique object NP (i.e., object of a preposition that is not an indirect object)
> genitive (i.e., possessive) NP
> object NP of a comparison (least accessible or least able to become a relative pronoun)

This hierarchy claims (among other things) that in cross-linguistic terms, subject NPs are easier to relativize than direct object NPs, which in turn are easier to relativize than indirect object NPs, and so on. This means that all languages that have relative clauses can relativize subjects, but it also implies that there are some languages, such as Tagalog, that can relativize only subjects (or topics). Furthermore, any language like Slovenian that can relativize object NPs of comparisons can also relativize all the other five types of NPs that are higher in the hierarchy.

English has a rich system of relativization with only a few restrictions on the kind of noun phrase that can be relativized or replaced by a relative pronoun; for example:

subject NP—The book *that* is on the coffee table was written by Wallace.

direct object NP—The authors *that* he mentioned are well known.

indirect object NP—The girl $\left\{ \begin{array}{l} \textit{(to) whom} \text{ we gave the message} \\ \textit{who} \text{ we gave the message } \textit{to} \end{array} \right\}$ is not here.

oblique object NP—The child $\left\{ \begin{array}{l} \text{from } \textit{whom} \text{ you took the candy} \\ \textit{whom} \text{ you took the candy from} \end{array} \right\}$ is crying.

genitive NP—The man *whose name* you wanted to know is Cal North.

object NP of comparison— $\begin{cases} \text{?The only person } that \text{ I was shorter than was Fritz.} \\ \text{*The only person than } whom \text{ I was shorter was Fritz.} \end{cases}$

Reviewing the NP accessibility hierarchy, we can see that the only marginal NP function for relativization in English is "object of a comparison." The other five functions are fully acceptable. This means that speakers of Tagalog and related languages that relativize only subjects (or topics) (e.g., Malay, Indonesian) may have some difficulty with the variety of NPs that can be relativized in English.

Being aware of these differences among languages will hopefully help you understand what background your students are bringing with them and allow you to be better prepared in presenting and practicing relative clause formation in English.

PROBLEMS FOR ESL/EFL STUDENTS

J. Schachter (1974:202–208), in discussing the work of Keenan and Comrie (1972), identifies three main dimensions along which relative clauses can differ. The first dimension has to do with the position of the relative clause with respect to the head noun, i.e., the noun being modified. As should be clear from the examples above, English relative clauses follow the head noun. This is also true of relative clauses in most European languages and also in languages such as Farsi and Arabic. Not all languages, however, adhere to this syntactic pattern. Japanese, Chinese, and Korean, for instance, all require that the relative clause occur before the head noun. Students who are native speakers of these languages will have to grasp this fundamental ordering difference.

Schachter's second dimension involves how relative clauses are marked. English uses a relative pronoun (for example, *who*) to mark that what follows is a relative clause. Persian, Arabic, and Chinese employ other kinds of markers between the head noun and the relative clause. For speakers of these languages, the concept of a relative pronoun should not cause undue hardship in learning English. Japanese, on the other hand, uses particles in the relative clause itself to mark its restrictive function. Japanese students of ESL/EFL may thus require additional practice with English relative pronouns in order for them to become comfortable in using relative clauses in English.

The third dimension along which languages differ with respect to relative clause formation is the presence or absence of a pronominal reflex. In English the relative pronoun substitutes for the identical NP in the embedded sentence. For example, in the sentence:

Shirley called out to the boy that she knew.

the "that" replaces "the boy" in the embedded sentence, "she knew the boy." In other languages—for instance, Arabic, Hebrew, and Persian—a relative clause marker is introduced, but the object noun in the embedded sentence that is identical to the head noun is often retained in a form called a pronominal reflex. Thus, speakers of these languages tend to commit errors in English such as the following:

*Shirley called out to the boy that she knew *him*.

Chinese and Arabic also allow pronominal reflexes to occur as objects of prepositions; so speakers of these languages sometimes err in producing English sentences such as:

*The man who you were talking to *him* is my uncle.

THE RELATIVIZATION OF THE SUBJECT IN THE EMBEDDED SENTENCE

Subject-subject Relatives

There is a great diversity in English relative clause types. We will first treat those in which the subject of the embedded sentence becomes relativized. Consider the following sentence:

> The girl who speaks Basque is my cousin.

We understand that the "who" refers to the "girl." We understand this as speakers of English despite the fact that *who* can refer to persons of either sex in the singular or plural.

> The boy who speaks Basque is my cousin.
> The girls who speak Basque are my cousins.

Who is the relative pronoun in all these sentences. We know that it has the same referent as the head NP which directly precedes it. Thus, the basic structure for the first sentence above is:

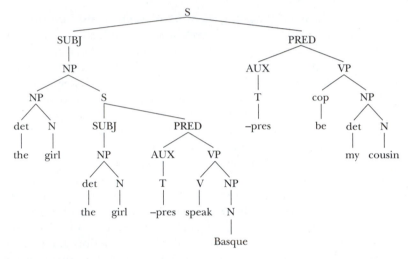

To account for sentences that are embedded within NPs, we have had to expand our phrase structure rule for rewriting the NP to include:

$$NP \rightarrow NP \; [S]$$

In order to function as a relative clause, the embedded sentence must contain an NP that is identical in form and reference to the NP in the main clause. When this condition exists, a mapping rule called "relative pronoun substitution" replaces this NP in the embedded sentence with the appropriate relative pronoun. In order to arrive at the surface structure for our example sentence, then, the following mapping rules would be necessary:

> output of base: the girl [the girl -pres speak Basque] -pres be my cousin
> copy s/t: the girl [the girl -pres [+ 3 + sg] speak Basque] -pres [+ 3 + sg] be my cousin
> relative pronoun substitution: the girl [who -pres [+ 3 + sg] speak Basque] -pres [+ 3 + sg] be my cousin
> morphological rules: The girl who speaks Basque is my cousin.

Object-subject Relatives

The sentence we have just examined has an embedded sentence that modifies the subject NP of the main clause. It is also possible to have an embedded sentence with a relativized subject modifying an NP that is the object of the main clause; for example:

> I know the girl who speaks Basque.

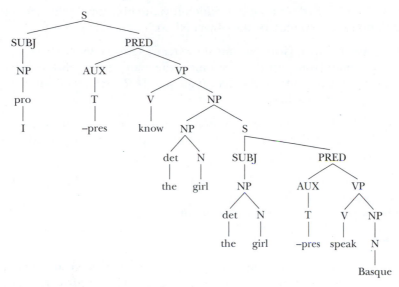

The mapping rules we applied to our first sentence would also apply here to give us the desired surface structure.

Next we will consider sentences in which the object NP of the embedded relative clause is identical to some NP in the main clause; that is, the object of the embedded sentence is relativized.

THE RELATIVIZATION OF THE OBJECT
IN THE EMBEDDED SENTENCE

Subject-object Relatives

In this type of relative clause, the object NP of the embedded sentence is affected. Consider the following:

The man whom you met is my teacher.

What is the embedded sentence in this example? At first glance the relative clause in this sentence appears no different from the first two we looked at. Upon closer examination, however, we realize that the underlying embedded sentence is "you met the man" and that, therefore, in the basic structure the two identical NPs will not be adjacent as they were in the two previous sentences we have discussed.

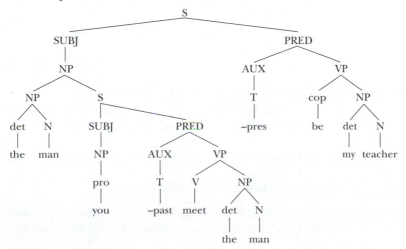

Notice that with embedded sentences in which it is the object NP that refers to the head noun, it won't do to merely replace the object NP with a relative pronoun.

> output of base: the man [you -past meet the man] -pres be my teacher
> copy s/t: The man [you -past [+ 2 + sg] meet the man] -pres [+ 3 + sg] be my teacher
> relative pronoun substitution: the man (you -past [+ 2 + sg] meet whom[1]) -pres
> [+ 3 + sg] be my teacher

What is necessary at this point is for us to move the relative pronoun to initial position in the embedded clause. This is accomplished by a mapping rule referred to as "relative pronoun fronting."

> relative pronoun fronting: the man [whom you -past [+ 2 + sg] meet] -pres
> [+ 3 + sg] be my teacher
> morphological rules: The man whom you met is my teacher.

Object-object Relatives

Earlier you saw that an embedded sentence with a relativized subject could modify the object as well as the subject of the main clause. This is also true of embedded sentences with relativized objects; for example:

I read the book that you mentioned.

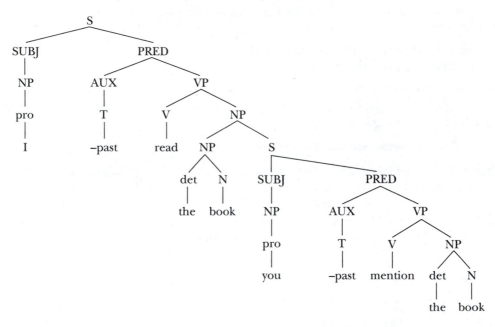

output of base: I -past read the book [you -past mention the book]
copy s/t: I -past [+ 1+ sg] read the book [you -past [+ 2 + sg] mention the book]
relative pronoun substitution: I -past [+ 1 + sg] read the book [you -past [+ 2 + sg] mention that]
relative pronoun fronting: I -past [+ 1 + sg] read the book [that you -past [+ 2 + sg] mention]
morphological rules: I read the book that you mentioned.

Besides the need for relative pronoun fronting, another characteristic of embedded sentences with relativized objects is that the relative pronoun may be optionally deleted without affecting the grammaticality of the sentence. To capture this fact, we can have an optional relative pronoun deletion rule operate after relative pronoun fronting.

> relative pronoun fronting: I -past [+ 1 + sg] read the book [that you -past [+ 2 + sg] mention]
> relative pronoun deletion: I -past [+ 1 + sg] read the book [you -past [+ 2 + sg] mention]

After the morphological rules apply, we get:

> I read the book you mentioned.

If we had had the relative pronoun deletion rule apply to the other sentence with a relativized object that we discussed above, we would have produced:

> The man you met is my teacher.

Relative pronoun deletion applies only to relativized objects; it does not apply to embedded sentences with relativized subjects:

> *The girl speaks Basque is my cousin.   *I know the girl speaks Basque.

THE ORDER OF DIFFICULTY OF RELATIVE CLAUSES

So far we have examined four basic types of relative clauses:

SS   Subject of the embedded sentence is identical to the subject of the main clause; for example:

> The girl who speaks Basque is my cousin.

OS   Subject of the embedded sentence is identical to the object of the main clause; for example:

> I know the girl who speaks Basque.

SO   Object of the embedded sentence is identical to the subject of the main clause; for example:

> The man who(m) you met is my teacher.

OO   Object of the embedded sentence is identical to the object of the main clause; for example:

> I read the book that you mentioned.

In 1974, Kuno hypothesized that OS and OO relative clause types would be easier to acquire than SS and SO types. He reasoned that when the embedded relative clauses interrupted the sentence by coming directly after the subject of the main clause,[2] they would be more difficult to process than those relative clauses that modified the object of the main sentence and thus came at the end of the sentence. Studies in the field of second language acquisition by Ioup and Kruse (1977) and Schumann (1978) seem to support Kuno's hypothesis.

Schumann, for example, examined the production data of seven ESL learners and observed the following acquisition order. (The numbers represent the percentage of times the seven subjects used relative clauses of each type):

OS   0.53
OO   0.35
SS   0.06
SO   0.04

(0.02 of the clauses could not be unambiguously assigned to any one of the four types.)

In a subsequent study of the English written production of 170 Cantonese speakers, Wong (1991) found an acquisition order similar to that of Schumann: OS 47 percent, OO 26 percent, SS 15 percent, SO 10 percent (2 percent unidentifiable).

Stauble (1978) examined the frequency of these four relative clause types in samples of native speaker discourse drawn from three different discourse types: informal speech, spontaneous writing, and published writing. By calculating the number of instances and the frequency percentages for the four types of clauses, she obtained the following totals for the three combined discourse types:[3]

	Instances	Percentage
OS	234	55
OO	108	25
SS	52	12
SO	30	7
Total	424	99 (does not equal 100 because percentages were rounded off)

There is an obvious correlation between the rank order and frequency of occurrence of the different types of relative clauses used by native speakers and the observed second language acquisition order. However, Stauble also points out that the structural complexity and location of the various clause types may explain the order as well. The OS type may be the easiest simply because it requires only one major obligatory rule, whereas SS sentences require one rule plus center embedding, and OO sentences require two obligatory rules. Finally, SO types require two mapping rules with the added difficulty of their being center embedded.

ESL/EFL teachers, of course, may eventually have to deal with the teaching of all four types of relative clauses. However, since the OS and OO types are much more frequent, they clearly deserve priority from a pedagogical perspective.

THE DIVERSITY OF RELATIVE CLAUSE TYPES

So far we have dealt only with relative clauses modifying the subjects and direct objects of main clauses. Such a perspective belies the complexity that actually exists. The chart on page 579 illustrates the diversity of English relative clause structures.

THE RELATIVIZATION OF THE OBJECT OF THE PREPOSITION IN THE EMBEDDED SENTENCE

One of the relative clause types apparent in the chart that we have yet to examine is the one in which the object of the preposition in the embedded sentence is relativized. If we analyze one such example sentence from the chart, such as

I know the place which you spoke about.

we see that its basic structure is:

Example Sentences for the Various Relative Clause Structures in English*

Function of head noun in main clauses	Function of identical (i.e., relativized) noun in relative clauses			
	Subject	*Direct object*	*Indirect object*	*Object of a preposition*
Subject	The girl *who* speaks Basque is my cousin.	The man *who(m)* you met is my teacher.	The man *that* I gave the book to is over there.	The place *which* you spoke about is Denver.
Direct object	I know the girl *who* speaks Basque.	I know the place *that* you mentioned.	I gave the man *that* you mentioned the book.	I know the place *which* you spoke about.
Indirect object	We gave the boy *who* broke the window a warning.	I sent the boy *that* Mary saw a letter.	I told the boy *that* you gave the book to a story.	I gave the boy *that* you were talking about the book.
Object of the preposition	I talked with the girl *who* speaks Basque.	I work for the man *that* you met.	Mary knows about the boy *that* I gave the book to.	I know of the place *which* John spoke about.
Predicate noun	Mr. Thomas is a teacher *who* prepare his lessons.	Latin is the subject *that* Mr. Thomas teaches.	He's the boy *that* I gave the present to.	Denver is a place *which* you'll want to go to.

*Note that in addition to the above structures the possessive determiner *whose* can relativize any noun functioning as a subject, direct object, indirect object, object of a preposition, or predicate noun, giving us in effect 40 distinct relative clause structures in English.

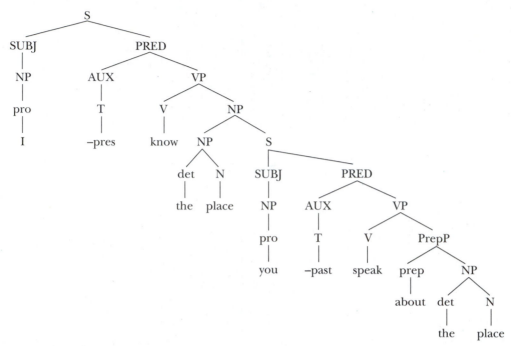

We have already seen how the rules of relative pronoun substitution and relative pronoun fronting operate on this sentence:

> output of base: I -pres know the place [you -past speak about the place]
>
> copy s/t: I -pres [+ 1 + sg] know the place [you -past [+ 2 + sg] speak about the place]
>
> relative pronoun substitution: I -pres [+ 1 + sg] know the place [you -past [+ 2 + sg] speak about which]
>
> relative pronoun fronting: I -pres [+ 1 + sg] know the place [which you -past [+ 2 + sg] speak about]

and actually this is all that would be necessary—other than morphological rules—to arrive at the desired surface structure. Another surface structure possibility, however, involves fronting the preposition along with its relativized object. If we were to do this, we would get:

> **I know the place about which you spoke.**

What results is a rather formal version of the sentence. Such a sentence is rarely appropriate in informal spoken discourse; however Stauble (1978) found that in both published writing and the quick first-draft writing of American graduate students, the preposition is almost always fronted along with the relative pronoun. Thus, this appears to be a systematic stylistic difference between written exposition and informal spoken English.

One final point in keeping with this topic is that the relative pronoun *that* cannot be used to replace the relativized object of a proposition, if the preposition is fronted with the pronoun; that is, *who(m)* and *which* are obligatory in this environment.

> ***The person with that you were**   ***The chair on that you were**
> **talking is the principal.**   **sitting broke.**

The relative pronoun *that* can be used, however, if the preposition is not fronted along with the relative pronoun:

> **The person that you were**   **The chair that you were**
> **talking with is the principal.**   **sitting on broke.**

Finally, we have already learned that the relative pronoun that replaces an object can be deleted. This is the case even for relative pronouns that substitute for objects of prepositions; however, remember that deletion is possible only if the preposition has not been fronted along with the relativized object NP:

> The place which you spoke about is Denver.   The place about which you spoke is Denver.
>
> The place you spoke about is Denver.   *The place about you spoke is Denver.

We should add a note of caution, however, in that Stauble found that retention of the relative pronoun was preferred over deletion for all three discourse types she sampled. In those cases where deletion of the relative pronoun was more frequent than retention, the head noun was almost always nonhuman. However, Stauble's data were limited; thus further research on the issue of deletion or retention of the relative pronoun is clearly needed.

THE RELATIVIZATION OF THE POSSESSIVE DETERMINER IN THE EMBEDDED SENTENCE

A relative clause type not illustrated in the chart on page 579 is the relative clause that results when a noun marked for possession in the embedded sentence is the noun that refers to a noun in the main clause. The basic structure for a sentence of this type follows:

The man whose wife you are admiring is a wrestler.

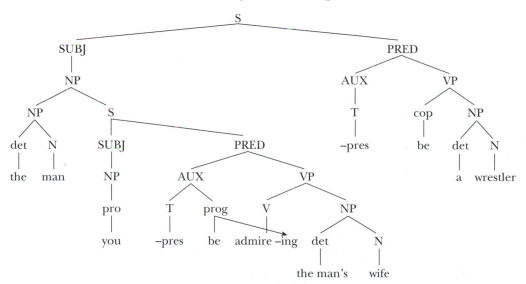

The mapping process would proceed as usual but with the relative determiner (*whose* in this case) substituting only for the possessive determiner rather than for the entire NP; that is, the rule becomes relative determiner substitution, not relative pronoun substitution.

> output of base: the man [you -pres be admire -ing the man's wife] -pres be a wrestler
> copy s/t: the man [you -pres [+ 2 + sg] be admire -ing the man's wife] -pres be [+ 3 + sg] a wrestler
> relative determiner substitution: the man [you -pres [+ 2 + sg] be admire -ing whose wife] -pres [+ 3 + sg] be a wrestler

At this point a difference emerges. Since the relative determiner is replacing the possessive determiner, when the relative determiner is fronted, the noun it modifies must also be fronted.[4]

relative determiner fronting: the man [whose wife you -pres [+ 2 + sg] be admire -ing]
    -pres [+ 3 + sg] be a wrestler
morphological rules: The man whose wife you are admiring is a wrestler.

THE MEANING OF RELATIVIZED NOUN PHRASES

Recall from the introduction that restrictive relative clauses modify head nouns and are thus sometimes called adjectival or limiting clauses since they serve to restrict and identify the head noun to that subset of individuals that the speaker wishes to refer to.

RELATIVE PRONOUN FEATURES

We have thus far been substituting relative pronouns for NPs without really being specific about the rules governing their use. Every relative pronoun is entered in the lexicon together with its semantic (and other) features. The feature specifications allow us to select the appropriate relative pronoun depending upon the features of the NP it replaces and the discourse context in which it will be used. The following are the relative pronouns in English and some of their salient semantic and syntactic features:

who + subject NP	*which* ± subject NP
+ human	− human
whom + object NP	*that* ± subject NP
+ human	± human
	whose + human
	+ possessive
	+ determiner

THE USE OF RELATIVE PRONOUNS AND RELATIVE CLAUSES

RELATIVE PRONOUN USE

Although it would always be prescriptively correct to use *whom* to replace a relativized human NP in object position—or the object of a preposition without a fronted preposition—native speakers do not generally use it this way. Often they opt for the simpler subject case form, *who*, instead:

- *who/whom*

    I spoke with the student who(m) I loaned the book to.

On the other hand, if the *who(m)* is replacing the object of the preposition and the preposition is fronted with the relative pronoun, *whom* will occur much more frequently:

   I know the student to $\left\{ \begin{array}{l} \text{whom} \\ \text{?who} \end{array} \right\}$ you loaned the book.

- *that/ who or which*

    In informal conversational discourse, *that* is often preferred over either *which* or *who(m)*. In written discourse, *who(m)* is preferred for human antecedents; *which* and *that* are both used to indicate a nonhuman head noun (Stauble, 1978).[5]

- *whose*

    Whose generally refers to a human head noun, but sometimes sentences like the following occur where *whose* refers to an inanimate noun:

    I found an old coin whose date has become worn and illegible.

This use of *whose* helps the speaker/writer avoid using a more awkward paraphrase:

   I found an old coin the date $\left\{ \begin{array}{l} \text{of} \\ \text{on} \end{array} \right\}$ which has become worn and illegible.

THE USE OF RELATIVE CLAUSES

Summary of Earlier Points

A few observations on relative pronoun use were briefly mentioned above when their form and meaning were discussed; they are restated here as a starting point for our discussion on the use of relative clauses:

- The relative pronouns that replace relativized objects are optionally deletable; however, generally speaking, retention of the relative pronoun is preferred over deletion in writing, with a higher frequency of deletion occurring in informal speech. Stauble (1978) found that deletion was preferred when the relative pronoun had a nonhuman antecedent. For example:

   The latest novel he wrote is excellent.

- When prepositional objects are relativized, the relative pronoun is either deleted or fronted and the preposition is left behind in speech, whereas in writing the preposition is fronted along with the relative pronoun and must be *which* (Stauble, 1978):

   Speech: *War and Peace* is the book (that) he was referring to.
   Writing: *War and Peace* is the book to which he was referring.

Use of Relative Clauses in Conversation

By far the most interesting research on the use of relative clauses has been the work of Fox and Thompson (1990), who show that in American English conversation there are clearly preferred patterns of use according to the following criteria: (1) the syntactic roles of the head noun and the relative pronoun, (2) the definiteness and specificity (or identifiability) of the referent, (3) the animacy or humanness of the referent, and (4) the discourse function of the relative clause—that is, whether it functions to give background, or new information.

- **Grounding**

   One of the striking patterns that Fox and Thompson found in their conversation data—illustrated in the following two examples—was the tendency for nonhuman head nouns functioning as subjects to strongly prefer relativized objects:[6]

   | The only thing *you'll see* is the table. | SO |
   | The car *that she borrowed* had a low tire. | SO |

In such cases the head noun tends to be definite but not fully grounded or established in the ongoing discourse with the relative clause serving the function of grounding (or anchoring) the head noun in the discourse through use of a context-relevant subject pronoun. For instance, the first example above had deictic *you* (the interlocutor) as subject of the relative clause, and the subject in the second example has anaphoric *she* (the reference is clear from prior discourse).

- **Characterizing**

   When nonhuman head NPs function as objects, Fox and Thompson found that there was a strong tendency for these heads to occur with relativized subjects in relative clauses that characterize or describe (instead of functioning to anchor or ground the head noun):

   | They're selling these candies *that explode when you chew on them.* | OS |
   | I don't like the pants *that come down narrow and then bell out.* | OS |

The object noun heads tend to be definite and already grounded in the discourse, so these relative clauses simply provide additional information to characterize and narrow down the scope of the head nouns.

- **Giving new information**

   Fox and Thompson also found some interesting tendencies with "existential" head nouns (i.e., logical subjects) following nonreferential *there* subjects (see Chapter 23).

These logical subject head nouns tend overwhelmingly to have indefinite determiners but are specific in reference as well as being human; furthermore, they strongly favor relativized subjects over relativized objects: In the two cases below the italicized locatives *there* and *In the U.S.* ground the head nouns in the discourse.[7] The relative clause moves the discourse forward—that is, it gives new information that contributes to the development of the discourse:

> There were two people *there* who were constantly on stage.   ExS (Logical SS)

> *In the U.S.* there are over a hundred thousand people who
> are over a hundred years old.   ExS (Logical SS)

- **Ordering**

A final observation made by Fox and Thompson was the overwhelming tendency for head nouns modified by two relative clauses to have the preferred relative clause type occur first and the less typical relative clause pattern to occur second. (Recall the preferred patterns: inanimate subject head nouns prefer relativized objects; inanimate object head nouns prefer relativized subjects; existential human head nouns following *there* subjects prefer relativized subjects).

> One thing *they said in the article that was really interesting* was that in the U.S. there are over a hundred thousand people who are over a hundred years old.

Here the first relative clause after "One thing" follows the preferred SO pattern "(that) they said in the article," while the second relative clause, "that was really interesting," is the less preferred SS pattern for an inanimate subject head noun.

Fox and Thompson conclude that communicative factors determine, to a large extent, the tendencies they uncovered in the combinations of head NP and relative clause that were significant in their oral data. For example, the speaker grounds new NPs in the ongoing discourse by showing their relationship to contextually clear or previously mentioned NPs.

Use of Relative Clauses in Writing

In another study, this one a large-scale corpus analysis of three written registers or genres (editorials, fiction, letters), Biber, Conrad, and Reppen (1994) found that relative clauses and participles are not nearly as frequent as prepositional phrases if all postnominal adjectivals are examined. These researchers thus argue against any extensive decontextualized instruction of difficult grammatical constructions such as relative clauses when there may be other simpler constructions that might be more frequent and more useful to learners. They suggest that it is important to teach intermediate and advanced learners the linguistic patterns that occur in the registers or genres the students will encounter in actual language use since no single set of linguistic features will be appropriate for all students.

There have been other corpus-based studies of relative clauses in written English such as Olofsson (1981), who used the Brown University corpus to uncover some oddities of lexical co-occurrence in relative clauses. For example, when *every* modifies the head noun, the relativized object is virtually always deleted; for example:

> Every man *we saw* had a tattoo.

When body parts function as head nouns, the relativized subject is *that* rather than *which* significantly more frequently than with other types of lexical items functioning as head nouns; for example:

> She was a girl in a sunbonnet with eyes *that flashed at the guests.*

Olofsson's corpus analysis finds that the following syntactic environments favor certain relative pronouns:

relativized nonhuman subjects: *that*
relativized nonhuman objects: no relative pronoun (it's normally deleted)
relativized prepositional objects: *which*

(Note that the final environment reflects a grammatical rule observed in written English rather than a usage tendency or preference, since prepositions are generally fronted along with relativized prepositional objects in writing and since only *which* can occur after prepositions.)

Using a completely different approach, Lapaire and Rotgé (1996) suggest that the relative pronouns *that* and *which*, though often appearing to be interchangeable after inanimate head nouns, codify different psycho-grammatical strategies. They quote a sentence taken from a *New York Times* obituary on George Balanchine, which used *that* in the original text:

George Balanchine was the foremost exponent of "abstract" or plotless ballet . . . But ballet *that told no story* did not always win favor with the public.

(Lapaire and Rotgé, p. 38)[8]

The authors claim that the use of the relative pronoun *that* clearly marks the relative clause as being presupposed because "ballet that told no story" is a paraphrase of "abstract or plotless ballet." Had the obituary writer used *which* instead of *that*, they argue, he would not have treated the information as given but would have been refreshing the reader's memory. *Which* is explanatory and fact-finding for Lapaire and Rotgé, while *that* signals something the speaker/writer regards as preestablished. Invoking the notion of "mental paths," the authors propose that *that* is "smooth and easy" while *which* is "slower and a little rougher." Finally, they claim that the relative clause is more tightly fastened to the head noun with *that* than with *which*, something Olofsson (1981) had also argued in his discussion of the example "She was a girl . . . with eyes that flashed at the guests." Olofsson had suggested that changing *that* to *which* in this sentence would force a looser connection between the head noun and the relative clause.

CONCLUSION

In this chapter we explored the syntactic diversity of restrictive relative clauses in English. Without considering the use of *whose* as a relative determiner, there are at least 20 different structural types of restrictive relative clause, as exemplified in the chart on page 579:

OO (12 types)
OS (4 types)
SO (3 types)
SS (1 type)

If we superimpose the relativized determiner *whose* on these, there are at least 40 different types. Learners clearly face formidable challenges of form when trying to master relative clauses: where to place the relative clause in relation to the head noun, which relative pronoun to choose, the internal structure of relative clauses, and so on. However, the studies on use that we have reported above strongly suggest that instead of trying to teach all possible patterns for relative clauses we would do well to discover which patterns our learners are most likely to need for their own oral or written discourse in English. Carrying out a relevant corpus-based study of relative clauses that would reveal syntactic, lexical, and discourse-functional patterns such as those that Fox and Thompson (1990) found for conversation and Olofsson (1981) and Biber, Conrad, and Reppen (1994) found for written discourse would be a useful way for ESL/EFL teachers to decide what to teach about relative clauses and when and how to present the information. Usage tendencies seem to be linked very specifically to given discourse genres, topics, and also to modality (speech vs. writing). Much more research is needed along the lines of the studies reported here if we are to establish better informed pedagogical priorities in this area.

Finally, some cross-linguistic research using parallel written texts in Chinese and English (Yan 1985) reveals that in written texts that deal with the same topic and that are of approximately the same length, Chinese uses one-third fewer relative clauses than English. The difference is particularly significant in view of the fact that Chinese exhibits a structural diversity similar to English in its inventory of relative clause types. This suggests that Chinese and English may use relative clauses for different discourse functions, making it all the more imperative that ESL/EFL teachers present relative clauses to learners in rich and clearly defined discourse contexts rather than simply at the sentence level.

TEACHING SUGGESTIONS

1. Form. It has been our experience that presenting students with a generative grammar analysis of relative clauses can be very enlightening. Ordinarily we don't recommend introducing tree diagrams and rules; however, for this particular construction, it has proved helpful for our ESL/EFL students to be able to see how relative clauses are formed in English. You may not wish to draw trees or to call the rules by the names we have used here, but introducing the concept of an embedded sentence and showing how relative pronouns replace an NP in the embedded sentence seems to be a useful first step for many ESL/EFL students. For instance, give students handouts with sentences in brackets embedded within a main clause; for example:

The students [the students arrived late] missed the announcement.

Show them how the *who* is substituted for the coreferential NP. Have them do exercises of a similar nature on their own.

2. Form. Once students have some idea of how to form relative clauses, they will need abundant practice to be able to do so with fluency. You may start by having students read a passage in class. Next divide them into small groups. The group's task is to bracket all the relative clauses in the passage. They are to underline all the relative pronouns they can find and determine to which head noun the relative pronoun refers. Finally, they should star all the relative clauses in which the relative pronoun has been deleted.

3. Form. Begin oral production using fairly tightly controlled contexts and perhaps only concentrating on one relative pronoun at a time. For instance, use a class information sheet to practice producing relative clauses with *who*. The students can make sentences to identify one of their fellow students who has some unique attribute; for example:

> The student who comes from Romania is _____.
> The student who speaks French is _____.
> The student who studies economics is _____.

4. Form/Meaning. A more conversational way of using student information is suggested by Sandra Elbaum (personal communication). Students work in groups and each one says something unique or interesting about themselves or their activities. Then each student has to describe a fellow student in terms of the information that was shared using a relative clause.

> "Mario is the person who visited the Grand Canyon last week."
> "Keiko is the one who has been to Disneyland three times."

5. Form/Meaning. Cuisenaire rods can be used for giving students practice in both listening to and producing sentences containing relative clauses. Winn-Bell Olsen (1977) suggests that teachers give commands and ask questions such as the following, encouraging students to think up their own as soon as they are able to:

> Give Dumduan the green rod that is beside the pink one. (student (a) does action)
> Dumduan, which rod did Phetsamone just give you? (student (b) answers question)
> Pheng, put the yellow rod that is under the black rod in the box. (student (c) does action)
> Sampong, which rod did Pheng just put in the box? (student (d) answers question)

6. Form/Meaning. Pictures are useful tools when a teacher is attempting to elicit one type of relative clause using a variety of relative pronouns from the class. Ask students to make meaningful statements describing some aspect of a picture you show them. For instance, students may make statements with relativized subjects in embedded sentences like the following about a beach scene:

> It's like a beach that is near my house.
> The boy who is wearing a red bathing suit is the same age as my brother.
> I see three people who are swimming too far from the beach.
> I would like to ride in the boat that is near the dock.

7. Form/Meaning. Have students play a game in which they try to identify the name of a person or thing you or another student is thinking of. You may wish to use a "Twenty Questions" format with the modification that questions must contain a restrictive relative clause. Students ask questions such as:

> Is this person someone who once was president of the United States?
> Is this thing something (that) I would use in the kitchen?

8. Use. As another good practice exercise, have students write about some topics that would be likely to entail their using relative clauses. Including compositions of this sort would be important, since we have claimed in this chapter that there are differences in the use of relative clauses depending upon whether one is using them in informal speech or in writing. For example, ask your students to describe "The Most Interesting Person That I Have Ever Met." A topic such as this one would probably prompt them to use some relative clauses.

EXERCISES

Test your understanding of what has been presented.

I. Provide an original sentence that illustrates each of the following terms. Underline the pertinent word(s) in your examples.

   a. restrictive relative clause   **d.** relative pronoun substitution
   b. relativized object of a preposition   **e.** relative pronoun deletion
   c. relativized subject   **f.** relativized possessive determiner

2. Give tree diagrams and mapping rules for the following sentences:

   a. The boy who spoke with John is my brother   **d.** Ann wrote the story you like.

   b. The boat that he is building is large.   **e.** The family with whom I am staying lives in town.

   c. I know the student whose article was published.

3. Why are the following sentences ungrammatical?

   a. *The river who is wide is the Mississippi.

   b. *The woman with that you were working quit.

   c. *I thought about the man whose we heard story.

Test your ability to apply what you know.

4. If your students produce the following sentences, what errors have they made? How will you make them aware of the errors, and what exercises will you prepare to correct the errors?

   a. *The woman whom is walking towards us is my aunt.

   b. *The boy who John hit him is on the ground.

   c. *The student sits next to me is sick.

   d. *That she is wrapping the package is for Christmas.

   e. *I like people they are friendly.

5. An ESL/EFL student asks you to explain the difference between the following two sentences:

   a. The person that called to you was a stranger.

   b. The person that you called to was a stranger.

   How would you answer?

6. Assume the following excerpt had appeared as part of an editorial in a small town newspaper:

. . . a week earlier, this state's education commissioner, Bob Smith, reported that the state's fourth- and eighth-graders cannot write well. . . . "It's a rare student that writes really well with a sense of personal expression, or what teachers call voice," Smith said. (Grammar probably isn't a strong point, either, especially if students are taking their cue from Smith. The Commish, if he were speaking proper English, would have said, "It's a rare student who writes really well. . . ." The pronoun "that" refers to things; "who" refers to people.

Is the writer of this editorial correct in what he says about Smith's grammar?

BIBLIOGRAPHY

References

Biber, D., S. Conrad, and R. Reppen (1994). "Corpus-Based Approaches to Issues in Applied Linguistics." *Applied Linguistics 15*(2): 169–189.

Fox, B. A., and S.A. Thompson (1990). "A Discourse Explanation of the Grammar of Relative Clauses." *Language 66*(2): 297–316.

Gustafson, L. (1992). "Relative Clause Type and Other Relative Construction Frequency in Talk Show Conversation." Unpublished Linguistics 5741 paper. University of Minnesota, Minneapolis.

Ioup, G., and A. Kruse (1977). "Interference Versus Structural Complexity in Second Language Acquisition: Language Universals as a Basis for Natural Sequencing." In H. D. Brown, C. A. Yorio, and R. H. Crymes (eds.), *On TESOL 77: Teaching and Learning English as a Second Language: Trends in Research and Practice*. Washington, D.C.: TESOL.

Keenan, E., and B. Comrie (1972). "Noun Phrase Accessibility and Universal Grammar." Paper delivered at LSA Annual Meeting, Atlanta. (Published in *Linguistic Inquiry 8*, 1977, 63–99.

Kuno, S. (1974). "The Position of Relative Clauses and Conjunctions." *Linguistic Inquiry V*(1): 117–136.

Lapaire, J-R., and W. Rotgé (1996). "Towards a Psycho-Grammatical Description of the English Language." *The Journal of TESOL France 3*(1): 35–51.

Loch, B. (1992). "Relative Clauses in Published Writing." Unpublished 5741 paper. University of Minnesota, Minneapolis.

Olofsson, A. (1981). "Relative Junctions in Written American English." Göteborg: Acta Universitatis Gothoburgensis. (Gothenburg Studies in English, 50).

Olsen, J. Winn-Bell (1977). *Communication Starters and Other Activities for the ESL Classroom*. San Francisco: The Alemany Press.

Schachter, J. (1974). "An Error in Error Analysis." *Language Learning 24*(2): 205–214.

Schumann, J. (1980). "The Acquisition of English Relative Clauses by Second Language Learners." In R. C. Scarcella and S. D. Krashen (eds.), *Research in Second Language Acquisition*. Rowley, Mass.: Newbury House.

Stauble, A. (1978). "A Frequency Study of Restrictive Relative Clause Types and Relative Pronoun Usage in English." Unpublished English 215 paper, UCLA, Fall, 1978.

Wong, J. (1991). "Learnability of Relative Clauses: A Hong Kong Case." *Working Papers of the Department of English 3*(1): 108–117. City Polytechnic of Hong Kong.

Yan, G. (1985). "A Contrastive Textological Analysis of Restrictive Relative Clauses in Chinese and English Written Text." Unpublished M. A. Thesis in Teaching English as a Second Language, UCLA.

Suggestions for further reading

For other second language acquisition studies that examine the effect of native language background on the acquisition of relative clauses by ESL learners, see:

Chiang, D. (1980). "Predictors of Relative Clause Production." In R. C. Scarcella and S. D. Krashen (eds.), *Research in Second Language Acquisition*. Rowley, Mass. Newbury House.

Gass, S. (1980). "An Investigation of Syntactic Transfer in Adult Second Language Learners." In R. C. Scarcella and S. D. Krashen (eds.), *Research in Second Language Acquisition*. Rowley, Mass. Newbury House.

For more syntactically sophisticated analyses of relative clauses than the one we provide, see:

Baker, C. L. (1989). *English Syntax*. Cambridge, Mass. MIT Press.

Jacobs, R. (1995). *English Syntax: A Grammar for English Language Professionals*. New York: Oxford University Press.

Stockwell, R., P. Schachter, and B. Partee (1973). *The Major Syntactic Structures of English*. New York: Holt, Rinehart and Winston, Ch. 7.

van Riemsdijk, H., and E. Williams (1989). *Introduction to the Theory of Grammar*. Cambridge, Mass. MIT Press.

For information on relative clause formation for many different languages, consult:

Keenan, E., and B. Comrie (1979), "Data on the Noun Phrase Accessibility Hierarchy." *Language 55*(2): 333–351.

Maxwell, D. N. (1979). "Strategies of Relativization and NP Accessibility." *Language 55*(2): 352–371.

For texts with exercises designed to give ESL/EFL students practice in forming and using relative clauses, consult:

Danielson, D., and P. Porter (1990). *Using English: Your Second Language* (2d ed.). Englewood Cliffs, N.J.: Prentice-Hall, pp. 360–370.

Frank, M. (1972). *Modern English: Part II: Sentences and Complex Structures.* Englewood Cliffs, N.J.: Prentice-Hall, Ch. 3 (she calls them adjective clauses).

Frodesen, J., and J. Eyring (1997). *Grammar Dimensions.* Book 4 (2d ed.). Boston: Heinle & Heinle, pp. 117–143.

Pennington, M. C. (ed.) (1995). Part II: Relative Clauses, pp. 25–37 in *New Ways in Teaching Grammar.* Alexandria, Va.: TESOL.

Riggenbach, H., and V. Samuda (1997). *Grammar Dimensions.* Book 2 (2d ed.). Boston: Heinle & Heinle, pp. 362–367.

Rutherford, W. (1975). *Modern English.* Vol 1 (2d ed.). New York: Harcourt Brace Jovanovich, pp. 240–242, 246–247.

Thewlis, S. (1997). *Grammar Dimensions.* Book 3 (2d ed.). Boston: Heinle & Heinle, pp. 195–208.

ENDNOTES

1. Note that since it is the object that is being replaced; *whom,* the objective form of the relative pronoun *who,* is inserted. This, however, represents formal usage. In informal usage many speakers of English use *who,* even in this environment.

2. This is called center embedding.

3. The percentages that emerge depend to a large extent on the data one uses. Examining exclusively oral TV talk show data in English, Gustafson (1992) found more OO clauses and fewer SS and SO clauses than Stauble, but the overall rank order remained the same.

4. If we were to omit this condition, ungrammatical sentences such as the following would be generated:

> *The man whose you are admiring wife is a wrestler.

5. Very often professional editors change all *which* restrictive relative pronouns referring to nonhuman antecedents to *that.* This serves to further distinguish restrictive and nonrestrictive relative clauses. This is in fact the pattern found by Loch (1992) when she analyzed relative pronouns occurring in the Feb. 3, 1992 issue of *Newsweek.* There are other differences between these relative pronouns that we will call attention to in the next chapter.

6. We have used examples adapted from those given in Fox and Thompson (1990) to illustrate their generalizations.

7. Fox and Thompson also show cases where propositional linking or propositional coherence provides the grounding, but these examples are longer and more complex.

8. No date was given for *New York Times* quote.

Chapter 29

MORE ON RELATIVE CLAUSES

INTRODUCTION

In the previous chapter we described restrictive relative clauses. In this chapter we consider nonrestrictive relative clauses. Then we treat reductions that occur in both types of relative clauses—restrictive and nonrestrictive. In the last chapter you saw how a restrictive relative clause can be reduced by deleting a relativized object in the embedded sentence. In this chapter we discuss another way to reduce both types of relative clauses that accounts for a variety of surface structures. Finally, we examine relative adverbials, which are additional relative constructions in English that are formed by means other than relativizing a noun phrase or a possessive determiner.

NONRESTRICTIVE VERSUS RESTRICTIVE RELATIVE CLAUSES

Thus far, the relative clauses we have been examining limit or characterize the meaning of the noun phrases they modify. Not all relative clauses have such a limiting function, however. For instance, in the following sentence we could just as easily do without the relative clause yet remain sure of the identity of the head noun in the main clause:

> Mrs. Jensen, who lives next door, is a Girl Scout troop leader.

The relative clause in this sentence is called a nonrestrictive relative clause since it merely supplies additional information about Mrs. Jensen; it is not necessary for telling us which woman is a Girl Scout troop leader in the same way that the restrictive relative clause is in the following sentence:

> The woman who lives next door is a Girl Scout troop leader.

Perhaps a contrastive example would be useful at this point. Compare the two following sentences:

> The climbers who reached the summit were exhausted.
> The climbers, who reached the summit, were exhausted.

As you already know, the first sentence contains a restrictive relative clause. We interpret the head noun in this sentence as representing some portion of the group of climbers who began the ascent: those who were successful at reaching the summit. Since the nonrestrictive clause in the second sentence does not restrict the meaning of the head noun, we understand that the head noun refers to the entire group of climbers. In other words, they were all successful in reaching the summit and were all exhausted from their efforts.

THE FORM OF SENTENCES WITH NONRESTRICTIVE RELATIVE CLAUSES

Notice that we have just paraphrased the second sentence above—the one with the nonrestrictive relative clause—in the form of two underlying sentences. By hypothesizing that sentences containing nonrestrictive relative clauses are derived from two underlying sentences, we are able to capture the fact that their base structures (and meanings) are essentially different from those of restrictive relative clauses and that both the main clause and the nonrestrictive clause supply somewhat independent bits of information.[1] On the other hand, by positing two sentences in the base structure, we seem to be implying that the two clauses are of approximately equal status. Since this is misleading, we shall adopt the convention of labeling the main clause S1 and the nonrestrictive clause S2 at the base structure level. Thus, two underlying sentences with upper nodes labeled S1 and S2 that meet certain conditions[2] and that are not joined by an explicit conjunction would motivate the optional application of the nonrestrictive embedding process. This process would embed the incidental, nonrestrictive information (i.e., the second clause) into the main clause. In other words, the nonrestrictive clause is a *derived* relative clause rather than an underlying embedded one.

Let us now examine the underlying structure and the mapping rules for a sentence containing a nonrestrictive relative clause.

The climbers, who reached the summit, were exhausted.

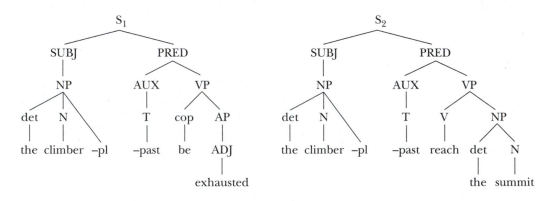

output of base: the climber -pl -past be exhausted [the climber -pl -past reach the summit]

copy s/t: the climber -pl -past [+ 3 + pl] be exhausted [the climber -pl -past [+ 3 + pl] reach the summit]

nonrestrictive embedding: the climber -pl [,the climber -pl -past [+ 3 + pl] reach the summit,] -past[+ 3 + pl] be exhausted

(Note the commas in the mapping rules that distinguish relative clauses with a derived nonrestrictive source from those with an underlying restrictive, embedded source. Phonological features also mark nonrestrictive relative clauses: Such clauses are (1) accompanied by a drop in pitch and (2) preceded and followed by brief pauses. (The intonation can also go down, then up before each "comma"; this seems a bit exaggerated and formal). These phonological features are captured in writing by the use of commas, which set off the nonrestrictive relative clause(s) from the main clause in the sentence.)

The rest of the derivation would be essentially the same as the one we followed for restrictive relative clauses:

relative pronoun substitution: the climber -pl [,who -past [+ 3 + pl] reach the summit,] -past [+ 3 + pl] be exhausted
morphological rules: The climbers, who reached the summit, were exhausted.

The two nonrestrictive relative clauses that we have discussed so far have contained noun phrases that are identical to noun phrases present in the main clause:

Mrs. Jensen, who lives next door, is a Girl Scout troop leader.
The climbers, who reached the summit, were exhausted.

This type of nonrestrictive relative clause is sometimes called an appositive clause, i.e. a clause that refers to and elaborates on the head noun referred to in the main clause.

The other type of nonrestrictive relative clause has a relative pronoun (always *which*) that refers to the entire preceding clause instead of just one noun phrase. For instance, in the following sentence the relative pronoun *which* refers to an event (Jason's getting off work early) and the nonrestrictive relative clause is a comment on the event reported in the main clause:

Jason got off work early, which was nice.

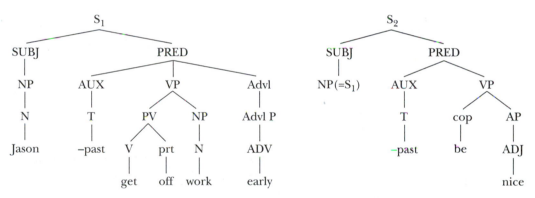

Since the entire proposition "Jason's getting off work early" is what is being commented on, we use the symbol NP (= S1) to represent that proposition in the second sentence in the tree. The mapping rules can then proceed as follows:

output of base: Jason -past get off work early [NP = S1 -past be nice]
copy s/t: Jason -past [+ 3 + sg] get off work early [NP = S1 -past [+ 3 + sg] be nice]
nonrestrictive embedding: Jason -past [+ 3 + sg] get off work early [,NP = S1 -past
 [+ 3 + sg] be nice,]

As mentioned earlier, when the subject of the nonrestrictive clause refers to the entire preceding clause, we always use the relative pronoun *which* as a substitute:

relative pronoun substitution: (Jason -past [+ 3 + sg] get off work early [, which -past
 [+ 3 + sg] be nice,]]
morphological rules: Jason got off work early, which was nice.

In addition to the differences already mentioned, a number of other characteristics serve to distinguish restrictive and nonrestrictive relative clauses. The chart below provides a summary of these differences, adapted from the analysis provided in Stockwell, Schachter, and Partee (1973):

Chart 1 Summary of Differences Between Restrictive and Nonrestrictive Relative Clauses

Restrictive

1. Provides information needed to identify or limit a noun in the main clause.
2. Derived from an underlying embedded source.
3. No pauses or special punctuation (commas, parentheses, dashes) to set off the relative clause from the main clause.
4. May not modify an entire proposition, only a head noun.
5. *That* is freely used as a relative pronoun as well as *who(m), which*, etc.
6. Does not usually modify proper nouns.*
7. May modify a head noun with a generic determiner like *any* or *every*.

Nonrestrictive

1. Provides additional information that is nonessential to determining the identity of a noun in the main clause.
2. Derived from two independent underlying sentences.
3. Commas (or parentheses or dashes) in writing and special pauses and lower pitch in speech set the relative clause off from the main clause.
4. May modify either a head noun or an entire proposition in the form of a comment.
5. *That* cannot be used as a relative pronoun. Only *wh-*pronouns are possible.
6. May modify proper nouns as well as common nouns.
7. May not modify a head noun with a generic determiner like *any* or *every*.

*It is possible for a restrictive relative clause to modify a proper noun if there is more than one person or thing that could be referred to by the name, e.g. "I'm talking about the Marsha who's in our class, not the one who works at the store." In such cases, the so-called proper noun is functioning as a common noun.

REDUCTION OF RESTRICTIVE AND NONRESTRICTIVE RELATIVE CLAUSES

In the last chapter we saw that relative pronouns that replaced some sort of object in the relative clause could be deleted. For example—

> The curry that I cooked was too hot.

—allows deletion of the relativized object *that* by application of the relative pronoun deletion rule:

> The curry I cooked was too hot.

We also noted that relative pronouns replacing the subject of the embedded relative clause could not be deleted:

> The ice skater who is in the show looks familiar.
> *The ice skater is in the show looks familiar.

While this is true enough, there is a way for relative clauses in such sentences to be reduced. Deletion is possible when the relativized subject is followed by a *be* verb.[3]

Prepositional Phrases

This *be* verb may function as either a copula or an auxiliary (progressive aspect, passive voice). When such a condition exists, the relative pronoun, the tense auxiliary, and the verb *be* may all be optionally deleted by the "relative pronoun + *be*" deletion rule. If we apply this rule to the above sentence, we get:

The ice skater in the show looks familiar.

Not all prepositional phrases that appear in the surface structure can be derived from embedded relative clauses that have been reduced. We have already seen that many prepositional phrases function as adverbials in the base structure in sentences such as "Mary jogs *through Central Park.*"

Also, not all postnominal prepositional phrases can be derived from reduced relative clauses; recall that in Chapters 5 and 6 we have an independent means of generating postnominal prepositional phrases to account for such expressions as these: *the city of New York, a man of means, a lady of leisure,* and so on.

Potential Ambiguity

It is sometimes the case that a surface structure prepositional phrase may be ambiguous as to whether its source is adverbial or adjectival (i.e., a reduced relative clause):

Carla drew the picture in the den.

We may interpret the prepositional phrase "in the den" as telling us where Carla drew the picture, in which case the prepositional phrase would be adverbial and the tree structure would look like this:

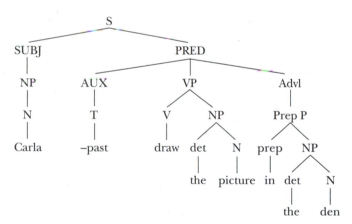

Alternatively, we may interpret the prepositional phrase as telling us which picture it was that Carla drew (i..e., the one in the den as opposed to the one in the dining room). This latter interpretation requires a base structure of a different sort, one where the prepositional phrase is adjectival, originating in a restrictive relative clause which is subsequently reduced:

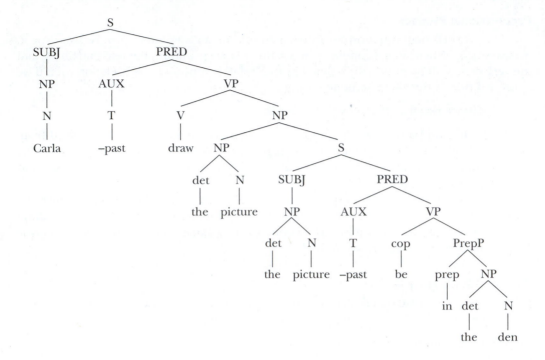

output of base: Carla -past draw the picture [the picture -pres be in the den]

copy s/t: Carla -past [+ 3 + sg] draw the picture [the picture -pres [+ 3 + sg] be in the den]

relative pro substitution: Carla -past [+ 3 + sg] draw the picture [which -pres[+ 3 + sg] be in the den]

rel pro + *be* deletion: Carla -past [+ 3 + sg] draw the picture [in the den][4]

morphological rules: Carla drew the picture in the den.

Appositives

Relative pronoun + *be* deletion can also operate on some of the nonrestrictive relative clauses that contain a noun phrase identical to one in the main clause:

> Mr. Langstrom, who is our new neighbor, comes from Providence.
> → Mr. Langstrom, our new neighbor, comes from Providence.

> Lansing, which is the capital of Michigan, has a population of 200,000.
> → Lansing, the capital of Michigan, has a population of 200,000.

The resulting phrase is what traditional grammarians refer to as an appositive—that is a group of words following an expression that further defines that expression. These phrasal appositives are reduced forms of the appositive clauses we described earlier on page 593.

Present or Passive Participle Phrases

The relative pronoun + *be* deletion rule also provides us with a way of relating a number of sentences with present participle phrases to synonymous sentences with full relative clauses. When this rule is applied to a restrictive relative clause containing a relativized subject and a verb in the progressive aspect, we are left with a present participle phrase modifying the head noun in the surface structure:

> How does the rodeo star who is riding the gray horse stay on? → How does the rodeo star riding the gray horse stay on?

The rule can also apply to a relative clause containing a relativized subject and a verb in the passive voice:

> Which cowboy was the one who was thrown by that horse? → Which cowboy was the one thrown by that horse?

Complex Postnominal Adjective Phrases

The final type of sentence in which relative pronoun + *be* deletion can occur is when relativized subjects are followed by the *be* copula and a complex adjective phrase. For example, this sentence—

> The editorial that was favorable to the project appeared yesterday.

—can be reduced to the following via application of this rule:

> The editorial favorable to the project appeared yesterday.

PARTICIPLES THAT DO NOT DERIVE FROM RELATIVE CLAUSES

Our discussion of this topic is incomplete unless we point out that there are also adjectival *-ing* participles that could not possibly be accounted for via the relative pronoun + *be* deletion rule. Recall that verbs which are stative rather than dynamic (e.g., *be, know, hear, measure*, etc.) rarely take progressive aspect, yet stative verbs can and do occur as adjectival participles:

> Max built an additional room, *measuring* 12 by 12 feet.

This *-ing* participle cannot be derived from a reduced relative clause:

> *Max built an additional room, which is measuring 12 by 12 feet.

How to account for the structure of such adjectival participles remains an unsolved problem in need of further research.

THE FORM OF RELATIVE ADVERBIAL CLAUSES

Another relative construction that we have yet to discuss is the relative clause that begins with a relative adverb. Consider the following:

> Sam knows the place *where we're meeting* and the time *when we're meeting*, but he doesn't know the reason *why we're meeting*.

We claim that each of the italicized clauses above are related to and therefore analyzable in a manner similar to restrictive relative clauses of the sort we have already analyzed in the preceding chapter. To support this position, let us examine the basic structure and mapping rules for one of these clauses.

Sam knows the place where we are meeting.

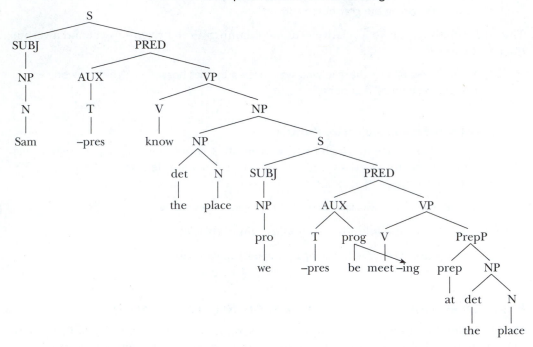

output of base: Sam -pres know the place [we -pres be meet -ing at the place]

copy s/t: Sam -pres [+ 3 + sg] know the place [we -pres[+ 1 + pl] be meet -ing at the place]

rel. pro. substitution: Sam -pres[+ 3 + sg] know the place [we -pres [+ 1 + pl] be meet -ing at which]

rel. pro. fronting: Sam -pres [+ 3 + sg] know the place [at which we -pres [+ 1 + pl] be meet -ing]

At this point we could simply complete the process by applying the morphological rules and produce:

> Sam knows the place at which we are meeting.

However, another possibility also exists. We could produce a less formal variant of this sentence by applying the "relative adverb substitution" rule, which substitutes the relative adverb *where* for the locative prepositional phrase *at which*.

rel. adverb substitution: Sam -pres [+ 3 + sg] know the place [where we -pres [+ 1 + pl] be meet -ing]

morphological rules: Sam knows the place where we are meeting.

The function of the relative adverb substitution rule, therefore, is to substitute the semantically related relative adverb for the corresponding preposition and relative pronoun combination, as follows:

prep + *which* [+ place] → *where*
prep + *which* [+ time] → *when*
prep + *which* [+ reason] → *why*

There is also one other combination that we will examine shortly:

prep + *which* [+ manner/way] → *how*

This rule allows us to show how the other two clauses in our original sentence are produced. They are less formal variants of clauses in which the preposition and the relative pronoun are retained:

> Sam knows the time at which we are meeting → Sam knows the time when we're meeting.

> Sam does not know the reason for which we are meeting → Sam doesn't know why we're meeting.

HEAD NOUN DELETION

You may have noticed that although it is perfectly grammatical to say *the place where* in *Sam knows the place where we are meeting*, it does seem redundant. A less redundant and less formal variant of such a statement is:

> Sam knows where we are meeting.

Here we apply an optional rule called "head noun deletion" to delete the head noun where the use of both the head noun and the relative adverb is redundant. Such a structure is often called a "free relative" since it allows a relative adverbial clause to exist without a head noun in the surface structure. It could apply to our other example sentences as well:

> Sam knows the time when we are meeting. → Sam knows when we are meeting.
> Sam knows the reason why we are meeting.→ Sam knows why we are meeting.

Although deletion of the head noun is optional in all three instances above, it becomes obligatory if the relative adverb is *how:*

> *That is the way how he writes.

With the application of the head noun deletion rule, this sentence becomes grammatical:

> That is how he writes.

It is interesting to note that the sequence "the way how" was acceptable in earlier forms of Standard English and still is acceptable in some dialects—but not in current Standard English. ESL/EFL students predictably have trouble with this exception and will have to learn to consistently delete the head noun in order to produce a grammatical sentence when the relative adverb *how* is used.

Of course, while we say that the head noun deletion rule is optional except for the relative adverb *how*, the head noun cannot be deleted without a concomitant loss of information in those cases where it is more specific than the general nouns *the place, the time, the reason, the way/manner.*

> She returned to (the village) where she was born.
> He can never remember (the day of the week) when he was married.

In such cases, the head noun deletion rule, while seeemingly optional, would result in a sentence that is less precise semantically.

RELATIVE ADVERB DELETION

Another way to make sentences of "the way how" type acceptable is to delete the relative adverb:

> That is the way he writes.

This rule can also be applied to the other relative adverbs we have discussed:

> (why) The reason I voted "no" was my opposition to the project.
> (when) I remember the time I tried to make a soufflé.

It is not clear, however, what the exact conditions on relative adverb deletion are. For instance, the relative adverb *where* cannot always be easily deleted for all native speakers of English:

> ?Jersey City is the place I was born.

If the preposition is retained, full grammaticality is restored:

> Jersey City is the place I was born in.

Or, if the head noun is deleted but the relative adverb retained, the sentence is also grammatical:

> Jersey City is where I was born.

Further study is needed to determine precisely when it is appropriate to delete the relative adverb as opposed to deleting the head noun. In fact we mention this topic again along with some related issues of use at the end of this chapter.

Nonrestrictive Use of Relative Adverbial Clauses

Although we have not discussed this possibility thus far, we should acknowledge Eyring's finding (1988) that relative adverbials can occasionally occur in nonrestrictive relative clauses (although the vast majority of relative adverbial clauses are restrictive). Eyring found several tokens, such as the following, with *where* functioning as the relativized constituent in a nonrestrictive clause:

> This is . . . a very precise hierarchy chart . . . , where each level of the hierarchy is composed of one or more of the following. . . .
>
> > (Eyring 1988:22)

Since Eyring did not discuss in her paper the one token of the relative adverb *when* used nonrestrictively, we have constructed our own example (similar examples could also be constructed for the other relative adverbs):

> John F. Kennedy was assassinated in 1963, when Anne was studying at Kansas State University.

FREE RELATIVE CLAUSES VIA SPECIAL SUBSTITUTION

In our preceding discussion of the head noun deletion rule, we indicated that its function is to delete a head noun when it is semantically redundant with the relative adverb. This process also appears to occur in the absence of any adverbial phrase or clause when the head noun is functioning as a subject, object, or predicate noun:

> The new teacher is just (the one/person) who we're looking for. → The new teacher is just who we're looking for.

However, with certain combinations of head nouns and relative pronouns, simple deletion of the head noun cannot take place:

> The new teacher is just the person that we're looking for. → *The new teacher is just that we're looking for.

If we also consider examples where the head noun is nonhuman, we get additional data that will help us solve this problem since the free relative pronoun surfacing as a substitute is *what* rather than *which* or *that*:

> Painting is the thing (that/which) he does best. → Painting is what he does best.

Therefore, the best solution appears to be a special substitution rule ("free relative substitution") that substitutes *who* for *the person/one who/that* and substitutes *what* for *the thing that/which*. In other words, the free relative pronoun replaces both the head noun and the relative pronoun when this substitution rule applies to subject, object, and predicate head nouns that are followed by relative pronouns. The following examples are provided to show that such free relatives also can easily occupy subject position:

> The thing that he does can harm us. → What he does can harm us.

> The person that you are tells us how you were raised.
> → Who you are tells us how you were raised.

In summary, free relative clauses have no head noun in the main clause and are the result of either the head noun deletion rule (for adverbial relative clauses) or the free relative substitution rule that allows *who* or *what* to replace a head noun and relative pronoun in subject, object or predicate position.

USE OF RELATIVE CLAUSES

USE OF THE "RELATIVE PRONOUN + *BE*" DELETION RULE

Earlier we indicated that the relative pronoun+ *be* deletion rule is optional. By now you understand that when we use the term "optional" we mean that the sentence is grammatical with or without the application of the particular rule. We do not mean that the rule is arbitrarily applied. Presumably, there are discourse constraints limiting the application of this rule to appropriate contexts. While definite rules for when a relative clause may be reduced remain to be worked out, we suggest that reduction might be favored in contexts where a number of relative clauses appear in sequence. Even within a single sentence, for instance, it is likely that reduction would occur in a relative clause when it is embedded within another relative clause; for example:

> I've forgotten the name of the contractor who submitted the bid that is now being considered by the Board. → I've forgotten the name of the contractor who submitted the bid now being considered by the Board.

On the other hand, the reduction of a relative clause might not be favored in those cases where an ambiguous sentence would result (cf. *Carla painted the picture in the den*). Clearly, more research is needed on this topic.

USE OF NONRESTRICTIVE RELATIVE CLAUSES

The Restrictive-Nonrestrictive Distinction in Spoken English

Taglicht (1977) examined relative clauses in an oral British database and suggested that in spoken English the restrictive-nonrestrictive distinction should be viewed as a continuum rather than a strict binary classification. He gives examples like the following, which were generated in the course of a job interview situation, to support his proposal (the use of a comma indicates a pause and/or a drop in pitch):

Primary/restrictive: I'd prefer a young man who had no experience.
>   (i.e., like a regular restrictive relative)
Secondary: I'd prefer an older man, who had more experience.
>   (i.e., intermediate between restrictive and nonrestrictive)
Nonrestrictive: I prefer the older man, who certainly has more experience.

Nonrestrictive Relative Clauses in Writing

Frodesen (1985) examined relative clauses in a corpus of written Chemical Engineering texts and found that most (77 percent) were restrictive with the remainder being nonrestrictive. Eyring (1988) focused in depth on the use of nonrestrictive relative clauses in scientific writing to determine the forms that they normally take (we know from the preceding chapter that the high-to-low frequency order for restrictive relative clauses is OS, OO, SS, SO).

Eyring examined a total of 330 nonrestrictive relative clauses drawn from the following written sources:

> Interoffice memos (in a computer firm): 110 tokens (informal)
> Articles from popular computer magazines: 111 token (semiformal)
> Published articles in computer research journals: 109 tokens (formal)

The construction did not have high frequency in Eyring's database (8.1 tokens per 10,000 words); however, when she compared her results with Stauble's, the same rank ordering of structural types emerged despite the fact that nonrestrictives have one additional structural type—the commentary-type relative clause (e.g. *John didn't come, which was unfortunate*).

TABLE 1 A COMPARISON OF FREQUENCY OF RESTRICTIVE AND NONRESTRICTIVE RELATIVE CLAUSE TYPES

Frequency of RRCs (informal speech, spontaneous writing, and published writing)—Stauble (1978)			Frequency of NRRCs (office memos, popular magazines, journals)		
Type	*Instances*	*Percent**	*Type*	*Instances*	*Percent**
OS	234	55	OS	189	57
OO	108	25	OO	59	18
SS	52	12	SS	33	10
SO	30	7	SO	8	2
			Clause + comment on clause	41	12
Total	424	99	Total	330	99

*Percentages do not add up to 100 percent because the numbers have been rounded off.

Furthermore, Eyring found that in her database the prototypical nonrestrictive relative clause had a head noun that was an identifiable inanimate common noun occurring in object position followed by the relative pronoun *which* functioning as subject of the nonrestrictive relative clause:

> Very high-level languages . . . allow people to . . . leave the details to the machine, which must then search its database of domain-specific knowledge to complete the task.

> It has several subdirectories, one of which has ARC500.EXE and DQC . . .

> (Eyring 1988:33)

Eyring's findings thus argue against the traditional presentation of nonrestrictive relative clauses as being prototypically center-embedded SS appositive constructions. Although such appositive constructions do occur, the most frequent and typical nonrestrictive relative clause (and restrictive relative clause also) is the OS type, where the relative clause functions to add new information or a comment to what has already been written or said about the head noun or the main clause.

Interestingly, in the most informal writing in her database (the interoffice memos), Eyring found a few tokens of relative clauses that seemed to be reminiscent of the intermediate cases that Taglicht (1977) had found in his oral data (those tokens that fall somewhere between a prototypical restrictive and a prototypical nonrestrictive relative clause):

> I have hit a couple of minor glitches, that are probably pilot error . . .
>
> (Eyring 1998:8)

This is very likely a result of the informal, somewhat oral nature of the interoffice memos in Eyring's database. Here the relative clause seems like an afterthought.

USE OF RELATIVE ADVERBS

With reference to their use, Snow (1978) has observed that relative adverbs seem to occur most frequently in sentences that refer to a previously mentioned notion. For example, relative adverbs are commonly used in a sentence beginning with *this* or *that:*

> This is the time of year when I like to think about my goals in life, and this is also the place where I can think best.

Register Differences

With the addition of the rules we have discussed in this chapter, we can now consider the possibility that there could be as many as six surface variants[5] for a sentence in which a relative adverb may occur:

1. 1950 is the year (which/that) I was born in. (relative pronoun fronted without preposition)
2. 1950 is the year I was born in. (relative pronoun deletion)
3. 1950 is the year in which I was born. (preposition is fronted with relative pronoun)
4. 1950 is the year when I was born. (relative adverb substitution)
5. 1950 is when I was born. (head noun deletion)
6. 1950 is the year I was born. (relative adverb deletion)

Using a database to compare the frequencies of the latter three sentence types, Snow (1978) concluded that the full form (i.e., head noun + relative adverb, exemplified in 4 above) occurred with greatest frequency in written or formal contexts. Sentences with free relatives, such as in 5, occurred most frequently in spoken or informal contexts. Sentences with the head noun alone (e.g. 6 above) were found to be the least frequent type in both written and spoken data for relative adverbs of time, place, and reason. However, a strong preference for use of the head noun alone was demonstrated when the relative adverb was *how*.

We need additional studies to confirm these tendencies toward use of one pattern or another based on level of formality, head noun, or discourse context. It would be useful also to include the first three patterns in such a study. However, what Snow has observed provides a starting point, and it may be useful to make advanced learners aware of these observed tendencies.

Some Comments on Unresolved Issues

The line between use of a relative adverb and use of a regular relative pronoun is sometimes rather fuzzy. In certain environments either form seems possible without obvious differences in meaning:

> Four in the afternoon is the time (when/that/ø) he always reads.

Also, as the "zero pronoun" option above indicates, we could delete either overt relativized element and still have a grammatical sentence. However, if we delete the head noun, only the relative adverb remains a grammatical option:

> Four in the afternoon is (when/ *that/ *ø) he always reads.

When the head noun occurs as the object of a preposition, there seems to be a strong preference for *that* or no pronoun at all over use of a relative adverb, which seems unacceptable here:

> My father will have arrived by the time (*when/ that/ ø) the train gets to town.

Why these preferences emerge is not completely clear. We do know that relative adverbs work best if they replace a preposition + *which* in the relative clause. This is why the following sentence is odd:

> ?The school where I attended is going to be demolished.

Here the proposition underlying the relative clause is simply *I attended the school*, not *I attended at/in the school*; that is, there is no locative prepositional phrase with a relativized *which* as its object that *where* can replace. Therefore we have to say instead:

> The school (that) I attended is going to be demolished.

The relativized object is, of course, optional in this sentence.

Finally, the fact that *the way that* but not *the way how* can occur in modern English—

> Can you show me the way (that/*how) this corkscrew works?

—suggests that some adverbial relative clauses that were previously only adverbial may be shifting to NP [S] adjectival-type relative clauses, so perhaps we should add a seventh pattern to the preceding six to allow for this possibility. It would be useful to have a unified treatment of these residual issues; for now, they remain topics for further research.

CONCLUSION

In this chapter we further explored relative clauses to account for nonrestrictive as well as restrictive relative clauses. The formal differences between restrictive and nonrestrictive relative clauses reflect differences in meaning that are often unclear to nonnative speakers. In fact, we recently asked some advanced EFL learners to distinguish the meaning of contrastive pairs of restrictive and nonrestrictive relative clauses, and most were unable to do this accurately. Also, many nonnative speakers have never before been introduced to the largely oral commentary-type nonrestrictive relative clause that modifies or makes a comment on the entire preceding main clause. A final problem involves the use of commas in writing; many writers (native and nonnative) omit commas when the meaning is clearly nonrestrictive. Therefore, these are challenges in form and meaning for learners.

We have shown that for both restrictive and nonrestrictive relative clauses the proto-typical form in naturalistic data is OS. This is something that needs to be addressed in language pedagogy, where there has long been a traditional preference for presenting and teaching SS type relative clauses (both restrictive and nonrestrictive) to the exclusion of other more frequently occurring combinations of head nouns and relative pronouns.

Once the various possible patterns for relative adverbials have been made clear to learners, the relative adverbials discussed in this chapter present challenges primarily in use. When should one substitute a relative adverb for "preposition + *which*," and when should the head noun or the relative adverb be deleted? We admit that our own answers to these questions are not complete and that more research is needed. This also applies to deciding when one should retain the head noun and relative pronoun (*the person who/that*; *the thing which/that*) or substitute a free relative: *who* or *what*. We look forward to seeing further research that will elucidate the use of all the various types of relative clauses along the lines of the research on restrictive relative clauses by Fox and Thompson (1990) that we reported in the previous chapter.

TEACHING SUGGESTIONS

1. Form/Meaning. One way of presenting the difference between restrictive and nonre-strictive relative clauses was suggested by Walter Goodwin (personal communication). There are three steps in all:

   a. The teacher says, "If you do not speak Japanese, stand up." With the help of the other students and the teacher, one student writes a sentence on the board about the students who speak Japanese, such as:

      The students who speak Japanese are seated.

   b. The teacher then tells the class, "If you speak some English, remain seated." One student, with the help of the others, writes the following on the board about the students who speak English:

      The Japanese-speaking students, who also speak English, are seated.

   c. The teacher now asks the students to make an explicit comparison between the two sentences. After doing this, students in small groups create sentences using each type of relative clause to express information about the class or about class member(s).

2. Form. To practice reduced forms of relative clauses, bring lots of "action" pictures to class—pictures of people doing things like skiing, surfing, hiking, and swimming.

   a. First, elicit sentences with restrictive relative clauses reduced to prepositional phrases by asking students to make observations about where the people are performing the actions:

      I see a woman in a swimming pool.
      I see the climber on top of the mountain.
      I see the man on the ski slope.

   b. Next, have the students pair up and practice producing statements using present participles about who (in the pictures) they would like to be and why, such as:

      I'd like to be the woman in the swimming pool because . . .
      I'd like to be the boy surfing in Hawaii because . . .
      I'd like to be one of those people hiking in the mountains because . . .

3. Form. To practice reductions of nonrestrictive relative clauses, distribute small maps of the United States (or any country/region) or display a large map that everyone can see. Have students make statements containing appositives, such as:

> Rhode Island, the smallest state, is located in the Northeast.
> Lake Superior, one of the Great Lakes, is the largest of the group.
> Florida, the southeastern-most state, is a popular vacation spot.

4. Form. Students can be given some fairly mechanical written drills asking them to replace prepositions and relative pronouns with the appropriate relative adverbs. These sentences could then be further reduced by asking students to (a) delete the head noun, and (b) delete the relative adverb. They are told to signal if any ungrammatical string results as these substitutions and reductions take place.

5. Use. Once students feel comfortable manipulating the forms practiced in exercise 4 above, they should be given some experience to help them become sensitive to register variation. Rutherford (1977:184) uses an exercise that could easily be adapted for practice of register with relative adverbs. He provides a series of sentences written in an informal register and asks the students to put them into a more formal register by moving the preposition to a position before the relative pronoun (e.g., *This is the house they live in.* → *This is the house in which they live.*). Snow (1978) suggests the same type of exercise could be used effectively to teach the degrees of formality of clauses with relative adverbs (e.g., *This is the park where I play tennis.* → *This is the park in which I play tennis.*). Now we have a formality continuum with three points that students can refer to:

> Formal/Written: This is the park in which I play tennis.
> Semiformal: This is the park where I play tennis.
> Informal/Spoken: This is the park I play tennis in.

6. Meaning. Frodesen & Eyring (1997:47) suggest that students be given a worksheet of sentences with relative clauses but no punctuation. They would have to decide whether the relative clause was restrictive or nonrestrictive and why. Then they would have to explain their decision to a partner and add punctuation as needed. For example:
  a. the teacher who got married in June will not be returning next year
  b. in New York I'm going shopping at Saks Fifth Avenue which is located in downtown Manhattan

7. Form/Meaning. Frodesen & Eyring (1997:150) suggest giving the students a list of evaluative adjectives, such as *annoying, disappointing, exasperating, expensive, frightening, surprising, boring,* and *stressful,* and asking students to use one of these adjectives in a nonrestrictive clause in order to make a comment on the main clause. The students should be told to comment on something that has happened to them; for example:

> I had to wait in line for 30 minutes at the post office, which was very annoying.
> My nephew broke my favorite vase, which was very disappointing.

8. Form. Frodesen & Eyring (1997:168) suggest that students first practice relative adverbs by completing sentences such as these:

> I'd like to know the date (day, year, century) when . . .
> I'd like to know the place (city, country, etc.) where . . .
> I wish I knew the reason(s) why . . .
> I'm interesting in finding out how . . .

9. Use. Students can be asked to videotape TV news and then to transcribe several segments using nonrestrictive relative clauses to share with classmates:

> "The President of the United States, who visited the Middle East this week, met with the Prime Minister of Israel to discuss the issue of settlements on the West Bank . . ."

They should be asked to describe and imitate the intonation of the TV news anchor when they report the examples they have found to the class.

EXERCISES

Test your understanding of what has been presented.

1. Give an example sentence to illustrate each of the following terms. Underline the pertinent word(s) in your examples.
   a. relative adverb substitution
   b. free relative substitution
   c. relative pronoun + *be* deletion
   d. head noun deletion
   e. relative adverb deletion
   f. appositive
   g. nonrestrictive relative clause
      (i) appositive type
      (ii) commentary type

2. Give the tree diagrams and mapping rules for the following sentences:
   a. Dr. Graber, who(m) you know, will lecture next week.
   b. The place where he lived is unknown.
   c. Marilyn lent me her car, which was very thoughtful.
   d. The boys running in the marathon were very athletic.
   e. This is the time we will do it.

3. Why are the following sentences ungrammatical?
   a. *Christmas is the time at which when he's busiest.
   b. *Any teacher, who is dedicated, must work hard.
   c. *This is the office I work.
   d. *Engineers, many of which have never met Kilbey, are very proud of his work.
   e. *Burt will have raised $20,000 by the time when the fund-raising drive ends.

Test your ability to apply what you know.

4. If your students produce the following sentences, what errors have they made? How will you make them aware of the errors, and what exercises will you prepare to correct the errors?
   a. *I took that course with Mr. Hall, which is an excellent teacher.
   b. *That is the way how he drives.
   c. *Cooking is the thing what he enjoys.

5. One of your students asks you to explain the difference in meaning between the following two sentences. How will you respond?

> My sister, who lives in Chicago, has two children.
> My sister who lives in Chicago has two children.

6. Try to order the following sentences along a formality/register continuum according to what has been discussed in this chapter as well as using your own intuitions. How could you make your students aware of the register differences among these sentence types?

> Do you recall why he resigned?
> Do you recall the reason why he resigned?
> Do you recall the reason he resigned?
> Do you recall the reason for which he resigned?

BIBLIOGRAPHY

References

Eyring, J. (1988). "Nonrestrictive Relative Clauses in Scientific Discourse. "Unpublished Ph.D. qualifying paper in Applied Linguistics, UCLA.

Fox, B. A., and S. A. Thompson, (1990). "A Discourse Explanation of the Grammar of Relative Clauses in English Conversation." *Language* 66:2, 297–316.

Frodesen, J. (1986). "Rhetorical and Grammatical Structures in Chemical Engineering Texts." Unpublished paper. Program in Applied Linguistics, UCLA.

Frodesen, J., and J. Eyring (1997). *Grammar Dimensions*. Book 4 (2d ed.). Boston: Heinle & Heinle.

Rutherford, W. E. (1977). *Modern English*. Vol. 2 (2d ed.). New York: Harcourt, Brace, Jovanovich.

Snow, M. A. (1978). "The Where, When, Why, and How of Relative Clauses." Unpublished English 215 paper, UCLA.

Stauble, A. (1978). "A Frequency Study of Restrictive Relative Clause Types and Relative Pronoun Usage in English." Unpublished English 215 paper, UCLA.

Stockwell, R., P. Schachter, B. Partee (1973). *The Major Syntactic Structures of English*. New York: Holt, Rinehart, and Winston.

Taglicht, J. (1977). "Relative Clauses as Postmodifiers: Meaning, Syntax, and Intonation."In W-D Bald and R. Ilson (eds.), *Studies in English Usage: The Resources of a Present-Day English Corpus for Linguistic Analysis*, 73–108. Frankfurt: Peter Lang.

Suggestions for further reading

For a good reference on the analysis of nonrestrictive relative clauses that supplements Stockwell, Schachter, Partee (1973) in the references above, see:

Thompson, S. A. (1971). "The Deep Structure of Relative Clauses." In C. J. Fillmore and D. T. Langendoen (eds.), *Studies in Linguistic Semantics*. New York: Holt, Rinehart, and Winston.

For an alternative analysis of relative clauses that accounts for the usual data as well as idioms like "the headway that John made" refer to:

Schachter, P. (1973). "Focus and Relativization." *Language* 49:1, 14–46.

For suggestions regarding the teaching of nonrestrictive relative clauses, see:

Bland, S. K. (1996). *Intermediate Grammar: From Form to Meaning and Use.* New York: Oxford University Press, 262–268.

Frodesen, J., and J. Eyring (1997). *Grammar Dimensions.* Book 4 (2d ed.). Boston: Heinle & Heinle, 144–154.

Rutherford, W. E. (1975). *Modern English.* Vol.1 (2d ed.). New York: Harcourt, Brace, Jovanovich, 248–249.

For suggestions on how to teach relative adverbial clauses, see:

Frodesen, J., and J. Eyring (1997). *Grammar Dimensions.* Book 4 (2d ed.). Boston: Heinle & Heinle,155–169.

ENDNOTES

1. The bits of information are, of course related to one another, but the meaning of one clause is not dependent upon the other as is the case with sentences containing restrictive relative clauses.

2. There are two types of conditions corresponding to the two types of nonrestrictive relative clauses. One type requires a coreferential noun in the incidental clause—just as restrictive relative clauses do; the other type requires that the nonrestrictive clause be a comment on the event or fact expressed in the main clause.

3. Other verbs may also be involved in this reduction, but *be* is far and away the most frequent (cf. The objection [that they *made*] to the proposal; the man [who *lives*] down the street).

4. As noted earlier, tense and subject person and number features are also deleted as part of this rule.

5. We have already noted several times above that not all six variants are possible for all relative adverbs; for example, sentences like type 4 would not be possible if the relative adverb were *how* in the phrase *the way how.*

Chapter 30

FOCUS AND EMPHASIS

INTRODUCTION

In English, focus and emphasis are related notions; however, the structures used for focus center primarily on issues of use, whereas the words and structures used to express emphasis are primarily concerned with meaning. Focus and emphasis can be expressed in three different ways: (1) phonologically (through special stress and intonation), (2) lexically or nonphonologically (through special words and phrases), and (3) syntactically (through marked word order or special focus constructions). We will present the form, meaning, and use of these devices in this chapter, giving particular emphasis to the syntactic means for conveying focus and emphasis in English.

THE FORMS THAT FOCUS AND EMPHASIS CAN TAKE

PHONOLOGICAL FORM

Consider the following sentence:

> John cooked the dinner.

When produced in a normal, unmarked style, the speaker stresses the accented syllable of the last content word and uses this syllable as a pivot for the rising-falling intonation contour that normally accompanies a declarative English sentence:

> John cooked the dinner.

However, a nonemphatic sentence such as this one may contain an emphatic constituent if the speaker assigns special stress or prominence to one of the constituents (see also our earlier discussion of stress-focused yes/no questions in Chapter 11):

> JOHN cooked the dinner. (not someone else)

> John COOKED the dinner. (as opposed to doing something else with respect to the dinner)

> John cooked the DINner. (not something else)

In these cases, the stressed (or prominent) syllable also serves as the pivot for a marked intonation contour.

MORPHOLOGICAL AND LEXICAL DEVICES

English also has several morphological and lexical means for expressing special emphasis.

Emphatic *Do*

An entire sentence receives greater emphasis if the auxiliary is stressed. *Do* is introduced when no auxiliary verb is present to carry emphatic stress:

> That *wóuld* be nìce![1]   It *doés* taste nìce!

Do occurs as a marker of emphasis in affirmative declarative sentences (like the second one above) that have no *be* copula or auxiliary verb to serve as the stress bearing operator. It also occurs in the two following constructions:

- Affirmative *wh*-questions that ask about the subject (other auxiliary verbs may occur with stress here too)

> What *díd* hàppen?   Who $\left\{ \begin{array}{l} do\acute{e}s \\ c\acute{a}n \end{array} \right\}$ earn that kind of mòney?

> What wás hàppening?

- Emphatic affirmative imperatives (even for those with the copula, *do* is the only auxiliary used here)

> Dó come ìn!   Dó be cìvil this time.

Emphatic Reflexive Pronouns

Emphatic reflexive pronouns generally follow the nouns they refer to:

> The owner himself built the house.
> The victims themselves can't explain how the accident occurred.
> I saw the president himself.

However, it is also possible to postpose the reflexive pronoun emphasizing the subject and have it at the end of the sentence:

> I saw the president myself.

This use of reflexives is different from their referential use, which was discussed in Chapter 16 (e.g., John cut himself) in that they do not replace a coreferential noun phrase but occur after a noun phrase and refer back to it to make it more emphatic. They are also different from the adverbial use of reflexives that means "all alone; without assistance." When used with the latter meaning, the reflexive pronoun is often preceded by the preposition *by*:

> The owner built this house (by) himself.

Emphatic *Own*

Possessive determiners (and sometimes nouns with a possessive inflection) that modify a head noun can be made emphatic by the addition of *own*, which in turn can be intensified by the addition of very:

> (After having accepted Chomsky's analysis of comparative sentences for several years), I later developed my own analysis for such sentences.

> Is that Johnny's very own Ferrari? (I didn't know he had the money to buy such a car.)

Emphatic Adjectives and Adverbs

Emphatic adjectives, a subcategory of reference adjectives, occur only in attributive position (see Chapter 20):

a pure fabrication	*That fabrication is pure.
an outright lie	*This lie is outright.
a mere child	*The child is mere.

We distinguish these emphatic adjectives from amplifying adjectives, which may occur in both attribute and predicate position:

a complete victory	(The victory was complete.)
their extreme condemnation	(Their condemnation was extreme.)
his great folly	(His folly was great.)

Emphatic Logical Connectors

Halliday and Hasan (1976) suggest that some logical connectors are more emphatic than others. Thus, for expressing addition, *and* is a nonemphatic connector whereas *furthermore, moreover*, and some others are emphatic and thus not appropriate unless the discourse context merits special emphasis with respect to the logic of the connection (see Chapter 26 for more discussion on when to use *furthermore* and *moreover*):

John went to the store, and he bought some bread.

?John went to the store; $\left\{ \begin{array}{l} \text{furthermore} \\ \text{moreover} \end{array} \right\}$, he bought some bread.

John talked us into going out for dinner; moreover, he insisted on paying the bill.

SYNTACTIC MEANS FOR EXPRESSING FOCUS AND EMPHASIS

MARKED WORD ORDER

Marked word order can be defined as the movement of a constituent into a position in the sentence where we would not ordinarily expect to find it (i.e., it would *not* be generated by the phrase structure rules in that position). Sometimes other syntactic elements present in the sentence must be moved around to produce a grammatical sentence. The reasons for employing word-order focus that have most frequently been identified and described are: discourse constraints (e.g. the management of given and new information) and the expression of counterexpectancy, contrast, or emphasis.

Next, we outline several different types of marked word order.

Object-Subject-Verb Word Order

Fronting the object to first position in a sentence tends to be a stylistic feature of spoken rather than written English, and it can appear in contexts where a strong contrast is being made:

Him I like; her I don't. (I like him but I don't [like] her.)

John I can comprehend; the others speak gibberish. (I can comprehend John—but as for the others, they speak gibberish.)

Predicate Adjectival/Nominal-Subject-Copula Word Order

Fronting a predicate adjective or noun to initial position is also a possibility in certain written genres, such as fiction:

Ambitious she must have been, or she wouldn't have come.
A professor he was, but in name only.

In addition to an appropriate discourse context explicitly or implicitly mentioning the fronted item, all such orderings seem to require a clause or phrase that follows the sentence with the inversion. The following clause or phrase is needed to make explicit the counter-expectation or contrast implied by the inversion.

Fronting with Subject-Operator Inversion

In some instances, fronting a negative adverbial constituent or an adverbial constituent expressing extent, degree, or comparison gives a more emphatic or exclamatory reading to the sentence as a whole; in such cases, subject-operator inversion accompanies the constituent fronting:

Negative fronting:

Never have I seen such a mess!
Under no circumstances will he enter this house again!

Extent/degree/comparison fronting:

So absurd was his manner that everyone laughed at him.
Even more roguish was John's younger brother.

Several constituents other than noun phrases, adjectives, and adverbials regularly get fronted in a similar manner; in these cases, subject/operator inversion also occurs:

Present participle fronting:

Sitting at the kitchen table was our missing uncle.

Past participle fronting:

Hidden in the cellar were several barrels of wine.

However, as Bresnan (1994) correctly points out, the locative element in such participle fronting examples is often quite strong (*at the kitchen table; in the cellar*) and if the locative adverbial is deleted, the sentence becomes less grammatical:

?Sitting was our missing uncle.
?Hidden were several barrels of wine.

But if there is no participle, the sentences seem fine; they are simply cases of an initial adverbial prepositional phrase with required inversion of the subject and operator[2]:

At the kitchen table was our missing uncle.   *At the kitchen our uncle was.
In the cellar were several barrels of wine.   *In the cellar the barrels were.

Fronting with or without Subject-Verb Inversion

Two other instances of fronting occur that seem somewhere between the two categories above; i.e., they involve fronted adverbials and are grammatical whether or not the subject and main verb (not the operator, but the verb) are also inverted. Thus, for these two following instances of adverbial fronting, two types of adverbial fronting are possible:

Adverbials of direction

John ran into the house. { a. Into the house John ran.
                          { b. Into the house ran John.

Adverbials of position

An elm tree stands in the garden.
$$\begin{cases} \text{a. In the garden an elm tree } \begin{cases} \text{stands} \\ \text{*is}^2 \end{cases}. \\[2em] \text{b. In the garden } \begin{cases} \text{stands} \\ \text{is} \end{cases} \text{ an elm tree.} \end{cases}$$

In both of these cases the (a) version, which could in fact be directly generated by our phrase structure rules, seems to signal discourse emphasis or contrast of the initial adverbial element, whereas the (b) version of the two sentences appears to give focus to the delayed subject of the sentence. It is the inverted (b) versions that are of particular interest to us here and will be discussed again later in the use section.

SPECIAL FOCUS CONSTRUCTIONS

A focus construction is a structure that frames (i.e., gives explicit grammatical focus to) the constituent appearing in the focus slot. The two most important focus constructions in English are passive voice and nonreferential *there*, which have already been discussed in Chapters 18 and 23, respectively. Two other important focus constructions that we discuss next are *it*-clefts and *wh*-clefts.

It-Clefts

An *it*-cleft is a specially marked construction that puts some constituent, typically an NP, into focus. The construction implies contrast. (Note that contrastive stress alone without the cleft transformation could signal the same meaning as the cleft.)

Neutral: John wants a car.
Cleft: It's a car that John wants (not a house).
Neutral: The manager mows the lawn.
Cleft: It's the manager who mows the lawn (not a gardener).

It is difficult to formulate a rule that would generate all *it*-clefts since many different constituents such as subject NPs, object NPs, and even prepositional phrases and adverbial clauses can be put into the focus slot that follows *it* + *be*:

It's the teacher who corrects the papers (not the aide).
It's power that the president wants (not money).
It's in the kitchen that I study (not in the den).
It was because he was jealous that Bobby lied about his sister's prize. (not for some other reason).

In each case, not only can the negative presupposition be expressed overtly, but if it is, it can be moved forward; for example, *It's the teacher, not the aide, who corrects the papers*. Note that a negated version of this construction yields sentences like the following (i.e., if the focus is negative, the affirmative presupposition is contrastive and is often expressed in a phrase marked by *but*):

It's not the gardener who mows the lawn (but the manager).

Again, the contrastive presupposition may be moved forward if it is expressed overtly:

It's not the gardener, but the manager, who mows the lawn.

The following formula is, therefore, an approximation for describing an *it*-cleft:

$$S \rightarrow It + AUX + be + (Not) + \triangle + \left\{ \begin{array}{c} who \\ that \end{array} \right\} + S$$

focused   (minus focused
constituent   constituent)

In particular, our use of the "AUX" symbol in the cleft formula is a gross approximation. It has been suggested to us that only the "tense" constituent of the auxiliary be used in the *It + be* segment of the rule rather than the entire auxiliary. The logic behind this suggestion is that in Standard North American English the *It + be* segment of the cleft can never take a phrasal modal, a *have . . . -en* (perfective), or a *be . . . -ing* (progressive):

> It's in the kitchen that I am able to study.
> *It is able to study that I am in the kitchen.

> It's these books that Peter has written.
> *It's have written these books that Peter has done.

> It's the teacher who was correcting the papers.
> *It's correcting the papers that the teacher was (doing).

(In other dialects of English some of the starred sentences are possible).

It is, however, possible for the *It + be* segment of a cleft to contain a modal auxiliary (logical use) in standard North American:

> It might be Marty who stole the money.
> It must be the butler who killed Mr. Smith.

Also, it has been claimed that the tense of the *It + be* segment is merely a copy of the tense used in the main sentence. This claim is not always true, however, because clefts such as the following occur, where different tenses are used in the *It + be* segment and the main sentence:

> So, it's the butler who killed Mr. Smith (not his wife).
>   pres   past

Thus, until all these complex factors have been resolved, we will continue to use the symbol "AUX" in this rule—with the added condition that the AUX may contain only a tense or a logical (i.e., epistemic) modal. Furthermore, if a modal and *not* are both present in the *It + be* segment, the *not* will follow the modal and precede the *be*:

> It can't be Peter who wrote this book. (someone else did)

Note that *who* may come between the focused constituent and the S only if the former refers to a person. Otherwise, *that* is used to refer to objects and prepositional phrases as well as to persons when the register is informal.

Except for the presence of contrastive stress in cleft sentences, they sometimes resemble relative clauses. For example, note the ambiguity of the following sentence, cited by Schachter (1973) in his discussion of cleft sentences as focus constructions that sometimes resemble relative clauses:

> It's the woman $\left\{ \begin{array}{c} that \\ who \end{array} \right\}$ cleans the house.

> (answer to "Who's that?" = relative clause)
> (answer to "Who cleans the house—the man or the woman?" = *it*-cleft)

When spoken, however, the sentence would have different stress patterns since the *it*-cleft reading would give special stress to *woman* and the relative clause reading would not.

Wh-Clefts

Wh-clefts (also referred to as "pseudoclefts") are the other important focus construction in English. Consider the following examples:

> What he is, is a complete fool.
> Where we found the key was in the flowerpot.
> What I said was that we shouldn't go there.
> What he does is get himself in trouble.[3]

Now compare these *wh*-clefts with their neutral counterparts:

> He is a complete fool.
> We found the key in the flowerpot.
> I said that we shouldn't go there.
> He gets himself in trouble.

The *wh*-cleft sentences give special emphasis to the constituent(s) following some form of the copula *be*:

> *What he is* | IS | a complete fool.
> presumed shared knowledge: "he is something"　　(element receiving focus, emphasis)

As the examples above demonstrate, the constituent receiving special focus can be a noun phrase, a verb phrase, a prepositional phrase, or an embedded noun clause (see Chapters 31 and 33). If there are two forms of the verb *be* present, the second one is the pivotal *be* structure.

  Wh-clefts should not be confused with the less emphatic free relative clause construction discussed in the preceding chapter.

> *Wh*-cleft:
> 　　What I said was that we shouldn't go there.
> Free relative:
> 　　What he said doesn't concern me.

In the free relative, the *what* = *the thing that,* and there is no pivotal form of *be*. Also, in the free relative, *what he said* functions as the subject of the sentence. In the *wh*-cleft, there is a pivotal form of *be* (i.e., *was*), and the initial *wh*-clause, *what I said,* gets elaborated and put into focus in the material that comes after the pivot, *that we shouldn't go there.*

  Free relatives can occur wherever NPs normally occur, so they can occur as objects of verbs or prepositions as easily as they can occur as subjects:

> I'm not interested in what he said. (free relative)

Wh-clefts can be reversed, although they occur primarily in initial position, as our examples above have shown:

> We shouldn't go there was what I said.
> A complete fool is what he is.

MEANING AND USE OF SOME EMPHATIC FORMS

EMPHATIC USE OF DO

Emphatic *do* is used in at least five contexts, according to Frank (1993:94):[4]

  1. Affirmative contradictions of negative statements (often used with *but):*

> My teacher claims that I didn't turn in my paper but I *did* turn it in.

2. Emphasis of a verb used with a preverbal adverb (see Chapter 25):

> The horse he bet on always *did* win.
> The guest we were waiting for never *did* arrive.

3. Emphasis of a positive outcome after some initial doubt.

> I'm relieved to know that he *does* like beef stroganoff.
> (because that's what we're having for dinner)

4. Strong concession bordering on contrast:

> Even though I dislike most nonclassical music, I *do* find myself drawn to Dixieland jazz.

5. Emphasis of a whole sentence (*do* often occurs with an intensifying adverb such as *certainly, really, definitely*):

> I certainly *do* like that color on you.
> They definitely *did* win the game.

Of course, when sentences contain auxiliary verbs that can be used as operators, the auxiliary verbs can be stressed in the same contexts as those identified above for emphatic use of *do*:

> **1.** You predict we won't win the match, but we *will* win. You wait and see!
> **2.** Aaron never *can* figure out problems like that.
> **3.** I'm happy to hear you *are* planning to be there.
> **4.** Although he hasn't made a donation this year, he *has* contributed generously in the past.
> **5.** We certainly *will* support your election to the board.

MEANING AND USE OF OWN

In nonemphatic sentences the possessive (or genitive) case can be used to express an agent (e.g., *Holbein's portrait of Henry VIII*), a possessor (e.g., *Al's house*), an event (e.g., *John's death*), and so on. (see Chapter 16); however, the use of emphatic *own* with a possessive determiner or noun usually signals the meaning of ownership or special interest rather than other possible meanings of the possessive. Thus, if we take the above example for the possessive expressing an agent and add *own* (e.g., *I prefer Holbein's own portrait of Henry VIII*), English speakers who are naive about the historical names and facts involved will tend to understand that Holbein is the owner of—rather than the artist who produced—the portrait. The use of *own* to emphasize an agent is appropriate only when the person referred to in the possessive form is both the agent and the possessor of the head noun. There is a special construction in English for expressing this double relationship:

> head noun + of + possessive form + own + gerund
>   possession   agency

> Examples: That's a problem of his own making.
>   You will have an escort of your own choosing.

In volume 7 of his multivolume grammar of the English language, Jespersen (1961) notes that emphatic reflexives and emphatic *own* often function as paraphrases of each other:[5]

> He cooks his own meals.   He cooks his meals himself.

COLLOQUIAL USE OF EMPHATIC *HERE* AND *THERE* WITH DEMONSTRATIVES

The English language also has many colloquial and dialectal markers of emphasis such as the use of *here* and *there* to emphasize the demonstratives *this/these* and *that/those*, respectively:

This $\left\{\begin{array}{l}\textbf{a.}\ \text{here cow}\\ \textbf{b.}\ \text{cow here}\end{array}\right\}$ has always given a lot of milk.

What do you think of that $\left\{\begin{array}{l}\textbf{a.}\ \text{there house?}\\ \textbf{b.}\ \text{house there?}\end{array}\right\}$

All the sequences above occur only in somewhat nonstandard colloquial usage; however, the (b) sentences represent a more acceptable variant than the (a) ones do.

USE OF MARKED WORD ORDER

What is the motivation for fronting adverbials of direction or position in sentences where subject-verb inversion also occurs?

> Into the house ran John.
> In the garden stands an elm tree.

A pilot study by Gary (1974) suggests that the speaker/writer has selected the subject NP— now in final position—to surprise the speaker/reader, create suspense, and specifically to go counter to the expectations of the listener/reader. For example, using texts such as the following, Gary claims that the counter-to-expectation function of the (b) version of the text-final sentence carries a special presupposition of counterexpectancy and that this contrasts with the neutral, noninverted (a) version, which has no special presuppositions:

> Keith Sebastian had given me detailed instructions on how to find his house; he was to meet me there with the money. I drove up the driveway and got out of my car. Just as the car door closed, I heard the main door to the house open.

a. $\left\{\begin{array}{l}\text{Keith Sebastian}\\ \text{Dan Carlyle}\\ \text{The Sheriff}\end{array}\right\}$ stepped out of the house.

b. Out of the house stepped $\left\{\begin{array}{l}\text{\#Keith Sebastian}\\ \text{Dan Carlyle}\\ \text{the Sheriff}\end{array}\right\}$.

(*Note:* # = not acceptable given the discourse context)

In the (b) version, *Keith Sebastian* is not acceptable as the postposed subject, according to Gary, because there is no counterexpectancy; that is, the reader would normally expect *Keith Sebastian* to be the subject just as he is in the first option of the (a) version, but given the use of the (b) construction, which signals counterexpectancy, the reader is invited to be surprised when someone else is the postposed subject.

Gary convincingly demonstrates that concepts such as definiteness versus indefiniteness or new information versus given information do not adequately explain this example—and the other examples he cites—as effectively as does the notion of counterexpectancy.

Gary provides evidence that use of present and past participle fronting may also signal surprise or counterexpectancy to the listener/reader in the same way that fronting of adverbials of direction and position do:[6]

> Sitting in the front seat of the car was my cousin Joe.
> Hidden at the back of my father's wine cellar was an old bottle of Chateau d'Yquem.

On the other hand, Gary does not feel that the fronting of negative or of degree or extent constituents accomplishes the same discourse function:

> Never have I seen such a mess!
> So absurd was his proposition that no one believed him.

We agree with Gary and feel that these last two cases of fronting express an emphatic exclamatory meaning. Use of negative or degree/extent/comparison fronting reflects exclamatory speaker/writer stance rather than signaling the possibility of surprise or counterexpectation on the part of the listener/reader.

Gary (1974) used fiction (i.e., paperback novels) as his source for examples. Yang (1989) used a larger and more diversified database that included transcribed speech, short stories, academic writing, and journalism. One interesting finding she made is that marked word order with inversion did not occur at all in her oral corpus (about 24,500 words), which had only one instance of direct object fronting: *John I like.* In her written corpus (about 70,000 words drawn from fiction, journalism, and academic writing), Yang found 29 instances of inverted word order, only five of which (17 percent) expressed contrast or counter expectation. However, she found 16 cases (55 percent) where the marked word order with inversion served to maintain thematic continuity and eight cases (28 percent) where it established or resumed a topic.[7]

In the following example, thematic continuity is maintained through use of marked word order and inversion:

> (A short *L.A. Times* article describes Mother Teresa's visit to South Africa. Having reported what Mother Teresa said upon arrival at the airport, the writer continues:)
>
> Accompanying her (Mother Teresa) were four nuns who will run the new mission. . . .
>
> (Yang 1989:23)

Here the present participle fronting and inversion serve to keep Mother Teresa as the initial noun phrase in the clause. The same goal could have been achieved, of course, by using passive voice (a focus construction we have discussed previously in Chapter 18).

> She was accompanied by four nuns who . . .

The following text begins a paragraph and is an example of using marked word order with inversion to introduce or present a character or participant:

> Across the aisle was an elderly woman, dressed resolutely in black—dress, scarf, stockings, shoes. [paragraph continues to describe the old woman]
>
> (Yang 1989:15)

Since the preceding paragraph had described another character in the short story, one might say that this construction is being used to express contrast in addition to introducing a new participant or topic. In fact, Yang acknowledges that the three discourse functions she identified can overlap and that often two occur in any one instance of marked and inverted word order.

There was at least one clear case of contrast (or counterexpectation) that Yang found in academic writing dealing with language acquisition:

> These clause types are followed by relative clauses modifying common nouns in object position. *Still missing at age 4 are relative clauses built on sentence subjects.*
>
> (Yang, 1989:20)

Birner (1994) also looked at a large number of naturally occurring tokens of sentences with inversion-type marked word order, and she proposes that "inversion serves an information-packaging function: that of presenting information which is more familiar in the discourse before information which is less familiar"(p. 255). She also felt it was significant that information inferrable from context was treated just as if it were given information (for purposes of inversion). Birner's account, however, does not fully explain those cases where a sense of emphasis or contrast seems to be achieved through the use of inversion, which several of the examples from Gary and Yang have illustrated.

DIFFERENCES IN THE DISTRIBUTION, MEANING, AND USE OF *IT*-CLEFTS AND *WH*-CLEFTS

Kim (1988) examined a database of over 500,000 words (about 230,000 spoken and 290,000 written) and found a strong preference for *wh*-clefts in the spoken data: 147 spoken versus 50 written tokens and a preference (through less marked) for *it*-clefts in the written data—68 written tokens versus 32 spoken. *Wh*-clefts occurred twice as frequently in Kim's database as *it*-clefts. Kim also found that definite NPs are frequently the focused element in *it*-clefts, which tend to have a contrastive function and to occur in planned discourse (Ochs 1979), whereas indefinite NPs are frequently the focused element in *wh*-clefts, which often function to present the speaker's perspective to the listener and tend to occur in unplanned discourse.

Kim was building on the work of Prince (1978), who did the earliest empirical research showing that *it*-clefts and *wh*-clefts were not at all synonymous in terms of presupposition and function and that neither one should be derived from the other. Prince pointed out that the presupposed part of *wh*-clefts contains given information that the speaker assumes the hearer is thinking about, while the presupposed part of *it*-clefts contains known information that the reader either knows or can deduce but is not thinking about. She also noted that in *it*-clefts the average length of the presupposed part is greater than the focused part, while the reverse is true for *wh*-clefts.

Use of *It*-Clefts in Writing

Prince (1978) distinguishes two types of *it*-cleft sentences in English—stressed focus (SF) and informative-presupposition (IP). The former contains known information in its presupposed part (i.e., the relative clause) and is used for emphasis, while the latter contains new information in its presupposed part and introduces this new information at the end of the sentence for rhetorical effect:

> *Stressed focus:* It isn't higher prices but changed expectations that have caused people to buy more at the present time.
> *Information-presupposition:* It was in 1979 that Piet Kornhof rather boldly announced, "Apartheid is dead."

Kim's (1988) corpus reveals that such *it*-clefts occur most frequently in written genres such as historical narrative, persuasive discourse, and journalistic writing. In his corpus, about three-quarters of the *it*-clefts were of the SF variety—that is, they were used to express the author's emphasis or focus rather than to provide a backdrop for rhetorically salient new information.

Celce-Murcia (1996) shows that a good source of data for *it*-clefts *is Time* magazine. For example, the May 22, 1995, U.S. edition had several tokens of *it*-clefts. The following one occurred on page 4 in the fourth paragraph of a short five-paragraph article titled "To our readers," which discussed two *Time* correspondents, Michael Duffy and Wendy Cole.

The article is clearly more about Cole than Duffy, since she is the topic of four of the paragraphs, including this one:

> It was Cole who chose Fargo as the microcosm for the debate on federal benevolence and intrusion. Says Duffy, who wrote the story, "She saw it as a fascinating mix of frontier and front page. Then she dissected the town until she knew more about it than Fargoans. Late last week, needing an anecdote, she ran down to a local bowling alley, did three interviews and delivered a freshly minted kicker for the story inside an hour."

The placement of Cole in the information focus of the paragraph initial, stress focus *it*-cleft sentence signals that Cole will be the topic of the paragraph. It also provides stylistic variation in that the other three paragraphs about Cole begin: *Cole has . . . , Wendy has . . . , Cole found . . . .*

Use of *Wh*-Clefts in Conversation

Kim (1995) has carried out one of the most complete studies of *wh*-clefts in English conversation. He found 76 instances of *wh*-clefts in naturally occurring conversations and found that all but seven of the tokens had four types of verbs in the *wh*-clause (Kim 1995:251):

1. Verbs expressing a speaker-internal state (29 tokens): *realize, want, feel, think, enjoy, know, object to,* etc.
2. Verbs expressing a metalinguistic dimension (22 tokens): *mean, say, ask,* etc.
3. Verbs marking meta-events (12 tokens): *happen* (e.g., *What does happen is (that) there's a tendency to forget this.*)
4. Verbs marking meta-actions (6 tokens): *do* (e.g., *What I'm doing right now is the vacuuming.*)

Therefore, the types of verbs used in the *wh*-clause are highly constrained and give us a good general sense of the interactional functions of *wh*-clefts, which according to Kim (1995:253) are:

1. Discourse-organization uses, such as marking a topic shift or expressing the gist of prior talk:

   (Context: The therapist, Dan, marks the gist of exchanges between two teenagers, Ken and Louise, about how parents never get over treating offspring as children):

   K: My father's 45 or 43, an' he'll go over to my grandmother's house, and insteada my grandmother offering him a drink of beer, she'll say
   L: Wanna glassa milk?

   [minor digression by K and L]

   K: Wouldja like a peanut butter an' jelly sandwich?
   D: So, in a way, what you're saying is you'll never get through *that*.
   (adapted from Kim, 1995:256)

2. Interactional management uses such as expressing or dealing with disagreement or initiating repair (see Schegloff, 1979):

   (context: A is Brad Crandall, a talk show host, and B is the caller. They are having a disagreement about the caller's Medicaid eligibility)

   A: They won't be taking you off Medicaid.
   B: They *will*!

> *A:* So you would still be eligible. It wouldn't change your eligibility.
>
> *B:* Well, what I know is they gave me a letter and they never sent me my Medicaid card.
>
> (adapted from Kim, 1995:258–259)

3. Display of speaker affect:

> (Context: Louise is telling a story, and she self-interrupts and reformulates with a *wh*-cleft as an aside to add her affective stance)
>
> . . . or like you come and they're talking—what I love is when they're talking about something—you know, "You had radio when you were a little girl?"
>
> (adapted from Kim, 1995:266)

Kim concludes (p. 268) that "these various interactional uses cannot be explained from the informational perspective alone in terms of presupposition/focus or given/new, because what is consciously involved in them is the speaker's interactional exploitation of the grammatical form and the function of the *wh*-cleft as a stance marker." *Wh*-clefts are used by speakers to accomplish interactional tasks in ways that serve to convey their attitude toward their interlocutor(s) and towards the topic.

CONCLUSION

There are problems from the outset in trying to define focus and emphasis in English because they overlap with other topics such as exclamation and intensification. In addition, it must be recognized that emphasis is essentially a semantic notion, and we have shown that it may be signaled in many ways, including use of special stress and intonation patterns, choice of words, choice of grammatical markers, and so on. Focus, on the other hand, seems to be a discourse-functional notion, related to what the speaker/writer wants to draw the listener/reader's attention to in the ongoing discourse or text. As we have tried to point out, such attention can be activated through the use of marked word order and special focus constructions. We make no claim to having provided an exhaustive treatment of focus and emphasis in English, but we hope to have drawn attention to this important area.

TEACHING SUGGESTIONS

1. Form/Meaning. For teaching *it*-cleft sentences, the teacher should give several examples showing how *it*-clefts embody certain presuppositions and differ from their normal affirmative and negative statement counterparts. For example:

Sam studies physics.	John doesn't drive a Ford.
(Cue: He doesn't study chemistry.)	(Cue: He drives a Buick.)
It's physics that Sam studies, not chemistry.	It's not a Ford that John drives, but a Buick.
-or-	-or-
It's physics, not chemistry, that Sam studies.	It's not a Ford, but a Buick, that John drives.

In groups of three, students should be given one 3 x 5 card, each with a false affirmative or negative statement as a cue. The statements will be about their fellow students. They should write a mini-dialog that makes natural use of an *it*-cleft construction.

On cue card: Kim comes from Hong Kong. (It's a false statement.)[8]
Sample student-generated dialog:

> A: Is anyone in this class from Hong Kong?
> B: Yes, Kim comes from Hong Kong.
>
> C: No, he doesn't. { It's Lee who comes from Hong Kong, not Kim.
> { It's Korea that Kim comes from, not Hong Kong.

These dialogues can then be presented to the class as a whole for evaluation and correction.

2. Meaning. You might want to try the following sequence of activities for teaching emphatic reflexives.

   a. Show the class sentences with emphatic reflexives:

Subject emphasis:
1. The owner himself built the house.   **2.** Did you yourself have a good time?

Object emphasis (all objects):
3. I met Troy Aikman himself.
4. We gave the President himself a copy of the proclamation.
5. Susan did her term paper on Einstein himself.

   b. Read these sentences and have the class repeat. Ask them to paraphrase the sentences and to describe the function of the reflexive pronoun.
   c. Point out the position of the reflexive and ask them to explain what is emphasized in each sentence.
   d. Show the class several picture cards with sentences and have students supply correct reflexive pronouns to emphasize the subjects, For example:

> Cue: Mary made the dress.
> S1: Mary herself made the dress.

   e. Then a student selects a card, and someone else in the class asks a yes/no question based on the card. The student who selected the card should give a meaningful response. For example:

> S1: Did you yourself make that dress?
> S2: Yes, I did. / No, I didn't. My mother did.

3. Meaning. Emphatic *do* might be introduced using the following context:
   a. The teacher can give the class practice in using emphatic *do* to contradict negative statements by giving some false negative statements as a cue and then putting an edited version of the dialogue on the board. For example:

> T: Ali, you didn't turn in your homework.
> Ali: That's not true. I *did* turn in my homework. I gave it to you a few minutes ago.

   b. The class should discuss the function of *do* in such a dialogue.
   c. The students are divided into small groups and asked to write a dialogue that incorporates use of emphatic *do* to contradict a false negative statement.
   d. The dialogues are performed in front of the class, evaluated, and corrected.

4. Use. Fronting directional adverbs. Read a short paragraph or anecdote to your class. For example:

> Everyone but Harry had arrived on time for the meeting. We waited 15 minutes. There still was no sign of Harry. We had just decided to proceed without him, when into the conference room dashed Harry!

Ask them about the word order of the last clause. Why does the adverbial come first? See if they can explain the fact that the others had decided Harry wouldn't come, and when he did, they were surprised because their expectation that Harry would not come turned out to be false.

Divide the class into small groups and give each group a sentence involving some class member(s) with the directional adverb fronted (e.g., Out of the house came Maria and Rosa). Have each group write a paragraph that uses the inverted cue sentence as the last sentence. Groups will then exchange paragraphs so that each group can judge the appropriateness and accuracy of another group's story.

5. Form/Use. Melinda Erickson (personal communication) suggests that pseudocleft sentences can be learned and practiced in the context of a small-town planning committee meeting. Each member of the committee is trying to present a different proposal.

Sample dialogue:

Chairman:	What our town needs is careful development. May I hear your proposals?
Head librarian:	What we see as important is a new library branch to supplement the main library.
High school principal:	What we need is better athletic facilities for the high school.
Businessman:	What we should have is a Chamber of Commerce like all the other towns in the area.

The class can be split into groups to practice and role-play the sample dialogue. The followup activity could be for each group to make one or more suggestions/proposals concerning their ESL/EFL class. For example:

> What we need is fewer exams.
> What we would like is less homework.
> What we would prefer is more conversation.

6. Use. Show intermediate or advanced students authentic excerpts from written texts containing *it*-clefts. Ask them to decide in pairs or groups what the *it*-clefts are doing in the written texts. Have each pair or group compose their own passage with an *it*-cleft.

EXERCISES

Test your understanding of what has been presented.

  I. Provide example sentences that illustrate the following terms. Underline the pertinent word(s) in your examples.

a. *wh*-cleft	**d.** emphatic *do*
b. *it*-cleft	**e.** emphatic reflexive
c. fronting of a directional adverbial	**f.** emphatic possessive

2. Why are the following sentences ungrammatical (or at best awkward)?

    a. *On his car a bumper sticker is: Have you hugged your kid today?

    b. *What we meant to say we are sorry.

    c. *He is Robert who wrote the letter. (not someone else)

3. Explain the ambiguity in the following sentences:

    a. It's the graduate student who corrects the papers in our class.

    b. Our chairman criticized the dean himself.

4. Do the following sentences illustrate *wh*-clefts or free relatives? Give reasons to support your choice of construction:

    a. I forgot what he said.   **c.** What he said is of little concern to us.

    b. A big lie is what he told.   **d.** What he said is that you are a jerk.

Test your ability to apply what you know.

5. If your students produce the following sentences, what errors have they made? How will you make them aware of the errors, and what exercises will you prepare to correct the errors?

    a. *Never I have tasted such a delicious sandwich!

    b. *Who you mean is that Oscar did it.

    c. *Sitting on the front porch my long-lost brother was.

6. Develop a mini-lesson for teaching appropriate use of sentence-initial negative constituents (e.g., *Under no circumstances will we tolerate that!*) to an advanced ESL/EFL class.

7. Describe differences in use of meaning, if any, in the following pairs of sentences:

    a. (1) What he said is that he wasn't coming.

         (2) He said that he wasn't coming.

    b. (1) The misbehaving child was standing in the corner.

         (2) Standing in the corner was the misbehaving child.

    c. (1) Come back again.

         (2) Do come back again.

    d. (1) Why doesn't Jim use his book?

         (2) Why doesn't Jim use his own book?

BIBLIOGRAPHY

References

Birner, B. J. (1994). "Information Status and Word Order: An Analysis of English Inversion. "*Language* 70:2, 232–259.

Bresnan, J. (1994). "Locative Inversion and the Architecture of Universal Grammar." *Language* 70:1, 71–131.

Celce-Murcia, M. (1996). "Describing and Teaching English Grammar with Reference to Written Discourse." *The Journal of TESOL France* 3:1, 5-18.

Frank, M. (1993). *Modern English: A Practical Reference Guide.* (2d ed.). Englewood Cliffs, N.J.: Prentice-Hall Regents.

Gary, N. (1974). "A Discourse Analysis of Certain Root Transformations in English." Unpublished paper. Department of Linguistics, UCLA. (Reproduced and distributed by the Indiana University Linguistics Club.)

Halliday, M., and R. Hasan (1976). *Cohesion in English.* London: Longman.

Jacobs, R. (1995). *English Syntax: A Grammar for English Language Professionals*. Oxford: Oxford University Press.

Jespersen, O. (1961). *A Modern English Grammar on Historical Principles* (Part VII) compiled and edited by Niels Haislund. London: Allen and Unwin.

Kim, K-H. (1988). "A Discourse Analysis of Cleft and Pseudocleft Constructions in American English." Unpublished M.A. thesis in TESL, UCLA.

Kim, K-H. (1995). "*Wh*-Clefts and Left-Dislocation in English Conversation." In P. Downing and M. Noonan (eds.), *Word Order in Discourse*. Amsterdam: John Benjamins, 245–296.

Ochs, E. (1979). "Planned and Unplanned Discourse." In T. Givón (ed.), *Syntax and Semantics* (vol. 12). New York: Academic Press, 51–80.

Prince, E. (1978). "A Comparison of *Wh*-Clefts and *It*-Clefts in Discourse." *Language* 54:4, 883–906.

Rutherford, W. (1974). "Pragmatic Syntax in the Classroom." *TESOL Quarterly* 8:2, 177–184.

Schachter, P. (1973). "Focus and Relativization." *Language* 49:1, 19–46.

Schegloff, E. (1979). "The Relevance of Repair to Syntax for Conversation." In T. Givón (ed.), *Syntax and Semantics* (vol. 12), 261–286.

Yang [He], A. W. (1989). "Marked Word Order in Clause-Initial Position." Unpublished Ph.D. qualifying paper. Applied Linguistics Program, UCLA.

Suggestions for further reading

For a discussion of it-*cleft sentences, relative clauses, and their similarities and differences, see:*
Schachter, P. (1973). "Focus and relativization." *Language* 49:1, 19–46.

The relationship between it-*cleft and pseudocleft (i.e.,* wh-*cleft) sentences is explored in the following sources:*
Gundell, J. K. (1977). "Where Do Cleft Sentences Come From?" *Language* 53:3, 343–359.

Prince, E. (1978). "A Comparison of *Wh*-Clefts and *It*-Clefts in Discourse. *Language* 54:4, 883–906.

Jacobs, R. (1995). *English Syntax*. Oxford: Oxford University Press, 171–183.

The discourse significance of several adverbial fronting and participle fronting rules is explored in the following source:
Gary, N. (1974). "A Discourse Analysis of Certain Root Transformations in English." Unpublished paper. Department of Linguistics, UCLA. (Reproduced and distributed by the Indiana University Linguistics Club.)

For an excellent description of the use of wh-*clefts in English conversation, see:*
Kim, K-H. (1995). "*Wh*-Clefts and Left-Dislocation in English Conversation." In P. Downing and M. Noonan (eds.), *Word Order in Discourse*. Amsterdam: John Benjamins, 245–296.

For a discussion of (1) emphatic do, *(2) emphatic adjectives and/or adverbs, and (3) emphatic use of reflexives, see the following sources:*
Frank, M. (1993). *Modern English: A Practical Reference Guide* (2d ed.). Englewood Cliffs, N.J.: Prentice Hall Regents.

Quirk, R., and S. Greenbaum (1973). *A Concise Grammar of Contemporary English*. New York: Harcourt Brace Jovanovich. (1) p. 427, (2) pp. 122, 132, 409–410, (3) pp. 424–426.

For a discussion of emphatic logical connectors, see:
Halliday, M., and R. Hasan (1976). *Cohesion in English*. London: Longman, 246, 249.

For some useful information about focus and emphasis in general, see:
Leech, G., and J. Svartvik (1975). *A Communicative Grammar of English.* London: Longman, 175–185.

For useful discussions of the inverted sentences discussed in this chapter, see:
Emonds, J. (1976). *A Transformational Approach to English Syntax: Root, Structure Preserving, and Local Transformations.* New York: Academic Press.
Birner, B. J. (1994). "Information Status and Word Order." *Language* 70:2, 233–259.

Teaching materials for the topics covered in this chapter are rare. For some exercises for teaching emphatic reflexives, see:
Frank, M. (1975). *Modern English: Exercises for Nonnative Speakers. Part I: Parts of Speech.* Englewood Cliffs, N.J.: Prentice-Hall, 25.

For a suggestion on teaching emphatic own, *see:*
Rutherford, W. (1977). *Modern English.* Vol. 2 (2d ed.). New York: Harcourt Brace Jovanovich, 34.

For a general overview of emphasis and focus with exercises, see:
Danielson, D., and P. Porter (1990). *Using English: Your Second Language.* (2d ed.). Englewood Cliffs, N.J.: Prentice Hall Regents, 338–345.

For an excellent unit treating it-*clefts and* wh-*clefts, see:*
Frodesen, J., & J. Eyring (1997). *Grammar Dimensions.* Book 4 (2d ed.). Boston: Heinle & Heinle, 394–408.

ENDNOTES

1. The accent marks used in these examples and some of those that follow refer to primary sentence stress (´) and secondary sentence stress (`).

2. Note that in such cases the copula *be* is not grammatical in final position because *be* is not a full lexical verb, and therefore, subject-verb inversion or subject-auxiliary inversion must occur if adverbial fronting or sentence initial generation occurs with *be* as the verb. Note that the lexical verbs in such sentences must be intransitive.

3. As Jacobs (1995:178) points out, when the constituent in focus is a verb phrase, the *wh*-clause ends with a form of *do* instead of another verb if there is no auxiliary verb. His example is:

> What Henry has done is develop a better mousetrap.

Jacobs also points out that if a noun phrase referring to a person is the focused item, the *wh*-clause is often embedded in a noun phrase beginning with *the person who, the one who,* etc.:

> The one who advocated stronger action was Palmerston (Jacobs 1995:179).

4. As Frank (1993:94) notes, Elizabethan English also used *do* in nonemphatic affirmative sentences in variation with the simple present:

> Thus conscience does make cowards of us all. (Shakespeare)

5. Jespersen (1961) goes so far as to suggest that *own* is the genitive form of *-self*.

6. As Bresnan (1994) points out, the locative prepositional phrase in such participles is critical; the words *sitting* and *hidden* could be deleted.

7. Bresnan (1994) also discusses presentation or resumption of participants as a motivation for using such a construction.

8. This type of exercise is a version of Rutherford's (1974) false presupposition drill.

COMPLEMENTATION

INTRODUCTION

You have seen in Chapters 28 and 29 how relative constructions can place one clause within the structure of another larger clause of which it forms a part. For example, the vast majority of relative clauses function as modifiers of NPs within a sentence. However, as will become clear in this and the next two chapters, relative constructions are not the only possible type of clause-within-clause in English.

This chapter is concerned with English clausal *complementation*. Complements, which are constituents needed to complete the meaning of a verb or an adjective, are often distinguished from *adjuncts*, which are perceived not to be central to the propositional meaning of the sentence and which are never required to occur with a verb or adjective:

> John believed *that Jill was coming.*
> (complement)

> John *(almost)* believed that Jill was coming.
> adjunct

The verb *believe* must take some sort of object. This object may be an NP (*John believed the report*), or it may be an embedded complement clause as in the first example above. By contrast, the adverbial *almost* in the second example is not a structurally obligatory constituent; it is an optional adjunct. Ordinary relative clauses, too, are a type of adjunct: for example, there is no noun in English that is required in every instance to be followed by a relative clause. Relative clauses are typically just *modifiers* of nouns.

In this chapter we discuss clausal complements that include, at least, a verbal element with an assumed subject, and often an expressed subject as well. These complements fall naturally into five types:

1. full clausal *that*-complements with tensed verbs
2. tenseless subjunctive complements
3. infinitives
4. gerunds
5. noun-participle constructions

These five types of clausal complements tend to be strictly associated with the occurrence of certain verbs. Because there are many types of clausal complements and because the relation of verb to complement type often seems arbitrary, the grammar of clausal complementation is somewhat complex to learn. An ESL/EFL teacher may expect many errors here even at advanced levels of instruction, so it is well worth a teacher's time to be aware of the structural variations and difficulties.

THE FORM OF COMPLEMENTS

ORDINARY *THAT*-COMPLEMENTS

Tensed *that*-clauses are one of the most frequent types of clausal complement:

> Scientists claim [that the globe is getting warmer].
> We long expected [that nothing worthwhile would come from our effort].
> People generally know [that bears don't make good pets].

In each case, we have a complete sentence. Notice that the material inside the brackets looks exactly like an ordinary clause except that it is prefaced by *that*. In each bracketed clause there is a subject and a verb, and there may be various types of additional information such as one would find in an ordinary sentence. The first auxiliary verb may appear in the present or past tense, or it may be a modal auxiliary. What is different is that these bracketed clauses cannot stand by themselves as acceptable sequences as long as they begin with *that*:

> *That the globe is getting warmer.
> *That nothing worthwhile would come from our effort.
> *That bears don't make good pets.

As with the adverbial clauses discussed in Chapter 25, such clauses are called "dependent" clauses because they depend on, or require the presence of, another clause to which they are attached in some way. Moreover, in each full sentence above, the dependent *that*-clause seems to stand in a position in which an NP might ordinarily stand. The verbs *claim, expect,* and *know* may under other circumstances take simple NPs as objects:

> Scientists often claim [great discoveries].
> We expected [nothing else].
> Everyone knows [the answer].

This suggests that we should regard these dependent clauses as noun-like in nature and say that they are *embedded* into larger, independent clauses, forming an integral part of them—in these cases, as direct objects. Additional evidence to support the belief that the embedded clauses are noun-like is the fact that they behave like the corresponding NPs: in all the cases above, the bracketed material can appear in a passive sentence as the subject—that is, in another position where NPs occur:

> [Great discoveries] are often claimed by scientists.
> [That the earth is getting warmer] is claimed by scientists.
>
> [Nothing else] was expected by us.
> [That nothing worthwhile would come from our effort] was long expected by us.
>
> [The answer] is known by everyone.
> [That bears don't make good pets] is generally known (by people).[1]

A third piece of evidence for the NP status of these clauses is that each *that*-clause above answers the typical noun-like question *what?* just as does each case of a simple NP object:

Question	Answer
What do scientists often claim?	→ Great discoveries.
What do scientists often claim?	→ That the earth is getting warmer.

One way to incorporate this new possibility into our grammar is to rewrite the phrase-structure rule for the expansion of NPs:

$$NP \rightarrow \begin{Bmatrix} \text{(det)(AP) N (-pl)(PrepP)} \\ \text{pro} \\ \text{S} \end{Bmatrix}$$

We will now say that it is possible for an S to function as an NP.[2]

What sort of word is *that*, and where do we place it in the tree? It should be clear that this use of *that* is not the same as the word *that* in relative clauses (see Chapters 28 and 29): it does not replace a full NP in the same way as relative *that*:

> This is the shop *that* I told you about. (*that* = shop)
> Scientists claim *that* the globe is getting warmer. (*that* = ?)

Nor is *that* in the above complement clauses identical to the demonstrative determiner *that* (see Chapter 16); not only does it not replace an NP, but it also cannot receive emphatic or contrastive stress in the same way that a demonstrative can:

> *That's* the type of bird I was telling you about.
> We should pay attention to *this* sign, not *that* one.
> ?Scientists claim *that* the globe is getting warmer.

Indeed, it is hard to see what sort of contrast could possibly be intended in the last example. Thus, in the case of complement clauses, it seems we have a third type of *that*, one we shall call a "complementizer," a signal of a complement clause. This complementizer is neither of the noun/pronoun category nor of any other grammatical category we have introduced so far in the book. We will abbreviate it in the tree as "comp"; we will place it under S, in a position adjacent to (and to the left of) S':

Scientists claim that the globe is getting warmer.

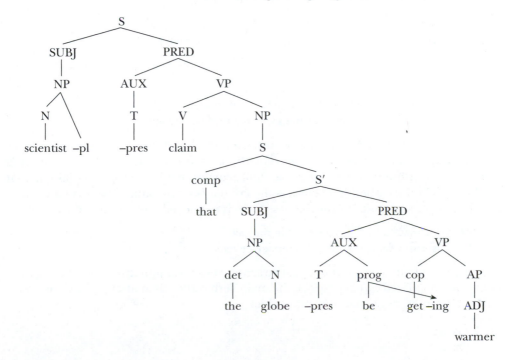

We also have to expand the options for rewriting the rule for S to include an optional complementizer as follows:

$$S \rightarrow (comp)\ (sm^n)\ S'$$

We must leave the complementizer optional both because simple, single-clause sentences do not require them and because it is possible for complement clauses like those above to appear without *that*:

> Scientists often claim the globe is getting warmer.
> People generally know bears don't make good pets.

Later in this chapter we will discuss some reasons why *that* might be included or omitted in such clauses.

There are many verbs that permit or require tensed *that*-complements as objects. Besides *believe, claim, expect,* and *know,* among the more common are *assume, discover, explain, find, find out, imagine, learn, perceive, point out, promise, prove, see, show, think,* and *understand.* For example,

> The lecturer explained that the source of the error was human.
> The dealer promised that my car would be fixed for free.
> New evidence shows that broccoli sprouts are more healthful than broccoli.

SUBJUNCTIVE COMPLEMENTS

An additional type of *that*-clause is superficially similar to the type above but different in that the form of the verb in the embedded clause does not vary, regardless of whether the subject is first, second, or third person or singular/plural, and regardless of time reference. Such clauses are called *subjunctive complements,* as in the cases below:

> They insist [that all the students *sign up* for counselors].
> They insist [that this student *sign up* for a counselor].
>
> The customer is demanding [that the store *return* his money].
> The customer demanded [that the store *return* his money].

The third person singular present tense *-s* is absent, and past-tense forms are ungrammatical, as the following examples show:

> *They insist that this student *signs up* for a counselor.
> *The customer demanded that the store *returned* his money.

The fact that the embedded verb is never inflected or altered in any other way suggests that in forming a subjunctive, one uses only the base form of the verb; the resulting clauses are then without any sort of tense at all. Further evidence for this claim is that where the verb in the embedded clause is the copula *be* or the auxiliary *be* (in a passive, progressive, or phrasal modal) only the base form is employed after *insist* and *demand*:

> We insist that he *be* the one to make the call.
> The customer demanded that his money *be returned.*

Even stronger evidence comes from negative sentences. In subjunctive clauses, a negation element is always placed directly before the main verb rather than after an auxiliary verb; thus, no addition of the *do* operator is possible:

We insist that he *not make* the telephone call.

*We insist that he $\left\{\begin{array}{l} do \\ does \end{array}\right\}$ *not make* the telephone call.

Without present or past tense in the clause, it should be clear that our expansion rule for AUX will have to allow for the possibility of a tenseless AUX node. Fortunately, we already have such a possibility in the [-imper] option for imperative sentences, which also lack tenses. The tree for a subjunctive sentence would then look like that below:

The customer demanded that the store return his money.

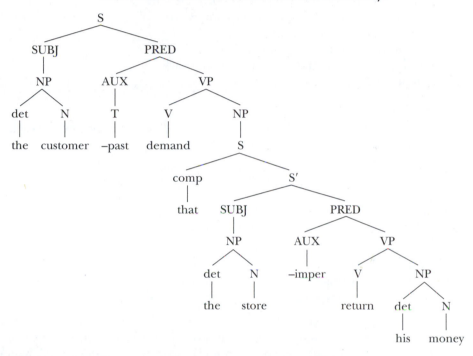

According to the PS rules, modal auxiliaries will not appear in subjunctive clauses; in general, this holds true in native-speaker use, although many people do accept *should* or *had to* rather than imperative mood after *insist*, perhaps in an attempt to achieve a softening effect:

> We insisted that he (should/had to) take the test again.
> The customer demanded that the store (?must/?had to) return his money.

Besides occurring after *insist* and *demand*, the subjunctive appears in embedded-clause verbs after such main-clause verbs of urging and advice such as *ask* (meaning "request"), *prefer, propose, recommend, request, require,* and *suggest*:

> We ask/request that you please keep a little quieter.
> The members prefer that the constitution not be changed this year.
> The city proposed that the land be returned to the farmers.
> We recommend that you order the fish.

INFINITIVE COMPLEMENTS

We have now expanded our notion of "clause" somewhat, to include subject-verb sequences without tenses. Infinitives (so called because they are not "finite," or tensed) are an additional, and far more common, type of tenseless clause than subjunctives. Unlike the other complement clauses we have discussed, they have five sub-types, each of which we discuss in turn.

> Infinitive Complements
> **1.** *believe* type: The students believe their professor to be amazing.
> **2.** *advise* type: We advised them to play baseball outside.
> **3.** *attempt* type: I attempted to avoid the ice on the road.
> **4.** *want* type: I want to clean the house.
>   (*for/to* infinitive) I want (for) him to clean the house.
> **5.** *let* type: The teacher let the students go home early.
>   (bare stem)

Believe-type Infinitives

The first type of infinitive follows main-clause verbs like *believe* and *imagine*. The bracketed parts of the sentences below seem to show no evidence of tense:

> a. The students believed [their professor to be amazing].
> b. The citizens imagined [the politician to have led an honest life].

If the above, past-tense main verbs are changed to indicate future time or present-habitual time, for example, nothing inside the brackets will change:

> c. The students will believe [their professor to be amazing].
> d. The students always believe [their professor to be amazing].
> e. The citizens will imagine [the politician to have led an honest life].
> f. The citizens currently imagine [the politician to have led an honest life].

In what sense, then, can infinitives be considered clauses? Like other clauses that we have considered, they seem to possess both subjects and verbs (and in the (b) example above, a direct object as well). While there may be no marking of tense under the AUX node, there does seem to be a marker—the AUX *to*—which stands roughly in the position in which auxiliary elements usually occur. If we place the *to* under AUX, we will need an additional expansion option for the AUX rule:

$$\text{AUX} \rightarrow \left\{ \left\{ \begin{matrix} \text{T} \\ \text{M} \\ to \end{matrix} \right\} \text{(perf)(prog)(pass)} \\ \text{-imper} \right\}$$

This new expansion suggests that we cannot have infinitive *to* co-occurring with a modal verb but that we can have perfect, progressive, and perfect progressive infinitives. In fact, these claims are validated by data such as the following. (We cover passive infinitives in Chapter 32):

> *The students believe [their professor to can do almost anything].
> The students believe [their professor to be able to do good research].
> The students believe [their professor to be correcting their homework].
> The students believe [their professor to have been lecturing too much lately].

The next question to answer is what position these infinitives occupy in the structure of the whole sentence. Are they direct object NPs, as we argued for *that*-clauses? The answer seems doubtful if we use the notional test that says that a direct object answers the question *what?* about a main verb. The answers below seem odd:

Question   Answer
What did the students believe? → ??Their professor to be amazing.
What did the citizens imagine? → ??The politician to have led an honest life.

Moreover, if these infinitival clauses are NPs, we might expect them to appear in other NP positions, such as subject position. Yet they cannot appear as subjects of passive verbs in the way that "that" complement clauses can:

*[Their professor to be amazing] was believed by all the students.
*[The politician to have led an honest life] was imagined by the citizens.

These facts then suggest that we add an S option to the phrase-structure expansion for VP to include infinitives (the optional NP before the S will be explained shortly):

$$
VP \rightarrow \left\{ \begin{array}{ll} cop & \left\{ \begin{array}{l} NP \\ AP \\ PrepP \end{array} \right\} \\ V & \left\{ \begin{array}{l} (NP^2)\ (PrepP) \\ (NP)\ S \end{array} \right\} \end{array} \right\}
$$

VPs will now be able to include the option [V+S]. This type of infinitive has a peculiar characteristic: although we have argued that the infinitive has an overt subject, this "subject" has some of the characteristics of a direct object within the main clause VP. If we make the subject of the infinitive a pronoun, it will be of the object type, not the subject type, perhaps because of the preceding main verb:

The students believe [*her* to be amazing].
*The students believe [*she* to be amazing].
The citizens imagine [*him* to have led an honest life].
*The citizens imagine [*he* to have led an honest life].

For example, the sentence *The students believe **she** to be amazing* is ungrammatical. At the same time, we cannot really view the pronouns above (or the NPs for which they substitute) as true direct objects of the verbs *believe* and *imagine*, in spite of the fact that the pronouns occur in the objective case. We cannot ask the question,

Who(m) do the students believe?

and get as our answer, *Her, to be amazing*. Nor can we ask the question,

Who do the citizens imagine?

and receive the answer, *Him, to have led an honest life*. In fact, it hardly matters whether the infinitive in the second example appears in the active or the passive voice, for the meaning comes out approximately the same in either case (though the sentence becomes stylistically awkward):

The citizens imagine [honest lives to have been led by their politicians].

The fact that verbs like *believe* take complements that may have object-pronoun subjects has made the analysis of this type of infinitive difficult for linguists, but we will assume the amended PS rule as it stands.[3] The related tree structure is as follows:

The students believed their professor to be amazing.

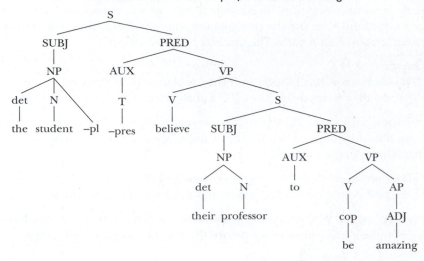

Some other mental cognition verbs of this type include *assume, find, know, perceive, prove, show, think,* and *understand*:

> The players assumed their opponents to have practiced more.
> They found the box to contain more money than they had expected.
> The geologists knew the hills to contain gold deposits.
> We perceived them to be uninterested in our proposal.

Advise-type Infinitives

There is a second similar, though not exactly structurally identical, class of verbs followed by infinitives. Consider the following sentences:

> We advised the children to play baseball outside.
> The police officer ordered my friend to move his car.

Let us assume as before that the infinitives here have no tense and that the *to* is to be analyzed as an element under AUX. In these cases, we get better results when we ask *who*-type questions:

> Question: Who(m) did we advise?
> Answer: The children. (We advised them to play outside.)

> Question: Who(m) did the police officer order?
> Answer: My friend. (He ordered him to move his car.)

In these cases, it does seem to matter whether the infinitive is presented in the active or passive; the sentences below—to the degree that they are acceptable—show no synonymy with those above:

> ?We advised baseball to be played outside (by the children).
> ?The police officer ordered my friend's car to be moved (by him).

We cannot "advise" or "order" an inanimate object to do anything.

As in the case of the first type of infinitive—the type that occurs in embedded clauses after verbs like *believe*—we can substitute an object pronoun by making use of the optional NP that appears before S in the revised VP rule on p. 635:

> We advised *them* to play baseball outside.
> The police officer ordered *him* to move his car.

However, since the main clauses here seem to have real objects (whereas the *believe-* and *expect*-clauses did not), then we must ask what the status of the rest of the infinitive is. We could analyze the remainder of the infinitive as a complement to this object, and reflect the difference in the PS rules. However, if we wish to say that all infinitives are clauses, and since we have presented all clauses in the past as bearing subjects, then we must ask what occupies the subject position of these infinitives. Following recent generative theory, we will say that there is an empty subject position whose identity is *controlled*, or determined, in this case by the object of the main clause and is identical to that object. We call this empty element PRO; it is not a lexical pronoun and does not show up on the surface. It merely signals that some NP in the main clause functions semantically as the subject of the complement clause. The tree for the sentence *We advised the children to play baseball outside* is then:

We advised the children to play baseball outside.

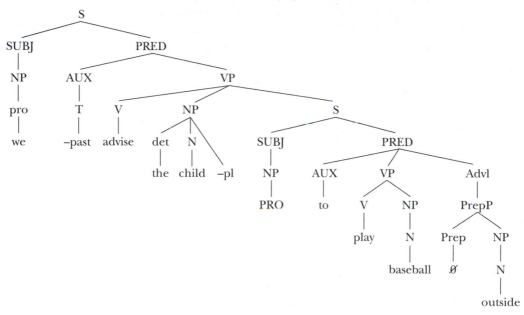

We will then have to allow this PRO element as an option for the expansion of NP in our phrase structure rules:

$$NP \rightarrow \begin{cases} \text{(det)(AP) N (-pl)(PrepP)} \\ \text{pro} \\ \text{S} \\ \text{PRO} \end{cases}$$

Other verbs that fit this infinitive pattern are manipulative verbs like *allow, cause, force, help, permit, persuade,* and *urge:*

> Our parents allowed us to stay up late.
> The wind caused the canopy to fall down.
> Bad luck forced us to leave Las Vegas early.
> I helped my sister to find the answer.

Note that the "to" AUX is optional after the verb *help*.

Attempt-type Infinitives

A third type of infinitive also involves a type of control. In this case the control comes not from the object of the main clause but instead from its subject. Two main-clause verbs that require this infinitive type are *attempt* and *tend*:

> The driver attempted to avoid the ice on the road.
> Bears tend to eat voraciously in the spring.

As before, the infinitive seems tenseless, and *to* is present; in this case, there is clearly no object at all. Infinitives following the verbs *attempt*[4] and *tend* certainly cannot be construed as direct objects:

> Question: What did the driver attempt? → Answer: ??To avoid the ice on the road.
> Question: *What do bears tend? → Answer: ??To eat voraciously in the spring.

How shall we represent this type of infinitive in a tree? In the case of the first sentence, the driver is the agent who is both "attempting" and, hopefully, "avoiding." It is not possible that the agents who *avoid* or *eat* in these sentences could be anyone other than the main-clause subjects. For example, the following make no sense at all:

> *The driver attempted her to avoid the ice on the road.
> *Bears tend chipmunks to eat voraciously in the spring.

Following the pattern of the object control infinitive type, we could say that in these cases the main-clause subject controls the identity of the missing infinitival subject, which we will again call PRO:

The driver attempted to avoid the ice on the road.

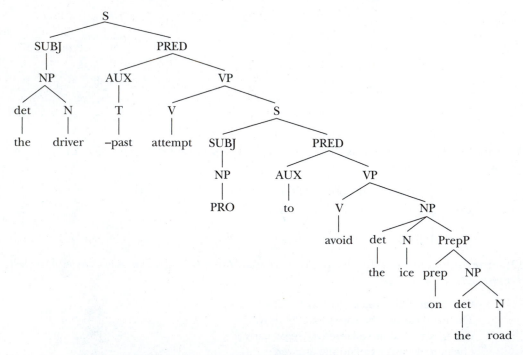

Our two recently revised PS rules expanding VP and NP will work to permit the generation of infinitives that are complements to this class of main verb; the class also includes the verbs *begin, continue, decide, fail, forget, manage, offer, proceed, promise, refuse, regret, remember, start, try,* and *vow*. Some example sentences are:

That radio station continues to play horrible music.
We proceeded to sell off most of our furniture.
She forgot to buy her books.
I promised (him) to work harder next time.
I refuse to travel any farther tonight.

They are nearly all intransitive verbs when they appear with infinitives following them; however, the verb *promise* is an exception for many speakers.[5]

Want-type Infinitives (*For/To* Infinitives)

A fourth class of main-clause verbs taking infinitive complements permits the option of either the subject or object of the main clause providing the infinitive with a logical subject. In the latter case, the object is overtly expressed, and some of the subjects of the infinitives may be introduced with *for*:

1. a. I want to refinish the furniture.
   b. I want (for) him to refinish the furniture.

2. a. She intends to clean the house.
   b. She intends (for) him to clean the house.

In the (a) sentences in each pair, it is *I* and *She* who are doing the refinishing and cleaning; in these cases, we might assign the same tree structure as we did with the subject-control verbs above like *attempt*. The (b) sentences, which optionally introduced their infinitives with *for*, are clearly somehow different; we do not seem to have a tree type that these will fit. Let us apply the same tests that we did earlier. We can attempt to ask the usual *Who/What* question that is normally associated with NP objects:

Question: What do you want? → Answer: { ?Him to refinish the furniture.
                                        { For him to refinish the furniture.

Question: What does she intend? → Answer; { ?Him to clean the house.
                                           { For him to clean the house.

Native speakers tend to find the *for*-infinitive somewhat acceptable here, suggesting that at least the *for*-infinitive may be seen as an NP object of the main-clause verb. At the same time, if we ask the *Who*-question, we come up with unfavorable results, suggesting that the pronoun *him* is not by itself the direct object of the verbs *want* and *intend*:

Question: Who(m) do you want? → Answer: ??Him (to refinish the furniture).
Question: Who(m) do you intend? → Answer: ??Him (to clean the house).

In fact, as was true with the *believe*-class of verbs, if the infinitives appear in the passive voice the sentences are equally grammatical and convey the same general idea:

I want (for) the furniture to be refinished by him.
She intends (for) the house to be cleaned by him.

This suggests that these verbs are much like *believe* when they occur without subject control. What, then, do we make of the word *for*, which is in other environments a preposition? Since it appears in much the same position as the complementizer *that* in tensed clauses, we will treat it as such, following the tradition established in generative grammar. The relevant tree structure is then as follows:

I want (for) him to refinish the furniture.

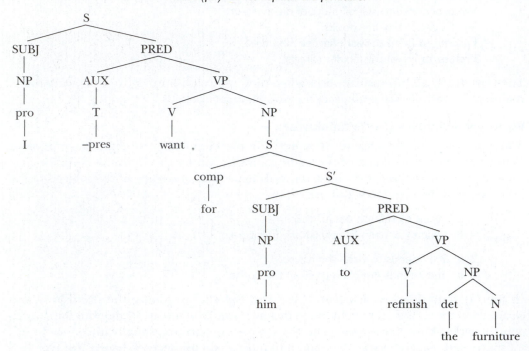

With some verbs such as *want, expect,* and *hope,* some native speakers find the *for*-phrase either overly colloquial, dialectal, or both, and simply use other means to express the same meaning; the factors that bear on this choice merit further research. Other future-oriented and affective verbs in this class which more readily occur with *for* include *arrange, desire, expect, hate, hope, intend, like, love, plan,* and *prefer;* for example,

> The travel agent arranged (for us) to take another trip.
> I would hate (for you) to be stranded in the cabin this winter.
> The doctor would like (for me) to try some new pills.
> I would love (for you) to visit Paris next year.
> The tour leaders plan (for us) to visit more museums.

The subject of the infinitive will, of course, vary depending on the presence or absence of the *for*-complementizer. When the *for* is present, the following NP represents the subject of the infinitive; when there is no *for*-phrase, the subject of the main clause represents the subject of the infinitive, which is represented as PRO in the tree.

Let-type (Bare-Stem) Infinitives

There is one more important class of infinitive that must be distinguished, although the main-clause verbs with which it occurs are quite limited. This type is often called the *bare-stem* infinitive, where the usual *to* is either optionally or obligatorily absent:

> The teacher let the students go home early.
> We saw our friend leave the station.

Applying the usual test to determine whether bare-stem infinitives are objects of the main-clause verb, we get unacceptable results:

> Question: *What did the teacher let? → Answer: *The students go home early.
> Question: What did you see? → Answer: *Our friend leave the station.

Applying the test to see if the NPs *the students* and *our friend* are direct objects of the main-clause verb, we again get odd results:

> *Who(m) did the teacher let? → Answer: *The students (go home early).
> Who(m) did you see? → Answer: ?Our friend (leave the station).

As with infinitives that follow instances of verbs of the *let/see* class, we cannot say that bare-stem infinitives are NP objects; we will assume that they are simply clausal complements to the main-clause verb. Since they include no expressed *to*, the AUX position will show the tenseless [-imper], as it does in the case of subjunctive complements. The tree structure for such sentences will be like the following:

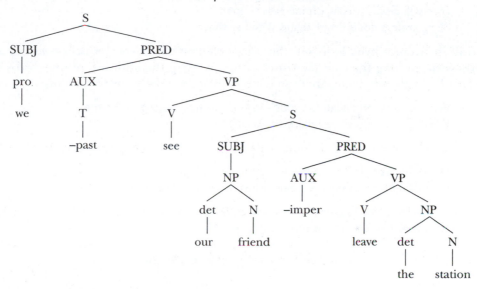

We saw our friend leave the station.

Other verbs in this class include *feel, have, hear, help,*[6] *make, observe,* and *watch*:

> We felt the door close behind us.
> The teacher had us repeat the exercise.
> They heard the bell ring twice.
> Please help us move our furniture.

GERUND COMPLEMENTS

While *that*-clauses and infinitives cover a large range of verbal complements in English, there is an additional type of complement, sometimes called the *-ing* complement or *gerund*, which must also be discussed. Consider, then, an additional pair of sentences:

> Fred disliked [making phone calls to John].
> Mary preferred [doing other things with her time].

The bracketed parts of the two sentences have some of the earmarks of other clauses we have seen—specifically, subject-control infinitives like those that follow the verb *attempt*. We seem to have a verb-object order of elements, with the logical subject of the bracketed material being the same as the subject of the whole sentence:

> [(Fred) making phone calls to John] → Fred made phone calls to John.
> [(Mary) doing other things with her time] → Mary did other things with her time.

So it appears that the missing subject in these clauses is like the PRO-type subject for some infinitives. Also, we seem to have an auxiliary element in the inflection *-ing*; though it is not the *-ing* of the progressive, it is an affix that attaches itself to a verb stem. It is possible in fact to have both perfect and progressive forms in sequences like those above:

> having made phone calls to John
> having been making phone calls to John

However, there are differences between these sequences and normal clauses, just as there were with infinitives. As with infinitives, there does not seem to be any tense present. If we change the tense of *dislike* and *prefer* in the sentences above, the complement does not change at all:

> Fred will dislike making phone calls to John.
> Mary prefers doing other things with her time.

In contrast to infinitives, however, the verbal elements in the sequences—*making* and *doing*—seem to have the characteristics of nouns. With the addition of *-ing*, verbs can regularly be made into nouns that can serve as subjects and objects of sentences:

> What is most enjoyable for you? → Hiking is most enjoyable for me.
> What do you enjoy? → I enjoy swimming.

The "*what*-ness" of these verbal nouns, called *gerunds*, extends to gerund clauses as well:

> What did Fred dislike? → Making phone calls to John.
> What did Mary prefer? → Doing other things with her time.

We conclude that these gerund clauses are NP objects which happen also to have the status of a clausal (S). The relevant tree structure is

Fred disliked making phone calls to John.

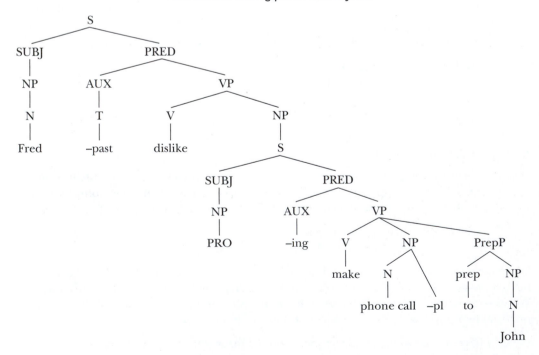

It is also possible to have a gerund phrase that has something that looks like an expressed subject, one different from the logical PRO subject exemplified in the sentences above. We can also have sentences like these:

Fred disliked [Susan's making phone calls to John].
Mary prefers [his doing other things with his time].

In each pair, we have what looks like an [NP + possessive morpheme or a possessive determiner] before the gerund noun. In both cases, it looks as if we have the basic structure of clauses with subjects. Thus the tree representation above must be amended to accommodate such cases by replacing the PRO in the subject position with *Susan* or *he* and positing a possessive *'s* morpheme as a third type of complementizer. In this case the complementizer combines with the embedded subject during the mapping rules to yield the surface possessive form.

Other verbs that take gerund complements include *admit, appreciate, avoid, begin, continue, defend, deny, enjoy, feel, finish, forget, hate, hear, like, love, prefer, quit, recall, regret, remember, resume, risk, see, smell, start, stop,* and *try.* Some occur only with PRO-NP subjects (e.g., *begin, continue*), some require NP subjects—preceded by *'s* complementizers that may be different from the subject of the whole sentence (e.g., *appreciate, see*), and some may occur either way (e.g., *enjoy, remember*).

Fred disliked Susan's making phone calls to John.

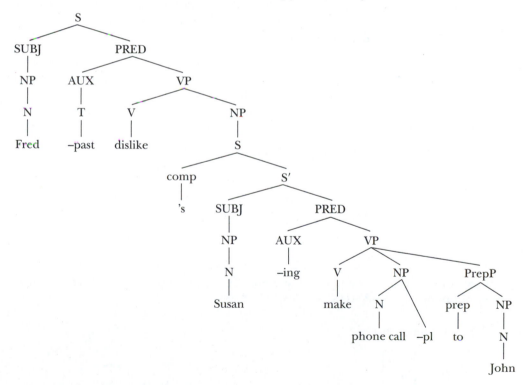

Just as the *that* complementizer was optional in informal speech, so is the *'s* complementizer that accompanies subjects of gerunds for some speakers (but see following page):

Fred disliked Susan making phone calls to John.

THE SUBJECT-PARTICIPLE COMPLEMENT

There is one additional complement type in which -ing appears, one which is superficially similar to the possessive gerund complement but which has an NP or object pronoun in place of the possessive form. These may be statistically more frequent than the possessive gerund; while some of the following sentences (the first three) can be viewed as colloquial simplifications of the possessive gerund construction, others (the last three) cannot; so we once again have a new structure here, i.e., the subject-participle complement:

> Fred disliked [Susan making phone calls to John].
> Mary prefers [him doing other things with his time].
> I didn't like [him coming in here like that].
> He doesn't want [his employees sitting around with nothing to do].
> I watched [the ice melting in the sun].
> The teacher had [the students drawing trees] yesterday.

Once again, we have what looks like the general structure of a clause without a tense. In this case, it seems we have a stable element to place in subject position, and it is plausible to say that the entire bracketed clause functions as a unit as a noun object, much as free relative clauses were viewed in Chapter 29 to function as nouns in subject and object positions. Often this type of clause is found as the object of the preposition *with*:

> With [Susan making phone calls to John], Fred was miserable.
> With [the employees sitting around with nothing to do], the firm won't survive.
> With [the ice melting in the sun], there won't be any cold drinks left.
> With [the students drawing trees], the kindergarten teacher could relax.

We may draw the tree representation for this type of construction in a way similar to the first one for gerunds, (page 642), except that no PRO is required, since an overtly expressed subject is present to fill the same position.

Other verbs taking this sort of complement include *discover, feel, hate, have, hear, like, love, observe, prefer, recall, remember, see,* and *watch*. For example,

> The authorities discovered the dog hiding behind the bushes.
> We could feel the weather turning cold.
> The tour leaders had us visiting museums day and night.
> We observed the doves making their nest.
> I remember John telling me the same story last year.

SUMMARY

In this part of the chapter, we have revised our set of phrase-structure rules by adding a number of options to S, NP, AUX, and VP as follows:

1. $S \rightarrow (\text{comp}) \ (\text{sm}) \ S'$

2. $\text{comp} \rightarrow \begin{Bmatrix} that \\ for \\ 's \end{Bmatrix}$

3. $NP \rightarrow \begin{Bmatrix} (\text{det}) (\text{AP}) \ N \ (\text{-pl}) (\text{PrepP}) \\ \text{pro} \\ S \\ PRO \end{Bmatrix}$

4. $\text{AUX} \rightarrow \left\{ \left\{ \begin{matrix} \text{T} \\ \text{M} \\ to \\ \text{-}ing \\ \text{-imper} \end{matrix} \right\} (\text{perf})\,(\text{prog})\,(\text{pass}) \right\}$

5. $\text{VP} \rightarrow \left\{ \begin{matrix} \text{cop} \left\{ \begin{matrix} \text{NP} \\ \text{AP} \\ \text{PrepP} \end{matrix} \right\} \\ \\ \text{V} \left\{ \begin{matrix} (\text{NP}^2)\ (\text{PrepP}) \\ (\text{NP})\text{S} \end{matrix} \right\} \end{matrix} \right\}$

These revisions allow us to generate all the *that*-clauses, infinitives, gerunds, and subject-participle constructions that we have discussed in this chapter.

THREADS OF COMMON MEANING WITHIN COMPLEMENT TYPES

As the presentation above clearly shows, there are many clausal complementation options for English verbs. This situation is the source of numerous ESL/EFL errors. The most common source of error is that while students have learned the various forms of complements, they often couple the wrong complement with the wrong main verb. They do this for understandable reasons: a student who generalizes by using some kind of meaning-analogy may find the errors on the right below somewhat puzzling given the grammatically similar models on the left:

> The general commanded him to leave. → *My father demanded me to study harder.
> I like to study history. → *I dislike to study math.
> My sister advised me to go abroad. → *My friend recommended me to stay home.
> The teacher let us go home early. → *Our parents allowed us stay up late.

A frequency count in written text by Butoyi (1977) showed that there is considerable variation in the actual occurrence of the various types of complement, with *that*-type complement clauses constituting 46 percent of the total, subject-control infinitives (*I want to leave, I tried to leave*) constituting another 45 percent, with other complement types distributed among the remaining 9 percent. Interestingly, while structures akin to *that*-clauses and infinitives are frequent in the world's languages, gerund phrases are far less common. All else being equal, we might expect ESL/EFL learners to experience the greatest difficulty with gerund complement use. Indeed, further research by Butoyi (1978) and a study by Anderson (1976) both indicate that this is true for speakers of a variety of languages acquiring English.

Much does seem idiosyncratic about the [verb + complement] combinations, and it would be false to claim that no arbitrariness exists in student mastery in this area of grammar. However, there is also fortunately some regularity within this seemingly complex array of possibilities, and to a certain extent teachers can exploit these regularities pedagogically.

SEMANTIC SIMILARITIES OF VERBS TAKING *THAT*-COMPLEMENTS AND INFINITIVE CLAUSES

Up to now, we have said that certain verbs take a certain type of complement exclusively, while some verbs may occur with more than one. We have said little about whether any sense can be made of the fact that *claim* takes a tensed *that*-complement, *insist* a subjunctive complement, *believe* either a *that*-complement or an infinitival one, *try* either an infinitival or a gerund complement, and *make* a bare infinitive. In fact, a loose correlation does seem to exist between the semantics of the main-clause verb and the type of complement it takes. The correlation has been sketched by Givón (1980; 1990, Chapter 13).

Verbs Taking *That*-Complements

The main verbs that take ordinary tensed *that*-complements tend mostly to denote mental states or attitudes regarding the truth of the proposition in the complement clause. Thus, to say

$$
I \left\{ \begin{array}{l} \text{think} \\ \text{assume} \\ \text{imagine} \\ \text{know} \\ \text{understand} \\ \text{say} \end{array} \right\} \text{that it will rain today.}
$$

is to say something about the nature of the particular belief—its relative strength, among other things (a topic which we will return to in the next chapter). Givón places such verbs in the "cognition-utterance" category and says that a clause in which such a verb occurs is (1) more "loosely" connected syntactically with the complement clause, and (2) not necessarily well integrated semantically with the complement clause. The first quality means, for instance, that it is easy to detach a *that*-complement from its main clause, omit the complementizer, and be left with a perfectly well-formed sentence; the second quality means that it is not at all necessary for the subject of the complement clause to be identical to any noun in the main clause.

Verbs Taking Infinitive Complements

We may contrast cognition-utterance verbs with those which Givón calls more *manipulative*; typically, these verbs take infinitival complements. "Manipulative" here means, in effect, that an agent named in the main clause is in some way related to, or has some interest in, the real or hypothetical occurrence of the event that is depicted in the complement clause. Thus, in the sentences, *Mary wanted John to return sooner* or *The teacher allowed the students to leave*, Mary and the teacher have an interest in John's returning or the students' leaving. In accordance with Givón's criteria, such infinitives tend to be more integrated syntactically with their main clauses in that an infinitive cannot stand by itself as a sentence; it is "more dependent" syntactically on its main clause. The main clause and infinitive are also much more likely to share an NP referent in common—as with the PRO category, where the identity of the logical subject of the infinitive (*Mary wanted [PRO] to go*) is controlled by an NP in the main clause. In the case of bare-stem infinitives (*Mary made John stay, John had the thief arrested*), there is even more integration since there is no *to* present and since a stronger sort of control or involvement is depicted: indeed, verbs like *let, make,* and *have* together with their complements are often called *causative* verbs or constructions since one agent is (to one degree or another) "causing" another to act.

Givón's correlations are very rough—there are many exceptional cases—and may have limited pedagogical value for language teachers who seek to present the English complement options systematically to their students. However, Givón's description is of some value to teachers who wish to understand why English complement options pattern as they do. For a few cases, the schema does make predictions in cases where options exist in use, and here ESL/EFL learners might benefit from explanation. Consider the following two sentences:

She helped them to pick cherries.
She helped them pick cherries.

In the first case, the woman mentioned may have provided a ladder to the cherry-pickers, while in the second case we are more likely led to believe that she was actually picking the fruit together with the others. Her greater involvement is reflected in the use of a bare-stem infinitive. It thus makes sense that a corpus study like that of Lind (1983) would find bare-stem infinitives appearing six times more frequently with animate subjects than inanimate when compared with *to*-infinitives.[7]

THE MEANING OF SUBJUNCTIVE VERBS

As pointed out in Chapter 2, the subjunctive is one of the five moods of English—one of the five sentence types that systematically exhibit the speaker/writer's attitude toward the proposition expressed in a sentence. Just as the interrogative involves the questioning of a proposition and the imperative marks a command, so the subjunctive exhibits the speaker/writer's orientation toward bringing a certain state of affairs into being. Verbs that take subjunctive *that*-clauses are highly manipulative in a semantic sense, if not in Givón's syntactic sense. We have said that subjunctive clauses occur with a relatively restricted set of verbs, which include *advise, ask, demand, insist, recommend, request,* and *urge,* and argued that subjunctives have no tense forms. These forms will be particularly difficult for ESL/EFL students since they have most likely been told that every clause in English contains a tense, most often a tense which is overtly marked in some distinguishing way. Yet the verbs that take subjunctive complements fit a special frame in which an agent, expressed or implied, in the main clause attempts to exert some control over the occurrence of the event in the embedded clause, usually through the action of a different agent that is the subject of the subjunctive clause. The verbs may express "weak" control (*suggest, recommend*), "strong" control suggesting the existence of one individual's authority over the other (*insist, demand, require*), or control of an in-between sort (*ask, request*).[8] Thus, we get:

> We suggest that you stay one more day.
> The committee recommended that the plan be reconsidered.
> The college requires that freshmen live in dormitories.
> We ask that you not smoke near this building.
> He requested that they give him an extra week to finish the project.

Verbs that simply express a *desire* for some event to occur—that is, without any evidence of influence or control at all—tend not to take subjunctive complements. Thus we get no subjunctive complement with *hope*:

> *She hoped that her husband get a better job.

The relevant semantic characteristic shows up also in the fact that the subjunctive is used in dependent clauses following certain main-clause adjectives like *important, imperative,* and *vital* but not following other adjectives such as *understandable* in main clauses:

> It is important that she *be* given another chance.
> It was imperative that we *act* immediately.
> What is vital is that we not *become* overly anxious.
> *It is understandable that she *be* given another chance.

Subjunctive clauses do not seem to fit Givón's strength-of-bond scale perfectly in that while there seems to be strong manipulation, the syntax is almost as "loose" as with cognition-utterance verbs like *believe* except that the verbs are tenseless. However, sentences in which subjunctives occur exhibit a common semantic theme.

THE MEANING OF VERBS TAKING GERUNDS

Verbs that require gerunds such as *enjoy, risk, deny, avoid, appreciate, defend, quit,* and *stop,* among others, encode actions in the gerund complement that are vivid, real, ongoing in the present or completed in the past. They represent the success of the subject of the main verb—or the gerund—in accomplishing some outcome, which may be positive or negative:

> Bob enjoys going to the movies.
> > (= Bob succeeds in going to movies.)
>
> Sue avoided talking to Barry.
> > (= Sue succeeded in not talking to Barry.)

This is very different from those main verbs taking infinitives which encode future unfulfilled projections rather than past or present accomplishments in the complement.

> Mary wanted to see the play.
> > (≠ Mary saw the play.)

We discuss this distinction further in the next section.

INFINITIVE *TO*-COMPLEMENTS VERSUS GERUND *-ING* COMPLEMENTS

There is considerable overlap across the class of verbs that permit subject-control infinitive complements and those that permit gerund *-ing* complements. The overlap is illustrated in the italicized forms in the lists below:

> **Verbs taking infinitives:** *begin,* choose, *continue,* dare, expect, fail, *forget, hate,* hope, intend, *like, love,* manage, *prefer,* proceed, promise, refuse, *regret, remember, start,* tend, *try,* want, vow
>
> **Verbs taking gerund** *-ing:* admit, appreciate, avoid, *begin, continue,* defend, deny, dislike, enjoy, finish, *forget, hate,* intend, *like, love, prefer,* quit, recall, *regret, remember,* resume, risk, *start,* stop, *try*

In many of the cases of overlap, there is a distinct meaning difference implied, one which is worth focusing on here and pointing out to learners. In some cases, the difference is substantial. Consider the options with *forget*:

> He forgot to buy the books.
> He forgot buying the books.

In the case where the infinitive is chosen, no books were bought (because of forgetfulness), while the action described in the second sentence above actually happened (but was subsequently forgotten). Likewise with *remember*:

> She remembered to do her homework.
> She remembered doing her homework.

In the first case, the meaning may be paraphrased by saying "She did not forget that she had to do her homework, so she did it," while in the second, the intention is to say, "She did her homework, and then later she remembered that she had done it."

Some degree of correlation exists between the choice of infinitives with events that are "hypothetical, future, unfulfilled" and the choice of gerunds with events that are "real, vivid, fulfilled," a fact that was first pointed out by Bolinger (1968). In the case of "forgetting" above, this principle is substantiated. It is also supported in the case of the verb *try*. Compare the two sentences below:

> Peter tried to go to Oxford.
> Peter tried going to Oxford.

In the first instance, native speakers tend to interpret the sentence to mean that Peter wanted to go to Oxford but did not in fact attend the school; in the second, the preferred interpretation is that Peter did go to Oxford but did not complete his studies. Compare the additional two sentences below:

> I tried to call you, but there was no phone anywhere.
> I tried calling you, but your line was busy.

In the first instance, no calling took place; in the second, at least one (unsuccessful) call was made.

It is also worthwhile to look at how Bolinger's principle holds up with the extremely frequent verb *like*. When someone expresses a desire to do something that he/she has not done before, it is common to use the modal construction *would like* and follow it with an infinitive. A gerund is much less acceptable:

> I would like to go bungee-jumping someday.
> ?I would like going bungee-jumping someday.

On the other hand, if someone has already done bungee-jumping and wishes to express an affection for that activity, the gerund form is strongly preferred:

> I like going bungee-jumping. (I just did it last week, in fact.)

While the Bolinger principle does not yield such clear distinctions for all of the overlapping pairs in the lists above, it does provide teachers with a partial explanation for students who want to understand the meaning differences with verbs taking both types of complements.

ASPECTUAL OPTIONS IN INFINITIVES AND GERUNDS

We have argued that infinitives have no tense markings and therefore do not by themselves express past versus nonpast time. However, infinitives do express aspectual relationships of the sort discussed in Chapters 7 and 9. These include the full range of aspectual categories with the exception that the distinction between habitual (i.e., durative) and punctual (i.e., "one time") is lost in the simple form of the verb, as in the case of *drink* below:

> I want to drink espresso (regularly).
> I want to drink espresso (tonight).

The sense of a specific ongoing activity is expressible with the progressive form:

> I would prefer to be drinking espresso (right now).
> She expected to be doing homework during the time that her roommate was out.

The sense of the completion of one event prior to the occurrence of another may be expressed with the perfect form:

> I would prefer not to have drunk so much espresso this evening.

In the above case, the "drinking" occurs prior to the "preferring." Progressive and perfect may be combined, just as they may in ordinary main clauses:

> I'm surprised to have been making so much progress these days.

In this case, the ongoing condition, the "making of much progress," is (at least to some extent) temporally prior to the "surprise."

For main verbs that express attitudinal states, the sense of future-in-past is conveyed with a main verb in the past tense plus a simple infinitive:

> She wanted to go to Europe the following year.
> We didn't expect the weather to change soon.

Where contrary-to-fact conditions exist (see Chapter 27), there are two options available. One can encode the counterfactuality either in the main verb through a perfect modal or in the infinitive through use of a perfect infinitive:

> She would have liked to visit Munich on her trip.
> She would like to have visited Munich on her trip.

An exacting attention to tense and aspect here may lead to two different interpretations— the first in which the "liking" expressed by the person in question existed *prior to* the moment of speaking and may not exist *at* that moment, and the second in which the "liking" does exist at the moment of speaking. However, the two forms seem interchangeable, at least in oral production. To add to the profusion of options, one frequently finds the same meaning conveyed in colloquial speech through the use of a doubly-marked perfect, though this use is frowned on by prescriptive grammarians:

> She would have liked to have visited Munich on her trip.

The meaning normally intended in such cases is not one in which one past event or state (the "visiting") is set temporally prior to another past event or state (the "liking"), although again that meaning may be conveyed when the forms are emphatically stressed.

Gerund forms are likewise not marked for tense, but they too may express aspectual distinctions. When a simple gerund is used, the distinction between perfective, habitual, and progressive may be lost:[9]

> She remembered drinking espresso (that night).
> She remembered drinking espresso (during her three years in Italy).
> She remembered drinking espresso (while the music was playing).

Where the gerund is in the perfect form, however, one may distinguish the progressive from the perfect through the presence or absence respectively of *-ing* on the verb in the complement:

> She remembers having been listening to a Grieg concerto (all evening).[10]
> She remembers having listened to a Grieg concerto (at least once in her life).

Once again, actual use may blur the distinction here, just as the distinction between *I have lived here for ten years* and *I have been living here for ten years* lies more in what is implied than what is necessarily expressed by the forms themselves.

It may be said with certainty that if tense and aspect in English is difficult for ESL/EFL students to master in simple clauses, the juxtaposition of tense and aspect in multi-clausal sentences is even more difficult to accomplish in a nativelike way. As we have seen, even native speakers exhibit considerable variation in their own production in this area and are often seen almost struggling to express intended tense-aspect relationships, often rephrasing something that has already been said to make a relationship more precise. We therefore do not recommend close attention to these relationships in multi-clausal sentences until learners of English are well advanced.

ORDINARY INFINITIVES VERSUS PURPOSE INFINITIVES

In our discussion of infinitive types, we omitted mention of one additional type of infinitive. This type is distinct in not being regularly associated with any main-clause verb and hence is not a true complement infinitive; it is called the *purpose infinitive*, illustrated in the following sentences:

> They covered the porch to shield out the sun.
> This drill bit is used to drill holes in metal.

It is easy to distinguish purpose infinitives from other infinitives by attempting to substitute *in order to* (or *so as to*) for *to*. You may also try to move the infinitive to first position in the sentence and see if an acceptable sentence results:

> We used a wrench to fix the sink. → To fix the sink, we used a wrench.
> We hope to take our vacation soon. → *To take our vacation soon, we hope.

Purpose infinitives, which are adverbial, may be moved, while ordinary infinitives may not.

Easily one of the most confusing alternations for learners concerns the verb *stop*, which takes a gerund complement in one context but often appears with a purpose infinitive following. Note the difference in meaning below:

> a. The man should stop drinking. (His drinking should cease.)
>
> b. The man should stop to drink. (He should stop $\begin{Bmatrix} \text{walking} \\ \text{driving} \\ \text{etc.} \end{Bmatrix}$ to drink some water.)

We have said that gerund-type complements are not well represented in the world's languages while infinitives are common. This fact undoubtedly contributes to the frequency of errors where the (b) sentence pattern above is substituted for the (a) pattern. Teachers should expect frequent errors of this type and perhaps address the issue directly during class time.

THE BARE INFINITIVE VERSUS THE SUBJECT-PARTICIPLE COMPLEMENT

There is considerable overlap in the class of verbs that take bare-infinitive complements and those that take subject-participle complements. The overlap is illustrated in the italicized forms below:

> **Verbs taking bare infinitives:** *feel, have, hear,* help, let, make, *see, watch*
>
> **Verbs taking subject + participle:** dislike, enjoy, *feel,* hate, *have, hear,* like, love, observe, prefer, recall, remember, *see,* want, *watch*

It may be noticed that most of the overlap concerns sensory perception verbs. One view (advanced by Kirsner and Thompson 1976) of the crucial difference between pairs like

> I saw him break the branch.
> I saw him breaking the branch.
>
> They heard the door close.
> They heard the door closing.
>
> They watched the boat disappear over the horizon.
> They watched the boat disappearing over the horizon.

reflects a difference between perfective and imperfective aspect: the simple form marks an event seen as punctual, limited and bounded or perfective; in contrast, the *-ing* form marks an imperfective event which is represented as durative, ongoing, or iterative, seen without focus on its beginning or end. This account explains why a main verb in the simple present tense may occur with an *-ing* form but not a bare infinitive:

> Look! I see him leaving the building.
> *Look! I see him leave the building.

Since the simple present is not used to mark discrete, punctual events (but instead states or ongoing or repeated actions), it makes sense that it would not take a bare infinitive incompatible by nature with this viewpoint. The account also explains why a perception verb like *observe* can appear with a [subject + participle] complement but not a bare-infinitive complement even in the simple past tense: part of the inherent meaning of "observing" involves the visual perception of something over an extended period of time without focus on the event as a completed whole; one "observes" an action in progress. We can "observe" the painting of a picture as it progresses, but we would not normally speak of "observing" a sudden, momentary event such as the switching on of a light. Thus we are likely to hear sentences like:

> We observed them eating dinner at Spago.

but are unlikely to hear ones like:

> ?We observed them sit down.

Likewise, the capacity for independent action on the part of the subject was also noted by Kirsner and Thompson to account for pairs such as these:

> I saw the sunglasses $\left\{ \begin{array}{l} \text{lying} \\ \text{*lie} \end{array} \right\}$ by the side of the road.

Since "sunglasses" cannot act independently, the bare infinitive is not possible.

  We can also extend Kirsner and Thompson's proposal to a nonperception verb, the causative verb *have*:

> The boss had me turn off the light (a moment ago).
> ?The boss had me turning off the light (a moment ago).
> The boss had me turning off the light (as part of my daily routine).

The second sentence, in order to be fully acceptable, would have to mean that the speaker's task—in itself a momentary, punctual event—was repeated over an unspecified period of time, as in the more normal-sounding third sentence.

GERUND COMPLEMENTS VERSUS SUBJECT-PARTICIPLE COMPLEMENTS

For some speakers of English there is a semantic contrast for verbs taking both the possessive gerund complement and the subject-participle construction:

> I appreciate his taking care of the dog.
> I appreciate him taking care of the dog.

Such speakers report a greater focus on the entire event in the possessive gerund complement and a greater focus on the agent NP in the subject-participle construction.

CAUSATIVE CONSTRUCTIONS

We have already spoken of *causative* constructions as those that depict one agent success-fully causing another agent to perform an action. Some verbs which enter into these constructions (*cause, force, get*) fall syntactically into the object-control category; others (*make, have*) take bare infinitive complements. How do they differ in meaning? Here we will address *have, get,* and *make,* drawing on the work of Martin (1981).

Have. The verb *have* suggests a routine hiring or selecting in which a relation of authority is implied, as between customer-businessperson or creditor-debtor:

> We had Ray mow the lawn. (He does it every week.)
> I had the barber trim my hair. (It is his profession.)
> Fred had John give him five dollars. (It was part of a debt that John owed Fred.)
> ?He had a stranger on the street give him directions.

The questioned example above is inappropriate since it suggests a relation of authority which does not exist between two strangers in a chance meeting. The action performed must also relate to the specific *area* of authority.

Get. The verb *get* often tends to convey the sense that some difficulty was involved; perhaps the subject of the main clause used persuasion or coercion on the subject of the embedded clause:

> I got Ray to give me five dollars. (He had refused earlier.)

Make. The verb *make* suggests that the subject of the main clause has coercive *power* (though not necessarily *authority* in any conventional sense) over the subject of the infinitive:

> He made a stranger on the street give him five dollars. (Threat was involved.)

Have and *get,* but not *make,* may also take passive complements in which these meanings carry over well:

> I finally had the lawn mowed.
> I finally got the lawn mowed.
> *I finally made the lawn mowed.

However, the *get*-sentence is now ambiguous as to whether the lawn was mowed by the speaker or by someone else.

Martin (1981), in a discourse analysis of causatives, provides support for the distinc-tions made above. In one of his native-speaker survey questionnaire items, 20 out of 23 respondents chose *get* when it was clear that some difficulty was involved:

> I had a lot of trouble finding someone to do it, but I finally
> (a) had the lawn mowed. (= 3)   (b) got the lawn mowed. (= 20)

On the other hand, he also found native speakers favoring *get* for some fairly routine activ-ities such as "cashing a check," which may have involved some unexpected difficulties. (I finally got the check cashed.)

THE USE OF COMPLEMENTS

THE PRESENCE VERSUS ABSENCE OF *THAT*

A question that ESL/EFL teachers will hear asked over and over again by students concerns the environments in which an expressed *that* is or is not required in object *that*-complement clauses.[11] The answer seems to be statable partially in syntactic terms and partially in terms of discourse conditions. Bolinger (1972) suggests that one determining factor is the relative formality of discourse: the more formal the register, the more likely it is for *that* to be expressed. Another factor concerns specific verbs: the greater the relative frequency of the main verb in discourse, the more likely it is that the complementizer will be absent:

1. He said he wasn't interested.
2. He conceded he wasn't interested.
3. ?He snarled he wasn't interested.

A third factor is that the presence of intervening material between the verb and the complement tends to increase the likelihood that *that* will be present:

He said he wasn't interested.
He said in a recent report he wasn't interested.
?He said in a report released yesterday by UPI he wasn't interested.

In the second and third case above, occurrence of *that* would resolve any possible processing problem. A fourth factor mentioned by Bolinger concerns whether the verb in the main clause "operates" on the verb in the complement clause in a causative sense:

The court decided that wiretapping must stop.
I decided I was too old.

In the first sentence, the court's power to stop the wiretapping makes the use of *that* more likely than in the second case, where no power over events or conditions is apparent.

Underhill (1986) suggests several other interesting factors, including relative degree of elaborate "speaker endorsement" of the truth value of the complement clause. The idea is that the greater the degree of speaker endorsement, the more likely that the complementizer will be absent. This may partially contribute to why *that* is so often absent where the main clause begins with *I think*, as in *I think I want to go home*: speakers are presumably most certain about their own mental states.

According to recent corpus-based research (Biber 1998), the deletion of the complementizer *that* does indeed appear to be sensitive to register differences. For example, *that* is omitted most frequently in conversation and least frequently in academic prose, with fiction and news reportage falling between the two extremes.

USE OF *THAT* COMPLEMENTS

Biber (1998) also provides information on the frequency of *that* complements according to register: they are most frequent in conversation, next most frequent in fiction, then news reportage, and least frequent in academic writing. He also reports that the most common verbs controlling *that* complements in both conversation and news reports are *think, say, know, see, believe, show, find,* and *feel*. These are verbs of cognition, perception, and speech often related to the speaker's or writer's stance. Such corpus-based information can be of great use to language teachers for it indicates the verbs to emphasize when introducing *that* complements.

CONCLUSION

In this chapter, we have presented what we believe to be fairly uncontroversial analyses of most of the English clausal complement types. In the following two chapters, we will carry the discussion further. It should be clear by now that much of what is required of a learner in mastering complementation is similar to what is involved in learning noun gender in most Indo-European languages or noun classes in Chinese or Bantu languages: a certain amount of feel for the logic of semantic regularities, and a certain amount of simple memorization. It would be unrealistic for an ESL/EFL teacher to expect students to master all of the verb-complement pairs that exist in English in the course of a term, but with systematic teacher attention, students can be brought to the point where they are conscious of the many options before them.

TEACHING SUGGESTIONS

1. Form. Students who wish to learn the information in this chapter simply through a form of rote memorization should be advised that the most effective way to do this is probably *not* to make lists of which verbs take which complements and then to memorize the lists. Rather, a more effective self-drill method would be for students to make up their own [verb + complement] sentences on a verb-class-by-verb-class basis and—after verifying the grammaticality and idiomaticity of these sentences—to reread or, better, recite their sentences orally at home, attending to their meaning. By making the relevant association of verb with complement type in this way, students will at least approach something resembling actual language in use.

2. Form. At lower class levels, and for review at higher class levels, a useful teaching technique that will cue students to proper forms and give them practice in using verbs meaningfully is for the teacher to model questions that incorporate the complement type in the question itself, and then for the students to practice these forms with verb + verb forms written on the board. What follows is an outline of four lesson plans in the spirit of suggestions made by Rosenzweig (1973).

Lesson 1. *Attempt*-type infinitives (*attempt, tend, fail, proceed, manage, refuse, promise, offer, decide*)

The teacher asks questions that elicit model sentences that can be put on the board:

> What will you attempt to do this weekend?
> Where have you decided to go on your vacation next year?

The teacher then leads a drill in which students generate sentences based on pairs of verbs provided by the teacher, such as *refuse/accept:*

> *Student:* I refuse to accept your offer.

Students can then work in small groups with pairings such as *manage/finish, fail/do, offer/help, refuse/eat,* and so on.

Lesson 2. *Want*-type infinitives (*want, intend, expect, prefer, hate, like, love, hope, desire, love*)

The *want*-class of verbs, which may or may not have objects, make a good focus for students interviewing other students. Most of these verbs give students ample opportunity to express their feelings on topics which concern them directly. The teacher may begin with:

> What do you hate/love most to do?
> What do you hate/love most for someone else to do?

A drill follows based on pairs provided, such as *intend/study:*

> *Teacher:* What do you intend to study?
> *Student:* I intend to study engineering.
> *Teacher:* What does your family intend (for) you to study?
> *Student:* My family intends (for) me to study engineering, too.

Student-to-student questioning follows with additional pairs: *prefer/eat, hope/spend the coming vacation,* and so on, adding direct object forms where reasonable, as above.

Lesson 3. *Verbs taking only gerund objects (stop, quit, recall, dislike, enjoy, avoid, admit, deny, defend)*

The lesson continues to follow essentially the same pattern as above.

Lesson 4. *Verbs taking both gerunds and infinitives (forget, remember, try, like, start, begin, continue, love)*

At this stage, the teacher may find it useful to present Bolinger's principle distinguishing gerunds from infinitives, supplying verbs where the distinction is most clearly exhibited:

Teacher: What do you remember doing yesterday?
What did you remember to do yesterday?

With each student answer, the teacher should make sure to confirm that the student intended to convey that he or she actually did or did not do the activity mentioned.

The lesson then continues to follow the same pattern as above but with student questioners cued to elicit alternating pairs, such as *forget* + gerund, *forget* + infinitive, *would like* + infinitive, *like* + gerund or infinitive, and so on.

Lesson 5. *Encourage integration and transfer of rules learned in the preceding lessons.*

At this point, teachers may mix different types of [verb + complement] pairs and either continue an activity like the above or have students write compositions or carry out role-plays in which various [verb-verb] pairs suggested by the teacher are used.

3. Meaning. For verbs that take both infinitives and gerunds—but with a difference in meaning—Bill Gaskill has suggested that explicit time sequences be used to teach the differences between infinitives and gerunds with main verbs such as *remember* and *forget.* The teacher introduces these verbs along with a number of situations that can appropriately serve as complements:

call my parents   lock the door
tell you the news   smoke cigars

Then the notion of time sequence is introduced and an example provided to show that if the action in the main verb *precedes* the action in the complement, the infinitive is used:

This happened earlier   This happened later
I remembered   I called my parents
(main clause)   (complement clause)

→ I remembered to call my parents.

The teacher must also show the reverse. That is, if the action in the main clause *follows* the action in the complement, the gerund is used:

This happened earlier   This happened later
I called my parents.   I remembered.
(complement)   (main clause)

→ I remembered calling my parents.

Students can then generalize this activity to the verb *forget*.

4. Meaning. The distinction in use between verbs that alternate between taking bare infinitives and [subject + participle] complements (*see, hear, watch, feel, have*) can be modeled to some extent in the classroom by the teacher or by other students. Someone can close the door slowly and incompletely while asking,

What do you see? (Answer: "I see you closing the door.")

Someone can then close the door quickly and completely and ask,

What did you see? (Answer: "I saw you close the door.")

Teachers can use their imaginations in coming up with ideas for other verbs. This sort of activity can, incidentally, be done in conjunction with a review contrasting the simple present/present progressive and simple past/past progressive in main clauses (*What am I doing? What did I do? What was I doing?* and so on).

5. Meaning/Use. A good role-play situation for practicing the causative *have* is to role-play a beauty parlor/barbershop scene. A role-play for three will include two customers and a beautician/barber. The beautician/barber will ask one customer, "What do want to have done today?" The customer can then answer in a variety of ways using *have:* "I want to have my hair permed," "I want to have my sideburns cut," and so on. This customer can then ask the other customer what he or she wants to have done, and so on. It has even been suggested (by Jill Rosenheim and Sue Weingarten) that students actually visit a beauty salon or barbershop as a type of field experience and make an inventory of services available at the business.

6. Form. Frodesen and Eyring (1997:352) suggest that students role-play the solving of a problem to practice the use of subjunctive *that*-clauses. Two or more students take opposite sides of an issue. For example:

A young man would like to attend an all-female college. The president of the college wants to maintain the 100-year tradition of an all-female campus.

Students then use the following frames to make their arguments:

I propose that . . .
I suggest that . . .
We recommend that . . .

7. Use. Find a news article containing many examples of *that* complements with several clauses having the *that* complementizer present and several others having it absent. Ask your students to work in groups and underline all the *that* complements and circle all the *that* complementizers. Ask them to come up with generalizations about why *that* appears before some of complement clauses but not others. If they have difficulties, give them Bolinger's (1972) observations and see if they can apply these to the text they are analyzing.

EXERCISES

Test your understanding of what has been presented.

1. Give sentences that illustrate the following terms:
   - **a.** complement
   - **b.** complementizer
   - **c.** tensed *that*-clause
   - **d.** subjunctive clause
   - **e.** infinitive
   - **f.** subject control
   - **g.** PRO
   - **h.** gerund
   - **i.** subject + participle construction
   - **j.** purpose infinitive
   - **k.** object control
   - **l.** progressive infinitive
   - **m.** perfect infinitive
   - **n.** the Bolinger principle (for gerunds vs. infinitives)

2. Draw trees for the following sentences:
   - **a.** The sign told drivers to proceed slowly.
   - **b.** The players continued playing bridge.
   - **c.** We suggested that he return on the following day.
   - **d.** Let my dog go.
   - **e.** Some students wanted us to help on the project.
   - **f.** The teacher made everyone return to their seats.
   - **g.** I would hate for you to refuse the offer.
   - **h.** I have found my pickup truck to be useful.

3. Account for the ungrammaticality of the following sentences:
   - **a.** *I want that my brother will come home for New Year's.
   - **b.** *My friends insisted me to come with them.
   - **c.** *The teacher forced us drink hot chocolate.
   - **d.** *I understood for me to be the winner.
   - **e.** *They disagreed over to go to that movie.

4. Based on the various types of complement we have outlined in the chapter, which category or categories of complement types would the following verbs appear with? These verbs were not included in any of the lists given in the chapter. Use your intuitions (or consult a dictionary) about the use of the verbs in ordinary English sentences together with your knowledge of the categories of complement, and provide example sentences.

agree	beg	notice
argue	dare	resist
assist	keep	suspect

Test your ability to apply what you know.

5. How would you teach ESL/EFL students to use infinitives and gerunds correctly with the verb *try*? Suggest a context and a teaching strategy.

6. In our discussion of *get,* we did not contrast this verb in the following two frames:

   > The teacher got the students to draw pictures.
   > The teacher got the students drawing pictures.

   A student asks which of the two is the correct form. You say that both are correct, but how would you explain the difference between them?

7. Another student asks you to explain the difference between the two sentences below:

   > I expect to leave by 4:15.
   > I expect to have left by 4:15.

How would you respond to the question?

8. One ESL teacher said he had his students memorize the verbs that take gerund complements and told them to use infinitives everywhere else. Do you think that this is a good teaching strategy? Why or why not?

9. Suppose you are presented with the following sentences in an ESL composition and wish to make explicit oral feedback on them. What would you tell the student?
   a. *The kindergarten teacher made them to lie down.
   b. *She told us that where the restaurant was located.
   c. *We will go overseas for visiting our parents.
   d. *The officer demanded that I had to show him my license.

BIBLIOGRAPHY

References

Anderson, J. I. (1976). "A Comparison of the Order of Difficulty of English Sentential Complements between Native Speakers of Spanish and Native Speakers of Persian." Paper presented at the Los Angeles Second Language Research Forum, UCLA, 1976.

Biber, D. (1998). Teaching Actual Use in Conversation and Writing. Presentation at TESOL '98 in Seattle, March, 1998.

Bolinger, D. (1968). "Entailment and the Meaning of Structures," *Glossa* 2:2, 119–127.

Bolinger, D. (1972). *That's That.* The Hague: Mouton.

Bolinger, D. (1975). "About Questions." Lecture, UCLA Linguistics Colloquium, February 12, 1975.

Bresnan, J. (1970). "On Complementizers: Towards a Syntactic Theory of Complement Types." *Foundations of Language* 6, 297–321.

Butoyi, C. (1977). *The Accuracy Order of Sentential Complements by ESL Learners.* Unpublished M.A. thesis in TESL, UCLA.

Duffley, Patrick (1992). *The English Infinitive.* London: Longman.

Frodesen, J., and J. Eyring (1997). *Grammar Dimensions: Form, Meaning, and Use.* Book 4 (2d ed.). Boston: Heinle & Heinle.

Givón, T. (1980). "The Binding Hierarchy and the Typology of Complements." *Studies in Language* 4:3, 333–377.

Givón, T. (1990). *Syntax: A Functional-Typological Introduction* (vol. 2). Amsterdam: John Benjamins.

Kirsner, R. and S. Thompson (1976). "The Role of Pragmatic Inference in Semantics: A Study of Sensory Verb Complements in English." *Glossa* 10:2.

Lind, A. (1983). "The Variant Forms *Help to/Help ø*." *English Studies* 64:3, 263–273.

Martin, W. (1981). "Causative Verbs in English." Unpublished Independent Professional Project, School for International Training, Brattleboro, Vt.

Quirk, R., S. Greenbaum, G. Leech, and J. Svartvik (1985). *A Comprehensive Grammar of Contemporary English.* London: Longman.

Rosenzweig, F. (1973). "A Strategy for Teaching Gerunds and Infinitives to Advanced ESL Students." Unpublished English 215 paper, UCLA, Fall 1973.

Underhill, R. (1986). "The Discourse Conditions for *that*-Deletion." Manuscript, California State University at San Diego.

Suggestions for Further Reading

Generative grammar has undergone many changes over the years with regard to treatment of complement types. Two books that cover most of the constructions mentioned in this chapter are:

Baker, C. L. (1995). *English Syntax*. Cambridge: MIT Press.

Radford, A. (1988). *Transformational Grammar: A First Course*. Cambridge: Cambridge University Press.

A very clear treatment in an older generative framework may be found in:

Akmajian, A. and F. Heny (1975). *An Introduction to the Principles of Transformational Syntax:* Cambridge, MA: MIT Press.

Traditional non-generative treatments may be found in:

Joos, M. (1964). *The English Verb: Form and Meaning*. Madison, WI: University of Wisconsin Press.

Poutsma, H. (1923). *The Infinitive, the Gerund and the Participles of the English Verb*. Groningen: Noordhoff.

For a good review and discussion of factors bearing on whether that *is present or absent see:*

Lisovsky, K. (1988). A Discourse Analysis of Nominal *That* Clauses in English. Unpublished master's thesis, UCLA.

For a more complete inventory of English verbs and their complement options, see:

Quirk, R. et al. (1985). *A Comprehensive Grammar of the English Language*. London: Longman (see Chapter 16).

This reference may also be consulted for a discussion of tense and aspect in infinitive and gerund complements (see Chapter 3).

Most ESL/EFL grammar texts at the intermediate level and above cover infinitives, gerunds, and that-*clauses. For many, however, the treatment of infinitives is usually a highly simplified one that does not carefully distinguish types in the way we have done in this chapter. Two of the better recent treatments at the high intermediate level are:*

Elbaum, S. (1996). *Grammar in Context*. Book 3 (2nd ed.). Boston: Heinle & Heinle (Lessons 7 and 8.)

Thewlis, S. (1997). *Grammar Dimensions: Form, Meaning, and Use*. Book 3 (2nd ed.). Boston: Heinle & Heinle. (Units 6 & 7.)

A treatment at the advanced level is in:

Frodesen, J. and Eyring, J. (1997). *Grammar Dimensions: Form, Meaning, and Use*. Book 4 (2nd ed.). Boston: Heinle & Heinle.

ENDNOTES

1. Clausal *that*-complements differ from ordinary phrasal NPs in that they cannot appear after prepositions as prepositional objects:

> Scientists are often surprised by [great discoveries].
> *Scientists are disturbed by [that the globe is getting warmer].

However, if the *that*-clause appears at the beginning of the sentence and the preposition is stranded, i.e. left at the end of its clause with no object following, this restriction does not hold:

> [That the globe is getting warmer] is something scientists are disturbed by.

2. We choose to expand S rather than S' because of the possibility of embedded sentence modifiers, at least in the case of some of the clausal complements discussed in this chapter. We would want to generate sentences like the following:

She said that, unfortunately, she could not make the appointment.

3. In recent generative grammar, infinitives occurring with main clause verbs like *believe, know, report* are called "exceptional clauses" partly because of this chameleonlike property of "subjects looking like objects," and also because their structural analysis differs from that of other infinitive types.

4. The verb *attempt* can, of course, be used in other contexts in which it takes a normal NP object, as in *She attempted a quick exit from the building.* In that case, the *What*-question would be appropriate. Most linguists would say that in the lexicon, the verb *attempt* is listed with two possible syntactic frames: one in which the verb takes a non-clausal NP object, and another in which it takes an infinitival complement.

5. Some speakers find it odd to say, *She promised me to fix the problem;* others do not. Those who reject this construction find an acceptable paraphrase in *She promised me that she would fix the problem.*

6. When *help* occurs without *to,* the AUX is [-imper] as in the tree on page 641; however, when *help* occurs with *to,* the AUX is *to* as in the earlier trees for infinitives.

7. Duffley (1992) is a book-length treatment of the "verb + to" versus "verb + ø" alternation which offers accounts of other such parallel forms not discussed here.

8. Note that some of these verbs occur in other environments in which they do not convey this subjunctive sense. *Insist* may mean "strongly assert," as in *She insisted that the Indians won the World Series in 1949;* in this case, the embedded verb is in past tense. *Ask* may mean "inquire," in which case it takes a tensed *if/whether* complement, discussed in Chapter 33. In addition, many of these verbs (*ask, require*) may also take infinitival complements, which are by nature tenseless; finally, some verbs with similar meanings take only infinitival complements (*command, urge*).

9. Recall that the *-ing* of the gerund (which formally marks a nominal form) is not the same as the *-ing* of the progressive (which marks an ongoing activity).

10. Many native speakers would simplify such a sentence to:

She remembers listening to a Grieg concerto (all evening).

11. This problem arises with the relative pronoun *that* as well; see Chapters 28 and 29 for discussion.

Chapter **32**

Other Aspects of Complementation and Embedded Clauses

Introduction

In this chapter we continue our discussion of issues related to complementation from Chapter 31. We also look at some clausal constructions where embedded clauses function in ways other than as complements to verbs, and return to a discussion of passive voice. Finally, we introduce some additional semantic distinctions among complement types; namely, factive versus nonfactive predicates and implicative verbs.

The six new constructions we discuss in this chapter are:

- raising to subject: the subject of the complement becomes the subject of the higher clause.

  It seems [that they have succeeded].
  They seem [to have succeeded].

- complex-NP complements: the *that*-clause or infinitive functions as a complement to an NP.

  The news [that a hurricane is coming] is worrisome.
  This is a good time [to open a bottle of champagne].

- adjective complements: the fact that adjectives, like verbs and nouns, can also take complements.

  Joan is eager [to see you].

- extraposition of complements: the tendency of non-final heavy or dominant constituents to move to the end of the sentence.

  [That he left without any money] is unfortunate.
  It is unfortunate [that he left without any money].

- constructions like *easy-to-please*: the object of the complement becomes the subject of the main clause.

  It is important [to solve the problem].
  The problem is important [to solve].

- complex passives: either the main clause or complement clause is in the passive voice, thus making different word orders and structures possible.

> [That he has won the tournament] is rumored.
> It is rumored [that he has won the tournament].
> He is rumored to have won the tournament.

RAISING TO SUBJECT

Every sentence in English must have some overt element in subject position. However, in certain constructions the subject position is filled with a word that does not fit our intuitive notion of what a subject "should be." We have already seen in Chapter 23 that *there* in the *there*-construction has very general meaning and is placed in subject position primarily to allow for new information to appear in predicate position. We also saw in Chapter 23 that the word *it* in the sentence *It is raining* has no real-world referent. In this and the following sections of this chapter, we will look at some additional instances in which *it* is used in nonreferential ways.

STRUCTURAL ASPECTS OF RAISING

In Chapter 31, we discussed verb classes that are associated with certain types of complement. One additional type of verb that takes an obligatory complement is a copular verb, exemplified here by the verb *seem*. This verb commonly appears in three frames:

> The offer seems good.
> They seem to have succeeded.
> It seems that they have succeeded.

In the first case, we have a sentence that we can already generate by the base rule for VP, one of whose possible expansions is [cop + AP]. The other sentences cannot be so easily generated. We follow a standard analysis by which the second type of sentence is generated through a rule called *raising-to-subject,* which generates the subject of the main clause in the embedded sentence and then moves it forward and up into the main clause subject position:

> [ ] seem [they to have succeeded] → *raising* →
> They seem [[ ] to have succeeded].

In one way, the verb *seem* is like the verb *hope* in cases where the latter is followed by an infinitive. Wherever the verb *seem* is used with an infinitive following, the infinitive has as its logical subject the subject of the main clause. We cannot have, for example:

> *They seem their friend to have succeeded.

However, the similarity ends there. One reason for the raising analysis is that this type of structure is not quite like that for verbs like *hope*, where the subject of the sentence controls a PRO in the dependent infinitive clause:

> They hope [PRO to win the game]
> (PRO = *they*)

The two structures are different because, among other things, it is possible to have the semantically vague *there* in subject position in the main clause if the main verb is *seem*, but not if the main verb is *hope*:

> There seems to be something wrong.
> *There hopes to be . . .

The idea is that something must be controlling the reference of the subject of the embedded infinitive if the main verb is *hope*, and the word *there* cannot fulfill this requirement since *there* does not refer to anything specific. With *seem*, however, control does not seem to be an issue; after all, we can say *There seems to be something wrong*. So an assumption in generative grammar, at least, has been that the subject of the main clause in these sentences is generated as an empty slot and, because every sentence in English must have an overt subject, the subject of the infinitive moves up to first position in the main clause:

What, then, of the third type of sentence? These are sentences such as:

> It seems that John is happy.

We cannot have raising here, since the result would be ungrammatical:[1]

> *John seems that [ ] is happy.
> ↑_____|

We may simply assume, then, that the *that*-clause in this case is a complement generated in the position after the verb and that the nonreferential subject *it* is placed in initial position to fulfill the requirement for a surface subject. Other verbs that follow the pattern of *seem* in the relevant respects include *turn out, happen,* and *appear:*

> It turned out that John got the promotion.
> John turned out to get the promotion.
> It happens/appears that you are right.
> You happen/appear to be right.

Three other verb-like constructions that are similar but not completely parallel are *seem like, sound like,* and *look like:*

> It seems like (*that) something is wrong.
> Something seems like it's wrong.

> It sounds like (*that) you don't agree.
> You sound like you don't agree.

> It looks like (*that) our roof is going to cave in.
> Our roof looks like it is going to cave in.

Here the unacceptability of the complementizer *that* is probably related to the fact that these verbs involve a prepositional construction; as we have already noted in chapter 31, a tensed *that* clause cannot be the object of a preposition.[2]

Raising is also sometimes held to operate in the case of certain adjective constructions such as *be (un)likely, be certain*. We get the same structural alternations as with verbs like *seem,* and the same patterns of ungrammaticality:

> It is unlikely/certain that we will be able to return the merchandise.
> *We are unlikely/certain that will be able to return the merchandise.

> We are unlikely/certain to return the merchandise.

We derive the last of these sentences exactly as we did *seem* + infinitive, by generating the subject NP in the embedded clause and then promoting it into subject position in the main clause.

ESL/EFL ISSUES WITH RAISING STRUCTURES

As with other instances in which *it* plays a mainly formal role in English sentences—namely, to fulfill the requirement that a surface subject be expressed—ESL/EFL teachers may find their students omitting the *it* in sentences with *seem* and similar verbs. This is because other languages may exhibit no such requirement, permitting sentences like

> Seems (that) John is sick today.
> Looks like we won't be able to do it.

In fact, in highly colloquial speech even native English speakers may omit *it* in these sentences. However, in more formal registers this is not an option, especially not in academic writing, and teachers may want to stress this fact in classes. Student learners will also produce sentences like these, which mix the possible syntactic frames for *seem* and *be certain:*

> *He seems like to be not very honest.
> (It seems like he is not very honest.)
> *I am certain for the assignment to be very easy.
> (I am certain that the assignment will be very easy.)

A teacher faced with sentences like the starred ones above should be aware of the structural options available to native speakers and the confusion that ESL/EFL learners may experience in trying to select among them.

OTHER TYPES OF CLAUSAL COMPLEMENTS

Up to now, all of the clausal complements we have presented have been complements to verbs. However, these are not the only types of complements: both nouns and adjectives may take complements as well.

COMPLEX-NP COMPLEMENTS

We have seen many cases in Chapter 31 of *that*-clauses that function as embedded complement objects of main verbs. *That*-clauses often function as complements of NPs as well, especially in conjunction with certain NPs that represent a cognitive stance or indicate the presumed truth value of the proposition expressed in the complement clause. Such NPs are often called *complex* NPs. Some example sentences include those below, with the head noun in italics:

> The *belief* [that petroleum reserves are infinite] is again common nowadays.
> I don't agree with the *notion* [that there is no future in electric cars].
> Do you believe the *claim* [that Sam is really a bigamist]?
> Her interest in Monet lies in the *fact* [that he was a French painter].
> The *news* [that a hurricane was coming our way] made us worry.
> It's *time* [to give up and go to bed].
> This is a good *occasion* [to open a bottle of champagne].

Each complex NP includes a simple NP plus a complement clause. Note carefully that although the *that*-clause examples look similar to relative clauses, they are grammatically distinct. For instance, the *that* at the beginning of the complement clause cannot be identified with any NP in the clause (as can the word *that* in a clause like *Mary saw the coat [that she wanted to buy [ ]]*, where *that* is moved forward from object position and is identical to *coat*). Our phrase structure rule for NP must be adapted again to permit an expansion of this type:

> NP → NP S
> S → comp S'

The tree structure will be the following:

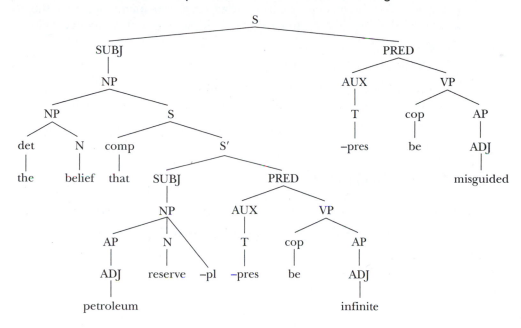

The belief that petroleum reserves are infinite is misguided.

Some types of noun complement with the phrase *the fact,* where the NP is a prepositional object, have become part of complex prepositional-phrase chunks which, when spoken, may be uttered so quickly that they seem like single words:

> I turned off the projector *because of the fact that* no one liked my movie.
> Parrots don't understand what they say *due to the fact that* they aren't smart.
> She was angry *on account of the fact that* he hadn't called her back.
> They left town *in spite of the fact that* they loved the place.

The formulaic nature of these sorts of sequences may partially be accounted for by the inability of a full *that*-clause to appear as the object of a preposition and the need for a grammatical means to serve the same function—a need that is fulfilled by NPs like *the fact.* Teachers will probably see the following sentence type produced by ESL/EFL students who are unaware of this restriction:

> *My friend drove me home in my car because of I was too tired to drive.
> *The principal scolded me in spite of I hadn't done anything wrong.

It is therefore worthwhile for a teacher to make students aware of expressions involving *the fact* and to provide them with examples in use, especially in written prose.[3]

As a final note, if NPs of urging or recommendation take *that*-clause complements, the verbs in these complements will appear in the subjunctive, just as they do for verbs of urging or recommendation taking subjunctive clauses:

Ordinary subjunctive verb complements:
We recommended that he *take* an early plane.
The government demanded that truck drivers *be* specially tested.

Sentences with complex NP subjunctive complements:
The recommendation that he *take* an early plane was a wise one.
The government's demand that truck drivers *be* specially tested was excessive.

ADJECTIVE COMPLEMENTS

Adjectives, like nouns and verbs, may also take clausal complements; they may be infinitival, or they may be tensed *that*-clauses, depending on the adjective. (We mentioned some subjunctive cases in Chapter 31.) You will recognize the idiomatic pairings in the sentences below:

> Susan is eager [to know your birthday].
> She was fascinated [to learn the truth].
>
> We're happy [that you could be here with us tonight].
> The students are disappointed [that they have to sit and watch another movie in class].

Such clauses can be said to branch from the AP node and will necessitate a revision of the AP phrase structure rule to read:

$$AP \rightarrow (\text{intens}) \; Adj \; (\begin{Bmatrix} PrepP \\ S \end{Bmatrix})$$

The resulting tree structure for the sentence *Susan is eager to know your birthday* is:

Susan is eager to know your birthday.

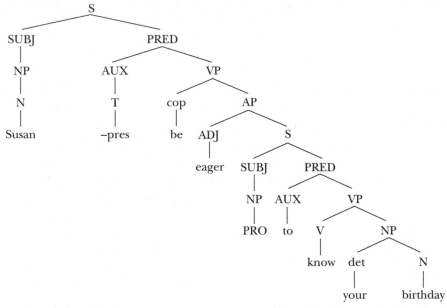

As with earlier infinitives, the analysis makes use of PRO, which suggests that some adjectives, like many verbs, incorporate a "control" type meaning. Other similar adjectives include *unwilling, willing, disappointed, inclined, anxious,* and *overjoyed;* most express emotional states. Most are not sources of many ESL/EFL errors, except for the occasional confusion of which type of complement—*that*-clause or infinitive—goes with which adjective.

COMPLEMENTS AND EXTRAPOSITION

THE FORMAL ASPECTS OF EXTRAPOSITION

There are instances other than *seem*-type sentences where *it* appears in subject position and an embedded clause follows the main verb. However, they are distinctly different in that in these cases, the embedded clause could replace the *it* in subject position and yield an acceptable paraphrase. For instance, we cannot have sentences like

*That John is happy seems.

With other verbs, the situation is much different. Consider the following related pairs:

[That he left without any money] is unfortunate.
It's unfortunate [that he left without any money].

[That he spent all day watching MTV] didn't help his grades.
It didn't help his grades [that he spent all day watching MTV].

[That someone would say that] indicates a complete lack of understanding.
It indicates a complete lack of understanding [that someone would say that].

Classical generative grammar (for example, Akmajian and Heny 1975) relates such sentence pairs by a rule of *extraposition,* where a clause is generated in subject position[4] and then moved, or extraposed, to the end of the sentence. The nonreferential subject *it* is then placed in subject position to satisfy the requirement for an overt subject in every English sentence. Note that when *that*-clauses are placed at the beginning of the sentence in this way, we cannot omit the complementizer *that* under any circumstances:

*He left without any money is unfortunate.

However, extraposed *that*-clauses may sometimes omit the complementizer, probably for some of the same reasons we noted concerning *that*-deletion in Chapter 31:

It's unfortunate he left without any money.

We see the same kind of alternative forms with infinitives as well as the free relatives discussed in Chapter 29:

Infinitives:

[For her to quit like that] was scandalous.
It was scandalous [for her to quit like that].

[To do that] would take more time than I have right now.
It would take more time than I have right now [to do that].

[To buy one of those cars] is well worth it.
It's well worth it [to buy one of those cars].

Free relatives:

[Who did that] is unknown.
It is unknown [who did that].

[Where we're going] is a mystery to me.
It's a mystery to me [where we're going].

Gerunds are less amenable to extraposition than *that*-clauses or infinitives; they do not extrapose well with possessive subjects, but they sometimes occur extraposed without expressed subjects in colloquial English:

[Her whistling old songs] woke up the neighborhood.
*It woke up the neighborhood [her whistling old songs].

[Spending the afternoon with you] is nice.
It's nice [spending the afternoon with you].

[Living without a car in this city] is not easy.
It's not easy [living without a car in this city].

[Watching the election results] made me angry.
It made me angry [watching the election results].

In our tree structure, extraposition involves the following structural change taking place:

That he left without his money is unfortunate.

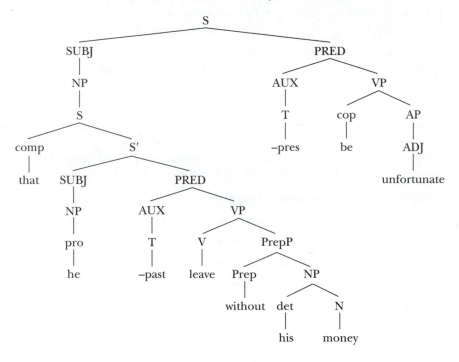

It is unfortunate that he left without his money.

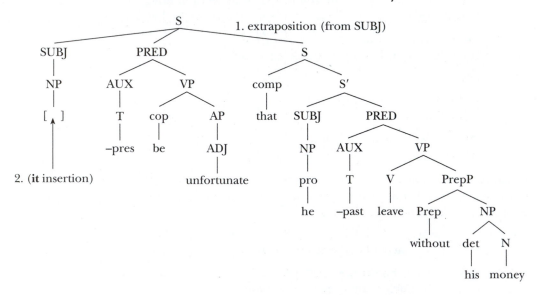

Extraposition, in these cases, shifts an entire subject clause[5] to the end of a sentence, where complements usually occur.

The same sort of movement seems to be taking place in sentences such as the following, where extraposition occurs from an object position. In these cases, the first alternative is clearly interpretable but may be awkward:

> ?I doubt [that she has the answer] very much.
> I doubt (it) very much [that she has the answer].
>
> ?We appreciate [that you had the time to help us] greatly.
> We appreciate (it) greatly [that you had the time to help us].

Note: the optional *it* in parentheses is a pronominal reflex for the extraposed *that* clause.

> We want [to go back to our dormitory] very much.
> We want very much [to go back to our dormitory].

An extraposition rule has been claimed to operate elsewhere as well. Sometimes just one part of a subject, such as a relative clause or a complement, may detach and move to sentence-final position; such movement in structures other than complements is most common in colloquial usage but is not considered good formal written style:

Extraposed NP complement:

> The fact [that you have won the lottery] is irrelevant.
> The fact is irrelevant [that you have won the lottery].

Extraposed relative clauses:

> The plan [which the president proposed] has been approved today.
> The plan has been approved today [which the president proposed].
>
> The problem [that I told you about] has been diagnosed.
> The problem has been diagnosed [that I told you about].

Extraposed participial phrase:

> Any questions [regarding the contract] should be dealt with immediately.
> Any questions should be dealt with immediately [regarding the contract].

Such movement is sometimes called *extraposition from NP*.[6]

THE USE OF EXTRAPOSITION

Extraposition is usually regarded as a stylistic rule. As we have seen in cases of extraposition from object position, the failure to extrapose can result in awkward constructions that may even cause interpretation difficulties.

English has a tendency for "heavy" or dominant elements to move to the end of a sentence, where heaviness or dominance is calculated mainly in terms of the length of a constituent. This movement is presumably a processing strategy since dominant NPs are harder to encode and decode in initial or medial position than in final position. This is true especially where subjects are concerned, but may occur even with other NPs in certain cases. NPs followed by relative clause modifiers, for example, are relatively long compared to other NPs and frequently undergo a shift toward the end of the sentence:

> We saw [the movie which she had spoken about] Sunday.
> We saw Sunday [the movie which she had spoken about].

Note that this would not be a possibility with shorter, simple NPs:

> We saw the movie **last** Sunday.
> *We saw **last** Sunday the movie.

Since NPs can in principle be of indefinite length, it should therefore not be surprising that a rule like extraposition regularly operates in English.

Extraposition may serve an additional function. As we have mentioned in earlier chapters, English tends to place old, given information in subject position and new information in the predicate. Since old information is typically encoded in brief form relative to the rest of the sentence (because known or assumed information requires no elaboration), a sentence like the following tends to sound better with an extraposed subject:

> *Unextraposed form:*
> That the governor will formally announce the new sales tax bill is likely.
> *Extraposed form:*
> It is likely that the governor will formally announce the new sales tax bill.

If the bill in question is already familiar to hearers/readers and is mentioned within the subject, it would be far more likely to appear in shorter form, approximately as follows:

> The governor's new sales tax bill is likely to be announced today.

Thus, the given/new distinction may play a considerable role in an utterer's decision to extrapose.

Conversely, we might ask why someone chooses *not* to extrapose—why a full clause might be retained in subject position. One fairly clear case is that in which the predicate of the main clause *itself* contains a clause. The operation of extraposition in such cases may present serious problems for sentence processing:

> That he always selects the correct answer shows that he has studied the material.
> ?It shows that he has studied the material that he always selects the correct answer.
>
> That you brought this matter to our attention helps us to see the real problem.
> ?It helps us to see the real problem that you brought the matter to our attention.

In fact, a careful discourse analysis of the use of clausal subjects would be useful since it might confirm that subject complements occur most frequently in cases exactly like these. In terms of where we find such structures, Lisovsky (1988) shows that formal writing has a significantly higher number of clausal *that* subjects than spoken or informal written genres.

THE *EASY-TO-PLEASE* CONSTRUCTION

A similar but distinct syntactic pattern, often called the *easy-to-please* construction,[7] causes frequent difficulties for ESL/EFL students, for reasons that we outline below.

STRUCTURAL ISSUES

The *easy-to-please* structure depends on the presence of certain adjectives denoting personal judgments about something: *easy, hard, challenging, difficult, annoying, important, (im)possible, safe, dangerous, nice, boring, interesting,* and *fun:*

> It's easy to please my friend John = My friend John is easy to please.
> It's fun to play this game. = This game is fun to play.
> It's impossible to solve the problem. = The problem is impossible to solve.
> It's not safe to eat those mushrooms. = Those mushrooms are not safe to eat.

The alternation may occur in embedded structures as well, as in the following bare-infinitive complement:

The teacher made it easy to follow the lectures.
The teacher made the lectures easy to follow.

This construction may appear with a *for*-phrase, similar to verbs like *prefer* (see Chapter 31). Where the *for*-phrase is present, the understood subject of the infinitive is the object of *for*:

It's easy for me to please my friend John.
The teacher made it easy for us to follow the lectures.

When there is no *for*-phrase, the understood PRO-type subject of *to* in all these cases is normally understood to be a rather vague "anyone" or "someone." While the *easy-to-please* construction is usually associated with infinitives, at least one very common verb-like construction, *be worth* V + *-ing*, seems to follow a similar pattern:

It's worth watching a good program. = A good program is worth watching.

Which of the structures is basic, and how is the derivation done? While there has been no consensus among linguists on this point, one possibility is to derive the second sentence in each pair from the first, by raising the embedded object to main clause subject in a manner reminiscent of *wh*-fronting:

[ ] is impossible to solve the problem →
[The problem] is impossible to solve [ ]
↑ _____|

The basic structure is then one in which the embedded clause originates as the complement to an adjective like *easy*, *difficult* or *impossible*. The relevant part of the tree is illustrated as follows:

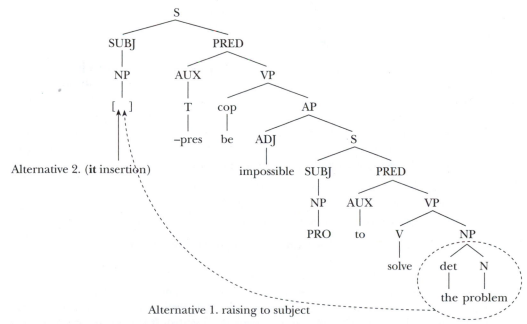

It is impossible to solve the problem.
(The problem is impossible to solve.)

If the object NP in the complement is raised to fill the empty slot in the main clause, *it* insertion does not take place: *The problem is impossible to solve*. Alternatively, if the embedded object NP is not moved out of the infinitive to serve as the higher subject, nonreferential *it* fills the subject slot: [*It*] *is impossible to solve this problem*.

Our earlier revision of AP to permit expansion with an optional complement S will accommodate this structure. As before, where no movement takes place, the semantically empty element *it* fills the subject position.

While the above movements are from direct object position, they may occur from a prepositional object position as well when the verb phrase of the main clause includes a PrepP, as for example,

> to work on *a computer* → Computers are fun to work on.
> to deal with *a problem* → This problem is hard to deal with.
> to play with *a toy* → That toy is dangerous to play with.
> to run around *a track* → The track is easy to run around.

and so on. In these cases, we are left with a stranded preposition after movement:

> [ ] be fun to work on computers →
> [Computers] are fun to work on [ ]
>   ↑_____|

ESL/EFL ISSUES WITH THE "EASY-TO-PLEASE" CONSTRUCTION

We know of no published work on raising based on an examination of a large corpus of utterances that can provide an explanation of native-speaker choice between the basic and the derived forms. It may be that relative focus is the key distinction here, just as it appears to be where raising occurs in *seem*-type structures. An unpublished study by Terry Santos does indicate that nonnative speakers tend to disprefer raising to subject in cases where native speakers would raise an NP. Consider the following example (adapted from *Time* 4/27/98, p. 33):

> Much has happened since Betty Currie first faced the Grand Jury back
> in January. Old friends who have been speaking with her say
> > a) it seems she is calm and unfazed about Round 2.
> > b) she seems to be calm and unfazed about Round 2.

In Santos' study nonnative speakers preferred sentences like version (a) with nonraised subjects whereas native speakers preferred sentences like (b) with raised subjects because they express better topic continuity, given the discourse context. Whatever might be the reason for this pattern of preferences, we do know that this type of structure occasions many ESL/EFL learner errors. There are several reasons for this. For one thing, when we consider that extraposition is also an option in some of these sentences, we are now faced with a situation of *three*-way synonymy among sets like those below:

> I am easy to please.   That is easy (for me) to do.
> It is easy to please me.   It is easy (for me) to do that.
> To please me is easy.   To do that is easy (for me).

Many learners seem to blend the structures, producing sentences like

> *I am easy to do that.

where the intended meaning is, *It is easy for me to do that.*[8] The confusion is understandable. A second problem is that there is also something passivelike in the sentence *I am easy to please*: it means that someone else, not the speaker, is doing the pleasing.[9] Since the underlying PRO that heads the infinitive is a vague, unnamed agent (rather than an easily inferrable one as in *She likes PRO to play tennis*), there is some learner logic in expecting a passive here. In fact, this logic is the source of another learner error type:

> *I am easy to be pleased.

Such an error is readily understood in view of the overall meaning of the sentence, but a passive infinitive is not acceptable here: the unnamed PRO makes the sentence active. A third source of error arises from a lack of awareness of the fact that with raising an NP is moved to the left in a manner similar to relative pronoun fronting, where there can be no pronominal reflex in the original NP position; thus the ungrammaticality of the underlined pronouns:

> *I am easy to please <u>me</u>.
> *The movie is worth watching <u>it</u>.

Teachers working at intermediate to advanced levels would do well to help students sort out the difficulties in these structures, whose similarities of syntax and meaning make them highly confusing. Though they are syntactically marked constructions, they are frequent in everyday speech and writing, and it makes sense to devote some attention to them.

COMPLEX PASSIVES

At this point it is useful to return to a structure that was covered in Chapter 18 on the passive voice and to see how the structure and its uses integrate into the grammar of multiclausal sentences. As you recall from Chapter 18, a passive structure has a patient or recipient in the subject position of the sentence and places the agent of the sentence into a secondary position, appearing (if at all) in a *by*-phrase in the VP.

We will treat reported speech and writing in the next chapter; however, it is worth mentioning at this point that passives frequently appear in reports where the agent—that is, the reporter—is of no particular interest, and the report, or message, is the focus. Rather than saying *People believe that . . .* with a clause following, it is more common to see sentences like those below:

> It is believed that weather patterns are changing worldwide.
> It is not known for certain who Homer was.
> It is rumored that Dick has been fired.

As you will recall from the discussion in Chapter 18, the passive construction is a means to topicalize the receiver of an action or the patient of the sentence rather than the agent. In the case of the sentences above there are no real "actions," hence no real agents. However, the "logical" subjects of *believe/know/rumor* are unstated, possibly because they are unknown or not being divulged but also because they seem relatively irrelevant to the main message, which is the information in the embedded clauses. As we noted in Chapter 18, the verb *rumored* does not even have an active counterpart, as in

> *People have rumored that Dick has been fired.

In these sentences extraposition of the subject clauses also seems to have taken place, as elsewhere seemingly for the reasons (a) that heavier, lengthier constituents tend to be placed at the end of the sentence and (b) that new information tends to fall within the predicate. In these commonly employed ways of reporting others' utterances, then, we see the functional interaction of two grammatical structures.

Passives may occur *within* embedded clauses as well and are presumably subject to the same conditions of use in discourse. However, the syntactic options are somewhat more limited, depending on which type of complement among those outlined in Chapter 31 is present. We will mention some of the possibilities here. Passives may occur with cognition-utterance verbs taking tensed or infinitival complements:

> Mary believed (that) her son had been given the grand prize.
> Mary thought her son to have been treated unfairly.

The choice of the passive in the second sentence above seems motivated by a desire to focus on the receiver/patient (i.e., *her son*) rather than the agent. Note that while passives may occur in infinitival clauses as well, the forms of *be* must be untensed in such cases: *be/been/being* occur, but *am/is/are/was/were* do not. For *want*-type verbs, for example, we may have:

> Mary wanted her son *to be given* the grand prize.

Again, the passive seems preferable to its active counterpart. In the case of *allow*-type verbs (*allow, cause, order, persuade*), the choice of passive may sometimes be required, since the active would have a completely different meaning:

> Mary persuaded her son to be examined by a podiatrist.
> Mary persuaded a podiatrist to examine her son.

In the case of bare-infinitive or NP + participle complements, passives may occur, bearing in mind the usual conditions of use. Recall that these complement types follow verbs of perception (*see, hear, watch, notice*) and manipulation (*make, let, have*). While the syntax of the following two pairs of sentences is identical, they differ decidedly in terms of naturalness:

> We saw a squirrel eating a nut.
> ?We saw a nut being eaten by a squirrel.

> We saw a bear chasing a man.
> We saw a man being chased by a bear.

The reason is that we would normally find it odd for a speaker observing the event depicted in the first pair of sentences to focus on the nut; however, we would not find it at all strange in the second pair to focus either on the bear or on the man, i.e. the animacy of the noun phrase is highly relevant here.

MORE COMPLEMENT SEMANTICS: FACTIVES AND IMPLICATIVES

In this and the last chapter we have talked about complements in terms of syntactic types, verbal frames, and the semantic classes of verbs that pattern with one or another of these frames. One dimension we have not explored involves the issue of truth versus falsity of complements.

FACTIVE VERSUS NONFACTIVE PREDICATES

Kiparsky and Kiparsky (1968) distinguished verbs and adjectival predicates according to whether they carry *presuppositions,* or inherent assumptions, regarding the factual status of their complements. Some examples are listed below:

Factive	*Nonfactive*
comprehend	believe
regret	claim
bear in mind	maintain
be significant	seem
be odd	be likely
be clear	be possible

A factive complement clause is a clause that is true regardless of whether the higher clause is affirmative, negative, or interrogative:

> John regrets that he committed the crime.
> John does not regret that he committed the crime.
> Does John regret that he committed the crime?

In all three examples, it remains a presumed truth that John committed the crime. In a courtroom trial, the defense attorney would likely object if the question above were posed directly to the defendant as "Do you regret that you committed the crime?" Whether the question is answered "yes" or "no," the response amounts to an admission of guilt. The same quality holds with the other words and expressions on the above list of factives: Whether the sentence *It is odd that our friend disappeared* is negated, questioned, or left in the affirmative, it remains true that *our friend disappeared*.

Compare now a nonfactive complement, which yields different results:

> The police maintain that John committed the crime.
> The police do not maintain that John committed the crime.
> Do the police maintain that John committed the crime?

In these sentences, there is no presumption about whether John did or did not commit the crime, regardless of whether the police have strong beliefs about John's guilt or innocence. In a similar way, to say *It is likely that the Yankees won the game* does not presume that the Yankees won or did not win; nor is this presumed if the sentence is made negative or cast as a question.

Factivity carries over to NP complements as well. Complements of the NP *the fact* are, obviously, factive:

> the fact that the President is elected every four years
> ?the fact that the President is elected every month

Complements of *the claim, the supposition, the belief,* and other nouns are not factive:

> the belief that the earth is round
> the claim that the earth is flat

In Chapter 31 we spoke of the Bolinger principle, which says that gerunds tend to depict events which are "vivid, real, fulfilled" while infinitives tend to depict events which are "hypothetical, future, and unfulfilled." As it turns out, gerunds—especially those with possessive subjects—and infinitives pattern to a large extent along the factive-nonfactive dimension as well. The use of gerunds in subject position, for example, involves a presumption that the event asserted in the gerund is true; if the event is asserted not (yet) to have occurred, the sentence is slightly odd:

> [John('s) doing that] annoyed me.
> ?John's doing that would annoy me.

If the event has not (yet) occurred, the far more idiomatic construction would be an infinitive:

> For John to do that would annoy me.

The same holds for gerunds in object position. If a gerund is used with *hate,* we expect that the event is fulfilled and thus find use of the infinitive less idiomatic:

> I hate his having talked like that.
> ?I hate for him to have talked like that.

With the conditional *would,* indicating an unfulfilled condition, we get the opposite results:

> I would hate for him to say that.
> ?I would hate his saying that.

The same distinctions may be observed with the verbs *like* and *love.*

IMPLICATIVE VERBS

Karttunen (1971) identified a further distinction among verbs in which the factuality or nonfactuality of the complement depends both on the verb itself and on whether the main clause asserts or denies the complement. These verbs can be "positive implicatives" or "negative implicatives" as follows:

Positive implicative	*Negative implicative*
manage	fail
succeed	neglect
remember	forget

If we say, *Mary managed to finish her work,* we assume that Mary did in fact finish it. If we say, *Mary failed to finish her work,* we assume that she did not. The same holds for the other verbs on the list. When implicatives are negated, however, the situation reverses:

> Mary did not manage to finish her work. (She did not finish it.)
> Mary did not fail to finish her work. (She finished it.)

In the first case (a negated positive implicative) Mary did not finish her work, while in the second (a negated negative implicative) she did.

Though the above examples are infinitival, it should be pointed out that the majority of verbs taking infinitives are not of the implicative type. Most tend simply to be ordinary nonfactives: the use of *allow, believe, prefer, hate,* or *imagine* with the infinitives following them presupposing nothing about the truth of the event expressed in the complement, regardless of whether the sentence is affirmed or denied. Factive verbs like *regret* and factive adjectival predicates such as *be odd* tend to take *that*-clause complements, though a great many nonfactive verbs take *that*-clause complements as well.

CONCLUSION

In this chapter we have focused most strongly on a number of structures in which stylistic variation comes into the picture—that is, where one has the choice of using one syntactic form or another when the options produce roughly synonymous sentences but when discourse considerations tend to dictate a certain form for certain functions. These structures include:

a. Raising to subject in a *seem*-type clause or using a tensed *seem*-complement
b. Extraposing or not extraposing
c. Moving or not moving an *easy-to-please* object into main clause subject position
d. Using a complex passive or using the roughly synonymous active form

The fact of rough synonymy here means that issues of use as well as form come to the fore as elements of ESL/EFL teaching. High-intermediate as well as advanced writing students may benefit tremendously from a knowledge of the options available to them once they master the more basic syntactic structures of the language.

In the next chapter you will see how complex sentences are put to use in reported speech and writing. We also carry the discussion of factive versus nonfactive verbs further to see what bears on choosing one or the other in the course of reporting others' utterances.

TEACHING SUGGESTIONS

1. Form/Use. Learning the rules for raising, extraposition, *easy-to-please,* and complex passives help students to become aware of a variety of syntactic forms that share essentially the same meaning. Because the variations are roughly synonymous, there is some value simply in presenting students with one form and having them transform sentences into roughly synonymous variants, as for example:

> That Seattle is so rainy does not bother me.
> (> It does not bother me that Seattle is so rainy.)
> To work with clay is interesting.
> (> It's interesting to work with clay. / Clay is interesting to work with.)
> People believe that electric cars may soon be popular.
> (> It is believed that electric cars may soon be popular.)
> The fact that John passed the exam is not surprising.
> (> John's passing the exam is not surprising.)

However, it is also of immense value where more complex constructions are concerned for students to see how the constructions pattern in naturally occurring discourse. After covering the constructions and their functions in class, teachers should present whole paragraphs from written texts they have collected and ask students why a writer may have chosen one structure over the other. (In many cases, of course, no definitive answer may be obvious.) Another option would be for students to collect their own example paragraphs containing one or more of these structures from the opinion section of the daily newspaper (where syntax tends to be somewhat more complex) and to present them to the class, offering their own explanations of why the writer chose to write the sentences in the way that they appeared.

2. Form. Practicing *easy-to-please* constructions might go hand-in-hand with practice in stranding prepositions in a nativelike way (see Chapter 21). Both might be practiced in the context of small groups, with each student having to solve a relatively quickly solvable problem such as a scrambled-word sentence or a small crossword puzzle. Each group works in pairs or threes to perform their tasks. The teacher then writes the alternative grammatical forms on the board and proceeds to model questions in both forms for the first group of students approximately as follows:

> T: What was Ali working on?
> S1: He was working on a crossword puzzle.
> T: Was it hard for Ali to solve the puzzle, or was the puzzle easy to solve? Ask him.
> S1: Was it hard for you to solve the puzzle, or was it easy to solve?
> Ali: It was very hard for me to solve. It was impossible to solve.

The teacher can then present a larger range of adjectives—*fun, interesting, boring, challenging,* and *impossible*—and have students query each other in their groups as to the difficulty of their tasks. They can then report their results to the class as a whole.

An alternative to this task might be a question-and-verification sequence in which the teacher models the first question and the verification question, using alternative forms in each sentence. The students then reply directly to the form of each type of question:

> *Teacher:* Alicia, is it hard to drive a car?
> *Student 1:* Yes, it is hard to drive a car.
> *Teacher:* Grace, is a car *really* hard to drive?
> *Student 2:* No, a car is really not hard to drive.

Students can then work in groups, taking turns asking each other such questions while using the adjectives on the blackboard as options.

3. Form. A clause-combining exercise may help students integrate some of the constructions in this chapter and the last in such a way as to allow them not only to master the formal aspects but also the stylistic ones. It is important to point out the usefulness of expressions like *the fact (that . . .)* in clause combining in view of the impossibility of *that-*clauses occurring after prepositions. With these things in mind, teachers can set sentences like those below side by side and have students turn them into all the possible grammatical sentences they can think of, allowing them to bring in other clause types they know (such as relative clauses and adverbial clauses, for example). The resulting sentences may or may not express identical ideas:

  a. My brother sleeps late.
     That bothers me.
     I can't play my music.
     That is a fact.

    1) It bothers me that my brother sleeps late because of the fact that I can't play my music.
    2) The fact that my brother sleeps late bothers me because I can't play my music.
    3) My brother's sleeping late means that I can't play my music, and that fact bothers me.

  b. It's unfortunate.
     You won't be able to join me for lunch.
     My friend is in town.
     You wanted to meet my friend.

    1) (The fact) that you won't be able to join me for lunch is unfortunate because my friend who(m) you wanted to meet is in town.
    2) It's unfortunate that you won't be able to join me for lunch because my friend is in town who(m) you wanted to meet.

  c. Something is (not) likely.
     My brother will remember something.
     Next Friday is my birthday.
     My parents will call my brother.
     My parents will remind my brother.

    1) It is not likely that my brother will remember my birthday, which is next Friday, even though my parents will call him to tell him that.
    2) It is likely that my parents will call my brother to remind him that next Friday is my birthday, but my brother will not remember.

One advantage of this kind of activity is that teachers have the opportunity to guide students away from the less felicitous combinations that result and toward more natural-sounding ones. At the same time, however, students often come up with quite sensible combinations that the teacher would never have thought of!

    There is an alternative, more contextualized way of doing this sort of exercise, but it will somewhat constrain the possible combinations. With some integration, individual combined clause sets may be sequenced in such a way as to form a coherent story or other text, provided the right combinations are chosen. Teachers choosing this option may select paragraphs from newspapers or magazines and adapt them for the purpose of the exercise, creating three- and four-sentence sets of short clauses to combine.

4. Use. The form of raising structures, as well as their use, can be practiced with the help of a series of pictures that depict a progression of events (see, for example, the *Longman Picture Series,* which provides ready-made materials for this sort of activity). The teacher can tell students that they cannot be absolutely certain of what is happening in the pictures, so they will have to hedge their descriptions with verbs like *seem, appear,* and *look like.* This can be a good opportunity for students to practice relatively focused raising structures and relatively unfocused *it*-structures. The teacher can ask a general question first:

> What is happening in this picture?

Appropriate responses might be,

> It seems that it is a very windy day.
> It looks like it is a very windy day in the mountains.

The teacher can then zero in on individuals in the picture and ask,

> What is *the man* doing?

An appropriate response which focuses on the man would be,

> The man seems to be holding onto his hat.

This sort of questioning can continue for the other pictures, until the last picture:

> *Teacher:* How did the story turn out?
> *Student:* It turned out that everyone was safe inside a cabin.
> *Teacher:* Who did the man turn out to be?
> *Student:* He turned out to be a very famous movie star.

The task is also easily adaptable as a written exercise involving narration and description.

5. Form/Meaning. Complex-NP complement structures like *the fact that, the recommendation that,* and so on can be practiced by providing students with a list of possible NPs like the following:

the fact	the news
the claim	the belief
the idea	the announcement/report
the possibility/chance	the recommendation/proposal
the likelihood/probability	the demand
the suggestion	the argument

Students are then given sentences to be turned into complements of suitable NPs chosen from the list; these may include NPs that take subjunctive complements. The sentences represent controversial statements likely to elicit inspired responses of different types:

   a. It has just been announced on the news that engineering students will pay higher college tuition because they will make higher salaries in the future.

   Possible responses:
   1) The idea that engineering students should pay higher tuition is ridiculous because they will not necessarily make higher salaries.
   2) There is no possibility that engineering students will pay higher tuition.
   3) I am surprised to hear the news that engineering students will pay higher tuition, because it does not seem fair.

  b. Cars should be banned completely from the downtown area.

   Possible responses:
   1) I completely agree with the recommendation that cars be banned from the downtown area because it will reduce traffic.
   2) The proposal that cars be banned from the downtown area will cause big problems.
   3) There is no likelihood that cars will be banned from the downtown area because people need to drive through this area.

This exercise can be adapted to an essay-writing task in which students develop an argumentative response to one or another of the statements.

EXERCISES

Test your ability to understand what has been presented.

 1. Identify the following terms and provide an example sentence in which each occurs.
  a. raising to subject   **g.** *easy-to-please* constructions
  b. complex NP   **h.** complex passive
  c. adjective complement   **i.** factive verb
  d. clausal subject   **j.** nonfactive verb
  e. extraposition   **k.** implicative verb
  f. extraposition from NP

 2. State why the following sentences are ungrammatical:
  a. *It seems John to be a successful businessman.
  b. *They avoided that hotel due to it was so expensive.
  c. *To watch Tanya skate it's interesting.
  d. *Nobody ever complains proves this is a happy office.

 3. Draw trees for the base forms of the following sentences and show, where necessary, how mapping rules produce the surface forms.
  a. The fact that our car has broken down forces us to change our plans.
  b. That the record was a smashing success helped to make the singer famous.
  c. It seems clear that someone has made a mistake.
  d. John disagreed with the claim that his senator was unsympathetic to motorists.
  e. The idea is preposterous that parrots are linguistic geniuses.
  f. It is usually assumed that parrots do not understand what they say.
  g. A sponge cake is simple to make with this new recipe.

Test your ability to apply what you know.

 4. Suppose that a writing student who has produced the following sentences asks why you have identified them as incorrect. How would you answer?

  Is not true that Olivia missed her train.
  I thought I was easy to walk that far.
  This kind of movie is boring to be watched.

 5. One way has been mentioned in this chapter for distinguishing between relative clauses with *that* and noun complements with *that:* the word *that* at the beginning of the complement clause cannot be identified with an NP in the clause the way the relative pronoun *that* can. Can you think of another test that can serve to distinguish them?

6. In this chapter we have presented the categories "factive" and "nonfactive" to classify verbs. How would you classify the verbs *see* and *understand* based on the following example sentences?

> I see that you've bought a new car.
> The drunken sailor saw snakes crawling on the floor.
>
> I now understand that there is a faster route to Houston.
> I understood Mary to say that she was from Houston.

Explain your answer based on the criteria presented in the chapter.

BIBLIOGRAPHY

References

Akmajian, A., and F. Heny (1975). *An Introduction to the Principles of Transformational Syntax*. Cambridge: MIT Press.

Baker, C. L. (1989). *English Syntax*. Cambridge: MIT Press.

Emonds, J. E. (1976). *A Transformational Approach to English Syntax*. New York: Academic Press.

Givón, T. (1990). *Syntax: A Functional-Typological Introduction* (vol. 2). Philadelphia: John Benjamins.

Karttunen, L. (1971). "Implicative Verbs," *Language* 47:2, 340–358.

Kiparsky, P., and C. Kiparsky (1970). "Fact." In M. Bierwisch and K. Heidolph (eds.), *Progress in Linguistics*. The Hague: Mouton.

Koster, J. (1978). "Why Subject Sentences Don't Exist." In S. J. Keyser (ed.), *Recent Transformational Studies in European Languages*, Cambridge: MIT Press, 53–64.

Lisovsky, K. (1988). A Discourse Analysis of Nominal *That*-clauses in English. Unpublished Master's thesis, UCLA.

Santos, T. (undated). "The Frequency and Usage of Raised and Non-Raised Structures in English Discourse." Unpublished paper, UCLA.

Suggestions for further reading

Raising to subject and extraposition are discussed in a traditional generative framework in Chapters 8 and 9 of:
Akmajian, A. and F. Heny (1975). Full reference above and in a more recent framework in Chapter 8 of:
Radford, A. (1988). *Transformational Grammar: A First Course*. Cambridge: Cambridge University Press.

A functional discussion of raising, including the easy-to-please *construction appears in Chapter 17 of:*
Givón, T. (1990). Full reference above.

The types of extraposition outlined here and some additional proposed types are discussed in:
Baltin, M (1981). "Strict Bounding" in C. L. Baker & J. J. McCarthy (eds.) *The Logical Problem of Language Acquisition*. Cambridge, MA: MIT Press.

Quirk, R. et al. (1985). *A Comprehensive Grammar of the English Language*. London: Longman (see Chapter 18).

Radford, A. (1988). Full reference above. Chapters 7 and 8; also pays considerable attention to passives within clausal complements.

Grammar textbooks for ESL/EFL students seldom distinguish raising-type infinitives from other types previously discussed in Chapter 31; nor do they normally treat extraposition as a whole, though many books have sections on subject extraposition, that is, moving subject noun clauses to the end of the sentences and then inserting it *whenever a surface subject is required. Some of the texts teaching subject extraposition are:*

Thewlis, S. (1997). *Grammar Dimensions*. Book 3 (2d ed.). Boston: Heinle & Heinle (Unit 6).

Elbaum, S. (1996). *Grammar in Context*. Book 3 (2d ed.). Boston: Heinle & Heinle (Lesson 10).

A presentation of *the fact that and other noun complement structures appear in:*

Frodesen, J. and J. Eyring (1997). *Grammar Dimensions*. Book 4 (2d ed.). Boston: Heinle & Heinle (Unit 23).

A presentation of adjective complements also appears in Unit 20 of the above book. For a variety of suggestions for teaching complements, see:

Danielson, D. and Porter, P. (1990). *Using English: Your Second Language*. Englewood Cliffs, NJ: Prentice-Hall Regents. (Chapters 13 and 14).

ENDNOTES

1. Recent generative grammar has accounted for the ungrammaticality of this sentence by the Empty Category Principle, which says, among other things, that one cannot remove subjects out of embedded *that*-clauses.

2. In more formal register, we have *as if* appearing in place of *like* in these sentences. Since *as if* is already an adverbial subordinator, the addition of the complementizer *that* would result in ungrammatical sentences here as well. In fact, one could argue that *like* is also functioning as an adverbial subordinator in these sentences.

3. It is of course also worthwhile to show that there are less wordy alternatives to sentences like these. As style manuals have long pointed out, the expression *because of the fact that* can be replaced simply with *because.*

4. There is some evidence that these clauses are actually generated not in subject position but in an adjacent position sometimes called "topic." Some evidence for this argument (in Emonds 1976 and Koster 1978) lies in the generally bad results obtained when such clauses are questioned through subject-operator inversion:

> ?Is [that he left without any money] a reason to be distressed?
> ?Did [for her to quit like that] seem as scandalous as you say?

Other possible evidence is that gerunds in the first position in the sentence, which behave more like prototypical subject NPs, cannot extrapose:

> [His watching MTV all day long] did not help his grades.
> *It did not help his grades [**his** watching MTV all day long].

5. Baker (1989) calls these clauses *pseudocomplements* in that they are understood as moved sentential subjects even though they appear in a part of the sentence where clausal complements tend to be.

6. In some cases, more than one type of extraposition may even occur in one and the same sentence:

It's odd that the customers were so dissatisfied who ate the lobster.

In simplified form, the derivation would look like this:

Base structure: [That the customers [who ate the lobster] were so dissatisfied] is odd
Extraposition 1: [ ] is odd [that the customers [who ate the lobster] were dissatisfied]
Extraposition 2: [ ] is odd [that the customers were dissatisfied [who ate the lobster]]

With the addition of *it* to function as the surface subject, the sentence is structurally complete.

7. Sometimes this construction is called "object raising"; see Emonds (1976:77–78).

8. A possible additional source of blending might be the construction *too* + adj *to* + verb, as in *I am too tired to talk* (see Chapter 35).

9. This characteristic, incidentally, distinguishes this construction from other similar-looking ones where the alternation with *it* is not possible:

Mary is happy to help.   *It is happy to help Mary.
Kim is too tired to go out.   *It is too tired to go out Kim.

Chapter

REPORTED SPEECH AND WRITING

INTRODUCTION

Grammar and rhetoric books generally recognize three ways for a speaker or writer to attribute statements or thoughts to other people: *direct quotation, indirect reported speech,* and *paraphrase.* The first of these does not seem to merit extensive discussion from a formal point of view: one simply copies original material (whether full sentences or constituent parts of sentences) verbatim, adds quotation marks, and attributes the quotation to its source through use of a suitable reporting device (most often a verb such as *said* or an expression such as *according to*):

> *Original source* (J. Smith): School budgets will not be cut during this recession.
> *Quotation:* According to Smith, "School budgets will not be cut during this recession."

With indirect reported speech, where one wishes to report the content of the original source without necessarily repeating sentences exactly as they were originally uttered, there are many more options available as well as certain rules of conversion. For example:

Original source (Smith):
> "School budgets will not be cut during this recession."

Indirect reported speech:
a. Smith reports that no school budget cuts will occur during this recession.
b. Smith said that school budgets would not be cut during this recession.
c. Smith claimed that during this/that recession, there would be no reduction in school budgets.
d. Smith predicted that no school budget cuts would occur during this/that recession.

Indirect reported speech plays an important role in everyday conversations (see, for example, Goodwin [1990]). For this reason alone, it justifies attention in an ESL/EFL class. Also, the grammar and vocabulary involved in reported speech are particularly important for students who plan to attend college or university since a great deal of what is done in college-level writing involves paraphrase and summary of research sources, both of which play a central role in academic paper writing. ESL/EFL students must have a firm grasp of the categorical distinction between proper quotation and true paraphrase and how each is done; failure to appreciate the distinction can, after all, lead to charges of plagiarism (when quoted or paraphrased material is not properly cited), distortion of words (when quoted material is inaccurately reproduced), or distortion of ideas (when a source's ideas are inaccurately represented in a paraphrase). While the difference between quoted and paraphrased material may seem straightforward to teachers, it may not be so simple for students; in some areas of the world, presenting uncited quotations as if they were one's own work is simply not considered in the same negative light as it is in English-speaking countries.

In paraphrasing, students must be aware of an author's cognitive stance toward what he or she utters: is the author presenting his or her material as established fact, as conjecture, as proof? Is the student, in presenting the author's ideas, presenting them in such a way as to show the student's agreement with the author, or only as a secondhand report of what the author has said? For all of these reasons, it is important for students to know how reporting is done.

THE FORM OF INDIRECT SPEECH STRUCTURES

THAT-CLAUSES

Reported material can appear in several grammatical frames, but reporting most commonly involves creating complements to a reporting verb such as *say* or *report*. We discuss these frames and verbs more fully later; for the present, we note that ordinary *that*-clauses are probably the most common way in which reporting is done. Recall that the *that* complementizer is structurally optional and that pragmatic factors govern its presence or absence (see the "use" section below).

That-clauses were presented in Chapter 31 as objects of a higher verb. We can thus use this analysis for those indirect reports that have *that* clauses:

Smith reports that budget cuts may occur during this recession.

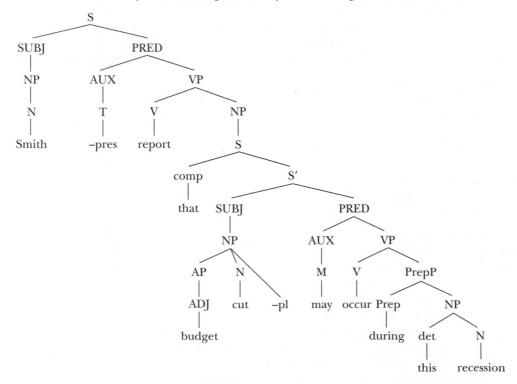

THE SEQUENCE OF TENSES

When tensed, indirect reported clauses are traditionally subject to a rule referred to as *sequence of tenses* or *backshifting*, which is described below.

Backshifting

The standard textbook treatment of the sequence-of-tenses rule, in both descriptive and pedagogical grammars, says that the tense in reported clauses is in some sense controlled by the tense in the reporting clause such that when the reporting verb is in the past tense, the verb in the reported clause must "backshift." The paradigm below illustrates the contexts in which this phenomenon traditionally does and does not occur:

1. Original sentence: "I **am leaving** tomorrow." *(= present progressive)*
    Report:
    Simple present—no backshifting:
      She **says** that she **is leaving tomorrow.**
    Present perfect—no backshifting:
      She **has said** that she **is leaving** tomorrow.
    Simple past + backshifting to past progressive:
      She **said** that she **was leaving** tomorrow/the next day.

2. Original sentence: "I **left** yesterday." *(= simple past)*
    Report:
    Simple present—no backshifting:
      She **says** that she **left** yesterday.
    Present perfect—no backshifting:
      She **has said** that she **left** yesterday.
    Simple past + backshifting to past perfect:
      She **said** that she **had left** yesterday/the day before.

3. Original sentence: "I **have left** already." *(= present perfect)*
    Report:
    Simple present—no backshifting:
      She **says** that she **has left** already.
    Simple past + backshifting to past perfect:
      She **said** that she **had left** already.

4. Original sentence: "I **had left** earlier." *(= past perfect)*
    Report:
    Simple present—no backshifting:
      She **says** that she **had left** earlier.
    Simple past—no backshifting possible:
      She **said** that she **had left** earlier.

5. Original sentence: "I **will leave** soon." *(modal, future)*
    Report:
    Simple present—no backshifting:
      She **says** that she **will leave** soon.
    Simple past + backshifting:
      She **said** that she **would leave** soon.

6. Original hypothetical sentence, not yet uttered: "I **have** the answer."
  Report:
  Modal, future—no backshifting[1]:
    She **will say** that she **has** the answer.

As the examples illustrate, tense shifting occurs only when the main verb is in a past tense; otherwise the tense remains as in the original quotation. What is most important to notice is that the tense in the reported clause bears no necessary relation to whether the actual event described is in the past at the time the spoken or written report is made. That is, if one says on March 11, "She said today that she *was* leaving on March 15," the listener will interpret the woman's date of departure to be in four days—that is, four days in the future from the listener/speaker's perspective—rather than a March date in some previous year. What is happening here seems to be a shift in *perspective* with regard to the time of the utterance reported on, which is of necessity in the past.

The traditional tense switch is accompanied by:
  a. the changing of pronouns from first-person to third-person forms, and
  b. the changing of *tomorrow* to *the next day* and the changing of *yesterday* to *the day before.*

Such changes are called *deictic shifts,* from the Greek word *deixis* meaning "to point," a term previously mentioned elsewhere in this book. These shifts will be described in the course of this chapter.

Many ESL/EFL students will find the sequence-of-tenses rule rather bizarre. It is not a feature found in every language, not even in languages that have rich systems of verb tense. The reason for the difficulty is that in constructions of reporting, English tends to index tense to the time at which the reported utterance was originally made rather than to the time that the utterance is reported. While some other languages (German being one of them) exhibit a similar tendency, many others do not. For example, Comrie (1984:109) reports that in Russian, while there is a deictic shift for adverbials, tenses in reported speech remain identical to those in the original utterance. Other languages, such as Yoruba, have no tense shift because they do not encode grammatical tense at all (Coulmas 1986:14). For such reasons, a teacher should expect learners to have difficulties.

Exceptions to Backshifting

What makes the backshifting rule even more difficult is that there are exceptions in use—a fact to which most descriptive and ESL/EFL grammar books are sensitive, and one which calls the "rule" into question. Unfortunately, research has not yet revealed a completely satisfying unity among these exceptions. We list three standard exceptions here:

State-event remains true. Thompson (1994:109ff.), drawing on a corpus database, suggests that present tense is retained in reported clauses when the author wishes to emphasize that the state or event in question still holds true at the time of reporting and/or is not presented as something temporary. He offers as illustration the following example, where the first sentence deals with a general on-going policy (no tense shift) and the second sentence deals with a specific situation (tense shift):

> A Foreign Ministry spokesman *said* government policy *is* not to sell arms to sensitive areas. But he *said* his country *needed* the income to convert arms factories to non-military production.

Perceived general truths. Many sources such as Quirk et al. (1985:1027f.) mention as a chief source of exceptions cases of general truths, as in their examples,

> Their teacher told them that the earth *moves* around the sun.
> Socrates said that nothing *can* harm a good man.

To put this more precisely, it seems that the key lies in what is *perceived* to be general or timeless truth; in such cases, we hold that we cannot imagine a state of affairs in the world other than the one we have mentally committed ourselves to. As a hypothetical contrastive case in point, consider the case of a child who is told by a trusted older sister that, for example, seven plus four equals twelve. The child might say, "My sister told me that seven plus four is twelve." Upon hearing otherwise from a (more trusted) teacher and committing inwardly to this new answer, the child might say to the sister (perhaps in disappointment or anger), "You told me that seven plus four *was* twelve." The actual sum presumably remains constant regardless of anyone's belief, but the child's mental *commitment* to the general truth of a certain sum has changed.

Immediate reports. A third case in which tense shifting tends not to occur involves a specific discourse context. When a statement is reported to a third person by a second person immediately following its utterance by a first person, it will often tend to be repeated with its original tenses unchanged[2]:

> *Speaker A:* We will be having polenta for lunch.
> *Speaker B:* What did he say?
> *Speaker C:* He said we'll be having polenta for lunch.

Let us now look at reported speech that involves constructions other than ordinary *that*-clauses.

SUBJUNCTIVES

We have already outlined the nature of subjunctive clauses in Chapter 31 on complementation. Where subjunctive reporting verbs are concerned, the same general features exist as with other subjunctives. First, there is no tense in the complement, which means that backshifting does not apply:

> *Speaker A:* I recommend that you leave tomorrow.
> She recommends that we leave tomorrow.
> She recommended that we leave tomorrow/the next day.
> She had recommended that we leave tomorrow/the next day.

Deictic shifts in pronouns and time adverbials, however, do apply as with ordinary *that*-clauses, as the examples illustrate. Second, as we showed in Chapter 31, the verbs that take subjunctive complements all involve one agent who is oriented toward inducing another agent to perform an act. These verbs might usefully be ordered along a scale from weak to strong: *suggest, propose, recommend, urge, ask* (in the sense of *request*), *require, demand.* The fact that subjunctive complements typically do not take modal verbs such as *must* (** She demanded that I must go*) might be accounted for if we assume that verbs which take subjunctives already have the notions of *should* or *must* as part of their meaning, thus rendering the use of modals redundant. Teachers should expect many second-language problems in the production of these verbs, which learners tend very strongly to produce with modals following them or with infinitival complements, as in **She recommended me to go.* Since these really represent only a small subset of English verbs, students tend to overgeneralize the more commonly occurring complement frames to subjunctives.

INDIRECT IMPERATIVES

Many imperative sentences can be reported accurately with verbs such as *demand* or *insist* that take subjunctive *that*-clause complements:

> "Please go away!" → He asked/insisted that I (please) go away.

Imperatives can also be reported with ordinary *that*-clauses (the presence of the indirect object with verbs like *tell* is dealt with later in the chapter):

> "Please go away!" → He said that I should go away.
> → He told me that I should go away.

However, it is probably most common for imperatives to be paraphrased with infinitival complements using the main-clause verbs *tell, order, ask*:

> "Please go away!" → He told (asked, ordered) me to (please) go away.

Imperatives can, of course, be used for purposes other than outright commands. They can, for instance, be used for invitations as in

> "Stop by for some dessert and coffee tonight!"
> → She asked (= invited) us to stop by for some dessert and coffee tonight.

Indirect imperatives with *to* tend to be much less problematical for ESL/EFL students than subjunctive forms, perhaps because they are simpler and also occur much more frequently in native speaker discourse and thus in the input the learners are likely to receive.

INDIRECT QUESTIONS

An *indirect question* (or *embedded question*) is so called because the utterer is typically not asking a question but reporting a real or hypothetical question.[3] The difference between direct and hypothetical questions may be illustrated with the following pair of sentences:

> Is anyone interested in the movie?
> She wants to know *whether/if* anyone is interested in the movie.

In the first case, the speaker is asking the question, while in the second case, the speaker may simply wish to state a fact about someone else's wishes and does so with *whether* or *if* plus a dependent clause. Just as we have placed the complementizer *that* into a comp position directly under the embedded S, just to the left of the S' position, so will we place *whether/if* into comp in yes/no indirect questions. In all other respects, the trees are identical.

Word Order

We covered the formation, meaning, and use of direct yes/no and *wh*-questions in Chapters 11 and 13. There, we discussed the fact that direct questions involve subject-operator inversion and the need in certain cases to add a form of the operator *do*. Thus we get pairs like

> Susan can come with us. → Can Susan come with us?
> It is raining in Fresno. → Is it raining in Fresno?
> She has bought a new car. → What has she bought?
> We arrived before noon. → When did you arrive?

But as the sentences below show, indirect yes/no questions involve no movement at all; clauses follow normal declarative subject-verb-object order:

> Mary asked [whether Susan could come with us].
> (*Mary asked whether could Susan come with us.)
> I wonder [if it is raining in Fresno].
> (*I wonder if is it raining in Fresno.)
> They inquired [whether she had bought a new car].
> (*They inquired whether had she bought a new car.)

Since there is no movement of an operator, there is also no need for addition of the *do* operator in indirect *wh*-questions that have no inherent operator:

> They asked us [when we arrived].
>
> (*They asked us when $\begin{Bmatrix} \text{we did} \\ \text{did we} \end{Bmatrix}$ arrive.)

While *do* may be used in the uninverted word order with heavy stress to mark special emphasis, it cannot be used in the normal way simply as a syntactic operator.

The rule of non-inversion in embedded questions, which is standard, is complicated by the fact that speakers of some ethnic dialects, such as Black English Vernacular and of some regional dialects such as the one spoken in the New York City area, often invert subject and operator in embedded *wh*-questions as they would in unembedded questions:

> ?She asked where was I going.
> ?They asked what was the time.

Further research is needed to show the extent of such inversion and whether or not there are pragmatic factors such as length of the embedded question that help explain the environments in which such inversion most often occurs.

Main-Verb Choices and Complementizer Types

There is a much smaller range of main-clause verb choices in indirect question structures than in indirect declarative statements. The most common are *ask, inquire,* and *wonder*. All are capable of taking either tensed-clause or subject-controlled infinitival complements. In the case of complements with a tense or modal, where the indirect question is of a yes/no type, either *whether* or *if* may appear as the complementizer; for infinitives, only *whether* may appear:

> John asked (whether/if) he should bring dessert.
> John asked (whether/*if) to bring dessert.

There are periphrastic methods of introducing such questions such as

> Cindy wanted to know whether to bring dessert.
> They did not know whether/if they would return.
> It's an interesting question whether/if the global climate is really getting warmer.

It is also possible to have indirect informational *wh*-questions, as below:

> **a.** We wondered [what we should do] in case of an emergency.
> **b.** We wondered [what to do] in case of an emergency.
> **c.** We wondered [which plants we should water].
> **d.** We wondered [which plants to water].

In such cases, the *wh*-word or expression gets fronted to serve in place of *whether/if* as a complementizer. In the infinitival cases, above (*b* and *d*), the logical subject of the infinitive will be PRO—that is, the same as the subject of the sentence as a whole.[4]

There are also a number of other verbs which may take either *that*-complements or infinitives containing *wh*-words where no actual direct or indirect question is involved. These are free relatives and relative adverbials. Some verbs associated with such cases are *discover, explain, find out, know, learn, show, teach,* and *tell*:

> We discovered [*what* the cause of the leak was].
> We discovered by accident [*how* to get to our destination].
> We found out [*who* we should call].
> We found out [*where* to look for eagles].
> The students learned [*which Europeans* had visited America first].
> The students learned [*how* to do subtraction problems].

An electrician should know [*how* one fixes an electrical short].
An electrician should know [*what* to do about our problem].
Our guide showed us [*which way* we should go].
Our guide showed us [*which way* to go].

The difference between an embedded indirect *wh*-question and a free relative or relative adverbial is often quite subtle. Tests of paraphrasing can be helpful; if the *wh*-word can best be paraphrased in the following manner

what = the thing that
who = the person who
how = the way that
where = the place where

and other minor adjustments yield a good sentence, then we have a relative clause of sorts:

We discovered what the cause of the leak was.
= We discovered the thing that was the cause of the leak.

If the *wh*-clause can best be paraphrased as a direct question with minor adjustments, then we have an embedded indirect question.

He asked what we were doing.
He asked, "What are you doing?"

Notice that if we reverse these paraphrase tests on these two sentences, the results are awkward and do not yield good paraphrases:

?We discovered, "What was the cause of the leak?"
?He asked the thing that we were doing.

To sum up this section, the tree for an indirect yes/no question with *whether* or *if* is as follows:

John asked whether he should bring dessert.

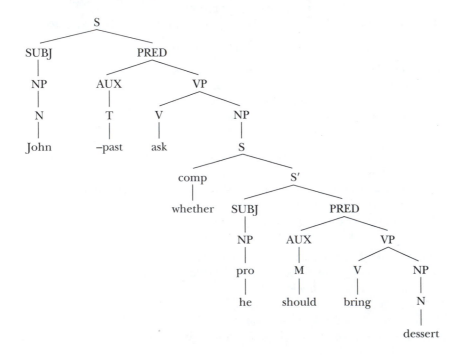

The tree for an infinitival embedded yes/no question with *whether* will be:

John asked whether to bring dessert.

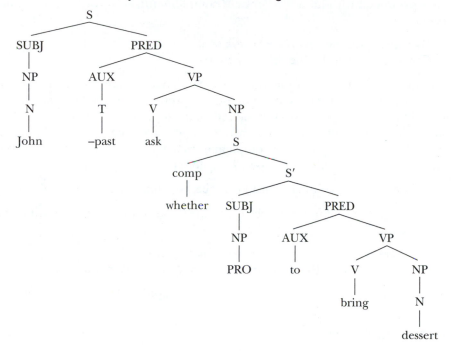

The tree for an embedded indirect *wh*-question, after *wh*-fronting applies, is:

They asked what we were doing.

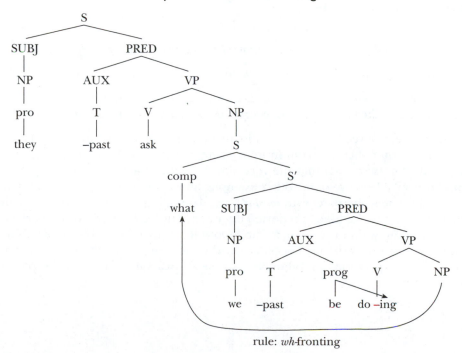

rule: *wh*-fronting

Special ESL/EFL Issues with Indirect Questions

ESL/EFL students often have trouble with embedded yes/no questions. Typically, such clauses are produced without a *whether* or *if* complementizer and with direct-question word order:

> *My friend asked me did I really believe that.
> *Can you tell me is this the right way to go?

There is some irony in this type of learner error. Students typically have some initial difficulty producing properly inverted direct questions, producing instead normal declarative word order. Once the proper order is mastered, many students then understandably tend to transfer it to indirect questions, where inversion produces ungrammatical results!

In some languages, two adjacent complementizers may occur in embedded "yes/no" questions, resulting in the following type of transfer error:

> *My friend asked me whether that I really believed the story.

Also in some languages, but not in English, a complementizer may co-occur with an information question:

> *The woman asked us that how we could fix the flat tire.
> *She wants to know that when would be a good time to visit you.

It must simply be pointed out that English never has the option of double complementizers.

OTHER DEICTIC SHIFTS

As was illustrated in the beginning of this chapter, the use of indirect speech may require not only shifts in tense but also shifts in time and place adverbials and in personal and demonstrative pronouns.

Time/Place Adverbial Shifts

In the example given at the beginning of this chapter,

> "School budgets will not be cut during this recession."—Smith

a good paraphrase might contain either *this* or *that,* but the implications will be different:

> Smith predicted that no school budget cuts would occur during *this* recession.
> Smith predicted that no school budget cuts would occur during *that* recession.

In the first case, the reader or hearer will assume that the recession in question is still ongoing at the time that the paraphrase is written; in the second case, one might easily assume with the use of *that* that the recession is over at the time of writing. Likewise, options are available in two of the other examples above where *tomorrow* alternates with *the next day* and *yesterday* alternates with *the day before,* depending on the relation of the time of original utterance to the time of reported utterance. Such shifts in time are marked quite systematically and without overlap, as the following comparative tables show. Table 33.1 contains expressions with speaker-time, i.e. the moment of speaking, as the point of reference; the expressions in Table 33.2 are used with some point in the past as the reference-point:

Table 33.1 *Expressions used with reference to time of speaking*

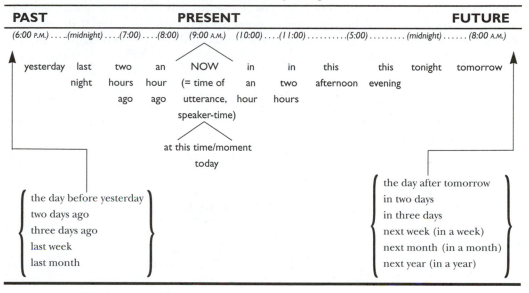

PAST				PRESENT						FUTURE
(6:00 P.M.).....(midnight)....(7:00)....(8:00)				(9:00 A.M.)	(10:00)....(11:00).........(5:00)........ midnight......(8:00 A.M.)					
yesterday	last night	two hours ago	an hour ago	NOW (= time of utterance, speaker-time)	in an hour	in two hours	this afternoon	this evening	tonight	tomorrow
				at this time/moment						
				today						

the day before yesterday
two days ago
three days ago
last week
last month

the day after tomorrow
in two days
in three days
next week (in a week)
next month (in a month)
next year (in a year)

Table 33.2 *Expressions used with reference to shifted time*[5]

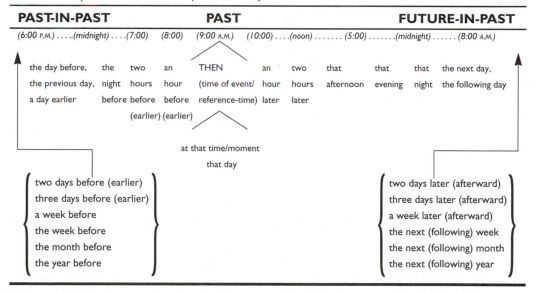

PAST-IN-PAST				PAST						FUTURE-IN-PAST
(6:00 P.M.).....(midnight)....(7:00)			(8:00)	(9:00 A.M.)	(10:00)....(noon).......(5:00).......(midnight)......(8:00 A.M.)					
the day before, the previous day, a day earlier	the night before	two hours before (earlier)	an hour before (earlier)	THEN (time of event/ reference-time)	an hour later	two hours later	that afternoon	that evening	that night	the next day, the following day
				at that time/moment						
				that day						

two days before (earlier)
three days before (earlier)
a week before
the week before
the month before
the year before

two days later (afterward)
three days later (afterward)
a week later (afterward)
the next (following) week
the next (following) month
the next (following) year

The parallel between these adverbials and tense-backshifting is evident; however, there are no "exceptions" as there was with tense choice. One cannot use the adverb *tomorrow* to talk about the day after the day that is talked about in a reported (dependent) clause unless the condition for using *tomorrow* still prevails in the main clause as well. Likewise, one cannot use *the next day* in an utterance to refer to the day after the utterance, unless the condition for using this expression still obtains in the main clause.

The same considerations apply to place-deictics, although the range of distinctions is not as large: the adverb *here* becomes *there* (or vice versa), but this shift is again subject to consideration of whether the reported utterance was or was not uttered in the same location as the report. If the two places remain identical, then there is no shift; if there is no identity, there is a shift:

Original quote:

"I have been cleaning $\left\{ \begin{array}{l} \text{here} \\ \text{this room} \end{array} \right\}$ all day."

Report (uttered in the same room):

She said she had been cleaning $\left\{ \begin{array}{l} \text{here} \\ \text{this room} \end{array} \right\}$ all day.

Report (uttered elsewhere):

She said she had been cleaning $\left\{ \begin{array}{l} \text{there} \\ \text{that room} \end{array} \right\}$ all day.

Deictic Shifts in Pronouns

Just as time and place adverbials shift, pronominal forms also change as necessary. Most commonly, first- and second-person forms change to third-person forms:

Original quote:
   "*I* hope that a solution to the problem will soon be found."
Reported utterance:
   Smith said that *he* hoped for a quick solution to the problem.

Under the proper circumstances, of course, quoted third-person forms can be shifted to first- and second-person forms, if the reference of the form is to the reporter or the reader/hearer of the report:

Original quote by Mary:
   "I hope that Fred gets better soon."
Report by Fred:
   Mary says that she hopes that *I* get better soon.
Report by someone speaking/writing to Fred:
   Mary says that she hopes that *you* get better soon.

In another set of circumstances, a first-person form might be properly paraphrased by a second-person form, and vice versa, when interlocutors are reporting on their own and each other's speech:

Original quote:
   I am your best friend.
Report:
   You said you were my best friend.
Response to report:
   Yes, I said I was your best friend.

   In general, it can be said that time/place adverbial shifts and pronoun shifts seldom leave the reporter with more than a single proper choice among forms. In this they contrast with backshifts in verb tense, which frequently permit real options. While pronoun shifts pose relatively few problems for ESL/EFL students, it is worthwhile for a teacher to spend some time focusing on adverbial shifts because, as with tense shift, the required changes are not always reflected in exactly the same ways in other languages' conventions for encoding time and place expressions.

SHIFTING AND PARTIAL QUOTATIONS

We have presented the complementizer *that* as a specific signal of indirect speech—that is, of a genuine paraphrase. It is not used to preface full quotations. Thus, a sequence like the following is not acceptable:

> *He said that, "The strong economy is likely to improve still further this year."

A full quotation requires the absence of *that*. However, it is often the case that what follows the complementizer is a mixture of quotation and paraphrase, and the quotation does not directly follow *that*, in which case *that* may become acceptable:

> He said that the economy, which has been strong, "is likely to improve still further this year."

However, there are limits to such mixing that are imposed as a result of the need for the various shifts we have discussed. For example,

> *Direct quotation:*
> The mayor told me, "I am impressed at the level of your commitment this year to the betterment of our city."
> *Full indirect report:*
> The mayor told me that he was impressed with the level of my commitment that year to the betterment of my home town.
> *Partial indirect reports:*
> *The mayor told me that he was impressed with "the level of your commitment this year to the betterment of our city."
> *The mayor told me that "I am impressed at the level of your commitment" that year to the betterment of my home town.

The problem in the last two examples is related to the need for complete deictic shifts throughout the report. Without these shifts, the references of *I, you/your, our,* and *this/that year* become unclear enough to cause severe comprehension problems for readers. The conclusion to draw is that where deictic shifts are possible in reporting, a writer has three choices: (a) full quotation, (b) full paraphrase, or (c) the use of shifted deictics in square brackets within quotations to replace the original, unshifted ones:

> The mayor told me that he was "impressed with the degree of [my] commitment [that] year to the betterment of our city."

REPORTING NOUNS AND OTHER METHODS OF ATTRIBUTION

So far, most of this chapter has covered the use of main-clause verbs to perform attributions in complement clause constructions. It should not, however, be assumed that indirect speech need always be marked in this way. For example, many of the verbs used for reporting have related noun forms which can also serve as reporting devices. Thompson (1994:115ff.) provides a substantial list of reporting nouns. To give one example, the content of the clause below may be incorporated into a corresponding noun phrase:

> Smith believed that school budgets should not be cut.
> . . . Smith's belief that school budgets should not be cut . . .

Other examples involve alternations between *notify/notification, reveal/revelation,* and *complain/complaint*. Predicated adjectives can also be used to alternate with verbs, provided other necessary changes occur:

> The politician insisted that taxes be cut.
> The politician was insistent on taxes being cut.

There are also a number of conventional ways that prepositional phrases are used in citation. The most common is probably the phrase *according to X*; others include *in the opinion of X, in X's view,* and so on.

Still other citation options that are used frequently in monologic narrative and conversation have been called *free indirect discourse* (Rimmon-Kenan 1983) and *zero-quotatives* (Yule, Mathis, and HopKins 1992). In the first option, the identity of the reporting author often seems to phase into the identity of the person reported on, thereby producing what seems closer to direct than to indirect speech. Often, what is reported in this way are thoughts:

> Little Red Riding Hood objected to her mother's advice. Why should she always take the same path to Gran[d]ma's? She might see something different if she could cut through the woods.   (Yule, Mathis, and HopKins 1992:247)

The second and third sentences cannot be direct quotations given the use of the third person pronoun *she*. Sometimes the standard textbook rule that says that no subject-operator inversion may occur in embedded clauses seems violated, as in a further example from the authors cited above:

> Mr. H. asked didn't the town get 2% of sales from the company and wasn't it a 15-year contract with a 10-year pension.   (1992:247)

Given appropriate discourse contexts and adequate contrast and texture in voice quality (i.e., Yule (1995)), even entire dialogues can be represented without conventional markers of speaker-change, as in the following text with two zero-quotatives which also makes use of the expression *be like* (a predicate now current among younger speakers with the meaning of "say something approximately like") in the context of a speaker's conversation with her mother:

> She's like, "*So what time did you get in?*" "We got in at two-thirty." "*Well I got home a little after one*". . .   (1992:249)

Two other expressions, both current among younger speakers are the verb *go* and the predicate *be all*, as illustrated in the following constructed example:

> I said, "What are we gonna do, then?" And she goes, "What are you asking me for?" And I go, "You're the one who made the suggestion," and she's all, "Yeah, but you're the one with the money". . .

Yule, Mathis, and HopKins note that everyday reporting in conversation is full of such devices unlikely to be found in textbooks and that ESL/EFL students ought to be made aware of them not so much in order to produce them as to avoid misunderstanding them when they encounter such reporting strategies in everyday conversation.

THE MEANING OF REPORTING DEVICES

THE COMPLEMENTS OF REPORTING VERBS

As should be obvious by now, verbs used for reporting do not all share identical complement types. Verbs like *say* require tensed *that*-clause complements, verbs like *wonder* take question complements (i.e. both yes/no and *wh-*), verbs like *order* take infinitives, and others take tenseless subjunctive clauses. While some of these verbs could also be cross-listed in the lexicon for either one type of complement or another with virtually the same meaning, other cases involve identical verbs whose meaning changes according to the type of complement following them. We list three cases here. Complements to the verb *insist* can be either ordinary declarative or subjunctive, with a marked difference in meaning:

> Jack insists that we have visited that place.
> Jack insists that we visit that place.

In the first case, Jack expresses his certainty that we have been at that place before, while in the second, he strongly recommends our visiting that place at some time in the future.

The verb *ask* can accompany either subjunctives or interrogatives, again with a meaning change:

> The conductor asked that we give him our tickets. *(asked = requested)*
> The conductor asked us where we were going. *(asked = queried)*

Second, many verbs used in reporting such as *notice, remember, forget, see,* and *know* do not change their meaning when negated, but there may be a change in the presumed factual status of the complement depending on which complementizer is chosen:

> They noticed/remembered/knew that those birds flew south in the fall.
> **a.** They did not notice/remember/know that those birds flew south in the fall.
> **b.** They did not notice/remember/know whether those birds flew south in the fall.

In example (a), it is still presumed true that the birds fly south in fall. In example (b), it does not necessarily hold true; in this case, the factive presupposition ceases to hold.

Finally, some verbs require either direct or indirect objects, some cannot take them, and some take them optionally. A few examples are listed below:

> No indirect object: *agree, realize, conclude, think, believe, say, prove, wonder*
> I agreed (*him) that it was true.
> They said (*him) that it was time to go.
> Obligatory indirect object: *tell, assure, convince, persuade, remind, inform*
> She told us the way to San Jose.
> The magician convinced the audience of his powers.
> Optional indirect object: *promise, show, warn, ask*
> You showed (us) what the results would be.
> Please ask (me) if you have any questions.

This is information that students will have to learn one verb at a time; since there does not seem to be any reason for why a verb like *inform* must take an overt indirect object, teachers should expect to see errors in this area even at advanced stages of learning.

Choice of *If* Versus *Whether*

Many traditional grammarians claim that the difference between *if* and *whether* is one of register, *whether* being used when a more formal register is desired. This observation, however, does not give us the whole picture.

Bolinger (1975) has suggested that there is a difference between these two complementizers in that *if* marks true yes/no questions, whereas *whether* implies the existence of alternatives. Although this distinction is subtle, it may be true that *whether* would be more frequently selected in situations where the listener is being asked to make a choice:

> Margaret: Do you prefer Mexican or Greek food?
> Margaret asked whether I preferred Mexican or Greek food.

Further support for Bolinger's hypothesis might be the fact that only *whether* can be immediately followed by *or not:*

I wondered $\left\{ \begin{array}{l} \text{whether} \\ \text{*if} \end{array} \right\}$ or not Helen was coming.

The subordinator *if,* however, may also be followed by *or not,* provided that there is a short clause intervening:

I wondered if Helen was coming or not.

A co-occurrence restriction that always distinguishes between *if* and *whether* is that only *whether* can occur after prepositions or participial *-ing* forms functioning like prepositions:

I inquired as to $\left\{ \begin{array}{l} \text{whether} \\ \text{*if} \end{array} \right\}$ there were any new developments.

We asked them regarding $\left\{ \begin{array}{l} \text{whether} \\ \text{*if} \end{array} \right\}$ there were any new developments.

Brown Ssensalo (1991) carried out a data-based study of *if* vs. *whether* as complementizers of reported yes/no questions in written English discourse and found that usage was genre sensitive. College textbooks and professional journals strongly preferred *whether* (91%), newspapers had a modest preference for *whether* (63%), and children's literature tended to use *if* (67%). Among the frequently occurring main verbs that preferred *if* were *ask, see,* and *wonder,* in order of frequency. The most frequently occurring verbs that selected *whether* (again in order of frequency) were *decide, question, determine,* and *know.* Brown Ssensalo concluded that verbs of interrogation tended to select *if* whereas verbs of mental activity tended to select *whether;* a main verb's semantic category tended to override the genre in which it occurred and accounted twice as often as genre for the use of these two complementizers in writing.

Further research is needed to determine whether the same trends obtain in oral discourse.

THE SEMANTICS OF REPORTING VERBS

It must be said from the beginning that the distinction between reporting verbs and other verbs is often a matter of the way they are used in a given set of circumstances, not a matter of inherent verbal semantics. The term "reporting verb" is used here rather broadly: we mean any verb used in a context where someone else's statements or thoughts are being commented on, much as a journalist would report.

Simple Declarative Reporting Verbs

There are a host of possible verbs with which to mark reported utterances. Quirk et al. (1985:1181) list over 150 of them, many of which overlap in meaning. They divide these into several categories, including those they call "public" and "private" types—that is, those in which the person reported on has actually said or written something publicly observable—and those in which only an inner "intellectual state" is reported. For ESL/EFL teachers, Quirk et al.'s distinctions may be of less importance than the distinction mentioned in Chapter 31 on complementation, which we revisit now: the factive-nonfactive distinction. Below is a listing of some of the more common factive/nonfactive reporting verbs and a capsule description of their relative complexity. We might adopt Quirk et al.'s feature [public] as basic and develop further features in the manner below, taking the verb *believe* as an understood primitive:

Nonfactive
believe
say, assert = [*believe* + public]
claim = [*say* + nonobvious]
argue = [*claim* + reasons]
assume = [*believe* + no reasons]
suspect = [*believe* + doubt]
suggest = [*say* + doubt]
be certain = [*believe* + no doubt]

Factive
know, be aware = [*believe* + FACT]
reveal, show, point out = [*know* + public]
prove, demonstrate = [*show* + reasons]
realize, notice = [come to *know*]
discover = [*realize* + nonobvious]

Students may be surprised to hear that *to be certain* about something says nothing definitive about the actual truth-value of the proposition that one is certain about; it merely reflects a person's cognitive state. Some verbs, such as *explain* or *understand*, may be somewhat more ambiguous with regard to the factive-nonfactive distinction.

> *understand*
> factive: He understood (the fact) that $4^2 = 16$.
>   ("$4^2 = 16$" even if one questions or negates the higher verb.)
> nonfactive: The children understood that their uncle would come later.
>   (i.e., Their understanding was misguided, inaccurate.)

However, there is a decisive difference in such a large majority of cases that the distinction is worth noting. Other verbs may be somewhat more difficult to present in terms of simple features. (For instance, to *mention* something is to *say* it, but the two verbs are not completely interchangeable.)

Emotional-State Reporting Verbs

There is a subclass of declarative reporting verbs that reveal not only a cognitive but also an affective state. These include verbs such as *complain, exclaim, rejoice, lament;* if we represent these verbs as well with semantic features, we might do so as follows:

complain = [*say* + anger]
exclaim = [*say* + surprise]
rejoice = [*say* + joyfulness]
lament = [*say* + sadness]

Interrogative Reporting Verbs

The factive-nonfactive distinction does not seem to apply when the truth of a proposition is being questioned. However, some of the same other distinctions mentioned do apply. For example, *to wonder* seems to differ from *to ask* in the feature [public]:

wonder [not know] + [desire to know]
ask [not know] + [desire to know] + [public]

One can "wonder" without making public one's wonder, but "asking" seems to imply a "public" wonder.

ESL/EFL writers, even at the advanced levels, tend to rely heavily on "simple" verbs such as *say* and *think* to indicate what another speaker or author has said. This may reflect a certain reluctance to use verbs with more complex semantic features whose informational content is more precise. Indeed, such verbs may prove difficult to use in a nativelike way, and there may not always be near-exact equivalents in students' native languages. For this reason, developing student writers may appreciate an analysis using semantic features such as those above.

ISSUES OF USE IN REPORTING

QUOTATION VERSUS INDIRECT REPORTING IN WRITING

In spoken language, one is seldom expected to report others' oral utterances in a fully accurate way by quoting directly, for the simple reason that it is in most cases impossible to do so. In those cases where it is possible—such as when one reads directly from a written source—ESL/EFL students should be aware of the convention of beginning a spoken quotation by uttering "quote" or "and I quote" prior to the first word of the quotation and uttering "unquote" after the last word. This convention is the oral equivalent of proper written citation.

In writing that utilizes written sources, however, students are constantly faced with the choice of whether or not to quote. Nearly all rhetoric manuals cover this topic, and we see no reason to alter or elaborate on the usual guidelines. One current source says, for example,

> As a general rule, quote only in these situations: (1) the wording of the source is particularly memorable or vivid and expresses a point so well that you cannot improve it without destroying the meaning; (2) the words of reliable or respected authorities would lend support to your position; (3) you wish to highlight the author's opinions; (4) you wish to cite an author whose opinions challenge or vary greatly from other experts'. Paraphrase those passages whose details you wish to note completely but whose language is not particularly striking. (R. E. Axelrod and C. R. Cooper (1994), *St. Martin's Guide to Writing,* Fourth Short Edition. New York: St. Martin's Press, 494–495)

We will not attempt to determine here how a seasoned native writer might come to the decision that one or another of these conditions is actually met. We would like to point out, however, that guidelines such as these are written on the assumption that a writer will know what counts as "memorable or vivid" and that he/she will in most other cases be able to paraphrase without "destroying the meaning" of a text. For an ESL/EFL writer, it will often not be possible to distinguish what represents highly personalized writing in a given text from what is simply ordinary, everyday prose. For example, one college ESL student was presented with the following passage to paraphrase:

> Pure monopoly is at the opposite end of the market continuum from pure competition in the sense that pure competition has many firms and pure monopoly has but one . . . (from R. C. Ammacher and H. H. Ulbrich (1989). *Principles of Microeconomics.* Cincinnati: South-Western)

The student's paraphrase was as follows:

> According to Ammacher and Ulbrich, there is a continuum in the types of markets. Pure monopoly is at one end with one firm, and pure competition is at the other end with many firms.

The ESL student has repeated the words *continuum, pure monopoly, firm,* and *pure competition* without quotation marks, and it is likely that no professor would object to her doing so. Though they are not among the most frequently used words in everyday speech, these four expressions have predictable and regular uses in the field of economics and are so presented in classes. Contrast this now with another passage that the same ESL writer was called upon to paraphrase:

> It ought to be obvious that homelessness cannot be the result of a 'festering value system,' or 'free-market capitalism,' or a 'system firmly rooted in competition or self-interest,' or any other long-term systemic feature of American society, for the simple reason that all these have remained more or less what they always have been, and so cannot explain the rise of homelessness *now*. (from T. Main, "What We Know about the Homeless." *Commentary*, May 1988)

The ESL writer paraphrased the first part of this passage as follows:

> Main says that homelessness is not the result of a system of values that is festering.

The original author's choice of the word *festering* was a metaphorical one; as an economic conservative, he appears to be imitating the sort of language that he perceives as typical of liberals (as suggested by his own single-quoting of phrases), and perhaps doing so with the intention of providing color to his writing. A paraphrase of this passage that retains the word *festering* would seem to call for the word to be placed in quotation marks. However, it may not be at all obvious to the student why quotation is called for in this instance but not in the first. One reason for this is that the unusual "vividness" of the word *festering* may not be at all apparent to an ESL/EFL student; another reason is that a grasp of the political-cultural context of the original writer's word choice may be beyond the student's reach.

The overuse of long quotations is common in ESL/EFL writing based on written sources; the reasons for this overuse surely overlap only partially with the reasons why native-speaker writers might also quote more than is necessary. The task of paraphrasing another writer may be particularly difficult for an ESL writer. For a native writer, the vocabulary and syntactic patterns in the original text have in most cases already been internalized prior to the reading of the text; the average native writer's linguistic competence already permits multiple alternative means to recast the original text in alternative words and structures in such a way that the paraphrases will not be judged as distortions of the original author's meaning or as plagiarism. For a developing ESL/EFL writer, this may not be the case at all: each reading of a text may present a wealth of linguistic challenges, especially for writers whose exposure to English study has been limited to classes in formal aspects of the language. For this reason, student ESL/EFL writers will likely need extensive practice in the techniques of para-phrasing, in conjunction with the active development of other language skills.

PRESENCE AND ABSENCE OF *THAT* WITH *SAID*

In Chapter 31 we discussed the presence or absence of the complementizer *that* with respect to all verbs taking *that* complements. Here we restrict our observations to the co-occurrence of *that* with the verb *said* in written American English.

Using 150 tokens of "*said* + *that* clause," Huang (1993) found that 76 percent of the tokens occurred without *that*. This was explained by Huang based on the following:

a. Ninety one percent of tokens without *that* had personal pronoun subjects, which favored deletion of *that*.

> Doctors at the hospital said he was partially paralyzed.

b. When the main verb subject and *that* clause subject were co-referential, deletion of *that* occurred in 94 percent of such tokens.

> The president *said* he was representing her.

Does any variable favor the retention of *that*? Huang found that when an adverb inter-vened between the verb *said* and the complement clause, *that* was retained 65 percent of the time (23 tokens).

> Mr. W. said yesterday *that* work continued through the week.

More research along these lines with other reporting verbs would be useful.

PRESENT VERSUS PAST TENSE WITH REPORTING VERBS

While much has been said about the sequence of tenses in complex sentences when a main verb occurs in a past tense, we have said nothing about how a writer chooses between present and past tense in main clauses—i.e., *Smith says* X versus *Smith said* X.

Vividness

One criterion mentioned by Thompson (1994:110ff.) that bears on tense choice is the desire to achieve a "vividness effect," a desire mentioned in Chapters 7 and 9 in connection with historical present tense in general. The difference in effect can be seen below:

> The newspaper said the shop windows downtown are/were all decorated for the holidays.

> The newspaper says the shop windows downtown are all decorated for the holidays.

The choice of present tense in the second sentence may reflect the speaker's sense of immediacy and vividness.

Present Relevance

Another criterion mentioned by Thompson has already been noted in connection with a condition where sequence-of-tenses can be overridden: the case in which the reporter wishes to emphasize that a statement is still true or somehow of present relevance. Thompson offers the following as examples:

> The shopkeeper says he won't be able to carry on if the population drops any further.

> It helps that your friend's handy with a pistol. She tells me that she actually got in some target practice in the woods yesterday morning.

Presumably the shopkeeper and the friend, if asked, would repeat the same statements at the time that the reporting occurs.

Speaker/Writer Stance

Indirectly related to the notion of "present relevance" is the idea that speakers/writers may convey personal stance with regard to a reported proposition through the choice of verb tense. Batstone (1995) illustrates this with the following invented quotation:

> Smith (1980) *argued* that Britain *was* no longer a country in which freedom of speech *was* seriously *maintained*. Johnson (1983), though, *argues* that Britain *remains* a citadel of individual liberty.

Although the writer of the passage may be writing more than a decade after both quotations were made, he/she has chosen to cast the 1980 report in the past tense and the 1983 quote in the present. While it is not impossible to argue that a writer might make these choices in order to emphasize time sequence, Batstone interprets the tense distinction as a means for the writer to show "subjective distribution of approval and disapproval" (1995:198); in effect, the writer juxtaposes the two tenses to indicate personal agreement with the idea in the 1983 quotation. While Batstone does not support his claim with a corpus of evidence, it seems likely that the choice of tense often does convey stance in the way described. Further research along these lines would be very useful.

Published Sources

In general, there is a strong tendency for reporting to occur in the present whenever the source is a written, published one. This may be partially accounted for by the fact that once something is published, it is permanently "present" to the public. Perhaps some of the most noteworthy examples of these involve paraphrases or quotations from famous works regardless of antiquity:

> The Bible says that the meek shall inherit the earth.
> Pope says that no man is an island.
> Plato tells us that all learning is recollection.

The appropriateness of present tense in such statements is probably strengthened to the degree that they are presented (and accepted) as general truths; we find a parallel in the fact that sequence-of-tenses can be overridden in such cases. Yet the use of present tense in formal writing is far from limited to such cases. In a journal article published in 1996, we read, with reference to a study published in 1988, that

> This article further explores an insider's perspective on teaching by examining teachers' understanding of teaching. . . . It seeks to explain the basis for teachers' interventions. . . . (Jack Richards (1996), "Teachers' Maxims in Language Teaching," *TESOL Quarterly* 30:2, 282)

As long as Richards' statements about the article cited were true at the time his own article was written, it seems that nothing necessitates their being recast into the past tense at any point in the future: it will always be true that the article does the things which Richards claims of it. Similarly, what was already in the past for the original author at the time of publication is also in the past for the reporter. On the same page of his article, Richards cites a different author in this way:

> Connors (1978) studied elementary school teachers and found that all nine teachers in her study used three overarching principles of practice to guide and explain their interactive teaching behavior.

Connors' study and findings were temporally prior to the publication of her article, thus Richards presents in past tense events that were seen as past even at the time Connors' paper was written.

Politeness

Finally, we may note that verbs reporting the speaker's thoughts are often used to express politeness. The *Collins Cobuild English Grammar* (1990:330) mentions expressions like

> I wonder if I could ask you a question.
> Don't you think we'd better wait and see?
> I don't suppose you could stay an hour or two longer?

as a means of softening an utterance which might otherwise sound too direct, as in

> Could I ask you a question?
> We'd better wait and see.
> Could you stay an hour or two longer?

Reporting structures seem to be used here in a way parallel to and in combination with modals (Chapter 8): asking the question *May I offer you a drink?* is seen as more polite than *Do you want a drink?* Also relevant is the use of negation (Chapter 10): *Don't you think . . . ?* makes a stronger appeal than *Do you think . . . ?*

READER INFERENCES IN EXTENDED REPORTING

Where reporting is done in academic writing, writers must not only be careful about conveying their stance and personal commitment to the (non)factuality of statements reported on; they must also be scrupulous about making certain that readers are able to discern the difference between the reporter's assertions and those of the speaker/author reported on. For this purpose, all of the means mentioned in this chapter are at the writer's disposal. Obviously, one sure way for a writer to distance himself/herself (both cognitively and affectively) from the assertions of the original source is to preface every sentence with an explicit reporting device. However, naturalistic reporting, even in more formal writing, is not always done this way. Students who are simply taught, first, that reporting is always done with reporting verbs, and second, that it is necessary to attribute the content of every sentence by naming the source explicitly, are faced with a stylistic dilemma that is impossible to escape ("The author says X . . . Then the author claims Y . . . And then he says Z . . . "). Yet practiced native writers do, in fact, manage to properly differentiate the contribution of the reporter from that of the reportee by a variety of means, as textual analysis shows. In the following passage, only one reporting verb (shown in boldface) is used; there are no other explicit reporting expressions. Yet it is clear that the entire statement following the reporting verb is to be attributed to Barrett Seaman:

> While the journalists interviewed for this article didn't express much concern over the possibility of competitors or hackers breaching their computer security, some worried about the danger of foreign governments. *Time*'s Barrett Seaman, for instance, **says** his magazine takes precautions in certain countries. Instead of sending electronic mail to the bureau's open computer system where it might be printed out on hard copy, *Time* uses personal electronic mail boxes accessible only with the correspondent's personal code. (Gib Johnson, "The Compel Reporter." *Washington Journalism Review*, May 1990)

Nothing, of course, absolutely guarantees that the content of the last sentence is fully attributable to Seaman as a source. The author, Gib Johnson, could have unearthed this information himself through personal investigation. However, Johnson mentions in the second sentence that Seaman has said that *Time* "takes precautions in certain countries"; a specific precaution is then described in the following sentence. Ultimately, readers derive an adequately solid inference that Seaman is the source of the information about "personal electronic mail boxes."

Likewise, a reporting device (the word "premise," which indirectly indicates another's opinion) is used in the initial attribution in the following passage about alcohol advertising:

> All these ads illustrate the major premise of alcohol advertising's mythology: alcohol is magic, a magic carpet that can take you away. It can make you successful, sophisticated, sexy. Without it, your life would be dull, mediocre, and ordinary. (Jean Kilbourne, "Deadly Persuasion." *Media and Values*, Spring/Summer 1991)

How do we achieve reasonable certainty that the ideas in the second and third sentences are attributable to the alcohol advertisers and not to Kilbourne's personal opinions about alcohol? It is not impossible that she could share such opinions. Yet we find this an implausible inference for several reasons. First, from what we know about alcohol from our own observations, it seems clear that alcohol is not likely to effect such permanent, "magical" changes on a person; it is hence unlikely that a serious author would attempt to persuade us otherwise. Second, anything that could actually effect these changes really *would* seem to be magical; there is an ideational and lexical cohesion among the expressions *magic, make successful, make sophisticated, make sexy,* and so on that seems to carry further the advertisers' claims mentioned in the first sentence. Since most of us do not believe in magic and would regard it as odd if someone else were to express such a belief in an academic journal, we infer that Kilbourne does not believe in magic. Third, if one is already aware of the larger context of the discussion in the essay, one presumes that Kilbourne is not working as an advocate for companies that advertise alcohol; rather, she is a critic of these companies. We are therefore led to infer that the content of the second and third sentences may be properly attributed to the advertisers.

The point of looking at such examples is simply to illustrate that doing effective indirect or reported speech and writing is not simply a matter of grammar but of pragmatics—of permitting readers to draw correct conclusions about "who believes what" based on inferences from the immediate context (the text which is being read) and of general knowledge about the world. Students should be exposed to a variety of such naturalistic texts as well as to the explicit grammar of reporting in order to get a realistic picture of how native speakers do attributions.

CONCLUSION

Reporting the ideas of others presents challenges to ESL/EFL students at the levels of form, meaning, and use. The strictly grammatical structures provide a challenge largely from the standpoint of selecting the proper complement type; the challenge of meaning lies mainly in the proper choice of reporting terms. By far the greatest challenge at the higher levels of instruction comes from the use to which students put these structures and terms in written work, where the careful attention required in the process of combining sentences into larger units of discourse will necessitate that the teacher give attention to all three areas many times at nearly all class levels.

TEACHING SUGGESTIONS

Few grammatical phenomena are as easily amenable to teaching speaking or writing as indirect speech. This is true for speaking activities because there is a wealth of possible communicative activities in which one learner can be asked to relate what someone has said; it is true for composition activities since much academic writing crucially involves paraphrase and summary of others' work.

1. Form. One relatively elementary activity that can be used as a way for students to introduce themselves can involve the entire class as a group. The students focus on a particular question—students' countries of origin, for example. The first student can say, "I am Hideko, and I come from Japan." The adjacent student can say, "She says she is Hideko, and she comes from Japan. I am Carlos, and I was born in Argentina," and so on.

2. Form. Another, somewhat more complicated, activity has one student asking a second student a question. The second student answers, and a third student then is asked to report on what has been asked and answered. For example:

> *Song:* How many brothers and sisters do you have?
> *Li:* I have two sisters and no brothers.
> *Teacher:* Hiroki, what did they say?
> *Hiroki:* Song asked how many brothers and sisters Li had, and Li said he had two
> sisters and no brothers.

The activity can be further expanded to include four students—the third reporting on the question, and the fourth on the answer.

3. Form. Indirect questions of all types can be practiced as repetitions: Student A asks Student B a question, which Student B pretends not to hear. Student B asks, "I'm sorry. What did you say?" Student A then produces indirect speech ("I asked you whether/ how/when . . . ").

4. Meaning. An activity that can in principle cover all the constructions presented in this chapter involves the teacher's providing written dialogues to be paraphrased by the students. These dialogues might contain statements, questions, and commands. Students might be asked to paraphrase the dialogues using more informal, present-tense reporting or a more formal, past-tense type of reporting.

5. Meaning. An activity that can be used for either speaking or writing activities involves students listening to short monologues on audiotape or video. These might be news reports or excerpts from famous speeches. After listening to the monologues, students can cast themselves into the role of reporters and take turns attempting to paraphrase exactly what was said.

6. Form/Meaning/Use. In multiskills classrooms, one excellent writing activity that involves the use of indirect speech is based on students' doing an extended interview. Students can pair off and probe each other for a topic area in which each is an "expert." This can be a hobby, an area of academic or vocational study, an aspect of the student's native culture such as a holiday custom or a method of preparing food, or a particular area of life experience (parenthood, the experience of being a refugee, the experience of living in another country, etc.). Students can be asked to take exhaustive notes during the interview and, from these notes, write an essay or give a talk in which each reports, as a journalist would, on what his or her partner has related.

7. Form/Meaning/Use. At the high-intermediate level and above, summary writing is a good activity for ESL/EFL students to practice reported speech patterns while breaking away from a rigid pattern of making attributions at the beginning of each sentence. Students may be given a short piece to read as many times as they like. Without looking back at the text, they should then be encouraged to use a variety of devices—reporting verbs, *according to the author*-type expressions, and contextual cues—to convey the content of the piece to an audience. After finishing the summary, students may look back briefly at the text to check for accuracy.

Students might then exchange their summaries; each student will read a classmate's summary with the goal in mind of determining whether the writer has actually ensured that the reader will view the piece as a summary of someone else's writing, rather than as a mixture of summary plus personal contribution of ideas. (Depending on the class level, the teacher may choose to become the final judge of students' success on the task.)

8. Form/Meaning/Use. At a higher and more formal level of writing—one that is very frequent in university settings—the writing of critiques provides an excellent opportunity to focus on reported speech. In a critique, a writer must do two things: (a) report another's ideas in a faithfully accurate and adequate way, and (b) provide an intelligent response to these ideas. Moreover, it is crucial that these two tasks be performed in a transparent way and kept distinct; a reader must know at every stage of the process whether statements reflect the beliefs of the author of the critique or those of the author being critiqued. The student's choice of reporting verbs makes an important contribution here: should the student choose the verb *show* or *prove* rather than *claim* or *argue* to report someone's assertions, the student will be seen to be taking a cognitive stance toward the original author's ideas.

To emphasize the effect of cognitive stance, a teacher might present a paragraph to students in which the ideas expressed are highly questionable or patently absurd, and then ask the students to paraphrase it. In the following paragraph taken from a century-old book that claims that the earth is flat and that the sun is much smaller than is now assumed, students are presented with a challenge for paraphrase:

> The globe theory [of the earth] teaches us that the diameter of the sun is **888,646** miles. [In fact,] the sun is only thirty miles in diameter, and I can prove it beyond a doubt to anyone who wishes to believe the truth. The way I measured the diameter of the sun is as follows: by finding out how far north and south one can travel from the equator on the 21st day of March, when the sun is directly over the equator, and still look directly up at it, or in other words how far one can travel north and south without casting a shadow. I find that distance to be about thirty miles either way, which proves that the sun is only about thirty miles in diameter. (Orlando Ferguson, *The Latest Discoveries in Astronomy*, 1891)

Should a student write, "Ferguson has proven that the sun is only thirty miles in diameter," the student will be seen to be committing himself/herself to the truth of this claim; the amusing effect should be sufficient to underscore the effects of using factive verbs in reporting. At this point, students might be introduced to the concept of "scare quotes"—the selective and often repeated quoting of individual words and phrases, sometimes with an air of sarcasm, for the purpose of showing that the writer wishes to distance himself/herself from particular assertions made:

> In this book, the author "proves" that the sun is just thirty miles wide.

(The use of scare quotes as they are replicated in native oral production can be graphically illustrated with two upraised fingers on each hand in imitation of the marking of quotation marks, while the quoted word or expression is pronounced.) Likewise, the student can be made aware of the possibility of combining nonfactive with factive verbs to create a less embarrassing effect:

> In this book, the author *claims to prove* that the sun is thirty miles wide.
> The author *believes that he has shown* that the sun has a very small diameter.

Such activities can provide interesting and clear illustrations of the importance of accuracy in reporting.[6]

In doing critiques and simple summaries alike, students will quickly be faced with the problem of how much explicit attribution must take place, and how much can be left to the devices by which ordinary pragmatic inferences are made. Here, the precision of grammar blends into some less easily explicated issues in rhetoric; the teacher must often make fairly subtle judgments about whether the student has adequately shown who is "speaking" in the text—the student writer or the original author.

Exercises

Test your understanding of what has been presented.

1. Create an original sentence in which each of the following terms is illustrated:
   - **a.** reported *that*-clause
   - **b.** indirect imperative
   - **c.** indirect information question
   - **d.** indirect yes/no question
   - **e.** backshifting
   - **f.** deictic time-adverbial shift
   - **g.** deictic place-adverbial shift
   - **h.** deictic pronoun shift
   - **i.** reporting noun
   - **j.** factive reporting verb
   - **k.** nonfactive reporting verb
   - **l.** emotional-state reporting verb
   - **m.** free indirect discourse
   - **n.** zero-quotation

2. Draw trees for the following sentences:
   - **a.** This book argues that a political shift is occurring.
   - **b.** The recipe says to add one cup of melted butter to the mixture.
   - **c.** The author claims she has shown why parrots imitate humans.
   - **d.** They asked if we had seen John.
   - **e.** The reviewer wondered where Ann had found her evidence.

3. Why are the following sentences unacceptable in standard English?
   - **a.** *We were asked did we have the time?
   - **b.** *The bureaucrat informed John his license to have expired.
   - **c.** *The owner asked the customer to do not shop at another store.
   - **d.** *They asked whether that it would be possible to do it another way.

4. A type of error made with one intended interpretation of the following sentences is frequently found both in ESL and native writing. What is that intended interpretation, and what is the problem with the following sentences, given that intention? What is the alternative acceptable interpretation?

   *In Smith's opinion, he believes that there is no alternative to petroleum.
   *According to Smith, he says that DNA cannot account for these facts.

   Does the same problem occur in the following sentence? If not, can you suggest the reason why?

   Smith says that in his opinion, DNA cannot account for these facts.

5. The verbs *complain, rejoice, exclaim, lament* were mentioned as verbs that illustrate the emotional state of the person reported on. Nothing was said, however, about their status as factive or nonfactive verbs. Can these verbs be said to be either factive or nonfactive? Give arguments and illustrations to support your answer for each verb.

6. Explain as fully as possible the difference between the following two sentences:

   John said that he would be leaving next week.
   John said that he would be leaving the next week.

Test your ability to apply what you know.

7. Suppose that you wish to conduct a survey to determine the extent to which native speakers follow the sequence-of-tenses rule. How would you proceed in your survey?

8. Suppose that a student writes the following sentences in an essay. How would you explain the problems to the student?
   - **a.** *I'm not sure do I go or not.

    b. *My mother asked me that how I planned to raise my grades.

    c. *My father insisted for me to work harder.

    d. *My friend said that, "Can you please help me?"

    e. *I told to him that it wouldn't be possible now.

9. Suppose that a student has handed in an essay, part of which includes the following summary of an article from the newspaper. Assuming that the summary reflects honest paraphrase of the original author's words and ideas, how might you provide feedback on the student's way of presenting the summary?

> In this article, Richard Walter gives his opinion on violence in movies. He says that violence in movies is not as bad as many people think. He tells us that there are several reasons for this. The first reason that he gives is that strong emotion and tension are a part of everyday life. Then he says that famous plays since antiquity have been full of violence, and says that nobody objects to those plays. He also says that it is wrong for people to think that violence in movies causes violence in the real world, because in his opinion, movie violence is just a reflection of the real world. He does not think it is a cause of violence at all. So he tells us that he is not able to understand why people are so emotional about this issue.

10. Locate direct quotations in five or six separate periodical articles in the context of paraphrased reporting. Do these quotations tend to appear in consistent places in the reporting (at the beginning, in the middle, at the end, after indirect statements have been made, etc.)? Can you make any inference as to why the author of the article chose to quote rather than to paraphrase?

BIBLIOGRAPHY

References

Axelrod, R. E., and C. R. Cooper (1994). *The St. Martin's Guide to Writing* (4th short ed.). New York: St. Martin's Press.

Batstone, R. (1995). "Grammar in Discourse: Attitude and Deniability." In G. Cook and B. Seidlhofer (eds.), *Principles and Practice in Applied Linguistics: Studies in Honour of H. G. Widdowson.* Oxford: Oxford University Press. 197–213.

Brown Ssensalo, D. (1991). On wondering if they'll choose *whether* or whether they'll choose *if.* Unpublished paper, TESL & Applied Linguistics, UCLA.

Collins Cobuild English Grammar (1990). London: Collins.

Comrie, B. (1985). *Tense.* Cambridge: Cambridge University Press.

Coulmas, F. (1986). "Reported speech." In F. Coulmas (ed.), 1–28.

Coulmas, F. (ed.) (1986). *Direct and Indirect Speech.* Berlin: De Gruyter.

Goodwin, M. H. (1990). *He-Said-She-Said: Talk as Social Organization Among Black Children.* Bloomington, IN: Indiana University Press.

Harman, I. (1990). "Teaching Indirect Speech: Deixis Points the Way." *ELT Journal* 44:3 (July 1990): 230–238.

Huang, C. (1993). A Contextual Analysis of *that* Retention/Deletion with the Reporting Verb *Said.* Unpublished paper, UCLA.

Quirk, R., S. Greenbaum, G. Leech, and J. Svartvik (1985). *A Comprehensive Grammar of the English Language.* London: Longman.

Rimmon-Kenan, S. (1983). *Narrative Fiction: Contemporary Poetics.* London: Methuen.

Thompson, G. (1994). *Collins Cobuild English Guides 5: Reporting.* London: HarperCollins.

Yule, G., T. Mathis, and M. F. HopKins. "On Reporting What Was Said." *ELT Journal* 46:3 (July 1992):245–251.

Yule, G. (1995). The Paralinguistics of Reference: Representation in Reported Discourse. In *Principle and Practice in Applied Linguistics*. Cook, G. and B. Seidlhofer, (eds). Oxford, Oxford University Press, 185–196.

Suggestions for further reading

One highly accessible source with a wealth of detail about reporting is:
Thompson, G. (1994). *Collins Cobuild English Guide 5: Reporting.* London: Collins.

Another good source that also gives a comprehensive list of reporting verbs (p. 314) is:
Collins Cobuild English Grammar (1990). London: Collins. (See Chapter 7.)

Two useful papers written from a linguistic perspective—one on quotation in general, the other a cross-linguistic treatment of verbs like "say" are:
Partee, B. (1973) The Syntax and Semantics of Quotation. In *A Festschrift for Morris Halle*, Kiparsky, P., and S. Anderson (eds.). New York: Holt, Rinehart, and Winston, 410–418.
Munro, P. (1987). On the Transitivity of "Say" Verbs. In *Syntax and Semantics*. Vol. 15. P. Hopper and S. Thompson (eds.). New York: Academic Press, 301–318.

For a treatment of reported speech as part of reflexive language in general, see:
Lucy, J. A. (ed.) (1993). Reflexive Language: *Reported Speech and Metapragmatics.* Cambridge: Cambridge University Press.

For treatment of tense usage and backshifting in reported indirect speech, see:
Harman, I. (1990). Reference above.
Salkie, R., and S. Reed, (1997). Time Reference in Reported Speech. *English Language and Linguistics* 1:2, 319–348.

For an article that classifies reporting signals beyond the traditional types of signal presented in grammer books, see:
Thompson, J. (1996). Voices in the Text: Discourse Perspectives on Language Reports. *Applied Linguistics* 17:4, 501–530.

For a classification of reporting verbs that writers use to evaluate the work of others in research-based writing, see:
Thompson, J., and C. Ye, (1991). Evaluation in the Reporting Verbs Used in Academic Papers. *Applied Linguistics* 17:4, 501–530.

Some of the linguistic devices by which writers can achieve cohesion to assist readers in making proper inferences about reporter vs. reportee are found in:
Halliday, M. (1994). *Introduction to Functional Grammar.* (2d ed.). London: Edward Arnold, Chapter 7.

For a variety of approaches on techniques of reporting and shifting perspectives in natural oral discourse and literature, see:
Tannen, D. (1989). *Talking Voices.* Cambridge: Cambridge University Press.
Yule, G. (1995). The Paralinguistics of Reference: Representation in Reported Discourse. In *Principle and Practice in Applied Linguistics*. Cook, G., and B. Seidhofer (eds.). Oxford: Oxford University Press, 185–196.
Short, M. (1994). Understanding Texts: Point of View. In *Language and Understanding*, Brown, G., M. Kristen, A. Pollitt, and J. Williams (eds). Oxford: Oxford University Press, 170–190.

For a nontraditional view of the function of quotations, see also:
Clark, H.H., and R.J. Gehrig (1990). Quotations as Demonstrations. *Language* 66: 4, 764–805.

Many higher-level ESL/EFL textbooks offer chapters or sections on the form of reported speech. Two of the better sources are:

Oshima, A., and A. Hogue (1991). *Writing Academic English.* (2d ed.). Menlo Park, CA: Addison Wesley. (See Chapters 9 and 12).

Raimes, A. (1990). *How English Works.* New York: St. Martin's. (Chapter 25)

Two textbook treatments that cover the various aspects of indirect speech are:

Thewlis, S. (1997). *Grammar Dimensions.* Book 3 (2d ed.). Boston: Heinle & Heinle. (See Unit 25.)

Bland, S. K. (1996). *Intermediate Grammar: From Form to Meaning and Use.* Oxford: Oxford University Press.

One article directed at ESL/EFL teachers that proposes an alternative pedagogical approach for teaching reported speech is:

Goodell, E. W. (1987). Integrating Theory with Practice: An Alternative Approach to Reported Speech in English. *TESOL Quarterly* 21:2, 305–325.

ENDNOTES

1. There is a possibility of shift in modals as in other verbs; recall from Chapter 8 that historically, modals had both present and past forms. However, the shift is somewhat less than systematic. Although *will* becomes *would* and *can* becomes *could* in a regular way, *may* becomes *might* only when *may* expresses possibility, not permission; otherwise, only *could* is possible:

> "The children may (= are allowed to) go to the circus."
> → Father said that the children **could** go to the circus.

Likewise, *shall* does not become *should,* since such a shift would alter meaning considerably.

2. The immediate repetition could also be from the first person, who would then be repeating him/herself—B: *What did you say?* A: *I said we'll be having polenta for lunch.*

3. One can, of course, ask direct questions that contain indirect questions, such as *Who knows what will happen?* or *Who asked whether we could drive them home?* It is also possible to ask highly polite questions by phrasing them as indirect questions; see the section on use in this chapter.

4. Because *whether, if,* and *for* all function as complementizers and English cannot have double complementizers, it is not possible to have *for/to* infinitives in indirect questions, as for example, **They asked whether for John or Mary to do the job.*

5. Distinctions such as those in the second chart on page 697 arise, incidentally, not only in reported speech but also in cases in which comparison of two sequential events or states in the past or future are compared. For example:

> She finally picked up the car. She had paid for it **a month before.**
> She is finally picking up the car today. She paid for it **a month ago.**
> They will leave next January 16. They will return **a month later.**
> They are leaving now. They will return **in a month.**

6. We refer teachers to Donna Kossy (1994), *Kooks: A Guide to the Outer Limits of Human Belief* (Portland, Ore.: Feral House) for many useful examples of such scientific claims that have not been borne out by later investigation.

34

DEGREE— COMPARATIVES AND EQUATIVES

INTRODUCTION

One of the most basic and powerful of human cognitive processes is the ability to comprehend and express the fact that two things are similar or different. Often such a similarity or difference is expressed in terms of degree, extent, or quantity. This chapter describes the two most important English constructions used to express similarities or differences of degree or extent—that is, the equative and comparative constructions, respectively. We also briefly discuss the major ways in which the languages of the world express degree-type comparison.

From the outset, it is important that we distinguish the absolute use of adjectives and adverbs from the relative use of such words.

Absolute Use: John is tall.
John runs fast.
Relative Use: John is taller than Susan.
John runs faster than Bill.

There are important semantic differences in these two underlying uses. For example, if we negate the assertion with the absolute form and conjoin the resulting negative statement with the affirmative statement, we produce a contradiction:

*John is tall, but he isn't tall.

A contradiction does not result, however, when we conjoin the same negative absolute assertion with the sentence containing the affirmative relative usage:

John is taller than Susan, but he isn't tall.

The reason for this difference is that words such as *tall(er)* and *fast(er)* can be used in a relative sense without making any absolute assertion about the referent's height or speed.

In this chapter we discuss comparative and equative constructions, which involve the relative rather than the absolute use of such words. It is important to note, as we did in Chapter 20, that there are nongradable adjectives and adverbs, such as *parliamentary, true, false,* and so on; such adjectives and adverbs cannot be compared, intensified, or used in a relative sense (Bolinger, 1972).

THE FORMS OF COMPARISON

A TYPOLOGICAL OVERVIEW

There seem to be at least four different ways in which the languages of the world express comparison. We will use English words below to exemplify these different construction types.[1]

Comparison by Juxtaposition[2]

Some languages express comparison by mere juxtaposition of clauses and have no explicit syntactic device or construction for expressing comparison. For example:

> My boat (is) big.
> +
> Your boat (is) very big.   (= "Your boat is bigger than mine.")

Limited Scope Comparison

Some languages, such as Chinese and Japanese, compare by limiting the scope of an adjective—or some other part of speech—so that it has a relative rather than an absolute meaning:

> $\left\{ \begin{array}{l} \text{Compare(d) (to)} \\ \text{From} \end{array} \right\}$ Mary, John (is) tall.   ("John is taller than Mary.")
>
> John, compare(d) to Mary, (is) tall.

"Surpass" Comparatives

Still other languages, such as many West African or Bantu languages, express comparison using a verb that means "to pass" or "to surpass":

> John $\left\{ \begin{array}{l} \text{pass} \\ \text{surpass} \end{array} \right\}$ Mary (in) $\left\{ \begin{array}{l} \text{tallness} \\ \text{height} \end{array} \right\}$.   ("John is taller than Mary.")

Many languages of this type cannot directly express the reverse of such a statement—that is, Mary is shorter than John.[3]

Comparison Using Degree Morphemes

Finally, there are languages like English (i.e., most Indo-European languages) that have developed verbs, adjectives or quantifiers—words like *more* and *less*—or inflections like *-er* that use these words or morphemes to directly express comparison:

> John (is) tall MORE than Mary.   ("John is taller than Mary.")
>
> Mary (is) $\left\{ \begin{array}{l} \text{short MORE} \\ \text{tall LESS} \end{array} \right\}$ than John.   ("Mary is shorter/less tall than John.")

In such languages, comparisons can always be reversed, but one form is usually preferred over the other in any given discourse context for semantic and/or pragmatic reasons. As we shall see below, the unmarked or positive form occurs most frequently.

TYPICAL LEARNER PROBLEMS

In the preceding section we noted that all languages have ways of expressing comparison but that the devices used can differ greatly from one language to another. Depending on the type(s) of comparison used in the native language of your students, different types of problems will occur, especially at the initial stage of learning. Then as students become more advanced, developmental errors occur that have nothing at all to do with first language interference.

Here are some of the common errors:

1. Omission of the comparative inflection—and perhaps also the copula:

> John (is) tall than Mary.

2. Substitution of some other function word for *than* (a) or inappropriate use of *than* (b):

> **a.** *John is tall(er) from Mary. **b.** *Paul is as tall than John.

3. Use of *more* where *-er* is required or vice versa:

> *John is $\begin{Bmatrix} \text{tall more} \\ \text{more tall} \end{Bmatrix}$ than Mary.   *Mary is beautifuller than Karen.

4. Use of a regular pattern where an irregular form is required.

> *His handwriting is badder than mine.

5. Double marking of the comparative:

> *Jim runs more faster than Paul.   *This car is more better than that one.

While the first three errors may be explained in terms of negative transfer, in that they reflect the learner's native language, the last two are developmental errors that young English-speaking children also produce during first language acquisition.

WHAT MAKES COMPARISON IN ENGLISH DIFFICULT?

Partly related to the developmental errors discussed above, there are a number of other factors, such as the range of construction types and the variations in choosing *more* versus *-er*, that the ESL/EFL teacher must be aware of in order to teach comparison effectively.

The Range of Comparative Construction Types

Most reference grammars and ESL/EFL texts center their discussion of comparison in English around adjectives and adverbs. Actually, every major part of speech in English (i.e., nouns, verbs, adjectives, adverbs) permits comparison.

Recall that when we formulate a comparison, we presuppose a difference of degree or extent; for example:

$$X \begin{Bmatrix} \text{is} \\ \text{has} \\ \text{other} \\ \text{verbs} \end{Bmatrix} \begin{Bmatrix} \text{MORE} \\ \text{LESS} \end{Bmatrix} \text{A than Y}$$

(presupposes "X is different from Y with respect to A")

As the following examples illustrate, each major part of speech in English can be used with some version of the formula above to make comparisons. (This must be made clear to ESL/EFL learners, since many languages do not have as large an inventory of comparative constructions as does English.)

Adjective: John is taller than Mary (is).
Joe is less intelligent than Sam (is).

Adverb: Bill runs faster than Peter ($\begin{Bmatrix} \text{runs} \\ \text{does} \end{Bmatrix}$).

Judy dances less gracefully than Sally ($\begin{Bmatrix} \text{dances} \\ \text{does} \end{Bmatrix}$).

Noun: Jack has more money than Harry ($\begin{Bmatrix} \text{has} \\ \text{does} \end{Bmatrix}$).

Max $\begin{Bmatrix} \text{has fewer books} \\ \text{less money} \end{Bmatrix}$ than I ($\begin{Bmatrix} \text{have} \\ \text{do} \end{Bmatrix}$).

Verb: Paul weighs more than Alex (does).
This book costs less than that one (does).

The ESL/EFL teacher must make sure that his or her students practice all of these patterns, not just the adjective and adverb patterns illustrated in the first two sets of examples above.

Collectively, these examples raise a number of problems and questions that we discuss in the following section.

The Choice of *-Er* Versus *More* with Adjectives and Adverbs

There is a metrical tendency based on English syllable structure that in many cases helps native speakers decide when to apply the *-er* inflection and when to use the periphrastic comparative form *more* with adjectives and adverbs.[4] We discuss counterexamples to this tendency below under use of comparatives.

First, adjectives and adverbs of one syllable take the inflectional ending, as do two-syllable adjectives with a final unstressed *-y* ending:[5]

Base Form	-er
big	bigger
tall	taller
soon	sooner
hard	harder
happy	happier
noisy	noisier

Second, many other two-syllable adjectives that have a stressed first syllable and an unstressed second syllable ending in *-ly*, *-ow*, or *-le* (syllabic [l])[6] also take the inflection, although it is certainly possible to use the periphrastic form in certain contexts, such as when contrastive emphasis is being placed on the comparative element *(Ann is friendly but Beth is MORE friendly)*.

Base Form	-er
friendly	friendlier
	(more friendly)
narrow	narrower
	(more narrow)
gentle	gentler
	(more gentle)

Note also that even if these two-syllable adjectives add derivational prefixes, they still take the same inflections as the base form (e.g., *unhappier, unfriendlier*, etc.).

Third, all two-syllable adverbs ending in *-ly* that do not have an adjective homonym also ending in *-ly* take periphrastic *more:*

Base Form	"More"	
slowly	more slowly	(*not* slowlier)
brusquely	more brusquely	(*not* brusquelier)
sharply	more sharply	(*not* sharplier)

Fourth, some adjectives that seem more suited to the periphrastic comparative form may also occur with an inflectional ending, especially in informal use. These include two-syllable adjectives that (a) end in *-er* or *-ure,* such as *tender, mature,* (b) end in a weakly stressed vowel followed by nothing more than a final /d/ or /t/, such as *stupid, quiet,* and (c) end in a weakly stressed syllable with final /m/ or /n/, such as *handsome, awesome, common.*

Base Form	"More"
tender	more tender
	(tenderer)
stupid	more stupid
	(stupider)
handsomer	more handsome
	(handsomer)
common	more common
	(commoner)

Fifth, adjectives and adverbs with two syllables having any ending other than those described previously, as well as all adjectives and adverbs of three or more syllables, take only the periphrastic form *more:*

	Base Form	"More"
Adjective	curious	more curious
	pleasant	more pleasant
	beautiful	more beautiful
Adverb	skillfully	more skillfully
	cautiously	more cautiously
	independently	more independently

The "rules" above for the comparative inflection are not as rigid as those for the plural or past-tense inflections. We regularly hear English speakers use a periphrastic form for emphasis (e.g., *Before this happened, I didn't believe I could be more sad*) when the "rule" would predict the inflection. There is also some individual variation, and thus some speakers may prefer *quieter* and *stupider* over *more quiet* and *more stupid.* Thus we speak of a tendency rather than a rule when discussing this phenomenon; the variation that occurs among English speakers can be partially explained by the fact that the second and fourth groups of adjectives and adverbs listed above can take both the periphrastic and the inflectional forms.

Nonnative speakers should be taught the general tendencies and should also be alerted to the fact that the comparative affix *-er* is sometimes used by native speakers for specific effect (i.e., to get attention) in literature or other forms of creative writing. These are cases where the normal rules would not lead us to expect an *-er* comparative. One of the most famous examples of this is when Lewis Carroll made Alice say "curiouser and curiouser!" in *Alice in Wonderland.* (We would normally use *more,* not *-er,* with an adjective that ends in *-ous,* such as *curious,* and nonnative speakers should avoid using *-er* where it is not expected). Other aspects of variation will be discussed below under the use of comparatives.

Use of *Less* Versus *Fewer*

A much less complicated rule accounts for the distribution of *less* and *fewer,* the negative counterparts of *more.* In contrast to *more,* which may occur before both count and noncount nouns, *less* changes to *fewer* when modifying plural count nouns in formal contexts:

$$\text{I have more} \begin{Bmatrix} \text{money} \\ \text{books} \end{Bmatrix} \text{than Mr. Sims (does).}$$

$$\text{Mr. Sims has} \begin{Bmatrix} \text{less money} \\ \text{fewer books} \end{Bmatrix} \text{than I (do).}$$

We will have more to say about the distribution of *less* and *fewer* in informal contexts later when we turn our attention to the use of comparatives.

Clause Reductions and Case Adjustments

By now you may have noticed that the constituent following *than* sometimes resembles a reduced clause:

$$\text{She has more books than I} \begin{Bmatrix} \text{have} \\ \text{do} \end{Bmatrix}.$$

and sometimes a noun phrase:

> She has more books than John.

In the latter situation, if a pronoun follows *than,* it tends to change from subject to object form (i.e., a subject form standing alone seems a bit awkward):

$$\text{She has more books than} \begin{Bmatrix} \text{?I} \\ \text{me} \end{Bmatrix}.$$

In other words, if no verb or auxiliary follows the noun phrase, English speakers tend to analyze the pronoun as an object of a preposition because even though *than* is a complementizer (much like *that* in Chapter 31), it also has prepositional force.

Irregular Comparative Forms

A number of irregular comparative adjective and adverb forms in English cannot be explained with reference to the *-er* inflection or the periphrastic form *more:*

Base Form	Irregular Comparative Form
$\begin{Bmatrix} \text{much} \\ \text{many} \end{Bmatrix}$	more
little	less
good	better
bad	worse
far	farther (distance)
	further (nonspatial progression)
	elder (comparing ages of siblings)
old	(*older* is the regular form used elsewhere)

In informal usage, *further* is often used instead of *farther* to compare distance, and in all contexts *older* is now generally used to refer to a sibling of greater age—that is, *elder* is becoming somewhat archaic even in this function.[7] The most common irregular comparative forms, *better* and *worse,* must be presented and practiced apart from the regular forms to help avoid errors such as these:

*I'm speaking English $\begin{Bmatrix} \text{more better} \\ \text{gooder} \end{Bmatrix}$ now.

Substitute Expressions Used with Comparatives

Another source of difficulty to be aware of are the nominal substitute expressions commonly used in comparative constructions. Since English comparative constructions often involve two clauses, the second of which has been greatly reduced, certain substitute expressions commonly occur as part of a comparison. The possessive pronouns are one such type of substitute expression (Halliday and Hasan 1976):

> This car is bigger than mine (is). (mine = my car)

However, when a possessive pronoun is not appropriate, the substitute expressions *one* and *ones* are often used along with an appropriate determiner such as the definite article or demonstrative:

> This car is bigger than that one.[8] (one = car)
> The blue books are cheaper than the red ones. (ones = books)

The nominal substitutes *one* and *ones* may also occur without a definite determiner to replace a modified noun with indefinite or generic reference:

> A wool garment is warmer than a cotton *one*.
> Wool garments are warmer than cotton *ones*.

In more formal contexts, the demonstrative pronouns *that* and *those* may be used in a comparison to introduce the second of two prepositional phrases; possessive constructions formed with *of* are especially common in this type of construction.

> The financial resources of Mr. Jones are greater than those of Mr. Johnson.

A common error committed by both native and nonnative speakers is deletion of the demonstrative and the *of* in such a context:

> *The financial resources of Mr. Jones are greater than Mr. Johnson.

The demonstratives *that* and *those* also introduce relative clauses as part of a comparison:

$\begin{Bmatrix} \text{Food} \\ \text{Foods} \end{Bmatrix}$ which we cook at home $\begin{Bmatrix} \text{is} \\ \text{are} \end{Bmatrix}$ often better than $\begin{Bmatrix} \text{that} \\ \text{those} \end{Bmatrix}$ which we eat in a restaurant.

Again, there is a tendency on the part of both native and nonnative speakers to erroneously simplify such a construction. The result is an error such as the following:

Food $\begin{Bmatrix} \text{which} \\ \text{that} \end{Bmatrix}$ we cook at home is often better than in a restaurant.

In both cases cited above—the possessive phrase and the relative clause—the speaker/writer must maintain parallel structure in the reduced clause following $\begin{Bmatrix} \textit{more} \\ \textit{-er} \end{Bmatrix}$ ... *than* in order to produce a grammatical sentence. The demonstrative pronouns *that* and *those* help satisfy the parallelism condition in such contexts.

The possessive pronouns and the substitutes *one* and *ones* tend to occur in informal language, whereas the demonstrative pronouns *that* and *those* are more typical of formal usage. When they refer to countable nouns, either form can be used, the only difference being one of register.

Informal: The stories she wrote 10 years ago are more interesting than the ones she is writing now.

Formal: The stories (that) she wrote 10 years ago are more interesting than those (that) she is writing now.

However, when the substitute refers to mass (noncount) nouns, only demonstrative *that* is possible since the use of *one(s)* requires a countable noun antecedent:

The coffee on the stove is fresher than $\begin{Bmatrix} \text{that} \\ \text{*the one} \end{Bmatrix}$ on the counter.

OTHER COMPARATIVE CONSTRUCTIONS

In addition to the four major types of comparative constructions outlined above, there are a number of other types of comparatives that the ESL/EFL teacher should be aware of, such as the following.

Type of Comparison	*Example*
Comparison of two different properties of the same object rather than one property of two different objects	The river is wider than it is deep.
Comparison involving two or more properties as well as two or more objects	John enjoys movies more than I enjoy the theater.
Comparison with a partitive noun rather than another object used as the standard of comparison	Mark is more than six feet tall. The book weighs more than two kilos.
Comparison with an absolute adjective used as the standard of comparison (used a lot in advertising)	Shaq is taller than tall (i.e., he's gigantic!) This product is newer than new. (i.e., it's the very latest.)
Comparison with the comparative morpheme modifying a cardinal number	Ben has $\begin{Bmatrix} \text{more} \\ \text{fewer} \end{Bmatrix}$ than three brothers.[9]
Comparison with a partitive noun modifying the comparative morpheme	Mark is two inches taller than Phil. Danny is three years older than Alice.
Comparison expressing a progressive change of state[10]	Arlene is getting prettier (and prettier).
Comparison with *of* plus a predicate noun	He's more of a fool than $\begin{Bmatrix} \text{Alec (is).} \\ \text{I thought.} \end{Bmatrix}$
Comparison expressing a conditional relationship	The greater the pressure, the higher the temperature. The more you learn, the less you know.
Comparison expressing preference (i.e. *more than = rather than*)[11]	Peter looks for danger more than adventure.
Comparisons expressing a denial (*more than = instead of*)	He's more friendly than helpful. That looks more like an eel than a snake.

These 11 additional comparative constructions combine with the four basic types outlined above to yield 15 different semantic and syntactic combinations. Intermediate and advanced ESL/EFL students will ultimately also need to become familiar with the 11 constructions listed above. Beginners should concentrate on the four basic patterns.

ISSUES OF MEANING WITH RESPECT TO COMPARATIVES

COMPARATIVE FORM BUT SUPERLATIVE MEANING

True comparatives involve relative differences between two or more entities, two or more sets, two or more quantities, or two or more properties. A number of English constructions superficially appear to be comparatives but in fact function semantically as superlatives (thus, they are only mentioned here but are discussed further in the following chapter on superlatives):

Type of Comparative Form	*Example*
Comparatives used as suppletive variants of superlatives when there are only two members in a set	Clem is the taller of the two boys. Compare: Clem is the tallest of the $\left\{\begin{array}{l}\text{three}\\\text{four}\\\text{etc.}\end{array}\right\}$ boys.
Comparatives with (*n*)*ever*, which express a superlative meaning	That's more people than I've ever seen. (= That's the most people (that) I've ever seen.)
Comparatives with *any other*, which express a superlative meaning	This play is better than any other play I've seen. (= This play is the best one (that) I've seen.)

OTHER FORMS USED TO EXPRESS COMPARISON IN ENGLISH

The English language also has a number of other syntactic and lexical means to express comparison. Some of these are reminiscent of the dominant comparative construction types found in other languages (see the discussion of language typology on page 718):

Type	*Example*
Some constructions limit the scope of an adjective or adverb, thereby making its meaning relative rather than absolute (see above).	Mary is tall for a girl. John is tall compared to Joey.
Sometimes special verbs are used to express a superior degree or extent (see above).	John's height $\left\{\begin{array}{l}\text{exceeds}\\\text{surpasses}\end{array}\right\}$ Mary's (height).
As an extension of the preceding type, some derived verbs using *out-*, *under-*, and *over-* as prefixes are also inherently comparative.	Bill *outplayed* his opponents. The professor $\left\{\begin{array}{l}\textit{over-}\\\textit{under-}\end{array}\right\}$ rated his own worth.
One of the meanings of prepositions such as *over* and *under* is inherently comparative (i.e., is equivalent to *more than* or *less than*).	The temperature rose to over 80°F. Bob's annual salary is under $20,000.

Today, ESL/EFL teachers often use some sort of semantically based syllabus rather than a strictly structurally based one. This means that these other forms expressing comparison should also be introduced (to learners) under the topic of comparison in English.

THE USE OF COMPARATIVES

MARKEDNESS AND THE USE OF COMPARATIVE FORMS

As discussed in Chapter 20, many adjectives and adverbs that are commonly used to express comparison in English form oppositions.

$$
\textit{Positive polarity} \; (+) \atop \text{(unmarked form)}
\left\{
\begin{array}{l}
\text{tall—short} \\
\text{old—young} \\
\text{heavy—light} \\
\text{fast—slow}
\end{array}
\right\}
\textit{Negative polarity} \; (-) \atop \text{(marked form)}
$$

The existence of such paired positive and negative polarity forms gives us a way to avoid the use of *less* (which sounds awkward in many contexts) and to encourage the use of *more* or *-er* as often as possible in the expression of comparison:

> John is taller than Mary.   Mary is shorter than John
> (Mary is less tall than John.)

Psycholinguists call *more* and the positive polarity forms listed above "unmarked" because they are used more frequently in any given language,[12] are learned first by children, and occur with greater frequency in the languages of the world. The unmarked forms also tend to be used in neutral questions that have no special presuppositions:

> How old (?young) are you?
> How tall (?short) is John?
> What more (?less) do you want?

Psycholinguists call *less* and the negative polarity forms listed above "marked" because they are used less frequently in any given language, learned later by children,[13] and used only in highly marked contexts.

When Are Marked Comparative Forms Used?

In an attempt to determine when and why marked comparatives are used, Ssensalo (1976) examined the *White House Transcripts* and also a large number of advertisements. In both databases the unmarked forms predominated significantly; however, Ssensalo found that two major principles explained many of the marked or negative comparatives in the *White House Transcripts:*

1. The marked form best expresses the speaker's message or point of view; for example:

> They will have to redesign it as a *narrower* action (saying *narrower* is more direct and specific instead of simply saying it is *too broad*).

2. The marked form was cued by the proximity of a related word or idea; for example:

> In the *Post* article, we're so *low* now we can't go any *lower*. (*Lower* cannot easily be changed to *higher* in a paraphrase.)

In the advertisements, Ssensalo found that marked comparatives were used only about 20 percent of the time. When they occurred, they were used to indicate either the poorer quality of a rival product (e.g., the same amount of the other detergent will do *fewer* dishes) or because the marked form signals something desirable to the potential buyer (e.g., Look *younger!* We have *lower* prices.).

USE OF *LESS* VERSUS *FEWER*

Above, we gave the formal rule for the distribution of *less* and *fewer* in negative comparisons of noun quantity:

1. Use *less* before uncountable nouns:

> He has less furniture than you do.

2. Use *fewer* before plural countable nouns:

> He has fewer chairs than you do.

However, anyone who has been closely observing informal English speech will have noticed that *less* is often used with plural countable nouns:

> He has less chairs than you do.

Also, for some time now, written uses of *less* modifying countable nouns have been attested. Here are two examples written in 1958 that Chen (1982) found:

> "Out of the 170 million people in the country, less than 81 million have IQs that are high."
> (*Harper's,* March, 1958)
> "Rejoice then that no less than 34 of the 81 past volumes . . . are back in print."
> (N.Y. *Times* Book Review Sections, March 30, 1958)

Chen (1982) examined a corpus of more than 180,000 spoken words and a control corpus of about 50,000 written words. In these corpora he found 26 tokens of *less* and 2 tokens of *fewer*. Both tokens of fewer occurred in the written corpus. In the spoken corpus, *less* occurred in six tokens where traditional grammar would have prescribed *fewer:*

> . . . less people (two tokens)
> . . . less than 300 people
> . . . less such fellows
> . . . less than one person in four
> . . . the number of farmers is less every day

Because neither form was particularly frequent in his corpora, Chen administered a written fill-in-the-blank questionnaire and an oral elicitation task to native English speakers (the oral task involved people looking at pictures of two apple trees, one having more apples or two desks, one having more books on it, etc.). He found that 16 percent of the responses on the written task used *less* where *fewer* was predicted by the traditional rule but that slightly over 50 percent of the responses on the oral elicitation task used *less* where *fewer* was predicted. No one used *fewer* where *less* was predicted. This suggests that the college students Chen used as consultants tended to monitor their use of *less* and *fewer* on the written questionnaire but did this much less often on the oral tasks.

On the basis of his various sources of data, Chen identified four factors that seem to influence the use of *less* rather than *fewer:*

1. English speakers are much less likely to use *fewer* in informal speech than in formal writing.

2. Partitive nouns (see Chapter 17) are even less likely to be preceded by *fewer* than plural countable nouns:

> less *bushels* of apples (rather than *fewer*)
> (partitive noun)
> fewer apples/less apples (both occur)
> (plural countable noun)

3. Separation of *fewer* from the head noun encourages the use of *less:*

> less than 50 people

4. Ellipsis of constituents following *less* or *fewer* encourages the use of *less* (i.e., *fewer* is rarely used pronominally):

> They told us 300 people would come to the rally, but we had less.

Chen's results are reinforced by the fact that *less* occurs in all syntactic environments where a negative comparison is possible:

> *Adjective:* to be less extravagant than
> *Adverb:* to dance less gracefully than
> *Verb:* to weigh less than
> *Noun:* less money than

But *fewer* can only occur in the last environment—with nouns—and then only if the noun is countable and plural (e.g., *fewer dollars than*). Thus *fewer* seems to be a suppletive[14] form of *less* that can occur only as a modifier of plural countable nouns. Chen speculates that because *less* can encode a smaller-than-other quantity with no regard at all for countability and plurality while *fewer* must explicitly take these features into account, it is sometimes hard (even for native speakers) to use *fewer,* and this is especially true when the modifier and the head noun are not adjacent.

USE OF *-ER* VERSUS *MORE*

Solomon (1994) compares the use of naturally occurring tokens of inflected *(-er)* and periphrastic comparatives in spoken American English and finds that periphrastic *more* is being used in many cases where the *-er* form is expected. Some of the discourse-sensitive reasons she has isolated to explain this are the following:

1. The speaker changes from the inflectional form to the periphrastic form because she/he needs to emphasize the positive comparison (one can stress *more* but not *-er*):

> My instructor told me to come up with a clearer thesis statement, but I don't see how I can make it any MORE clear.

2. Periphrasis is used with the base form in some cases where the positive form of the base word occurred in the preceding clause (no special emphasis):

> It's easy to catch this disease. . . . It's more easy to catch than AIDS.

3. Some collocations frequently occur with *more: a (whole) lot more, way more, even more, a (little) bit more, much more,* and so on. If one has started using one of these strong collocates, there may be pressure to use periphrastic *more:*

> I'm way more funny than he is.

4. In some environments, the choice of either periphrasis (a) or inflection (b) seems to depend on an earlier comparative form occurring in a more or less parallel structure, and this seems to happen much more often with periphrasis:

> a.   I'm more aware of pressures . . . so I'm more tense, like now.
> b.   There's been a lot of influence from English, in a briefer but intenser manner.

Sometimes Solomon's examples seem to reflect two or more of the above tendencies. For example, the following has both the emphatic stress illustrated in (1) and the repetition of forms mentioned in (2) above:

> It's gonna be tough with him. . . . It's gonna be MORE tough without him.

Finally, we should note that Solomon found five tokens of double marking produced by native speakers, two of which involved irregular forms:

> I am way more funnier than he is.
> It seems to taste more better when it's oily and fried.
> She didn't make the problem worser, she made it better.
> And it made her a little more sneakier. (two tokens from same speaker)

This suggests that double marking of comparatives is a developmental phenomenon that never completely disappears in the informal speech of some English users.

FORM AND MEANING OF EQUATIVE CONSTRUCTIONS

PATTERNS FOR EQUATIVES

In many respects (i.e., both semantically and syntactically) equative constructions are similar to comparatives. However, when we formulate an equative construction, we presuppose a degree of similarity or identity (as opposed to the degree of difference we presuppose when we formulate a comparison). For example:

$$X \left\{ \begin{array}{l} \text{is} \\ \text{has} \\ \text{other} \\ \text{verbs} \end{array} \right\} \text{ as (MUCH) A as Y}$$

$$\text{``X is } \left\{ \begin{array}{l} \text{similar} \\ \text{identical} \end{array} \right\} \text{ to Y with respect to A''}$$

The equative construction—like the comparative—occurs with all four major parts of speech:

> *Adjective:* Mel is as tall as George (is).
> *Adverb:* Joe runs as fast as Bill (runs/does).
> *Noun:* Ed has as (much money/many books) as Jack (has/does).
> *Verb:* Roger weighs as much as Paul (weighs/does).

Also, the complementizer *as*—like the complementizer *than*—can be followed by a reduced clause:

$$\text{She has as many books as I } \left\{ \begin{array}{l} \text{have} \\ \text{do} \end{array} \right\}. \text{[15]}$$

Or simply a noun phrase:

> She has as many books as John.

In the latter context, if a pronoun follows *as* instead of a lexical noun, it once again tends to change from subject to object form in informal conversation:

$$\text{She has as many books as } \left\{ \begin{array}{l} \text{me} \\ \text{?I} \end{array} \right\}.$$

In other words, if no verb or auxiliary follows the noun phrase, English speakers tend to treat that noun as the object of a preposition. Thus the complementizer *as*—like the complementizer *than*—appears to have some of the features of a preposition.

Surface Variations

Notice that the underlying *much* in the formula "as (MUCH) … as" changes to *many* before plural count nouns and that the *much* must be deleted before adjectives and adverbs. The failure of some ESL/EFL students to observe these syntactically motivated alternations produces errors like these:

> *Sam has as much books as Harry.   *Jill types as much fast as Jack.

The Negative Equative

The equative construction has a negative form, which is equivalent semantically to a negative or marked comparative:

> Paul doesn't have as much money as Peter. = Paul has less money than Peter.

The Occurrence of "So (MUCH) . . . As"

The form *so* may replace the first *as* of the equative formula when it is immediately preceded by *not*.

> Mary is not $\left\{ \begin{array}{l} \text{so} \\ \text{as} \end{array} \right\}$ tall as John (is).

This is not possible in affirmative equatives:

> Mary is $\left\{ \begin{array}{l} \text{as} \\ \text{*so} \end{array} \right\}$ tall as Susan (is).

Certain negative words other than *not* also account for some of the variation of *so* with *as*:

> Nothing is $\left\{ \begin{array}{l} \text{so} \\ \text{as} \end{array} \right\}$ exciting as this!

> I've never seen anyone $\left\{ \begin{array}{l} \text{so} \\ \text{as} \end{array} \right\}$ happy as Sue.

In addition to sentences like those above with overtly negative words such as *not, nothing,* and *never, so* may also occur instead of *as* in at least two other types of sentences that have the potential for negative (as well as positive) implication:

> *Wh-questions:* What is $\left\{ \begin{array}{l} \text{so} \\ \text{as} \end{array} \right\}$ rare as a day in June?

> ("There is nothing $\left\{ \begin{array}{l} \text{so} \\ \text{as} \end{array} \right\}$ rare as a day in June.")

> *Conditionals:* I'll be happy $\left\{ \begin{array}{l} \text{so} \\ \text{as} \end{array} \right\}$ long as I have you.

> ("If I don't have you, I won't be happy.")

We say more about the use of *so* versus *as* later.

THE MEANING OF EQUATIVES VIS-A-VIS COMPARATIVES

Mitchell (1990) has pointed out that equatives are not constructions of strict identity but convey instead a sense of "same or more." He uses these following example sentences to make his point in that (3) is a contradiction, but (4) and (5) are fine (numbers are ours, not from Mitchell 1990:59):

1. Mary is as tall as her father.
2. Mary and her father are identical in height.
3. ?Mary is as tall as her father. In fact, she's shorter than him.
4. Mary is as tall as her father. In fact, she's taller than him.
5. Mary is as tall as her father. In fact, they're identical in height.

Mitchell says that most people treat (1) and (2) as synonymous, yet the possibility of (4), the contradiction in (3), and the somewhat tautological but still possible (5) show that equatives are more like comparatives than most grammars would indicate.

Further, if comparison with respect to quantity *(much/more; little/less)* is combined with negation, we get the following equivalences between comparatives and equatives (Mitchell 1990:63):

Comparative		*Equative*
X costs more than Y	=	X doesn't cost as little as Y
X costs less than Y	=	X doesn't cost as much as Y
X costs no more than Y	=	X costs as little as Y
X costs no less than Y	=	X costs as much as Y

If one adds the possibility of using gradable adjectives with positive and negative polarity *(tall/short)*, then the following equivalences are available (Mitchell 1990:67).

Comparative		*Equative*
[taller than] less short than	=	not as short as
less tall than [shorter than]	=	not as tall as
no taller than no less short than	=	[as short as]
no less tall than no shorter than	=	[as tall as]

Thus, as Mitchell shows us, comparatives and equatives have an inverse relationship such that the cognitively less demanding form (i.e., the forms in square brackets in the above lists) will tend to be used most often to express a given meaning.

The Potential Ambiguity of *As Well As*

Because of the deletions that occur in degree constructions, sometimes these constructions are ambiguous. Consider, for example, a sentence such as the following:

Jane can type as well as Sarah.

In one interpretation—"Jane is as good a typist as Sarah"—*as well as* expresses the similarity in their degrees of proficiency as typists. The other meaning for this sentence is "In addition to Sarah, Jane can also type," which could also be paraphrased as "Sarah types and Jane does as well." In these cases, *as well (as)* is functioning as a prepositional logical connector expressing addition; that is, no element of degree is being expressed.

ISSUES CONCERNING THE USE OF EQUATIVE CONSTRUCTIONS

MORE ON *SO*/*AS* VARIATION

A number of factors other than an adjacent negative form must be considered in accounting for *so*/*as* variation in equatives. First of all, the acceptability of *so* greatly diminishes when other lexical items intervene between the negative word and *so*/*as:*

Joe does not speak $\left\{ \begin{array}{l} \text{as} \\ \text{?so} \end{array} \right\}$ well as Mark.

However, the probability of *so* occurring increases when an adverb with negative associations such as *nearly* (= not exactly) directly precedes the equative construction:

Joe $\left\{ \begin{array}{l} \text{doesn't} \\ \text{does not} \end{array} \right\}$ speak nearly $\left\{ \begin{array}{l} \text{so} \\ \text{as} \end{array} \right\}$ well as Mark.

Also, since *so* is perceived as somewhat formal—perhaps even literary or slightly archaic—when used in equatives, its use diminishes when *not* is contracted and no negative adverb like *nearly* is present:

Mary isn't $\left\{ \begin{array}{l} \text{as} \\ \text{?so} \end{array} \right\}$ tall as John.

USING NEGATIVE EQUATIVES VERSUS MARKED NEGATIVE COMPARATIVES

In many cases an equative is preferable to a negative comparative with *less* or negative adjective plus *-er* because it is perceived as being less direct or blunt. Negative equatives are also often preferred over comparatives with negative polarity adjectives because they seem to be less awkward stylistically or—as already mentioned in Chapter 10—more tactful and polite. For example:

Mary is not $\left\{ \begin{array}{l} \text{so} \\ \text{as} \end{array} \right\}$ tall as John (is).

(Mary is $\left\{ \begin{array}{l} \text{?less tall} \\ \text{shorter} \end{array} \right\}$ than John.)

Joe doesn't run as fast as Burt ($\left\{ \begin{array}{l} \text{runs} \\ \text{does} \end{array} \right\}$).

(Joe runs $\left\{ \begin{array}{l} \text{?less fast} \\ \text{slower} \end{array} \right\}$ than Burt [$\left\{ \begin{array}{l} \text{runs} \\ \text{does} \end{array} \right\}$].)

A complete statement of when to use the negative equative rather than a *less/fewer* comparative or a marked comparative with *-er* is not available (to our knowledge) and further research on this topic would thus be useful. However, the ESL/EFL teacher must be aware of the problem so that sentences such as those cited above as potentially questionable are not presented and practiced in class as normal, preferred usage. (We have observed such sentences being used as models or being elicited in drills—in inappropriate ways—in ESL/EFL classrooms and textbooks.) In the meantime, using the bracketed equivalent forms indicated on page 731 in the lists adapted from Mitchell (1990) seems to be a good rule of thumb.

CONCLUSION

This chapter has in no way exhausted all that could be said about comparative and equative constructions in English. We have not provided a syntactic analysis (i.e., the tree diagrams and derivations) because the available descriptions were either inadequate or too complicated to incorporate here. Furthermore, it is obvious that a number of important questions of usage (e.g., *-er* vs. *more*, equative vs. negative comparative) deserve additional careful future study. Depending on how comparison is expressed in the learner's native language, the learning challenge could involve all three dimensions: form, meaning, and use.

TEACHING SUGGESTIONS

1. Form/Meaning. A good way to introduce comparison of adjectives (the simplest pattern) is to give your students information about people and ask them to make comparisons:

	Age	Height	GPA	Number of pounds he can press
Hamid	22	5'8"	3.7	150
Mario	19	5'10"	3.1	200

> Examples: Mario is taller than Hamid.
> Hamid is older than Mario.

2. Form/Meaning. To introduce comparison of noun quantities, have your students compare the amount of coins and money that two people have in their wallets:

	Pennies	Nickels	Dimes	Quarters	Dollars	Total money
Greta	3	2	4	2	5	$6.03
Christine	2	4	1	3	4	$5.07

> Example: Greta has more pennies than Christine.
> (or Greta has one more penny than Christine.)

3. Form/Meaning. One of the best ways to integrate different patterns of comparison is to give a variety of data concerning two people such that the data naturally elicit a variety of comparative structures:

	Age	Height	Weight	Year in College	Number of classes this term	Can run the mile in:
Pablo	20	6'	170 lb	Junior	4	4½ minutes
Marc	21	6'2"	180 lb	Senior	3	5 minutes

> Examples: Marc weighs more than Pablo.
> Pablo runs (the mile) faster than Marc.

4. Form/Meaning/Use. A realistic environment for eliciting negative polarity (or marked) comparatives is to show students objects—or present them with situations where both things are, for example, smaller, shorter, or less than normal. In such a case, it makes sense to use a negative polarity form. Here are a few examples:

    a. Two pencils—both short but one more so than the other: "The blue pencil is shorter than the yellow one."

    b. Two cars—both new but one newer than the other (Last year George bought his car March 1st and Alice bought her car April 15th): "Alice's car is newer than George's (car)."

    c. Stick figures of Stan and Bill (Stan is short; Bill is very short): "Bill is shorter than Stan."

5. Form/Meaning. To introduce equatives, use the concept of identical twins so that the equatives can be practiced naturally.

	Age	Height	Weight	Number of brothers and sisters	Year in college
Sandra	18	5'5"	115 lbs.	3	Freshman
Sheila	18	5'5"	115 lbs.	3	Freshman

Examples: Sandra is as $\begin{Bmatrix} \text{old} \\ \text{tall} \end{Bmatrix}$ as Sheila.

Sheila weighs as much as Sandra.

6. Form/Meaning/Use. Comparatives and equatives can often be combined if information about cities, states, or countries can be assembled for purposes of comparison:

	Area	Population	Year of statehood	State bird	Highest point
Kentucky	about 40,000 sq. miles	3,500,000	1792	Cardinal	4,150 ft.
Virginia	about 40,000 sq. miles	5,000,000	1788	Cardinal	5,730 ft.

Examples: Kentucky is the same size as Virginia.
Virginia has a larger population than Kentucky.

7. Form/Meaning. One way of teaching free comparatives is to present information about an individual over a period of time:

Sally	Age	5	7	9	11
	Height	3'	3'9"	4'5"	5'2"

Example: Sally $\begin{Bmatrix} \text{is} \\ \text{has been} \end{Bmatrix}$ getting taller and taller.

Harvey	Age	10	13	16	19	21
	GPA	2.5	2.9	3.3	3.6	3.8

Example: Harvey $\begin{Bmatrix} \text{is} \\ \text{has been} \end{Bmatrix}$ getting smarter and smarter.

(or) Harvey $\begin{Bmatrix} \text{is} \\ \text{has been} \end{Bmatrix}$ studying harder and harder.

8. Use. You can present the use of *-er* versus *more* to your students by contrasting short, informal adjectives with longer, more formal adjectives in a context where both types of adjectives are being used to make similar comparisons.

> Situation:
> Mrs. Harrison owns a public relations firm. She is creating a new position and asks her manager if she should promote Ms. Franklin or Ms. Thomas.
>
> Manager (on the phone with Mrs. Harrison):
> Oh, I'd hire Ms. Thomas. She's *smarter*, *works harder*, and is much *friendlier*.
>
> Manager (in a written memo to Mrs. Harrison):
> I recommend Ms. Thomas for the promotion because she is *more intelligent* and *more industrious* than the other person being considered. Also, Ms. Thomas is *more personable*, which will also be an important asset to bring to the new position.

EXERCISES

Test your understanding of what has been presented.

1. Provide an original example sentence for each of the following terms. Underline the pertinent word(s) in your examples.

    a. the comparative construction   **e.** use of adverb to express degree
    b. the equative construction   **f.** free comparative
    c. irregular comparative adverb   **g.** unmarked adjective
    d. absolute use of adjectives

2. Describe the ambiguity in the following sentences:
    a. Phyllis likes Carol more than Sue.   **b.** Mark teaches Sam as well as Ralph.

3. What part of speech is being compared in the following sentences?
    a. Harry throws the ball farther than Ned does.
    b. John has more than two cars.
    c. I bought more oranges than we can eat.
    d. This book costs more than I want to pay.
    e. This movie is more interesting than the one we saw last week.

4. Why is the following sentence awkward or questionable?
    ?Joan sings less well than Sally.

Test your ability to apply what you know.

5. If your students produce the following sentences, what errors have they made? How will you make them aware of their errors? What exercises will you prepare to correct them?
    a. *To make the story more short, I'll just tell the ending.
    b. *I like this book more better than that one.
    c. *I was lucky than my little brother.
    d. *Their prediction about empathy was not as realistic than they had thought.
    e. *The newspapers in Los Angeles have better international coverage than in San Diego.

6. Many languages express the free comparative with its meaning of progressive change in a way that more clearly parallels more formal English constructions like these:

> He grew ever taller.   It became progressively more overcast.

To learners who are only familiar with such a construction, how would you present the more frequent and more colloquial English construction? For example:

> He grew taller and taller.   It became more and more overcast.

7. Consider the following sentences:
  a. I've seen monkeys more intelligent than Herbert.
  b. I've seen more intelligent monkeys than Herbert.

What's the difference in meaning?

8. A student brings you a magazine article that contains the following:

> Benjamin Franklin was both smarter and loyaler than...

He asks you why the writer used *loyaler* instead of *more loyal*. He thinks *loyaler* may be a mistake and wants your opinion. What would you say to the student?

BIBLIOGRAPHY

References

Bolinger, D. (1972). *Degree Words*. The Hague: Mouton.
Browne, W. (1964). "On Adjectival Comparisons and Reduplication in English." Unpublished paper, Department of Linguistics, MIT.
Celce-Murcia, M. (1972). "A Syntactic and Psycholinguistic Study of Comparison in English." Unpublished Ph.D. dissertation in Linguistics, UCLA.
Celce-Murcia, M., D. Brinton, and J. Goodwin (1996). *Teaching Pronunciation*. Cambridge: Cambridge University Press.
Chen, Z. (1982). An Analysis of *Less* vs. *Fewer*. Unpublished paper, Department of TESL and Applied Linguistics, UCLA.
Donaldson, M., and G. Balfour (1968). "Less is More: A Study of Language Comprehension in Children." *British Journal of Psychology* 59:461–472.
Halliday, M. A. K. & R. Hasan (1976). *Cohesion in English*. London: Longman.
McCawley, J. D. (1964). "Quantitative and Qualitative Comparison in English." Paper presented at the annual LSA winter meeting, New York, Dec. 29, 1964.
Mitchell, K. (1990). "On Comparisons in a Notional Grammar." *Applied Linguistics* 11:1, 5202.
Solomon, G. (1994). "A More Closer Look at Comparatives and Superlatives." Unpublished paper. Department of TESL and Applied Linguistics, UCLA.
Ssensalo, D. A. (1976). "Markedness and the Usage of Comparatives." Unpublished M.A. thesis in TESL, UCLA.

Suggestions for further reading

For useful accounts of the English comparative, see:
Bresnan, J. (1973). Syntax of the Comparative Construction in English. *Linguistic Inquiry* 3:3, 275-343.

Jespersen, O. (1964). *Essentials of English Grammar.* University, Ala.: University of Alabama Press.

Quirk, R., and S. Greenbaum (1973). *A Concise Grammar of Contemporary English.* New York: Harcourt Brace Jovanovich.

For a transformational analysis of the comparative and the equative construction in English, see Celce-Murcia (1972) in the references above, pp. 35–84.

For useful treatments of semantic opposition and markedness, see:

Kruse, D. A. (1986). *Lexical Semantics.* Cambridge: Cambridge University Press.

Mettinger, A (1994). *Aspects of Semantic Opposition in English.* Oxford: Clarendon Press.

For ESL/EFL texts with good ideas for teaching the comparative and equative constructions, see:

Danielson, D., and P. Porter (1990). *Using English: Your Second Language* (2d ed.). Englewood Cliffs, N.J.: Prentice-Hall Regents.

Riggenbach, H., and V. Samuda (1997). *Grammar Dimensions.* Book 2 (2d ed.). Boston: Heinle & Heinle., 107–122.

Thewlis, S. (1997). *Grammar Dimensions.* Book 3 (2d ed.). Boston: Heinle & Heinle, 159–173.

For two units especially designed for introducing comparison of adjectives and adverbs to beginners, see units 22 and 23 in:

Badalamenti, V., and C. Henner Stanchina (1997). *Grammar Dimensions.* Book 1 (2d ed.). Boston: Heinle & Heinle.

ENDNOTES

1. For some examples of these constructions in other languages, see Celce-Murcia (1972:160–167).

2. We had been unaware of this typological pattern until R. Longacre (personal communication) informed us that several languages of New Guinea expressed comparison this way. Then later, Bonnie Glover (personal communication) confirmed that this mode of comparing also occurs in some American Indian languages.

3. Martin Mould (personal communication) has told us, for example, that Igbo and most Bantu languages cannot reverse such a "surpass" comparison to directly express the notion that "Mary is shorter than John"; i.e., the *pass* verb can only be used to compare in a positive direction. However, not all languages having a "surpass" comparative are quite so restricted. Dolly Meyers (personal communication) has informed us that in Yoruba it is possible to say "Mary surpasses John in shortness." At the moment we do not know whether Yoruba always had this flexibility or whether it acquired flexibility through internal change or through contact with other languages of the type discussed under "Comparison using degree morphemes."

4. The rule presented here is adapted from Celce-Murcia, Brinton, and Goodwin (1996).

5. There are a few one-syllable adjectives that are exceptional in that they take only periphrastic *more* or *most: real, right, wrong,* and *like* (= similar to).

6. Syllabic [ḷ] in this context generally becomes consonantal and begins a new syllable when the inflection is added *(gent·ler).*

7. The adjective *elder* does, however, occur in certain fixed collocations such as *elder statesman.*

8. In standard English the plural substitute *ones* does not follow a plural demonstrative:

>   These cars are bigger than those (*ones).

9. Note that in this example a determiner (not a noun, verb, adjective, or adverb) is being compared.

10. This is sometimes called a "free comparative," terminology that was first suggested by Browne (1964).

11. This type is not a comparative of degree or extent like the others. McCawley's term (1964) for this type of construction is "qualitative comparison."

12. See Celce-Murcia (1972) for empirical evidence that unmarked comparatives are produced significantly more frequently in English than are marked ones.

13. Donaldson and Balfour (1968), for example, have demonstrated that young English-speaking children cannot correctly distinguish *less* from *more* (i.e., they consistently interpret *less* as *more*) until they have reached a certain cognitive developmental stage that occurs somewhere around the age of 5.

14. Recall that suppletive forms are grammatically related forms that are not historically related morphemes:

>   e.g., *go-went; bad-worse,* etc.

15. Charles Fillmore (personal communication) has pointed out to us that only literal equatives can take a redundant verb or operator. Figurative equatives cannot:

>   Washington is as hot as Tokyo is.
>   *Washington is as hot as hell is.
>   *You are as dead as a doornail is.

35

DEGREE— COMPLEMENTS AND SUPERLATIVES

INTRODUCTION

In this chapter we continue the discussion of degree constructions that we began in the preceding chapter, which covered comparatives and equatives. First of all, we discuss several degree complements expressing notions such as "excess" *(too much/too many)*, "insufficiency" *(too little/too few)*, and "sufficiency" *(enough)*, with infinitive complements; and "causality" *(so much/so many; so little/so few; or such)* + *that* complements. Then we briefly examine the absolute use of *too* and *so*, with attention to contexts where they function as emphatic counterparts of the intensifier *very*.

The final degree construction that we consider is the English superlative *(-est, most, least)*. We comment on the highly marked nature of this form since many languages of the world do not have a superlative degree that is morphologically distinct from their comparative degree. We also contrast the superlative with the comparative degree because this contrast is the crux of many of the teaching-learning problems encountered when superlatives are presented in the ESL/EFL classroom.

FORM AND MEANING OF DEGREE COMPLEMENTS

There are several degree complements that resemble comparatives and equatives in that they make relative (rather than absolute) use of the four major parts of speech.

TOO (MUCH/LITTLE) PLUS INFINITIVE COMPLEMENT

$$
too \; + \;
\left\{
\begin{array}{l}
\text{ADJ} \\
\text{ADV} \\
\left\{ \begin{array}{l} much \\ little \end{array} \right\} \; (\text{N noncount}) \\
\left\{ \begin{array}{l} many \\ few \end{array} \right\} \; (\text{N count})
\end{array}
\right\}
\; + \; (for\;\text{NP}) \; + \; \text{infinitive complement}
$$

Examples: He's *too* old to join the Army.
She left *too* quickly for me to thank her.

Burt has *too* $\begin{Bmatrix} \textit{much money} \\ \textit{many investments} \end{Bmatrix}$ to understand what it's like to be poor.

I have *too little time* to watch TV.
There were *too few examples* in his paper to support his hypothesis.
Martha *weighs too much* to work as a flight attendant.

Semantically, this construction indicates either an excess or an insufficiency of some quality or of something measurable. When *much* or *many* occurs, the meaning of excess is explicit. Likewise, when *little* or *few* occurs, the meaning of insufficiency is overtly expressed. None of these quantifiers, however, occurs before an adjective or an adverb. In such cases, an adjective or an adverb with positive polarity would express excess (e.g., *too tall*), whereas an adjective or an adverb with negative polarity would express insufficiency (e.g., *too small*). Note that *much* and *little* precede noncount nouns, while *many* and *few* are the related forms preceding count nouns.

SO (*MUCH/LITTLE*) PLUS *THAT* CLAUSE

$$
so \quad \left\{ \begin{array}{l} \text{ADJ} \\ \text{ADV} \\ \begin{Bmatrix} much \\ little \end{Bmatrix} \ (\text{N noncount}) \\ \begin{Bmatrix} many \\ few \end{Bmatrix} \ (\text{N count}) \end{array} \right\} \quad (to\ \text{VP}) \ (that) + \text{complement S}
$$

Examples: They're *so noisy* (that) we can't sleep.
He ran *so fast* (that) no one could catch him.

I have *so* $\begin{Bmatrix} \textit{much work} \\ \textit{many errands} \end{Bmatrix}$ to do (that) I'll never finish.

Bess has *so* $\begin{Bmatrix} \textit{little ability} \\ \textit{few skills} \end{Bmatrix}$ (that) she won't find a good job.

He runs *so little* (that) it won't help him get in shape.

When *so (much/little)* is used in this construction, the notion of "causality" is conveyed; that is, the degree, extent, or amount—positive or negative—expressed in the main clause is sufficient to bring about the result expected in the complement clause preceded by *that*. Just as in the previous construction, *much* and *little* occur before noncount nouns and after verbs, while *many* and *few* occur before countable nouns. Also, none of these quantifiers precedes an adjective or an adverb; the *so* occurs alone in such environments.

SUCH (*A/AN*) (*ADJ*) NOUN PLUS *THAT* CLAUSE

$$
such \quad \left\{ \begin{array}{l} \begin{Bmatrix} a \\ an \end{Bmatrix} \ (\text{adj}) \ \text{N count} \\ \\ \emptyset \begin{Bmatrix} (\text{adj}) \ \text{N plural} \\ \\ (\text{adj}) \ \text{N noncount} \end{Bmatrix} \end{array} \right\} \quad (that) + \text{complement S}
$$

Examples: Bobby was *such a nuisance* (that) he was sent to his room.
They are *such racists* (that) they would rather close down their schools than integrate.
The victim was in *such agony* (that) she was taken to the hospital.

This construction closely parallels the one above in meaning and structure. In both constructions, causality is expressed in the clause containing *so* or *such,* and a result is expressed in the *that* clause. Unlike *so,* however, *such* modifies only nouns or noun phrases. *Such* is used instead of *so (much/little),* and so on when the degree or extent of a noun is being conveyed rather than its quantity or amount. When *such* modifies a singular countable noun, the indefinite article *a/an* must follow *such.* In other environments, *such* may directly precede the noun it modifies. Note, however, that an adjective frequently occurs between *such (a/an)* and the noun:

>   such an unusual incident...   such easy questions...

There is often a near-paraphrase relationship between *so* and *such* in those cases where semantically parallel nouns and adjectives exist:

>   Jane is such an athlete that all the boys want her to play on the varsity team.
>   Jane is so athletic that all the boys want her to play on the varsity team.

>   The test had such easy questions that I finished it early.
>   The questions were so easy that I finished the test early.

ENOUGH PLUS INFINITIVE COMPLEMENT

$$\left\{ \begin{array}{l} \text{ADJ} \\ \text{ADV} \\ \text{verb} \\ <\text{noun}_x>^1 \end{array} \right\} \textit{enough}<\text{noun}_x>^1 \; (\textit{for}\,\text{NP})\,)\;(\text{infinitive complement})$$

Examples: She's *qualified enough* for them to hire her.
He ran *fast enough* to win the race.
He *weighs enough* to compete as a heavyweight.

I have $\left\{ \begin{array}{l} \text{enough money} \\ \text{money enough} \end{array} \right\}$ to get by for a while.

Enough, unlike the two previous degree complements we have discussed, follows adjectives and adverbs as well as verbs. It expresses "sufficiency" and it usually precedes nouns; however, there is a less frequent variant of the *enough* + NOUN construction where *enough* may follow the noun instead. (See the last example above.) Another difference is that *enough* simply doesn't occur with the quantifiers *much/many/little*[2]*/few.*

Semantically, of course, *not* + *enough* is similar to *too* + *little/few* since, in both cases, the meaning of "insufficiency" is conveyed:

>   He doesn't have enough time to watch TV.   He has too little time to watch TV.

There are some important differences we should mention with regard to infinitive complements and *that* clause complements occurring with degree constructions. When *not* + *enough* is used to paraphrase so *little/few,* any *not* occurring in the *that* clause complement following the *so* must be deleted in the corresponding infinitive complement following *not enough:*

>   He exercises so little that he is not in good shape.

He doesn't exercise enough $\left\{ \begin{array}{l} \text{to be in good shape} \\ \text{*not to be in good shape} \end{array} \right\}$.

The same thing happens when *too (much/little) (for NP)* (infinitive complement) is used to paraphrase *so (much/little) that* or *such (a/an) (adj) N that*. In other words, any overt negative in the *that* clause following *so* or *such* must be deleted in the parallel infinitive complement following *too (much/little)*:

> He is so weak that he can't speak coherently.
>
> He is too weak $\left\{ \begin{array}{l} \text{to speak coherently} \\ \text{*not to speak coherently} \end{array} \right\}$.

Thus, the ESL/EFL teacher must make it clear that the infinitive complements following *not enough* or *too (much/little)* are implicitly negative since this fact is not always obvious to ESL/EFL learners.

Another detail to be pointed out to learners is a fact already established in Chapter 31, i.e., when there is a *for* phrase preceding the infinitive, it provides a subject for the infinitive complement. When there is no *for* phrase, the subject of the main clause controls the reference of the unexpressed subject of the infinitive.

> The soup is too hot for me [PRO] to eat.
>
> John exercises enough [PRO] to stay healthy.

A NOTE ON THE USE OF *SO*, *TOO*, AND *VERY*

Quirk et al. (1985) have pointed out that *so* is sometimes used absolutely as an emphatic form of *very:*

> I'm *so* tired!   The party was *so* delightful!

They add that this usage is more typical of women's speech than men's. To these observations we add that in environments where *so* does not precede an adjective or adverb, *so much/many* may also be used absolutely as emphatic forms of *very much/many:*

> I enjoyed this book *so much*!   They have *so many* friends!

Quirk et al. also mention that *too* is sometimes used absolutely as a colloquial emphatic counterpart of *very:*

> He isn't *too* bright.   I don't feel *too* good.

They add that this use is more typical of informal American English than of the British variety. Note, however, that this informal use of *too* as an intensifier is acceptable only in semantically negative contexts. When ESL/EFL learners overgeneralize this absolute use of *too* to affirmative contexts, errors result:

> ?This food is too good.

What such learners want to say, of course, is "This food is very good."

In all dialects of English *too much* and *too little* can be used "absolutely," but again only in contexts where a negative meaning is implied:[3]

> He smokes too much.   They study too little.

Some ESL/EFL learners incorrectly extend this pattern to affirmative contexts and produce errors such as this:

> *We like you too much.

when what they mean to say is "We like you very much."

THE SUPERLATIVE CONSTRUCTION

HOW OTHER LANGUAGES EXPRESS THE SUPERLATIVE DEGREE

ESL/EFL teachers should be aware of the fact that most languages do not have morphologically distinct comparative and superlative forms; however, English and other related languages (i.e., other Germanic languages such as German, Dutch, Swedish, and Danish) are somewhat idiosyncratic, in having distinct superlative forms. Languages without a distinct superlative form often express a superlative meaning by using either a definite article or some other defining word(s) with a comparative morpheme; for example:

(literally) Ben is the more intelligent student in the class.
(meaning) "Ben is the most intelligent student in the class."

or by using a construction that excludes all other members of the set to which the subject belongs:

(literally) The VW is more economical than any other car.
(meaning) "The VW is the most economical car."

Using examples like the sentences above, Jespersen (1924) points out that the superlative does not necessarily indicate a higher degree than the comparative but rather that it expresses degree from a different point of view. For this reason, Jespersen feels that many languages are able to make do without superlative forms. Furthermore, some languages, such as those in the Romance family (e.g., French, Italian, Spanish), which formerly possessed a distinct superlative, have since discarded their superlative form and have simply extended the semantic domain of their comparative forms. In other words, many languages have no distinct superlative form either because they have never developed one or because they had one but discarded it over time—that is, they found it unnecessary.

In addition, in his work on language universals, Greenberg (1966) has pointed out that superlatives are more "marked" than comparatives. That is to say, comparatives occur more frequently than superlatives in any language that has both forms. He also noted that if a language has a superlative form, it must also have a comparative form; however, the reverse is not necessarily true. Solomon's (1994) data-based analysis of English comparative and superlative forms in spoken American English seems to support Greenberg's claim. She found 561 tokens of inflected, periphrastic, and irregular comparatives and superlatives in her oral corpus. Only 180 (32 percent) of these tokens were superlatives (i.e., marked forms occur less frequently than unmarked ones). Of these 180 superlatives, 76 tokens (42 percent) occurred with the *-est* inflection, 55 tokens (31 percent) occurred with periphrastic *most*, and 49 tokens (27 percent) were irregular (e.g., *best, worst*).

All this evidence suggests that the English superlative may be harder for most ESL/EFL students to learn than the comparative, and that the two forms will frequently be confused. Neuman (1977) did, in fact, find errors in compositions written by intermediate-level ESL students, verifying our prediction that these forms will be confused even by learners who are well beyond the beginning level in their acquisition of English:

*I am the younger in my family.
*That food is worst than the food for the pig.

(ESL errors from Neuman 1977:131)

SIMILARITIES AND DIFFERENCES BETWEEN COMPARATIVES AND SUPERLATIVES

In terms of distribution, the *-est* and *most* forms of the superlative behave exactly like the *-er* and *more* of the comparative. The following is a brief, simplified restatement of the morphological rule that was given in somewhat greater detail for the comparative in the preceding chapter.

Superlative Inflectional Endings[4]

First, adjectives and adverbs of one syllable take the inflectional ending as do two-syllable adjectives with a final *-y* suffix (pronounced as unstressed /i/).[5]

Base Form	*-est*
big	biggest
tall	tallest
soon	sooner
hard	hardest
happy	happiest
noisy	noisiest

Second, many other two-syllable adjectives that have a stressed first syllable and an unstressed second syllable ending in *-ly*/li/, *-ow*/o/, or *-le* (syllabic [ḷ])[6] also take the inflection, although it is certainly possible to use the periphrastic form in specific contexts, such as when extra emphasis is being placed on the comparative or superlative element ("She is the MOST friendly person I know").

Base Form	*-est*
friendly	friendliest
	(most friendly)
narrow	narrowest
	(most narrow)
gentle	gentlest
	(most gentle)

Note also that these two-syllable adjectives can add derivational prefixes and still take the same inflections as the base form (e.g., *unhappiest, unfriendliest,* etc.).

Third, all two-syllable adverbs ending in *-ly* that do not have an adjective homonym also ending in *-ly* take only the periphrastic form.

Adverbs Taking the Periphrastic Form

Base Form	*most*	
slowly	most slowly	(*not* slowliest)
brusquely	most brusquely	(*not* brusqueliest)
sharply	most sharply	(*not* sharpliest)

Fourth, there are adjectives that seem more suited to the periphrastic superlative form but that also may occur with the inflectional ending, especially in informal use. These include two-syllable adjectives that (a) end in *-er* or *-ure*, such as *tender, mature;* (b) end in a weakly stressed vowel followed by nothing more than a final /d/ or /t/, such as *stupid, quiet;* and (c) end in a weakly stressed syllable ending in /m/ or /n/, such as *handsome, awesome, common:*

Base Form	*"Most"*
tender	most tender
	(tenderest)

	Base Form	"Most"
	stupid	most stupid
		(stupidest)
	handsome	most handsome
		(handsomest)
	common	most common
		(commonest)

Fifth, adjectives and adverbs of two syllables having any ending other than those described previously, and all adjectives and adverbs of three or more syllables, tend to take only the periphrastic form:

	Base Form	"Most"
Adjective	curious	most curious
	pleasant	most pleasant
	beautiful	most beautiful
Adverb	skillfully	most skillfully
	cautiously	most cautiously
	independently	most independently

Also, the same adjectives and adverbs that were morphologically irregular in the comparative (see the preceding chapter) are also irregular in the superlative (e.g., *good-better-best*). These morphological similarities are probably the main reason why so many people erroneously believe that comparative and superlative constructions are essentially the same, with the only difference being the number of persons or objects compared; that is, they believe that when two things are being compared, one should use the comparative, and when three or more things are being compared, one should use the superlative. This, in fact, is the rule given in most ESL/EFL texts as well as the rule cited in most reference grammars. If we do nothing else in this chapter, we hope to dispel this misleading oversimplification.

THE MEANING OF SUPERLATIVES

Comparatives are often used quite appropriately when three or more persons, objects, or properties are involved:

Jack is taller than John $\left\{ \begin{array}{l} \text{and} \\ \text{or}^7 \end{array} \right\}$ Bill.

Jill and Ann have more A's than B's $\left\{ \begin{array}{l} \text{and} \\ \text{or}^7 \end{array} \right\}$ C's.

Likewise, many speakers of English feel comfortable about using superlatives informally when only two objects or properties are being compared, even though use of the comparative form is considered to be formally more accurate in such cases, for example:

Bill is 6 feet tall and Joe is 6 feet 2 inches tall.
Who's the tallest?

In fact, if we ask, "Who's the taller (of the two)?" which would be the prescriptively correct form here, we are merely using a comparative form in a superlative sense. This is because the semantic function of the superlative is to select one or more members out of a set because they rank first or last (with respect to other members of the set) on a scale that measures a particular attribute (i.e., height, size, weight, age, intelligence, speed). This is why superlatives, like ordinals, tend to co-occur with a definite determiner and to be following by *of* phrases or *that* clauses which describe the whole set out of which the subject of the superlative has been selected. (The subject may be singular or plural.) For example:

$$\left\{\begin{array}{l}\text{Clem is}\\\text{Clem and Bob are}\end{array}\right\}\quad\text{the tallest}\quad\left\{\begin{array}{l}\text{(one[s]) of the four boys}\\\text{boy(s) in my class}\end{array}\right\}.$$

The superlative thus concerns itself with the extremes of a given scale with regard to a specific set, whereas the comparative ignores the extremes and looks at two points anywhere on the scale with regard to two or more individuals, objects, and so on. The number of persons or objects involved in a comparison is therefore not the most important thing that a native speaker of English considers when deciding whether to use a comparative or a superlative form.

This distinction of the extremes versus any two intermediate points on a scale gets muddied, however, since it's a fact that English comparative forms are sometimes used to express a superlative meaning. One example of this was given above (i.e., "Who's the taller of the two boys?"), and at least two other situations exist where comparative forms are used to express a superlative meaning:

1. Comparatives with *(n)ever*

> I've never seen more people.
> or
> That's more people than I've ever seen.   ("That's the most people I've ever seen.")

2. Comparatives with *any (other)*

> This play is better than any other play I've seen   ("This is the best play (that) I've ever seen.")

As a rule, if a sentence containing a comparative form can be paraphrased using a sentence with a superlative form, then we can say that the comparative form is being used to express a superlative meaning. In fact, all superlative sentences in English can be paraphrased using a comparative form. Superlative forms, on the other hand, are rarely used to paraphrase a comparative meaning.

THE USE OF SUPERLATIVES

OTHER USES OF SUPERLATIVE FORMS

Note that the word *most* is often used absolutely as an intensifier, with a meaning similar to *very*, to express a strong degree:

> He was a most gracious host.   That was most thoughtful of you.

The use of the indefinite article in the first of the two preceding examples demonstrates that *most* is not being used to express a superlative meaning,[8] since a true superlative almost always selects the definite article (if it occurs with an article).

A colloquial use of the superlative involves using it absolutely without explicitly specifying any set. In such cases, a superlative meaning is intended nonetheless:

> You're $\left\{\begin{array}{l}\text{the greatest!}\\\text{the most!}\end{array}\right\}$ Joe still thinks Ali's the greatest!

Another type of abbreviated superlative that occurs in colloquial usage are sentences like the following, which end in *ever*:

> That book was his best ever. (i.e., "That was the best book that he ever wrote.")
> The play was the most resounding flop ever. (i.e., "The play was the most resounding flop of any play ever performed.")

The presence of *ever* makes such sentences more emphatic because the proposition holds true over a period of time.

Co-occurrence of Superlatives with the Definite Article

Superlatives usually co-occur with the definite article or some other definite determiner or defining word; however, the underlying *the* can be omitted if *-est*, *most*, or *least* is not followed by a noun or a noun substitute[9] in the surface structure—that is, if the underlying noun has been deleted.[10] For example:

the obligatory:	*the* optional:
Which is the highest mountain?	Which mountain is (the) highest?
Which mountain is the highest one?	Who climbed (the) highest?

The Use of Marked and Unmarked Superlatives

In the preceding chapter and in Chapter 20, we stated that there were semantically related adjectives that had positive and negative polarity and that the positive forms were unmarked while the negative forms were marked; here we add *most* to the unmarked forms and *least* to the marked forms:

	Most	Least	
	tall	short	
	big	little	
(+) "unmarked"	old	young	(−) "marked"
	deep	shallow	

These oppositions are as valid for superlatives as they are for comparatives, with the added caveat (noted earlier in this chapter) that superlatives are inherently more marked than comparatives.

The superlative form *least* is the most highly marked of all these forms. In other words, we tend not to say phrases such as "the least tall":

?Bob is the least tall of all the boys.

but prefer to use *most*—or its morphological variant *-est*—if we have a negative polarity word such as *short*, which we can combine with *most* or *-est*:

Bob is the shortest of all the boys.

Thus, whenever there are negative and positive polarity adjectives and adverbs available for English speakers to combine with *most* or *-est*, the form *least* tends not to occur.

So when does the form *least* occur? It is used frequently as the opposite of *most* whenever the ranking or scaling of items is involved. For example:

$$\text{the most/least} \begin{cases} \text{likely[11]} \\ \text{expensive} \\ \text{important} \end{cases}$$

The other environment in which *least* occurs is a negative one, where the use of *least* indicates the least negative (i.e. most nearly positive) member(s) of a set that is viewed as being completely negative; for example:

$$\text{the least} \begin{cases} \text{objectionable} \\ \text{sinister} \\ \text{reprehensible} \end{cases}$$

There is, of course, the related comparative form *lesser,* which also can be used in negative contexts with this special type of superlative meaning if the set described has only two members:

$$\text{the lesser} \begin{cases} \text{of two evils} \\ \text{evil} \end{cases}$$

Lesser, however, has more semantic flexibility than *least* since it can also be used in a comparative sense that has no superlative counterpart:

> a lesser punishment   (= "a less severe punishment")

We should also briefly mention *fewest,* the suppletive variant of *least* that occurs before countable nouns in formal or prescriptively correct usage. (In informal usage *least* often occurs in this environment instead of *fewest.*) Semantically, *fewest* is like *least* in that it occurs as the opposite of *most* when items are being ranked or scaled:

> Of all the children in the class, Barbara seems to have the most friends and Jennifer the fewest (friends). (informal: the least ([friends]))

Fewest also occurs in predominantly negative contexts to indicate the least negative (or most nearly positive) member of a set that is viewed as having only negative members:

> Paul has reservations about all the proposals; however, he has the fewest reservations about the third one.

Again, *least* may be used as an informal variant of *fewest* here.

DIFFERENCES BETWEEN REGULAR QUANTIFIERS AND SUPERLATIVES

In Chapter 17 we presented *least* and *fewest* as superlative forms of the quantifiers *little* and *few;* however, there are grammatical and semantic differences we should note between the quantifiers *(little, few)* and the superlative forms *(least, fewest).* The quantifiers can be used to make assertions about small quantities that the speaker perceives negatively (and that do not imply any specific comparison):

> They have little money.
> They have few friends.

The superlative forms, on the other hand, take the definite article and specify (or imply) a relevant set for which the extreme negative quantity is being asserted:

> They have the least money of anyone I know.
> They have the fewest friends of anyone I know.

ARGUMENTS FOR PRESENTING COMPARATIVES AND SUPERLATIVES SEPARATELY

Part of the general confusion between comparatives and superlatives no doubt stems from the fact that most ESL/ EFL textbooks present them in the same lesson or chapter. From a semantic point of view, it seems more sensible to present comparatives and equatives along with verbs, adjectives, nominals, and prepositions, such as the following, all of which express similarity or difference:

Verbs	Adjectives	Nominals	Prepositions
to differ from NP	to be different from (than[12]) NP	to be the same as NP	(to be) like NP
to $\left\{\begin{array}{c}\text{sound}\\\text{feel}\\\text{look}\\\text{taste}\\\text{seem}\end{array}\right\}$ like NP	to be similar to NP to be taller than NP to be as tall as NP to be equal/equivalent to NP to be identical to NP		(to be) unlike NP
to behave like NP	to be alike		

Examples: John is different from Bill.   John is taller than Bill (is).

Comparatives, in our opinion, can usefully be considered a complex type of transitive adjective.

Superlatives, on the other hand, should be presented in the context of ordinals and ordinal-like prenominal modifiers that occur in the postdeterminer position:

Definite Core Determiner   Post Determiner   Head Noun

$$\left\{\begin{array}{c}\text{the}\\\text{my}\\\text{this}\end{array}\right\} \quad + \quad \left\{\begin{array}{c}\text{first}\\\text{second}\\\text{third}\\\\\text{next}\\\text{last}\end{array}\right\} \quad + \quad \left\{\begin{array}{l}\text{NOUN }(that + \text{S})\\\text{NOUN (prep NP)}\end{array}\right\}$$

core post head noun   core post head noun
Examples: This is my first course. / This is the best course (that) I have taken.

core   post   head noun   core   post
This exercise is your next assignment. / This exercise is the hardest

head noun
assignment of the semester.

In other words, it is useful to classify superlatives as a type of postdeterminer.

LACK OF DOUBLE MARKING WITH SUPERLATIVES

Solomon's (1994) findings for the use of superlatives in spoken data produced by native English speakers show some differences with comparatives in that no tokens of double marking occurred with superlatives whereas six double-marked tokens occurred with comparatives (e.g., *more sneakier*). She also found only one token of the periphrastic *most* superlative with a one-syllable adjective (vs. 17 tokens of *more* with one-syllable adjectives for comparatives), and this token was a case where *most* was stressed:

It's one of the MOST grand sights in New York City.

(Solomon 1994:17)

The 62 other one-syllable adjectives and adverbs took the *-est* inflection; for example:

> At the very deepest level of awareness . . . .
> (Solomon 1994:17)

For two-syllable adjectives and adverbs, Solomon found 21 periphrastic forms versus 14 inflected forms. However, the periphrastic forms included both tokens where *-est* would be predicted (*most corny*) as well as tokens where *most* would be predicted (*most frequent*) by the morphological rules we gave earlier in this chapter:

> That is the most corny thing I've ever done.
> (Solomon 1994:6)
> If I say "black," the most frequent response is "white."
> (Solomon 1994:18)

All three-syllable adjectives and adverbs (33 tokens) occurring in superlative form in Solomon's corpus took periphrastic *most*.

Thus there appears to be some variation in the use of superlatives but not nearly as much as Solomon detected in the case of comparatives. We speculate that this is due to the differences in the syntax of superlatives and comparatives: superlatives function as a complex modifier (postdeterminer or intensifier) within some other constituent, whereas comparatives function as a higher order connector of two clauses or phrases and seem to have a freer distribution.

Therefore, given all these differences—syntactic and semantic—we feel that it is important for the ESL/EFL student to practice first the comparative and then, at some later time, the superlative, each in different contexts and in conjunction with the semantically and syntactically related patterns, which we have cited above. Once the two forms have been fairly well established, the teacher can combine them in contexts where the students must learn to properly distinguish the use of the comparative and superlative.

One noteworthy exception to this suggestion has been brought to our attention by Werner Kruse (personal communication). Kruse points out that when ESL/EFL students are speakers of German or some other Germanic language, they are already familiar with comparative and superlative forms similar to the English ones and use them in their own language in much the same way that they are used in English. For such students the main learning problem is a morphological one—that is, they need to learn when to use *-er* versus *more* and when to use *-est* versus *most*. We agree with Kruse that for such students our reasons for strict segregation of the two constructions at the initial stage of instruction no longer apply. The teacher of such students should concentrate on presenting and practicing, in communicative contexts, the distributional differences between the inflectional forms (*-er, -est*) and the corresponding periphrastic ones (*more, most*).

CONCLUSION

This chapter concludes our discussion of degree constructions in English. Certainly there is much more to say about comparatives, equatives, superlatives, and the other degree complements than we have been able to cover in these two chapters. However, we do feel the chapters provide essential background for the ESL/EFL teacher and a point of departure for further research on degree constructions in English. One obvious suggestion for additional research is that a contemporary analysis of the distribution and functions of *least* versus *fewest* would provide ESL/EFL teachers with valuable information.

This chapter also concludes our treatment of selected areas in English grammar. Needless to say, there are topics and problems in English grammar that are of interest to

ESL/EFL teachers and that we have not covered adequately here, such as discourse markers (Schiffrin 1987), the many types of ellipsis in English, the grammar of complex referring forms such as *else,* the grammar of complex nominalizations, and so forth. Our work in this area will not end; however, our textbook must.

The following and final chapter is a closing statement that summarizes what we have done and attempts to put our work into the larger context of current issues in language learning and language teaching.

TEACHING SUGGESTIONS

1. Form/Meaning. To elicit superlatives, you can provide your students with data on several people—for example, four brothers (you may want to use similar data representing four of your students):

	Jack	*Bill*	*Tom*	*Henry*
Height	6'	5'9"	6'2"	5'10"
Weight	200 lbs.	150 lbs.	180 lbs.	170 lbs.
Age	25	23	21	19

The students' task is to generate all the possible superlative sentences:

Jack is the oldest.	Tom is the tallest.	Jack weighs the most.
Henry is the youngest.	Bill is the shortest	Bill weighs the least.

2. Form/Meaning. Comparing statistics about places such as states can also elicit authentic use of superlatives:

	Alaska	*California*	*Texas*	*Vermont*
Area (square miles)	586,412	158,693	263,338	9,609
Population	407,000	21,896,000	12,830,000	483,000
Highest point	Mt. McKinley 20,320	Mt. Whitney 14,494 feet	Guadalupe Peak 8,751 feet	Mt. Mansfield 4,393 feet
Year of statehood	1959	1850	1845	1791

> Examples: Alaska is the largest of the four states.
> Vermont is the oldest/smallest of the four states.

3. Form/Meaning. For presenting a variety of superlative forms in context, Paul Le Vasseur (personal communication) suggests that ESL/EFL teachers give their students a handout consisting of several advertisements extracted from newspapers and magazines. In groups, students are instructed first to identify all the superlative forms and meanings and then to ask each other questions (and to answer them) about the content of the ads. For example:

    a. "The Gillette TRAC II Shaving System. The closest thing to a perfect shave."

    b. "Everyone agrees the only rums worth coming back to are the Rums of Puerto Rico. The best-tasting, best-selling rums made."

    c. "New York Life's Best-Seller Policy. It's not our least expensive policy. But, then again, no other life insurance can do quite as many things for you."

4. Form/Meaning. To introduce *so (much)* . . . *that* degree constructions, the ESL/EFL teacher can present contexts like this one to students:

> Salwa is having a bad day at school.
> > She's sleepy. She can't pay attention to the lecture.
> > She's hungry. She can't concentrate on the quiz.
> > It's hot (i.e., the weather). She can't study.

> Later in the day Salwa goes home and tells her roommate about her bad day:
> > "I was so sleepy (that) I couldn't pay attention to the lecture."
> > (Students continue using this pattern to describe Salwa's day.)

5. Form/Meaning. Students can practice *"too (much)* . . . *to"* and *"enough* . . . *to"* degree constructions if the teacher gives each pair (or small group of students) a situation like this written on a card:

> You have to be 18 years old to vote.
> Harry is 17 years old.
> Ned is 20 years old.

The students must then write down at least one sentence with *too,* one with *enough,* and one with *not enough:*

> Harry is too young to vote.
> Harry isn't old enough to vote.
> Ned is old enough to vote.

6. Meaning/Use. To learn differences in the meaning and distribution of *so, too,* and *very,* students should work with two types of modified "cloze" exercises—(a) informal conversation and (b) expository writing.

> a. X: I'm not hungry today. It's (1) _____ hot.
> > Y: Why don't you try this salad? It's (2) _____ good.
> > X: I have (3) _____ much work to do. I'll just skip lunch.
> > Y: Don't rush off (4) _____ fast. You could get sick if you skip _____ many meals.

> b. The results of yesterday's election are (1) _____ ambiguous at this point that we don't know who won. Both candidates are still making (2) _____ optimistic statements, and even the experts feel that the race is (3) _____ close to call.

7. Meaning/Use. Ultimately, the ESL/EFL teacher will need to focus on exercises that will help students discriminate between comparative and superlative forms. Here are some suggestions:

> a. Modified "cloze" exercises in dialog or story form where the correct degree must be supplied for each word indicated.

> > X: Are you ___, or am I?
> >   (1) tall

> > Y: I don't know. Let's ask Lars. He's _____ than either of us.
> >   (2) tall

> > X: Yeah. He's the ___ one in the class.
> >   (3) tall

Note that irregular forms can be practiced this way too.

> Mr. Jenkins was asked to judge the apple pies at the fair. So he started, and each
> new one tasted ____ than the previous one. He had a very hard time picking the
>   (1) good
> _____ one.
> (2) good

b. Three-term problems can be used to test comprehension of comparative and superlative forms. The teacher can provide the problems orally or in writing and the students can give a name (orally or in writing) to indicate their answer:

> (1) If Bob is taller than Joe and Joe is taller than Mike, who's the tallest?
> (2) If Mary is younger than Nancy, and Nancy is older than Judy, who's the oldest?

c. To bring out the similarity of content but difference of form and focus between comparatives and superlatives, the teacher can use data such as were presented in the first and second teaching suggestions above. The students would be asked to generate either comparative or superlative sentences using the data and then to paraphrase using the other form (if possible); for example:

> *S1:* Tom is taller than his three brothers.
> *S2:* Tom is the tallest of the four brothers.
> *S1:* Alaska is the largest state (largest of the 50 states).
> *S2:* Alaska is larger than the other 49 states.

It should be emphasized that while all superlatives can be paraphrased with a comparative form, not all comparatives (e.g., *Ann runs faster than Harry*) can be paraphrased with a superlative.

EXERCISES

Test your understanding of what has been presented.

1. Provide original sentences that illustrate the following terms. Underline the pertinent word(s) in your examples.
   - **a.** a comparative used in a superlative sense
   - **b.** the negative import of *too (much/little)*
   - **c.** intensifying, nonsuperlative use of *most*
   - **d.** a marked superlative
   - **e.** absolute use of *too*
   - **f.** comparative and superlative uses of *lesser*

2. Why are the following sentences ungrammatical?

   a. *She's the $\left\{ \begin{array}{l} \text{boringest} \\ \text{boredest} \end{array} \right\}$ person I know.

   b. *John $\left\{ \begin{array}{l} \text{lives the fartherest away} \\ \text{is the elderest} \end{array} \right\}$ of all.

3. In each of the following cases, decide whether the sentence should be completed with a comparative or a superlative form or could be completed with either, and explain why. If both forms are possible, is there a difference in meaning?
   a. Alex has financial problems, but Joe and Robert don't because they have _____ money.
   (more, the most)

    b. Of the five candidates for president, I voted for Sheila because I definitely think she's _____.
            (the best, better)

    c. After examining several books I finally bought this novel because I felt that it was

    _____.

    (the most interesting one, more interesting than the others)

4. What's the difference?
    a. She's very young to be a pro tennis player.
    b. She's too young to be a pro tennis player.

Test your ability to apply what you know.

5. If your students produce the following sentences, what errors have they made? How will you make them aware of the errors, and what exercises will you prepare to help your students avoid these errors?
    a. *Joe is the older child in a big family.
    b. *February is the most cold month in my country.
    c. *The first and important thing of all is studying English.
    d. *I was worst than my roommate at making friends.
    e. *This food is too tasty.

6. If you are using an ESL/EFL textbook that presents comparatives and superlatives in the same lesson, what will you do?

7. You are using an ESL/EFL textbook that tells your students to use the comparative for two persons or objects and the superlative for three or more persons or objects. One of your students asks you if this rule always works. What will you say?

8. In a newspaper article entitled "The 'Usefulest' Adjectives," William Safire (1980) quotes two famous authors:

> Thomas Carlyle—"Surely of all the 'rights of man' this right of the ignorant to be guided by the wiser . . . is the indisputablest."
> Mark Twain—" . . . the confoundedest, brazenest, ingeniousest piece of fraud."

What point do you think Safire was trying to make in this article?

BIBLIOGRAPHY

References

Celce-Murcia, M., D. Brinton, and J. Goodwin (1996). *Teaching Pronunciation*. New York: Cambridge University Press.

Greenberg, J. H. (1966). *Language Universals*. The Hague: Mouton.

Jespersen, O. (1924). *The Philosophy of Grammar*. London: Allen and Unwin.

Neuman, R. A. (1977). "An Attempt to Define through Error Analysis the Intermediate ESL Level at UCLA." Unpublished M.A. thesis in TESL, UCLA.

Quirk, R., S. Greenbaum, G. Leech, and J. Svartvik (1985). *A Comprehensive Grammar of the English Language*. London: Longman.

Safire, W. (1980, June 22). "The 'usefulest' adjectives." *New York Times,* Sec. 6, p.10.

Schiffrin (1987). *Discourse Markers*. Cambridge: Cambridge University Press.

Solomon, G. (1994). "A More Closer Look at Comparatives and Superlatives." Unpublished paper. TESL and Applied Linguistics, UCLA.

Suggestions for further reading

For useful descriptive information about degree words and the English superlative, see:
Bolinger, D. (1972). *Degree Words*. The Hague: Mouton.
Jespersen, O. (1964). *Essentials of English Grammar*. University, Ala: University of Alabama Press, Ch. 22.

For a transformational analysis of most of the degree complements discussed in this chapter, see:
Celce-Murcia, M. (1972). "A Syntactic and Psycholinguistic Study of Comparison in English." Unpublished Ph.D. dissertation in Linguistics, UCLA.

For a good discussion of the degree complements formed with so, such, too, *and* enough, *see:*
Gary, E. N. (1979). "Extent in English: A Unified Account of Degree and Quantity." Unpublished Ph.D. dissertation in Linguistics, UCLA, pp. 129–178.

For ESL/ EFL textbooks that offer good suggestions for practicing superlatives, see:
Badalamenti, V. and C. Henner Stanchina (1997). *Grammar Dimensions*. Book 1 (2d ed.), pp. 371–384. Boston: Heinle & Heinle.

For exercises integrating the use of comparative and superlative, see:
Bland, S.K. (1996). *Intermediate Grammar*. New York: Oxford University Press, pp. 313–338.
Fingado, G., L. J. Freeman, M. R. Jerome, and C. V. Summer (1981). *The English Connection*, pp. 171–178. Cambridge, Mass: Winthrop.

For good lessons dealing with degree complements, see:
Bland, S.K. (1996). *Intermediate Grammar*. New York: Oxford University Press, pp. 313–338.
Riggenbach, H. and V. Samuda (1997). *Grammar Dimensions*. Book 2 (2d ed.), pp. 139–153. Boston: Heinle & Heinle.
Thewlis, S. (1997). *Grammar Dimensions*. Book 3 (2d ed.), pp. 117–138. Boston: Heinle & Heinle.

ENDNOTES

1. This notation (i.e., < >) indicates that a given noun (i.e., $noun_x$) may occur either before or after *enough* but not in both positions at the same time.

2. There is one fixed expression where we find *enough* modified by *little*: e.g., "I have little enough time as it is, and now they tell me to do more!" In this idiomatic usage, *little enough* means something like *too little*.

3. We use the term "absolutely" in a very guarded sense here because these *too*'s are not like *very* in that there is always an infinitive complement implied, and this implied complement always expresses a negative implication:

He smokes too much ($\left\{ \begin{array}{l} \text{to have good health} \\ \text{for his own good} \end{array} \right\}$). (= He is not in good health).

They study too little (to succeed academically). (= They are not succeeding.)

4. This rule is adapted from Celce-Murcia, Brinton, and Goodwin (1996:256–257).

5. There are a few one-syllable adjectives that are exceptional in that they take only periphrastic *more* or *most*: *real*, *right*, *wrong*, and *like* (= similar to).

6. Syllabic [l] in this context generally becomes consonantal when the inflection is added, often changing the syllable structure (gen·tle; gent· lest).

7. Note that in most such cases it does not seem to make much difference whether *and* or *or* is used as the conjunction following *than,* although a difference in meaning is possible, and additional modifiers are sometimes used to suggest an additive rather than an alternative meaning; for example:

Jill and Ann have more A's than B's and C's put together.

8. Another meaning of the form *most* that is not strictly superlative is the meaning of the quantifier *most* when used to express the notion of majority; e.g., "Most (of the) voters were in favor of the measure" (i.e., more voters were in favor than those who were not in favor).

9. The forms *one* and *ones* are the noun substitutes that occur most frequently with superlatives; e.g.:

the best one(s)

10. The only case where it is difficult to reconstruct an underlying noun is with adverbial use of the superlative; e.g.:

Roger behaves the most politely (of all the boys).

Ultimately, one might perhaps argue that such a sentence is related to one with a noun paraphrase and that this relationship accounts for the presence of *the:*

Roger exhibits the most polite behavior (of all the boys).

However, exploring such an analysis in detail is beyond the scope of this textbook.

11. Adverbs or adjectives that use *un-* or some other negative prefix to derive their negative polarity form are different from adjectives and adverbs that have preexisting polar opposites that are lexically distinct (e.g., *big—little).* Whenever such overt negative prefixes are needed, the tendency is to avoid the derived negative and to use *least* with the stem form (e.g., *least important)* rather than *most* with the derived negative (e.g., *most unimportant);* however, the latter pattern does occasionally occur:

Lester always seems to dwell on the most $\begin{Bmatrix} \text{unimportant} \\ \text{uninteresting} \end{Bmatrix}$ details.

12. The phrase *different than* is acceptable in colloquial American English. In formal situations, *different from* is preferred. Many speakers of British English do not find *different than* grammatically acceptable and some use *different to,* which is ungrammatical to American ears. All dialects seem to accept *different from.* Also, some nonnative speakers confuse the patterns: "X is different from Y" and "The difference between X and Y" in their English production. The teacher should thus be alert to such errors.

Chapter 36

CONCLUSION

One of our concerns in writing such a lengthy book is that we run the risk of discouraging teachers who may feel overwhelmed by the level of grammatical detail we have included here. However, we felt that we needed to take this risk for two reasons. First, readers of the first edition have told us that after being students in courses where the *The Grammar Book* was the course text, they would refer to it again and again as grammatical questions arose while they were teaching. In other words, although we had not intended the book to be used as a reference grammar, that is indeed what many teachers were using it for. We have kept this in mind in writing this second edition. Second, one of the not-so-subtle, implicit messages of our text is that language is complex. We felt that we would neither be honoring the complexity of the subject matter nor contributing to the professionalization of teachers if we were to oversimplify our treatment of grammar.

What we would like, therefore, is for our readers to appreciate the complexity without feeling discouraged by it. Perhaps it will help to know that we do not expect you to master all the material we have presented here. It is our intention that you come away from your reading of *The Grammar Book* having gained a way to look at language, a knowledge of some basic facts concerning English grammar, and the awareness and skill necessary to be able to analyze language from a linguistic perspective. You will learn the details about English grammar as you teach English. Indeed, those of you who are native speakers of English and who are beginning your teaching careers should derive comfort from an old axiom with which experienced teachers are well acquainted—that you will learn English grammar (and a lot more!) by teaching it.

As you may recall, we said in the first chapter that grammar is both an abstract system and a socially constructed practice. As an abstract system, grammar can be characterized by certain rules below the level of the sentence—that is, morphological rules (e.g., formation of plurals, subject-verb agreement, and so forth), sentence-level syntactic rules (e.g., those necessary for specifying unmarked and marked sentence word order), and rules above the level of the sentence, discourse rules, which contribute to thematic coherence and cohesion of oral and written texts.

The socially constructed view of grammar applies when we consider what grammatical devices speakers/writers employ to convey what they mean to their listeners/readers—for example, what presupposition they intend to convey by using a negative yes/no question rather than using an unmarked question form, or by using an uninverted question rather than an inverted one. Finally, we have seen many instances where social factors affect the appropriateness of the choice of lexicogrammatical structures that users of the language make when, for example, they want to demonstrate their alliance with a particular discourse community. To address the issue of speaker preference in using particular grammar structures, we have provided the results of discourse analyses, contextual analyses, and usage studies, including native English speaker preferences solicited through questionnaires. Undergirding all this effort has been our assumption that a pedagogical grammar is not just a compilation of decontextualized rules. As we put it in the first chapter of this book, "Think of reasons, not rules" when teaching English grammar.

We don't wish to leave the impression, however, that grammar and communication are isomorphic. We believe, in fact, that there is a nonhierarchial relationship between grammar and communication (Celce-Murcia 1992; Larsen-Freeman 1992). It seems to us that both are in need of attention in an ESL/EFL classroom. But both need attention in ways that are complementary. That is why we have proposed here a view of grammar that takes into consideration the three dimensions of form, meaning, and use. Grammar structures not only have morphosyntactic form; they are also used to express meaning in context-appropriate use. As such, the three-dimensional nature of grammar should be honored when thinking about teaching practice. We believe that the three dimensions are learned differently and therefore need to be taught through a multifaceted teaching approach. Above all, what is important is not that learners should learn the grammar rules in the abstract but rather that they should acquire the ability to use them automatically in real acts of communication. Thus, it is "grammaring," not grammar, that should be taught.

We also want to reinforce the need to remember that the learning challenge for different students and different groups of students may vary. Thus, where possible, we have included contrastive information about language typology. It is our hope that such information will help teachers to better understand what linguistic background learners are bringing with them to their classes and what the nature of the learners' linguistic experience will be as they strive to master English.

Another recurring theme in this book has been that grammar is organic, evolving in a nonlinear way (Larsen-Freeman 1997), which is why traditional rules don't always work. An example of its mutable nature was given when we noted the discrepancy between the prescribed form of the verb in a sentence beginning with nonreferential *there* and the fact that native speakers of English often say the contracted *there's* form regardless of the number of the logical subject.

Of course, another reason that the rules don't always work is that the perspective that led to their formulation was not wide enough. We have tried to provide a very wide perspective on grammar, continually reinforcing the need to seek explanations at all levels of language, most definitely including the level of discourse. While it may make good science to limit the scope of one's investigation, as teachers we can't afford to limit the scope of our understanding. Further, we need to use whatever knowledge and tools are at our disposal. As such, we have drawn upon many different schools of linguistic thought for the insights they afford.

Since it is in the nature of any science to change, doubtless the findings and analyses that we have reported here will be challenged and/or expanded by additional research. Such challenges are welcome; we certainly do not claim to have written the last word on English grammar. Indeed, as we have indicated many times in this text, there is much yet to be discovered, and we welcome the contributions of researchers working within all of schools of thought. We also hope that we have dispelled the myth that all linguistic research is complete and that all is known about English grammar. Much remains to be learned, and we welcome you to the quest. Indeed, encouraging you to conduct your own original research is one of the reasons we have given you a framework and provided practice in investigating grammar rather than simply supplying you with a compendium of facts about English.

Finally, it is our sincere wish that you have developed the skill of being able to apply what you have learned in detecting and diagnosing students' grammatical errors. We also hope that you will feel more confident in your ability to answer your students' grammar questions. Perhaps most importantly, through your adaptations of our teaching suggestions and through your own creative endeavors, we hope that you feel prepared to work with your students on English grammar in pedagogically useful and satisfying ways.

REFERENCES

Celce-Murcia, M. (1992). "A Nonhierarchical Relationship Between Grammar and Communication. Part II: Insights from Discourse Analysis." In J. E. Alatis (ed.), *Georgetown University Round Table on Languages and Linguistics 1992.* Washington, D.C.: Georgetown University Press, pp. 166–173.

Larsen-Freeman, D. (1992). "A Nonhierarchical Relationship Between Grammar and Communication. Part I: Theoretical and Methodological Considerations." In J. E. Alatis (ed.), *Georgetown University Round Table on Languages and Linguistics 1992.* Washington, D.C.: Georgetown University Press, pp. 158–165.

Larsen-Freeman, D. (1997). "Chaos/Complexity Science and Second Language Acquisition." *Applied Linguistics 18:2,* 141–165.

APPENDIX

SUGGESTED ANSWERS TO THE CHAPTER EXERCISES

Chapter 1: Introduction
(No exercises)

Chapter 2: Grammatical Metalanguage

1.
a.	noun	This <u>book</u> is good.
b.	verb	I <u>walk</u> to school.
c.	adjective	Have a <u>nice</u> day!
d.	adverb	They work <u>quickly</u>.
e.	pronoun	<u>She</u> is a teacher.
f.	determiner	<u>The</u> world is round.
g.	preposition	The book is <u>on</u> the table.
h.	conjunction	The weather was rainy <u>but</u> warm.
i.	phrase/clause	<u>The quick brown fox is jumping</u> <u>over the lazy dog</u>.
		clause phrase
j.	subject/predicate	<u>Studying grammar</u> <u>is lots of fun</u>.
		subject predicate
k.	simple sentence	I like ice cream.
l.	coordination	I like ice cream <u>and so does John</u>.
m.	subordination	David doesn't eat ice cream <u>because it is fattening</u>.
n.	embedding	<u>The fact that most people like ice cream</u> is not surprising.
o.	genre	Chop the onions finely. (genre: recipe)
p.	register	Why don't you come over for a drink? (informal)
		versus
		We would like to invite you to join us for drinks. (formal)
q.	given-new	<u>This grammar book</u> <u>is very comprehensive</u>.
		given new

2. a.

Word	Part of Speech	Criteria
John	noun	semantic (name of a person); functional (part of a phrase that forms the subject of a verb); structural (position in sentence—part of the phrase that precedes the verb)
and	conjunction	functional (coordinates "John" and "Paul")
Paul	noun	same criteria as for "John"
were	verb	structural (position in sentence—after a noun; inflections for number and past tense)
fighting	verb	semantic (describes an action); structural (verbal inflection *-ing*)

b.

John	noun	same as for "John" in 2a.
gave	verb	semantic (an action); structural (position—after a noun; inflection for past tense)
Paul	noun	semantic (name of a person); functional (indirect object of a verb)
a	determiner	structural (precedes an adjective and noun)
black	adjective	semantic (describes a quality); structural (between a determiner and a noun)
eye	noun	semantic (name of an object); structural (follows a determiner and adjective); functional (direct object of a verb)

c.

The	determiner	structural (precedes a noun)
principal	noun	semantic (name of a type of person); structural (position—after a determiner); functional (subject of the verb)

Word	Part of Speech	Criteria
sent	verb	semantic (an action); structural (position—after a noun; inflection for past tense)
them	pronoun	semantic (replaces a noun); structural (same position as a noun—after a verb; inflection for number and person)
to	preposition	structural (connects a following noun phrase to a verb)
his	determiner	semantic (refers to a person, possession); structural (inflection for number, person, and gender; precedes noun)
office	noun	semantic (name of an object); structural (preceded by a determiner); functional (object of a preposition)
immediately	adverb	semantic (manner); structural (derivational inflection of manner *-ly*); functional (modifies a verb)

3. declarative (indicative)   e.g., My dog has fleas.
   interrogative   e.g., Are you rich?
   imperative   e.g., Go to your room!

4. A pragmatic function (e.g., request) does not always correspond to a particular sentence type because there are many different linguistic means of performing a pragmatic function with varying levels of politeness, formality, directness, and so on, which utilize different sentence types. For example:

   Open the window, please. (imperative)
   Could you open the window? (interrogative)
   I'd like you to open the window. (declarative)

5. reference: The woman entered the room. <u>She</u> looked around.
   ellipsis: *A:* When did you arrive?
                       B: <u>Yesterday</u>. (= I arrived yesterday.)
   substitution: *A:* I'll do all my homework this evening.
                       B: I hope <u>so</u>.
   conjunction: I haven't done my homework yet; <u>however</u>, I plan to do it soon.
   lexical cohesion: The <u>fruit</u> is wonderful in Indonesia. The <u>mangos</u> and <u>pineapples</u> are really sweet, and there are so many kinds of <u>bananas</u>.

6. The theme is less important than the rheme in terms of its information-bearing status: the theme only identifies what the sentence will be about, while the rheme contains what the speaker wants to say about the theme and thus carries more information. Also, the theme contains old information, the rheme new.

7. Answers will vary.

8. Answers will vary.

9. **a.** "Out of nowhere" is the theme of the sentence, making the unexpectedness of the event the focus of the sentence. This unusual (rather literary) word order (PrepP V S) makes it a marked sentence, since the subject of the sentence is not the theme and, in fact, follows the verb.

   b. The theme in this sentence is neither the agent nor the subject of the sentence but the recipient of the action. The passive voice is used to achieve this effect.

   c. The phrase "concerning homework" has been used to place the object of the sentence in the theme position, thus achieving a topic-comment structure similar to that found in some Asian languages. The object of the sentence (homework) is then repeated as a pronoun (it) in the main clause. In this case, the passive voice would sound very unnatural as a means to achieve this effect.

10. Answers will vary.

Chapter 3: The Lexicon

1. **a.** verb requiring a locative prepositional phrase   I <u>placed</u> the cup <u>on the table</u>.
    b. determiner requiring a mass noun   He doesn't have <u>much</u> patience.
    c. conversion   I already <u>salted</u> the vegetables.
    d. change-of-state verb   The stores <u>close</u> early on Saturday.
    e. compound word   We saw a <u>flying saucer</u> last night.
    f. derivational affix   David could use some excite<u>ment</u>.
    g. inflectional affix   He like<u>s</u> me.
    h. transitive adjective   Susan is <u>attracted</u> to Jim.
    i. semantic field   The university <u>students</u> helped the local elementary school <u>pupils</u> with their homework.
    j. transitive verb   We <u>enjoy</u> spicy food.
    k. verb with three arguments   Jane <u>sent</u> a letter to her mother.
    l. irregular plural   There are millions of <u>sheep</u> in New Zealand.

m. lexical phrase   I teach <u>English as a second language</u>.

n. durative verb   I <u>sleep</u> in the same room as my sister.

o. verb–direct object collocation   I was <u>given advice</u> on how to apply.

p. co-occurrence with a preposition   She is <u>married to</u> Henry.

q. adjective-noun collocation   He's a very <u>handsome man</u>.

r. polysemy   She's too <u>soft</u> with the students. This is a very <u>soft</u> pencil.

2. a. *Lurk* is a verb that requires an adverb of location (e.g., *in the alley*)—a syntactic problem.

b. *Fascinate* requires an animate object (a higher-order animal or human)—a semantic problem.

c. The determiner *these* modifies plural nouns only—a syntactic problem (agreement).

d. The plural ending has been attached to the part of the compound word that can be a noun on its own (*break*). Once a compound is formed, it should be treated as a single unit; thus, the plural ending should be attached as usual to the end of the word.

e. An adjective from the verb *trust* has been generated by attaching the suffix *-ful*. While *-ful* is an adjectival suffix that can be used with *trust*, it is inappropriate in this context. Adjectives with the suffix *-ful* usually mean that the noun described by the adjective is the agent associated with the verb that forms the base of the adjective. However, in this example, the noun described (*friend*) would be the object in the intended meaning (i.e., "can be trusted," rather than "trusts"). *Trustworthy* would be the correct choice.

f. This is an attempt to create a new noun from *favorite* in a sentence structure where *preference* would be the correct choice. Although *favoritism* is a correct noun form, it carries a strong negative connotation and belongs to a different semantic field (concerning the treatment of humans).

3. a. *Information* is a mass noun in English and therefore does not take the plural *-s* or the determiner *many*.

b. *From my point of view* is the usual idiom. However, *in my opinion* may also be used. These are fixed lexical phrases.

c. *Remodeling* is questionable here since it is usually used in the context of houses, rooms, or buildings, but not streets.

d. *Firecrackers* is the correct word, since "pyrotechnics" is referred to here. Although *crackerfires* follows the rules of compounding, it is not a word in English. If there were such a word, it might refer to fires made by people burning crackers, since for noun/noun compounds, the first noun usually functions as a descriptor of the second noun.

e. The student may have been trying to form a verb from the noun *passion*. The only verb that can be so formed is *impassioned*, which may be too strong for the context. *Fascinated* may be a better choice (and may have been intended but phonologically confused). Rephrasing is another alternative: *Photography has been a passion of mine since I was a child.*

f. *Solutions* collocates with *found*, not *met*.

g. The correct preposition collocation for *aware* is *of*, not *to*.

h. *By pure chance* would be the more idiomatic lexical phrase, but *fortune* is a close synonym of *chance*, making it marginally acceptable.

4. These verbs are all in the same semantic field but have distinct differences in their exact meanings. For example, *look* is more intentional than *see*, which can be nonvolitional. *Look* also differs grammatically since it co-occurs with the preposition *at*. *Watch* implies some duration; *stare* also does, but often with a negative connotation. A simplified semantic feature analysis in the form of a chart would be useful to summarize the differences for students. These particular words also lend themselves well to mime to illustrate the differences.

5. *Pretty* is polysemous, and therefore students need to know that this same word can have different meanings in different contexts. While *pretty* is often used in the semantic field of beauty, it can also be used as an intensifier with words like *soon*, *quickly*, or *good*. It is not as strong as *very* but belongs to the same semantic field.

6. Both *owing to* and *due to* have the same meaning, being used to give a reason. Both can be used in initial position in a sentence; for example,

> Owing to unforeseen circumstances, I will not be able to make the meeting.
> Due to unforeseen circumstances, I will not be able to make the meeting.

However, only *due to* can be used following *be* in a sentence; for example,

> My failure was due to laziness.
> *My failure was owing to laziness.

Chapter 4: The Copula and Subject-Verb Agreement

1. a. the copular function of *be*   Marina Del Rey <u>is</u> an attractive harbor.

b. a copular verb other than *be*   She <u>seems</u> nice enough.

c. an auxiliary function of *be*   David <u>was</u> allowed to conduct research on the patients who were in a coma.

d.	collective noun subject	The <u>committee</u> is composed of three employers and three employees.
		The <u>committee</u> are all against the bill.
e.	noncount noun subject	<u>Oil</u> floats on <u>water</u>.
f.	third person singular present inflection	Fiona <u>likes</u> Philip to walk her home.
g.	the proximity principle	Either Tom or <u>you are</u> to sign this contract.
h.	the nonintervention principle	The <u>discrepancy</u> found in his pilot studies <u>was</u> ascribed to a computer bug.
i.	subject-verb agreement with a clausal subject	<u>What we need to do</u> / <u>is</u> to choose a qualified director for the project.

2. (1) Unlike other verbs in English, the copula *be* may be followed by adjective phrases. (2) Copula *be* behaves differently than other verbs in question formation and negation in that it behaves like an auxiliary verb and does not require the use of a *do* auxiliary.

3. Subject-verb agreement applies to all the forms of *be*. For all other verbs, only third person singular forms in the present tense show an overt inflection.

4. The traditional subject-verb agreement rule is often not maintained in the following cases:

(1) the *neither . . . nor* construction with personal pronouns; for example,

Neither you nor her *were* (rather than *was*) supposed to contact them.

(2) in informal sentences beginning with *there;* for example,

There *is* (rather than *are*) a desk and two chairs in the room.

5. a. *Be* often poses difficulties because it is an irregular verb. The form *are* is used to agree with both singular and plural second person pronoun subjects in English and thus should be used here.

    b. There should be subject-verb agreement in the present tense with a third person singular subject. In this example, the third person singular present tense morpheme is realized as *-es* in spelling and, phonetically, as the sound [z].

    c. All English sentences have a copula before a predicate adjective phrase. In this case, the first person singular verb *am* is needed.

    d. Subject-verb agreement does not apply to modal auxiliaries.

    e. Only third person singular subjects agree overtly with present tense verbs. In this example, the subject is third person plural and thus does not take *-s*.

    f. In negative sentences the copula *be* eliminates the need for the auxiliary *do*. Thus this sentence should be *I am not angry anymore.*

6. An ESL/EFL student who claims that this sentence breaks the proximity rule for the use of *is* instead of *are* would be correct in terms of the prescriptive rule. However, especially in informal English, native speakers do not always follow prescriptive rules, which often do not reflect the actual use of language as it changes over time. Nevertheless, students might be well advised to stick to the rules in their written English since written forms of a language tend to be more conservative, and rules are followed more strictly when writing than when speaking.

7. After having established that mass noun subjects take singular verbs and that plural subjects take plural verbs, while collective noun subjects take either singular or plural verbs depending on the meaning, you can then introduce fractions and percentages. Explain that the number of the verb agrees with the noun that is modified by the fraction/percentage (if there is such as noun); for example,

Half of the *tomatoes are* rotten.
Ninety percent of the *water was* contaminated.

Almanacs are good sources of contexts for working in this area. Recipes are good contexts for fractions and census data for percentages. If students are taking other courses, problems in their math books or tables/diagrams/charts in social studies texts may be consulted. Remember also that if arithmetical operations are being done without a specific head noun in the context, subject-verb agreement is third person singular; for example,

Ten percent of 50 <u>is</u> 5.
Two-thirds of 9 <u>is</u> 6.

8. It is a good idea to review a list of count nouns that show the same transformation for plurals. For example, you can begin with nouns that end with *f* in the singular form and change into *-ves* in the plural form. Maclin (1981) contains many rules for forming irregular plural nouns along with examples. After a brief review of the form, you can provide contexts where students can practice plural noun formation. For example:

My closet has one shelf, but yours has two _____. (shelves)

Chapter 5: Introduction to Phrase Structure Rules

1.
  a. noun phrase — <u>A short, sharp shock</u> is usually sufficient.
  b. adverbial of reason — I study English <u>because I want to get a good job</u>.
  c. adverbial of frequency — I go to church <u>regularly</u>.
  d. adverbial of manner — They looked at us <u>superciliously</u>.
  e. adverbial of direction — I walked <u>to the bathroom</u>.
  f. subject — <u>The student</u> completed the exercises at home.
  g. predicate — The student <u>completed the exercises at home</u>.
  h. sentence modifier — <u>Surprisingly</u>, the whole class passed.
  i. adverbial clause of time — We went home <u>after the show had finished</u>.
  j. intensifier — That's an <u>extremely</u> good question.
  k. prepositional phrase — I walked the guests <u>to the door</u>.
  l. deletable preposition — I've waited <u>(for)</u> four months for that letter.
  m. adjective phrase — I put the <u>outrageously colorful</u> flowers on the table.

2. a.

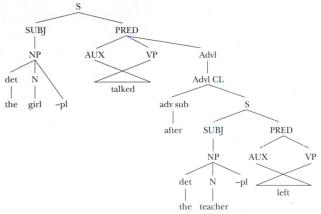

2. b.

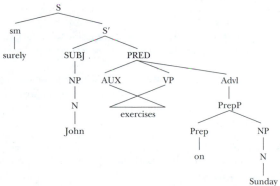

2. c.

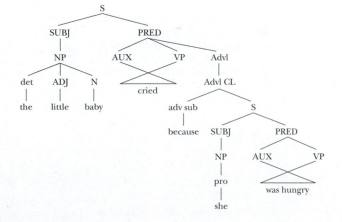

2. d.

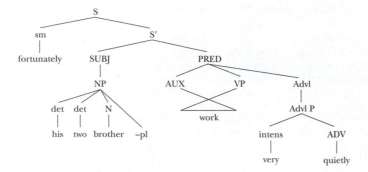

2. e.

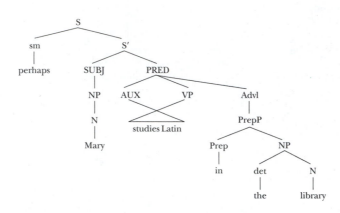

3. a. Time adverbials (such as *yesterday*) follow directional adverbials (such as *to the store*).

  b. The plural determiner *those* can precede only a plural noun, and the verb also has a plural inflection; therefore, the noun *woman* should be in the plural form, *women.*

  c. After the conjunction *because*, a complete clause or a prepositional phrase (such as *of the rain*) is required. In the absence of a preposition, a subject (*it*) is needed to make a complete clause following *because.*

4. All three time adverbials are derived from prepositional phrases. The difference is the presence or absence of the preposition. In (a), the preposition is obligatory (with the structure Prep NP); in (b), it is optionally present; and in (c), it is obligatorily not present (with the structure Ø NP). We discuss the reasons for these differences in Chapter 21.

5. The locative noun *home* (as well as a few other locative nouns like *uptown, downtown,* and *overseas*) is not preceded by a preposition when it follows a verb of motion or direction such as *go, walk,* etc. It may, however, take a preceding preposition when the verb describes a state, as in *I stayed (at) home.*

Chapter 6: More Phrase Structure Rules

1.	**a.**	imperative	<u>Leave</u> it alone!
	b.	modal	I <u>might</u> stay home and study tonight.
	c.	verb with two objects	He <u>showed me the basement</u>.
	d.	phrasal modal	I <u>have to</u> return a book to the library.
	e.	perfect aspect	Sue <u>has</u> work<u>ed</u> here for seven years.
	f.	progressive aspect	We <u>are</u> talk<u>ing</u> about the accident.
	g.	object noun predicate	I now pronounce you <u>husband and wife</u>.

2. a.

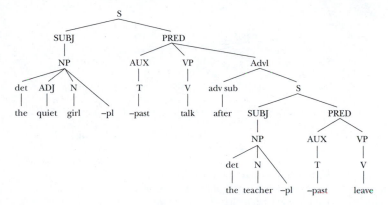

output of base: the quiet girl -pl -past talk after the teacher -pl -past leave
copy s/t: the quiet girl -pl -past [+ 3 + pl] talk after the teacher -pl -past [+3 + pl] leave.
morphological rules: The quiet girls talked after the teachers left.

2. b.

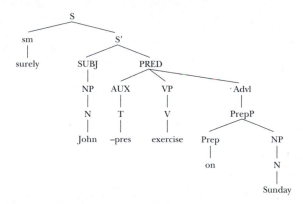

output of base: surely John -pres exercise on Sunday
copy s/t: surely John -pres [+ 3 + sg] exercise on Sunday
morphological rules: Surely John exercises on Sunday.

2. c.

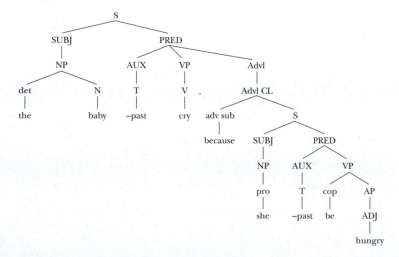

output of base: the baby -past cry because she -past be hungry
copy s/t: the baby -past [+ 3 + sg] cry because she -past [+ 3 + sg] be hungry
morphological rules: The baby cried because she was hungry.

2. d.

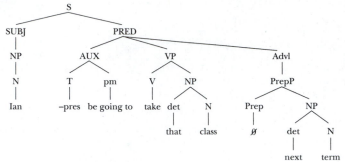

output of base: Ian -pres be going to take that class next term
copy s/t: Ian -pres [+ 3 + sg] be going to take that class next term
morphological rules: Ian is going to take that class next term.

2. e.

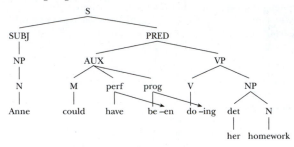

output of base: Anne could have be -en do -ing her homework
morphological rules: Anne could have been doing her homework.

2. f.

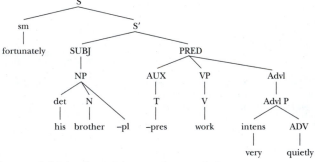

output of base: fortunately his brother -pl -pres work very quietly
copy s/t: fortunately his brother -pl -pres [+ 3 + pl] work very quietly
morphological rules: Fortunately his brothers work very quietly.

2. g.

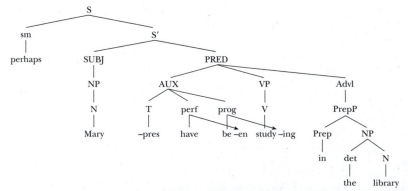

output of base: perhaps Mary -pres have be -en study -ing in the library
copy s/t: perhaps Mary -pres [+ 3 + sg] have be -en study -ing in the library
morphological rules: Perhaps Mary has been studying in the library.

2. h.

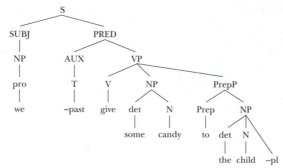

output of base: we -past give some candy to the child -pl
copy s/t: we -past [+ 1 + pl] give some candy to the child -pl
morphological rules: We gave some candy to the children.

2. i.

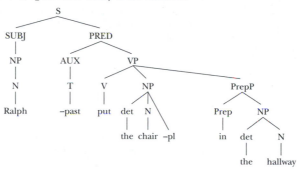

output of base: Ralph -past put the chair -pl in the hallway
copy s/t: Ralph -past [+3 + sg] put the chair -pl in the hallway
morphological rules: Ralph put the chairs in the hallway.

3. **a.** Verbs in sentences with modal auxiliaries are tenseless.
   b. Progressive aspect consists of two components: a form of *be* and the suffix *-ing*, which should be attached to the main verb (here, *jump* → *jumping*).
   c. Modal verbs are always followed by the infinitive form of the verb without *to*.
   d. Perfective aspect consists of two components: a form of *have* and the past participle. The *have* auxiliary is missing from this sentence.
   e. *Put* is a verb that requires an adverbial of location after the direct object.

4. Both learners need to learn that the progressive has two parts: *be* + *-ing*. The required form of *be* precedes the verb, and the *-ing* is attached to the next verb in the sentence. Learner (a) needs to have the use of *be* empha-sized, and learner (b) needs to have the use of the *-ing* suffix emphasized.

5. English can, of course, express future time, but has no "future tense" in the structural sense since verbs are not inflected in English for future as they are for present (*-s* or *Ø*) and past (*-ed*). English has a number of ways to express the future, including *will*, *be going to*, and the simple present or present progressive with future time adverbials (e.g., *tomorrow*).

Chapter 7: The Tense and Aspect System

1. **a.** simple future — I <u>will stay</u> here until I find a permanent apartment.
   b. present perfect — He <u>has tried</u> every means possible to get the door open.
   c. past progressive — Stella <u>was making</u> a lemon pie when I called her.
   d. past perfect — I <u>had finished</u> typing the documents one hour before my boss came to check them.
   e. stative verb — This small box <u>contains</u> all the jewelry that she <u>has</u>.
   f. simple present — I <u>smell</u> garlic in this salad.
   g. accomplishment verb — He has <u>written</u> two novels in two months.
   h. present perfect progressive — She <u>has been making</u> the opening speech at the association's annual meeting for four years.

2. No. Both sentences have the same ordering of events. The use of *before* makes the order explicit without necessitating the use of the past perfect. It is in the absence of such clear temporal markers that the past perfect becomes essential to express the order. Used here, it does place more emphasis on the prior nature of "finishing homework."

3. The use of *since* implies that something started at a definite time in the past and has continued until now. This notion of such duration is what the present perfect expresses and is what distinguishes it from the simple past.

> *I did this since 1960.
> I have done this since 1960.

4. **a.** The first sentence with the present perfect talks about an experience that was completed, but the second one with the present perfect progressive implies that the action of reading is still an ongoing process.

  b. The present tense here is used for a permanent situation—that is, this is Stan's permanent job—while the sentence with present progressive suggests that Stan is doing the job only on a short-term basis.

  c. The question in the past tense is a definite query and requires some shared knowledge of the timeline on which the event in the question occurred. For example, such a question could be asked of somebody who was speaking about the time when they were in New York.

   The second question uses the present perfect of the same verb (*go*) and could thus be assumed to be the indefinite equivalent of the same question without presuming shared knowledge. However, *go* behaves irregularly in this respect; in fact, the appropriate indefinite question would be *Have you been to . . . ?* In contrast, the question *Have you gone to . . . ?* implies that the person is still there and thus is unlikely to be asked of the person who may have gone. Compare the following sentences, which could appear in written notes:

   > I've gone to the mall. (I haven't returned yet; I am still there)
   > I've been to the mall. (I went and returned)

5. **a.** Present perfect is incompatible with a specific past time adverbial like *last Saturday*, which should go with the past tense since it reports a specific action at a specific time in the past.

  b. Stative verbs do not normally take the progressive unless the verb implies agency, such as in *You're being a fool*, or a gradual change of state, such as *I'm hearing the music better now*.

  c. This sentence sounds strange because *will* expresses future intention at the moment of speaking. In this case, the speaker has no control over the action. The use of *be going to* would be correct since it refers to an imminent action related to the evidence available in the present.

  d. Even though it may not seem logical, the present tense is conventionally required (i.e., *When Larry comes . . .*) in subordinate clauses of time or condition when the main clause contains a future time verb.

  e. It is difficult to know what the student intended here, but in any case, the intransitive verb *live* has incorrectly been used in a passive construction (*was lived*). The correct structure depends on the meaning intended: if Phyllis is still living with her parents, the present perfect (*has lived*) should be used; if Phyllis no longer lives with her parents, the past progressive (*was living*) or the simple past (*lived*) could be used; the first would make it sound more temporary and the latter more permanent.

6. In the first sentence, *now* refers to the time when he habitually goes to the store. In the second sentence, the present perfect entails a resultant state: *you* did something that has relevance now, hence the use of *now*.

7. By definition, stative verbs do not involve change; they imply a stable situation that is assumed to last more or less indefinitely. The four verbs mentioned here, however, usually refer to a limited duration of time and commonly occur with progressive aspect, as shown in the following two examples, which convey the same proposition:

> [A: What's wrong?]
> B: My nose itches. versus My nose is itching.

While the first response describes the situation more objectively and the second one sounds more interactive, personal, and affective, there may be no real difference in terms of time duration, which is why these four verbs cannot be classified as stative verbs in the strict sense.

8. For some speakers of American English, these sentences are synonymous; however, other speakers feel that the first sentence reflects the speaker's point of view (i.e., the speaker just heard the news and wants to know if the listener just heard it too). On the other hand, the second sentence is more likely spoken with the listener's perspective in mind (i.e., the listener looks surprised or shocked, so the speaker tries to show empathy and asks if the listener has just heard the news). A discourse analysis would have to be conducted to determine whether this analysis is supported and whether there are other differences.

9. In the first example, the two forms both express the meaning of *surviving* or *overcoming*. In the second example, *has got* signals stative possession, whereas in the third, *has gotten* means *has obtained* and conveys the sense of an accomplishment.

10. The first sentence uses the stative verb *hear* and thus implies that the perception of the melody is not the result of an action on the part of the person but something that has been happening to the person involuntarily. For example, it may be a popular melody that is playing on every radio and in every store. The unusual use of the present progressive with a stative verb emphasizes the repetitiveness of the state rather than reporting a current state.

The verb *listen* is the active counterpart of *hear* and thus implies that the person has made a point of listening to the melody repeatedly—that is, has taken some action so as to hear it. For example, the person may have bought a new CD, or may have been studying the melody, and for this reason is intentionally playing it over and over.

Chapter 8: Modal Auxiliaries and Related Phrasal Forms

1. a. phrasal modal   I <u>am about to</u> go now.
   b. social use of a modal   <u>Would</u> you close the window?
   c. logical probability meaning of a modal   This bridge <u>may</u> collapse in an earthquake.
   d. a combination of more than one modal or phrasal modal   You <u>may have to</u> arrive early.
   e. polite form of a request   <u>Could</u> you drop me off at my apartment?
   f. literal question with a phrasal modal   <u>Are</u> you <u>able to</u> read that sign?

2. The sentence is ambiguous since *may* could mean either that his mother has given her <u>permission</u> for him to go or that his mother was commenting on the <u>possibility</u> of his going.

3. a. *Must be* makes a present inference; *must have been* makes a past inference.
   b. *Would you* is a softer, more polite form of the request than *will you*, which could also be a literal question (i.e., are you willing to help?).
   c. The first sentence implies that the action took place; the second implies that it did not.
   d. *May* expresses possibility. *Must* expresses strong inference—the speaker is sure of the conclusion drawn.
   e. *Should* implies advisability. *Had better* is more insistent, almost a threat, with overtones of unpleasant consequences if the suggestion is not complied with.

4. "That might not be important" expresses low probability of the truth of the negative statement (as do both the affirmative sentences); in contrast, "That couldn't be important" expresses high probability that the negative statement is true.

5. a. A modal verb followed by a modal verb is not a grammatical sequence in English (although some modal + modal combinations occur in some regional dialects in the United States).
   b. In questions, *may* is used to ask for permission. If the pronoun were changed from *you* to *I*, the sentences would be grammatical because the speaker is seeking permission to do something. As it stands, *can* (asking about the possibility of performing the action) and *will* (asking about the willingness of the person to perform the action) are possibilities for this request.
   c. *Should* is used to give advice for future action. The perfect form, *should have studied*, is needed here because the past time adverbial *last term* indicates the advice is "hindsight"—referring to past time.
   d. The common co-occurrence of modal verbs with *be* leads some students to overgeneralize and to insert *be* after every modal. In addition, the main lexical verb must follow the modal, without *to*, although an adverb may be interposed (*easily*), unless the passive, perfect, or progressive is used; for example, "They could easily reach the goal."
   e. A modal verb must be followed by the main lexical verb without *to*.
   f. A modal verb must be followed directly by a verb. The copula *be* needs to precede the adjective *good*.
   g. The choice of register is the problem here. With the polite markers of *excuse me* and *Mr.*, the choice of *gotta* is too informal. The modal *should* or the phrasal modal *have to* would be more appropriate.
   h. *Would* is used in the question as a politeness marker, but it cannot take this meaning in a declarative sentence (where it carries a conditional meaning). The correct response would be simply *Of course* or *Of course I will*, if a modal is used.

6. Both (a) and (b) are polite requests for information, but in question (a), the speaker is asking whether the addressee is able to fulfil the request, whereas (b) assumes the addressee is able to comply and is querying his or her willingness to do so.

Sentence (c) is the speaker's own suggestion that Sam introduce the guest, whereas (d) presupposes that Sam has already been asked or has even agreed to introduce the guest but expresses some doubt that he will actually do so.

Sentence (e) is ambiguous in the same way as the sentence in Exercise 2 above (probability or permission), whereas (f) is unambiguously expressing logical probability referring to the past (i.e. that it is possible that Joe went).

7. *Need* and *dare* are really archaic modals that now often function like regular verbs; nevertheless, they have retained some of their modal qualities: they can function like other negative modals without *do*, such as in (b); and invert as an AUX in a question (again without *do*), such as in (d). In (c) there is a *do* verb in the question, but *dare* has retained the characteristic of other modals in not requiring the *to*-infinitive between *dare* and the main verb *think*.

In (a), *need* could be seen as a lexical verb, parallel to "I want to see him," or as a phrasal modal, parallel to "I have to see him."

In (e), *dare* functions like an ordinary lexical verb.

Thus *need* and *dare* are shifting in their functions and presently represent a mixture of forms.

8. *Could* is not used to refer to ability or possibility with a human agent performing a specific punctual action with a specific recent past time adverbial, such as *last night*. It is possible, however, to use it if the subject is a perceiver or experiencer:

I $\left\{\begin{array}{l}\text{could}\\\text{was able to}\end{array}\right\}$ see many stars in the sky last night.

Moreover, it is possible to use *could* with both specific and general time adverbials in the remote past:

I could read when I was 3 years old.

Note that where a preceding main clause clearly establishes past time, *could* can function like *be able to* in an embedded clause in a way that it cannot in an independent clause:

Compare:	*I could visit him last week.
	I was able to visit him last week.
with:	I was glad I could visit him last week.
	I was glad I was able to visit him last week.

In the negative, these distribution problems are not as complicated. In all the contexts, *couldn't* and *wasn't able to* are possible paraphrases. We can say "I couldn't pick up the tickets last night" because the specific, punctual action referred to was not accomplished.

Chapter 9: The Tense-Aspect-Modality System in Discourse

1. **a.** historical present   . . . and suddenly, I <u>fall</u> down an open manhole.
   b. backgrounding tense   I went to the Grand Canyon last year. It<u>'s</u> immense.
   c. past time axis   Cynthia <u>had worked</u> on her thesis for two years before she finally <u>finished</u> it. Then, she <u>got</u> a good job almost immediately.
   d. future time plus progressive aspect   I <u>will be staying</u> there for three years.
   e. interactive use of present perfect   I saw *Gone with the Wind* last night. <u>Have</u> you ever <u>seen</u> it?
   f. frame-elaboration pattern for:

   - specific past events   I<u>'ve visited</u> Indonesia three times now. The first time, I <u>went</u> to study music.
   - past habitual narrative   I <u>used to</u> talk on the phone for hours. I<u>'d</u> phone all my friends and talk for an hour to each one. Dave<u>'d</u> get really angry.
   - future scenario   I<u>'m going to</u> take night classes next year. I<u>'ll</u> enroll for one or two. I<u>'ll</u> have to get my husband to do more cooking.

2. *I see him* in sentence (a) expresses present habitual activity, whereas in (b) it is the historical present and thus expresses an event in the past.

3. Usually a clause with *used to* will precede one with *would* in a past habitual narrative episode. The first and second sentences are phrased in the past, but the third jumps without justification into the present axis with the present perfect and the present habitual, resulting in a sequence that lacks coherence.

4. Bull's framework—past axis
   Basic axis time (simple past)   In those days we <u>went</u> into the wild to hunt.
   Time before the axis time   I <u>had come</u> from the city . . . , and I<u>'d</u> already <u>made</u> some friends.
          (*The perfect tense used here also functions as a frame for the following.*)

   Past habitual: details—"would" alternating with simple past

   . . . Chidra, the half-breed Mayan, <u>would</u> first <u>go</u> to call for Crispin. When he <u>reached</u> the house, he <u>gave</u> a long whistle and out Crispin <u>came</u>. . . . Then they <u>came</u> to fetch me. . . .

   When they <u>got</u> to our farm, Chidra <u>whistled</u> again, and my grandfather <u>would come</u> to the door to let them in.

   Bull's framework—past axis
   Basic axis time (simple past)   Chidra <u>lived</u> in the wild,
   Time before the axis time   and <u>had eaten</u> no food. Not so Crispin.
   Basic axis time (simple past)   He <u>lived</u> a few streets away
   Time before the axis time   and I knew he <u>had had</u> a good breakfast.
   Basic axis time (simple past)   Both . . . <u>accepted</u> the hot chocolate. . . . While we <u>ate</u>, my grandfather . . . <u>joked</u> gravely with us . . . the old man <u>was</u> very fond of Crispin.

   Suh's past habitual frame-elaboration
   Frame   He <u>used to call</u> him "don Crispin" and every now
   Elaboration   and then he<u>'d suggest</u> jobs for him . . .

5.

Present description	There's a man . . . It is five years to the day
Change to simple past to describe past event	since he began hitting me on the head. . . .
Change to past habitual	At first I couldn't stand it;
Present perfect frame for previous past sequence	now I've grown accustomed to it.
	(signalling change from past to present)
Return to present description	I don't know his name. I know he's an ordinary man . . .
Change to simple past for past narrative	I met him one sultry morning five years ago.
Change to past continuous to provide	I was sitting peacefully on a bench . . .
	setting for past narrative (background)
Return to simple past to continue past narrative	All of a sudden I felt something touch my head. It was this same man
Return to present description (background)	who now . . . keeps striking me blows with his umbrella.
Change to simple past to continue past narrative	That first time I turned around full of indignation
Change to generic present tense to describe writer's general stance (background)	(I become terribly annoyed when I'm bothered while reading the paper);
Return to simple past to continue past narrative	he went right on, calmly hitting me.

6. There is a greater feeling of intimacy when the simple past is changed to the historical present, which would reflect a closer relationship between the mother and daughter than is expressed in the original, where the simple past indicates psychological distance.

7. The present perfect ("The gas company's really been good.")—shift in topic from baseball to gas company pay.

8. a. Past axis (past perfect: *had won*) and present axis (present continuous: *is going to*) are mixed. Both should be either in the present axis (present perfect and present continuous) or in the past axis (past perfect and past continuous).

   b. The use of the past perfect (instead of the present perfect or simple present) makes it sound as if the effect of the film occurred before the film, which is of course ridiculous. However, the sentence would be acceptable if the basic time axis were a later time, after a second change had occurred in the writer's thinking (i.e., the film had affected the way the writer thought about marriage until something else happened, which changed the writer's way of thinking again).

   c. The past axis (*could* and *was introduced*) suddenly jumps to the future axis (*will*) in the second sentence.

   d. The past and present axes are mixed. All the verbs should be in the past.

   e. The present perfect (*I have come*) can be used as a frame to introduce a past narrative, but here it is used to give a specific detail (the year of arrival) rather than provide a transition from the moment of speaking.

      The present perfect should be used in the next clause (*I have been here*) with the stative verb (*be*) to signal that the state has not ended at the time of speech (see Chapter 7). This clause might be better at the beginning of the paragraph as a present perfect frame.

      The present axis set up by *I have some problems* is not followed up in the next sentence, which jumps to the past axis (*was English*).

      Used to has been overused. The more usual frame-elaboration pattern with *used to* and *would* needs to be explained.

      Will in the last sentence would be better replaced by *am going to* since it expresses an intention based on a prior decision (see Chapter 7).

9. Her tense usage is correct here. She needs to understand the justification for the different tenses that she has used so that she can feel more confident. The details in the first sentence are correctly given in the past tense, since a specific past time (the period following 1978) is referred to. The perfect tense in the second sentence is correct since a stative verb (*become*) is used to signal that the state has not ended at the time of speech; it also functions as a frame for the habitual present tense narrative (*are oppressed, do not need, do not even have to be*).

10. *Be going to* in the second clause of (b) expresses more personal engagement; *will* in sentence (a) seems to express the purpose, while *be going to* in (b) seems to express more confidently the outcome expected by the speaker.

Chapter 10: Negation

1. a. sentence-level negation   I was not sure about the outcome.
    b. phrasal negation   Fiona decided not to call Richard again.
    c. lexical negation   Nobody was listening to the hackneyed lecture.
    d. operator addition   She doesn't care about her appearance.
    e. *not* contraction   The experiment wasn't satisfactory.
    f. *no* determiner   They had no hope of success.
    g. negative equative   My book is not as thick as yours.
    h. negative indefinite pronoun   Her performance leaves nothing to be desired.

2. a.

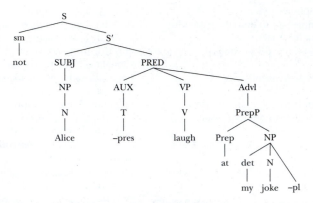

Mapping rules that apply are: copy s/t, operator addition, *not* placement, *not* contraction, and morphological rules.

2. b.

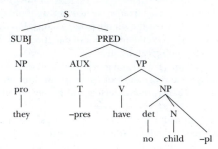

Mapping rules that apply are: copy s/t and morphological rules.

2. c.

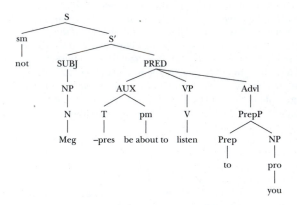

Mapping rules that apply are: copy s/t, *not* placement, and morphological rules.

2. d.

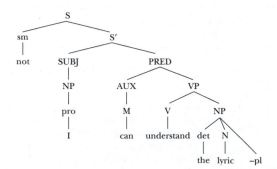

Mapping rules that apply are: *not* placement, *not* contraction and morphological rules.

2. e.

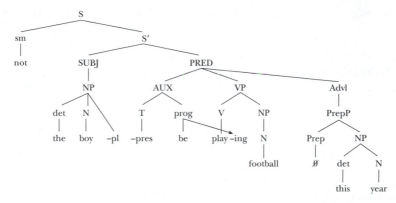

Mapping rules that apply are: copy s/t, *not* placement, *not* contraction, and morphological rules.

3. a. All three sentences are examples of sentential negation and convey the same proposition—"It is not the case that Sam is working these days,"—but the uncontracted version is used mainly in formal contexts, such as in written English, and gives prominence to the negative. On the other hand, the contracted ones can be heard in more informal contexts, such as in spoken English, where sentences with uncontracted *not* are marked for emphasis of the negation.

b. The first sentence with a negative polarity adjective in a comparative sounds more direct than the other with a positive polarity adjective in a negative equative, which can be used by writers/speakers wishing to be more tactful.

c. Sentences with *not*-negation (like the first sentence) are more prevalent in speech, while *no* negation appears more often in formal or written contexts.

d. The first sentence is more prevalent in writing than in speech. In speech nonaffixal negation is more common.

4. a. Operator addition (of *do*) is required in this negative sentence, and the negative particle should be *not* instead of *no*.

b. The correct negative particle, *not*, is used here, but operator addition (*do*), inflected for the tense intended, is required before the particle.

c. The wrong prefix has been selected for lexical negation; that is, *unpatient* should be changed into *impatient*.

d. The subject number has not been copied onto the tense of the operator. Third person present singular subjects require *does* instead of *do* in Standard English.

e. The sentence contains a double negative, which is ungrammatical in Standard English. In Standard English, *some* → *any*, changing *something* to *anything* (rather than to *nothing*).

f. *Not any* cannot occur at the beginning of a sentence to negate a noun phrase, since *not*-negation is used to negate verbs. *No* is needed here to negate a noun.

5. The difference is extremely subtle in this case. In the first sentence, *not* negates *might have tried before*, whereas in the second sentence it is narrower in scope, negating only *tried before*. Thus, the first sentence expresses a negative possibility that they tried, whereas the second sentence expresses a possibility that they didn't try.

6. Standard English conventionally places the negative particle (*not*) after AUX, while in some other languages (e.g., Korean), AUX with a negative particle is placed at the end of a sentence, in which case one must wait until the sentence is complete to see if it is positive or negative. The form shown here also delays the negative particle to the end of the sentence, which has the effect of delaying the negation and thus surprising the listener.

7. *Some* changes to *any* in the environment of a negative like *not* only if the *some* refers to an indefinite nonspecific entity. When the entity that *some* refers to is an indefinite quantity but a specific entity (i.e., identifiable), then *some* → *any* does not take place. Thus, *I can't recall any of their names* means the teacher has forgotten all of them, but *I can't recall some of their names* means the teacher has forgotten only some of the them.

8. Perhaps making your students aware of the frequency with which native English speakers use contractions would encourage them to use them in informal speech and writing. In an ESL context, students might be given an assignment to canvas native speakers with a list of questions that would be likely to elicit negative responses. They could be instructed to listen not only to the content of the answers but also to the frequency of contracted forms versus uncontracted forms. For demonstration of the use of contracted forms in written informal language, the teacher could bring in a letter from a friend and have the students look for the contracted forms. Students could also be assigned to look for the contractions in a page of comic strips or to listen to an informal taped conversation between two native speakers.

9. An inherently negative verb such as *fail*, which occurs with an infinitive phrase, can be paraphrased with a negator. For example:

> He <u>failed to</u> do it.
> He <u>didn't</u> do it.

Chapter 11: Yes/No Questions

1. a. unmarked yes/no question — Did you like the recital?

b. negative yes/no question — Weren't you going to say something to me?

c. *some* in a yes/no question — Would you like <u>some</u> biscuits?

d. uncontracted negative yes/no question — <u>Did</u> it <u>not</u> have anything to do with the law of gravity?

e. yes/no question with *do* — <u>Do</u> you like to go swimming?

f. uninverted question — You almost hit the bicycle?

g. focused yes/no question — Did <u>YOU</u> turn on the computer?

h. standard short-form answer — [Is she from China?] <u>No, she isn't.</u>

i. formulaic short answer — [Will he take the risk?] <u>I doubt it</u>. / <u>I'm afraid so.</u>

j. yes/no question with phrasal modal and *do* operator — Do you <u>have to</u> pay for the brochure?

k. echo question (showing surprise) — [Nancy is leaving L.A. tonight.] <u>She's leaving L.A. tonight?</u>

l. elliptical yes/no question — (Are) You going out for lunch?

m. nonclausal question as a next turn repair initiator — [She is so attractive.] <u>The girl you just met in the hall?</u>

2. a.

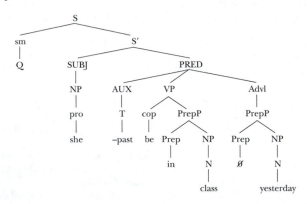

Mapping rules that apply are: copy s/t, subject-operator inversion and morphological rules.

2. b.

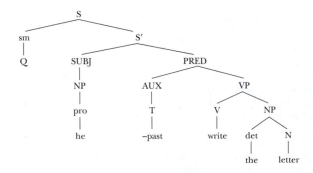

Mapping rules that apply are: copy s/t, operator addition, subject-operator inversion and morphological rules.

2. c.

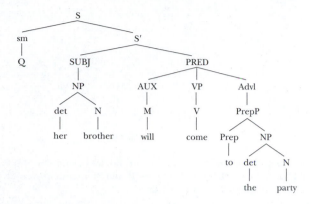

Mapping rules that apply are: subject-operator inversion and morphological rules.

2. d.

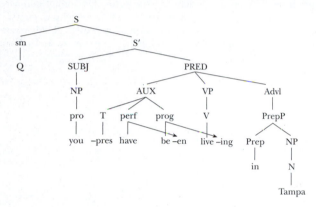

Mapping rules that apply: copy s/t, subject-operator inversion and morphological rules.

3. a. The past tense in the auxiliary was not inverted with the subject and was therefore mistakenly attached to the main verb. The verb *do* has to carry the past tense (i.e., "<u>Did</u> she go?").

b. The subject-operator inversion rule was violated. Only the first auxiliary verb and tense (if present) should be inverted with the subject (i.e., "Could he have gone?").

c. The operator addition rule must be applied when a sentence has no auxiliary verb and no *be* copula. Also, the tense should be separated from the main verb and attached to the verb *do* (i.e., "Does he run fast?").

d. The operator addition rule should not be applied when a sentence has a *be* copula, which serves as the operator in the subject-operator inversion rule (i.e., "Are they happy?").

4. The first auxiliary verb or copula *be* verb—and the tense constituent if there is one—is involved in both of them. These elements are either followed by *not* in the case of the *not* placement rule or inverted with the subject in the case of the subject-operator inversion rule. If there is neither an auxiliary verb nor a *be* copula in the sentence, both require operator addition.

5. a. The main verb (other than a *be* copula) is not inverted with the subject in English question formation. Operator addition would be applied in this case (i.e., "Did you see . . . ?").

b. Tense should be marked only once. In sentences with a *do* verb, the *do* acts as the tense carrier, while the main verb takes the base form without tense.

c. If *not* comes before the subject in the sentence, it should be contracted with the verb (i.e., "Isn't she intelligent?"); if *not* comes after the subject, it should be uncontracted (i.e., "Is she not intelligent?").

d. If there is no auxiliary verb or copula *be* in the sentence, then the *do* verb is used in short answers to yes/no questions:

> Do you like ice cream?   Yes, I do.

Alternatively, since *like* is a transitive verb, if a full-form answer were given, *like* must be followed by an NP:

> Do you like ice cream?   { Yes, I like it.
>   Yes, I like ice cream.

6.

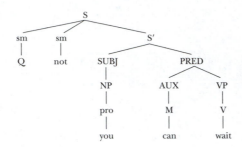

Not placement followed optionally by *not* contraction and, lastly, subject-operator inversion generates the two acceptable negative yes/no question forms. If subject-operator inversion is done before *not* placement, the third (unacceptable) form results.

7. He is correct because native speakers do produce uninverted yes/no questions. You should point out, however, that native speakers do so only when they have certain expectations about the answer they will receive. Since inverting yes/no questions is definitely the norm, this student's uninverted questions will often seem inappropriate (i.e., aggressive, presumptuous, and rude) to his listeners.

8. This humor is possible because the function and the form of utterances do not always go together. Here, B has treated A's indirect request for the time as if it were a literal request for information as the form suggests (i.e., whether B has a watch).

Chapter 12: Imperatives

1. a. imperative
  (i) affirmative   <u>Get</u> something to drink.
  (ii) negative   <u>Don't touch</u> the light bulb.
 b. inclusive imperative   <u>Let's go</u> roller-blading this afternoon.
 c. diffuse imperative   <u>Somebody help</u> me!
 d. *let* (noninclusive) imperative <u>Let</u> her choose her own way.
 e. elliptical imperative   (Get me) Three plates.
 f. *you* retention   Mike, <u>you</u> read the first half.
 g. *you* deletion   Close the window.
 h. imperative with *please*   Please pass the salt.
 i. emphatic *do* to add politeness <u>Do</u> join our party tomorrow.

2. a.

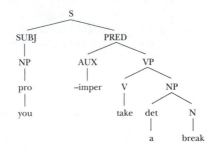

Mapping rules that apply are subject deletion and morphological rules.

2. b.

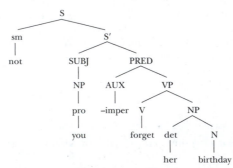

Mapping rules that apply are: operator addition, *not* placement, *not* contraction, subject deletion and morphological rules.

2. c.

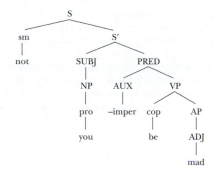

Mapping rules that apply are: operator addition, *not* placement, *not* contraction, subject deletion and morphological rules.

2. d.

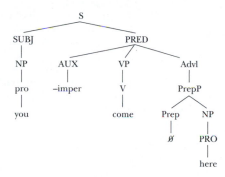

The only mapping rule that applies is morphological rules.

3. **a.** Pronouns other than the second person pronoun, *you*, cannot be the subjects of imperatives.
　　b. A negative imperative requires the verb *do* along with a negative particle before a main verb. But a main verb such as *be* or *get* is missing in this sentence.
　　c. Imperatives are tenseless—that is, they never take an inflection.
　　d. If *not* is uncontracted in a negative imperative, *you* must be omitted.

4. Evidence for the fact that imperatives are tenseless is that there is never any inflection even for the third person diffuse imperative:

　　　Somebody help (*helps) me.

One piece of syntactic evidence for the argument that a subject of an unmarked imperative is *you* is that the form of the reflexive pronoun in object position in imperatives is always *yourself* or *yourselves*:

　　　Wash yourself/yourselves.
　　　Wash *myself/*himself/*herself/*itself/*ourselves/*themselves.

5. These other subjectless utterances occur only in highly informal contexts, whereas the subjectless imperatives are much more frequent and conventionalized than are imperatives with subjects. Additionally, the other elliptical utterances often need more context to be properly interpreted: enough clues must be provided to easily identify the deleted subject (different contexts can force an interpretation different from the ones provided in the parentheses). On the other hand, deleted subjects of imperatives are easily identifiable since they always refer to the addressee—*you*.

6. Show students various contexts where imperatives are appropriate. These would include situations where imperatives are polite, such as offers and invitations, especially with *please* and emphatic *do;* and situations where cooperation is assumed, such as requests for items at the table (*"Please pass the butter."*); and warnings (*"Watch out!"*). In addition, it can be a good idea to illustrate some situations in which they may want to be forceful to counteract rudeness or attempts to take advantage of them.

7. Adding *please* to an imperative or using the emphatic *do* are the ways already mentioned. In addition, embedding an imperative within a conditional can make it sound more polite—for example, "If you have the time, bring me the files." Adding tags may also increase politeness: "Bring me the files, would you?" Another way is to use tags that imply that the recipient is already aware of the need for the action expressed in the imperative, such as "Watch that bar line, OK?" or "Snatch a breath there, right?" Using a personal form of address may increase politeness. Intonation is crucial in determining exactly how polite these imperatives sound.

8. Semantically, *You will be quiet* conveys the meaning of what is sometimes called the "peremptory future," which is different from an imperative in that it expresses a prediction along with the speaker's authority to ensure that the addressee will carry out the prediction. These assumptions are not necessarily true for imperatives.

   Syntactically, if *You will be quiet* were the underlying structure, then the negative form would be ** Won't be quiet*, rather than *Don't be quiet*. In addition, the proposal to derive *Be quiet* from *You will be quiet* seems to rest on the fact that *won't you* can be used as the tag, as in *Be quiet, won't you!* However, syntactically, *won't you* is not a tag derived from the imperative that precedes it. Other tags are also possible, such as *Be quieter, can't you?*, and thus *won't you* is not a systematic tag. It is an arbitrary and formulaic tag serving as a gap filler for imperatives, which are tenseless.

Chapter 13: *Wh*-Questions

I.
  a. *wh*-question focusing on the subject   <u>Who</u> wrote this poem?
  b. *wh*-question focusing on an object   formal—To whom did you send this report?
          of a preposition   informal—Who did you sent this report to?
  c. *wh*-question focusing on a determiner:
          (i) possessive   <u>Whose</u> pen is this?
          (ii) demonstrative   <u>Which</u> color do you like better?
          (iii) quantifier   <u>How many</u> articles did you find on that topic?
  d. uninverted *wh*-question   You went there with whom?
  e. negative *wh*-question:
          (i) contracted   Why didn't he answer you?
          (ii) uncontracted   Why did he not answer you?
  f. formulaic *wh*-question (lexicalized unit)   How are you doing? / How's it going?
  g. *wh*-question with ellipsis of the auxiliary Who (are) you going with?

2. a.

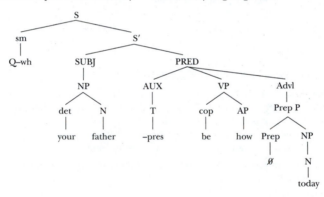

Mapping rules that apply are: copy s/t, *wh*-fronting, subject-operator inversion and morphological rules.

2. b.

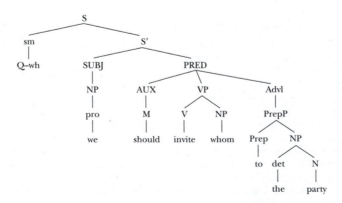

Mapping rules that apply are: *wh*-fronting, subject-operator inversion and morphological rules.

2. c.

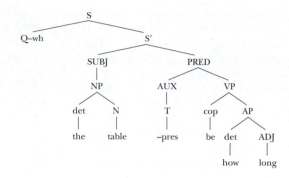

Mapping rules that apply are: copy s/t, *wh*-fronting, subject-operator inversion and morphological rules.

2. d.

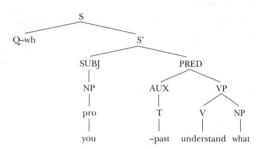

Mapping rules that apply are: copy s/t, *wh*-fronting, operator addition, subject-operator inversion and morphological rules.

2. e.

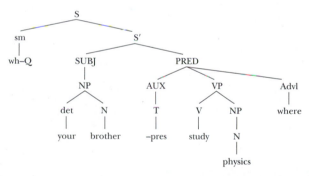

Mapping rules that apply are: copy s/t, *wh*-fronting, operator addition, subject-operator inversion and morphological rules.

3. When a determiner is the focus of a *wh*-question, the head noun constituent it modifies must be moved, along with the determiner (e.g., *which car, whose handbag*).

4. More specific *wh*-questions can be:

> What street do you live on?
> Which shelf is the sugar on?
> How far back is it?

5. a. Subject-operator inversion should be applied when the *wh*-question focuses on something in the predicate (i.e., "Where are you going?").

   b. This question lacks operator addition, which is necessary if a question has no auxiliary verb or copula and it focuses on something in the predicate. (This could, of course, also be an elliptical question if used appropriately as such.)

   c. The preposition *to* should either be fronted with the *wh*-question word (i.e., "To whom did he say that?") or it should remain behind when the *wh*-question is fronted (i.e., "Who did he say that to?"). It should not occur in both places.

   d. English sentences require a verb. In this sentence, *be* (correct form: *is*) has been omitted.

6. <u>Structure</u>: With *why*, the normal rules for *wh*-question formation apply. They also apply for the *what . . . for* structure, except that *for* cannot be fronted with the *what*; it must stay behind. For example:

> *For what did he say that?

With *how come*, the word order of the following elements is the same as for an affirmative statement—that is, there is no subject-operator inversion.

<u>Meaning</u>: All three can be used to ask for a reason; however, unless questions with *why* are given a particular intonation pattern, they appear to be more neutral than do *what . . . for* and *how come*. One can imagine the latter two being used as challenges; for example,

> What did you do that for? (surely there was a better alternative!)

Another difference may be that *why* and *how come* can be used to ask about the cause of something, whereas *what . . . for* seems to ask about purpose; for example,

> Why is the sky blue? (cause)
> How come the sky is blue? (cause)
> What is the sky blue for? (purpose)

<u>Register</u>: *Why* questions appear to be the most formal, with *how come* and *what . . . for* being used informally. *How come* is probably the least formal of the three.

In addition to these differences, another instance where they cannot be paraphrases of each other is in the formation of negative questions. *What . . . for* cannot be used as a negative paraphrase of the other two:

> Why didn't he say that?
> How come he didn't say that?
> *What didn't he say that for?

7. In the questions with *did* [i.e., (a), (b), and (e)] the question focuses on information contained in the predicate. In these questions, the subject and operator must be inverted, and the *do* operator has been added to carry the tense. In the questions without *did* [i.e., (c) and (d)], the question focuses on information contained in the subject. In such cases, no inversion and, therefore, no *do* operator are required.

8.

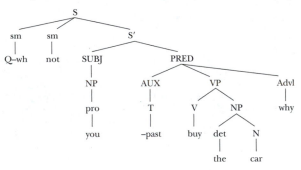

Output of base: Q-wh not you -past buy the car why
Copy s/t: Q-wh not you -past [+ 2 + sg] buy the car why
Operator addition: Q-wh not you -past [+ 2 + sg] do buy the car why
not placement: Q-wh you -past [+ 2 + sg] do not buy the car why
not contraction: Q-wh you -past [+ 2 + sg] do + n't buy the car why
wh-fronting: Why you -past [+ 2 + sg] do + n't buy the car
subject-operator inversion: why -past [+ 2 + sg] do + n't you buy the car
morphological rules: Why didn't you buy the car?

9. The second *do* is lexical and, therefore, meaningful. The first *do* is inserted only to allow subject-operator inversion in the question form; it does not carry any meaning.

Chapter 14: Other Structures That Look Like Questions

1.

a.	tag question	
	(i) unmarked	You're going to give me back that money I lent you, <u>aren't you</u>?
	(ii) idiosyncratic	I'm subtle, <u>aren't I</u>?
	(iii) marked	So you're going to pay me back next week, <u>are you</u>?
b.	alternative question	Do you want to go to a movie tonight or the concert?
c.	*wh*-/alternative question combination	What do you want to do tonight—a movie or the concert?
d.	exclamatory "question"	Aren't you lucky!
e.	rhetorical question	Are you here to worry about grades or to learn something?

2. **a.** The tense should be the same in both the main verb and the tag. The main verb and the tag should be either both present (*wants* and *doesn't*) or both past (*wanted* and *didn't*).

   b. Since the main clause is negative (negated by the preverbal adverb *never*) the tag needs to be affirmative (i.e., *does she*).

   c. Just as with negative yes/no questions and negative *wh*-questions, the *not* in a negative tag question must be contracted if it is to precede the subject in the tag (i.e., *didn't he*). Otherwise, *not* should follow the subject (i.e., *did he not*).

   d. The exclamatory question follows the same grammatical rules as other negative questions (as in (c) above); when the *not* is placed before the subject (i.e., *that*), it must be contracted (i.e., *isn't*).

3. **a.** Is Janet blue-eyed or is she not blue-eyed?

   b. You're looking forward to vacation, aren't you?

   c. Was it Bill who wrote this letter, or was it Bob who wrote this letter?

4. **a.** If there is an auxiliary verb in the main sentence, the tag question is formed using the same auxiliary verb. The subject in the main sentence and the tag must refer to the same entity as well, although the latter is pronominalized if necessary. Thus, the tag must be *aren't we* rather than *isn't it* (which is a common transfer error among speakers of other languages).

   b. *Yes* is never an appropriate tag question in English, although native speakers will sometimes use *no* as a tag with a rising intonation in informal situations.

   c. This has the intonation pattern of an alternative question; the listener is being asked to make a choice between two alternatives. Since it is not a yes/no question, the response *yes* is inappropriate, as would be *no*.

5. **a.** These two utterances differ with regard to the presupposition of the speaker. Sentence (2) would be uttered by the speaker if he or she did not expect it to rain, whereas (1) signals that rain is expected by the speaker.

   b. Analysis of the wider discourse context, including intonation, would be needed to be certain of the difference. It may be that (2) is more formal than (1) or more emphatic; for example, one can imagine (2) being uttered by a speaker who is losing patience with his or her listener.

   c. The speaker of (1) expects that the listener has carried out the action. In (2) (depending on stress and intonation), the speaker may be expressing displeasure or annoyance that the action was performed; or the speaker may be trying to ascertain whether or not the action was performed. The second interpretation for (2) is more characteristic of British than American usage.

   d. In (1), the speaker is raising a genuine question about the truth of the proposition and either has no presuppositions about the listener's thoughts or suspects the listener may disagree. In (2), the speaker is seeking confirmation and expects the listener to agree with the proposition.

   e. The speaker in (1) expects disagreement with the proposition or has doubt about the listener's position (the listener may have given some indication—verbal or otherwise—of disagreement), whereas the speaker in (2) is expressing an exclamation, not asking a question.

   f. (1) is able to be used to express doubt or certainty (as in (d) depending on the intonation used. (2) can be used only in seeking confirmation from the listener (i.e., expecting agreement). Also, (2) puts greater pressure on the interlocutor to respond than does (1).

6. The author used a question for his title as a rhetorical device to introduce his topic and gain the reader's attention. The question is, of course, rhetorical, and the reader can expect to find the author's answer in the essay. The question is also likely to make readers think of their own answers, which they can then compare to the author's answer.

7. Both are fairly informal requests. The first is more polite because it is the usual (i.e., unmarked) use of the tag question (i.e., the tag is negative when the main clause is affirmative). The second is less common (marked) and implies some impatience or directness, which might also signal rudeness or irritation.

Chapter 15: Articles

1. **a.** noncount noun

     (i) mass noun   <u>Water</u> is composed of oxygen and hydrogen.

     (ii) abstract noun   <u>Cleanliness</u> is next to <u>Godliness</u>.

   b. count noun   Have a <u>seat</u>.

   c. definite article

     (i) with textual coreference   I read a great novel last week.   <u>The</u> imagery was fantastic.

     (ii) with situational/cultural reference   Let's go to <u>the library</u>.

     (iii) with structural reference   <u>The end</u> of the world is nigh.

   d. first mention–subsequent mention   Once upon a time, there was <u>a little girl</u>. <u>The girl</u> lived with
     principle   her mother and father.

    e. indefinite article
        (i) with generic usage   A tiger is a large cat.
        (ii) with predicate noun   This is a warm day.
    f. indefinite noun
        (i) specific   I'm looking for a pen that I misplaced.
        (ii) nonspecific   If I don't find it, I'll have to buy a new pen.
    g. idiomatic article usage   She is in hospital. (U.K.) versus She is in the hospital. (U.S.)
    h. zero article use with generic meaning   Dreams are free.
    i. null article use with definite meaning   Lunch was served on the terrace.

2. Listener and speaker specific referent   Can you find the page?
    Listener nonspecific, speaker specific   I read a great book last week.
    Listener specific, speaker nonspecific   I believe you own a house in Malibu.
    Listener and speaker nonspecific   I'm looking for an apartment.

3. a. textual coreference—associative anaphoric use ("the traffic" refers to "the traffic in New York")
    b. situational/cultural use—local use (general knowledge—e.g., for a family)
    c. textual coreference ("the course" in sentence 2 refers back to "a grammar course" in sentence 1)
    d. structural reference ("on the corner" postmodifies "house")

4. a. *Coffee* is a mass noun here and does not take an article. *A coffee* means a serving/cup of coffee. If the coffee were spilled, it would no longer be contained within a cup and therefore could not be referred to with the indefinite article.
    b. *Information* is a mass noun in English; it is therefore noncount and cannot take a plural ending or the determiner *many*.
    c. *Examination* is a singular count noun and must therefore take an article. The indefinite article is required because in this case the noun has a specific referent for the speaker but not for the listener.

5. a. The indefinite article *a* or *an* can precede only a singular noun. However, *time* is a noun that can be used in a number of different ways: noncount and in singular or plural count forms, with different meanings. In order to avoid the error of *long times, take a long time* is probably best learned as a lexical phrase (i.e., a single unit).
    b. *Taiwan travel industry* has a specific referent for both speaker and listener, and thus the definite article is required.
    c. The definite article is used only with a noun that has a specific referent for both speaker and listener. If the plan has not been made yet, then it cannot be specific to either, and the indefinite article is required instead.
    d. *Computer* is a singular count noun, so it cannot occur without an article. A generic statement is intended here, so the student should be advised to use the zero article (being the most flexible pattern for generic use) with a plural noun and to make the necessary number adjustment (i.e., *aren't* and *luxuries*).
    e. *Europe* is a proper noun, so it takes no article.
    f. Here *poetry* is a mass noun used non-specifically. No article should be used.
    g. Singular predicate nominals that classify the subject noun are preceded by an indefinite article.

6. An indefinite article used in object position may be ambiguous with regard to whether it modifies a specific or nonspecific noun in the speaker's mind. *A car* could be nonspecific to both speaker and listener—that is, any car; or it could be specific to the speaker—that is, a particular car that John has in mind.

7. In the first sentence, the frame of reference is likely to be different types of drugs in a generic sense. In the second sentence, the range of possible drinks is the frame of reference. The third sentence refers to the coffee in a particular place (café, country, etc.) in contrast to coffee in other places. In the last sentence, different types of coffee in a single place are referred to.

8. You would probably write *the beach* if there was only one possible beach for you to go to, if you had previously written about a particular beach (that consequently did not need identification), or if you were referring to the activity of "going to the beach" as something familiar to your family, a local use within Hawkins' location theory. Conversely, you would use the indefinite article if none of the assumptions above held.

Chapter 16: Reference and Possession

1. a. subject pronoun   She loves the man.
    b. object pronoun   The man loves her.
    c. possessive pronoun   I thought the car outside the apartment was theirs.
    d. possessive determiner   Their apartment was small and cluttered.
    e. demonstrative pronoun   The last exercises were harder than these.
    f. demonstrative determiner   These exercises are easy.
    g. reciprocal pronoun   We bought each other presents for Christmas.

   h. reflexive pronoun   I bought <u>myself</u> a new dress.
   i. indefinite compound pronoun   <u>No one</u> likes a poor loser.
   j. singular "they"   Anyone using the beach after 5 P.M. does so at <u>their</u> own risk.
   k. *'s* possessive   <u>Erin's</u> voice was the loudest in the room.
   l. *of* possessive   The title <u>of the story</u> was "The Lottery."

2. **a.** The *of* possessive is preferred here because *the room* is inanimate and does not perform an action.
    b. *Him* is an object pronoun being used where the subject pronoun *he* should be used.
    c. *Mines* is the incorrect form of this possessive pronoun. It should be *mine*. This is perhaps an overgeneralization error since the other possessive pronouns end in *s*.
    d. The last pronoun in the sentence should be the object pronoun *me* since it is the object of the preposition *besides*.

3. **a.** *My friend's house* is the correct form of an animate possessor, especially here where the possessor is not a long or complex NP.
    b. The third person singular masculine reflexive pronoun is *himself*. This is perhaps an overgeneralization error, since other reflexive pronouns are formed with the possessive determiner followed by *self* or *selves*, such as *myself* or *ourselves*.
    c. The student neglected to use the *'s* possessive form to mark *Mary* as the possessor.
    d. The subject *Everybody*, like all the other compound indefinite pronouns, requires a singular verb.
    e. The reflexive pronoun *themselves* has been used, implying that Leo hit himself and Hugo hit himself, when presumably the reciprocal pronoun *each other* is what was intended (i.e., Leo hit Hugo and vice versa, unless self-flagellation was the intended meaning!).

4. Since the *'s* morpheme and the plural morpheme are both suffixed to NPs, and since both pattern the same way phonetically, their similarity may cause some confusion. Also, *'s* is unstressed and may not therefore be perceived by students. (In other words, *'s* has low perceptual saliency.) On the other hand, some students may perceive *'s* but not be able to produce it because their native language has few or no consonant clusters.

5. Spanish speakers may use the *of* possessive incorrectly in place of the *'s* possessive:

     *the garden of Milly

They may also omit the *'s* possessive altogether by analogy with nouns modifying other nouns:

     *Milly garden   (cf. stone wall, summer garden)

6. Other pronouns in English that can also mean "everyone in general" are:

     you—You gotta study hard to get good grades.
     we—We should study hard if we want to get good grades.
     everyone (everybody)—Everyone should learn a foreign language.

7. Two ways of avoiding the usage of *he, his,* and *him* when these forms are used in a general sense are:
    a. to use plurals

      A student should plan his schedule wisely.
      →Students should plan their schedules wisely.

    b. to use *one*

      A person should not reveal his deepest thoughts to total strangers.
      →One should not reveal one's deepest thoughts to total strangers.

Of course, both these ways have drawbacks. Sometimes using the plural will not work, such as when you simply want to discuss an individual's doing something. And the use of *one* can easily be overdone, resulting in stilted (or overly formal) language.

8. Native speakers sometimes do violate the prescriptive rules of pronoun usage and use subject pronouns where object pronouns are called for; for example, **The book is by she and Professor Hansen*. Native speakers also sometimes use object pronouns where the prescriptive rule says subject pronouns are necessary: for example, **Me and Mark are going to the store.*

    You can explain to your ESL/EFL students that they won't be wrong in following the prescriptive rules, even though not all native speakers abide by them all the time.

Chapter 17: Partitives, Collectives, and Quantifiers

1. **a.** partitive noun   a <u>bowl</u> of rice
    b. idiomatic partitive noun   a <u>gaggle</u> of geese
    c. collective noun   The <u>jury</u> brought in its decision.
    d. collective noun derived from adjective   The <u>disabled</u> are well cared for here.
    e. quantifier   I'll have to give this one <u>a little</u> thought.

f. quantifier with negative connotation   They had <u>little</u> success in solving the problem.

g. quantifier for count nouns   There are <u>many</u> questions one could ask.

h. phrasal quantifier   A <u>lot of</u> people love grammar.

2. a. *Chalk* is a mass noun. It can be used without any preceding determiner in sentences that express a general characteristic (e.g., *Chalk is dusty.*) However, when used specifically, as here, it is necessary to use a determiner such as the definite article, the partitive (*a*) *piece*(*s*) *of* (e.g., *a piece of chalk, three pieces of chalk*), a quantifier, or a demonstrative determiner. Regardless of the choice, a singular verb is required.

b. *A lot of* and *lots of* always take the *of* unless they are functioning as nouns or pronouns.

c. *Few* is a quantifier with a negative connotation. Since *although* signals a contrast, you would expect a quantifier with a positive connotation to be used. Here, the correct quantifier is *a few;* alternatively, the logical connector *because* should replace *although* if *few* is truly intended to convey a negative connotation.

d. The quantifiers *a great deal* and *a good deal* always occur with the adjective *good* or *great* as part of them.

e. *Almost* can be used with the quantifier *all*, but it is not by itself a quantifier. The quantifier needed here is *most* or, alternatively, *almost all.*

3. a. *Many* is followed by *of* only when the noun it quantifies is definite. In (2), *workers* is not definite as it is in (1).

b. *Class* is a collective noun. In (1), *class* refers to a collective whole, while in (2), it refers to the individuals that make up the collective whole.

c. *Lots* seems more informal than *a lot*. It also seems to signify a greater amount, perhaps because it can be reduplicated (i.e., *lots and lots and lots*) whereas *a lot* cannot.

d. *Speck* is the idiomatic partitive for *dust*. *Piece* is not ungrammatical; however, it implies an unusually large piece.

4. a. *Problem* is a count noun and must have the *-s* ending for plural. *Much* is used before noncount nouns, not plural count nouns. *Many* is the correct form; that is, the correct NP is *many problems*. (*Much difficulty*—a noncount NP—would also be correct.)

b. *A dozen* is a numerical expression, rather than a quantity such as *pound*. It therefore does not take *of*.

c. *Information* is a noncount noun and cannot take *-s*. *Some* is still correct because it can be used with either count or noncount nouns.

d. *A lot of* is preferred over *much* in positive assertions, especially in informal language.

e. When followed by another determiner such as *my*, which makes the noun specific, *some* takes *of*.

f. Noun-based numerical words remain in the singular even when modified by a number greater than one. The correct phrase would be "Five Hundred Miles."

g. The student would appear to be relying on aural evidence, since the phrase *a couple of minutes* is often pronounced as written in the example. The student needs to learn the nonspecific quantifier *a couple of* as a chunk, although in North American English it is increasingly common to hear people say (and even see them write) *a couple minutes*. In addition, the difference between *a dozen* and *a couple of* may be noted—*a dozen* is a precise numerical expression, whereas *a couple of* is more imprecise, which explains the use of *of*.

h. When *some* is used with *of*, the definite article is needed before the noun phrase to make it specific.

5. Both partitive nouns refer to a single item. Structurally, they are different in that *cattle* is a plural count noun and *lettuce* is a singular count noun or noncount noun. Thus, *head of cattle* can also be used as the plural form, whereas you would have to add *-s* to make the plural *heads of lettuce*.

6. It is grammatical to use the plural when the number-based noun is used with a general rather than specific number reference. In this case, the number of centuries is not specified. However, it would be ungrammatical to say

    *a Five-centuries-old Framework

because the number is specified. The same pattern occurs with phrases like *four million dollars* (specific) but *millions of stars* (general).

7. Quantifiers are used with *of* only when the noun being quantified is specific. In this case, *several offspring* is the first mention of the offspring, and therefore *offspring* is not specific. In the second mention, the offspring are now specific, and the use of *several of the offspring* denotes that only a specific subset of the group are now being referred to.

8. When the definite determiner is before the partitive noun, it specifies the exact identity of the item referred to. When the definite determiner is before the following noun, it specifies the set of such things. For example, *this carton of milk* refers to only one possible carton (e.g., the one in my hand), whereas *a carton of this milk* could refer to any carton of the specified milk (e.g., any one from a shelf of nonfat milk).

Chapter 18: The Passive Voice

1. **a.** active voice — Two million people <u>watch</u> the program every week.
    b. passive voice — The mail <u>is delivered</u> daily.
    c. passive voice with agent — "The Road Not Taken" <u>was written</u> by <u>Robert Frost</u>.
    d. the *get*-passive — The dog <u>got hit</u> on its way home.
    e. a verb that is always passive — Jonathan <u>was born</u> in Japan.
    f. a verb that is never passive — Water <u>consists</u> of hydrogen and oxygen.
    g. the agentless middle voice (i.e., ergative) construction — The boat <u>sailed</u> away.
    h. an intransitive verb with a nonagent subject — Prices <u>rose</u> dramatically this year.

2. a.

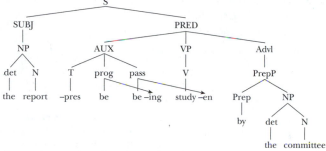

Mapping rules that apply are: copy s/t and morphological rules.

2. b.

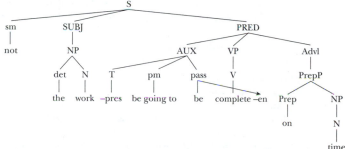

Mapping rules that apply are: copy s/t, *not* placement, *not* contraction and morphological rules.

2. c.

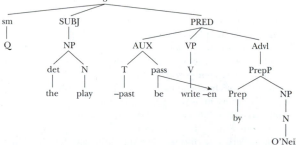

Mapping rules that apply are: copy s/t, subject-operator inversion and morphological rules.

2. d.

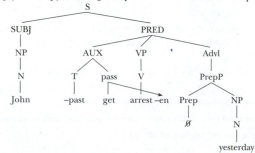

Mapping rules that apply are: copy s/t and morphological rules.

3. a. The student has confused the order of the auxiliary elements, and inflected *have* incorrectly. The *be . . . en* of the passive follows all the other elements of the auxiliary and, unless it is the first element in the auxiliary, *have* is always the correct form within such an auxiliary; for example, "Horace will have been tested on his Spanish." Alternatively, the intended sentence may have been "Horace will be tested on his Spanish." In this case, the *had* is unnecessary and should be deleted.

b. *Contain* is one of those verbs like *weigh* and *have* that normally do not occur in a passive form. Quirk and Greenbaum (1973:359–360) indicate that there are four such categories of verbs:

    (i) "Reciprocal" verbs (e.g., *resemble, look like, equal, agree with*)

        *Her sister is resembled by Nancy.

    (ii) Verbs of "containing" (e.g., *contain, hold, comprise, lack*)

        *Confidence is lacked by him.

    (iii) Verbs of "suiting" (e.g., *suit, fit, become*)

        *I am suited by this arrangement.

    (iv) Verbs of measurement (e.g., *weigh, cost, contain*)

        *$15 is cost by the shirt.

Many of these categories overlap with the stative verbs discussed in Chapter 7. Thus, many verbs that do not take progressive aspect also do not occur in the passive.

c. Unlike as in some languages (such as some Bantu languages) a locative expression, such as *in the bus*, cannot be the subject of a passive clause in English. The object of the action must precede the verb in subject position; that is, in this case *a sandwich* must precede the verb *was eaten*.

d. The use of the definite article before *customer* makes this NP the known information in the sentence, whereas *three cars* (lacking such a marker) is the new information. The active word order would thus reverse the order of these NPs, putting them in the more acceptable order where the new information comes second.

4. The second *be* in a sentence with two *be* verbs in a row is the passive. The passive *be* takes the *-en* ending, (here on *prepare*).

5. "A deck of cards that has been shuffled"—the passive is used here in a relative clause to maintain the deck of cards as the focus of this part of the sentence.

    "Both cards get turned face down"—the use of the passive here emphasizes the shift in focus away from the student who failed to produce a correct sentence; in addition, the *get*-passive is used to convey more of a sense of action, since the *be*-passive ("are turned over") has a strong stative reading here.

    "Until all the pairs have been matched"—the passive enables the focus to be on the pairs of cards, the status of which is the criterion for the game being over, rather than anything to do with the agents involved.

6. a. *To be born* always occurs in the passive. The student has omitted the obligatory *be* auxiliary.

b. The student has used *sang*, the simple past tense of the verb *sing*, instead of the correct (irregular) form of the passive participle—that is, *sung*.

c. *Brazil* is the agent, and active word order is used, so the passive voice is incorrect. An active verb form should be used, such as *Brazil has slowed down its inflation.*

d. The incorrect participle for *hurt* has been used (it should be simply *hurt*). This is a case of main verb *get* being followed by an adjective in its past participle form.

e. *Die* is always intransitive and therefore can never occur in the passive. The transitive verb *kill* is probably intended here, since an agent is expressed.

f. *Disappear* is an intransitive verb, and thus the receiver of the action is the subject without the use of the passive. Given the absence of an expressed agent, deleting *was* is the best way to correct the sentence rather than changing the verb (to *lose*, for example).

7. *Rise, lie,* and *sit* are all intransitive verbs and therefore can never occur in the passive. They each have transitive counterparts given here (which can occur in the passive), however, that are very similar in form and thus are easily confused.

8. Although the differences are not glaring, English speakers tend to use the *be*-passive when the agent is at least understood:

    Sheila and Steven were married on August 28 (by the rabbi).

The *get*-passive tends to be used informally when there is no expressed or understood agent:

    Sheila and Steven got married on August 28.

In addition, the *be*-passive is used whenever the speaker or writer wants to express a stative passive:

> Sheila and Steven are married. (i.e., they are not single)

The *get*-passive can never be used in this meaning.

> The active form, *have married*, is punctual and can be used to express repetitive action, as in
>
> Sheila and Steven have married each other seven times.

or to express the action of the officiator:

> The rabbi has married many couples this year.

Have been married (like *are married*) is a *be* + adjective construction:

> Sheila and Steven have been married for seven years.
>
> or
>
> Sheila and Steven have both been married before.

9. A lengthy *by* phrase will presumably mean that there is important information contained in it. If this is the case, then the passive is a good choice because it means that the important information will come later in the sentence, in the comment (rheme) position.

Chapter 19: Sentences with Indirect Objects

1. a. direct object — He gave her <u>a diamond ring</u>.
b. eliciting indirect object — Debbie requested a favor <u>of Penny</u>.
c. benefactive indirect object — She bought a valentine <u>for her boyfriend</u>.
d. dative indirect object — I will loan <u>you</u> my car.
e. passive with indirect object as subject — <u>The expectant parents</u> were given a shower.
f. dominance — Wait! You're giving the money to the wrong person. Give that money <u>to me</u>.
g. indirect object alternation — The kindergarten teacher read the story to his class.
→The kindergarten teacher read his class the story.
h. benefactive *for* — She planned a surprise party <u>for him</u>.
i. proxy *for* — Then she became ill, so her sister was hostess <u>for her</u>.
j. verb of transfer — She <u>rolled</u> the ball <u>across</u> the table to her friend.
k. verb of future possession — The Immigration Department <u>denied</u> me a visa.

2. a.

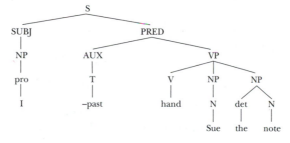

Mapping rules that apply are: copy s/t, and morphological rules.

2. b.

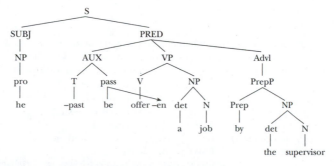

Mapping rules that apply are: copy s/t, and morphological rules.

2. c.

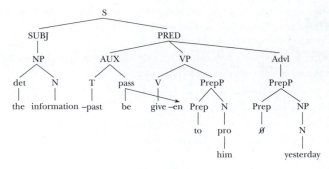

Mapping rules that apply are: copy s/t, and morphological rules.

2. d.

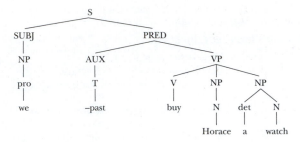

Mapping rules that apply are: copy s/t, and morphological rules

2. e.

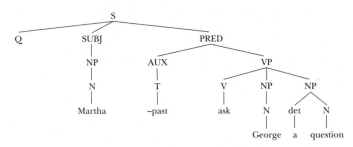

Mapping rules that apply are: copy s/t, operator addition, subject-operator inversion, and morphological rules.

3. a. The direct object is a pronoun, while the indirect object is a noun. Under these conditions, the rules of dominance tell us that indirect object alternation shouldn't take place. This sentence should be:

John hasn't sent it to his brother.

b. When indirect object alternation takes place (i.e., the dative meaning is intended), the preposition is deleted:

Mary bought me the book.

Alternatively, if the proxy meaning is intended, the prepositional phrase would not move forward, since the direct object is not long and complex enough to merit movement of the PrepP.

c. With eliciting verbs, the preposition *of* precedes the indirect object, not the preposition *to*.

4. a.

active	Mother sent the parcel to Bob.
with indirect object alternation	Mother sent Bob the parcel.
passive (direct object as subject)	The parcel was sent to Bob by Mother.
with no agent expressed	The parcel was sent to Bob.
passive (indirect object as subject)	Bob was sent the parcel by Mother.
with no agent expressed	Bob was sent the parcel.

b.

active	Bill brought some flowers for Agnes.
with indirect object alternation	Bill brought Agnes some flowers.
passive (direct object as subject)	Some flowers were brought for Agnes by Bill.
with no agent expressed	Some flowers were brought for Agnes.

5. **a.** *Explain* is a verb that does not allow indirect object alternation (i.e., *explain that rule to me*).
   b. With indirect object alternation, the preposition is deleted (i.e., *give me an answer*).
   c. *Open* is a verb that allows indirect object alternation only when the deleted *for* is benefactive, not when it is the proxy *for*. Thus one can say:

   > Open him a can of beer. (benefactive: the can of beer is <u>for</u> him)
   > *Open him the door.   (proxy: the door is not <u>for</u> him, but being opened for him)

   d. Since *ask* is an eliciting verb, the underlying preposition in this sentence is *of*:

   > We asked something of Harry.

   But even if the student had used *of*, he or she would have been incorrect here since no preposition can be used if the direct object is deleted.

   e. *Excuse* does not take an indirect object. Either *me* or *my poor English* may function as the direct object, but one cannot use both.

   > Please excuse me. or Please excuse my poor English.

6. With the exception of the verb *say*, Fraser is correct in stating that one-syllable verbs that take indirect objects may optionally undergo indirect object alternation. They can do this whether their indirect objects are marked by *to*, *for*, or *of*. Although Fraser did not explicitly mention this, it is also important to note that no verb of three or more syllables may take indirect object movement:

   > *Educate us these children.   *Evaluate NSF this proposal.
   > *Communicate your father this message.

   The real problem arises with two-syllable verbs. Except for the two-syllable eliciting verbs, which never take indirect object movement, it appears that neither the stress pattern nor the co-occurring preposition is a good predictor of indirect object alternation:

	to "dative"	for "benefactive"	of "eliciting"
stress on first syllable	*mention offer	*open scramble (i.e., the eggs)	
stress on second syllable	*explain award	*perform reserve	the two-syllable eliciting verbs do not take indirect object movement: *demand; *request

   We hope that future research will reveal some system in what now appears to be rather arbitrary behavior.

7. In conversation, *giving* is usually reduced to *givin'*, making the present and passive participles hard to distinguish. You would therefore want to have your students concentrate on listening for the differences in the prepositional phrases. The *by* phrase always marks the agent, and the whole phrase is often deleted. On the other hand, the *to* phrase is obligatorily present with many directional or dative verbs.

8. *Beg* can take an indirect object only when it is an eliciting verb:

   > I beg this favor of you.

   When it is used in this way, it cannot undergo indirect object alternation:

   > *I beg you this favor.

   For other uses, *beg* does not take an indirect object. It does, however, take a direct object which could be phrasal (e.g., I beg *your pardon*), containing within itself an indirect object. As a different example, in the following sentence, all that follows *beg* is the direct object:

   > I beg *you to stop*.
   >   direct object

   If the direct object is a phrase, it might have an indirect object embedded within it:

   > I beg *you to do something for me*.
   >   direct object

   But here, the benefactive indirect object phrase belongs to the verb *do*, not *beg*.

   A few eliciting verbs also occur in another frame with *for*. For example:

   > He begged/asked for money/help (of someone).

   In this case, *for* is neither benefactive nor proxy, but a prepositional phrase, and the verb is still eliciting.

Chapter 20: Adjectives

I. **a.** attributive adjective   What a <u>beautiful</u> day it is!
   b. predicate adjective   The sky is clear <u>blue</u>.

c.	postnominal adjective	Jack accepted the only job <u>available</u>.
d.	reference adjective	They were in <u>total</u> accord.
e.	present participle adjective	Jurassic Park is a <u>thrilling</u> ride.
f.	past participle adjective	We were <u>thrilled</u> to see you there.
g.	restrictive adjective	Stuart wrote an <u>apologetic</u> letter.
h.	gradable adjective	She is a very <u>skilled</u> musician.

2. a. *Asleep* functions exclusively as a predicate adjective and thus can never occur in attributive position as it does here.

 b. *Main* is a "reference" adjective that can occur only in attributive position, not in predicate position as in this sentence.

 c. The adjective phrase "overly fond of chocolate" is complex and is therefore restricted to postnominal or predicative position, not prenominal position as in this sentence.

 d. When measure phrases are used adjectivally, the singular form of the noun is always used; thus *thirteen-year-old* is the correct form. The exception to this is when more general expressions are used, such as *centuries-old* as in Chapter. 17, Exercise 6.

3. The *-ing* participle here can be interpreted either as a verb, in which case the sentence is elliptical of what Hazel is trying to do (e.g., *Hazel is trying to open the jar*), or as an adjective, in which case *trying* describes Hazel (i.e., *Hazel tries one's patience*).

4. When *white* is in the postnominal position, it refers more to the action and thus implies that the fence was not white before it was painted. In the attributive position, *white* refers to a more permanent state and therefore implies that the fence was white before it was painted.

5. a. Opinion adjectives normally come before size adjectives. *Nice* should therefore precede *big* in this sentence.

 b. The *-en* participle form *haired* is the correct form of the adjective here, although it is never used as a verb form.

 c. The *-en* participle, rather than the *-ing* participle, is needed to express the idea that the subject ("I") is the experiencer of the boredom. The *-ing* participle implies that "I" am the cause of the experience of boredom.

6. Speaker A uses *good* as a gradable adjective and inquires where on the scale (which presumably could run from "not good" upwards) the Red Sox should be placed. However, speaker B interprets *good* as an opinion adjective, and the response implies that the Red Sox would not even get onto the scale denoted by the word *good*, proposing a separate scale (*bad*) that they could be placed on.

7. The word order is derived from a relative clause, *things that are unfamiliar*, and is a rare (marked) but grammatical word order. This particular example sounds rather poetic and emphasizes the adjective by placing it at the end of the sentence where new information is typically placed.

8. *Quite* can be used to intensify predicate adjectives in the same way as the other intensifiers. However, when used to intensify an attributive adjective, it is placed before the indefinite article.

9. In *be used to*, the *-en* participle can be viewed as an adjective. The test for this would be to place an intensifier in front of *used to*:

> ?I am very used to spicy Indian food.

This sentence is questionable, but in the second sentence it would be impossible (**I very used to eat spicy Indian food*). In *used to*, the *-en* participle is a verb phrase, modal in character.

> Another test is to look at what follows each expression: *be used to* is followed by a noun (as adjectives are), whereas *used to* is followed by a verb, as other modals are.

Chapter 21: Prepositions

1. a.	verb + preposition co-occurrence	I have <u>adapted to</u> life in this country now.
b.	deletable preposition	
	(i) optional	<u>On</u> Thursday, softball practice began late.
	(ii) obligatory	Most of us just wanted to go Ø̲ home.
c.	co-occurring nonadjacent prepositions	<u>Out of</u> the frying pan, <u>into</u> the fire.
d.	complex preposition	I found it <u>at the bottom of</u> the drawer.
e.	source preposition	I drew a number <u>from</u> the hat.
f.	metaphorical extension of *in*	He was <u>in</u> a bad mood.
g.	genitive use of *of*	I came here on the advice <u>of</u> my school teacher.
h.	collocation with preposition	We received a <u>loan for</u> the <u>purpose of</u> buying a computer.

2. a. The verb *rely* must always be followed by the preposition *on*.

 b. A measured amount of time after which something will occur (as in this sentence) is indicated by the preposition *in*. *During* indicates that an action or actions occur within the span of time mentioned.

c. *Interested* co-occurs with *in*, not *by*.

d. *Beneath* is the correct preposition in this expression, although *underneath* has the same core meaning. This is possibly because *beneath*, being more formal, is more inclined to take metaphorical meanings, whereas *underneath* usually retains a more literal meaning. *Beneath one's dignity* has also become a lexicalized unit.

3. a. *Discuss* requires no preposition (unlike *talk about*, *argue about*). One might say that the meaning of *about* is already part of the meaning of *discuss*.

   b. *On* is used for the street alone (*on* Western Avenue); *at* is used for the number and street together because they indicate a specific point.

   c. *Because of* must be followed by a noun phrase, not a clause as here. Thus the sentence could be changed to *Because of all the homework I have, I can't go*. Alternatively, the *of* could be deleted, leaving *because* correctly followed by a complete clause. In this case the *because* is an adv sub, not part of the complex preposition *because of*.

   d. Locative nouns, such as *home*, *downtown*, and *overseas*, never occur with *to* with a verb of motion or direction.

   e. When *here* or *there* occur with stative verbs and with *in*, they do so only when *in* is interpreted in its core meaning of being enclosed by something—for example, *It's in here* (meaning "in this room" or "in this cupboard"). In its more metaphorical senses, such as *in this city*, *here* or *there* are used alone, even when substituting for a locative phrase using *in*, such as *in Washington*.

4. In this sentence, *of* is used in a partitive expression to divide a noncount noun (*paper*) into units.

5. To be done on your own. Answers will vary.

6. Five such prepositions are described below:

Preposition	Space	Time	Degree	Other
after	My house is after the big barn as you are heading south.	after 9:00 A.M. after 10 minutes	---	after all
beside	beside the still waters	---	---	beside himself
forward	Forward of aft is the bow.	Let's move the clocks forward an hour.	---	He was rather forward.
into	She crawled into the cave.	As we came into the twentieth century	divide 21 into 207	He's really into TM.
within	You should reach the rest stop within two miles.	. . .within an hour	. . . within 5° of boiling	within reason

7. The ambiguity lies in the two possible interpretations of *in*. It could be used in the sense of "after five minutes has elapsed" (i.e., the storytelling will start after five minutes), or it could be used to mean that the telling of the story will be completed within a span of five minutes (i.e., the storytelling will start now and be finished after five minutes).

Chapter 22: Phrasal Verbs

1. a. verb + preposition — Alice <u>fell down</u> the hole.
   b. transitive phrasal verb — Lois is always <u>making up</u> stories.
   c. intransitive phrasal verb — Last night I just <u>fooled around</u>.
   d. separable phrasal verb — We <u>put</u> our coats <u>on</u>.
   e. inseparable phrasal verb — I'll <u>go over</u> those problems in class tomorrow.
   f. phrasal verb + preposition — I am really <u>put off by</u> a pushy salesperson.
   g. literal phrasal verb — Please <u>pick up</u> your clothes.
   h. aspectual phrasal verb — I <u>fixed up</u> my car.
   i. idiomatic phrasal verb — They all <u>turned up</u> on my doorstep.
   j. phrasal verb that is always separated — The little girl cried her eyes out.

2. a.

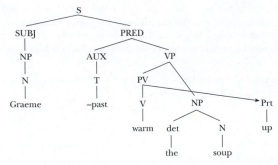

2. b.

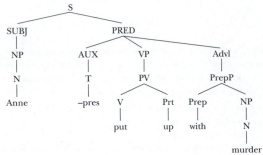

2. c.

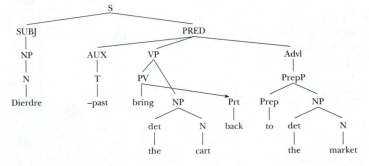

2. d.

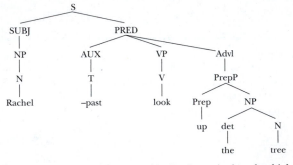

This sentence is ambiguous. A literal reading would be V + Prep via the adverbial option.

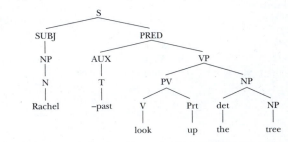

A phrasal reading (i.e. she looked the tree up in a book) would be a phrasal verb (V + Prt), as above.

3. **a.** If *call on* means "to pay an informal visit," it is an inseparable phrasal verb. Alternatively, the wrong form of the particle may have been used. For example, if the meaning of "to telephone" was intended, *up* should have been used.

   b. Even though the particle *over* can be separated from its verb *look*, the direct object is long and complex; so the particle should follow the verb directly.

   c. Indirect object alternation has already been applied to this sentence, implying that the indirect object (*Larry*) is nondominant. In such a case, the verb and its particle will not occur together because it would be in conflict with the fact that the indirect object is nondominant and is being moved forward in the sentence to indicate this. Thus, *I gave Larry back the money* would be correct, as would *I gave Larry the money back*, although the latter reduces the dominance of the direct object slightly since it is no longer sentence-final.

   d. *Show* is occasionally used in this sense (meaning "to appear"), but is ambiguous with the transitive verb. The completive phrasal verb *show up* is more common in this sense.

   e. *Put* would be a more likely verb for this sentence than *place*.

4. **a.** *Put up* is a phrasal verb that occurs with the preposition *with*, which thus needs to be inserted after *up*.

   b. *Discontinued* is a rather formal way of expressing the idea, which would be more typically expressed with a phrasal verb: *broke off*.

   c. The problem here is the particle. We *turn off* (or *put off*, *switch off*, *flick off*) lights, but a candle *burns out* or is *put out* or is *blown out*. A candle can also *burn down*.

   d. *Work out* is an intransitive phrasal verb. Thus the sentence could be *Kim worked out at the gym*, or, if the muscles were important to mention, the noun form should be used: *Kim gave her muscles a workout at the gym*.

   e. A pronoun always goes before the particle of a separable phrasal verb because of its nondominant status (it must refer to something previously mentioned in the discourse).

5. The term "two-word verb" is somewhat inaccurate since some phrasal verbs have three components.

6. Tests for whether it is a verb + preposition:

adverb insertion	*When we got quickly to the station . . .
phrase fronting	*when to the station we got . . .
wh-fronting	*to what did we get?

   Got to fails all these tests and thus is not a verb + preposition.

   Tests for whether it is a phrasal verb:

passivization	*When the station was got to . . .
verb substitution	When we reached the station . . .
NP insertion	*When we got the station to . . .

   Given that *got to* does not pass any of the tests for being a verb + preposition but passes some of those for a phrasal verb, it would appear to be a phrasal verb.

   If we focus on the two tests recommended at the bottom of page 340, *got to* does not pass the first test (NP insertion), meaning that it may be either an inseparable phrasal verb or a verb + preposition (since this test does not distinguish between the two but only eliminates separable phrasal verbs). *Got to* also does not pass the second test (*wh*-fronting) and thus must be an inseparable phrasal verb.

   Fight over passes the adverb insertion test,

   > My brother and I always fought furiously over the prize.

   the phrase fronting test,

   > Over the prize we fought.

   and the *wh*-fronting test

   > Over what did you fight?

   so *fight over* is a verb + preposition.

7. In some poetic or archaic phraseology, it is possible to place certain prepositions after the verb when they are adverbial in nature. In this case, it could be said that English has something resembling postpositions.

8. Library routine:

   I want to take a book out of the library. I finish off my coffee before going into the building. I look the book up on the computer catalog and jot down the call number. I look at the library map to find out where that call number is. I go up the elevator and look for the book on the shelves. The stacks are dark, so I turn on the light. It's hard to pick out the book I want from all the others. After I find the book, I take it to the front desk and check it out. Before I go out, I decide to visit the newspaper section because I like to keep up with events around the world. On my way there, I notice there's going to be a seminar on using the Internet soon, so I sign up for it.

9. check in (to a hotel); grow up (in a place); stand by (your friend); shop around

Chapter 23: Nonreferential *It* and *There* as Subjects

I.
 a. nonreferential *it*   How far is <u>it</u> to the beach?
 b. referential *it*   Have you seen my house key? I can't find <u>it</u>.
 c. deictic *there*   Let's go to the mountains. It's so peaceful <u>there</u>.
 d. nonreferential *there*   <u>There</u> are several issues we need to discuss.
 e. ontological use of *there*   <u>There</u> is a God.
 f. narrative use of *there*   Yesterday, <u>there</u> was this really funny man here.

2.
 a. Nonreferential *it* always uses a singular verb regardless of whether a singular or plural noun follows (in contrast to *there*).
 b. Pronouns in a list following *there* are always object pronouns; thus *I* should be *me* (although native speakers who have been admonished to avoid using the object pronouns in such phrases in subject position may hypercorrect to produce a sentence like this).
 c. *There* should be *it*; nonreferential *it* is used when describing the weather with verbs or adjectives. (However, *There is some sunshine today* would be grammatical—though less common—since it uses a noun phrase.)
 d. Only locative prepositional phrases can be moved to initial position without the use of *there*. Thus, *There are 28 days in the month of February* or *In the month of February there are 28 days* would be more natural.

3. While the transformation works for the example given, it does not always work. For example, there is no corresponding sentence that could have undergone transformation for a sentence like:

> There is no need for that.
> *No need for that is.

Moreover, while such transformations would work for such a sentence if the verb was *exist* (*No need for that exists*), such an option does not exist for the use of *there* in lists or suggestions. For the following example:

> Where's he going to sleep?   Well, there's the couch.

The couch exists is not a suitable paraphrase. Besides the paraphrase problem, the sentences have different uses.

4.
 a. This sentence lacks a surface subject, which every nonimperative, nonelliptical sentence in English requires. Nonreferential *it* is needed here as the subject.
 b. This word order is possible in certain contexts for more concrete descriptions, such as *A pen is on the table*. However, since *a lot of noise* is more abstract, nonreferential *there* is required, in accordance with Bolinger's observation that "The less vividly on stage an action is, the more necessary [nonreferential] *there* becomes."
 c. At first glance, it appears that there is a missing relative pronoun *who*, and indeed the sentence could be corrected in this way. However, if this is produced by a speaker of a topic-comment language, such as Mandarin Chinese, it is possible that the student is using *there* as a topic introducer. Since it is not necessary in English to have a topic introducer, another way to correct the sentence would be to omit *there are* altogether, leaving only *Many tourists visit there*.
 d. *There are a lot of people in my family* would be more appropriate. This sentence may have been produced by a native speaker of Japanese as a way to maintain topic-comment word order.
     By way of comparison, when the object of the sentence is a noun phrase that does not include all members of the subject NP, the sentence is more acceptable; for example,

> Our company has a lot of employees.

 e. *There* and *it* are used in different contexts. *It* is the nonreferential term used in time expressions and should be used in this sentence instead of *there*.

5.
 a. The difference here is one of discourse context: (i) and (ii) could be one piece of information in a longer description where the writer is setting the reader up to expect something to happen. Both sentences are marked; (ii) places more emphasis on the ball by placing it in sentence-final position. (iii) also achieves this latter effect through the use of *there* and may simply be a description without any accompanying expectation being aroused in the reader. It is the more common structure.
 b. The first sentence is more formal than the second and is more likely to be heard on radio or TV than in other contexts. The second sentence, especially in its contracted form, occurs far more frequently and represents the typical usage. (Contraction of *it is* would make it more informal.)

6. This is an area where the language seems to be changing. Many native speakers will accept and even produce *there is* in contracted form (i.e., *there's*) regardless of whether the logical subject of the sentence is singular or plural. This is particularly true in informal speech.

7. In sentences (a) and (b), the sentence is literally locative in meaning, referring more to the "here and now"; it is the type of sentence that could be used as a stage instruction. For this type of utterance, either form expresses the meaning grammatically. However, sentences (c) and (d) are more ontological since *is* could conceivably be replaced by *exists*. The only way to express this grammatically is with nonreferential *there*. This is further evidence against the transformational analysis of nonreferential *there*.

Chapter 24: Coordinating Conjunction

I. a. coordination
My friends bought me dinner and paid for my movie ticket.
John and Mary wanted to visit the ocean.

b. coordinating conjunction
My friends bought me dinner <u>and</u> paid for my movie ticket.
John <u>and</u> Mary wanted to visit the ocean.

c. conjunct
My friends <u>bought me dinner</u> and <u>paid for my movie ticket</u>.
Both <u>John</u> and <u>Mary</u> wanted to visit the ocean.

d. correlative conjunction
My friends <u>both</u> bought me dinner <u>and</u> paid for my movie ticket.
<u>Both</u> John <u>and</u> Mary wanted to visit the ocean.

e. correlative movement
My friends bought me dinner and paid for my movie ticket <u>both</u>.
John and Mary <u>both</u> wanted to visit the ocean.

f. *respectively*-addition
Elizabeth I and Peter the Great ruled England and Russia, <u>respectively</u>.

g. ellipsis
Harry isn't going, and Fred isn't going either.
Harry isn't going, and Fred isn't Ø, either.

h. gapping
She bought a cappuccino, and he Ø an espresso.
She left in a Ford, and he Ø in a Mercedes.

2. a.

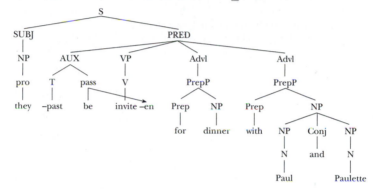

Mapping rules that apply are: copy s/t, and morphological rules.

2. b.

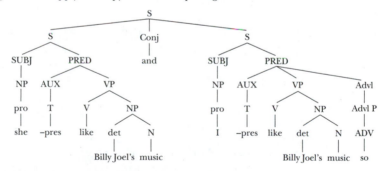

To map to the surface structure, the following rules apply:
copy s/t;
then in the second clause only: ellipsis of VP, operator addition, *so* fronting, and subject-operator inversion.
Finally, morphological rules apply to both clauses.

2. c.

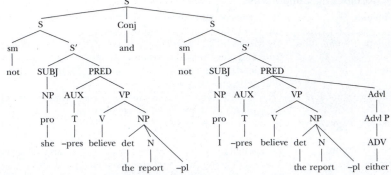

To map to the surface structure, the following rules apply:

> copy s/t for both clauses;
>
> then for the the second clause: ellipsis, operator addition, *not* + *either; neither*-fronting and subject-operator inversion;
>
> then for the first clause: operator addition and *not*-placement.
>
> Finally, morphological rules are applied to the whole sentence.

2. d.

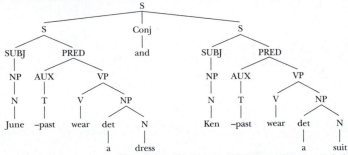

Mapping rules which apply are: copy s/t; gapping (deletion of AUX and V in second clause); and morphological rules.

3. The ambiguity lies in the fact that the sentence may be interpreted either as phrasal conjunction: Pam drinks [coffee and milk] (i.e., mixed together):

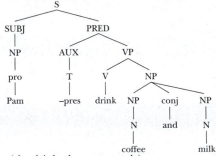

or as sentential conjunction (she drinks them separately):

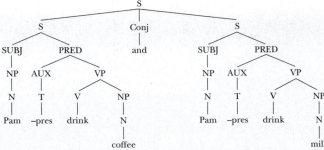

In this second case, ellipsis of the redundant elements in the second clause is required to map the tree onto the surface structure.

4. *Do* can be used to stand for an entire VP, not just a verb, in sentences like the following:

> She [believes the reports that the politician was lying about his involvement with space aliens during his first term of office], and I <u>do</u> too.

5. **a.** Since the conjunction *or* presents alternatives, the sentence will be true as long as one of the alternatives enters into a true statement. In this case, each alternative is a singular proper name. Also in this case, the meaning of the sentence makes it fairly clear that *or* will be interpreted exclusively—that is, it cannot be the case that both Helen and Judy will be the president this year.

    The student who produced this sentence might be told simply that when he/she uses *or* to coordinate NPs and when agreement is an issue, *or* should be accompanied by a singular verb in the sentence as long as the final of the two (or more) conjuncts appears as a singular NP. (Recall that in cases where singular NPs are coordinated with plural NPs, the proximity principle tends to make the verb plural in naturalistic discourse: *Either my mother or my cousins are taking me to the mall.*)

    A supplementary, meaning-based teacher response to this particular error would be to ask the student how many presidents a club or a company is likely to have in one year. Getting "one" as the response, the teacher can then point out that the student has used a plural verb form, which suggests more than one actual president.

    b. The error here lies in the fact that *too*, an adverb that accompanies coordinated affirmative clauses, should be replaced by its negative counterpart, *either*. Students need to become aware that the patterns are "Yes → too," and "No → (n)either."

    The error is somewhat though not completely parallel to what happens to *some* when it appears in a negative sentence and becomes *any*. Since students at the intermediate level are likely to have a fairly good mastery of *some/any* environments, the teacher might exploit the parallel in giving feedback to a student at this level.

    c. Ellipsis here has eliminated not only the VP (as it normally does) but also the AUX (since *could* is not repeated in the second clause), and the result receives mixed acceptability reports from native speakers when AUX is deleted in this way.

    d. *Nor* can act as a simple coordinating conjunction, while *neither* cannot. The proper form here is *nor*, which then requires subject-operator inversion. Students might be given this information and presented with a few examples in spoken use, where *nor* will be heard to coordinate either after rising intonation or after a full stop (falling intonation), but where *neither* will be heard only after falling intonation, as in *You didn't ask me. Neither did I ask you.*

    e. The error is simply that where ellipsis of this sort occurs, there must be some form of adverbial—*too* or *as well*—to complete the proper coordination.

    f. The student has identified the wrong set of relations holding between multiple sentence elements that permit the addition of *respectively*. This adverbial requires the relationship [A & B . . . A & B, respectively], where the first and second items mentioned in the second conjoined set of constituents apply in that order to the first and second items mentioned in the first set of constituents. (The adverbial *conversely* could be used properly, before "Bill paid Fred" in the sentence that the student has produced.)

    The student could be shown what sort of pattern he/she would need to produce in order to use *respectively* properly. Taking the student's own sentence and changing it substantially might get, for example, "Fred and Bill paid Mary and Julie, respectively." The student can compare the semantic relations here with those in their original sentence and see the differences.

6. Yes, they can. For example:

> They cleaned both inside and outside the house.
> They looked up and down the street.
> This is a government of, for, and by the people.
> Drinks will be served before, after, and during the show.
> I've been in and out of the house all day.

7. **a.** The following categories can all be co-ordinated with *not only . . . but also*:

V + V	They not only hiked but also skied on their trip.
VP + VP	They not only hiked in the Ardennes but also skied in the Alps.
AP + AP	The hotel was not only very expensive but also hard to reach.
Prep + Prep	The guests were not only inside but also outside the house.
PrepP + PrepP	The guests were not only in our house but also on the veranda.
AdvP + AdvP	The guests left not only very quickly but also very quietly.

N + N cannot be successfully co-ordinated with *not only . . . but also*; only NPs can be. For example:

N + N	*We have not only a truck but also station wagon.
NP + NP	We have not only a truck but also a station wagon.

Sentences/clauses may not be coordinated in this way without additional changes, as discussed under (b):

    S' + S'   *Not only you helped me out but also you gave me some new ideas.

b. An example that is truly clause-to-clause requires subject-operator inversion because of the presence of negation in the first correlative:

Not only could you comfort me but also you could help me.
Not only did she get a scholarship but she also got a teaching job.

In addition, the sentence sounds more natural if *also* is moved to follow the subject.

8. In both sentences, it appears that two unlike constituents are being coordinated. In the first sentence, it looks as if an AP is being coordinated with a PP; in the second, we seem to have a [VP + AdvP] coordination.

For the first sentence, our PS rules will permit VP to expand with a copula followed by one of three types of constituents:

$$VP \rightarrow cop \begin{Bmatrix} NP \\ AP \\ PrepP \end{Bmatrix} \begin{matrix} \text{Example: Mary is an architect.} \\ \text{Example: John is penniless.} \\ \text{Example: John is without visible means of support.} \end{matrix}$$

It seems possible to place any two of these three constituents side by side when followed by a copula and get a fairly good-sounding sentence as a result:

Mary is an architect, and very knowledgeable. (NP + AP)
The kitten is a Persian, and of very pure breeding. (NP + PrepP)
John was penniless and without visible means of support. (AP + PrepP)

If coordination of these pairs of constituents is possible, there seems a violation of the rule that only like constituents can be coordinated.

One solution might be to somehow revise the PS rules in order to make these constituents into "identical types" of constituent. Another solution might be to loosen the requirements for coordination somewhat. However, a third solution is available if we entertain the idea that we do not actually have the types of phrasal coordination noted above. The fact that the first two sentences above sound better with pauses (which are at least partially suggested by the use of commas) following the words *architect* and *Persian* makes them distinct, since we do not see a comma (or hear a pause) in sentences with simple NP coordination like

    *Mary, and John went to the circus

or AP coordination like

    *This friendly, and intelligent woman has just given me some advice.

A plausible explanation is that a type of ellipsis not discussed in this chapter has taken place in all these cases. This type of ellipsis would delete all identical material toward the beginning of sentences rather than at the end under VP.

[Mary is] an architect, and [Mary is] very knowledgeable.
[The kitten is] a Persian, and [the kitten is] of very pure breeding.
[John was] penniless, and [John was] without visible means of support.

This kind of ellipsis would likely have to take place in at least two steps each time. The reason becomes clear when trees are drawn for the relevant coordinated full clauses: we will need to delete an element from subject position and an element from the AUX position under PRED—rather than following a simple rule like "delete the VP," which we saw for other ellipsis. It has been traditionally assumed in syntactic theory that a single rule will not involve operations both on full constituents and parts of other, different constituents at the same time.

If we assume that ellipsis operates on the sentences above, then we have a way to explain the other problem sentence in the exercise, *They finished the freeway construction, and quickly.* For this sentence, we get the base construction:

[They finished the freeway construction], and [they finished the freeway construction] quickly.

Since the only element not common to the two sentences is the word *quickly*, a series of deletions occurs to cut the sentence down considerably, leaving a comma in its wake.

9. The most reasonable explanation might be to say that since *and* alternates with *or* in affirmative/negative structures, native speakers already take the *or* here to be negative and tend to reserve *nor* for more formal discourse contexts such as writing.

10. For a student at the intermediate level of instruction, a teacher might not want to respond at all to issues of cohesion, since the entire text is quite clearly written. However, for a student in a writing class who is planning to go on to higher levels of writing instruction, the student should know that the stringing together of multiple uses of *and* and its synonyms from sentence to sentence does not produce normal-sounding academic prose. At the very least, there are many other cohesive devices more specific than *and* to the functions that the writer is trying to perform in the narrative. Specifically, these include relative clauses. The sequence

> We began our bicycle trip from my brother's house, and he lived not so far from the mountains . . .

can be changed to

> We began our bicycle trip from the house of my brother, who lived not far from the mountains . . .

Likewise, the sequence

> . . . after about one half-hour we reached the mountains, and it was cooler there . . .

can be changed to read

> . . . after about one half-hour we reached the mountains, where it was cooler . . .

The teacher can explain to the student that while the prose is grammatical, it is difficult to derive the full effect of a word such as *and* if it is repeated endlessly.

Chapter 25: Adverbials

1. **a.** sentence-initial
   - (i) adverbial phrase   <u>Reluctantly</u>, I went through the records.
   - (ii) prepositional phrase   <u>To please Henry</u>, I went through the records.
   - (iii) adverbial clause   <u>When no one else agreed to</u>, I went through the records.

   b. sentence-final
   - (i) adverbial phrase   I went through the records <u>methodically</u>.
   - (ii) prepositional phrase   I went through the records <u>in the office</u>.
   - (iii) adverbial clause   I went through the records <u>when I was asked to</u>.

   c. specific or general adverbial of frequency
   - specific   Lorraine jogs five miles <u>every week</u>.
   - general   Lorraine jogs <u>on occasion</u>.

   d. preverbal adverb of frequency
   - (i) positive   I <u>often</u> see her brother on campus.
   - (ii) negative   He <u>rarely</u> comes to visit.

   e. phrasal preverbal adverb of frequency
   - (i) positive   Beth is <u>almost always</u> on time.
   - (ii) negative   She is <u>not usually</u> late.

   f. adverbial participle   <u>Having been up all night</u>, Beth was late this morning.

2. **a.** It should be *Isn't he ever . . .* or *Is he not ever. . . . Not ever* placement patterns like *not* placement; only if contracted does the *not* stay together with the operator in subject-operator inversion.

   b. The preverbal adverb of frequency can separate only an auxiliary verb that occurs in the nucleus or the *be* copula from *not*. Since in this case neither of these underlying forms is present, only two orders are possible:

   > Marvin does not often dance.   Marvin often does not dance.

   c. The answer is not given in a full sentence; rather, it occurs in a reduced clause. In such cases, preverbal adverbs of frequency cannot be the final constituent. The order should be *I never am.* Alternatively, the response could be even further reduced to "No, never" or simply "No" or "Never" without the subject pronoun and copula being present.

3. **a.** If the nucleus contains an unstressed auxiliary verb, place the preverbal adverb of frequency after it. Thus, this sentence should be:

   > José can sometimes play handball after work.

   b. If a negative preverbal adverb of frequency has been fronted, subject/auxiliary inversion must take place:

   > Rarely can we eat outside in the garden!

   Alternatively, the preverbal adverb of frequency could be placed after the first auxiliary verb in the nucleus:

   > We can rarely eat outside in the garden.

   This second form should be used if emphasis (i.e., exclamation) is not intended.

   c. *Fluently* is a sentence-final adverbial. A correct sentence would be either *I speak French fluently,* or *I speak fluently.*

   d. Adverbials of direction or goal (*to seafood restaurants*) come before adverbs of position (*in Boston*).

   e. This is the classic "dangling participle" since the subject of the adverbial participle is not the same as the subject of the main clause (presumably, it is the little girl who is crying hysterically). Since the main clause of this sentence cannot be very easily expressed in the passive, the adverbial participle would have to be changed to a more explicit adverbial clause such as *As the little girl was crying hysterically, the mother tried to calm her down*. Alternatively, the main clause would have to be changed to a different proposition to enable *the little girl* to become the subject: *Crying hysterically, the little girl resisted all attempts by her mother to calm her down*.

4. **a.** The second sentence emphasizes the absolute frequency with which Alice uses dental floss, although both sentences indicate her use of dental floss is habitual.

   b. There is no difference in meaning between these sentences since adverbs of frequency modify the whole sentence regardless of their position, but there is a subtle difference in emphasis and likely use. The sentence-initial position makes *sometimes* more salient since it more often occurs medially, especially in conversation.

   c. Again, there is little if any difference in meaning between these two sentences, with the sentence-initial position for the adverbial clause giving more salience to it. The sentence-final position is more common in conversation. The sentence-initial position can also be used to tie the utterance back to previous discourse or to signal a shift in topic.

5. **a.** Probably speaker A expects more specific information about the frequency of B's trips to the beach. B should preferably use an adverb expressing specific or at least general frequency. For example:

   (best) specific   *B:* Every weekend.
   (acceptable) general   *B:* Whenever I have the time.

   b. Speaker A is asking a yes/no question. Appropriate answers would be:

   No, but I hope to go there some day.   Yes, I've been there twice.

6. In sentence (b), the preverbal adverb of frequency precedes the auxiliary verb, which means that the auxiliary carries emphatic or contrastive stress. In sentence (a), the auxiliary verb has reduced stress, and the sentence is in the unmarked form; that is, it is not emphatic.

7. Time adverbials (*at 10 p.m.*) usually come before adverbials of frequency (*every day*) so sentence (a) is the more common. Sentence (b) is not incorrect, however, but it is more unusual and makes the time adverbial sound more like an afterthought. The student should be advised to keep to the order in sentence (a) if in doubt.

Chapter 26: Logical Connectors

1. **a.** Adverbial subordinator   She attends dance class *because* she likes the exercise.

   b. Conjunctive adverbial   She likes basketball; *however*, she prefers volleyball.

   c. Concessive connector   *Although* she is late, I still believe she'll be here.

   d. Time connector   *Whenever* vacation comes, I get a cold.

   e. Purpose connector   He went to summer camp *so that* he would learn to play basketball well.

   f. Causal connector   *Consequently*, he got a basketball scholarship.

   g. Inferential connector   They had a lot in common *so* they became good friends.

2. a.

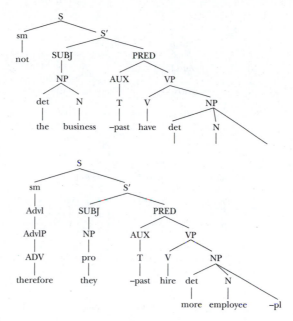

Note: The redundant head noun in the final NP of the second sentence is deleted through ellipsis when mapping to the surface structure.

2. b.

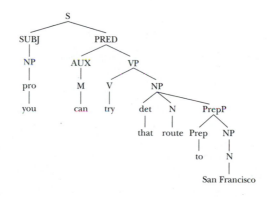

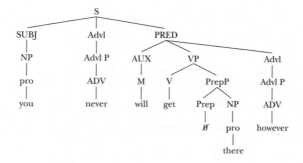

Note: In the second sentence, adverbial movement (of *never* to follow *will*) is needed for mapping to the surface structure.

2. c.

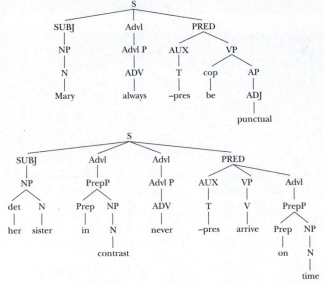

Note: In the first sentence, adverbial movement of *always* to follow *be* is needed for mapping to the surface structure.

2. d.

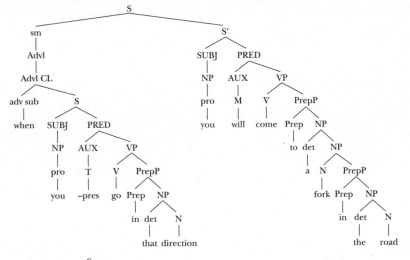

2. e.

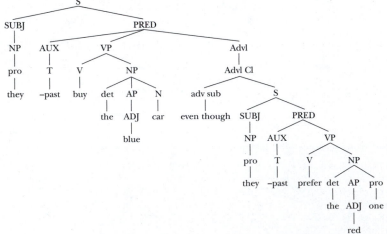

3. a. The error is one of meaning/use. *On the contrary* is not appropriate here since it most often signals that there is a contradiction between the truth of some proposition expressed in an initial sentence and the truth of that in the following sentence in which the adverbial occurs. The contradictory proposition is implied more often than stated: *This is not a Burgundy; on the contrary, it is a Beaujolais.* The speaker seems to be implying that someone believes or has believed the contradictory proposition (that the wine is a Burgundy).

b. The error is one of form. Specifically, the comma after the word *class* suggests that there is rising intonation at the end of this clause, but in fact the normal reading is one with falling, end-of-sentence intonation. The comma should be replaced by a period (full stop).

c. The error is again one of form, related to the implications of punctuation for intonation. There is normally no rising intonation before the word *although*, and there is no rising intonation after *although;* and so no commas should be used.

d. The error is one of meaning/use. The use of *nevertheless* suggests that there is a denial of expectations created in the first clause by the content of the second clause. However, no expectations are reasonably created by the first clause: to say that crystal glasses break very easily suggests nothing about the fragility of plastic glasses.

e. The error is one of form. *While* is an adverbial subordinator, and thus the clause that follows it is a subordinate clause, which can't stand alone.

4. In the two examples given, *plus* cannot be an adverbial subordinator, since the period at the end of the prior sentence marks falling intonation, and adverbial clauses do not normally stand alone as full sentences. Moreover, we could not reverse the order of the two clauses, beginning the sentence with *plus*, and get an acceptable sentence as a result.

It is also doubtful that *plus* is a conjunctive adverbial. This is so because it does not seem that we can insert the *plus* at any point other than S-initial position and get an acceptable sentence as a result:

> They had to drive five miles out of the way.
> ?They, plus, had to drive through the mud.
> ?They had to drive through the mud, plus.

(However, if native speakers actually judge these sequences as acceptable, that constitutes evidence of conjunctive adverbial status.)

If *plus* fails these two tests, we are led to classify the word as a coordinating conjunction.

5. a. A student who produces this sort of sequence may be told that there are both form and meaning reasons to avoid it. Formally, an *although*-clause is grammatically subordinate to the other clause; formally, a *but*-clause is grammatically equal to the other clause. There is, therefore, a formal contradiction when *although* and *but* are used together in this way.

As far as meaning is concerned, the student can be told that while one can express simple additive relationships with correlative conjunctions, one cannot express contrastive relationships in this way. The effect of juxtaposing *although* and *but* is a highly confusing one for native speakers, since it seems as if two contrasts are somehow involved, when only one is actually intended.

b. It might be worthwhile to explain orally to a student that commas are regularly associated with a single kind of intonation in most structural positions—specifically a rising intonation, which is not used with *as a result* by native speakers. If the student is fairly fluent in the spoken language, a teacher can model the sentence with a somewhat exaggerated intonation contour and then ask the student if they actually hear this intonation in this context (just prior to *as a result*). If the student is not very fluent in the spoken language, the teacher can at least explain and model the relationship between intonation and punctuation.

c. The error here is that the wrong connector is used. The student can be told that when *on the contrary* is used, we expect some overt marker of negation to occur in the first clause, and we also expect there to be some implication of falsehood associated with the first clause. If the student simply wants to contrast two people or things, a proper connector would be *in contrast*.

d. The error here is similar to that in sentence (a): while *if* is a subordinating word, *so* is a coordinating word. To connect the clauses in this way creates a formal contradiction, although the effect on meaning does not seem so severe as in sentence (a).

e. The student seems to understand the contribution of *even* to the sentence but may not be aware that when it occurs before a clause, *even* must appear in the combination *even if, even when, even after, even before*, prefacing an adverbial clause. It may simply be pointed out that there is a syntactic difference between *even* and *even if*, and a few contrastive model sentences may be shown to the student:

> Even my friend is here.　　We work even on Sundays.
> (even + NP)　　　　　　　　(even + PrepP)
> Even before you left,　　I was worried about you.
> (*even before* + adverbial clause)

Even if my friend is here,   I won't be happy.
(*even* + adverbial clause)

6. It is not necessarily easy to explain to a student why advertisers, novelists, or news columnists may take liberties that student writers are not supposed to take in academic writing. One reason for punctuating sentence fragments in this way may be to highlight or stress both clauses for dramatic effect. In the deodorant ad, both the product and the reason for using it are stressed by means of short, pointed statements; one does not feel that the reason-clause is subordinated in the same way as *because*-clauses are normally subordinated. Why is it not possible for a writer of formal academic discourse to follow the same pattern of writing adverbial clauses? It simply seems to be the case that effecting a sense of equal stress in this way is not a prescriptive option in formal academic writing.

Another reason for punctuating in this way may be to achieve the effect of an afterthought clause, a clause which was not originally planned for when the clause prior to it was written. In such cases, a teacher might point out to students that in highly planned discourse, writers do not usually present clauses with the intention of signaling to the reader that a certain clause was intended as an unplanned afterthought.

7. Such student writing, overfilled with cohesive expressions, is commonly seen where teachers have overstressed the need for such devices to mark meaning relationships among sentences. One way to begin would be to ask the student to eliminate exactly half of the expressions, asking with each eliminated expression whether the intended meaning relationship is adequately conveyed without the expression. (Of course the teacher's personal judgement will be of great value here.) It would also be worthwhile to point out to the student that one does not normally use the expression *moreover* in simple lists of items; there must be a more complicated relationship, one most often involving evidential support, for this expression to be used effectively.

Another possibility would be to present the writer with a page or two of fairly formal expository prose and ask the student to locate all of the "logical connectors" or "transitional expressions" in the sample text. After underlining them, the student might calculate the relative frequency-per-page of these expressions and see that it is quite possible to be a coherent writer without using them to excess.

Chapter 27: Conditional Sentences

1. **a.** factual conditional
     (i) generic   Water freezes if the temperature gets to $0°C$.
     (ii) implicit inference   If it's 9 o'clock, the library is closed.
   b. future conditional
     (i) weakened result clause   If the snow keeps melting so fast, <u>there may be a flood</u>.
     (ii) weakened *if* clause   <u>If it happens to be nice on Friday</u>, we can always go sailing.
   c. counterfactual conditional   If there had been less snow cover, the bulbs would have suffered greater damage.
   d. contrastive use of a conditional   I'll let you off this time, but <u>if you do it again, you're really in for it</u>.
   e. subjunctive use of *were*   If that dog <u>were</u> here now, you would know it.
   f. *then* insertion   If you don't think that's funny, <u>then</u> you missed the point.
   g. *if* deletion with subject/ auxiliary inversion   <u>Had we</u> only known, we would have been there.
   h. conditional clause pro-form   Do you have a reservation? <u>If so</u>, go right in.
   i. sarcastic use of conditional   If you had any brains, you'd be dangerous.
   j. hypothetical conditional   If I felt more energetic, I would weed the garden.

2. **a.**

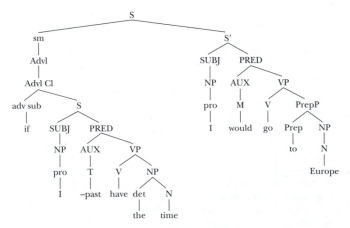

Mapping rules which apply are: copy s/t and morphological rules.

2. b.

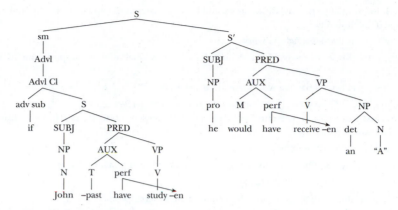

Mapping rules which apply are: copy s/t; *then* addition and morphological rules.

3. c.

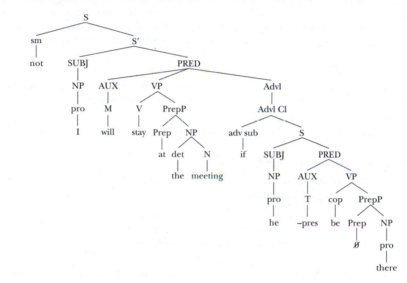

Mapping rules which apply are: copy s/t, *not* placement, and morphological rules.

3. d.

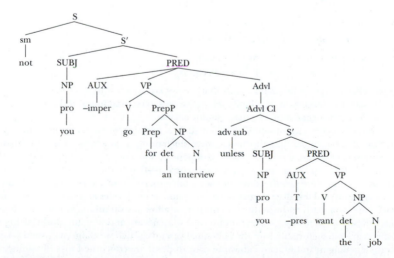

Mapping rules which apply are: copy s/t; operator addition; *not* placement; *not* contraction; subject deletion and morphological rules.

3. a. Implicit inferential factual conditionals should have the same tense and aspect or modal in both clauses. This should be:

> If she was there, she did the work.

Alternatively, this sentence may be a counterfactual conditional referring to past time, in which case it should be:

> If she had been there, she would have done the work.

where the main clause should contain *would* + the present perfect tense.

b. The normal pattern for future conditionals is to have a present tense in the *if* clause. Thus, this sentence should read:

> If John is free, I'll invite him.

Alternatively, the conditional clause could be weakened by using *should,* not *might:*

> If John should be free, I'll invite him.

c. The *if* clause almost always precedes the result clause in sarcastic speech.

d. This *if* clause really does not mean "on the condition" so much as "on the assumption." In such cases of "strong deductions," the *if* clause precedes the *then* clause. Even if the *if* clause is not fronted, *then* does not typically begin a conditional sentence; that is, the *then* insertion rule should not have been applied. The only circumstance in which this sentence might be acceptable is a conversation in which the speaker is trying to elicit a deduction from the other person, and in this context the sentence would be an uninverted yes/no question:

> Then he'll keep his word if he made a promise?

4. a. The subjunctive *were* does not occur in a main clause. In counterfactual conditionals such as this, the students need to be aware of the necessity to use *would* in the result clause:

> If I were an American, I would be speaking better English.

b. In hypothetical conditional sentences, the modal *would* is used in the main clause, even when the sentence refers to present time:

> What would happen if I pushed this button?

Another possibility is that this sentence could contain a generic factual conditional:

> What happens if I push this button?

c. The same tense should be used in both clauses of this factual conditional. Since this is a habitual factual, and the "habit" still obtains, present tense should be used:

> Why do some Americans say "Gesundheit" if someone sneezes?

d. There are three possible ways to correct this sentence:

> **(i)** Since the *only if* adverbial clause has been fronted, subject/operator inversion is necessary in the main clause:
>
>> Only if you help me will I study for the quiz.

> **(ii)** Do not front the *only if* adverbial clause:
>
>> I will study for the quiz only if you help me.

> **(iii)** Weaken the condition by dropping *only:*
>
>> If you help me, I will study for the quiz.

5. Both of these sentences are colloquial variants that are not consistent with what traditional grammar prescribes. Prescriptive usage would call for subjunctive *were* to be used in the *if* clause in the first sentence, since it is a present counterfactual conditional clause.

The second sentence is a hypothetical conditional. Prescriptive usage would lead one to expect a simple past tense in the *if* clause, rather than the modal *would* which results in a "double *would* construction."

Thus, your answer to your student's question depends upon a definition of correctness. The sentences your student reports are not prescriptively correct—that is, they do not adhere to the rules in a grammar book—but they are produced by, and acceptable to, native speakers in informal conversation.

We have encountered this discrepancy between grammar book rules and native speaker usage many times. Which rules you teach and whether you present or allow any variation from these will presumably depend upon how *you* use the language and who your students are and why they are studying English. For example, if you are uncomfortable with the colloquial variants, which we claim many native speakers use, and if you are teaching in an EFL context where your students are concerned with obtaining a high score on a standardized language proficiency examination, then perhaps only the prescriptive rules should be presented and practiced. On the other hand, if your students are adult immigrants in an ESL situation, perhaps you would choose to teach both the prescriptive rules and colloquial variants.

6. Answers will vary.
7. This is a future conditional. It is more complicated than those described in this chapter since the main clause contains both the *will* modal to signal future time and the *have to* phrasal modal to signal necessity. Phrasal modals may be used in the main clause of a conditional to express additional meaning—in this case, the phrasal modal expresses the necessity of father's mowing the lawn.

Chapter 28: Introduction to Relative Clauses

1. a. restrictive relative clause   She's the one <u>who has the books in her arms</u>.
    b. relativized object of a preposition   Isn't she the one about <u>whom</u> you asked?
    c. relativized subject   The teacher <u>who</u> left was unhappy.
    d. relative pronoun substitution   The package (<u>the package</u> arrived yesterday) is for Christmas. → The package (<u>which</u> arrived yesterday) is for Christmas.
    e. relative pronoun deletion   Sally raved about the sale <u>that</u> they are having downtown. → Sally raved about the sale <u>Ø</u> they are having downtown.
    f. relativized possessive determiner   Julie is the student <u>whose</u> birthday we'll be celebrating next week.

2. a.

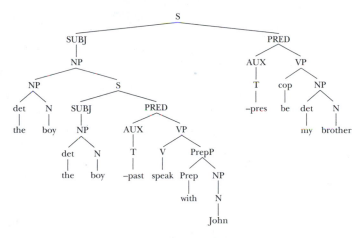

Mapping rules which apply are: copy s/t; relative pronoun substitution; and morphological rules.

2. b.

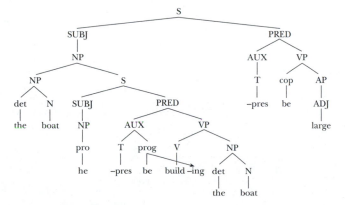

Mapping rules that apply are: copy s/t; relative pronoun substitution; relative pronoun fronting; relative pronoun deletion; and morphological rules.

2. c.

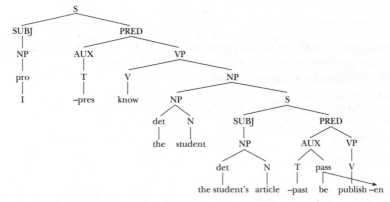

Mapping rules which apply are: copy s/t; relative determiner substitution; and morphological rules.

2. d.

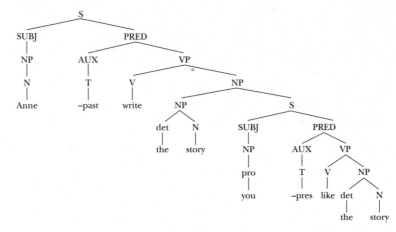

Mapping rules which apply are: copy s/t; relative pronoun substitution; relative pronoun fronting; relative pronoun deletion; and morphological rules.

2. e.

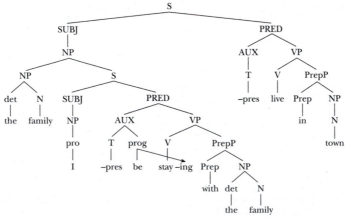

Mapping rules which apply are: copy s/t; relative pronoun substitution; relative pronoun (and preposition) fronting; and morphological rules.

3. a. *Who* is a relative pronoun that substitutes for NPs marked (+ human). *Which* or *that* would be appropriate relative pronouns to substitute for the (− human) subject *river.*

　　b. The relative pronoun *that* cannot be used to replace the relativized object of a preposition if the preposition is fronted with, and thus precedes, the relative pronoun. *Whom* should be used as the relative pronoun in this sentence since the antecedent is (+ human).

c. The noun *story* must be fronted along with the relativized determiner *whose* when relative pronoun fronting takes place since *whose* modifies the head noun *story*.

4. a. *Whom* should be *who* or *that*, since the relative pronoun that is being replaced in the embedded sentence is the subject. *Whom* replaces (+ human) NPs only in object position.

b. The pronoun *him* should be deleted since *who* (or more formally, *whom*) was substituted for *the boy* and was then fronted within the embedded sentence. Several languages can retain a pronominal reflex of a relative pronoun, and so this sentence may be the result of interference from the student's first language.

c. The relative pronoun *who*, which is the subject of the embedded sentence, has been deleted. Subject relative pronouns are not deletable; however, relativized objects are.

d. The embedded sentence *that she is wrapping* must be placed after the noun that it is modifying (i.e., *the package*). Not all languages have the relative clause following the noun it modifies as does English.

e. *They are friendly* could be an embedded sentence or a conjoined sentence; if it is an embedded sentence, its subject is coreferential with the object of the main sentence, *people*. Thus, the pronoun *they* should be replaced by the relative pronoun *who* or *that*.

5. In the first sentence, the person (the stranger) called you; and in the second sentence, you called the person (the stranger). Structurally, this means that in the first sentence, the relative pronoun replaced the subject of the embedded sentence; in the second sentence, the relative pronoun replaced the object of the embedded sentence.

6. The writer of the editorial may be confusing *that* with *which*. In fact, *that* can be used with either human or nonhuman antecedents, although in formal written English, *who* may be preferred for humans. Some confusion may also have arisen here due to the fact that the newspaper is quoting (in writing) what Smith produced when speaking; thus, while his use of *that* probably escaped notice during the actual interview (since it is common usage), once it is in the written form it has become subject to an overly prescriptive editorial standard.

Chapter 29: More on Relative Clauses

I. a. relative adverb substitution — If we only knew the place <u>where</u> we were going to stay, I would rest more easily.

b. free relative substitution — I had to think about <u>what</u> she had told me.

c. relative pronoun + *be* deletion — The boy doing handsprings is my son. (*who is* has been deleted before *doing*)

d. head noun deletion — I'm trying to remember where we met each other. (*the place* has been deleted before *where*)

e. relative adverb deletion — By the time (<u>when</u>) I arrived, the excitement was over.

f. appositive — Amherst, <u>a center of higher education</u>, is a home for several major colleges.

g. nonrestrictive relative clause
  (i) appositive type — Chris, <u>who is a Beethoven fan</u>, appreciates classical music.
  (ii) commentary type — He also likes jazz, which is lucky.

2. a.

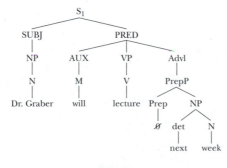
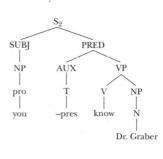

Mapping rules which apply are: copy s/t; nonrestrictive embedding, relative pronoun substitution; relative pronoun fronting; and morphological rules.

2. b.

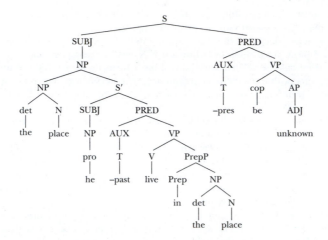

Mapping rules which apply are: copy s/t; relative pronoun substitution; relative pronoun fronting (with preposition); relative adverb substitution; and morphological rules.

2. c.

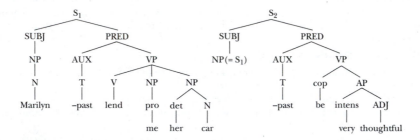

Mapping rules which apply are: copy s/t; nonrestrictive embedding; relative pronoun substitution; and morphological rules.

2. d.

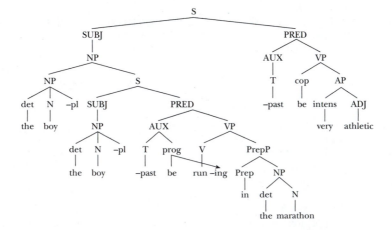

Mapping rules which apply are: copy s/t, relative pronoun substitution; relative pronoun + *be* deletion; and morphological rules.

2. e.

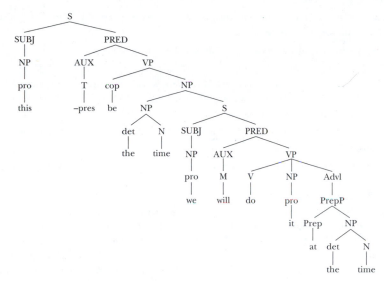

Mapping rules which apply are: copy s/t; relative pronoun substitution; relative pronoun fronting (with preposition), relative adverb substitution; relative adverb deletion; and morphological rules.

3. a. The relative adverb *when* is supposed to substitute for the preposition + relative pronoun. When relative adverb substitution is properly applied, the following sentence results:

> Christmas is the time when he's busiest.

If relative adverb substitution does not occur, the preposition + relative pronoun would be retained:

> Christmas is the time at which he's busiest.

One could have a sentence without either form (i.e., Christmas is the time he's busiest) but not one with both!

b. A nonrestrictive clause may not modify a head noun preceded by the generic determiner *any*. A restrictive clause should be used.

c. There are three possible reasons for the ungrammaticality:

(i) Relative pronoun deletion took place, and the preposition was incorrectly deleted along with the relative pronoun. If the preposition had not also been deleted, the following would have been produced:

> This is the office I work in.

(ii) Of course, if relative pronoun deletion had not occurred, a grammatical sentence would also have resulted:

> This is the office which I work in.   This is the office in which I work.

(iii) Finally, this sentence may be ungrammatical because the relative adverb *where*, which replaced *in + which*, was incorrectly deleted. If this had not occurred, the sentence would have been:

> This is the office where I work.

d. The inanimate relative pronoun *which* has been used to refer to human engineers; *whom* should be used instead.

e. When the head noun (*the time*) is the object of a preposition (*by*), the relative adverb (*when*) is ungrammatical. No pronoun, or *that* could be used here:

> Bert will have raised $20,000 by the time (that) the fundraising ends.

Alternatively, *when* could be used to replace the entire PrepP:

> Bert will have raised $20,000 when the fundraising ends.

4. a. *Which* is a relative pronoun that substitutes for NPs marked (– human) or for entire clauses. Since *Mr. Hall* is the antecedent for the relative pronoun, *who*, the relative pronoun marked (+ human), would be the correct substitution.

b. If the relative adverb substitution rule replaces the preposition + relative pronoun with *how*, then the head noun deletion rule must be applied:

> That is how he drives.

Alternatively, the head noun could be retained if the relative adverb substitution rule was not applied:

> That is the way in which he drives.

Or, the preposition + relative pronoun could be deleted to produce:

> That is the way he drives.

c.   The head noun deletion rule replaces *the thing (that/which)* with *what*. The student would have been correct if the head noun *the thing* had been retained with *that* or *which* as the relative pronoun:

> Cooking is the thing that he enjoys.

Another correct sentence would have resulted if the relative pronoun had been deleted:

> Cooking is the thing he enjoys.

Finally, the sentence would have been correct if the student had deleted the head noun and used *what*:

> Cooking is what he enjoys.

5.   The first sentence implies that the speaker has only one sister (or at least only one sister relevant to the discourse); the fact that she lives in Chicago is incidental information. The second sentence implies that the speaker has more than one sister relevant to the discourse, one of whom lives in Chicago; the fact that she lives in Chicago is a way of distinguishing her from the other sisters, rather than just giving extra information.

6.   The last sentence (with *the reason for which*) appears to be the most formal. The next most formal is the second sentence (with *the reason why*). The other two seem the least formal, with the first sentence (with *why*) occurring more frequently than the third (with *the reason*).

Chapter 30: Focus and Emphasis

1. **a.** *wh*-cleft   What we want is complete compliance.
    b. *it*-cleft   It's the coach that calls the shots.
    c. fronting of a directional adverbial   <u>Up the hill</u> they ran.
    d. emphatic *do*   The Thanksgiving turkey <u>did</u> look wonderful.
    e. emphatic reflexive   The author <u>himself</u> did not expect the acclaim his book received.
    f. emphatic possessive   She used up some of her <u>own</u> assets in her unsuccessful bid for state office.

2. **a.** The adverbial of position *on his car* has been fronted in this sentence, but the copula *be* is ungrammatical in sentence-final position. Thus subject/auxiliary inversion must take place to produce:

> On his car is a bumper sticker . . .

   b. A *wh*-cleft requires *be* after the *wh*-phrase; thus, the sentence should read: "What we meant to say was/is we are sorry."

   c. *He* cannot be used in fronting a cleft construction. Only *it* can be used as a pronoun in an *it*-cleft construction.

3. **a.** This could be either a cleft sentence or a sentence with a relative clause. If it is a cleft sentence, we understand that the speaker is underscoring the fact that the graduate student corrects the papers; the professor doesn't. If it is a sentence with a relative clause, we understand that we are singling out the graduate student who corrects the papers in our class from all other graduate students.

   b. The ambiguity involves the antecedent of *himself*. Does *himself* emphasize our chairman (acting on his own) or the dean (someone presumably above reproach)? Of course, if the dean were known to be a woman, the ambiguity would not be there.

4. **a.** This is a sentence with a free relative. In *wh*-clefts, the *wh*-word can occur only sentence-initially. Free relatives can occur in any NP position.

   b. This is a *wh*-cleft. The emphasis is on the NP that follows the copula *be*. Notice that this is an emphatic counterpart to the neutral sentence: He told a big lie.

   c. This is a sentence with a free relative. What follows the *be* does not identify "what he said" but merely comments on it. Furthermore, this could not come from the neutral sentence:

> *He said of little concern to us.

   d. This is a *wh*-cleft. What follows the copula *be* is emphasized. We can easily reconstruct an equivalent neutral sentence:

> He said that you are a jerk.

5. **a.** When a negative preverbal adverb of frequency is fronted, subject-auxiliary inversion must take place. This sentence should be:

> Never have I tasted such a delicious sandwich!

b. This is an incorrect form of a *wh*-cleft. The emphatic constituent following the *be* copula is not a person; therefore the *wh*-word should not be *who*. The *wh*-word should be *what* instead:

What you mean is that Oscar did it.

c. When a participle phrase is fronted, subject-operator inversion is required:

Sitting on the front porch was my long-lost brother.

6. Answers will vary.

7. a. Sentence (1) is the emphatic or *wh*-cleft equivalent of sentence (2). One could imagine (1) being said after the speaker had already said (2), and the listener then asked for repetition.

b. In sentence (2), the adverbial has been fronted as compared with sentence (1). In sentence (2) the delayed subject receives more focus than the normal subject does in sentence (1). Gary (1974) suggests that a sentence like (2) would be more apt to be chosen when the speaker or writer has made the listener or reader expect that someone other than the missing child would be standing in the corner.

c. Sentence (1) is a normal affirmative imperative; sentence (2) is an imperative with emphatic *do*. The *do* receives strong stress and gives affirmative emphasis to the invitation.

d. Sentence (2) contains emphatic *own* before the object NP; sentence (1) is unmarked in this respect. One could imagine sentence (2) being uttered in a context in which the speaker was annoyed that Jim was always borrowing the speaker's (or someone else's) book.

Chapter 31: Complementation

1. a.	complement	John thinks that Bob is funny.
b.	complementizer	John thinks that Bob is funny.
c.	tensed *that*-clause	Everyone knows that the earth is round.
d.	subjunctive clause	I urged that he go there.
e.	infinitive	He wanted to go there.
f.	subject control	We failed to finish the job.
g.	PRO	We asked the professor [PRO] to repeat the question.
h.	gerund	I regret telling her the news.
i.	subject + participle construction	I saw John crossing the street.
j.	purpose infinitive	We stopped to see my cousin.
k.	object control	I advised John to stay home.
l.	progressive infinitive	It's a good time to be working.
m.	perfect infinitive	She wants to have finished the project by next week.
n.	the Bolinger principle (for gerunds vs. infinitives)	I regret to inform you that you didn't pass. I regret informing you that you didn't pass.

2. a.

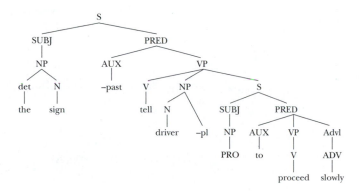

2. b.

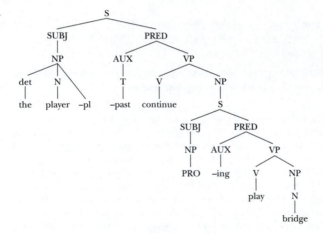

2. c.

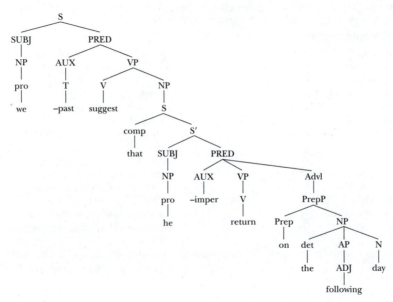

2. d.

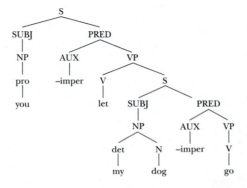

Note: By applying the *you* deletion rule and morphological rules, the surface structure is realized.

2. e.

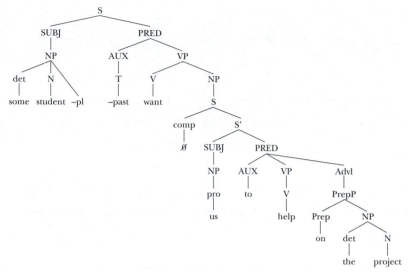

2. f.

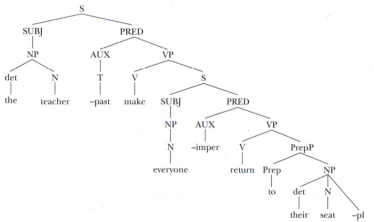

2. g.

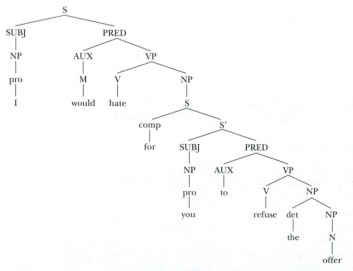

2. h.

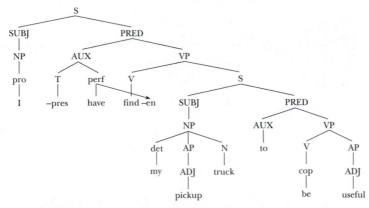

3. a. The verb *want* requires an infinitival complement; it cannot take a *that*-complement.

  b. The verb *insist* requires a *that*-clause complement—in this case, a subjunctive clause.

  c. The verb *force*, although it is a semantically highly manipulative verb, requires a *to*-infinitive as its complement.

  d. The verb *understand* falls into the *believe*-type class of verbs, not the *want*-class. It requires either a tensed *that*-complement or an infinitival complement with *myself* instead of *for me*.

  e. The word *over* is a preposition that requires an NP object. Only a gerund can appear as the object of a preposition; therefore, the required form is *going*, not *to go*.

4. Agree:

She agreed to make a salad.	subject control inf. (*attempt*-type)
She agreed that she would make a salad.	tensed *that*-clause

Argue:

They argued that nothing could be done.	tensed *that*-clause

Assist:

They assisted me to climb the stairs.	object control inf. (*advise*-type)
They assisted me in climbing the stairs.	prep. *in* + gerund

Beg:

They begged Mr. Day to give easier homework.	object control inf. (*advise*-type)
They begged to enter the castle.	subject control inf. (*attempt*-type)

Dare:

Will you dare to jump over the canyon?	subject control inf. (*attempt*-type)

Keep:

They kept me waiting.	subject-participle
They kept making me wait.	gerund

Notice:

John noticed that Mary was running.	tensed *that*-clause
John noticed Mary running.	subject-participle

Resist:

He couldn't resist eating more chocolate.	gerund

Suspect:

The police suspected that John was guilty.	tensed *that*-clause

5. The essential informational difference between *try to* + V and *try* V + *-ing* is that with the infinitive, the action referred to is generally thought not to actually happen, while with the gerund, it does—even if for only a short duration. Teachers can exploit these differences within single sentences by juxtaposing situations where someone *tried to* + V but did not *try* V + *-ing*. For instance,

> I have tried to live in Cairo many times, but I have never tried living in Cairo.
> I tried to learn bungee jumping, but I never actually tried doing it.

Since hearers will not wish to accept a contradiction in meaning here—and many will think there is, in fact, a contradiction—they will likely seek the only interpretations of *try* in which the entire sentence could be true.

Other sequences can be presented to students where two clauses are coordinated, and where the second clause clearly indicates whether the action was hypothetical or fulfilled:

> You can try to open this lock, but you won't succeed.
> You can try opening this lock; then you can see what's inside the box.
> I tried working on my car, but I just couldn't get started.
> I tried working on my car, but I got tired halfway through the job.

After looking at such examples, students can get together in groups and make lists of things which they have *tried to do* but not actually *tried doing.* This may be largely a list of their own heroic failures! It will include (perhaps) schools to which they have applied but at which they have not been accepted, sports that were too formidable to engage in, long-term projects that either were or were not ever begun, and so on. It may also simply be a recent school assignment. The students can then read their lists to the class as a whole.

6. From the first sentence, most native speakers get the idea that the students in question engaged in a discrete act with a beginning and an end—the act of drawing pictures from beginning to end. From the second sentence, we get instead a picture of students in the *process* of drawing pictures, with no commitment as to whether the pictures necessarily were completed. The student can be told that the difference is mainly one of what is *focused* on—the completed act or the process.

7. In *I expect to leave by four o'clock,* a speaker may be focusing on the exact moment of four o'clock and intends to convey, "When the clock strikes four, I will leave." It might also be possible to mean, "At the point when the clock strikes four, or at some point before that, I will leave." In *I expect to have left by four o'clock,* a speaker conveys the idea, "When the clock strikes four, you will not find me there: I will already be gone." Thus the crucial difference lies in the question of whether the speaker may be, or will definitely not be, in a certain place at four.

8. This strategy may have some value as a heuristic strategy at lower levels of instruction to get students using a large percentage of verbs with the correct complements. The reason is that *-ing* complements are the least common type of clausal complement. However, as this chapter has shown, the facts of English complementation are not this simple. First, many verbs can take *either* a gerund or an infinitive complement, as with the verb *try* in Exercise 5 above, and as with *continue, begin, like, regret,* and many others. Second, many verbs take neither infinitive nor gerund but instead *that*-complements. Finally, there are a variety of infinitive types that may be unnecessarily confused if infinitives are lumped together in one category.

9. a. The error in this case is a natural one since there are both syntactic and semantic reasons for adding a *to* to the sentences. The student may be following the pattern of *force* or *cause,* both manipulative verbs which take *to*-complements. But in the case of the verbs *make, let,* and *have,* no *to* is possible. Students might be told that no *to* occurs mostly when there is a closely interactive relationship between two persons—where both are intimately engaged in the fulfillment of an event. Then, verbs like *force* and *cause* might be presented as more the exceptional cases—where close interaction is present, but where *to* is present.

   b. This error is very likely a transfer error from certain languages that permit two constituents in the initial complementizer position of sentences. A student can be told simply that English does not permit two words of this sort at the beginning of the sentence and that the student should choose the more descriptive of the two words—in this case, the word *where,* which conveys place. (In contrast, *that* is more or less semantically empty.)

   c. This is an extremely common error. English has [V + *-ing*] patterns with *go* like the following:

   > We will go swimming.
   > They went singing through the streets.

   English also has purpose infinitive—V + infinitive—patterns like the following:

   > We will go to the stockbroker to check on our investments.
   > We will go overseas to visit our parents.

   The student may be blending these two patterns in ungrammatical examples like those above. In this case, students can be told that where they are expressing a purpose, they should use an infinitive. They might also be told to test what they are saying by asking themselves whether *in order to* would fit in the place of the simple infinitive.

   d. Such errors might be addressed in terms of the redundancy present in them. By saying that the officer demanded something, it follows that I had to do something, since police officers are normally deputed to demand certain types of behavior of people. Saying this sentence is (at least in the easiest possible reading) saying the same thing twice.

Chapter 32: Other Aspects of Complementation and Embedded Clauses

1. **a.** raising to subject — John seems to be sick today.
    b. complex NP — The landlord threw the tenants out due to <u>the fact that they were making too much noise.</u>
    c. adjective complement — She is willing <u>to help us out today.</u>
    d. clausal subject — <u>To do that now</u> would be a mistake.
    <u>That she couldn't make the trip</u> disappointed everyone.
    e. extraposition — [That he won't give us better leads] is too bad. → It is too bad [that he won't give us better leads].
    f. extraposition from NP — The people [who called us up] were not very friendly. → The people were not very friendly [who called us up]. (This is often not acceptable in formal writing)
    g. *easy-to-please* constructions — It's hard to crack black walnuts. → Black walnuts are hard to crack.
    h. complex passives — It is believed that the swindler has escaped to France.
    It would be a shame for this painting to be ignored.
    i. factive verb — We <u>noticed</u> that John had bought a new car.
    j. nonfactive verb — John <u>claimed</u> that he had bought a new car.
    k. implicative verb — John <u>managed</u> to leave. (affirmative, positive implicative, complement true)
    John did not <u>manage</u> to leave. (negative, positive implicative, complement false)
    John <u>failed</u> to leave. (affirmative, negative implicative, complement false)
    John did not <u>fail</u> to leave. (negative, negative implicative, complement true)

2. **a.** In this sentence, raising to subject, which is obligatory, has not taken place.
    b. The prepositional construction *due to* requires an NP object complement. In this sentence, a full clause illegitimately takes the place of an NP.
    c. The problem here seems to be that there are two constituents in subject position—the infinitive and the semantically empty *it*. Either the infinitive must be extraposed, or the *it* must be deleted.
    d. When a tensed *that*-clause appears in subject position, it is not possible to delete the complementizer; *that* must be present in the surface form of the sentence: *That nobody ever complains. . . .*

3. **a.**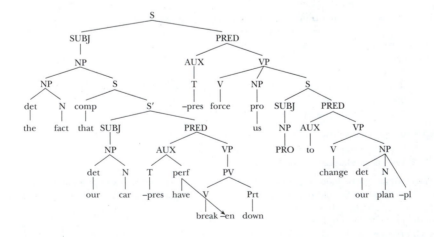

3. b.

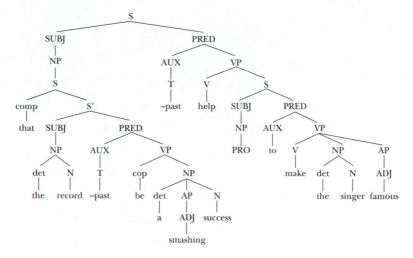

3. c.

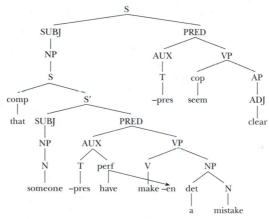

Note: to obtain the surface structure, it is necessary to apply extraposition from SUBJ and then apply *it* insertion (in addition to the usual copy s/t and morphological rules).

3. d.

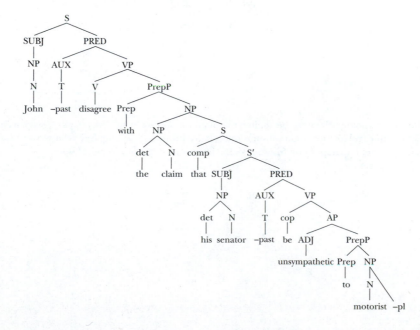

3. e.

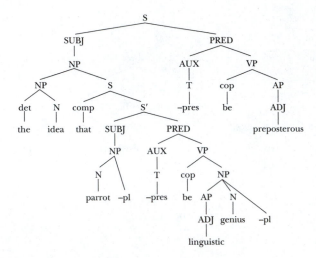

Note: Extraposition of the NP complement "that parrots are linguistic geniuses" is required to obtain the surface structure.

3. f.

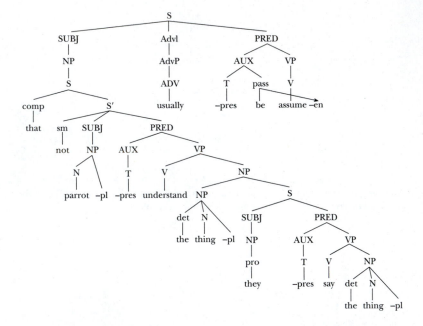

The following mapping rules must be applied to obtain the surface structure: copy s/t; *not* placement; operator addition; relative pronoun substitution; relative pronoun fronting; free relative substitution; adverbial movement; extraposition from subject; *it* insertion; and morphological rules.

3. g.

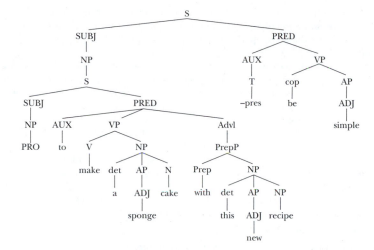

To obtain the surface structure we need extraposition of the embedded sentence from subject position, and then raising of the embedded direct object NP "a sponge cake" to subject position.

4.   *Is not true that Olivia missed her train.

The teacher can point out to the student that in English, (a) every clause with a tense has an expressed subject, or (b) every main clause has an expressed subject. Since the student will probably recognize that the word *it* contributes little if anything to the meaning of the sentence, the teacher can exploit this knowledge in explaining that the subject requirement is so strong that even where the full meaning of the sentence is conveyed without a lexical subject, a subject must be "brought in from outside" to fulfill the requirement.

   *I thought I was easy to walk that far.

There is a strong likelihood that the student is producing this pattern along the analogy of grammatical sentences like *I was happy to see my friend*. In view of that, a teacher might set the two types of sentences side by side and contrast them, asking the following questions:

   ?was easy to walk that far.
   Question: *Who* or *what* was easy? Answer: *Walking* was easy.

   ?was happy to see my friend.
   Question: *Who* or *what* was happy? Answer: *I* was happy.

The semantic differences associated with the two constructions should then be clear.

   Part of the reason such sentences are produced may be that English pronouns are nearly always unstressed. This means that when a nonnative speaker hears native speakers produce the sentence *I thought it was easy to walk that far*, the learner may hear *I* where the native speaker says *it*. A teacher might then contrast for the student the phonetic difference between the two words in such contexts: if the word were *I*, it would be pronounced quickly as [ai] or [a], while the word *it* would be pronounced as [It] or [ət].

   *This kind of movie is boring to be watched.

One possibility is for the teacher to point out the similarity of this sentence to what one usually finds in passive constructions—which makes the student's error look somewhat logical. Both here and in passives, an NP that is not an agent—not a performer of an action—is being focused. However, the focused constituents are in different types of syntactic construction. The student can be shown the equivalent paraphrase *It is boring to watch this kind of movie*, which is the base structure; the student will probably recognize that it is not possible to say *It is boring to be watched this kind of movie*. Then the student can be told that whenever he/she produces this construction, he/she should also be able to produce the other simply by moving the NP into subject position.

5. One way would be to try to substitute the relative pronoun *which* or *who(m)* for *that*. Compare:

   We saw clouds that looked like feathers. (. . . *which* looked like feathers.)
   We heard the news that rain was coming. (* . . . *which* rain was coming.)

Another way would be to isolate the embedded clause and try substituting a pronoun like *it/he/she/they* for *that*. The results should work for the relative clause but not for the complex NP clause:

   They looked like feathers.
   *It/*He/*She/*They rain was coming.

6. The verb *see*, as normally used, is factive. If someone says, "Today I saw President Clinton on the street in Houston," another person who knows of the president's whereabouts might answer, "No, you didn't see him in Houston, because the newspaper says he's in Japan this week. You <u>thought</u> you saw him." This is a standard test for factivity.

However, it is common to speak of drunken or delirious people "seeing things" like snakes. Perhaps because we are not talking of a "normal" state of consciousness, the normal factive quality of the verb seems to be suspended; at least, no one considers it a viable possibility that snakes are actually present in such cases, so there is nothing misleading about using the phrase "to see snakes."

One use of the verb *understand* seems factive. If someone says, "I now understand that the earth is flat after all," a likely answer would be, "No, you <u>don't</u> understand that, because the earth <u>isn't</u> flat." If the first person later changes his/her mind, he/she would likely say, "I <u>thought</u> I understood that the earth was flat, but I was wrong." (It would be far less likely to hear him/her say, "I <u>used</u> to understand that the earth is flat.")

At the same time, it is common to report on what one has heard someone say in terms of what one has "understood." It is a common hedging device to say things like, "I understood Mary to say that she was from Houston; was I right?"; it leaves open the possibility that the speaker may have been mistaken about what Mary said. In this use, *understand* might be taken to be nonfactive.

Chapter 33: Reported Speech and Writing

1. a. reported *that*-clause — The president announced <u>that taxes would be cut this year</u>.
  b. indirect imperative — The teacher said <u>to finish the homework by Monday</u>.
  c. indirect information question — My friend wanted to know how much the car cost.
  d. indirect yes/no question — My friend wanted to know if the car had air bags.
  e. backshifting — She asked me whether I had time to help her tomorrow.
  f. deictic time-adverbial shift — ("Do you have time now?") → She asked me if I had time then.
  g. deictic place-adverbial shift — ("Can you come over here?") → He asked me if I could go over there.
  h. deictic pronoun shift — ("Are you busy?") → She asked me if I was busy.
  i. reporting noun — The reporter's <u>claim</u> that the couple was marrying was false.
  j. factive reporting verb — Meteorologists have <u>shown</u> that the globe is getting warmer.
  k. nonfactive reporting verb — Meteorologists have <u>argued</u> that the globe is getting warmer.
  l. emotional-state reporting verb — My friend <u>complained</u> that it was getting hotter every year in the desert.
  m. free indirect discourse — She said to me, why should she be the one to ask the question first?
  n. zero-quotation — "Do you want to meet after class?" "Sure, why not." "Then where are we going to go?" "I don't know, you tell me."

2. a.

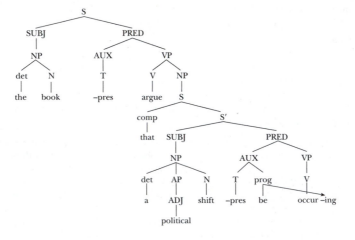

2. b.

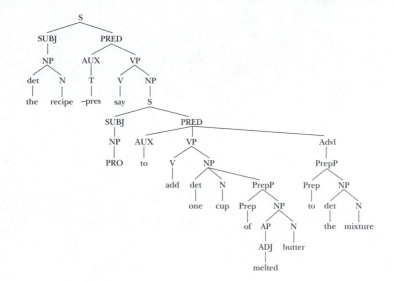

2. c.

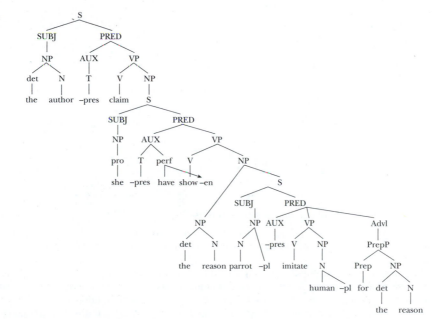

Note: relative pronoun substitution and fronting, and relative adverb substitution are required to map this tree to the surface structure.

2. d.

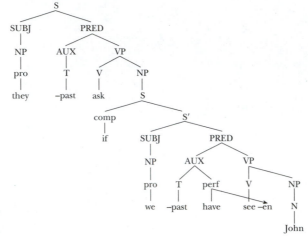

2. e.

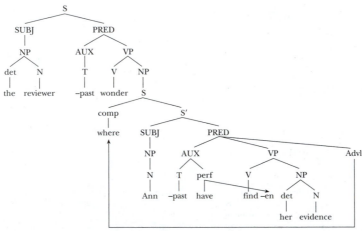

Note: this tree shows *wh*-fronting having already occurred

3. a. In Standard English, indirect questions require normal, uninverted subject-verb-object word order. The sentence as written exhibits main-clause question word order, in which subject-operator inversion has applied.

b. The verb *inform* requires a *that*-clause complement, not an infinitival one.

c. The choice of infinitive complement is correct, but the speaker/writer has inserted a tense-carrying *do* into the infinitive; infinitives are tenseless and do not take operator addition.

d. English permits only one complementizer per clause. Here, two complementizers have been chosen (*whether* and *that*).

4. The intended interpretation is (a) that Smith believes that no alternative to petroleum exists and (b) that DNA cannot account for the facts in question. However, in each sentence two reporting devices are used. This makes it seem as if *Smith* and *he* are two different persons and that Smith is reporting on what the second man believes or has said. Each sentence therefore sounds like a "report-on-a-report," but this is not likely to be the intention of the writer of the report.

There are at least two possible explanations for the fact that it sounds more acceptable to see *in his opinion* following the *say/believe*-attribution. One explanation is that the original quotation began, "In my opinion . . . "; in that case, the expression *in his opinion* constitutes a paraphrase of his exact words. A second possibility is that this is an example of "free indirect discourse," in which case the paraphraser is "taking on the identity" of Smith in a semi-indirect, semi-direct fashion, and expressing what he believes is Smith's opinion.

5. The factive or nonfactive status of these verbs can be tested by creating sentences that involve clearly false complements and then checking native-speaker intuitions regarding the oddity of the entire statement with the emotional-state verbs. For example, it was argued in the chapter that one cannot say *Smith knows that the earth is flat* if the earth is not, in fact, flat. We may carry over this sort of example to *complain, rejoice, exclaim,* and *lament* as follows:

> Smith complained/exclaimed that the earth is flat.
> ?Smith lamented/rejoiced that Tokyo was no longer the capital city of Japan.

We may also attempt a classification based on exposing contradictions in the following type of sentence:

> I complained/exclaimed that she was harassing me, but she was actually not harassing me.
> ?I rejoiced/lamented that my team had won the World Series, but they had not won it after all.

The probable answer (based on our intuitions) is that *complain/exclaim* are nonfactive, while *rejoice/lament* are factive.

6. The difference is that in the first sentence, one is projecting forward from the time of speaking, while in the second, one is projecting forward from a point in the past that has already been established in prior discourse. Thus, *next week* is in the real future from the point of view of the speaker/writer; for that person, *next week* has not occurred yet. *The next week* may or may not be in the real future for the speaker/writer, depending on how far distant in the past the established reference point is; if this point is (say) a month previous to the moment of utterance, then *the next week* is already three weeks past.

7. One possibility is to do audiotaped interviews of native speakers talking about conversations they have had about their own or others' plans, asking them to recount as fully as possible what these plans were. This may elicit the desired type of structures. A more direct method would be to tape news broadcasts of newscasters talking about events; some of these events should be in the past, and some of them should be projected in the future by the newscaster. The researcher should then have native speakers watch these broadcasts and have the respondents give as full an accounting as possible of what they heard the newscasters say. The following time-categories should be looked for:
   a. events in the past for both newscaster(s) and your native-speaker reporter
   b. events in the future for the newscaster(s) and in the past for the reporter
   c. event in the future for both newscaster(s) and reporter

   In looking at the data given by respondents, the researcher should see whether the sequence-of-tenses rules are followed consistently across all three categories. If they are not followed consistently, the researcher should check to see whether some pattern exists in the inconsistencies. It may be that the respondents exhibit a tendency to pattern certain tenses with certain types of verbs. It may be that the respondents fail to follow the rules in just those cases listed in this chapter as exceptions—where general truths are expressed, for example. It may be that the researcher can detect inconsistencies wherever a respondent seems to exhibit excitement or other emotional involvement in making a report. It may be that no pattern at all can be detected—that there may seem to be "free variation." It is certainly possible that previously undiscovered patterns, together with explanations for them, may emerge from a data-based study of this type.

8. a. There are two problems in this sentence. The first is that the predicate *be not sure* takes a *whether/if* complement that requires uninverted (subject-verb) constituent order; there is no need for operator addition in embedded clauses with this order. The second problem is that if the verb in the main clause is in present tense, the tense in the embedded clause should probably be cast in the future, not the present.
   b. *That* introduces an indirect declarative and cannot be followed by a *wh*-question word such as *how*. In addition, the verb *ask* must be followed by a subjunctive *that* complement (e.g., *My mother asked that I plan to raise my grades*). If the embedded question begins with *how*, however, *that* should be deleted leaving the *wh*-word in the comp position.

   A tense or modal must also be added, (e.g. My mother asked how I $\left\{ \begin{matrix} \text{could plan} \\ \text{planned} \end{matrix} \right\}$ to raise my grades).

   c. The verb *insist* takes a subjunctive complement, not an infinitive complement. The correct form is *My father insisted (that) I work harder.*
   d. Only indirect quotations are introduced by *that*. This is a fully direct quotation and cannot be prefaced by *that*.
   e. The verb *tell* cannot take an indirect object with *to*; only a simple NP recipient may follow *tell*. Sequence-of-tenses would also seem to dictate that *now* be replaced with *at that time* or the like.

9. This student is careful to indicate that all of the information reported on comes directly from Mr. Walter's article. In that respect, it is a competent paraphrase/summary. However, it can be explained to the student that the number of overt citations can be cut back considerably without losing the sense that citation is taking place. For example, the third sentence, *He tells us that there are several reasons for this*, can be simplified as *He gives us three reasons*. Then, these three reasons can be enumerated without any explicit reference to Walter; readers of the paraphrase/summary will properly infer that the reasons are Walter's, not those of the student, since any alternative interpretation would be unreasonable in the context of the paraphrase. The writer can then be advised to return to a direct reference to Walter in the last sentence.

10. Answers will vary.

Chapter 34: Degree: Comparatives and Equatives

1.
  a. the comparative construction   Sam has <u>more clothes than</u> Evelyn.
  b. the equative construction   He has <u>as many clothes as</u> Ben.
  c. irregular comparative adverb   Margaret sings <u>better</u> than her brother.
  d. absolute use of adjectives   That's a <u>beautiful</u> painting.
  e. use of adverb to express degree   The "bullet" train travels <u>faster</u> than any other train in Japan.
  f. free comparative   The pumpkins are growing <u>bigger (and bigger)</u> every day.
  g. unmarked adjective   How <u>old</u> is your daughter?

2.
  a. The ambiguity comes from the fact that there is a reduced clause following the complementizer *than*. The full clause could be either:

> Phyllis likes Carol more than Sue likes Carol.
>
>   or
>
> Phyllis likes Carol more than Phyllis likes Sue.

  b. The ambiguity derives from the two possible meanings of the phrase *as well as*. It could be expressing the degree of similarity in their teaching ability; that is, they both teach Sam equally well. *As well as* could also mean *in addition to*, which in turn has two possible readings:

> Mark teaches Sam. In addition, Ralph teaches Sam.
> Mark teaches Sam. In addition, Mark teaches Ralph.

3.
  a. adverb   *far*
  b. determiner   *two*
  c. noun   *oranges*
  d. verb   *costs*
  e. adjective   *interesting*

4. *Less* is a marked form that often sounds rather awkward. The usual way to avoid it is to use the negative polarity form with the comparative when such a form is available—in this case, the adverb *worse*:

> Joan sings worse than Sally.

or to use a negative equative:

> Joan doesn't sing as well as Sally.

Another possibility is to make *Sally* the subject of the sentence and to use a positive polarity adverb:

> Sally sings better than Joan.

5.
  a. Since *short* is a one-syllable adjective, the *-er* suffix should be used when making comparisons: *shorter* rather than *more short*.
  b. *Better* is the irregular comparative form of the adjective *good*. There is no need for *more*, since it unnecessarily and incorrectly marks the comparative a second time.
  c. This comparative construction is incomplete. While *than* is present, the sentence contains neither *-er* nor *more*. Two-syllable adjectives ending in *-y*, like *lucky*, take the *-er* suffix in the comparative; that is, *lucky* should be *luckier*.
  d. The equative construction (*as X as*) and the comparative (*more X than*, or *X-er than*) have been confused. The negative equative construction here should be *not as X as*, instead of *not as X *than*. Thus the construction should read "not as realistic as."
  e. The structure of the reduced clause must be parallel to that of the main clause. Adding the demonstrative *those* to the reduced clause will bring about the necessary parallelism and thus achieve grammaticality:

> The newspapers in Los Angeles have better international coverage than *those* in San Diego.

6. Answers will vary.

7. From (a), where the comparative construction has been derived from a restrictive relative clause, we understand that Herbert's intelligence is being compared with that of certain monkeys. However, sentence (a) does not imply that Herbert himself is a monkey.

    One interpretation of (b) is that the speaker has seen other monkeys that are more intelligent than the monkey known as Herbert. Another interpretation is that both the speaker and Herbert have seen monkeys but that the speaker has seen more intelligent monkeys than Herbert has seen. In fact, even the phrase "more intelligent monkeys" is ambiguous in (b). It could refer either to the number of intelligent monkeys or to their degree of intelligence.

8. The decision whether to use *more* or *-er* is very complicated. The rules outlined in this chapter would lead one to expect that *loyal* should be made comparative with a preceding *more*. However, it is possible that in the interests of parallelism with *smart*, the author chose to use the affix *-er* with *loyal*. Since there are many two-syllable adjectives that can take either *-er* or *more* there is considerable variation—and some aesthetic license—involved in such decisions.

Chapter 35: Degree: Complements and Superlatives

1. a. a comparative used in a superlative sense — This is <u>a longer</u> Indian summer than any other on record.

   b. the negative import of *too (much/little)* — It was such an old bridge that it couldn't support vehicles. → The bridge was too old to support vehicles.

   c. intensifying, nonsuperlative use of *most* — The fireworks made for a <u>most</u> dazzling spectacle.

   d. a marked superlative — This is the <u>shallowest</u> part of the river.

   e. absolute use of *too* — I can't say that I care <u>too</u> much for their attitude.

   f. comparative and superlative uses of *lesser*

      comparative — A <u>lesser</u> mind could not have accomplished what Einstein did.

      superlative — The compromise was the <u>lesser</u> of many evils.

2. a. If we wish to say that she is the cause of the boredom, we would say *most boring*. *Boring* is a two-syllable adjective that takes *most* to form the superlative construction.

      But if we wish to say that she is the experiencer of the boredom, we would say *most bored*. Most adjectives ending in derivational suffixes use *most* in the superlative construction.

   b. The speaker has added the superlative suffix *-est* to an adverb/adjective that is already in the comparative form with an *-er* ending. The *-est* should be added to *base* form. Here this would give us *farthest* and *eldest*. In addition, *furthest* and *oldest* would probably be used more frequently these days.

3. a. *More* should be used here. Even though there are three people involved, Alex is being compared with the other two together; that is, *he* has financial problems but *they* don't, since they both have more money.

   b. *The best* would probably be used here. Sheila is at the "end of the scale" of candidates for the speaker. Notice, however, the comparative form would be appropriate if Sheila was being compared with the other candidates as a group.

      Of the five candidates for president, I voted for Sheila because I definitely

      think she's better than $\begin{cases} \text{the others.} \\ \text{the rest.} \end{cases}$

   c. Either form could be used here. The difference would be whether the speaker found his or her choice superior to the other books along an interest scale (in which case the superlative form would be appropriate) or whether the speaker was comparing his or her choice with all the other books as a group for the quality of "interesting" (in which case the comparative form would be correct).

4. *Very* is an intensifier that may or may not have a negative connotation, depending on the intonation. *Too* is a degree complement that expresses the idea of "excess" and thus has a firm negative connotation.

5. a. The error is in the use of the comparative form *older* where the superlative form *oldest* is more appropriate. The use of the superlative form *oldest* follows the definite article and indicates that Joe is at the extreme of the scale for age of children in his family.

   b. Both *most* and the superlative suffix *-est* have been used, so that the superlative is marked twice. Only the *-est* superlative form is required, since *cold* is a one-syllable word, unless some special effect is the intention.

   c. The syntactic context (a preceding *the*) and the semantic context (an indication that something is first on a scale of importance) necessitate the use of a superlative form:

      The first and *most* important thing . . .

   d. The student has used the incorrect form of this irregular adjective. The comparative form *worse* is required here.

   e. The student has used *too*, which is used to express excess, when the semantic context (the positively evaluative adjective *tasty*) suggests that the intensifier *very* is what is intended. This may be due to overgeneralization from the colloquial use of *too* as a counterpart to *very* in negative contexts. Note that very exaggerated intonation could also make the utterance acceptable in some colloquial contexts, but the more common usage should be highlighted to students.

6. If you agree with us that comparatives and superlatives are quite different semantically, you may choose to teach the comparative form at one time and then come back to the superlative form at a later time. This problem is greatest if your students speak languages without distinctive comparative and superlative forms.

7. As we have tried to indicate, this is an oversimplification of the difference between comparatives and superlatives. Whether a speaker chooses to use a comparative or superlative to a large extent depends upon the speaker's perspective, not upon the number of things/people being compared.

8. He is perhaps making the point that the rules of superlative formation are complicated, variable, and not universally adhered to and therefore can be violated when an author is striving to achieve a certain effect.

Chapter 36: Conclusion (No exercises)

Index of Names

Index of Languages and Language Groups

Index of Words and Phrases

Note: The symbol "f" means "and following pages" and the symbol "n" means that the information about the form is in an endnote rather than in the main text.

Index of Topics

Marianne Celce-Murcia and Diane Larsen-Freeman have long been leaders in the field of second language pedagogy.

Marianne Celce-Murcia is Professor of Applied Linguistics and TESL at the University of California, Los Angeles. In addition to co-authorship of *The Grammar Book,* Marianne is editor of *Teaching English as a Second or Foreign Language,* and *Beyond Basics: Issues and Research in TESOL.* She is also co-author of *Techniques and Resources in Teaching Grammar* (with Sharon Hilles) and *Teaching Pronunciation* (with Donna Brinton and Janet Goodwin), as well as series consultant for *Grammar Dimensions: Form, Meaning, and Use.*

Diane Larsen-Freeman is a Professor of Applied Linguistics in the Department of Language Teacher Education at the School for International Training in Brattleboro, Vermont. In addition to her co-authorship of *The Grammar Book,* Diane is the editor of *Discourse Analysis in Second Language Research,* author of *Techniques and Principles in Language Teaching,* co-author (with Michael Long) of *An Introduction to Second Language Acquisition Research,* and Series Director for *Grammar Dimensions: Form, Meaning, and Use.*

Other Heinle & Heinle titles by the co-authors:

Grammar Dimensions, Diane Larsen-Freeman, Series Director; Marianne Celce-Murcia, Series Consultant

This four-level ESL series with accompanying workbooks, tapes, and a website systematically addresses the form, meaning, and use of each grammar structure. It focuses learners' attention on the greatest challenges for each structure to help students communicate accurately, meaningfully, and appropriately.

Also by Marianne Celce-Murcia

Teaching English as a Second or Foreign Language

This comprehensive introduction to teaching ESL/EFL gives both experienced and prospective teachers the theoretical background and practical applications they need to succeed.

Beyond Basics: Issues and Research in TESOL

Designed as a complement to *Teaching English as a Second or Foreign Language,* this text surveys research issues and related pedagogical problems central to TESOL such as acquisition, assessment, role of culture, and language policy.

Also by Diane Larsen-Freeman

Grammar 3D, CD-ROM

A dynamic program for high beginning through advanced level students that can be used alone or as a supplement to any grammar text. It addresses the three dimensions of grammar—form, meaning, and use—in order to provide abundant meaningful grammar practice.

Teaching Language: From Grammar to Grammaring (1999)

This book treats the three dimensions of grammar from the perspective of second language acquisition, English linguistics, and language pedagogy. It offers a coherent and empirically sound approach to teaching grammar.